Inside the Bible

Inside the Bible

An Introduction to
Each Book of the Bible

IGNATIUS PRESS   SAN FRANCISCO

Cover design by Roxanne Mei Lum

© 1998 Ignatius Press, San Francisco
All rights reserved
ISBN 0-89870-665-3
Library of Congress catalogue number 98-71260
Printed in the United States of America ∞

Contents

THE NEW TESTAMENT

Introduction

The Bible contains the word of God. It is a collection of letters that God has written to us to tell us where we came from, why we are here, and where we are going. God is the primary author of the Bible, but he used human beings as his instruments to produce it — men like Moses, David, Amos, Isaiah, Matthew, Mark, Luke, John, Paul, and the other prophets and wise men. In all they wrote they were protected from error by the assistance of the Holy Spirit.

The Catholic Bible contains forty-five books in the Old Testament, or forty-six if Lamentations is separated from Jeremiah. The New Testament has twenty-seven books, fourteen, or over half of them, by St. Paul.

A believer who wants to read and study the Bible should realize that it takes effort to come to a good understanding of the contents of the Greatest Book ever written. It takes effort because the Bible was composed by many different persons over a period of more than a thousand years. It was written in ancient languages — the Old Testament in Hebrew, and the New Testament in Koine Greek. Also it was written in the Near East and reflects a culture flourishing two thousand years ago that is now foreign to Americans and Europeans. Many of its words and concepts seem strange to us, and the way of thinking is often different from Western logical categories.

The Bible is the Greatest Book in the world because it has God as its author. One might look upon the seventy-two books as so many chapters of one book because there is one author. Since God is the author, we say that Holy

Scripture is "inspired", that is, God caused it to be written, and so it has a divine origin. Consequently, the Bible is free from all errors because God can neither deceive nor be deceived. Apparent contradictions can be attributed to problems with the transmission of the ancient text through the centuries or to the fact that we do not adequately understand the context and cultural situation of the matter reported.

We learn from the Bible that God created everything that exists; he is the Master of the world and of history. We also learn that he is absolute goodness and that he freely created the world in order to communicate his own goodness to others. In various ways he has manifested or revealed himself to us.

God's revelation of himself occurs in two ways: in nature and by speaking to us through the patriarchs and prophets of Israel, and especially through his Son, Jesus Christ. The Bible contains revelation in the second sense — God has spoken to us, and his word has been recorded in writing. That writing is what we have in the Bible in both Testaments — Old and New.

My main reason for producing the present book is to make available to those who want to understand the Bible simple, clear, and short introductions to each book of the Bible. It can profitably be used as a companion volume to the *Ignatius Bible* (Revised Standard Version, Catholic Edition) or to any other approved Catholic Bible. I have tried to include in a few pages enough information about each book so that the daily or occasional reader can quickly find the essential information on the book he is reading or wants to read. The goal is to have a bird's-eye view of any book in the Bible.

All the introductions are composed the same way: (1) title of the book; (2) a quote that catches a main point in the book; (3) the location of the book in the Bible; (4) date and author, that is, who wrote it and when; (5) the theme of the book; (6) summary of the contents and a few comments about the context in which it was written; (7) the theology of the book; (8) an outline; (9) a reflection taken from the book.

The purpose of each chapter and of the whole book is to help you, the reader, to grow in the knowledge and love of God's word as it is contained in the Bible — and through that word to grow in knowledge and love of God himself, the author. For the Bible is not a closed book; it should not be the special preserve of biblical scholars and university classrooms. This is God's word, and it is intended for all his children — for all those who believe, no matter what their level of education might be, but also for his children who are not yet believers.

Please note that *Inside the Bible* is not intended to be a comprehensive treatment of the Bible. Not at all. Many important aspects of the study of Scripture have been omitted, for example, text, source, and redaction criticism; very little is noted about the influence on Israel of the surrounding cultures — Canaanite, Egyptian, Assyrian, Persian, Greek, and Roman. What I have tried to do, for the sake of clarity and brevity, is to cut everything to the bone.

For the most part, I have avoided giving various opinions about the sources of each book and the different opinions about the date and author. These opinions are often contradictory and help little or not at all to an understanding of the book as it has been handed down to us. My purpose has been to explain the *meaning* of each book as briefly as possible for the ordinary reader who is not familiar with biblical scholarship. If some are inspired by this little work to study the Bible in more depth, then I will consider the book a success.

The study of the Bible is a major enterprise. Each year hundreds of new books on the Bible are published. Every Sunday millions of Catholics hear sermons or homilies on passages from the Bible. Most universities and colleges have courses on the Bible; all the Christian churches promote it. So every year millions of copies of the Bible are sold and innumerable books and articles about the Bible are printed — covering everything from textual criticism to suggestions on how to pray with the Bible.

With regard to the *interpretation* of the Bible, the Catholic Church insists that the fundamental meaning of the text is the literal meaning, that is, the meaning intended by the author. That meaning might be historical, poetic, a song, a prayer, a curse, and so forth. A second type of meaning is what is known as the "spiritual meaning" of the text. This applies mostly to the Old Testament, which, after the Paschal Mystery of the death and Resurrection of Jesus Christ, is seen by Christians in a different light. An example can be found in Matthew 1:23, where the author applies the word "virgin" from Isaiah 7:14 to the Blessed Virgin Mary. Isaiah was thinking about the wife of the king, but Matthew saw the word as a reference to Mary and the Virgin Birth.

The unity of the Bible comes from the fact that the Logos is the author of the Bible. He wrote all of it in such a way that earlier books foreshadow later events. As some of the Fathers of the Church said, everything in the Old Testament points to Jesus and the New Testament *in some way*. St. Augustine expressed the same idea: The New Testament is hidden in the Old Testament, and the Old Testament is made manifest in the New Testament. The Second Vatican Council in the Constitution on Divine Revelation quoted this insight of Augustine (*Dei Verbum*, no. 16).

The nature of God is hidden from us. Because of his spirituality and infinity, he is wrapped in mystery as far as we are concerned. His intelligibility exceeds our power of understanding, just as the light of the sun is too bright for our eyes to look at it directly. Since God wrote the Bible, and much of it is about him, it is a treasure of knowledge about God. In fact, it is an inexhaustible treasure that can never be totally comprehended. That is why so many books on the Bible are now and will continue to be printed each year.

The Bible is the Church's own book, and only she is the final and authentic interpreter of the meaning of any passage (see *Dei Verbum*, no. 10). The 1993 Vatican document "The Interpretation of the Bible in the Church" in one sentence sums up what the Bible is and what its purpose is: "The Bible is a text inspired by God which has been entrusted to the Church for the nourishment of faith and for the guidance of Christian life" (3, D, 1).

The Bible, therefore, is directed by God to man's mind and also to his will or heart. In addition to the instruction we find in the Bible, it also offers us an abundance of prayers. The 150 psalms are called "the prayer book of the Church". Many other beautiful prayers are scattered throughout the books of the Bible besides the Psalms.

St. Teresa of Avila offers some sage advice on how to use Scripture during times of prayer. Her method of prayer has four steps: (1) choose a passage; (2) be aware of the presence of God; (3) read and reflect; (4) respond with acts of faith, hope, and love. The passage chosen should not be long—it could be one verse or a chapter of a book, but not more than that. A good example is the passage in Luke 1:26–38, which recounts the Annunciation of the angel Gabriel to Mary that she is to be the Mother of God.

The Bible achieves its purpose in each one of us when we can pray with it and so grow in the knowledge and love of God and of our neighbor. I hope and pray that this little book will help the reader to do just that.

The Old Testament

The Five Books of Moses

The first five books of the Bible are commonly called the "Pentateuch", which is a Greek word meaning "five books". The five books are: Genesis, Exodus, Leviticus, Numbers, and Deuteronomy. They function as an introduction to the whole Bible, Old Testament and New Testament, and as the historical and theological foundation of all the other books of the Bible, all the way to the end in the book of Revelation by St. John. If one does not understand the basic ideas contained in these five books, then it is impossible to understand fully the following books in the Old Testament and all the implications of the story of Jesus in the New Testament.

According to many biblical passages, Moses was the author of the Pentateuch. Modern scholars have modified that assertion considerably by showing how parts were contributed by other authors over the centuries and how the final edition or the form we now have of the Pentateuch was completed during the time of the Jewish exile in Babylon about 550 B.C. But still most of the basic ideas in the books go back to Moses. In the Bible itself the first five books are referred to simply as "Moses", or as the "Book of Moses", or as "Torah" — a Hebrew word that means "instruction", "teaching", or "law".

The Pentateuch is extremely important and critical to understanding the Bible because it tells the story of how the world as we know it came to be, where mankind came from, why man is here on this earth, and what his destiny is. It also tells the story of how God chose the Hebrew people, or Israel, as the instrument he would use to reveal his will to mankind. So the Pentateuch contains a message from God to each one of us about who we are and why we are on this earth.

It might help one who is trying to get "inside" the Bible to look upon the Pentateuch as one book with five chapters. The chapters consist almost exclusively of narrative (or story) and laws governing divine worship and community life. The "plan" or "plot" goes like this, in very simple outline: God creates the world; he gives special attention to Adam and Eve and their children, who are supposed to praise his goodness, but they are disobedient and fall into sin (Gen 1—11); in order to remedy the fall, God chooses Abraham and his descendants (Israel) as a faithful people who will be a light to all other nations (Gen 12—50); through suffering in Egypt and deliverance from bondage, under the inspired leadership of Moses (Exodus), they learn the lesson of God's goodness and eventually become God's holy people united to him by an everlasting Covenant (Ex 19—24; Lev; and Num 1—10); then God will lead them into the Promised Land (Num 10—36); but there is a condition — they will have peace and permanent possession of the land if they are obedient to the Torah and worship only the Lord God of Israel (Deuteronomy).

That is a simple outline of what the reader will find in the first five books of the Bible. Is this history or myth? It is not myth in the sense of an imaginative story like a novel; the narrative and the laws are based on events that really happened in the past. Biblical history, however, is not like modern scientific, "objective" history. The biblical authors did not try to tell everything — to be comprehensive. They told only part of what really happened because the Bible is about God's dealings with man; it is about "salvation history", or how God intervened in history to save mankind; so every sentence and every word is theological, that is, it has to do either with God himself in his inner nature or with his relations to the world and to mankind.

Perhaps we could put it another way and say that these stories were composed in order to make a point, like editorials in the local newspaper. So the Bible tells us about God—who he is, what he wants from us, and what will happen to us if we reject his offer of love. Therefore, this type of history is more interested in explaining *why* things happened in the past than it is in giving all the details; so the *message* is more important than mathematical accuracy. This type of history is more interested in telling the reader how to live now and to be happy than it is in giving a complete picture of everything that happened.

If you can approach the Pentateuch with this frame of mind, you will not be unduly disturbed by the many omissions and apparent inconsistencies in the Holy Bible, which is the word of God. The purpose in reading the Bible is to grow in the knowledge and love of God; it is not to become a historian or a scientist.

So what we find in the Pentateuch briefly is: creation (Adam and Eve), sin, choice of a people (Abraham), a Covenant (Moses), a Law to be obeyed, and guidance through the wilderness to the Promised Land (Israel). In a sense, the life of each human being reflects or imitates the story told in the five books of Moses.

The main ideas or themes that run through the Pentateuch are: (1) God created the world, and it is good; (2) sin and death entered into the world because of the disobedience of Adam and Eve; (3) God wants to save man from his sinful self so he makes a promise to Abraham, chooses a people, and makes a binding, everlasting Covenant with them; (4) God gives his people a holy Law for worship and for governance of the community; (5) God liberates his people from the slavery of Egypt and guides them to the Promised Land; (6) even though God is not seen by his people with their eyes, he is always with them to guide them and protect them.

Finally, for us Catholics and Christians it is important to realize that everything in the Old Testament refers to Christ and his Church in one way or another. So Christ and his Church are hidden in every sentence and every word of the Old Testament. The partial revelation of the Old Testament foreshadows the full revelation of the New Testament. The Old Testament promises the Messiah, presents and proclaims him. His name is Jesus Christ.

Genesis

In the beginning God created the heavens and the earth. . . .
And God saw everything that he had made, and behold,
it was very good (1:1, 31).

PLACE IN THE BIBLE: Genesis is the first book of the Bible. It takes first place in the "Pentateuch", which means the first five books. The Pentateuch is also called the "Torah", a Hebrew word that means "Law".

DATE AND AUTHOR: The first draft was written in the tenth century B.C.; the final editing of the book took place in the sixth century B.C. Jewish and Catholic tradition traces the origins of this book back to Moses, but inspired editors worked on it after he did to give it the form in which we now have it.

THEME: "Genesis" means beginning or origin. So Genesis is about the creation of the universe and everything in it — sun, moon, stars, earth, plants, animals, and man — and the origins of the Hebrew people. It describes how God out of sheer goodness and love created the first man and woman. They sinned or rebelled against God and were punished by expulsion from Paradise. Their sin affects not only them but all their descendants. It is a classic story of good and evil and also of God's justice and mercy. Sin infects all mankind, but God's love and mercy work to bring good out of evil. God chooses Abraham and makes him a promise; he fulfills that promise in Isaac, Jacob, and the twelve sons of Jacob. In spite of man's perversity, God always remains faithful.

SUMMARY: Even people who know very little about the Bible know something about the book of Genesis. This is because it contains many interesting stories that are filled with concrete details.

The book is divided into two main parts. The first part deals with the creation of the world and of our first parents, Adam and Eve, and what happened to their descendants. It tells the story of how the world got started and how the human race began. The second part deals with the three great patriarchs who were the ancestors of the Hebrew people: Abraham, Isaac, and Jacob. Genesis covers the longest time span of any book in the Bible, since it stretches from the creation of the world by God to the presence of the Hebrews in Egypt about 1700 B.C. It lays the groundwork, so to speak, for the great events that will take place in Egypt under Moses — liberation and sojourn in the wilderness, as they are described in the book of Exodus.

The dominant figure in Genesis is the Lord God. He is described directly and indirectly as good, loving, and merciful, but he is also a God of wrath and punishment for those who violate his Law. He is completely above this world, but at the same time he is concerned about his creatures, especially man. But his wrath is always tempered by his mercy and his loving concern for his creatures, even when they turn against him.

In the first eleven chapters the author tells us about the creation of the world, and especially of the first parents, Adam and Eve. God showers gifts on them; he tests them, and they fall into sin, being tempted by Satan in the guise of a serpent. They are expelled from Paradise and now must work for their food; the relationship between the man and his wife is marred by their sin — they feel shame before one another's nakedness; the woman will be subject to the man, and she will bear her children in pain; sin ushers into the world suffering and death. Sin spreads among their first descendants; for example, Cain murders his brother, Abel. Sin spreads, and so God sends a flood to destroy all human flesh but saves Noah and his family in the famous ark. When Noah's children multiply, they become arrogant and try to build the tower of Babel reaching to heaven — an attempt to challenge the supremacy of the Lord God. God confounds them by confusing their language so they can no longer communicate. One of the sons of Noah is the ancestor of Abraham. When we get to Abraham, we arrive at the first link in the chain that will lead to the Hebrews in Egypt and eventually to the people of Israel.

In chapters 12 to 50 we find the stories of the three patriarchs — Abraham, Isaac, and Jacob — and the twelve sons of Jacob, especially Joseph. They are important in the Bible because from them the whole House of Israel is descended. The chief person is Abraham. Born in a pagan family and culture in Mesopotamia (modern Iraq), he is called by God to leave his family and home and to go to a distant land. God promises him that he will make him the father of many nations (chaps. 12, 15, and 17).

This promise from God to Abraham is a theme that runs through the whole Bible and all of revelation. The final fulfillment will come at the Second Coming of Christ on the Last Day.

Abraham is distinguished for his absolute faith in the promises of God to him. For this reason in the First Eucharistic Prayer at Mass he is called "our father in faith". He is humble and obedient to God. For this reason he is a type or model of Jesus Christ himself, who was obedient unto death. Therefore God blesses Abraham and establishes a Covenant (agreement, contract) with him. God promises him many descendants; the key one, of course, is the Messiah, who would come about eighteen hundred years later. Today all the members of the Church worldwide, those who believe in Jesus Christ, are descendants of Abraham in a spiritual sense.

Abraham's most difficult trial is the Lord's command to him to sacrifice his son, Isaac; the purpose is to test his faith. Abraham does not hesitate to do it, and at the last minute the angel of the Lord prevents him from killing his son. And Isaac is the son of promise.

The story about Isaac is rather short (25:19—26:35). He marries Rebekah, who gives him twin sons—Esau the elder and Jacob the younger son. Through the trickery and collusion of Rebekah and Jacob, Isaac gives his blessing to Jacob (thinking he is Esau), so the birthright passes to Jacob and from him to his twelve sons.

There is real character development in the Bible in the case of Jacob (27:1—37:1). He is clever and scheming and does not seem to have any remorse about lying to get his way. But God makes use of him to achieve his end. In every way God is portrayed as the Lord of history. In the case of evil, he tolerates it; in order to achieve his will, at crucial points he directly intervenes in history.

The key point in the Jacob story is the *blessing* he receives from his father, Isaac. It is presented as an objective reality, and once it is given, it cannot be taken back. So it is through him and his children that the *promise* made to Abraham will be fulfilled, namely, the creation of a new people — the nation of Israel. The rest of the Old Testament, in one way or another, will be concerned with the fortunes of that people.

The cycle of stories about Joseph, next-to-youngest son of Jacob, is perhaps, from a literary point of view, the most artistically written story in the Old Testament (37:2 — 50:26). The point to look for here is the working out of divine *providence* in human history. Out of sheer jealousy, Joseph's brothers sell him into slavery. Taken to Egypt and thrown into prison, he languishes for a few years, but God favors him by giving him the gift of interpreting dreams. After correctly interpreting two dreams of the Pharaoh, he is made the master of all Egypt. He amasses immense stores of grain and food for the coming famine. His brothers come down from Canaan in search of food. He recognizes them, favors them, forgives them, and is reconciled to them. He has them bring his father, Jacob, down to Egypt, where he can care for him.

Before his death, Jacob blesses his twelve sons and makes certain predictions about the future of the twelve tribes of Israel, which will descend from the twelve sons. The Joseph story explains how the Hebrew people happened to be in Egypt. The beginning of the next book of the Bible, Exodus, finds them in a state of slavery and great suffering about four hundred years after Joseph. The date would be approximately 1290 B.C.

THEOLOGY: The book of Genesis is perhaps the most commented on book in the Bible because its fascinating pages bristle with themes and ideas about God that resound from one end of the Bible to the other, culminating in the final book of Revelation.

The first eleven chapters express several basic truths that are the foundation of God's whole plan of salvation. Some of the truths are: the creation of all things by God at the beginning of time; God's special concern in the creation of man and woman; the unity of the human race; God's institution of marriage between a man and a woman; the sin of our first parents, Adam and Eve; the fall from divine grace; and the consequences of that sin, namely, suffering and death. We also see the dire effects of sin on the human family with the arrival of murder (Cain and Abel), idolatry, and many other evils.

For their sin Adam and Eve are punished severely, but God offers them the hope of eventual reconciliation through the various promises he makes to Abraham and his descendants. In fulfillment of his *promise* to Abraham, God raises up Moses to be the leader of his people. Moses will lead them out of Egypt into the wilderness and eventually to the land of Canaan — the Promised Land. There the People of God thrive and multiply.

Genesis also teaches us about the absolute transcendence of God above all material things. We see his wisdom and goodness and the immensity of his power, through which all things were made.

The second part of Genesis includes chapters 12 to 50. Here we get into the stories about the patriarchs Abraham, Isaac, Jacob, and Jacob's son Joseph, who saves his people and gives them a place of refuge in Egypt. The story about Abraham stresses God's *promise* of a land of his own and many descendants. The real fulfillment of that promise is found in Christ and the Church founded by him. The story about Jacob fulfills the prophecy made to Abraham and highlights God's abundant *blessing*. The story about Joseph describes the working of divine *providence* in history. In spite of the evil intentions of men, God achieves his own purposes in creation; for, the evil done to Joseph by his brothers brings him to Egypt, where he becomes a man of great political power so that, later, he is able to save his whole family from starvation. So the underlying principle in the story of the patriarchs is: one God, one people, one land.

The New Testament quotes Genesis or refers to it several times. Christ is the new Adam — sin and death come through Adam, while justification and life come through Jesus Christ (Rom 5:12–21). Noah's ark is a symbol of the Church by which men are saved by the water of Baptism (1 Pet 3:20ff.). Abraham is praised for his faith and obedience; the sacrifice of his son, Isaac, foreshadows the sacrifice of Jesus, who is the Son of the Father.

D. Joseph sold into slavery; down to Egypt
   (37:2—50:26)

   1. Joseph meets his brothers in Egypt

   2. Jacob goes down to Egypt

   3. Jacob blesses his sons

   4. Burial of Jacob and last days of Joseph

REFLECTION

"Blessed be Abram by God Most High, maker of heaven and earth; and blessed be God Most High, who has delivered your enemies into your hand!" (14:19–20).

Exodus

God said to Moses, "I AM WHO I AM." And he said, "Say this to the people of Israel, 'I AM has sent me to you'" (3:14).

PLACE IN THE BIBLE: The book of Exodus is the second book in the Old Testament and the second book of the Pentateuch. The word "Exodus" means "departure", that is, the departure of the Israelite people from Egypt to Mount Sinai and thence to a period of forty years in the desert before they entered into Canaan, or the Promised Land. The book contains forty chapters.

DATE AND AUTHOR: The time of these events was about 1290 to 1250 B.C. The original draft of the book was probably written under King David in the tenth century B.C. The final editing of the book took place in the sixth century, during the exile in Babylon, so about 550 B.C. The basic content and inspiration of the book came from Moses.

THEME: There are two major themes in Exodus: The first major theme is that Yahweh, the God of Israel (also called "Lord"), through a series of miracles or "mighty works", brought Israel out from the slavery of Egypt. The second major theme is the theophany or self-revelation of the

Lord at Sinai and the making of the Covenant with Israel. This is the heart or essence of Exodus.

SUMMARY AND MAIN POINTS: Exodus takes up where Genesis left off: the Israelites, who are the inheritors of the promise to Abraham, are in Egypt. They have greatly increased in number over a period of about four hundred years. A new king, or Pharaoh, is now in charge, and he reduces them to a state of oppressive slavery. In answer to their prayers for liberation, God raises up Moses, son of a Levite family but raised as an Egyptian by the Pharaoh's daughter. In defense of his people, he kills an Egyptian and then is forced to flee for his life to the east.

The Lord God (Yahweh) reveals himself to Moses in the land of Midian, which is in the Sinai peninsula. He orders him to return to Egypt and to ask the Pharaoh to let his people go. Moses complies, with the help of his brother, Aaron. It takes ten plagues or miracles to force Pharaoh to let them go. The tenth plague is the death of all the firstborn, human beings and animals, in the kingdom. The Israelites are spared because of the blood of the paschal lamb; every year this miraculous event is celebrated on the feast of Passover, for the avenging angel "passed over" the dwellings of the Israelites where he saw traces of the blood of the lamb on the doorposts.

Pharaoh lets them go; his people are so happy to see them go that they load them down with gifts of gold and silver. The Israelites head for the Red Sea. Having changed his mind about releasing them, Pharaoh decides to pursue them with his army. The Lord performs a great miracle at the Red Sea—he parts the water so that the Israelites, led by Moses, can cross over to the other side on dry land with a wall of water to the right and to the left. Pharaoh's army goes after them; when all the Israelites have safely arrived on the other side, Moses lifts his rod and commands the sea to return to its natural state. It does so at his word, and all the Egyptians perish in the sea.

It takes the people about two months to get to Mount Sinai. There God appears to Moses and gives him the Ten Commandments and the more detailed laws for governing the community; this is called the "Book of the Covenant" (20:22—23:33). Then the people ratify or accept the Covenant, that is, they agree to live by its laws or requirements.

Chapters 25 to 31 give detailed instructions on the building of the sanctuary that they will carry with them in the wilderness, for they are a nomadic people now.

While Moses is spending forty days on the top of Mount Sinai in communion with the Lord, the people become impatient and force Aaron to make a golden calf for them, which they then worship. This of course is a serious violation of the First Commandment. When Moses comes down from the mountain and discovers what is going on, in his anger he breaks the two stone tablets that contain the writing of the Ten Commandments; he destroys the golden calf and rebukes the people. He again ascends the mountain, asking pardon for the people. God forgives them and gives him the Commandments again. When he descends a second time, the people renew the Covenant and agree to live by its terms. From now on, Yahweh is their God, for he is the only God, and they are his people.

Chapters 35 to 40 are basically a repetition of 25 to 31, this time describing the actual building of the sanctuary and its contents and the vestments of the priests. The book ends with the Lord once again blessing Israel with a sign of the divine presence: his glory fills the sanctuary and covers it with a cloud by day and fire by night (40:34–38).

THEOLOGY: The book of Exodus is the heart and soul of the Old Testament. In fact, "testament" is just another word for the Covenant that the Lord made with Moses and Israel at Mount Sinai. The two themes of liberation and covenant reverberate, in one way or another, through all the books of the Old Testament. They are also present in all the books of the New Testament, with the exception of James and Jude. Many of the psalms sing praise to the Lord for his deliverance of Israel; his Covenant is mentioned often, especially in the longest psalm of all, Psalm 119, which refers to God's Law in each of its 176 verses.

In Exodus God reveals himself to Moses and even gives him his name — YAHWEH, that is, "I AM" or "HE WHO IS". So the God of Israel is the source of all being — the Creator of heaven and earth. By his almighty power, he liberates his people from the bondage of Egypt. Later that liberation becomes a symbol or type of liberation from sin by the grace of Jesus Christ. And Moses is a type of Christ himself. Moses the lawgiver of Sinai is a type of Jesus, who proclaims the new law of love of God and neighbor as found in the Sermon on the Mount in St. Matthew and in the rest of the New Testament.

The ideas of promise and election also run through Exodus. We recall God's promises to Abraham, Isaac, and Jacob. In Exodus the promise is partially fulfilled in the formation of the People of Israel; the second part will be fulfilled when they cross over the Jordan River and occupy the land of Canaan, which is the Promised Land. Election is found in the fact that God freely chooses Israel as his people. He does not choose them for a special role in the history of mankind because of any merit on their part — it is a pure gift. Please note that the initiative in all of this comes from God alone — not from Moses or the people. They are favored, but they are a bit reluctant to accept God's favor.

The notion of "covenant" is prominent in Exodus. Basically, it means an agreement or contract between two parties. In Exodus, it means an agreement between the Lord and his people Israel. The terms of the agreement are the Ten Commandments. If the people keep them, they will be protected and rewarded by the Lord; if they violate them, they will be punished. The most important one is the first: "I am the LORD your God . . . you shall have no other gods before me." In a certain way, this First Commandment contains, as in a seed, all the rest. The definitive and final Covenant between God and all mankind was made by Jesus through his life, death, and Resurrection. So the Christian sacred writings are called the "New Testament".

OUTLINE

I. Liberation from Egypt (1:1—15:21)

    A. Israel in Egypt (ties in with the end of Genesis)

    B. Early life of Moses

    C. The call of Moses

    D. The plagues of Egypt

    E. Passover

    F. Departure from Egypt and deliverance at the Red Sea

II. Journey in the wilderness (15:22—18)

III. God's Covenant with Israel (19—24)

    A. The Covenant and the Decalogue

    B. The book of the Covenant

    C. Ratification of the Covenant

IV. Instructions on building the sanctuary and on its ministers (25—31)

V. Golden calf: Sin and renewal of the Covenant (32—34)

VI. Furnishing and building of the sanctuary (35—40)

REFLECTION

"I will sing to the LORD, *for he has triumphed gloriously; the horse and his rider he has thrown into the sea. The* LORD *is my strength and my song, and he has become my salvation; this is my God, and I will praise him, my father's God, and I will exalt him"* (15:1–2).

Leviticus

"You shall be holy; for I the LORD *your God am holy"*
(19:2).

PLACE IN THE BIBLE: The book of Leviticus is the third
book in the Old Testament and the third book of the Pentateuch. The name is taken from the tribe of Levi, whose
male members were responsible for taking care of the sacrifices and worship of the people of Israel. The book contains twenty-seven chapters.

DATE AND AUTHOR: Like that of all five books in the Pentateuch, the basic content and inspiration of the book
come from Moses during the time of the wandering in the
wilderness in the first half of the thirteenth century B.C.
Many scholars place the final editing of the book around
the time of the exile, since the prophet Ezekiel seems to
be aware of it; the finishing touches probably date from
the time of Ezra, about 450 B.C.

THEME: Leviticus is the main liturgical book of the Old
Testament. It gives detailed directions for divine worship
as well as regulations for priests and for national and personal holiness. It gives rules for the different kinds of sacrifices, that is, who does what, which sacrifices are acceptable and which are not. Because of the majesty of the
Lord God, only things and persons who are ritually clean

37

can be engaged in the divine worship. The overall theme of the book is summarized in the admonition from the Lord: "*You shall be holy; for I the LORD your God am holy*" (19:2).

SUMMARY: The last verses of Exodus describe the descent of the Glory of the Lord on the Tabernacle (Ex 40:34–38). Man must bow down in worship when he encounters the revelation of God's Glory. So it makes sense that the directives on how to worship God correctly should follow right after Exodus. The book of Leviticus then teaches the Israelites how to worship God properly, how he wants to be worshipped. The first part deals with different kinds of sacrifices of animals and cereals. The chief animals mentioned are young bulls, lambs, rams, goats, and turtledoves or pigeons; the latter can be offered at times by the poor, who cannot afford the cost of a larger animal. In a holocaust, the whole animal is burned on the altar as a sign of submission to God; the cereal offerings are also a form of holocaust.

In the other sacrifices (sin offering, guilt offering, and peace offering), only part of the animal is burned on the altar, and the rest goes to the priests and the offerers. When they eat the rest, it symbolizes fellowship or communion between the Israelites and God; that is, he is in their midst and has concern for them.

Chapters 8 to 10 give the rules for the consecration of Aaron and his four sons as the first priests, since they were from the tribe of Levi. Right at the beginning two of Aaron's four sons, Nadab and Abihu, are killed by fire, as an act of God, because they have violated one of the rules. This action brings home to all that the Lord is serious about how he is to be worshipped by Israel.

The third part presents the laws of purity—what is "clean" and what is "unclean". This refers both to what is acceptable in divine worship, for example, clean and unclean animals, and to how the people should keep themselves clean because they are a "holy people" and a "royal nation". Legal purity extends to childbirth, leprosy (various diseases of the skin), and sexual relations.

The fourth part gives the rules for the Day of Atonement (Yom Kippur), the most important festival of the year. On this day atonement is made for all the people by a series of special sacrifices and ceremonies; its importance is similar to that which Christians give to the services of Holy Week. Yom Kippur is still the most important Jewish holy day of the year.

The Holiness Code (chaps. 17—26) spells out many rules for the people to observe so that they may remain in ritual purity. Some of the rules cover the sacredness of blood and sex, others concern personal conduct, priestly sanctity, how to observe the liturgical year (Pentecost, New Year's Day, and so on), holy years, sabbatical years, and jubilee years. "Holiness" has the meaning of otherness, distinctiveness, and separation from all that is ordinary or profane; so God is the one who is primarily "holy", for he is transcendent and totally other. Communion with God in the Sinai Covenant makes God's people holy. So they are set apart from the profane world and are required to live according to the Ten Commandments, that is, in a way that reflects the glory of the Lord who is in their midst.

The last part in chapter 27 deals with the laws governing release from vows that one has made to the Lord but that now cannot be fulfilled for one reason or another, in other words, laws governing what the Church would call indults or dispensations.

THEOLOGY: By his mighty hand the Lord brought his people out of the bondage of Egypt into the Promised Land. The land was his, and the people were his, for he had formed them. So in a sense they were only tenants of the land; they were caretakers, and as such they were responsible to God for how they used the land.

The book of Leviticus spells out in great detail how the people of Israel were to worship God, originally in the desert under Moses and then later in the great Temple in Jerusalem. By their daily sacrifices and worship, they gave expression to their total dependence on the Lord for their life and their livelihood. The sacrifices of animals and cereals were intended to be external signs of the inner disposition of the heart, which was not always the case, as we see from Jesus' stern denunciation of the externalism and formalism of the Scribes and Pharisees of his time.

The worship of God is serious business; failure in this regard can result in instant death, as we see in the case of Nadab and Abihu. The purpose of all these rules is to produce and maintain a holy people who have a special relationship to the all-holy Lord God.

The liturgical laws of Leviticus were provisional for the people of Israel until the final revelation that God made of himself in Christ Jesus. The Ten Commandments are universal and so binding then and always on all men; the liturgical laws of Leviticus were abolished by the sacrificial death of Jesus on Calvary—the true Lamb of God. So all the sacrifices of the Old Law were really foreshadowings or types that pointed to the fullness of worship of God in Jesus, true God and true Man, the only begotten Son of the Father.

For the modern reader, Leviticus is difficult reading unless he sees all of it as pointing ultimately to Christ and his sacrifice once and for all. However, the seriousness of it brings home to us how much God demanded of his Chosen People and should be a clear warning to us not to be casual or nonchalant in our worship of God.

One of the most profound theological treatises in the New Testament is to be found in the book of Hebrews. It is impossible to understand fully what the author is talking about when he speaks of the tabernacle, the high priest, the blood of sacrifices, and so forth, unless one is familiar with the teaching of the book of Leviticus. So the payoff for a careful study of Leviticus is a deeper understanding of the high priesthood of Jesus as it is explained in Hebrews.

OUTLINE

I. Laws governing sacrifice (1:1—7:38)

   A. Types of sacrifice: holocausts, cereal offerings, peace offerings, sin offerings, guilt offerings

   B. The priest and sacrifice (6:1—7:38)

II. The ceremony of ordination (8:1—10:20)

III. Legal purity (11:1—15:33)

REFLECTION

"*I am the* LORD *who sanctify you, who brought you out of the land of Egypt to be your God: I am the* LORD" (22:32–33).

Numbers

And the LORD spoke to Moses in the wilderness of Sinai (9:1).

PLACE IN THE BIBLE: The book of Numbers is the fourth book of the Bible. The name is taken from the census, or counting of the people, that takes place in chapters 1 and 26. The book contains thirty-six chapters.

DATE AND AUTHOR: Numbers contains many ancient traditions, some of which go back to Moses himself. But Moses is always referred to in the third person. The book was composed over a period of about one thousand years. Many later laws and liturgical norms from the time of the monarchy and beyond were retrojected by the authors back to Moses. There is a strong influence by the so-called "priestly" authors, who are concerned about the tabernacle, sacrifices, and genealogies. The final edition we now have was probably finished in the fifth century in the time of Ezra.

THEME: The theme of Numbers works on two levels: (1) It tells the story of thirty-eight years of wandering of the People of God from Sinai to the Plains of Moab just before the invasion of Canaan under Joshua; (2) on a deeper level, it is a story of how God acted in *history* to guide and protect his Chosen People from Sinai to the Jordan River.

He was always in their midst to protect them, to teach them, to help them in their difficulties, and to punish them when they rebelled against him.

SUMMARY: The story of the journey of the Chosen People from Egypt to the Promised Land was interrupted at Exodus 19. The Covenant, laws, and the book of Leviticus take place while the people are at Sinai. Numbers takes up the story again of the progress of the community of Israel from Sinai to the Plains of Moab, just prior to invading and capturing the Promised Land. The census of 600,000 men, not counting women and children, is probably the census taken up by King David in the tenth century; the numbers are then attributed to the people in the desert. For, if we count women and children, we would come up with a figure in the neighborhood of two million people out in the desert, along with flocks and herds. That is unrealistic. What the sacred author is affirming is that the promise of God to Abraham of a large progeny has been fulfilled; they are a populous and fruitful nation of twelve tribes.

The story of the march in the wilderness is interspersed with various laws and liturgical directions, parallel to many of the norms already given in Exodus and Leviticus. These may come from other oral traditions, with an ancient history going back to Moses.

The Israelites spent thirty-eight years in the area of Kadesh, which had abundant water and grazing land to support them. During that time the older generation, which refused to follow the Lord's command to go up and take possession of the Promised Land, died off and was replaced by a new generation under the leadership of Joshua and Caleb, who wanted to follow the Lord's command and occupy the land.

During that time there was much murmuring and rebellion against the leadership of Moses. Even his own sister and brother, Miriam and Aaron, turned against him. Moses, however, trusted in God and was vindicated in each case. When the Lord was angry and wanted to destroy the people and raise up a new people from Moses, Moses protested and prayed for the people. There is a good lesson here of the power of intercessory prayer.

Moses himself was guilty of a serious fault — a certain lack of faith in God. For this he was punished by the Lord in that he was not allowed to enter into the Promised Land. He was able to see it from the top of Mount Nebo, but he was not allowed to enter. What fault he committed is not perfectly clear, but it seems that he showed a certain doubt of God's promise and power when he struck the rock two times to bring forth water; the Lord had told him just to command it.

The thirty-eight years in the wilderness was a time of discipline and of educating the people about what it meant to be the People of God. He was instructing them in his ways. If they were faithful, he would reward them; if they abandoned the Covenant and sinned, he would punish them.

After thirty-eight years at Kadesh, the Lord gave the command to march north in order to conquer the land of Canaan. When they came out of Moab, east of the Dead Sea, they defeated two kings, Sihon and Og, in battle. The king of Moab, Balak, hired the prophet Balaam to come and curse Israel; he tried to do it three times, but the Lord would not let him — each time he uttered a blessing on Israel, much to the consternation and anger of Balak.

After a few other battles, they moved into the area east of the Jordan River, the site of the modern state of Jordan, and prepared for the invasion of Canaan. Three of the tribes, Reuben, Gad, and Mannasseh, persuaded Moses to let them settle on the east side of the river, with the solemn proviso that they send their warriors across the river to help their brothers subdue the land from the Canaanites. The stage was now set for the invasion under Joshua and the conquest of the first city, Jericho.

THEOLOGY: Numbers presents the priestly version of the history of Israel in the wilderness on the way from Sinai to the Plains of Moab. It is part of a continuous story that links up Exodus with what is to come in the conquest of Canaan as described in the book of Joshua.

The author does not intend to give an exact history of everything that took place; he is not writing modern precise history. His real concern is with living in history under the influence of the Lord God. He is trying to communicate to the reader the divine meaning contained in the events he relates.

The main point the sacred author wants to make is that everything related should be understood in the context of the Sinai Covenant, which was described in Exodus 19. The wise men and leaders of Israel were convinced that God reveals himself in history — in the events of everyday life. They see the hand of God behind everything.

So Numbers teaches us about the one God who acts in history. He is the living God who has chosen Israel for a special mission in the history of the world.

Here is a good summary of the *meaning* of the book:

> God dwells among his people, who are the object of his steadfast love. Man is bound to obey the Lord; disobedience will be countered by divine punishment, but God will never totally abandon his people. Numbers is a striking testimonial to the Lord's providential care of the Israelites. Despite their constant grumbling, he guided them through the desert, he sustained them with nourishment in the most barren wastes, and he led them to victory in the face of hostile forces. Despite all their recalcitrance, the Lord was able to bring them to the Promised Land. Numbers gives the assurance also that the Lord listens to the prayers of men; oftentimes Moses interceded with the Lord on behalf of Israel (see Philip King, *Old Testament Reading Guide*, ed. William G. Heidt [Collegeville, Minn.: Liturgical Press, 1960–1968], vol. 3, p. 5).

In the New Testament both Jesus and the apostles make reference to events in the book of Numbers — for example, the bronze serpent (Jn 3:14), the rebellion of Korah and its consequences (1 Cor 10:10), the prophecies of Balaam (2 Pet 2:15f.), and the water rushing forth from the rock at the touch of Moses (1 Cor 10:4) — and derive useful lessons from them.

REFLECTION

"The LORD bless you and keep you: The LORD make his face to shine upon you, and be gracious to you: The LORD lift up his countenance upon you, and give you peace" (6:24–26).

Deuteronomy

"Hear, O Israel: The LORD *our God is one* LORD*; and you shall love the* LORD *your God with all your heart, and with all your soul, and with all your might"* (6:4).

PLACE IN THE BIBLE: The book of Deuteronomy is the fifth book of the Bible and the last book of the Pentateuch. The name is derived from two Greek words: *deuteros* + *nomos* (= second law). The first law is that given by Moses in Exodus 19ff. The book contains thirty-four chapters.

DATE AND AUTHOR: Containing traditions that go back to Moses, it was probably composed in Israel, in the northern Kingdom, in the eighth century B.C. and brought to Jerusalem after the fall of the north in 721, where it was revised and finally edited by the Levites associated with the Temple.

THEME: Israel was chosen by the Lord (Yahweh) to be his people, and he made a Covenant with them. In order to be blessed and so to prosper in all ways, the people must keep his laws and statutes. They must reject all foreign gods and worship the Lord at one place, namely, Jerusalem, by offering sacrifices. The book gives expression to the joy of observing the laws of the Lord and of relying on his power to protect them. The distinctive style of the book is *oratorical*, and the author uses many set phrases over and over again to get his point across.

SUMMARY: Deuteronomy is basically a series of sermons given by Moses — sermons on the Law and Covenant as an essential part of God's salvific plan for Israel. The book is a proclamation of God's free choice of Israel and his love for it, not based on any merit on its part. The book is a moving exhortation to keep the Law. According to God's word, obedience will be rewarded and disobedience will be punished. And that is exactly what happened in Israel's later history.

A special characteristic of Deuteronomy is the command to centralize the worship of the Lord Yahweh in one place — namely, in Jerusalem. Other places of worship, such as Dan, Bethel, and Shechem, are to be abolished.

Moses' first sermon in Deuteronomy (1:1—4:43) gives a brief history of God's dealings with Israel: God's choice and love of Israel, the liberation from the slavery in Egypt, wandering in the desert, the victories on the Plains of Moab, opposite Jericho. He urges the people to keep the Ten Commandments of the Covenant, especially the First Commandment. If they do, they will prosper. If they do not, they will suffer disaster.

Moses' second sermon is the heart of Deuteronomy (4:44—28:69). He proclaims the Great Commandment to love God with all one's heart and strength (6:5) and repeats the Ten Commandments of Exodus 19. Then he states many laws governing worship and public and private life. Moses concludes with the blessings for obedience and the curses for disobedience.

Moses' third sermon repeats the main points of the previous two, with special emphasis on the blessings and curses. Again, the emphasis is on the First Commandment — avoid all idolatry. Blessings are the reward of obedience, and curses the reward of violating the Covenant.

Deuteronomy concludes with four appendices. It recounts that Joshua succeeded Moses as leader of the people. There follow the song of Moses and his blessings on the twelve tribes and the account of the death of Moses on Mount Nebo. Before he died, Moses saw the Promised Land from the other side of the Jordan River, but because of a previous fault the Lord does not allow him to enter into it.

THEOLOGY: The book of Deuteronomy offers a theological evaluation of God's dealings with Israel over a period of about seven hundred years. It recalls his gratuitous choice of Israel above all other peoples and his long-suffering kindness to his people. Moses insists, over and over again, on the importance of keeping the laws and statutes of the Covenant. The people must repudiate all foreign gods and offer worship and sacrifice to the Lord Yahweh in only one place, namely, Jerusalem.

The idea of temporal reward for keeping the Law and punishment for violating it appears often. This is a theme that runs all through the so-called Deuteronomic history —Joshua, Judges, 1 and 2 Samuel, 1 and 2 Kings. The same idea is expressed in the colorful but threatening blessings and curses.

Deuteronomy is cited explicitly in the New Testament. Jesus quotes the book three times in Matthew 4 in rejecting the three temptations of Satan. He also quotes Deuteronomy 6:5 when he answers the lawyers' question about the first and greatest commandment (see Mt 22:35–39).

OUTLINE

I. Moses' first sermon (1:1—4:43)

    A. Survey of God's past dealings with Israel

    B. Moses' exhortation to the people

II. Moses' second sermon (4:44—28:69)

    A. The commandments of the Lord

        1. The Covenant and the Ten Commandments

        2. The great Commandment of Love

    B. The Deuteronomic Law Code (12:1—26:19)

        1. Laws governing worship

        2. Laws governing the officials of Israel

        3. Criminal law

        4. Laws governing holy war

    C. Covenant ceremony at Shechem

    D. Blessings and curses (28:1–69)

III. Moses' third sermon (29:1—30:20)

    A. A Covenant appeal

REFLECTION

"I will proclaim the name of the LORD. *Ascribe greatness to our God! The Rock, his work is perfect; for all his ways are justice. A God of faithfulness and without iniquity, just and right is he"* (32:3–4).

Joshua

"The LORD your God is providing you a place of rest, and will give you this land" (1:13).

PLACE IN THE BIBLE: Joshua is the sixth book of the Bible. It follows the Pentateuch and precedes Judges. The name is taken from the main character in the book, Joshua, close associate of Moses during the forty years of wandering in the desert and then his successor as the leader of the People of God. The book contains twenty-four chapters.

DATE AND AUTHOR: The occupation of the Promised Land probably took place between 1250 and 1200 B.C. The book seems to be a compilation of reports and stories; some of the material comes from that time, but it was worked on for centuries and probably attained its present form during the time of the Deuteronomic reform in the seventh and sixth centuries B.C. It is one of the books in the part of the Bible known as the "Deuteronomic history" because it illustrates the Deuteronomic theological principle of reward for keeping the Covenant and punishment for abandoning it. The attribution of the book to Joshua himself has been abandoned by most modern scholars.

THEME: The book of Joshua tells the story of the conquest, division, and initial settlement of the land of Canaan or Palestine, which lies on the eastern coast of the Mediterranean Sea, stretches from Sinai and Egypt in the south to Lebanon in the north, and reaches east to present-day Jordan and Iraq. The Lord God had promised this land to the patriarchs, and the conquest was carried out, with the help of the Lord, in fulfillment of his promise. Joshua was the inspired leader and warrior who led the conquest and oversaw the division of the land among the twelve tribes of Israel.

SUMMARY: After the death of Moses, Joshua became the leader of the Israelites. It was his task actually to capture Canaan, eliminate the people living there, and install the twelve tribes of Israel — all of this in fulfillment of the promises made to Abraham, Isaac, and Jacob (chaps. 1 — 12). First he sent spies to reconnoiter Jericho. They were befriended and helped by Rahab, the prostitute, in return for the promise that she and her family would be spared when the city was overrun.

Just as the people crossed the Red Sea on dry land, so also, by the power of God working through the Ark of the Covenant, the waters of the Jordan River were stopped and backed up so the Israelites could cross over on dry ground. They attacked and captured Jericho. Then they went on to take the city of Ai. They were tricked by the Gibeonites into signing a treaty with them, so the Gibeonites were spared. The story is presented as a series of rapid raids both south and north that resulted in conquering most of the land, but the Israelites did not conquer all of the land, for some of the Canaanite cities were too strong for them. These were bypassed and allowed to stand.

First the Israelites had to capture the land. Next came the distribution of the land among the twelve tribes (chaps. 13—21). The tribes of Reuben, Gad, and the half-tribe of Mannasseh were assigned to the area east of the Jordan River. All the other tribes settled west of the Jordan; no land was assigned to the tribe of Levi because they were to serve the Lord and take care of tribal worship. The other tribes had the obligation to support the Levites. Five cities of refuge were designated for those guilty of the unintentional death of another to protect them from the revenge of the offended families; also, the Levites were assigned a few cities of their own, but they did not control grazing land for flocks.

At the end of the book, in chapters 23 and 24, Joshua gives two stirring sermons or exhortations in which he urges his people to be obedient to the Covenant, that is, to obey God's laws, especially with respect to idolatry and going after strange gods. At Shechem he renews the Covenant with the Lord, and all Israel joins him in this. The book closes with the account of the death of Joshua at the age of 110.

THEOLOGY: Through many stories of the conquest, the author(s) emphasize that God is *faithful*, for he had solemnly promised to give the land to the Israelites, and now it has become a reality. Also, the conquest is viewed, not as a human work, but as the work of God — one that reflects the Exodus from Egypt and the crossing of the Red Sea, for the Lord said to Joshua as he had said to Moses, "I will be with you" (1:5).

A lesson inculcated over and over again is that fidelity

to the Lord and observance of his Law are rewarded, while disobedience is severely punished. Joshua is a faithful leader in imitation of his great mentor, Moses. As such, he is the model for the kings of the future, such as David, Solomon, and Josiah.

The book of Joshua teaches that the people must listen to and obey the word of God, that they must avoid all worship of false idols, and that they must renew the Covenant with the Lord and rededicate themselves to the Lord so that he will bless them in the future and guarantee their continued possession of the land.

Joshua is not quoted in the New Testament, but the book does provide some types of New Testament personalities, especially Jesus himself and St. John the Baptist. The name "Joshua" is a variant form of "Jesus", and it means "Yahweh saves." "The manner in which Joshua leads Israel into the Promised Land and mediates the renewal of the Covenant between God and his people foreshadows how Jesus forms the new People of God through the ministry of his word and then establishes the new Covenant in his blood on the night before he dies" (Michael Duggan, *The Consuming Fire* [San Francisco: Ignatius Press, 1991], p. 165). In the broad sense of typology, Joshua's conquest of the Promised Land is a prophecy of the spiritual conquest of the world by Jesus and his Church, which is his Mystical Body.

OUTLINE

I. The conquest of Canaan (1:1—12:24)

  A. Joshua's instructions

  B. Rahab and the spies

  C. Crossing the Jordan River

  D. The capture of Jericho

  E. The capture of Ai

  F. Proclamation of the Law on Mount Ebal

  G. The pact with the Gibeonites

  H. Victories in the south and north

  I. Summary of the conquest

II. Division of the Holy Land among the twelve tribes (13:1—21:42)

  A. The Lord speaks to Joshua

  B. Division of land east and west of the Jordan

  C. Cities of refuge and Gentile cities

III. Final events and last counsels (21:43—24:33)

  A. Transjordanian tribes return to their land

  B. Joshua's exhortation to the Israelites regarding their life in the Holy Land

  C. Covenant at Shechem (24:1–28)

  D. Death of Joshua (24:29–33)

"Sun, stand thou still at Gibeon, and thou Moon in the valley of Aijalon." And the sun stood still, and the moon stayed, until the nation took vengeance on their enemies (10:12–13).

Judges

Then the Lord raised up judges, who saved them out of the power of those who plundered them (2:16).

PLACE IN THE BIBLE: Judges is the seventh book of the Bible, part of the Deuteronomic history. The name is derived from the description of the local leaders of the Israelites, who were charismatic figures and primarily military chiefs. The book, which follows Joshua and precedes Ruth, contains twenty-one chapters.

DATE AND AUTHOR: Between the occupation of the Promised Land and the coming of the first king, Saul, there was a period of about two hundred years, from 1200 to 1000 B.C. There were several charismatic leaders, like Deborah, Gideon, and Samson. Both written and oral traditions from this period were gathered together during the reign of David and in subsequent centuries. The Deuteronomic writers probably finished the book in the seventh or sixth century B.C. Thus the composition of the book took place over a period of about six hundred years.

THEME: The general theme is that fidelity to God brings blessing, while infidelity to him brings punishment and misery. God, however, is always infinitely merciful, and at the first sign of repentance he comes to the aid of his people by raising up a new judge or leader. A fourfold cycle is clearly spelled out in the book: sin, punishment, repentance, and then deliverance. It goes like this: the people fall away from the true worship of Yahweh and worship local idols; God punishes them by allowing them to be conquered by an enemy; in their suffering they recognize their sin and ask for forgiveness; in response, God raises up a new Judge, who delivers them from their enemies. Then there is peace for a while, until the next generation sins again and the cycle is repeated.

SUMMARY: Judges tells the story of what happened to the twelve tribes from the time of the conquest until the advent of the kings. The stories of the different judges offer traditions from various tribes and probably overlap, for it does not seem that the judges ruled over all the tribes — they were quite independent of one another. Samson, of course, is the most famous of the judges. The basic outlines of his life are known to people who have never read the Bible; his life story is part of Western popular culture. In addition to Samson, the main judges are Deborah, Gideon, and Jephthah.

The last chapters of the book present the view several times that "In those days there was no king in Israel, and everyone did as he pleased" (for example, 17:6; 18:1; 19:1; 21:25). It was a period in which there was no centralized government of the twelve tribes; it was more a theocracy than a kingdom. So the book leads naturally into 1 Samuel, where the story of the selection of the first king, Saul, is told.

THEOLOGY: Like the other books of the Bible, Judges is a religious treatise about God's dealings with his people. Some of the stories are not very edifying, but they do manifest a basic religious concern of the time, even though it was not very lofty. The religious life of the time appears not to be well organized, and Shiloh seems to be the religious center, even though the book does not state how it was selected. Priests and Levites make their appearance, but they do not seem to be well instructed or very effective with the people. Responsibility and punishment are more collective and community oriented than personal. A basic faith in Yahweh is present in the book, but it is imperfect. The purpose of the book is to show that the good or bad fortune of Israel depended on the obedience or disobedience of the people to God's Law, especially the First Commandment.

The one explicit reference to Judges in the New Testament is found in the Letter to the Hebrews 11:32–34, where the author praises the *faith* of the judges. The story of Samson's conception and birth (Judg 13:1–25) is similar to that of St. John the Baptist. There are many types of Mary, the Mother of Jesus, in the Old Testament. The angel greets her as he did Gideon (Judg 6:12), and Elizabeth's praise of Mary reflects Deborah's words about Jael as the "most blessed of women" (Judg 5:24; Lk 1:42).

OUTLINE

I. Introduction (1:1 — 3:6)

    A. Recalling the settlement in Canaan

    B. An overall picture of the period of the judges

II. The judges (3:7—16:31): Othniel, Ehud, Shamgar, Deborah and Barak, Gideon and Abimelech, Tola, Jair, Jephthah, Ibzan, Elon, Abdon, Samson

III. Appendices (17:1—21:25)

    A. Micah's shrine

    B. The migration of the Danites and their sanctuary

    C. The crime at Gibeah and the war against Benjamin

REFLECTION

"Hear, O kings; give ear, O princes; to the Lord *I will sing, I will make melody to the* Lord, *the God of Israel"* (5:3).

Ruth

But Ruth said, "Entreat me not to leave you or to return from following you; for where you go I will go, and where you lodge I will lodge; your people shall be my people, and your God my God" (1:16).

PLACE IN THE BIBLE: The book of Ruth is the eighth book in the Old Testament, coming after Judges and before 1 and 2 Samuel. It contains four chapters.

DATE AND AUTHOR: According to the first verse of the book, the story about Ruth takes place in the time of the judges, therefore no later than 1025 B.C. This literary masterpiece was probably written between the tenth and eighth centuries B.C. The genealogical appendix (4:18–22) was added later, probably by one of the priestly editors after the exile. Who wrote the original story is not known.

THEME: The Moabites were traditional enemies of the Israelites. Ruth, who is a Moabitess, leaves her home and pagan gods, goes with her mother-in-law, Naomi, to Bethlehem in Judah, embraces Yahweh as the only God, and seeks incorporation into the people of Israel. She marries Boaz and so becomes the great-grandmother of David, the great king and founder of the Davidic dynasty. So the author gives expression to the universal reach of God's love to all, not just to Israel, for Ruth the Moabitess by divine providence becomes an ancestor of Jesus the Messiah.

SUMMARY: Ruth is a story about an Israelite woman named Naomi who, with her husband and two sons, because of famine migrated from Bethlehem in Judah to the land of Moab on the eastern side of the Jordan river and the Dead Sea. There her husband died and left her a widow with two sons; then the two sons took Moabite wives, Orpah and Ruth. After ten years the two sons also died. Naomi decided to return to Bethlehem, and so she told the two daughters-in-law to return to their own families. Orpah did, but Ruth wanted to stay with Naomi, to worship her God and go with her to Bethlehem.

When they arrived, they had no way to support themselves, so Naomi sent Ruth out to glean barley from the fields of Boaz, a relative; this was not stealing but was allowed by the Law for widows, orphans, and the destitute. Boaz was friendly and generous to Ruth. Naomi advised Ruth to make known to Boaz that she was available as a wife, even though he was an older man. He liked the idea, but first he had to offer her to another kinsman who was more closely related to Ruth than he was. Since the closer kinsman was not interested in marriage with Ruth, he ceded his prior right to Boaz, who then married Ruth. She conceived and bore a son, whose name was Obed. In the last verses we are told that Obed became the father of Jesse, who was the father of David, the future king. So Ruth, a Gentile, was the great-grandmother of King David.

THEOLOGY: The book of Ruth presents an interesting story. It has been called a "historical novel" or historical romance. It also has the characteristics of a morality play. Ruth abandons her pagan family and country to join the people of Israel and to worship the true God, who is the God of Israel. So the book makes very clear that God's love and grace extend to those outside of Israel, even to the hated Moabites. Therefore, a key theological notion of the book is the universal love of the Lord God for all peoples. His revelation comes through Israel, but his love is directed to all his children. Another idea is *fidelity*. Ruth remains faithful to her mother-in-law in good times and in bad.

The book is also concerned with genealogy. One of the main points is to show that one of the ancestors of King David was a Gentile and Moabite woman. This reaffirms the theme of universalism in the book. There is no reason to doubt the basic historical accuracy of the story, since it deals with historical persons, namely, the ancestors of David, who became king about the year 1000 B.C. The story illustrates God's fidelity to his people and that he blesses those who trust in him.

By the working of God's providence, Ruth the Moabitess becomes the great-grandmother of David. St. Matthew mentions Ruth in the genealogy of Christ because she participated in the plan of God as one who foreshadows Mary of Nazareth, chosen by God to be the Mother of his only Son. Just as God chose a Gentile to be the great-grandmother of David, so he defied human expectation by having his Son born of a virgin.

I. Naomi and Ruth move from Moab to Bethlehem (1:1–22)

    A. The hardships: Migration, famine, and death

    B. Ruth's oath of fidelity to Naomi

II. Ruth gleans barley in the field of Boaz (2:1–23)

    A. In the field: Ruth and Boaz

    B. At home: Ruth and Naomi

III. Ruth meets Boaz at the threshing floor (3:1–18)

    A. At home: Ruth and Naomi

    B. At the threshing floor: Ruth and Boaz

    C. At home: Ruth and Naomi

IV. Boaz marries Ruth: The birth of Obed (4:1–17)

    A. At the city gate: Boaz, the kinsman

    B. In the town: Naomi's joy at the birth of a grandson

V. Genealogical appendix: David, the grandson of Obed (4:18–22) (see *The Consuming Fire*, by Michael Duggan, [San Francisco: Ignatius Press, 1991] p. 458).

REFLECTION

"The LORD recompense you for what you have done, and a full reward be given you by the LORD, the God of Israel, under whose wings you have come to take refuge!" (2:12).

1 and 2 Samuel

The prophet Nathan to David: *"Your house and your kingdom shall be made sure for ever before me; your throne shall be established for ever"* (2 Sam 7:16).

PLACE IN THE BIBLE: The first and second books of Samuel are the ninth and tenth books of the Bible. They come after the book of Ruth and before the two books of Kings. First Samuel contains thirty-one chapters, and 2 Samuel contains twenty-four chapters.

DATE AND AUTHOR: It is probable that most of the two books was written by the court scribe(s) during the reigns of King David and King Solomon, from about 1000 B.C. to 930 B.C. Later editorial refinements were probably added by the Deuteronomist in the seventh or sixth century B.C. The names of the author or authors are not known.

THEME: The theme of the two books of Samuel is the origin of the Davidic monarchy. It begins with Samuel, who is both a judge, in the sense of the book of Judges, and also a prophet, in the sense that will become common later on. At the direction of the Lord, Samuel anoints Saul as the first king; Saul is not faithful, so then Samuel anoints David to replace him. There is conflict between Saul and David. Saul dies in battle, and then David is named king in Hebron. Most of the second book deals with the reign of David and the problems he had in government and in his family. With the death of his son Absalom, the way is open for the appointment of Solomon as David's successor—this will be narrated in the next book, 1 Kings.

SUMMARY: The two books of Samuel begin with the miraculous conception of Samuel by his previously sterile mother and then his divine call to be a judge/prophet. They tell the story of the change of Israel from a twelve-tribe confederacy, in which the tribes were independent, to a monarchy in which power from God was now exercised by a human ruler—the king. The period covered is approximately one hundred years from about 1070 to 970 B.C. The twelve tribes are harassed by their enemies and are disorganized, so they plead with Samuel to give them a king. By divine guidance he chooses Saul of the tribe of Benjamin. Saul is a great warrior who defeats the enemies of Israel, but he is moody and selfish. He does not follow God's will, so Samuel is directed to anoint David as king. Saul persecutes David and tries to kill him, until he loses a battle and kills himself by falling on his own sword. The first part of book one is about Samuel and Saul; the second half relates the conflict between Saul and David.

The second book of Samuel is about David, his rule over Israel, his family problems, which are a result of his sin with Bathsheba, and the question of the succession to the kingship. At the end of the book, after the death of David's favorite son, Absalom, the stage is set for Solomon to succeed his father as king of Israel. This is related in 1 Kings 1—2. These books contain some of the most vivid and memorable historical writing in the Old Testament: the call of Samuel; Saul, Jonathan and David, Goliath, Bathsheba and Uriah, Absalom, and David's mourning for his dead son.

THEOLOGY: Yahweh is the Lord of history. He is the main agent in the two books of Samuel, working his will through fallible and sinful human beings. The basic idea is that God gave the Israelites what they wanted, namely, a king like the kings in the tribes around them. In the time of the judges, Yahweh was king — it was a type of theocracy, but the people were not satisfied with that. They wanted a human king. So God gave it to them. There is a train of thought in the first book that is definitely opposed to the kingship; there is also another train of thought that is highly favorable to the Davidic kings. The author was probably looking at the kingship from different points of view.

David is the main character, and everything leads up to his being named king. Theologically, the most important passage is found in 2 Samuel 7, in which God promises David that his descendants will rule forever. The prophecy of Nathan found there is the basis of the Messianism that runs through the rest of the Bible and finds its fulfillment in the birth, life, death, and Resurrection of Jesus the Christ, or Messiah (see Acts 2:30; Heb 1:5; Ps 2:7). Even though most of the kings who succeeded David for about four hundred years were not very good, God never totally rejected them. One of Jesus' major titles is "Son of David". He is the "seed", as St. Paul says, who is the fulfillment of the promises to Israel through Noah, Abraham, Isaac, and Jacob.

The two books contain a clear theological statement about the effects of sin on a family. David's sin of adultery with Bathsheba and the murder of her husband Uriah in order to cover up the adultery and conception of a child bring upon him and his family a punishment of disorder and violence. For Amnon rapes his half-sister Tamar; Absalom, her brother, kills Amnon; Absalom rebels against his father and tries to kill him; Absalom is killed by Joab.

In the New Testament, the narrative about the conception of Samuel (1 Sam 1:1—2:11) is reflected in St. Luke's account of the Annunciation to Mary. And Hannah's song of praise and thanksgiving in the sanctuary at Shiloh foreshadows Mary's Magnificat in Luke 1:46–55.

OUTLINE

I. Eli, Samuel, Saul, and David (1 Sam 1:1—31:13)

   A. Eli and Samuel

   B. Establishment of the monarchy in Israel; Samuel and Saul

   C. Saul and David (13:1—31:13)

II. David King of Israel and Judah (2 Sam 1:1—24:25)

   A. Turmoil and strife in the house of David (9:1—20:26)

   B. Appendices: The lessons of history (21:1—24:25)

      1. Revenge on the house of Saul

      2. David's heroes

REFLECTION

"There is none holy like the LORD, *there is none besides thee; there is no rock like our God"* (1 Sam 2:2).

1 and 2 Kings

The Lord said to Solomon: *"Behold, I give you a wise and discerning mind, so that none like you has been before you and none like you shall arise after you"* (1 Kings 3:12).

PLACE IN THE BIBLE: The first and second book of Kings follow the two books of Samuel and precede the two books of Chronicles. First Kings contains twenty-two chapters, and 2 Kings contains twenty-five chapters.

DATE AND AUTHOR: The first version of 1 and 2 Kings may have been composed under King Josiah (640–609 B.C.) by the Deuteronomists, a few years before the fall of Jerusalem in 587 B.C. The final version was completed in exile about 550 B.C., because book two recounts the release from captivity of King Jehoiakim in 562 B.C. The sources used were the chronicles of the kings of Israel and Judah, plus some Temple history and two accounts of the lives of the prophets Elijah and Elisha.

THEME: The theme of the two books of Kings is the history of the monarchy from Solomon in 970 B.C. to the destruction of Jerusalem in 587 B.C. After the death of Solomon, the united kingdom is divided into the northern Kingdom of Israel and the southern Kingdom of Judah. Each king, both in the north and in the south, is judged by the author(s) according to whether or not he abided by the Covenant of the Lord with Israel, especially as this relates to the centralization of worship in Jerusalem in the Temple — the worship of Yahweh, and not the idol worship that was common among the local inhabitants who were called "Canaanites".

SUMMARY: As indicated in the outline below, the two books are conveniently divided into three parts — Solomon's reign over a united kingdom, after his death the division into the northern Kingdom of Israel and the southern Kingdom of Judah, and finally the small kingdom of Judah from 722 B.C. to the fall of Jerusalem. The first eleven chapters report the death of David and Solomon's succession to the throne with the help of his mother, Bathsheba. Here we learn about Solomon's wisdom, his wealth, how he built the magnificent Temple in Jerusalem, his fame, and his faults because of his weakness for foreign women.

The second part narrates the story of the two kingdoms from the death of Solomon in about 930 B.C. to the destruction of Israel by the Assyrians in 722 B.C. The judgment of the author is that most of the kings were not good because they either encouraged or permitted pagan idol worship in their territory. In this account we find two cycles of miracle stories surrounding the great early prophets Elijah and Elisha.

The third part recounts what happened in Judah from 722 to 587 B.C., when the Babylonians conquered the country and destroyed Jerusalem and the Temple. Two of the kings are praised for their promotion of the worship of the true God, namely, Hezekiah and Josiah.

THEOLOGY: While reading these two books, it is important to remember that the author is writing *theology* primarily, though it is based on real history. His primary concern is God's activity in history and the revelation of his holy will. He is not writing secular, objective history. He is trying to prove a theological point, namely, that the fall of Israel in the north in 722 B.C. and the catastrophic destruction of Jerusalem and the Temple in the south in 587 B.C. were the result of the Chosen People's infidelity to the Covenant with Yahweh.

The author reminds his readers often of the divine promise to David in 2 Samuel 7 that his kingdom would last forever. God always keeps his promises. At the time of the writing, the Davidic kingdom had been destroyed, and there seemed to be no hope of a restoration. What was one to think of the divine promise to David? The author wants to convince his post-exilic audience in 550 B.C. that they should have hope, that God will fulfill his promise. That promise was abundantly fulfilled in the coming of Jesus Christ, the Son of God and the Son of David — the Redeemer of all mankind.

The theological message of the book can be expressed in three propositions: (1) the catastrophe can be explained by the continual infidelity of the kings of Israel and Judah to both the Covenant and the Temple; (2) the word of God is infallible and always attains its end. Thus in the two books there are more than forty prophetic prediction-fulfillment stories; (3) the promise made by God to David in 2 Samuel 7 that his dynasty would be eternal is a promise that must be fulfilled because God is faithful.

Also, Elijah and Elisha combine their preaching with many miracles, and in this they foreshadow Jesus, who announces the Kingdom of God in power and miracles. During his ministry many people thought that Jesus was a new Elijah (see Mk 6:15; 8:28). His prophecies of the destruction of the Temple and of Jerusalem remind us of the predictions of the prophets in the two books of Kings. To help us understand the Lord's plan of salvation, St. Paul in his Letter to the Romans appeals to the Lord's promise to Elijah on Mount Horeb (Rom 11:2).

OUTLINE

I. Solomon's reign: The united kingdom (1 Kings 1:1—11:43)

II. Israel and Judah: Divided kingdom (1 Kings 12:1—2 Kings 17:41)

    A. Revolt of the northern tribes

    B. Kings of Israel and Judah

    C. The Elijah cycle (1 Kings 17:1 to 2 Kings 1:18)

    D. The Elisha cycle (2 Kings 2:1—8:29)

    E. Kings from Jehu to Samaria's destruction (2 Kings 9:1—17:41)

III. Kingdom of Judah (2 Kings 18:1—25:30); King Hezekiah and his reform to the destruction of Jerusalem in 587 B.C. and the aftermath

Prayer of Solomon at the dedication of the Temple: *"O LORD, God of Israel, there is no God like thee, in heaven above or on earth beneath, keeping covenant and showing steadfast love to thy servants who walk before thee with all their heart; who hast kept with thy servant David my father what thou didst declare to him; yea, thou didst speak with thy mouth, and with thy hand hast fulfilled it this day"* (1 Kings 8:23–24).

1 and 2 Chronicles

Give thanks to the LORD, for his steadfast love endures for ever (2 Chron 20:21).

PLACE IN THE BIBLE: The first and second book of Chronicles follow the two books of Kings and cover much of the same material, but from a different point of view. They precede the book of Ezra. First Chronicles contains twenty-nine chapters, and 2 Chronicles has thirty-six chapters.

DATE AND AUTHOR: The author gives a genealogy of the descendants of David down to about 400 B.C., so he must have written after that. The two books, which were originally one in the Hebrew Bible, were therefore written about 400 to 350, with perhaps some editorial revisions added later. The author is called the "Chronicler", but his true identity is not known. Because of his preoccupation with the Temple, genealogies, and Temple music, he probably was a Levite cantor associated with the Temple liturgy.

THEME: The theme of the two books of Chronicles is the Messianic promise made to David by the prophet Nathan in 2 Samuel 7. In the view of the Chronicler (the author), God's promise to David is infallibly valid, even though he does not know how it will be realized. Over a four-hundred-year period he judges each king of Judah in the light of David, and he finds most of them failures because they did not promote the worship of the Lord as David did and as they should have done. The two whom he does praise are Hezekiah and Josiah in the seventh century B.C., shortly before the destruction of Jerusalem in 587 B.C. The Chronicler ignores the kings of the north in Israel because they fell away from the true worship of Yahweh with the first king, Jeroboam. So for him they simply do not count.

The Chronicler is especially interested in the centralization of the worship at the Temple in Jerusalem. He sees all other worship, especially at Bethel and Dan in the north, as violations of the Covenant God made with David.

The two books offer a rereading of the books of Samuel and Kings from a special theological point of view. So the books contain a special type of theological history; some scholars refer to them as a type of "midrash", that is, a retelling of the biblical story with certain alterations in order to bring out the hidden meaning and to make some practical applications to the religious/political situation of the author at the time of composition.

SUMMARY: In a summary fashion, the Chronicler retells the story of the Bible from the creation of the world up to his own time, which was about 400 B.C. He gives genealogies of many different individuals, from Adam to King David. The real history begins in 1 Chronicles 10 with the story of David and then Solomon, followed by all the kings of the southern Kingdom of Judah from 930 B.C. to the disaster of 587 B.C. He goes into much detail about the reigns of David and Solomon, but he idealizes them and does not mention their sins, such as David's adultery with Bathsheba or Solomon's setting up altars to pagan gods in order to please his foreign wives. He uses regular formulas to introduce each of the kings of Judah, telling who his father was, how old he was when he started to rule, how many years he ruled, and where he was buried after his death. Each king is judged according to how well he imitated his ancestor David. Most of them are condemned for failing to abide by the Davidic Covenant. All of the kings from Rehoboam, the son of Solomon, to the end of the exile in 538 are covered in the last part of the second book of Chronicles. The last two verses of chapter 36 bring in an aspect of hope for the future, so the history closes on a positive note.

THEOLOGY: While reading these two books, it is important to remember that the author is offering us, not scientific modern history, but a theology of history based on a few strong theological convictions. He covers much of the same matter contained in the books of Samuel and Kings, but he does it from a different perspective from that of the Deuteronomist author(s) of those books.

The first thing to note is that for the Chronicler, history begins with David and his Covenant with the Lord Yahweh. In addition, the Lord ordered him to gather materials for the building of the Temple of Jerusalem. David drew up the plans but left the actual construction of the Temple to his son Solomon, who succeeded him on the throne of Judah. So the relation between David and the Temple and the proper worship in the Temple is a key point in the theology of Chronicles. The author idealizes

David and Solomon; he omits their faults and speaks only of their virtues.

Secondly, there is a strong note of divine retribution in this theology of history. Simply put, it comes to this: The few kings who promoted the true worship of Yahweh in Jerusalem and destroyed all the pagan temples in the country were rewarded by God. Those kings who failed to do that (and that was most of them) were punished by God sooner or later. A few started out as good kings but then ended as bad ones.

Thirdly, the author gives prominence to the Levites as musicians and servers in the Temple. This is one of his main preoccupations. Many scholars conclude from this that the Chronicler was a member of that group.

The final two verses end on a note of hope — the restoration of the Temple at the order of the Persian emperor, Cyrus. The author is convinced that God will keep his promise to David of a successor and an eternal kingdom. He hints that this fulfillment will come in the spiritual order rather than in the order of politics and earthly government.

The books of Chronicles are not quoted in the New Testament. But the author's emphasis on the importance of the Temple prepares our minds for the relation between Jesus and the Temple. St. Paul speaks about both the community and the body of each Christian as being a "temple of the Holy Spirit", that is, both should be treated with the same reverence that the Chronicler showed toward the holy Temple in Jerusalem. And we should not forget that Jesus pointed to his own body and said, "Destroy this temple and in three days I will raise it up", thus establishing a connection between the "temple" of his body and the Resurrection.

REFLECTION

O give thanks to the LORD, call on his name, make known his deeds among the peoples! Sing to him, sing praises to him, tell of all his wonderful works! Glory in his holy name; let the hearts of those who seek the LORD rejoice! (1 Chron 16:8–10).

Ezra and Nehemiah

Cyrus, king of Persia, says: *"Whoever is among you of all his people, may his God be with him, and let him go up to Jerusalem, which is in Judah, and rebuild the house of the LORD, the God of Israel—he is the God who is in Jerusalem"* (Ezra 1:3).

PLACE IN THE BIBLE: The two books of Ezra and Nehemiah, which were originally one book in the Hebrew Bible and in the Septuagint, follow 1 and 2 Chronicles and precede the book of Tobit. They belong to the historical books of the Old Testament. Ezra contains ten chapters, and Nehemiah contains thirteen chapters.

DATE AND AUTHOR: The period covered by the two books is from the return from exile in 538 B.C. to about 410 B.C. Most scholars date them shortly after the year 400. The author is the same scholar who wrote the two books of Chronicles, since the four books make up one complete unit of Jewish history. Some scholars think the author was Ezra, but there is not conclusive evidence to support this.

THEME: The theme of these two books is the restoration of the Jewish religion, based on the Law of Moses and the worship of Yahweh in the Temple in Jerusalem. Both books are written with the assumption that the reader knows about the Covenant with Moses and David, that he knows about the history of the kings from David to the destruction of Jerusalem in 587 B.C., that he knows about the painful exile of the Jewish people in Babylon from 587 to 538 B.C., when Cyrus the Persian allowed them to return home from Babylon.

Key elements of the restoration are the rebuilding of the Temple, which was completed in 515 B.C., the rebuilding of the walls of Jerusalem under Nehemiah during the years 445 to 433 B.C., and the establishment by Ezra and Nehemiah of the Torah, or the Law of Moses, as the law of the land. A unifying theme that runs through the books is that Israel has been chosen by God to be a theocratic people whose hope of survival does not lie in military strength but in fidelity to their God and to the Torah.

SUMMARY: After destroying the Babylonian empire, Cyrus the Persian in 538 B.C. gave permission to the Jewish exiles to return to their homeland. The books of Ezra and Nehemiah are about that return and what happened during the next hundred years. Jerusalem was a mass of ruins, like Cologne and Berlin after World War II. The first thing the returnees did was to rebuild the Temple in Jerusalem on the site of the first Temple of Solomon. The job was completed and the Temple dedicated in 515 B.C.

But religious practice among the Jews was at a low ebb. Ezra, the wise scribe, was sent by the Persian emperor to help restore the Jewish religion and practice, including the worship and singing in the Temple. The two books show a special interest in the roles and functions of priests, Levites, singers, and other Temple personnel.

In 445 B.C. the Persian emperor sent a Jewish nobleman

named Nehemiah to organize Judea politically and to rebuild the city of Jerusalem, especially the walls, which, up to that time, had not been restored. He encountered a lot of opposition from some of the people who had been left in the land by the Babylonians, especially the Samaritans. The latter did not want to see the resurgence of a strong Jerusalem.

Ezra and Nehemiah worked together to restore Israel both religiously and politically. Ezra proclaimed the Law of Moses, and Nehemiah saw to it that it was observed. For example, they forbade marriage with non-Jews and dissolved the marriages that had taken place previously.

THEOLOGY: The two books do recount history from 538 to 410 B.C., but they are not a work of scientific history in the modern sense. They are primarily a work of *theology*; they continue the story told in the previous historical books and, like them, focus primarily on God's dealings with Israel or on how God acts in history. As we saw in the Deuteronomic history, there is emphasis on the connection between sin and punishment, on the one hand, and fidelity and reward, on the other.

The author is telling his contemporaries (and us) that Israel's future depends on faithful worship in the Temple in Jerusalem, the only place of legitimate sacrifice, and on cutting off contact with corrupting alien influences, such as that of the Philistines, Samaritans, and Egyptians.

Ezra and Nehemiah gave cohesion and spiritual unity to their people, which saved them from disintegration under the strong influence of Hellenism that followed in the next century. In fact, Ezra was the founder of Judaism as it existed in the time of Jesus Christ and as it persists even to this day. That which identifies the Jewish way of life is fidelity to the Law of Moses. Both Ezra and Nehemiah contributed to the establishment of Judaism. Nehemiah was the builder of the wall of Jerusalem, and he was the architect of administrative reform. Ezra was the religious reformer who succeeded in making the Torah, or Law of Moses, the constitutional basis of the restored Jewish community in Jerusalem and the surrounding territory.

There are no direct references in the New Testament to Ezra-Nehemiah, but the two men are important because they were the real creators of the Judaism of the Scribes, Pharisees, and Sadducees that was the cultural milieu into which Jesus of Nazareth was born and lived. It was also the culture out of which the Christian Church grew and spread to the rest of the world. So we Christians also are indebted to the two men. Finally, the religious zeal of Ezra-Nehemiah persists to the present day in Orthodox Judaism.

OUTLINE

I. Return of the exiles from Babylon to Judea (Ezra 1—2)

A. Rebuilding the Temple in Jerusalem (Ezra 3—6)

B. Mission of Ezra and his reforms (Ezra 7—10)

II. Rebuilding the walls of Jerusalem; opposition encountered and overcome by Nehemiah and his followers (Neh 1—7)

A. Ezra teaches from the Book of the Law (Neh 8—9)

B. The transformation of Jerusalem under Nehemiah (Neh 10—13)

REFLECTION

"Stand up and bless the LORD your God from everlasting to everlasting. Blessed be thy glorious name which is exalted above all blessing and praise" (Neh 9:5).

Tobit

"Righteous art thou, O Lord; all thy deeds and all thy ways are mercy and truth, and thou dost render true and righteous judgment for ever" (3:2).

PLACE IN THE BIBLE: The book of Tobit is placed in the historical books and comes after Nehemiah and before Judith. The book contains fourteen chapters.

DATE AND AUTHOR: The most likely date is about 200 B.C. It was probably composed in Aramaic in Jerusalem. The identity of the author is not known.

THEME: God's providence is with us every day and every hour, whether we recognize it or not; God blesses families who remain faithful to him while living in the pagan world. The righteous and believing man should be patient in times of trouble, confident that God will deliver him. God protects and rewards the man who observes the Law and practices works of mercy such as almsgiving, burying the dead, prayer of thanksgiving to God.

SUMMARY: Tobit is a pious Jew who is deported from Israel to Nineveh in Assyria after the fall of Samaria in 722 B.C. There he is persecuted for practicing the good works of a pious man, such as burying the dead. One night he returns home after burying a dead man and cannot enter the house because he is unclean, so he sleeps outside against the wall of the house. Bird droppings fall on his eyes, and he is blinded. He accepts this in patience. At the same time, far away in Ecbatana in Persia, Sarah, a young relative, is afflicted by the demon Asmodeus, who causes the death of seven husbands in a row. Like Tobit, she prays that God will take her life from her. Thinking he will die soon, Tobit sends his son Tobias to collect a debt from his kinsman Gabael, which he intends to give to his son as his inheritance. Tobias meets the angel Raphael, whom he thinks is his cousin Azarias, and Raphael agrees to accompany him on the journey to Rages. Tobias catches a big fish, and Raphael tells him how to use the fish to cure both Sarah and Tobit, his father. Tobias falls in love with Sarah, marries her, and drives out the demon; then he returns home and cures his father's blindness with the gall of the fish. Raphael reveals who he is and refuses any reward. Tobit sings a song of praise and thanksgiving to God and prophesies a glorious future for Jerusalem.

THEOLOGY: The book of Tobit is an edifying domestic tale about a pious Jew who believes in God, diligently observes the Law of Moses, and is a model family man. The story appears to be a historical account, but the mixed-up historical and geographic facts indicate that the author does not intend to present factual history as we understand it. The book is more like one of Jesus' parables; there may be some basis in history for such a family experience, but we do not know what it is. So the book of Tobit is a wisdom book; that is, it offers instruction and encouragement to the reader on how to live in relation to God and to one's fellow men. Theological points to look for in the book are: (1) God is nearer to us than we think, and he is ready to assist us if we remain faithful to him; (2) love for God must be shown in virtuous deeds and not just in words; (3) God rewards filial piety; (4) we should think highly of burying the dead properly, remaining chaste before marriage, being faithful to one's wife or husband, prayer, fasting, and almsgiving; (5) finally, the book offers an advanced angelology — more developed than anything previously found in the Old Testament. Here we meet a devil, Asmodeus, who harasses human beings, and a good angel, Raphael, who guides, protects, and assists Tobias. Both are presented as personal beings and not just as impersonal extensions of the power of God.

The book of Tobit is not quoted explicitly in the New Testament, but the man Tobit exemplifies the manner of life typical of the "just" who depend on the Lord to meet all their needs. In this sense, he is a precursor of Zechariah and Elizabeth, of Simeon and Anna, and also of St. Joseph. Some of Tobit's instructions to his son about charity and almsgiving were taken up later by Jesus and developed further. Tobit begins a tradition that later develops into the Golden Rule, when he says to his son, "and what you hate, do not do to any one" (4:15; see Mt 7:12).

REFLECTION

"Blessed art thou, O God of our fathers, and blessed be thy holy and glorious name for ever. Let the heavens and all thy creatures bless thee" (8:5).

Judith

God is not like man, to be threatened, nor like a human being, to be won over by pleading (8:16).

PLACE IN THE BIBLE: The book of Judith comes after Tobit and before Esther. The book contains sixteen chapters.

DATE AND AUTHOR: Although the story takes place during the time of the Assyrian domination of the Near East, the ideas and language indicate a date closer to about 100 B.C. The author was a master storyteller, but his identity is not known.

THEME: God works mysteriously in history through the agency of human beings, both good and bad. The example of Judith teaches us that trust in God, piety, prayer, worship of God and obedience to his Commandments result in divine protection and salvation from one's enemies, no matter how powerful they might seem to be according to the judgment of the world.

SUMMARY: The historical setting presented by the author does not square with recorded history, so this is an indication that the author is not writing history, at least not in the sense in which we understand it. The story goes like this: Nebuchadnezzar, king of Assyria, decides to invade Israel because it refused to help him in his war with the Medes. He sends his general Holofernes with an army of 120,000 soldiers and 12,000 cavalry to the west. They camp near Bethulia in Israel (there is no record of any city there of that name). The Israelites refuse to surrender. Achior the Ammonite explains to Holofernes that he cannot defeat the Israelites unless they have sinned against their God; in this he functions as a prophet. Holofernes takes this as treason, and so he sends Achior to Bethulia to perish (as he thinks) with all its inhabitants when he captures it. Holofernes besieges Bethulia and captures the water supply. Judith, a young widow of Bethulia, argues with the elders against surrender, urges trust in God, and promises to deliver the city. Judith prays before entering the camp of Holofernes; she flatters him and wins his affection because of her outstanding beauty and grace. Holofernes invites Judith to a sumptuous banquet with him alone in his tent; he drinks too much wine, and then she cuts off his head with his own sword, which seems to be an allusion to David and Goliath. Judith and her maid take the head in a sack to Bethulia and show it to the elders. Seeing this, Achior is converted to Israel and the true God. Then the Israelites attack the leaderless Assyrians and defeat them utterly. The story ends with a canticle of Judith. She lives in honor and dies still a widow at the ripe old age of 105.

THEOLOGY: There may be a historical basis for the story, but we do not know that for sure. It depends on the literary form of Judith. Is the book of Judith intended to be history? Or is it more like a parable or a historical romance or a short story that teaches some lessons about the Jewish faith? The names and historical data given are all mixed up and do not fit any period of Israelite history; this is a hint that we are not dealing with history such as we find in the books of Samuel and Kings. Let us say that it is a historical romance, with perhaps a basis in history that is unknown to us.

The story of Judith has tremendous appeal because it dramatizes the confrontation between faith in the true God and the powers of this world in every age. There is more than just a military conquest at stake, for Holofernes intends to destroy the Temple in Jerusalem and to force the Israelites to abandon the worship of Yahweh, the true God, and to worship a mere man, Nebuchadnezzar, and the gods of the Gentiles. So underlying the story are the questions: Who is the true God, and which God created the world and rules history? The point in the book of Judith is that the God of Israel is the true God and that he protects those who recognize and worship him, such as Judith and the people of her town. The cult of Nebuchadnezzar, like the later cult of the Caesars in Rome, represents the recurring heresy of the human race when it worships man as God (see Gen 3:5).

What saves Bethulia, Jerusalem, and all Israel, in this story, is the faith, prayer, and obedience to the Law practiced by a young, beautiful widow by the name of Judith (which means, in Hebrew, "Jewess"). Trusting completely in the Lord, she uses her beauty and her wisdom to defeat the mighty Holofernes and his Gentile army. Judith's wisdom comes from her trust in God and from her firm determination to submit herself to God in all circumstances. Her strength and courage come from her faith and obedience. So her story demonstrates how God uses the weak things of this world to overcome the mighty (see 13:15). There is a powerful lesson here for everyone who reads the book of Judith with faith and understanding.

In the context of the whole Bible, Judith is a type of the Blessed Virgin Mary. As a model of faith, she foreshadows Mary insofar as she submits herself to the will of God for the sake of her people. She is a model of true Judaism, just as Mary is a model of the Church.

OUTLINE

REFLECTION

"You are the exaltation of Jerusalem, you are the great glory of Israel, you are the great pride of our nation" (15:9).

Esther

"The Lord has saved his people; the Lord has delivered us from all these evils" (10:9).

PLACE IN THE BIBLE: The book of Esther is placed after Judith and before the book of Job. The book contains ten chapters in the Hebrew text; another six chapters were added in the Greek version in the Septuagint.

DATE AND AUTHOR: The Hebrew text probably comes from about 400 B.C. The Greek additions and the final text as we now have it came from the post-Maccabean period about 125 B.C. The identity of the authors is not known.

THEME: The main theme of the book is the providence of God, who watches over his Chosen People and saves them from annihilation through two human agents, Queen Esther and her cousin/foster father, Mordecai. The purpose of the book seems to be to give an explanation, based on God's intervention in history on behalf of his people, for the Jewish feast of Purim. Secondary themes are the superiority of the wisdom of Israel over that of the Gentiles and also a lesson on how Jewish believers should conduct themselves when they live in a pagan, often hostile culture.

SUMMARY: The book is named for a beautiful Jewish woman, Esther, who rose from obscurity to become the Queen of Persia some time after the fall of Babylon in 538 B.C. The story begins when the king of Persia, Ahasuerus (Greek: Xerxes), decides to put away his queen, Vashti, because of her insubordination. Another queen is sought among all the beautiful maidens of the empire, and the Hebrew maiden Hadassa, cousin of Mordecai, is chosen. They give her the Persian name of Esther. Her uncle finds out about a conspiracy against the life of the king and reveals it to him through Esther. But Mordecai is hated by the grand vizier, or chief minister of state, Haman, because he will not bow down to him. So Haman, out of hatred of the Jews, gets the king to sign a decree stating that all Jews are to be executed on a certain day. Determined to get rid of Mordecai, he erects a scaffold seventy-five feet in height on which to hang his enemy.

Mordecai, however, asks Esther to appeal to the king on behalf of her people; in order to do this, she has to take her life into her hands. But through prayer and fasting she wins the favor of the king, obviously helped in this by the power of God, who is not mentioned in the Hebrew account of the story. Esther makes her appeal at a banquet that she prepares for the king and for Haman.

When the king grants Esther's request at the banquet, she reveals that Haman is the enemy of the Jews. At this, Haman throws himself at the feet of Esther to plead for mercy. The king interprets this as indecent and orders Haman to be executed on the scaffold he has prepared for Mordecai. The king then issues another decree giving the Jews permission to kill all their enemies in the empire.

This great victory is celebrated on the feast of Purim, and Mordecai replaces Haman as the grand vizier of the empire.

To what extent the book has a historical base is hard to say. Many modern Scripture experts consider it a wisdom story or a "historical romance", that is, more as a parable than factual history. But one should not lightly dismiss all historical foundations for this edifying story.

THEOLOGY: A few distinctions should be made between the theology of the Hebrew shorter version and the Greek longer version. The name of God is not mentioned in the Hebrew text, but the underlying idea is that God's providence is working in history to preserve his Chosen People; it is often hidden and unnoticed, but it is there. There is a certain similarity between the rise of Esther to be queen and the rise of Joseph in the court of Pharaoh in Egypt in Exodus and the rise of Daniel in the court in Babylon. The theological idea here is that God is watching out for his own people, especially when they are faithful to him. Also, he answers the prayers for help of those Jews who trust in him and keep his Covenant.

The Greek longer version of Esther mentions God in many places and makes explicit what is only implicit in the Hebrew version.

In addition to the idea of divine providence, the book also instills the idea that prayer and fidelity to the Lord are efficacious. God will never abandon those who trust in him. Further, the book also offers advice to Jews anywhere in the world about how they should conduct themselves when they live in the midst of a hostile cultural environment. The book gives a theological rationale, based on salvation history, for the Jewish feast of Purim.

There are no direct quotes from the book of Esther in the New Testament, but there may be an allusion to it in the words of King Herod to the young dancer Salome, when he tells her at the banquet, "I will give you anything you ask, even half my kingdom" (Mk 6:23; see Esther 5:3, 6; 7:2).

OUTLINE

I. Prologue: Mordecai's dream (11:2—12:6)

II. King Ahasuerus names Esther Queen of Persia (1:1—2:23)

III. Haman: Threatens oppression of the Jews (3:1—7:10)

    A. Edict for the annihilation of the Jews (3:1–15)

    B. Plans and prayers of Esther and Mordecai (4:1–17)

    C. Esther's audience with the king (5:1–14)

    D. The outcome for Mordecai and Haman (6:1—7:10)

IV. The guarantee of Jewish civil rights (8:1—10:3)

    A. Mordecai replaces Haman (8:1–17)

    B. The Feast of Purim (9:1–32)

    C. Conclusion: Mordecai's greatness (10:1–3)

V. Epilogue: Recalling Mordecai's dream (10:4–13)

VI. The Greek scribal signature (11:1)

REFLECTION

"O God, whose might is over all, hear the voice of the despairing, and save us from the hands of evildoers. And save me from my fear!" (14:19).

Wisdom in the Old Testament

A major section of the Old Testament is composed of what are known as the "wisdom books". Wisdom runs through most of the books in the Old Testament, but it is found in a concentrated form in the following: Proverbs, Job, Ecclesiastes, Sirach, Wisdom, Song of Solomon, and some psalms.

What does wisdom mean in the Old Testament? It is a very rich concept that grew in content as the centuries passed. Basically it means: knowledge of human relations and how to deal with others—wife, children, parents, public officials, business associates. In this sense it is very *practical*, for it teaches one how to relate to others without offending them and to promote one's own self-interest. In a deeper sense, the wise person is one who fears God, lives in harmony with him, and obeys his law. A recurring refrain in these books is found in the statement: "The fear of the Lord is the beginning of wisdom" (Ps 111:10). "Fear" in this context does not mean trepidation and anxiety but rather awe and respect before the majesty of Almighty God. In this sense it is close to what we mean by "love" and is sometimes called "filial fear".

Practical wisdom was the result of experience and observation of the human scene. The ancients believed that wisdom in this sense could be taught to the young by their parents and by older people who had seen much of life—both good and evil. In some passages, for example, in Leviticus and 1 Kings, wisdom means skill in making things, like that of goldsmiths, carpenters, architects, and engineers of all sorts. Some passages regard these skills also as gifts of God. In this sense also God is said to be all-wise because he created the heavens and the earth. In other passages wisdom has a moral dimension, and it refers to the right way of acting in relation to others, basically by being honest, upright, sincere, chaste, and faithful. A curious characteristic of wisdom in the Old Testament is that it has little to do with the great events of Israel's salvation history — the Lord Yahweh as the Master of history and Savior of Israel, worship and cult in the Temple, and the coming of the Messiah. So the main concern is with the conduct of daily life. After the exile, however, Sirach identifies wisdom with the Torah, the Law of Moses, and sees the fullness of wisdom in keeping the Law.

The wisdom literature takes human nature seriously and recognizes that there is something crooked in man, although it may be disguised under a veneer of smiles, friendliness, and smooth words. Therefore, there are many warnings about being on guard against wicked individuals and false friends. Also, there are many warnings about folly or foolishness; one should associate with the wise and avoid fools like the plague.

Another contrast that is rather frequent is that between the just or wise man and the wicked man. The just man obeys God's law and does not offend against his neighbor; the wicked man is selfish, deceives others, and has no regard for the rights of God. This idea is spelled out clearly in the very first psalm, which talks about the two ways — the way of the wise and the way of the wicked: "Blessed is the man who walks not in the counsel of the wicked."

The authors of the wisdom books shared the Deuteronomic view of retribution: God rewards the good and punishes the evil. Reward and punishment, however, take place in this life. The good enjoy a long life, riches, many descendants, honor among friends; the wicked die young and do not prosper in this life. But especially after the exile in Babylon, the sages saw that things do not always work out that way. Often the good die young and suffer terribly, while the wicked prosper. This problem is dealt with in a profound way in Job and Ecclesiastes (Qoheleth). It was through wrestling with this problem, under the inspiration of the Holy Spirit, that they gradually came to see that full justice is found only in the next life, where God will reward the just and punish the wicked — what we call heaven and hell. For in the book of Wisdom we find clear assertions of the immortality of the soul, while Daniel and 2 Maccabees affirm the resurrection of the body in the future.

The focus in the historical and prophetic books is on the community rather than on the individual and his problems. The wisdom literature directs attention to the individual person and shows concern for him.

Sometimes wisdom is treated almost as a person and is actually personified; you will find this in Proverbs 8:22–36, Sirach 24:1—22, and Wisdom 7:24—8:1. This literary form foreshadows and prepares the way for St. Paul in the New Testament to refer to Christ as "the wisdom of God" (1 Cor 1:24) because he is the full revelation of God, who is infinite wisdom.

Job

And Job said: *"Naked I came from my mother's womb, and naked shall I return; the LORD gave, and the LORD has taken away; blessed be the name of the LORD"* (1:21).

PLACE IN THE BIBLE: The book of Job is the first of the wisdom books. In the Catholic edition of the Revised Standard Version, it is located after the book of Esther and before the Psalms. The book contains forty-two chapters.

DATE AND AUTHOR: The author of Job is unknown, but he was learned, profound, and a poet. The problem dealt with and the language point to a time of composition after the exile, that is, after 538 B.C. The most probable date of composition is between 500 and 400 B.C.

THEME: The book of Job offers the most profound treatment of the problem of evil that is to be found in world literature. The basic theme is the justice or goodness of God within the context of the suffering of the good man. The author questions the traditional view found in some psalms and in the Deuteronomic history that the good prosper and the wicked are punished in this life. Our author sees that life does not always work out that way, for often the wicked prosper and the good suffer. If God is good, which he is, then how is this possible?

SUMMARY: In the prose prologue in the first two chapters, we learn that Job, a wealthy and pious man (a saint in his own way), has been deprived of his children and all his possessions and afflicted with a serious disease in order that a dispute between Yahweh and Satan about the sincerity of Job's virtue might be settled. No matter what happens to Job, he refuses to blame God for his misfortunes.

There follows a long dialogue between Job and his three wise friends — Eliphaz, Bildad, and Zophar — about whether or not Job's sufferings are the result of his sins. Job protests his innocence from beginning to end. His friends argue that he must have sinned because he is now being punished.

A fourth friend shows up in chapters 32 to 37, younger than the others. Basically he repeats the arguments of the other three and makes no substantial contribution to the argument.

The climax of the book of Job is reached in chapter 38, when Yahweh speaks twice and Job answers and submits to God totally. The story ends happily when God blesses Job, restores him to his former state of prosperity, and increases his wealth twofold.

THEOLOGY: The book of Job is a reflection or dialogue on the problem of evil, specifically, why the just suffer in this world. So it is also a question about the providence of God. The author intends to probe deeper than the older biblical belief that God rewards those who keep his Law and punishes those who violate it. He has seen that often the good suffer and die young, while the wicked prosper in this life and live to a ripe old age.

The great poet who wrote Job presents the problem, but he does not offer a theologically argued conclusion. He does come to see, however, that the justice of God cannot be defended by affirming that it is realized in this world. This leads him to suspect that God's justice will triumph in the next life. He is not clear about this, but he does prepare the way for the later biblical prophets to speak about eternal life and the resurrection of the body. If justice is not attained in this life, it will be achieved in the next.

Job comes to the realization that human reason and wisdom cannot solve the riddle of evil. The end of Job's spiritual journey is the appearance of God, who confronts Job with the mysteries of the visible world. God stresses the point to Job that, if he cannot fathom the mysteries of the visible creation, then it should be clear that he cannot understand God's mysterious ways with man. What is clear is that God is in charge of his world, and it functions in an orderly way according to his will.

So the book does not offer a theoretical solution to the problem of evil. Job's experience is presented, not as a way to understand evil, but as a way to live with it.

As a result of his experience of God, Job is able to live with evil. The conclusion of the book of Job is that only faith in God and his goodness makes evil tolerable. From nature and revelation man can know something about God, but ultimately God and his ways with man are and remain mysterious. Faith with complete trust in God is the only way to bridge the gap between the temporal world of man and the eternal life of God.

The complete answer to the problem Job raises is to be found in Jesus Christ, who died and rose again for the salvation of all mankind. Jesus revealed clearly that man is immortal and that after this life there are two possibilities: The wicked who reject God's offer of love will be damned in hell for all eternity, while those who love him in return and do his will in this life will attain eternal life with the Father, the Son, and the Holy Spirit. Thus it remains true that the good will be rewarded and the wicked will be punished; the new revelation of Jesus is that this does not necessarily happen in this life but surely will happen in the next life.

OUTLINE

I. Prologue (1:1—2:13)

II. The dialogue (3:1—31:40)

    A. Eliphaz, Bildad, and Zophar each speak to Job three times, and he replies to them all

    B. A short interlude: The search for wisdom (28:1–28)

III. Elihu's three speeches (32:1—37:40)

IV. God's two speeches and Job's two answers (38:1—42:6)

V. Epilogue (42:7–17)

    A. Job's friends expiate their faults (42:7–10a)

B. God blesses Job and restores him to his former
    good fortune twofold (42:10b–17)

REFLECTION

Then Job answered the LORD: *"I know that thou canst do
all things, and that no purpose of thine can be thwarted.
'Who is this that hides counsel without knowledge?' Therefore I have uttered what I did not understand, things too
wonderful for me, which I did not know. . . . I had heard
of thee by the hearing of the ear, but now my eye sees thee;
therefore I despise myself, and repent in dust and ashes"*
(42:1–6).

Psalms

Thy word is a lamp to my feet and a light to my path
(119:105).

PLACE IN THE BIBLE: The book of Psalms occupies a central place in the Bible. It is found between Job and Proverbs. There are 150 psalms, and each one is an independent unit.

DATE AND AUTHOR: The psalms are lyrical or poetic hymns of praise of the God of Israel. Some of them come from the time of King David, about 1000 B.C. The most recent psalms are post-exilic and reflect the liturgy of the Second Temple, which was dedicated in 515 B.C. The book of Psalms as we now have it was finished by about 250 B.C., when it was translated into Greek and incorporated into the Septuagint (LXX).

THEME: The main theme of the psalms is that the Lord God of Israel reigns supreme and almighty over the heavens and the earth; he is the Lord of history and shows special care for his people Israel, whom he saves from their enemies, so he is the Savior of Israel. There are two types of human beings: the good and the wicked, the just and the unjust. The former keep God's Law as known through the Covenant with Moses; the latter trust in themselves and ignore God and his Commandments.

SUMMARY: The 150 Psalms were the hymnbook of the Jewish people, especially at the services in the Temple in Jerusalem. They give expression to every sentiment of the human heart, from joy and adoration to fear and despair. As you can see from the brief outline below, they fall into certain identifiable categories. The four main ones are: hymns of praise of the God of Israel, lamentations and pleas for deliverance, hymns of thanksgiving, and royal psalms about King David and the Davidic kings who followed him.

The basic structure of most of the psalms is quite simple: (1) state the theme of praise or thanks or lament; (2) give the reason(s) for the invocation; (3) state what God has or has not done for the one invoking him; (4) repeat the theme with the assurance that God will respond favorably.

It is important to note that the psalms are hymns or songs that were written to be sung with musical accompaniment, so they fit into what we would call poetry rather than prose. In one way or another they are all *prayers* that are directed to God in the sense of adoration, thanksgiving, petition, or satisfaction. It is for this reason that they have been adopted by the Church and converted into her own prayer book.

THEOLOGY: The psalms are hymns and prayers to God that cover the whole range of human experience, from happiness to despair. The dominant idea of the psalter is that the Lord reigns; God is supreme and sovereign; he is in control of heaven and earth, and he disposes all things sweetly for the good of his creatures, especially the people of the Covenant.

How does this affect human beings? The first word of Psalm 1 gives us a clue: Blessed is the man who walks not in the counsel of the wicked . . . his delight is in the law of the Lord, and on his law he meditates day and night. So the man whose mind and heart and actions are guided by God's will, will enjoy happiness and fulfillment in life. Likewise, the person who puts his trust in God, who relies on him, who makes him his "refuge" and "fortress", will be happy and blessed (see Ps 2:12). This idea is found often in the psalms.

The fundamental idea here is dependence on God for life, food, and security. This same notion is found in the word "righteous" or "just". Thus the righteous are those who acknowledge their basic dependence on God by obeying his Law, especially the First Commandment of giving worship to the Lord alone. The psalms repeat often the idea that God will not abandon those who trust in him.

The righteous are those who live by the grace of God, and they are contrasted with the "wicked" in Psalm 1 (also Ps 119). The wicked or sinners are those who neglect God and live in radical dependence on self rather than on God. They are the autonomous ones who do not follow God's Law but adhere to their own law and will.

The most important theological concept in the psalms is that of "steadfast love" or "unfailing love", which is expressed by the Hebrew word *hesed*. This idea is found in all five books of the psalter and is often paired with "faithfulness" (Hebrew: *'emet*).

The overall theological picture of God in the psalms

is that he is sovereign over all, but he is no tyrant. He is described as compassionate, gracious, loving, and faithful. This does not by any means indicate that he is weak or overly indulgent; God can also get angry at arrogant sinners and at times is a God of wrath (Ps 2:5, 12; 6:1; 56:7). But the dominant note is that he is a God of love —a point that is stated explicitly by St. John (1 Jn 4:8) in the New Testament.

The psalms are quoted in the New Testament more frequently than any other book of the Old Testament. Jesus quotes them as referring to himself (for example, Ps 8:2 in Mt 21:16); the evangelists apply many psalms to Jesus, especially in reference to his royal dignity and his Passion (see Ps 2, 8, 16, 22, 69, 110, 118). The early Christian Church adopted and adapted the psalms for her own use. Some psalms are interpreted in the New Testament in a Messianic sense (Ps 2, 22, 89, 110); others were understood in an eschatological way because they sing of the Lord's reign as King over the whole world on the Last Day (Ps 47, 93, 96–99). The 150 psalms were the hymnbook of the Old Testament and for two thousand years have been the prayer book of the Church of the New Testament. The psalms are used in the liturgy of the Church—at Mass and in the Breviary, or the Liturgy of the Hours, which priests, religious, and laity pray every day.

Here we cannot give an "outline" as in the other books of the Bible, since each of the 150 psalms is unique. Instead we will offer a *classification* of the psalms into different groups that manifest similar characteristics:

I. Hymns of praise:

    A. These can be either of the community or of individuals: Psalms 8, 19, 29, 33, 65, 67—68, 76, 84, 87, 105, 111, 113—14, 117, 122, 135, 145—50

    B. The kingship of the Lord: Psalms 47, 93, 96—99

    C. The songs of Zion: Psalms 46, 48, 76, 84, 87, 122

II. Psalms of lamentation and plea for deliverance:

    A. Collective: Psalms 44, 60, 74, 79-80

    B. Individual: Psalms 3, 5—7, 13, 22, 26, 27:7-14, 28, 31, 35, 38—39, 42—43, 51, 54—55, 57, 59, 61, 63—64, 69—71, 80, 88, 102, 109, 120, 130, 140—43

    C. Penitential: Psalms 32, 38, 51

III. Psalms of thanksgiving and confidence:

    A. Collective: 67, 124, 129, 136

    B. Individual: 30, 32, 34, 40:2-12, 66:13-20, 107, 116, 138

IV. Royal psalms: Psalms 2, 18, 20—21, 45, 72, 101, 110, 132, 144

V. Wisdom psalms: 1, 14, 19:8–14, 37, 49, 53, 73, 112, 119, 127, 128

VI. Other types:

    A. Liturgical: Psalms 15, 24, 134

    B. Prophetic: Psalms 50, 75, 82

    C. Historical meditations: 78, 105—6

REFLECTION

Blessed be the LORD, *the God of Israel, who alone does wondrous things. Blessed be his glorious name for ever; may his glory fill the whole earth! Amen and Amen* (72:18–19).

Proverbs

The fear of the LORD is the beginning of knowledge; fools despise wisdom and instruction (1:7).

PLACE IN THE BIBLE: The book of Proverbs is located after the book of Psalms and before Ecclesiastes. The book contains thirty-one chapters.

DATE AND AUTHOR: The book as we now have it was most probably finished in the fifth century B.C. The two collections of "sayings" of Solomon probably go back to the time of the famous wise king of Israel, for the second collection of 128 sayings was already well known in the time of Hezekiah (about 700 B.C.). The prologue and epilogue were added in the post-exilic times in the fifth century.

THEME: The main theme of the book is that the "fear of the Lord" is the beginning of wisdom. "Fear" in this context means reverence, awe, and respect for the almighty God, who is the creator of heaven and earth. It consists primarily in keeping God's Law as revealed through Moses and in observing the law of nature.

SUMMARY: The book begins with a nine-chapter poem on the great value of wisdom. It is written in the form of instructions of a father to his son, or a teacher to his pupil. The heart of the book is contained in the two collections of sayings or proverbs of Solomon (III and V in Outline). Around those sayings, others have been collected and added. The book closes with a beautiful portrait of the ideal wife and a description of what a treasure she is to the man who is married to her. The book of Proverbs is the Bible's compendium of practical wisdom spanning five or six centuries, from the time of Solomon (970–931 B.C.) to the era of Nehemiah (445–410 B.C.). Reading leisurely through the book is like walking in a lovely garden with exotic flowers, shrubs, and trees on all sides.

THEOLOGY: Proverbs are wise sayings, usually brief, that communicate knowledge or insight about right living. Hebrew proverbs often consist of two lines of equal length. The synonymous proverb expresses the same basic thought in both lines; the antithetical proverb offers a contrast, such as good and evil, wise and foolish, virtuous and corrupt.

Proverbs are not theoretical statements; rather, they are affirmations of practical wisdom that help a person to live at peace with himself, with God, and with his fellow man. So they correspond to what we today call morality, both natural and that which is inspired by divine revelation.

All true wisdom comes ultimately from God, but it is found in the laws of nature and in the Torah, or Law of Moses. As mentioned above under Theme, "fear of the Lord" is the foundation of all true wisdom. "Fear" here does not mean fright and trepidation before God; rather, it means respect and reverence for the Creator of the world, who is infinitely powerful and can do all things. This wisdom is necessary for a meaningful human existence. It is a quality that distinguishes a prudent homemaker, a brave warrior, and a just king.

Certain themes keep recurring in the individual proverbs: One should respect one's parents and teachers; one should keep the tongue under control and be sparing in words; one should not easily trust others but should be careful about one's friends; one should avoid women of loose morals, excessive drinking of wine, and the company of fools; one should practice all the virtues, especially humility, prudence, justice, temperance, and obedience. Family values are stressed; both father and mother should be involved in the instruction of their children (1:8).

One of the high points of the book is the personification of wisdom found in the poems in the first nine chapters. There wisdom is described as a companion of God from the beginning — this is a personification of the wisdom of God and prepares the People of God for Jesus' revelation that he is indeed the wisdom of God in Person, the second Person of the Blessed Trinity.

The book of Proverbs is quoted fourteen times in the New Testament and is alluded to in about twenty other passages. It influenced the construction of the Beatitudes in Matthew 5; in St. John's Gospel Jesus presents himself as the wisdom of God; the Letter of St. James uses Proverbs, since it offers much practical advice, especially regarding the use of the tongue. Also, the letters of St. Peter and St. Paul offer practical advice for virtuous living, some of it borrowed from the book of Proverbs.

Finally, it should be noted that the personification of wisdom that is found in Proverbs 8:22–35 is applied to the Blessed Virgin Mary in the liturgy of the Church. The ancient Latin Mass applied this text to her in the Epistle for the Mass of the birth of Mary on September 8.

OUTLINE

I. Poems on wisdom (1:1—9:18)

II. First Solomonic collection of 375 sayings (10:1—22:16)

III. Thirty "sayings of the sages" (22:17—24:22)

IV. More sayings of the sages (24:23–34)

V. Second Solomonic collection of 128 sayings transcribed under King Hezekiah (25:1—29:27)

VI. The words of Agur (30:1–14)

VII. Numerical proverbs (30:15–33)

VIII. The words of Lemuel (31:1–9)

IX. Portrait of the ideal wife (31:10–31)

REFLECTION

"He who finds me [wisdom] finds life and obtains favor from the LORD; *but he who misses me injures himself; all who hate me love death"* (8:35–36).

Ecclesiastes

Vanity of vanities, says the Preacher, vanity of vanities!
All is vanity. What does man gain by all the toil at which
he toils under the sun? (1:2–3).

PLACE IN THE BIBLE: The book of Ecclesiastes is one of the
wisdom books of the Old Testament and is located after
the book of Proverbs and before the Song of Solomon.
The book contains twelve chapters.

DATE AND AUTHOR: The book's doctrine, vocabulary, and
style date it after the exile, probably about 300 B.C. The
author is unknown. Most likely, there was one author of
the book, but there is reason to think that minor additions were made later by an editor. The book was written
originally in Hebrew. In verse 1 the author identifies himself as "Qoheleth" or "the Preacher" and says he is a "son
of David" and "king in Jerusalem", that is, Solomon. This
is generally understood as a literary device that was common to Hebrew authors of the time, that is, the attribution of a new work to a well-known author such as David
or Solomon.

THEME: The theme is the purpose and value of human life.
It is stated briefly in the opening three verses, "Vanity of
vanities! All is vanity." The author stresses the *emptiness*
of human life because death may come at any time and

deprive a man of everything he has. The same fate awaits both the good man and the wicked man — death. His advice is to work hard and to enjoy life in moderation by eating and drinking. The present moment is all man has, so he should enjoy it the best way he can but should never forget that it will all end in death. Man should honor God and accept life as his gift.

SUMMARY: The content of the book of Ecclesiastes consists in the author's reflections on life. He uses many contrasts, even some contradictions, to see life from many different points of view.

The order or structure of the book is not clear, but the author offers reflections on things that affect all men: the world, the sun, the ocean, the season of the year, human speech, wisdom, enjoyment of food, drink, and sex, hard work, wealth, living for the present moment, suffering, death, women, unfulfilled desires.

Because the author does not see clearly how the sufferings of this life will be rewarded in the next life, he recommends moderate enjoyment of the pleasures of life right now, because no one knows what happens to man after death.

The author tends toward pessimism, but not without a certain sense of humor. In all things he is respectful of God, but God's purpose in human life is mysterious to him. For him, human life is empty because he is not able to see the fullness of Christ. That part of revelation will come later.

THEOLOGY: The author of Ecclesiastes is looking for meaning in human life. Since he is searching for wisdom, he is a wise man. The key to understanding this practical book of the Bible is to be found in the theme that human life is empty (= vain). Why is life empty? For Ecclesiastes, it is empty because nothing is permanent, nothing lasts. What has been will come again; the mighty will fall and will be replaced by others who, in their turn, will pass away.

The author sees earthly advantage in wisdom, but he is also troubled that, in the long run, the wise man is no better off than the evil man. Why? Because they both end up in the grave, and no one knows what will happen to them after death.

Qoheleth is mildly pessimistic, but at the same time he places his trust in God. He sees all creation as good and says that one should enjoy the good things of life while one is alive and has time. For, soon death will come, and then man can no longer enjoy food, drink, sex, and friendship. Qoheleth's view, however, is incomplete because he does not know about eternal life, which will be clearly taught and given by Jesus Christ.

Like Job, the author questions the traditional biblical wisdom that the just or good man will be rewarded in this life and that the wicked will be punished. He has seen that life does not always work out that way, for often the wicked prosper, while the good suffer and die young. We are dealing here with a *transitional stage* in the theological development of Israel. The new revelation of Jesus Christ will answer all of the hard questions raised by Ecclesiastes, especially with regard to eternal life for the just man and eternal damnation for the wicked.

The Preacher sees that nothing in this life — none of the following or all of them put together: love, power, wealth, food, drink, sex, long life, many children, even wisdom itself—fully satisfies the craving of the human heart. This profound insight prepared for the revelation of Jesus Christ about the resurrection of the body and life everlasting.

OUTLINE

I. Qoheleth's world view (1:1—4:3)
    A. Nature's constant and aimless toil (1:1–11)
    B. Human life with no purpose (1:12—2:26)
    C. Futility of human effort (3:1–15)
    D. The lack of morality in nature (3:16—4:3)

II. A wise man's experiences (4:4—9:16)
    A. The wise conduct of life (4:4—5:20)
    B. Frustration of hopes and desires (6:1–12)
    C. Source of wisdom (7:1–29)
    D. History is going nowhere (8:1–17)
    E. Death awaits all (9:1–16)

III. Advice to disciples (9:17—12:14)
    A. Several maxims (9:17—10:20)
    B. Need for action (11:1–8)
    C. Live for the moment (11:9—12:7)
    D. Epilogue (12:8–14)

REFLECTION

Fear God, and keep his commandments; for this is the whole duty of man. For God will bring every deed into judgment, with every secret thing, whether good or evil (12:13).

The Song of Solomon

O that you would kiss me with the kisses of your mouth!
(1:2).

PLACE IN THE BIBLE: The Song of Solomon, also known
for centuries as the Canticle of Canticles or the Song of
Songs, which means the best song or the greatest song, is
found after the book of Ecclesiastes and before the book
of Wisdom. It contains eight chapters.

DATE AND AUTHOR: The language and content suggest a
date after the exile, therefore after 538 B.C., probably in
the fifth or fourth centuries B.C. The author is not known.
In the first verse it is attributed to Solomon, but this is
a literary device common among the ancients, just as the
books of Proverbs, Ecclesiastes, and Wisdom are ascribed
to him by inspired authors of a later generation. The author, however, may have incorporated some ancient lyrics
going back to the time of Solomon.

THEME: The Song of Solomon is a celebration of the loyal
and mutual love that leads to marriage. Human sexual
love is prized in the Song as a great good and is implicitly
looked upon as a gift of God, who, by the way, is never
mentioned explicitly in the Song. In a fuller sense, the
Song is about the love of God for his people and their

love for him. It is for this reason that it is included in the Bible.

SUMMARY: The Song of Solomon does not follow any definite or logical plan of development. It is rather a collection of songs or poems united by a common theme of love. One could describe it as a "lyric dialogue", since the text alternates between the female beloved, the male lover, and the daughters of Jerusalem, who function as a chorus that provides bridges from one poem to the next.

The Song is a hymn to spousal love, and, like all good poetry, it makes extensive use of symbolism and sensual figures of speech, for example, "I am a rose of Sharon, a lily of the valleys" (2:1). The young man is referred to as "king" and "shepherd". The young woman is called a "garden". The theme of seeking and finding stands out; the idea of sleep and awakening occurs several times. A common way of interpreting the Song is to see it as a hymn to spousal love leading to fulfillment in marriage. Both before and after the Christian era, the Jewish people used the Song to celebrate human love at wedding feasts.

THEOLOGY: The two basic and traditional ways of interpreting the Song of Solomon are the literal and the allegorical. Literally, it is a love poem, full of powerful imagery and symbolism, singing the praises of human sexual love between a man and a woman. If that is so, the question naturally arises: Why is it in the Bible, which has to do with sin and salvation? On the first level, the answer is that romantic love between man and woman was created by God, and everything he made is good (see Gen 1). On a deeper level, it symbolizes the love that God has for his faithful people and the love they have for him. In the literal sense, therefore, it is more a parable than an allegory in which each phrase has a hidden meaning.

In the Christian era, however, the Song has been given an allegorical interpretation by several mystics and masters of the spiritual life, such as St. Bernard of Clairvaux and St. John of the Cross, whose *Spiritual Canticle* is based on it. From this point of view, the lover and his beloved stand for God and his people, or Christ and the Church, or Christ and the individual soul.

There are many ambiguities in the Song, so it lends itself to a variety of interpretations. Commentaries on the Song abound and are still being written, especially by those who are concerned about the love of God for man and man for God. After all, St. John tells us that "God is love" (1 Jn 4:8).

Describing the relation between God and his people in terms of married love has a valid pedigree in the Old Testament, for example, in Hosea, Isaiah, Jeremiah, and Ezekiel. The use of marriage as a symbol is found also in the New Testament (Mt 9:15; 25:1–13; Jn 3:29; Eph 5:23–32; Rev 19:7ff.). In the liturgy of the Catholic Church, passages from the Song of Solomon are frequently applied to the Blessed Virgin Mary.

I. Title: Solomon's Song of Songs (1:1)

II. Prelude: Love's desire (1:2–4)

III. Dialogue of affection between the beloved and her lover (1:5—2:7)

IV. Courtship in springtime (2:8—3:5)

V. Solomon's wedding procession (3:6–11)

VI. The fairest of maidens (4:1—5:1)

VII. She searches everywhere for him (5:2—6:3)

VIII. The union of spouses (6:4—8:4)

IX. Summary: The strength of committed love (8:5–7)

X. Appendices (8:8–14)

(Adapted from Michael Duggan, *The Consuming Fire* [San Francisco: Ignatius Press, 1991].)

REFLECTION

Behold, you are beautiful, my love; behold, you are beautiful; your eyes are doves! (1:15).

The Wisdom of Solomon

But the souls of the righteous are in the hand of God, and no torment will ever touch them. In the eyes of the foolish they seemed to have died, . . . but they are at peace (3:1–3).

PLACE IN THE BIBLE: The book of Wisdom is located after the Song of Solomon and before the book of Sirach. It contains nineteen chapters.

DATE AND AUTHOR: Written in Greek and coming to terms with Hellenistic culture, the language and content indicate that the book was written about the year 50 B.C. in Alexandria, Egypt, by a Greek-speaking Jew who was familiar with Greek culture. The identity of the author is not known. The book gives the impression of being written by Solomon in the tenth century B.C., but this is a literary device to give some authority to the writing, since Solomon was considered the model of all wise men.

THEME: Wisdom means fidelity to the Law of God as revealed to Israel through Moses and the other prophets. Wisdom is a gift of God. The wise man leads a righteous life in this world, and for this he will be rewarded by God in the next life with immortality.

SUMMARY: As understood in this divinely inspired book, wisdom means, among other things, fidelity to the Law of Moses. The author says that this fidelity is superior to all the earthly wisdom or "philosophy" of the Greeks and other Gentile intellectuals. So the book of Wisdom is an apology for the superiority of the revealed religion of Israel over all other religions and philosophies.

The book contains three main parts. The first five chapters offer a meditation on immortality. The main point here is that the godless will perish and will be destroyed by God, but the righteous, that is, those who practice the true religion of Israel, will be rewarded by God with eternal life, and they will live forever.

The next four chapters, 6 to 9, are an attempt to define and describe the true wisdom of Israel, which leads to immortality. Our author presents the advantages of this wisdom as he tries to motivate the reader to give up everything else in order to hold on to this pearl of great price.

The final section, chapters 10 to 19, offers a theology of history from Adam to Moses, showing how God protected and saved those who were faithful to the Law. In the middle of it there is a lengthy attack on the idolatry of the pagans; the purpose here is to warn the Jews against getting involved in pagan idol worship. Apparently this was a recurring problem for those Jews, young and old, who wanted to be fashionable and up-to-date.

THEOLOGY: The book of Wisdom is the last book written in the Old Testament. Some very important religious truths are asserted here in virtue of divine revelation. The most important point made by the author is that the human soul is immortal and will be judged after death by God: the godless and wicked will be punished, and the just will be rewarded by God by a blessed immortality — what we now mean by heaven or the face-to-face vision of God. The just man is the "wise" man who remains faithful to the God of Israel in all cultural circumstances. But the book does not say anything about the resurrection of the body — an idea that is touched on in the books of Daniel and Maccabees.

In the second part of the book (chaps. 6—9), wisdom is personified and made an associate of God in the creation of the world. This idea also occurs in the book of Proverbs and is a divine preparation for the full revelation in the New Testament that Jesus Christ, the second Person of the Blessed Trinity, is the wisdom of God and the image of God. In the Middle Ages this personification of wisdom was applied to the Blessed Virgin Mary by some theologians, and eventually it was incorporated into the Saturday Votive Masses of the Virgin Mother of God.

The third part (chaps. 10—19) offers a powerful meditation on the activity of God in history. As mentioned above, it is in the form of a theology of history, showing how God protected the believing and faithful Jews from all their enemies. This is a further development of the Deuteronomic principle of punishment for sin and reward for fidelity.

In summary, the book of Wisdom offers a strong polemic for the faithful Jew (and Christian) against paganism and secularism. The main ideas are: (1) immortality is the fruit of fidelity; (2) wisdom is a gift of God, who bestows it on those who pray for it; (3) the Lord alone is God, and so the worship of idols is utter foolishness and stupidity; (4) the Lord God of Israel is the Master of history and protects those who are faithful to him.

The New Testament does not quote Wisdom directly, but the latter book did influence some New Testament thinking. Thus, there is a connection between the statement in Wisdom that death came into the world through the "envy" of the devil and Paul's attributing death to the power of sin (see Rom 5:12–21). And like the author of Wisdom, Paul sees that idolatry of any kind is the root source of immorality (Rom 1:24–32). In addition, Paul's assertion that the contemplation of creation can, should, and does give everyone some knowledge that God is Creator (Rom 1:18–22) is rooted in the same argument that is found in Wisdom 13:1–9. The suffering just man of Wisdom 2:12–24 is a foreshadowing of the fate of Christ. Also Paul's notion in Colossians 1:15–20 that Christ is the "Wisdom" of God was probably influenced by the book of Wisdom. The Letter to the Hebrews (1:3) borrows a term from Wisdom when it describes Christ as the "reflection" of God's glory (see Wis 7:25–26).

The warnings in this book about the dangers to faith of living in a hostile, secular culture can be applied today to the situation of the believing Catholic who tries to preserve his faith in a culture shot through with atheism and materialism. Read in this light, the book of Wisdom offers guidance right now to every sincere Christian.

REFLECTION

Wisdom is more mobile than any motion; because of her pureness she pervades and penetrates all things. For she is a breath and the power of God, and a pure emanation of the glory of the Almighty; therefore nothing defiled gains entrance into her. For she is a reflection of eternal light, a spotless mirror of the working of God and an image of his goodness (7:24–26).

Sirach
(Ecclesiasticus)

To fear the Lord is the beginning of wisdom; she is created with the faithful in the womb (1:14).

PLACE IN THE BIBLE: The book of Sirach is placed after the book of Wisdom and before the prophecy of Isaiah. Thus it is the last of the wisdom books of the Old Testament. The book contains fifty-one chapters.

DATE AND AUTHOR: The author gives us his name as Jesus, son of Sirach, son of Eleazar (50:27). He lived at the beginning of the second century B.C.; the most likely date for the composition is about 180 B.C. He lived and wrote before the reign of King Antiochus IV Epiphanes and the Maccabean revolt.

THEME: As with the book of Proverbs, the theme of this book is the great value of "wisdom", which consists primarily in the fear of the Lord. Wisdom for Sirach is found primarily in the Law of Moses and in keeping the Ten Commandments of the Covenant. Also as in Proverbs, wisdom is personified in several places in the book.

SUMMARY: The translator of the Hebrew original into Greek (about 132 B.C.) prefixed his own foreword to the book. The prologue in chapter 1 shows that wisdom comes ultimately from God and consists in "fear of the Lord", which means awe, reverence, and respect for the Almighty God of creation. Chapters 2 to 23 and 25 to 42 offer practical advice for wise living; much of it is based on and borrowed from the book of Proverbs. But Sirach develops his ideas more at length than does the book of Proverbs, for he offers short little essays or treatises on various practical subjects, such as how to train children, how to choose friends, how to guard one's speech and tongue; there are warnings against excess in anything, sloth, foolishness, drunkenness, associating with evil companions, and the company of loose living women. The advice is all very practical and useful.

Chapter 24, about the middle of the book, offers a beautiful hymn to wisdom in which wisdom is personified and made a companion of God from the beginning. This personification helped prepare the way for the revelation of Jesus that there are three Persons in one God and that he, Jesus, is Wisdom incarnate. The liturgy of the Church applies this chapter to the Blessed Virgin Mary because of her intimate association with Jesus.

Chapters 44 to 50 are based on the history of the great men of Israel, from Enoch to Nehemiah. They are praised and presented as models to be imitated in the pursuit of wisdom. At the end of chapter 50, the author identifies himself (vv. 27–29); this is something very unusual in the Old Testament. The book closes with two short psalms — the first one offers thanksgiving to God (51:1–12), and the second one is a hymn to wisdom (51:13–30).

THEOLOGY: The key to understanding the book of Sirach is the author's identification of wisdom with the fear of the Lord; this is repeated several times in chapter 1. But what is new in Sirach is the author's further statement that wisdom is to be found in the observance of the Law of Moses, that is, in keeping the Ten Commandments and in living by the Mosaic Covenant with the Lord.

As in the book of Proverbs, personified wisdom holds an important place; this foreshadows the revelation in the New Testament that the second Person of the Blessed Trinity is Wisdom itself and the Word of God, that Wisdom is found in human history in the Person of Jesus Christ. Further reflection by Fathers of the Church on the divine decree by which God created Mary as the Mother of the Incarnate Wisdom led the Church to apply chapter 24 to the Blessed Virgin Mary and to use it for the Epistle of the Saturday Votive Masses. This passage, as well as those in the books of Proverbs and Wisdom that have been applied to Mary, is the basis for the Marian title *Sedes Sapientiae* (Seat of Wisdom).

The general purpose of the book is indicated at the beginning and at the end (foreword; 50:27–29). After much reflection on Proverbs and the other wisdom books, Ben Sirach decided to write about wisdom and discipline so that lovers of learning and wisdom might make greater progress in living according to the Law of Israel.

The doctrine in Sirach is traditional: there are two classes of men — the wise and the foolish, the good and the wicked. With regard to the retribution for good and evil, he is quite traditional and seems to hold that it takes place in this life. He is not clear about reward and punishment in the next life. His identification of wisdom with the Law of Moses is something new (19:17; 24:22).

The book of Sirach is not quoted directly in the New Testament, but many influences can be detected in the Gospels and in the Letter of James, especially with respect to such ideas as wisdom, correct living, and prayer. The author is unique in the Old Testament in calling upon God as "my Father" (23:1; 51:10), an invocation that was used frequently by Jesus and bequeathed to us by him in the Our Father.

For many centuries this book was called "Ecclesiasticus", that is, the book used in the Church. It was given this name because of its frequent use in the early Church in the instruction of the people. Many readings in the liturgy of the Mass are taken from Sirach; also many readings from the book are included in the Liturgy of the Hours, or Breviary, which priests, religious, and laity pray every day.

OUTLINE

   I. Translator's prologue (vv. 1–35)

  II. Wisdom and the fear of the Lord (1:1—2:18)

 III. Practical advice for wise living (3:1—23:27)

 IV. Wisdom lives in Jerusalem and in the Law of Moses (24:1–34)

  V. More practical advice for wise living (25:1—42:14)

 VI. The majesty of God revealed in creation (42:15—43:33)

REFLECTION

Wisdom says: "*Come to me, you who desire me, and eat your fill of my produce. For the remembrance of me is sweeter than honey, and my inheritance sweeter than the honeycomb. Those who eat me will hunger for more, and those who drink me will thirst for more*" (24:19–21).

Prophets

A prophet is one who speaks for another. In the Bible the term is applied to those men and women, such as Amos, Hosea, Isaiah, Jeremiah, and Ezekiel, who proclaimed the word and therefore the will of God to their fellow Israelites. So the prophet is one who has had an immediate experience of God; in fact, we could call him a "mystic". God has chosen and called him and revealed to him his own holiness and his will. The prophet sees the present and the future through the eyes of God. He is also sent by God to men to remind them of their duties to God and to bring them back to obedience and love. But the key idea here in the Old Testament is that God spoke through the prophets (for example, Mt 1:22; Heb 1:1).

The prophet's two main functions are to proclaim the word of God that he has received directly from on high and also to foretell future events that depend on human free will and that only God knows. A proof that the prophet is authentic and truly sent by God is shown when predictions, such as that of the fall of Samaria to the Assyrians (721 B.C.) and that of the fall of Jerusalem to the Babylonians (587 B.C.), actually take place. If he wanted to, the prophet then could say to his people: "See, I told you so, but you would not listen to me!" But predicting future events is a secondary function of the prophet; his main role is to proclaim God's word and to call the people back from sin and rebellion to obedience to the Torah, or God's Law.

Sin is the main obstacle that the prophet opposes. His

oracles and messages are marked by two characteristics: threats of disaster because of sin and promises of blessing for repentance and obedience. The situation in the Old Testament is something like this: God chose Abraham and his descendants as his special people. He loved them, revealed his will to them on Mount Sinai, and made a Covenant with them. Their duty is to love him in return by keeping the terms of the Covenant, namely, the Ten Commandments. But over and over again they abandon the worship of the true God and give themselves to manmade idols and sensuality. So God raises up a prophet to call them to repentance and observance of the Law. Each prophet over a period of about eight hundred years from 1200 B.C. to 400 B.C. prophesies in the context of the political and religious situation of the place and time in which he lives. In the name of God, he threatens his co-religionists with disaster if they do not repent, and he promises them blessings, peace, and prosperity if they do repent and mend their ways.

In the Bible there are sixteen books of prophecy — four major prophets (Isaiah, Jeremiah, Ezekiel, Daniel) and twelve minor prophets. The latter are called "minor" because their recorded message is relatively short. The title "prophet", in the sense given above of one who experiences God and speaks for him, is also given in the Bible to Abraham, Moses, Aaron, Miriam, Nathan, and many others. In the New Testament Jesus is called a prophet by others, but he rarely applies the term to himself (see Lk 4:24; 13:33). The reason for this is obvious: Jesus is God and speaks to us directly, while the human prophets receive the word from God and then speak it (see Heb 1:1–2).

The prophets played an essential role in the development of the religion of Israel. They tried to keep the people faithful to the true religion of Yahweh the Lord as given to them through Moses. But they were also instruments especially chosen by God to reveal his will in more detail and to prepare his people for the coming of the future Messiah, who would be the Savior of the world, that is, for the coming of Jesus Christ. In our terms, we could say that they contributed to the development of the doctrine contained in biblical religion.

The message of the prophets elaborates the three main features of Old Testament religion: monotheism, morality, and future salvation. The religion of the Bible is often called "ethical monotheism". For, the Hebrew people gradually came to realize, under the guidance of the prophets, that Yahweh, the God of Israel, is the only God there is and that the gods of the surrounding nations are nothing but human creations. That is what is meant by "monotheism". The religion of the Old Testament is "ethical" because it makes moral demands on the people: they must love God and keep his commandments; the God of Israel is never satisfied with mere external ritualism or animal sacrifices.

Biblical morality means this: God alone is pure *holiness*, and human beings are unclean because they are sinners. The prophets are opposed to sin because it is sin that separates man from God, who is man's true end and happiness. For sin is an offense against the God of holiness, justice, and love.

Sin and punishment are not the last word of the prophets. God promises, through his prophets, salvation in the future for those who remain faithful to him, especially to the "holy remnant" — those who obey his will and survive every disaster. God never abandons his people but always remains with them — he is Immanuel ("God with us", Is 7:14).

John the Baptist is a prophet in the New Testament, and he is also the bridge, the connecting link, between the two Covenants. There were also prophets in the early Christian communities (Acts 11:27), but prophecy disappeared after New Testament times as it was absorbed by the development of the hierarchical offices of bishop and priest.

In order to get "inside the Bible", to understand the Bible and especially the relationship between the Old Testament and the New Testament of Jesus Christ, it is necessary to have a good grasp of the message of the Old Testament prophets. The following outlines have been composed as a guide to help you understand the prophets as you read them prayerfully.

Isaiah

And I said, "Woe is me! For I am lost; for I am a man of unclean lips, and I dwell in the midst of a people of unclean lips; for my eyes have seen the King, the LORD of hosts!" (6:5).

PLACE IN THE BIBLE: Isaiah is the first and the greatest of the Old Testament prophets. In the Old Testament the Pentateuch comes first, then the historical books, then the wisdom books, and then the prophets. Isaiah is first among the prophets. The book contains sixty-six chapters.

DATE AND AUTHOR: Isaiah was a man of the city, and the city was Jerusalem. He seems to have had good contacts with the royal family and the leaders of the city, so he probably came from a noble family. He was born about 765 B.C. and began to prophesy in 740. His last prophecy is dated in 701, so he died some time after that.

Most contemporary scholars hold that a gifted prophet during the exile, about 550 to 540 B.C., and whom they name "Deutero-Isaiah", or Second Isaiah, wrote chapters 40 to 55. Some of the same scholars hold for a "Trito-Isaiah", or Third Isaiah, as the author of chapters 56 to 66, although there is less certainty about this. It is not known who these gifted prophets were, if in fact they did exist. There is no external evidence for these opinions;

they are based on internal criticism, that is, literary and historical analysis of the text. Sometimes these presumed authors are referred to as "disciples" of Isaiah who closely studied him and wrote in his style. The traditional view, which held sway until the advent of the "higher criticism" of the nineteenth century, was that the whole book was written by Isaiah of Jerusalem.

THEME: The book of Isaiah contains many different prophecies given at different times and in different circumstances over a period of forty years. It has been called "a collection of collections". Most scholars are of the opinion that Isaiah did not write the book as we now have it; they think his disciples collected his various oracles and put them together as we have them and that they added some of their own material to what Isaiah had said, thus producing the book as it now stands and as it has been at least since 200 B.C. Several themes stand out and should be carefully noted:

1. There is only one God — Yahweh, the God of Israel. The idols worshipped by their surrounding neighbors are not gods at all. The special characteristic of God, which was revealed to Isaiah, is the *holiness* or transcendence of God. He often refers to God as "the Holy One of Israel".

2. God's perfections are reflected in his creation, so that the whole earth is filled with his glory. Yahweh is the sole Master of history, and he may intervene when and as he wishes.

3. The relations between Yahweh and Israel are regulated by the Sinai Covenant made with Moses and Israel. The Covenant promised material prosperity for the ful-

fillment of its precepts and punishment for their neglect. Isaiah often reminds his people that God's Law cannot be violated with impunity.

4. God's holiness and justice led him to punish the sins of his people, but he would not wipe them out completely. His punishment was intended to be corrective; his goal was not to destroy but to purify them. So he left a holy remnant, faithful to the Covenant, after the sinners had been destroyed. This idea of the *remnant* is a central teaching of Isaiah.

5. Isaiah speaks about the new and glorious age that would come for Israel in the future. He tends to emphasize the new age more than the person of the Messiah who will be acting on behalf of God. He does not think in terms of the divinity of the Messiah but of the Messiah as God's agent.

6. Isaiah teaches that Jerusalem enjoyed special privileges from God, because Yahweh rules from the Temple in Jerusalem. This idea is used by St. John in the book of Revelation where he describes his vision of the New Jerusalem coming down from heaven (21:2).

In chapters 40 to 66, we find the four famous Servant Songs in the following passages: 42:1–4; 49:1–7; 50:4–9; 52:13—53:12. The last one is called the Song of the Suffering Servant. Many books and articles have been written about the identity of the Servant. Most scholars today seem to think that the Servant stands in a *collective* sense for the people of Israel and in an *individual* sense for the Messiah.

Some of the principal themes of this section are the universalism of God's salvation; he is the Creator of the world and directs world history with a special concern for Israel and Jerusalem. He will send a Messiah and has prepared a glorious future for those who remain faithful to him and keep his Covenant.

SUMMARY: The oracles of Isaiah were uttered in response to political and religious situations of the time in which he lived in Jerusalem. Basically what he said was that the king and the people should trust in God, abide by the Covenant, avoid all idol worship, and not get involved in foreign treaties and wars. He did have some access to the king and his advisors, but in general they ignored him and tried to solve their political problems by making treaties with Assyria and Egypt and some of the small neighboring cities. This turned out to be a disaster for Jerusalem and Judah.

In order to understand the various oracles it is necessary to have some knowledge of the historical situation, since the oracles are related to that. The prophetic ministry of Isaiah over forty years can be divided into three main periods: (1) the reign of Jotham (742–735); (2) the reign of Ahaz (735–715); and (3) the reign of Hezekiah (715–687). The early oracles belong to the first period (chaps. 1–5); under King Ahaz, Judah was threatened by an attack from an alliance of Syria and Israel in the north. Isaiah urged faith and courage and trust in Yahweh, but the king opted instead for a treaty with Assyria. Most of Isaiah's Messianic prophecies come from this period (chaps. 6–12).

Hezekiah was one of the better kings. He undertook religious reform, but he still entered into treaties with Egypt against the advice of Isaiah. The later prophecies (13–39) come from this period. Isaiah's basic message is: Trust in God, not in military alliances with unbelievers.

All of the above refers primarily to the first thirty-nine chapters of Isaiah.

From the text it is clear that chapters 40 to 55 deal with the period of the exile, especially toward the end of it. The prophet even mentions the name of the Persian emperor, Cyrus, who defeated the Babylonians and permitted the Israelites to return home to Jerusalem. There are some indications in chapters 56 to 66 that they deal with the time of the return after 537 B.C. and before the rebuilding of the new Temple, which was completed in 515.

THEOLOGY: The most basic idea in the theology of Isaiah is his idea of the *holiness* of Yahweh. This is spelled out clearly in the account of his call to be a prophet when he had a vision of the glory of God (6:1ff.). This concept of holiness means the absolute transcendence of God, which makes him infinitely different from man. It is reflected in God's hatred of sin, especially as manifested in injustice and idol worship.

Yahweh's plan for Israel and for all mankind is based on his holiness and is unfathomable to man. The divine plan cannot be frustrated by human activity or conniving; he and not man is responsible for the course of human history — he can intervene when and as he likes. The proper response of man to God's holiness and his divine plan is *faith*, by which Isaiah means the acceptance of God's plan and his will and his power to accomplish it. The genuineness of this faith is shown by refusing to rely on human means — military or political, such as alliances with Assyria or Egypt. This faith is a complete surrender to the wisdom and plan of God. The fundamental sin for Isaiah is the refusal to put its faith in Yahweh. And this unbelief is the source of all the vices that Isaiah saw in his society, both individual and social.

The plan of Yahweh leads either to judgment, that is, punishment, or to salvation. The given effect depends on how individuals respond to his plan and will.

Another key idea in the teaching of Isaiah is that of the *remnant*. When the Lord punishes his people, he spares a small group of faithful Israelites who will carry on the tradition of the Covenant. Out of them will come the future leaders of the people — and ultimately the Messiah.

The influence of Isaiah on the thought of the New Testament is very profound. After the Psalms, Isaiah is the most frequently quoted book of the Old Testament in the New Testament. This is evident from the fact that forty-one different passages are quoted either explicitly or implicitly in sixty-six different places in the New Testament.

The author (or authors?) of the second part of the prophecy in chapters 40 to 66 repeat many of the same ideas and phrases of Isaiah mentioned above. In addition, Second Isaiah stresses the Israelite belief that Yahweh is the Creator of the universe, that he governs history completely and is leading it to the end he has chosen, and that the divine will is for the salvation of mankind. The tone of Second Isaiah is not one of threat and condemnation but one of consolation and hope. He sees the return from Babylon as a New Creation and projects the same idea on the end time for the Day of the Lord. In chapters 56 to

66 there is a strong note of consciousness of sin and guilt that is not present in the previous parts of the book.

REFLECTION

"*Holy, holy, holy is the* LORD *of hosts; the whole earth is full of his glory*" (6:3).

Jeremiah

The LORD said to me, "Behold, I have put my words in your mouth. See, I have set you this day over nations and over kingdoms, to pluck up and to break down, to destroy and to overthrow, to build and to plant" (1:9–10).

PLACE IN THE BIBLE: Jeremiah, a major prophet, is located after the prophecy of Isaiah and before the book of Lamentations. The book contains fifty-two chapters.

DATE AND AUTHOR: Jeremiah was born about 645 B.C. and was called by God to be a prophet in the year 627. He prophesied on and off from that date until the fall of Jerusalem in 587 B.C. Jeremiah lived in a time of war, intrigue, and great social turmoil. He lived to see the destruction of Jerusalem and the Temple, his people being carried off to exile in Babylon. It was a time of darkness and despair.

THEME: The dominant theme of Jeremiah is the devastating consequences of sin. Sin inevitably brings sorrow. Even if God pardons sin, one must still suffer the consequences of it. But God punishes the sinner in order to heal him — to bring him to repentance and a change of heart. So the punishments of God are purifying. Jeremiah was deeply moved by the knowledge of Yahweh, who is utter mystery but at the same time is goodness beyond comprehension.

Jeremiah is the prophet of the interior life. For him the true religion of the future must be primarily interior. He speaks of circumcision of the heart and of a new Covenant (31:31–34) that God will write on the fleshy tablets of the heart.

SUMMARY: The many oracles of Jeremiah, which in the book are not arranged according to their historical setting, concern two major points: (1) oracles about the political and social situations of his time and (2) oracles about himself and his relationship with Yahweh. He is the most personal and the most self-revealing of all the prophets.

Jeremiah began to prophesy during the reign of King Josiah (640–609 B.C.). This period saw the collapse of the mighty Assyrian empire and the rise of Babylon. There was excitement about the Deuteronomic reform at Jerusalem when the book of the Law was found in the Temple in 622 and read to the people. Josiah began a real religious reform the following year.

Jehoiakim succeeded his father, Josiah (609–597 B.C.). He was a ruthless, crafty tyrant who was despised by Jeremiah. Against the advice of Jeremiah, he revolted against Babylon and brought another invasion and the capture of Jerusalem. This was a disaster. The Babylonians installed Zedekiah as king in his place (597–587 B.C.). He was the last king of Judah, who entered into foreign alliances against the advice of Jeremiah and thereby brought ruin on himself and the whole nation when the Babylonian army came and destroyed them.

Jeremiah was given the choice by the Babylonians of either going into exile or staying in Judah. He chose to stay but was forced by his compatriots to go into Egypt. He died there, probably about 582. There is a Jewish tradition that he was murdered there by his fellow Jews.

THEOLOGY: A special characteristic of the theology of Jeremiah is his proclamation of a "new Covenant" inscribed in the heart of each believer; this new Covenant was to be the fulfillment and completion of the Mosaic Covenant of Exodus. The main passage relating to this is found in 31:31–34. Jeremiah's Covenant was "new" only to the extent that it emphasized points in the old Covenant that were being neglected, that is, interior conviction and love to go along with external worship. The new Covenant finds its final fulfillment in the life, death, and Resurrection of Jesus.

Jeremiah declares forcefully that sin brings on its own sorrow. Like other prophets, he condemns idol worship and injustice in dealings with others, especially the poor and defenseless. There is a close similarity between Jeremiah's grasp of the connections: sin, suffering, repentance, forgiveness and new life, and the Deuteronomic theology found in the books of Joshua, Judges, 1 and 2 Samuel, and 1 and 2 Kings.

There is a strong emphasis on prayer and conversation with God in Jeremiah's prophecies. He has the boldness to question God on his dealings with man in what are called his "confessions"; they are found in 12:1–5; 15:10–21; 17:12–18; 18:18–23; 20:7–18. He never wavers in faith, but he is bold in questioning God; this same approach will be taken up by the author of the book of Job.

Jeremiah offers a few criteria for determining the difference between true and false prophets. The main criteria are: (1) fulfillment of prophecy, for if prophecies do not come true, that is a sign they are not from God; (2) avoidance of attempts to contact the other world, such as those offered by mediums, fortune-tellers, and necromancers; (3) living a personal moral life (the false prophets, because of their own wicked ways, did not warn the people or rebuke them because of their injustices and sensuality); (4) acceptance of the prophet by the community. Jeremiah is a classic example of a prophet who was rejected by his own contemporaries, because they did not want to hear what he had to say. But subsequent generations saw that he was a true prophet and incorporated his immortal words in what was to become the Bible.

In the New Testament Jeremiah is quoted seven times. In a broader sense, he prefigures Jesus in certain aspects of his life: (1) his call to prophetic celibacy (16:1–4); (2) his rejection in his native village; (3) his prophecy of the destruction of the Temple; (4) his prophecy about the destruction of Jerusalem; (5) his trial because of his preaching about the Temple. He suffers at the hands of his own people, like the "Suffering Servant" of Isaiah 53, and in this foreshadows Jesus, who is the true Servant of the Lord. The Letter to the Hebrews twice quotes Jeremiah's oracle about the new Covenant (Heb 8:8–12; 10:16). Also, St. Paul alludes to Jeremiah three or four times in his letters.

OUTLINE

REFLECTION

"This is the covenant which I will make with the house of Israel after those days, says the LORD: I will put my law within them, and I will write it upon their hearts; and I will be their God, and they shall be my people" (31:33).

Lamentations

How lonely sits the city that was full of people! How like a widow has she become, she that was great among the nations! She that was a princess among the cities has become a vassal (1:1).

PLACE IN THE BIBLE: The book of Lamentations comes after Jeremiah as a kind of "attachment" to the great prophecy and before the book of Baruch. The book contains five chapters, each of which is a distinct psalm.

DATE AND AUTHOR: Since the point of the book is to lament and bemoan the destruction of Jerusalem that occurred in 587 B.C., these psalms were written shortly after that date by a person or persons who witnessed the devastation of the city. It is not known whether one poet wrote the five psalms or whether they were composed by several. The book has often been attributed to Jeremiah, but the content of the psalms seems to argue against that.

THEME: The book offers a sustained lament over the destruction of the city of Jerusalem and the Temple by the Babylonians. The destruction does not prove that Yahweh was too weak to stop it. Rather, it was the Lord himself who brought this disaster on his people because of their sins. But it is not an expression of despair. Because of the Lord's promises to Moses and David, the psalmist is certain that, if Israel repents, confesses its guilt, and trusts in the Lord, it can count on his mercy and forgiveness. There will come a time of restoration.

SUMMARY: Each of the five psalms is a complete unit by itself. The first four are "acrostic", that is, each of the twenty-two sets of verses begins with the same letter of the Hebrew alphabet, one after the other — AA, BB, CC, and so on. The purpose of this acrostic device seems to be to establish some sense of divine order in the midst of suffering and social chaos.

Here is the general movement of each psalm: (1) two speakers, the psalmist and Zion itself, lament the destruction of Jerusalem; (2) the psalmist and Zion describe the Day of the Lord that has happened; (3) an individual laments and expresses his hope for deliverance; (4) the people express a communal lament in which they survey the desolate city; (5) the community humbly appeals to the Lord from its present pitiable state.

One should note that the individual, personal lament in psalm 3 is the middle and heart of the book.

THEOLOGY: Lamentations shows some affinity to the theology of the Deuteronomist, to Jeremiah, and to Second Isaiah. It is a prayer book for the people who survived the ravages of war; also these psalms are lyrics that are intended for chanting or singing.

The psalms express the viewpoint of someone who is standing in the desolate city, in the midst of the ruins of the Temple, and raises his sorrowing heart to the Lord. They recognize the prophetic truth that there is a direct connection between sin and suffering. Because Judah was not faithful to the Covenant with the Lord, it is punished with destruction. The prophets, like Jeremiah, had warned it again and again, but to no avail. But the Lord punishes to purify, to bring to repentance and conversion. In a sense the destruction of Jerusalem is another proof of God's love for Judah and Israel because it shows that he cares for them and loves them. He had threatened disaster for violation of the Covenant; they violated it, so here is the punishment. But the Lord is faithful; he is merciful and compassionate and will restore his favor to his people when they have a change of heart. So the poem is not all despair; it contains an undercurrent of hope and trust in God, which becomes explicit in the fifth chapter or psalm.

The psalmist refers to Jerusalem as "Daughter Zion" (1:6) and "Daughter Jerusalem" (2:15). This is a tender, affectionate title for the city borrowed from Isaiah and Jeremiah. It expresses the note of a familial relationship between God and Jerusalem. So the book of Lamentations, by calling desolate Jerusalem "daughter", expresses the conviction that the city and its people never cease to belong to the Lord — no matter what!

In the New Testament there are no explicit references to Lamentations. But for centuries Christians have been in the habit of praying the psalms of Lamentations during Holy Week as the lessons of Matins in a solemn liturgy called "*Tenebrae*" (Latin = "darkness") because they were celebrated in the night before Holy Thursday, Good Friday, and Holy Saturday. In the course of the celebration, the special candles for the event were extinguished, one after the other, as the psalms were sung.

REFLECTION

The steadfast love of the LORD never ceases, his mercies never come to an end; they are new every morning; great is thy faithfulness (3:22–23).

Baruch

*" 'O Lord Almighty, God of Israel, the soul in anguish
and the wearied spirit cry out to thee. Hear, O Lord, and
have mercy, for we have sinned before thee. For thou art en-
throned for ever, and we are perishing for ever' "* (3:1–3).

PLACE IN THE BIBLE: The book of Baruch is closely associated with Jeremiah. In most Bibles it comes after the book
of Lamentations, which follows Jeremiah, and before the
prophet Ezekiel. The book contains six chapters.

DATE AND AUTHOR: Because of the historical references, the
literary style, and the theology, most scholars agree that
the book is a composite of writings by three or four different authors, but it is attributed to Baruch, the secretary and companion of Jeremiah. The characteristics of
the book point to a composition in the latter part of the
second century B.C., sometime after the Maccabean revolt. Baruch is the associate of Jeremiah who transmit-
ted the prophet's words to King Jehoiakim in 605 B.C. He
took down dictation from Jeremiah and composed some
of the biographical sections of the book of Jeremiah. He
was taken with the prophet into Egypt about 587 when
the people fled there.

THEME: This book helps us to understand the inner spiritual life of the Jews in the diaspora, especially in Baby-

lon and Egypt. There is no one theme in the book, but it does give expression to the following beliefs and sentiments: loyalty to and love for Jerusalem and the Temple; obedience to the Law of Moses and to the distant authority of Jerusalem; emphasis on prayer; hope for the future and determined resistance to pagan influences of idolatry.

SUMMARY: After a brief introduction, which names Baruch and locates him in Babylon, there is a lengthy prayer that contains a confession of national guilt, a plea for forgiveness, and a hope for the restoration of Israel in accordance with God's promises in the past.

The heart of the prophecy is found in the poem that praises wisdom as a unique gift that the Lord has bestowed on his people Israel (3:9—4:4).

This is followed by a psalm (4:5—5:9) in which a personified Jerusalem addresses her children. She reminds them of their sins and encourages them with the hope of the Messianic blessings of the future.

The final section contains what is called "Jeremiah's Letter" addressed to the exiles in Babylon. It is a fierce polemic against idol worship that is not so much a letter as it is a type of sermon ridiculing idolatry and paganism (6:1–72).

THEOLOGY: The purpose of the scribal editor of Baruch is to call his people to repentance, conversion, and faith. The Deuteronomic theology appears here again: sin, punishment, repentance, prayer, and restoration to God's favor. The various parts of the prophecy assume that the Jewish people are spiritual exiles in this world. They are exiles and dispersed because of their past sins and the sins of their ancestors. Now they must repent, rekindle their faith in God's revelation and his great promises, and abandon all forms of idolatry.

The opening prayer is a confession of guilt and a plea for mercy. The prophet is certain that the Lord will deliver Israel because it alone bears his name and is the object of his promises.

The poem in praise of wisdom is the center of the book. It seems to be influenced by Job 28 and Sirach 24, which offer lavish praise of wisdom. This wisdom is unfathomable for man; it is not the intellectual speculation of philosophers but is actually identified with the Law of Moses as found in the Pentateuch. Other nations come and go — they perish for a lack of real wisdom, but Israel lives on by conforming itself to the wisdom of the Law of Moses, basically the Ten Commandments.

In the final psalm (4:5—5:9), Jerusalem is personified and pleads with her children to put their trust in the goodness of the Lord. God is using present suffering to chasten his people, to teach them humility, so that he may bless them in his own good time. God will reveal his glory and gather his people together from all corners of the world.

The final chapter is "Jeremiah's Letter" to the exiles in Babylon. In strong terms he ridicules idol worship, warns the Jews in exile to avoid it, while saying over and over again, "they evidently are not gods; so do not fear them" (6:16).

The book of Baruch is not quoted in the New Testament, but the description of wisdom descending to earth in the form of the Law of Moses in a veiled way anticipates St. John's account of the Incarnation of the Word of God in Jesus Christ (Jn 1:1–18).

REFLECTION

"Take courage, my children, cry to God, and he will deliver you from the power and hand of the enemy" (4:21).

Ezekiel

As I was among the exiles by the river Chebar, the heavens were opened, and I saw visions of God (1:1).

PLACE IN THE BIBLE: The book of Ezekiel is located after Baruch and before Daniel; after Daniel come the twelve minor prophets who, with 1 and 2 Maccabees, conclude the Old Testament. The book contains forty-eight chapters.

DATE AND AUTHOR: The prophet Ezekiel was active between the years of 593 and 571 B.C. The book was given its final form a few years after that by his disciples, so we can date the book of Ezekiel about 550 B.C.

THEME: Ezekiel is profoundly aware of the majesty and transcendence of God. He emphasizes the glory of the Lord, his holiness, his utter otherness. He is preoccupied with the Temple and its liturgy, and he makes a sharp distinction between the sacred and the profane. The main theme of his book is the need for inner conversion on the part of each person. Men must attain a new heart and a new spirit (18:31) in order to be acceptable to God. He goes so far as to say that God himself will bestow a new heart and a new spirit on his people (11:19; 36:26).

SUMMARY: In the first three chapters Ezekiel describes his calling to be a prophet; in the process he offers a powerful and graphic description of God Almighty. The body of the book is easily and clearly divided into four parts: (1) Chapters 4 to 24 contain prophecies of threats and reproaches directed against Jerusalem and Judah for their sins; (2) chapters 25 to 32 contain the oracles against the surrounding pagan nations, a feature common to the other major prophets; (3) chapters 33 to 39 offer comfort and a promise of a better future to the Israelites during the siege of Jerusalem and afterward; (4) chapters 40 to 48 describe the new community and the new Temple that will be established in Palestine in the future.

THEOLOGY: Ezekiel, as a priest, was deeply concerned about the Temple and Temple worship. He has a lofty notion of the transcendence of God and speaks of his overpowering presence in terms of the "glory of the Lord" and his "holiness". He holds the Law in veneration and repeatedly accuses the people of "profaning the Sabbaths". Ezekiel is very conscious of the guilt of Israel — it is a point he keeps repeating. When he reviews the past history of Israel, he sees it as an unbroken series of infidelities (see chaps. 16, 20, 23).

Ezekiel was a prophet of action, and more than the other prophets he uses symbolic gestures to get across his message, such as building a model of Jerusalem under siege, lying on his side for long periods of time, cutting off his hair and shaving his beard, joining two sticks together to make one — symbolizing the future union of Israel and Judah.

To a great extent Ezekiel was a *visionary*. His visions bring the reader into a new and fantastic world: the four living creatures of Yahweh's chariot, the dry bones in the desert that come to life, and the mighty river that flows from the new Temple to produce a fertile land like the Garden of Eden in Genesis 1–3.

Ezekiel does not have much to say about the Messiah, and there are only a few references to the Covenant with Moses. He repeats and develops an idea of Jeremiah (31:29–30) when he stresses the principle of individual retribution over collective: each person is responsible for his own good and evil deeds and will be rewarded by God accordingly (see chaps. 18 and 33). In the following prophets this insight leads gradually to the realization that full justice and retribution will take place in the next life. In this connection he teaches the need for inner conversion, putting on a new spirit and a new heart. This idea achieves its full realization in Jesus, who is the Good Shepherd foretold by Ezekiel. He is the one who establishes true worship "in spirit", which is preached here by Ezekiel.

Ezekiel influenced Jesus' frequent use of the term "Son of Man", the most common title Jesus uses to refer to himself in the Gospels. Ezekiel also influenced the book of Revelation, since St. John took over some of his powerful images: the four living creatures, a voice like the sound of many waters, Gog from the land of Magog, and the prophet's being carried to a high mountain.

Finally, it should be noted that what is called "apocalyptic" literature, such as is found in prophets like Haggai, Zechariah, Joel, and Malachi in the Old Testament and in the book of Revelation in the New Testament, originated in the prophecies of Ezekiel.

OUTLINE

I. Introduction: The vision of God's glory and the call of the prophet (1:1—3:27)

II. Prophecies of judgment on Jerusalem and Judah (4:1—24:27)

III. Oracles against the nations (25:1—32:31)

IV. Prophecies of restoration and promise for the future (33:1—39:29)

V. The new Temple and the new community (40:1—48:35)

REFLECTION

"A new heart I will give you, and a new spirit I will put within you; and I will take out of your flesh the heart of stone and give you a heart of flesh. And I will put my spirit within you, and cause you to walk in my statutes and be careful to observe my ordinances" (36:26–27).

Daniel

I saw in the night visions, and behold, with the clouds of heaven there came one like a son of man, and he came to the Ancient of Days and was presented before him. And to him was given dominion and glory and kingdom . . . which shall not pass away (7:13–14).

PLACE IN THE BIBLE: The book of Daniel comes after Ezekiel and before Hosea and the other eleven minor prophets. The book contains fourteen chapters.

DATE AND AUTHOR: The book is written as taking place during the time of the exile in Babylon, 587–537 B.C. But detailed information concerning the reign of the Greek King Antiochus IV Epiphanes (173–164), about the time of the Maccabees, indicates that the book was written about 165 B.C. The author is unknown.

THEME: Through stories about the wisdom of Daniel and his visions, the author says that God is the Master of history, which he directs to the goal he has set for it. He further affirms that those who trust in God and avoid all forms of idol worship will be blessed by God; and if this blessing does not happen in this life, the faithful one will be blessed in the next life. There is the added notion that the idol worship of the Gentiles is vain and stupid.

SUMMARY: The first part consists of six stories about Daniel. Daniel and his three companions, Hananiah, Mishael, and Azariah, are chosen for service in the household of the king of Babylon. Their refusal to eat unclean foods results in their becoming stronger and fairer than their pagan associates. The king, Nebuchadnezzar, dreams about a statue with a head of gold, breast and arms of silver, and so on. Daniel interprets the dream for him. Next, Nebuchadnezzar makes a huge statue of gold and commands all to adore it. Daniel's three companions refuse and are cast into the fiery furnace but are saved by a miracle. Next, the king dreams of a tree that is cut down; Daniel interprets this as a sign that the king will suffer from madness for seven years, which he does. Belshazzar, the last king, puts on a big banquet at which he and his guests profane the sacred vessels of the Jerusalem Temple. A hand appears and writes three words on the wall "mene, tekel, peres" (measured, weighed, divided). That night the king is killed by the Persians. Finally, Daniel violates a law of the Persians against praying to the God of Israel; he is cast into the lions' den, but he remains unharmed.

The second part deals with the visions of Daniel. Daniel saw four beasts coming from the sea, which signify four empires. The ten horns of the fourth beast signify ten kings of the Seleucid dynasty, and the little horn is Antiochus IV Epiphanes. The "son of man" probably refers to the people of Israel as a whole. Next is the vision of the ram and the goat. The ram with two horns signifies the kingdoms of the Medes and Persians; the great horn is Alexander the Great.

Next, Daniel prays in chapter 9 to understand the meaning of the seventy years mentioned by Jeremiah. The angel Gabriel appears to him in a vision and explains that it is seventy weeks of years; there will be great tribulations, but in the end Israel will triumph over its enemies. Next, Daniel sees as in a vision the current history from the time of Alexander down to his own time under Antiochus IV. This is called "apocalyptic literature" because it relates contemporary events in the form of a revelation made to a great man long ago. It also invokes all kinds of natural disasters with the final result of the wicked being judged and punished by God; the other side of this is the triumph of the just (chaps. 10 and 11). In chapter 12 Daniel sees that after a period of trials the dead will rise, some to life and some to everlasting suffering. This is the first expression in the Old Testament of belief in the resurrection of both the good and the wicked.

Chapters 13 and 14 contain three stories: The innocent Susanna, accused of adultery by two lecherous old men, is rescued by Daniel, who shows great wisdom. Daniel proves that the food and drink set before the idol of Bel was really taken and eaten secretly by the priests of Bel. Finally, Daniel kills a huge snake worshipped in Babylon. As a result he is cast into the lions' den again, but God saves him; this leads Cyrus the king to admit that the God of Israel is the true God.

THEOLOGY: The book of Daniel is a book of resistance and a book of martyrdom. It was addressed to the youth in the time of persecution under the tyrant Antiochus IV Epiphanes, the Seleucid king who tried to Hellenize the Jewish people. He banned the Jewish religion and persecuted even to death those who remained faithful to the Law of Moses. The stories in Daniel are edifying lessons that were intended to cultivate a sense of identity in Jewish youth. Our author uses the persuasive power of storytelling and poetry to try to convince them to resist the corruption of their religion. In their resistance they may suffer, like Daniel and his three companions, but God is all-powerful and will save them, if not in this world, then in the next life.

Chapters 7 to 12, which recount the visions of Daniel, are apocalyptic literature. This type of literature uses symbols and bizarre figures of imagination in order to explain the unfolding of God's plan for the world; it predicts a final intervention of God into human history, which will take the form of judgment.

The phrase "son of man" in 7:13–14 is important for future development in the Bible. In this context it probably does not mean the Messiah; rather it seems to refer to the whole people of Israel, who, by the power of God, will triumph over all their enemies. In the fuller sense of the Bible, this is a prediction of the triumph of the Church, which is the Mystical Body of Christ.

The first clear assertion of the resurrection of the body in the Old Testament is found in chapter 12. The final three stories about Susanna, Bel, and the Dragon, are intended to show the wisdom of Daniel — a wisdom he has received as a free gift from the God of Israel. His wisdom is much greater than that of the wise men of Babylon, the point being that the gods of the Babylonians are nothing, mere creations of man made out of gold, silver, and bronze. Since they are nothing, there is no reason to fear them.

In the New Testament, Daniel is quoted only once by our Lord, in reference to the "abomination of desolation" set up in the Temple by the pagan conquerors (Mt 24:15; Mk 13:14); this probably refers to setting up the image of a Roman god or emperor in the Temple. The resurrection of the dead is described in Matthew 25:46 in terms influenced by Daniel 12:2. But the most important borrowing from Daniel is the expression "son of man", which Jesus uses frequently to describe himself, in the process giving new meaning to the phrase.

OUTLINE

REFLECTION

"Bless the Lord, all works of the Lord, sing praise to him and highly exalt him for ever" (3:35).

Hosea

I desire steadfast love and not sacrifice, the knowledge of God, rather than burnt offerings (6:6).

PLACE IN THE BIBLE: The book of Hosea comes first in the list of the twelve minor prophets and after the book of Daniel. Hosea contains fourteen chapters.

DATE AND AUTHOR: Hosea was a contemporary of Amos (see p. 186) and lived in the northern Kingdom of Israel under Jeroboam II (786–746 B.C.). He began to prophesy in the last years of Jeroboam, about 745, and may have prophesied until 730 approximately.

THEME: The theme of the book is the love and fidelity of the Lord Yahweh for his people. This love is exemplified in the marital situation and problems of Hosea and his wife, Gomer. Gomer is unfaithful to her husband, Hosea, so he divorces her. He later relents and takes her back, but not before disciplining her. Hosea uses his marital trials as a symbol of the relationship between God and Israel. The people of the north worship false gods and violate the Covenant with the Lord in many ways. They reject his love, but he does not give up on them. His love for them is everlasting. He is about to punish them by the hands of the Assyrians and carry them off to exile, but a remnant will remain faithful and will eventually be brought back to their own land. The prophecy is also a metaphor of God's dealings with each one of us.

The second part of the prophecy, chapters 4 to 14, deals with Israel's crimes and infidelity and the punishment it will receive because of them.

SUMMARY: The prophecy reveals that Hosea is a very sensitive, emotional man who can pass quickly from anger to tenderness. The story revolves around his unfortunate marriage to Gomer, who is unfaithful to him. He loves her very much, and she betrays him by giving herself to a life of harlotry.

Gomer bears three children for him, and he gives them names that symbolize God's rejection of Israel because of its infidelity. Gomer is rejected by the prophet, but later he takes her back after punishing her for her sins.

The prophecy is most likely based on a true life experience of the prophet; under the influence of the Holy Spirit, Hosea sees that his experience with Gomer is a symbol or replica of the relationship between Israel (Gomer) and the Lord God (Hosea). All of the above is spelled out in the first three chapters of the prophecy.

In chapters 4 to 14 Hosea rebukes Israel for its crimes against God and the poor — for idolatry, for injustice, and for oppression of the poor and defenseless.

The book ends on a note of hope and reconciliation with God after Israel has been punished for its sins and has repented. God's love is everlasting, and he will never abandon his people.

THEOLOGY: Like Amos, Hosea was a prophet of doom, but he balanced his condemnation of Israel with the promise of restoration and renewal. So the prophecy manifests a certain optimism — an optimism based on the constancy of Yahweh's love for his people.

The key to understanding Hosea is the story of his marriage to Gomer, the separation, and finally the reconciliation. It is not fully clear whether he is talking about one woman or two women, but most scholars now think he is talking about one woman only, Gomer by name.

Gomer's adultery and desertion of Hosea symbolize the violation by the people of Israel of their Covenant with the Lord. For that, they will be punished and rejected — this will take place when Samaria is overrun by the Assyrians and the people are carried off into captivity.

What God expects of Israel is covenant love, or "steadfast love", which involves loyalty and fidelity; he also wants them to know him in a way that includes commitment of mind and will. This is summed up in the famous quote in 6:6, "For I desire steadfast love and not sacrifice, the knowledge of God, rather than burnt offerings."

Hosea is telling us how God acts in history. He proclaims that God's anger or judgment is for our own salvation. His purpose is not to destroy but to heal. Just as Hosea's love for Gomer was greater than her infidelity, so also God's love for Israel is greater than its waywardness.

In chapter 2 the theme of discipline through suffering is developed at some length. Israel is to be brought out into the desert again, as it was after the exodus from Egypt; this will take place in the coming exile in 721 B.C. But in the wilderness it will be purified and will respond to God's offer of love. It will once again enter into a permanent Covenant with the Lord.

The marriage symbol introduced by Hosea to describe the relationship between the Lord and his people was developed by the later prophets and was used in the New Testament. Thus, Jesus refers to himself as the Bridegroom (Mk 2:19–20) and performs his first miracle at a wedding feast (Jn 2:1–11).

St. Paul describes Christian marriage as a symbol of Christ's eternal love for the Church in Ephesians 5:21–33. Jesus' solidarity with the People of God throughout history is affirmed when Matthew refers to Hosea 11:1 — God calling Israel out of Egypt in the exodus; he applies the text to the return of the Holy Family from Egypt to Israel (Mt 2:13–23) and sees it as the fulfillment of the prophecy. A further use of Hosea in the New Testament is found in Matthew 9:13 and 12:7, where Jesus refutes the accusations of his enemies by referring to Hosea's statement that the Lord desires love rather than sacrifice (Hos 6:6).

OUTLINE

I. Hosea's marriage: God and Israel (1:1—3:5)

    A. Hosea's family: God's people

    B. Husband and wife: The Lord and Israel (2:4–25)

        1. A husband's accusation against his unfaithful wife

        2. Reconciliation between husband and wife

    C. Remarriage of husband and wife (3:1–5)

REFLECTION

Sow for yourselves righteousness, reap the fruit of steadfast love; break up your fallow ground, for it is the time to seek the LORD, *that he may come and rain salvation upon you* (10:12).

Joel

"I will pour out my spirit on all flesh; your sons and your daughters shall prophesy, your old men shall dream dreams, and your young men shall see visions" (2:28).

PLACE IN THE BIBLE: The book of Joel is second in the list of the twelve minor prophets, coming after Hosea and before Amos. The book contains three chapters.

DATE AND AUTHOR: Nothing is known about the author except that he wrote this book. It seems to have been written after Ezra-Nehemiah and before the world conquest of the Greeks in the fourth century B.C. So a probable date for the book is about 400 B.C.

THEME: The dominant theme of the book is the coming of the Day of the Lord. The expression "the Day of the Lord" first occurs in Amos 5:18–20, and it has meaning on two levels. Its fundamental meaning is that God is the Lord of history and that he can, and will, intervene in the course of history in favor of his people Israel. In the first sense, he will intervene in current history to overcome the enemies of Israel, for example, to give a military victory to Joshua or to the Maccabees; in the second sense, it means the end of the world, when God will destroy all human pride and will punish the wicked and reward the just.

SUMMARY: The book of Joel is divided into two parts. The first chapter and the first part of the second deal with a severe plague of locusts. That plague was most probably a true historical event of the times that was considered in the eyes of faith to be a punishment from God for the sins of the people. The second part of the second chapter and the third chapter describe the Messianic Day of the Lord, which is understood by the prophet as the end of history, the triumph of Judah, and the punishment of her enemies. Joel sees the plague of locusts as a type or foreshadowing of the eschatological or final intervention of God into human history at the end of the world. It is this idea of the "foreshadowing" of the end time that binds the two parts of the book together.

THEOLOGY: What makes the prophecy of Joel stand out in the Bible is the graphic apocalyptic description of the Day of the Lord. The nations will attack Israel, but they will be overcome by the power of God and will be punished. In the new era that follows, Israel will enjoy the blessings of God in abundance.

An outstanding aspect of the prophet's description of the new era is the pouring out of the Spirit (2:28–29). The Spirit will be given to all the members of the community, but Joel understands this only with regard to Israel. His vision is not broad enough to include all the nations of the world.

Like Haggai, Zechariah, and Malachi, Joel tends to stress the importance of the liturgy of the Temple in Jerusalem. In the first section he mentions that the plague of locusts, with the ensuing poverty and distress, caused a cessation in the Temple sacrifices. When the plague is over, prosperity returns, so the sacrifices can again be offered. In the second section the blessings of the final period have their source in the Temple, the dwelling place of the Lord.

Joel is quoted in two places in the New Testament. At the beginning of the first sermon in the Acts of the Apostles, which is the first Christian sermon ever given, St. Peter quotes Joel 2:28–32 about the gift of the Spirit to show that this prophecy has now been fulfilled in the pouring out of the Spirit on the apostles at Pentecost (Acts 2:17–21). A second quote occurs in Romans 10:13, where St. Paul quotes Joel 2:32 to the effect that "all who call upon the name of the LORD shall be delivered."

OUTLINE

I. The plague of locusts (1:1 — 2:27)

    A. The desolation of the land (1:1–12)

    B. Call to penance and prayer (1:13–20)

    C. The locust plague and the Day of the Lord (2:1–11)

    D. Call to penance and prayer (2:12–17)

    E. Removal of the plague and restoration of fertility (2:18–27)

II. The eschatological Day of the Lord (2:28 — 3:21)

    A. Eschatological blessings for Israel (2:28–32)

    B. Judgment upon the nations (3:1–16)

    C. The blessings of Israel (3:17–21)

REFLECTION

"Spare thy people, O LORD, *and make not thy heritage a reproach, a byword among the nations. Why should they say among the peoples, 'Where is their God?'"* (2:17).

Amos

"I am no prophet, nor a prophet's son; but I am a herds-
man, and a dresser of sycamore trees, and the LORD took
me from following the flock, and the Lord said to me, 'Go,
prophesy to my people Israel'" (7:14).

PLACE IN THE BIBLE: The book of Amos is third among
the twelve minor prophets, after Hosea and Joel and before Obadiah. Amos is the oldest of the written prophetic
books. It contains nine chapters.

DATE AND AUTHOR: The prophecies of Amos were delivered
during the reign of Jeroboam II (786–746 B.C.) at Bethel
in the northern Kingdom of Israel. The most likely date is
between 760 and 750. Amos was a shepherd from Tekoa in
the southern Kingdom of Judea who cared for sheep and
sycamore trees. He was not a professional prophet (7:14)
but received a personal call from God to go to the north
and proclaim the word of the Lord.

THEME: Amos is perhaps the most severe among all the
prophets. In very strong and poetic language, from beginning to end, he condemns external religious ceremony
and practice that camouflages social corruption and is not
accompanied by internal conversion of heart to the Lord.
He is the Old Testament prophet of social justice par excellence. Because of the Israelites' empty worship and tol-

eration of injustice, Amos prophesies that those in the north will be conquered and carried off into exile. That is exactly what happened a generation later when the Assyrians destroyed Samaria in 721 B.C.

SUMMARY: In the first two chapters Amos utters condemnations of the surrounding nations and also Judea and Israel: he names Damascus, Gaza, Tyre, Edom, Ammon, and Moab. He rebukes them because of their practices of injustice and immorality. In chapters 3 to 6 he strongly attacks the corruption in Israel and says that the Israelites are more to blame than the surrounding nations because God has spoken to them through Moses and they know the will of the Lord — they know that they are doing evil and still persist in it.

In chapters 3 to 6 Amos admonishes Israel for its empty worship, its social corruption and its toleration of injustices against the poor on a large scale. He warns them about the "Day of Yahweh" and the coming doom.

In chapters 7 to 9 the prophet describes five symbolic visions (locusts, fire, plumb-line, basket of ripe fruit, sanctuary) given to him by the Lord, which signal the coming destruction of Israel and Samaria because of their transgressions against the Lord and against the poor.

The conclusion promises a restoration of Israel from exile and the rebuilding of the fallen house of David, followed by the prosperity and glory of the Messianic age. So the book of Amos, after many dire threats, ends on a note of hope.

THEOLOGY: Amos is the first prophet to have a whole book of the Bible named after him. He is called by God to leave his flock and his sycamore trees and travel north to Bethel, the shrine in Israel built by the first Jeroboam in the tenth century B.C. Amos emphasizes the threatening dimension of God's word rather than the aspect of love, mercy, and forgiveness. The reason for this is that the people of the north are blessed with prosperity and peace, but their religious practice is purely externalistic — it does not affect the way they live. And the way they live is by exploitation of others and oppression of the poor.

Because of their sins and their neglect of the Law of Moses, Amos sees their impending doom. God is about to punish them for their sins. He introduces the concept of the "Day of Yahweh", when God will visit his people. The people of Samaria have deceived themselves into thinking that the "Day" will be a time of reward; Amos says that it will be a time of divine judgment and terror for the unjust. It will produce lamentation, not joy.

Amos instructs the people on how to interpret the coming Assyrian invasion. It will be the fulfillment of God's word and will bring about divine punishment for injustice. So in a certain sense we are dealing here with a prophetic theology of history.

It is not all gloom. Amos knows that the Lord will preserve "a remnant of Joseph" that will continue to practice justice. This remnant will be the basis of hope for the future restoration. God's action in history, therefore, is to save and not to destroy. The book ends on a note of hope.

REFLECTION

Seek good, and not evil, that you may live; and so the LORD, God of hosts, will be with you, as you have said. Hate evil, and love good, and establish justice in the gate; it may be that the LORD, the God of hosts, will be gracious to the remnant of Joseph (5:14).

Obadiah

For the violence done to your brother Jacob, shame shall cover you, and you shall be cut off for ever (10).

PLACE IN THE BIBLE: The book of Obadiah is the fourth of the twelve minor prophets, following Amos and before Jonah; the prophecy contains only one chapter.

DATE AND AUTHOR: The date is around 450 B.C. Nothing is known about the author except that he composed this brief prophecy against Edom.

THEME: The theme of the first half is the destruction of the country of Edom, south and east of Judah, an ancient enemy of Israel. The theme of the second half is the Day of the Lord and the restoration of Israel.

SUMMARY: The people of Edom were descended from Esau, the twin brother of Jacob, who stole the birthright from him. There was intense rivalry between them — and this continued for many generations among the descendants of the two brothers. When the Babylonians destroyed Jerusalem in 587 B.C., they were assisted by the Edomites; they also took the occasion of the fall of Judah to occupy some of the territory of Judah. The people of Judah deeply resented that, and it is reflected in this prophecy, which expresses much bitterness against Edom.

The short prophecy consists of two parts—the first announces God's judgment on Edom (1–15), and the second proclaims the salvation of Jerusalem (16–18). There is an appendix that describes the full extent of Israel's borders at the end of the world when God completes his work (19–21).

THEOLOGY: Obadiah expresses a passionate appeal for vengeance against an ancient enemy who took advantage of Judah when it was weak and down. The prophet reminds us of the terrible justice and power of God, who is the defender of what is right and the avenger of the oppressed poor. Obadiah reinterprets the earlier prophetic traditions that had threatened Judah and Israel with punishment for their crimes. He prophesies that "on the Day of Yahweh" the Lord will overthrow Israel's oppressors and will reveal his salvation to his own people. The prophet asserts God's judgment on human arrogance and his vindication of the poor and oppressed. In the final analysis, tyrants will suffer from their own tyranny; they will fall into the pit they have dug for others. Because God is the Lord of history, he will save his own people and bring his judgment upon the hostile nations.

The prophecy of Obadiah is not cited explicitly in the New Testament.

OUTLINE

I. The destruction of Edom (1–15)

II. The Day of the Lord (16–18)

III. Appendix: The promised land of the end time
(19–21)

REFLECTION

The day of the LORD is near upon all the nations. As you have done, it shall be done to you, your deeds shall return on your own head (15).

Jonah

"Arise, go to Nineveh, that great city, and proclaim to it the message that I tell you" (3:2)

PLACE IN THE BIBLE: The book of Jonah is fifth in the list of twelve minor prophets, after Obadiah and before Micah. The book contains four chapters.

DATE AND AUTHOR: The exact date of composition is not known, but Tobit refers to Jonah, so the book must have existed before the fourth century B.C. The Hebrew is like that of Ezra and Nehemiah, so it was probably written in the fifth century around 450 B.C. Nothing is known about the author except his name. There is mention of a Jonah, son of Amittai, in 2 Kings 14:25 (see Jon 1:1), but he was not the author of the book.

THEME: The theme is God's compassionate love for all mankind, Jew and Gentile. The author tries to reassure his fellow Jews that the divine oracles against their pagan neighbors, especially those contained in Isaiah, Jeremiah, and Ezekiel, were conditional, that is, conditioned by their repentance and conversion. God does not hate any of the peoples he has made.

SUMMARY: Jonah is unlike any of the other prophets, for the book does not contain oracles. It is an interesting, and sometimes humorous, story about a reluctant prophet who is called by God to go to Nineveh, the capital city of Assyria, which has always been hostile and cruel to Israel, to preach conversion to them and faith in Yahweh, the God of Israel. Jonah does not like the call, so he tries to flee from God by taking a Gentile ship to Tarshish, perhaps a place far away in Spain. God pursues him with a great storm; the pagan sailors discover that Jonah is the reason for the danger, so they throw him overboard. Immediately he is swallowed by a big fish, and the storm stops. After three days the fish disgorges him on the shore near Nineveh. Jonah goes to Nineveh and preaches repentance. All the people, including the king, do penance and are converted. Jonah leaves the city and climbs a hill nearby to see whether or not God will destroy the pagan city. God spares the city out of mercy and compassion.

THEOLOGY: The meaning of the book of Jonah depends on its literary form. Basically the question comes down to this: Is the book of Jonah factual history, or is it a parable, or some kind of story made up with the idea of teaching some divine truth? Opinions on this matter are divided.

1. Until the twentieth century, for about 2500 years, Jews and then Christians understood Jonah to be a historical account. It is so much a part of Western culture that virtually everyone has heard about "Jonah and the whale". Evangelical and Fundamentalist Christians hold that it is a true historical account of events that actually took place. The weight of history is on the side of this interpretation. The plus side of this view is that it avoids pitfalls in-

volved with a "symbolic" or "mythical" view of historical events related in the Bible, which, in the hands of some interpreters, destroys the historical value of the Bible and makes it all "myth". The problem with this interpretation is that it ignores the literary form of "parable", which is present in both the Old Testament and the New Testament —Jesus himself used it frequently in his teaching (see the parables of the good Samaritan, the prodigal son, Mt 13, and so on).

2. Liberal Protestant interpreters in the twentieth century, and currently most Catholic biblical scholars, interpret the book of Jonah as a parable or "didactic fiction", or even as allegory. They may interpret it differently, but they all agree that it is not a historical account. This view raises difficulties with some of the words of Jesus, because he seems to quote from Jonah as if it were a historical account, saying that just as Jonah was in the belly of the big fish for three days so would the Son of Man be in the underworld for three days, and then he would rise again from the dead, just as Jonah was deposited on the shore by the fish.

But what does the book of Jonah mean? The main point was expressed above under Theme: God's love and compassion extend to all human beings, Jew and Gentile. Jonah himself is an example of the narrowness and particularism found among many Jews of the time. This means that they thought God loved only Israel and had mercy only on it; they thought that God hated their pagan neighbors and had only punishment in store for them. So the book is a rejection of that type of Jewish narrowness. In this sense, the book of Jonah is a giant step forward in biblical religion, seeing that God's love and salvation are meant for all mankind but comes to them *through* Israel, the Chosen People.

In the New Testament, Jesus makes reference to "the sign of Jonah" as a type of his three days of death before his Resurrection (see Mt 12:39 and Lk 11:30).

OUTLINE

I. Jonah's first mission (1:1—2:11)

   A. Jonah's flight from his call onto the Gentile boat (1:1–16)

   B. His prayer for life and deliverance from the fish (2:1–11)

II. Jonah's second mission (3:1—4:11)

   A. Jonah preaches, and the pagan city of Nineveh repents (3:1–10)

   B. His prayer for death; deliverance by the tree (4:1–11)

REFLECTION

"I called to the LORD, out of my distress, and he answered me; out of the belly of Sheol I cried, and thou didst hear my voice" (2:2).

Micah

What does the LORD require of you but to do justice, and to love kindness, and to walk humbly with your God? (6:8).

PLACE IN THE BIBLE: The book of Micah is the sixth of the twelve books of minor prophets. It contains seven chapters.

DATE AND AUTHOR: Micah was a contemporary of Isaiah, so he prophesied during the years 740 to 701 B.C. Some of his oracles precede the destruction of Samaria in 721, and some come after that. He came from the town of Moresheth in southwest Judah, west of the city of Hebron. Like Amos, he lived in the country and rebuked the corrupt ways of city dwellers in Samaria and Jerusalem.

THEME: The book bounces back and forth from threats to promises. Micah threatens Israel and Judah with punishment and destruction if they do not repent of their sins of injustice. If they do repent, God will be gracious to them and promises to bless them abundantly. The prophet sees the Assyrians as the instruments in the hands of God to punish his people. But a remnant will remain to be the carriers of God's promises to his people; he will not destroy them completely, as he did the Assyrians and the Babylonians.

THEOLOGY: Micah proclaims that the political and military disasters that threaten Israel and Judah come from the anger of the Lord, which the people have aroused by their sins. The crimes that he denounces include: oppression of the poor and dishonesty; superstitious worship of Yahweh, that is, merely external works without internal conversion; the lack of genuine morality.

Micah views the coming punishment as something through which Israel must pass in order to survive. The reason for the punishment is to save and not to destroy. He will preserve a faithful remnant, and from that remnant a new David will arise who will restore the nation in a way that surpasses its former glory (5:1–3).

Micah predicts the destruction of Jerusalem in 3:12. He knows that he is a true prophet, not like those false prophets who tell the people what they want to hear. For him the charisma of the prophet is power and the spirit of Yahweh, judgment and strength to denounce sin and injustice. Micah practically summarizes the teachings of the prophets when he says bluntly what the Lord asks of his people, only this, "To do justice, and to love kindness, and to walk humbly with your God" (6:8).

St. Matthew in 2:5–6 quotes Micah 5:1–3 to prove that Jesus is the Messiah because the prophet had predicted he would be born in Bethlehem. There is also an allusion to Micah 7:20 in the Canticle of Zechariah in Luke 1:72.

OUTLINE

I. Punishment of Israel's sins (1:1—2:13)
   A. Judgment: On Judah
      1. Samaria and Jerusalem condemned
      2. Social injustice
   B. Promise: A remnant (2:12–13)
II. The New Israel (3:1—5:14)
   A. Judgment: On rulers, prophets, and kings
   B. Promise: Zion's dignity restored
   C. The remnant and the conquest of sin
III. The Lord's lawsuit and Israel's repentance (6:1—7:20)
   A. Judgment: The Lord's case against Judah (6:1—7:7)
   B. Promise: The liturgy of repentance and new life (7:8–20)

REFLECTION

As for me, I will look to the Lord, I will wait for the God of my salvation; my God will hear me (7:7).

Nahum

The LORD is slow to anger and of great might, and the LORD will by no means clear the guilty (1:3).

PLACE IN THE BIBLE: The book of Nahum is the seventh of the twelve books of minor prophets, following Micah and preceding Habakkuk. The book contains three chapters.

DATE AND AUTHOR: Nothing is known of Nahum except his name and that he is from the town of Elkosh; the site of the town is not known, and it is not mentioned elsewhere in the Bible. The book was most probably written either during or shortly after the siege of Nineveh by the Babylonians in 612 B.C.

THEME: The theme of the book is very simple: the fall of Nineveh, the capital city of the cruel and oppressive Assyrian Empire. The Assyrians had harassed and devastated Israel and Judah for over one hundred years. Now they were to be repaid for all the evil they had done to God's people. God does not allow sin and injustice to go unpunished.

SUMMARY: It is important to note that the Assyrians had invaded Israel and Judah several times in the eighth and seventh centuries. They were extremely cruel to the conquered peoples and deported them to other lands. They had destroyed the ten tribes of Israel in the north and had brought in foreign peoples to settle there and mingle with the few Israelites left; together they became the semi-pagan Samaritans who were despised by faithful Jews. Nahum utters oracles of doom and exultation over the destruction of the chief enemy of Judah and Jerusalem.

THEOLOGY: The prophecy seems to be quite secular and political; the prophet exults over the destruction of Nineveh and the fall of the Assyrian Empire. There are no threats here directed against his own people. The name of Yahweh is mentioned twice (2:13; 3:5). But Nahum sees Yahweh as the real agent in the destruction of Nineveh; he makes use of the Babylonians to achieve his goal in history. The prophet sees the fall of Nineveh as proof of the principle of Israelite belief that the Lord will eventually punish the wicked and those who oppress others. So he sees God acting in history. The past and present tyrant is destroyed. Nahum does not reflect on the possibility of a new tyrant rising to take the place of the Assyrians, namely, the Babylonians. They will be the next tyrant to oppress Judah and eventually to destroy Jerusalem.

From a literary point of view, the oracles of Nahum reach a high poetic level. Some scholars consider Nahum to be among the best written books in the Old Testament.

In the New Testament St. John seems to have made use of Nahum's portrayal of the ruin of Nineveh as a model for his description of the destruction of Rome under the symbol of Babylon the Great (Rev 17—18).

OUTLINE

I. The Lord, Assyria, and Judah (1:1—2:1)

    A. Introductory psalm: The Lord's wrath

    B. Judgment on Assyria and promises for Judah

II. Nineveh's desolation (2:2—3:19)

    A. The final assault on Nineveh

    B. Meditation on Nineveh's ruin and futility

REFLECTION

The Lord is good, a stronghold in the day of trouble; he knows those who take refuge in him. But with an overflowing flood he will make a full end of his adversaries, and will pursue his enemies into darkness (1:7).

Habakkuk

"Behold, he whose soul is not upright in him shall fail, but the righteous shall live by his faith" (2:4).

PLACE IN THE BIBLE: The book of Habakkuk is the eighth of the twelve books of the minor prophets, following Nahum and preceding Zephaniah. The book contains three chapters.

DATE AND AUTHOR: Because the author sharply attacks the hated Babylonians before they attacked Jerusalem in 597 B.C., it is very likely that the prophecy was composed between 605 and 597. Nothing is known of Habakkuk's life and person except that he seems to have been associated with the Temple in Jerusalem in some way.

THEME: In the context of the oppression of Judah by the Babylonians, the theme of the book is the problem of evil, and specifically how God permits his ends to be accomplished by evil and unbelieving oppressors.

SUMMARY: The book contains three main parts: (1) a dialogue between the prophet and God about injustice (1:1–2:4); (2) the proclamation of five woes on the Babylonian invaders (2:5–20); (3) a final psalm announcing the revelation and victory of God (3:1–19).

THEOLOGY: There is an inner unity and progression of the text that points to one author. It moves from complaint about injustice to a vision of God's judgment on the wicked and finally to a revelation of the glory of God. The book moves from a certain doubt about the evil around us to a vision of how God will deal with it and finally to a basic trust in God no matter how bad things may appear to be.

The first step in the answer to the problem of evil is that God brings down one oppressing nation (Assyria) by another (Babylon). The next step is that in the rise and fall of nations the just or righteous man will survive by his fidelity to Yahweh (2:4). The final step is that Yahweh himself is the one who saves the just man (chap. 3).

In this prophecy for the first time in Israelite literature a man questions the ways of God. For Habakkuk calls him to account for his governance of the world. God replies that he is using Babylon to punish the wicked, but he reassures the prophet that the just Israelite will not perish in the coming disaster. There is a hint here again of the "remnant", even though the word is not mentioned.

Because there are several obscurities and ambiguities in the book of Habakkuk, it has stimulated many commentaries over the centuries.

In developing his idea of faith, St. Paul quotes Habakkuk in saying that the just man lives by faith (Gal 3:11; Rom 1:17; cf. Hab 2:4). Because all of us have sinned, we cannot be justified by works alone. Justification comes only through faith in Jesus Christ, who has redeemed us by shedding his blood for us (cf. Rom 3:20–28). The author of Hebrews quotes the same text in order to stress the importance of faith and perseverance in times of persecution (Heb 10:38; cf. Hab 2:3–4). Finally, in her Magnificat, Mary, the Mother of Jesus, is an example of the faith and confidence in God foreshadowed in Habakkuk when she prays, "My spirit rejoices in God my Savior" (Lk 1:47; cf. Hab 3:18).

OUTLINE

I. Dialogue between the prophet and God (1:1—2:4)

    A. Concerning injustice (1:2–11)

    B. Concerning the Babylonian victory (1:12—2:4)

II. Five woes proclaimed against the oppressors (2:5–20)

III. A psalm: Divine revelation and deliverance (3:1–19)

REFLECTION

God, the Lord, is my strength; he makes my feet like hinds' feet, he makes me tread upon my high places (3:19).

Zephaniah

"I will leave in the midst of you a people humble and lowly.
They shall seek refuge in the name of the LORD, those who
are left in Israel" (3:12).

PLACE IN THE BIBLE: The book of Zephaniah is the ninth
book in the collection of the minor prophets, following
Habakkuk and preceding Haggai, and contains three chapters.

DATE AND AUTHOR: Zephaniah prophesied under King Josiah but before his religious reform, so about 635–630 B.C.
He seems to have been a native of Jerusalem with connections to the royal court. He was the first important
prophet to arise in Judah in the approximately fifty years
following the death of Isaiah.

THEME: Zephaniah lived at the end of the period of the
kings of Judah and just before the destruction of Jerusalem
in 587 B.C., the exile, and the restoration. Two themes
stand out in the prophecy that he got from his predecessors, Amos and Isaiah: (1) the Day of the Lord is coming
soon, and (2) a remnant will survive in Judah.

THEOLOGY: The sins Zephaniah attacks are the superstitions and idol worship practiced under Mannasseh, Amon,
and the early Josiah in the seventh century B.C.; he does
condemn social sins, but his main concern is superstitions.

He is aware that the oppressive Assyrian empire is about to fall to the Babylonians. The coming fall of Judah and Jerusalem will be the Day of Yahweh (1:7, 14–17), which will be an intervention of Yahweh in history in a theophany of power and judgment.

Zephaniah is faithful to the prophetic tradition in his conception of judgment and punishment as the result of sin, especially the sins of idolatry and injustice to one's neighbor; because Judah has sinned, it will be severely punished. He is one of the less original prophets, since he borrows heavily from Amos and Isaiah, especially the key notions of the Day of Yahweh, the holy remnant, and the deliverance and the glory of Israel.

The punishment of the surrounding nations should serve as a warning (3:7) to bring God's people to obedience and humility; salvation is promised only to a humble and submissive "remnant" (3:12–13). This is as far as Zephaniah's Messianism goes. The Day of Yahweh will destroy the pride and arrogance of Judah, and it will bring forth a holy remnant, which will prosper because of its faith, humility, and submission to the ways of God.

There are no direct quotes of Zephaniah in the New Testament, but the graphic description of the dreaded Day of Yahweh in 1:14–18 inspired the opening words of the famous medieval dirge *Dies Irae*.

REFLECTION

Sing aloud, O daughter of Zion; shout, O Israel! Rejoice and exult with all your heart, O daughter of Jerusalem! The LORD has taken away the judgments against you, he has cast out your enemies (3:14–15).

Haggai

" 'I am with you, says the LORD of hosts, according to the promise that I made you when you came out of Egypt' " (2:4–5).

PLACE IN THE BIBLE: The book of Haggai is among the minor prophets and usually comes after Zephaniah, in the tenth place, and preceding Zechariah. The book contains two chapters and is one of the shortest books in the Old Testament.

DATE AND AUTHOR: The book was written between August and December in 520 B.C., the second year of the reign of Darius I of Persia. Nothing is known about the life and person of Haggai, but he is mentioned as a prophet, along with Zechariah, in Ezra 5:1 and 6:14.

THEME: The theme of the book is an exhortation by the prophet to the leaders and people of Jerusalem *to rebuild the Temple,* which had been destroyed by the Babylonians in 587 B.C.

SUMMARY: In 587 B.C. the conquering Babylonians had destroyed Jerusalem and the surrounding towns in Judah. Some of the leaders were executed, and the rest were taken into exile in Babylon. Poor people were left in the land to survive as best they could.

In 539 B.C. the Persians under Cyrus conquered the Babylonians. Cyrus decreed that the conquered peoples could return home, so in 537 the first group of Judean exiles returned to a devastated Jerusalem/Judah. They immediately began to rebuild the Temple but soon gave up the project because of a lack of funds and personnel.

In 520 God raised up the prophet Haggai to give the people heart and to urge them to finish the job of building the Temple in 515 B.C., when it was consecrated and dedicated to the worship of the Lord Yahweh.

THEOLOGY: The Temple in Jerusalem is very important in the Jewish religion because it locates the presence of God with his people (Hag 1:13; 2:4). Those who returned from the exile are the *remnant* of Israel, that is, the small group that God would use to fulfill his promises to David and his descendants. By mentioning the remnant, Haggai reminds us of the promise to David in 2 Samuel 7 (cf. Ps 89), which is essential in understanding the role of David in salvation history; for Jesus is the "Son of David", who fulfills all the promises. So even though the prophecy is mainly an exhortation to the people to rebuild the Temple, it has a very strong Messianic tone. In the context of the whole Bible, Old Testament and New Testament, it points to Jesus as the Messiah.

The prophet says that the reason for the poverty and suffering of the people is that they have not rebuilt the Temple (1:9). When they begin work on the Temple, he will bless them with abundance of food — grapes, figs, pomegranates, and olives.

The book ends on a very positive note with a promise

to Zerubbabel, the current ruler and descendant of David. The prophet says that the Messianic hope of Israel will be fulfilled through Zerubbabel, who is a type of the Messiah (that is, Jesus) whom God will send in the future to restore and save all Israel.

REFLECTION

" *'For thus says the Lord of hosts: Once again, in a little while, I will shake the heavens and the earth and the sea and the dry land; and I will shake all nations, so that the treasures of all nations shall come in, and I will fill this house with splendor, says the Lord of hosts'* " (2:6–7).

Zechariah

"Sing and rejoice, O daughter of Zion; for lo, I come and I will dwell in the midst of you, says the Lord" (2:10).

PLACE IN THE BIBLE: The book of Zechariah is eleventh in the list of the minor prophets, after Haggai and before Malachi, who is the last of the prophets. The book contains fourteen chapters.

DATE AND AUTHOR: Zechariah was a contemporary of Haggai and prophesied during the years 520–518 B.C., that is, after the return of the exiles from Babylon and before the rebuilding of the Temple was complete. He was the son of Iddo, who had returned from exile with Zerubbabel and Joshua. He was a priest and so shows special attention to the Temple.

THEME: The main theme of the prophecy is the rebuilding of the Temple in Jerusalem, which had been totally destroyed by the Babylonians in 587 B.C. In this he is closely associated with the prophet Haggai. But a very strong feature of the book is its Messianism, especially in the second half.

SUMMARY: In 587 B.C. the Babylonians had conquered and destroyed Jerusalem and the surrounding towns in Judah. Some of the leaders were executed, and the rest were taken into exile in Babylon. A few poor people were left in the land to survive as best they could.

In 539 B.C. the Persians under Cyrus conquered the Babylonians. Cyrus decreed that the conquered peoples could return home, so in 537 the first group of exiles returned to a devastated Jerusalem/Judah. They immediately began to rebuild the Temple but soon gave up the project because of a lack of funds and personnel.

In 520 B.C. God raised up the prophets Haggai and Zechariah to give them heart and to urge them to finish the job of building the Temple, for the Temple localizes and gives a certain visibility to the presence of God in the midst of his people. As a result of the prodding of the two prophets, the people went to work again and finished the Temple in 515 B.C., when it was consecrated and dedicated to the worship of the Lord Yahweh.

THEOLOGY: Because of the sharp differences in language and content between chapters 1 to 8 and 9 to 14, the vast majority of scholars hold that the last six chapters were added in the late fourth century to the earlier prophecy of Zechariah.

The dominant idea in both parts is Messianism, that is, predicting the future coming of the Son of David, who would save his people Israel. Messianic significance is attributed to the new Temple and also to the governor, Zerubbabel, who was the last member of the house of David to rule over Judah and Jerusalem.

Zechariah also stresses the notion of *universalism* in the sense that the salvation promised to Israel is to be offered to all the nations. In addition, he often refers to the importance of moral conversion as a necessary preparation for the inauguration of the new era.

The absolute transcendence of God is brought out in this book by the developed theology of angels. God usually does not speak directly to Zechariah; he communicates with him through angels and visions.

The second part of Zechariah, often called "Deutero-Zechariah", in addition to being Messianic is also heavily apocalyptic — a special type of biblical writing that interprets events in the present world by reference to what is taking place in heaven. Thus the prophet speaks of the defeat of the foreign oppressors of Israel and the "Messianic woes" that will usher in the final triumph of the Messiah. Jerusalem is mentioned frequently. The Messianism of Deutero-Zechariah plus the emphasis on the "new age" are the reason for the number of quotes of Zechariah found in the four Gospels (for example, Mt 21:4–5; Jn 19:37). Zechariah also influenced St. John in the writing of the last book of the Bible, the book of Revelation.

OUTLINE

I. Call to conversion (1:1–6)

II. Eight visions (1:7—6:15)

    A. The four horsemen (1:7–17)

    B. Four horns and four blacksmiths (2:1–4)

    C. The angel with the measuring line (2:5–17)

    D. Joshua the high priest (3:1–10)

    E. The lampstand and the two olive trees (4:1–14)

Rejoice greatly, O daughter of Zion! Shout aloud, O daughter of Jerusalem! Lo, your king comes to you; triumphant and victorious is he, humble and riding on an ass, on a colt the foal of an ass (9:9).

Malachi

"For from the rising of the sun to its setting my name is great among the nations, and in every place incense is offered to my name, and a pure offering; for my name is great among the nations, says the LORD of hosts" (1:11).

PLACE IN THE BIBLE: The book of Malachi is the last book of the twelve minor prophets, coming after Zechariah and before 1 and 2 Maccabees. The book contains four chapters.

DATE AND AUTHOR: The contents indicate that the book was written after the founding of the restored Temple in 515 B.C. and before the advent of Ezra about 445. So a reasonable date is the middle of the fifth century B.C. — about 450. Details about the author are not given. The name of the prophet, "Malachi", means "my messenger", and the word occurs in 3:1. It could be either a proper name or a title; it is probably a proper name.

THEME: Malachi is a prophet who proclaims God's word to a people who have become self-centered and neglectful of the pure worship of God. They have fallen into a state of spiritual complacency and lack of zeal for God and his commands. Their religious practice has become an empty ritual that reflects lives devoid of personal reverence. His task is to stir them up to fervor and zeal for God and for

God's Commandments. He tries to cultivate in the people a lively faith based on reverence for God and the Temple worship, fidelity to the Commandments, and a holy fear of divine judgment, which will surely come.

SUMMARY: The book contains six messages or oracles: (1) The Lord loves Israel in spite of her faults; (2) the priests and Levites have been unfaithful by neglecting the standards related to the offering of sacrifices and teaching the Law; (3) God hates divorce and marriage with foreigners; (4) the Lord will surely come to purify the Temple and the Levites; (5) prosperity of the land will return when honest tithing at the Temple is restored; (6) those who fear the Lord and keep his commandments will be saved on the day of judgment. A later editor, probably around 300 B.C., added two appendices; one refers to Moses (4:4) and the other to Elijah as the precursor of the Day of the Lord (4:5–6).

THEOLOGY: Malachi, like Haggai, Zechariah, and Joel before him, lays much stress on matters of worship. He regards the Temple, the priesthood, and the liturgy as central elements in the restored community and in the Messianic age to come. He confronts the spiritual aridity and mere externalism of his people with a call to fidelity to the Law of God, to reverence for holy things, to reverent awe before the living God. He warns them that the Day of the Lord is coming, when God will reward the just and punish the wicked, a theme that is borrowed from the Deuteronomic history.

Beginning with the Fathers of the Church, Christians have seen a prediction of the Holy Eucharist in the remarkable words found in 1:11: "For from the rising of the sun to its setting, my name is great among the nations, and in every place incense is offered to my name, and a pure offering." This is a good example of the "fuller sense" of Holy Scripture and a prophecy that the true worship of God as found in the Church will spread throughout the world.

The prophet condemns social evils, especially divorce, which is explicitly rejected in 2:16: "For I hate divorce, says the LORD, the God of Israel."

In the final verses the prophet says that God will send "Elijah the prophet before the great and terrible day of the LORD comes". Jesus interpreted this to mean the coming of John the Baptist before his own appearance (Mt 17:10–13). Malachi's understanding of divorce is based on Genesis rather than on Moses' permission of divorce in Deuteronomy 24:1–4. This establishes a precedent for Jesus' rejection of divorce in Matthew 19:3–9 (see Mal 2:15–16).

By ending his book on the positive note of the coming of the precursor before the Day of the Lord, the last prophecy of the Old Testament leads directly to the New Testament with the preaching of John the Baptist and his pointing out Jesus as the Lamb of God.

OUTLINE

I. Six prophetic oracles (1:1—4:3)

   A. God's love for Israel (1:1–5)

   B. Unfaithfulness of the priests in the Temple (1:6—2:9)

   C. The sin of divorce and marriage to foreigners (2:10–16)

   D. The Lord's messenger will purify the Temple (2:17—3:5)

   E. Repentance, tithes, and blessings (3:6–12)

   F. Those who reverence the Lord will survive judgment (3:13—4:3)

II. Two appendices (4:4–5)

   A. Moses and the Law at Sinai (4:4)

   B. Elijah and the coming Day of the Lord (4:5–6)

REFLECTION

"Behold, I send my messenger to prepare the way before me, and the Lord whom you seek will suddenly come to his temple; the messenger of the covenant in whom you delight, behold, he is coming, says the LORD *of hosts"* (3:1).

1 Maccabees

Then Mattathias cried out in the city with a loud voice, saying: "Let every one who is zealous for the law and supports the covenant come out with me!" And he and his sons fled to the hills and left all that they had in the city (2:27–28).

PLACE IN THE BIBLE: First Maccabees comes after Malachi and, with 2 Maccabees, concludes the Old Testament. It contains sixteen chapters.

DATE AND AUTHOR: First Maccabees was written around the year 100 B.C. It is not known who the author was, but the content of the book indicates that he was a Palestinian Jew, very familiar with the geography and customs of the Jews in second-century Israel. The book exists only in Greek but was written originally in Hebrew.

THEME: The theme of the book is that God was with Mattathias and his sons in their struggles to liberate Israel from foreign, Greek occupation. The purpose of 1 Maccabees is clearly to defend the legitimacy of the Hasmonean dynasty, that is, the Maccabees and their descendants, who ruled Israel and Jerusalem in the second and first centuries B.C. Since they were not descended from Aaron (and so priests) nor from David (and so kings), there was some question about their legitimacy. First Maccabees responds to that problem.

SUMMARY: To understand the books of Maccabees it is necessary to know something of the political situation of the time. The action takes place between 175 and 134 B.C. in Palestine. After the death of Alexander the Great in 323 B.C., his huge empire was divided between his generals. Seleucus took Syria and the Near East; Ptolemy took Egypt —Palestine is located between the two. They fought with each other, on and off, for control of what we call the Holy Land. From the death of Alexander to the beginning of our story, Greek culture became dominant in the whole area; this is called "Hellenism" or "Hellenization". Many Jews were affected by Hellenism and, in order to be "modern", abandoned Judaism to adopt the Greek ways. What was going on was what we now call a "culture war".

A new Seleucid king came on the scene in 175. He was Antiochus IV Epiphanes. He began a campaign to outlaw Judaism and to persecute all practicing Jews. He even set up a pagan god on the altar of sacrifice in the Temple in Jerusalem.

A family of devout Jews, led by Mattathias and his three sons, resolved to fight a guerilla war against the occupying Greek force. To do this they took to the mountains and began a series of raids against the enemy. These Jews are called the Maccabees, which means "hammer". When Mattathias was killed in battle, he was followed by his sons Judas, Jonathan, and Simon. They were very successful in defeating the pagans and eventually captured Jerusalem and the Temple, which they purified and rededicated to the Lord God of Israel. The period of 175 to 134 was a time of turmoil and war. The book of 1 Maccabees is therefore a historical account of the leadership and battles of the Maccabees. By 134 the faithful Jews were in control of most of Palestine. Then the son of Simon and the grandson of Mattathias, John Hyrcanus I, took over from his father as high priest and ethnarch of Palestine. He ruled until 104 B.C., and his reign was marked as a time of peace. What was peculiar about the Maccabees was that they joined in the person of the leader both religious and political power because the military leader was also the high priest of the Temple in Jerusalem.

THEOLOGY: At first sight, 1 Maccabees seems to be a secular history of political intrigue, power struggles, and guerilla warfare. The literary genre is history — and religious history, for the author intends to tell us what happened to the Jewish people in Palestine during most of the second century B.C. The dominant idea running through the story is that God is the Master of history, as we have seen before in the older historical books of the Old Testament. In the present case he works through the family of Mattathias and his three sons, Judas, Jonathan, and Simon. They are successful, our author tells us, in defeating the Hellenizers or pagans because they are faithful to the Covenant and the Law of Moses. In fact, they are victorious against vastly superior armies. In this he is implicitly comparing them to the judges of old and to Saul and David. The theology is similar to that of the Deuteronomist, that is, God rewards in this life those who obey the Covenant, and he punishes those who violate it.

So the author of 1 Maccabees attributes their success to their prayer and spirituality.

The Maccabees fought for the purity of the Temple worship and for a strict observance of the Law. In this they were the forerunners of the Pharisees and Sadducees we are familiar with in the Gospels.

First Maccabees is not quoted directly in the New Testament, but some of the ideas contained in the book had an influence on the Jewish culture into which Jesus was born over a century later. For, the success of the Hasmoneans in achieving liberation by the sword and violence contributed to the thinking during the time of Jesus that the promised Messiah would be a great military leader like Judas Maccabeus. They also highlight the importance of Jerusalem and the Temple — an attitude reflected in the Gospels, especially in St. Luke. Jesus himself rejected the violent ways of the Maccabees in order to establish the Kingdom of God. Jesus taught the primacy of meekness, humility, avoiding revenge, accepting of suffering, and love for one's enemies. This was a teaching that was totally new. It was distinctive of the apostles and the early Christian Church.

OUTLINE

I. Antiochus Epiphanes: Brutal suppression of Judaism (1:1–64) (175–164 B.C.)

II. Mattathias: Priest and beginner of the revolt against the Hellenists (2:1–70) (166 B.C.)

III. Judas Maccabeus: Commander of the holy war
(3:1—9:22) (166–160 B.C.)

IV. Jonathan: High priest and statesman (9:23—12:53)
(160–143 B.C.)

V. Simon: High priest and architect of the Hasmonean
dynasty (13:1—16:17) (143–134 B.C.)

VI. John Hyrcanus I, successor to the Maccabees
(16:18–24) (134–104 B.C.)

REFLECTION

"Blessed art thou, O Savior of Israel, who didst crush the attack of the mighty warrior by the hand of thy servant David. . . . So do thou hem in this army by the hand of thy people Israel, and let them be ashamed of their troops and their cavalry. . . . Strike them down with the sword of those who love thee, and let all who know thy name praise thee with hymns" (4:30–33).

2 Maccabees

And when he was at his last breath, he said, "You accursed wretch, you dismiss us from this present life, but the King of the universe will raise us up to an everlasting renewal of life, because we have died for his laws" (7:9).

PLACE IN THE BIBLE: Second Maccabees is the last book of the Old Testament. The book contains fifteen chapters.

DATE AND AUTHOR: The book was written after 124 B.C. — about twenty-five years before 1 Maccabees. The author is unknown, but he is a different person from the one who wrote 1 Maccabees. The author was most probably a Palestinian Jew; his main source was a five-volume work by Jason of Cyrene (2:23–26) in North Africa, who wrote in Greek.

THEME: The author sets out to show how the events of Jewish history from the time of Onias the high priest to the time of Judas Maccabeus (from 180 to 160 B.C.) reveal a God who cares for the Jewish people by rewarding those who are faithful to the Covenant and by punishing evildoers. He has great regard for the Temple and Temple worship and for fidelity to the Torah, or Law, of the Jews. In a sense, it is a story of God's divine providence guiding and protecting his faithful Jewish people when they are attacked by pagan Hellenizers. It is a story of those who are militarily weak overcoming the mighty because they pray to God, trust in him, and obey his laws.

SUMMARY: The story begins with two letters from Jerusalem to the Jews in Alexandria, Egypt (the intellectual center of Hellenism), urging them to celebrate the rededication of the Temple in Jerusalem; this is the feast of Hanukkah, or feast of lights. The author then adds a brief foreword in which he explains that, in his own way, he will summarize the five-volume work of Jason of Cyrene about the exploits of Judas Maccabeus and his family.

The body of the book has three main parts: (1) the story about the miraculous conversion of Heliodorus in the Temple (chap. 3); (2) the desecration of the Temple and its rededication by Judas during the reign of Antiochus IV (4–10); (3) the final military campaigns and victories of Judas Maccabeus during the reigns of Antiochus V and Demetrius I (10:9–15:36). The author then adds a personal note at the end as epitomizer of Jason's five volumes.

The book is very theological and spiritual. The author deals explicitly with God's intervention in history in order both to discipline his people Israel and to protect them from their enemies. The Temple predominates the story; the soldiers pray and fast before going into battle, and when they are victorious, they offer prayers of thanksgiving and attribute the victory to the Lord. The book emphasizes the high value of suffering and martyrdom for the faith; the motivation for this is the belief in the resurrection of the body and that God will reward his faithful people in the next life.

THEOLOGY: Second Maccabees is a story of dramatic, even rhetorical, history, sounding at times like the book of Deuteronomy. The book is loaded with theology and spiritual insight; these are indications of why the book is included in the canon of Holy Scripture. The book is not primarily an apology for the Hasmonean rulers, but rather it seeks to illustrate the theological point that God rewards the faithful and punishes the impious. Like 1 Maccabees, 2 Maccabees rejects any compromise with Hellenism and the secularism and idolatry connected with it, but the main idea is that God is active in history on behalf of his people.

The author is passionately supportive of the Torah and the Temple. Judas and his companions are successful against the vastly more powerful Syrians because they are fighting for God and his Temple, because they trust in him and obey his laws, including the observance of the Sabbath, and because they pray and ask for divine assistance.

In the suffering of the Jewish mother and her seven sons (chap. 7) and in the suicide of the elderly Razis (chap. 14), the author says that suffering can have a positive value as a kind of divine education or discipline; God may discipline his people, but he never abandons them (6:12–16). Further, the suffering of the innocent leads the author to affirm his belief in the resurrection of the dead (7:9, 11, 14, 23; 14:46). One of the strongest affirmations of the resurrection in the Old Testament is found in these passages in 2 Maccabees.

Through his victories, Judas brings salvation to the persecuted Jewish community. In this he is a model of the just man in the Old Testament and as such is a type of Jesus Christ, who saved all men by his Passion, death, and Resurrection.

The author of 2 Maccabees wants to edify his readers. The accent throughout the book is on divine activity on behalf of the faithful. Important theological points in the book that are part of the theology of the Catholic Church are: (1) the resurrection of the body (chaps. 7 and 14); (2) belief that the living can help the dead by their prayers and sacrifices (12:38–45); (3) the creation of the world by God alone, who produced it from nothing (7:28); (4) the efficacy of intercessory prayer on the part of the saints in heaven, like the prophet Jeremiah (15:13–16).

There are no direct quotes from 2 Maccabees in the New Testament, but some of the ideas in the book are reflected there. For example, the vivid portrayal of martyrdom in the book established a norm for witnessing to the faith that inspired Christians who faced persecution two hundred years later (see Heb 11:35–38; Acts 7:54–8:1). Also, belief in the resurrection was taken up by the Pharisees and helped to prepare the minds of the Jewish people to accept the full revelation about the resurrection and eternal life from Jesus, the Messiah.

REFLECTION

"I beseech you, my child, to look at the heaven and the earth and see everything that is in them, and recognize that God did not make them out of things that existed" (7:28).

The New Testament

Matthew

"Blessed are the poor in spirit, for theirs is the kingdom of heaven" (5:3).

PLACE IN THE BIBLE: The Gospel according to St. Matthew is the first book in the New Testament. The book contains twenty-eight chapters.

DATE AND AUTHOR: Scholars of the past hundred years have tended to place Matthew late in the first century, after A.D. 70 and the fall of Jerusalem. A good case can be made from ancient tradition and from the language and ideas in the Gospel that it is early and indeed the first of the four Gospels. If we locate it at A.D. 43, it would have been composed about ten years after the death and Resurrection of Jesus.

Ancient Christian tradition tells us that the author was St. Matthew, one of the apostles (also called Levi). The text itself shows us that the book was written by a Jewish Christian for Jewish Christians. The original language was Aramaic, the language that Jesus and his disciples spoke in Palestine at the time. At an early date it was translated into Koine Greek, the language in which it has come down to us. The Aramaic original has not been preserved.

THEME: Matthew's theme is that Jesus was the Messiah whom the Jews were looking for; the leaders of the people recognized him but rejected him and so cut themselves off from the Messianic Kingdom. Jesus did not come to destroy the Law but to fulfill it; this notion of fulfillment runs through the whole Gospel. Jesus is also presented as the Savior of the world, the Son of God, the Son of David, and the New Moses; he is Emmanuel, or God-with-us, now and until the end of the world in his Church (chaps. 1 and 28).

SUMMARY: Matthew begins his careful account of Jesus' life and death by giving his genealogy and then beginning with his miraculous birth and infancy. Along the way he cites the Old Testament to show that Jesus is the fulfillment of the prophecies about the Messiah. When Jesus appears as an adult of about thirty years of age at the Jordan, he is baptized by John the Baptist and then is tempted in the wilderness by the devil. He begins to proclaim the imminent coming of the heavenly Kingdom (concretely realized for Matthew in the Church).

On the Mount of Beatitude, like a New Moses, Jesus sketches the Kingdom's constitution and describes it as a more interior reality than the religion of the Old Testament. He performs many miracles as a sign of his divine power, and the crowds flock to him. Next, Jesus chooses the Twelve to help him in the work of evangelization; he gives them power to perform miracles and sends them on a tour of the Galilean villages.

In short order he encounters strong opposition from the religious and intellectual leaders of Judaism, while the crowds do not understand him. He begins to teach them in parables in order to stir up their curiosity. The Scribes and Pharisees become more hostile and demand a miracle from him as proof of his claims. He rebukes them sharply but still promises the future sign of his redemptive death and Resurrection.

From this point on, Jesus concentrates on the formation of his disciples. He is always on the move — an itinerant preacher — and even goes north to the pagan lands near Tyre and Sidon. He has compassion on the crowds and the infirm, but he no longer speaks to them at length. The faith and devotion of the disciples grow until a climax is reached with Peter's profession of faith at Caesarea Philippi (chap. 16).

When he arrives in Jerusalem to give his life for the salvation of all, Jesus condemns the religious leaders (23:13ff.). They in turn are determined to see that he is put to death. In a reserved and dispassionate way, Matthew tells the story of Jesus' Passion — condemnation, scourging, carrying of the Cross, and crucifixion on Calvary. He then gives a glimpse of the joyful meeting of the disciples with the risen Christ (chap. 28) and concludes his Gospel with Jesus' command to his disciples to convert the whole world (28:16–20).

THEOLOGY: The Gospel of Matthew tells the story of Jesus from a particular point of view. Each of the four evangelists sees Jesus from a particular perspective; each therefore has his own theology. In studying the Gospels, it is important to note the differences and the similarities between them. Matthew presupposes that the reader is familiar with the Old Testament, which he quotes forty-one times, usually with the formula "that it might be fulfilled"

(1:23). He presents Jesus in the first verse as the Son of David and the Son of God. The words of the angel to Joseph in chapter 1 give a clue to the whole Gospel: Jesus is begotten of the Holy Spirit, he will "save his people from their sins", he will be born of a virgin, and he will be called "Emmanuel" or "God with us".

Matthew presents Jesus, from the beginning of his public life, as a teacher like Moses; he is also the Messiah but is rejected by the religious leaders of the people — just as the prophets before him were rejected. But he has not come to destroy the Law of Moses but to fulfill it (5:17–19); so the notion of "fulfillment" is a key to the proper understanding of what Matthew is saying.

Because the Jews rejected Jesus, the Kingdom is given to the Gentiles (21:33–46; 23). There is no room for him in the inn, but the magi (2:1–12), who are Gentiles, are among the first worshippers of Jesus. This incident gives us an indication of Matthew's universal view that Jesus has come to save all mankind. The same idea is contained at the end of the Gospel in his great missionary command to convert all nations.

Matthew can be described as the Gospel of the Kingdom, since he uses that word so often. As it is used in the Gospel, "Kingdom" means the reign of God over the heart of man; so the members of the Kingdom are those who are humble, obey God, worship him alone, observe his Law, and believe in Jesus as the Messiah — the fulfillment of all the prophecies. They are the ones who belong to the Kingdom, which is not a place but a quality of life or being in reference to God and his will. Jesus calls all to enter into his Kingdom. The originality of Matthew lies in his explicit identification of the Kingdom with the Church (16:18 and 18:17).

In Matthew the Kingdom is not just a future reality; rather it is present right now as an existing society. This is clear from the parables of the weeds (13:24–30, 36–43) and the net (13:47–50). That the Kingdom-Church is a hierarchical society, of which the disciples are the present existing reality and the future governing body, is clear from the "ecclesial discourse" in chapter 18.

Matthew's Jesus has a dignity and majesty that is very attractive. He is a great teacher and shows infinite compassion for the sorry plight of sinful man. Perhaps that is why the Gospel of Matthew was quoted by the Fathers of the Church more often than any other Gospel. Also, it is quoted frequently in the liturgy of the Church. It is said that St. Dominic, the founder of the Dominican Order, carried a copy of St. Matthew's Gospel with him wherever he went.

From the above it should be clear that there is a close relationship between Matthew and the Old Testament. He quotes it forty-one times explicitly, and there are many other direct and indirect allusions. For Matthew sees Jesus as the *fulfillment* of the Law of Moses, the prophets, and the psalms. The reason for their existence is to point to Jesus as Messiah, Savior, Son of God, and God-with-us.

OUTLINE

I. Introduction: Birth and infancy of Jesus (1:1—2:23)

II. Foundation of the Kingdom (3:1—7:29)

    A. Narrative section (3:1—4:25)

    B. Sermon on the Mount (5:1—7:29)

III. The Kingdom of Heaven is proclaimed (8:1—10:42)

    A. Narrative (8:1—9:37)

    B. Instructions to the Twelve (10:1—11:1)

IV. Mystery of the Kingdom of Heaven (11:2—13:53)

    A. Narrative (11:2—12:50)

    B. Discourse of parables (13:1-53)

V. The Kingdom in the Christian community (13:54—19:1)

    A. Narrative (13:54—17:27)

    B. Discourse on the Church (18:1—19:1)

VI. Jesus prophesies the coming of the Kingdom (19:2—25:46)

    A. Narrative (19:2—23:39)

    B. The end and the Second Coming (24:1—25:46)

VII. Passion and Resurrection of Jesus (26:1—28:20)

REFLECTION

"Come to me, all who labor and are heavy laden, and I will give you rest. Take my yoke upon you, and learn from me; for I am gentle and lowly in heart, and you will find rest for your souls. For my yoke is easy, and my burden is light" (11:28–30).

Mark

"The time is fulfilled, and the kingdom of God is at hand; repent, and believe in the gospel" (1:15).

PLACE IN THE BIBLE: The book of Mark is the second Gospel in the New Testament, after Matthew and before Luke. The book contains sixteen chapters.

DATE AND AUTHOR: Ancient witnesses attribute the second Gospel to John Mark, a cousin of Barnabas who was a companion of St. Paul. He is mentioned several times in the New Testament (Acts 12:12; Col 4:10; 2 Tim 4:11; 1 Pet 5:13, and elsewhere). The book was written near the year A.D. 60, while Peter was in Rome. Tradition agrees that Mark was an interpreter or translator for St. Peter and that the Gospel was written in Rome for Gentile Christians. This is shown by Mark's use of language, by the rarity of quotes from the Old Testament, and the fact that conflicts between Jesus and the Pharisees are downplayed in comparison to the other Gospels.

THEME: The theme of the Gospel is that Jesus is the Son of God and that he is the Messiah promised by the prophets in the Old Testament, but Mark puts special emphasis on the fact that Jesus is a *suffering Messiah*. Because of this, he is misunderstood by his disciples and rejected by the leaders of Judaism because they were expecting a powerful political Messiah who would, like Moses of old, liberate them from the power of the hated Roman conquerors. Jesus uses the obscure term "Son of Man" to refer to himself, rather than "Messiah", which would tend to give the wrong impression of his Person and his mission. Only after his death does he accept the title of "Messiah", which means "Christ", or the Anointed One.

SUMMARY: The basic outline of the story of Jesus as told by Mark is quite simple when compared to Matthew and Luke. The book begins with the preaching of John the Baptist, the baptism of Jesus, and his temptation by the devil. Next comes a period of ministry in which Jesus visits the town and villages of Galilee, preaches, and performs miracles (1:14 — 7:23). From the very beginning he is greeted with envy and hostility on the part of the Jewish religious leaders. So he departs for the Gentile districts of Tyre and Sidon, which are west and north of Galilee; then he goes to the Ten Cities over near the present Golan Heights, east of the Sea of Galilee and Caesarea Philippi, which is at the headwaters of the Jordan River, which flows into the northern end of the Sea of Galilee. Here the confession of faith in him by Peter and the other disciples is a high point of the Gospel and also a turning point (7:24 — 8:38).

This is followed by Jesus' Transfiguration on Mount Tabor and the final journey through Jericho near the Dead Sea and on up to Jerusalem. There he confronts the Jewish leaders; this is followed by his Passion, death, and Resurrection.

Like Matthew and Luke, Mark describes only one trip

of Jesus to Jerusalem, while John lists at least three journeys there. Of course, Mark is writing a Gospel, which is "preached history" or a story of faith directed to those who have faith. He gives us the broad outlines of Jesus' life, not a day-by-day diary. At first the crowds receive Jesus warmly, especially when they see the miracles he works and personally profit from them. But their enthusiasm wanes when they begin to understand that this humble man does not fulfill their hopes of a Messiah who will be a political liberator. Therefore, Jesus leaves Galilee and devotes himself to the further training of his small group of faithful followers. Once he has received their profession of faith at Caesarea Philippi, he turns his attention to Jerusalem, where he will offer his life for the salvation of the world and attain the triumph of his Resurrection from the dead.

THEOLOGY: From the very first verse, Mark sets out to proclaim the good news of Jesus Christ, the Son of God (1:1). In Matthew, Jesus stands forth strongly as a teacher and preacher; in Mark the narrative is more concerned with Jesus' mighty deeds than it is with his words. The person of Jesus stands at the center of the Gospel. The primary question Mark sets out to answer is: Who is Jesus of Nazareth? The answer he gives is that Jesus is the Son of God, the Messiah, and the Son of Man. These are the main titles he applies to Jesus in his short Gospel.

That Jesus is divine and is the Son of God is revealed less in dogmatic statements than in the exercise by Jesus of divine power and authority: for example, in the forgiveness of sins (2:10–12), expulsion of demons (1:28; 3:11), knowledge of the secrets in men's hearts (2:8; 12:15), and predictions of free future events (8:31ff.). Also, the title "Son of God" occurs at critical points: in the very first verse (1:1), in the Transfiguration (9:7), and in the confession of the centurion at the death of Jesus (15:39).

In addition to describing Jesus as divine, Mark also stresses his humanity — in fact he does this more than the other evangelists. He says that Jesus is a carpenter (6:3); he attributes many human emotions to Jesus: anger (3:5), grief (3:50), pity (6:34), indignation (10:14), fondness for children (10:16). Jesus also asks several questions in Mark's Gospel, indicating that he does not know everything in his human knowledge (5:30; 8:5; 9:16–21; 13:32).

The most explicit doctrinal feature of Mark is the idea of the coming of the Kingdom of God or the reign of God over the hearts and minds of men. But in Mark this idea is more eschatological than it is present. He does not mention the Church, nor does he explicitly identify the Church with the Kingdom, but he does not exclude this connection either.

Many modern commentators on Mark point out what is known as "the Messianic secret", that is, Jesus tries to conceal the fact that he is the Messiah (1:34, 44; 3:12; 5:43; 7:36; 8:26; 8:30; 9:9). The reason for this is that the people had a false notion of what the Messiah should be — a political and national leader. Jesus identified himself as the rather obscure Son of Man and the humble Suffering Servant of Isaiah 52–53.

The secret is this: The Messiah is a *suffering Messiah* (8:27–34; 9:30–32; 10:32–34). So the Jesus of Mark is the Jesus of the Passion. In order to be true to him and to understand him, one must see his glory in his suffering and his crown in and through his Cross.

The truth about who and what Jesus is, is revealed progressively in the Gospel, key points being the profession of faith in him by Peter in chapter 8, the middle point of the Gospel, and the proclamation by the centurion under the Cross that he is truly the Son of God (15:39).

OUTLINE

   I. Prologue: Preaching of John, baptism, and temptation of Jesus (1:1–13)

  II. The Galilean ministry (1:14—6:6a)

    A. Capernaum and the surrounding district (1:14–45)

    B. Conflict between Jesus and religious leaders (2:1—3:6)

    C. Success of Jesus and more conflicts (3:7–35)

    D. Parables (4:1–34)

    E. Four miracles at the Sea of Galilee (4:35—5:43)

    F. Conclusion of Galilean ministry; rejection in his hometown of Nazareth (6:1–6a)

 III. The journeys of Jesus (6:6—10:52)

    A. Mission of the apostles (6:6b–29)

    B. Journey and return; feeding of the five thousand (7:1–23)

    C. Journey and return; miracles and controversy (7:24—8:12)

REFLECTION

"Abba, Father, all things are possible to thee; remove this cup from me; yet not what I will, but what thou wilt" (14:36).

Luke

"Behold, this child is set for the fall and rising of many in Israel, and for a sign that is spoken against" (2:34).

PLACE IN THE BIBLE: Luke is the third Gospel; it is located after Mark and before John. The book contains twenty-four chapters.

DATE AND AUTHOR: Ancient tradition going back to Irenaeus, Tertullian, Clement of Alexandria, Origen, Eusebius, and Jerome attributes the third Gospel (and also the Acts of the Apostles) to Luke. He appears in the New Testament as a companion of St. Paul in Colossians 4:14; 2 Timothy 4:11; Philemon 24. The book was written about A.D. 64, before the death of St. Paul. The literary form and the theology of the book clearly show that it is the work of a Gentile Christian written for Gentile Christians.

THEME: The theme is that Jesus of Nazareth is the Messiah promised to the Jews in the Old Testament; by his suffering and death he has entered into the glory of God the Father and thereby has effected the salvation of all mankind from sin and death. It has been called a Gospel of mercy and universal salvation because Luke stresses the fact that the redemption merited by Jesus is intended for everyone, not just for the Jews.

SUMMARY: Luke tells us in his prologue what he intends to do — to give an "ordered account" of the life of Jesus. He begins his story with the Annunciation to Mary that she is to be the Mother of God, the birth of John the Baptist, the birth of Jesus, and his infancy. Then he follows the traditional outline as found in Matthew and Mark: After being tempted by the devil, Jesus first preaches, works miracles, and gathers disciples in Galilee. The turning point is found in 9:51, when Jesus decides to go to Jerusalem to preach and to die. On the way he teaches his disciples that he must die and rise again on the third day, but they do not understand what he means. Much of Jesus' teaching and many of his parables are found in this journey narrative. Having arrived in Jerusalem, he stirs up the animosity of the leaders of Judaism, so they plot to put him to death. Then follows the account of his suffering, death, and Resurrection. In the final chapter he appears to his disciples and before their very eyes ascends into heaven.

Over the centuries many commentators have pointed out the excellence of Luke's composition and the elegance of his literary style in Greek. But this is not just a brief "history" of Jesus. It is more than that. It is a Gospel that sets out, while giving us many details of the life of Jesus, including his deeds and words, to persuade us that Jesus is the Savior of the world. In the prologue, that is what he says he intends to do, and careful study of the Gospel shows that he accomplishes his goal.

THEOLOGY: The Gospel of St. Luke is very artistically put together, not only with regard to the way the story of Jesus is told but also with regard to the theology. Luke abides by the tradition that Jesus preached the Kingdom of God, that he is the Messiah and the Son of God, but he puts his own special emphasis on the Person and message of Jesus.

The first thing the reader should note is that the Gospel begins in Jerusalem and ends in the same Holy City. During most of the Gospel Jesus is on his way to Jerusalem. So the Holy City is central to the thinking of Luke in the sense that man's salvation is accomplished in Jerusalem, and, after the Resurrection of Jesus, the apostles go out from Jerusalem to bring the good news to the whole world.

The concrete events of Jesus' life, his infancy and public life, are viewed by Luke in the light of the mystery of the Passion and Resurrection of Jesus, because that is the will of his heavenly Father (24:26).

Luke sees Jesus' salvific death and its merits as directed to the benefit of all men, not just to Jews. The old man Simeon calls Jesus "the light of the nations" (2:32), and Jesus himself before his Ascension tells his apostles to preach repentance for the forgiveness of sins "to all nations", beginning from Jerusalem (24:47).

Luke also stresses the gentleness, mercy, and compassion of Jesus more than Matthew and Mark do. More women appear in Luke than in the other Gospels; so Luke avoids the Jewish attitude of disdain toward women, which was common at that time. In the same vein, Luke portrays Jesus often as the friend of sinners and outcasts, as in the case of Zacchaeus (19:1ff.); the same idea finds expression in the parables of the lost sheep (15:1–7), the lost drachma (15:8–10), and the prodigal son (15:11–32).

Another outstanding example of this is Jesus' promise of heaven to the good thief (23:40–43).

The Holy Spirit is one of the main actors in the Gospel, beginning with the first two chapters. He is active in the Incarnation of the Son of God, and he is with Jesus throughout his public life. This produces a sense of joy, as we see in the Benedictus (1:66–79) of Zechariah and Mary's Magnificat (1:46–55). The coming of salvation in Jesus creates an atmosphere of prayer in Luke's Gospel, in which Jesus and others are frequently described as being at prayer.

Finally, Luke emphasizes the importance of poverty and detachment from material things. He brings this out in his version of the Beatitudes (6:20–26), in the parable of the rich man and Lazarus (16:19–31), and the story about the rich fool (12:13–21). He also repeats several times that the followers of Jesus must abandon all things in imitation of him (for example, 5:11, 28; 11:41; 12:13–33).

There is an old tradition that Luke was a physician. He may have been, but efforts to prove it just from the text of the Gospel have not been successful. Luke does quote from the Old Testament but not nearly as much as Matthew does. The reason is obvious: Luke was writing for Gentile Christians, most of whom would not have been familiar with the Law and the prophets, and so he could not presume that they would see the force of the argument. Luke is the last of the synoptic Gospels (so called because of their quite visible [syn-optic = with the eye] similar structure). Luke is followed by the Gospel according to St. John, a Gospel that is very different from the synoptics.

REFLECTION

"Father, hallowed be thy name. Thy kingdom come. Give us each day our daily bread; and forgive us our sins, for we ourselves forgive every one who is indebted to us; and lead us not into temptation" (11:2–4).

John

These [signs] are written that you may believe that Jesus is the Christ, the Son of God, and that believing you may have life in his name (20:31).

PLACE IN THE BIBLE: St. John's Gospel is the fourth book in the New Testament, coming after Luke and before the Acts of the Apostles. The book contains twenty-one chapters.

DATE AND AUTHOR: The almost unanimous testimony of the early Church is that John the Apostle, brother of James, is the author of the Gospel. He is the "disciple whom Jesus loved". There is no unanimity today among scholars on the date of composition. Most place it about A.D. 90, when John was an old man, but there are also persuasive arguments that St. John's Gospel was written before the destruction of Jerusalem in A.D. 70. There are two traditions about the place of composition—Antioch and Ephesus; the former is more likely. The book was written in Greek, but since John also spoke Aramaic and Jesus spoke that language, there is of necessity an Aramaic influence on the book. Detailed knowledge of Jewish language, customs, and geography prove beyond any doubt that the author was a Palestinian Jew.

THEME: The theme of the Gospel is that Jesus of Nazareth is the Messiah who was promised by God to the Old Testament patriarchs and prophets and that he is the only Son of God the Father. Belief in him is the only way to eternal life. (See 20:31, quoted above.)

SUMMARY: John begins with a prologue in which he asserts that Jesus of Nazareth is the eternal Word of God, who became man in order to save those who believe in him. Here John asserts the divinity of Jesus and that Jesus existed eternally before he became man. Jesus is pointed out as the Messiah by John the Baptist at the Jordan, and he gathers disciples around himself. Gradually he reveals himself and his divinity to his disciples by the majesty of his teaching and Person and by the miracles or "signs" he worked at Cana, the multiplication of the loaves, walking on water, curing the man born blind, and raising Lazarus from the dead.

Jesus reveals himself as light and life, as the true Bread of Life that replaces the manna of the Old Testament, as the Good Shepherd. He is also the source of the Holy Spirit, which he refers to as "living water". He cures the man born blind (chap. 9) and in doing so shows that those who believe in him can see, while those who reject him are spiritually blind.

When Jesus raises Lazarus from the dead (chap. 11), he so infuriates the Jewish leaders that they decide to have him put to death. This seals his fate. At this point in the story the public ministry of Jesus comes to an end.

Chapters 13 to 17 present the Last Supper, with Jesus washing the feet of his apostles and speaking eloquently about eternal life, faith, his Father, the Holy Spirit. There is heavy emphasis on love for God and for one another, the consoling and strengthening activity of the Holy Spirit, and the need for unity among all the believers.

John's account of the Passion is traditional and is similar to the stories of the other evangelists.

After his Resurrection, Jesus appears to the holy women who followed him and to his disciples. There are two conclusions to the Gospel. In between the two is the account of Jesus' appearance to his apostles at the Sea of Galilee. Here he confers special authority in the community on Peter by saying to him, "Feed my sheep" (21:17).

THEOLOGY: When you pass from reading the first three "synoptic" Gospels and come to John, you will notice immediately that John is different from Matthew, Mark, and Luke. The story does not follow the same lines, and Jesus does not talk the same way he does in the other Gospels. Here we get a very different view of him. It is a new world.

St. John's Gospel is full of talks or discourses in which Jesus enters into a kind of dialogue with his audiences. There are frequent interruptions and questions from his adversaries; this does not happen in the synoptic Gospels.

There is no "Messianic secret" in John because in this Gospel the author stresses the divine transcendence of Jesus: He is the Word of God who reveals his glory in his words and in his miracles, like changing water into wine at Cana, curing the man born blind, and raising Lazarus from the dead. In John Jesus is presented as very aggressive in his preaching and whole manner of life.

The main themes or topics are also different. John rarely mentions the Kingdom of God (twice). Instead he speaks of life and eternal life; love, truth, and light; he refers to himself in the "I am" formula fifty-four times; he speaks of bearing witness, judging, dwelling; he talks about the world often, about Jews, and he speaks of God as Father 118 times.

John is not intensely interested in eschatology, that is, the question of the end of the world and the Second Coming of Christ. The focus is more on Jesus being present and active in his Church right now; for John, the end of the history of the world is already basically attained in the resurrected Christ, who has triumphed over Satan, sin, and death. Those who believe in him share in that victory in a spiritual way now.

John emphasizes the divinity and glory of Jesus. He sees through external appearances to the reality that is hidden in Christ Jesus, the Son of God and Savior of the world.

The Gospel is also sacramental in its approach, that is, there are many subtle references to the sacraments: the water changed into wine points to the Eucharist; the discussion with Nicodemus is about the necessity of Baptism; the water and wine flowing from the pierced side of Jesus on the Cross symbolize Baptism and Eucharist; after his Resurrection Jesus gives his apostles the power to forgive sins (Sacrament of Penance).

The Gospel of St. John is a treasure hidden just under the surface. The deeper you dig, the more treasure you find. The book is full of symbolism — Jesus is the source of light and life and truth.

John does not contradict the synoptics; rather, what he

does is *complement* them by giving us a different view of Jesus. Because Jesus is God, he is the divine mystery that can never be exhausted. John, himself a mystic, tries to help us to see just a little bit of that mystery.

The eagle soars high in the sky and has an amazing power of vision. There is a just reason for calling St. John "the Divine" and for using the eagle as his symbol.

OUTLINE

REFLECTION

"Father, the hour has come; glorify thy Son that the Son may glorify thee, since thou hast given him power over all flesh, to give eternal life to all whom thou hast given him. And this is eternal life, that they know thee the only true God, and Jesus Christ whom thou hast sent" (17:1–3).

The Acts of the Apostles

"You shall be my witnesses in Jerusalem and in all Judea and Samaria and to the end of the earth" (Acts 1:8).

PLACE IN THE BIBLE: Acts comes after the Gospel of St. John and before Paul's great letter to the Romans. The book contains twenty-eight chapters.

DATE AND AUTHOR: The author is St. Luke the evangelist, who wrote the third Gospel. Acts is the second volume of a two-volume work and continues the story of Jesus in the community or Church he founded before his death and Resurrection. Since it is closely linked to the Gospel, it was written shortly after St. Luke's Gospel, probably about A.D. 65.

THEME: The theme of Acts is the lively story of the growth of the Church of Jesus Christ, after his Resurrection from the dead and under the impulse of the Holy Spirit, and the expansion of the Church from Jerusalem to the known civilized world and even to Rome, the capital of the Empire.

SUMMARY: Acts is a fast-moving historical account of the first beginnings of the Christian Church and her rapid spread to the whole civilized world. The story comes to an end when Paul of Tarsus, one of the heroes of the story,

arrives in Rome in chains and is under arrest. In brief outline, here is the way the story develops.

It begins with the glorified Jesus commanding the apostles to evangelize the whole world, after which he ascends
into heaven. The apostles select Matthias by lot to replace
Judas the betrayer. In chapter 2, on Pentecost, Peter gives
the first Christian sermon and converts three thousand
Jews to Christ. The apostles preach Jesus in Jerusalem and
stir up opposition from the Jewish leaders. They are persecuted, put in jail, and rescued by divine intervention.
The sermons of Peter in the first five chapters spell out
how Christ was preached at that time.

Seven deacons are appointed by the apostles; Stephen
gives a lengthy address to the Sanhedrin, showing that
Jesus is the Messiah. He is stoned to death, with the
help of Saul of Tarsus. After this, many Christians flee
Jerusalem and go to other cities, especially Antioch. The
conversion of Saul to Paul the Apostle is narrated in chapter 9. This is a very significant event, since he will be the
hero of the second part of Acts, while Peter is the hero of
the first part.

In chapters 10 and 11 we read how Peter, inspired by
the Holy Spirit, enters the house of the pagan Cornelius
and preaches to him and his household; the Holy Spirit
descends on them, and they are baptized. This is a turning
point, for it reveals God's will that the salvation of Jesus
is destined for all peoples.

At this point Barnabas and Paul come on the scene and
begin, slowly, their work of evangelizing the nearby pagan
peoples. To their surprise, the Gentiles believe in Christ,
and the Jews, for the most part, reject him. Another cli-

max of the story is reached in chapter 15 at the Council of Jerusalem, when the apostles decide that Gentiles do not have to observe the Jewish Law of Moses in order to be accepted into the Christian community. From that point on, Paul, Barnabas, and his other associates, like Timothy and Titus, are turned loose to spread the good news of salvation in Jesus Christ everywhere. They establish local churches in many of the major cities of the time, like Thessalonica, Ephesus, Corinth, Philippi, and so forth.

Paul goes to Jerusalem in the late fifties and is arrested for being a disturber of the peace. He appeals to Caesar and so is sent to Rome. On the way he is shipwrecked, but through his prayers all on board the ship are saved. Finally he arrives in Rome and is placed under house arrest. There, undisturbed, he preaches the gospel and disputes with the local Jews, trying to persuade them that Jesus is the Messiah. So the book comes to an end, and we are not told what the final fate of Paul is.

THEOLOGY: Many important theological themes run through the Acts of the Apostles. The book is history, but it is also theology; so in its own way it is a theology of history during the first four decades after the death and Resurrection of Jesus. Here we will consider the major points made by the author:

1. The infant Church grows through the impulse and guidance of the Holy Spirit. The descent of the Holy Spirit on the apostles on Pentecost signals a total change in the conduct of the Twelve. Whereas before they were fearful and cowardly in the face of opposition, now they become fearless proclaimers of the word of God. Peter gives the

first Christian sermon on Pentecost; there is a miracle of tongues so that all understand him and three thousand ask for Baptism. It is the Spirit that directs Peter and Philip and John and Paul and Barnabas and others in preaching salvation in the name of Jesus Christ. So the Acts has justly been called "The Gospel of the Holy Spirit", because he is the one who directs the apostolic activity from beginning to end.

2. Peter is the main actor in the first half of the book; he takes the initiative in the selection of Matthias, in proclaiming that Jesus is the Messiah, in defending the infant Church before the Jewish leaders, and especially in taking in the first Gentiles in the person of Cornelius and his household (chaps. 10–11). This was approved by the Council of Jerusalem (chap. 15), so the way was open to Paul to bring the Gospel to all the nations of the known world. Paul is the great hero for Luke in the second half of the book, because he traveled all over the Mediterranean world making converts and establishing new churches.

3. Acts puts heavy emphasis on Jesus as the Christ who alone brings salvation to mankind. This salvation is opened to all because of the crucifixion and glorification of Jesus; repentance is required for the forgiveness of sins; salvation is applied to each individual by faith in Jesus accompanied by Baptism.

4. The reader should note the many speeches in Acts — there are eighteen of them; they take up about one-fourth of the whole book. The speeches of Peter in the early chapters (2, 3, 4, 5, 10, 11) tell us how the gospel was preached at the beginning in Jerusalem. Briefly, it goes like this: Jesus was a good man, approved by God, a descendant of

David, who fulfilled all the prophecies of the Old Law. After being baptized by John, he was anointed with the Holy Spirit and with power. He went about healing and doing good, and the apostles witnessed all he did. Because of the hatred of the Jewish leaders, he was crucified under Pontius Pilate and laid in a tomb. On the third day he was raised from the dead and was seen by many witnesses. Ascended into heaven, he is the Lord of all, and from heaven he has poured forth the Holy Spirit on those who believe in him, granting them forgiveness of sins. Therefore, he is the Savior of the world and will come again at the end of the world to judge both the living and the dead. Here Luke is telling the Church of all times: "Here is how Peter preached; you should do the same."

5. Acts presents the first beginnings of the Church as a hierarchical community. The apostles are the leaders, but they appoint deacons, presbyters, and bishops, or *episcopoi*. At this point, the powers or roles of the various groups are not spelled out. Also, it is a sacramental community, since Baptism is the all-important rite of initiation into the Church. But we also find mention of Confirmation (8:15–17) and the Eucharist (2:42, 46; 20:7–11).

6. At the Council of Jerusalem in chapter 15, Peter and Paul get the fundamental principle of salvation through faith in Jesus Christ recognized. This dispenses pagans from circumcision and observance of the Mosaic Law. Thus the Christian Church throws open her doors to all, Jew and Gentile. Entrance depends on repentance, faith in Jesus, and Baptism.

1. Paul's arrest and address to the Jews (21:27 — 22:29)

2. Paul before the Sanhedrin; transfer to Caesarea and his defense before Agrippa II (22:30 — 26:32)

3. Voyage to Italy and shipwreck (27:1 — 28:16)

4. Paul's two-year imprisonment in Rome (28:17–31)

REFLECTION

"*And now, Lord, look upon their threats, and grant to thy servants to speak thy word with all boldness, while thou stretchest out thy hand to heal, and signs and wonders are performed through the name of thy holy servant Jesus*" (4:29–31).

Romans

I am not ashamed of the gospel: it is the power of God for salvation to every one who has faith, to the Jew first and also to the Greek (1:16).

PLACE IN THE BIBLE: Romans comes after the Acts of the Apostles and is the first of all Paul's epistles; it is followed by 1 Corinthians. The letter contains sixteen chapters.

DATE AND AUTHOR: Romans was written by St. Paul, and it is the most important of all his letters. It was written from Corinth in the year A.D. 58.

THEME: The theme is that justification, which makes one pleasing to God and merits eternal salvation, is available to all, both Jew and Gentile, through faith in Jesus Christ.

SUMMARY: Romans is an important doctrinal treatise that Paul sent to the church in Rome. He had not evangelized the Romans, so he was not known there personally, even though he was acquainted with some of the members, as is clear from the greetings in chapter 16. The letter is a type of recommendation that Paul makes for himself since he hopes to visit them in the near future. By this time Paul was well known, and he had many enemies who had spread false reports about his doctrine. So Paul writes to explain to the Romans in detail the basic points of the gospel he preached.

Right at the beginning he states his theme: The gospel of Jesus Christ is the power of God unto salvation for all those who believe in him. The body of the letter from 1:16 to 11:36 treats of the justice of God. In this context "justice" means the holiness of God, his divine grace, his gift of eternal salvation, which he offers to those who have faith in him. Paul points out in chapters 2 and 3 that neither pagans nor Jews have been able to obtain God's justice — the pagans because of their vices and the Jews because of their superficiality, hardness of heart, and lack of faith.

It is Jesus Christ who brought God's justice into the world and made it available to all through faith; Abraham was justified by his faith in God before he was circumcised (chaps. 3 and 4). Paul stresses that God gives his justice gratuitously to all who have faith in him — it is not the result of observing the external rites of the Mosaic Law. When a person through faith has attained God's justice or grace, he is changed into a new person and is liberated from sin, from death, and from the Mosaic Law (6:1 – 7:25). The positive side of justification is that the justified person now lives a life in the Holy Spirit and possesses the conviction and hope of sharing in God's life forever (8:1–19).

This raises a question about God's fidelity to the Jews because they have rejected Christ. Paul says that God has made use of their rejection to call all the Gentiles to salvation, but he insists that a "remnant" of Jews (as always in the past) has remained faithful to God and has believed in Jesus. Further, he expresses his belief that before the Second Coming of Christ the Jews as a nation, not necessarily each individual, will come over to Christ and accept him as the promised Messiah (chaps. 9—11).

The justice of God makes serious moral demands on the person who believes in Christ. He must keep the Commandments, practice love of God and love of neighbor, and in all things give good example to the Gentiles. He gives special instructions stating that those who have a "strong" or certain conscience should not scandalize those who are weak or uncertain (12:1—15:13).

Paul concludes by telling the Romans that he will visit them on his way to Spain; he commends his co-worker Phoebe to them, warns them against false teachers (probably Judaizers who said that Christians must observe the Law of Moses), and sends greetings to twenty-six individuals by name. The last three verses offer a lofty praise of God.

THEOLOGY: Romans has been the center of discussion and controversy almost from the time it was written. When St. Peter says in his second letter that some of Paul's statements are obscure, more than likely he was referring to this letter. Many of the Fathers of the Church commented on it and preached on it. Martin Luther in the sixteenth century based his new and heretical doctrine of "faith alone" (*sola fides*) on Paul's letter to the Romans.

Let us admit that the letter is profound and difficult, but it is also extremely rich in theological reflection on the mystery of Christ and the salvation he offers to all who have faith in him.

A main point in the letter is that man, no matter who he is, cannot save himself, that is, he cannot be acceptable to God or a friend of God by his own efforts. He cannot, as they say, lift himself up by his own bootstraps. Gentiles cannot do it, and Jews cannot do it by diligently observing the Law of Moses. So justification (= salvation, redemption, divine grace) is a free gift from God to those who have faith in him and in his Son, Jesus Christ.

After Paul states his theme and exemplifies it by the example of Abraham in the book of Genesis, he gets to the heart of the matter in chapters 3 to 8. This is where you will find the central core of his teaching. Briefly, it comes to this: God offers his salvation to all men in Jesus Christ (chaps. 3—4). We are saved gratuitously through the merits and grace of Jesus — it is a gift of God, not something owed to us (chap. 5).

What is the justice of God? It is a divine quality that transforms man interiorly into a new creature pleasing to God; it frees man from sin, death, and the Law of Moses; it makes one a child of God and an heir of heaven; it is a completely new and higher type of life that entitles one, at death, to enter into heaven and to see God face to face for all eternity (chaps. 6—8).

Paul was constantly concerned about the fate of his own Jewish people who had rejected Christ (that is, the leaders of the Jewish people; many of the first Christians, like the apostles and Paul, were Jews). So he explains how God makes use of the rejection of the Jews to spread the gospel to all the Gentiles — this makes Christianity into a world religion. But God always keeps his promises, so eventually the Chosen People of the Jews as a nation will accept Jesus as their Messiah and become Christian (chaps. 9—11).

The final chapters offer an exhortation, based on the doctrine expressed, to keep the Commandments, to avoid sin and scandal of others, and above all to practice a universal charity.

REFLECTION

May the God of hope fill you with all joy and peace in believing, so that by the power of the Holy Spirit you may abound in hope (15:13).

1 Corinthians

For I decided to know nothing among you except Jesus Christ and him crucified (2:2).

PLACE IN THE BIBLE: First Corinthians is the second letter in the Pauline corpus, coming after the Epistle to the Romans and before 2 Corinthians. The book contains sixteen chapters.

DATE AND AUTHOR: St. Paul, the Apostle of the Gentiles, wrote this letter in the spring of A.D. 57 while he was staying at Ephesus in the course of his third missionary journey.

THEME: It has been reported to Paul that there is division and dissension in the church he founded in the pagan city of Corinth. The theme of the letter is that there should be order and unity in the Corinthian church because all Christians are united to Christ, in one body, and therefore should be united with one another. In the course of the long letter, he answers several questions they have put to him about moral and doctrinal matters.

SUMMARY: First Corinthians is an important and key letter for anyone who wants to understand the thinking of St. Paul, who often speaks in language difficult for us to grasp. The reader should note that the Apostle is writing to converts he knows well, for Paul is the one who brought them to faith in Jesus Christ. It also helps to note that this is a "friendly" letter, in the sense that he is trying to teach them more about what it is they have embraced when they became Christians or followers of Jesus Christ.

The overall argument goes like this: Members of the Corinthian church have traveled to Ephesus to see Paul, their father in the faith, in order to ask him some questions about matters troubling the community. Paul writes that it has been reported to him that there are divisions, immorality, excesses, and some doubts about basic Christian teaching. One reason for this is that they have not yet grasped the difference between the wisdom of God, which is expressed in the folly of the Cross, and worldly wisdom. The Corinthians have sent him a letter with some questions (7:1), perhaps in response to Paul's previous letter (5:9). He then answers their serious questions about the proper attitude to marriage and virginity, about eating meat that has been offered to pagan idols, about the Lord's Supper, or the Eucharist, about the extraordinary gifts of the Holy Spirit, like speaking in tongues and prophesying, and especially about the resurrection of the dead.

The problem is that the Corinthians have recently converted from paganism and a corrupt way of life to a life of grace and holiness in Christ Jesus. But they have not fully converted in their minds, because they are still infected with many of the errors of the Hellenists or Greek intellectuals. In one sense, therefore, the letter deals with the differences between the Christian way of life and the Hellenistic pagan way of life. This has led to divisions, because the wisdom of the Greek world is opposed to the wisdom of God and Jesus Christ.

Paul says that there should not be divisions in the Church because we who believe in Jesus Christ are all one in him. We are united to him, who now lives in the glory of his resurrected body at the right hand of the Father, through faith and Baptism with water in the Holy Spirit. Therefore there should be no division or disunity in the community, but all should be one in mind and heart and share what they have with one another.

THEOLOGY: It is amazing how St. Paul in this letter brings the essential elements of Christian thought and conduct to bear on the practical everyday problems of the church in Corinth. By his faith and Baptism, the Christian is liberated from pagan superstition and Jewish legalism. Being justified by Christ, he is a new creature, a member of his Body and a temple of the Holy Spirit. Thus he is freed from sin and from all human servitude; he comes under the influence of Christ and becomes subject to his law, which is a law of love and peace. The new ethics requires of the Christian that he live a life of love of God and love of neighbor. This love governs everything, including the charisms that are granted for the good of the community. The ultimate purpose of these charisms is the glory of God.

The wisdom of this world, which is a wisdom of pride and selfishness, is opposed to the wisdom of God and the folly of the Cross. The presentation of this divine wisdom permeates the whole letter. God's wisdom was manifested in the way he saved the world through the Cross of

Christ, which is a stumbling block to the Jews and folly to the Gentiles. Power is manifested in human weakness so that no one will glorify himself but that all will find their happiness in God alone. This is an important part of St. Paul's gospel.

So that the Corinthians may properly understand the Christian way of life, Paul stresses the value of the unique authority of the apostles and the traditions coming from them regarding doctrine, morals, and liturgical worship. He says that he is merely handing on the traditions he has received (11:23; 15:3). As faithful Christians, they are to observe those traditions.

Paul emphasizes the significance and importance of the Lord's Supper in chapter 11:23–34. This is based on the command of Christ, which he states two times, "Do this in remembrance of me." The Eucharist occurs now—between the historical fact of the Cross that it recalls and the Second Coming of Christ at the end of the world that it announces. By giving us his Body and Blood under the appearances of bread and wine, Jesus makes us Christians one Body with him through love. Because of this unity with Christ, the Corinthians must be united among themselves in the charity of Christ. In the matter of the liturgy, they must submit themselves to the traditions of the Church of Jerusalem, which regulates the liturgical celebration everywhere (11:23ff.). The notions of love, order, and submission run through the whole letter.

An important theological point made by Paul in 1 Corinthians has to do with the "Body of Christ". He uses the expression first of all to refer to the resurrected body of Christ (11:24, 27, 29). Since Christians are alive spiritually through Christ's life of grace, they are united to him in a special way; Paul says that they are members of his Body. In this sense the "Body of Christ" has a communitarian meaning and refers to the Church. Thus he writes in chapter 12, "by one Spirit we were all baptized into one body" (v. 13) and "Now you are the body of Christ and individually members of it" (v. 27). The idea of all Christians as members of the Body of Christ is basic to the theology of St. Paul.

Finally, in chapter 15 Paul clearly states the Church's teaching on the resurrection of the body. Apparently some of the Hellenistic converts, influenced by Platonism, Gnostic sects, and the mystery religions, reinterpreted the Christian teaching about the Resurrection of Jesus and of all the faithful at his Second Coming. Paul reminds them of the many witnesses to the Resurrection of Jesus. So he stresses the fact and then gives a brief explanation that the risen body, like that of Jesus, is no longer a material body such as we now have but is a "spiritual body" with powers and qualities we do not understand. He leaves no doubt that, at the end of the world, those who have persevered in the grace of Christ will rise from the dead with their own bodies and be united with him forever. He concludes his teaching on a note of hope.

REFLECTION

Grace to you and peace from God our Father and the Lord Jesus Christ (1:3).

2 Corinthians

We are ambassadors for Christ, God making his appeal through us (5:20).

PLACE IN THE BIBLE: Second Corinthians follows 1 Corinthians and is before Galatians. The letter contains thirteen chapters.

DATE AND AUTHOR: The letter was written by St. Paul from Macedonia or Northern Greece in A.D. 57, about six months after his first letter.

THEME: The theme of the epistle is the grandeur of the apostolic ministry in general and, in particular, a vigorous defense of Paul's own ministry as Christ's chosen apostle to the Gentiles.

SUMMARY: In order to understand 2 Corinthians, it must be read in connection with 1 Corinthians. We conclude from 2 Corinthians that his first letter had the effect of correcting abuses and restoring peace to the community. But around this time some Jewish Christians arrived in Corinth and stirred up more trouble by attacking the person and authority of Paul. Apparently they said that Paul was not a real apostle like the Twelve because he had not seen Christ in the flesh; they said he was arrogant, boastful, and fickle — and he exploited his converts; they said his appearance was shabby, that he was courageous when absent and writing letters to them, but that he was afraid to meet his adversaries face to face.

Paul reacted strongly to these accusations and answered each one of them. We learn from 2 Corinthians that he had written them a sharp letter (which we do not have) and had made a quick visit to Corinth some time during the six months after he wrote 1 Corinthians.

The argument of the letter is not easy to understand because it does not follow a logical development. It is very impassioned, personal, sarcastic, and hard-hitting. The main point to remember while reading 2 Corinthians is that Paul is defending his apostolic authority against false and devious accusers: in strong terms he says that he is equal to the other apostles, for he saw the risen Christ and was commissioned by him to preach the gospel.

There is no clear plan of the letter, but it can be divided into three parts: (1) in chapters 1 to 7 Paul reviews his relationship with the Corinthians and defends his actions and his conduct with regard to them; (2) in chapters 8 and 9 he politely asks them to take up a collection to help the impoverished Christians in Jerusalem, the mother church; (3) in chapters 10 to 13 he suddenly launches into a violent attack on his accusers in Corinth and argues for the authenticity of his apostolate, while rejecting them as "false apostles".

Because the three parts do not fit nicely together, many scholars have theorized that parts of two or three other Pauline letters have been joined together to give us 2 Corinthians. These theories are based, not on any external evidence, but solely on literary criticism. All the good manuscripts record the letter as one composition of St. Paul, and that is also the testimony of tradition. A man of strong emotions and character, it is possible that his moods changed as he dictated the letter, so he jumped from one topic to another. The best approach for a Catholic is to maintain the unity of the letter until the contrary has been proved; up till now, the arguments supporting the contention that several letters were joined together are not convincing.

This letter is the most personal of all Paul's writings and gives us many precious insights into his life and his apostolic ministry.

THEOLOGY: We have seen above that 2 Corinthians is a strong defense by Paul of his apostolic ministry. The letter tells us a lot about one of the first Christian communities that we do not find in the Acts of the Apostles. There were problems, abuses, sinners, false teachers, adversaries of St. Paul who had to be dealt with. The letter offers us a personal response of a great apostle to a serious crisis that he faced in his ministry. In replying to his critics, he tells us much about his travels, his sufferings, his disappointments, the persecutions he endured, his mystical experiences, and visions. So 2 Corinthians reveals the mind and heart of the Apostle of the Gentiles in a way the other letters do not. The letter shows that he is a very loving and sensitive person, but he also displays strong emotions. He even boasts of his weakness, his sufferings, and his visions, but he does it without being proud, "For it is when I am weak that I am strong" (12:1–10). In fact, he tells us that

God gave him a lasting affliction in order to keep him humble.

The secret of his apostolate is the love of Christ that urges him on. His mind is so filled with Christ that he judges all things from the viewpoint of Christ Jesus. So the letter abounds in profound insights on the basic truths of the Catholic faith such as: the mystery of the Blessed Trinity, the role of the Holy Spirit in the life of the Christian, Jesus Christ as the redeemer of all mankind, the glory of the New Covenant that has replaced the Old Law of Moses. The letter also gives an exposition of the nature of the apostolate and a short essay on almsgiving in which Paul explains why the Christian should be charitable and generous in helping others, especially members of the faith.

OUTLINE

REFLECTION

The grace of the Lord Jesus Christ and the love of God and the fellowship of the Holy Spirit be with you all (13:14).

Galatians

*We . . . know that a man is not justified by works of the
law but through faith in Jesus Christ* (2:16).

PLACE IN THE BIBLE: The Epistle of Paul to the Galatians
comes after 2 Corinthians and before Ephesians. The book
contains six chapters.

DATE AND AUTHOR: St. Paul the Apostle of the Gentiles
wrote the letter to the Galatians in A.D. 54; he wrote the
letter while he was staying in Ephesus, which is on the
Mediterranean coast of the modern country of Turkey.
Galatia was not a city but a Roman province inland about
220 miles east of Ephesus, near the present city of Ankara.

THEME: The main theme of the book is that to be a Christian it is necessary to have faith in Jesus Christ, to be
baptized, and to practice the works of charity. Circumcision according to the Law of Moses and observance of
the liturgical and dietary laws of Israel are not necessary
for the Christian. Christ has freed the Christian from the
burden of the Old Law. A secondary theme, treated in
the first two chapters, concerns the apostolic authority of
Paul himself: He is equal to the original twelve apostles
because he was called directly by the Lord Jesus Christ
when he appeared to him on the road to Damascus.

SUMMARY: Paul's writing in Galatians is filled with emotion and feeling. He writes with controlled anger. The letter contains many personal and autobiographical details about Paul and the beginnings of the Church. His authority as an apostle has been challenged; he has been accused of misrepresenting the gospel of Jesus Christ in order to deceive and so win over the Galatians to Christ. Some of the Jewish converts are saying that Christian converts from paganism must be circumcised according to the Law of Moses and that they must become practicing Jews in order to be Christians. Paul writes to refute them and to assure the Galatians that he (Paul) has the same authority as the other apostles. He stresses the point repeatedly that faith and Baptism in Christ Jesus free one from the requirements of the Law of Moses.

In the opening lines Paul states the purpose of the letter: to lead the Galatians back to the true gospel and to prove that his own apostolic authority and his teaching come from God. Paul then says that his teaching does not come from men—it comes directly from God by divine revelation. Twice in fourteen years he went to Jerusalem to consult with the apostles (James, Peter, and John); they approved of his teaching and confirmed his mission to the Gentiles. In chapter 2 Paul defends his gospel of freedom from the Jewish Law and records that he rebuked Peter to his face for not being consistent with regard to observance of the Law. In that, he was right and Peter was wrong in a practical matter of proper Christian behavior.

Paul sets out to prove that justification comes from faith in God and Jesus Christ and not from the observance of the Law of Moses. By "justification" here he means what we mean by holiness, sanctifying grace, and being pleasing to God so that one is worthy of heaven. He argues from the charismatic gifts they received when they were baptized; he argues from the life of Abraham (Genesis) that the Gentiles receive the promised blessing through faith and not from the Law, which came 430 years later; divine blessing has been promised to Abraham and his offspring (namely, Christ) — and the Law that came later cannot change this (3:15–18); he points out that the Law was temporary, imperfect, bound up in sin — it served as a preparation for Christ; when Christ came, the Law was no longer binding (3:19–29). The former state was like being a minor or servant; the latter stage of faith in Christ is like those who are free and independent adults (4:1–11). So a Christian, whether a Jewish or a pagan convert, is not subject to the Law of Moses.

Because he was so close to them and they had such love for him, Paul wonders how the Galatians could listen to such calumnies about him. Then he goes on to speak of Christian liberty. The allegory of the two wives of Abraham illustrates the difference between the slavery of the Old Law and the freedom of the New Law of Jesus Christ. He also warns the Galatians against the sins of the flesh and following the spirit of the world, which is another kind of slavery.

In his conclusion Paul says that he has no other interest but Christ and him crucified. The one who believes in Christ becomes a "new creation". Since Paul preaches only Christ and carries his "marks" in his body (6:17), the one who opposes Paul by that very fact opposes Christ.

THEOLOGY: Some of the Jewish converts to Christ who continued to practice the Jewish religion thought and taught that one had to be a Jew in order to be a Christian. This was a very serious problem in the primitive Church. This doctrine had been preached to the Galatians after Paul left them, and apparently some of his converts had had themselves circumcised and had begun to live according to Jewish customs. These adversaries of Paul were called "Judaizers" for that reason. They argued that Paul's gospel was a heresy; that the Law had not been repealed by Christ; that salvation was open to the Gentiles only on condition that they became Jews. They claimed that Paul was not a real apostle because he had not seen Jesus in the flesh or been one of his disciples; only the Twelve were real apostles, and they had said nothing about the repeal of the Law of Moses. Further, they denied that Paul had received a mission from Jesus; he was only a representative of the Twelve from whom he had learned about Jesus and on whom he depended. They probably represented themselves as preachers of the true Christianity that was practiced in Jerusalem, the mother of all churches.

This serious problem gave Paul the opportunity to work out theologically his gospel on the freedom of Christianity from Judaism and the complete efficacy of the salvation offered through Christ. This led him to see that all, Jews and Gentiles, are called to unity in the one Body of Christ. It also gave him a chance to explain why he was an apostle on the same level as the Twelve who walked with Jesus before his death and Resurrection.

Paul's solution of this grave problem in favor of Christian liberty from the Law of Moses opened up the possibility of converting the whole world to Christ by making faith in Christ more appealing to Gentiles the world over. It must be remembered, however, that Paul's theology of freedom is not an antinomian libertarianism, for he says that Christians must serve one another through love and learn the difference between the works of the flesh and the fruits of the Spirit (see 5:13–26). His solution also shows us indirectly that Jesus did not give his disciples pat answers to all problems. They had to work out the solutions to new problems themselves on the basis of the principles he had given them; that process is still going on.

REFLECTION

Grace to you and peace from God the Father and our Lord Jesus Christ, who gave himself for our sins to deliver us from the present evil age, according to the will of our God and Father; to whom be the glory for ever and ever. Amen (1:3–5).

Ephesians

He [God] has made known to us in all wisdom and insight the mystery of his will, according to his purpose which he set forth in Christ as a plan for the fulness of time, to unite all things in him, things in heaven and things on earth (1:9–10).

PLACE IN THE BIBLE: Ephesians is placed after Galatians and before Philippians. The letter contains six chapters.

DATE AND AUTHOR: The letter was written by St. Paul from Rome during his captivity, 61 to 63 A.D. The letter might have been written to all the churches in Asia as a circular letter, but it has come down to us as addressed to the Christians at Ephesus.

THEME: The theme of the letter is that Jesus Christ, since he is God, possesses the fullness of all reality. Therefore we are all united in him. The Church is his Body — he is the Head, and we are his members. The mystery has been revealed to us that eternal salvation is offered to all who believe in him, both Jews and Gentiles. He has reconciled all mankind to the Father and ranks supreme in the whole universe.

SUMMARY: Ephesians is bristling with important points of Christian doctrine and is a further development of Paul's thought as expressed in his letter to the Colossians. He does not state the special occasion for writing the letter, but from its contents we can conclude that it has to do with the same problem he deals with in Colossians, namely, certain syncretistic ideas of a Gnostic nature coming from the Greek mystery religions and also from Judaism that challenge the primacy of Christ in all creation. The point is that Christians were being urged to show divine worship to angels or "principalities and powers" and in so doing to downplay the role of Christ in salvation and in the universe.

In a profound opening section (1:3–14), Paul praises God for the great blessings of the Christian faith: our election by God, our redemption by Christ, the gift of knowledge of the mystery of salvation in Christ Jesus, the choice of the apostles, and the call of the Gentiles to faith.

The "mystery" of the divine plan of salvation, including the call of the Gentiles to faith, finds its reality in the Christian Church, which is the Body of Christ, and this mystery has been revealed to the Gentiles through Paul, who has been sent to them. For all of this Paul thanks God profusely (3:14–19) and glorifies him for his goodness (3:20–21).

Because we are all united in Christ and in the Church, there are many practical consequences. It follows, therefore, that Christians should avoid the vices of the pagans and live a life of virtue — especially practicing love of neighbor. He makes particular applications to the relations between husbands and wives, parents and children, masters and slaves. Paul concludes with an exhortation to be prepared for spiritual combat with the devil, making use in a figurative way of the usual equipment of the Roman soldier of the time, such as breastplate, shield, helmet, and sword (6:10–20).

THEOLOGY: Paul was at the peak of his theological powers when he composed his letter to the Ephesians. He had seen Christ; he had suffered incredibly for him; he had preached Christ for thirty years as the Creator and Redeemer of mankind; he had prayed and meditated constantly on the meaning of what had been communicated to him by revelation. So a growth in his understanding of the Christian faith is recognizable from his earliest letters (Thessalonians) to his later ones.

Ephesians therefore offers a synthesis of the key ideas of St. Paul. Here he does not speak about his "gospel"; rather, he talks about the "mystery" that had been hidden in God from all eternity and revealed to him. What is this mystery? It is that God in his infinite freedom decreed that his Son would become incarnate in Jesus of Nazareth, that Jesus would die for the salvation of all men — not just for the Chosen People of the Old Testament; that this mystery would be revealed to the apostles and to Paul in order that they might proclaim it throughout the world.

In Ephesians Paul briefly touches on the main point of his letters to the Galatians and the Romans about justification by faith, but he does not linger on it. Also, there is not much here about the last things — the Second Coming of Christ and the end of the world, such as we find in the two letters to the Thessalonians.

In addition to his explanation of the "mystery", he develops the notion that all those who are baptized into Christ are members of his Body, the Church. Christ possesses the "fullness" of all things — grace, wisdom, and power — and Christians share in it by being united to him in faith, hope, and love.

An important conclusion of this is that we are all united in Christ and make one (spiritual or mystical) body with him. This has some practical consequences in the moral and social orders. It means that the Christian must avoid the vices of the pagans and dedicate himself to a life of prayer and to constant practice of the love of God and love of neighbor in imitation of Christ and St. Paul. He applies this specifically to family relations.

St. Paul's letter to the Ephesians is an outstanding example of deep theological thought touching on the Trinity, Christ, the Church, the sacraments, and Christian life. The letter is optimistic — inspiring and uplifting from beginning to end. It stimulates the devout reader to set his mind and heart on heavenly and eternal things. The person who can understand what Paul is saying in Ephesians will have a good grasp of the fundamental pillars of Catholic theology.

OUTLINE

I. Salutation (1:1–2)

II. Doctrine: The mystery of the unity of all things in Christ (1:3—3:21)

    A. The mystery decreed from eternity (1:3–14)

B. The mystery fulfilled in the Church
   (1:15—2:22)

C. The mystery revealed to the Gentiles (3:1–13)

D. Prayer and doxology (3:14–21)

III. Morality: Christian life in the world (4:1—6:20)

A. General principles (4:1–24)

B. Application to all Christians (4:25—5:21)

C. Family life (5:22—6:9)

D. Spiritual warfare (6:10–20)

IV. Conclusion: News and final blessing (6:21–24)

REFLECTION

Now to him who by the power at work within us is able to do far more abundantly than all that we ask or think, to him be glory in the church and in Christ Jesus to all generations, for ever and ever. Amen (3:20–21).

Philippians

*Being found in human form he humbled himself and be-
came obedient unto death, even death on a cross. Therefore God has highly exalted him and bestowed on him the
name which is above every name* (2:8–9).

PLACE IN THE BIBLE: The Epistle of Paul to the Philippians
is found after Ephesians and before Colossians. The letter
contains four chapters.

DATE AND AUTHOR: The letter was written by St. Paul in
A.D. 54 from Ephesus while he was on his second missionary journey. Philippians is known as one of the "captivity epistles" because Paul composed it while he was "in
chains" or in prison (1:13).

THEME: Paul wrote the letter to encourage his converts in
Philippi, a large seaport in northern Greece, to persevere
in the true faith, which they had received through him.
He urges them to pray constantly in the joy of Christ,
to imitate the humility and obedience of Jesus, to avoid
those who distort the gospel in any way, and finally to be
models of charity.

SUMMARY: Paul was very fond of his converts in Philippi,
and they were fond of him. They showed their love for
him by sending him gifts to sustain him in his labors and

in prison. The warmth of his feeling for them shines forth throughout the letter. Normally, Paul would not accept gifts from his converts and even worked as a tent-maker to support himself when he settled down for lengthy periods. The occasion of this letter was a gift sent to him by the Philippians. It was brought by one of their own, Epaphroditus, who became ill in Ephesus and almost died. When he recovered, Paul decided to send him back to Philippi. Epaphroditus was the one who carried this letter with him on his return journey from Ephesus to Philippi, which took about six or seven days. In his letter Paul congratulated the Philippians on their spiritual progress in the faith of Christ; he thanked them for their generous gift, encouraged them to resist their persecutors and to avoid false teachers, and finally urged them to persevere in the faith they had accepted. He also told them that he would soon send his beloved Timothy to them — to assist them in any way he could. There is a suggestion that Paul himself might come to see them when he is released from prison.

THEOLOGY: Philippians is a joyful and hopeful epistle. Again and again Paul urges his converts to rejoice because they are united with Christ through faith and the grace of God. The letter contains clear statements about the uselessness of the Law of Moses for justification and eternal salvation; he states that we all need the grace of God not only to do good but even to will it (2:12–13); he asserts the union of the soul with Christ at the moment of death (1:23) and his conviction that he will rise from the dead through the transforming power of Christ (3:12). Paul also gives many valuable counsels regarding Christian living: that one must live in peace with others, be humble like Jesus, strive for perfection, and trust in Christ, in whom we can do all things (4:13).

With respect to Christian doctrine, the most important passage in the letter is found in the christological "hymn" in 2:6–11. Tightly packed in six short verses, we find a brief summary of Paul's basic understanding of who Jesus Christ is. The six verses affirm the following about Christ: (1) his divine preexistence, that is, he is God and existed for all eternity before assuming flesh in the womb of the Virgin; (2) he abased or "emptied" himself by becoming man; (3) he further humiliated himself by accepting death on a cross; (4) God the Father glorified him; (5) the whole universe worships and adores him; (6) the glorified Christ has won a new Name, that is, the Name of God himself. So Paul urges the Philippians, and us, to imitate the humility and obedience of Christ Jesus our Lord as we strive to do good to all and to work out our salvation "in fear and trembling" (2:12). But Paul is not talking about servile fear or the fear of slaves, because God is always near to help us, as he affirms in the following verse, which should be pondered over and over again: "For God is at work in you, both to will and to work for his good pleasure."

REFLECTION

Rejoice in the Lord always; again I will say, Rejoice. Let all men know your forbearance. The Lord is at hand (4:4–5).

Colossians

*He [Christ] is the image of the invisible God, the first-born
of all creation* (1:15).

PLACE IN THE BIBLE: Colossians is located after Philippians
and before 1 Thessalonians. It is often referred to as one
of the "captivity epistles", that is, written while he was in
prison. The letter contains four chapters.

DATE AND AUTHOR: St. Paul wrote his letter to the Colossians from Rome during his first imprisonment there —
between A.D. 61 and 63. The city was about one hundred
miles east of Ephesus in the interior of the modern country of Turkey.

THEME: The theme is that the Colossians must remain
faithful to the traditional faith that has been given to
them, and they must avoid all false teaching and false
philosophies, whether pagan or Jewish. He opposes the
current errors by teaching the primacy of Christ as the
Creator and Redeemer of the whole world.

SUMMARY: The church at Colossae was founded by Epa-
phras, a native of the city and a co-worker with Paul in
the apostolate. It was reported to Paul that false teachers
were disturbing the community there. The errors arose
from some sort of pre-Gnosticism, that is, esoteric or eli-

tist "knowledge" that (supposedly) gives the one who has it an assurance of salvation. Also, there may have been some Judaizers involved. The heart of the error was belief in the "elements" or the "powers" (2:15) of the world; these were intermediate beings between God and man who were thought to have power over men. Basically, they were thought to be angelic beings who operated independently of God, the Supreme Being.

It seems from the Letter that some of the Colossians were involved in this error and had even offered some kind of worship to these "elements" or "powers". Paul reacts strongly to this, since the error was an implicit denial of the primacy of Jesus Christ as the only redeemer and mediator between God and man. He not only rejects this error, but he positively explains the unique role of Christ in creation and redemption.

Paul then exhorts the Colossians to live a life of virtue in accordance with the faith they have adopted. They are to avoid all immorality and lust; they are to reject anger, malice, and abusive language. Since all are now one in Christ Jesus, because they are members of his Body, they should be models of mercy, kindness, humility, meekness, and patience. But above all these things they must have charity, "which binds everything together in perfect harmony" (3:14). Then he offers domestic advice for husbands, wives, parents, children, slaves, and masters. Since they are new creatures "in Christ", they must treat each other with respect as children of God made in his image.

THEOLOGY: In refuting the errors being spread among the Colossians, Paul penetrates to the heart of the Christian faith by explaining who Jesus Christ is. The main passage is found in chapter 1, verses 15 to 23. This passage is often referred to as a "christological hymn", singing the praises and glory of Christ. Paul's point in this important passage is to show that Jesus Christ is God Almighty, "He is the image of the invisible God, the first-born of all creation" (1:15). Paul says Jesus is the Creator of all things, including the elements and powers — whatever they might be. They are subject to Christ, so there is no reason to fear them or worship them — they are creatures.

Next he says that Christ is "the head of the body, the church" (1:18). Christ is the first one to rise from the dead: He is "the first-born from the dead", and in all things he has the first place. Jesus possesses the fullness of the divinity, and by the blood of his Cross he has reconciled all things with the Father.

Paul is so consumed by his love for Christ that he wants to suffer with and for Christ in order to be more like him. So he rejoices in his sufferings (1:24) and offers them up for those who refuse to suffer for Christ: "I complete what is lacking in Christ's afflictions for the sake of his body, that is, the church" (1:24).

Paul says he has been sent by God to preach the word, that is, "the *mystery* hidden for ages and generations but now made manifest to his saints" (1:26; emphasis added). What is this mystery? The mystery is that by faith and Baptism Christ comes to dwell in the soul of every believer — whether Jew or Gentile; the gospel and the divine grace it communicates are intended for the whole world so that all may become one in Christ Jesus: "Christ in you, the hope of glory" (1:27). This is the heart of Paul's gospel and the key to understanding his letter to the Colossians.

The "elements" of this world, the principalities and powers, whatever they are, are nothing in comparison with Christ. So Paul tells the Colossians to reject all that false teaching and to embrace Christ with all their might.

Since the Christian is spiritually and mystically united to Christ in his Baptism, he dies to sin and rises to a new life of grace because Christ is within him. That being the case, the mind and heart of the Christian should be in heaven and not on earth: "Set your minds on things that are above, not on things that are on earth. For you have died [to sin], and your life is hid with Christ in God" (3:2–3). From this Paul concludes that the Christian should mortify his flesh in imitation of Christ, and he should practice all the virtues as seen in the life of Christ and in the example of Paul himself, who closely imitates Christ.

OUTLINE

I. Introduction (1:1–14)

II. Paul's doctrinal teaching (1:15–23)

    A. Excellence of Christ the Creator (1:15–18)

    B. Excellence of Christ the Redeemer (1:19–23)

III. Paul's warnings (1:24 — 3:4)

    A. Paul's zeal for souls (1:24 — 2:3)

    B. The danger of false teachers (2:4–23)

    C. True Christian spirituality (3:1–4)

IV. Paul's moral teaching (3:5—4:6)

    A. General principles (3:5–17)

    B. Domestic duties of family members (3:18—4:1)

    C. Prayer, vigilance, and wisdom (4:2–6)

V. Conclusion (4:7–18)

REFLECTION

If then you have been raised with Christ, seek the things that are above, where Christ is, seated at the right hand of God. Set your minds on things that are above, not on things that are on earth. For you have died, and your life is hid with Christ in God. When Christ who is our life appears, then you also will appear with him in glory (3:1–4).

1 Thessalonians

For since we believe that Jesus died and rose again, even so, through Jesus, God will bring with him those who have fallen asleep (4:14).

PLACE IN THE BIBLE: First Thessalonians will be found after the epistle of St. Paul to the Colossians and before 2 Thessalonians. The letter contains five chapters.

DATE AND AUTHOR: First Thessalonians is the earliest of St. Paul's letters to be found in the New Testament. It was written to his new converts in Thessalonica, about a hundred miles north of Athens and some distance west of Philippi in northern Greece. Thessalonica, an excellent seaport, was at the time the second largest city of Greece after Athens. The letter was written from Corinth, a major seaport not far from Athens, during Paul's second missionary journey in either A.D. 51 or 52.

THEME: St. Paul encourages his new converts, who are being persecuted by Jewish zealots who consider them to be heretics. Watching for the coming of the Lord means living a moral life and fulfilling one's daily tasks. Paul hopes to see the coming of the Lord, but the exact time of the Parousia is not part of divine revelation. He urges them to be faithful and to persevere in prayer.

SUMMARY: After wishing grace and peace to his converts, he thanks God for the work of the Holy Spirit among them in promoting the virtues of faith, hope, and charity in the midst of much opposition. Their faith is already well known in Greece and is a model for others. Paul handed on the gospel to them free of charge, in sincerity and truth, and he gives expression to great affection for them.

When Paul first went to Thessalonica, as usual he proclaimed Jesus to the Jews in the synagogue. Since they rejected him and Jesus, he turned to the Gentiles. Now the Jews are persecuting the new Christians just as they formerly persecuted Jesus and put him to death and then persecuted the first Jewish Christians in Jerusalem. Paul wants to return to them to comfort them, but he has been impeded by Satan.

Wanting to know how they were doing, Paul sent Timothy to visit them. Timothy has returned and reported that the community is persevering in faith and charity in the midst of troubles. Paul rejoices at this news and tells them how much he wishes to see them again and strengthen them in their faith.

Next he urges them to avoid all immorality and to strive for holiness, because God wants them to be saints. He then assures them that the living will have no advantage over the dead at the coming of the Lord. The dead will rise, and both the living and the dead will meet the Lord Jesus and enter with him into glory. He intends to comfort them with these words.

The time of the Parousia of the Lord is not known, but he will come suddenly, like a thief in the night. So all should be always prepared for his coming. Being prepared means to avoid all immorality and to practice faith, hope, and charity to all. He urges them to rejoice always and to pray without ceasing.

THEOLOGY: The converts Paul is writing to are primarily Gentiles who have accepted faith in Christ and Baptism. Since Paul spent only a few months in Thessalonica, they were not well instructed. The reason for writing the letter is problems in the community — problems concerning perseverance in doing good, avoiding pagan customs and idol worship, and especially concern about the end of the world and the Second Coming of Christ. Paul teaches them that the divine gift of salvation has been brought by Christ to those who believe in him. This salvation must be accepted in a spirit of humility and docility. Also, they are to be submissive to the authority of the Apostle Paul and faithful to the traditions that go back to the community in Jerusalem and to the Lord Jesus.

The main point of the epistle, however, has to do with eschatology, or the teaching about the end of the world or "the Day of the Lord", when Jesus will come in glory to judge the living and the dead.

The good news is that Jesus Christ, whom God raised from the dead, will save all those who believe in him from eternal damnation. Those who have lived in faith and died in Christ will be joined to him when he comes again in glory, and they will share in his everlasting happiness.

Throughout the letter Paul stresses the importance of leading a life of faith, hope, and charity, including love of neighbor, and of avoiding all forms of immorality and paganism. In writing this letter he shows his profound grasp of the mystery of Christ, that the salvation of Christ is meant for all peoples and that one must humbly accept the offer of grace in order to be joined to Christ and so be saved.

OUTLINE

REFLECTION

May the God of peace himself sanctify you wholly; and may your spirit and soul and body be kept sound and blameless at the coming of our Lord Jesus Christ. He who calls you is faithful, and he will do it (5:23).

2 Thessalonians

We beg you, brethren, not to be quickly shaken in mind or excited, either by spirit or by word, or by letter purporting to be from us, to the effect that the day of the Lord has come (2:1–2).

PLACE IN THE BIBLE: Second Thessalonians follows 1 Thessalonians and comes before 1 Timothy. The book contains three chapters.

DATE AND AUTHOR: The author is St. Paul, who also wrote 1 Thessalonians. Since it was written a few months after 1 Thessalonians and is Paul's second earliest letter in the New Testament, the date of composition was A.D. 51 or 52.

THEME: The main point is that the Parousia has not yet come. We now live in the intermediate time between Christ's glorification at the right hand of the Father and his Parousia, or Second Coming in glory to judge the living and the dead. No one knows when that will happen. In the meantime, all must persevere in faith, hope, and charity and good works toward the neighbor.

SUMMARY: Paul wishes the Thessalonians grace and peace and then thanks God for their faith and perseverance in the face of persecution. He assures them that God will punish those who afflict them when the Lord Jesus comes in glory. He prays earnestly and constantly for them that God may make them worthy of his call.

Paul insists that the Day of the Lord has not yet come, for there are certain signs that will precede his coming, and those signs are not yet in evidence. Although Paul's meaning here is obscure, he says that first there will be a great apostasy and a "man of sin" who will lead many astray. For now the Antichrist is being "restrained" by some power. When the man of sin does come, the Lord Jesus "will slay him with the breath of his mouth". So he urges them to stand firm and remain faithful to the traditional teaching of the Church.

Finally, Paul reminds them that the Lord is faithful and that they should persevere in prayer and good works. They should avoid those who fall away from the faith and abandon Christ, but they should not be hostile to them. Everyone should work and avoid idleness. Here Paul makes his famous statement: "If any one will not work, let him not eat" (3:10). He concludes by wishing them the grace and peace of Christ.

THEOLOGY: Both epistles to the Thessalonians have to do with *eschatology*, that is, with those things that will happen at the end of time when Christ comes again in glory to judge the living and the dead. In 2 Thessalonians Paul teaches them and us that the Parousia has not happened yet and that only God knows when it will occur. Now we live between the "already" of Christ's glorification and the "not yet" of his Second Coming. When he does come, he will totally defeat Satan, and all those who have done his will and been faithful to him will be welcomed into his everlasting Kingdom.

The Thessalonians have embraced Christ, but they are being persecuted for his sake. Paul urges them to fidelity, perseverance, and good works. Two terms in 2 Thessalonians need some clarification. The "Adversary" or "lawless one" (2:8), who is also called the Antichrist in the New Testament, stands for all those forces in the moral order that are aligned with Satan; they constantly oppose God and the establishment of his Kingdom among men. The "restrainer" is one who shows strength and firmness in opposing evil. Since the restrainer is opposed to the work of the devil, the word stands for those forces that are aligned with the Messiah.

These terms are part of biblical "apocalyptic" literature, which means something that is hidden and mysterious. We should not look for particular persons in history designated by these terms. Rather, the terms refer to those forces in all ages until the end of time that oppose God and all those who fight on the side of God.

It should be noted Paul did not teach that the Parousia was near, in spite of what some interpreters have said and do say now. While he lived a life of intense faith and activity, Paul hoped that the Parousia was near so that he could be united with Christ.

What Paul is saying in these two letters is also directed to us. He passes on to us the warning he received from the Lord Jesus, namely, that we should live worthily in the sight of God so that we may one day share in his glorious Kingdom and be with Christ forever.

REFLECTION

May our Lord Jesus Christ himself, and God our Father, who loved us and gave us eternal comfort and good hope through grace, comfort your hearts and establish them in every good work and word (2:16–17).

1 Timothy

O Timothy, guard what has been entrusted to you (6:20).

PLACE IN THE BIBLE: First Timothy comes after 2 Thessa-lonians and before 2 Timothy. First Timothy, 2 Timothy, and Titus are usually referred to as the "Pastoral Epistles". The letter contains six chapters.

DATE AND AUTHOR: The letter was written by St. Paul from Macedonia in northern Greece to Timothy, Paul's close associate in the apostolate, about the year A.D. 65. At the time Timothy was in charge of the church at Ephesus.

THEME: The theme of the letter is the pastoral care of the Church. This includes teaching sound doctrine coming from the apostles, guarding the deposit of faith and pro-tecting it against false teachers, governing the Church with wisdom and charity, and giving good example in word and deed to all.

SUMMARY: Timothy was a co-worker with St. Paul and is mentioned in several of his letters. When Paul departed from Ephesus about the year A.D. 64 for Macedonia, he left Timothy in charge of the church there. It has come to Paul's attention that the church is troubled with some false teachers. He does not say clearly who they were, but he hints that they were Jewish Christians with strange doctrines about genealogies (some of them were commentaries on Genesis) and also Gentile Christians who are bothering others with fables from the Greek mystery cults. This matter comes up three times in the letter, so it was very much on Paul's mind. He exhorts Timothy to correct them, refute them, and require them to adhere to the "sound doctrine" of the apostles. Paul insists again and again on the importance of preserving the tradition or "trust", the deposit of faith, that has been given to them from the apostles, that is, the true teaching about Jesus Christ, the Father, and the Holy Spirit.

Another major concern of the letter is Church discipline. Paul gives directions for liturgical worship and spells out the qualities those men should have who are chosen as bishops, deacons, and presbyters. He tells Timothy to avoid the vices of the pagans and to give good example to all, Christians and pagans, in his actions and in his teaching.

First Timothy contains many precious gems of practical advice for pastors of souls and is quoted often in the liturgy of the Church for the feasts of bishops and confessors. So the primary focus of this letter is Church organization, sound teaching, good morals, and good works.

THEOLOGY: As should be clear from the above summary, the thrust of 1 Timothy is pastoral theology — good government and good morals, with a strong emphasis on teaching "sound doctrine" and opposing false teachers. In short, Paul exhorts Timothy to guard the *deposit of faith* (6:20). Apparently the church in Ephesus is endangered by false teachers who cause division in the community and promote loose morals (6:4–5). Paul uses strong language, calling these Judaizers seducers, hypocrites, vain babblers, insubordinate, and absorbed by "foolish fables and old wives' tales" (4:7).

Paul is very concerned about the qualities that should be present in those who are named as bishops, presbyters, and deacons. He also gives directives on the ordering of Christian life and the duties of different classes of the faithful: old people, young people, slaves, widows, and women in public gatherings of the faithful.

One of Paul's main concerns in the letter is handing on the true faith, which is the "word of God", the "word of truth", and the sound instruction of our Lord Jesus Christ (6:3).

At this stage of the Church there does not seem to be a clear distinction between bishop and elder (or priest: *presbyteros*). There is some hierarchical organization, but at this point in time all are still under the authority of Paul as the founder of the community.

On the side of doctrine, Paul stresses that God the Father is our "Savior" (through his Son, Jesus), and he says explicitly that God desires the salvation of all men (2:4). As the reason for the Incarnation, he states that "Jesus Christ came into the world to save sinners" (1:15). So the Christology of the letter is soteriological, since Jesus also is presented in his role as Savior and Mediator (2:5).

In sum, we find in 1 Timothy a marvelous blend of practical advice from the Apostle of the Gentiles on how to organize and govern a local church. But these practical norms are based upon the Pauline doctrine of the primacy of Christ, the mercy of God the Father, and the holiness of the Spirit that we find in his major epistles. Shining throughout the letter is Paul's insight that the Church is the Body of Christ and that all Christians are animated by his life and his Spirit.

Since it was first written almost two thousand years ago, this letter has been a guide for pastors of souls throughout the world and will continue to be so until Christ comes again in glory to judge the living and the dead.

OUTLINE

REFLECTION

To the King of ages, immortal, invisible, the only God, be honor and glory for ever and ever. Amen (1:17).

2 Timothy

I charge you in the presence of God and of Christ Jesus who is to judge the living and the dead, and by his appearing and his kingdom: preach the word, be urgent in season and out of season, convince, rebuke, and exhort, be unfailing in patience and in teaching (4:1–2).

PLACE IN THE BIBLE: This letter is located between 1 Timothy and Titus as the second of the three "Pastoral Epistles". The letter contains four chapters.

DATE AND AUTHOR: St. Paul wrote this letter in A.D. 66, shortly before his execution, during his second imprisonment in Rome. It was written to his beloved convert and co-worker Timothy, who, at the time, was in charge of the church in Ephesus. It is something like his last will and testament because it is his last letter before his death.

THEME: The theme of the letter is the same as the other two Pastoral Letters: it is a powerful exhortation to Timothy to teach sound doctrine and to be faithful to the apostolic tradition; he is to oppose false teachers and refute their errors; he is to be a model of virtue, a vigorous preacher of the gospel, and he is to urge the members of his church to put the gospel into practice in their daily lives.

SUMMARY: This letter is very much like Paul's first letter to Timothy, though a bit shorter. It has the added feature of being his "last will and testament", since it was his last letter to his close associate and friend. Paul knows that his death is approaching (4:6), so he sends one final exhortation to Timothy, urging him "to stir up the grace of God" that he has received through the laying on of Paul's hands (1:6), in other words, the grace of his ordination as a priest of Jesus Christ.

St. Paul exhorts Timothy to spare no personal efforts in proclaiming the gospel of salvation in Jesus Christ; he tells him how to oppose the false teachers in Ephesus successfully; he then concludes the letter with some personal requests, greetings, and a final salutation.

THEOLOGY: Second Timothy is a jewel of a letter. In its own way, it is a brief summary of the gospel preached by Paul. It also contains some biographical information about Paul—how he has fought the good fight for Christ, how he has kept the faith, how he has suffered for Jesus Christ. He reminds Timothy that "all who desire to live a godly life in Christ Jesus will be persecuted" (3:12), and in that way they will be imitating him.

The theology of this letter is the same as that of 1 Timothy, with a few minor variations. Paul mentions "the laying on of my hands" (1:6), which is what came later to be called priestly ordination. As in 1 Timothy and Titus, Paul emphasizes the importance of sound teaching and handing on the true faith. A consequence of that is the necessity of opposing error and false teachers. And in this letter there is more emphasis on eschatology, that is, the end of the world and the Second Coming of Christ.

In a well-known passage, Paul charges Timothy to "preach the word, be urgent in season and out of season, convince, rebuke, and exhort" (4:2). The same concern about teaching sound doctrine and correcting errors is found in the other two Pastoral Letters, but here it is stated more forcefully. In 2 Timothy, however, Paul does not list the qualities of bishops, presbyters, and deacons. The letter presents a convincing combination of Pauline theology along with its practical requirements. It is an outstanding example of biblical moral and pastoral theology.

Finally a word about Holy Scripture. Paul urges Timothy to be faithful to the tradition he has learned since his childhood from his mother Eunice and his grandmother Lois. He was raised on the Bible, and he should use his knowledge of Scripture in preaching and governing the church. Here we find Paul's understanding of Scripture: "All scripture is inspired by God and profitable for teaching, for reproof, for correction, and for training in righteousness, that the man of God may be complete, equipped for every good work" (3:16). St. Paul was so equipped, and he urges Timothy to follow the same path.

OUTLINE

REFLECTION

The saying is sure: If we have died with him, we shall also live with him; if we endure, we shall also reign with him; if we deny him, he also will deny us; if we are faithless, he remains faithful—for he cannot deny himself (2:11–13).

Titus

But as for you, teach what befits sound doctrine (2:1).

PLACE IN THE BIBLE: The letter to Titus will be found after 2 Timothy and before Philemon. The letter contains three chapters.

DATE AND AUTHOR: In the year 65, while he was in Macedonia, St. Paul wrote to Titus; at the time Titus was in charge of the church on the island of Crete as Paul's representative.

THEME: The theme of this letter is the same as that of 1 Timothy, that is, Paul exhorts Titus to teach sound doctrine coming from the apostles. He is to appoint worthy bishops and presbyters in each city and see to it that all give good example in word and deed. Also he must oppose and refute the false teachers who are disturbing the church for the sake of monetary gain.

SUMMARY: This letter was written by St. Paul about the same time he composed 1 Timothy. Since the problems and situation are similar in Ephesus and Crete, the content of the two letters is very similar. What was said in the previous outline on 1 Timothy also applies to Titus. In short, Paul stresses the importance of teaching sound doctrine, and Titus is to exhort the Christians to put the doctrine into practice in their daily lives.

In almost the same language that he used in 1 Timothy, Paul spells out the qualities that should be present in men who are appointed leaders of the community, that is, bishops and presbyters. They should be free of serious vice, and they should be models for others of virtuous Christian family life. An important task for Titus is to refute the false teachers who specialize in Jewish fables, genealogies, and Greek mystery religions. Their teaching is in error, and they spread division among Christians, and this in turn leads to immorality.

Briefly what Paul says is this: Root out error and immorality, and promote orthodoxy and good works. If he does that, Titus will be a good bishop worthy of the name.

THEOLOGY: The moral and pastoral theology of Titus is almost identical to that of 1 Timothy. Again the emphasis is on teaching—that is what Titus is supposed to do: Teach sound doctrine, refute errors, encourage good works among Christians. The stress is on "the rule of faith", the sound instruction of the apostles.

Eschatology is mentioned (2:13) but not stressed in this letter. The emphasis is more on soteriology—God the Father as Savior (2:11) and Jesus Christ as Savior (2:13). There is mention of all three Persons of the Blessed Trinity. The Father's motive in saving us is his mercy—his goodness and kindness (3:4).

Titus contains one of the few direct statements in the New Testament that call Jesus "God": ". . . awaiting our blessed hope, the appearing of the glory of our great God and Savior Jesus Christ, who gave himself for us to redeem us from all iniquity" (2:13–14). There is another important doctrinal summary in 3:4–7. Both of these passages are familiar to most Catholics because they are read every year during the first two Masses on Christmas day.

This letter and the two letters to Timothy are called "Pastorals" because they offer abundant pastoral advice to bishops and priests on how to conduct themselves in their ministry. The three letters of Paul offer priests of all times a clear guide or map on how to be a true shepherd of souls in imitation of Jesus himself, the first and chief Pastor.

OUTLINE

I. Greeting (1:1–4)

II. Duties of Titus (1:5–16)

    A. What to look for in bishops (1:5–9)

    B. Work against false teachers (1:10–16)

III. Problems of discipline (2:1—3:11)

    A. Duties of various groups (2:1–10)

    B. The grace of God imposes Christian virtues (2:11–15)

    C. Duties toward superiors and others (3:1–3)

    D. Regeneration leads to a new life and good works (3:4–8)

REFLECTION

Grace and peace from God the Father and Christ Jesus our Savior (1:4).

Philemon

I appeal to you for my child, Onesimus, whose father I have become in my imprisonment (10).

PLACE IN THE BIBLE: Philemon is located after the letter to Titus, which is the last of the Pastoral Letters, and it comes before Hebrews. A very short letter, it contains only twenty-five verses and is not broken into chapters.

DATE AND AUTHOR: The letter was written by St. Paul during his first Roman imprisonment, in A.D. 61 to 63.

THEME: Paul pleads with Philemon, master of the runaway slave Onesimus, to receive him back as a brother and not to punish him.

SUMMARY: Philemon is a warmly personal letter written to one person to ask a favor. Philemon was a wealthy man from Colossae whom Paul had converted in Ephesus. His slave, Onesimus, had run away and eventually came to Rome, where he met Paul in prison and was converted to Christ. His name in Greek means "useful", so Paul makes a pun by pointing out that he has been useful to him during his imprisonment. But he has persuaded him to return to his master in the company of Tychicus, who, at the same time, is carrying Paul's epistle to the Colossians. The main point is that Paul begs Philemon to receive his slave kindly as a brother in Christ. He says Philemon owes him this favor, since he (Philemon) has received the supernatural life of the soul through the ministry of Paul. The letter is very artistically written. Paul is polite in dealing with Philemon, whom he knows and respects. The letter is what we today would call "a letter of recommendation".

THEOLOGY: The short letter illustrates some of the main points of Paul's gospel: the dignity of the Christian, the love of Christians for one another, and their union in the one Body of Christ, who is the Head. Paul does not condemn the prevalent institution of slavery, but he does imply that Philemon should set Onesimus free because he is now a brother in Christ. So the groundwork is laid for the eventual abolition of slavery.

OUTLINE

I. Greeting (1–3)

II. Thanksgiving for Philemon's faith and fraternal love (4–7)

III. Request that Philemon should welcome back Onesimus, his slave, as a brother in Christ; Paul will pay for any damage done by Onesimus (8–21)

IV. Request for lodgings and final greeting (22–25)

REFLECTION

Grace to you and peace from God our Father and the Lord Jesus Christ (3).

Hebrews

Jesus Christ is the same yesterday and today and for ever (13:8).

PLACE IN THE BIBLE: Hebrews comes after St. Paul's letter to Philemon and before the letter of James. The book contains thirteen chapters.

DATE AND AUTHOR: For about fifteen hundred years Hebrews was attributed to St. Paul. But because of the differences in thought, language, and style between Hebrews and the known Pauline letters, most scholars now say it was not written by Paul. Many of them think it was written by a disciple of Paul who was a Hellenistic Jew, well versed in Greek thought, and a master of the Old Testament. The author might have been in Italy when the letter was written (see 13:24). The exact date of composition is not known either, but it was probably about the time of the destruction of Jerusalem in A.D. 70.

THEME: The theme centers on Jesus Christ — Son of God, Savior, and eternal High Priest — who was sent into the world by the Father to die for us, rise from the dead, and enter gloriously into heaven, where he reigns now eternally with the Father and the Holy Spirit. Jesus and the New Covenant he inaugurated are superior to the angels, to Abraham, to Moses, and to the old Covenant of Sinai;

331

Jesus has entered into heaven, where he intercedes for us and waits for us. In order to share in his eternal triumph, we must persevere and remain faithful to him.

SUMMARY: The problem addressed by Hebrews is how to attain heaven, the everlasting city, where Christ reigns eternally with the Father and the Holy Spirit. First the author stresses the great dignity of Christ: He is superior to the angels, to Abraham, and to Moses. His gospel is addressed to each one of us, and he promises eternal "rest" with him if we are faithful to him.

Christ is the true High Priest, for his priesthood is universal, effective, and everlasting. He was foreshadowed in Genesis 14 by Melchizedek, who blessed Abraham and his descendants. The high priesthood in the Old Testament was temporary; the high priests had to offer sacrifices for their own sins and for the sins of the people. The priesthood of Jesus is superior to the Gentile priesthood of the Old Law and has replaced it. Jesus offered himself and shed his blood once for all; his was a perfect sacrifice. Because of it he has entered into heaven, which is the eternal sanctuary, infinitely superior to the sanctuary in the tent in the desert and to the sanctuary in the Temple in Jerusalem. So Christ has established a New Covenant, a new sanctuary, a new cult, and a new sacrifice—all of which surpass the similar arrangements in the Old Law. The old cult was mainly external in its effects; the new cult of Jesus reaches to the heart of man and transforms him from within, making him a son of God and heir of heaven.

The last four chapters deal with moral counsels to persevere in the faith, to practice fraternal charity, to be chaste, detached from the world, and prayerful. Perhaps the most famous passage from the letter is in chapter 11, where the author gives many examples of faith from the heroes of the Old Testament—such as Abraham, Moses, Gideon, David, and others.

THEOLOGY: Hebrews is a theological interpretation of the Old Testament. It is not possible to understand the thinking of the author of Hebrews without a basic knowledge of the Old Testament. The letter is primarily a treatise on Christology, for Christ is the heart and center of the book. The letter presents profound ideas about the risen Jesus Christ. It goes something like this:

1. Jesus Christ, true God and true Man, was sent into this world to suffer and die in order to destroy sin and the power of the devil. He rose from the dead and entered into heaven, where he reigns at the right hand of the Father. In the heavenly sanctuary he intercedes for us, that we will remain faithful and avoid all sin. Much of the development from chapters 3 to 10 revolves around the notion of Christ being the eternal "High Priest", who offers the sacrifice of his own Body and Blood in reparation for all the sins of mankind. In the Old Testament the high priest entered the Holy of Holies once a year to sprinkle blood and ask God for pardon for sins; it was an imperfect gesture that had to be repeated every year. In contrast, Christ offered himself as a perfect sacrifice, died, and entered heaven or the "heavenly sanctuary" once for all, where he waits for the faithful on earth to join him. The high priesthood of Jesus is infinitely superior to that

of the Gentile priests because Jesus is not a mere man like Moses, who stood between God and the people; rather, as God and Man he participates in both sides of the mediation process (see 4:14—5:10). So his sacrifice and his "liturgy" are unique, eternal, and infinitely superior to that of the Old Law.

All through the letter there is a comparison between the New Testament and the cult and persons of the Old Testament. The author stresses that all the provisions of the Old Testament were temporary and provisional—that they were all shadows or weak images pointing to the real thing, which is the New Covenant inaugurated by Christ. To prove his thesis, he quotes scores of texts from the Old Testament, especially from the Pentateuch, the Psalms, and the prophets. He characterizes the Gentile priesthood and the Temple worship as earthly, visible, and temporary. Christ has instituted the New Covenant, and its worship is heavenly, invisible, and eternal. So everything in the Old Testament was, in a sense, unreal and foreshadowed the true worship of God, which is found only in Christ Jesus.

2. The contrast between the superiority of the New Covenant to the Old permeates the whole letter. Because the author is dealing with the notions of priest, cult, and sanctuary, there is a heavy emphasis on the proper worship of God. The author, of course, sees that fulfilled only by Christians. For the Law of Moses has been superseded by the Law of Jesus Christ, the eternal High Priest.

3. The vision of Christ in this letter is very lofty. He is presented as reigning gloriously in heaven but in constant contact through the Holy Spirit with the suffering faithful on earth.

4. It is hard to say whether the letter is a sermon or a theological treatise because the author moves back and forth from exposition of doctrine to exhortation to virtue and perseverance in faith.

5. From beginning to end there is much emphasis on faith and fidelity. Certainly a key idea in the letter is the encouragement that it offers to Christians to keep their eyes on Christ, not to lose hope, and to persevere in the faith no matter what obstacles they encounter. Chapter 11 on the heroes of the faith is an example of this.

6. Finally, there is a pastoral theme in the letter in the author's view of the People of God. For the faithful are viewed as a community on a march toward God's "rest". The goal of the Israelites wandering in the wilderness was the "rest" of the Promised Land. The goal of the new People of God is "eternal rest" with Christ in the heavenly sanctuary. If they persevere in the faith, they will surely enter it and be with Christ forever.

OUTLINE

I. The Son higher than the angels (1:1—2:18)

    A. Christ is superior to the angels (1:1–14)

    B. Exhortation to fidelity to him (2:1–18)

II. Faithful and compassionate High Priest (3:1—5:10)

    A. Jesus is superior to Moses (3:1–19)

    B. The sabbath rest (4:1–13)

    C. A compassionate High Priest (4:14–16)

REFLECTION

May the God of peace who brought again from the dead our Lord Jesus, the great shepherd of the sheep, by the blood of the eternal covenant, equip you with everything good that you may do his will, working in you that which is pleasing in his sight, through Jesus Christ; to whom be glory for ever and ever. Amen (13:20–21).

James

Blessed is the man who endures trial, for when he has stood the test he will receive the crown of life which God has promised to those who love him (1:12).

PLACE IN THE BIBLE: The letter of James follows the letter to the Hebrews and comes before 1 Peter. The letter contains five chapters.

DATE AND AUTHOR: There is a long Catholic tradition that the author is James "the brother of the Lord" (Gal 1:19; Mk 6:3; brother here = cousin/relative) who was a "pillar" of the Church (Gal 2:9) and leader of the Christian community in Jerusalem (Acts 12:17; 21:18ff.). It is not James the brother of John, son of Zebedee (Mk 3:17), because he was martyred in A.D. 42. The exact date of composition is not known, but it was probably about A.D. 57: James the author died in 62.

THEME: The true and wise Christian is the one who has faith in Jesus Christ as the Messiah and Son of God and puts his faith into practice by living a life of love of God and love of neighbor. For, faith without works is dead; the "works" meant here are not external rites but keeping the Commandments and living the Beatitudes — works of love.

SUMMARY: The reader should not look for a clear, logical outline of the letter of St. James, because there is none. The letter contains a series of moral exhortations to avoid vice and practice virtue, but the author moves from one topic to another with no real connection or development.

The letter is addressed to "the twelve tribes that are in the Dispersion" (1:1). By this he means the Christians who are the New Israel and who are dispersed in the Mediterranean world. He urges them to accept their trials patiently and use them to come closer to God. He says that all are subject to temptations, but these do not come from God.

One idea that runs through the letter is that of true wisdom, which comes not only from hearing God's word but also from doing it (1:22). Both rich and poor should be treated equally by the community — no favors for the rich. For, the truly rich are the poor who are close to God and will inherit an everlasting reward in the heavenly Jerusalem.

One of the most famous passages in the letter comes in the second chapter where James establishes the principle that faith without works is dead (2:17, 20, 26). This principle is only *apparently* in conflict with St. Paul's doctrine of justification by faith and not by works. By "works", Paul means not just the external rituals of Judaism but also and especially following the Commandments of the Law as a purely human achievement — something I can boast of as "mine" independently of God's assisting grace. Faith for Paul, however, must include the works of charity in order to be alive — and that is what James means here.

James speaks about the sins of the tongue and controlling it in chapter 3. This is difficult for most people, so he says, "If any one makes no mistakes in what he says, he is a perfect man" (3:2). Next he speaks about "true wisdom" that comes from God: it is chaste, peaceable, moderate, docile, and so on (3:13–18).

Not controlling one's passions leads to discord and division in the community, while self-control leads to peace and a just society. Next James warns the rich to avoid arrogance, and he exhorts his fellow Christians to patience in the midst of trials (4:13 — 5:11). He concludes with an exhortation to be faithful in prayer. Here one will find the short passage on the anointing of the sick by the presbyters of the Church (5:14–15) that is the biblical basis of the Church's teaching about the Sacrament of the Anointing of the Sick (formerly: Extreme Unction).

The letter is a practical exhortation to do good and to avoid evil. This is a direct consequence of faith in Jesus Christ. The thinking of James is like that of the great wisdom literature of the Old Testament — Proverbs, Ecclesiastes, Sirach, and Wisdom. It also reflects the teaching of Jesus, especially as it is found in the Beatitudes and the Sermon on the Mount in Matthew 5 — 7.

THEOLOGY: Though the letter of St. James is primarily concerned with good moral conduct, it nevertheless contains some doctrinal points that serve as a basis for moral living. The letter is not a treatise on any one point of morality or doctrine. Rather, it offers a lot of sage advice to do good and avoid evil, but the sections that follow one upon the other are only loosely connected, if at all.

It is clear from the letter that the author is a Jewish

Christian and that he is writing for Jewish Christians. The theology is very similar to Old Testament thinking, with the addition of belief in Jesus Christ as Lord, Savior, and Messiah. The author directly asserts that there is only one God (2:19) but does not give a hint of belief in the Holy Trinity. This is an indication that the letter was written very early, as we said above, in the mid-fifties of the first century. God is spoken of as the Creator of the stars, the Author of all good and of wisdom. As the Father of all men, he showers his grace on them, hears their prayers, and remits their sins. He does not cause evil temptations (1:13), and he is the sovereign judge of all (4:12; 5:1–11).

Man who is made in the image of God is a sinner and is inclined to evil by his own nature and by the devil. Born again by faith and Baptism, he is destined for eternal life (1:12). Ultimately he is saved, not by faith as an act of the mind, but by putting into practice the principles of the gospel of Jesus Christ (1:21ff.).

The Church is considered both as the local assembly (2:2) and the communion of all Christians in the dispersion (1:1). There is a beginning of hierarchical organization because the local church has both presbyters and teachers.

The main doctrinal point concerns the Sacrament of the Anointing of the Sick. For the Council of Trent in 1551 decreed that this sacrament is meant by the anointing of the sick on the part of the presbyters in 5:14–15.

If there is any overarching unity to the letter, it would have to do with Christian wisdom in the sense of good morals, borrowing from the Old Testament, namely, that the good Christian is the one who leads an upright life by obeying the Commandments; the one who does that will be rewarded by God with eternal happiness. On the other hand, the foolish Christian is the one who abandons the faith and lives like a pagan; such a person will be judged by God "without mercy" (2:13; see also 5:1–12).

REFLECTION

Every good endowment and every perfect gift is from above, coming down from the Father of lights with whom there is no variation or shadow due to change (1:17).

1 Peter

You are a chosen race, a royal priesthood, a holy nation, God's own people, that you may declare the wonderful deeds of him who called you out of darkness into his marvelous light (2:9).

PLACE IN THE BIBLE: First Peter is located after the letter of St. James and before 2 Peter. The letter contains five chapters.

DATE AND AUTHOR: First Peter was written by St. Peter, the prince of the apostles and the first Vicar of Christ on earth. It was written at Rome about A.D. 64.

THEME: The theme is that Christians through faith and Baptism now share in the salvation provided by the death and Resurrection of Jesus. They therefore should lead lives of virtue and uprightness in conformity with the Scriptures, and they should be prepared, in imitation of Jesus, for trials and persecution from the devil and the enemies of God.

SUMMARY: The first letter of St. Peter is like the letter of James, but it is richer in doctrinal content. Peter is writing to the Christians in Asia Minor, but he does not specify whether they are Jewish or Gentile Christians — they were probably a combination of both. He reminds them of the great gift they have received in being called to be members of the Church and that they should live holy lives because they have been redeemed by the precious blood of Christ. Because of what Christ has done for them, they should be outstanding in the practice of love of God and love of neighbor. He invites them to draw near to Christ, who is the cornerstone of the Church, but they must abandon their former attachment to sin. Following from this are particular counsels for different types of Christians — citizens, servants, wives, and husbands. He warns them that they will be called upon to suffer, but they will be rewarded only if they suffer for doing good; there is no advantage in suffering for wrongdoing.

As the leading shepherd, St. Peter urges the local presbyters to be faithful to their duties — to be humble and not greedy. He urges all to practice humility and to be wary of the devil, who roams about "like a roaring lion" ready to devour them if they are not careful. He concludes with a note of greeting and wishes the grace of Christ to all.

THEOLOGY: First Peter is a moral exhortation that is based on doctrinal truths. The main theological point Peter makes is that Christians all over the world have been redeemed by the precious blood of Christ (1:18–19; also 1:2). Once they were sinners and given over to the vices of the pagans, but now they have been chosen for a life of grace and holiness in union with Jesus Christ, who rose from the dead and has sanctified them. God the Father planned the mode of their salvation even before the creation of the world. The plan was revealed to the prophets of the Old Testament, and they spoke about it. Christ came in the flesh and fulfilled the plan in history; the effect of his suffering and death was the expiation of man's sins. Through Baptism, man dies to sin and is reborn to a new life because of the merits of Jesus. By submission to Christ and by faith in him, Christians can hope for an eternal reward in heaven. To obtain this reward, Christians must identify with Christ and be holy. They do this, according to Peter, by resisting the devil, by rejecting past sins, by accepting the trials and sufferings of this life, by practicing the virtues that pertain to their present state in life, and by devoting themselves to fraternal charity.

OUTLINE

REFLECTION

Blessed be the God and Father of our Lord Jesus Christ! By his great mercy we have been born anew to a living hope through the resurrection of Jesus Christ from the dead, and to an inheritance which is imperishable, undefiled, and unfading, kept in heaven for you, who by God's power are guarded through faith for a salvation ready to be revealed in the last time (1:3–5).

2 Peter

For we did not follow cleverly devised myths when we made known to you the power and coming of our Lord Jesus Christ, but we were eyewitnesses of his majesty (1:16).

PLACE IN THE BIBLE: Second Peter follows 1 Peter and comes before 1 John. The letter contains three chapters.

DATE AND AUTHOR: Since the third century there has been a dispute over whether or not St. Peter is the author of 2 Peter. But Origen in the third century and many scholars since, considering all the facts, still attribute the letter to Peter. It was definitively accepted as belonging to the canon of Scripture by the Council of Trent in the sixteenth century. There is no indication in the letter of the date it was composed; a probable date is shortly before A.D. 70.

THEME: The theme of the letter is the certainty of the Parousia, or Second Coming of Jesus, even though now it seems to be delayed. A secondary theme is the refutation of false teachers and their errors about Christ and the Parousia.

SUMMARY: Like James and 1 Peter, this letter gives the appearance of being a letter, but it is better characterized as an exhortation or homily in the style of the Hellenized

Jewish Christians of the time. So the letter is intended for all Christians, including us, rather than directed to one small group.

In the first chapter the author exhorts his readers to strive for virtue in imitation of Christ, because by our calling we have been summoned to be "partakers of the divine nature" by Baptism and grace (1:4). He assures them of the truth of the Second Coming of Christ (1:16), even though, for now, it is delayed. In verse 21 he offers an important definition of prophecy by saying that it is speech of holy men of God who "were moved by the Holy Spirit".

In the second chapter he tells his audience to be on their guard against false teachers. He seems to be thinking of definite errors but does not say exactly what they are. These false heretics follow their own sensuality and in effect deny true faith in Jesus Christ. They fall into all kinds of vices. To bring home the point, he refers to fallen angels and sinners in the Old Testament who were severely punished by God for similar offenses. These false teachers once were pagans and then converted to Christ; now they have fallen away from the true faith — and they know better, so their responsibility is greater. Peter says that their last state is worse than the first (2:20–22).

In the last chapter Peter takes up the arguments of those who deny the Parousia and refutes them. He says the Lord is surely coming, but no one knows when it will happen, because "the day of the Lord will come like a thief" (3:10). He gives a vivid description of the coming of Jesus, and, because the time is unknown, he urges his readers to persevere in virtue and to be always ready for the coming of Christ. He goes on to say that St. Paul also has written about these things, but what he has written is difficult to understand. The unlearned and the unstable have distorted them to their own destruction (3:16), that is, they have tried to interpret them independently of the tradition of the Church and have fallen into error. Then he concludes with another warning and a doxology like the one in 1 Peter 5:10–11.

THEOLOGY: The letter contains a well-developed Christology. In the very first verse Jesus is called God and Savior; by his divine power (1:3) he has called us to faith and to become "partakers of the divine nature" (1:4). The Christian convert, who once was enmeshed in sin and error, has been bought and redeemed by Jesus Christ, who is rightly called "Savior" and also "Lord", a title in the Old Testament given only to God.

Jesus has given man all he needs to share in the divine promises; among the major gifts is that of faith that is based on the knowledge of Christ. Both faith and knowledge are increased by the practice of virtue and the avoidance of vice (1:5–8). Following the way of sin leads to a denial of Christ and eventually to eternal damnation (2:3, 17).

False teachers and their errors lead one away from faith in Jesus Christ and terminate in moral deviancy. God will severely punish sinners of this type, just as he punished sinners in the Old Testament, as we learn from the examples of the fallen angels, Sodom and Gomorrah, and the foreign prophet Balaam.

One of the main theological points of the letter is the

certainty of the Parousia. The coming of Jesus may be delayed, but he will surely come. This is a powerful motive for men to lead a life of virtue while they wait for him to come again in glory. In asserting the certainty of the Parousia, Peter is apparently refuting an error being spread abroad by the false teachers he attacks in chapter 2.

Two other theological points should be noted. The first one is that the Christian, through the gift of divine grace, becomes a sharer or partaker of the divine nature (1:4). This is an important addition to St. Paul's doctrine that Christians compose the Body of Christ, while he is the Head. The second one has to do with the nature of Scripture, inspiration, and the interpretation of the Bible — all very important issues. Peter says that the Scriptures do not come from fallible men but from God, for it is the Holy Spirit who moves holy men to speak in his name (we now call this motion "inspiration") (2:20–21). So God is the origin of Scripture, not man. Also, interpretation is not a personal or private thing; Peter implies that the Church is the authentic interpreter of the Bible and has the last word on the meaning of any part of it.

Peter also offers a comment on the letters of St. Paul. He says that Paul speaks about the Parousia, but some of his writings are difficult to understand. One must be careful to interpret them in terms of the traditional faith (3:15–16). If we Catholics find it hard to understand all that Paul is saying, we are in good company and should not be discouraged. For even St. Peter, the Vicar of Christ on earth, found some of Paul's writings "difficult to understand".

Finally, the three Persons of the Holy Trinity are mentioned in the letter: Father (1:17), Son (1:17), and the Holy Spirit (1:21). This suggests a belief in the Trinity even though the word and the doctrine were not fully elaborated in the first century.

REFLECTION

You therefore, beloved, knowing this beforehand, beware lest you be carried away with the error of lawless men and lose your own stability. But grow in the grace and knowledge of our Lord and Savior Jesus Christ. To him be the glory both now and to the day of eternity. Amen (3:17–18).

1 John

God is love, and he who abides in love abides in God, and God abides in him (4:16).

PLACE IN THE BIBLE: First John comes after 2 Peter and before 2 John. The letter contains five chapters.

DATE AND AUTHOR: The letter was written by St. John, the author of the Fourth Gospel. In thought and vocabulary the letter resembles the Gospel of John, so it was probably written about the same time, that is, around A.D. 90, according to most contemporary scholars.

THEME: The theme of the letter is that everyone who believes that Jesus is the Son of God by that very fact possesses eternal life within himself. As a consequence, he must avoid all sin and errors spread by Antichrists. If he does that, he will live in the light of God's love and not in the darkness of the evil one.

SUMMARY: The prologue reminds us of the prologue to St. John's Gospel, but this one emphasizes not only the divinity of Jesus but also, and especially, his humanity (1:1-4). If the Christian remains faithful and steadfast in the faith, he has fellowship or communion with God. He is living in the light, that is, in the truth and goodness of God, because God is light. We know and love Jesus by keeping his commandments; they include the Ten Commandments of the Old Testament and especially the love of God and love of neighbor. All are warned not to love the world or the things of the world (2:15). In John's terms, "world" here means those powers opposed to God and his Kingdom.

Next, the author warns his community to beware of the Antichrists, that is, those who deny that Jesus is the Christ and reject his Father. Scripture has predicted that they will appear in the time before the Second Coming, but all are warned to avoid them and reject their false doctrine about Christ and eternal life.

Those who remain in Christ are by that fact children of God and heirs of eternal life. Since we are children of God, we must love not only God our Father but also our brother and sister Christians and all men. His commandment is that we should believe in Jesus Christ and love one another. Those who do that "remain" or "abide" in him, and he in them, through the Holy Spirit.

St. John offers a test to find out whether or not a spirit is good and a test for false prophets: Those who acknowledge that Jesus Christ has come in the flesh are of God.

We should love one another because we are begotten of God by faith and Baptism, and God is love itself. That is St. John's definition. Again, to remain in love, one must acknowledge that Jesus is the Son of God (4:15). Christian faith, rooted in love, overcomes the world and conquers the evil one who is the master of the world (5:19).

THEOLOGY: The theology of 1 John is similar to that of St. John's Gospel. Ideas that are common to both include:

emphasis on the word, light and darkness, life and death, truth and falsehood, the new birth of the Christian, children of God, the world (in a hostile sense), the Holy Spirit of God, the intimate relationship between the Father and the Son. From the very beginning the author stresses the full humanity of Jesus — this truth is repeated many times in the letter. He also emphasizes the divinity of Christ, and it is probably Christ whom he calls "God" in 5:20.

A key theological idea in the letter is that the faithful Christian is in real communion with God; he is born of God and so his child; he possesses God within himself; he knows God, and he dwells in him. This is a very mysterious reality that the Christian knows by faith. But as a result he has become a new creature and must keep the Commandments and love the brothers.

Different qualities of God are affirmed without qualification when the author says that God is light, God is just, God is love. That God is infinite goodness is shown by the fact that he sent his only begotten Son into the world to die for us on the Cross. Christian life is communion with the Father and the Son and should be reflected in lives that are free of sin and motivated by faith and love — for God and for one another.

The Father and the Son are truth (light) and life. Those who abide in their love already have eternal life living within them. The source of all these gifts to men is the love of God. Since God is love and we are united to him and he made us for himself, the purpose of our existence is love. Therefore, we are bound to do his will by keeping his Commandments, by walking in his light. If we do that, we will abide in love and share in his eternal life.

OUTLINE

REFLECTION

Beloved, let us love one another; for love is of God, and he who loves is born of God and knows God. He who does not love does not know God; for God is love (4:7–8).

2 John

This is love, that we follow his commandments (6).

PLACE IN THE BIBLE: Second John follows 1 John and precedes 3 John. The letter contains thirteen verses and is the shortest book in the Bible.

DATE AND AUTHOR: The letter was written by St. John, the author of the Fourth Gospel and of 1 John. The thought and vocabulary resemble the Gospel of St. John and also the First Epistle, so it was probably written about the same time, that is, around A.D. 90, according to most modern scholars.

THEME: The theme is that the addressees of the letter, whoever they are, should remain faithful to the teaching they have received from the apostles. They are to avoid those who deny the coming of Christ in the flesh (7); these false teachers are deceivers and Antichrists. They are to practice love for one another as they were taught; in the concrete, this means keeping the Commandments.

SUMMARY: Unlike 1 John, which is more like a treatise, this is a real letter. The author identifies himself as the "elder", which seems to mean in this context a man of some authority over the community. The "elect lady" he writes to is not an individual woman but the particular church he is addressing; "her children" are the members of the community.

In the first three verses he greets them, and then he thanks God that they are faithfully following the will of God. He urges them to love one another and to keep the Commandments. Then he warns them to avoid and reject the heretics who distort the true gospel about Jesus Christ. "He who abides in the doctrine has both the Father and the Son" (9). Because of the danger of being contaminated by the false teachers, they should not welcome them into their homes and should avoid them. He excuses himself for the shortness of the letter and says he will visit them soon. The final greeting from "the children of your elect sister" are the members of the elder's church—probably in Ephesus.

THEOLOGY: This letter sounds like a brief summary of 1 John. St. John wishes the "elect lady" grace, mercy, and peace from God the Father and from his Son, Christ Jesus. The main theological point of the letter is that the addressees persevere in the true faith by living the commandment of love of God and love of neighbor; they do this by keeping the Commandments. They are to avoid false teachers like the plague, because false teaching and the errors it conveys lead to immoral living, and immoral living results in a denial of God and merits eternal damnation.

The reference to "going ahead" in verse 9 probably refers to the esoteric doctrine of the false teachers who claimed to know a better way to serve God than the one they had learned from the true apostles. Those who fall for that no longer "have God" within them; that is, they have lost the grace of God.

John tells them that, if any itinerant preachers come with a new doctrine, they are not to receive them into their house and they are not even to greet them. In this we see that the early Church had very little or no tolerance for dissenters and heretics.

OUTLINE

I. The presbyter greets the elect lady and her children (1–3)

II. Exhortation (4–12)

    A. Joy because some are faithful (4)

    B. The commandment of love (5–6)

    C. Beware of deceivers and the Antichrist (7)

    D. Heretics have fallen from the grace of God (8–9)

    E. Avoid heretics (10–11)

    F. Soon I will visit you (12)

III. Final greetings (13)

REFLECTION

Grace, mercy and peace will be with us, from God the Father and from Jesus Christ the Father's Son, in truth and love (3).

3 John

No greater joy can I have than this, to hear that my children follow the truth (4).

PLACE IN THE BIBLE: The third letter of John comes after 2 John and before Jude. The letter contains fifteen verses; it is therefore the second shortest book in the Bible after 2 John.

DATE AND AUTHOR: The letter was written by St. John, the author of the Fourth Gospel and of 1 and 2 John. It was written about the same time as 2 John, namely, around A.D. 90, according to most contemporary scholars.

THEME: The theme is that all Christians should live the truth of the Christian faith, do good to all, and especially offer hospitality to the brethren.

SUMMARY: The author calls himself "the elder" and addresses the letter to a certain "Gaius", who was probably an important person in the local community. The elder praises Gaius for being a faithful Christian and for offering hospitality and friendship to the missionaries he sent to him. St. John strongly criticizes Diotrephes for rejecting his authority and refusing to welcome missionaries. He recommends Demetrius, who is faithful to the truth.

He excuses himself for the brevity of the letter but assures Gaius that he will come to see him in the near future.

THEOLOGY: The third letter of John deals with matters of administration in a local church. There is no question of heresy in this letter, as there is in 1 and 2 John. Here it is rather a matter of personal relations and an overbearing, arrogant leader of the community who is insubordinate to the Apostle, who is above him in authority. In typical Johannine terminology, the author praises Gaius for "following" the truth and Demetrius for living the truth. In both cases "truth" means the gospel of Jesus Christ. Emphasis on the truth of the gospel dominates the letter, since it is mentioned seven times in fifteen verses.

OUTLINE

   I. Greeting to Gaius (1)

  II. Exhortation (2–14)

     A. Joy because Gaius "follows the truth", that is, lives the Gospel (2–4)

     B. Gaius' help for missionaries praised (5–8)

     C. Diotrephes rejects us and hinders the brethren (9–10)

     D. Do good and avoid evil (11)

     E. Faithfulness of Demetrius (12)

     F. Soon I will visit you (13–14)

 III. Final greeting and salutation (15)

REFLECTION

Beloved, I pray that all may go well with you and that you may be in health; I know that it is well with your soul (2).

Jude

Keep yourselves in the love of God; wait for the mercy of our Lord Jesus Christ unto eternal life (21).

PLACE IN THE BIBLE: The letter of Jude is the last of the "Catholic Epistles", coming after 3 John and before the book of Revelation. The letter contains twenty-five verses.

DATE AND AUTHOR: The author identifies himself in the first verse as "Jude . . . brother of James". That James is the author of the letter of St. James, head of the church in Jerusalem and a cousin of Jesus, so Jude is also a cousin of the Lord. There is no consensus about the date of composition, but a probable date is about A.D. 70. The author is a Jewish Christian writing to various communities, probably most of whose members are Gentiles or converts from paganism.

THEME: The theme of the letter is an exhortation to fidelity to the unchangeable deposit of faith from the apostles, in spite of the enticements of the false teachers.

SUMMARY: The Epistle of St. Jude is more like a homily or exhortation than it is like a letter. It is addressed to "the called", that is, to baptized Christians, but the author does not say where they are. Right at the beginning he states his theme: "contend for the faith" (3). He is strongly attacking certain "ungodly persons" (4), but it is not clear precisely what they are teaching. In any event, their doctrine has led to a loosening of Christian morals, and Jude is incensed about that.

Jude reminds his audience in strong terms that God punishes those who violate his law, and he offers some examples from the Old Testament (Cain; Sodom and Gomorrah; the Egyptians; Balaam; and the rebellion of Korah in Numbers 16). He even cites the non-inspired and non-biblical book of Enoch relative to a prophecy (14–16).

Next he reminds his audience that the apostles predicted there would be false teachers before the Second Coming of the Lord and told them that they should protect themselves against them. Finally, he concludes the letter with an admonition to be faithful to the tradition and with a beautiful doxology, saying that to God alone belong "glory, majesty, dominion, and authority, before all time and now and for ever. Amen" (25).

THEOLOGY: Like the letter of James, Jude is primarily a moral exhortation to keep the faith pure and inviolate in the face of dissenters who are upsetting the faithful, especially in the matter of upright moral living. But in spite of its practical purpose, the letter does contain references to some basic Christian truths. God the Father is the only God; he is all-powerful, glorious, and the initiator of man's salvation through Jesus Christ (1, 25). Jesus Christ is "our only Master and Lord" (4), who speaks through the apostles (17). The letter expresses belief in the existence of angels — good angels like Michael and bad angels like the devil (6, 9).

Christians are those "called" by God; their faith is the unchangeable instruction received from the apostles, and it is the foundation of their life (20). There is even a hint of the Trinity of three Divine Persons in verses 20–21, where the Holy Spirit, God the Father, and Jesus Christ are mentioned in close proximity. Finally the absolute transcendence of God Almighty and his glorious majesty are affirmed in the powerful and beautiful doxology that concludes the letter (24–25). Even though the letter is very short, it is not hard to see why it was included in the canon of inspired Scriptures.

OUTLINE

I. Address and greetings (1–2)

II. Statement of the theme (3–4)

III. Warning about false teachers (5–19)

    A. Warning from the past (5–7)

    B. Description (8–13)

    C. Enoch's prophecy (14–16)

    D. Heed the apostles' warning (17–19)

IV. Admonitions (20–23)

V. Concluding doxology (24–25)

REFLECTION

Now to him who is able to keep you from falling and to present you without blemish before the presence of his glory with rejoicing, to the only God, our Savior through Jesus Christ our Lord, be glory, majesty, dominion, and authority, before all time and now and for ever. Amen (24–25).

Revelation

Blessed is he who reads aloud the words of the prophecy, and blessed are those who hear, and who keep what is written therein; for the time is near (1:3).

PLACE IN THE BIBLE: The book of Revelation (Apocalypse) is the last book of the Bible, and it contains twenty-two chapters.

DATE AND AUTHOR: In the history of the Church the book of Revelation has been attributed to St. John the Evangelist. Aspects of both style and content are both similar to and different from the Gospel; this has led many scholars to suggest that the version we now have was drafted by a disciple of John, but no one knows for certain. Two dates have been proposed, both during times of persecution of Christians: A.D. 68 and 95.

THEME: The theme of the book is the war between God and Satan for the souls of men. Satan and his human agents (dragon, beasts, false prophet) persecute and kill those who believe in Christ, but Christ is God and is armed with divine power. Christ conquers and binds Satan, but he permits him to tempt Christians until the Parousia, or Second Coming of Christ and the end of the world as we now know it. From beginning to end, it is certain that Satan will be defeated, God will triumph, and the faithful ones will enter into his Kingdom.

SUMMARY: The book of Revelation is perhaps the most difficult of all the books in the Bible for modern Catholics to read and understand. The book fits into a type of literature that was current from 200 B.C. to A.D. 200. This is known as "apocalyptic" literature. Some of the characteristics of apocalyptic writing are: material things are used as symbols for spiritual, intellectual, or unseen realities. Almost everything is symbolic. Some of the things mentioned in this book include: lampstands, stars, colors, seals, trumpets, bowls, colored horses, numbers, animals with ten heads and seven horns, eyes inside and out. A good rule of thumb here is to realize that almost every material thing mentioned stands for something else. Also the story progresses as a series of visions, and many of the statements have to do with future events.

"Apocalypse" means "uncovering something hidden". One reason for hiding the meaning of the book was so that the Roman persecutors of Christians, if they got a copy of the book, could not understand it: the meaning was hidden from them. The book was written in a time of persecution when Christians were being put in jail, tortured, and brutally killed by lions or crucifixion because of their faith in Jesus Christ. The main purpose of the book was to encourage Christians to stand fast, to avoid all sin and paganism, to die for the faith.

God is presented as the absolute Lord of history; he is in control. For his own unstated reasons he allows Christians to suffer, but at the same time he assures them that, if they remain faithful, they will triumph over Satan and death and will reign with Christ in heaven forever. The book ends on a joyous, hopeful, triumphant note. Revelation restates, in symbolic language, truths found elsewhere in the Bible, so there is no "secret truth" here that is open only to biblical scholars.

The first three chapters present seven letters to seven churches in Asia: Ephesus, Smyrna, Thyatira, Pergamum, Sardis, Philadelphia, and Laodicea (in present day Turkey). The Lord Jesus praises them for some things, but he also finds fault with them and urges them to repent.

The body of the letter offers four series of seven signs in heaven; most of them have to do with God's punishment of the wicked on earth. He does not destroy them immediately, because he wants to give them time to repent of their sins; if they do not repent, they will be cast into hell or the pool of fire (= the second death). Here you will find the seven seals, the seven trumpets, the seven signs, and the seven bowls of wrath.

Chapters 17 to 20 deal with the destruction of Babylon —here "Babylon" stands for the Roman Empire, which persecuted the Christians and promoted worship of the emperor. The final two chapters present the revelation of the heavenly Jerusalem, that is, the Second Coming of Christ and the great joy of heaven granted to all who remain faithful to God and the Lamb (Christ).

THEOLOGY: God is presented in the book of Revelation as absolutely transcendent over all material and created things. He is the Lord God Almighty—he who was, who is, and who is to come. As such, he is the Lord of history—he guides history and human events according to his own divine will. This is mysterious to man, but since God is infinitely good, we know that his government is good and just. After reading this book, one knows the certainty of divine judgment—the wicked will be punished, there is no doubt about that; and the good will be fabulously rewarded, there is no doubt about that.

Jesus Christ is presented as God Almighty, equal to God the Father, and he is active all through the story. One point to stress is his presence in the Church: He is in the midst of the seven lampstands, which represent the churches. In his right hand he holds the seven stars, which are "the angels of the seven churches" (1:20).

Much of the book has to do with the war against the devil, or Satan. He has been conquered by Christ through his death and Resurrection and chained down, but he still retains some power to deceive men until the time of the Second Coming of Christ, when he and his minions will be cast into hell forever. Along with him human sinners will also be cast into hell. There is some very sobering material here for reflection for the many modern Catholics who think that God is "nice" and everyone is going to heaven (see 14:9–11 and 21:8). It is important for the contemporary Catholic reading the book of Revelation to realize that the book does not speak directly to the particular historical circumstances of our time, as some fundamentalists claim. Like all apocalyptic literature, Revelation addresses the issues of the time in which it was written through symbols that were commonly understood by those to whom it was addressed. But the struggle be-good and evil, between God and Satan, will continue until the Second Coming of Christ, so in that sense it can be applied to every age.

The existence of angels, or good spirits, is asserted again and again. St. John speaks of "myriads of myriads and thousands of thousands" of angels around the throne of God (5:11; 12:7).

Just as in the book of Hebrews, there is a close connection between Revelation and the Old Testament. The author sees God in Christ Jesus fulfilling all of his promises that were made in the Old Testament. So the Church is the new People of God, which is protected by him as he guides it to the final coming of the Lord on the Last Day.

Even though the book of Revelation speaks often of destruction, death, and disasters, it is fundamentally an optimistic and hopeful book. For the Lamb of God, Jesus Christ the Savior, triumphs over the power of Satan, sin, and death and grants eternal life and happiness to all those who remain faithful to him. It is for that reason that the book, and the whole Bible, ends on a note of expectation, joy, hope, and calling upon the Lord to come soon.

OUTLINE

A. The seven seals (6:1—8:1)

B. The seven trumpets (8:2—11:18)

C. The seven signs (11:19—15:4)

D. The seven bowls of wrath (15:5—16:21)

V. The punishment of Babylon (Rome) and the destruction of the pagan nations (17:1—20:15)

VI. The new creation (21:1—22:5)

A. The voice from the throne (21:1-8)

B. Vision of the heavenly Jerusalem (21:9—22:5)

VII. Epilogue and final blessing (22:6-21)

REFLECTION

"Holy, holy, holy, is the Lord God Almighty, who was and is and is to come! . . . Worthy art thou, our Lord and God, to receive glory and honor and power, for thou didst create all things, and by thy will they existed and were created" (4:8, 11).

Bibliography

Bible. Revised Standard Version, Catholic edition. *The Holy Bible*. San Francisco: Ignatius Press, 1994.

Brown, Raymond E., Joseph A. Fitzmyer, and Roland A. Murphy, editors. *The Jerome Biblical Commentary*. Englewood Cliffs, N.J.: Prentice-Hall, 1968.

Duggan, Michael. *The Consuming Fire: A Christian Introduction to the Old Testament*. San Francisco: Ignatius Press, 1991.

Heidt, William G., general editor. *Old Testament Reading Guide*. 31 volumes. Collegeville, Minn.: Liturgical Press, 1960–1968.

———. *New Testament Reading Guide*. 14 volumes. Collegeville, Minn.: Liturgical Press, 1960–1965.

McKenzie, John L., S.J. *Dictionary of the Bible*. Milwaukee: Bruce Publishing Co., 1965.

Most, William G. *The Thought of St. Paul. A Commentary on the Pauline Epistles*. Front Royal, Va.: Christendom Press, 1994.

Robert, A., and A. Feuillet. *Introduction to the New Testament*. New York: Desclee Company, 1965.

>>>

SIXTEEN FAMOUS
EUROPEAN PLAYS

>>>>>>>>>>>>>>>>>>>>>>>>>>>>>>>>>>>

The publishers will be pleased to send, upon request, an illustrated folder setting forth the purpose and scope of THE MODERN LIBRARY, *and listing each volume in the series. Every reader will find titles he has been looking for, handsomely printed, in unabridged editions, and at an unusually low price.*

>>>>>>>>>>>>>>>>>>>>>>>>>>>>>>>>>>>

SIXTEEN
FAMOUS EUROPEAN
PLAYS

>>>

Compiled by

BENNETT A. CERF *and* VAN H. CARTMELL

With an Introduction by JOHN ANDERSON

>>>

THE MODERN LIBRARY
NEW YORK

THE MODERN LIBRARY

IS PUBLISHED BY

RANDOM HOUSE, INC.

BENNETT A. CERF · DONALD S. KLOPFER · ROBERT K. HAAS

Manufactured in the United States of America
By H. Wolff

ACKNOWLEDGMENTS

For permission to include the following plays, acknowl·edgment is here made to the authors of the plays and the publishers under whose imprint they were originally issued:

Amphitryon 38 by Jean Giraudoux, copyright, 1938, by S. N. Behrman; *The Playboy of the Western World* by John M. Synge, copyright, 1907, by John M. Synge; *Shadow and Substance* by Paul Vincent Carroll, copyright, 1937, by Random House, Inc.; *Tovarich* by Jacques Deval, copyright, 1937, by Random House, Inc.; reprinted by permission of Random House, Inc.

Anatol by Arthur Schnitzler, copyright, 1925, by the Modern Library, Inc., reprinted by permission of the Modern Library, Inc.

The Cradle Song by G. Martinez Sierra, copyright, 1922, by E. P. Dutton & Co., Inc., and *Six Characters in Search of an Author* by Luigi Pirandello, copyright, 1922, by E. P. Dutton & Co., Inc., reprinted by permission of E. P. Dutton & Co., Inc.

Cyrano de Bergerac by Edmond Rostand, copyright, 1923, by Henry Holt and Company, reprinted by permission of Henry Holt and Company.

Grand Hotel by Vicki Baum, copyright, 1930, by Georg Marton, reprinted by permission of Curtis Brown, Ltd.

Liliom by Ferenc Molnar, copyright, 1921, by United Plays, Inc., and *The Dybbuk* by S. Ansky, copyright, 1926, by Henry G. Alsberg, reprinted by permission of Liveright Publishing Corporation.

R. U. R. by Karel Capek, copyright, 1923, by Doubleday,

Page and Company, reprinted by permission of Samuel French.

The Weavers by Gerhart Hauptmann, copyright, 1913, 1940, by the Viking Press, Inc., reprinted by permission of the Viking Press, Inc.

The Wild Duck by Henrik Ibsen, revised and edited by William Archer. Copyright, 1907, by Charles Scribner's Sons; renewal copyright 1935 by Frank Archer. Used by permission of Charles Scribner's Sons.

FOREWORD

In 1941, the editors of this volume undertook a collection of *Sixteen Famous American Plays* that proved gratifyingly successful both in Garden City and Modern Library Giant editions. In 1942, we prepared a companion volume of *Sixteen Famous British Plays*. Both of these editorial tasks proved to be comparatively smooth sailing, conceding the definite limitations that governed our selection.

These were our rules:

1. Only one play by any one author.

2. Every selection to have the endorsement of a successful presentation on Broadway.

3. Only "modern" plays to be considered: nothing earlier than the eighties; seventy-five percent of the selections, in fact, to be chosen from the wealth of material written in the past ten years—"the golden decade of the modern theatre."

4. An introduction by a well-known dramatic critic, who was to feel free to criticize our selections as harshly as he chose. (Brooks Atkinson and John Mason Brown wrote the respective introductions and they certainly "chose!".)

This new collection of sixteen famous European plays presents new and more difficult problems. The question of translation is not the least of them. And whether foreign playwrights are more prolific than native products, or whether they maintain a higher general average of excellence, we are not prepared to say, but certainly we had the devil's own time deciding just which single play we would select of certain of the European masters. Consider the case of Henrik Ibsen, for example. It is generally accepted by outstanding students of the drama that Ibsen is the father of the modern theatre, and the logical point of departure for our new collection was one of his plays. But which one? How is one to choose among *A Doll's House, Hedda Gab-*

ler, Ghosts and *The Wild Duck*—to name the four most popular of his works? All would certainly qualify as famous and characteristic Ibsen plays! Our ultimate selection of *The Wild Duck* was frankly influenced by the fact that earlier—and dare we say stodgier—anthologists almost invariably ignored it. A similar difficulty presented itself in the case of Molnar. We chose *Liliom* because it was his greatest success in this country, and because a recent revival proved that the years had shorn it of none of its lustre.

Another difficulty in preparing this collection lay in the fact that some of the greatest European plays had never been produced in this country. Either they would have lost too much in translation, or their themes would have been unacceptable to an American audience. Many plays that have become famous abroad are known here only as titles that are tossed about by a George Jean Nathan intent on proving his erudition to the readers of "Esquire." That is why we have omitted entirely certain German playwrights whose names are well known here but whose plays are not.

There is a tendency on the part of European dramatists, bravely resisted by our own more commercially-minded authors, to write plays that are virtually unproduceable— "closet drama," masques, poetic pageants. We feel that they do not belong in a volume of this kind. Accept that, if you will, as the explanation for the absence of a play by the vastly overrated—to us, at any rate—Mr. Maeterlinck.

We included no Irish plays in our British collection; it is a pleasure to welcome them into the European group. They are among the best we have to offer! If the French selections seem frivolous and lightweight in comparison to the others, we ask you: what would you have chosen in their place? The Russian plays, we think, speak for themselves.

To the various publishers and authors who have made this volume possible by their consent to the use of their copyrights we are most grateful. A number of the plays

included have never appeared in any other anthology, and
one of them, *Grand Hotel,* has never before appeared in
print.

As usual, the selection of plays was made without consulting the victim whom we elected to introduce the book
for us. Mr. Anderson will not, we trust, disagree too heartily, but in any case he is not to be held liable for our vagar-
ies as editors. We still stand ready to take what raps may be
in store. After two previous anthologies our heads are a bit
bruised but only to flatteries are they bowed.

VAN H. CARTMELL
BENNETT A. CERF

CONTENTS

CONTENTS

INTRODUCTION

BY JOHN ANDERSON

Like all great drama, most of the plays in this collection spring from the finest impulses of free creation, in spiritual pride and humane understanding; so there is an immediate grimness at this date in celebrating them as *Sixteen Famous European Plays*. Their connection with contemporary Europe, their currently obscured force as expressions of European civilization are part of a guarantee older than the rootless usurper that they, and not he, will survive.

Of them we know that Hitler gave whatever he uses for laughter to *Tovarich* and saw it three times after twisting the ending and after careful assurance that its author was suitably Aryan. But if his fatuous star-gazing extended more liberally to the constellation of the theatre, and especially to these plays, he could find things in them to suggest the futility of his dream. He is not only "loosely educated," to use Mr. Churchill's magnificently contemptuous phrase, but he is apparently a careless playgoer.

He could learn the fate of fanatical reformers in the carbolic wrath of *The Wild Duck;* he could find happy personal clues to his own destiny in the madness and impotence which overtake the sheer bully of *The Jest.* He could capture some fearful suggestions, worse than his own nightmares, on the matter of regimented automatons in *R.U.R.* And he could learn from *Liliom* the glory and permanence of the intractable spirit of man which can go through hell, even Hitler's hell, and come out intact.

From nearly all of the others he could, within his own barren spiritual limits, discover the instinctive and unflinching faith men place upon love, honor, and individual integrity. He could observe, even if he could not understand, the common ideals, expressed in so many of the plays, which impel free men to oppose tyranny and to defend their liberties with their lives. He could see them in these plays, as he will be ultimately forced to see them, since they are the powers of his defeat.

So these sixteen plays are part of a European testament, already inherited and richly enjoyed, as proven by the enormous popularity they attained not only in the countries of origin, but, in the benediction of handclaps across the sea, in our own theatre and in spite of the fact that they have often suffered sadly in translation.

Quite by accident in selection they fall into two nearly equal groups: nine of them belong to the pre-World War I, Cherry-Orchard-Heartbreak-House Europe, and seven belong to that ominously quiet but superficially frantic period between 1918 and 1937, the intermezzo of our false security. By a tragic irony, undetected at the time, the last of them carried a French-comedy salute to classical Greek legend at the moment Austria found itself Anschlussed out of existence.

In viewpoint and technique they range from the realistic social theme of *The Wild Duck* to the subjective discussion of illusion and reality in *Six Characters in Search of an Author;* from the bitter comedy of *The Playboy* to the lyric, but static, beauty of *The Cradle Song,* from the cynical sex pattern of *Anatol* to the ecstatic love song of *The Dybbuk.*

To suggest that there is a close and detailed relationship among all these plays, out of such diverse countries and of such widely different treatment, is to embark upon a critical trapeze act which would make the Flying Codonas seem mere ground moles.

Yet most of them are linked in one way or another to the mainsprings of European thought, to the mid-nineteenth-century revolution of ideas, and finally to the free theatre movement which carried the ideas into the playhouses. The theatre responded not only with new drama, but with a new stagecraft, wrought in its image and designed to emphasize the change.

The actual moment of the change which was to color all of our thinking may be set as it has been at 1859, the almost too convenient moment of coincidence when Darwin published *The Origin of Species,* Marx his *Critique* and Wagner *Tristan.* Many impulses contributed to these events, and many impulses have flowed out of them. It is safe to say, in any case, that the world has never been the same again, and the two major impulses are now at death grips all over the world.

The world of romanticism, the world of Shelley and Byron, had passed away, amid the loud outcries and ululations of men who decried the new order in the scornful epithet "materialism." Industrialism spread; the machines were on the march; and instead of trying to realize that the earth shakers were simply facing rationally a fundamental problem, the Laodiceans arose and declared that the three prophets of science, art and economics had, as if in conspiracy, wiped out the individual and left him enslaved to his own glands and the serfdom of collectivist politics—without a soul or a penny or a God to call his own.

Since "realism" was the word that frightened them, they were naturally in no position to borrow it for the calm analysis of what had happened to their world. Their world was overturned, not by the isolated work of three men, but by the forces which had quietly gathered to make the work of those three men not only possible, but inevitable. They solidified the unstable, half-understood, drifting impulses they found around them and, by the catalysis of realism, suggested methods for dealing with them.

It is always painful to remove the rose-colored glasses from people addicted to them, especially when the wearers are afflicted at the same time with astigmatism. If people were moved by silver wires running up to Heaven, and could prove it, it would be useful information from any realistic point of view. If their conduct is based on physical and economic, spiritual or aesthetic facts they are ignorant of, then it is sensible to try to discover the facts, and to discard false notions which are deeply irrational. That is a fundamental concept of the inquiring spirit of man.

But by confusing this impulse to know the forces of human behavior with the ridiculous notion that it debased the individual, the romanticists merely clouded the issues. If anything can debase the individual more than industrial,

political and religious oligarchies have, it has yet to be discovered. It will get a profitable patent quickly enough.
Man's illusion of freedom was merely the keystone of the
whole fabulous structure. It was this illusion that was the
point of attack in the drama that came with Ibsen as its
spearhead. In the theatre it provoked the apparent paradox
of an art of illusion being used to contradict itself. The
dramatists vaulted that one neatly by restoring to the playhouse its ancient privilege of expressing life. If truth itself
turned out to be an illusion, at least the theatre could move
it nearer the common denominator of reality, and leave to
the fascinating speculation of Pirandello's *Six Characters in
Search of an Author* the probing of that rarefied problem
of consciousness that lies beyond.

By a stroke of ironic emphasis Ibsen was just the man to
do the job. His contempt for dramatic lollipops and romantic soothing syrup had the full-bodied strength of a
man revolted by stuff he had worked in himself. Scribe's
influence had infected him with the carpentry ideals of the
well-made play and the intrigue of the romantic drama. His
own early work clearly showed his allegiance, and even
A Doll's House once had a happy ending.

But when Ibsen had isolated the target he was shooting
at, he hit it with relentless precision and unflagging fury.
As a blasting reformer he was to come ultimately face to
face with the illusions of a reformer, the poisonous distor-
tion which stealthily undoes the reason at the moment it
tries to be most rational. Against the people who will make
a cult out of anything and reduce a living attitude to inhuman stencils, he aimed *The Wild Duck*, with the wry
knowledge that some of the blows were bound to fall on
his own head.

Of all his plays *The Wild Duck* is the most deceptive for
the reader, which in the illiteracy of the theatre possibly accounts for its infrequent production. When all its carefully
orchestrated values fall into place on the stage, when you
sit through a surface comedy scene waiting in agony for the
shot that is to come from the rabbit hutch, you have the

jangled and wrenching force of great drama. The effect is bound to escape the printed page, since it is cunningly and beautifully wrought for the physical juxtaposition possible only in a theatre.

By showing the ruin of a family that was happy only in its romantic illusions, Ibsen, however much he has been scorned by late comers as a "bourgeois revolutionary," sounded the harsh but inspiring theme of the new salvation. By the beard of Ibsen's prophet Shaw, it was sworn that men must free themselves; they cannot be freed from without.

Gorky's somberly magnificent *The Lower Depths* repeats the theme on a larger canvas in brilliant strokes and with deeper compassion. His outcasts, whose counterparts the slumming Stanislavsky found in the cellars and caves of the Khitrov Market, are the lowest of the low—thieves, prostitutes and murderers. Their lustily vivid misery is invaded by a gentle Pilgrim Luka who offers them the old comfort of illusion and a gospel of pity and hope.

But it is Satine, the heroic and unwinking realist, who flings out Gorky's passionate conviction in the memorable scene of Act Four, when the Pilgrim has fled.

"I understand the old man, yes!" he shouts to the cringing inmates of the dive. "He lied—but lied out of sheer pity for you. God damn you! Lots of people lie out of pity for their fellow beings! I know. I've read about it. They lie—oh, beautifully, inspiringly, stirringly. Some lies bring comfort and others bring peace—a lie alone can justify the burden which crushed a workman's hand and condemns those who are starving. I know what lying means. The weakling and the one who is a parasite through his very weakness—they both need lies—lies are their support, their shield, their armor. But the man who is strong, who is his own master, who is free and does not have to suck his neighbor's blood—he needs no lies. To lie—it's the creed of slaves and masters of slaves. Truth is the religion of the free man!"

By putting these words into the mouth of a self-proclaimed murderer and crook, Gorky really struck home.

There was no doubt thereafter where the line of cleavage lay between the alleged "debasers of men" and the debasers of truth.

"Man must be respected—not degraded with pity—" says Satine, "but respected, respected." There is the Big Theme.

This doesn't seem to fit very well into the theory that the "materialists" and the realists were debasing anything except the spurious currency of pietistic cant and the convenient but ill-concealed economic slavery for which it was an appropriate front.

Actually, of course, as all but the self-appointed righteous could see, the drama, under the stinging impact of realism, had dropped its solo hero and made a common hero of the human race. It celebrated the courage and the wisdom and the noble impulse that stand revealed, without illusion, in a race which, knowing its own weaknesses, goes staunchly on to fulfil its own inner faith, a faith that needs, in the finest glimpses we have of it, no narcotics of make-believe in or out of the theatre.

The thought that all men may some day and somehow fulfil that faith in actual living, freed of superstition and fear and want, is a dream of heroic grandeur. You may identify it simply as man's faith in God, or his faith in himself as he evolves, but there is in it the instinctive belief that in all the values of life there is something beyond living— even if it is someone's else future.

All through the plays in this book, the great and the lesser, you will find this theme repeated. In the almost impalpable meshes of Tchekov's masterpiece *The Sea Gull* (I wish the Editors had used Stark Young's brilliant translation, but they decided otherwise) we see the haze of grief and futility of people without purpose in living, defeated by their own lack of responsibility, irresolute and anguished. It is an unforgettable picture of the selfish and conscienceless delusion which made *The Cherry Orchard* the symbol of a feudal society, lost in the dead dream of its past, and cracking up against reality. The individual must accept the responsibility as well as the privilege of freedom. Tchekov haunts us with the insistent challenge.

It was Hauptmann, however, who put the challenge into blunt drama in *The Weavers*. He created the mass hero in his angry picture of a group of Silesian peasants, oppressed by their masters and threatened by the machines, and he brought vividly into the theatre the most violent social conflict of the times. As Huneker said: "He paints the picture; his audience finds the indictment."

It is a picture so brutal and unsparing that it makes *Tobacco Road* seem almost cheerful by comparison. Much of it is bound to seem repetitious to modern readers, accustomed now to take for granted the field in which Hauptmann was a pathfinder, but the reality of his observation and the heat of his righteous wrath keep alive the strength of its compassion and the vigor of its protest. Our view of Hauptmann is bound to be colored by his senile lip-service to the Nazis, but our view of his masterpiece need not be clouded by that. If he is a weathervane, as Ashley Dukes called him, at least his greatest play pointed into the heart of the storm.

Liliom is one of the few fantasies in dramatic literature that has real iron in its soul. Molnar's roughneck carnival barker, who beats his wife cruelly because he is ashamed of the tenderness of his love and who steals for her because he hates to see her cry, is a wonderful symbol of the toughness of the human spirit, of the indestructible soul of man. When he is killed in a hold-up, he goes to hell and returns unregenerate to earth (stealing a star on the way) to perform the one good deed that can release him from the eternal bonfires, and he winds up slapping his little daughter.

"It is possible," says Julie to the startled child in the triumphant last line of the play, "it is possible for someone to beat you, and beat you, and beat you, and never hurt you at all."

Here, I take it, is the transcendent point of the play: that the human spirit endures beyond the judgment of heaven and the pain of hell, and that in the mute and hurting passion of these two lovers, nothing here or hereafter shall save them from one another.

The deadly and inhuman power of a lie, the readiness of people to deceive themselves with false values, is made so uproariously funny in Synge's *Playboy* that the caustic meaning of the play seems sometimes lost in laughter. But the vivid characters, the singing richness of the language, the humor and life of all the scenes are subordinate finally to the statement the play makes—that even the crime of murder may be invested with romantic illusion, if it seems far enough away; that an impostor, who brags of his evil deed, is scorned when it turns out that he didn't commit it, and that finally when he does commit murder, the people who admired him for his distant and imagined wrong are revolted by the reality of one that touches them nearly.

Between *The Playboy* and *Shadow and Substance* lies most of the history of Dublin's Abbey Theatre, with all its ups and downs. Paul Vincent Carroll is a newcomer to the ranks of the world's foremost dramatists, and his later work has by no means maintained the standards of his first, which is incontestably his best. Though *Shadow and Substance* has the witty line, the relish of character, the soothing speech, and what Mr. Nathan calls "the emotional candor" of Irish drama, it produced some cloudy interpretations even from its enthusiastic admirers—and none cloudier than the mystical explanations by its own author. Yet its obvious values are clear enough, and its human contrast of the emptiness and austerity of dogmatism as opposed to the goodness and naturalness of simple faith is as far as we need to look for the qualities which draw it into this anthology.

I objected strenuously to *The Jest* when the Messrs. Cerf and Cartmell proposed it for this table of contents, in spite of my personal affection for it as a colorful and romantic melodrama, made unforgettable (even in a version which emasculated the play instead of its protagonist) by the brilliant performances of John and Lionel Barrymore and Louis

Wolheim, and by the Renaissance magnificence of Robert Edmond Jones settings in Arthur Hopkins' superb production. And I must confess that I am a little sorry now, for while I lost the argument, as prefators ever lose them to their editors, they found the publication rights inextricably tied up in, among other things, Mr. Barrymore's confusing estate. The play, let it be said in its absence, has the sheen and incandescence of sheer theatre.

It would be difficult, searching the world around, to find much more dissimilar dramas than *The Jest* and *Six Characters in Search of an Author*. To find them in one country, written within two years of one another, is to measure not only the range of modern Italian plays, but the centripetal forces of the post-war theatre in Europe, as the world moved unconsciously out of one war toward new but then indistinct barricades.

Pirandello's masterpiece is not only an assault on the theatre and the falsity of art, but the ultimate negation of reality, the play, as John Gassner has described it, to end plays. Yet I suspect that Stark Young comes nearer a true identification when he sees it in terms of the *Commedia dell'Arte*. It is an honest tenant of the playhouse of the mind, a cerebral improvisation, wrought in intellectual impromptu, full of subtle meanings and mischievous implications, elusive, fascinating, disquieting and profound. How can we know truth, Pirandello asks from the depths of his pessimism, when we do not even know what reality is? And yet, unless I am grievously mistaken, he suggests that even imagined characters have rights and lives of their own beyond the control of their creator. However much he yielded late in a difficult and troubled life to the grim incentive of Benito ("the utensil"), Pirandello was no Fascist. He started out by hating D'Annunzio, who was Benelli's pattern-maker, and his disenchantment with life had every private justification in personal grief.

The matters of production should not obtrude themselves on these pages devoted to drama off-stage, but I feel it is necessary in the case of *The Dybbuk*, a strange, ecstatic love story, with special qualities which make it one of the outstanding plays of the Jewish theatre. Its tale of a young girl whose body was inhabited by the spirit of a youth who died when he found that her father was forcing her to marry another seemed more completely captured, with weird emphasis and suitable ghostliness, by the great Vachtangov's production for the Habimah Players, than in our local production at the Neighborhood Playhouse. I believe the conception is spooky, as well as lyrical, that while it has a racial background it holds a universal fascination, and that if this notion colors the reading, the curious and compelling values of a unique drama will be enhanced.

From the other end of Europe comes another drama of high spiritual intensity, also religious in concept, and certainly a perfect example of what has been identified with a certain contradiction in terms as "static drama." Almost nothing happens in any dramatic sense in *The Cradle Song*, yet its conventual atmosphere is so strong, its characters are so clearly drawn, its little pattern of movement is so quietly right for the material, that it creates a world of its own, strong, tender, innocent, and deeply touching.

Over the presence of three of the plays in this volume your prefator held strong but losing arguments with the Messrs. Editors, who warned that they would make final choices, though adding honorably that I was at liberty to dissent in my remarks. The three that I would like to throw out are *Amphitryon 38, Anatol* and *Grand Hotel*.

In spite of S. N. Behrman's brilliant and in some passages wittily penetrating adaptation of Giraudoux's original and presumably thirty-eighth treatment of the *Amphitryon* legend, it still seems to me to be merely an expanded smoking-car story, neatly classicized, which never quite lives up to the bright audacity of its prologue. It did give the Lunts a magnificent field day, and so justifies its inclusion herein as a "famous European play," but I cling to the suspicion that its fame rests not on its authorship, but upon its players.

There can be no such exception taken to *Grand Hotel*,

which was solidly popular. Its casual sketches of life in a
big European hotel, pieced together and caught up in a
general pattern, make, on its own record, effective theatre.
The characters meet and entangle one another's lives in the
enormous impersonality of the hotel, and there is a minor
irony in the transience of the whole thing as they all go
out at the end, and a new set of hotel guests comes in, for
what you might call the revolving-door drama in excelsis.
Elmer Rice caught the same tone, with far greater effect
and meaning in his human rondo, in the final moments of
Street Scene.

Anatol, though I know it is *lèse majesté* to say it, strikes
me as being violently overestimated. I know that it is ur-
bane, ultra-civilized in its somewhat clinical attitude
towards sex, and that it is accepted as a complete expression of what the world considers the spirit of old Vienna,
with its light intrigue, its air of amorous banter, and, to my
way of thinking as far as Dr. Schnitzler is concerned, its
tiresome preoccupation with *l'amour.* My eminent and
knowing senior, Mr. Nathan, assures me that my disaffec-
tion for the play may be attributed to the slovenly transla-
tions that have been made of it, and that its true quality can
be tasted only in the original.

Besides *Amphitryon 38,* there are two other French plays
in the collection, and the fact that they were written nearly
forty years apart emphasizes a curious fact about the
French theatre. Since France has always been supposed to
be headquarters of *logique,* and was actually the birthplace
of the *théatre libre,* one would reasonably expect to find
material there equal at least to the theatres of the rest of
Europe.

But actually the modern French drama presents many
fights and nothing much worth fighting over. Bourdet's
tragedy of abnormal sexuality, *La Prisonnière,* might well
represent the brilliance of a classical tradition wrought into
a modern idiom, but the editors thought it unsuitable for
an anthology of general appeal. Vildrac suggested a talent
that was never realized and while Jules Romain's *Knock* is a

hilarious satire, and ran for four years at the Comédie des Champs Elysées, with the incomparable Jouvet in the name part, it has never succeeded elsewhere and therefore is not, for our present bi-lingual purposes, famous.

Though Pagnol is probably the strongest of the modern French dramatists, his best work has never been popular outside France, and he long ago transferred his allegiance to the movies. But *Marius*, especially as played by Pierre Fresney, had genuine quality, and *Marchands de Gloire* (it was presented in New York by the Theatre Guild) a healthy and vigorous contempt for warmongers in general, and the self-delusion of French heroics in particular.

Topaze is a caustic examination of some of the traits which made France so vulnerable in the final clash of European wills, but in spite of my personal fondness for it, I cannot, by the wildest stretch of a willing imagination, call its brief Broadway career "fame."

So we have Rostand, with *Cyrano*, A.D. 1897, and a classic in anybody's calendar, and *Tovarich*. There are some plays that go so directly to the human heart that there is no use quarreling about the catalogue. *Cyrano* is one of those plays. I suppose it represents a brief flaring up of the romantic theatre, and its language, its period, its costumes, and its sentiments could be cited to confirm the category. It is lovely and swashbuckling and bathed in beautiful twilight, and it represents people living and loving and grieving and dying under the old compulsions of illusion. But Cyrano is a realist knowing both the strength and futility of illusion, trapped by the romantic convention.

Tovarich rippled with a wave of laughter around the world. At one time in Europe you could hear, as Mr. Sherwood, its adapter, amusingly points out, only two sounds— the great international armorers and the sound of people laughing at this *papier-mâché* comedy, pasted up out of old stencils, but somehow gay and touching and delightful. The sounds were directly antithetical. Besides being the one about the upper-class couple hiring out as servants, *Tovarich* is a pretty lesson in tolerance, so much so in fact that while Der Fuehrer was delighted with it, he had the scene of the transfer of the money from the Czar's regime to the Soviet Commissar changed so that when Prince Sergei handed the millions of rubles to Holy Russia, in the person of Gorotchenko, he said, in the Nazi version: "You may take these so-and-so million rubles: and you may take this (striking him in the face) from me."

I have saved *R.U.R.* for the last not only to emphasize the contribution of Czechoslovakia, but because it puts into dramatic form a reply, and the only possible reply, to the people who feared that the prophets of materialism had abolished the individual. It turned out that that sin was committed only in the name of Wagner, and that the two other apostles of modern thought in Europe fought only for the dignity and prestige of man, man with his delusions shed, his eyes open only for the truth, and the personal reality of his own destiny.

Capek's play is an interesting, often fascinating play, and while its ending may seem a little forced, there is the credo. The automatons, men of machinery, made by Rossum's Universal Robots, were about to conquer the human race and drive it from the face of the earth. But they didn't. Instead the Robots became human.

As a symbol of man's conquest of the machine, even the physical machine of his own existence, it is parable enough. All this may be all we have. There may be no "Heaven, too." Wherefore the individual is the cornerstone of the universe. It is his life, in living freedom, his world and what he, not a tyrant, wishes to make of it; it is his eternity, if God wills it for the glory of man. Centuries have brought this free faith into the human heart. It is here in these oncoming pages. We have seen nothing that can safely deny it.

Stepney Depot
November 1, 1942.

The Wild Duck

BY HENRIK IBSEN

CHARACTERS

WERLE, *a merchant, manufacturer, etc.*
GREGERS WERLE, *his son.*
OLD EKDAL.
HIALMAR EKDAL, *his son, a photographer.*
GINA EKDAL, *Hialmar's wife.*
HEDVIG, *their daughter, a girl of fourteen.*
MRS. SÖRBY, *Werle's housekeeper.*
RELLING, *a doctor.*
MOLVIK, *student of theology.*
GRÅBERG, *Werle's bookkeeper.*
PETTERSEN, *Werle's servant.*
JENSEN, *a hired waiter.*
A FLABBY GENTLEMAN.
A THIN-HAIRED GENTLEMAN.
A SHORT-SIGHTED GENTLEMAN.
SIX OTHER GENTLEMEN, *guests at Werle's dinner-party.*
SEVERAL HIRED WAITERS.

The first act passes in WERLE's *house, the remaining acts at* HIALMAR EKDAL's.

Pronunciation of Names: GREGERS WERLE = Grayghers Verlë; HIAL-MAR EKDAL = Yalmar Aykdal; GINA = Cheena; GRÅBERG = Groberg JENSEN = Yensen.

THE WILD DUCK

ACT ONE

...use. A richly and comfortably furnished study; bookcases ...d furniture; a writing-table, with papers and documents, ...f the room; lighted lamps with green shades, giving a sub-... the back, open folding doors with curtains drawn back. ... a large and handsome room, brilliantly lighted with lamps ...g candlesticks. In front, on the right (in the study), a small ...ds into WERLE's *office. On the left, in front, a fireplace with ...al fire, and farther back a double door leading into the dining*

...RLE's *servant,* PETTERSEN, *in livery, and* JENSEN, *the hired waiter, ...black, are putting the study in order. In the large room, two or three other hired waiters are moving about, arranging things and lighting more candles. From the dining room, the hum of conversation and laughter of many voices are heard; a glass is tapped with a knife; silence follows, and a toast is proposed; shouts of "Bravo!" and then again a buzz of conversation.*

PETTERSEN (*lights a lamp on the chimney-place and places a shade over it*). Hark to them, Jensen! now the old man's on his legs holding a long palaver about Mrs. Sörby.

JENSEN (*pushing forward an armchair*). Is it true, what folks say, that they're—very good friends, eh?

PETTERSEN. Lord knows.

JENSEN. I've heard tell as he's been a lively customer in his day.

PETTERSEN. May be.

JENSEN. And he's giving this spread in honour of his son, they say.

PETTERSEN. Yes. His son came home yesterday.

JENSEN. This is the first time I ever heard as Mr. Werle had a son.

PETTERSEN. Oh, yes, he has a son, right enough. But he's a fixture, as you might say, up at the Höidal works. He's never once come to town all the years I've been in service here.

A WAITER (*in the doorway of the other room*). Pettersen, here's an old fellow wanting——

PETTERSEN (*mutters*). The devil —who's this now?

(OLD EKDAL *appears from th... right, in the inner room. He ... dressed in a threadbare overco... with a high collar; he wears wo... len mittens, and carries in his h... a stick and a fur cap. Under ... arm, a brown paper parcel. I...*

5

*red-brown wig and small grey
moustache.*)

PETTERSEN (*goes towards him*).
Good Lord—what do you want
here?

EKDAL (*in the doorway*). Must get
into the office, Pettersen.

PETTERSEN. The office was closed
an hour ago, and——

EKDAL. So they told me at the front
door. But Gråberg's in there still.
Let me slip in this way, Pettersen;
there's a good fellow. (*Points towards the baize door*) It's not the
first time I've come this way.

PETTERSEN. Well, you may pass.
(*Opens the door*) But mind you
go out again the proper way, for
we've got company.

EKDAL. I know, I know—h'm!
Thanks, Pettersen, good old friend!
Thanks! (*Mutters softly*) Ass!
*He goes into the office; PETTER-
sen shuts the door after him.*)

EN. Is he one of the office
?

EN. No he's only an out-
that does odd jobs of
ut he's been a tip-topper
has old Ekdal.

can see he's been

he was an army

y so?

e about it.
the timber

trade or something of the sort. They
say he once play ed Mr. Werle a
very nasty trick. They were part-
ners in the Höida works at the
time. Oh, I know old well, I
do. Many a nip of
bottle of ale we two ha
Madam Eriksen's.

JENSEN. He don't look as
much to stand treat with.

PETTERSEN. Why, bless you,
sen, it's me that stands treat. I
ways think there's no harm in bei
a bit civil to folks that have see
better days.

JENSEN. Did he go bankrupt then?

PETTERSEN. Worse than that. He
went to prison.

JENSEN. To prison!

PETTERSEN. Or perhaps it was the
Penitentiary. (*Listens*) Sh! They're
leaving the table.
(*The dining-room door is thrown
open from within, by a couple of
waiters.* MRS. SÖRBY *comes out conversing with two gentlemen. Gradually the whole company follows,
amongst them* WERLE. *Last come*
HIALMAR EKDAL *and* GREGERS
WERLE.

MRS. SÖRBY (*in passing, to the servant*). Tell them to serve the coffee
in the music room, Pettersen.

PETTERSEN. Very well, Madam.
(*She goes with the two gentlemen
into the inner room, and thence out
to the right.* PETTERSEN *and* JENSEN
go out the same way.)

A FLABBY GENTLEMAN (*to a* THIN-
HAIRED GENTLEMAN). Whew! What

a dinner!—It was no joke to do it justice!

THE THIN-HAIRED GENTLEMAN. Oh, with a little good will one can get through a lot in three hours.

THE FLABBY GENTLEMAN. Yes, but afterwards, afterwards, my dear Chamberlain!

A THIRD GENTLEMAN. I hear the coffee and maraschino are to be served in the music room.

THE FLABBY GENTLEMAN. Bravo! Then perhaps Mrs. Sörby will play us something.

THE THIN-HAIRED GENTLEMAN (*in a low voice*). I hope Mrs. Sörby mayn't play us a tune we don't like, one of these days!

THE FLABBY GENTLEMAN. Oh no, not she! Bertha will never turn against her old friends.
(*They laugh and pass into the inner room.*)

WERLE (*in a low voice, dejectedly*). I don't think anybody noticed it, Gregers.

GREGERS (*looks at him*). Noticed what?

WERLE. Did you not notice it either?

GREGERS. What do you mean?

WERLE. We were thirteen at table.

GREGERS. Indeed? Were there thirteen of us?

WERLE (*glances towards* HIALMAR EKDAL). Our usual party is twelve.

(*To the others*) This way, gentlemen!
(WERLE *and the others, all except* HIALMAR *and* GREGERS, *go out by the back, to the right.*)

HIALMAR (*who has overheard the conversation*). You ought not to have invited me, Gregers.

GREGERS. What! Not ask my best and only friend to a party supposed to be in my honour——?

HIALMAR. But I don't think your father likes it. You see I am quite outside his circle.

GREGERS. So I hear. But I wanted to see you and have a talk with you, and I certainly shan't be staying long.—Ah, we two old schoolfellows have drifted far apart from each other. It must be sixteen or seventeen years since we met.

HIALMAR. Is it so long?

GREGERS. It is indeed. Well, how goes it with you? You look well. You have put on flesh, and grown almost stout.

HIALMAR. Well, "stout" is scarcely the word; but I daresay I look a little more of a man than I used to.

GREGERS. Yes, you do; your outer man is in first-rate condition.

HIALMAR (*in a tone of gloom*). Ah, but the inner man! That is a very different matter, I can tell you! Of course you know of the terrible catastrophe that has befallen me and mine since last we met.

GREGERS (*more softly*). How are things going with your father now?

HIALMAR. Don't let us talk of it, old fellow. Of course my poor unhappy father lives with me. He hasn't another soul in the world to care for him. But you can understand that this is a miserable subject for me.—Tell me, rather, how you have been getting on up at the works.

GREGERS. I have had a delightfully lonely time of it—plenty of leisure to think and think about things. Come over here; we may as well make ourselves comfortable. (*He seats himself in an arm-chair by the fire and draws* HIALMAR *down into another alongside of it.*)

HIALMAR (*sentimentally*). After all, Gregers, I thank you for inviting me to your father's table; for I take it as a sign that you have got over your feeling against me.

GREGERS (*surprised*). How could you imagine I had any feeling against you?

HIALMAR. You had at first, you know.

GREGERS. How at first?

HIALMAR. After the great misfortune. It was natural enough that you should. Your father was within an ace of being drawn into that—well, that terrible business.

GREGERS. Why should that give me any feeling against you? Who can have put that into your head?

HIALMAR. I know it did, Gregers; your father told me so himself.

GREGERS (*starts*). My father! Oh indeed. H'm.—Was that why you never let me hear from you?—not a single word.

HIALMAR. Yes.

GREGERS. Not even when you made up your mind to become a photographer?

HIALMAR. Your father said I had better not write to you at all, about anything.

GREGERS (*looking straight before him*). Well, well, perhaps he was right.—But tell me now, Hialmar: are you pretty well satisfied with your present position?

HIALMAR (*with a little sigh*). Oh yes, I am; I have really no cause to complain. At first, as you may guess, I felt it a little strange. It was such a totally new state of things for me. But of course my whole circumstances were totally changed. Father's utter, irretrievable ruin,—the shame and disgrace of it, Gregers——

GREGERS (*affected*). Yes, yes; I understand.

HIALMAR. I couldn't think of remaining at college; there wasn't a shilling to spare; on the contrary, there were debts—mainly to your father I believe——

GREGERS. H'm——

HIALMAR. In short, I thought it best to break, once for all, with my old surroundings and associations. It was your father that specially urged me to it; and since he interested himself so much in me——

GREGERS. My father did?

HIALMAR. Yes, you surely knew that, didn't you? Where do you suppose I found the money to learn photography, and to furnish a studio and make a start? All that costs a pretty penny, I can tell you.

GREGERS. And my father provided the money?

HIALMAR. Yes, my dear fellow, didn't you know? I understood him to say he had written to you about it.

GREGERS. Not a word about his part in the business. He must have forgotten it. Our correspondence has always been purely a business one. So it was my father that——!

HIALMAR. Yes, certainly. He didn't wish it to be generally known; but he it was. And of course it was he, too, that put me in a position to marry. Don't you—don't you know about that either?

GREGERS. No, I haven't heard a word of it. (Shakes him by the arm) But, my dear Hialmar, I can't tell you what pleasure all this gives me—pleasure, and self-reproach. I have perhaps done my father injustice after all—in some things. This proves that he has a heart. It shows a sort of compunction——

HIALMAR. Compunction——?

GREGERS. Yes, yes—whatever you like to call it. Oh, I can't tell you how glad I am to hear this of father.—So you are a married man, Hialmar! That is further than I shall ever get. Well, I hope you are happy in your married life?

HIALMAR. Yes, thoroughly happy.

She is as good and capable a wife as any man could wish for. And she is by no means without culture.

GREGERS (rather surprised). No, of course not.

HIALMAR. You see, life is itself an education. Her daily intercourse with me—— And then we know one or two rather remarkable men, who come a good deal about us. I assure you, you would hardly know Gina again.

GREGERS. Gina?

HIALMAR. Yes; had you forgotten that her name was Gina?

GREGERS. Whose name? I haven't the slightest idea——

HIALMAR. Don't you remember that she used to be in service here?

GREGERS (looks at him). Is it Gina Hansen——?

HIALMAR. Yes, of course it is Gina Hansen.

GREGERS. ——who kept house for us during the last year of my mother's illness?

HIALMAR. Yes, exactly. But, my dear friend, I'm quite sure your father told you that I was married.

GREGERS (who has risen). Oh, yes, he mentioned it; but not that—— (Walking about the room) Stay— perhaps he did—now that I think of it. My father always writes such short letters. (Half seats himself on the arm of the chair) Now, tell me Hialmar—this is interesting—how did you come to know Gina—your wife?

HIALMAR. The simplest thing in the world. You know Gina did not stay here long, everything was so much upset at that time, owing to your mother's illness and so forth, that Gina was not equal to it all; so she gave notice and left. That was the year before your mother died—or it may have been the same year.

GREGERS. It was the same year. I was up at the works then. But afterwards——?

HIALMAR. Well, Gina lived at home with her mother, Madam Hansen, an excellent hard-working woman, who kept a little eating-house. She had a room to let too; a very nice comfortable room.

GREGERS. And I suppose you were lucky enough to secure it?

HIALMAR. Yes; in fact, it was your father that recommended it to me. So it was there, you see, that I really came to know Gina.

GREGERS. And then you got engaged?

HIALMAR. Yes. It doesn't take young people long to fall in love—— h'm——

GREGERS (rises and moves about a little). Tell me: was it after your engagement—was it then that my father—I mean was it then that you began to take up photography?

HIALMAR. Yes, precisely. I wanted to make a start, and to set up house as soon as possible; and your father and I agreed that this photography business was the readiest way. Gina thought so too. Oh, and there was another thing in its favour, by-the-

bye: it happened, luckily, that Gina had learned to retouch.

GREGERS. That chimed in marvellously.

HIALMAR (pleased, rises). Yes, didn't it? Don't you think it was a marvellous piece of luck?

GREGERS. Oh, unquestionably. My father seems to have been almost a kind of providence for you.

HIALMAR (with emotion). He did not forsake his old friend's son in the hour of his need. For he has a heart, you see.

MRS. SÖRBY (enters, arm-in-arm with WERLE). Nonsense, my dear Mr. Werle; you mustn't stop there any longer staring at all the lights. It's very bad for you.

WERLE (lets go her arm and passes his hand over his eyes). I daresay you are right.
(PETTERSEN and JENSEN carry round refreshment trays.)

MRS. SÖRBY (to the guests in the other room). This way, if you please, gentlemen. Whoever wants a glass of punch must be so good as to come in here.

THE FLABBY GENTLEMAN (comes up to MRS. SÖRBY). Surely, it isn't possible that you have suspended our cherished right to smoke?

MRS. SÖRBY. Yes. No smoking here, in Mr. Werle's sanctum, Chamberlain.

THE THIN-HAIRED GENTLEMAN. When did you enact these stringent amendments on the cigar law, Mrs Sörby?

MRS. SÖRBY. After the last dinner, Chamberlain, when certain persons permitted themselves to overstep the mark.

THE THIN-HAIRED GENTLEMAN. And may one never overstep the mark a little bit, Madame Bertha? Not the least little bit?

MRS. SÖRBY. Not in any respect whatsoever, Mr. Balle.
(*Most of the guests have assembled in the study; servants hand round glasses of punch.*)

WERLE (*to* HIALMAR, *who is standing beside a table*). What are you studying so intently, Ekdal?

HIALMAR. Only an album, Mr. Werle.

THE THIN-HAIRED GENTLEMAN (*who is wandering about*). Ah, photographs! They are quite in your line of course.

THE FLABBY GENTLEMAN (*in an armchair*). Haven't you brought any of your own with you?

HIALMAR. No, I haven't.

THE FLABBY GENTLEMAN. You ought to have; it's very good for the digestion to sit and look at pictures.

THE THIN-HAIRED GENTLEMAN. And it contributes to the entertainment, you know.

THE SHORT-SIGHTED GENTLEMAN. And all contributions are thankfully received.

MRS. SÖRBY. The Chamberlains think that when one is invited out to dinner, one ought to exert oneself a little in return, Mr. Ekdal.

THE FLABBY GENTLEMAN. Where one dines so well, that duty becomes a pleasure.

THE THIN-HAIRED GENTLEMAN. And when it's a case of the struggle for existence, you know——

MRS. SÖRBY. I quite agree with you! (*They continue the conversation, with laughter and joking.*)

GREGERS (*softly*). You must join in, Hialmar.

HIALMAR (*writhing*). What am I to talk about?

THE FLABBY GENTLEMAN. Don't you think, Mr. Werle, that Tokay may be considered one of the more wholesome sorts of wine?

WERLE (*by the fire*). I can answer for the Tokay you had today, at any rate; it's one of the very finest seasons. Of course you would notice that.

THE FLABBY GENTLEMAN. Yes, it had a remarkably delicate flavour.

HIALMAR (*shyly*). Is there any difference between the seasons?

THE FLABBY GENTLEMAN (*laughs*). Come! That's good!

WERLE (*smiles*). It really doesn't pay to set fine wine before you.

THE THIN-HAIRED GENTLEMAN. Tokay is like photographs, Mr. Ekdal: they both need sunshine. Am I not right?

HIALMAR. Yes, light is important no doubt

MRS. SÖRBY. And it's exactly the same with Chamberlains—they, too, depend very much on sunshine,* as the saying is.

THE THIN-HAIRED GENTLEMAN. Oh fie! That's a very threadbare sarcasm!

THE SHORT-SIGHTED GENTLEMAN. Mrs. Sörby is coming out——

THE FLABBY GENTLEMAN. ——and at our expense, too. (*Holds up his finger reprovingly*) Oh, Madame Bertha, Madame Bertha!

MRS. SÖRBY. Yes, and there's not the least doubt that the seasons differ greatly. The old vintages are the finest.

THE SHORT-SIGHTED GENTLEMAN. Do you reckon me among the old vintages?

MRS. SÖRBY. Oh, far from it.

THE THIN-HAIRED GENTLEMAN. There now! But me, dear Mrs. Sörby——?

THE FLABBY GENTLEMAN. Yes, and me? What vintage should you say that we belong to?

MRS. SÖRBY. Why, to the sweet vintages, gentlemen.
(*She sips a glass of punch. The gentlemen laugh and flirt with her.*)

WERLE. Mrs. Sörby can always find a loop-hole—when she wants to. Fill your glasses, gentlemen! Pettersen, will you see to it——!

* The "sunshine" of Court favour.

Gregers, suppose we have a glass together. (*Gregers does not move*) Won't you join us, Ekdal? I found no opportunity of drinking with you at table.
(GRÅBERG, *the Bookkeeper, looks in at the baize door.*)

GRÅBERG. Excuse me, sir, but I can't get out.

WERLE. Have you been locked in again?

GRÅBERG. Yes, and Flakstad has carried off the keys.

WERLE. Well, you can pass out this way.

GRÅBERG. But there's some one else——

WERLE. All right; come through, both of you. Don't be afraid.
(GRÅBERG *and* OLD EKDAL *come out of the office.*)

WERLE (*involuntarily*). Ugh!

(*The laughter and talk among the guests cease.* HIALMAR *starts at the sight of his father, puts down his glass, and turns towards the fireplace.*)

EKDAL (*does not look up, but makes little bows to both sides as he passes, murmuring*). Beg pardon, come the wrong way. Door locked —door locked. Beg pardon.
(*He and* GRÅBERG *go out by the back, to the right.*)

WERLE (*between his teeth*). That idiot Gråberg.

GREGERS (*open-mouthed and staring, to* HIALMAR). Why surely that wasn't——!

THE FLABBY GENTLEMAN. What's the matter? Who was it?

GREGERS. Oh, nobody, only the bookkeeper and some one with him.

THE SHORT-SIGHTED GENTLEMAN (to HIALMAR). Did you know that man?

HIALMAR. I don't know—I didn't notice——

THE FLABBY GENTLEMAN. What the deuce has come over every one? (He joins another group who are talking softly.)

MRS. SÖRBY (whispers to the servant). Give him something to take with him—something good, mind.

PETTERSEN (nods). I'll see to it. (Goes out.)

GREGERS (softly and with emotion, to HIALMAR). So that was really he!

HIALMAR. Yes.

GREGERS. And you could stand there and deny that you knew him!

HIALMAR (whispers vehemently). But how could I——!

GREGERS. ——acknowledge your father?

HIALMAR (with pain). Oh, if you were in my place——
(The conversation amongst the guests, which has been carried on in a low tone, now swells into constrained joviality.)

THE THIN-HAIRED GENTLEMAN (approaching HIALMAR and GREGERS in a friendly manner). Aha! Reviving old college memories, eh? Don't you smoke, Mr. Ekdal? May I give you a light? Oh, by-the-bye, we mustn't——

HIALMAR. No, thank you, I won't ——

THE FLABBY GENTLEMAN. Haven't you a nice little poem you could recite to us, Mr. Ekdal? You used to recite so charmingly.

HIALMAR. I am sorry I can't remember anything.

THE FLABBY GENTLEMAN. Oh, that's a pity. Well, what shall we do, Balle?
(Both gentlemen move away and pass into the other room.)

HIALMAR (gloomily). Gregers—I am going! When a man has felt the crushing hand of Fate, you see —— Say good-bye to your father for me.

GREGERS. Yes, yes. Are you going straight home?

HIALMAR. Yes. Why?

GREGERS. Oh, because I may perhaps look in on you later.

HIALMAR. No, you mustn't do that. You must not come to my home. Mine is a melancholy abode, Gregers; especially after a splendid banquet like this. We can always arrange to meet somewhere in the town.

MRS. SÖRBY (who has quietly approached). Are you going, Ekdal?

HIALMAR. Yes.

MRS. SÖRBY. Remember me to Gina.

HIALMAR. Thanks.

MRS. SÖRBY. And say I am coming up to see her one of these days.

HIALMAR. Yes, thank you. (*To* GREGERS) Stay here; I will slip out unobserved.
(*He saunters away, then into the other room, and so out to the right.*)

MRS. SÖRBY (*softly to the servant, who has come back*). Well, did you give the old man something?

PETTERSEN. Yes; I sent him off with a bottle of cognac.

MRS. SÖRBY. Oh, you might have thought of something better than that.

PETTERSEN. Oh no, Mrs. Sörby; cognac is what he likes best in the world.

THE FLABBY GENTLEMAN (*in the doorway with a sheet of music in his hand*). Shall we play a duet, Mrs. Sörby?

MRS. SÖRBY. Yes, suppose we do.

THE GUESTS. Bravo, bravo!
(*She goes with all the guests through the back room, out to the right.* GREGERS *remains standing by the fire.* WERLE *is looking for something on the writing-table, and appears to wish that* GREGERS *would go; as* GREGERS *does not move,* WERLE *goes towards the door.*)

GREGERS. Father, won't you stay a moment?

WERLE (*stops*). What is it?

GREGERS. I must have a word with you.

WERLE. Can it not wait till we are alone?

GREGERS. No, it cannot; for perhaps we shall never be alone together.

WERLE (*drawing nearer*). What do you mean by that?
(*During what follows, the pianoforte is faintly heard from the distant music room.*)

GREGERS. How has the family been allowed to go so miserably to the wall?

WERLE. You mean the Ekdals, I suppose.

GREGERS. Yes, I mean the Ekdals. Lieutenant Ekdal was once so closely associated with you.

WERLE. Much too closely; I have felt that to my cost for many a year. It is thanks to him that I—yes *I*—have had a kind of slur cast upon my reputation.

GREGERS (*softly*). Are you sure that he alone was to blame?

WERLE. Who else do you suppose——?

GREGERS. You and he acted together in that affair of the forests ——

WERLE. But was it not Ekdal that drew the map of the tracts we had bought—that fraudulent map! It was he who felled all that timber illegally on Government ground. In fact, the whole management was in his hands. I was quite in the dark as to what Lieutenant Ekdal was doing.

GREGERS. Lieutenant Ekdal himself seems to have been very much in the dark as to what he was doing.

WERLE. That may be. But the fact remains that he was found guilty and I acquitted.

GREGERS. Yes, I know that nothing was proved against you.

WERLE. Acquittal is acquittal. Why do you rake up these old miseries that turned my hair grey before its time? Is that the sort of thing you have been brooding over up there, all these years? I can assure you, Gregers, here in the town the whole story has been forgotten long ago —so far as I am concerned.

GREGERS. But that unhappy Ekdal family——

WERLE. What would you have had me do for the people? When Ekdal came out of prison he was a broken-down being, past all help. There are people in the world who dive to the bottom the moment they get a couple of slugs in their body, and never come to the surface again. You may take my word for it, Gregers, I have done all I could without positively laying myself open to all sorts of suspicion and gossip——

GREGERS. Suspicion——? Oh, I see.

WERLE. I have given Ekdal copying to do for the office, and I pay him far, far more for it than his work is worth——

GREGERS (without looking at him). H'm; that I don't doubt.

WERLE. You laugh? Do you think I am not telling you the truth? Well, I certainly can't refer you to my books, for I never enter payments of that sort.

GREGERS (smiles coldly). No, there are certain payments it is best to keep no account of.

WERLE (taken aback). What do you mean by that?

WERLE (mustering up courage). Have you entered what it cost you to have Hialmar Ekdal taught photography?

WERLE. I? How "entered" it?

GREGERS. I have learned that it was you who paid for his training. And I have learned, too, that it was you who enabled him to set up house so comfortably.

WERLE. Well, and yet you talk as though I had done nothing for the Ekdals! I can assure you these people have cost me enough in all conscience.

GREGERS. Have you entered any of these expenses in your books?

WERLE. Why do you ask?

GREGERS. Oh, I have my reasons. Now tell me: when you interested yourself so warmly in your old friend's son—it was just before his marriage, was it not?

WERLE. Why, deuce take it—after all these years, how can I——?

GREGERS. You wrote me a letter about that time—a business letter, of course; and in a postscript you mentioned—quite briefly—that Hialmar Ekdal had married a Miss Hansen.

WERLE. Yes, that was quite right. That was her name.

GREGERS. But you did not mention that this Miss Hansen was Gina Hansen—our former housekeeper.

WERLE (*with a forced laugh of derision*). No; to tell the truth, it didn't occur to me that you were so particularly interested in our former housekeeper.

GREGERS. No more I was. But (*Lowers his voice*) there were others in this house who were particularly interested in her.

WERLE. What do you mean by that? (*Flaring up*) You are not alluding to me, I hope?

GREGERS (*softly but firmly*). Yes, I am alluding to you.

WERLE. And you dare——! You presume to——! How can that ungrateful hound—that photographer fellow—how dare he go making such insinuations!

GREGERS. Hialmar has never breathed a word about this. I don't believe he has the faintest suspicion of such a thing.

WERLE. Then where have you got it from? Who can have put such notions in your head?

GREGERS. My poor unhappy mother told me; and that the very last time I saw her.

WERLE. Your mother! I might have known as much! You and she—you always held together. It was she who turned you against me, from the first.

GREGERS. No, it was all that she had to suffer and submit to, until she broke down and came to such a pitiful end.

WERLE. Oh, she had nothing to suffer or submit to; not more than most people, at all events. But there's no getting on with morbid, overstrained creatures—that I have learned to my cost.—And you could go on nursing such a suspicion—burrowing into all sorts of old rumours and slanders against your own father! I must say, Gregers, I really think that at your age you might find something more useful to do.

GREGERS. Yes, it is high time.

WERLE. Then perhaps your mind would be easier than it seems to be now. What can be your object in remaining up at the works, year out and year in, drudging away like a common clerk, and not drawing a farthing more than the ordinary monthly wage? It is downright folly.

GREGERS. Ah, if I were only sure of that.

WERLE. I understand you well enough. You want to be independent; you won't be beholden to me for anything. Well, now there happens to be an opportunity for you to become independent, your own master in everything.

GREGERS. Indeed? In what way ——?

WERLE. When I wrote you insisting on your coming to town at once— h'm——

GREGERS. Yes, what is it you really want of me? I have been waiting all day to know.

WERLE. I want to propose that you should enter the firm, as partner.

GREGERS. I! Join your firm? As partner?

WERLE. Yes. It would not involve our being constantly together. You could take over the business here in town, and I should move up to the works.

GREGERS. You would?

WERLE. The fact is, I am not so fit for work as I once was. I am obliged to spare my eyes, Gregers; they have begun to trouble me.

GREGERS. They have always been weak.

WERLE. Not as they are now. And, besides, circumstances might possibly make it desirable for me to live up there—for a time, at any rate.

GREGERS. That is certainly quite a new idea to me.

WERLE. Listen, Gregers: there are many things that stand between us; but we are father and son after all. We ought surely to be able to come to some sort of understanding with each other.

GREGERS. Outwardly, you mean, of course?

WERLE. Well, even that would be something. Think it over, Gregers. Don't you think it ought to be possible? Eh?

GREGERS (looking at him coldly). There is something behind all this.

WERLE. How so?

GREGERS. You want to make use of me in some way.

WERLE. In such a close relationship as ours, the one can always be useful to the other.

GREGERS. Yes, so people say.

WERLE. I want very much to have you at home with me for a time. I am a lonely man, Gregers; I have always felt lonely, all my life through; but most of all now that I am getting up in years. I feel the need of some one about me——

GREGERS. You have Mrs. Sörby.

WERLE. Yes, I have her; and she has become, I may say, almost indispensable to me. She is lively and even-tempered; she brightens up the house; and that is a very great thing for me.

GREGERS. Well then, you have everything just as you wish it.

WERLE. Yes, but I am afraid it can't last. A woman so situated may easily find herself in a false position, in the eyes of the world. For that matter it does a man no good, either.

GREGERS. Oh, when a man gives such dinners as you give, he can risk a great deal.

WERLE. Yes, but how about the woman, Gregers? I fear she won't accept the situation much longer; and even if she did—even if, out of attachment to me, she were to take her chance of gossip and scandal and all that——? Do you think, Gregers—you with your strong sense of justice——

GREGERS (*interrupts him*). Tell me in one word: are you thinking of marrying her?

WERLE. Suppose I were thinking of it? What then?

GREGERS. That's what I say: what then?

WERLE. Should you be inflexibly opposed to it?

GREGERS. Not at all. Not by any means.

WERLE. I was not sure whether your devotion to your mother's memory——

GREGERS. I am not overstrained.

WERLE. Well, whatever you may or may not be, at all events you have lifted a great weight from my mind. I am extremely pleased that I can reckon on your concurrence in this matter.

GREGERS (*looking intently at him*). Now I see the use you want to put me to.

WERLE. Use to put you to? What an expression!

GREGERS. Oh, don't let us be nice in our choice of words—not when we are alone together, at any rate. (*With a short laugh*) Well, well. So this is what made it absolutely essential that I should come to town in person. For the sake of Mrs. Sörby, we are to get up a pretence at family life in the house—a tableau of filial affection! That will be something new indeed.

WERLE. How dare you speak in that tone!

GREGERS. Was there ever any family life here? Never since I can remember. But now, forsooth, your plans demand something of the sort. No doubt it will have an excellent effect when it is reported that the son has hastened home, on the wings of filial piety, to the grey-haired father's wedding feast. What will then remain of all the rumours as to the wrongs the poor dead mother had to submit to? Not a vestige. Her son annihilates them at one stroke.

WERLE. Gregers—I believe there is no one in the world you detest as you do me.

GREGERS (*softly*). I have seen you at too close quarters.

WERLE. You have seen me with your mother's eyes. (*Lowers his voice a little*) But you should remember that her eyes were—clouded now and then.

GREGERS (*quivering*). I see what you are hinting at. But who was to blame for mother's unfortunate weakness? Why you, and all those ——! The last of them was this woman that you palmed off upon Hialmar Ekdal, when you were—— Ugh!

WERLE (*shrugs his shoulders*). Word for word as if it were your mother speaking!

GREGERS (*without heeding*). And there he is now, with his great, confiding, childlike mind, compassed about with all this treachery—living under the same roof with such a creature, and never dreaming that what he calls his home is built upon a lie! (*Comes a step nearer*) When I look back upon your past, I seem to see a battle-field with shattered lives on every hand.

WERLE. I begin to think the chasm that divides us is too wide.

GREGERS (*bowing, with self-command*). So I have observed; and therefore I take my hat and go.

WERLE. You are going! Out of the house?

GREGERS. Yes. For at last I see my mission in life.

WERLE. What mission?

GREGERS. You would only laugh if I told you.

WERLE. A lonely man doesn't laugh so easily, Gregers.

GREGERS (*pointing towards the background*). Look, father,—the Chamberlains are playing blindman's-buff with Mrs. Sörby.— Good night and good-bye.
(*He goes out by the back to the right. Sounds of laughter and merriment from the company, who are now visible in the outer room.*)

WERLE (*muttering contemptuously after* GREGERS). Ha——! Poor wretch—and he says he is not overstrained!

ACT TWO

HIALMAR EKDAL'S *studio, a good-sized room, evidently in the top storey of the building. On the right, a sloping roof of large panes of glass, half-covered by a blue curtain. In the right-hand corner, at the back, the entrance door; farther forward, on the same side, a door leading to the sitting room. Two doors on the opposite side, and between them an iron stove. At the back, a wide double sliding door. The studio is plainly but comfortably fitted up and furnished. Between the doors on the right, standing out a little from the wall, a sofa with a table and some chairs; on the table a lighted lamp with a shade; beside the stove an old armchair. Photographic instruments and apparatus of different kinds lying about the room. Against the back wall, to the left of the double door, stands a bookcase containing a few books, boxes, and bottles of chemicals, instruments, tools, and other objects. Photographs and small articles, such as camel's-hair pencils, paper, and so forth, lie on the table.*

GINA EKDAL *sits on a chair by the table, sewing.* HEDVIG *is sitting on the sofa, with her hands shading her eyes and her thumbs in her ears, reading a book.*

GINA (*glances once or twice at* HEDVIG, *as if with secret anxiety; then says*): Hedvig!

HEDVIG (*does not hear*).

GINA (*repeats more loudly*). Hedvig!

HEDVIG (*takes away her hands and looks up*). Yes, mother?

GINA. Hedvig dear, you mustn't sit reading any longer now.

HEDVIG. Oh mother, mayn't I read a little more? Just a little bit?

GINA. No, no, you must put away your book now. Father doesn't like it; he never reads hisself in the evening.

HEDVIG (*shuts the book*). No, father doesn't care much about reading.

GINA (*puts aside her sewing and takes up a lead pencil and a little account-book from the table*). Can you remember how much we paid for the butter today?

HEDVIG. It was one crown sixty-five.

GINA. That's right. (*Puts it down*) It's terrible what a lot of butter we get through in this house. Then there was the smoked sausage, and the cheese—let me see—(*Writes*) —and the ham—(*Adds up*) Yes, that makes just——

HEDVIG. And then the beer.

GINA. Yes, to be sure. (*Writes*) How it do mount up! But we can't manage with no less.

HEDVIG. And then you and I didn't need anything hot for dinner, as father was out.

GINA. No; that was so much to the good. And then I took eight crowns fifty for the photographs.

HEDVIG. Really! So much as that?

GINA. Exactly eight crowns fifty. (*Silence.* GINA *takes up her sewing again,* HEDVIG *takes paper and pencil and begins to draw, shading her eyes with her left hand.*)

HEDVIG. Isn't it jolly to think that father is at Mr. Werle's big dinner-party?

GINA. You know he's not really Mr. Werle's guest. It was the son invited him. (*After a pause*) We have nothing to do with that Mr. Werle.

HEDVIG. I'm longing for father to come home. He promised to ask Mrs. Sörby for something nice for me.

GINA. Yes, there's plenty of good things going in that house, I can tell you.

HEDVIG (*goes on drawing*). And I believe I'm a little hungry too. (OLD EKDAL, *with the paper parcel under his arm and another parcel in his coat pocket, comes in by the entrance door.*)

GINA. How late you are today, grandfather!

EKDAL. They had locked the office door. Had to wait in Gråberg's room. And then they let me through —h'm.

HEDVIG. Did you get some more copying to do, grandfather?

EKDAL. This whole packet. Just look.

GINA. That's capital.

HEDVIG. And you have another parcel in your pocket.

EKDAL. Eh? Oh never mind, that's nothing. (*Puts his stick away in a corner*) This work will keep me going a long time, Gina. (*Opens one of the sliding doors in the back walls a little*) Hush! (*Peeps into the room for a moment, then pushes the door carefully to again*) Hee-hee! They're fast asleep, all the lot of them. And she's gone into the basket herself. Hee-hee!

HEDVIG. Are you sure she isn't cold in that basket, grandfather?

EKDAL. Not a bit of it! Cold? With all that straw? (*Goes towards the farther door on the left*) There are matches in here, I suppose.

GINA. The matches is on the drawers.
(EKDAL *goes into his room.*)

HEDVIG. It's nice that grandfather has got all that copying.

GINA. Yes, poor old father; it means a bit of pocket-money for him.

HEDVIG. And he won't be able to sit the whole forenoon down at that horrid Madam Eriksen's.

GINA. No more he won't.
(*Short silence.*)

HEDVIG. Do you suppose they are still at the dinner table?

GINA. Goodness knows; as like as not.

HEDVIG. Think of all the delicious things father is having to eat! I'm certain he'll be in splendid spirits when he comes. Don't you think so, mother?

GINA. Yes; and if only we could tell him that we'd got the room let——

HEDVIG. But we don't need that this evening.

GINA. Oh, we'd be none the worst of it, I can tell you. It's no use to us as it is.

HEDVIG. I mean we don't need it this evening, for father will be in a good humour at any rate. It is best to keep the letting of the room for another time.

GINA (*looks across at her*). You like having some good news to tell father when he comes home in the evening?

HEDVIG. Yes; for then things are pleasanter somehow.

GINA (*thinking to herself*). Yes, yes, there's something in that.
(OLD EKDAL *comes in again and is going out by the foremost door to the left.*)

GINA (*half turning in her chair*). Do you want something out of the kitchen, grandfather?

EKDAL. Yes, yes, I do. Don't you trouble. (*Goes out.*)

GINA. He's not poking away at the fire, is he? (*Waits a moment*) Hedvig, go and see what he's about. (EKDAL *comes in again with a small jug of steaming hot water.*)

HEDVIG. Have you been getting some hot water, grandfather?

EKDAL. Yes, hot water. Want it for something. Want to write, and the ink has got as thick as porridge—h'm.

GINA. But you'd best have your supper, first, grandfather. It's laid in there.

EKDAL. Can't be bothered with supper, Gina. Very busy, I tell you. No one's to come to my room. No one—h'm.
(*He goes into his room;* GINA *and* HEDVIG *look at each other.*)

GINA (*softly*). Can you imagine where he's got money from?

HEDVIG. From Gråberg, perhaps.

GINA. Not a bit of it. Gråberg always sends the money to me.

HEDVIG. Then he must have got a bottle on credit somewhere.

GINA. Poor grandfather, who'd give him credit?
(HIALMAR EKDAL, *in an overcoat and grey felt hat, comes in from the right.*)

GINA (*throws down her sewing and rises*). Why, Ekdal, is that you already?

HEDVIG (*at the same time jumping up*). Fancy your coming so soon, father!

HIALMAR (*taking off his hat*). Yes, most of the people were coming away.

HEDVIG. So early?

HIALMAR. Yes, it was a dinner party, you know.
(*Is taking off his overcoat.*)

GINA. Let me help you.

HEDVIG. Me too.
(*They draw off his coat;* GINA *hangs it up on the back wall.*)

HEDVIG. Were there many people there, father?

HIALMAR. Oh, no, not many. We were about twelve or fourteen at table.

GINA. And you had some talk with them all?

HIALMAR. Oh yes, a little; but Gregers took me up most of the time.

GINA. Is Gregers as ugly as ever?

HIALMAR. Well, he's not very much to look at. Hasn't the old man come home?

HEDVIG. Yes, grandfather is in his room, writing.

HIALMAR. Did he say anything?

GINA. No, what should he say?

HIALMAR. Didn't he say anything about——? I heard something about his having been with Gråberg. I'll go in and see him for a moment.

GINA. No, no, better not.

HIALMAR. Why not? Did he say he didn't want me to go in?

GINA. I don't think he wants to see nobody this evening——

HEDVIG (making signs). H'm—h'm!

GINA (not noticing). ——he has been in to fetch hot water——

HIALMAR. Aha! Then he's——

GINA. Yes, I suppose so.

HIALMAR. Oh God! my poor old white-haired father!—Well, well; there let him sit and get all the enjoyment he can.
(OLD EKDAL, in an indoor coat and with a lighted pipe, comes from his room.)

EKDAL. Got home? Thought it was you I heard talking.

HIALMAR. Yes, I have just come.

EKDAL. You didn't see me, did you?

HIALMAR. No, but they told me you had passed through—so I thought I would follow you.

EKDAL. H'm, good of you, Hialmar.—Who were they, all those fellows?

HIALMAR. Oh, all sorts of people. There was Chamberlain Flor, and Chamberlain Balle, and Chamberlain Kaspersen, and Chamberlain —this, that, and the other—I don't know who all——

EKDAL (nodding). Hear that, Gina! Chamberlains every one of them!

GINA. Yes, I hear as they're terrible genteel in that house nowadays.

HEDVIG. Did the Chamberlains sing, father? Or did they read aloud?

HIALMAR. No, they only talked nonsense. They wanted me to recite something for them; but I knew better than that.

EKDAL. You weren't to be persuaded, eh?

GINA. Oh, you might have done it.

HIALMAR. No; one mustn't be at everybody's beck and call. (Walks about the room) That's not my way, at any rate.

EKDAL. No, no; Hialmar's not to be had for the asking, he isn't.

HIALMAR. I don't see why I should bother myself to entertain people on the rare occasions when I go into society. Let the others exert themselves. These fellows go from one great dinner table to the next and gorge and guzzle day out and day in. It's for them to bestir themselves and do something in return for all the good feeding they get.

GINA. But you didn't say that?

HIALMAR (humming). Ho-ho-ho ——faith, I gave them a bit of my mind.

EKDAL. Not the Chamberlains?

HIALMAR. Oh, why not? (*Lightly*) After that, we had a little discussion about Tokay.

EKDAL. Tokay! There's a fine wine for you!

HIALMAR (*comes to a standstill*). It may be a fine wine. But of course you know the vintages differ; it all depends on how much sunshine the grapes have had.

GINA. Why, you know everything, Ekdal.

EKDAL. And did they dispute that?

HIALMAR. They tried to; but they were requested to observe that it was just the same with Chamberlains—that with them, too, different batches were of different qualities.

GINA. What things you do think of!

EKDAL. Hee-hee! So they got that in their pipes too?

HIALMAR. Right in their teeth.

EKDAL. Do you hear that, Gina? He said it right in the very teeth of all the Chamberlains.

GINA. Fancy——! Right in their teeth!

HIALMAR. Yes, but I don't want it talked about. One doesn't speak of such things. The whole affair passed off quite amicably of course. They were nice, genial fellows; I didn't want to wound them—not I!

EKDAL. Right in their teeth, though ——!

HEDVIG (*caressingly*). How nice it is to see you in a dress-coat! It suits you so well, father.

HIALMAR. Yes, don't you think so? And this one really sits to perfection. It fits almost as if it had been made for me—a little tight in the armholes perhaps—help me, Hedvig (*Takes off the coat*). I think I'll put on my jacket. Where is my jacket, Gina?

GINA. Here it is. (*Brings the jacket and helps him.*)

HIALMAR. That's it! Don't forget to send the coat back to Molvik first thing tomorrow morning.

GINA (*laying it away*). I'll be sure and see to it.

HIALMAR (*stretching himself*). After all, there's a more homely feeling about this. A free-and-easy indoor costume suits my whole personality better. Don't you think so, Hedvig?

HEDVIG. Yes, father.

HIALMAR. When I loosen my necktie into a pair of flowing ends—like this—eh?

HEDVIG. Yes, that goes so well with your moustache and the sweep of your curls.

HIALMAR. I should not call them curls exactly; I should rather say locks.

HEDVIG. Yes, they are too big for curls.

HIALMAR. Locks describes them better.

HEDVIG (*after a pause, twitching his jacket*). Father!

HIALMAR. Well, what is it?

HEDVIG. Oh, you know very well.

HIALMAR. No, really I don't——

HEDVIG (*half laughing, half whispering*). Oh, yes, father; now don't tease me any longer!

HIALMAR. Why, what do you mean?

HEDVIG (*shaking him*). Oh what nonsense; come, where are they, father? All the good things you promised me, you know?

HIALMAR. Oh—if I haven't forgotten all about them!

HEDVIG. Now you're only teasing me, father! Oh, it's too bad of you! Where have you put them?

HIALMAR. No, I positively forgot to get anything. But wait a little! I have something else for you, Hedvig.
(*Goes and searches in the pockets of the coat.*)

HEDVIG (*skipping and clapping her hands*). Oh mother, mother!

GINA. There, you see; if you only give him time——

HIALMAR (*with a paper*). Look, here it is.

HEDVIG. That? Why, that's only a paper.

HIALMAR. That is the bill of fare, my dear; the whole bill of fare.

Here you see: "Menu"—that means bill of fare.

HEDVIG. Haven't you anything else?

HIALMAR. I forgot the other things, I tell you. But you may take my word for it, these dainties are very unsatisfying. Sit down at the table and read the bill of fare, and then I'll describe to you how the dishes taste. Here you are, Hedvig.

HEDVIG (*gulping down her tears*). Thank you.
(*She seats herself, but does not read;* GINA *makes signs to her;* HIALMAR *notices it.*)

HIALMAR (*pacing up and down the room*). It's monstrous what absurd things the father of a family is expected to think of; and if he forgets the smallest trifle, he is treated to sour faces at once. Well, well, one gets used to that too. (*Stops near the stove, by the old man's chair*) Have you peeped in there this evening, father?

EKDAL. Yes, to be sure I have. She's gone into the basket.

HIALMAR. Ah, she has gone into the basket. Then she's beginning to get used to it.

EKDAL. Yes; just as I prophesied. But you know there are still a few little things——

HIALMAR. A few improvements, yes.

EKDAL. They've got to be made, you know.

HIALMAR. Yes, let us have a talk about the improvements, father. Come, let us sit on the sofa.

EKDAL. All right. H'm—think I'll just fill my pipe first. Must clean it out, too. H'm.
(*He goes into his room.*)

GINA (*smiling to* HIALMAR). His pipe!

HIALMAR. Oh yes, yes, Gina; let him alone—the poor shipwrecked old man.—Yes, these improvements —we had better get them out of hand tomorrow.

GINA. You'll hardly have time tomorrow, Ekdal.

HEDVIG (*interposing*). Oh, yes, he will, mother!

GINA. ——for remember them prints that has to be retouched; they've sent for them time after time.

HIALMAR. There now! those prints again! I shall get them finished all right! Have any new orders come in?

GINA. No, worse luck; tomorrow I have nothing but those two sittings, you know.

HIALMAR. Nothing else? Oh no, if people won't set about things with a will——

GINA. But what more can I do? Don't I advertise in the papers as much as we can afford?

HIALMAR. Yes, the papers, the papers; you see how much good they do. And I suppose no one has been to look at the room either?

GINA. No, not yet.

HIALMAR. That was only to be expected. If people won't keep their eyes open——. Nothing can be done without a real effort, Gina!

HEDVIG (*going towards him*). Shall I fetch you the flute, father?

HIALMAR. No; no flute for me; I want no pleasures in this world. (*Pacing about*) Yes, indeed I will work tomorrow; you shall see if I don't. You may be sure I shall work as long as my strength holds out.

GINA. But my dear good Ekdal, I didn't mean it in that way.

HEDVIG. Father, mayn't I bring in a bottle of beer?

HIALMAR. No, certainly not. I require nothing, nothing—— (*Comes to a standstill*) Beer? Was it beer you were talking about?

HEDVIG (*cheerfully*). Yes, father; beautiful fresh beer.

HIALMAR. Well—since you insist upon it, you may bring in a bottle.

GINA. Yes, do; and we'll be nice and cosy.
(HEDVIG *runs towards the kitchen door.*)

HIALMAR (*by the stove, stops her, looks at her, puts his arm around her neck and presses her to him*). Hedvig, Hedvig!

HEDVIG (*with tears of joy*). My dear, kind father!

HIALMAR. No, don't call me that. Here have I been feasting at the rich man's table—battening at the groaning board——! And I couldn't even——!

GINA (*sitting at the table*). Oh, nonsense, nonsense, Ekdal.

HIALMAR. It's not nonsense! And yet you mustn't be too hard upon me. You know that I love you for all that.

HEDVIG (*throwing her arms round him*). And we love you, oh, so dearly, father!

HIALMAR. And if I am unreasonable once in a while—why then—you must remember that I am a man beset by a host of cares. There, there! (*Dries his eyes*) No beer at such a moment as this. Give me the flute.
(HEDVIG *runs to the bookcase and fetches it.*)

HIALMAR. Thanks! That's right. With my flute in my hand and you two at my side—ah——!
(HEDVIG *seats herself at the table near* GINA; HIALMAR *paces backwards and forwards, pipes up vigorously, and plays a Bohemian peasant dance, but in a slow plaintive tempo, and with sentimental expression.*)

HIALMAR (*breaking off the melody, holds out his left hand to* GINA, *and says with emotion*). Our roof may be poor and humble, Gina; but it is home. And with all my heart I say: here dwells my happiness.
(*He begins to play again; almost immediately after, a knocking is heard at the entrance door.*)

GINA (*rising*). Hush, Ekdal—I think there's some one at the door.

HIALMAR (*laying the flute on the bookcase*). There! Again!
(GINA *goes and opens the door.*)

GREGERS WERLE (*in the passage*). Excuse me——

GINA (*starting back slightly*). Oh!

GREGERS. ——does not Mr. Ekdal, the photographer, live here?

GINA. Yes, he does.

HIALMAR (*going towards the door*). Gregers! You here after all? Well, come in then.

GREGERS (*coming in*). I told you I would come and look you up.

HIALMAR. But this evening——? Have you left the party?

GREGERS. I have left both the party and my father's house.—Good evening, Mrs. Ekdal. I don't know whether you recognise me?

GINA. Oh yes; it's not difficult to know young Mr. Werle again.

GREGERS. No, I am like my mother; and no doubt you remember her.

HIALMAR. Left your father's house, did you say?

GREGERS. Yes, I have gone to a hotel.

HIALMAR. Indeed. Well, since you're here, take off your coat and sit down.

GREGERS. Thanks.
(*He takes off his overcoat. He is now dressed in a plain grey suit of a countrified cut.*)

HIALMAR. Here, on the sofa. Make yourself comfortable.
(GREGERS *seats himself on the sofa;* HIALMAR *takes a chair at the table.*)

GREGERS (*looking around him*). So these are your quarters, Hialmar—this is your home.

HIALMAR. This is the studio, as you see——

GINA. But it's the largest of our rooms, so we generally sit here.

HIALMAR. We used to live in a better place; but this flat has one great advantage: there are such capital outer rooms——

GINA. And we have a room on the other side of the passage that we can let.

GREGERS (*to* HIALMAR). Ah—so you have lodgers too?

HIALMAR. No, not yet. They're not so easy to find, you see; you have to keep your eyes open. (*To* HEDVIG) What about that beer, eh? (HEDVIG *nods and goes out into the kitchen.*)

GREGERS. So that is your daughter?

HIALMAR. Yes, that is Hedvig.

GREGERS. And she is your only child?

HIALMAR. Yes, the only one. She is the joy of our lives, and—(*lowering his voice*)—at the same time our deepest sorrow, Gregers.

GREGERS. What do you mean?

HIALMAR. She is in serious danger of losing her eyesight.

GREGERS. Becoming blind?

HIALMAR. Yes. Only the first symptoms have appeared as yet, and she may not feel it much for some time. But the doctor has warned us. It is coming, inexorably.

GREGERS. What a terrible misfortune! How do you account for it?

HIALMAR (*sighs*). Hereditary, no doubt.

GREGERS (*starting*). Hereditary?

GINA. Ekdal's mother had weak eyes.

HIALMAR. Yes, so my father says; I can't remember her.

GREGERS. Poor child! And how does she take it?

HIALMAR. Oh, you can imagine we haven't the heart to tell her of it. She dreams of no danger. Gay and careless and chirping like a little bird, she flutters onward into a life of endless night. (*Overcome*) Oh, it is cruelly hard on me, Gregers. (HEDVIG *brings a tray with beer and glasses, which she sets upon the table.*)

HIALMAR (*stroking her hair*). Thanks, thanks, Hedvig. (HEDVIG *puts her arm round his neck and whispers in his ear.*)

HIALMAR. No, no bread and butter just now. (*Looks up*) But perhaps you would like some, Gregers.

GREGERS (*with a gesture of refusal*). No, no thank you.

HIALMAR (*still melancholy*). Well, you can bring in a little all the same. If you have a crust, that is all I want. And plenty of butter on it, mind.

(HEDVIG *nods gaily and goes out into the kitchen again.*)

GREGERS (*who has been following her with his eyes*). She seems quite strong and healthy otherwise.

GINA. Yes. In other ways there's nothing amiss with her, thank goodness.

GREGERS. She promises to be very like you, Mrs. Ekdal. How old is she now?

GINA. Hedvig is close on fourteen; her birthday is the day after tomorrow.

GREGERS. She is pretty tall for her age, then.

GINA. Yes, she's shot up wonderful this last year.

GREGERS. It makes one realise one's own age to see these young people growing up.—How long is it now since you were married?

GINA. We've been married—let me see—just on fifteen years.

GREGERS. Is it so long as that?

GINA (*becomes attentive; looks at him*). Yes, it is indeed.

HIALMAR. Yes, so it is. Fifteen years all but a few months. (*Changing his tone*) They must have been long years for you, up at the works, Gregers.

GREGERS. They seemed long while I was living them; now they are over, I hardly know how the time has gone.

(OLD EKDAL *comes from his room*

without his pipe, but with his old-fashioned uniform cap on his head; his gait is somewhat unsteady.*)

EKDAL. Come now, Hialmar, let's sit down and have a good talk about this—h'm—what was it again?

HIALMAR (*going towards him*). Father, we have a visitor here—Gregers Werle.—I don't know if you remember him.

EKDAL (*looking at* GREGERS, *who has risen*). Werle? Is that the son? What does he want with me?

HIALMAR. Nothing; it's me he has come to see.

EKDAL. Oh! Then there's nothing wrong?

HIALMAR. No, no, of course not.

EKDAL (*with a large gesture*). Not that I'm afraid, you know; but——

GREGERS (*goes over to him*). I bring you a greeting from your old hunting-grounds, Lieutenant Ekdal.

EKDAL. Hunting-grounds?

GREGERS. Yes, up in Höidal, about the works, you know.

EKDAL. Oh, up there. Yes, I knew all those places well in the old days.

GREGERS. You were a great sportsman then.

EKDAL. So I was, I don't deny it. You're looking at my uniform cap. I don't ask anybody's leave to wear it in the house. So long as I don't go out in the streets with it——

(HEDVIG *brings a plate of bread and butter, which she puts upon the table.*)

HIALMAR. Sit down, father, and have a glass of beer. Help yourself, Gregers.

(EKDAL *mutters and stumbles over to the sofa.* GREGERS *seats himself on the chair nearest to him,* HIALMAR *on the other side of* GREGERS. GINA *sits a little way from the table, sewing;* HEDVIG *stands beside her father.*)

GREGERS. Can you remember, Lieutenant Ekdal, how Hialmar and I used to come up and visit you in the summer and at Christmas?

EKDAL. Did you? No, no, no; I don't remember it. But sure enough I've been a tidy bit of a sportsman in my day. I've shot bears too. I've shot nine of 'em, no less.

GREGERS (*looking sympathetically at him*). And now you never get any shooting?

EKDAL. Can't just say that, sir. Get a shot now and then perhaps. Of course not in the old way. For the woods you see—the woods, the woods——! (*Drinks*) Are the woods fine up there now?

GREGERS. Not so fine as in your time. They have been thinned a good deal.

EKDAL. Thinned? (*More softly, and as if afraid*) It's dangerous work, that. Bad things come of it. The woods revenge themselves.

HIALMAR (*filling up his glass*). Come—a little more, father.

GREGERS. How can a man like you —such a man for the open air— live in the midst of a stuffy town, boxed within four walls?

EKDAL (*laughs quietly and glances at* HIALMAR). Oh, it's not so bad here. Not at all so bad.

GREGERS. But don't you miss all the things that used to be a part of your very being—the cool sweeping breezes, the free life in the woods and on the uplands, among beasts and birds——?

EKDAL (*smiling*). Hialmar, shall we let him see it?

HIALMAR (*hastily and a little embarrassed*). Oh, no, no, father; not this evening.

GREGERS. What does he want to show me?

HIALMAR. Oh, it's only something —you can see it another time.

GREGERS (*continues, to the old man*). You see I have been thinking, Lieutenant Ekdal, that you should come up with me to the works; I am sure to be going back soon. No doubt you could get some copying there too. And here, you have nothing on earth to interest you—nothing to liven you up.

EKDAL (*stares in astonishment at him*). Have *I* nothing on earth to——!

GREGERS. Of course you have Hialmar; but then he has his own family. And a man like you, who has always had such a passion for what is free and wild——

EKDAL (*thumps the table*). Hialmar, he shall see it!

HIALMAR. Oh, do you think it's worth while, father? It's all dark.

EKDAL. Nonsense; it's moonlight. (*Rises*) He shall see it, I tell you. Let me pass! Come and help me, Hialmar.

HEDVIG. Oh, yes, do, father!

HIALMAR (*rising*). Very well then.

GREGERS (*to* GINA). What is it?

GINA. Oh, nothing so very wonderful, after all.
(EKDAL *and* HIALMAR *have gone to the back wall and are each pushing back a side of the sliding door;* HEDVIG *helps the old man;* GREGERS *remains standing by the sofa;* GINA *sits still and sews. Through the open doorway a large, deep irregular garret is seen with odd nooks and corners; a couple of stove-pipes running through it, from rooms below. There are skylights through which clear moonbeams shine in on some parts of the great room; others lie in deep shadow.*)

EKDAL (*to* GREGERS). You may come close up if you like.

GREGERS (*going over to them*). Why, what is it?

EKDAL. Look for yourself. H'm.

HIALMAR (*somewhat embarrassed*). This belongs to father, you understand.

GREGERS (*at the door, looks into the garret*). Why, you keep poultry, Lieutenant Ekdal.

EKDAL. Should think we did keep poultry. They've gone to roost now. But you should just see our fowls by daylight, sir!

HEDVIG. And there's a——

EKDAL. Sh—sh! don't say anything about it yet.

GREGERS. And you have pigeons too, I see.

EKDAL. Oh yes, haven't we just got pigeons! They have their nest-boxes up there under the roof-tree; for pigeons like to roost high, you see.

HIALMAR. They aren't all common pigeons.

EKDAL. Common! Should think not indeed! We have tumblers, and a pair of pouters, too. But come here! Can you see that hutch down there by the wall?

GREGERS. Yes; what do you use it for?

EKDAL. That's where the rabbits sleep, sir.

GREGERS. Dear me; so you have rabbits too?

EKDAL. Yes, you may take my word for it, we have rabbits! He wants to know if we have rabbits, Hialmar! H'm! But now comes the thing, let me tell you! Here we have it! Move away, Hedvig. Stand here; that's right,—and now look down there.—Don't you see a basket with straw in it?

GREGERS. Yes. And I can see a fowl lying in the basket.

EKDAL. H'm--"a fowl"——

GREGERS. Isn't it a duck?

EKDAL (*hurt*). Why of course it's a duck.

HIALMAR. But what kind of duck, do you think?

HEDVIG. It's not just a common duck——

EKDAL. Sh!

GREGERS. And it's not a Muscovy duck either.

EKDAL. No, Mr.—Werle; it's not a Muscovy duck; for it's a wild duck!

GREGERS. Is it really? A wild duck?

EKDAL. Yes, that's what it is. That "fowl" as you call it—is the wild duck. It's our wild duck, sir.

HEDVIG. My wild duck. It belongs to me.

GREGERS. And can it live up here in the garret? Does it thrive?

EKDAL. Of course it has a trough of water to splash about in, you know.

HIALMAR. Fresh water every other day.

GINA (*turning towards* HIALMAR). But my dear Ekdal, it's getting icy cold here.

EKDAL. H'm, we had better shut up then. It's as well not to disturb their night's rest, too. Close up, Hedvig.
(HIALMAR *and* HEDVIG *push the garret doors together.*)

EKDAL. Another time you shall see her properly. (*Seats himself in the armchair by the stove*) Oh, they're curious things, these wild ducks, I can tell you.

GREGERS. How did you manage to catch it, Lieutenant Ekdal?

EKDAL. *I* didn't catch it. There's a certain man in this town whom we have to thank for it.

GREGERS (*starts slightly*). That man was not my father, was he?

EKDAL. You've hit it. Your father and no one else. H'm.

HIALMAR. Strange that you should guess that, Gregers.

GREGERS. You were telling me that you owed so many things to my father; and so I thought perhaps——

GINA. But we didn't get the duck from Mr. Werle himself——

EKDAL. It's Hakon Werle we have to thank for her, all the same, Gina. (*To* GREGERS) He was shooting from a boat, you see, and he brought her down. But your father's sight is not very good now. H'm; she was only wounded.

GREGERS. Ah! She got a couple of slugs in her body, I suppose.

HIALMAR. Yes, two or three.

HEDVIG. She was hit under the wing, so that she couldn't fly.

GREGERS. And I suppose she dived to the bottom, eh?

EKDAL (*sleepily, in a thick voice*). Of course. Always do that, wild ducks do. They shoot to the bottom as deep as they can get, sir—and bite themselves fast in the tangle and seaweed—and all the devil's own mess that grows down there. And they never come up again.

GREGERS. But your wild duck came up again, Lieutenant Ekdal.

EKDAL. He had such an amazingly clever dog, your father had. And that dog—he dived in after the duck and fetched her up again.

GREGERS (*who has turned to HIALMAR*). And then she was sent to you here?

HIALMAR. Not at once; at first your father took her home. But she wouldn't thrive there; so Pettersen was told to put an end to her——

EKDAL (*half asleep*). H'm—yes—Pettersen—that ass——

HIALMAR (*speaking more softly*). That was how we got her, you see; for father knows Pettersen a little; and when he heard about the wild duck he got him to hand her over to us.

GREGERS. And now she thrives as well as possible in the garret there?

HIALMAR. Yes, wonderfully well. She has got fat. You see, she has lived in there so long now that she has forgotten her natural wild life; and it all depends on that.

GREGERS. You are right there, Hialmar. Be sure you never let her get a glimpse of the sky and the sea——. But I mustn't stay any longer; I think your father is asleep.

HIALMAR. Oh, as for that——

GREGERS. But, by-the-bye—you said you had a room to let—a spare room?

HIALMAR. Yes; what then? Do you know of anybody——?

GREGERS. Can *I* have that room?

HIALMAR. You?

GINA. Oh no, Mr. Werle, you——

GREGERS. May I have the room? If so, I'll take possession first thing tomorrow morning.

HIALMAR. Yes, with the greatest pleasure——

GINA. But, Mr. Werle, I'm sure it's not at all the sort of room for you.

HIALMAR. Why, Gina! how can you say that?

GINA. Why, because the room's neither large enough nor light enough, and——

GREGERS. That really doesn't matter, Mrs. Ekdal.

HIALMAR. I call it quite a nice room, and not at all badly furnished either.

GINA. But remember the pair of them underneath.

GREGERS. What pair?

GINA. Well, there's one as has been a tutor——

HIALMAR. That's Molvik—Mr. Molvik, B.A.

GINA. And then there's a doctor, by the name of Relling.

GREGERS. Relling? I know him a little; he practised for a time up in Höidal.

GINA. They're a regular rackety pair, they are. As often as not, they're out on the loose in the evenings; and then they come home at all hours, and they're not always just——

GREGERS. One soon gets used to that sort of thing. I daresay I shall be like the wild duck——

GINA. H'm; I think you ought to sleep upon it first, anyway.

GREGERS. You seem very unwilling to have me in the house, Mrs. Ekdal.

GINA. Oh, no! What makes you think that?

HIALMAR. Well, you really behave strangely about it, Gina. (To GREGERS) Then I suppose you intend to remain in the town for the present?

GREGERS (putting on his overcoat). Yes, now I intend to remain here.

HIALMAR. And yet not at your father's? What do you propose to do, then?

GREGERS. Ah, if I only knew that, Hialmar, I shouldn't be so badly off! But when one has the misfortune to be called Gregers——! "Gregers"—-and then "Werle" after it; did you ever hear anything so hideous?

HIALMAR. Oh, I don't think so at all.

GREGERS. Ugh! Bah! I feel I should like to spit upon the fellow that answers to such a name. But when a man is once for all doomed to be Gregers—Werle in this world, as I am——

HIALMAR (laughs). Ha, ha! If you weren't Gregers Werle, what would you like to be?

GREGERS. If I should choose, I should like best to be a clever dog

GINA. A dog!

HEDVIG (involuntarily). Oh, no!

GREGERS. Yes, an amazingly clever dog; one that goes to the bottom after wild ducks when they dive and bite themselves fast in tangle and sea-weed, down among the ooze.

HIALMAR. Upon my word now, Gregers—I don't in the least know what you're driving at.

GREGERS. Oh, well, you might not be much the wiser if you did. It's understood, then, that I move in early tomorrow morning. (To GINA) I won't give you any trouble; I do everything for myself. (To HIALMAR) We can talk about the rest tomorrow. — Good night, Mrs. Ekdal (Nods to HEDVIG) Good night.

GINA. Good night, Mr. Werle.

HEDVIG. Good night.

HIALMAR (who has lighted a candle). Wait a moment; I must show you a light; the stairs are sure to be dark.

(GREGERS *and* HIALMAR *go out by the passage door.*)

GINA (*looking straight before her, with her sewing in her lap*). Wasn't that queer-like talk about wanting to be a dog?

HEDVIG. Do you know, mother—I believe he meant something quite different by that.

GINA. Why, what should he mean?

HEDVIG. Oh, I don't know; but it seemed to me he meant something different from what he said—all the time.

GINA. Do you think so? Yes, it was sort of queer.

HIALMAR (*comes back*). The lamp was still burning. (*Puts out the candle and sets it down*). Ah, now one can get a mouthful of food at last. (*Begins to eat the bread and butter*) Well, you see, Gina—if only you keep your eyes open——

GINA. How, keep your eyes open ——?

HIALMAR. Why, haven't we at last had the luck to get the room let? And just think—to a person like Gregers—a good old friend.

GINA. Well, I don't know what to say about it.

HEDVIG. Oh, mother, you'll see; it'll be such fun!

HIALMAR. You're very strange. You were so bent upon getting the room

let before; and now you don't like it.

GINA. Yes, I do, Ekdal; if it had only been to some one else—— But what do you suppose Mr. Werle will say?

HIALMAR. Old Werle? It doesn't concern him.

GINA. But surely you can see that there's something amiss between them again, or the young man wouldn't be leaving home. You know very well those two can't get on with each other.

HIALMAR. Very likely not, but——

GINA. And now Mr. Werle may fancy it's you that has egged him on——

HIALMAR. Let him fancy so, then! Mr. Werle has done a great deal for me; far be it from me to deny it. But that doesn't make me everlastingly dependent upon him.

GINA. But, my dear Ekdal, maybe grandfather'll suffer for it. He may lose the little bit of work he gets from Gråberg.

HIALMAR. I could almost say: so much the better! Is it not humiliating for a man like me to see his grey-haired father treated as a pariah? But now I believe the fulness of time is at hand. (*Takes a fresh piece of bread and butter*) As sure as I have a mission in life, I mean to fulfil it now!

HEDVIG. Oh, yes, father, do!

GINA. Hush! Don't wake him!

HIALMAR (*more softly*). I will fulfil it, I say. The day shall come when—— And that is why I say it's a good thing we have let this room; for that makes me more independent. The man who has a mission in life must be independent. (*By the armchair, with emotion*) Poor old white-haired father! Rely on your Hialmar. He has broad shoulders—strong shoulders, at any rate. You shall yet wake up some fine day and—— (*To* GINA) Do you not believe it?

GINA (*rising*). Yes, of course I do; but in the meantime suppose we see about getting him to bed.

HIALMAR. Yes, come.
(*They take hold of the old man carefully.*)

ACT THREE

HIALMAR EKDAL'S *studio. It is morning: the daylight shines through the large window in the slanting roof; the curtain is drawn back.*

HIALMAR *is sitting at the table, busy retouching a photograph; several others lie before him. Presently* GINA, *wearing her hat and cloak, enters by the passage door; she has a covered basket on her arm.*

HIALMAR. Back already, Gina?

GINA. Oh, yes, one can't let the grass grow under one's feet.
(*Sets her basket on a chair, and takes off her things.*)

HIALMAR. Did you look in at Gregers' room?

GINA. Yes, that I did. It's a rare sight, I can tell you; he's made a pretty mess to start off with.

HIALMAR. How so?

GINA. He was determined to do everything for himself, he said; so he sets to work to light the stove, and what must he do but screw down the damper till the whole room is full of smoke. Ugh! There was a smell fit to——

HIALMAR. Well, really!

GINA. But that's not the worst of it; for then he thinks he'll put out the fire, and goes and empties his water-jug into the stove, and so makes the whole floor one filthy puddle.

HIALMAR. How annoying!

GINA. I've got the porter's wife to clear up after him, pig that he is! But the room won't be fit to live in till the afternoon.

HIALMAR. What's he doing with himself in the meantime?

GINA. He said he was going out for a little while.

HIALMAR. I looked in upon him, too, for a moment—after you had gone.

GINA. So I heard. You've asked him to lunch.

HIALMAR. Just to a little bit of early lunch, you know. It's his first day —we can hardly do less. You've got something in the house, I suppose?

GINA. I shall have to find something or other.

HIALMAR. And don't cut it too fine, for I fancy Relling and Molvik are coming up, too. I just happened to meet Relling on the stairs, you see; so I had to——

GINA. Oh, are we to have those two as well?

HIALMAR. Good Lord—a couple more or less can't make any difference.

EKDAL (*opens his door and looks in*). I say, Hialmar——(*Sees* GINA.) Oh!

GINA. Do you want anything, grandfather?

EKDAL. Oh, no, it doesn't matter. H'm!
(*Retires again.*)

GINA (*takes up the basket*). Be sure you see that he doesn't go out.

HIALMAR. All right, all right. And, Gina, a little herring salad wouldn't be a bad idea; Relling and Molvik were out on the loose again last night.

GINA. If only they don't come before I'm ready for them——

HIALMAR. No, of course they won't; take your own time.

GINA. Very well; and meanwhile you can be working a bit.

HIALMAR. Well, I am working! I am working as hard as I can!

GINA. Then you'll have that job off your hands, you see.
(*She goes out to the kitchen with her basket.* HIALMAR *sits for a time pencilling away at the photograph, in an indolent and listless manner.*)

EKDAL (*peeps in, looks round the studio, and says softly*): Are you busy?

HIALMAR. Yes, I'm toiling at these wretched pictures——

EKDAL. Well, well, never mind,— since you're so busy—h'm!
(*He goes out again; the door stands open.*)

HIALMAR (*continues for some time in silence; then he lays down his brush and goes over to the door*). Are you busy, father?

EKDAL (*in a grumbling tone, within*). If you're busy, I'm busy, too. H'm!

HIALMAR. Oh, very well, then.
(*Goes to his work again.*)

EKDAL (*presently, coming to the door again*). H'm; I say, Hialmar, I'm not so very busy, you know.

HIALMAR. I thought you were writing.

EKDAL. Oh, devil take it! can't Gråberg wait a day or two? After all, it's not a matter of life and death.

HIALMAR. No; and you're not his slave either.

EKDAL. And about that other business in there——

HIALMAR. Just what I was thinking of. Do you want to go in? Shall I open the door for you?

EKDAL. Well, it wouldn't be a bad notion.

HIALMAR (*rises*). Then we'd have that off our hands.

EKDAL. Yes, exactly. It's got to be ready first thing tomorrow. It is tomorrow, isn't it? H'm?

HIALMAR. Yes, of course it's tomorrow.
(HIALMAR *and* EKDAL *push aside each his half of the sliding door. The morning sun is shining in through the skylights; some doves are flying about; others sit cooing, upon the perches; the hens are heard clucking now and then, further back in the garret.*)

HIALMAR. There; now you can get to work, father.

EKDAL (*goes in*). Aren't you coming, too?

HIALMAR. Well, really, do you know—— I almost think—— (*Sees* GINA *at the kitchen door.*) I? No; I haven't time; I must work. —But now for our new contrivance——
(*He pulls a cord, a curtain slips down inside, the lower part consisting of a piece of old sailcloth, the upper part of a stretched fishing net. The floor of the garret is thus no longer visible.*)

HIALMAR (*goes to the table*). So! Now, perhaps I can sit in peace for a little while.

GINA. Is he rampaging in there again?

HIALMAR. Would you rather have had him slip down to Madam Eriksen's? (*Seats himself*) Do you want anything? You know you said——

GINA. I only wanted to ask if you think we can lay the table for lunch here?

HIALMAR. Yes; we have no early appointment, I suppose?

GINA. No, I expect no one today except those two sweethearts that are to be taken together.

HIALMAR. Why the deuce couldn't they be taken together another day!

GINA. Don't you know, I told them to come in the afternoon, when you are having your nap.

HIALMAR. Oh, that's capital. Very well, let us have lunch here then.

GINA. All right; but there's no hurry about laying the cloth; you can have the table for a good while yet.

HIALMAR. Do you think I am not sticking at my work? I'm at it as hard as I can!

GINA. Then you'll be free later on, you know.
(*Goes out into the kitchen again. Short pause.*)

EKDAL (*in the garret doorway, behind the net*). Hialmar!

HIALMAR. Well?

EKDAL. Afraid we shall have to move the water-trough, after all.

HIALMAR. What else have I been saying all along?

EKDAL. H'm—h'm—h'm.
(*Goes away from the door again.* HIALMAR *goes on working a little; glances towards the garret and half rises.* HEDVIG *comes in from the kitchen.*)

HIALMAR (*sits down again hurriedly*). What do you want?

HEDVIG. I only wanted to come in beside you, father.

HIALMAR (*after a pause*). What makes you go prying around like that? Perhaps you are told off to watch me?

HEDVIG. No, no.

HIALMAR. What is your mother doing out there?

HEDVIG. Oh, mother's in the middle of making the herring salad. (*Goes to the table*) Isn't there any little thing I could help you with, father?

HIALMAR. Oh, no. It is right that I should bear the whole burden—so long as my strength holds out. Set your mind at rest, Hedvig; if only your father keeps his health——

HEDVIG. Oh, no, father! You mustn't talk in that horrid way.
(*She wanders about a little, stops by the doorway and looks into the garret.*)

HIALMAR. Tell me, what is he doing?

HEDVIG. I think he's making a new path to the water-trough.

HIALMAR. He can never manage that by himself! And here am I doomed to sit——!

HEDVIG (*goes to him*). Let me take the brush, father; I can do it, quite well.

HIALMAR. Oh, nonsense; you will only hurt your eyes.

HEDVIG. Not a bit. Give me the brush.

HIALMAR (*rising*). Well, it won't take more than a minute or two.

HEDVIG. Pooh, what harm can it do then? (*Takes the brush*) There! (*Seats herself*) I can begin upon this one.

HIALMAR. But mind you don't hurt your eyes! Do you hear? *I* won't be answerable; you do it on your own responsibility—understand that.

HEDVIG (*retouching*). Yes, yes, I understand.

HIALMAR. You are quite clever at it, Hedvig. Only a minute or two, you know.
(*He slips through by the edge of the curtain into the garret.* HEDVIG *sits at her work.* HIALMAR *and* EKDAL *are heard disputing inside.*)

HIALMAR (*appears behind the net*). I say, Hedvig—give me those pincers that are lying on the shelf. And the chisel. (*Turns away inside*) Now you shall see, father. Just let me show you first what I mean!
(*HEDVIG has fetched the required tools from the shelf, and hands them to him through the net.*)

HIALMAR. Ah, thanks. I didn't come a moment too soon.

(*Goes back from the curtain again; they are heard carpentering and talking inside.* HEDVIG *stands looking in at them. A moment later there is a knock at the passage door; she does not notice it.*)

GREGERS WERLE (*bareheaded, in indoor dress, enters and stops near the door*). H'm——!

HEDVIG (*turns and goes towards him*). Good morning. Please come in.

GREGERS. Thank you. (*Looking towards the garret*) You seem to have workpeople in the house.

HEDVIG. No, it is only father and grandfather. I'll tell them you are here.

GREGERS. No, no, don't do that; I would rather wait a little.
(*Seats himself on the sofa.*)

HEDVIG. It looks so untidy here——
(*Begins to clear away the photographs.*)

GREGERS. Oh, don't take them away. Are those prints that have to be finished off?

HEDVIG. Yes, they are a few I was helping father with.

GREGERS. Please don't let me disturb you.

HEDVIG. Oh, no.
(*She gathers the things to her and sits down to work;* GREGERS *looks at her, meanwhile, in silence.*)

GREGERS. Did the wild duck sleep well last night?

HEDVIG. Yes, I think so, thanks.

GREGERS (*turning towards the garret*). It looks quite different by day from what it did last night in the moonlight.

HEDVIG. Yes, it changes ever so much. It looks different in the morning and in the afternoon; and it's different on rainy days from what it is in fine weather.

GREGERS. Have you noticed that?

HEDVIG. Yes, how could I help it?

GREGERS. Are you, too, fond of being in there with the wild duck?

HEDVIG. Yes, when I can manage it——

GREGERS. But I suppose you haven't much spare time; you go to school, no doubt.

HEDVIG. No, not now; father is afraid of my hurting my eyes.

GREGERS. Oh; then he reads with you himself?

HEDVIG. Father has promised to read with me; but he has never had time yet.

GREGERS. Then is there nobody else to give you a little help?

HEDVIG. Yes, there is Mr. Molvik; but he is not always exactly— quite——

GREGERS. Sober?

HEDVIG. Yes, I suppose that's it!

GREGERS. Why, then you must have any amount of time on your hands. And in there I suppose it is a sort of world by itself?

HEDVIG. Oh, yes, quite. And there are such lots of wonderful things.

GREGERS. Indeed?

HEDVIG. Yes, there are big cupboards full of books; and a great many of the books have pictures in them.

GREGERS. Aha!

HEDVIG. And there's an old bureau with drawers and flaps, and a big clock with figures that go out and in. But the clock isn't going now.

GREGERS. So time has come to a standstill in there--in the wild duck's domain.

HEDVIG. Yes. And then there's an old paint-box and things of that sort; and all the books.

GREGERS. And you read the books, I suppose?

HEDVIG. Oh, yes, when I get the chance. Most of them are English though, and I don't understand English. But then I look at the pictures.—There is one great big book called "Harrison's History of London."* It must be a hundred years old; and there are such heaps of pictures in it. At the beginning there is Death with an hourglass and a woman. I think that is horrid. But then there are all the other pictures of churches, and castles, and streets, and great ships sailing on the sea.

GREGERS. But tell me, where did all those wonderful things come from?

* A New and Universal History of the Cities of London and Westminster, by Walter Harrison. London, 1775, folio.

HEDVIG. Oh, an old sea captain once lived here, and he brought them home with him. They used to call him "The Flying Dutchman." That was curious, because he wasn't a Dutchman at all.

GREGERS. Was he not?

HEDVIG. No. But at last he was drowned at sea; and so he left all those things behind him.

GREGERS. Tell me now—when you are sitting in there looking at the pictures, don't you wish you could travel and see the real world for yourself?

HEDVIG. Oh, no! I mean always to stay at home and help father and mother.

GREGERS. To retouch photographs?

HEDVIG. No, not only that. I should love above everything to learn to engrave pictures like those in the English books.

GREGERS. H'm. What does your father say to that?

HEDVIG. I don't think father likes it; father is strange about such things. Only think, he talks of my learning basket-making and straw-plaiting! But I don't think that would be much good.

GREGERS. Oh, no, I don't think so either.

HEDVIG. But father was right in saying that if I had learned basket-making I could have made the new basket for the wild duck.

GREGERS. So you could; and it was you that ought to have done it, wasn't it?

HEDVIG. Yes, for it's my wild duck.

GREGERS. Of course it is.

HEDVIG. Yes, it belongs to me. But I lend it to father and grandfather as often as they please.

GREGERS. Indeed? What do they do with it?

HEDVIG. Oh, they look after it, and build places for it, and so on.

GREGERS. I see; for no doubt the wild duck is by far the most distinguished inhabitant of the garret?

HEDVIG. Yes, indeed she is; for she is a real wild fowl, you know. And then she is so much to be pitied; she has no one to care for, poor thing.

GREGERS. She has no family, as the rabbits have——

HEDVIG. No. The hens too, many of them, were chickens together; but she has been taken right away from all her friends. And then there is so much that is strange about the wild duck. Nobody knows her, and nobody knows where she came from either.

GREGERS. And she has been down in the depths of the sea.

HEDVIG (*with a quick glance at him, represses a smile and asks*): Why do you say "depths of the sea"?

GREGERS. What else should I say?

HEDVIG. You could say "the bottom of the sea." *

GREGERS. Oh, mayn't I just as well say the depths of the sea?

HEDVIG. Yes; but it sounds so strange to me when other people speak of the depths of the sea.

GREGERS. Why so? Tell me why?

HEDVIG. No, I won't; it's so stupid.

GREGERS. Oh, no, I am sure it's not. Do tell me why you smiled.

HEDVIG. Well, this is the reason: whenever I come to realise suddenly—in a flash—what is in there, it always seems to me that the whole room and everything in it should be called "the depths of the sea."—But that is so stupid.

GREGERS. You mustn't say that.

HEDVIG. Oh, yes, for you know it is only a garret.

GREGERS (*looks fixedly at her*). Are you so sure of that?

HEDVIG (*astonished*). That it's a garret?

GREGERS. Are you quite certain of it?
(HEDVIG *is silent, and looks at him open-mouthed.* GINA *comes in from the kitchen with the table things.*)

GREGERS (*rising*). I have come in upon you too early.

* Gregers here uses the old-fashioned expression "havsens bund," while Hedvig would have him use the more commonplace "havets bund" or "havbunden."

GINA. Oh, you must be somewhere; and we're nearly ready now, anyway. Clear the table, Hedvig.

(HEDVIG *clears away her things; she and* GINA *lay the cloth during what follows.* GREGERS *seats himself in the armchair, and turns over an album.*)

GREGERS. I hear you can retouch, Mrs. Ekdal.

GINA (*with a side glance*). Yes, I can.

GREGERS. That was exceedingly lucky.

GINA. How—lucky?

GREGERS. Since Ekdal took to photography, I mean.

HEDVIG. Mother can take photographs, too.

GINA. Oh, yes; I was bound to learn that.

GREGERS. So it is really you that carry on the business, I suppose?

GINA. Yes, when Ekdal hasn't time himself——

GREGERS. He is a great deal taken up with his old father, I daresay.

GINA. Yes; and then you can't expect a man like Ekdal to do nothing but take car-de-visits of Dick, Tom and Harry.

GREGERS. I quite agree with you; but having once gone in for the thing——

GINA. You can surely understand, Mr. Werle, that Ekdal's not like one of your common photographers.

GREGERS. Of course not; but still ——

(*A shot is fired within the garret.*)

GREGERS (*starting up*). What's that?

GINA. Ugh! now they're firing again!

GREGERS. Have they firearms in there?

HEDVIG. They are out shooting.

GREGERS. What! (*At the door of the garret*) Are you shooting, Hialmar?

HIALMAR (*inside the net*). Are you there? I didn't know; I was so taken up—— (*To* HEDVIG) Why did you not let us know?
(*Comes into the studio.*)

GREGERS. Do you go shooting in the garret?

HIALMAR (*showing a double-barrelled pistol*). Oh, only with this thing.

GINA. Yes, you and grandfather will do yourselves a mischief some day with that there pigstol.

HIALMAR (*with irritation*). I believe I have told you that this kind of firearm is called a pistol.

GINA. Oh, that doesn't make it much better, that I can see.

GREGERS. So you have become a sportsman, too, Hialmar?

HIALMAR. Only a little rabbit-shooting now and then. Mostly to please father, you understand.

GINA. Men are strange beings; they must always have something to pervert theirselves with.

HIALMAR (*snappishly*). Just so; we must always have something to divert ourselves with.

GINA. Yes, that's just what I say.

HIALMAR. H'm. (*To* GREGERS) You see the garret is fortunately so situated that no one can hear us shooting. (*Lays the pistol on the top shelf of the bookcase*) Don't touch the pistol, Hedvig! One of the barrels is loaded; remember that.

GREGERS (*looking through the net*). You have a fowling-piece too, I see.

HIALMAR. That is father's old gun. It's of no use now; something has gone wrong with the lock. But it's fun to have it all the same; for we can take it to pieces now and then, and clean and grease it, and screw it together again.—Of course, it's mostly father that fiddle-faddles with all that sort of thing.

HEDVIG (*beside* GREGERS). Now you can see the wild duck properly.

GREGERS. I was just looking at her. One of her wings seems to me to droop a bit.

HEDVIG. Well, no wonder; her wing was broken, you know.

GREGERS. And she trails one foot a little. Isn't that so?

HIALMAR. Perhaps a very little bit.

HEDVIG. Yes, it was by that foot the dog took hold of her.

HIALMAR. But otherwise she hasn't the least thing the matter with her; and that is simply marvellous for a creature that has a charge of shot in her body, and has been between a dog's teeth——

GREGERS (*with a glance at* HEDVIG). ——and that has lain in the depths of the sea—so long.

HEDVIG (*smiling*). Yes.

GINA (*laying the table*). That blessëd wild duck! What a lot of fuss you do make over her.

HIALMAR. H'm—will lunch soon be ready?

GINA. Yes, directly. Hedvig, you must come and help me now.
(GINA *and* HEDVIG *go out into the kitchen.*)

HIALMAR (*in a low voice*). I think you had better not stand there looking in at father; he doesn't like it. (GREGERS *moves away from the garret door*) Besides, I may as well shut up before the others come. (*Claps his hands to drive the fowls back*) Shh—shh, in with you! (*Draws up the curtain and pulls the doors together*) All the contrivances are my own invention. It's really quite amusing to have things of this sort to potter with, and to put to rights when they get out of order. And it's absolutely necessary, too; for Gina objects to having rabbits and fowls in the studio.

GREGERS. To be sure; and I suppose the studio is your wife's special department?

HIALMAR. As a rule, I leave the everyday details of business to her; for then I can take refuge in the parlour and give my mind to more important things.

GREGERS. What things may they be, Hialmar?

HIALMAR. I wonder you have not asked that question sooner. But perhaps you haven't heard of the invention?

GREGERS. The invention? No.

HIALMAR. Really? Have you not? Oh, no, out there in the wilds——

GREGERS. So you have invented something, have you?

HIALMAR. It is not quite completed yet; but I am working at it. You can easily imagine that when I resolved to devote myself to photography, it wasn't simply with the idea of taking likenesses of all sorts of commonplace people.

GREGERS. No; your wife was saying the same thing just now.

HIALMAR. I swore that if I consecrated my powers to this handicraft, I would so exalt it that it should become both an art and a science. And to that end I determined to make this great invention.

GREGERS. And what is the nature of the invention? What purpose does it serve?

HIALMAR. Oh, my dear fellow, you mustn't ask for details yet. It takes time, you see. And you must not think that my motive is vanity. It is not for my own sake that I am working. Oh, no; it is my life's mission that stands before me night and day.

GREGERS. What is your life's mission?

HIALMAR. Do you forget the old man with the silver hair?

GREGERS. Your poor father? Well, but what can you do for him?

HIALMAR. I can raise up his self-respect from the dead, by restoring the name of Ekdal to honour and dignity.

GREGERS. Then that is your life's mission?

HIALMAR. Yes. I will rescue the shipwrecked man. For shipwrecked he was, by the very first blast of the storm. Even while those terrible investigations were going on, he was no longer himself. That pistol there —the one we use to shoot rabbits with—has played its part in the tragedy of the house of Ekdal.

GREGERS. The pistol? Indeed?

HIALMAR. When the sentence of imprisonment was passed—he had the pistol in his hand——

GREGERS. Had he——?

HIALMAR. Yes; but he dared not use it. His courage failed him. So broken, so demoralised was he even then! Oh, can you understand it? He, a soldier; he, who had shot nine bears, and who was descended from two lieutenant colonels—one after the other, of course. Can you understand it, Gregers?

GREGERS. Yes, I understand it well enough.

HIALMAR. I cannot. And once more the pistol played a part in the history of our house. When he had put on the grey clothes and was under lock and key—oh, that was a terrible time for me, I can tell you. I kept the blinds drawn down over both my windows. When I peeped out, I saw the sun shining as if nothing had happened. I could not understand it. I saw people going along the street, laughing and talking about indifferent things. I could not understand it. It seemed to me that the whole of existence must be at a standstill—as if under an eclipse.

GREGERS. I felt that, too, when my mother died.

HIALMAR. It was in such an hour that Hialmar Ekdal pointed the pistol at his own breast.

GREGERS. You, too, thought of——!

HIALMAR. Yes.

GREGERS. But you did not fire?

HIALMAR. No. At the decisive moment I won the victory over myself. I remained in life. But I can assure you it takes some courage to choose life under circumstances like those.

GREGERS. Well, that depends on how you look at it.

HIALMAR. Yes, indeed, it takes courage. But I am glad I was firm: for now I shall soon perfect my invention; and Dr. Relling thinks, as I do myself, that father may be allowed to wear his uniform again. I will demand that as my sole reward.

GREGERS. So that is what he meant about his uniform——?

HIALMAR. Yes, that is what he most yearns for. You can't think how my heart bleeds for him. Every time we celebrate any little family festival—Gina's and my wedding day, or whatever it may be—in comes the old man in the lieutenant's uniform of happier days. But if he only hears a knock at the door—for he daren't show himself to strangers, you know—he hurries back to his room again as fast as his old legs can carry him. Oh, it's heart-rending for a son to see such things!

GREGERS. How long do you think it will take you to finish your invention?

HIALMAR. Come now, you mustn't expect me to enter into particulars like that. An invention is not a thing completely under one's own control. It depends largely on inspiration—on intuition—and it is almost impossible to predict when the inspiration may come.

GREGERS. But it's advancing?

HIALMAR. Yes, certainly, it is advancing. I turn it over in my mind every day; I am full of it. Every afternoon, when I have had my dinner, I shut myself up in the parlour, where I can ponder undisturbed. But I can't be goaded to it; it's not a bit of good; Relling says so, too.

GREGERS. And you don't think that all that business in the garret draws you off and distracts you too much?

HIALMAR. No, no, no; quite the contrary. You mustn't say that. I cannot be everlastingly absorbed in the same laborious train of thought. I must have something alongside of it to fill up the time of waiting. The inspiration, the intuition, you see—when it comes, it comes, and there's an end of it.

GREGERS. My dear Hialmar, I almost think you have something of the wild duck in you.

HIALMAR. Something of the wild duck? How do you mean?

GREGERS. You have dived down and bitten yourself fast in the undergrowth.

HIALMAR. Are you alluding to the well-nigh fatal shot that has broken my father's wing—and mine, too?

GREGERS. Not exactly to that. I don't say that your wing has been broken; but you have strayed into a poisonous marsh, Hialmar; an insidious disease has taken hold of you, and you have sunk down to die in the dark.

HIALMAR. I? To die in the dark? Look here, Gregers, you must really leave off talking such nonsense.

GREGERS. Don't be afraid; I shall find a way to help you up again. I, too, have a mission in life now; I found it yesterday.

HIALMAR. That's all very well; but you will please leave me out of it. I can assure you that—apart from my very natural melancholy, of course—I am as contented as any one can wish to be.

GREGERS. Your contentment is an effect of the marsh poison.

HIALMAR. Now, my dear Gregers, pray do not go on about disease and poison; I am not used to that sort of talk. In my house nobody ever speaks to me about unpleasant things.

GREGERS. Ah, that I can easily believe.

HIALMAR. It's not good for me, you see. And there are no marsh poisons here, as you express it. The poor photographer's roof is lowly, I know —and my circumstances are narrow. But I am an inventor, and I am the breadwinner of a family. That exalts me above my mean surroundings.—Ah, here comes lunch!

(GINA and HEDVIG bring bottles of ale, a decanter of brandy, glasses, etc. At the same time, RELLING and MOLVIK enter from the passage; they are both without hat or overcoat. MOLVIK is dressed in black.)

GINA (placing the things upon the table). Ah, you two have come in the nick of time.

RELLING. Molvik got it into his head that he could smell herring salad, and then there was no holding him. —Good morning again, Ekdal.

HIALMAR. Gregers, let me introduce you to Mr. Molvik. Doctor—— Oh, you know Relling, don't you?

GREGERS. Yes, slightly.

RELLING. Oh, Mr. Werle, junior! Yes, we two have had one or two little skirmishes up at the Höidal works. You've just moved in?

GREGERS. I moved in this morning.

RELLING. Molvik and I live right under you; so you haven't far to go for the doctor and the clergyman, if you should need anything in that line.

GREGERS. Thanks, it's not quite un-likely; for yesterday we were thir-teen at table.

HIALMAR. Oh, come now, don't let us get upon unpleasant subjects again!

RELLING. You may make your mind easy, Ekdal; I'll be hanged if the finger of fate points to you.

HIALMAR. I should hope not, for the sake of my family. But let us sit down now, and eat and drink and be merry.

GREGERS. Shall we not wait for your father?

HIALMAR. No, his lunch will be taken in to him later. Come along! (*The men seat themselves at table, and eat and drink.* GINA *and* HEDVIG *go in and out and wait upon them.*)

RELLING. Molvik was frightfully screwed yesterday, Mrs. Ekdal.

GINA. Really? Yesterday again?

RELLING. Didn't you hear him when I brought him home last night?

GINA. No, I can't say I did.

RELLING. That was a good thing, for Molvik was disgusting last night.

GINA. Is that true, Molvik?

MOLVIK. Let us draw a veil over last night's proceedings. That sort of thing is totally foreign to my better self.

RELLING (*to* GREGERS). It comes over him like a sort of possession, and then I have to go out on the loose with him. Mr. Molvik is dæmonic, you see.

GREGERS. Dæmonic?

RELLING. Molvik is dæmonic, yes.

GREGERS. H'm.

RELLING. And dæmonic natures are not made to walk straight through the world; they must meander a little now and then.—Well, so you still stick up there at those horrible grimy works?

GREGERS. I have stuck there until now.

RELLING. And did you ever manage to collect that claim you went about presenting?

GREGERS. Claim? (*Understands him*) Ah, I see.

HIALMAR. Have you been pre-senting claims, Gregers?

GREGERS. Oh, nonsense.

RELLING. Faith, but he has, though! He went round to all the cotters' cabins presenting something he called "the claim of the ideal."

GREGERS. I was young then.

RELLING. You're right; you were very young. And as for the claim of the ideal—you never got it hon-oured while *I* was up there.

GREGERS. Nor since either.

RELLING. Ah, then you've learnt to knock a little discount off, I expect.

GREGERS. Never, when I have a true man to deal with.

HIALMAR. No, I should think not, indeed. A little butter, Gina.

RELLING. And a slice of bacon for Molvik.

MOLVIK. Ugh; not bacon!
(*A knock at the garret door.*)

HIALMAR. Open the door, Hedvig; father wants to come out.
(HEDVIG *goes over and opens the door a little way;* EKDAL *enters with a fresh rabbit-skin; she closes the door after him.*)

EKDAL. Good morning, gentlemen! Good sport today. Shot a big one.

HIALMAR. And you've gone and skinned it without waiting for me ——!

EKDAL. Salted it, too. It's good tender meat, is rabbit; it's sweet; it tastes like sugar. Good appetite to you, gentlemen! (*Goes into his room.*)

MOLVIK (*rising*). Excuse me——; I can't—— I must get downstairs immediately——

RELLING. Drink some soda water, man!

MOLVIK (*hurrying away*). Ugh— ugh! (*Goes out by the passage door.*)

RELLING (*to* HIALMAR). Let us drain a glass to the old hunter.

HIALMAR (*clinks glasses with him*). To the undaunted sportsman who has looked death in the face!

RELLING. To the grey-haired—— (*Drinks*) By-the-bye, is his hair grey or white?

HIALMAR. Something between the two, I fancy; for that matter, he has very few hairs left of any colour.

RELLING. Well, well, one can get through the world with a wig. After all, you are a happy man, Ekdal; you have your noble mission to labour for——

HIALMAR. And I do labour, I can tell you.

RELLING. And then you have your excellent wife, shuffling quietly in and out in her felt slippers, with that see-saw walk of hers, and making everything cosy and comfortable about you.

HIALMAR. Yes, Gina—(*nods to her*) —you were a good helpmate on the path of life.

GINA. Oh, don't sit there cricketising me.

RELLING. And your Hedvig, too, Ekdal!

HIALMAR (*affected*). The child, yes! The child before everything! Hedvig, come here to me. (*Strokes her hair*) What day is it tomorrow, eh?

HEDVIG (*shaking him*). Oh, no, you're not to say anything, father.

HIALMAR. It cuts me to the heart when I think what a poor affair it will be; only a little festival in the garret——

HEDVIG. Oh, but that's just what I like!

RELLING. Just you wait till the wonderful invention sees the light, Hedvig!

HIALMAR. Yes, indeed—then you shall see——! Hedvig, I have resolved to make your future secure. You shall live in comfort all your days. I will demand—something or other—on your behalf. That shall be the poor inventor's sole reward.

HEDVIG (*whispering, with her arms round his neck*). Oh, you dear, kind father!

RELLING (*to* GREGERS). Come now, don't you find it pleasant, for once in a way, to sit at a well-spread table in a happy family circle?

HIALMAR. Ah, yes, I really prize these social hours.

GREGERS. For my part, I don't thrive in marsh vapours.

RELLING. Marsh vapours?

HIALMAR. Oh, don't begin with that stuff again!

GINA. Goodness knows there's no vapours in this house, Mr. Werle; I give the place a good airing every blessed day.

GREGERS (*leaves the table*). No airing you can give will drive out the taint I mean.

HIALMAR. Taint!

GINA. Yes, what do you say to that, Ekdal!

RELLING. Excuse me—may it not be you yourself that have brought the taint from those mines up there?

GREGERS. It is like you to call what I bring into this house a taint.

RELLING (*goes up to him*). Look here, Mr. Werle, junior: I have a strong suspicion that you are still carrying about that "claim of the ideal" large as life, in your coat-tail pocket.

GREGERS. I carry it in my breast.

RELLING. Well, wherever you carry it, I advise you not to come dunning us with it here, so long as *I* am on the premises.

GREGERS. And if I do so none the less?

RELLING. Then you'll go head-foremost down the stairs; now I've warned you.

HIALMAR (*rising*). Oh, but Relling ——!

GREGERS. Yes, you may turn me out——

GINA (*interposing between them*). We can't have that, Relling. But I must say, Mr. Werle, it ill becomes you to talk about vapours and taints, after all the mess you made with your stove.

(*A knock at the passage door.*)

HEDVIG. Mother, there's somebody knocking.

HIALMAR. There now, we're going to have a whole lot of people!

GINA. I'll go—— (*Goes over and opens the door, starts, and draws back*) Oh—oh, dear!
(WERLE, *in a fur coat, advances one step into the room.*)

WERLE. Excuse me; but I think my son is staying here.

GINA (*with a gulp*). Yes.

HIALMAR (*approaching him*). Won't you do us the honour to ——?

WERLE. Thank you, I merely wish to speak to my son.

GREGERS. What is it? Here I am.

WERLE. I want a few words with you, in your room.

GREGERS. In my room? Very well —— (*About to go.*)

GINA. No, no, your room's not in a fit state——

WERLE. Well then, out in the passage here; I want to have a few words with you alone.

HIALMAR. You can have them here, sir. Come into the parlour, Relling.
(HIALMAR *and* RELLING *go off to the right.* GINA *takes* HEDVIG *with her into the kitchen.*)

GREGERS (*after a short pause*). Well, now we are alone.

WERLE. From something you let fall last evening, and from your coming to lodge with the Ekdals, I can't help inferring that you intend to make yourself unpleasant to me, in one way or another.

GREGERS. I intend to open Hialmar Ekdal's eyes. He shall see his position as it really is—that is all.

WERLE. Is that the mission in life you spoke of yesterday?

GREGERS. Yes. You have left me no other.

WERLE. Is it I, then, that have crippled your mind, Gregers?

GREGERS. You have crippled my whole life. I am not thinking of all that about mother—— But it's thanks to you that I am continually haunted and harassed by a guilty conscience.

WERLE. Indeed! It is your conscience that troubles you, is it?

GREGERS. I ought to have taken a stand against you when the trap was set for Lieutenant Ekdal. I ought to have cautioned him; for I had a misgiving as to what was in the wind.

WERLE. Yes, that was the time to have spoken.

GREGERS. I did not dare to, I was so cowed and spiritless. I was mortally afraid of you—not only then, but long afterwards.

WERLE. You have got over that fear now, it appears.

GREGERS. Yes, fortunately. The wrong done to old Ekdal, both by me and by—others, can never be undone; but Hialmar I can rescue from all the falsehood and deception that are bringing him to ruin.

WERLE. Do you think that will be doing him a kindness?

GREGERS. I have not the least doubt of it.

WERLE. You think our worthy photographer is the sort of man to appreciate such friendly offices?

GREGERS. Yes, I do.

WERLE. H'm—we shall see.

GREGERS. Besides, if I am to go on living, I must try to find some cure for my sick conscience.

WERLE. It will never be sound. Your conscience has been sickly from childhood. That is a legacy from your mother, Gregers—the only one she left you.

GREGERS (*with a scornful half-smile*). Have you not yet forgiven her for the mistake you made in supposing she would bring you a fortune?

WERLE. Don't let us wander from the point.—Then you hold to your purpose of setting young Ekdal upon what you imagine to be the right scent?

GREGERS. Yes, that is my fixed resolve.

WERLE. Well, in that case I might have spared myself this visit; for, of course, it is useless to ask whether you will return home with me?

GREGERS. Quite useless.

WERLE. And I suppose you won't enter the firm either?

GREGERS. No.

WERLE. Very good. But as I am thinking of marrying again, your share in the property will fall to you at once.*

GREGERS (*quickly*). No, I do not want that.

WERLE. You don't want it?

GREGERS. No, I dare not take it, for conscience's sake.

WERLE (*after a pause*). Are you going up to the works again?

GREGERS. No; I consider myself released from your service.

WERLE. But what are you going to do?

GREGERS. Only to fulfil my mission; nothing more.

WERLE. Well but afterwards? What are you going to live upon?

GREGERS. I have laid by a little out of my salary.

WERLE. How long will that last?

GREGERS. I think it will last my time.

WERLE. What do you mean?

GREGERS. I shall answer no more questions.

WERLE. Good-bye then, Gregers.

* By Norwegian law, before a widower can marry again, a certain proportion of his property must be settled on his children by his former marriage.

GREGERS. Good-bye.
(WERLE *goes*.)

HIALMAR (*peeping in*). He's gone, isn't he?

GREGERS. Yes.

(HIALMAR *and* RELLING *enter; also* GINA *and* HEDVIG *from the kitchen*.)

RELLING. That luncheon-party was a failure.

GREGERS. Put on your coat, Hialmar; I want you to come for a long walk with me.

HIALMAR. With pleasure. What was it your father wanted? Had it anything to do with me?

GREGERS. Come along. We must have a talk. I'll go and put on my overcoat.
(*Goes out by the passage door*.)

GINA. You shouldn't go out with him, Ekdal.

RELLING. No, don't you do it. Stay where you are.

HIALMAR (*gets his hat and overcoat*). Oh, nonsense! When a friend of my youth feels impelled to open his mind to me in private——

RELLING. But devil take it—don't you see that the fellow's mad, cracked, demented!

GINA. There, what did I tell you! His mother before him had crazy fits like that sometimes.

HIALMAR. The more need for a friend's watchful eye. (*To* GINA)

Be sure you have dinner ready in good time. Good-bye for the present.
(*Goes out by the passage door*.)

RELLING. It's a thousand pities the fellow didn't go to hell through one of the Höidal mines.

GINA. Good Lord! what makes you say that?

RELLING (*muttering*). Oh, I have my own reasons.

GINA. Do you think young Werle is really mad?

RELLING. No, worse luck; he's no madder than most other people. But one disease he has certainly got in his system.

GINA. What is it that's the matter with him?

RELLING. Well, I'll tell you, Mrs. Ekdal. He is suffering from an acute attack of integrity.

GINA. Integrity?

HEDVIG. Is that a kind of disease?

RELLING. Yes, it's a national disease; but it only appears sporadically. (*Nods to* GINA) Thanks for your hospitality.
(*He goes out by the passage door*.)

GINA (*moving restlessly to and fro*). Ugh, that Gregers Werle—he was always a wretched creature.

HEDVIG (*standing by the table, and looking searchingly at her*). I think all this is very strange.

ACT FOUR

HIALMAR EKDAL's *studio. A photograph has just been taken; a camera with the cloth over it, a pedestal, two chairs, a folding table, etc., are standing out in the room. Afternoon light; the sun is going down; a little later it begins to grow dusk.*

GINA *stands in the passage doorway, with a little box and a wet glass plate in her hand, and is speaking to somebody outside.*

GINA. Yes, certainly. When I make a promise I keep it. The first dozen shall be ready on Monday. Good afternoon.

(*Someone is heard going downstairs.* GINA *shuts the door, slips the plate into the box, and puts it into the covered camera.*)

HEDVIG (*comes in from the kitchen*). Are they gone?

GINA (*tidying up*). Yes, thank goodness, I've got rid of them at last.

HEDVIG. But can you imagine why father hasn't come home yet?

GINA. Are you sure he's not down in Relling's room?

HEDVIG. No, he's not; I ran down the kitchen stair just now and asked.

GINA. And his dinner standing and getting cold, too.

HEDVIG. Yes, I can't understand it. Father's always so careful to be home to dinner!

GINA. Oh, he'll be here directly, you'll see.

HEDVIG. I wish he would come; everything seems so queer today.

GINA (*calls out*). There he is!
(HIALMAR EKDAL *comes in at the passage door.*)

HEDVIG (*going to him*). Father! Oh, what a time we've been waiting for you!

GINA (*glancing sidelong at him*). You've been out a long time, Ekdal.

HIALMAR (*without looking at her*). Rather long, yes.
(*He takes off his overcoat;* GINA *and* HEDVIG *go to help him; he motions them away.*)

GINA. Perhaps you've had dinner with Werle?

HIALMAR (*hanging up his coat*). No.

GINA (*going towards the kitchen door*). Then I'll bring some in for you.

HIALMAR. No; let the dinner alone. I want nothing to eat.

HEDVIG (*going nearer to him*). Are you not well, father?

HIALMAR. Well? Oh, yes, well enough. We have had a tiring walk, Gregers and I.

GINA. You didn't ought to have gone so far, Ekdal; you're not used to it.

HIALMAR. H'm; there's many a thing a man must get used to in this world. (*Wanders about the room*) Has any one been here while I was out?

GINA. Nobody but the two sweethearts.

HIALMAR. No new orders?

GINA. No, not today.

HEDVIG. There will be some tomorrow, father, you'll see.

HIALMAR. I hope there will; for tomorrow I am going to set to work in real earnest.

HEDVIG. Tomorrow! Don't you remember what day it is tomorrow?

HIALMAR. Oh, yes, by-the-bye——. Well, the day after, then. Henceforth I mean to do everything myself; I shall take all the work into my own hands.

GINA. Why, what can be the good of that, Ekdal? It'll only make your life a burden to you. I can manage the photography all right; and you can go on working at your invention.

HEDVIG. And think of the wild duck, father—and all the hens and rabbits and——!

HIALMAR. Don't talk to me of all that trash! From tomorrow I will never set foot in the garret again.

HEDVIG. Oh, but father, you promised that we should have a little party——

HIALMAR. H'm, true. Well, then, from the day after tomorrow. I should almost like to wring that cursed wild duck's neck!

HEDVIG (*shrieks*). The wild duck!

GINA. Well I never!

HEDVIG (*shaking him*). Oh, no, father; you know it's my wild duck!

HIALMAR. That is why I don't do it. I haven't the heart to—for your sake, Hedvig. But in my inmost soul I feel that I ought to do it. I ought not to tolerate under my roof a creature that has been through those hands.

GINA. Why, good gracious, even if grandfather did get it from that poor creature, Pettersen——

HIALMAR (*wandering about*). There are certain claims—what shall I call them?—let me say claims of the ideal—certain obligations, which a man cannot disregard without injury to his soul.

HEDVIG (*going after him*). But think of the wild duck—the poor wild duck!

HIALMAR (*stops*). I tell you I will spare it—for your sake. Not a hair of its head shall be—I mean, it shall be spared. There are greater problems than that to be dealt with. But you should go out a little now, Hedvig, as usual; it is getting dusk enough for you now.

HEDVIG. No, I don't care about going out now.

HIALMAR. Yes, do; it seems to me your eyes are blinking a great deal;

all these vapours in here are bad for you. The air is heavy under this roof.

HEDVIG. Very well, then, I'll run down the kitchen stair and go for a little walk. My cloak and hat?— oh, they're in my own room. Father —be sure you don't do the wild duck any harm while I'm out.

HIALMAR. Not a feather of its head shall be touched. (*Draws her to him*) You and I, Hedvig—we two ——! Well, go along.
(HEDVIG *nods to her parents and goes out through the kitchen.*)

HIALMAR (*walks about without looking up*). Gina.

GINA. Yes?

HIALMAR. From tomorrow—or, say, from the day after tomorrow—I should like to keep the household account-book myself.

GINA. Do you want to keep the accounts too, now?

HIALMAR. Yes; or to check the receipts at any rate.

GINA. Lord help us! that's soon done.

HIALMAR. One would hardly think so; at any rate you seem to make the money go a very long way. (*Stops and looks at her*) How do you manage it?

GINA. It's because me and Hedvig, we need so little.

HIALMAR. Is it the case that father is very liberally paid for the copying he does for Mr. Werle?

GINA. I don't know as he gets anything out of the way. I don't know the rates for that sort of work.

HIALMAR. Well, what does he get about? Let me hear!

GINA. Oh, it varies; I dare say it'll come to about as much as he costs us, with a little pocket-money over.

HIALMAR. As much as he costs us! And you have never told me this before!

GINA. No, how could I tell you? It pleased you so much to think he got everything from you.

HIALMAR. And he gets it from Mr. Werle.

GINA. Oh, well, he has plenty and to spare, he has.

HIALMAR. Light the lamp for me, please!

GINA (*lighting the lamp*). And, of course, we don't know as it's Mr. Werle himself; it may be Gråberg ——

HIALMAR. Why attempt such an evasion?

GINA. I don't know; I only thought ——

HIALMAR. H'm!

GINA. It wasn't me that got grandfather that copying. It was Bertha, when she used to come about us.

HIALMAR. It seems to me your voice is trembling.

GINA (*putting the lamp-shade on*). Is it?

HIALMAR. And your hands are shaking, are they not?

GINA (*firmly*). Come right out with it, Ekdal. What has he been saying about me?

HIALMAR. Is it true—can it be true that—that there was an—an understanding between you and Mr. Werle, while you were in service there?

GINA. That's not true. Not at that time. Mr. Werle did come after me, that's a fact. And his wife thought there was something in it, and then she made such a hocus-pocus and hurly-burly, and she hustled me and bustled me about so that I left her service.

HIALMAR. But afterwards, then?

GINA. Well, then I went home. And mother—well, she wasn't the woman you took her for, Ekdal; she kept on worrying and worrying at me about one thing and another—for Mr. Werle was a widower by that time.

HIALMAR. Well, and then?

GINA. I suppose you've got to know it. He gave me no peace until he'd had his way.

HIALMAR (*striking his hands together*). And this is the mother of my child! How could you hide this from me?

GINA. Yes, it was wrong of me; I ought certainly to have told you long ago.

HIALMAR. You should have told me at the very first—then I should have known the sort of woman you were.

GINA. But would you have married me all the same?

HIALMAR. How can you dream that I would?

GINA. That's just why I didn't dare tell you anything, then. For I'd come to care for you so much, you see; and I couldn't go and make myself utterly miserable——

HIALMAR (*walks about*). And this is my Hedvig's mother. And to know that all I see before me— (*Kicks at a chair*)—all that I call my home—I owe to a favoured predecessor! Oh, that scoundrel Werle!

GINA. Do you repent of the fourteen—the fifteen years we've lived together?

HIALMAR (*placing himself in front of her*). Have you not every day, every hour, repented of the spider's-web of deceit you have spun around me? Answer me that! How could you help writhing with penitence and remorse?

GINA. Oh, my dear Ekdal, I've had all I could do to look after the house and get through the day's work——

HIALMAR. Then you never think of reviewing your past?

GINA. No; Heaven knows I'd almost forgotten those old stories.

HIALMAR. Oh, this dull, callous contentment! To me there is something revolting about it. Think of it—

never so much as a twinge of remorse!

GINA. But tell me, Ekdal—what
would have become of you if you
hadn't had a wife like me?

HIALMAR. Like you——!

GINA. Yes; for you know I've always been a bit more practical and
wide-awake than you. Of course
I'm a year or two older.

HIALMAR. What would have become of me!

GINA. You'd got into all sorts of
bad ways when first you met me;
that you can't deny.

HIALMAR. "Bad ways" do you call
them? Little do you know what a
man goes through when he is in
grief and despair—especially a man
of my fiery temperament.

GINA. Well, well, that may be so.
And I've no reason to crow over
you, neither; for you turned a moral
of a husband, that you did, as soon
as ever you had a house and home
of your own.—And now we'd got
everything so nice and cosy about
us; and me and Hedvig was just
thinking we'd soon be able to let
ourselves go a bit, in the way of
both food and clothes.

HIALMAR. In the swamp of deceit,
yes.

GINA. I wish to goodness that detestable thing had never set his
foot inside our doors!

HIALMAR. And I, too, thought my
home such a pleasant one. That
was a delusion. Where shall I now

find the elasticity of spirit to bring
my invention into the world of
reality? Perhaps it will die with me;
and then it will be your past, Gina,
that will have killed it.

GINA (nearly crying). You mustn't
say such things, Ekdal. Me, that has
only wanted to do the best I could
for you, all my days!

HIALMAR. I ask you, what becomes
of the breadwinner's dream? When
I used to lie in there on the sofa
and brood over my invention, I had
a clear enough presentiment that it
would sap my vitality to the last
drop. I felt even then that the day
when I held the patent in my hand
—that day—would bring my—release. And then it was my dream
that you should live on after me,
the dead inventor's well-to-do
widow.

GINA (drying her tears). No, you
mustn't talk like that, Ekdal. May
the Lord never let me see the day
I am left a widow!

HIALMAR. Oh, the whole dream has
vanished. It is all over now. All
over!

(GREGERS WERLE opens the passage
door cautiously and looks in.)

GREGERS. May I come in?

HIALMAR. Yes, come in.

GREGERS (comes forward, his face
beaming with satisfaction, and
holds out both his hands to them).
Well, dear friends——! (Looks
from one to the other, and whispers to HIALMAR) Have you not
done it yet?

HIALMAR (aloud). It is done.

GREGERS. It is?

HIALMAR. I have passed through the bitterest moments of my life.

GREGERS. But also, I trust, the most ennobling.

HIALMAR. Well, at any rate, we have got through it for the present.

GINA. God forgive you, Mr. Werle.

GREGERS (*in great surprise*). But I don't understand this.

HIALMAR. What don't you understand?

GREGERS. After so great a crisis— a crisis that is to be the starting-point of an entirely new life—of a communion founded on truth, and free from all taint of deception——

HIALMAR. Yes, yes, I know; I know that quite well.

GREGERS. I confidently expected, when I entered the room, to find the light of transfiguration shining upon me from both husband and wife. And now I see nothing but dulness, oppression, gloom——

GINA. Oh, is that it?
(*Takes off the lamp-shade.*)

GREGERS. You will not understand me, Mrs. Ekdal. Ah, well, you, I suppose, need time to——. But you, Hialmar? Surely you feel a new consecration after the great crisis.

HIALMAR. Yes, of course I do. That is——in a sort of way.

GREGERS. For surely nothing in the world can compare with the joy of forgiving one who has erred, and raising her up to oneself in love.

HIALMAR. Do you think a man can so easily throw off the bitter cup I have drained?

GREGERS. No, not a common man, perhaps. But a man like you——!

HIALMAR. Good God! I know that well enough. But you must keep me up to it, Gregers. It takes time, you know.

GREGERS. You have much of the wild duck in you, Hialmar.
(RELLING *has come in at the passage door.*)

RELLING. Oho! is the wild duck to the fore again?

HIALMAR. Yes; Mr. Werle's wing-broken victim.

RELLING. Mr. Werle's——? So it's him you are talking about?

HIALMAR. Him and—ourselves.

RELLING (*in an undertone to* GREGERS). May the devil fly away with you!

HIALMAR. What is that you are saying?

RELLING. Only uttering a heartfelt wish that this quack-salver would take himself off. If he stays here, he is quite equal to making an utter mess of life, for both of you.

GREGERS. These two will not make a mess of life, Mr. Relling. Of course I won't speak of Hialmar— him we know. But she, too, in her innermost heart, has certainly something loyal and sincere——

GINA (*almost crying*). You might have let me alone for what I was, then.

RELLING (*to* GREGERS). Is it rude to ask what you really want in this house?

GREGERS. To lay the foundations of a true marriage.

RELLING. So you don't think Ekdal's marriage is good enough as it is?

GREGERS. No doubt it is as good a marriage as most others, worse luck. But a true marriage it has yet to become.

HIALMAR. You have never had eyes for the claims of the ideal, Relling.

RELLING. Rubbish, my boy!—but excuse me, Mr. Werle: how many —in round numbers—how many true marriages have you seen in the course of your life?

GREGERS. Scarcely a single one.

RELLING. Nor I either.

GREGERS. But I have seen innumerable marriages of the opposite kind. And it has been my fate to see at close quarters what ruin such a marriage can work in two human souls.

HIALMAR. A man's whole moral basis may give away beneath his feet; that is the terrible part of it.

RELLING. Well, I can't say I've ever been exactly married, so I don't pretend to speak with authority. But this I know, that the child enters into the marriage problem. And you must leave the child in peace.

HIALMAR. Oh—Hedvig! my poor Hedvig!

RELLING. Yes, you must be good enough to keep Hedvig outside of all this. You two are grown-up people; you are free, in God's name, to make what mess and muddle you please of your life. But you must deal cautiously with Hedvig, I tell you; else you may do her a great injury.

HIALMAR. An injury!

RELLING. Yes, or she may do herself an injury—and perhaps others, too.

GINA. How can you know that, Relling?

HIALMAR. Her sight is in no immediate danger, is it?

RELLING. I am not talking about her sight. Hedvig is at a critical age. She may be getting all sorts of mischief into her head.

GINA. That's true—I've noticed it already! She's taken to carrying on with the fire, out in the kitchen. She calls it playing at house-on-fire. I'm often scared for fear she really sets fire to the house.

RELLING. You see; I thought as much.

GREGERS (*to* RELLING). But how do you account for that?

RELLING (*sullenly*). Her constitution's changing, sir.

HIALMAR. So long as the child has me——! So long as *I* am above ground——!
(*A knock at the door.*)

GINA. Hush, Ekdal; there's some one in the passage. (*Calls out*) Come in!

(MRS. SÖRBY, *in walking dress, comes in.*)

MRS. SÖRBY. Good evening.

GINA (*going towards her*). Is it really you, Bertha?

MRS. SÖRBY. Yes, of course it is. But I'm disturbing you, I'm afraid?

HIALMAR. No, not at all; an emissary from that house——

MRS. SÖRBY (*to* GINA). To tell the truth, I hoped your men-folk would be out at this time. I just ran up to have a little chat with you, and to say good-bye.

GINA. Good-bye? Are you going away, then?

MRS. SÖRBY. Yes, tomorrow morning—up to Höidal. Mr. Werle started this afternoon. (*Lightly to* GREGERS) He asked me to say good-bye for him.

GINA. Only fancy——!

HIALMAR. So Mr. Werle has gone? And now you are going after him?

MRS. SÖRBY. Yes, what do you say to that, Ekdal?

HIALMAR. I say: beware!

GREGERS. I must explain the situation. My father and Mrs. Sörby are going to be married.

HIALMAR. Going to be married!

GINA. Oh, Bertha! So it's come to that at last!

RELLING (*his voice quivering a little*). This is surely not true?

MRS. SÖRBY. Yes, my dear Relling, it's true enough.

RELLING. You are going to marry again?

MRS. SÖRBY. Yes, it looks like it. Werle has got a special licence, and we are going to be married quite quietly, up at the works.

GREGERS. Then I must wish you all happiness, like a dutiful stepson.

MRS. SÖRBY. Thank you very much —if you mean what you say. I certainly hope it will lead to happiness, both for Werle and for me.

RELLING. You have every reason to hope that. Mr. Werle never gets drunk—so far as I know; and I don't suppose he's in the habit of thrashing his wives, like the late lamented horse-doctor.

MRS. SÖRBY. Come now, let Sörby rest in peace. He had his good points, too.

RELLING. Mr. Werle has better ones, I have no doubt.

MRS. SÖRBY. He hasn't frittered away all that was good in him, at any rate. The man who does that must take the consequences.

RELLING. I shall go out with Molvik this evening.

MRS. SÖRBY. You mustn't do that, Relling. Don't do it—for my sake.

RELLING. There's nothing else for it. (*To* HIALMAR) If you're going with us, come along.

GINA. No, thank you. Ekdal doesn't go in for that sort of dissertation.

HIALMAR (*half aloud, in vexation*). Oh, do hold your tongue!

RELLING. Good-bye, Mrs.—Werle. (*Goes out through the passage door.*)

GREGERS (*to* MRS. SÖRBY). You seem to know Dr. Relling pretty intimately.

MRS. SÖRBY. Yes, we have known each other for many years. At one time it seemed as if things might have gone further between us.

GREGERS. It was surely lucky for you that they did not.

MRS. SÖRBY. You may well say that. But I have always been wary of acting on impulse. A woman can't afford absolutely to throw herself away.

GREGERS. Are you not in the least afraid that I may let my father know about this old friendship?

MRS. SÖRBY. Why, of course, I have told him all about it myself.

GREGERS. Indeed?

MRS. SÖRBY. Your father knows every single thing that can, with any truth, be said about me. I have told him all; it was the first thing I did when I saw what was in his mind.

GREGERS. Then you have been franker than most people, I think.

MRS. SÖRBY. I have always been frank. We women find that the best policy.

HIALMAR. What do you say to that, Gina?

GINA. Oh, we're not all alike, us women aren't. Some are made one way, some another.

MRS. SÖRBY. Well, for my part, Gina, I believe it's wisest to do as I've done. And Werle has no secrets either, on his side. That's really the great bond between us, you see. Now he can talk to me as openly as a child. He has never had the chance to do that before. Fancy a man like him, full of health and vigour, passing his whole youth and the best years of his life in listening to nothing but penitential sermons! And very often the sermons had for their text the most imaginary offences—at least so I understand.

GINA. That's true enough.

GREGERS. If you ladies are going to follow up this topic, I had better withdraw.

MRS. SÖRBY. You can stay as far as that's concerned. I shan't say a word more. But I wanted you to know that I had done nothing secretly or in an underhand way. I may seem to have come in for a great piece of luck; and so I have, in a sense. But after all, I don't think I am getting any more than I am giving. I shall stand by him always, and I can tend and care for him as no one else can, now that he is getting helpless.

HIALMAR. Getting helpless?

GREGERS (*to* MRS. SÖRBY). Hush, don't speak of that here.

MRS. SÖRBY. There is no disguising it any longer, however much he would like to. He is going blind.

HIALMAR (*starts*). Going blind? That's strange. He, too, going blind!

GINA. Lots of people do.

MRS. SÖRBY. And you can imagine what that means to a business man. Well, I shall try as well as I can to make my eyes take the place of his. But I mustn't stay any longer; I have heaps of things to do.—Oh, by-the-bye, Ekdal, I was to tell you that if there is anything Werle can do for you, you must just apply to Gråberg.

GREGERS. That offer I am sure Hialmar Ekdal will decline with thanks.

MRS. SÖRBY. Indeed? I don't think he used to be so——

GINA. No, Bertha, Ekdal doesn't need anything from Mr. Werle now.

HIALMAR (*slowly, and with emphasis*). Will you present my compliments to your future husband, and say that I intend very shortly to call upon Mr. Gråberg——

GREGERS. What! You don't really mean that?

HIALMAR. To call upon Mr. Gråberg, I say, and obtain an account of the sum I owe his principal. I will pay that debt of honour—ha, ha, ha! a debt of honour, let us call it! In any case, I will pay the whole with five per cent. interest.

GINA. But, my dear Ekdal, God knows we haven't got the money to do it.

HIALMAR. Be good enough to tell your future husband that I am working assiduously at my invention. Please tell him that what sustains me in this laborious task is the wish to free myself from a torturing burden of debt. That is my reason for proceeding with the invention. The entire profits shall be devoted to releasing me from my pecuniary obligations to your future husband.

MRS. SÖRBY. Something has happened here.

HIALMAR. Yes, you are right.

MRS. SÖRBY. Well, good-bye. I had something else to speak to you about, Gina; but it must keep till another time. Good-bye.
(HIALMAR *and* GREGERS *bow silently.* GINA *follows* MRS. SÖRBY *to the door.*)

HIALMAR. Not beyond the threshold, Gina!
(MRS. SÖRBY *goes;* GINA *shuts the door after her.*)

HIALMAR. There now, Gregers; I have got that burden of debt off my mind.

GREGERS. You soon will, at all events.

HIALMAR. I think my attitude may be called correct.

GREGERS. You are the man I have always taken you for.

HIALMAR. In certain cases, it is impossible to disregard the claim of the ideal. Yet, as the breadwinner of a family, I cannot but writhe and groan under it. I can tell you it is no joke for a man without capital to attempt the repayment of a long-standing obligation, over which, so to speak, the dust of oblivion had gathered. But it cannot be helped: the Man in me demands his rights.

GREGERS (*laying his hand on* HIALMAR'S *shoulder*). My dear Hialmar —was it not a good thing I came?

HIALMAR. Yes.

GREGERS. Are you not glad to have had your true position made clear to you?

HIALMAR (*somewhat impatiently*). Yes, of course I am. But there is one thing that is revolting to my sense of justice.

GREGERS. And what is that?

HIALMAR. It is that—but I don't know whether I ought to express myself so unreservedly about your father.

GREGERS. Say what you please, so far as I am concerned.

HIALMAR. Well, then, is it not exasperating to think that it is not I, but he, who will realise the true marriage?

GREGERS. How can you say such a thing?

HIALMAR. Because it is clearly the case. Isn't the marriage between your father and Mrs. Sörby founded upon complete confidence, upon entire and unreserved candour on both sides? They hide nothing from each other, they keep no secrets in the background; their relation is based, if I may put it so, on mutual confession and absolution.

GREGERS. Well, what then?

HIALMAR. Well, is not that the whole thing? Did you not yourself say that this was precisely the difficulty that had to be overcome in order to found a true marriage?

GREGERS. But this is a totally different matter, Hialmar. You surely don't compare either yourself or your wife with those two——? Oh, you understand me well enough.

HIALMAR. Say what you like, there is something in all this that hurts and offends my sense of justice. It really looks as if there were no just providence to rule the world.

GINA. Oh, no, Ekdal; for God's sake don't say such things.

GREGERS. H'm; don't let us get upon those questions.

HIALMAR. And yet, after all, I cannot but recognise the guiding finger of fate. He is going blind.

GINA. Oh, you can't be sure of that.

HIALMAR. There is no doubt about it. At all events there ought not to be; for in that very fact lies the righteous retribution. He has hoodwinked a confiding fellow creature in days gone by——

GREGERS. I fear he has hoodwinked many.

HIALMAR. And now comes inexorable, mysterious Fate, and demands Werle's own eyes.

GINA. Oh, how dare you say such dreadful things! You make me quite scared.

HIALMAR. It is profitable, now and then, to plunge deep into the night side of existence.

(HEDVIG, *in her hat and cloak, comes in by the passage door. She is pleasurably excited and out of breath.*)

GINA. Are you back already?

HEDVIG. Yes, I didn't care to go any farther. It was a good thing, too; for I've just met some one at the door.

HIALMAR. It must have been that Mrs. Sörby.

HEDVIG. Yes.

HIALMAR (*walks up and down*). I hope you have seen her for the last time.

(*Silence.* HEDVIG, *discouraged, looks first at one and then at the other, trying to divine their frame of mind.*)

HEDVIG (*approaching, coaxingly*). Father.

HIALMAR. Well—what is it, Hedvig?

HEDVIG. Mrs. Sörby had something with her for me.

HIALMAR (*stops*). For you?

HEDVIG. Yes. Something for to-morrow.

GINA. Bertha has always given you some little thing on your birthday.

HIALMAR. What is it?

HEDVIG. Oh, you mustn't see it now. Mother is to give it to me to-morrow morning before I'm up.

HIALMAR. What is all this hocus-pocus that I am to be in the dark about!

HEDVIG (*quickly*). Oh, no, you may see it if you like. It's a big letter. (*Takes the letter out of her cloak pocket.*)

HIALMAR. A letter, too?

HEDVIG. Yes, it is only a letter. The rest will come afterwards, I suppose. But fancy—a letter! I've never had a letter before. And there's "Miss" written upon it. (*Reads*) "Miss Hedvig Ekdal." Only fancy—that's me!

HIALMAR. Let me see that letter.

HEDVIG (*hands it to him*). There it is.

HIALMAR. That is Mr. Werle's hand.

GINA. Are you sure of that, Ekdal?

HIALMAR. Look for yourself.

GINA. Oh, what do I know about such-like things?

HIALMAR. Hedvig, may I open the letter—and read it?

HEDVIG. Yes, of course you may, if you want to.

GINA. No, not tonight, Ekdal; it's to be kept till tomorrow.

HEDVIG (*softly*). Oh, can't you let him read it! It's sure to be something good; and then father will be glad, and everything will be nice again.

HIALMAR. I may open it then?

HEDVIG. Yes, do, father. I'm so anxious to know what it is.

HIALMAR. Well and good. (*Opens the letter, takes out a paper, reads it through, and appears bewildered*) What is this——!

GINA. What does it say?

HEDVIG. Oh, yes, father—tell us!

HIALMAR. Be quiet. (*Reads it through again; he has turned pale, but says with self-control:*) It is a deed of gift, Hedvig.

HEDVIG. Is it? What sort of gift am I to have?

HIALMAR. Read for yourself. (HEDVIG *goes over and reads for a time by the lamp.*)

HIALMAR (*half aloud, clenching his hands*). The eyes! The eyes— and then that letter!

HEDVIG (*leaves off reading*). Yes, but it seems to me that it's grandfather that's to have it.

HIALMAR (*takes letter from her*). Gina—can you understand this?

GINA. I know nothing whatever about it; tell me what's the matter.

HIALMAR. Mr. Werle writes to Hedvig that her old grandfather need not trouble himself any longer with the copying, but that he can henceforth draw on the office for a hundred crowns a month——

GREGERS. Aha!

HEDVIG. A hundred crowns, mother! I read that.

GINA. What a good thing for grandfather!

HIALMAR. ——a hundred crowns a month so long as he needs it— that means, of course, so long as he lives.

GINA. Well, so he's provided for, poor dear.

HIALMAR. But there is more to come. You didn't read that, Hedvig. Afterwards this gift is to pass on to you.

HEDVIG. To me! The whole of it?

HIALMAR. He says that the same amount is assured to you for the whole of your life. Do you hear that, Gina?

GINA. Yes, I hear.

HEDVIG. Fancy—all that money for me! (*Shakes him*) Father, father, aren't you glad——?

HIALMAR (*eluding her*). Glad! (*Walks about*) Oh what vistas— what perspectives open up before me! It is Hedvig, Hedvig that he showers these benefactions upon!

GINA. Yes, because it's Hedvig's birthday——

HEDVIG. And you'll get it all the same, father! You know quite well I shall give all the money to you and mother.

HIALMAR. To mother, yes! There we have it.

GREGERS. Hialmar, this is a trap he is setting for you.

HIALMAR. Do you think it's another trap?

GREGERS. When he was here this morning he said: Hialmar Ekdal is not the man you imagine him to be.

HIALMAR. Not the man——!

GREGERS. That you shall see, he said.

HIALMAR. He meant you should see that I would let myself be bought off——!

HEDVIG. Oh mother, what does all this mean?

GINA. Go and take off your things. (HEDVIG *goes out by the kitchen door, half crying.*)

GREGERS. Yes, Hialmar—now is the time to show who was right, he or I.

HIALMAR (*slowly tears the paper across, lays both pieces on the table, and says*): Here is my answer.

GREGERS. Just what I expected.

HIALMAR (*goes over to* GINA, *who stands by the stove, and says in a low voice*): Now please make a clean breast of it. If the connection between you and him was quite over when you—came to care for me, as you call it—why did he place us in a position to marry?

GINA. I suppose he thought as he could come and go in our house.

HIALMAR. Only that? Was not he afraid of a possible contingency?

GINA. I don't know what you mean.

HIALMAR. I want to know whether —your child has the right to live under my roof.

GINA (*draws herself up; her eyes flash*). You ask that!

HIALMAR. You shall answer me this one question: Does Hedvig belong to me—or——? Well!

GINA (*looking at him with cold defiance*). I don't know.

HIALMAR (*quivering a little*). You don't know!

GINA. How should I know. A creature like me——

HIALMAR (*quietly turning away from her*). Then I have nothing more to do in this house.

GREGERS. Take care, Hialmar! Think what you are doing!

HIALMAR (*puts on his overcoat*). In this case, there is nothing for a man like me to think twice about.

GREGERS. Yes, indeed, there are endless things to be considered. You three must be together if you are to attain the true frame of mind for self-sacrifice and forgiveness.

HIALMAR. I don't want to attain it. Never, never! My hat! (*Takes his hat*) My home has fallen in ruins about me. (*Bursts into tears*) Gregers, I have no child!

HEDVIG (*who has opened the kitchen door*). What is that you're saying? (*Coming to him*) Father, father!

GINA. There, you see!

HIALMAR. Don't come near me, Hedvig! Keep far away. I cannot bear to see you. Oh! those eyes ——! Good-bye.
(*Makes for the door.*)

HEDVIG (*clinging close to him and screaming loudly*). No! no! Don't leave me!

GINA (*cries out*). Look at the child, Ekdal! Look at the child!

HIALMAR. I will not! I cannot! I must get out—away from all this! (*He tears himself away from HEDVIG, and goes out by the passage door.*)

HEDVIG (*with despairing eyes*). He is going away from us, mother! He is going away from us! He will never come back again!

GINA. Don't cry, Hedvig. Father's sure to come back again.

HEDVIG (*throws herself sobbing on the sofa*). No, no, he'll never come home to us any more.

GREGERS. Do you believe I meant all for the best, Mrs. Ekdal?

GINA. Yes, I daresay you did; but God forgive you, all the same.

HEDVIG (*lying on the sofa*). Oh, this will kill me! What have I done to him? Mother, you must fetch him home again!

GINA. Yes, yes, yes; only be quiet, and I'll go out and look for him. (*Puts on her outdoor things*) Perhaps he's gone in to Relling's. But you mustn't lie there and cry. Promise me!

HEDVIG (*weeping convulsively*). Yes, I'll stop, I'll stop; if only father comes back!

GREGERS (*to* GINA, *who is going*). After all, had you not better leave him to fight out his bitter fight to the end?

GINA. Oh, he can do that afterwards. First of all, we must get the child quieted. (*Goes out by the passage door.*)

HEDVIG (*sits up and dries her tears*). Now you must tell me what all this means. Why doesn't father want me any more?

GREGERS. You mustn't ask that till you are a big girl—quite grown-up.

HEDVIG (*sobs*). But I can't go on being as miserable as this till I'm grown-up.—I think I know what it is.—Perhaps I'm not really father's child.

GREGERS (*uneasily*). How could that be?

HEDVIG. Mother might have found me. And perhaps father has just got to know it; I've read of such things.

GREGERS. Well, but if it were so ——

HEDVIG. I think he might be just as fond of me for all that. Yes, fonder almost. We got the wild duck in a present, you know, and I love it so dearly all the same.

GREGERS (*turning the conversation*). Ah, the wild duck, by-the-bye! Let us talk about the wild duck a little, Hedvig.

HEDVIG. The poor wild duck! He doesn't want to see it any more, either. Only think, he wanted to wring its neck!

GREGERS. Oh, he won't do that.

HEDVIG. No; but he said he would like to. And I think it was horrid of father to say it; for I pray for the wild duck every night, and ask that it may be preserved from death and all that is evil.

GREGERS (*looking at her*). Do you say your prayers every night?

HEDVIG. Yes.

GREGERS. Who taught you to do that?

HEDVIG. I myself; one time when father was very ill, and had leeches on his neck, and said that death was staring him in the face.

GREGERS. Well?

HEDVIG. Then I prayed for him as I lay in bed; and since then I have always kept it up.

GREGERS. And now you pray for the wild duck too?

HEDVIG. I thought it was best to bring in the wild duck; for she was so weakly at first.

GREGERS. Do you pray in the morning, too?

HEDVIG. No, of course not.

GREGERS. Why not in the morning as well?

HEDVIG. In the morning it's light, you know, and there's nothing in particular to be afraid of.

GREGERS. And your father was going to wring the neck of the wild duck that you love so dearly?

HEDVIG. No; he said he ought to wring its neck, but he would spare it for my sake; and that was kind of father.

GREGERS (*coming a little nearer*). But suppose you were to sacrifice the wild duck of your own free will for his sake.

HEDVIG (*rising*). The wild duck!

GREGERS. Suppose you were to make a free-will offering, for his sake, of the dearest treasure you have in the world!

HEDVIG. Do you think that would do any good?

GREGERS. Try it, Hedvig.

HEDVIG (*softly, with flashing eyes*). Yes, I will try it.

GREGERS. Have you really the courage for it, do you think?

HEDVIG. I'll ask grandfather to shoot the wild duck for me.

GREGERS. Yes, do. But not a word to your mother about it.

HEDVIG. Why not?

GREGERS. She doesn't understand us.

HEDVIG. The wild duck! I'll try it tomorrow morning.
(GINA *comes in by the passage door.*)

HEDVIG (*going towards her*). Did you find him, mother?

GINA. No, but I heard as he had called and taken Relling with him.

GREGERS. Are you sure of that?

GINA. Yes, the porter's wife said so. Molvik went with them too, she said.

GREGERS. This evening, when his mind so sorely needs to wrestle in solitude——!

GINA (*takes off her things*). Yes, men are strange creatures, so they are. The Lord only knows where Relling has dragged him to! I ran over to Madam Eriksen's, but they weren't there.

HEDVIG (*struggling to keep back her tears*). Oh, if he should never come home any more!

GREGERS. He will come home again. I shall have news to give him to-morrow; and then you shall see how he comes home. You may rely upon that, Hedvig, and sleep in peace. Good night. (*He goes out by the passage door.*)

HEDVIG (*throws herself sobbing on* GINA's *neck*). Mother, mother!

GINA (*pats her shoulder and sighs*). Ah, yes; Relling was right, he was. That's what comes of it when crazy creatures go about presenting the claims of the—what-you-may-call-it.

ACT FIVE

HIALMAR EKDAL's *studio. Cold, grey morning light. Wet snow lies upon the large panes of the sloping roof-window.*

GINA *comes from the kitchen with an apron and bib on, and carrying a dusting-brush and a duster; she goes towards the sitting-room door. At the same moment* HEDVIG *comes hurriedly in from the passage.*

GINA (*stops*). Well?

HEDVIG. Oh, mother, I almost think he's down at Relling's——

GINA. There, you see!

HEDVIG. ——because the porter's wife says she could hear that Relling had two people with him when he came home last night.

GINA. That's just what I thought.

HEDVIG. But it's no use his being there, if he won't come up to us.

GINA. I'll go down and speak to him at all events.

(OLD EKDAL, *in dressing-gown and slippers, and with a lighted pipe, appears at the door of his room.*)

EKDAL. Hialmar—— Isn't Hialmar at home?

GINA. No, he's gone out.

EKDAL. So early? And in such a tearing snowstorm? Well well; just as he pleases; I can take my morning walk alone. (*He slides the garret door aside;* HEDVIG *helps him; he goes in; she closes it after him.*)

HEDVIG (*in an undertone*). Only think, mother, when poor grandfather hears that father is going to leave us.

GINA. Oh, nonsense; grandfather mustn't hear anything about it. It was a heaven's mercy he wasn't at home yesterday in all that hurlyburly.

HEDVIG. Yes, but——
(GREGERS *comes in by the passage door.*)

GREGERS. Well, have you any news of him?

GINA. They say he's down at Relling's.

GREGERS. At Relling's! Has he really been out with those creatures?

GINA. Yes, like enough.

GREGERS. When he ought to have been yearning for solitude, to collect and clear his thoughts——

GINA. Yes, you may well say so.
(RELLING *enters from the passage.*)

HEDVIG (*going to him*). Is father in your room?

GINA (*at the same time*). Is he there?

RELLING. Yes, to be sure he is

HEDVIG. And you never let us know!

RELLING. Yes; I'm a brute. But in the first place I had to look after the other brute; I mean our dæmonic friend, of course; and then I fell so dead asleep that——

GINA. What does Ekdal say today?

RELLING. He says nothing whatever.

HEDVIG. Doesn't he speak?

RELLING. Not a blessed word.

GREGERS. No, no; I can understand that very well.

GINA. But what's he doing, then?

RELLING. He's lying on the sofa, snoring.

GINA. Oh is he? Yes, Ekdal's a rare one to snore.

HEDVIG. Asleep? Can he sleep?

RELLING. Well, it certainly looks like it.

GREGERS. No wonder, after the spiritual conflict that has rent him——

GINA. And then he's never been used to gadding about out of doors at night.

HEDVIG. Perhaps it's a good thing that he's getting sleep, mother.

GINA. Of course it is; and we must take care we don't wake him up too early. Thank you, Relling. I must get the house cleaned up a bit now, and then—— Come and help me, Hedvig. (GINA *and* HEDVIG *go into the sitting room.*)

GREGERS (*turning to* RELLING). What is your explanation of the spiritual tumult that is now going on in Hialmar Ekdal?

RELLING. Devil a bit of a spiritual tumult have *I* noticed in him.

GREGERS. What! Not at such a crisis, when his whole life has been placed on a new foundation——? How can you think that such an individuality as Hialmar's——?

RELLING. Oh, individuality—he! If he ever had any tendency to the abnormal developments you call individuality, I can assure you it was rooted out of him while he was still in his teens.

GREGERS. That would be strange indeed—considering the loving care with which he was brought up.

RELLING. By those two high-flown, hysterical maiden aunts, you mean?

GREGERS. Let me tell you that they were women who never forgot the claim of the ideal—but of course you will only jeer at me again.

RELLING. No, I'm in no humour for that. I know all about those ladies; for he has ladled out no end of rhetoric on the subject of his "two soul-mothers." But I don't think he has much to thank them for. Ekdal's misfortune is that in his own circle he has always been looked upon as a shining light——

GREGERS. Not without reason, surely. Look at the depth of his mind!

RELLING. *I* have never discovered it. That his father believed in it I don't so much wonder; the old lieutenant has been an ass all his days.

GREGERS. He has had a child-like mind all his days; that is what you cannot understand.

RELLING. Well, so be it. But then, when our dear, sweet Hialmar went to college, he at once passed for the great light of the future amongst his comrades too. He was handsome, the rascal—red and white— a shop-girl's dream of manly beauty; and with his superficially emotional temperament, and his sympathetic voice, and his talent for declaiming other people's verses and other people's thoughts——

GREGERS (*indignantly*). Is it Hialmar Ekdal you are talking about in this strain?

RELLING. Yes, with your permission; I am simply giving you an inside view of the idol you are grovelling before.

GREGERS. I should hardly have thought I was quite stone blind.

RELLING. Yes, you are—or not far from it. You are a sick man, too, you see.

GREGERS. You are right there.

RELLING. Yes. Yours is a complicated case. First of all there is that plaguey integrity-fever; and then— what's worse—you are always in a delirium of hero-worship; you must always have something to adore, outside yourself.

GREGERS. Yes, I must certainly seek it outside myself.

RELLING. But you make such shocking mistakes about every new phœnix you think you have discovered. Here again you have come to a cotter's cabin with your claim of the ideal; and the people of the house are insolvent.

GREGERS. If you don't think better than that of Hialmar Ekdal, what pleasure can you find in being everlastingly with him?

RELLING. Well, you see, I'm supposed to be a sort of a doctor— save the mark! I can't but give a hand to the poor sick folk who live under the same roof with me.

GREGERS. Oh, indeed! Hialmar Ekdal is sick too, is he!

RELLING. Most people are, worse luck.

GREGERS. And what remedy are you applying in Hialmar's case?

RELLING. My usual one. I am cultivating the life-illusion * in him.

GREGERS. Life—illusion? I didn't catch what you said.

RELLING. Yes, I said illusion. For illusion, you know, is the stimulating principle.

GREGERS. May I ask with what illusion Hialmar is inoculated?

RELLING. No, thank you; I don't betray professional secrets to quacksalvers. You would probably go and muddle his case still more than you have already. But my method is infallible. I have applied it to Mol-

* "Livslögnen," literally "the life-lie."

vik as well. I have made him "dæmonic." That's the blister I have to put on his neck.

GREGERS. Is he not really dæmonic then?

RELLING. What the devil do you mean by dæmonic! It's only a piece of gibberish I've invented to keep up a spark of life in him. But for that, the poor harmless creature would have succumbed to self-contempt and despair many a long year ago. And then the old lieutenant! But he has hit upon his own cure, you see.

GREGERS. Lieutenant Ekdal? What of him?

RELLING. Just think of the old bearhunter shutting himself up in that dark garret to shoot rabbits! I tell you there is not a happier sportsman in the world than that old man pottering about in there among all that rubbish. The four or five withered Christmas trees he has saved up are the same to him as the whole great fresh Höidal forest; the cock and the hens are big game-birds in the fir-tops; and the rabbits that flop about the garret floor are the bears he has to battle with—the mighty hunter of the mountains!

GREGERS. Poor unfortunate old man! Yes, he has indeed had to narrow the ideals of his youth.

RELLING. While I think of it, Mr. Werle, junior—don't use that foreign word: ideals. We have the excellent native word: lies.

GREGERS. Do you think the two things are related?

RELLING. Yes, just about as closely as typhus and putrid fever.

GREGERS. Dr. Relling, I shall not give up the struggle until I have rescued Hialmar from your clutches!

RELLING. So much the worse for him. Rob the average man of his life-illusion, and you rob him of his happiness at the same stroke. (*To* HEDVIG, *who comes in from the sitting room*) Well, little wild-duck-mother, I'm just going down to see whether papa is still lying meditating upon that wonderful invention of his. (*Goes out by passage door.*)

GREGERS (*approaches* HEDVIG). I can see by your face that you have not yet done it.

HEDVIG. What? Oh, that about the wild duck! No.

GREGERS. I suppose your courage failed when the time came.

HEDVIG. No, that wasn't it. But when I awoke this morning and remembered what we had been talking about, it seemed so strange.

GREGERS. Strange?

HEDVIG. Yes, I don't know—— Yesterday evening, at the moment, I thought there was something so delightful about it; but since I have slept and thought of it again, it somehow doesn't seem worth while.

GREGERS. Ah, I thought you could not have grown up quite unharmed in this house.

HEDVIG. I don't care about that, if only father would come up——

GREGERS. Oh, if only your eyes had been opened to that which gives life its value—if you possessed the true, joyous, fearless spirit of sacrifice, you would soon see how he would come up to you.—But I believe in you still, Hedvig. (*He goes out by the passage door.* HEDVIG *wanders about the room for a time; she is on the point of going into the kitchen when a knock is heard at the garret door.* HEDVIG *goes over and opens it a little; old* EKDAL *comes out; she pushes the door to again.*)

EKDAL. H'm, it's not much fun to take one's morning walk alone.

HEDVIG. Wouldn't you like to go shooting, grandfather?

EKDAL. It's not the weather for it today. It's so dark there, you can scarcely see where you're going.

HEDVIG. Do you never want to shoot anything besides the rabbits?

EKDAL. Do you think the rabbits aren't good enough?

HEDVIG. Yes, but what about the wild duck?

EKDAL. Ho-ho! are you afraid I shall shoot your wild duck? Never in the world. Never.

HEDVIG. No, I suppose you couldn't; they say it's very difficult to shoot wild ducks.

EKDAL. Couldn't! Should rather think I could.

HEDVIG. How would you set about it, grandfather?—I don't mean with my wild duck, but with others?

EKDAL. I should take care to shoot them in the breast, you know; that's the surest place. And then you must shoot against the feathers, you see—not the way of the feathers.

HEDWIG. Do they die then, grandfather?

EKDAL. Yes, they die right enough —when you shoot properly. Well, I must go and brush up a bit. H'm—understand—h'm. (*Goes into his room.*)
(HEDVIG *waits a little, glances towards the sitting-room door, goes over to the bookcase, stands on tiptoe, takes the double-barrelled pistol down from the shelf, and looks at it.* GINA, *with brush and duster, comes from the sitting room.* HEDVIG *hastily lays down the pistol, unobserved.*)

GINA. Don't stand raking amongst father's things, Hedvig.

HEDVIG (*goes away from the bookcase*). I was only going to tidy up a little.

GINA. You'd better go into the kitchen, and see if the coffee's keeping hot; I'll take his breakfast on a tray, when I go down to him. (HEDVIG *goes out.* GINA *begins to sweep and clean up the studio. Presently the passage door is opened with hesitation, and* HIALMAR EKDAL *looks in. He has on his overcoat, but not his hat; he is unwashed, and his hair is dishevelled and unkempt. His eyes are dull and heavy.*)

GINA (*standing with the brush in her hand, and looking at him*). Oh, there now, Ekdal—so you've come after all?

HIALMAR (*comes in and answers in a toneless voice*). I come—only to depart again immediately.

GINA. Yes, yes, I suppose so. But, Lord help us! what a sight you are!

HIALMAR. A sight?

GINA. And your nice winter coat too! Well, that's done for.

HEDVIG (*at the kitchen door*). Mother, hadn't I better——? (*Sees* HIALMAR, *gives a loud scream of joy, and runs to him*) Oh, father, father!

HIALMAR (*turns away and makes a gesture of repulsion*). Away, away, away! (*To* GINA) Keep her away from me, I say!

GINA (*in a low tone*). Go into the sitting room, Hedvig.
(HEDVIG *does so without a word.*)

HIALMAR (*fussily pulls out the table-drawer*). I must have my books with me. Where are my books?

GINA. Which books?

HIALMAR. My scientific books, of course; the technical magazines I require for my invention.

GINA (*searches in the bookcase*). Is it these here paper-covered ones?

HIALMAR. Yes, of course.

GINA (*lays a heap of magazines on the table*). Shan't I get Hedvig to cut them for you?

HIALMAR. I don't require to have them cut for me. (*Short silence.*)

GINA. Then you're still set on leaving us, Ekdal?

HIALMAR (*rummaging amongst the books*). Yes, that is a matter of course, I should think.

GINA. Well, well.

HIALMAR (*vehemently*). How can I live here, to be stabbed to the heart every hour of the day?

GINA. God forgive you for thinking such vile things of me.

HIALMAR. Prove——!

GINA. I think it's you as has got to prove.

HIALMAR. After a past like yours? There are certain claims—I may almost call them claims of the ideal——

GINA. But what about grandfather? What's to become of him, poor dear?

HIALMAR. I know my duty; my helpless father will come with me. I am going out into the town to make arrangements—— H'm——(*hesitatingly*)—has any one found my hat on the stairs?

GINA. No. Have you lost your hat?

HIALMAR. Of course I had it on when I came in last night; there's no doubt about that; but I couldn't find it this morning.

GINA. Lord help us! where have you been to with those two ne'er-do-weels?

HIALMAR. Oh, don't bother me about trifles. Do you suppose I am in the mood to remember details?

GINA. If only you haven't caught cold, Ekdal—— (*Goes out into the kitchen.*)

HIALMAR (*talks to himself in a low tone of irritation, while he empties the table-drawer*). You're a scoundrel, Relling!—You're a low fellow! —Ah, you shameless tempter!—I wish I could get some one to stick a knife into you! (*He lays some old letters on one side, finds the torn document of yesterday, takes it up and looks at the pieces; puts it down hurriedly as* GINA *enters.*)

GINA (*sets a tray with coffee, etc., on the table*). Here's a drop of something hot, if you'd fancy it. And there's some bread and butter and a snack of salt meat.

HIALMAR (*glancing at the tray*). Salt meat? Never under this roof! It's true I have not had a mouthful of solid food for nearly twenty-four hours; but no matter.—My memoranda! The commencement of my autobiography! What has become of my diary, and all my important papers? (*Opens the sitting-room door but draws back*) She is there too!

GINA. Good Lord! the child must be somewhere!

HIALMAR. Come out. (*He makes room,* HEDVIG *comes, scared, into the studio.*)

HIALMAR (*with his hand upon the door-handle, says to* GINA). In these, the last moments I spend in my former home, I wish to be spared from interlopers—— (*Goes into the room.*)

HEDVIG (*with a bound towards her mother, asks softly, trembling*). Does that mean me?

GINA. Stay out in the kitchen, Hedvig; or, no—you'd best go into your own room. (*Speaks to* HIALMAR *as she goes in to him.*) Wait a bit, Ekdal; don't rummage so in the drawers; I know where everything is.

HEDVIG (*stands a moment immovable, in terror and perplexity, biting her lips to keep back the tears; then she clenches her hands convulsively, and says softly*). The wild duck. (*She steals over and takes the pistol from the shelf, opens the garret door a little way, creeps in, and draws the door to after her.*) (HIALMAR *and* GINA *can be heard disputing in the sitting room.*)

HIALMAR (*comes in with some manuscript books and old loose papers, which he lays upon the table*). That portmanteau is of no use! There are a thousand and one things I must drag with me.

GINA (*following with the portmanteau*). Why not leave all the rest for the present, and only take a shirt and a pair of woollen drawers with you?

HIALMAR. Whew!—all these exhausting preparations——! (*Pulls off his overcoat and throws it upon the sofa.*)

GINA. And there's the coffee getting cold.

HIALMAR. H'm. (*Drinks a mouthful without thinking of it, and then another.*)

GINA (*dusting the backs of the chairs*). A nice job you'll have to find such another big garret for the rabbits.

HIALMAR. What! Am I to drag all those rabbits with me too?

GINA. You don't suppose grandfather can get on without his rabbits.

HIALMAR. He must just get used to doing without them. Have not I to sacrifice very much greater things than rabbits!

GINA (*dusting the bookcase*). Shall I put the flute in the portmanteau for you?

HIALMAR. No. No flute for me. But give me the pistol!

GINA. Do you want to take the pigstol with you?

HIALMAR. Yes. My loaded pistol.

GINA (*searching for it*). It's gone. He must have taken it in with him.

HIALMAR. Is he in the garret?

GINA. Yes, of course he's in the garret.

HIALMAR. H'm—poor lonely old man. (*He takes a piece of bread and butter, eats it, and finishes his cup of coffee.*)

GINA. If we hadn't have let that room, you could have moved in there.

HIALMAR. And continued to live under the same roof with——! Never—never!

GINA. But couldn't you put up with the sitting room for a day or two? You could have it all to yourself.

HIALMAR. Never within these walls!

GINA. Well then, down with Relling and Molvik.

HIALMAR. Don't mention those wretches' names to me! The very thought of them almost takes away my appetite.—Oh no, I must go out into the storm and the snow-drift— go from house to house and seek shelter for my father and myself.

GINA. But you've got no hat, Ekdal! You've been and lost your hat, you know.

HIALMAR. Oh those two brutes, those slaves of all the vices! A hat must be procured. (*Takes another piece of bread and butter*) Some arrangements must be made. For I have no mind to throw away my life, either. (*Looks for something on the tray.*)

GINA. What are you looking for?

HIALMAR. Butter.

GINA. I'll get some at once. (*Goes out into the kitchen.*)

HIALMAR (*calls after her*). Oh it doesn't matter; dry bread is good enough for me.

GINA (*brings a dish of butter*). Look here; this is fresh churned. (*She pours out another cup of coffee for him; he seats himself on the sofa, spreads more butter on the already buttered bread, and eats and drinks awhile in silence.*)

HIALMAR. Could I, without being subject to intrusion—intrusion of any sort—could I live in the sitting-room there for a day or two?

GINA. Yes, to be sure you could, if you only would.

HIALMAR. For I see no possibility of getting all father's things out in such a hurry.

GINA. And, besides, you've surely got to tell him first as you don't mean to live with us others no more.

HIALMAR (*pushes away his coffee cup*). Yes, there is that too; I shall have to lay bare the whole tangled story to him—— I must turn matters over; I must have breathing-time; I cannot take all these burdens on my shoulders in a single day.

GINA. No, especially in such horrible weather as it is outside.

HIALMAR (*touching* WERLE's *letter*). I see that paper is still lying about here.

GINA. Yes, I haven't touched it.

HIALMAR. So far as I am concerned it is mere waste paper——

GINA. Well, I have certainly no notion of making any use of it.

HIALMAR. ——but we had better not let it get lost all the same—in all the upset when I move, it might easily——

GINA. I'll take good care of it, Ekdal.

HIALMAR. The donation is in the first instance made to father, and it rests with him to accept or decline it.

GINA (*sighs*). Yes, poor old father ——

HIALMAR. To make quite safe—— Where shall I find some gum?

GINA (*goes to the bookcase*). Here's the gum-pot.

HIALMAR. And a brush?

GINA. The brush is here too. (*Brings him the things.*)

HIALMAR (*takes a pair of scissors*). Just a strip of paper at the back ——(*Clips and gums*) Far be it from me to lay hands upon what is not my own—and least of all upon what belongs to a destitute old man—and to—the other as well.—There now. Let it lie there for a time; and when it is dry, take it away. I wish never to see that document again. Never!
(GREGERS WERLE *enters from the passage.*)

GREGERS (*somewhat surprised*). What—are you sitting here, Hialmar?

HIALMAR (*rises hurriedly*). I had sunk down from fatigue.

GREGERS. You have been having breakfast, I see.

HIALMAR. The body sometimes makes its claims felt too.

GREGERS. What have you decided to do?

HIALMAR. For a man like me, there is only one course possible. I am just putting my most important things together. But it takes time, you know.

GINA (*with a touch of impatience*). Am I to get the room ready for you, or am I to pack your portmanteau?

HIALMAR (*after a glance of annoyance at* GREGERS). Pack—and get the room ready!

GINA (*takes the portmanteau*). Very well; then I'll put in the shirt and the other things. (*Goes into the sitting room and draws the door to after her.*)

GREGERS (*after a short silence*). I never dreamed that this would be the end of it. Do you really feel it a necessity to leave house and home?

HIALMAR (*wanders about restlessly*). What would you have me do?—I am not fitted to bear unhappiness, Gregers. I must feel secure and at peace in my surroundings.

GREGERS. But can you not feel that here? Just try it. I should have thought you had firm ground to build upon now—if only you start afresh. And, remember, you have your invention to live for.

HIALMAR. Oh don't talk about my invention. It's perhaps still in the dim distance.

GREGERS. Indeed!

HIALMAR. Why, great heavens, what would you have me invent? Other people have invented almost everything already. It becomes more and more difficult every day ——

GREGERS. And you have devoted so much labour to it.

HIALMAR. It was that blackguard Relling that urged me to it.

GREGERS. Relling?

HIALMAR. Yes, it was he that first made me realise my aptitude for making some notable discovery in photography.

GREGERS. Aha—it was Relling!

HIALMAR. Oh, I have been so truly happy over it! Not so much for the sake of the invention itself, as because Hedvig believed in it—believed in it with a child's whole eagerness of faith.—At least, I have been fool enough to go and imagine that she believed in it.

GREGERS. Can you really think Hedvig has been false towards you?

HIALMAR. I can think anything now. It is Hedvig that stands in my way. She will blot out the sunlight from my whole life.

GREGERS. Hedvig! Is it Hedvig you are talking of? How should she blot out your sunlight?

HIALMAR (without answering). How unutterably I have loved that child! How unutterably happy I have felt every time I came home

to my humble room, and she flew to meet me, with her sweet little blinking eyes. Oh, confiding fool that I have been! I loved her unutterably—and I yielded myself up to the dream, the delusion, that she loved me unutterably in return.

GREGERS. Do you call that a delusion?

HIALMAR. How should I know? I can get nothing out of Gina; and besides, she is totally blind to the ideal side of these complications. But to you I feel impelled to open my mind, Gregers. I cannot shake off this frightful doubt—perhaps Hedvig has never really and honestly loved me.

GREGERS. What would you say if she were to give you a proof of her love? (Listens) What's that? I thought I heard the wild duck ——?

HIALMAR. It's the wild duck quacking. Father's in the garret.

GREGERS. Is he? (His face lights up with joy) I say you may yet have proof that your poor misunderstood Hedvig loves you!

HIALMAR. Oh, what proof can she give me? I dare not believe in any assurance from that quarter.

GREGERS. Hedvig does not know what deceit means.

HIALMAR. Oh Gregers, that is just what I cannot be sure of. Who knows what Gina and that Mrs. Sörby may many a time have sat here whispering and tattling about? And Hedvig usually has her ears open, I can tell you. Perhaps the deed of gift was not such a surprise to her, after all. In fact, I'm not sure but that I noticed something of the sort.

GREGERS. What spirit is this that has taken possession of you?

HIALMAR. I have had my eyes opened. Just you notice;—you'll see, the deed of gift is only a beginning. Mrs. Sörby has always been a good deal taken up with Hedvig; and now she has the power to do whatever she likes for the child. They can take her from me whenever they please.

GREGERS. Hedvig will never, never leave you.

HIALMAR. Don't be so sure of that. If only they beckon to her and throw out a golden bait——! And oh! I have loved her so unspeakably! I would have counted it my highest happiness to take her tenderly by the hand and lead her, as one leads a timid child through a great dark empty room!—I am cruelly certain now that the poor photographer in his humble attic has never really and truly been anything to her. She has only cunningly contrived to keep on a good footing with him until the time came.

GREGERS. You don't believe that yourself, Hialmar.

HIALMAR. That is just the terrible part of it—I don't know what to believe—I never can know it. But can you really doubt that it must be as I say? Ho-ho, you have far too much faith in the claim of the ideal, my good Gregers! If those others came, with the glamour of wealth about them, and called to the child:—"Leave him: come to us: here life awaits you——!"

GREGERS (quickly). Well, what then?

HIALMAR. If I then asked her: Hedvig, are you willing to renounce that life for me? (Laughs scornfully) No thank you! You would soon hear what answer I should get. (A pistol shot is heard from within the garret.)

GREGERS (loudly and joyfully). Hialmar!

HIALMAR. There now; he must needs go shooting too.

GINA (comes in). Oh Ekdal, I can hear grandfather blazing away in the garret by hisself.

HIALMAR. I'll look in——

GREGERS (eagerly, with emotion). Wait a moment! Do you know what that was?

HIALMAR. Yes, of course I know.

GREGERS. No you don't know. But I do. That was the proof!

HIALMAR. What proof?

GREGERS. It was a child's free-will offering. She has got your father to shoot the wild duck.

HIALMAR. To shoot the wild duck!

GINA. Oh, think of that——!

HIALMAR. What was that for?

GREGERS. She wanted to sacrifice to you her most cherished possession;

for then she thought you would surely come to love her again.

HIALMAR (*tenderly, with emotion*). Oh, poor child!

GINA. What things she does think of!

GREGERS. She only wanted your love again, Hialmar. She could not live without it.

GINA (*struggling with her tears*). There, you can see for yourself, Ekdal.

HIALMAR. Gina, where is she?

GINA (*sniffs*). Poor dear, she's sitting out in the kitchen, I dare say.

HIALMAR (*goes over, tears open the kitchen door, and says*). Hedvig, come, come in to me! (*Looks around*) No, she's not here.

GINA. Then she must be in her own little room.

HIALMAR (*without*). No, she's not here either. (*Comes in*) She must have gone out.

GINA. Yes, you wouldn't have her anywheres in the house.

HIALMAR. Oh, if she would only come home quickly, so that I can tell her—— Everything will come right now, Gregers; now I believe we can begin life afresh.

GREGERS (*quietly*). I knew it; I knew the child would make amends. (OLD EKDAL *appears at the door of his room; he is in full uniform, and is busy buckling on his sword.*)

HIALMAR (*astonished*). Father! Are you there?

GINA. Have you been firing in your room?

EKDAL (*resentfully, approaching*). So you go shooting alone, do you, Hialmar?

HIALMAR (*excited and confused*). Then it wasn't you that fired that shot in the garret?

EKDAL. Me that fired? H'm.

GREGERS (*calls out to* HIALMAR). She has shot the wild duck herself!

HIALMAR. What can it mean? (*Hastens to the garret door, tears it aside, looks in and calls loudly*): Hedvig!

GINA (*runs to the door*). Good God, what's that!

HIALMAR (*goes in*). She's lying on the floor!

GREGERS. Hedvig! lying on the floor! (*Goes in to* HIALMAR.)

GINA (*at the same time*). Hedvig! (*Inside the garret*) No, no, no!

EKDAL. Ho-ho! does she go shooting, too, now?
(HIALMAR, GINA *and* GREGERS *carry* HEDVIG *into the studio; in her dangling right hand she holds the pistol fast clasped in her fingers.*)

HIALMAR (*distracted*). The pistol has gone off. She has wounded herself. Call for help! Help!

GINA (*runs into the passage and calls down*). Relling! Relling! Doc·

tor Relling; come up as quick as you can!

(HIALMAR *and* GREGERS *lay* HEDVIG *down on the sofa.*)

EKDAL (*quietly*). The woods avenge themselves.

HIALMAR (*on his knees beside* HEDVIG). She'll soon come to now. She's coming to——; yes, yes, yes.

GINA (*who has come in again*). Where has she hurt herself? I can't see anything——

(RELLING *comes hurriedly, and immediately after him* MOLVIK; *the latter without his waistcoat and necktie, and with his coat open.*)

RELLING. What's the matter here?

GINA. They say Hedvig has shot herself.

HIALMAR. Come and help us!

RELLING. Shot herself! (*He pushes the table aside and begins to examine her.*)

HIALMAR (*kneeling and looking anxiously up at him*). It can't be dangerous? Speak, Relling! She is scarcely bleeding at all. It can't be dangerous?

RELLING. How did it happen?

HIALMAR. Oh, we don't know——

GINA. She wanted to shoot the wild duck.

RELLING. The wild duck?

HIALMAR. The pistol must have gone off.

RELLING. H'm. Indeed.

EKDAL. The woods avenge themselves. But I'm not afraid, all the same. (*Goes into the garret and closes the door after him.*)

HIALMAR. Well, Relling—why don't you say something?

RELLING. The ball has entered the breast.

HIALMAR. Yes, but she's coming to!

RELLING. Surely you can see that Hedvig is dead.

GINA (*bursts into tears*). Oh my child, my child——

GREGERS (*huskily*). In the depths of the sea——

HIALMAR (*jumps up*). No, no, she must live! Oh, for God's sake, Relling—only a moment—only just till I can tell her how unspeakably I loved her all the time!

RELLING. The bullet has gone through her heart. Internal hemorrhage. Death must have been instantaneous.

HIALMAR. And I! I hunted her from me like an animal! And she crept terrified into the garret and died for love of me! (*Sobbing*) I can never atone to her! I can never tell her——! (*Clenches his hands and cries, upwards*) O thou above——! If thou be indeed! Why hast thou done this thing to me?

GINA. Hush, hush, you mustn't go on that awful way. We had no right to keep her, I suppose.

MOLVIK. The child is not dead, but sleepeth.

RELLING. Bosh.

HIALMAR (*becomes calm, goes over to the sofa, folds his arms, and looks at* HEDVIG). There she lies so stiff and still.

RELLING (*tries to loosen the pistol . She's holding it so tight, so tight.*

GINA. No, no, Relling, don't break her fingers; let the pigstol be.

HIALMAR. She shall take it with her.

GINA. Yes, let her. But the child mustn't lie here for a show. She shall go to her own room, so she shall. Help me, Ekdal.
(HIALMAR *and* GINA *take* HEDVIG *between them.*)

HIALMAR (*as they are carrying her*). Oh, Gina, Gina, can you survive this!

GINA. We must help each other to bear it. For now at least she belongs to both of us.

MOLVIK (*stretches out his arms and mumbles*). Blessed be the Lord; to earth thou shalt return; to earth thou shalt return——

RELLING (*whispers*). Hold your tongue, you fool; you're drunk.
(HIALMAR *and* GINA *carry the body out through the kitchen door.* RELLING *shuts it after them.* MOLVIK *slinks out into the passage.*)

RELLING (*goes over to* GREGERS *and says*). No one shall ever convince me that the pistol went off by accident.

GREGERS (*who has stood terrified, with convulsive twitchings*). Who can say how the dreadful thing happened?

RELLING. The powder has burnt the body of her dress. She must have pressed the pistol right against her breast and fired.

GREGERS. Hedvig has not died in vain. Did you not see how sorrow set free what is noble in him?

RELLING. Most people are ennobled by the actual presence of death. But how long do you suppose this nobility will last in him?

GREGERS. Why should it not endure and increase throughout his life?

RELLING. Before a year is over, little Hedvig will be nothing to him but a pretty theme for declamation.

GREGERS. How dare you say that of Hialmar Ekdal?

RELLING. We will talk of this again, when the grass has first withered on her grave. Then you'll hear him spouting about "the child too early torn from her father's heart"; then you'll see him steep himself in a syrup of sentiment and self-admiration and self-pity. Just you wait!

GREGERS. If you are right and I am wrong, then life is not worth living.

RELLING. Oh, life would be quite tolerable, after all, if only we could be rid of the confounded duns that keep on pestering us, in our poverty, with the claim of the ideal.

GREGERS (*looking straight before him*). In that case, I am glad that my destiny is what it is.

RELLING. May I inquire—what is your destiny?

GREGERS (*going*). To be the thirteenth at table.

RELLING. The devil it is.

The Weavers

A DRAMA OF THE FORTIES

BY GERHART HAUPTMANN

TRANSLATED FROM THE GERMAN
BY MARY MORISON

CHARACTERS

DREISSIGER, *fustian manufacturer.*
MRS. DREISSIGER.
PFEIFER, *manager*
NEUMANN, *cashier*
AN APPRENTICE } *in* DREISSIGER'S *employment.*
JOHN, *coachman*
A MAID
WEINHOLD, *tutor to* DREISSIGER'S *sons.*
PASTOR KITTELHAUS.
MRS. KITTELHAUS.
HEIDE, *Police Superintendent.*
KUTSCHE, *policeman.*
WELZEL, *publican.*
MRS. WELZEL.
ANNA WELZEL.
WIEGAND, *joiner.*
A COMMERCIAL TRAVELER.
A PEASANT.
A FORESTER.
SCHMIDT, *surgeon.*
HORNIG, *rag dealer.*
WITTIG, *smith.*

WEAVERS

BERKER
MORITZ JAEGER
OLD BAUMERT
MOTHER BAUMERT
BERTHA } BAUMERT
EMMA
FRITZ, EMMA'S *son (four years old)*
AUGUST BAUMERT
OLD ANSORGE

MRS. HEINRICH
OLD HILSE
MOTHER HILSE
GOTTLIEB HILSE
LUISE, GOTTLIEB'S *wife*
MIELCHEN, *their daughter*
REIMANN, *weaver*
HEIBER, *weaver*
A WEAVER'S WIFE

A number of weavers, young and old, of both sexes.
The action passes in the Forties, at Kaschbach, Peterswaldau and Langenbielau, in the Eulengebirge.

THE WEAVERS

ACT ONE

A large whitewashed room on the ground floor of DREISSIGER'S *house at Peterswaldau, where the weavers deliver their finished webs and the fustian is stored. To the left are uncurtained windows, in the back wall there is a glass door, and to the right another glass door, through which weavers, male and female, and children, are passing in and out. All three walls are lined with shelves for the storing of the fustian. Against the right wall stands a long bench, on which a number of weavers have already spread out their cloth. In the order of arrival each presents his piece to be examined by* PFEIFER, DREISSIGER'S *manager, who stands, with compass and magnifying-glass, behind a large table, on which the web to be inspected is laid. When* PFEIFER *has satisfied himself, the weaver lays the fustian on the scale, and an office apprentice tests its weight. The same boy stores the accepted pieces on the shelves.* PFEIFER *calls out the payment due in each case to* NEUMANN, *the cashier, who is seated at a small table.*

It is a sultry day towards the end of May. The clock is on the stroke of twelve. Most of the waiting workpeople have the air of standing before the bar of justice, in torturing expectation of a decision that means life or death to them. They are marked, too, by the anxious timidity characteristic of the receiver of charity, who has suffered many humiliations, and, conscious that he is barely tolerated, has acquired the habit of self-effacement. Add to this an expression on every face that tells of constant, fruitless brooding. There is a general resemblance among the men. They have something about them of the dwarf, something of the schoolmaster. The majority are flat-breasted, short-winded, sallow, and poor looking— creatures of the loom, their knees bent with much sitting. At a first glance the women show fewer typical traits. They look over-driven, worried, reckless, whereas the men still make some show of a pitiful self-respect; and their clothes are ragged, while the men's are patched and mended. Some of the young girls are not without a certain charm, consisting in a wax-like pallor, a slender figure, and large, projecting, melancholy eyes.

NEUMANN (*counting out money*). Comes to one and sevenpence halfpenny.

WEAVER'S WIFE (*about thirty, emaciated, takes up the money with trembling fingers*). Thank you, sir.

NEUMANN (*seeing that she does not move on*). Well, something wrong this time, too?

WEAVER'S WIFE (*agitated, imploringly*). Do you think I might have a few pence in advance, sir? I need it that bad.

89

NEUMANN. And I need a few pounds. If it was only a question of needing it—! (*Already occupied in counting out another weaver's money, shortly*) It's Mr. Dreissiger who settles about pay in advance.

WEAVER'S WIFE. Couldn't I speak to Mr. Dreissiger himself, then, sir?

PFEIFER (*now manager, formerly weaver. The type is unmistakable, only he is well fed, well dressed, clean-shaven; also takes snuff copiously. He calls out roughly*). Mr. Dreissiger would have enough to do if he had to attend to every trifle himself. That's what we are here for. (*He measures, and then examines through the magnifying-glass*) Mercy on us! what a draught! (*Puts a thick muffler round his neck*) Shut the door, whoever comes in.

APPRENTICE (*loudly to* PFEIFER). You might as well talk to stocks and stones.

PFEIFER. That's done!—Weigh! (*The weaver places his web on the scales*) If you only understood your business a little better! Full of lumps again. . . . I hardly need to look at the cloth to see them. Call yourself a weaver, and "draw as long a bow" as you've done there! (BECKER *has entered. A young, exceptionally powerfully-built weaver; offhand, almost bold in manner.* PFEIFER, NEUMANN, *and the* APPRENTICE *exchange looks of mutual understanding as he comes in.*)

BECKER. Devil take it! This is a sweating job, and no mistake.

FIRST WEAVER (*in a low voice*). This blazing heat means rain. (OLD BAUMERT *forces his way in at*

the glass door on the right, through which the crowd of weavers can be seen, standing shoulder to shoulder, waiting their turn. The old man stumbles forward and lays his bundle on the bench, beside BECKER'S. He sits down by it, and wipes the sweat from his face.*)

OLD BAUMERT. A man has a right to a rest after that.

BECKER. Rest's better than money.

OLD BAUMERT. Yes, but we *needs* the money, too. Good mornin' to you, Becker!

BECKER. Morning, Father Baumert! Goodness knows how long we'll have to stand here again.

FIRST WEAVER. And what does that matter? What's to hinder a weaver waitin' for an hour, or for a day if need be? What else is he there for?

PFEIFER. Silence there! We can't hear our own voices.

BECKER (*in a low voice*). This is one of his bad days.

PFEIFER (*to the weaver standing before him*). How often have I told you that you must bring cleaner cloth? What sort of mess is this? Knots, and straw, and all kinds of dirt.

REIMANN. It's for want of a new picker, sir.

APPRENTICE (*has weighed the piece*). Short weight, too.

PFEIFER. I never saw such weavers. I hate to give out the yarn to them. It was another story in my day! I'd have caught it finely from my master for work like that. The business was carried on in different style then. A man had to know his trade —that's the last thing that's thought of nowadays. Reimann, one shilling.

REIMANN. But there's always a pound allowed for waste.

PFEIFER. I've no time. Next man!— What have you to show?

HEIBER (*lays his web on the table. While* PFEIFER *is examining it, he goes close up to him; eagerly in a low tone*). Beg pardon, Mr. Pfeifer, but I wanted to ask you, sir, if you would perhaps be so very kind as do me the favor an' not take my advance money off this week's pay.

PFEIFER (*measuring and examining the texture; jeeringly*). Well! What next, I wonder? This looks very much as if half the weft had stuck to the bobbins again.

HEIBER (*continues*). I'll be sure to make it all right next week, sir. But this last week I've had to put in two days' work on the estate. And my missus is ill in bed. . . .

PFEIFER (*giving the web to be weighed*). Another piece of real slop-work. (*Already examining a new web*) What a selvage! Here it's broad, there it's narrow; here it's drawn in by the wefts goodness knows how tight, and there it's torn out again by the temples. And hardly seventy threads weft to the inch. What's come of the rest? Do you call this honest work? I never saw anything like it.

(HEIBER, *repressing tears, stands humiliated and helpless.*)

BECKER (*in a low voice to* BAUMERT). To please that brute you would have to pay for extra yarn out of your own pocket.

(*The* WEAVER'S WIFE, *who has remained standing near the cashier's table, from time to time looking round appealingly, takes courage and once more comes forward.*)

WEAVER'S WIFE (*to cashier imploringly*). I don't know what's to come of me, sir, if you won't give me a little advance this time—O Lord, O Lord!

PFEIFER (*calls across*). It's no good whining, or dragging the Lord's name into the matter. You're not so anxious about Him at other times. You look after your husband and see that he's not to be found so often lounging in the public house. We can give no pay in advance. We have to account for every penny. It's not our money. People that are industrious, and understand their work, and do it in the fear of God, never need their pay in advance. So now you know.

NEUMANN. If a Bielau weaver got four times as much pay, he would squander it four times over and be in debt into the bargain.

WEAVER'S WIFE (*in a loud voice, as if appealing to the general sense of justice*). No one can't call me idle, but I'm not fit now for what I once was. I've twice had a miscarriage. And as to John, he's but a poor creature. He's been to the shepherd at Zerlau, but he couldn't do him no good, and . . . you can't do more than you've strength for. . . . We works as hard as ever we can. This many a week I've been at it till far on into the night. An' we'll keep our heads above water right enough if I can just get a bit of strength into me. But you must have pity on us, Mr. Pfeifer, sir. (*Eagerly, coaxingly*) You'll please be so very kind as to let me have a few pence on the next job, sir?

PFEIFER (*paying no attention*). Fielder, one and twopence.

WEAVER'S WIFE. Only a few pence, to buy bread with. We can't get no more credit. We've a lot of little ones.

NEUMANN (*half aside to the AP-PRENTICE, in a serio-comic tone*). "Every year brings a child to the linen-weaver's wife, heigh-ho, heigh-ho, heigh."

APPRENTICE (*takes up the rhyme, half singing*). "And the little brat it's blind the first weeks of its life, heigh-ho, heigh-ho, heigh."

REIMANN (*not touching the money which the cashier has counted out to him*). We've always got one and fourpence for the web.

PFEIFER (*calls across*). If our terms don't suit you, Reimann, you have only to say so. There's no scarcity of weavers—especially of your sort. For full weight we give full pay.

REIMANN. How anything can be wrong with the weight is past . . .

PFEIFER. You bring a piece of fustian with no faults in it, and there will be no fault in the pay.

REIMANN. It's not possible that there's too many knots in this web.

PFEIFER (*examining*). If you want to live well, then be sure you weave well.

HEIBER (*has remained standing near PFEIFER, so as to seize on any favorable opportunity. He laughs at PFEIFER's little witticism, then steps forward and again addresses him*). I wanted to ask you, sir, if you would perhaps have the great kindness not to take my advance of sixpence off today's pay? My missus has been bedridden since February. She can't do a hand's turn for me, and I've to pay a bobbin girl. And so . . .

PFEIFER (*takes a pinch of snuff*). Heiber, do you think I have no one to attend to but you? The others must have their turn.

REIMANN. As the warp was given me I took it home and fastened it to the beam. I can't bring back better yarn than I get.

PFEIFER. If you are not satisfied, you need come for no more. There are plenty ready to tramp the soles off their shoes to get it.

NEUMANN (*to REIMANN*). Do you not want your money?

REIMANN. I can't bring myself to take such pay.

NEUMANN (*paying no further attention to REIMANN*). Heiber, one shilling. Deduct sixpence for pay in advance. Leave sixpence.

HEIBER (*goes up to the table, looks at the money, stands shaking his head as if unable to believe his eyes, then slowly takes it up*). Well, I never!—(*Sighing*) Oh, dear, oh, dear!

OLD BAUMERT (*looking into* HEIBER's *face*). Yes, Franz, that's so! There's matter enough for sighing.

HEIBER (*speaking with difficulty*). I've a girl lying sick at home, too, an' she needs a bottle of medicine.

OLD BAUMERT. What's wrong with her?

HEIBER. Well, you see, she's always been a sickly bit of a thing. I don't know. . . . I needn't mind tellin' you—she brought her trouble with her. It's in her blood, and it breaks out here, there, and everywhere.

OLD BAUMERT. It's always the way. Let folks be poor, and one trouble comes to them on the top of another. There's no help for it and there's no end to it.

HEIBER. What are you carryin' in that cloth, Father Baumert?

OLD BAUMERT. We haven't so much as a bite in the house, and so I've had the little dog killed. There's not much on him, for the poor beast was half starved. A nice little dog he was! I couldn't kill him myself. I hadn't the heart to do it.

PFEIFER (*has inspected* BECKER's *web—calls*). Becker, one and threepence.

BECKER. That's what you might give to a beggar: it's not pay.

PFEIFER. Everyone who has been attended to must clear out. We haven't room to turn round in.

BECKER (*to those standing near, without lowering his voice*). It's a beggarly pittance, nothing else. A man works his treadle from early

morning till late at night, an' when he has bent over his loom for days an' days, tired to death every evening, sick with the dust and the heat, he finds he's made a beggarly one and threepence!

PFEIFER. No impudence allowed here.

BECKER. If you think I'll hold my tongue for your telling, you're much mistaken.

PFEIFER (*exclaims*). We'll see about that! (*Rushes to the glass door and calls into the office*) Mr. Dreissiger, Mr. Dreissiger, will you be good enough to come here?
(*Enter* DREISSIGER. *About forty, full-bodied, asthmatic. Looks severe.*)

DREISSIGER. What is it, Pfeifer?

PFEIFER (*spitefully*). Becker says he won't be told to hold his tongue.

DREISSIGER (*draws himself up, throws back his head, stares at* BECKER; *his nostrils tremble*). Oh, indeed!—Becker. (*To* PFEIFER) Is he the man? . . .
(*The clerks nod.*)

BECKER (*insolently*). Yes, Mr. Dreissiger, yes! (*Pointing to himself*) This is the man. (*Pointing to* DREISSIGER) And that's a man, too!

DREISSIGER (*angrily*). Fellow, how dare you?

PFEIFER. He's too well off. He'll go dancing on the ice once too often, though.

BECKER (*recklessly*). You shut up, you Jack-in-the-box. Your mother must have gone dancing once too often with Satan to have got such a devil for a son.

DREISSIGER (*now in a violent passion, roars*). Hold your tongue this moment, sir, or . . . (*He trembles and takes a few steps forward.*)

BECKER (*holding his ground steadily*). I'm not deaf. My hearing's quite good yet.

DREISSIGER (*controls himself, asks in an apparently cool business tone*). Was this fellow not one of the pack . . . ?

PFEIFER. He's a Bielau weaver. When there's any mischief going, they are sure to be in it.

DREISSIGER (*trembling*). Well, I give you all warning: if the same thing happens again as last night— a troop of half-drunken cubs marching past my windows singing that low song . . .

BECKER. Is it "Bloody Justice" you mean?

DREISSIGER. You know well enough what I mean. I tell you that if I hear it again I'll get hold of one of you, and—mind, I'm not joking— before the justice he shall go. And if I can find out who it was that made up that vile doggerel . . .

BECKER. It's a beautiful song, that's what it is!

DREISSIGER. Another word and I send for the police on the spot, without more ado. I'll make short work with you young fellows. I've got the better of very different men before now.

BECKER. I believe you there. A real thoroughbred manufacturer will get the better of two or three hundred weavers in the time it takes you to turn round—swallow them up, and not leave as much as a bone. He's got four stomachs like a cow, and teeth like a wolf. That's nothing to him at all!

DREISSIGER (*to his clerks*). That man gets no more work from us.

BECKER. It's all the same to me whether I starve at my loom or by the roadside.

DREISSIGER. Out you go, then, this moment! . . .

BECKER (*determinedly*) Not without my pay.

DREISSIGER. How much is owing to the fellow, Neumann?

NEUMANN. One and threepence.

DREISSIGER (*takes the money hurriedly out of the cashier's hand, and flings it on the table, so that some of the coins roll off onto the floor*). There you are, then; and now, out of my sight with you!

BECKER. Not without my pay.

DREISSIGER. Do you not see it lying there? If you don't take it and go . . . It's exactly twelve now . . . The dyers are coming out for their dinner . . .

BECKER. I get my pay into my hand —here. (*Points with the fingers of his right hand at the palm of his left.*)

DREISSIGER (*to the* APPRENTICE). Pick up the money, Tilgner.

(*The* APPRENTICE *lifts the money and puts it into* BECKER's *hand.*)

BECKER. Everything in proper order. (*Deliberately takes an old purse out of his pocket and puts the money into it.*)

DREISSIGER (*as* BECKER *still does not move away*). Well? Do you want me to come and help you? (*Signs of agitation are observable among the crowd of weavers. A long, loud sigh is heard, and then a fall. General interest is at once diverted to this new event.*)

DREISSIGER. What's the matter there?

CHORUS OF WEAVERS AND WOMEN. "Someone's fainted."—"It's a little sickly boy."—"Is it a fit, or what?"

DREISSIGER. What do you say? Fainted? (*He goes nearer.*)

OLD WEAVER. There he lies, anyway.
(*They make room. A boy of about eight is seen lying on the floor as if dead.*)

DREISSIGER. Does anyone know the boy?

OLD WEAVER. He's not from our village.

OLD BAUMERT. He's like one of Weaver Heinrich's boys. (*Looks at him more closely*) Yes, that's Heinrich's little Philip.

DREISSIGER. Where do they live?

OLD BAUMERT. Up near us in Kaschbach, sir. He goes round playin' music in the evenings, and all day he's at the loom. They've nine children an' a tenth a-coming.

CHORUS OF WEAVERS AND WOMEN. "They're terrible put to it."—"The rain comes through their roof."—"The woman hasn't two shirts among the nine."

OLD BAUMERT (*taking the boy by the arm*). Now then, lad, what's wrong with you? Wake up, lad.

DREISSIGER. Some of you help me, and we'll get him up. It's disgraceful to send a sickly child this distance. Bring some water, Pfeifer.

WOMAN (*helping to lift the boy*). Surely you're not going to die, lad!

DREISSIGER. Brandy, Pfeifer, brandy will be better.

BECKER (*forgotten by all, has stood looking on. With his hand on the door-latch, he now calls loudly and tauntingly*). Give him something to eat, an' he'll soon be all right. (*Goes out.*)

DREISSIGER. That fellow will come to a bad end.—Take him under the arm, Neumann. Easy now, easy; we'll get him into my room. What?

NEUMANN. He said something, Mr. Dreissiger. His lips are moving.

DREISSIGER. What—what is it, boy?

BOY (*whispers*). I'm h—hungry.

WOMAN. I think he says . . .

DREISSIGER. We'll find out. Don't stop. Let us get him into my room. He can lie on the sofa there. We'll hear what the doctor says.

(DREISSIGER, NEUMANN, *and the woman lead the boy into the office. The weavers begin to behave like school-children when their master has left the classroom. They stretch themselves, whisper, move from one foot to the other, and in the course of a few moments are conversing loudly.*)

OLD BAUMERT. I believe as how Becker was right.

CHORUS OF WEAVERS AND WOMEN. "He did say something like that." —"It's nothing new here to fall down from hunger."—"God knows what's to come of them in winter if this cutting down of wages goes on."—"An' this winter the potatoes aren't no good at all."—"Things'll get worse and worse till we're all done for together."

OLD BAUMERT. The best thing a man could do would be to put a rope round his neck and hang hisself on his own loom, like Weaver Nentwich. (*To another old weaver*) Here, take a pinch. I was at Neurode yesterday. My brother-in-law, he works in the snuff factory there, and he give me a grain or two. Have you anything good in your handkercher?

OLD WEAVER. Only a little pearl barley. I was coming along behind Ulbrich the miller's cart, and there was a slit in one of the sacks. I can tell you we'll be glad of it.

OLD BAUMERT. There's twenty-two mills in Peterswaldau, but of all they grind, there's never nothing comes our way.

OLD WEAVER. We must keep up heart. There's always something comes to help us on again.

HEIBER. Yes, when we're hungry, we can pray to all the saints to help us, and if that don't fill our bellies we can put a pebble in our mouths and suck it. Eh, Baumert?

(*Re-enter* DREISSIGER, PFEIFER, *and* NEUMANN.)

DREISSIGER. It was nothing serious. The boy is all right again. (*Walks about excitedly, panting*) But all the same it's a disgrace. The child's so weak that a puff of wind would blow him over. How people, how any parents can be so thoughtless is what passes my comprehension. Loading him with two heavy pieces of fustian to carry a good six miles! No one would believe it that hadn't seen it. It simply means that I shall have to make a rule that no goods brought by children will be taken over. (*He walks up and down silently for a few moments*) I sincerely trust such a thing will not occur again.—Who gets all the blame for it? Why, of course the manufacturer. It's entirely our fault. If some poor little fellow sticks in the snow in winter and goes to sleep, a special correspondent arrives posthaste, and in two days we have a blood-curdling story served up in all the papers. Is any blame laid on the father, the parents, that send such a child?—Not a bit of it. How should they be to blame? It's all the manufacturer's fault—he's made the scapegoat. They flatter the weaver, and give the manufacturer nothing but abuse—he's a cruel man, with a heart like a stone, a wicked fellow, at whose calves every cur of a journalist may take a bite. He lives on the fat of the land, and pays the poor weavers starvation wages. In the flow of his eloquence the writer forgets to mention that such a man has his cares too and his sleepless nights; that he runs risks of which the workman never dreams; that he is often driven distracted by all the calculations he has to make, and all the different things he has to take into account; that he has to struggle for his very life against competition; and that no day passes without some annoyance or some loss. And think of the manufacturer's responsibilities, think of the numbers that depend on him, that look to him for their daily bread. No, no! none of you need wish yourselves in my shoes—you would soon have enough of it. (*After a moment's reflection*) You all saw how that fellow, that scoundrel Becker, behaved. Now he'll go and spread about all sorts of tales of my hardheartedness, of how my weavers are turned off for a mere trifle, without a moment's notice. Is that true? Am I so very unmerciful?

CHORUS OF VOICES. No, sir.

DREISSIGER. It doesn't seem to me that I am. And yet these ne'er-do-wells come round singing low songs about us manufacturers—prating about hunger, with enough in their pockets to pay for quarts of bad brandy. If they would like to know what want is, let them go and ask the linen-weavers: they can tell something about it. But you here, you fustian-weavers, have every reason to thank God that things are no worse than they are. And I put it to all the old, industrious weavers present: Is a good workman able to gain a living in my employment, or is he not?

MANY VOICES. Yes, sir; he is, sir.

DREISSIGER. There now! You see! Of course such a fellow as that Becker

can't. I advise you to keep these young lads in check. If there's much more of this sort of thing, I'll shut up shop—give up the business altogether, and then you can shift for yourselves, get work where you like—perhaps Mr. Becker will provide it.

FIRST WEAVER'S WIFE (*has come close to* DREISSIGER, *obsequiously removes a little dust from his coat*). You've been an' rubbed ag'in' something, sir.

DREISSIGER. Business is as bad as it can be just now, you know that yourselves. Instead of making money, I am losing it every day. If, in spite of this, I take care that my weavers are kept in work, I look for some little gratitude from them. I have thousands of pieces of cloth in stock, and don't know if I'll ever be able to sell them. Well, now, I've heard how many weavers hereabouts are out of work, and—I'll leave Pfeifer to give the particulars—but this much I'll tell you, just to show you my good will. . . . I can't deal out charity all round; I'm not rich enough for that; but I can give the people who are out of work the chance of earning at any rate a little. It's a great business risk I run by doing it, but that's my affair. I say to myself Better that a man should work for a bite of bread than that he should starve altogether. Am I not right?

CHORUS OF VOICES. Yes, yes, sir.

DREISSIGER. And therefore I am ready to give employment to two hundred more weavers. Pfeifer will tell you on what conditions. (*He turns to go.*)

FIRST WEAVER'S WIFE (*comes between him and the door, speaks hurriedly, eagerly, imploringly*). Oh, if you please, sir, will you let me ask you if you'll be so good . . . I've been twice laid up for . . .

DREISSIGER (*hastily*). Speak to Pfeifer, good woman. I'm too late as it is. (*Passes on, leaving her standing.*)

REIMANN (*stops him again. In an injured, complaining tone*). I have a complaint to make, if you please, sir. Mr. Pfeifer refuses to . . . I've always got one and twopence for a web . . .

DREISSIGER (*interrupts him*). Mr. Pfeifer's my manager. There he is. Apply to him.

HEIBER (*detaining* DREISSIGER; *hurriedly and confusedly*). O sir, I wanted to ask if you would p'r'aps, if I might p'r'aps . . . if Mr. Pfeifer might . . . might . . .

DREISSIGER. What is it you want?

HEIBER. That advance pay I had last time, sir; I thought p'r'aps you would kindly . . .

DREISSIGER. I have no idea what you are talking about.

HEIBER. I'm awful hard up, sir, because . . .

DREISSIGER. These are things Pfeifer must look into—I really have not the time. Arrange the matter with Pfeifer. (*He escapes into the office. The suppliants look helplessly at one another, sigh, and take their places again among the others.*)

PFEIFER (*resuming his task of inspection*). Well, Annie, let us see what yours is like.

OLD BAUMERT. How much are we to get for the web, then, Mr. Pfeifer?

HEIBER. One shilling a web.

OLD BAUMERT. Has it come to that! (*Excited whispering and murmuring among the weavers.*)

ACT TWO

A small room in the house of WILHELM ANSORGE, *weaver and houseowner in the village of Kaschbach, in the Eulengebirge.*

In this room, which does not measure six feet from the dilapidated wooden floor to the smoke-blackened rafters, sit four people. Two young girls, EMMA *and* BERTHA BAUMERT *are working at their looms;* MOTHER BAUMERT, *a decrepit old woman, sits on a stool beside the bed, with a winding-wheel in front of her; her idiot son* AUGUST *sits on a foot-stool, also winding. He is twenty, has a small body and head, and long, spiderlike legs and arms.*

Faint, rosy evening light makes its way through two small windows in the right wall, which have their broken panes pasted over with paper or stuffed with straw. It lights up the flaxen hair of the girls, which falls loose on their slender white necks and thin bare shoulders, and their coarse chemises. These, with a short petticoat of the roughest linen, form their whole attire. The warm glow falls on the old woman's face, neck, and breast—a face worn away to a skeleton, with shriveled skin and sunken eyes, red and watery with smoke, dust, and working by lamp-light; a long goitre neck, wrinkled and sinewy; a hollow breast covered with faded, ragged shawls.

Part of the right wall is also lighted up, with stove, stove-bench, bed-stead, and one or two gaudily colored sacred prints. On the stove rail rags are hanging to dry, and behind the stove is a collection of worthless lumber. On the bench stand some old pots and cooking-utensils, and potato-parings are laid out on it, on paper, to dry. Hanks of yarn and reels hang from the rafters; baskets of bobbins stand beside the looms. In the back wall there is a low door without fastening. Beside it a bundle of willow wands is set up against the wall, and beyond them lie some damaged quarter-bushel baskets.

The room is full of sound—the rhythmic thud of the looms, shaking floor and walls, the click and rattle of the shuttles passing back and forward, and the steady whir of the winding-wheels, like the hum of gigantic bees.

MOTHER BAUMERT (*in a querulous, feeble voice, as the girls stop weaving and bend over their webs*). Got to make knots again already, have you?

EMMA (*the elder of the two girls, about twenty-two, tying a broken thread*). It's the plaguyest web, this!

BERTHA (*fifteen*). Yes, it's real bad yarn they've given us this time.

EMMA. What can have happened to father? He's been away since nine.

MOTHER BAUMERT. You may well ask. Where in the wide world can he be?

BERTHA. Don't you worry yourself, mother.

MOTHER BAUMERT. I can't help it, Bertha lass.
(EMMA *begins to weave again.*)

BERTHA. Stop a minute, Emma!

EMMA. What is it!

BERTHA. I thought I heard someone.

EMMA. It'll be Ansorge coming home.
(*Enter* FRITZ, *a little, barefooted, ragged boy of four.*)

FRITZ (*whimpering*). I'm hungry, mother.

EMMA. Wait, Fritzel, wait a bit! Gran'-father will be here very soon, an' he's bringin' bread along with him, an' coffee too.

FRITZ. But I'm awful hungry, mother.

EMMA. Be a good boy now, Fritz. Listen to what I'm tellin' you. He'll be here this minute. He's bringin' nice bread an' nice corn-coffee; an' when we stop working mother'll take the tater peelin's and carry them to the farmer, and the farmer'll give her a drop o' good skim milk for her little boy.

FRITZ. Where's grandfather gone?

EMMA. To the manufacturer, Fritz, with a web.

FRITZ. To the manufacturer?

EMMA. Yes, yes, Fritz; down to Dreissiger's at Peterswaldau.

FRITZ. Is it there he gets the bread?

EMMA. Yes; Dreissiger gives him money, and then he buys the bread.

FRITZ. Does he give him a heap of money?

EMMA (*impatiently*). Oh, stop that chatter, boy. (*She and* BERTHA *go on weaving for a time, and then both stop again.*)

BERTHA. August, go and ask Ansorge if he'll give us a light. (AUGUST *goes out accompanied by* FRITZ.)

MOTHER BAUMERT (*overcome by her childish apprehension, whimpers*). Emma! Bertha! where can father be?

BERTHA. He'll have looked in to see Hauffen.

MOTHER BAUMERT (*crying*). What if he's sittin' drinkin' in the public house?

EMMA. Don't cry, mother! You know well enough father's not the man to do that.

MOTHER BAUMERT (*half distracted by a multitude of gloomy forebodings*). What . . . what . . . what's to become of us if he doesn't come home?—if he drinks the money, and brings us nothin' at all? There's not so much as a handful of salt in the house—not a bite o' bread, nor a bit o' wood for the fire.

BERTHA. Wait a bit, mother! It's moonlight just now. We'll take August with us and go into the wood and get some sticks.

MOTHER BAUMERT. Yes, an' be caught by the forester.
(ANSORGE, *an old weaver of gigantic stature, who has to bend down to get into the room, puts his head and shoulders in at the door. Long, unkempt hair and beard.*)

ANSORGE. What's wanted?

BERTHA. Light, if you please.

ANSORGE (*in a muffled voice, as if speaking in a sick-room*). There's good daylight yet.

MOTHER BAUMERT. Are we to sit in the dark next?

ANSORGE. I've to do the same myself. (*Goes out.*)

BERTHA. It's easy to see that he's a miser.

EMMA. Well, there's nothin' for it but to sit an' wait his pleasure. (*Enter* MRS. HEINRICH, *a woman of thirty, enceinte; an expression of torturing anxiety and apprehension on her worn face.*)

MRS. HEINRICH. Good-evenin' t' you all.

MOTHER BAUMERT. Well, Jenny, and what's your news?

MRS. HEINRICH (*who limps*). I've got a piece o' glass into my foot.

BERTHA. Come an' sit down, then, an' I'll see if I can get it out.
(MRS. HEINRICH *seats herself*. BERTHA *kneels down in front of her, and examines her foot.*)

MOTHER BAUMERT. How are you all at home, Jenny?

MRS. HEINRICH (*breaks out despairingly*). Things is in a terrible way with us! (*She struggles in vain against a rush of tears; then weeps silently.*)

MOTHER BAUMERT. The best thing as could happen to the likes of us, Jenny, would be if God had pity on us an' took us away out o' this weary world.

MRS. HEINRICH (*no longer able to control herself, screams, still crying*). My children's starvin'. (*Sobs and moans*) I'm at my wits' ends. Let me work till I fall down—I'm more dead than alive—it's all no use. Am I able to fill nine hungry mouths? We got a bit o' bread last night, but it wasn't enough even for the two smallest ones. Who was I to give it to, eh? They all cried: Me, me, mother! give it to me! . . . An' if it's like this while I'm still on my feet, what'll it be when I've to take to bed? Our few taters was washed away. We haven't a thing to put in our mouths.

BERTHA (*has removed the bit of glass and washed the wound*). We'll put a rag round it. Emma, see if you can find one.

MOTHER BAUMERT. We're no better off than you, Jenny.

MRS. HEINRICH. You have your girls, anyway. You've a husband as can work. Mine was taken with one of his fits last week again—so bad that I didn't know what to do with him, and was half out o' my mind with fright. And when he's had a turn like that, he can't stir out of bed under a week.

MOTHER BAUMERT. Mine's no better. His breathin' 's bad now as well as his back. An' there's not a farthin' nor a farthin's worth in the house. If he don't bring a few pence with him today, I don't know what we're to do.

EMMA. It's the truth she's tellin' you, Jenny. We had to let father take the little dog with him today, to have him killed, that we might get a bite into our stomachs again!

MRS. HEINRICH. Have you not got as much as a handful of flour to spare?

MOTHER BAUMERT. And that we have not, Jenny. There's not as much as a grain of salt in the house.

MRS. HEINRICH. Oh, whatever am I to do? (*Rises; stands still, brooding*) I don't know what'll be the end of this! It's more nor I can bear. (*Screams in rage and despair*) I would be contented if it was nothin' but pigs' food!—But I can't go home again empty-handed —that I can't. God forgive me, I see no other way out of it. (*She limps quickly out.*)

MOTHER BAUMERT (*calls after her in a warning voice*). Jenny, Jenny!

don't you be doin' anything fool-ish, now!

BERTHA. She'll do herself no harm, mother. You needn't be afraid.

EMMA. That's the way she always goes on. (*Seats herself at the loom and weaves for a few seconds.*)
(AUGUST *enters, carrying a tallow candle, and lighting his father,* OLD BAUMERT, *who follows close behind him, staggering under a heavy bundle of yarn.*)

MOTHER BAUMERT. Oh, father, where have you been all this long time? Where have you been?

OLD BAUMERT. Come now, mother, don't fall on a man like that. Give me time to get my breath first. An' look who I've brought with me.
(MORITZ JAEGER *comes stooping in at the low door. Reserve soldier, newly discharged. Middle height, rosy-cheeked, military carriage. His cap on the side of his head, hussar fashion, whole clothes and shoes, a clean shirt without collar. Draws himself up and salutes.*)

JAEGER (*in a hearty voice*). Good-evening, Auntie Baumert!

MOTHER BAUMERT. Well, well, now! And to think you've got back! An' you've not forgotten us? Take a chair, then, lad.

EMMA (*wiping a wooden chair with her apron, and pushing it toward* MORITZ). An' so you've come to see what poor folks are like again, Moritz?

JAEGER. I say, Emma, is it true that you've got a boy nearly old enough

to be a soldier? Where did you get hold of him, eh?
(BERTHA, *having taken the small supply of provisions which her father has brought, puts meat into a saucepan, and shoves it into the oven, while* AUGUST *lights the fire.*)

BERTHA. You knew Weaver Finger, didn't you?

MOTHER BAUMERT. We had him here in the house with us. He was ready enough to marry her; but he was too far gone in consumption; he was as good as a dead man. It didn't happen for want of warning from me. But do you think she would listen? Not she. Now he's dead an' forgotten long ago, an' she's left with the boy to provide for as best she can. But now tell us how you've been gettin' on, Moritz.

OLD BAUMERT. You've only to look at him, mother, to know that. He's had luck. It'll be about as much as he can do to speak to the likes of us. He's got clothes like a prince, an' a silver watch, an' thirty shil-lings in his pocket into the bargain.

JAEGER (*stretching himself conse-quentially, a knowing smile on his face*). I can't complain. I didn't get on at all badly in the regiment.

OLD BAUMERT. He was the major's own servant. Just listen to him—he speaks like a gentleman.

JAEGER. I've got so accustomed to it that I can't help it.

MOTHER BAUMERT. Well, now, to think that such a good-for-nothing as you were should have come to be a rich man. For there wasn't nothing to be made of you. You would never sit still to wind more than a hank of yarn at a time, that you wouldn't. Off you went to your tom-tit boxes an' your robin redbreast snares—they was all you cared about. Is it not the truth I'm telling?

JAEGER. Yes, yes, auntie, it's true enough. It wasn't only redbreasts. I went after swallows, too.

EMMA. Though we were always tellin' you that swallows were poison.

JAEGER. What did I care?—But how have you all been getting on, Auntie Baumert?

MOTHER BAUMERT. Oh, badly, lad, badly these last four years. I've had the rheumatics—just look at them hands. And it's more than likely as I've had a stroke o' some kind, too, I'm that helpless. I can hardly move a limb, an' nobody knows the pains I suffers.

OLD BAUMERT. She's in a bad way, she is. She'll not hold out long.

BERTHA. We've to dress her in the mornin' an' undress her at night, an' to feed her like a baby.

MOTHER BAUMERT (speaking in a complaining, tearful voice). Not a thing can I do for myself. It's far worse than bein' ill. For it's not only a burden to myself I am, but to everyone else. Often and often do I pray to God to take me. For oh! mine's a weary life. I don't know . . . p'r'aps they think . . . but I'm one that's been a hard worker all my days. An' I've always been able to do my turn too; but now, all at once (she vainly attempts to rise), I can't do nothing.—I've a good husband an' good children, but to have to sit here and see them . . . ! Look at the girls! There's hardly any blood left in them—faces the color of a sheet. But on they must work at these weary looms whether they earn enough to keep theirselves or not. What sort o' life is it they lead? Their feet never off the treadle from year's end to year's end. An' with it all they can't scrape together as much as'll buy them clothes that they can let theirselves be seen in; never a step can they go to church, to hear a word of comfort. They're liker scarecrows than young girls of fifteen and twenty.

BERTHA (at the stove). It's beginnin' to smoke again!

OLD BAUMERT. There now; look at that smoke. And we can't do nothin' for it. The whole stove's goin' to pieces. We must let it fall, and swallow the soot. We're coughin' already, one worse than the other. We may cough till we choke, or till we cough our lungs up—nobody cares.

JAEGER. But this here is Ansorge's business; he must see to the stove.

BERTHA. He'll see us out of the house first; he has plenty against us without that.

MOTHER BAUMERT. We've only been in his way this long time past.

OLD BAUMERT. One word of complaint an' out we go. He's had no rent from us this last half-year.

MOTHER BAUMERT. A well-off man like him needn't be so hard.

OLD BAUMERT. He's no better off than we are, mother. He's hard put to it, too, for all he holds his tongue about it.

MOTHER BAUMERT. He's got his house.

OLD BAUMERT. What are you talkin' about, mother? Not one stone in the wall is the man's own.

JAEGER (*has seated himself, and taken a short pipe with gay tassels out of one coat pocket, and a quart bottle of brandy out of another*). Things can't go on like this. I'm dumbfounded when I see the life the people live here. The very dogs in the towns live better.

OLD BAUMERT (*eagerly*). That's what I say! Eh? eh? You know it, too! But if you say that here, they'll tell you that it's only bad times. (*Enter* ANSORGE, *an earthenware pan with soup in one hand, in the other a half-finished quarter-bushel basket.*)

ANSORGE. Glad to see you again, Moritz!

JAEGER. Thank you, Father Ansorge —same to you!

ANSORGE (*shoving his pan into the oven*). Why, lad, you look like a duke!

OLD BAUMERT. Show him your watch, Moritz! An' he's got a new suit of clothes besides them he's on, an' thirty shillings in his purse.

ANSORGE (*shaking his head*). Is that so? Well, well!

EMMA (*puts the potato-parings into a bag*). I must be off; I'll maybe get a drop o' skim milk for these. (*Goes out.*)

JAEGER (*the others hanging on his words*). You know how you all used to be down on me. It was always: Wait, Moritz, till your soldiering time comes—you'll catch it then. But you see how well I've got on. At the end of the first half-year I had got my good-conduct stripes. You've got to be willing—that's where the secret lies. I brushed the sergeant's boots; I groomed his horse; I fetched his beer. I was as sharp as a needle. Always ready, accoutrements clean and shining— first at stables, first at rollcall, first in the saddle. And when the bugle sounded to the assault—why, then, blood and thunder, and ride to the devil with you!! I was as keen as a pointer. Says I to myself: There's no help for it now, my boy, it's got to be done; and I set my mind to it and did it. Till at last the major said before the whole squadron: There's a hussar now that shows you what a hussar should be! (*Silence. He lights his pipe.*)

ANSORGE (*shaking his head*). Well, well, well! You had luck with you, Moritz. (*Sits down on the floor, with his willow twigs beside him, and continues mending the basket, which he holds between his legs.*)

OLD BAUMERT. Let's hope you've brought some of it to us.—Are we to have a drop to drink your health in?

JAEGER. Of course you are, Father Baumert. And when this bottle's done, we'll send for more. (*He flings a coin on the table.*)

ANSORGE (*open-mouthed with amazement*). Oh, my! Oh, my! What goings on to be sure! Roast meat frizzlin' in the oven! A bottle o' brandy on the table! (*He drinks out of the bottle*) Here's to you, Moritz!—Well, well, well! (*The bottle circulates freely after this.*)

OLD BAUMERT. If we could anyway have a bit o' meat on Sundays and holidays, instead of never seein' the sight of it from year's end to year's end! Now we'll have to wait till another poor little dog finds its way into the house like this one did four weeks gone by—an' that's not likely to happen soon again.

ANSORGE. Have you killed the little dog?

OLD BAUMERT. We had to do that or starve.

ANSORGE. Well, well!

MOTHER BAUMERT. A nice, kind little beast he was, too!

JAEGER. Are you as keen as ever on roast dog hereabouts?

OLD BAUMERT. My word, if we could only get enough of it!

MOTHER BAUMERT. A nice little bit o' meat like that does you a lot o' good.

OLD BAUMERT. Have you lost the taste for it, Moritz? Stay with us a bit, and it'll soon come back to you.

ANSORGE (*sniffing*). Yes, yes! That will be a tasty bite—what a good smell it has!

OLD BAUMERT (*sniffing*). Splendid!

ANSORGE. Come, then, Moritz, tell us your opinion, you that's been out and seen the world. Are things at all like improving for us weavers, eh?

JAEGER. They would need to.

ANSORGE. We're in an awful state here. It's not livin' an' it's not dyin'. A man fights to the bitter end, but he's bound to be beat at last—to be left without a roof over his head, you may say without ground under his feet. As long as he can work at the loom he can earn some sort o' poor, miserable livin'. But it's many a day since I've been able to get that sort o' job. Now I tries to put a bite into my mouth with this here basket-makin'. I sits at it late into the night, and by the time I tumbles into bed I've earned three-halfpence. I put it to you if a man can live on that, when everything's so dear? Nine shillin' goes in one lump for house tax, three shillin' for land tax, nine shillin' for mortgage interest—that makes one pound one. I may reckon my year's earnin' at just double that money, and that leaves me twenty-one shillin' for a whole year's food, an' fire, an' clothes, an' shoes; and I've to keep up some sort of a place to live in. Is it any wonder if I'm behindhand with my interest payments?

OLD BAUMERT. Someone would need to go to Berlin an' tell the King how hard put to it we are.

JAEGER. Little good that would do, Father Baumert. There's been plenty written about it in the newspapers. But the rich people, they can turn and twist things round . . . as cunning as the devil himself.

OLD BAUMERT (*shaking his head*). To think they've no more sense than that in Berlin!

ANSORGE. And is it really true, Moritz? Is there no law to help us? If a man hasn't been able to scrape together enough to pay his mortgage interest, though he's worked the very skin off his hands, must his house be taken from him? The peasant that's lent the money on it, he wants his rights—what else can you look for from him? But what's to be the end of it all, I don't know.—If I'm put out o' the house . . . (*In a voice choked by tears*) I was born here, and here my father sat at his loom for more than forty year. Many was the time he said to mother: Mother, when I'm gone, the house'll still be here. I've worked hard for it. Every nail means a night's weaving, every plank a year's dry bread. A man would think that . . .

JAEGER. They're quite fit to take the last bite out of your mouth—that's what they are.

ANSORGE. Well, well, well! I would rather be carried out than have to walk out now in my old days. Who minds dyin'? My father, he was glad to die. At the very end he got frightened, but I crept into bed beside him, an' he quieted down again. I was a lad of thirteen then. I was tired and fell asleep beside him—I knew no better—and when I woke he was quite cold.

MOTHER BAUMERT (*after a pause*). Give Ansorge his soup out o' the oven, Bertha.

BERTHA. Here, Father Ansorge, it'll do you good.

ANSORGE (*eating and shedding tears*). Well, well, well! (OLD BAUMERT *has begun to eat the meat out of the saucepan.*)

MOTHER BAUMERT. Father, father, can't you have patience an' let Bertha serve it up properly?

OLD BAUMERT (*chewing*). It's two years now since I took the sacrament. I went straight after that an' sold my Sunday coat, an' we bought a good bit o' pork, an' since then never a mouthful of meat has passed my lips till tonight.

JAEGER. How should *we* need meat? The manufacturers eat it for us. It's the fat of the land *they* live on. Whoever doesn't believe that has only to go down to Bielau and Peterswaldau. He'll see fine things there—palace upon palace, with towers and iron railings and plateglass windows. Who do they all belong to? Why, of course, the manufacturers! No signs of bad times there! Baked and boiled and fried—horses and carriages and governesses—they've money to pay for all that and goodness knows how much more. They're swelled out to bursting with pride and good living.

ANSORGE. Things was different in my young days. Then the manufacturers let the weaver have his share. Now they keep everything to theirselves. An' would you like to know what's at the bottom of it all? It's that the fine folks nowadays believes neither in God nor devil. What do they care about commandments or punishments?

And so they steal our last scrap o' bread, an' leave us no chance of earnin' the barest living. For it's their fault. If our manufacturers was good men, there would be no bad times for us.

JAEGER. Listen, then, and I'll read you something that will please you. (*He takes one or two loose papers from his pocket*) I say, August, run and fetch another quart from the public-house. Eh, boy, do you laugh all day long?

MOTHER BAUMERT. No one knows why, but our August's always happy—grins an' laughs, come what may. Off with you, then, quick! (*Exit* AUGUST *with the empty brandy bottle*) You've got something good now, eh, father?

OLD BAUMERT (*still chewing; spirits rising from the effect of food and drink*). Moritz, you're the very man we want. You can read an' write. You understand the weavin' trade, and you've a heart to feel for the poor weavers' sufferin's. You should stand up for us here.

JAEGER. I'd do that quick enough! There's nothing I'd like better than to give the manufacturers round here a bit of a fright—dogs that they are! I'm an easy-going fellow, but let me once get worked up into a real rage, and I'll take Dreissiger in the one hand and Dittrich in the other, and knock their heads together till the sparks fly out of their eyes.—If we could only arrange all to join together, we'd soon give the manufacturers a proper lesson . . . without help from King or Government . . . all we'd have to do would be to say: We want this and that, and we don't want the other

thing. There would be a change of days then. As soon as they see that there's some pluck in us, they'll cave in. I know the rascals; they're a pack of cowardly hounds.

MOTHER BAUMERT. There's some truth in what you say. I'm not an ill-natured woman. I've always been the one to say as how there must be rich folks as well as poor. But when things come to such a pass as this. . . .

JAEGER. The devil may take them all, for what I care. It would be no more than they deserve.
(OLD BAUMERT *has quietly gone out.*)

BERTHA. Where's father?

MOTHER BAUMERT. I don't know where he can have gone.

BERTHA. Do you think he's not been able to stomach the meat, with not gettin' none for so long?

MOTHER BAUMERT (*in distress, crying*). There, now, there! He's not even able to keep it down when he's got it. Up it comes again, the only bite o' good food as he's tasted this many a day.
(*Re-enter* OLD BAUMERT, *crying with rage.*)

OLD BAUMERT. It's no good! I'm too far gone! Now that I've at last got hold of somethin' with a taste in it, my stomach won't keep it. (*He sits down on the bench by the stove crying.*)

JAEGER (*with a sudden violent ebullition of rage*). And yet there are people not far from here, justices they call themselves too, overfed brutes, that have nothing to do all the year round but invent new ways of wasting their time. And these people say that the weavers would be quite well off if only they weren't so lazy.

ANSORGE. The men as say that are no men at all, they're monsters.

JAEGER. Never mind, Father Ansorge; we're making the place hot for 'em. Becker and I have been and given Dreissiger a piece of our mind, and before we came away we sang him "Bloody Justice."

ANSORGE. Good Lord! Is that the song?

JAEGER. Yes; I have it here.

ANSORGE. They call it Dreissiger's song, don't they?

JAEGER. I'll read it to you.

MOTHER BAUMERT. Who wrote it?

JAEGER. That's what nobody knows. Now listen. (*He reads, hesitatingly like a schoolboy, with incorrect accentuation, but unmistakably strong feeling. Despair, suffering, rage, hatred, thirst for revenge, all find utterance.*)

The justice to us weavers dealt
    Is bloody, cruel, and hateful;
Our life's one torture, long drawn
        out:
    For Lynch law we'd be grateful.

Stretched on the rack day after day,
    Hearts sick and bodies aching,
Our heavy sighs their witness bear
    To spirits slowly breaking.

(*The words of the song make a strong impression on* OLD BAUMERT. *Deeply agitated, he struggles against the temptation to interrupt* JAEGER. *At last he can keep quiet no longer.*)

OLD BAUMERT (*to his wife, half laughing, half crying, stammering*). Stretched on the rack day after day. Whoever wrote that, mother, wrote the truth. You can bear witness . . . eh, how does it go? "Our heavy sighs their witness bear" . . . what's the rest?

JAEGER. "To spirits slowly breaking."

OLD BAUMERT. You know the way we sigh, mother, day and night, sleepin' and wakin'. (ANSORGE *has stopped working, and cowers on the floor, strongly agitated.* MOTHER BAUMERT *and* BERTHA *wipe their eyes frequently during the course of the reading.*)

JAEGER (*continues to read*).

The Dreissigers true hangmen are,
    Servants no whit behind them;
Masters and men with one accord
    Set on the poor to grind them.

You villains all, you brood of hell
    . . .

OLD BAUMERT (*trembling with rage, stamping on the floor*). Yes, brood of hell ! !

JAEGER (*reads*).

You fiends in fashion human,
A curse will fall on all like you,
    Who prey on man and woman.

ANSORGE. Yes, yes, a curse upon them!

OLD BAUMERT (*clenching his fist threateningly*). You prey on man and woman.

JAEGER (*reads*).

The suppliant knows he asks in
     vain,
     Vain every word that's spoken.
"If not content, then go and
     starve—
     Our rules cannot be broken."

OLD BAUMERT. What is it? "The suppliant knows he asks in vain"? Every word of it's true . . . every word . . . as true as the Bible. He knows he asks in vain.

ANSORGE. Yes, yes! It's all no good.

JAEGER (*reads*).

Then think of all our woe and
     want,
     O ye who hear this ditty!
Our struggle vain for daily bread
     Hard hearts would move to pity.

But pity's what you've never
     known—
     You'd take both skin and cloth-
     ing,
You cannibals, whose cruel deeds
     Fill all good men with loathing.

OLD BAUMERT (*jumps up, beside himself with excitement*). Both skin and clothing. It's true, it's all true! Here I stand, Robert Baumert, master-weaver of Kaschbach. Who can bring up anything against me? I've been an honest, hard-working man all my life long, an' look at me now! What have I to show for it? Look at me! See what they've made of me! Stretched on the rack day after day. (*He holds out his arms*) Feel that! Skin and bone! "You villains all, you brood of hell!!" (*He sinks down on a chair, weeping with rage and despair.*)

ANSORGE (*flings his basket from him into a corner, rises, his whole body trembling with rage, gasps*). And the time's come now for a change, I say. We'll stand it no longer! We'll stand it no longer! Come what may!

ACT THREE

The common room of the principal public-house in Peterswaldau. A large room with a raftered roof supported by a central wooden pillar, round which a table runs. In the back wall, a little to the right of the pillar, is the entrance door, through the opening of which the spacious lobby or outer room is seen, with barrels and brewing utensils. To the right of this door, in the corner, is the bar—a high wooden counter with receptacles for beer-mugs, glasses, etc.; a cupboard with rows of brandy and liqueur bottles on the wall behind, and between counter and cupboard a narrow space for the barkeeper. In front of the bar stands a table with a gay-colored cover, a pretty lamp hanging above it, and several cane chairs placed around it. Not far off, in the right wall, is a door with the inscription: Bar Parlor. Nearer the front on the same side an old eight-day clock stands *ticking. At the back, to the left of the entrance door, is a table with bottles and glasses and beyond this, in the corner, is the great stove. In the left wall there are three small windows. Below them runs a long bench; and in front of each stands a large oblong wooden table, with the end towards the wall. There are benches with backs along the sides of these tables, and at the end of each facing the window stands a wooden chair. The walls are washed blue and decorated with advertisements, colored prints and oleographs, among the latter a portrait of Frederick William III.*

WELZEL, *the publican, a good-natured giant, upwards of fifty, stands behind the counter, letting beer run from a barrel into a glass.*

MRS. WELZEL *is ironing by the stove. She is a handsome, tidily dressed woman in her thirty-fifth year.*

ANNA WELZEL, *a good-looking girl of seventeen, with a quantity of beautiful, fair, reddish hair, sits, nicely dressed, with her embroidery, at the table with the colored cover. She looks up from her work for a moment and listens, as the sound of a funeral hymn sung by schoolchildren is heard in the distance.*

WIEGAND, *the joiner, in his working clothes, is sitting at the same table, with a glass of Bavarian beer before him. His face shows that he understands what the world requires of a man if he is to attain his ends—namely, craftiness, sharpness, and relentless determination.*

A COMMERCIAL TRAVELER *is seated at the pillar-table, vigorously masticating a beefsteak. He is of middle height, stout and thriving-looking, inclined to jocosity, lively, and impudent. He is dressed in the fashion of the day, and his portmanteau, pattern-case, umbrella, overcoat, and traveling-rug lie on chairs beside him.*

WELZEL (*carrying a glass of beer to the* TRAVELER, *but addressing* WIEGAND). The devil's loose in Peterswaldau today.

WIEGAND (*in a sharp, shrill voice*). That's because it's delivery day at Dreissiger's.

MRS. WELZEL. But they don't generally make such an awful row.

WIEGAND. It's maybe because of the two hundred new weavers that he's going to take on.

MRS. WELZEL (*at her ironing*). Yes, yes, that'll be it. If he wants two hundred, six hundred's sure to have come. There's no lack of *them*.

WIEGAND. You may well say that. There's no fear of their dying out, let them be ever so badly off. They bring more children into the world than we know what to do with. (*The strains of the funeral hymn are suddenly heard more distinctly*) There's a funeral today, too. Weaver Nentwich is dead, as no doubt you know.

WELZEL. He's been long enough about it. He's been goin' about like a livin' ghost this many a long day.

WIEGAND. You never saw such a little coffin, Welzel; it was the tiniest, miserablest little thing I ever glued together. And what a corpse! It didn't weigh ninety pounds.

TRAVELER (*his mouth full*). What I don't understand's this. . . . Take up whatever paper you like and you'll find the most heart-rending accounts of the destitution among the weavers. You get the impression that three-quarters of the people in this neighborhood are starving. Then you come and see a funeral like what's going on just now. I met it as I came into the village. Brass band, schoolmaster, schoolchildren, pastor, and such a procession behind them that you would think it was the Emperor of China that was getting buried. If the people have money to spend on this sort of thing, well . . . ! (*He takes a drink of beer; puts down the glass; suddenly and jocosely*) What do you say to it, miss? Don't you agree with me?

(ANNA *gives an embarrassed laugh, and goes on working busily.*)

TRAVELER. Now, I'll take a bet that these are slippers for papa.

WELZEL. You're wrong, then; I wouldn't put such things on my feet.

TRAVELER. You don't say so! Now, I would give half of what I'm worth if these slippers were for me.

MRS. WELZEL. Oh, you don't know nothing about such things.

WIEGAND (*has coughed once or twice, moved his chair, and prepared himself to speak*). You were saying, sir, that you wondered to see such a funeral as this. I tell you, and Mrs. Welzel here will bear me out, that it's quite a small funeral.

TRAVELER. But, my good man . . . what a monstrous lot of money it must cost! Where does that all come from?

WIEGAND. If you'll excuse me for saying so, sir, there's a deal of foolishness among the poorer working-people hereabouts. They have a kind of inordinate idea, if I may say so, of the respect an' duty an' honor they're bound to show to such as are taken from their midst. And when it comes to be a case of parents, then there's no bounds whatever to their superstitiousness. The children and the nearest family scrapes together every farthing they can call their own, an' what's still wanting, that they borrow from some rich man. They run themselves into debt over head and ears; they're owing money to the pastor, to the sexton, and to all concerned. Then there's the victuals and the drink, an' such like. No, sir, I'm far from speaking against dutifulness to parents; but it's too much when it goes the length of the mourners having to bear the weight of it for the rest of their lives.

TRAVELER. But surely the pastor might reason them out of such foolishness.

WIEGAND. Begging your pardon, sir, but I must mention that every little place hereabouts has its church an' its respected pastor to support. These honorable gentlemen has their advantages from big funerals. The larger the attendance is, the larger the offertory is bound to be. Whoever knows the circumstances connected with the working classes here, sir, will assure you that the pastors are strong against quiet funerals.

(*Enter* HORNIG, *the rag-dealer, a little bandy-legged old man, with a strap around his chest.*)

HORNIG. Good-mornin', ladies and gentlemen! A glass of schnapps, if you please, Mr. Welzel. Has the young mistress anything for me to-day? I've got beautiful ribbons in my cart, Miss Anna, an' tapes, an' garters, an' the very best of pins an' hairpins an' hooks an' eyes. An' all in exchange for a few rags. (*He changes his voice*) An' out of them rags fine white paper's to be made, for your sweetheart to write you a letter on.

ANNA. Thank you, but I've nothing to do with sweethearts.

MRS. WELZEL (*putting a bolt into her iron*). No, she's not that kind. She'll not hear of marrying.

TRAVELER (*jumps up, affecting delighted surprise, goes forward to* ANNA's *table, and holds out his hand to her across it*). That's right, miss. You and I think alike in this matter. Give me your hand on it. We'll both remain single.

ANNA (*blushing scarlet, gives him her hand*). But you are married already!

TRAVELER. Not a bit of it. I only pretend to be. You think so because I wear a ring. I only have it on my finger to protect my charms against shameless attacks. I'm not afraid of you, though. (*He puts the ring into his pocket*) But tell me, truly, miss, are you quite determined never, never, never, to marry?

ANNA (*shakes her head*). Oh, get along with you!

MRS. WELZEL. You may trust her to remain single unless something very extra good turns up.

TRAVELER. And why should it not? I know of a rich Silesian proprietor who married his mother's lady's maid. And there's Dreissiger, the rich manufacturer, his wife is an innkeeper's daughter too, and not half so pretty as you, miss, though she rides in her carriage now, with servants in livery. And why not? (*He marches about, stretching himself, and stamping his feet*) Let me have a cup of coffee, please.

(*Enter* ANSORGE *and* OLD BAUMERT, *each with a bundle. They seat themselves meekly and silently beside* HORNIG, *at the front table to the left.*)

WELZEL. How are you, Father Ansorge? Glad to see you once again.

HORNIG. Yes, it's not often as you crawl down from that smoky old nest.

ANSORGE (*visibly embarrassed, mumbles*). I've been fetchin' myself a web again.

BAUMERT. He's goin' to work at a shilling the web.

ANSORGE. I wouldn't have done it, but there's no more to be made now by basket-weavin'.

WIEGAND. It's always better than nothing. He does it only to give you employment. I know Dreissiger very well. When I was up there taking out his double windows last week we were talking about it, him and me. It's out of pity that he does it.

ANSORGE. Well, well, well! That may be so.

WELZEL (*setting a glass of schnapps on the table before each of the weavers*). Here you are, then. I say, Ansorge, how long is it since you had a shave? The gentleman over there would like to know.

TRAVELER (*calls across*). Now, Mr. Welzel, you know I didn't say that. I was only struck by the venerable appearance of the master-weaver. It isn't often one sees such a gigantic figure.

ANSORGE (*scratching his head, embarrassed*). Well, well!

TRAVELER. Such specimens of primitive strength are rare nowadays. We're all rubbed smooth by civilization . . . but I can still take pleasure in nature untampered with. . . . These bushy eyebrows! That tangled length of beard!

HORNIG. Let me tell you, sir, that these people haven't the money to pay a barber, and as to a razor for themselves, that's altogether beyond them. What grows, grows. They haven't nothing to throw away on their outsides.

TRAVELER. My good friend, you surely don't imagine that I would. . . . (*Aside to* WELZEL) Do you think I might offer the hairy one a glass of beer?

WELZEL. No, no; you mustn't do that. He wouldn't take it. He's got some queer ideas in that head of his.

TRAVELER. All right, then, I won't. With your permission, miss. (*He seats himself at* ANNA'S *table*) I declare, miss, that I've not been able to take my eyes off your hair since I came in—such glossy softness, such a splendid quantity! (*Ecstatically kisses his fingertips*) And what a color! . . . like ripe wheat. Come to Berlin with that hair and you'll create no end of a sensation. On my honor, with hair like that you may go to Court. . . . (*Leans back, looking at it*) Glorious, simply glorious!

WIEGAND. They've given her a name because of it.

TRAVELER. And what may that be?

HORNIG. The chestnut filly, isn't it?

WELZEL. Come, now, we've had enough o' this. I'm not goin' to have the girl's head turned altogether. She's had a-plenty of silly notions put into it already. She'll hear of nothing under a count today, and tomorrow it'll be a prince.

MRS. WELZEL. You let her alone, father. There's no harm in wantin' to rise in the world. It's as well that people don't all think as you do, or nobody would get on at all. If Dreissiger's grandfather had been of your way of thinkin', they would be poor weavers still. And now they're rollin' in wealth. An look at old Tromtra. He was nothing but a weaver, too, and now he owns twelve estates, an' he's been made a nobleman into the bargain.

WIEGAND. Yes, Welzel, you must look at the thing fairly. Your wife's in the right this time. I can answer for that. I'd never be where I am, with seven workmen under me, if I had thought like you.

HORNIG. Yes, you understand the way to get on; that your worst enemy must allow. Before the weaver has taken to bed, you're gettin' his coffin ready.

WIEGAND. A man must attend to his business if he's to make anything of it.

HORNIG. No fear of you for that. You know before the doctor when death's on the way to knock at a weaver's door.

WIEGAND (*attempting to laugh, suddenly furious*). And you know better than the police where the thieves are among the weavers, that keep back two or three bobbins full every week. It's rags you ask for, but you don't say no, if there's a little yarn among them.

HORNIG. An' your corn grows in the churchyard. The more that are bedded on the sawdust, the better for you. When you see the rows of little children's graves, you pats yourself on the belly, and says you: This has been a good year; the little brats have fallen like cockchafers off the trees. I can allow myself a quart extra in the week again.

WIEGAND. And supposing this is all true, it still doesn't make me a receiver of stolen goods.

HORNIG. No; perhaps the worst you do is to send in an account twice to the rich fustian manufacturers, or to help yourself to a plank or two at Dreissiger's when there's building goin' on and the moon happens not to be shinin'.

WIEGAND (*turning his back*). Talk to anyone you like, but not to me. (*Then suddenly*) Hornig the liar!

HORNIG. Wiegand the coffin-jobber!

WIEGAND (*to the rest of the company*). He knows charms for bewitching cattle.

HORNIG. If you don't look out, I'll try one of 'em on you.
(WIEGAND *turns pale.*)

MRS. WELZEL (*had gone out; now returns with the* TRAVELER'S *coffee; in the act of putting it on the table*). Perhaps you would rather have it in the parlor, sir?

TRAVELER. Most certainly not! (*With a languishing look at* ANNA) I could sit here till I die.
(*Enter a* YOUNG FORESTER *and a* PEASANT, *the latter carrying a whip. They wish the others "Good Morning," and remain standing at the counter.*)

PEASANT. Two brandies, if you please.

WELZEL. Good morning to you, gentlemen. (*He pours out their beverage; the two touch glasses, take a mouthful, and then set the glasses down on the counter.*)

TRAVELER (*to* FORESTER). Come far this morning, sir?

FORESTER. From Steinseiffersdorf— that's a good step.
(*Two old* WEAVERS *enter, and seat themselves beside* ANSORGE, BAUMERT, *and* HORNIG.)

TRAVELER. Excuse me asking, but are you in Count Hochheim's service?

FORESTER. No. I'm in Count Keil's.

TRAVELER. Yes, yes, of course—that was what I meant. One gets confused here among all the counts and barons and other gentlemen. It would take a giant's memory to remember them all. Why do you carry an axe, if I may ask?

FORESTER. I've just taken this one from a man who was stealing wood.

OLD BAUMERT. Yes, their lordships are mighty strict with us about a few sticks for the fire.

TRAVELER. You must allow that if everyone were to help himself to what he wanted . . .

OLD BAUMERT. By your leave, sir, but there's a difference made here as elsewhere between the big an' the little thieves. There's some here as deals in stolen wood wholesale, and grows rich on it. But if a poor weaver . . .

FIRST OLD WEAVER (*interrupts* BAUMERT). We're forbid to take a single branch; but their lordships, they take the very skin off of us— we've assurance money to pay, an' spinning-money, an' charges in kind —we must go here an' go there, an' do so an' so much field work, all willy-nilly.

ANSORGE. That's just how it is— what the manufacturer leaves us, their lordships takes from us.

SECOND OLD WEAVER (*has taken a seat at the next table*). I've said it to his lordship himself. By your leave, my lord, says I, it's not possible for me to work on the estate so many days this year. For why— my own bit of ground, my lord, it's been next to carried away by the rains. I've to work both night and day if I'm to live at all. For oh, what a flood that was! . . . There I stood an' wrung my hands, an' watched the good soil come pourin' down the hill, into the very house! And all that dear, fine seed! . . . I could do nothing but roar an' cry until I couldn't see out o' my eyes for a week. And then I had to start an' wheel eighty heavy barrow-loads of earth up that hill, till my back was all but broken.

PEASANT (*roughly*). You weavers here make such an awful outcry. As if we hadn't all to put up with what Heaven sends us. An' if you *are* badly off just now, whose fault is it but your own? What did you do when trade was good? Drank an' squandered all you made. If you had saved a bit then, you'd have it to fall back on now when times is bad, and not need to be goin' stealin' yarn and wood.

FIRST YOUNG WEAVER (*standing with several comrades in the lobby or outer room, calls in at the door*). What's a peasant but a peasant, though he lies in bed till nine?

FIRST OLD WEAVER. The peasant an' the count, it's the same story with 'em both. Says the peasant when a weaver wants a house: I'll give you a little bit of a hole to live in, an' you'll pay me so much rent in money, an' the rest of it you'll make up by helpin' me to get in my hay an' my corn—an' if that doesn't please you, why, then you may go elsewhere. He tries another, and the second he says the same as the first.

BAUMERT (*angrily*). The weaver's like a bone that every dog takes a gnaw at.

PEASANT (*furious*). You starving curs, you're no good for anything. Can you yoke a plough? Can you draw a straight furrow or throw a bundle of sheaves onto a cart? You're fit for nothing but to idle about an' go after the women. A pack of scoundrelly ne'er-do-wells! (*He has paid and now goes out. The* FORESTER *follows, laughing.* WELZEL, *the joiner, and* MRS. WELZEL *laugh aloud; the* TRAVELER *laughs to himself. Then there is a moment's silence.*)

HORNIG. A peasant like that's as stupid as his own ox. As if I didn't know all about the distress in the villages round here. Sad sights I've seen! Four and five lyin' naked on one sack of straw.

TRAVELER (*in a mildly remonstrative tone*). Allow me to remark, my good man, that there's a great difference of opinion as to the amount of distress here in the Eulengebirge. If you can read . . .

HORNIG. I can read straight off, as well as you. An' I know what I've seen with my own eyes. It would be queer if a man that's traveled the country with a pack on his back these forty years an' more didn't know something about it. There was Fullern, now. You saw the children scrapping about among the dungheaps with the peasants' geese. The people up there died naked, on the bare stone floors. In their sore need they ate the stinking weavers' glue. Hunger carried them off by the hundred.

TRAVELER. You must be aware, since you are able to read, that strict investigation has been made by the Government, and that . . .

HORNIG. Yes, yes, we all know what that means. They send a gentleman that knows all about it already better nor if he had seen it, an' he goes about a bit in the village, at the lower end, where the best houses are. He doesn't want to dirty his shining boots. Thinks he to himself: All the rest'll be the same as this. An' so he steps into his carriage, an' drives away home again, an' then writes to Berlin that there's no distress in the place at all. If he had but taken the trouble to go higher up into a village like that, to where the stream comes in, or across the stream onto the narrow side—or, better still, if he'd gone up to the little out-o'-the-way hovels on the hill above, some of 'em that black an' tumble-down as it would be the waste of a good match to set fire to 'em—it's another kind of report he'd have sent to Berlin. They should have come to me, these government gentlemen that wouldn't believe there was no distress here. I would have shown them something. I'd have opened their eyes for 'em in some of these starvation holes. (*The strains of the Weavers' Song are heard, sung outside.*)

WELZEL. There they are, roaring at that devil's song again.

WIEGAND. They're turning the whole place upside down.

MRS. WELZEL. You'd think there was something in the air. (JAEGER *and* BECKER *arm in arm, at the head of a troop of young weavers, march noisily through the outer room and enter the bar.*)

JAEGER. Halt! To your places! (*The new arrivals sit down at the various tables, and begin to talk to other weavers already seated there.)*

HORNIG (*calls out to* BECKER). What's up now, Becker, that you've got together a crowd like this?

BECKER (*significantly*). Who knows but something may be going to happen? Eh, Moritz?

HORNIG. Come, come, lads. Don't you be a-gettin' of yourselves into mischief.

BECKER. Blood's flowed already. Would you like to see it? (*He pulls up his sleeve and shows bleeding tattoo-marks on the upper part of his arm. Many of the other young weavers do the same*) We've been at Father Schmidt's gettin' ourselves vaccinated.

HORNIG. Now the thing's explained. Little wonder there's such an uproar in the place, with a band of young rapscallions like you paradin' round.

JAEGER (*consequentially, in a loud voice*). You may bring two quarts at once, Welzel! I pay. Perhaps you think I haven't got the needful. You're wrong, then. If we wanted we could sit an' drink your best brandy an' swill coffee till tomorrow morning with any bagman in the land.
(*Laughter among the young weavers.*)

TRAVELER (*affecting comic surprise*). Is the young gentleman kind enough to take notice of me?
(*Host, hostess, and their daughter, WIEGAND, and the TRAVELER all laugh.*)

JAEGER. If the cap fits wear it.

TRAVELER. Your affairs seem to be in a thriving condition, young man, if I may be allowed to say so.

JAEGER. I can't complain. I'm a traveler in made-up goods. I go shares with the manufacturers. The nearer starvation the weaver is, the better I fare. His want butters my bread.

BECKER. Well done, Moritz! You gave it to him that time. Here's to you!
(WELZEL *has brought the corn-brandy. On his way back to the counter he stops, turns round slowly, and stands, an embodiment of phlegmatic strength, facing the weavers.*)

WELZEL (*calmly but emphatically*). You let the gentleman alone. He's done you no harm.

YOUNG WEAVERS. And we're doing him no harm.
(MRS. WELZEL *has exchanged a few words with the* TRAVELER. *She takes the cup with the remains of his coffee and carries it into the parlor. The* TRAVELER *follows her amidst the laughter of the weavers.*)

YOUNG WEAVERS (*singing*).

The Dreissigers the hangmen are,
Servants no whit behind them.

WELZEL. Hush-sh! Sing that song anywhere else you like, but not in my house.

FIRST OLD WEAVER. He's quite right. Stop that singin', lads.

BECKER (*roars*). But we must march past Dreissiger's, boys, and let them hear it once more.

WIEGAND. You'd better take care— you may march once too often.

(*Laughter and cries of Ho, ho!* WITTIG *has entered; a gray-haired old smith, bareheaded, with leather apron and wooden shoes, sooty from the smithy. He is standing at the counter waiting for his schnapps.*)

YOUNG WEAVER. Wittig, Wittig!

WITTIG. Here he is. What do you want with him?

YOUNG WEAVERS. "It's Wittig!"— "Wittig, Wittig!" — "Come here, Wittig."—"Sit beside us, Wittig."

WITTIG. Do you think I would sit beside a set of rascals like you?

JAEGER. Come and take a glass with us.

WITTIG. Keep your brandy to yourselves. I pay for my own drink. (*Takes his glass and sits down beside* BAUMERT *and* ANSORGE. *Clapping the latter on the stomach*) What's the weavers' food so nice? Sauerkraut and roasted lice!

OLD BAUMERT (*excitedly*). But what would you say now if they'd made up their minds as how they would put up with it no longer.

WITTIG (*with pretended astonishment, staring open-mouthed at the old weaver*). Heinerle! you don't mean to tell me that that's you? (*Laughs immoderately*) O Lord, O Lord! I could laugh myself to death. Old Baumert risin' in rebellion! We'll have the tailors at it next, and then there'll be a rebellion among the baa-lambs, and the rats and the mice. Damn it all, but we'll see some sport. (*He nearly splits with laughter.*)

OLD BAUMERT. You needn't go on like that, Wittig. I'm the same man I've always been. I still say 'twould be better if things could be put right peaceably.

WITTIG. Peaceably! How could it be done peaceably? Did they do it peaceably in France? Did Robespeer tickle the rich men's palms? No! It was: Away with them, every one! To the gilyoteen with them! Allongs onfong! You've got your work before you. The geese'll not fly ready roasted into your mouths.

OLD BAUMERT. If I could make even half a livin'——

FIRST OLD WEAVER. The water's up to our chins now, Wittig.

SECOND OLD WEAVER. We're afraid to go home. It's all the same whether we works or whether we lies abed; it's starvation both ways.

FIRST OLD WEAVER. A man's like to go mad at home.

OLD ANSORGE. It's that length with me now that I don't care how things go.

OLD WEAVERS (*with increasing excitement*). "We've no peace anywhere."—"We've no spirit left to work."—"Up with us in Steenkunzendorf you can see a weaver sittin' by the stream washin' hisself the whole day long, naked as God made him. It's driven him clean out of his mind."

THIRD OLD WEAVER (*moved by the spirit, stands up and begins to "speak with tongues," stretching out his hand threateningly*). Judgment is at hand! Have no dealings

with the rich and the great! Judgment is at hand! The Lord God of Sabaoth . . .
(*Some of the weavers laugh. He is pulled down onto his seat.*)

WELZEL. That's a chap that can't stand a single glass—he gets wild at once.

THIRD OLD WEAVER (*jumps up again*). But they—they believe not in God, not in hell, not in heaven. They mock at religion . . .

FIRST OLD WEAVER. Come, come now, that's enough!

BECKER. You let him do his little bit o' preaching. There's many a one would be the better for taking it to heart.

VOICES (*in excited confusion*). "Let him alone!"—"Let him speak!"

THIRD OLD WEAVER (*raising his voice*). But hell is opened, saith the Lord; its jaws are gaping wide, to swallow up all those that oppress the afflicted and pervert judgment in the cause of the poor.
(*Wild excitement.*)

THIRD OLD WEAVER (*suddenly declaiming schoolboy fashion*).

When one has thought upon it well,
It's still more difficult to tell
Why they the linen-weaver's work
    despise.

BECKER. But we're fustian-weavers, man.
(*Laughter.*)

HORNIG. The linen-weavers is ever so much worse off than you. They're wandering about among the hills like ghosts. You people here have still got the pluck left in you to kick up a row.

WITTIG. Do you suppose the worst's over here? It won't be long till the manufacturers drain away that little bit of strength they still have left in their bodies.

BECKER. You know what he said: It will come to the weavers working for a bite of bread.
(*Uproar.*)

SEVERAL OLD AND YOUNG WEAVERS. Who said that?

BECKER. Dreissiger said it.

A YOUNG WEAVER. The damned rascal should be hung up by the heels.

JAEGER. Look here, Wittig. You've always jawed such a lot about the French Revolution, and a good deal too about your own doings. A time may be coming, and that before long, when everyone will have a chance to show whether he's a braggart or a true man.

WITTIG (*flaring up angrily*). Say another word if you dare! Have you heard the whistle of bullets? Have you done outpost duty in an enemy's country?

JAEGER. You needn't get angry about it. We're comrades. I meant no harm.

WITTIG. None of your comradeship for me, you impudent young fool.
(*Enter KUTSCHE, the policeman.*)

SEVERAL VOICES. Hush—sh! Police!
(*This calling goes on for some time, till at last there is complete silence,*

amidst which KUTSCHE *takes his place at the central pillar-table.*)

KUTSCHE. A small brandy, please. (*Again complete silence.*)

WITTIG. I suppose you've come to see if we're all behaving ourselves, Kutsche?

KUTSCHE (*paying no attention to* WITTIG). Good morning, Mr. Wiegand.

WIEGAND (*still in the corner in front of the counter*). Good morning 'you, sir.

KUTSCHE. How's trade?

WIEGAND. Thank you, much as usual.

BECKER. The chief constable's sent him to see if we're spoiling our stomach on these big wages we're getting. (*Laughter.*)

JAEGER. I say, Welzel, you will tell him how we've been feasting on roast pork an' sauce an' dumplings and sauerkraut, and now we're sitting at our champagne wine. (*Laughter.*)

WELZEL. The world's upside down with them today.

KUTSCHE. An' even if you had the champagne wine and the roast meat, you wouldn't be satisfied. I've to get on without champagne wine as well as you.

BECKER (*referring to* KUTSCHE's *nose*). He waters his beet-root with brandy and gin. An' it thrives upon it, too. (*Laughter.*)

WITTIG. A p'liceman like that has a hard life. Now it's a starving beggar boy he has to lock up, then it's a pretty weaver girl he has to lead astray; then he has to get roarin' drunk an' beat his wife till she goes screamin' to the neighbors for help; and there's the ridin' about on horseback and the lyin' in bed till nine—nay, faith, but it's no easy job!

KUTSCHE. Jaw away; you'll jaw a rope round your neck in time. It's long been known what sort of a fellow you are. The magistrates know all about that dangerous tongue of yours. I know who'll drink wife and child into the poorhouse an' himself into jail before long, who it is that'll go on agitatin' and agitatin' till he brings down judgment on himself and all concerned.

WITTIG (*laughs bitterly*). It's true enough—no one knows what'll be the end of it. You may be right yet. (*Bursts out in fury*) But if it does come to that, I know who I've got to thank for it, who it is that's blabbed to the manufacturers an' all the gentlemen round, an' blackened my character to that extent that they never give me a hand's turn of work to do—an' set the peasants an' the millers against me, so that I'm often a whole week without a horse to shoe or a wheel to put a tire on. I know who's done it. I once pulled the damned brute off his horse, because he was givin' a little stupid boy the most awful flogging for stealin' a few unripe pears. But I tell you this, Kutsche, and you know me—if you get me put into prison, you may make your own will. If I hear as much as a whisper of it, I'll take the first thing as comes handy, whether it's a horseshoe or a hammer, a wheel-spoke or a pail; I'll get hold of you if I've to drag you out of bed from beside your wife, and I'll beat in your brains, as sure as my name's Wittig. (*He has jumped up and is going to rush at* KUTSCHE.)

OLD AND YOUNG WEAVERS (*holding him back*). Wittig, Wittig! Don't lose your head!

KUTSCHE (*has risen involuntarily, his face pale. He backs toward the door while speaking. The nearer the door the higher his courage rises. He speaks the last words on the threshold, and then instantly disappears*). What are you goin' on at me about? I didn't meddle with you. I came to say something to the weavers. My business is with them an' not with you, and I've done nothing to you. But I've this to say to you weavers: The Superintendent of Police herewith forbids the singing of that song—Dreissiger's song, or whatever it is you call it. And if the yelling of it on the streets isn't stopped at once, he'll provide you with plenty of time and leisure for going on with it in jail. You may sing there, on bread and water, to your hearts' content. (*Goes out.*)

WITTIG (*roars after him*). He's no right to forbid it—not if we were to roar till the windows shook an' they could hear us at Reichenbach —not if we sang till the manufacturers' houses tumbled about their ears an' all the Superintendents' helmets danced on the top of their heads. It's nobody's business but our own.
(BECKER *has in the meantime got up, made a signal for singing, and now leads off, the others joining in.*)

The justice to us weavers dealt
  Is bloody, cruel, and hateful;
Our life's one torture, long drawn
  out;
  For Lynch law we'd be grateful.

(WELZEL *attempts to quiet them but they pay no attention to him.* WIEGAND *puts his hands to his ears and rushes off. During the singing of the next verse the weavers rise and form into procession behind* BECKER *and* WITTIG, *who have given pantomimic signs for a general break-up.*)

Stretched on the rack, day after day,
  Hearts sick and bodies aching,
Our heavy sighs their witness bear
  To spirit slowly breaking.

(*Most of the weavers sing the following verse out on the street, only a few young fellows, who are paying, being still in the bar. At the conclusion of the verse no one is left in the room except* WELZEL *and his wife and daughter,* HORNIG, *and* OLD BAUMERT.)

You villains all, you brood of hell,
  You fiends in fashion human,
A curse will fall on all like you
  Who prey on man and woman.

WELZEL (*phlegmatically collecting the glasses*). Their backs are up to-day, and no mistake.

HORNIG (*to* OLD BAUMERT, *who is preparing to go*). What in the name of Heaven are they up to, Baumert?

BAUMERT. They're goin' to Dreissiger's to make him add something onto the pay.

WELZEL. And are you joining in these foolish ongoings?

OLD BAUMERT. I've no choice, Welzel. The young men may an' the old men must. (*Goes out rather shamefacedly.*)

HORNIG. It'll not surprise me if this ends badly.

WELZEL. To think that even old fellows like him are goin' right off their heads!

HORNIG. We all set our hearts on something!

ACT FOUR

Peterswaldau. Private room of DREISSIGER, *the fustian manufacturer—luxuriously furnished in the chilly taste of the first half of this century. Ceiling, doors, and stove are white, and the wall paper, with its small, straight-lined floral pattern, is dull and cold in tone. The furniture is mahogany, richly carved, and upholstered in red. On the right, between two windows with crimson damask curtains, stands the writing-table, a high bureau with falling flap. Directly opposite to this is the sofa, with the strong-box beside it; in front of the sofa a table, with chairs and easy-chairs arranged about it. Against the back wall is a gun-cupboard. All three walls are decorated with bad pictures in gilt frames. Above the sofa is a mirror with a heavily gilt rococo frame. On the left an ordinary door leads into the hall. An open folding door at the back shows the drawing-room, over-furnished in the same style of comfortless splendor. Two ladies,* MRS. DREISSIGER *and* MRS. KITTELHAUS, *the Pastor's wife, are seen in the drawing-room, looking at pictures.* PASTOR KITTELHAUS *is there too, engaged in conversation with* WEINHOLD, *the tutor, a theological graduate.*

KITTELHAUS (*a kindly little elderly man, enters the front room, smoking and talking to the tutor, who is also smoking; he looks round and shakes his head in surprise at finding the room empty*). You are young, Mr. Weinhold, which explains everything. At your age we old fellows held—well, I won't say the same opinions—but certainly opinions of the same tendency. And there's something fine about youth—youth with its grand ideals. But unfortunately, Mr. Weinhold, they don't last; they are as fleeting as April sunshine. Wait till you are my age. When a man has said his say from the pulpit for thirty years—fifty-

two times every year, not including saints' days—he has inevitably calmed down. Think of me, Mr. Weinhold, when you come that length.

WEINHOLD (*nineteen, pale, thin, tall, with lanky fair hair; restless and nervous in his movements*). With all due respect, Mr. Kittelhaus —I can't think—people have such different natures.

KITTELHAUS. My dear Mr. Weinhold, however restless-minded and unsettled a man may be—(*in a tone of reproof*)—and you are a case in point—however violently and wantonly he may attack the existing order of things, he calms down in the end. I grant you, certainly, that among our professional brethren individuals are to be found, who, at a fairly advanced age, still play youthful pranks. One preaches against the drink evil and founds temperance societies, another publishes appeals which undoubtedly read most effectively. But what good do they do? The distress among the weavers, where it does exist, is in no way lessened —but the peace of society is undermined. No, no; one feels inclined in such cases to say: Cobbler, stick to your last; don't take to caring for the belly, you who have the care of souls. Preach the pure Word of God, and leave all else to Him who provides shelter and food for the birds, and clothes the lilies of the field. But I should like to know where our good host, Mr. Dreissiger, has suddenly disappeared to. (MRS. DREISSIGER, *followed by* MRS. KITTELHAUS, *now comes forward. She is a pretty woman of thirty, of a healthy, florid type. A certain discordance is noticeable between her deportment and way of expressing herself and her rich, elegant toilette.*)

MRS. DREISSIGER. That's what I want to know, too, Mr. Kittelhaus. But it's what William always does. No sooner does a thing come into his head than off he goes and leaves me in the lurch. I've said enough about it, but it does no good.

KITTELHAUS. It's always the way with business men, my dear Mrs. Dreissiger.

WEINHOLD. I'm almost certain that something has happened downstairs.

(DREISSIGER *enters, hot and excited.*)

DREISSIGER. Well, Rosa, is coffee served?

MRS. DREISSIGER (*sulkily*). Fancy your needing to run away again!

DREISSIGER (*carelessly*). Ah! these are things you don't understand.

KITTELHAUS. Excuse me—has anything happened to annoy you, Mr. Dreissiger?

DREISSIGER. Never a day passes without that, my dear sir. I am accustomed to it. What about that coffee, Rosa?
(MRS. DREISSIGER *goes ill-humoredly and gives one or two violent tugs at the broad embroidered bell-pull.*)

DREISSIGER. I wish you had been downstairs just now, Mr. Weinhold. You'd have gained a little experience. Besides. . . . But now let us have our game of whist.

KITTELHAUS. By all means, sir. Shake off the dust and burden of the day, Mr. Dreissiger; forget it in our company.

DREISSIGER (*has gone to the window, pushed aside a curtain, and is looking out*). Vile rabble!! Come here, Rosa! (*She goes to the window*) Look . . . that tall redhaired fellow there! . . .

KITTELHAUS. That's the man they call Red Becker.

DREISSIGER. Is he the man that insulted you the day before yesterday? You remember what you told me—when John was helping you into the carriage?

MRS. DREISSIGER (*pouting, carelessly*). I'm sure I don't know.

DREISSIGER. Come now, what's the use of being cross? I must know. If he's the man, I mean to have him arrested. (*The strains of the Weavers' Song are heard*) Listen to that! Just listen!

KITTELHAUS (*highly incensed*). Is there to be no end to this nuisance? I must acknowledge now that it is time for the police to interfere. Permit me. (*He goes forward to the window*) See, see, Mr. Weinhold! These are not only young people. There are numbers of steady-going old weavers among them, men whom I have known for years and looked upon as most deserving and God-fearing. There they are, taking part in this intolerable uproar, trampling God's law under foot. Do you mean to tell me that you still defend these people?

WEINHOLD. Certainly not, Mr. Kittelhaus. That is, sir . . . *cum grano salis*. For after all, they are hungry and they are ignorant. They are giving expression to their dissatisfaction in the only way they understand. I don't expect that such people . . .

MRS. KITTELHAUS (*short, thin, faded, more like an old maid than a married woman*). Mr. Weinhold, Mr. Weinhold, how can you?

DREISSIGER. Mr. Weinhold, I am sorry to be obliged to . . . I didn't bring you into my house to give me lectures on philanthropy, and I must request that you will confine yourself to the education of my boys, and leave my other affairs entirely to me—entirely! Do you understand?

WEINHOLD (*stands for a moment rigid and deathly pale, then bows, with a strained smile. In a low voice*). Certainly, of course I understand. I have seen this coming. It is my wish too. (*Goes out.*)

DREISSIGER (*rudely*). As soon as possible then, please. We require the room.

MRS. DREISSIGER. William, William!

DREISSIGER. Have you lost your senses, Rosa, that you're taking the part of a man who defends a low, blackguardly libel like that song?

MRS. DREISSIGER. But, William, he didn't defend it.

DREISSIGER. Mr. Kittelhaus, did he defend it or did he not?

KITTELHAUS. His youth must be his excuse, Mr. Dreissiger.

MRS. KITTELHAUS. I can't understand it. The young man comes of such a good, respectable family. His father held a public appointment for forty years, without a breath on his reputation. His mother was overjoyed at his getting this good situation here. And now . . . he himself shows so little appreciation of it.

PFEIFER (*suddenly opens the door leading from the hall and shouts in*). Mr. Dreissiger, Mr. Dreissiger! they've got him! Will you come, please? They've caught one of them.

DREISSIGER (*hastily*). Has someone gone for the police?

PFEIFER. The Superintendent's on his way upstairs.

DREISSIGER (*at the door*). Glad to see you, sir. We want you here. (KITTELHAUS *makes signs to the ladies that it will be better for them to retire. He, his wife, and* MRS. DREISSIGER *disappear into the drawing-room.*)

DREISSIGER (*exasperated, to the* POLICE SUPERINTENDENT, *who has now entered*). I have at last had one of the ringleaders seized by my dyers. I could stand it no longer—their insolence was beyond all bounds—quite unbearable. I have visitors in my house, and these blackguards dare to . . . They insult my wife whenever she shows herself; my boys' lives are not safe. My visitors run the risk of being jostled and cuffed. Is it possible that in a well-ordered community incessant public insult offered to unoffending people like myself and my family should pass unpunished? If so . . . then . . . then I must confess that I have other ideas of law and order.

SUPERINTENDENT (*a man of fifty, middle height, corpulent, full-blooded. He wears cavalry uniform with a long sword and spurs*). No, no, Mr. Dreissiger . . . certainly not! I am entirely at your disposal. Make your mind easy on the subject. Dispose of me as you will. What you have done is quite right. I am delighted that you have had one of the ringleaders arrested. I am very glad indeed that a settling day has come. There are a few dis-turbers of the peace here whom I have long had my eye on.

DREISSIGER. Yes, one or two raw lads, lazy vagabonds, that shirk every kind of work, and lead a life of low dissipation, hanging about the public-houses until they've sent their last halfpenny down their throats. But I'm determined to put a stop to the trade of these professional blackguards once and for all. It's in the public interest to do so, not only my private interest.

SUPERINTENDENT. Of course it is! Most undoubtedly, Mr. Dreissiger! No one can possibly blame you. And everything that lies in my power . . .

DREISSIGER. The cat-o'-nine tails is what should be taken to the beggarly pack.

SUPERINTENDENT. You're right, quite right. We must make an example. (KUTSCHE, *the policeman, enters and salutes. The door is open, and the sound of heavy steps stumbling up the stair is heard.*)

KUTSCHE. I have to inform you, sir, that we have arrested a man.

DREISSIGER (*to* SUPERINTENDENT). Do you wish to see the fellow?

SUPERINTENDENT. Certainly, most certainly. We must begin by having a look at him at close quarters. Oblige me, Mr. Dreissiger, by not speaking to him at present. I'll see to it that you get complete satisfaction, or my name's not Heide.

DREISSIGER. That's not enough for me, though. He goes before the magistrates. My mind's made up.

(JAEGER *is led in by five dyers, who have come straight from their work —faces, hands, and clothes stained with dye. The prisoner, his cap set jauntily on the side of his head, presents an appearance of impudent gayety; he is excited by the brandy he has just drunk.*)

JAEGER. Hounds that you are!—Call yourselves workingmen!—Pretend to be comrades! Before I would do such a thing as lay my hands on a mate, I'd see my hand rot off my arm!

(*At a sign from the* SUPERINTENDENT, KUTSCHE *orders the dyers to let go their victim.* JAEGER *straightens himself up, quite free and easy. Both doors are guarded.*)

SUPERINTENDENT (*shouts to* JAEGER). Off with your cap, sir. (JAEGER *takes it off, but very slowly, still with an impudent grin on his face*) What's your name!

JAEGER. What's yours? I'm not your swineherd.

(*Great excitement is produced among the audience by this reply.*)

DREISSIGER. This is too much of a good thing.

SUPERINTENDENT (*changes color, is on the point of breaking out furiously, but controls his rage*). We'll see about this afterwards.—Once more, what's your name? (*Receiving no answer, furiously*) If you don't answer at once, fellow, I'll have you flogged on the spot.

JAEGER (*perfectly cheerful, not showing by so much as the twitch of an eyelid that he has heard the* SUPERINTENDENT'S *angry words, calls over the heads of those around*

him *to a pretty servant girl, who has brought in the coffee and is standing open-mouthed with astonishment at the unexpected sight*). Hullo, Emmy, do you belong to this company now? The sooner you find your way out of it, then, the better. A wind may begin to blow here, an' blow everything away overnight.

(*The girl stares at* JAEGER, *and as soon as she comprehends that it is to her he is speaking, blushes with shame, covers her eyes with her hands, and rushes out, leaving the coffee things in confusion on the table. Renewed excitement among those present.*)

SUPERINTENDENT (*half beside himself, to* DREISSIGER). Never in all my long service . . . such a case of shameless effrontery . .

(JAEGER *spits on the floor.*)

DREISSIGER. I'll thank you to remember that this is not a stable.

SUPERINTENDENT. My patience is at an end now. For the last time: What's your name?

(KITTELHAUS, *who has been peering out at the partly opened drawing-room door, listening to what has been going on, can no longer refrain from coming forward to interfere. He is trembling with excitement.*)

KITTELHAUS. His name is Jaeger, sir. Moritz . . . is it not? Moritz Jaeger. (*To* JAEGER) And, Jaeger, you know me.

JAEGER (*seriously*). You are Pastor Kittelhaus.

KITTELHAUS. Yes, I am your pastor, Jaeger! It was I who received you, a babe in swaddling clothes, into the Church of Christ. From my hands you took for the first time the body of the Lord. Do you remember that, and how I toiled and strove to bring God's Word home to your heart? Is this your gratitude?

JAEGER (*like a scolded schoolboy, in a surly voice*). I paid my half-crown like the rest.

KITTELHAUS. Money, money . . . Do you imagine that the miserable little bit of money . . . Such utter nonsense! I'd much rather you kept your money. Be a good man, be a Christian! Think of what you promised. Keep God's law. Money, money! . . .

JAEGER. I'm a Quaker now, sir. I don't believe in anything.

KITTELHAUS. Quaker! What are you talking about? Try to behave yourself, and don't use words you don't understand. Quaker, indeed! They are good Christian people, and not heathens like you.

SUPERINTENDENT. Mr. Kittelhaus, I must ask you . . . (*He comes between the* PASTOR *and* JAEGER) Kutsche! tie his hands!
(*Wild yelling outside:* "*Jaeger, Jaeger! come out!*")

DREISSIGER (*like the others, slightly startled, goes instinctively to the window*). What's the meaning of this next?

SUPERINTENDENT. Oh, I understand well enough. It means that they want to have the blackguard out among them again. But we're not going to oblige them. Kutsche, you

have your orders. He goes to the lock-up.

KUTSCHE (*with the rope in his hand, hesitating*). By your leave, sir, but it'll not be an easy job. There's a confounded big crowd out there— a pack of raging devils. They've got Becker with them, and the smith . . .

KITTELHAUS. Allow me one more word!—So as not to rouse still worse feeling, would it not be better if we tried to arrange things peaceably? Perhaps Jaeger will give his word to go with us quietly, or . . .

SUPERINTENDENT. Quite impossible! Think of my responsibility. I couldn't allow such a thing. Come, Kutsche! lose no more time.

JAEGER (*putting his hands together, and holding them out*). Tight, tight, as tight as ever you can! It's not for long.
(KUTSCHE, *assisted by the workmen, ties his hands.*)

SUPERINTENDENT. Now, off with you, march! (*To* DREISSIGER) If you feel anxious let six of the weavers go with them. They can walk on each side of him, I'll ride in front, and Kutsche will bring up the rear. Whoever blocks the way will be cut down.
(*Cries from below:* "*Cock-a-doodle-doo-oo-oo! Bow, wow, wow!*")

SUPERINTENDENT (*with a threatening gesture in the direction of the window*). You rascals, I'll cock-a-doodle-doo and bow-wow you! Forward! March! (*He marches out first, with drawn sword; the others, with* JAEGER, *follow.*)

JAEGER (*shouts as he goes*). An' Mrs. Dreissiger there may play the lady as proud as she likes, but for all that she's no better than us. Many a hundred times she's served my father with a half-penny-worth of schnapps. Left wheel—march! (*Exit laughing.*)

DREISSIGER (*after a pause, with apparent calmness*). Well, Mr. Kittelhaus, shall we have our game now? I think there will be no further interruption. (*He lights a cigar, giving short laughs as he does so; when it is lighted, bursts into a regular fit of laughing*) I'm beginning now to think the whole thing very funny. That fellow! (*Still laughing nervously*) It really is too comical: first came the dispute at dinner with Weinhold—five minutes after that he takes leave—off to the other end of the world; then this affair crops up—and now we'll proceed with our whist.

KITTELHAUS. Yes, but . . . (*Roaring is heard outside*) Yes, but . . . that's a terrible uproar they're making outside.

DREISSIGER. All we have to do is to go into the other room; it won't disturb us in the least there.

KITTELHAUS (*shaking his head*). I wish I knew what has come over these people. In so far I must agree with Mr. Weinhold, or at least till quite lately I was of his opinion, that the weavers were a patient, humble, easily led class. Was it not your idea of them, too, Mr. Dreissiger?

DREISSIGER. Most certainly that is what they used to be—patient, easily managed, peaceable people.

They were that as long as these so-called humanitarians let them alone. But for ever so long now they've had the awful misery of their condition held up to them. Think of all the societies and associations for the alleviation of the distress among the weavers. At last the weaver believes in it himself, and his head's turned. Some of them had better come and turn it back again, for now he's fairly set a-going there's no end to his complaining. This doesn't please him, and that doesn't please him. He must have everything of the best. (*A loud roar of "Hurrah!" is heard from the crowd.*)

KITTELHAUS. So that with all their humanitarianism they have only succeeded in almost literally turning lambs into wolves.

DREISSIGER. I won't say that, sir. When you take time to think of the matter coolly, it's possible that some good may come of it yet. Such occurrences as this will not pass unnoticed by those in authority, and may lead them to see that things can't be allowed to go on as they are doing—that means must be taken to prevent the utter ruin of our home industries.

KITTELHAUS. Possibly. But what is the cause, then, of this terrible falling off of trade?

DREISSIGER. Our best markets have been closed to us by the heavy import duties foreign countries have laid on our goods. At home the competition is terrible, for we have no protection, none whatever.

PFEIFER (*staggers in, pale and breathless*). Mr. Dreissiger, Mr Dreissiger!

DREISSIGER (*in the act of walking into the drawing-room, turns round, annoyed*). Well, Pfeifer, what now?

PFEIFER. Oh, sir! Oh, sir! . . . It's worse than ever!

DREISSIGER. What are they up to next?

KITTELHAUS. You're really alarming us—what is it?

PFEIFER (*still confused*). I never saw the like. Good Lord!—The Superintendent himself . . . they'll catch it for this yet.

DREISSIGER. What's the matter with you, in the devil's name? Is anyone's neck broken?

PFEIFER (*almost crying with fear, screams*). They've set Moritz Jaeger free—they've thrashed the Superintendent and driven him away—they've thrashed the policeman and sent him off to—without his helmet . . . his sword broken . . . Oh dear, oh dear!

DREISSIGER. I think you've gone crazy, Pfeifer.

KITTELHAUS. This is actual riot.

PFEIFER (*sitting on a chair, his whole body trembling*). It's turning serious, Mr. Dreissiger! Mr. Dreissiger, it's serious now!

DREISSIGER. Well, if that's all the police . . .

PFEIFER. Mr. Dreissiger, it's serious now!

DREISSIGER. Damn it all, Pfeifer, will you hold your tongue?

MRS. DREISSIGER (*coming out of the drawing-room with* MRS. KITTELHAUS). This is really too bad, William. Our whole evening's being spoiled. Here's Mrs. Kittelhaus saying that she'd better go home.

KITTELHAUS. You mustn't take it amiss, dear Mrs. Dreissiger, but perhaps, under the circumstances, it *would* be better . . .

MRS. DREISSIGER. But, William, why in the world don't you go out and put a stop to it?

DREISSIGER. Go you and try if you can do it. Try! Go and speak to them! (*Standing helplessly in front of the* PASTOR) Am I such a tyrant? Am I a cruel master? (*Enter* JOHN *the coachman.*)

JOHN. If you please, m'm, I've put to the horses. Mr. Weinhold's put Georgie and Charlie into the carriage. If it comes to the worst, we're ready to be off.

MRS. DREISSIGER. If what comes to the worst?

JOHN. I'm sure I don't know, m'm. But the crowd's gettin' bigger and bigger, an' they've sent the Superintendent an' the p'liceman to the right-about.

PFEIFER. It's serious now, Mr. Dreissiger! It's serious!

MRS. DREISSIGER (*with increasing alarm*). What's going to happen? —What do the people want?— They're never going to attack us, John?

JOHN. There's some rascally hounds among 'em, ma'am.

PFEIFER. It's serious now! serious!

DREISSIGER. Hold your tongue, fool! —Are the doors barred?

KITTELHAUS. I ask you as a favor, Mr. Dreissiger . . . as a favor . . . I am determined to . . . I ask you as a favor . . . (*To* JOHN) What demands are the people making?

JOHN (*awkwardly*). It's higher wages they're after, the blackguards.

KITTELHAUS. Good, good!—I shall go out and do my duty. I shall speak seriously to these people.

JOHN. Oh, sir, please, sir, don't do any such thing. Words is quite useless.

KITTELHAUS. One little favor, Mr. Dreissiger. May I ask you to post men behind the door, and to have it closed at once after me?

MRS. KITTELHAUS. O Joseph, Joseph! you're not really going out?

KITTELHAUS. I am. Indeed I am. I know what I'm doing. Don't be afraid. God will protect me.
(MRS. KITTELHAUS *presses his hand, draws back, and wipes tears from her eyes.*)

KITTELHAUS (*while the murmur of a great, excited crowd is heard uninterruptedly outside*). I'll go . . . I'll go out as if I were simply on my way home. I shall see if my sacred office . . . if the people have not sufficient respect for me left to . . . I shall try . . . (*He takes his hat and stick*) Forward, then, in God's name! (*Goes out accompanied by* DREISSIGER, PFEIFER, *and* JOHN.)

MRS. KITTELHAUS. Oh, dear Mrs. Dreissiger! (*She bursts into tears and embraces her*) I do trust nothing will happen to him.

MRS. DREISSIGER (*absently*). I don't know how it is, Mrs. Kittelhaus, but I . . . I can't tell you how I feel. I didn't think such a thing was possible. It's . . . it's as if it was a sin to be rich. If I had been told about all this beforehand, Mrs. Kittelhaus, I don't know but what I would rather have been left in my own humble position.

MRS. KITTELHAUS. There are troubles and disappointments in every condition of life, Mrs. Dreissiger.

MRS. DREISSIGER. True, true, I can well believe that. And suppose we have more than other people . . . goodness me! we didn't steal it. It's been honestly got, every penny of it. It's not possible that the people can be going to attack us! If trade's bad, that's not William's fault, is it?
(*Loud, confused yelling is heard outside. While the two women stand gazing at each other, pale and startled,* DREISSIGER *rushes in.*)

DREISSIGER. Quick, Rosa—put on something, and get into the carriage. I'll be after you this moment. (*He rushes to the strong-box, and takes out papers and various articles of value.*)
(*Enter* JOHN.)

JOHN. We're ready to start. But come quickly, before they get round to the back door.

MRS. DREISSIGER (*in a transport of fear, throwing her arms around*

JOHN's *neck*). John, John, dear, good John! Save us, John. Save my boys! Oh, what is to become of us?

DREISSIGER. Rosa, try to keep your head. Let John go.

JOHN. Yes, yes, ma'am! Don't be frightened. Our good horses'll soon leave them all behind; an' whoever doesn't get out of the way'll be driven over.

MRS. KITTELHAUS (*in helpless anxiety*). But my husband . . . my husband? But, Mr. Dreissiger, my husband?

DREISSIGER He's in safety now, Mrs. Kittelhaus. Don't alarm yourself; he's all right.

MRS. KITTELHAUS. Something dreadful has happened to him. I know it. You needn't try to keep it from me.

DREISSIGER. You mustn't take it to heart—they'll be sorry for it yet. I know exactly whose fault it was. Such a detestable, shameful outrage will not go unpunished. A community laying hands on its own pastor and maltreating him—abominable! Mad dogs they are—raging brutes—and they'll be treated as such. (*To his wife who still stands petrified*) Go, for my sake, Rosa, go quickly! (*The clatter of window panes being smashed on the ground floor is heard*) They've gone quite mad. There's nothing for it but to get away as fast as we can. (*Cries of "Pfeifer, come out!"— "We want Pfeifer!"—"Pfeifer, come out!" are heard.*)

MRS. DREISSIGER. Pfeifer, Pfeifer, they want Pfeifer!

PFEIFER (*dashes in*). Mr. Dreissiger, there are people at the back gate already, and the house door won't hold much longer. The smith's battering it in with a stable pail.

(*The cry sounds louder and clearer: "Pfeifer! Pfeifer! Pfeifer! come out!"* MRS. DREISSIGER *rushes off as if pursued.* MRS. KITTELHAUS *follows.* PFEIFER *listens, and changes color as he hears what the cry is. A perfect panic of fear seizes him; he weeps, entreats, whimpers, writhes, all at the same moment. He overwhelms* DREISSIGER *with childish caresses, strokes his cheeks and arms, kisses his hands, and at last, like a drowning man, throws his arms round him and prevents him moving.*)

PFEIFER. Dear, good, kind Mr. Dreissiger, don't leave me behind. I've always served you faithfully. I've always treated the people well. I couldn't give them more wages than the fixed rate. Don't leave me here—they'll do for me! If they find me, they'll kill me. O God! O God! My wife, my children!

DREISSIGER (*making his way out, vainly endeavoring to free himself from* PFEIFER's *clutch*). Can't you let me go, fellow? It'll be all right; it'll be all right.

(*For a few seconds the room is empty. Windows are broken in the drawing-room. A loud crash resounds through the house, followed by shouts of "Hurrah!" For an instant there is silence. Then gentle, cautious steps are heard on the stair, then timid, hushed ejaculations: "To the left!"—"Up with you!"—"Hush!"—"Slow, slow!"— "Don't shove like that!"—"It's a wedding we're goin' to!"—"Stop*

*that crowding!"—"You go first!"—
"No, you go!"*)

(*Young weavers and weaver girls
appear at the door leading from
the hall, not daring to enter, but
each trying to shove the other in.
In the course of a few moments
their timidity is overcome, and the
poor, thin, ragged or patched figures, many of them sickly looking,
disperse themselves through* DREIS-
SIGER'S *room and the drawing-
room, first gazing timidly and curiously at everything, then beginning
to touch things. Girls sit down on
the sofas, whole groups admire
themselves in the mirrors, men
stand up on chairs, examine the
pictures and take them down.
There is a steady influx of miser-
able-looking creatures from the
hall.*)

FIRST OLD WEAVER (*entering*). No,
no, this is carryin' it too far. They've
started smashing things downstairs.
There's no sense nor reason in that.
There'll be a bad end to it. No man
in his wits would do that. I'll keep
clear of such on-goings.

(JAEGER, BECKER, WITTIG *carrying
a wooden pail,* BAUMERT, *and a
number of other old and young
weavers, rush in as if in pursuit of
something, shouting hoarsely.*)

JAEGER. Where has he gone?

BECKER. Where's the cruel brute?

BAUMERT. If we can eat grass, he
may eat sawdust.

WITTIG. We'll hang him whenever
we catch him.

FIRST YOUNG WEAVER. We'll take
him by the legs and fling him out

at the window, onto the stones.
He'll never get up again.

SECOND YOUNG WEAVER (*enters*).
He's off!

ALL. Who?

SECOND YOUNG WEAVER. Dreissiger.

BECKER. Pfeifer too?

VOICES. Let's get hold of Pfeifer.
Look for Pfeifer!

BAUMERT. Yes, yes! Pfeifer! Tell
him there's a weaver here for him
to starve.
(*Laughter.*)

JAEGER. If we can't lay hands on
that brute Dreissiger himself . . .
we'll at any rate make a poor man
of him.

BAUMERT. As poor as a church
mouse . . . we'll see to that!
(*All, bent on the work of destruction, rush towards the drawing-
room door.*)

BECKER (*who is leading, turns
round and stops the others*). Halt!
Listen to me! This is nothing but a
beginning. When we're done here,
we'll go straight to Bielau, to Dittrich's, where the steam power-
looms are. The whole mischief's
done by these factories.

OLD ANSORGE (*enters from hall.
Takes a few steps, then stops and
looks round, bewildered; shakes his
head, taps his forehead*). Who am
I? Weaver Anton Ansorge. Has he
gone mad, Old Ansorge? My head's
goin' round like a humming-top,
sure enough. What's he doing here?
He'll do whatever he's a mind to.

Where is Ansorge? (*He taps his forehead repeatedly*) Something's wrong! I'm not answerable! I'm off my head! Off with you, off with you, rioters that you are! Heads off, legs off, hands off! If you take my house, I take your house. Forward, forward! (*Goes yelling into the drawing-room, followed by a yelling, laughing mob.*)

ACT FIVE

Langen-Bielau. OLD WEAVER HILSE'S *workroom. On the left a small window, in front of which stands the loom. On the right a bed, with a table pushed close to it. Stove, with stove-bench, in the right-hand corner. Family worship is going on.* HILSE, *his old, blind, and almost deaf wife, his son* GOTTLIEB, *and* LUISE, GOTTLIEB'S *wife, are sitting at the table, on the bed and wooden stools. A winding-wheel and bobbins on the floor between table and loom. Old spinning, weaving, and winding implements are disposed of on the smoky rafters; hanks of yarn are hanging down. There is much useless lumber in the low narrow room. The door, which is in the back wall, and leads into the big outer passage, or entry-room of the house, stands open. Through another open door on the opposite side of the passage, a second, in most respects similar, weaver's room is seen. The large passage, or entry-room of the house, is paved with stone, has damaged plaster, and a tumble-down wooden staircase leading to the attics; a washing-tub on a stool is partly visible; dirty linen of the most miserable description and poor household utensils lie about untidily. The light falls from the left into all three apartments.*

OLD HILSE *is a bearded man of strong build, but bent and wasted with age, toil, sickness, and hardship. He is an old soldier, and has lost an arm. His nose is sharp, his complexion ashen-gray, and he shakes; he is nothing but skin and bone, and has the deep-set, sore weaver's eyes.*

OLD HILSE (*stands up, as do his son and daughter-in-law; prays*). O Lord, we know not how to be thankful enough to Thee, for that Thou hast spared us this night again in thy goodness . . . an' hast had pity on us . . . an' hast suffered us to take no harm. Thou art the All-Merciful, an' we are poor, sinful children of men—that bad that we are not worthy to be trampled under thy feet. Yet Thou art our loving Father, an' Thou will look upon us an' accept us for the sake of thy dear Son, our Lord and Saviour Jesus Christ. "Jesus' blood and righteousness, Our covering is and glorious dress." An' if we're sometimes too sore cast down under Thy chastening—when the fire of Thy purification burns too raging hot—oh, lay it not to our charge; forgive us our sin. Give us patience, heavenly Father, that after all these sufferin's we may be made partakers of Thy eternal blessedness. Amen.

MOTHER HILSE (*who has been bending forward, trying hard to hear*). What a beautiful prayer you do say, father!

(LUISE *goes off to the wash-tub,* GOTTLIEB *to the room on the other side of the passage.*)

OLD HILSE. Where's the little lass?

LUISE. She's gone to Peterswaldau, to Dreissiger's. She finished all she had to wind last night.

OLD HILSE (*speaking very loud*). You'd like the wheel now, mother, eh?

MOTHER HILSE. Yes, father, I'm quite ready.

OLD HILSE (*setting it down before her*). I wish I could do the work for you.

MOTHER HILSE. An' what would be the good of that, father? There would I be, sittin' not knowin' what to do.

OLD HILSE. I'll give your fingers a wipe, then, so that they'll not grease the yarn. (*He wipes her hands with a rag.*)

LUISE (*at her tub*). If there's grease on her hands, it's not from what she's eaten.

OLD HILSE. If we've no butter, we can eat dry bread—when we've no bread, we can eat potatoes—when there's no potatoes left, we can eat bran.

LUISE (*saucily*). An' when that's all eaten, we'll do as the Wenglers did —we'll find out where the skinner's buried some stinking old horse, an' we'll dig it up an' live for a week or two on rotten carrion—how nice that'll be!

GOTTLIEB (*from the other room*). There you are, letting that tongue of yours run away with you again.

OLD HILSE. You should think twice, lass, before you talk that godless way. (*He goes to his loom, calls*) Can you give me a hand, Gottlieb? —there's a few threads to pull through.

LUISE (*from her tub*). Gottlieb, you're wanted to help father.

(GOTTLIEB *comes in, and he and his father set themselves to the troublesome task of "drawing and slaying," that is, pulling the strands of the warp through the "heddles" and "reed" of the loom. They have hardly begun to do this when* HORNIG *appears in the outer room.*)

HORNIG (*at the door*). Good luck to your work!

HILSE *and* GOTTLIEB. Thank you, Hornig.

GOTTLIEB. I say, Hornig, when do you take your sleep? You're on your rounds all day, and on watch all night.

HORNIG. Sleep's gone from me nowadays.

LUISE. Glad to see you, Hornig!

OLD HILSE. And what's the news?

HORNIG. It's queer news this mornin'. The weavers at Peterswaldau have taken the law into their own hands, an' chased Dreissiger an' his whole family out of the place.

LUISE (*perceptibly agitated*). Hornig's at his lies again.

HORNIG. No, missus, not this time, not today.—I've some beautiful pinafores in my cart.—No, it's God's truth I'm telling you. They've sent him to the right-about. He came down to Reichenbach last night, but, Lord love you! they daren't take him in there, for fear of the weavers—off he had to go again, all the way to Schweinitz.

OLD HILSE (*has been carefully lifting threads of the web and approaching them to the holes, through which, from the other side,* GOTTLIEB *pushes a wire hook, with which he catches them and draws them through*). It's about time you were stopping now, Hornig!

HORNIG. It's as sure as I'm a livin' man. Every child in the place'll soon tell you the same story.

OLD HILSE. Either your wits are a-wool-gatherin' or mine are.

HORNIG. Not mine. What I'm telling you's as true as the Bible. I wouldn't believe it myself if I hadn't stood there an' seen it with my own eyes—as I see you now, Gottlieb. They've wrecked his house from the cellar to the roof. The good china came flyin' out at the garret windows, rattlin' down the roof. God only knows how many pieces of fustian are lying soakin' in the river! The water can't get away for them—it's running over the banks, the color of washin'-blue with all the indigo they've poured out at the windows—it was flyin' like clouds of sky-blue dust. Oh, it's a terrible destruction they've worked! And it's not only the house—it's the dye-works, too —an' the stores! They've broken the stair rails, they've torn up the

fine flooring—smashed the lookin'-glasses—cut an' hacked an' torn an' smashed the sofas an' the chairs.— It's awful—it's worse than war.

OLD HILSE. An' you would have me believe that my fellow weavers did all that? (*He shakes his head incredulously. Other tenants of the house have collected at the door and are listening eagerly.*)

HORNIG. Who else, I'd like to know? I could put names to every one of 'em. It was me took the sheriff through the house, an' I spoke to a whole lot of 'em, an' they answered me back quite friendly like. They did their business with little noise, but my word! they did it well. The sheriff spoke to them, and they answered him mannerly, as they always do. But there wasn't no stoppin' of them. They hacked on at the beautiful furniture as if they were workin' for wages.

OLD HILSE. *You* took the sheriff through the house?

HORNIG. An' what would I be frightened of? Everyone knows me. I'm always turning up, like a bad penny. But no one has anything agin' me. They're all glad to see me. Yes, I went the rounds with him, as sure as my name's Hornig. An' you may believe me or not as you like, but my heart's sore yet from the sight—an' I could see by the sheriff's face that he felt queer enough, too. Not a living word did we hear—they were doin' their work and holdin' their tongues. It was a solemn an' a woeful sight to see the poor starving creatures for once in a way takin' their revenge.

LUISE (*with irrepressible excitement, trembling, wiping her eyes with her apron*). An' right they are! It's only what should be!

VOICES AMONG THE CROWD AT THE DOOR. "There's some of the same sort here."—"There's one no farther away than across the river."—"He's got four horses in his stable an' six carriages, an' he starves his weavers to keep them."

OLD HILSE (*still incredulous*). What was it set them off?

HORNIG. Who knows? Who knows? One says this, another says that.

OLD HILSE. What do they say?

HORNIG. The story as most of them tells is that it began with Dreissiger sayin' that if the weavers were hungry they might eat grass. (*Excitement at the door, as one person repeats this to the other, with signs of indignation.*)

OLD HILSE. Well, now, Hornig—if you was to say to me: Father Hilse, says you, you'll die tomorrow, I would answer back: That may be —an' why not? You might even go to the length of saying: You'll have a visit tomorrow from the King of Prussia. But to tell me that weavers, men like me an' my son, have done such things as that—never! I'll never in this world believe it.

MIELCHEN (*a pretty girl of seven, with long, loose, flaxen hair, carrying a basket on her arm, comes running in, holding out a silver spoon to her mother*). Mammy, mammy! look what I've got! An' you're to buy me a new frock with it.

LUISE. What d' you come tearing in like that for, girl? (*With increased excitement and curiosity*) An' what's that you've got hold of now? You've been runnin' yourself out o' breath, an' there—if the bobbins aren't in her basket yet? What's all this about?

OLD HILSE. Mielchen, where did that spoon come from?

LUISE. She found it, maybe.

HORNIG. It's worth its seven or eight shillin's at least.

OLD HILSE (*in distressed excitement*). Off with you, lass—out of the house this moment—unless you want a lickin'! Take that spoon back where you got it from. Out you go! Do you want to make thieves of us all, eh? I'll soon drive that out of you. (*He looks round for something to beat her with.*)

MIELCHEN (*clinging to her mother's skirts, crying*). No, grandfather, no! don't lick me! We—we did find them. All the other bob—bobbin . . . girls has . . . has them too.

LUISE (*half frightened, half excited*). I was right, you see. She found it. Where did you find it, Mielchen?

MIELCHEN (*sobbing*). At—at Peterswal—dau. We—we found them in front of—in front of Drei—Dreissiger's house.

OLD HILSE. This is worse an' worse! Get off with you this moment, unless you would like me to help you.

MOTHER HILSE. What's all the to-do about?

HORNIG. I'll tell you what, Father Hilse. The best way'll be for Gottlieb to put on his coat an' take the spoon to the police office.

OLD HILSE. Gottlieb, put on your coat.

GOTTLIEB (*pulling it on, eagerly*). Yes, an' I'll go right in to the office an' say they're not to blame us for it, for what can a child like that understand about it? an' I brought the spoon back at once. Stop your crying now, Mielchen! (*The crying child is taken into the opposite room by her mother, who shuts her in and comes back.*)

HORNIG. I believe it's worth as much as nine shillin's.

GOTTLIEB. Give us a cloth to wrap it in, Luise, so that it'll take no harm. To think of the thing bein' worth all that money! (*Tears come into his eyes while he is wrapping up the spoon.*)

LUISE. If it was only ours, we could live on it for many a day.

OLD HILSE. Hurry up, now! Look sharp! As quick as ever you can. A fine state o' matters, this! Get that devil's spoon out o' the house. (GOTTLIEB *goes off with the spoon.*)

HORNIG. I must be off now, too. (*He goes, is seen talking to the people in the entry-room before he leaves the house.*)

SURGEON SCHMIDT (*a jerky little ball of a man, with a red, knowing face, comes into the entry-room*). Good morning, all! These are fine goings on! Take care! Take care! (*Threatening with his finger*) You're a sly lot—that's what you are. (*At* HILSE'S *door without coming in*) Morning, Father Hilse. (*To a woman in the outer room*) And how are the pains, mother? Better, eh? Well, well. And how's all with you, Father Hilse? (*Enters*) Why the deuce! what's the matter with mother?

LUISE. It's the eye veins, sir—they've dried up, so as she can't see at all now.

SURGEON SCHMIDT. That's from the dust and weaving by candlelight. Will you tell me what it means that all Peterswaldau's on the way here? I set off on my rounds this morning as usual, thinking no harm; but it wasn't long till I had my eyes opened. Strange doings these! What in the devil's name has taken possession of them, Hilse? They're like a pack of raging wolves. Riot —why, it's revolution! they're plundering and laying waste right and left . . . Mielchen! where's Mielchen? (MIELCHEN, *her face red with crying, is pushed in by her mother*) Here, Mielchen, put your hand into my coat pocket. (MIELCHEN *does so*) The gingerbread nuts are for you. Not all at once, though, you baggage! And a song first! The fox jumped up on a . . . come, now . . . The fox jumped up . . . on a moonlight . . . Mind, I've heard what you did. You called the sparrows on the churchyard hedge a nasty name, and they're gone and told the pastor. Did anyone ever hear the like? Fifteen hundred of them agog—men, women, and children. (*Distant bells are heard*) That's at Reichenbach— alarm-bells! Fifteen hundred people! Uncomfortably like the world coming to an end!

OLD HILSE. An' is it true that they're on their way to Bielau?

SURGEON SCHMIDT. That's just what I'm telling you. I've driven through the middle of the whole crowd. What I'd have liked to do would have been to get down and give each of them a pill there and then. They were following on each other's heels like grim death, and their singing was more than enough to turn a man's stomach. I was nearly sick, and Frederick was shaking on the box like an old woman. We had to take a stiff glass at the first opportunity. I wouldn't be a manufacturer, not though I could drive my carriage and pair. (*Distant singing*) Listen to that! It's for all the world as if they were beating at some broken old boiler. We'll have them here in five minutes, friends. Good-bye! Don't you be foolish. The troops will be upon them in no time. Keep your wits about you. The Peterswaldau people have lost theirs. (*Bells ring close at hand*) Good gracious! There are our bells ringing too! Everyone's going mad. (*He goes upstairs.*)

GOTTLIEB (*comes back. In the entry-room, out of breath*). I've seen them, I've seen them! (*To a woman*) They're here, auntie, they're here! (*At the door*) They're here, father, they're here! They've got bean-poles, an' ox-goads, an' axes. They're standin' outside the upper Dittrich's kickin' up an awful row. I think he's payin' them money. O Lord! whatever's goin' to happen? What a crowd! Oh, you never saw such a crowd! Dash it all—if once they make a rush, our manufacturers'll be hard put to it.

OLD HILSE. What have you been runnin' like that for? You'll go racin' 'till you bring on your old trouble, and then we'll have you on your back again, strugglin' for breath.

GOTTLIEB (*almost joyously excited*). I had to run, or they would have caught me an' kept me. They were all roarin' to me to join them. Father Baumert was there too, and says he to me: You come an' get your sixpence with the rest—you're a poor starving weaver too. An' I was to tell you, father, from him, that you were to come an' help to pay out the manufacturers for their grindin' of us down. Other times is coming, he says. There's going to be a change of days for us weavers. An' we're all to come an' help to bring it about. We're to have our half-pound of meat on Sundays, and now and again on a holiday sausage with our cabbage. Yes, things is to be quite different, by what he tells me.

OLD HILSE (*with repressed indignation*). An' that man calls himself your godfather! and he bids you take part in such works of wickedness? Have nothing to do with them, Gottlieb. They've let themselves be tempted by Satan, an' it's his works they're doin'.

LUISE (*no longer able to restrain her passionate excitement, vehemently*). Yes, Gottlieb, get into the chimney corner, an' take a spoon in your hand, an' a dish of skim milk on your knee, an' put on a petticoat an' say your prayers, an' then father'll be pleased with you. And *he* sets up to be a man!
(*Laughter from the people in the entry-room.*)

OLD HILSE (*quivering with suppressed rage*). An' you set up to be a good wife, eh? You call yourself a mother, an' let your evil tongue run away with you like that? You think yourself fit to teach your girl, you that would egg on your husband to crime an' wickedness?

LUISE (*has lost all control of herself*). You an' your piety an' religion—did they serve to keep the life in my poor children? In rags an' dirt they lay, all the four—it didn't as much as keep them dry. Yes! I set up to be a mother, that's what I do—an' if you'd like to know it, that's why I would send all the manufacturers to hell—because I'm a mother!—Not one of the four could I keep in life! It was cryin' more than breathin' with me from the time each poor little thing came into the world till death took pity on it. The devil a bit you cared! You sat there prayin' and singin', and let me run about till my feet bled, tryin' to get one little drop o' skim milk. How many hundred nights have I lain an' racked my head to think what I could do to cheat the churchyard of my little one? What harm has a baby like that done that it must come to such a miserable end—eh? An' over there at Dittrich's they're bathed in wine an' washed in milk. No! you may talk as you like, but if they begin here, ten horses won't hold me back. An' what's more—if there's a rush on Dittrich's, you'll see me in the forefront of it—an' pity the man as tries to prevent me—I've stood it long enough, so now you know it.

OLD HILSE. You're a lost soul—there's no help for you.

LUISE (*frenzied*). It's you there's no help for! Tatter-breeched scarecrows—that's what you are—an' not men at all. Whey-faced gutterscrapers that take to your heels at the sound of a child's rattle. Fellows that say "thank you" to the man as gives you a hidin'. They've not left that much blood in you as that you can turn red in the face. You should have the whip taken to you, an' a little pluck flogged into your rotten bones. (*She goes out quickly.*)
(*Embarrassed pause.*)

MOTHER HILSE. What's the matter with Liesl, father?

OLD HILSE. Nothin', mother! What should be the matter with her?

MOTHER HILSE. Father, is it only me that's thinkin' it, or are the bells ringin'?

OLD HILSE. It'll be a funeral, mother.

MOTHER HILSE. An' I've got to sit waitin' here yet. Why must I be so long a-dyin', father?
(*Pause.*)

OLD HILSE (*leaves his work, holds himself up straight; solemnly*). Gottlieb!—you heard all your wife said to us. Look here, Gottlieb! (*He bares his breast*) Here they cut out a bullet as big as a thimble. The King knows where I lost my arm. It wasn't the mice as ate it. (*He walks up and down*) Before that wife of yours was ever thought of, I had spilled my blood by the quart fo' King an' country. So let her call what names she likes—an' welcome! It does me no harm.—Frightened? Me frightened? What would I be frightened of, will you tell me that? Of the few soldiers, maybe, that'll be comin' after the rioters? Good gracious me! That would be a lot to be frightened at! No, no, lad; I may be a bit stiff in the back, but there's some strength left in the old bones; I've got the stuff in me yet to make a stand against a few rubbishin' bay'nets. —An' if it came to the worst! Willin', willin' would I be to say good-bye to this weary world. Death would be welcome—welcomer to me today than tomorrow. For what is it we leave behind? That old bundle of aches an' pains we call our body, the care an' the oppression we call by the name of life. We may be glad to get away from it.—But there's something to come after, Gottlieb!—an' if we've done ourselves out of that too—why, then it's all over with us!

GOTTLIEB. Who knows what's to come after? Nobody's seen it.

OLD HILSE. Gottlieb! don't you be throwin' doubts on the one comfort us poor people have. Why have I sat here an' worked my treadle like a slave this forty year an' more?— sat still an' looked on at him over yonder livin' in pride an' wastefulness—why? Because I have a better hope, something as supports me in all my troubles. (Points out at the window) You have your good things in this world—I'll have mine in the next. That's been my thought. An' I'm that certain of it— I'd let myself be torn in pieces. Have we not His promise? There's a Day of Judgment coming; but it's not us as are the judges—no: vengeance is mine, saith the Lord. (A cry of "Weavers, come out!" is heard outside the window.)

OLD HILSE. Do what you will for me. (He seats himself at his loom) I stay here.

GOTTLIEB (after a short struggle). I'm going to work, too—come what may. (Goes out.)
(The Weavers' Song is heard, sung by hundreds of voices quite close at hand; it sounds like a dull monotonous wail.)

INMATES OF THE HOUSE (in the entry-room). "Oh, mercy on us! there they come swarmin' like ants!"— "Where can all these weavers be from?"—"Don't shove like that, I want to see too."—"Look at that great maypole of a woman leadin' on in front!"—"Gracious! they're comin' thicker an' thicker."

HORNIG (comes into the entry-room from outside). There's a theayter play for you now! That's what you don't see every day. But you should go up to the other Dittrich's an' look what they've done there. It's been no half work. He's got no house now, nor no factory, nor no wine-cellar, nor nothing. They're drinkin' out of the bottles—not so much as takin' the time to get out the corks. One, two, three, an' off with the neck, an' no matter whether they cut their mouths or not. There's some of them runnin' about bleedin' like stuck pigs.— Now they're goin' to do for this Dittrich.
(The singing has stopped.)

INMATES OF THE HOUSE. There's nothin' so very wicked-like about them.

HORNIG. You wait a bit! you'll soon see! All they're doin' just now is makin' up their minds where they'll begin. Look, they're inspectin' the palace from every side. Do you see that little stout man there, him with the stable pail? That's the smith from Peterswaldau—an' a dangerous little chap he is. He batters in the thickest doors as if they were made o' piecrust. If a manufacturer was to fall into his hands it would be all over with him!

INMATES OF THE HOUSE. "That was a crack!"—"There went a stone through the window!"—"There's old Dittrich, shakin' with fright."—"He's hangin' out a board."—"Hangin' out a board?"—"What's written on it?"—"Can you not read?"—"It would be a bad job for me if I couldn't read!"—"Well, read it, then!"—"'You—shall have—full—satisfaction! You—shall have full satisfaction.'"

HORNIG. He might ha' spared himself the trouble—*that* won't help him. It's something else they've set their minds on here. It's the factories. They're goin' to smash up the power-looms. For it's them that are ruinin' the hand-loom weaver. Even a blind man might see that. No! the good folks know what they're after, an' no sheriff an' no p'lice superintendent'll bring them to reason—much less a bit of a board. Him as has seen them at work already knows what's comin'.

INMATES OF THE HOUSE. "Did anyone ever see such a crowd?"—"What can these ones be wantin'?"—(*Hastily*) "They're crossin' the bridge!"—(*Anxiously*) "They're never comin' over on this side, are they?"—(*In excitement and terror*) "It's to us they're comin'!"—"They're comin' to us!"—"They're comin' to fetch the weavers out of their houses!"

(*General flight. The entry-room is empty. A crowd of dirty, dusty rioters rush in, their faces scarlet with brandy and excitement; tattered, untidy-looking, as if they had been up all night. With the shout: "Weavers, come out!" they disperse themselves through the house.* BECKER *and several other young weavers, armed with cudgels and poles, come into* OLD HILSE'S *room. When they see the old man at his loom they start, and cool down a little.*)

BECKER. Come, Father Hilse, stop that. Leave your work to them as wants to work. There's no need now for you to be doin' yourself harm. You'll be well taken care of.

FIRST YOUNG WEAVER. You'll never need to go hungry to bed again.

SECOND YOUNG WEAVER. The weaver's goin' to have a roof over his head and a shirt on his back once more.

OLD HILSE. An' what's the devil sendin' you to do now, with your poles an' axe?

BECKER. These are what we're goin' to break on Dittrich's back.

SECOND YOUNG WEAVER. We'll heat them red hot an' stick them down the manufacturers' throats, so as they'll feel for once what burnin' hunger tastes like.

THIRD YOUNG WEAVER. Come along, Father Hilse! We'll give no quarter.

SECOND YOUNG WEAVER. No one had mercy on us—neither God nor man.

Now we're standin' up for our rights ourselves.

(OLD BAUMERT *enters, somewhat shaky on the legs, a newly killed cock under his arm.*)

OLD BAUMERT (*stretching out his arms*). My brothers—we're all brothers! Come to my arms, brothers!
(*Laughter.*)

OLD HILSE. And that's the state you're in, Willem?

OLD BAUMERT. Gustav, is it you? My poor starvin' friend! Come to my arms, Gustav!

OLD HILSE (*mutters*). Let me alone.

OLD BAUMERT. I'll tell you what, Gustav. It's nothin' but luck that's wanted. You look at me. What do I look like? Luck's what's wanted. Do I not look like a lord? (*Pats his stomach*) Guess what's in there! There's food fit for a prince in that belly. When luck's with him a man gets roast hare to eat an' champagne wine to drink.—I'll tell you all something: We've made a big mistake—we must help ourselves.

ALL (*speaking at once*). We must help ourselves, hurrah!

OLD BAUMERT. As soon as we get the first good bite inside us we're different men. Damn it all! but you feel the power comin' into you till you're like an ox, an' that wild with strength that you hit out right an' left without as much as takin' time to look. Dash it, but it's grand!

JAEGER (*at the door, armed with an old cavalry sword*). We've made one or two first-rate attacks.

BECKER. We know how to set about it now. One, two, three, an' we're inside the house. Then, at it like lightning—bang, crack, shiver! till the sparks are flyin' as if it was a smithy.

FIRST YOUNG WEAVER. It wouldn't be half bad to light a bit o' fire.

SECOND YOUNG WEAVER. Let's march to Reichenbach and burn the rich folks' houses over their heads!

JAEGER. That would be nothing but butterin' their bread. Think of all the insurance money they'd get.
(*Laughter.*)

BECKER. No, from here we'll go to Freiburg, to Tromtra's.

JAEGER. What would you say to givin' all them as holds Government appointments a lesson? I've read somewhere as how all our troubles come from them birocrats, as they call them.

SECOND YOUNG WEAVER. Before long we'll go to Breslau, for more an' more'll be joining us.

OLD BAUMERT (*to* HILSE). Won't you take a drop, Gustav?

OLD HILSE. I never touches it.

OLD BAUMERT. That was in the old world; we're in a new world to-day, Gustav.

FIRST YOUNG WEAVER. Christmas comes but once a year.
(*Laughter.*)

OLD HILSE (*impatiently*). What is it you want in my house, you limbs of Satan?

OLD BAUMERT (*a little intimidated, coaxingly*). I was bringin' you a chicken, Gustav. I thought it would make a drop o' soup for mother.

OLD HILSE (*embarrassed, almost friendly*). Well, you can tell mother yourself.

MOTHER HILSE (*who has been making efforts to hear, her hand at her ear, motions them off*). Let me alone. I don't want no chicken soup.

OLD HILSE. That's right, mother. An' I want none, an' least of all that sort. An' let me say this much to you, Baumert: The devil stands on his head for joy when he hears the old ones jabberin' and talkin' as if they was infants. An' to you all I say—to every one of you: Me and you, we've got nothing to do with each other. It's not with my will that you're here. In law an' justice you've no right to be in my house.

A VOICE. Him that's not with us is against us.

JAEGER (*roughly and threateningly*). You're a cross-grained old chap, and I'd have you remember that we're not thieves.

A VOICE. We're hungry men, that's all.

FIRST YOUNG WEAVER. We want to live—that's all. An' so we've cut the rope we were hung up with.

JAEGER. And we were in our right! (*Holding his fist in front of the old man's face*) Say another word, and I'll give you one between the eyes.

BECKER. Come now, Jaeger, be quiet. Let the old man alone.—

What we say to ourselves, Father Hilse, is this: Better dead than begin the old life again.

OLD HILSE. Have I not lived that life for sixty years an' more?

BECKER. That doesn't help us—there's got to be a change.

OLD HILSE. On the Judgment Day.

BECKER. What they'll not give us willingly we're going to take by force.

OLD HILSE. By force. (*Laughs*) You may as well go an' dig your graves at once. They'll not be long showin' you where the force lies. Wait a bit, lad!

JAEGER. Is it the soldiers you're meaning? We've been soldiers, too. We'll soon do for a company or two of them.

OLD HILSE. With your tongues, maybe. But supposin' you did—for two that you'd beat off, ten'll come back.

VOICES (*call through the window*). The soldiers are comin'! Look out! (*General, sudden silence. For a moment a faint sound of fifes and drums is heard; in the ensuing silence, involuntary exclamation, "The devil! I'm off!" followed by general laughter.*)

BECKER. Who was that? Who speaks of running away?

JAEGER. Which of you is it that's afraid of a few paltry helmets? You have me to command you, and I've been in the trade. I know their tricks.

OLD HILSE. An' what are you goin' to shoot with? Your sticks, eh?

FIRST YOUNG WEAVER. Never mind that old chap; he's wrong in the upper story.

SECOND YOUNG WEAVER. Yes, he's a bit off his head.

GOTTLIEB (*has made his way unnoticed among the rioters; catches hold of the speaker*). Would you give your impudence to an old man like him?

SECOND YOUNG WEAVER. Let me alone. 'Twasn't anything bad I said.

OLD HILSE (*interfering*). Let him jaw, Gottlieb. What would you be meddlin' with him for? He'll soon see who it is that's been off his head today, him or me.

BECKER. Are you comin', Gottlieb?

OLD HILSE. No, he's goin' to do no such thing.

LUISE (*comes into the entry-room, calls*). What are you puttin' off your time with prayin' hypocrites like them for? Come quick to where you're wanted! Quick! Father Baumert, run all you can! The Major's speakin' to the crowd from horseback. They're to go home. If you don't hurry up, it'll be all over.

JAEGER (*as he goes out*). That's a brave husband of yours.

LUISE. Where is he? I've got no husband!
(*Some of the people in the entry-room sing.*)

Once on a time a man so small,
    Heigh-ho, heigh!
Set his heart on a wife so tall,
    Heigh diddle-di-dum-di!

WITTIG, THE SMITH (*comes downstairs, still carrying the stable pail; stops on his way through the entry-room*). Come on! all of you that are not cowardly scoundrels!—hurrah! (*He dashes out, followed by* LUISE, JAEGER, *and others, all shouting "Hurrah!"*)

BECKER. Good-bye, then, Father Hilse; we'll see each other again. (*Is going.*)

OLD HILSE. I doubt that. I've not five years to live, and that'll be the soonest you'll get out.

BECKER (*stops, not understanding*). Out o' what, Father Hilse?

OLD HILSE. Out of prison—where else?

BECKER (*laughs wildly*). Do you think I would mind that? There's bread to be had there anyhow! (*Goes out.*)

OLD BAUMERT (*has been cowering on a low stool, painfully beating his brains; he now gets up*). It's true, Gustav, as I've had a drop too much. But for all that I know what I'm about. You think one way in this here matter; I think another. I say Becker's right: even if it ends in chains an' ropes—we'll be better off in prison than at home. You're cared for there, an' you don't need to starve. I wouldn't have joined them, Gustav, if I could have let it be; but once in a lifetime a man's got to show what he feels. (*Goes slowly towards the door*) Good-bye,

GUSTAV. If anything happens, mind you put in a word for me in your prayers. (*Goes out.*)
(*The rioters are now all gone. The entry-room gradually fills again with curious onlookers from the different rooms of the house.* OLD HILSE *knots at his web.* GOTTLIEB *has taken an axe from behind the stove and is unconsciously feeling its edge. He and the old man are silently agitated. The hum and roar of a great crowd penetrate into the room.*)

MOTHER HILSE. The very boards is shakin', father—what's goin' on? What's goin' to happen to us? (*Pause.*)

OLD HILSE. Gottlieb!

GOTTLIEB. What is it?

OLD HILSE. Let that axe alone.

GOTTLIEB. Who's to split the wood, then? (*He leans the axe against the stove. Pause.*)

MOTHER HILSE. Gottlieb, you listen to what father says to you.
(*Someone sings outside the window.*)

Our little man does all that he can,
    Heigh-ho, heigh!
At home he cleans the pots an' the
    pan,
    Heigh-diddle-di-dum-di!

(*Passes on.*)

GOTTLIEB (*jumps up, shakes his clenched fist at the window*). Brute that you are, would you drive me crazy?
(*A volley of musketry is heard.*)

MOTHER HILSE (*starts and trembles*). Good, Lord! is that thunder again?

OLD HILSE (*instinctively folding his hands*). Oh, our Father in heaven! defend the poor weavers, protect my poor brothers!
(*A short pause ensues.*)

OLD HILSE (*to himself, painfully agitated*). There's blood flowing now.

GOTTLIEB (*had started up and grasped the axe when the shooting was heard; deathly pale, almost beside himself with excitement*). And am I to lie to heel like a dog still?

A GIRL (*calls from the entry-room*). Father Hilse, Father Hilse! get away from the window. A bullet's just flown in at our upstairs. (*Disappears.*)

MIELCHEN (*puts her head in at the window, laughing*). Gran'father, gran'father, they've shot with their guns. Two or three's been knocked down, an' one of them's turnin' round and round like a top, an' one's twistin' himself like a sparrow when its head's bein' pulled off. An' oh, if you saw all the blood that came pourin'—! (*Disappears.*)

A WEAVER'S WIFE. Yes, there's two or three'll never get up again.

AN OLD WEAVER (*in the entry-room*). Look out! They're goin' to make a rush on the soldiers.

A SECOND WEAVER (*wildly*). Look, look, look at the women!—skirts up, an' spittin' in the soldiers' faces already!

A WEAVER'S WIFE (*calls in*). Gottlieb, look at your wife. She's more pluck in her than you. She's jumpin' about in front o' the bay'nets as if she was dancin' to music.

(*Four men carry a wounded rioter through the entry-room. Silence, which is broken by someone saying in a distinct voice, "It's Weaver Ulbrich." Once more silence for a few seconds, when the same voice is heard again: "It's all over with him; he's got a bullet in his ear." The men are heard climbing the wooden stair. Sudden shouting outside: "Hurrah, hurrah!"*)

VOICES IN THE ENTRY-ROOM. "Where did they get the stones from?"—"Yes, it's time you were off!"—"From the new road."—"Tata, soldiers!"—"It's raining paving-stones."

(*Shrieks of terror and loud roaring outside, taken up by those in the entry-room. There is a cry of fear, and the house door is shut with a bang.*)

VOICES IN THE ENTRY-ROOM. "They're loading again."—"They'll fire another volley this minute."—"Father Hilse, get away from that window."

GOTTLIEB (*clutches the axe*). What! are we mad dogs? Are we to eat powder an' shot now instead of bread? (*Hesitating an instant: to the old man*) Would you have me sit here an' see my wife 'shot? Never! (*As he rushes out*) Look out! I'm coming!

OLD HILSE. Gottlieb, Gottlieb!

MOTHER HILSE. Where's Gottlieb gone?

OLD HILSE. He's gone to the devil.

VOICES FROM THE ENTRY-ROOM. Go away from the window, Father Hilse.

OLD HILSE. Not I! Not if you all go crazy together! (*To* MOTHER HILSE, *with rapt excitement*) My heavenly Father has placed me here. Isn't that so, mother? Here we'll sit, an' do our bounden duty—aye, though the snow was to go on fire. (*He begins to weave.*)

(*Rattle of another volley.* OLD HILSE, *mortally wounded, starts to his feet and then falls forward over the loom. At the same moment loud shouting of "Hurrah!" is heard. The people who till now have been standing in the entry-room dash out, joining in the cry. The old woman repeatedly asks: "Father, father, what's wrong with you?" The continued shouting dies away gradually in the distance.* MIELCHEN *comes rushing in.*)

MIELCHEN. Gran'father, gran'father, they're drivin' the soldiers out of the village; they've got into Dittrich's house, an' they're doin' what they did at Dreissiger's. Gran'father! (*The child grows frightened, notices that something has happened, puts her finger in her mouth, and goes up cautiously to the dead man.*) Gran'father!

MOTHER HILSE. Come now, father, can't you say something? You're frightenin' me.

CURTAIN

The Sea Gull

A COMEDY IN FOUR ACTS

BY ANTON TCHEKOV

TRANSLATED FROM THE RUSSIAN
BY CONSTANCE GARNETT

CHARACTERS

IRINA NIKOLAYEVNA ARKADIN, MADAME TREPLEV, *an Actress.*
KONSTANTIN GAVRILOVITCH TREPLEV, *her son, a young man.*
PYOTR NIKOLAYEVITCH SORIN, *her brother.*
NINA MIHAILOVNA ZARETCHNY, *a young girl, the daughter of a wealthy Landowner.*
ILYA AFANASYEVITCH SHAMRAEV, *a retired Lieutenant,* SORIN's *Steward.*
POLINA ANDREYEVNA, *his wife.*
MASHA, *his daughter.*
BORIS ALEXEYEVITCH TRIGORIN, *a literary man.*
YEVGENY SERGEYEVITCH DORN, *a Doctor.*
SEMYON SEMYONOVITCH MEDVEDENKO, *a Schoolmaster.*
YAKOV, *a Labourer.*
A MAN COOK.
A HOUSEMAID.

The action takes place in SORIN's *house and garden. Between the Third and Fourth Acts there is an interval of two years.*

THE SEA GULL

ACT ONE

Part of the park on SORIN'S *estate. Wide avenue leading away from the spectators into the depths of the park towards the lake is blocked up by a platform roughly put together for private theatricals, so that the lake is not visible. To right and left of the platform, bushes. A few chairs, a little table.*

The sun has just set. YAKOV *and other labourers are at work on the platform behind the curtain; there is the sound of coughing and hammering.* MASHA *and* MEDVEDENKO *enter on the left, returning from a walk.*

MEDVEDENKO. Why do you always wear black?

MASHA. I am in mourning for my life. I am unhappy.

MEDVEDENKO. Why? (*Pondering*) I don't understand . . . You are in good health; though your father is not very well off, he has got enough. My life is much harder than yours. I only get twenty-three roubles a month, and from that they deduct something for the pension fund, and yet I don't wear mourning. (*They sit down.*)

MASHA. It isn't money that matters. A poor man may be happy.

MEDVEDENKO. Theoretically, yes; but in practice it's like this: there are my two sisters and my mother and my little brother and I, and my salary is only twenty-three roubles. We must eat and drink, mustn't we? One must have tea and sugar. One must have tobacco. It's a tight fit.

MASHA (*looking round at the platform*). The play will soon begin.

MEDVEDENKO. Yes. Miss Zaretchny will act: it is Konstantin Gavrilitch's play. They are in love with each other and today their souls will be united in the effort to realise the same artistic effect. But your soul and mine have not a common point of contact. I love you. I am so wretched I can't stay at home. Every day I walk four miles here and four miles back and I meet with nothing but indifference from you. I can quite understand it. I am without means and have a big family to keep. . . . Who would care to marry a man who hasn't a penny to bless himself with?

MASHA. Oh, nonsense! (*Takes a pinch of snuff*) Your love touches me, but I can't reciprocate it—that's all. (*Holding out the snuffbox to him*) Help yourself.

MEDVEDENKO. I don't feel like it. (*A pause.*)

MASHA. How stifling it is! There must be a storm coming. . . . You're always discussing theories or talking about money. You think there is no greater misfortune than

151

poverty, but to my mind it is a thousand times better to go in rags and be a beggar than . . . But you wouldn't understand that, though. . . .

(SORIN *and* TREPLEV *enter on the right.*)

SORIN (*leaning on his walking-stick*). I am never quite myself in the country, my boy, and, naturally enough, I shall never get used to it. Last night I went to bed at ten and woke up this morning at nine feeling as though my brain were glued to my skull, through sleeping so long. (*Laughs*) And after dinner I accidentally dropped off again, and now I am utterly shattered and feel as though I were in a nightmare, in fact. . . .

TREPLEV. Yes, you really ought to live in town. (*Catches sight of* MASHA *and* MEDVEDENKO) When the show begins, my friends, you will be summoned, but you mustn't be here now. You must please go away.

SORIN (*to* MASHA). Marya Ilyinishna, will you be so good as to ask your papa to tell them to take the dog off the chain?—it howls. My sister could not sleep again last night.

MASHA. Speak to my father yourself; I am not going to. Please don't ask me. (*To* MEDVEDENKO) Come along!

MEDVEDENKO (*to* TREPLEV). So you will send and let us know before it begins. (*Both go out.*)

SORIN. So I suppose the dog will be howling all night again. What a business it is! I have never done

as I liked in the country. In old days I used to get leave for twenty-eight days and come here for a rest and so on, but they worried me so with all sorts of trifles that before I had been here two days I was longing to be off again. (*Laughs*) I've always been glad to get away from here. . . . But now I am on the retired list, and I have nowhere else to go, as a matter of fact. I've got to live here whether I like it or not. . . .

YAKOV (*to* TREPLEV). We are going to have a bathe, Konstantin Gavrilitch.

TREPLEV. Very well; but don't be more than ten minutes. (*Looks at his watch*) It will soon begin.

YAKOV. Yes, sir. (*Goes out.*)

TREPLEV (*looking round the stage*). Here is our theatre. The curtain, then the first wing, then the second, and beyond that—open space. No scenery of any sort. There is an open view of the lake and the horizon. We shall raise the curtain at exactly half-past eight, when the moon rises.

SORIN. Magnificent.

TREPLEV. If Nina is late it will spoil the whole effect. It is time she was here. Her father and her stepmother keep a sharp eye on her, and it is as hard for her to get out of the house as to escape from prison. (*Puts his uncle's cravat straight*) Your hair and your beard are very untidy. They want clipping or something. . . .

SORIN (*combing out his beard*). It's the tragedy of my life. Even as a young man I looked as though I had been drinking for days or something of the sort. I was never a favourite with the ladies. (*Sitting down*) Why is your mother out of humour?

TREPLEV. Why? Because she is bored. (*Sitting down beside him*). She is jealous. She is set against me, and against the performance, and against my play because Nina is acting in it, and she is not. She does not know my play, but she hates it.

SORIN (*laughs*). What an idea!

TREPLEV. She is annoyed to think that even on this little stage Nina will have a triumph and not she. (*Looks at his watch*) My mother is a psychological freak. Unmistakably talented, intelligent, capable of sobbing over a book, she will reel off all Nekrassov by heart; as a sick-nurse she is an angel; but just try praising Duse in her presence! O-ho! You must praise no one but herself, you must write about her, make a fuss over her, be in raptures over her extraordinary acting in "La Dame aux Camelias" or the "Ferment of Life"; but she has none of this narcotic in the country, she is bored and cross, and we are all her enemies—we are all in fault. Then she is superstitious—she is afraid of three candles, of the number thirteen. She is stingy. She has got seventy thousand roubles in a bank at Odessa—I know that for a fact—but ask her to lend you some money, and she will burst into tears.

SORIN. You imagine your mother does not like your play, and you are already upset and all that. Don't worry; your mother adores you.

TREPLEV (*pulling the petals off a flower*). Loves me, loves me not; loves me, loves me not; loves me, loves me not. (*Laughs*) You see, my mother does not love me. I should think not! She wants to live, to love, to wear light blouses; and I am twenty-five, and I am a continual reminder that she is no longer young. When I am not there she is only thirty-two, but when I am there she is forty-three, and for that she hates me. She knows, too, that I have no belief in the theatre. She loves the stage, she fancies she is working for humanity, for the holy cause of art, while to my mind the modern theatre is nothing but tradition and conventionality. When the curtain goes up, and by artificial light, in a room with three walls, these great geniuses, the devotees of holy art, represent how people eat, drink, love, move about, and wear their jackets; when from these commonplace sentences and pictures they try to draw a moral—a petty moral, easy of comprehension and convenient for domestic use; when in a thousand variations I am offered the same thing over and over again—I run away as Maupassant ran away from the Eiffel Tower which weighed upon his brain with its vulgarity.

SORIN. You can't do without the stage.

TREPLEV. We need new forms of expression. We need new forms, and if we can't have them we had better have nothing. (*Looks at his watch*) I love my mother—I love her very much—but she leads a senseless sort of life, always taken up with this literary gentleman, her name is always trotted out in the papers—and that wearies me. And sometimes the simple egoism of an ordinary mortal makes me feel sorry that my mother is a celebrated actress, and I fancy that if she were an ordinary woman I should be happier. Uncle, what could be more hopeless and stupid than my position? She used to have visitors, all celebrities—artists and authors—and among them all I was the only one who was nothing, and they only put up with me because I was her son. Who am I? What am I? I left the University in my third year—owing to circumstances "for which we accept no responsibility," as the editors say; I have no talents, I haven't a penny of my own, and on my passport I am described as an artisan of Kiev. You know my father was an artisan of Kiev, though he too was a well-known actor. So, when in her drawing-room all these artists and authors graciously noticed me, I always fancied from their faces that they were taking the measure of my insignificance—I guessed their thoughts and suffered from the humiliation. . . .

SORIN. And, by the way, can you tell me, please, what sort of man this literary gentleman is? There's no making him out. He never says anything.

TREPLEV. He is an intelligent man, good-natured and rather melancholy, you know. A very decent fellow. He is still a good distance off forty, but he is already celebrated and has enough and to spare of everything. As for his writings . . . what shall I say? They are charming, full of talent, but . . . after Tolstoy or Zola you do not care to read Trigorin.

SORIN. Well, I am fond of authors, my boy. At one time I had a passionate desire for two things: I wanted to get married, and I wanted to become an author; but I did not succeed in doing either. Yes, it is pleasant to be even a small author, as a matter of fact.

TREPLEV (listens). I hear steps. . . . (Embraces his uncle) I cannot live without her. . . . The very sound of her footsteps is lovely. . . . I am wildly happy. (Goes quickly to meet NINA ZARETCHNY as she enters) My enchantress—my dream. . . .

NINA (in agitation). I am not late. . . . Of course I am not late. . . .

TREPLEV (kissing her hands). No, no, no!

NINA. I have been uneasy all day. I was so frightened. I was afraid father would not let me come. . . . But he has just gone out with my stepmother. The sky is red, the moon is just rising, and I kept urging on the horse. (Laughs) But I am glad. (Shakes SORIN's hand warmly.)

SORIN (laughs). Your eyes look as though you have been crying. . . . Fie, fie! That's not right!

NINA. Oh, it was nothing. . . . You see how out of breath I am. I have to go in half an hour. We must make haste. I can't stay, I can't! For God's sake don't keep me! My father doesn't know I am here.

TREPLEV. It really is time to begin. We must go and call the others.

SORIN. I'll go this minute. (Goes to

the right, singing "To France two grenadiers." *Looks round*) Once I sang like that, and a deputy prosecutor said to me, "You have a powerful voice, your Excellency"; then he thought a little and added, "but not a pleasant one." (*Laughs and goes off.*)

NINA. My father and his wife won't let me come here. They say it is so Bohemian here . . . they are afraid I shall go on the stage. . . . But I feel drawn to the lake here like a sea gull. . . . My heart is full of you. (*Looks round.*)

TREPLEV. We are alone.

NINA. I fancy there is someone there.

TREPLEV. There's nobody. (*They kiss.*)

NINA. What tree is this?

TREPLEV. An elm.

NINA. Why is it so dark?

TREPLEV. It's evening; everything is getting dark. Don't go away early, I entreat you!

NINA. I must.

TREPLEV. And if I come to you, Nina, I'll stand in the garden all night, watching your window.

NINA. You can't; the watchman would notice you. Trésor is not used to you, and he would bark.

TREPLEV. I love you!

NINA. Sh-h. . . .

TREPLEV (*hearing footsteps*). Who is there? You, Yakov?

YAKOV (*behind the stage*). Yes, sir.

TREPLEV. Take your places. It's time to begin. Is the moon rising?

YAKOV. Yes, sir.

TREPLEV. Have you got the methylated spirit? Have you got the sulphur? When the red eyes appear there must be a smell of sulphur. (*To* NINA) Go, it's all ready. Are you nervous?

NINA. Yes, awfully! Your mother is all right—I am not afraid of her—but there's Trigorin . . . I feel frightened and ashamed of acting before him . . . a celebrated author. . . . Is he young?

TREPLEV. Yes.

NINA. How wonderful his stories are.

TREPLEV (*coldly*). I don't know. I haven't read them.

NINA. It is difficult to act in your play. There are no living characters in it.

TREPLEV. Living characters! One must depict life not as it is, and not as it ought to be, but as we see it in our dreams.

NINA. There is very little action in your play—nothing but speeches. And to my mind there ought to be love in a play. (*Both go behind the stage.*)
(*Enter* POLINA ANDREYEVNA *and* DORN.)

POLINA. It is getting damp. Go back and put on your goloshes.

DORN. I am hot.

POLINA. You don't take care of yourself. It's obstinacy. You are a doctor, and you know perfectly well that damp air is bad for you, but you want to make me miserable; you sat out on the verandah all yesterday evening on purpose. . . .

DORN (*hums*). "Do not say that youth is ruined."

POLINA. You were so absorbed in conversation with Irina Nikolayevna . . . you did not notice the cold. Own up . . . you are attracted by her.

DORN. I am fifty-five.

POLINA. Nonsense! That's not old for a man. You look very young for your age, and are still attractive to women.

DORN. Well, what would you have?

POLINA. All you men are ready to fall down and worship an actress, all of you!

DORN (*hums*). "Before thee once again I stand." If artists are liked in society and treated differently from merchants, for example, that's only in the nature of things. It's idealism.

POLINA. Women have always fallen in love with you and thrown themselves on your neck. Is that idealism too?

DORN (*shrugs his shoulders*). Well,

in the attitude of women to me there has been a great deal that was good. What they principally loved in me was a first-rate doctor. You remember that ten or fifteen years ago I was the only decent accoucheur in the district. Then, too, I have always been an honest man.

POLINA (*seizes him by the hand*). Dearest!

DORN. Sh-h! They are coming.
(*Enter* MADAME ARKADIN *surrounded by* SORIN, TRIGORIN, SHAMRAEV, MEDVEDENKO *and* MASHA.)

SHAMRAEV. In the year 1873 she acted marvellously at the fair at Poltava. It was a delight! She acted exquisitely! Do you happen to know, madam, where Pavel Semyonitch Tchadin, a comic actor, is now? His Rasplyuev was inimitable, even finer than Sadovsky's, I assure you, honoured lady. Where is he now?

MADAME ARKADIN. You keep asking me about antediluvians. How should I know? (*Sits down.*)

SHAMRAEV (*with a sigh*). Pashka Tchadin! There are no such actors now. The stage has gone down, Irina Nikolayevna! In old days there were mighty oaks, but now we see nothing but stumps.

DORN. There are few actors of brilliant talents nowadays, that's true; but the average level of acting is far higher than it was.

SHAMRAEV. I can't agree with you. But, of course, it's a matter of taste. *De gustibus aut bene aut nihil.*

(TREPLEV *comes out from behind the stage.*)

MADAME ARKADIN (*to her son*). My dear son, when is it going to begin?

TREPLEV. In a minute. I beg you to be patient.

MADAME ARKADIN (*recites from* "Hamlet").
"Oh, Hamlet, speak no more!
Thou turn'st mine eyes into my
very soul;
And there I see such black and
grained spots
As will not leave their tinct."

TREPLEV (*from* "Hamlet").
"And let me wring your heart, for
so I shall,
If it be made of penetrable stuff."
(*A horn is sounded behind the stage.*)

TREPLEV. Ladies and gentlemen, we begin! I beg you to attend. (*A pause*) I begin. (*Taps with a stick and recites aloud*) Oh, you venerable old shadows that float at night-time over this lake, lull us to sleep and let us dream of what will be in two hundred thousand years!

SORIN. There will be nothing in two hundred thousand years.

TREPLEV. Then let them present that nothing to us.

MADAME ARKADIN. Let them. We are asleep.
(*The curtain rises; the view of the lake is revealed; the moon is above the horizon, its reflection in the water;* NINA ZARETCHNY, *all in white, is sitting on a big stone.*)

NINA. Men, lions, eagles and part-ridges, horned deer, geese, spiders, silent fish that dwell in the water, starfishes and creatures which cannot be seen by the eye—all living things, all living things, all living things, having completed their cycle of sorrow, are extinct. . . . For thousands of years the earth has borne no living creature on its surface, and this poor moon lights its lamp in vain. On the meadow the cranes no longer waken with a cry, and there is no sound of the May beetles in the lime trees. It is cold, cold, cold! Empty, empty, empty! Dreadful, dreadful, dreadful! (*A pause*) The bodies of living creatures have vanished into dust, and eternal matter has transformed them into rocks, into water, into clouds, while the souls of all have melted into one. That world-soul I am—I. . . . In me is the soul of Alexander the Great, of Cæsar, of Shakespeare and of Napoleon, and of the lowest leech. In me the consciousness of men is blended with the instincts of the animals, and I remember all, all, all! And I live through every life over again in myself!
(*Will-of-the-wisps appear.*)

MADAME ARKADIN (*softly*). It's something decadent.

TREPLEV (*in an imploring and reproachful voice*). Mother!

NINA. I am alone. Once in a hundred years I open my lips to speak, and my voice echoes mournfully in the void, and no one hears. . . . You too, pale lights, hear me not. . . . The stagnant marsh begets you before daybreak and you wander until dawn, but without thought, without will, without the tremor of life. For fear that life should spring up in you the father of eternal matter, the devil, keeps the atoms in you, as in the stones and in the water, in continual flux, and you are changing perpetually. For in all the universe nothing remains permanent and unchanged but the spirit. (*A pause*) Like a prisoner cast into a deep, empty well I know not where I am and what awaits me. All is hidden from me but that in the cruel, persistent struggle with the devil—the principle of the forces of matter—I am destined to conquer, and, after that, matter and spirit will be blended in glorious harmony and the Kingdom of the Cosmic Will will come. But that will come only little by little, through long, long thousands of years when the moon and the bright Sirius and the earth are changed to dust. . . . Till then—terror, terror. . . . (*A pause; two red spots appear upon the background of the lake*) Here my powerful foe, the devil, is approaching. I see his dreadful crimson eyes. . . .

MADAME ARKADIN. There's a smell of sulphur. Is that as it should be?

TREPLEV. Yes.

MADAME ARKADIN (*laughs*). Oh, it's a stage effect!

TREPLEV. Mother!

NINA. He is dreary without man —

POLINA (*to* DORN). You have taken your hat off. Put it on or you will catch cold.

MADAME ARKADIN. The doctor has taken his hat off to the devil, the father of eternal matter.

TREPLEV (*firing up, aloud*). The play is over! Enough! Curtain!

MADAME ARKADIN. What are you cross about?

TREPLEV. Enough! The curtain! Let down the curtain! (*Stamping*) Curtain! (*The curtain falls*) I am sorry! I lost sight of the fact that only a few of the elect may write plays and act in them. I have infringed the monopoly. I . . . I . . . (*Tries to say something more, but with a wave of his hand goes out on left.*)

MADAME ARKADIN. What's the matter with him?

SORIN. Irina, you really must have more consideration for youthful vanity, my dear.

MADAME ARKADIN. What did I say to him?

SORIN. You hurt his feelings.

MADAME ARKADIN. He told us beforehand that it was a joke, and I regarded his play as a joke.

SORIN. All the same . . .

MADAME ARKADIN. Now it appears that he has written a great work. What next! So he has got up this performance and smothered us with sulphur not as a joke but as a protest. . . . He wanted to show us how to write and what to act. This is getting tiresome! These continual sallies at my expense—these continual pin-pricks would put anyone out of patience, say what you like. He is a vain, whimsical boy!

SORIN. He meant to give you pleasure.

MADAME ARKADIN. Really? He did not choose an ordinary play, however, but made us listen to this decadent delirium. For the sake of a joke I am ready to listen to delirium, but here we have pretensions to new forms and a new view of art. To my thinking it's no question of new forms at all, but simply bad temper.

TRIGORIN. Everyone writes as he likes and as he can.

MADAME ARKADIN. Let him write as he likes and as he can, only let him leave me in peace.

DORN. Jupiter! you are angry. . . .

MADAME ARKADIN. I am not Jupiter —I am a woman. (*Lights a cigarette*) I am not angry—I am only vexed that a young man should spend his time so drearily. I did not mean to hurt his feelings.

MEDVEDENKO. No one has any grounds to separate spirit from matter, seeing that spirit itself may be a combination of material atoms. (*With animation, to* TRIGORIN) But you know someone ought to write a play on how we poor teachers live, and get it acted. We have a hard, hard life.

MADAME ARKADIN. That's true, but don't let us talk either of plays or of atoms. It is such a glorious evening! Do you hear? There is singing! (*Listens*) How nice it is!

POLINA. It's on the other side of the lake.
(*A pause.*)

MADAME ARKADIN (*to* TRIGORIN). Sit down beside me. Ten or fifteen years ago there were sounds of music and singing on that lake continually almost every night. There are six country houses on the shores of the lake. I remember laughter, noise, shooting, and love affairs without end. . . . The *jeune premier* and the idol of all those six households was in those days our friend here, the doctor (*motions with her head towards* DORN), Yevgeny Sergeitch. He is fascinating still, but in those days he was irresistible. But my conscience is beginning to trouble me. Why did I hurt my poor boy's feelings? I feel worried. (*Aloud*) Kostya! Son! Kostya!

MASHA. I'll go and look for him.

MADAME ARKADIN. Please do, my dear.

MASHA (*going to the left*). Aa-oo! Konstantin Gavrilitch! Aa-oo! (*Goes off.*)

NINA (*coming out from behind the stage*). Apparently there will be no going on, and I may come out. Good evening! (*Kisses* MADAME ARKADIN *and* POLINA ANDREYEVNA.)

SORIN. Bravo! Bravo!

MADAME ARKADIN. Bravo! Bravo! We admired you. With such an appearance, with such a lovely voice, you really cannot stay in the country; it is a sin. You must have talent. Do you hear? It's your duty to go on the stage.

NINA. Oh, that's my dream! (*Sighing*) But it will never be realised.

MADAME ARKADIN. Who knows?

Here, let me introduce Boris Alexeyevitch Trigorin.

NINA. Oh, I am so glad. . . . (*Overcome with embarrassment*) I am always reading your . . .

MADAME ARKADIN (*making her sit down beside them*). Don't be shy, my dear. He is a celebrity, but he has a simple heart. You see, he is shy himself.

DORN. I suppose we may raise the curtain; it's rather uncanny.

SHAMRAEV (*aloud*). Yakov, pull up the curtain, my lad. (*The curtain goes up.*)

NINA (*to* TRIGORIN). It is a queer play, isn't it?

TRIGORIN. I did not understand it at all. But I enjoyed it. You acted so genuinely. And the scenery was delightful. (*A pause*) There must be a lot of fish in that lake.

NINA. Yes.

TRIGORIN. I love angling. There is nothing I enjoy so much as sitting on the bank of a river in the evening and watching the float.

NINA. But I should have thought that for anyone who has known the enjoyment of creation, no other enjoyment can exist.

MADAME ARKADIN (*laughing*). Don't talk like that. When people say nice things to him he is utterly floored.

SHAMRAEV. I remember one evening in the opera theatre in Moscow the celebrated Silva took the lower C! As it happened, there was sitting in the gallery the bass of our church choir, and all at once—imagine our intense astonishment—we heard from the gallery "Bravo, Silva!" a whole octave lower—like this: (*in a deep bass*) "Bravo, Silva!" The audience sat spellbound.
(*A pause.*)

DORN. The angel of silence has flown over us.

NINA. It's time for me to go. Goodbye.

MADAME ARKADIN. Where are you off to? Why so early? We won't let you go.

NINA. My father expects me.

MADAME ARKADIN. What a man, really. . . . (*Kisses her*) Well, there is no help for it. I am sorry—I am sorry to let you go.

NINA. If you knew how grieved I am to go.

MADAME ARKADIN. Someone ought to see you home, my little dear.

NINA (*frightened*). Oh, no, no!

SORIN (*to her, in an imploring voice*). Do stay!

NINA. I can't, Pyotr Nikolayevitch.

SORIN. Stay for an hour. What is there in that?

NINA (*thinking a minute, tearfully*). I can't! (*Shakes hands and hurriedly goes off.*)

MADAME ARKADIN. Unfortunate girl she is, really. They say her mother left her father all her immense property—every farthing of it—and now the girl has got nothing, as her father has already made a will leaving everything to his second wife. It's monstrous!

DORN. Yes, her father is a pretty thorough scoundrel, one must do him the justice to say so.

SORIN (*rubbing his cold hands*). Let us go too, it's getting damp. My legs ache.

MADAME ARKADIN. They seem like wooden legs, you can hardly walk. Let us go, unlucky old man! (*Takes his arm.*)

SHAMRAEV (*offering his arm to his wife*). Madame?

SORIN. I hear that dog howling again. (*To* SHAMRAEV) Be so kind, Ilya Afanasyitch, as to tell them to let it off the chain.

SHAMRAEV. It's impossible, Pyotr Nikolayevitch, I am afraid of thieves getting into the barn. Our millet is there. (*To* MEDVEDENKO *who is walking beside him*) Yes, a whole octave lower: "Bravo, Silva!" And he not a singer—simply a church chorister!

MEDVEDENKO. And what salary does a chorister get?
(*All go out except* DORN.)

DORN (*alone*). I don't know, perhaps I know nothing about it, or have gone off my head, but I liked the play. There is something in it. When that girl talked about loneliness and afterwards when the devil's eyes appeared, I was so excited that my hands trembled. It is fresh, naïve. . . . Here he comes, I believe. I want to say all the nice things I can to him.

TREPLEV (*enters*). They have all gone.

DORN. I am here.

TREPLEV. Mashenka is looking for me all over the park. Insufferable creature she is!

DORN. Konstantin Gavrilitch, I liked your play extremely. It's a strange thing, and I haven't heard the end, and yet it made a strong impression! You are a gifted man—you must persevere.
(TREPLEV *presses his hand warmly and embraces him impulsively.*)

DORN. Fie, what an hysterical fellow! There are tears in his eyes! What I mean is this. You have taken a subject from the realm of abstract ideas. So it should be, for a work of art ought to express a great idea. A thing is only fine when it is serious. How pale you are!

TREPLEV. So you tell me to persevere?

DORN. Yes. . . . But write only of what is important and eternal. You know, I have had varied experiences of life, and have enjoyed it: I am satisfied, but if it had been my lot to know the spiritual heights which artists reach at the moment of creation, I should, I believe, have despised my bodily self and all that appertains to it and left all things earthly as far behind as possible.

TREPLEV. Excuse me, where is Nina?

DORN. And another thing. In a work

of art there ought to be a clear definite idea. You ought to know what is your aim in writing, for if you go along that picturesque route without a definite goal you will be lost and your talent will be your ruin.

TREPLEV (*impatiently*). Where is Nina?

DORN. She has gone home.

TREPLEV (*in despair*). What am I to do? I want to see her . . . I must see her. . . . I must go. . . . (*Enter* MASHA.)

DORN (*to* TREPLEV). Calm yourself, my boy.

TREPLEV. But I am going all the same. I must go.

MASHA. Come indoors, Konstantin Gavrilitch. Your mother wants you. She is worried.

TREPLEV. Tell her that I have gone away. And I beg you—all of you—leave me in peace! Let me alone! Don't follow me about!

DORN. Come, come, come, dear boy. . . . You can't go on like that. . . . That's not the thing.

TREPLEV (*in tears*). Good-bye, doctor. Thank you. . . . (*Goes off.*)

DORN (*with a sigh*). Youth! youth!

MASHA. When people have nothing better to say, they say, "Youth! youth!" . . . (*Takes a pinch of snuff.*)

DORN (*takes her snuff-box from her and flings it into the bushes*). That's disgusting! (*A pause*) I believe they are playing the piano indoors. We must go in.

MASHA. Wait a little.

DORN. What is it?

MASHA. I want to tell you once more. I have a longing to talk. . . . (*Growing agitated*) I don't care for my father . . . but I feel drawn to you. For some reason I feel with all my heart that you are very near me. . . . Help me. Help me, or I shall do something silly, I shall make a mock of my life and ruin it. . . . I can't go on. . . .

DORN. What is it? Help you in what?

MASHA. I am miserable. No one, no one knows how miserable I am! (*Laying her head on his breast, softly*) I love Konstantin!

DORN. How hysterical they all are! How hysterical! And what a lot of love. . . . Oh, the sorcery of the lake! (*Tenderly*) But what can I do, my child? What? What?

CURTAIN

ACT TWO

A croquet lawn. The house with a big verandah in the background on the right, on the left is seen the lake with the blazing sun reflected in it. Flower beds. Midday. Hot. MADAME ARKADIN, DORN *and* MASHA *are sitting on a garden seat in the shade of an old lime tree on one side of the croquet lawn.* DORN *has an open book on his knee.*

MADAME ARKADIN (*to* MASHA). Come, let us stand up. (*They both get up*) Let us stand side by side. You are twenty-two and I am nearly twice as old. Yevgeny Sergeitch, which of us looks the younger?

DORN. You, of course.

MADAME ARKADIN. There! And why is it? Because I work, I feel I am always on the go, while you stay always in the same place and have no life at all. . . . And it is my rule never to look into the future. I never think about old age or death. What is to be, will be.

MASHA. And I feel as though I had been born long, long ago; I trail my life along like an endless train. . . . And often I have not the slightest desire to go on living. (*Sits down*) Of course, that's all nonsense. I must shake myself and throw it all off.

DORN (*hums quietly*). "Tell her, my flowers."

MADAME ARKADIN. Then I am as particular as an Englishman. I keep myself in hand, as they say, my dear, and am always dressed and have my hair done *comme il faut*. Do I allow myself to go out of the house even into the garden in a dressing-gown, or without my hair being done? Never! What has preserved me is that I have never been a dowdy, I have never let myself go, as some women do. . . . (*Walks about the lawn with her arms akimbo*) Here I am, as brisk as a bird. I could take the part of a girl of fifteen.

DORN. Nevertheless, I shall go on. (*Takes up the book*) We stopped at the corn merchant and the rats. . . .

MADAME ARKADIN. And the rats. Read. (*Sits down*) But give it to me, I'll read. It is my turn. (*Takes the book and looks in it*) And rats. . . . Here it is. . . . (*Reads*) "And of course for society people to spoil novelists and to attract them to themselves is as dangerous as for a corn merchant to rear rats in his granaries. And yet they love them. And so, when a woman has picked out an author whom she desires to captivate, she lays siege to him by means of compliments, flattery and favours . . ." Well, that may be so with the French, but there is nothing like that with us, we have no set rules. Among us, before a woman sets to work to captivate an author, she is generally head over ears in love herself, if you please. To go no further, take Trigorin and me. . . .

(*Enter* SORIN, *leaning on his stick*

and with him NINA; MEDVEDENKO *wheels an empty bath-chair in after them.*)

SORIN (*in a caressing tone, as to a child*). Yes? We are delighted, aren't we? We are happy today at last? (*To his sister*) We are delighted! Our father and stepmother have gone off to Tver, and we are free now for three whole days.

NINA (*sits down beside* MADAME ARKADIN *and embraces her*). I am happy! Now I belong to you.

SORIN (*sits down in his bath-chair*). She looks quite a beauty today.

MADAME ARKADIN. Nicely dressed and interesting. . . . That's a good girl. (*Kisses* NINA) But we mustn't praise you too much for fear of ill-luck. Where is Boris Alexeyevitch?

NINA. He is in the bathing-house, fishing.

MADAME ARKADIN. I wonder he doesn't get sick of it! (*Is about to go on reading.*)

NINA. What is that?

MADAME ARKADIN. Maupassant's "Sur l'eau," my dear. (*Reads a few lines to herself*) Well, the rest isn't interesting or true. (*Shuts the book*) I feel uneasy. Tell me, what's wrong with my son? Why is he so depressed and ill-humoured? He spends whole days on the lake and I hardly ever see him.

MASHA. His heart is troubled. (*To* NINA, *timidly*) Please, do read us something out of his play!

NINA (*shrugging her shoulders*). Would you like it? It's so uninteresting.

MASHA (*restraining her enthusiasm*). When he reads anything himself his eyes glow and his face turns pale. He has a fine mournful voice, and the gestures of a poet. (*There is a sound of* SORIN *snoring.*)

DORN. Good night!

MADAME ARKADIN. Petrusha!

SORIN. Ah?

MADAME ARKADIN. Are you asleep?

SORIN. Not a bit of it. (*A pause.*)

MADAME ARKADIN. You do nothing for your health, brother, and that's not right.

SORIN. I should like to take something, but the doctor won't give me anything.

DORN. Take medicine at sixty!

SORIN. Even at sixty one wants to live!

DORN (*with vexation*). Oh, very well, take valerian drops!

MADAME ARKADIN. It seems to me it would do him good to go to some mineral springs.

DORN. Well, he might go. And he might not.

MADAME ARKADIN. What is one to make of that?

DORN. There's nothing to make of it. It's quite clear. (*A pause.*)

MEDVEDENKO. Pyotr Nikolayevitch ought to give up smoking.

SORIN. Nonsense!

DORN. No, it's not nonsense. Wine and tobacco destroy the personality. After a cigar or a glass of vodka, you are not Pyotr Nikolayevitch any more but Pyotr Nikolayevitch plus somebody else; your ego is diffused and you feel towards yourself as to a third person.

SORIN (*laughs*). It's all very well for you to argue! You've lived your life, but what about me? I have served in the Department of Justice for twenty-eight years, but I haven't lived yet, I've seen and done nothing as a matter of fact, and very naturally I want to live very much. You've had enough and you don't care, and so you are inclined to be philosophical, but I want to live, and so I drink sherry at dinner and smoke cigars and so on. That's all it comes to.

DORN. One must look at life seriously, but to go in for cures at sixty and to regret that one hasn't enjoyed oneself enough in one's youth is frivolous, if you will forgive my saying so.

MASHA (*gets up*). It must be lunchtime. (*Walks with a lazy, lagging step*) My leg is gone to sleep. (*Goes off.*)

DORN. She will go and have a couple of glasses before lunch.

SORIN. She has no personal happiness, poor thing.

DORN. Nonsense, your Excellency.

SORIN. You argue like a man who has had all he wants.

MADAME ARKADIN. Oh, what can be more boring than this sweet country boredom! Hot, still, no one ever doing anything, everyone airing their theories. . . . It's nice being with you, my friends, charming to listen to you, but . . . to sit in a hotel room somewhere and learn one's part is ever so much better.

NINA (*enthusiastically*). Delightful! I understand you.

SORIN. Of course, it's better in town. You sit in your study, the footman lets no one in unannounced, there's a telephone . . . in the streets there are cabs and everything. . . .

DORN (*hums*). "Tell her, my flowers."
(*Enter* SHAMRAEV, *and after him* POLINA ANDREYEVNA.)

SHAMRAEV. Here they are! Good morning! (*Kisses* MADAME ARKADIN'S *hand and then* NINA'S) Delighted to see you in good health. (*To* MADAME ARKADIN) My wife tells me that you are proposing to drive into town with her today. Is that so?

MADAME ARKADIN. Yes, we are thinking of it.

SHAMRAEV. Hm! that's splendid, but how are you going, honoured lady? They are carting the rye today; all the men are at work. What horses are you to have, allow me to ask?

MADAME ARKADIN. What horses? How can I tell which?

SORIN. We've got carriage horses.

SHAMRAEV (*growing excited*). Carriage horses! But where am I to get collars for them? Where am I to get collars? It's a strange thing! It passes my understanding! Honoured lady! forgive me, I am full of reverence for your talent. I would give ten years of my life for you, but I cannot let you have the horses!

MADAME ARKADIN. But if I have to go! It's a queer thing!

SHAMRAEV. Honoured lady! you don't know what farming means.

MADAME ARKADIN (*flaring up*). That's the old story! If that's so, I go back to Moscow today. Give orders for horses to be hired for me at the village, or I'll walk to the station.

SHAMRAEV (*flaring up*). In that case I resign my position! You must look for another steward. (*Goes off.*)

MADAME ARKADIN. It's like this every summer; every summer I am insulted here! I won't set my foot in the place again. (*Goes off at left where the bathing shed is supposed to be; a minute later she can be seen entering the house.*)
(TRIGORIN *follows her, carrying fishing rods and tackle, and a pail.*)

SORIN (*flaring up*). This is insolence! It's beyond everything. I am thoroughly sick of it. Send all the horses here this minute!

NINA (*to* POLINA ANDREYEVNA). To refuse Irina Nikolayevna, the famous actress! Any wish of hers, any whim even, is of more consequence than all your farming. It's positively incredible!

POLINA (*in despair*). What can I do? Put yourself in my position: what can I do?

SORIN (*to* NINA). Let us go to my sister. We will all entreat her not to go away. Won't we? (*Looking in the direction in which* SHAMRAEV *has gone*) Insufferable man! Despot!

NINA (*preventing him from getting up*). Sit still, sit still. We will wheel you in. (*She and* MEDVEDENKO *push the bath-chair*) Oh, how awful it is!

SORIN. Yes, yes, it's awful. But he won't leave, I'll speak to him directly. (*They go out;* DORN *and* POLINA ANDREYEVNA *are left alone on the stage.*)

DORN. People are tiresome. Your husband ought to be simply kicked out, but it will end in that old woman Pyotr Nikolayevitch and his sister begging the man's pardon. You will see!

POLINA. He has sent the carriage horses into the fields too! And there are misunderstandings like this every day. If you only knew how it upsets me! It makes me ill; see how I am trembling. . . . I can't endure his rudeness. (*In an imploring voice*) Yevgeny, dearest, light of my eyes, my darling, let me come to you. . . . Our time is passing, we are no longer young, and if only we could lay aside concealment and lying for the end of our lives, anyway . . .
(*A pause.*)

DORN. I am fifty-five; it's too late to change my life.

POLINA. I know you refuse me because there are other women too who are as near to you. You can't take them all to live with you. I understand. Forgive me, you are tired of me.

(NINA *appears near the house; she is picking flowers.*)

DORN. No, it's all right.

POLINA. I am wretched from jealousy. Of course you are a doctor, you can't avoid women. I understand.

DORN (*to* NINA, *who comes up to them*). How are things going?

NINA. Irina Nikolayevna is crying and Pyotr Nikolayevitch has an attack of asthma.

DORN (*gets up*). I'd better go and give them both valerian drops.

NINA (*gives him the flowers*). Please take these.

DORN. *Merci bien.* (*Goes towards the house.*)

POLINA (*going with him*). What charming flowers! (*Near the house, in a smothered voice*) Give me those flowers! Give me those flowers! (*On receiving them tears the flowers to pieces and throws them away; both go into the house.*)

NINA (*alone*). How strange it is to see a famous actress cry, and about such a trivial thing! And isn't it strange? A famous author, adored by the public, written about in all the papers, his photographs for sale, his works translated into foreign languages—and he spends the whole day fishing and is delighted

that he has caught two gudgeon. I thought famous people were proud, unapproachable, that they despised the crowd, and by their fame and the glory of their name, as it were, revenged themselves on the vulgar herd for putting rank and wealth above everything. But here they cry and fish, play cards, laugh and get cross like everyone else!

TREPLEV (*comes in without a hat on, with a gun and a dead sea gull*). Are you alone here?

NINA. Yes.
(TREPLEV *lays the sea gull at her feet.*)

NINA. What does that mean?

TREPLEV. I was so mean as to kill this bird today. I lay it at your feet.

NINA. What is the matter with you? (*Picks up the bird and looks at it.*)

TREPLEV (*after a pause*). Soon I shall kill myself in the same way.

NINA. You have so changed, I hardly know you.

TREPLEV. Yes, ever since the day when I hardly knew you. You have changed to me, your eyes are cold, you feel me in the way.

NINA. You have become irritable of late, you express yourself so incomprehensibly, as it were in symbols. This bird is a symbol too, I suppose, but forgive me, I don't understand it. (*Lays the sea gull on the seat*) I am too simple to understand you.

TREPLEV. This began from that evening when my play came to grief so stupidly. Women never forgive failure. I have burnt it all; every scrap of it. If only you knew how miserable I am! Your growing cold to me is awful, incredible, as though I had woken up and found this lake had suddenly dried up or sunk into the earth. You have just said that you are too simple to understand me. Oh, what is there to understand? My play was not liked, you despise my inspiration, you already consider me commonplace, insignificant like so many others. . . . (*Stamping*) How well I understand it all, how I understand it! I feel as though I had a nail in my brain, damnation take it together with my vanity which is sucking away my life, sucking it like a snake. . . . (*Sees* TRIGORIN, *who comes in reading a book*) Here comes the real genius, walking like Hamlet and with a book too. (*Mimics*) "Words, words, words." . . . The sun has scarcely reached you and you are smiling already, your eyes are melting in its rays. I won't be in your way. (*Goes off quickly.*)

TRIGORIN (*making notes in his book*). Takes snuff and drinks vodka. Always in black. The schoolmaster is in love with her. . . .

NINA. Good morning, Boris Alexeyevitch!

TRIGORIN. Good morning. Circumstances have turned out so unexpectedly that it seems we are setting off today. We are hardly likely to meet again. I am sorry. I don't often have the chance of méeting young girls, youthful and charming; I have forgotten how one feels at eighteen or nineteen and can't picture it to myself, and so the young girls in my stories and novels are usually false. I should like to be in your shoes just for one hour to find out how you think, and altogether what sort of person you are.

NINA. And I should like to be in your shoes?

TRIGORIN. What for?

NINA. To know what it feels like to be a famous, gifted author. What does it feel like to be famous? How does it affect you, being famous?

TRIGORIN. How? Nohow, I believe. I have never thought about it. (*After a moment's thought*) It's one of two things: either you exaggerate my fame, or it never is felt at all.

NINA. But if you read about yourself in the newspapers?

TRIGORIN. When they praise me I am pleased, and when they abuse me I feel out of humour for a day or two.

NINA. What a wonderful world! If only you knew how I envy you! How different people's lots in life are! Some can scarcely get through their dull, obscure existence, they are all just like one another, they are all unhappy; while others— you, for instance—you are one out of a million, have an interesting life full of brightness and significance. You are happy.

TRIGORIN. I? (*Shrugging his shoulders*) Hm. . . . You talk of fame and happiness, of bright interesting life, but to me all those fine words, if you will forgive my saying so, are just like a sweetmeat which I never taste. You are very young and very good-natured.

NINA. Your life is splendid!

TRIGORIN. What is there particularly

nice in it? (*Looks at his watch*) I must go and write directly. Excuse me, I mustn't stay. . . . (*Laughs*) You have stepped on my favourite corn, as the saying is, and here I am beginning to get excited and a little cross. Let us talk though. We will talk about my splendid bright life. . . . Well, where shall we begin? (*After thinking a little*) There are such things as fixed ideas, when a man thinks days and night, for instance, of nothing but the moon. And I have just such a moon. I am haunted day and night by one persistent thought: I ought to be writing, I ought to be writing, I ought . . . I have scarcely finished one novel when, for some reason, I must begin writing another, then a third, after the third a fourth. I write incessantly, post haste, and I can't write in any other way. What is there splendid and bright in that, I ask you? Oh, it's an absurd life! Here I am with you; I am excited, yet every moment I remember that my unfinished novel is waiting for me. Here I see a cloud that looks like a grand piano. I think that I must put into a story somewhere that a cloud sailed by that looked like a grand piano. There is a scent of heliotrope. I hurriedly make a note: a sickly smell, a widow's flower, to be mentioned in the description of a summer evening. I catch up myself and you at every sentence, every word, and make haste to put those sentences and words away into my literary treasure-house—it may come in useful! When I finish work I race off to the theatre or to fishing; if only I could rest in that and forget myself. But no, there's a new subject rolling about in my head like a heavy iron cannon ball, and I am drawn to my writing table and must make haste again to go on writing and writing. And it's always like that, always. And I have no rest from myself, and I feel that I am eating up my own life, and that for the sake of the honey I give to someone in space I am stripping the pollen from my best flowers, tearing up the flowers themselves and trampling on their roots. Don't you think I am mad? Do my friends and acquaintances treat me as though I were sane? "What are you writing? What are you giving us?" It's the same thing again and again, and it seems to me as though my friends' notice, their praises, their enthusiasm—that it's all a sham, that they are deceiving me as an invalid and I am somehow afraid that they will steal up to me from behind, snatch me and carry me off and put me in a madhouse. And in those years, the best years of my youth, when I was beginning, my writing was unmixed torture. A small writer, particularly when he is not successful, seems to himself clumsy, awkward, unnecessary; his nerves are strained and overwrought. He can't resist hanging about people connected with literature and art, unrecognised and unnoticed by anyone, afraid to look anyone boldly in the face, like a passionate gambler without any money. I hadn't seen my reader, but for some reason I always imagined him hostile, and mistrustful. I was afraid of the public, it alarmed me, and when I had to produce my first play it always seemed to me that all the dark people felt hostile and all the fair ones were coldly indifferent. Oh, how awful it was! What agony it was!

NINA. But surely inspiration and the very process of creation give you moments of exalted happiness?

TRIGORIN. Yes. While I am writing I enjoy it. And I like reading my proofs, but . . . as soon as it is published I can't endure it, and I see that it is all wrong, a mistake, that it ought not to have been written at all, and I feel vexed and sick about it. . . . (*Laughing*) And the public reads it and says: "Yes, charming, clever. Charming, but very inferior to Tolstoy," or, "It's a fine thing, but Turgenev's 'Fathers and Children' is finer." And it will be the same to my dying day, only charming and clever, charming and clever—and nothing more. And when I die my friends, passing by my tomb, will say, "Here lies Trigorin. He was a good writer, but inferior to Turgenev."

NINA. Forgive me, but I refuse to understand you. You are simply spoiled by success.

TRIGORIN. What success? I have never liked myself; I dislike my own work. The worst of it is that I am in a sort of delirium, and often don't understand what I am writing. I love this water here, the trees, the sky. I feel nature, it arouses in me a passionate, irresistible desire to write. But I am not simply a landscape painter; I am also a citizen. I love my native country, my people; I feel that if I am a writer I am in duty bound to write of the people, of their sufferings, of their future, to talk about science and the rights of man and so on, and so on, and I write about everything. I am hurried and flustered, and on all sides they whip me up and are angry with me; I dash about from side to side like a fox beset by hounds. I see life and culture continually getting farther and farther away while I fall farther and farther be-

hind like a peasant too late for the train; and what it comes to is that I feel I can only describe scenes and in everything else I am false to the marrow of my bones.

NINA. You are overworked and have not the leisure nor the desire to appreciate your own significance. You may be dissatisfied with yourself, but for others you are great and splendid! If I were a writer like you, I should give up my whole life to the common herd, but I should know that there could be no greater happiness for them than to rise to my level, and they would harness themselves to my chariot.

TRIGORIN. My chariot, what next! Am I an Agamemnon, or what? (*Both smile.*)

NINA. For such happiness as being a writer or an artist I would be ready to endure poverty, disappointment, the dislike of those around me; I would live in a garret and eat nothing but rye bread, I would suffer from being dissatisfied with myself, from recognising my own imperfections, but I should ask in return for fame . . . real, resounding fame. . . . (*Covers her face with her hands*) It makes me dizzy. . . . Ough!
(*The voice of* MADAME ARKADIN *from the house.*)

MADAME ARKADIN. Boris Alexeyevitch!

TRIGORIN. They are calling for me. I suppose it's to pack. But I don't want to leave here. (*Looks round at the lake*) Just look how glorious it is! It's splendid!

NINA. Do you see the house and

garden on the other side of the lake?

TRIGORIN. Yes.

NINA. That house was my dear mother's. I was born there. I have spent all my life beside this lake and I know every little islet on it.

TRIGORIN. It's very delightful here! (*Seeing the sea gull*) And what's this?

NINA. A sea gull. Konstantin Gavrilitch shot it.

TRIGORIN. A beautiful bird. Really, I don't want to go away. Try and persuade Irina Nikolayevna to stay. (*Makes a note in his book.*)

NINA. What are you writing?

TRIGORIN. Oh, I am only making a note. A subject struck me. (*Putting away the note-book*) A subject for a short story: a young girl, such as you, has lived all her life beside a lake; she loves the lake like a sea gull, and is as free and happy as a sea gull. But a man comes by chance, sees her, and having nothing better to do, destroys her like that sea gull here.
(*A pause.* MADAME ARKADIN *appears at the window.*)

MADAME ARKADIN. Boris Alexeyevitch, where are you?

TRIGORIN. I am coming. (*Goes and looks back at* NINA. *To* MADAME ARKADIN *at the window*) What is it?

MADAME ARKADIN. We are staying. (TRIGORIN *goes into the house.*)

NINA (*advances to the footlights; after a few moments' meditation*). It's a dream!

CURTAIN.

ACT THREE

The dining-room in SORIN's *house. Doors on right and on left. A sideboard. A medicine cupboard. A table in the middle of the room. A portmanteau and hat-boxes; signs of preparation for departure.* TRIGORIN *is having lunch;* MASHA *stands by the table.*

MASHA. I tell all this to you as a writer. You may make use of it. I am telling you the truth: if he had hurt himself seriously I would not have gone on living another minute. But I have pluck enough all the same. I just made up my mind that I would tear this love out of my heart, tear it out by the roots.

TRIGORIN. How are you going to do that?

MASHA. I am going to be married. To Medvedenko.

TRIGORIN. That's the schoolmaster?

MASHA. Yes.

TRIGORIN. I don't understand what's the object of it.

MASHA. To love without hope, to spend whole years waiting for something. . . . But when I marry, there will be no time left for love, new cares will smother all the old feelings. And, anyway, it will be a change, you know. Shall we have another?

TRIGORIN. Won't that be too much?

MASHA. Oh, come! (*Fills two glasses*) Don't look at me like that! Women drink much oftener than you imagine. Only a small proportion drink openly as I do, the majority drink in secret. Yes. And it's always vodka or brandy. (*Clinks glasses*) My best wishes! You are a good-hearted man; I am sorry to be parting from you. (*They drink.*)

TRIGORIN. I don't want to go myself.

MASHA. You should beg her to stay.

TRIGORIN. No, she won't stay now. Her son is behaving very tactlessly. First, he shoots himself, and now they say he is going to challenge me to a duel. And whatever for? He sulks, and snorts, and preaches new forms of art. . . . But there is room for all—new and old—why quarrel about it?

MASHA. Well, there's jealousy too. But it is nothing to do with me. (*A pause.* YAKOV *crosses from right to left with a portmanteau.* NINA *enters and stands by the window.*)

MASHA. My schoolmaster is not very brilliant, but he is a good-natured man, and poor, and he is very much

in love with me. I am sorry for him. And I am sorry for his old mother. Well, let me wish you all happiness. Don't remember evil against me. (*Shakes hands with him warmly*) I am very grateful for your friendly interest. Send me your books and be sure to put in an inscription. Only don't write, "To my honoured friend," but write simply, "To Marya who belongs nowhere and has no object in life." Good-bye! (*Goes out.*)

NINA (*stretching out her arm towards* TRIGORIN, *with her fist clenched*). Odd or even?

TRIGORIN. Even.

NINA (*with a sigh*). Wrong. I had only one pea in my hand. I was trying my fortune whether to go on the stage or not. I wish someone would advise me.

TRIGORIN. It's impossible to advise in such a matter. (*A pause.*)

NINA. We are parting and . . . perhaps we shall never meet again. Won't you please take this little medallion as a parting gift? I had your initials engraved on one side of it . . . and on the other the title of your book, "Days and Nights."

TRIGORIN. How exquisite! (*Kisses the medallion*) A charming present!

NINA. Think of me sometimes.

TRIGORIN. I shall think of you. I shall think of you as you were on that sunny day—do you remember?—a week ago, when you were wearing a light dress . . . we were talking . . . there was a white sea gull lying on the seat.

NINA (*pensively*). Yes, a sea gull. . . . (*A pause*) We can't talk any more, there's someone coming. . . . Let me have two minutes before you go, I entreat you. . . . (*Goes out on the left.*)
(*At the same instant* MADAME ARKADIN, SORIN *in a dress coat with a star of some order on it, then* YAKOV, *occupied with the luggage, enter on the right.*)

MADAME ARKADIN. Stay at home, old man. With your rheumatism you ought not to go gadding about. (*To* TRIGORIN) Who was that went out? Nina?

TRIGORIN. Yes.

MADAME ARKADIN. *Pardon,* we interrupted you. (*Sits down*) I believe I have packed everything. I am worn out.

TRIGORIN (*reads on the medallion*). " 'Days and Nights,' page 121, lines 11 and 12."

YAKOV (*clearing the table*). Am I to pack your fishing things too, sir?

TRIGORIN. Yes, I shall want them again. You can give away the hooks.

YAKOV. Yes, sir.

TRIGORIN (*to himself*). Page 121, lines 11 and 12. What is there in those lines? (*To* MADAME ARKADIN) Are there copies of my books in the house?

MADAME ARKADIN. Yes, in my brother's study, in the corner bookcase.

TRIGORIN. Page 121. . . . (*Goes out.*)

MADAME ARKADIN. Really, Petrusha, you had better stay at home.

SORIN. You are going away; it will be dreary for me at home without you.

MADAME ARKADIN. And what is there in the town?

SORIN. Nothing particular, but still . . . (*laughs*) There will be the laying of the foundation-stone of the Zemstvo-hall, and all that sort of thing. One longs to shake oneself free from this stagnant existence, if only for an hour or two. I've been too long on the shelf like some old cigarette-holder. I have ordered the horses for one o'clock; we'll set off at the same time.

MADAME ARKADIN (*after a pause*). Come, stay here, don't be bored and don't catch cold. Look after my son. Take care of him. Give him good advice. (*A pause*) Here I am going away and I shall never know why Konstantin tried to shoot himself. I fancy jealousy was the chief cause, and the sooner I get Trigorin away from here, the better.

SORIN. What can I say? There were other reasons too. It's easy to understand; he is young, intelligent, living in the country, in the wilds, with no money, no position and no future. He has nothing to do. He is ashamed of his idleness and afraid of it. I am very fond of him indeed, and he is attached to me, yet in spite of it all he feels he is superfluous in the house, that he is a dependant, a poor relation. It's easy to understand, it's *amour propre.* . . .

MADAME ARKADIN. He is a great anxiety to me! (*Pondering*) He might go into the service, perhaps.

SORIN (*begins to whistle, then irresolutely*). I think that quite the best thing would be if you were to . . . let him have a little money. In the first place he ought to be able to be dressed like other people and all that. Just look at him, he's been going about in the same wretched jacket for the last three years and he has no overcoat. . . . (*Laughs*) It would do him no harm to have a little fun . . . to go abroad or something. . . . It wouldn't cost much.

MADAME ARKADIN. But all the same . . . I might manage the suit, perhaps, but as for going abroad . . . No, just at the moment I can't even manage the suit. (*Resolutely*) I have no money!
(SORIN *laughs*.)

MADAME ARKADIN. No!

SORIN (*begins to whistle*). Quite so. Forgive me, my dear, don't be cross. I believe you. . . . You are a generous, noble-hearted woman.

MADAME ARKADIN (*weeping*). I have no money.

SORIN. If I had money, of course I would give him some myself, but I have nothing, not a half-penny. (*Laughs*) My steward takes all my pension and spends it all on the land and the cattle and the bees, and my money is all wasted. The bees die, and the cows die, they never let me have horses. . . .

MADAME ARKADIN. Yes, I have money, but you see I am an actress;

my dresses alone are enough to ruin me.

SORIN. You are a kind, good creature . . . I respect you. . . . Yes . . . but there, I got a touch of it again. . . . (*Staggers*) I feel dizzy. (*Clutches at the table*) I feel ill and all that.

MADAME ARKADIN (*alarmed*). Petrusha! (*Trying to support him*) Petrusha, my dear! (*Calling*) Help! help!
(*Enter* TREPLEV *with a bandage round his head and* MEDVEDENKO.)

MADAME ARKADIN. He feels faint!

SORIN. It's all right, it's all right! (*Smiles and drinks some water*) It's passed off . . . and all that.

TREPLEV (*to his mother*). Don't be frightened, mother, it's not serious. Uncle often has these attacks now. (*To his uncle*) You must lie down, uncle.

SORIN. For a little while, yes. . . . But I am going to the town all the same. . . . I'll lie down a little and then set off. . . . It's quite natural. (*Goes out leaning on his stick.*)

MEDVEDENKO (*gives him his arm*). There's a riddle: in the morning on four legs, at noon on two, in the evening on three. . . .

SORIN (*laughs*). Just so. And at night on the back. Thank you, I can manage alone. . . .

MEDVEDENKO. Oh come, why stand on ceremony! (*Goes out with* SORIN.)

MADAME ARKADIN. How he frightened me!

TREPLEV. It is not good for him to live in the country. He gets depressed. If you would be generous for once, mother, and lend him fifteen hundred or two thousand roubles, he could spend a whole year in town.

MADAME ARKADIN. I have no money. I am an actress, not a banker.
(*A pause.*)

TREPLEV. Mother, change my bandage. You do it so well.

MADAME ARKADIN (*takes out of the medicine cupboard some iodoform and a box with bandaging material*). The doctor is late.

TREPLEV. He promised to be here at ten, and it is midday already.

MADAME ARKADIN. Sit down. (*Takes the bandage off his head*) It's like a turban. Yesterday a stranger asked in the kitchen what nationality you were. But you have almost completely healed. There is the merest trifle left. (*Kisses him on the head*) You won't do anything naughty again while I am away, will you?

TREPLEV. No, mother. It was a moment of mad despair when I could not control myself. It won't happen again. (*Kisses her hand*) You have such clever hands. I remember, long ago, when you were still acting at the Imperial Theatre—I was little then—there was a fight in our yard and a washerwoman, one of the tenants, was badly beaten. Do you remember? She was picked up senseless . . . you looked after her, took her remedies and washed her children in a tub. Don't you remember?

MADAME ARKADIN. No. (*Puts on a fresh bandage.*)

TREPLEV. Two ballet dancers lived in the same house as we did at the time. . . . They used to come to you and have coffee. . . .

MADAME ARKADIN. I remember that.

TREPLEV. They were very pious. (*A pause*) Just lately, these last days, I have loved you as tenderly and completely as when I was a child. I have no one left now but you. Only why, why do you give yourself up to the influence of that man?

MADAME ARKADIN. You don't understand him, Konstantin. He is a very noble character. . . .

TREPLEV. And yet when he was told I was going to challenge him, the nobility of his character did not prevent him from funking it. He is going away. Ignominious flight!

MADAME ARKADIN. What nonsense! It is I who am asking him to go.

TREPLEV. A very noble character! Here you and I are almost quarrelling over him, and at this very moment he is somewhere in the drawing-room or the garden laughing at us . . . developing Nina, trying to convince her finally that he is a genius.

MADAME ARKADIN. You take a pleasure in saying unpleasant things to me. I respect that man and beg you not to speak ill of him before me.

TREPLEV. And I don't respect him. You want me to think him a genius too, but forgive me, I can't tell lies, his books make me sick.

MADAME ARKADIN. That's envy. There's nothing left for people who have pretension without talent but to attack real talent. Much comfort in that, I must say!

TREPLEV (*ironically*). Real talent! (*Wrathfully*) I have more talent than all of you put together if it comes to that! (*Tears the bandage off his head*) You, with your hackneyed conventions, have usurped the supremacy in art and consider nothing real and legitimate but what you do yourselves; everything else you stifle and suppress. I don't believe in you! I don't believe in you or in him!

MADAME ARKADIN. Decadent!

TREPLEV. Get away to your charming theatre and act there in your paltry, stupid plays!

MADAME ARKADIN. I have never acted in such plays. Let me alone! You are not capable of writing even a wretched burlesque! You are nothing but a Kiev shopman! living on other people!

TREPLEV. You miser!

MADAME ARKADIN. You ragged beggar!
(TREPLEV *sits down and weeps quietly.*)

MADAME ARKADIN. Nonentity! (*Walking up and down in agitation*) Don't cry. . . . You mustn't cry. (*Weeps*) Don't. . . . (*Kisses him on the forehead, on the cheeks and on the head*) My dear child, forgive me. . . . Forgive your sinful mother. Forgive me, you know I am wretched.

TREPLEV (*puts his arms round her*). If only you knew! I have lost everything! She does not love me, and now I cannot write . . . all my hopes are gone. . . .

MADAME ARKADIN. Don't despair . . . Everything will come right. He is going away directly, she will love you again. (*Wipes away his tears*) Give over. We have made it up now.

TREPLEV (*kisses her hands*). Yes, mother.

MADAME ARKADIN (*tenderly*). Make it up with him too. You don't want a duel, do you?

TREPLEV. Very well. Only, mother, do allow me not to meet him. It's painful to me—it's more than I can bear. (*Enter* TRIGORIN) Here he is . . . I am going. . . . (*Rapidly puts away the dressings in the cupboard*) The doctor will do the bandaging now.

TRIGORIN (*looking in a book*). Page 121 . . . lines 11 and 12. Here it is. (*Reads*) "If ever my life can be of use to you, come and take it." (TREPLEV *picks up the bandage from the floor and goes out.*)

MADAME ARKADIN (*looking at her watch*). The horses will soon be here.

TRIGORIN (*to himself*). "If ever my life can be of use to you, come and take it."

THE SEA GULL

MADAME ARKADIN. I hope all your things are packed?

TRIGORIN (*impatiently*). Yes, yes. (*Musing*) Why is it that I feel so much sorrow in that appeal from a pure soul and that it wrings my heart so painfully? "If ever my life can be of use to you, come and take it." (*To* MADAME ARKADIN) Let us stay one day longer.
(MADAME ARKADIN *shakes her head.*)

TRIGORIN. Let us stay!

MADAME ARKADIN. Darling, I know what keeps you here. But have control over yourself. You are a little intoxicated, try to be sober.

TRIGORIN. You be sober too, be sensible and reasonable, I implore you; look at it all as a true friend should. (*Presses her hand*) You are capable of sacrifice. Be a friend to me, let me be free!

MADAME ARKADIN (*in violent agitation*). Are you so enthralled?

TRIGORIN. I am drawn to her! Perhaps it is just what I need.

MADAME ARKADIN. The love of a provincial girl? Oh, how little you know yourself!

TRIGORIN. Sometimes people sleep as they talk—that's how it is with me, I am talking to you and yet I am asleep and dreaming of her. . . . I am possessed by sweet, marvellous dreams. . . . Let me be free. . . .

MADAME ARKADIN (*trembling*). No, no! I am an ordinary woman, you can't talk like that to me. Don't torture me, Boris. It terrifies me.

TRIGORIN. If you cared to, you could be not ordinary. Love—youthful, charming, poetical, lifting one into a world of dreams—that's the only thing in life that can give happiness! I have never yet known a love like that. . . . In my youth I never had time, I was always hanging about the editors' offices, struggling with want. Now it is here, that love, it has come, it beckons to me. What sense is there in running away from it?

MADAME ARKADIN (*wrathfully*). You have gone mad!

TRIGORIN. Well, let me?

MADAME ARKADIN. You are all in a conspiracy together to torment me today! (*Weeps.*)

TRIGORIN (*clutching at his heart*). She does not understand! She won't understand!

MADAME ARKADIN. Am I so old and ugly that you don't mind talking of other women to me? (*Puts her arms round him and kisses him*) Oh, are you mad! My wonderful, splendid darling. . . . You are the last page of my life! (*Falls on her knees*) My joy, my pride, my bliss! . . . (*Embraces his knees*) If you forsake me even for one hour I shall not survive it, I shall go mad, my marvellous, magnificent one, my master. . . .

TRIGORIN. Someone may come in. (*Helps her to get up.*)

MADAME ARKADIN. Let them, I am not ashamed of my love for you.

(*Kisses his hands*) My treasure, you desperate boy, you want to be mad, but I won't have it, I won't let you. . . . (*Laughs*) You are mine . . . mine. . . . This forehead is mine, and these eyes, and this lovely silky hair is mine too . . . you are mine all over. You are so gifted, so clever, the best of all modern writers, you are the one hope of Russia. . . . You have so much truthfulness, simplicity, freshness, healthy humour. . . . In one touch you can give all the essential characteristics of a person or a landscape, your characters are living. One can't read you without delight! You think this is exaggerated? That I am flattering you? But look into my eyes . . . look. . . . Do I look like a liar? You see, I am the only one who can appreciate you; I am the only one who tells you the truth, my precious, wonderful darling. . . . Are you coming? Yes? You won't abandon me? . . .

TRIGORIN. I have no will of my own . . . I have never had a will of my own. . . . Flabby, feeble, always submissive—how can a woman care for such a man? Take me, carry me off, but don't let me move a step away from you. . . .

MADAME ARKADIN (*to herself*). Now he is mine! (*In an easy tone as though nothing had happened*) But, of course, if you like, you can stay. I'll go by myself and you can come afterwards, a week later. After all, why should you be in a hurry?

TRIGORIN. No, we may as well go together then.
(*A pause.* TRIGORIN *makes a note.*)

MADAME ARKADIN. What are you writing?

TRIGORIN. I heard a good name this morning, "The Maiden's Forest." It may be of use. (*Stretches*) So we are to go then? Again there will be railway carriages, stations, refreshment bars, mutton chops, conversations. . . .

SHAMRAEV (*enters*). I have the honour to announce, with regret, that the horses are ready. It's time, honoured lady, to set off for the station; the train comes in at five minutes past two. So please do me a favour, Irina Nikolayevna, do not forget to inquire what has become of the actor Suzdaltsev. Is he alive and well? We used to drink together at one time. . . . In "The Plundered Mail" he used to play incomparably . . . I remember the tragedian Izmaïlov, also a remarkable personality, acted with him in Elisavetograd. . . . Don't be in a hurry, honoured lady, you need not start for five minutes. Once they were acting conspirators in a melodrama and when they were suddenly discovered Izmaïlov had to say, "We are caught in a trap," but he said, "We are caught in a tap!" (*Laughs*) A tap!
(*While he is speaking* YAKOV *is busy looking after the luggage. The maid brings* MADAME ARKADIN *her hat, her coat, her umbrella and her gloves; they all help* MADAME ARKADIN *to put on her things. The man-cook looks in at the door on left and after some hesitation comes in. Enter* POLINA ANDREYEVNA, *then* SORIN *and* MEDVEDENKO.)

POLINA (*with a basket*). Here are some plums for the journey. . . . Very sweet ones. You may be glad to have something nice. . . .

MADAME ARKADIN. You are very kind, Polina Andreyevna.

POLINA. Good-bye, my dear! If anything has not been to your liking, forgive it. (*Weeps.*)

MADAME ARKADIN (*embraces her*). Everything has been nice, everything! But you mustn't cry.

POLINA. The time flies so fast!

MADAME ARKADIN. There's no help for it.

SORIN (*in a great-coat with a cape to it, with his hat on and a stick in his hand, enters from door on left, crossing the stage*). Sister, it's time to start, or you may be too late after all. I am going to get into the carriage. (*Goes out.*)

MEDVEDENKO. And I shall walk to the station . . . to see you off. I'll be there in no time. . . . (*Goes out.*)

MADAME ARKADIN. Good-bye, dear friends. . . . If we are all alive and well, we shall meet again next summer. (*The maid, the cook and* YAKOV *kiss her hand*) Don't forget me. (*Gives the cook a rouble*) Here's a rouble for the three of you.

THE COOK. We humbly thank you, madam! Good journey to you! We are very grateful for your kindness!

YAKOV. May God give you good luck!

SHAMRAEV. You might rejoice our hearts with a letter! Good-bye, Boris Alexeyevitch!

MADAME ARKADIN. Where is Konstantin? Tell him that I am starting; I must say good-bye. Well, don't remember evil against me. (*To* YAKOV) I gave the cook a rouble. It's for the three of you.

(*All go out on right. The stage is empty. Behind the scenes the noise that is usual when people are being seen off. The maid comes back to fetch the basket of plums from the table and goes out again.*)

TRIGORIN (*coming back*). I have forgotten my stick. I believe it is out there, on the verandah. (*Goes and, at door on left meets* NINA *who is coming in*) Is that you? We are going. . . .

NINA. I felt that we should see each other once more. (*Excitedly*) Boris Alexeyevitch, I have come to a decision, the die is cast, I am going on the stage. I shall be gone from here tomorrow; I am leaving my father, I am abandoning everything, I am beginning a new life Like you, I am going . . . to Moscow. We shall meet there.

TRIGORIN (*looking round*). Stay at the "Slavyansky Bazaar" . . . Let me know at once . . . Molchanovka, Groholsky House. . . . I am in a hurry. . . .
(*A pause.*)

NINA. One minute more. . . .

TRIGORIN (*in an undertone*). You are so lovely. . . . Oh, what happiness to think that we shall see each other soon! (*She sinks on his breast*) I shall see again those wonderful eyes, that inexpressibly beautiful tender smile . . . those soft features, the expression of angelic purity. . . . My darling. . . . (*A prolonged kiss.*)

CURTAIN

(*Between the Third and Fourth Acts there is an interval of two years.*)

ACT FOUR

One of the drawing-rooms in SORIN'S *house, which has been turned into a study for* KONSTANTIN TREPLEV. *On the right and left, doors leading to inner apartments. In the middle, glass door leading onto the verandah. Besides the usual drawing-room furniture there is, in corner on right, a writing-table, near door on left, a sofa, a bookcase and books in windows and on the chairs. Evening. There is a single lamp alight with a shade on it. It is half dark. There is the sound of trees rustling, and the wind howling in the chimney. A watchman is tapping. Enter* MEDVEDENKO *and* MASHA.

MASHA (*calling*). Konstantin Gavrilitch! Konstantin Gavrilitch! (*Looking round*) No, there is no one here. The old man keeps asking every minute, where is Kostya, where is Kostya? He cannot live without him. . . .

MEDVEDENKO. He is afraid of being alone. (*Listening*) What awful weather! This is the second day of it.

MASHA (*turns up the lamp*). There are waves on the lake. Great big ones.

MEDVEDENKO. How dark it is in the garden! We ought to have told them to break up that stage in the garden. It stands as bare and ugly as a skeleton, and the curtain flaps in the wind. When I passed it yesterday evening, it seemed as though someone were crying in it.

MASHA. What next. . . .
(*A pause.*)

MEDVEDENKO. Let us go home, Masha.

MASHA (*shakes her head*). I shall stay here for the night.

MEDVEDENKO (*in an imploring voice*). Masha, do come! Our baby must be hungry.

MASHA. Nonsense. Matryona will feed him.
(*A pause.*)

MEDVEDENKO. I am sorry for him. He has been three nights now without his mother.

MASHA. You are a bore. In old days you used at least to discuss general subjects, but now it is only home, baby, home, baby—that's all one can get out of you.

MEDVEDENKO. Come along, Masha!

MASHA. Go by yourself.

MEDVEDENKO. Your father won't let me have a horse.

MASHA. Yes, he will. You ask, and he will.

MEDVEDENKO. Very well, I'll ask. Then you will come tomorrow?

MASHA (*taking a pinch of snuff*). Very well, tomorrow. How you pester me.
(*Enter* TREPLEV *and* POLINA ANDREYEVNA; TREPLEV *brings in pillows and a quilt, and* POLINA ANDREYEVNA *sheets and pillow-cases; they lay them on the sofa, then* TREPLEV *goes to his table and sits down.*)

MASHA. What's this for, mother?

POLINA. Pyotr Nikolayevitch asked us to make a bed for him in Kostya's room.

MASHA. Let me do it. (*Makes the bed.*)

POLINA (*sighing*). Old people are like children. (*Goes up to the writing-table, and leaning on her elbow, looks at the manuscript; a pause.*)

MEDVEDENKO. Well, I am going then. Good-bye, Masha. (*Kisses his wife's hand*) Good-bye, mother. (*Tries to kiss his mother-in-law's hand.*)

POLINA (*with vexation*). Come, if you are going, go.

MEDVEDENKO. Good-bye, Konstantin Gavrilitch.
(TREPLEV *gives him his hand without speaking;* MEDVEDENKO *goes out.*)

POLINA (*looking at the MS.*). No one would have guessed or thought that you would have become a real author, Kostya. And now, thank God, they send you money from the magazines. (*Passes her hand over his hair*) And you have grown good-looking too. . . . Dear, good Kostya, do be a little kinder to my Mashenka!

MASHA (*as she makes the bed*). Leave him alone, mother.

POLINA (*to* TREPLEV). She is a nice little thing. (*A pause*) A woman wants nothing, you know, Kostya, so long as you give her a kind look. I know from myself.
(TREPLEV *gets up from the table and walks away without speaking.*)

MASHA. Now you have made him angry. What induced you to pester him?

POLINA. I feel so sorry for you, Mashenka.

MASHA. Much use that is!

POLINA. My heart aches for you. I see it all, you know, I understand it all.

MASHA. It's all foolishness. There is no such thing as hopeless love except in novels. It's of no consequence. The only thing is one mustn't let oneself go and keep expecting something, waiting for the tide to turn. . . . When love gets into the heart there is nothing to be done but to clear it out. Here they promised to transfer my husband to another district. As soon as I am there, I shall forget it all. . . . I shall tear it out of my heart.
(*Two rooms away a melancholy waltz is played.*)

POLINA. That's Kostya playing. He must be depressed.

MASHA (*noiselessly dances a few waltz steps*). The great thing, mother, is not to have him before one's eyes. If they only give my Semyon his transfer, trust me, I shall get over it in a month. It's all nonsense.

(*Door on left opens.* DORN *and* MEDVEDENKO *wheel in* SORIN *in his chair.*)

MEDVEDENKO. I have six of them at home now. And flour is two kopeks per pound.

DORN. You've got to look sharp to make both ends meet.

MEDVEDENKO. It's all very well for you to laugh. You've got more money than you know what to do with.

DORN. Money? After thirty years of practice, my boy, troublesome work during which I could not call my soul my own by day or by night, I only succeeded in saving two thousand roubles, and that I spent not long ago abroad. I have nothing.

MASHA (*to her husband*). You have not gone?

MEDVEDENKO (*guiltily*). Well, how can I when they won't let me have a horse?

MASHA (*with bitter vexation in an undertone*). I can't bear the sight of you.

(*The wheel-chair remains in the left half of the room;* POLINA ANDREYEVNA, MASHA *and* DORN *sit down beside it,* MEDVEDENKO *moves mournfully to one side.*)

DORN. What changes there have been here! The drawing-room has been turned into a study.

MASHA. It is more convenient for Konstantin Gavrilitch to work here. Whenever he likes, he can walk out into the garden and think there.

(*A watchman taps.*)

SORIN. Where is my sister?

DORN. She has gone to the station to meet Trigorin. She will be back directly.

SORIN. Since you thought it necessary to send for my sister, I must be dangerously ill. (*After a silence*) It's a queer thing, I am dangerously ill and here they don't give me any medicines.

DORN. Well, what would you like to have? Valerian drops? Soda? Quinine?

SORIN. Ah, he is at his moralising again! What an infliction it is! (*With a motion of his head towards the sofa*) Is that bed for me?

POLINA. Yes, it's for you, Pyotr Nikolayevitch.

SORIN. Thank you.

DORN (*hums*). "The moon is floating in the midnight sky."

SORIN. I want to give Kostya a subject for a story. It ought to be called "The Man who Wished"— *L'homme qui a voulu*. In my youth I wanted to become a literary man —and didn't; I wanted to speak well—and I spoke horribly badly, (*mimicking himself*) "and all the rest of it, and all that, and so on, and so forth" . . . and I would go plodding on and on, trying to sum up till I was in a regular perspiration; I wanted to get married—and

I didn't; I always wanted to live in town and here I am ending my life in the country—and so on.

DORN. I wanted to become an actual civil councillor—and I have.

SORIN (*laughs*). That I had no hankerings after. That happened of itself.

DORN. To be expressing dissatisfaction with life at sixty-two is really ungracious, you know.

SORIN. What a persistent fellow he is! You might understand that one wants to live!

DORN. That's just frivolity. It's the law of nature that every life must have an end.

SORIN. You argue like a man who has had enough. You are satisfied and so you are indifferent to life, nothing matters to you. But even you will be afraid to die.

DORN. The dread of death is an animal fear. One must overcome it. A rational fear of death is only possible for those who believe in eternal life and are conscious of their sins. And you, in the first place, don't believe, and, in the second, what sins have you to worry about? You have served in the courts of justice for twenty-five years—that's all.

SORIN (*laughs*). Twenty-eight. . . . (TREPLEV *comes in and sits down on a stool at* SORIN'S *feet.* MASHA *never takes her eyes off him.*)

DORN. We are hindering Konstantin Gavrilitch from working.

TREPLEV. Oh, no, it doesn't matter. (*A pause.*)

MEDVEDENKO. Allow me to ask you, doctor, what town did you like best abroad?

DORN. Genoa.

TREPLEV. Why Genoa?

DORN. The life in the streets is so wonderful there. When you go out of the hotel in the evening, the whole street is packed with people. You wander aimlessly zigzagging about among the crowd, backwards and forwards; you live with it, are psychologically at one with it and begin almost to believe that a world-soul is really possible, such as was acted by Nina Zaretchny in your play. And, by the way, where is she now? How is she getting on?

TREPLEV. I expect she is quite well.

DORN. I was told that she was leading a rather peculiar life. How was that?

TREPLEV. That's a long story, doctor.

DORN. Well, tell it us shortly. (*A pause.*)

TREPLEV. She ran away from home and had an affair with Trigorin. You know that?

DORN. I know.

TREPLEV. She had a child. The child died. Trigorin got tired of her and went back to his old ties, as might have been expected. Though, indeed, he had never abandoned them, but in his weak-willed way contrived to keep both going. As far as I can make out from what I have heard, Nina's private life was a complete failure.

DORN. And the stage?

TREPLEV. I fancy that was worse still. She made her début at some holiday place near Moscow, then went to the provinces. All that time I did not lose sight of her, and wherever she went I followed her. She always took big parts, but she acted crudely, without taste, screamingly, with violent gestures. There were moments when she uttered a cry successfully or died successfully, but they were only moments.

DORN. Then she really has some talent?

TREPLEV. It was difficult to make it out. I suppose she has. I saw her but she would not see me, and the servants would not admit me at the hotel. I understood her state of mind and did not insist on seeing her. (*A pause*) What more can I tell you? Afterwards, when I was back at home, I had some letters from her—warm, intelligent, interesting letters. She did not complain, but I felt that she was profoundly unhappy; every line betrayed sick overstrained nerves. And her imagination is a little unhinged. She signed herself the Sea gull. In Pushkin's "Mermaid" the miller says that he is a raven, and in the same way in her letters she kept repeating that she was a sea gull. Now she is here.

DORN. Here? How do you mean?

TREPLEV. In the town, staying at an inn. She has been there for five days. I did go to see her, and Marya Ilyinishna here went too, but she won't see anyone. Semyon Semyonitch declares he saw her yesterday afternoon in the fields a mile and a half from here.

MEDVEDENKO. Yes, I saw her. She went in that direction, towards the town. I bowed to her and asked why she did not come to see us. She said she would come.

TREPLEV. She won't come. (*A pause*) Her father and stepmother refuse to recognise her. They have put watchmen about so that she may not even go near the house. (*Walks away with the doctor towards the writing table*) How easy it is to be a philosopher on paper, doctor, and how difficult it is in life!

SORIN. She was a charming girl.

DORN. What?

SORIN. She was a charming girl, I say. Actual Civil Councillor Sorin was positively in love with her for a time.

DORN. The old Lovelace.
(SHAMRAEV's *laugh is heard.*)

POLINA. I fancy our people have come back from the station. . . .

TREPLEV. Yes, I hear mother.
(*Enter* MADAME ARKADIN, TRIGORIN *and with them* SHAMRAEV.)

SHAMRAEV (*as he enters*). We all grow old and dilapidated under the influence of the elements, while you, honoured lady, are still young . . . a light blouse, sprightliness, grace. . . .

MADAME ARKADIN. You want to bring me ill-luck again, you tiresome man!

TRIGORIN. How do you do, Pyotr Nikolayevitch! So you are still poorly? That's bad! (*Seeing* MASHA, *joyfully*) Marya Ilyinishna!

MASHA. You know me, do you? (*Shakes hands.*)

TRIGORIN. Married?

MASHA. Long ago.

TRIGORIN. Are you happy? (*Bows to* DORN *and* MEDVEDENKO, *then hesitatingly approaches* TREPLEV) Irina Nikolayevna has told me that you have forgotten the past and are no longer angry.
(TREPLEV *holds out his hand.*)

MADAME ARKADIN (*to her son*). Boris Alexeyevitch has brought the magazine with your new story in it.

TREPLEV (*taking the magazine, to* TRIGORIN). Thank you, you are very kind. (*They sit down.*)

TRIGORIN. Your admirers send their greetings to you. . . . In Petersburg and Moscow there is great interest in your work and I am continually being asked questions about you. People ask what you are like, how old you are, whether you are dark or fair. Everyone imagines, for some reason, that you are no longer young. And no one knows your real name, as you always publish under a pseudonym. You are as mysterious as the Iron Mask.

TREPLEV. Will you be able to make a long stay?

TRIGORIN. No, I think I must go back to Moscow tomorrow. I am obliged to. I am in a hurry to finish my novel, and besides, I have promised something for a collection of tales that is being published. It's the old story, in fact.
(*While they are talking* MADAME ARKADIN *and* POLINA ANDREYEVNA *put a card-table in the middle of the room and open it out.* SHAMRAEV *lights candles and sets chairs. A game of loto is brought out of the cupboard.*)

TRIGORIN. The weather has not given me a friendly welcome. There is a cruel wind. If it has dropped by tomorrow morning I shall go to the lake to fish. And I must have a look at the garden and that place where—you remember?—your play was acted. I've got a subject for a story, I only want to revive my recollections of the scene in which it is laid.

MASHA (*to her father*). Father, let my husband have a horse! He must get home.

SHAMRAEV (*mimicking*). Must get home—a horse! (*Sternly*) You can see for yourself: they have just been to the station. I can't send them out again.

MASHA. But there are other horses. (*Seeing that her father says nothing, waves her hand*) There's no doing anything with you.

MEDVEDENKO. I can walk, Masha Really. . . .

POLINA (*with a sigh*). Walk in such weather. . . . (*Sits down to the card-table*) Come, friends.

MEDVEDENKO. It is only four miles. Good-bye. (*Kisses his wife's hand*) Good-bye, mother. (*His mother-in-law reluctantly holds out her hand for him to kiss*) I wouldn't trouble anyone, but the baby. . . . (*Bows to the company*) Good-bye. . . . (*Goes out with a guilty step.*)

SHAMRAEV. He can walk right enough. He's not a general.

POLINA (*tapping on the table*). Come, friends. Don't let us waste time, we shall soon be called to supper.
(SHAMRAEV, MASHA *and* DORN *sit down at the table.*)

MADAME ARKADIN (*to* TRIGORIN). When the long autumn evenings come on, they play loto here. Look, it's the same old loto that we had when our mother used to play with us, when we were children. Won't you have a game before supper? (*Sits down to the table with* TRIGORIN) It's a dull game, but it is not so bad when you are used to it. (*Deals three cards to everyone.*)

TREPLEV (*turning the pages of the magazine*). He has read his own story, but he has not even cut mine. (*Puts the magazine down on the writing-table, then goes towards door on left; as he passes his mother he kisses her on the head.*)

MADAME ARKADIN. And you, Kostya?

TREPLEV. Excuse me, I would rather not . . . I am going out. (*Goes out.*)

MADAME ARKADIN. The stake is ten kopeks. Put it down for me, doctor, will you?

DORN. Right.

MASHA. Has everyone put down their stakes? I begin . . . Twenty-two.

MADAME ARKADIN. Yes.

MASHA. Three!

DORN. Right!

MASHA. Did you play three? Eight! Eighty-one! Ten!

SHAMRAEV. Don't be in a hurry!

MADAME ARKADIN. What a reception I had in Harkov! My goodness! I feel dizzy with it still.

MASHA. Thirty-four!
(*A melancholy waltz is played behind the scenes.*)

MADAME ARKADIN. The students gave me an ovation. . . . Three baskets of flowers . . . two wreaths and this, see. (*Unfastens a brooch on her throat and lays it on the table.*)

SHAMRAEV. Yes, that is a thing. . . .

MASHA. Fifty!

DORN. Exactly fifty?

MADAME ARKADIN. I had a wonderful dress. . . . Whatever I don't know, I do know how to dress.

POLINA. Kostya is playing the piano; he is depressed, poor fellow.

SHAMRAEV. He is awfully abused in the newspapers.

MASHA. Seventy-seven!

MADAME ARKADIN. As though that mattered!

TRIGORIN. He never quite comes off. He has not yet hit upon his own medium. There is always something queer and vague, at times almost like delirium. Not a single living character.

MASHA. Eleven!

MADAME ARKADIN (*looking round at* SORIN). Petrusha, are you bored? (*A pause*) He is asleep.

DORN. The actual civil councillor is asleep.

MASHA. Seven! Ninety!

TRIGORIN. If I lived in such a place, beside a lake, do you suppose I should write? I should overcome this passion and should do nothing but fish.

MASHA. Twenty-eight!

TRIGORIN. Catching perch is so delightful!

DORN. Well, I believe in Konstantin Gavrilitch. There is something in him! There is something in him! He thinks in images; his stories are vivid, full of colour and they affect me strongly. The only pity is that he has not got definite aims. He produces an impression and that's all, but you can't get far with nothing but an impression. Irina Nikolayevna, are you glad that your son is a writer?

MADAME ARKADIN. Only fancy, I have not read anything of his yet. I never have time.

MASHA. Twenty-six!
(TREPLEV *comes in quietly and sits down at his table.*)

SHAMRAEV (*to* TRIGORIN). We have still got something here belonging to you, Boris Alexeyevitch.

TRIGORIN. What's that?

SHAMRAEV. Konstantin Gavrilitch shot a sea gull and you asked me to get it stuffed for you.

TRIGORIN. I don't remember! (*Pondering*) I don't remember!

MASHA. Sixty-six! One!

TREPLEV (*flinging open the window, listens*). How dark it is! I don't know why I feel so uneasy.

MADAME ARKADIN. Kostya, shut the window, there's a draught.
(TREPLEV *shuts the window.*)

MASHA. Eighty-eight!

TRIGORIN. The game is mine!

MADAME ARKADIN (*gaily*). Bravo, bravo!

SHAMRAEV. Bravo!

MADAME ARKADIN. That man always has luck in everything. (*Gets up*) And now let us go and have something to eat. Our great man has not dined today. We will go on again after supper. (*To her son*) Kostya, leave your manuscripts and come to supper.

TREPLEV. I don't want any, mother, I am not hungry.

MADAME ARKADIN. As you like.

(*Wakes* SORIN) Petrusha, supper! (*Takes* SHAMRAEV'S *arm*) I'll tell you about my reception in Harkov. (POLINA ANDREYEVNA *puts out the candles on the table. Then she and* DORN *wheel the chair. All go out by door on left; only* TREPLEV, *sitting at the writing-table, is left on the stage.*)

TREPLEV (*settling himself to write; runs through what he has written already*). I have talked so much about new forms and now I feel that little by little I am falling into a convention myself. (*Reads*) "The placard on the wall proclaimed. . . . The pale face in its setting of dark hair." Proclaimed, setting. That's stupid. (*Scratches out*) I will begin where the hero is awakened by the patter of the rain, and throw out all the rest. The description of the moonlight evening is long and overelaborate. Trigorin has worked out methods for himself, it's easy for him now. . . . With him the broken bottle neck glitters on the dam and the mill-wheel casts a black shadow—and there you have the moonlight night, while I have the tremulous light, and the soft twinkling of the stars, and the far-away strains of the piano dying away in the still fragrant air. . . . It's agonising. (*A pause*) I come more and more to the conviction that it is not a question of new and old forms, but that what matters is that a man should write without thinking about forms at all, write because it springs freely from his soul. (*There is a tap at the window nearest to the table*) What is that? (*Looks out of window*) There is nothing to be seen. . . . (*Opens the glass door and looks out into the garden*) Someone ran down the steps. (*Calls*) Who is there? (*Goes out and can be heard walking rapidly along the verandah; returns half a minute later with* NINA ZARETCHNY) Nina, Nina!

(NINA *lays her head on his breast and weeps with subdued sobs.*)

TREPLEV (*moved*). Nina! Nina! It's you . . . you. . . . It's as though I had foreseen it, all day long my heart has been aching and restless. (*Takes off her hat and cape*) Oh, my sweet, my precious, she has come at last. Don't let us cry, don't let us!

NINA. There is someone here.

TREPLEV. No one.

NINA. Lock the doors, someone may come in.

TREPLEV. No one will come in.

NINA. I know Irina Nikolayevna is here. Lock the doors.

TREPLEV (*locks the door on right, goes to door on left*). There is no lock on this one. I'll put a chair against it. (*Puts an armchair against the door*) Don't be afraid, no one will come.

NINA (*looking intently into his face*). Let me look at you. (*Looking round*) It's warm, it's nice. . . . In old days this was the drawing-room. Am I very much changed?

TREPLEV. Yes . . . You are thinner and your eyes are bigger. Nina, how strange it is that I should be seeing you. Why would not you let me see you? Why haven't you come all this time? I know you have been here almost a week. . . . I have been to you several times every day; I stood under your window like a beggar.

NINA. I was afraid that you might hate me. I dream every night that you look at me and don't know me. If only you knew! Ever since I came I have been walking here . . . by the lake. I have been near your house many times and could not bring myself to enter it. Let us sit down. (*They sit down*) Let us sit down and talk and talk. It's nice here, it's warm and snug. Do you hear the wind? There's a passage in Turgenev, "Well for the man on such a night who sits under the shelter of home, who has a warm corner in safety." I am a sea gull. . . . No, that's not it. (*Rubs her forehead*) What was I saying? Yes . . . Turgenev . . . "And the Lord help all homeless wanderers!" . . . It doesn't matter. (*Sobs.*)

TREPLEV. Nina, you are crying again. . . . Nina!

NINA. Never mind, it does me good . . . I haven't cried for two years. Yesterday, late in the evening, I came into the garden to see whether our stage was still there. It is still standing. I cried for the first time after two years and it eased the weight on my heart and made it lighter. You see, I am not crying now. (*Takes him by the hand*) And so now you are an author. . . . You are an author, I am an actress. . . . We too have been drawn into the whirlpool. I lived joyously like a child—I woke up singing in the morning; I loved you and dreamed of fame, and now? Early tomorrow morning I must go to Yelets third-class . . . with peasants, and at Yelets the cultured tradesmen will pester me with attentions. Life is a coarse business!

TREPLEV. Why to Yelets

NINA. I have taken an engagement for the whole winter. It is time to go.

TREPLEV. Nina, I cursed you, I hated you, I tore up your letters and photographs, but I was conscious every minute that my soul is bound to yours for ever. It's not in my power to leave off loving you, Nina Ever since I lost you and began to get my work published my life has been unbearable—I am wretched. . . . My youth was, as it were, torn away all at once and it seems to me as though I have lived for ninety years already. I call upon you, I kiss the earth on which you have walked; wherever I look I see your face, that tender smile that lighted up the best days of my life. . . .

NINA (*distractedly*). Why does he talk like this, why does he talk like this?

TREPLEV. I am alone in the world, warmed by no affection. I am as cold as though I were in a cellar, and everything I write is dry, hard and gloomy. Stay here, Nina, I entreat you, or let me go with you! (NINA *rapidly puts on her hat and cape.*)

TREPLEV. Nina, why is this? For God's sake, Nina! (*Looks at her as she puts her things on; a pause.*)

NINA. My horses are waiting at the gate. Don't see me off, I'll go alone. . . . (*Through her tears*) Give me some water. . . .

TREPLEV (*gives her some water*) Where are you going now?

NINA. To the town. (*A pause*) Is Irina Nikolayevna here?

TREPLEV. Yes. . . . Uncle was taken worse on Thursday and we telegraphed for her.

NINA. Why do you say that you kissed the earth on which I walked? I ought to be killed. (*Bends over table*) I am so tired! If I could rest . . . if I could rest! (*Raising her head*) I am a sea gull. . . . No, that's not it. I am an actress. Oh, well! (*Hearing* MADAME ARKADIN *and* TRIGORIN *laughing, she listens, then runs to door on left and looks through the keyhole*) He is here too. . . . (*Turning back to* TREPLEV) Oh, well . . . it doesn't matter . . . no. . . . He did not believe in the stage, he always laughed at my dreams and little by little I left off believing in it too, and lost heart. . . . And then I was fretted by love and jealousy, and continually anxious over my little one. . . . I grew petty and trivial, I acted stupidly. . . . I did not know what to do with my arms, I did not know how to stand on the stage, could not control my voice. You can't understand what it feels like when one knows one is acting disgracefully. I am a sea gull. No, that's not it. . . . Do you remember you shot a sea gull? A man came by chance, saw it and, just to pass the time, destroyed it. . . . A subject for a short story. . . . That's not it, though. (*Rubs her forehead*) What was I saying? . . . I am talking of the stage. Now I am not like that. I am a real actress, I act with enjoyment, with enthusiasm, I am intoxicated when I am on the stage and feel that I am splendid. And since I have been here, I keep walking about and thinking, thinking and

feeling that my soul is getting stronger every day. Now I know, I understand, Kostya, that in our work—in acting or writing—what matters is not fame, not glory, not what I dreamed of, but knowing how to be patient. To bear one's cross and have faith. I have faith and it all doesn't hurt so much, and when I think of my vocation I am not afraid of life.

TREPLEV (*mournfully*). You have found your path, you know which way you are going, but I am still floating in a chaos of dreams and images, not knowing what use it is to anyone. I have no faith and don't know what my vocation is.

NINA (*listening*). 'Sh-sh . . . I am going. Good-bye. When I become a great actress, come and look at me. Will you promise? But now . . . (*presses his hand*) it's late. I can hardly stand on my feet. . . . I am worn out and hungry. . . .

TREPLEV. Stay, I'll give you some supper.

NINA. No, no. . . . Don't see me off, I will go by myself. My horses are close by. . . . So she brought him with her? Well, it doesn't matter. When you see Trigorin, don't say anything to him. . . . I love him! I love him even more than before. . . . A subject for a short story . . . I love him, I love him passionately, I love him to despair. It was nice in old days, Kostya! Do you remember? How clear, warm, joyous and pure life was, what feelings we had—feelings like tender, exquisite flowers. . . . Do you remember? (*Recites*) "Men, lions, eagles, and partridges, horned deer, geese, spiders, silent fish that dwell in the water, star-fishes, and creatures which cannot be seen by the eye—all living things, all living things, all living things, have completed their cycle of sorrow, are extinct. . . . For thousands of years the earth has borne no living creature on its surface, and this poor moon lights its lamp in vain. On the meadow the cranes no longer waken with a cry and there is no sound of the May beetles in the lime trees . . ." (*Impulsively embraces* TREPLEV *and runs out of the glass door.*)

TREPLEV (*after a pause*). It will be a pity if someone meets her in the garden and tells mother. It may upset mother. . . . (*He spends two minutes in tearing up all his manuscripts and throwing them under the table; then unlocks the door on right and goes out.*)

DORN (*trying to open the door on left*). Strange. The door seems to be locked. . . . (*Comes in and puts the armchair in its place*) An obstacle race.
(*Enter* MADAME ARKADIN *and* POLINA ANDREYEVNA, *behind them* YAKOV *carrying a tray with bottles;* MASHA; *then* SHAMRAEV *and* TRIGORIN.)

MADAME ARKADIN. Put the claret and the beer for Boris Alexeyevitch here on the table. We will play as we drink it. Let us sit down, friends.

POLINA (*to* YAKOV). Bring tea too at the same time. (*Lights the candles and sits down to the card-table.*)

SHAMRAEV (*leads* TRIGORIN *to the cupboard*). Here's the thing I was speaking about just now. (*Takes stuffed sea gull from the cupboard*) This is what you ordered.

TRIGORIN (*looking at the sea gull*). I don't remember it. (*Musing*) I don't remember.
(*The sound of a shot coming from right of stage; everyone starts.*)

MADAME ARKADIN (*frightened*). What's that?

DORN. That's nothing. It must be something in my medicine-chest that has gone off. Don't be anxious. (*Goes out at door on right, comes back in half a minute*) That's what it is. A bottle of ether has exploded. (*Hums*) "I stand before thee enchanted again. . . ."

MADAME ARKADIN (*sitting down to the table*). Ough, how frightened I was. It reminded me of how . . . (*Hides her face in her hands*) It made me quite dizzy. . . .

DORN (*turning over the leaves of the magazine, to* TRIGORIN). There was an article in this two months ago—a letter from America—and I wanted to ask you, among other things. (*Puts his arm round* TRIGORIN'S *waist and leads him to the footlights*) As I am very much interested in the question. . . . (*In a lower tone, dropping his voice*) Get Irina Nikolayevna away somehow. The fact is, Konstantin Gavrilitch has shot himself. . . .

CURTAIN

The Lower Depths

BY MAXIM GORKY

TRANSLATED FROM THE RUSSIAN
BY JENNIE COVAN

CHARACTERS

MIKHAIL IVANOFF KOSTILYOFF, *keeper of a night lodging.*
VASSILISA KARPOVNA, *his wife.*
NATASHA, *her sister.*
MIEDVIEDIEFF, *her uncle, a policeman.*
VASKA PEPEL, *a young thief.*
ANDREI MITRITCH KLESHTCH, *a locksmith.*
ANNA, *his wife.*
NASTYA, *a street-walker.*
KVASHNYA, *a vendor of meat-pies.*
BUBNOFF, *a cap-maker.*
THE BARON.
SATINE.
THE ACTOR.
LUKA, *a pilgrim.*
ALYOSHKA, *a shoemaker.*
KRIVOY ZOB ⎱ *Porters.*
THE TARTAR ⎰
NIGHT LODGERS, TRAMPS AND OTHERS.

The action takes place in a Night Lodging and in "The Waste," an area in its rear.

THE LOWER DEPTHS

ACT ONE

A cellar resembling a cave. The ceiling, which merges into stone walls, is low and grimy, and the plaster and paint are peeling off. There is a window, high up on the right wall, from which comes the light. The right corner, which constitutes PEPEL'S *room, is partitioned off by thin boards. Close to the corner of this room is* BUBNOFF'S *wooden bunk. In the left corner stands a large Russian stove. In the stone wall, left, is a door leading to the kitchen where live* KVASHNYA, *the* BARON, *and* NASTYA. *Against the wall, between the stove and the door, is a large bed covered with dirty chintz. Bunks line the walls. In the foreground, by the left wall, is a block of wood with a vise and a small anvil fastened to it, and another smaller block of wood somewhat further towards the back.* KLESHTCH *is seated on the smaller block, trying keys into old locks. At his feet are two large bundles of various keys, wired together, also a battered tin samovar, a hammer, and pincers. In the center are a large table, two benches, and a stool, all of which are of dirty, unpainted wood. Behind the table* KVASHNYA *is busying herself with the samovar. The* BARON *sits chewing a piece of black bread, and* NASTYA *occupies the stool, leans her elbows on the table, and reads a tattered book. In the bed, behind curtains,* ANNA *lies coughing.* BUBNOFF *is seated on his bunk, attempting to shape a pair of old trousers with the help of an ancient hat shape which he holds between his knees. Scattered about him are pieces of buckram, oilcloth, and rags.* SATINE, *just awakened, lies in his bunk, grunting. On top of the stove, the* ACTOR, *invisible to the audience, tosses about and coughs.*

It is an early Spring morning.

THE BARON. And then?

KVASHNYA. No, my dear, said I, keep away from me with such proposals. I've been through it all, you see—and not for a hundred baked lobsters would I marry again!

BUBNOFF (*to* SATINE). What are you grunting about?
(SATINE *keeps on grunting.*)

KVASHNYA. Why should I, said I, a free woman, my own mistress, enter my name into somebody else's passport and sell myself into slavery—no! Why—I wouldn't marry a man even if he were an American prince!

KLESHTCH. You lie!

KVASHNYA. Wha-at?

KLESHTCH. You lie! You're going to marry Abramka. . . .

THE BARON (*snatching the book out of* NASTYA'S *hand and reading the title*). "Fatal Love" . . . (*Laughs.*)

NASTYA (*stretching out her hand*). Give it back—give it back! Stop fooling!
(THE BARON *looks at her and waves the book in the air*.)

KVASHNYA (*to* KLESHTCH). You crimson goat, you—calling me a liar! How dare you be so rude to me?

THE BARON (*hitting* NASTYA *on the head with the book*). Nastya, you little fool!

NASTYA (*reaching for the book*). Give it back!

KLESHTCH. Oh—what a great lady . . . but you'll marry Abramka just the same—that's all you're waiting for . . .

KVASHNYA. Sure! Anything else? You nearly beat your wife to death!

KLESHTCH. Shut up, you old bitch! It's none of your business!

KVASHNYA. Ho-ho! can't stand the truth, can you?

THE BARON. They're off again! Nastya, where are you?

NASTYA (*without lifting her head*). Hey—go away!

ANNA (*putting her head through the curtains*). The day has started. For God's sake, don't row!

KLESHTCH. Whining again!

ANNA. Every blessed day . . . let me die in peace, can't you?

BUBNOFF. Noise won't keep you from dying.

KVASHNYA (*walking up to* ANNA). Little mother, how did you ever manage to live with this wretch?

ANNA. Leave me alone—get away from me. . . .

KVASHNYA. Well, well! You poor soul . . . how's the pain in the chest—any better?

THE BARON. Kvashnya! Time to go to market. . . .

KVASHNYA. We'll go presently. (*To* ANNA) Like some hot dumplings?

ANNA. No, thanks. Why should I eat?

KVASHNYA. You must eat. Hot food —good for you! I'll leave you some in a cup. Eat them when you feel like it. Come on, sir! (*To* KLESHTCH) You evil spirit! (*Goes into kitchen*.)

ANNA (*coughing*). Lord, Lord . . .

THE BARON (*painfully pushing forward* NASTYA'S *head*). Throw it away—little fool!

NASTYA (*muttering*). Leave me alone—I don't bother you . . .
(THE BARON *follows* KVASHNYA, *whistling*.)

SATINE (*sitting up in his bunk*). Who beat me up yesterday?

BUBNOFF. Does it make any difference who?

SATINE. Suppose they did—but why did they?

BUBNOFF. Were you playing cards?

SATINE. Yes!

BUBNOFF. That's why they beat you.

SATINE. Scoundrels!

THE ACTOR (*raising his head from the top of the stove*). One of these days they'll beat you to death!

SATINE. You're a jackass!

THE ACTOR. Why?

SATINE. Because a man can die only once!

THE ACTOR (*after a silence*). I don't understand——

KLESHTCH. Say! You crawl from that stove—and start cleaning house! Don't play the delicate primrose!

THE ACTOR. None of your business!

KLESHTCH. Wait till Vassilisa comes —she'll show you whose business it is!

THE ACTOR. To hell with Vassilisa! Today is the Baron's turn to clean. . . . Baron!
(THE BARON *comes from the kitchen.*)

THE BARON. I've no time to clean . . . I'm going to market with Kvashnya.

THE ACTOR. That doesn't concern me. Go to the gallows if you like. It's your turn to sweep the floor just the same—I'm not going to do other people's work . . .

THE BARON. Go to blazes! Nastya will do it. Hey there—fatal love! Wake up! (*Takes the book away from* NASTYA.)

NASTYA (*getting up*). What do you want? Give it back to me! You scoundrel! And that's a nobleman for you!

THE BARON (*returning the book to her*). Nastya! Sweep the floor for me—will you?

NASTYA (*goes to kitchen*). Not so's you'll notice it!

KVASHNYA (*to* THE BARON *through kitchen door*). Come on—you! They don't need you! Actor! You were asked to do it, and now you go ahead and attend to it—it won't kill you . . .

THE ACTOR. It's always I . . . I don't understand why. . . .
(THE BARON *comes from the kitchen, across his shoulders a wooden beam from which hang earthen pots covered with rags.*)

THE BARON. Heavier than ever!

SATINE. It paid you to be born a Baron, eh?

KVASHNYA (*to* ACTOR). See to it that you sweep up! (*Crosses to outer door, letting* THE BARON *pass ahead.*)

THE ACTOR (*climbing down from the stove*). It's bad for me to inhale dust. (*With pride*) My organism is poisoned with alcohol. (*Sits down on a bunk, meditating.*)

SATINE. Organism—organon. . . .

ANNA. Andrei Mitritch. . . .

KLESHTCH. What now?

ANNA. Kvashnya left me some

dumplings over there—you eat them!

KLESHTCH (*coming over to her*). And you—don't you want any?

ANNA. No. Why should I eat? You're a workman—you need it.

KLESHTCH. Frightened, are you? Don't be! You'll get all right!

ANNA. Go and eat! It's hard on me. . . . I suppose very soon . . .

KLESHTCH (*walking away*). Never mind—maybe you'll get well—you can never tell! (*Goes into kitchen.*)

THE ACTOR (*loud, as if he had suddenly awakened*). Yesterday the doctor in the hospital said to me: "Your organism," he said, "is entirely poisoned with alcohol . . ."

SATINE (*smiling*). Organon . . .

THE ACTOR (*stubbornly*). Not organon—organism!

SATINE. Sibylline. . . .

THE ACTOR (*shaking his fist at him*). Nonsense! I'm telling you seriously . . . if the organism is poisoned . . . that means it's bad for me to sweep the floor—to inhale the dust . . .

SATINE. Macrobistic . . . hah!

BUBNOFF. What are you muttering?

SATINE. Words—and here's another one for you—transcendentalistic . . .

BUBNOFF. What does it mean?

SATINE. Don't know—I forgot . . .

BUBNOFF. Then why did you say it?

SATINE. Just so! I'm bored, brother, with human words—all our words. Bored! I've heard each one of them a thousand times surely.

THE ACTOR. In Hamlet they say: "Words, words, words!" It's a good play. I played the grave-digger in it once. . . .
(KLESHTCH *comes from the kitchen.*)

KLESHTCH. Will you start playing with the broom?

THE ACTOR. None of your business. (*Striking his chest*) Ophelia! O—remember me in thy prayers!
(*Back stage is heard a dull murmur, cries, and a police whistle.* KLESHTCH *sits down to work, filing screechily.*)

SATINE. I love unintelligible, obsolete words. When I was a youngster—and worked as a telegraph operator—I read heaps of books. . . .

BUBNOFF. Were you really a telegrapher?

SATINE. I was. There are some excellent books—and lots of curious words . . . Once I was an educated man, do you know?

BUBNOFF. I've heard it a hundred times. Well, so you were! That isn't very important! Me—well—once I was a furrier. I had my own shop—what with dyeing the fur all day long, my arms were yellow up to the elbows, brother. I thought I'd never be able ever to get clean again—that I'd go to my grave, all yellow! But look at my hands now—they're plain dirty—that's what!

SATINE. Well, and what then?

BUBNOFF. That's all!

SATINE. What are you trying to prove?

BUBNOFF. Oh, well—just matching thoughts—no matter how much dye you get on yourself, it all comes off in the end—yes, yes——

SATINE. Oh—my bones ache!

THE ACTOR (sits, nursing his knees). Education is all rot. Talent is the thing. I knew an actor—who read his parts by heart, syllable by syllable—but he played heroes in a way that . . . why—the whole theatre would rock with ecstasy!

SATINE. Bubnoff, give me five kopecks.

BUBNOFF. I only have two——

THE ACTOR. I say—talent, that's what you need to play heroes. And talent is nothing but faith in yourself, in your own powers—

SATINE. Give me five kopecks and I'll have faith that you're a hero, a crocodile, or a police inspector—Kleshtch, give me five kopecks.

KLESHTCH. Go to hell! All of you!

SATINE. What are you cursing for? I know you haven't a kopeck in the world!

ANNA. Andrei Mitritch—I'm suffocating—I can't breathe——

KLESHTCH. What shall I do?

BUBNOFF. Open the door into the hall.

KLESHTCH. All right. You're sitting on the bunk, I on the floor. You change places with me, and I'll let you open the door. I have a cold as it is.

BUBNOFF (unconcernedly). I don't care if you open the door—it's your wife who's asking——

KLESHTCH (morosely). I don't care who's asking——

SATINE. My head buzzes—ah—why do people have to hit each other over the heads?

BUBNOFF. They don't only hit you over the head, but over the rest of the body as well. (Rises) I must go and buy some thread—our bosses are late today—seems as if they've croaked. (Exit.)
(ANNA coughs: SATINE is lying down motionless, his hands folded behind his head.)

THE ACTOR (looks about him morosely, then goes to ANNA). Feeling bad, eh?

ANNA. I'm choking——

THE ACTOR. If you wish, I'll take you into the hallway. Get up, then, come! (He helps her to rise, wraps some sort of a rag about her shoulders, and supports her towards the hall) It isn't easy. I'm sick myself—poisoned with alcohol . . .
(KOSTILYOFF appears in the doorway.)

KOSTILYOFF. Going for a stroll?

What a nice couple—the gallant cavalier and the lady fair!

THE ACTOR. Step aside, you—don't you see that we're invalids?

KOSTILYOFF. Pass on, please! (*Hums a religious tune, glances about him suspiciously, and bends his head to the left as if listening to what is happening in* PEPEL'S *room.* KLESHTCH *is jangling his keys and scraping away with his file, and looks askance at the other*) Filing?

KLESHTCH. What?

KOSTILYOFF. I say, are you filing? (*Pause*) What did I want to ask? (*Quick and low*) Hasn't my wife been here?

KLESHTCH. I didn't see her.

KOSTILYOFF (*carefully moving towards* PEPEL'S *room*). You take up a whole lot of room for your two rubles a month. The bed—and your bench—yes—you take up five rubles' worth of space, so help me God! I'll have to put another half ruble to your rent——

KLESHTCH. You'll put a noose around my neck and choke me . . . you'll croak soon enough, and still all you think of is half rubles——

KOSTILYOFF. Why should I choke you? What would be the use? God be with you—live and prosper! But I'll have to raise you half a ruble— I'll buy oil for the ikon lamp, and my offering will atone for my sins, and for yours as well. You don't think much of your sins—not much! Oh, Andrushka, you're a wicked man! Your wife is dying because of your wickedness—no one loves you,

no one respects you—your work is squeaky, jarring on everyone.

KLESHTCH (*shouts*). What do you come here for—just to annoy me? (SATINE *grunts loudly.*)

KOSTILYOFF (*with a start*). God, what a noise!
(THE ACTOR *enters.*)

THE ACTOR. I've put her down in the hall and wrapped her up.

KOSTILYOFF. You're a kindly fellow. That's good. Some day you'll be rewarded for it.

THE ACTOR. When?

KOSTILYOFF. In the Beyond, little brother—there all our deeds will be reckoned up.

THE ACTOR. Suppose you reward me right now?

KOSTILYOFF. How can I do that?

THE ACTOR. Wipe out half my debt.

KOSTILYOFF. He-ho! You're always jesting, darling—always poking fun . . . can kindliness of heart be repaid with gold? Kindliness—it's above all other qualities. But your debt to me—remains a debt. And so you'll have to pay me back. You ought to be kind to me, an old man, without seeking for reward!

THE ACTOR. You're a swindler, old man! (*Goes into kitchen.*)
(KLESHTCH *rises and goes into the hall.*)

KOSTILYOFF (*to* SATINE). See that squeaker——? He ran away—he doesn't like me!

SATINE. Does anybody like you besides the Devil?

KOSTILYOFF (*laughing*). Oh—you're so quarrelsome! But I like you all—I understand you all, my unfortunate, down-trodden, useless brethren . . . (*Suddenly, rapidly*) Is Vaska home?

SATINE. See for yourself——

KOSTILYOFF (*goes to the door and knocks*). Vaska!
(THE ACTOR *appears at the kitchen door, chewing something.*)

PEPEL. Who is it?

KOSTILYOFF. It's I—I, Vaska!

PEPEL. What do you want?

KOSTILYOFF (*stepping aside*). Open!

SATINE (*without looking at* KOSTILYOFF). He'll open—and she's there——

(THE ACTOR *makes a grimace.*)

KOSTILYOFF (*in a low, anxious tone*). Eh? Who's there? What?

SATINE. Speaking to me?

KOSTILYOFF. What did you say?

SATINE. Oh—nothing—I was just talking to myself——

KOSTILYOFF. Take care, brother. Don't carry your joking too far! (*Knocks loudly at door*) Vassily!

PEPEL (*opening door*). Well? What are you disturbing me for?

KOSTILYOFF (*peering into room*). I —you see——

PEPEL. Did you bring the money?

KOSTILYOFF. I've something to tell you——

PEPEL. Did you bring the money?

KOSTILYOFF. What money? Wait ——

PEPEL. Why—the seven rubles for the watch—well?

KOSTILYOFF. What watch, Vaska? Oh, you——

PEPEL. Look here. Yesterday, before witnesses, I sold you a watch for ten rubles, you gave me three—now let me have the other seven. What are you blinking for? You hang around here—you disturb people—and don't seem to know yourself what you're after.

KOSTILYOFF. Sh-h! Don't be angry, Vaska. The watch—it is——

SATINE. Stolen!

KOSTILYOFF (*sternly*). I do not accept stolen goods—how can you imagine——

PEPEL (*taking him by the shoulder*). What did you disturb me for? What do you want?

KOSTILYOFF. I don't want—anything. I'll go—if you're in such a state——

PEPEL. Be off, and bring the money!

KOSTILYOFF. What ruffians! I—I —— (*Exit.*)

THE ACTOR. What a farce!

SATINE. That's fine—I like it.

PEPEL. What did he come here for?

SATINE (*laughing*). Don't you understand? He's looking for his wife. Why don't you beat him up once and for all, Vaska?

PEPEL. Why should I let such trash interfere with my life?

SATINE. Show some brains! And then you can marry Vassilisa—and become our boss——

PEPEL. Heavenly bliss! And you'd smash up my household and, because I'm a soft-hearted fool, you'll drink up everything I possess. (*Sits on a bunk*) Old devil—woke me up —I was having such a pleasant dream. I dreamed I was fishing— and I caught an enormous trout— such a trout as you only see in dreams! I was playing him—and I was so afraid the line would snap. I had just got out the gaff—and I thought to myself—in a moment ——

SATINE. It wasn't a trout, it was Vassilisa——

THE ACTOR. He caught Vassilisa a long time ago.

PEPEL (*angrily*). You can all go to the devil—and Vassilisa with you ——

(KLESHTCH *comes from the hall.*)

KLESHTCH. Devilishly cold!

THE ACTOR. Why didn't you bring Anna back? She'll freeze, out there——

KLESHTCH. Natasha took her into the kitchen——

THE ACTOR. The old man will kick her out——

KLESHTCH (*sitting down to his work*). Well—Natasha will bring her in here——

SATINE. Vassily—give me five kopecks!

THE ACTOR (*to* SATINE). Oh, you— always five kopecks—Vassya—give us twenty kopecks——

PEPEL. I'd better give it to them now before they ask for a ruble. Here you are!

SATINE. Gibraltar! There are no kindlier people in the world than thieves!

KLESHTCH (*morosely*). They earn their money easily—they don't work——

SATINE. Many earn it easily, but not many part with it so easily. Work? Make work pleasant—and maybe I'll work too. Yes—maybe. When work's a pleasure, life's, too. When it's toil, then life is a drudge. (*To* THE ACTOR) You, Sardanapalus! Come on!

THE ACTOR. Let's go, Nebuchadnezzar! I'll get as drunk as forty thousand topers! (*They leave.*)

PEPEL (*yawning*). Well, how's your wife?

KLESHTCH. It seems as if soon—— (*Pause.*)

PEPEL. Now I look at you—seems to me all that filing and scraping of yours is useless.

KLESHTCH. Well—what else can I do?

PEPEL. Nothing.

KLESHTCH. How can I live?

PEPEL. People manage, somehow.

KLESHTCH. Them? Call them people? Muck and dregs—that's what they are! I'm a workman—I'm ashamed even to look at them. I've slaved since I was a child. . . . D'you think I shan't be able to tear myself away from here? I'll crawl out of here, even if I have to leave my skin behind—but crawl out I will! Just wait . . . my wife'll die . . . I've lived here six months, and it seems like six years.

PEPEL. Nobody here's any worse off than you . . . say what you like . . .

KLESHTCH. No worse is right. They've neither honor nor conscience.

PEPEL (indifferently). What good does it do—honor or conscience? Can you get them on their feet instead of on their uppers—through honor and conscience? Honor and conscience are needed only by those who have power and energy . . .

BUBNOFF (coming back). Oh—I'm frozen . . .

PEPEL. Bubnoff! Got a conscience?

BUBNOFF. What? A conscience?

PEPEL. Exactly!

BUBNOFF. What do I need a conscience for? I'm not rich.

PEPEL. Just what I said: honor and conscience are for the rich—right! And Kleshtch is upbraiding us because we haven't any!

BUBNOFF. Why—did he want to borrow some of it?

PEPEL. No—he has plenty of his own . . .

BUBNOFF. Oh—are you selling it? You won't sell much around here. But if you had some old boxes, I'd buy them—on credit . . .

PEPEL (didactically). You're a jackass, Andrushka! On the subject of conscience you ought to hear Satine —or the Baron . . .

KLESHTCH. I've nothing to talk to them about!

PEPEL. They have more brains than you—even if they're drunkards . . .

BUBNOFF. He who can be drunk and wise at the same time is doubly blessed . . .

PEPEL. Satine says every man expects his neighbor to have a conscience, but—you see—it isn't to anyone's advantage to have one— that's a fact.
(NATASHA enters, followed by LUKA who carries a stick in his hand, a bundle on his back, a kettle and a teapot slung from his belt.)

LUKA. How are you, honest folks?

PEPEL (twisting his mustache). Aha—Natasha!

BUBNOFF (to LUKA). I was honest —up to spring before last.

NATASHA. Here's a new lodger . . .

LUKA. Oh, it's all the same to me. Crooks—I don't mind them, either. For my part there's no bad flea— they're all black—and they all jump — . . . Well, dearie, show me where I can stow myself.

NATASHA (*pointing to kitchen door*). Go in there, grand-dad.

LUKA. Thanks, girlie! One place is like another—as long as an old fellow keeps warm, he keeps happy . . .

PEPEL. What an amusing old codger you brought in, Natasha!

NATASHA. A hanged sight more interesting than you! . . . Andrei, your wife's in the kitchen with us— come and fetch her after a while . . .

KLESHTCH. All right—I will . . .

NATASHA. And be a little more kind to her—you know she won't last much longer.

KLESHTCH. I know . . .

NATASHA. Knowing won't do any good—it's terrible—dying—don't you understand?

PEPEL. Well—look at me—I'm not afraid . . .

NATASHA. Oh—you're a wonder, aren't you?

BUBNOFF (*whistling*). Oh—this thread's rotten . . .

PEPEL. Honestly, I'm not afraid! I'm ready to die right now. Knife me to the heart—and I'll die without

making a sound . . . even gladly —from such a pure hand . . .

NATASHA (*going out*). Spin that yarn for someone else!

BUBNOFF. Oh—that thread is rotten —rotten——

NATASHA (*at hallway door*). Don't forget your wife, Andrei!

KLESHTCH. All right.

PEPEL. She's a wonderful girl!

BUBNOFF. She's all right.

PEPEL. What makes her so curt with me? Anyway—she'll come to no good here . . .

BUBNOFF. Through you—sure!

PEPEL. Why through me? I feel sorry for her . . .

BUBNOFF. As the wolf for the lamb!

PEPEL. You lie! I feel very sorry for her . . . very . . . very sorry! She has a tough life here—I can see that . . .

KLESHTCH. Just wait till Vassilisa catches you talking to her!

BUBNOFF. Vassilisa? She won't give up so easily what belongs to her— she's a cruel woman!

PEPEL (*stretching himself on the bunk*). You two prophets can go to hell!

KLESHTCH. Just wait—you'll see!

LUKA (*singing in the kitchen*). "In the dark of the night the way is black . . ."

KLESHTCH. Another one who yelps!

PEPEL. It's dreary! Why do I feel so dreary? You live—and everything seems all right. But suddenly a cold chill goes through you—and then everything gets dreary . . .

BUBNOFF. Dreary? Hm-hm——

PEPEL. Yes—yes——

LUKA (sings). "The way is black . . ."

PEPEL. Old fellow! Hey there!

LUKA (looking from kitchen door). You call me?

PEPEL. Yes. Don't sing!

LUKA (coming in). You don't like it?

PEPEL. When people sing well I like it——

LUKA. In other words—I don't sing well?

PEPEL. Evidently!

LUKA. Well, well—and I thought I sang well. That's always the way: a man imagines there's one thing he can do well, and suddenly he finds out that other people don't think so . . .

PEPEL (laughs). That's right . . .

BUBNOFF. First you say you feel dreary—and then you laugh!

PEPEL. None of your business, raven!

LUKA. Who do they say feels dreary?

PEPEL. I do.

(THE BARON enters.)

LUKA. Well, well—out there in the kitchen there's a girl reading and crying! That's so! Her eyes are wet with tears . . . I say to her: "What's the matter, darling?" And she says: "It's so sad!" "What's so sad?" say I. "The book!" says she. —And that's how people spend their time. Just because they're bored . . .

THE BARON. She's a fool.

PEPEL. Have you had tea, Baron?

THE BARON. Yes. Go on!

PEPEL. Well—want me to open a bottle?

THE BARON. Of course. Go on!

PEPEL. Drop on all fours, and bark like a dog!

THE BARON. Fool! What's the matter with you? Are you drunk?

PEPEL. Go on—bark a little! It'll amuse me. You're an aristocrat. You didn't even consider us human formerly, did you?

THE BARON. Go on!

PEPEL. Well—and now I am making you bark like a dog—and you will bark, won't you?

THE BARON. All right. I will. You jackass! What pleasure can you derive from it since I myself know that I have sunk almost lower than you. You should have made me drop on all fours in the days when I was still above you.

BUBNOFF. That's right . . .

LUKA. I say so, too!

BUBNOFF. What's over, is over. Remain only trivialities. We know no class distinctions here. We've shed all pride and self-respect. Blood and bone—man—just plain man—that's what we are!

LUKA. In other words, we're an equal . . . and you, friend, were you really a Baron?

THE BARON. Who are you? A ghost?

LUKA (*laughing*). I've seen counts and princes in my day—this is the first time I meet a Baron—and one who's decaying—at that!

PEPEL (*laughing*). Baron, I blush for you!

THE BARON. It's time you knew better, Vassily . . .

LUKA. Hey-hey—I look at you, brothers—the life you're leading . . .

BUBNOFF. Such a life! As soon as the sun rises, our voices rise, too—in quarrels!

THE BARON. We've all seen better days—yes! I used to wake up in the morning and drink my coffee in bed—coffee—with cream! Yes——

LUKA. And yet we're all human beings. Pretend all you want to, put on all the airs you wish, but man you were born, and man you must die. And as I watch I see that the wiser people get, the busier they get—and though from bad to worse, they still strive to improve—stubbornly——

THE BARON. Who are you, old fellow? Where do you come from?

LUKA. I?

THE BARON. Are you a tramp?

LUKA. We're all of us tramps—why —I've heard said that the very earth we walk on is nothing but a tramp in the universe.

THE BARON (*severely*). Perhaps. But have you a passport?

LUKA (*after a short pause*). And what are you—a police inspector?

PEPEL (*delighted*). You scored, old fellow! Well, Barosha, you got it this time!

BUBNOFF. Yes—our little aristocrat got his!

THE BARON (*embarrassed*). What's the matter? I was only joking, old man. Why, brother, I haven't a passport, either.

BUBNOFF. You lie!

THE BARON. Oh—well—I have some sort of papers—but they have no value——

LUKA. They're papers just the same —and no papers are any good——

PEPEL. Baron—come on· to the saloon with me——

THE BARON. I'm ready. Good-bye, old man—you old scamp——

LUKA. Maybe I am one, brother——

PEPEL (*near doorway*). Come on—come on! (*Leaves,* BARON *following him quickly.*)

LUKA. Was he really once a Baron?

BUBNOFF. Who knows? A gentleman—? Yes. That much he's even now. Occasionally it sticks out. He never got rid of the habit.

LUKA. Nobility is like smallpox. A man may get over it—but it leaves marks . . .

BUBNOFF. He's all right all the same—occasionally he kicks—as he did about your passport . . . (ALYOSHKA *comes in, slightly drunk, with a concertina in his hand, whistling.*)

ALYOSHKA. Hey there, lodgers!

BUBNOFF. What are you yelling for?

ALYOSHKA. Excuse me—I beg your pardon! I'm a well-bred man——

BUBNOFF. On a spree again?

ALYOSHKA. Right you are! A moment ago Medyakin, the precinct captain, threw me out of the police station and said: "Look here—I don't want as much as a smell of you to stay in the streets—d'you hear?" I'm a man of principles, and the boss croaks at me—and what's a boss anyway—pah!—it's all bosh —the boss is a drunkard. I don't make any demands on life. I want nothing—that's all. Offer me one ruble, offer me twenty—it doesn't affect me. (NASTYA *comes from the kitchen*) Offer me a million—I won't take it! And to think that I, a respectable man, should be ordered about by a pal of mine—and he a drunkard! I won't have it—I won't! (NASTYA *stands in the doorway, shaking her head at* ALYOSHKA.)

LUKA (*good-naturedly*). Well, boy, you're a bit confused——

BUBNOFF. Aren't men fools!

ALYOSHKA (*stretches out on the floor*). Here, eat me up alive—and I don't want anything. I'm a desperate man. Show me one better! Why am I worse than others? There! Medyakin said: "If you show yourself on the streets I smash your face!" And yet I shall go out—I'll go—and stretch out in the middle of the street—let them choke me—I don't want a thing!

NASTYA. Poor fellow—only a boy—and he's already putting on such airs——

ALYOSHKA (*kneeling before her*). Lady! Mademoiselle! *Parlez français—? Prix courrant?* I'm on a spree——

NASTYA (*in a loud whisper*). Vassilisa!

VASSILISA (*opens door quickly; to* ALYOSHKA). You here again?

ALYOSHKA. How do you do—? Come in—you're welcome——

VASSILISA. I told you, young puppy, that not a shadow of you should stick around here—and you're back —eh?

ALYOSHKA. Vassilisa Karpovna . . . shall I tune up a funeral march for you?

VASSILISA (*seizing him by the shoulders*). Get out!

ALYOSHKA (*moving towards the door*). Wait—you can't put me out this way! I learned this funeral march a little while ago! It's refreshing music . . . wait—you can't put me out like that!

VASSILISA. I'll show whether I can or not. I'll rouse the whole street against you—you foul-mouthed creature—you're too young to bark about me——

ALYOSHKA (*running out*). All right —I'll go——

VASSILISA. Look out—I'll get you yet!

ALYOSHKA (*opens the door and shouts*). Vassilisa Karpovna—I'm not afraid of you—— (*Hides.*) (LUKA *laughs.*)

VASSILISA. Who are you?

LUKA. A passer-by—a traveler . . .

VASSILISA. Stopping for the night or going to stay here?

LUKA. I'll see.

VASSILISA. Have you a passport?

LUKA. Yes.

VASSILISA. Give it to me.

LUKA. I'll bring it over to your house——

VASSILISA. Call yourself a traveler? If you'd say a tramp—that would be nearer the truth——

LUKA (*sighing*). You're not very kindly, mother!
(VASSILISA *goes to door that leads*

to PEPEL's *room.* ALYOSHKA *pokes his head through the kitchen door.*)

ALYOSHKA. Has she left?

VASSILISA (*turning around*). Are you still here?
(ALYOSHKA *disappears, whistling.* NASTYA *and* LUKA *laugh.*)

BUBNOFF (*to* VASSILISA). He isn't here——

VASSILISA. Who?

BUBNOFF. Vaska.

VASSILISA. Did I ask you about him?

BUBNOFF. I noticed you were looking around——

VASSILISA. I am looking to see if things are in order, you see? Why aren't the floors swept yet? How often did I give orders to keep the house clean?

BUBNOFF. It's the actor's turn to sweep——

VASSILISA. Never mind whose turn it is! If the health inspector comes and fines me, I'll throw out the lot of you——

BUBNOFF (*calmly*). Then how are you going to earn your living?

VASSILISA. I don't want a speck of dirt! (*Goes to kitchen; to* NASTYA) What are you hanging round here for? Why's your face all swollen up? Why are you standing there like a dummy? Go on—sweep the floor! Did you see Natalia? Was she here?

NASTYA. I don't know—I haven't seen her . . .

VASSILISA. Bubnoff! Was my sister here?

BUBNOFF. She brought him along.

VASSILISA. That one—was he home?

BUBNOFF. Vassily? Yes—Natalia was here talking to Kleshtch——

VASSILISA. I'm not asking you whom she talked to. Dirt everywhere—filth—oh, you swine! Mop it all up —do you hear? (*Exit rapidly.*)

BUBNOFF. What a savage beast she is!

LUKA. She's a lady that means business!

NASTYA. You grow to be an animal, leading such a life—any human being tied to such a husband as hers . . .

BUBNOFF. Well—that tie isn't worrying her any——

LUKA. Does she always have these fits?

BUBNOFF. Always. You see, she came to find her lover—but he isn't home——

LUKA. I guess she was hurt. Oh-ho! Everybody is trying to be boss—and is threatening everybody else with all kinds of punishment—and still there's no order in life . . . and no cleanliness——

BUBNOFF. All the world likes order —but some people's brains aren't fit for it. All the same—the room should be swept—Nastya—you ought to get busy!

NASTYA. Oh, certainly? Anything else? Think I'm your servant? (*Silence*) I'm going to get drunk to-night—dead-drunk!

BUBNOFF. Fine business!

LUKA. Why do you want to get drunk, girlie? A while ago you were crying—and now you say you'll get drunk——

NASTYA (*defiantly*). I'll drink—then I cry again—that's all there's to it!

BUBNOFF. That's nothing!

LUKA. But for what reason—tell me! Every pimple has a cause! (NASTYA *remains silent, shaking her head*) Oh—you men—what's to become of you? All right—I'll sweep the place. Where's your broom?

BUBNOFF. Behind the door—in the hall—— (LUKA *goes into the hall*) Nastinka!

NASTYA. Yes?

BUBNOFF. Why did Vassilisa jump on Alyoshka?

NASTYA. He told her that Vaska was tired of her and was going to get rid of her—and that he's going to make up to Natasha—I'll go away from here—I'll find another lodging-house——

BUBNOFF. Why? Where?

NASTYA. I'm sick of this—I'm not wanted here!

BUBNOFF (*calmly*). You're not wanted anywhere—and, anyway, all people on earth are superfluous——

(NASTYA *shakes her head. Rises and slowly, quietly, leaves the cellar.* MIEDVIEDIEFF *comes in.* LUKA, *with the broom, follows him.*)

MIEDVIEDIEFF. I don't think I know you——

LUKA. How about the others—d'you know them all?

MIEDVIEDIEFF. I must know everybody in my precinct. But I don't know you.

LUKA. That's because, uncle, the whole world can't stow itself away in your precinct—some of it was bound to remain outside . . . (*Goes into kitchen.*)

MIEDVIEDIEFF (*crosses to* BUBNOFF). It's true—my precinct is rather small—yet it's worse than any of the very largest. Just now, before getting off duty, I had to bring Alyoshka, the shoemaker, to the station house. Just imagine— there he was, stretched right in the middle of the street, playing his concertina and yelping: "I want nothing, nothing!" Horses going past all the time—and with all the traffic going on, he could easily have been run over—and so on! He's a wild youngster—so I just collared him—he likes to make mischief——

BUBNOFF. Coming to play checkers tonight?

MIEDVIEDIEFF. Yes—I'll come— how's Vaska?

BUBNOFF. Same as ever——

MIEDVIEDIEFF. Meaning—he's getting along——?

BUBNOFF. Why shouldn't he? He's able to get along all right.

MIEDVIEDIEFF (*doubtfully*). Why shouldn't he? (LUKA *goes into hallway, carrying a pail*) M-yes there's a lot of talk about Vaska. Haven't you heard?

BUBNOFF. I hear all sorts of gossip . . .

MIEDVIEDIEFF. There seems to have been some sort of talk concerning Vassilisa. Haven't you heard about it?

BUBNOFF. What?

MIEDVIEDIEFF. Oh—why—generally speaking. Perhaps you know—and lie. Everybody knows—(*Severely*) You mustn't lie, brother!

BUBNOFF. Why should I lie?

MIEDVIEDIEFF. That's right. Dogs! They say that Vaska and Vassilisa . . . but what's that to me? I'm not her father. I'm her uncle. Why should they ridicule me? (KVASHNYA *comes in*) What are people coming to? They laugh at everything. Aha—you here?

KVASHNYA. Well—my love-sick garrison——? Bubnoff! He came up to me again on the marketplace and started pestering me about marrying him . . .

BUBNOFF. Go to it! Why not? He has money and he's still a husky fellow.

MIEDVIEDIEFF. Me—? I should say so!

KVASHNYA. You ruffian! Don't you

dare touch my sore spot! I've gone through it once already, darling. Marriage to a woman is just like jumping through a hole in the ice in winter. You do it once, and you remember it the rest of your life . . .

MIEDVIEDIEFF. Wait! There are different breeds of husbands . . .

KVASHNYA. But there's only one of me! When my beloved husband kicked the bucket, I spent the whole day all by my lonely—just bursting with joy. I sat and simply couldn't believe it was true. . . .

MIEDVIEDIEFF. If your husband beat you without cause, you should have complained to the police.

KVASHNYA. I complained to God for eight years—and he didn't help.

MIEDVIEDIEFF. Nowadays the law forbids to beat your wife . . . all is very strict these days—there's law and order everywhere. You can't beat up people without due cause. If you beat them to maintain discipline—all right . . .

LUKA (comes in with ANNA). Well —we finally managed to get here after all. Oh, you! Why do you, weak as you are, walk about alone? Where's your bunk?

ANNA (pointing). Thank you, grand-dad.

KVASHNYA. There—she's married— look at her!

LUKA. The little woman is in very bad shape . . . she was creeping along the hallway, clinging to the wall and moaning—why do you leave her by herself?

KVASHNYA. Oh, pure carelessness on our part, little father—forgive us! Her maid, it appears, went out for a walk . . .

LUKA. Go on—poke fun at me . . . but, all the same, how can you neglect a human being like that? No matter who or what, every human life has its worth . . .

MIEDVIEDIEFF. There should be supervision! Suppose she died suddenly—? That would cause a lot of bother . . . we must look after her!

LUKA. True, sergeant!

MIEDVIEDIEFF. Well—yes—though I'm not a sergeant--ah--yet!

LUKA. No! But you carry yourself most martially!
(Noise of shuffling feet is heard in the hallway. Muffled cries.)

MIEDVIEDIEFF. What now—a row?

BUBNOFF. Sounds like it.

KVASHNYA. I'll go and see . . .

MIEDVIEDIEFF. I'll go, too. It is my duty! Why separate people when they fight? They'll stop sooner or later of their own accord. One gets tired of fighting. Why not let them fight all they want to—freely? They wouldn't fight half as often—if they'd remember former beatings . . .

BUBNOFF (climbing down from his bunk). Why don't you speak to your superiors about it?

KOSTILYOFF (throws open the door and shouts). Abram! Come quick—

Vassilisa is killing Natasha—come quick!
(KVASHNYA, MIEDVIEDIEFF, *and* BUBNOFF *rush into hallway;* LUKA *looks after them, shaking his head.*)

ANNA. Oh God—poor little Natasha . . .

LUKA. Who's fighting out there?

ANNA. Our landladies—they're sisters . . .

LUKA (*crossing to* ANNA). Why?

ANNA. Oh—for no reason—except that they're both fat and healthy . . .

LUKA. What's your name?

ANNA. Anna . . . I look at you . . . you're like my father—my dear father . . . you're as gentle as he was—and as soft. . . .

LUKA. Soft! Yes! They pounded me till I got soft! (*Laughs tremulously.*)

CURTAIN

ACT TWO

Same as Act I—Night.
   On the bunks near the stove SATINE, THE BARON, KRIVOY ZOB, *and* THE TARTAR *play cards.* KLESHTCH *and* THE ACTOR *watch them.* BUBNOFF, *on his bunk, is playing checkers with* MIEDVIEDIEFF. LUKA *sits on a stool by* ANNA's *bedside. The place is lit by two lamps, one on the wall near the card players, the other is on* BUBNOFF's *bunk.*

THE TARTAR. I'll play one more game—then I'll stop . . .

BUBNOFF. Zob! Sing! (*He sings*) *"The sun rises and sets . . ."*

ZOB (*joining in*).
"But my prison is dark, dark . . ."

THE TARTAR (*to* SATINE). Shuffle the cards—and shuffle them well. We know your kind——

ZOB AND BUBNOFF (*together*).
*"Day and night the wardens
   Watch beneath my window . . ."*

ANNA. Blows—insults—I've had nothing but that all my life long . . .

LUKA. Don't worry, little mother!

MIEDVIEDIEFF. Look where you're moving!

BUBNOFF. Oh, yes—that's right . . .

THE TARTAR (*threatening* SATINE *with his fist*). You're trying to palm a card? I've seen you—you scoundrel . . .

ZOB. Stop it, Hassan! They'll skin us anyway . . . come on, Bubnoff!

ANNA. I can't remember a single day when I didn't go hungry . . . I've been afraid, waking, eating, and sleeping . . . all my life I've trembled—afraid I wouldn't get another bite . . . all my life I've been in rags—all through my wretched life—and why . . . ?

LUKA. Yes, yes, child—you're tired —never you mind!

THE ACTOR (to ZOB). Play the Jack —the Jack, devil take you!

THE BARON. And we play the King!

KLESHTCH. They always win.

SATINE. Such is our habit.

MIEDVIEDIEFF. I have the Queen!

BUBNOFF. And so have I!

ANNA. I'm dying . . .

KLESHTCH. Look, look! Prince, throw up the game—throw it up, I tell you!

THE ACTOR. Can't he play without your assistance?

THE BARON. Look out, Andrushka, or I'll beat the life out of you!

THE TARTAR. Deal once more—the pitcher went after water—and got broke—and so did I!
(KLESHTCH shakes his head and crosses to BUBNOFF.)

ANNA. I keep on thinking—is it possible that I'll suffer in the other world as I did in this—is it possible? There, too?

LUKA. Nothing of the sort! Don't you disturb yourself! You'll rest there . . . be patient. We all suffer, dear, each in our own way. . . .

(Rises and goes quickly into kitchen.)

BUBNOFF (sings).
"Watch as long as you please . . ."

ZOB. "I shan't run away . . ."

BOTH (together).
"I long to be free, free—
  Alas! I cannot break my chains.
  . . ."

THE TARTAR (yells). That card was up his sleeve!

THE BARON (embarrassed). Do you want me to shove it up your nose?

THE ACTOR (emphatically). Prince! You're mistaken—nobody—ever . . .

THE TARTAR. I saw it! You cheat! I won't play!

SATINE (gathering up the cards). Leave us alone, Hassan . . . you knew right along that we're cheats —why did you play with us?

THE BARON. He lost forty kopecks and he yelps as if he had lost a fortune! And a Prince at that!

THE TARTAR (excitedly). Then play honest!

SATINE. What for?

THE TARTAR. What do you mean "what for"?

SATINE. Exactly. What for?

THE TARTAR. Don't you know?

SATINE. I don't. Do you?
(THE TARTAR spits out, furiously; the others laugh at him.)

ZOB (*good-naturedly*). You're a funny fellow, Hassan! Try to understand this; If they should begin to live honestly, they'd die of starvation inside of three days.

THE TARTAR. That's none of my business. You must live honestly!

ZOB. They did you brown! Come and let's have tea. . . . (*Sings*) "*O my chains, my heavy chains . . .*"

BUBNOFF (*sings*). "*You're my steely, clanking wardens . . .*"

ZOB. Come on, Hassanka! (*Leaves the room, singing*) "*I cannot tear you, cannot break you . . .*" (THE TARTAR *shakes his fist threateningly at* THE BARON, *and follows the other out of the room.*)

SATINE (*to* BARON, *laughing*). Well, Your Imperial Highness, you've again sat down magnificently in a mud puddle! You've learned a lot— but you're an ignoramus when it comes to palming a card.

THE BARON (*spreading his hands*). The Devil knows how it happened. . . .

THE ACTOR. You're not gifted— you've no faith in yourself—and without that you can never accomplish anything . . .

MIEDVIEDIEFF. I've one Queen— and you've two—oh, well . . .

BUBNOFF. One's enough if she has brains—play!

KLESHTCH. You lost, Abram Ivanovitch?

MIEDVIEDIEFF. None of your business—see? Shut up!

SATINE. I've won fifty-three kopecks.

THE ACTOR. Give me three of them . . . though, what'll I do with them?

LUKA (*coming from kitchen*). Well —the Tartar was fleeced all right, eh? Going to have some vodka?

THE BARON. Come with us.

SATINE. I wonder what you'll be like when you're drunk.

LUKA. Same as when I'm sober.

THE ACTOR. Come on, old man— I'll recite verses for you.

LUKA. What?

THE ACTOR. Verses. Don't you understand?

LUKA. Verses? And what do I want with verses?

THE ACTOR. Sometimes they're funny—sometimes sad.

SATINE. Well, poet, are you coming? (*Exit with* THE BARON.)

THE ACTOR. I'm coming. I'll join you. For instance, old man, here's a bit of verse—I forget how it begins —I forget . . . (*Brushes his hand across his forehead.*)

BUBNOFF. There! Your Queen is lost—go on, play!

MIEDVIEDIEFF. I made the wrong move.

THE ACTOR. Formerly, before my organism was poisoned with alcohol, old man, I had a good memory. But now it's all over with me, brother. I used to declaim these verses with tremendous success—thunders of applause . . . you have no idea what applause means . . . it goes to your head like vodka! I'd step out on the stage—stand this way—(*Strikes a pose*)—I'd stand there and . . . (*Pause*) I can't remember a word—I can't remember! My favorite verses—isn't it ghastly, old man?

LUKA. Yes—is there anything worse than forgetting what you loved? Your very soul is in the thing you love!

THE ACTOR. I've drunk my soul away, old man—brother, I'm lost . . . and why? Because I had no faith. . . . I'm done with . . .

LUKA. Well—then—cure yourself! Nowadays they have a cure for drunkards. They treat you free of charge, brother. There's a hospital for drunkards—where they're treated for nothing. They've owned up, you see, that even a drunkard is a human being, and they're only too glad to help him get well. Well—then—go to it!

THE ACTOR (*thoughtfully*). Where? Where is it?

LUKA. Oh—in some town or other . . . what do they call it—? I'll tell you the name presently—only, in the meanwhile, get ready. Don't drink so much! Take yourself in hand—and bear up! And then, when you're cured, you'll begin life all over again. Sounds good, brother, doesn't it, to begin all over again? Well—make up your mind!

THE ACTOR (*smiling*). All over again—from the very beginning—that's fine . . . yes . . . all over again . . . (*Laughs*) Well—then—I can, can't I?

LUKA. Why not? A human being can do anything—if he only makes up his mind.

THE ACTOR (*suddenly, as if coming out of a trance*). You're a queer bird! See you anon! (*Whistles*) Old man—*au revoir!* (*Exit.*)

ANNA. Grand-dad!

LUKA. Yes, little mother?

ANNA. Talk to me.

LUKA (*close to her*). Come on—let's chat . . .
(KLESHTCH, *glancing around, silently walks over to his wife, looks at her, and makes queer gestures with his hands, as though he wanted to say something.*)

LUKA. What is it, brother?

KLESHTCH (*quietly*). Nothing . . . (*Crosses slowly to hallway door, stands on the threshold for a few seconds, and exit.*)

LUKA (*looking after him*). Hard on your man, isn't it?

ANNA. He doesn't concern me much . . .

LUKA. Did he beat you?

ANNA. Worse than that—it's he who's killed me——

BUBNOFF. My wife used to have a lover—the scoundrel—how clever he was at checkers!

MIEDVIEDIEFF. Hm-hm——

ANNA. Grand-dad! Talk to me, darling—I feel so sick . . .

LUKA. Never mind—it's always like this before you die, little dove—never mind, dear! Just have faith! Once you're dead, you'll have peace—always. There's nothing to be afraid of—nothing. Quiet! Peace! Lie quietly! Death wipes out everything. Death is kindly. You die—and you rest—that's what they say. It is true, dear! Because—where can we find rest on this earth?
(PEPEL *enters. He is slightly drunk, dishevelled, and sullen. Sits down on bunk near door, and remains silent and motionless.*)

ANNA. And how is it—there? More suffering?

LUKA. Nothing of the kind! No suffering! Trust me! Rest—nothing else! They'll lead you into God's presence, and they'll say: "Dear God! Behold! Here is Anna, Thy servant!"

MIEDVIEDIEFF (*sternly*). How do you know what they'll say up there? Oh, you . . .
(PEPEL, *on hearing* MIEDVIEDIEFF's *voice, raises his head and listens.*)

LUKA. Apparently I do know, Mr. Sergeant!

MIEDVIEDIEFF (*conciliatory*). Yes—it's your own affair—though I'm not exactly a sergeant—yet——

BUBNOFF. I jump two!

MIEDVIEDIEFF. Damn—play!

LUKA. And the Lord will look at you

gently and tenderly and He'll say: "I know this Anna!" Then He'll say: "Take Anna into Paradise. Let her have peace. I know. Her life on earth was hard. She is very weary. Let Anna rest in peace!"

ANNA (*choking*). Grandfather—if it were only so—if there were only rest and peace . . .

LUKA. There won't be anything else! Trust me! Die in joy and not in grief. Death is to us like a mother to small . . .

ANNA. But—perhaps—perhaps I get well . . . ?

LUKA (*laughing*). Why—? Just to suffer more?

ANNA. But—just to live a little longer . . . just a little longer! Since there'll be no suffering hereafter, I could bear it a little longer down here . . .

LUKA. There'll be nothing in the hereafter . . . but only . . .

PEPEL (*rising*). Maybe yes—maybe no!

ANNA (*frightened*). Oh—God!

LUKA. Hey—Adonis!

MIEDVIEDIEFF. Who's that yelping?

PEPEL (*crossing over to him*). I! What of it?

MIEDVIEDIEFF. You yelp needlessly—that's what! People ought to have some dignity!

PEPEL. Block-head! And that's an uncle for you—ho-ho!

LUKA (*to* PEPEL, *in an undertone*). Look here—don't shout—this woman's dying—her lips are already grey—don't disturb her!

PEPEL. I've respect for you, granddad. You're all right, you are! You lie well, and you spin pleasant yarns. Go on lying, brother—there's little fun in this world . . .

BUBNOFF. Is the woman really dying?

LUKA. You think I'm joking?

BUBNOFF. That means she'll stop coughing. Her cough was very disturbing. I jump two!

MIEDVIEDIEFF. I'd like to murder you!

PEPEL. Abramka!

MIEDVIEDIEFF. I'm not Abramka to you!

PEPEL. Abrashka! Is Natasha ill?

MIEDVIEDIEFF. None of your business!

PEPEL. Come—tell me! Did Vassilisa beat her up very badly?

MIEDVIEDIEFF. That's none of your business, either! It's a family affair! Who are you anyway?

PEPEL. Whoever I am, you'll never see Natashka again if I choose!

MIEDVIEDIEFF (*throwing up the game*). What's that? Who are you alluding to? My niece by any chance? You thief!

PEPEL. A thief whom you were never able to catch!

MIEDVIEDIEFF. Wait—I'll catch you yet—you'll see—sooner than you think!

PEPEL. If you catch me, God help your whole nest! Do you think I'll keep quiet before the examining magistrate? Every wolf howls! They'll ask me: "Who made you steal and showed you where?" "Mishka Kostilyoff and his wife!" "Who was your fence?" "Mishka Kostilyoff and his wife!"

MIEDVIEDIEFF. You lie! No one will believe you!

PEPEL. They'll believe me all right —because it's the truth! And I'll drag you into it, too. Ha! I'll ruin the lot of you—devils—just watch!

MIEDVIEDIEFF (*confused*). You lie! You lie! And what harm did I do to you, you mad dog?

PEPEL. And what good did you ever do me?

LUKA. That's right!

MIEDVIEDIEFF (*to* LUKA). Well— what are you croaking about? Is it any of your business? This is a family matter!

BUBNOFF (*to* LUKA). Leave them alone! What do we care if they twist each other's tails?

LUKA (*peacefully*). I meant no harm. All I said was that if a man isn't good to you, then he's acting wrong . . .

MIEDVIEDIEFF (*uncomprehending*). Now then—we all of us here know each other—but you—who are you? (*Frowns and exit.*)

LUKA. The cavalier is peeved! Oh-ho, brothers, I see your affairs are a bit tangled up!

PEPEL. He'll run to complain about us to Vassilisa . . .

BUBNOFF. You're a fool, Vassily. You're very bold these days, aren't you? Watch out! It's all right to be bold when you go gathering mushrooms, but what good is it here? They'll break your neck before you know it!

PEPEL. Well—not as fast as all that! You don't catch us Yaroslavl boys napping! If it's going to be war, we'll fight . . .

LUKA. Look here, boy, you really ought to go away from here——

PEPEL. Where? Please tell me!

LUKA. Go to Siberia!

PEPEL. If I go to Siberia, it'll be at the Tsar's expense!

LUKA. Listen! You go just the same! You can make your own way there. They need your kind out there . . .

PEPEL. My way is clear. My father spent all his life in prison, and I inherited the trait. Even when I was a small child, they called me thief—thief's son.

LUKA. But Siberia is a fine country —a land of gold. Anyone who has health and strength and brains can live there like a cucumber in a hothouse.

PEPEL. Old man, why do you always tell lies?

LUKA. What?

PEPEL. Are you deaf? I ask—why do you always lie?

LUKA. What do I lie about?

PEPEL. About everything. According to you, life's wonderful everywhere—but you lie . . . why?

LUKA. Try to believe me. Go and see for yourself. And some day you'll thank me for it. What are you hanging round here for? And, besides, why is truth so important to you? Just think! Truth may spell death to you!

PEPEL. It's all one to me! If that— let it be that!

LUKA. Oh—what a madman! Why should you kill yourself?

BUBNOFF. What are you two jawing about, anyway? I don't understand. What kind of truth do you want, Vaska? And what for? You know the truth about yourself—and so does everybody else . . .

PEPEL. Just a moment! Don't crow! Let him tell me! Listen, old man! Is there a God?
(LUKA smiles silently.)

BUBNOFF. People just drift along— like shavings on a stream. When a house is built—the shavings are thrown away!

PEPEL. Well? Is there a God? Tell me.

LUKA (in a low voice). If you have faith, there is; if you haven't, there isn't . . . whatever you believe in, exists . . .

(PEPEL *looks at* LUKA *in staring surprise.*)

BUBNOFF. I'm going to have tea—come on over to the restaurant!

LUKA (*to* PEPEL). What are you staring at?

PEPEL. Oh—just because! Wait now—you mean to say . . .

BUBNOFF. Well—I'm off. (*Goes to door and runs into* VASSILISA.)

PEPEL. So—you . . .

VASSILISA (*to* BUBNOFF). Is Nastasya home?

BUBNOFF. No.
(*Exit.*)

PEPEL. Oh—you've come———?

VASSILISA (*crossing to* ANNA). Is she alive yet?

LUKA. Don't disturb her!

VASSILISA. What are you loafing around here for?

LUKA. I'll go—if you want me to . . .

VASSILISA (*turning towards* PEPEL*'s room*). Vassily! I've some business with you . . .
(LUKA *goes to hallway door, opens it, and shuts it loudly, then warily climbs into a bunk, and from there to the top of the stove.*)

VASSILISA (*calling from* PEPEL*'s room*). Vaska—come here!

PEPEL. I won't come—I don't want to . . .

VASSILISA. Why? What are you angry about?

PEPEL. I'm sick of the whole thing . . .

VASSILISA. Sick of me, too?

PEPEL. Yes! Of you, too! (VASSILISA *draws her shawl about her, pressing her hands over her breast. Crosses to* ANNA, *looks carefully through the bed curtains, and returns to* PEPEL) Well—out with it!

VASSILISA. What do you want me to say? I can't force you to be loving, and I'm not the sort to beg for kindness. Thank you for telling me the truth.

PEPEL. What truth?

VASSILISA. That you're sick of me —or isn't it the truth? (PEPEL *looks at her silently. She turns to him*) What are you staring at? Don't you recognize me?

PEPEL (*sighing*). You're beautiful, Vassilisa! (*She puts her arm about his neck, but he shakes it off*) But I never gave my heart to you. . . . I've lived with you and all that— But I never really liked you . . .

VASSILISA (*quietly*). That so? Well ———?

PEPEL. What is there to talk about? Nothing. Go away from me!

VASSILISA. Taken a fancy to someone else?

PEPEL. None of your business! Suppose I have—I wouldn't ask you to be my match-maker!

VASSILISA (*significantly*). That's too bad . . . perhaps I might arrange a match . . .

PEPEL (*suspiciously*). Who with?

VASSILISA. You know—why do you pretend? Vassily—let me be frank. (*With lower voice*) I won't deny it —you've offended me . . . it was like a bolt from the blue . . . you said you loved me—and then all of a sudden . . .

PEPEL. It wasn't sudden at all. It's been a long time since I . . . woman, you've no soul! A woman must have a soul . . . we men are beasts—we must be taught—and you, what have you taught me——?

VASSILISA. Never mind the past! I know—no man owns his own heart —you don't love me any longer . . . well and good, it can't be helped!

PEPEL. So that's over. We part peaceably, without a row—as it should be!

VASSILISA. Just a moment! All the same, when I lived with you, I hoped you'd help me out of this swamp—I thought you'd free me from my husband and my uncle— from all this life—and perhaps, Vassya, it wasn't you whom I loved —but my hope—do you understand? I waited for you to drag me out of this mire . . .

PEPEL. You aren't a nail—and I'm not a pair of pincers! I thought you had brains—you are so clever—so crafty . . .

VASSILISA (*leaning closely towards him*). Vassa—let's help each other!

PEPEL. How?

VASSILISA (*low and forcibly*). My sister—I know you've fallen for her. . . .

PEPEL. And that's why you beat her up, like the beast you are! Look out, Vassilisa! Don't you touch her!

VASSILISA. Wait. Don't get excited. We can do everything quietly and pleasantly. You want to marry her. I'll give you money . . . three hundred rubles—even more than that . . .

PEPEL (*moving away from her*). Stop! What do you mean?

VASSILISA. Rid me of my husband! Take that noose from around my neck . . .

PEPEL (*whistling softly*). So that's the way the land lies! You certainly planned it cleverly . . . in other words, the grave for the husband, the gallows for the lover, and as for yourself . . .

VASSILISA. Vassya! Why the gallows? It doesn't have to be yourself —but one of your pals! And supposing it were yourself—who'd know? Natalia—just think—and you'll have money—you go away somewhere . . . you free me forever—and it'll be very good for my sister to be away from me—the sight of her enrages me. . . . I get furious with her on account of you, and I can't control myself. I tortured the girl—I beat her up— beat her up so that I myself cried with pity for her—but I'll beat her —and I'll go on beating her!

PEPEL. Beast! Bragging about your beastliness?

VASSILISA. I'm not bragging—I speak the truth. Think now, Vassa. You've been to prison twice because of my husband—through his greed. He clings to me like a bedbug—he's been sucking the life out of me for the last four years—and what sort of a husband is he to me? He's forever abusing Natasha—calls her a beggar—he's just poison, plain poison, to everyone . . .

PEPEL. You spin your yarn cleverly . . .

VASSILISA. Everything I say is true. Only a fool could be as blind as you. . . .
(KOSTILYOFF enters stealthily and comes forward noisily.)

PEPEL (to VASSILISA). Oh—go away!

VASSILISA. Think it over! (Sees her husband) What? You? Following me?
(PEPEL leaps up and stares at KOSTILYOFF savagely.)

KOSTILYOFF. It's I, I! So the two of you were here alone—you were—ah—conversing? (Suddenly stamps his feet and screams) Vassilisa—you bitch! You beggar! You damned hag! (Frightened by his own screams which are met by silence and indifference on the part of the others) Forgive me, O Lord . . . Vassilisa—again you've led me into the path of sin. . . . I've been looking for you everywhere. It's time to go to bed. You forgot to fill the lamps—oh, you . . . beggar! Swine! (Shakes his trembling fist at her, while VASSILISA slowly goes to door, glancing at PEPEL over her shoulder.)

PEPEL (to KOSTILYOFF). Go away clear out of here——

KOSTILYOFF (yelling). What? I? The Boss? I get out? You thief!

PEPEL (sullenly). Go away, Mishka!

KOSTILYOFF. Don't you dare—I—I'll show you.
(PEPEL seizes him by the collar and shakes him. From the stove come loud noises and yawns. PEPEL releases KOSTILYOFF who runs into the hallway, screaming.)

PEPEL (jumping on a bunk). Who is it? Who's on the stove?

LUKA (raising his head). Eh?

PEPEL. You?

LUKA (undisturbed). I—I myself —oh, dear Jesus!

PEPEL (shuts hallway door, looks for the wooden closing bar, but can't find it). The devil! Come down, old man!

LUKA. I'm climbing down—all right . . .

PEPEL (roughly). What did you climb on that stove for?

LUKA. Where was I to go?

PEPEL. Why—didn't you go out into the hall?

LUKA. The hall's too cold for an old fellow like myself, brother.

PEPEL. You overheard?

LUKA. Yes—I did. How could I help it? Am I deaf? Well, my boy, happiness is coming your way. Real, good fortune I call it!

PEPEL (*suspiciously*). What good fortune——?

LUKA. In so far as I was lying on the stove . . .

PEPEL. Why did you make all that noise?

LUKA. Because I was getting warm . . . it was your good luck . . . I thought if only the boy wouldn't make a mistake and choke the old man . . .

PEPEL. Yes—I might have done it . . . how terrible . . .

LUKA. Small wonder! It isn't difficult to make a mistake of that sort.

PEPEL (*smiling*). What's the matter? Did you make the same sort of mistake once upon a time?

LUKA. Boy, listen to me. Send that woman out of your life! Don't let her near you! Her husband—she'll get rid of him herself—and in a shrewder way than you could—yes! Don't you listen to that devil! Look at me! I am bald-headed—know why? Because of all these women. . . . Perhaps I knew more women than I had hair on the top of my head—but this Vassilisa—she's worse than the plague. . . .

PEPEL. I don't understand . . . I don't know whether to thank you—or—well . . .

LUKA. Don't say a word! You won't improve on what I said. Listen: take the one you like by the arm, and march out of here—get out of here—clean out . . .

PEPEL (*sadly*). I can't understand people. Who is kind and who isn't? It's all a mystery to me . . .

LUKA. What's there to understand? There's all breeds of men . . . they all live as their hearts tell them . . . good today, bad tomorrow! But if you really care for that girl . . . take her away from here and that's all there is to it. Otherwise go away alone . . . you're young—you're in no hurry for a wife . .

PEPEL (*taking him by the shoulder*). Tell me! Why do you say all this?

LUKA. Wait. Let me go. I want a look at Anna . . . she was coughing so terribly. . . . (*Goes to* ANNA's *bed, pulls the curtains, looks, touches her.* PEPEL *thoughtfully and distraught, follows him with his eyes*) Merciful Jesus Christ! Take into Thy keeping the soul of this woman Anna, newcomer amongst the blessed!

PEPEL (*softly*). Is she dead? (*Without approaching, he stretches himself and looks at the bed.*)

LUKA (*gently*). Her sufferings are over! Where's her husband?

PEPEL. In the saloon, most likely . . .

LUKA. Well—he'll have to be told . . .

PEPEL (*shuddering*). I don't like corpses!

LUKA (*going to door*). Why should you like them? It's the living who demand our love—the living . . .

PEPEL. I'm coming with you . . .

LUKA. Are you afraid?

PEPEL. I don't like it . . .
(*They go out quickly. The stage is empty and silent for a few moments. Behind the door is heard a dull, staccato, incomprehensible noise. Then* THE ACTOR *enters.*)

THE ACTOR (*stands at the open door, supporting himself against the jamb, and shouts*). Hey, old man—where are you—? I just remembered — listen . . . (*Takes two staggering steps forward and, striking a pose, recites*)
"Good people! If the world cannot find
   A path to holy truth,
Glory be to the madman who will enfold all humanity
In a golden dream . . ."
(NATASHA *appears in the doorway behind* THE ACTOR) Old man! (*Recites*)
"If tomorrow the sun were to forget
   To light our earth,
Tomorrow then some madman's thought
Would bathe the world in sunshine. . . ."

NATASHA (*laughing*). Scarecrow! You're drunk!

THE ACTOR (*turns to her*). Oh—it's you? Where's the old man, the dear old man? Not a soul here, seems to me . . . Natasha, farewell—right—farewell!

NATASHA (*entering*). Don't wish me farewell, before you've wished me how-d'you-do!

THE ACTOR (*barring her way*). I am going. Spring will come—and I'll be here no longer——

NATASHA. Wait a moment! Where do you propose going?

THE ACTOR. In search of a town—to be cured—And you, Ophelia, must go away! Take the veil! Just imagine—there's a hospital to cure—ah—organisms for drunkards—a wonderful hospital—built of marble—with marble floors . . . light—clean—food—and all gratis! And a marble floor—yes! I'll find it—I'll get cured—and then I shall start life anew. . . . I'm on my way to regeneration, as King Lear said. Natasha, my stage name is . . . Svertchkoff—Zavoloushski . . . do you realize how painful it is to lose one's name? Even dogs have their names . . . (NATASHA *carefully passes* THE ACTOR, *stops at* ANNA's *bed and looks*) To be nameless—is not to exist!

NATASHA. Look, my dear—why—she's dead. . . .

THE ACTOR (*shakes his head*). Impossible . . .

NATASHA (*stepping back*). So help me God—look . . .

BUBNOFF (*appearing in doorway*). What is there to look at?

NATASHA. Anna—she's dead!

BUBNOFF. That means—she's stopped coughing! (*Goes to* ANNA's *bed, looks, and returns to his bunk*) We must tell Kleshtch—it's his business to know . . .

THE ACTOR. I'll go—I'll say to him—she lost her name—(*Exit.*)

NATASHA (*in center of room*). I, too—some day—I'll be found in the cellar—dead. . . .

BUBNOFF (*spreading out some rags on his bunk*). What's that? What are you muttering?

NATASHA. Nothing much . . .

BUBNOFF. Waiting for Vaska, eh? Take care—Vassilisa'll break your head!

NATASHA. Isn't it the same who breaks it? I'd much rather he'd do it!

BUBNOFF (*lying down*). Well—that's your own affair . . .

NATASHA. It's best for her to be dead—yet it's a pity . . . oh, Lord —why do we live?

BUBNOFF. It's so with all . . . we're born, live, and die—and I'll die, too—and so'll you—what's there to be gloomy about?
(*Enter* LUKA, THE TARTAR, ZOB, *and* KLESHTCH. *The latter comes after the others, slowly, shrunk up.*)

NATASHA. Sh-h! Anna!

ZOB. We've heard—God rest her soul . . .

THE TARTAR (*to* KLESHTCH). We must take her out of here. Out into the hall! This is no place for corpses —but for the living . . .

KLESHTCH (*quietly*). We'll take her out——
(*Everybody goes to the bed,* KLESHTCH *looks at his wife over the others' shoulders.*)

ZOB (*to* THE TARTAR). You think she'll smell? I don't think she will —she dried up while she was still alive . . .

NATASHA. God! If they'd only a little pity . . . if only someone would say a kindly word—oh, you . . .

LUKA. Don't be hurt, girl—never mind! Why and how should we pity the dead? Come, dear! We don't pity the living—we can't even pity our own selves—how can we?

BUBNOFF (*yawning*). And, besides, when you're dead, no word will help you—when you're still alive, even sick, it may. . . .

THE TARTAR (*stepping aside*). The police must be notified . . .

ZOB. The police—must be done! Kleshtch! Did you notify the police?

KLESHTCH. No—she's got to be buried—and all I have is forty kopecks——

ZOB. Well—you'll have to borrow then—otherwise we'll take up a collection . . . one'll give five kopecks, others as much as they can. But the police must be notified at once—or they'll think you killed her or God knows what not . . .
(*Crosses to* THE TARTAR's *bunk and prepares to lie down by his side.*)

NATASHA (*going to* BUBNOFF's *bunk*). Now—I'll dream of her . . . I always dream of the dead . . . I'm afraid to go out into the hall by myself—it's dark there . . .

LUKA (*following her*). You better fear the living—I'm telling you . . .

NATASHA. Take me across the hall, grandfather.

LUKA. Come on—come on—I'll take you across—
(*They go away. Pause.*)

ZOB (*to* THE TARTAR). Oh-ho! Spring will soon be here, little brother, and it'll be quite warm. In the villages the peasants are already making ready their ploughs and harrows, preparing to till . . . and we . . . Hassan? Snoring already? Damned Mohammedan!

BUBNOFF. Tartars love sleep!

KLESHTCH (*in center of room, staring in front of him*). What am I to do now?

ZOB. Lie down and sleep—that's all . . .

KLESHTCH (*softly*). But—she . . . how about . . .
(*No one answers him.* SATINE *and* THE ACTOR *enter.*)

THE ACTOR (*yelling*). Old man! Come here, my trusted Duke of Kent!

SATINE. Miklookha-Maklai is coming—ho-ho!

THE ACTOR. It has been decided upon! Old man, where's the town —where are you?

SATINE. Fata Morgana, the old man bilked you from top to bottom! There's nothing—no towns—no people—nothing at all!

THE ACTOR. You lie!

THE TARTAR (*jumping up*). Where's the boss? I'm going to the boss. If I can't sleep, I won't pay! Corpses— drunkards . . . (*Exit quickly.*)
(SATINE *looks after him and whistles.*)

BUBNOFF (*in a sleepy voice*). Go to bed, boys—be quiet . . . night is for sleep . . .

THE ACTOR. Yes—so—there's a corpse here. . . . "Our net fished up a corpse. . . ." Verses—by Béranger. . . .

SATINE (*screams*). The dead can't hear . . . the dead do not feel— Scream!—Roar! . . . the deaf don't hear!
(*In the doorway appears* LUKA.)

CURTAIN

ACT THREE

"The Waste," a yard strewn with rubbish and overgrown with weeds. Back, a high brick wall which shuts out the sight of the sky. Near it are elder bushes. Right, the dark, wooden wall of some sort of house, barn or stable. Left, the grey, tumbledown wall of KOSTILYOFF's *night asylum. It is built at an angle so that the further corner reaches almost to the centre of the yard. Between it and the wall runs a narrow passage. In the grey, plastered wall are two windows, one on a level with the ground,*

the other about six feet higher up and closer to the brick wall. Near the latter wall is a big sledge turned upside down and a beam about twelve feet long. Right of the wall is a heap of old planks. Evening. The sun is setting, throwing a crimson light on the brick wall. Early spring, the snow having only recently melted. The elder bushes are not yet in bud.

NATASHA *and* NASTYA *are sitting side by side on the beam.* LUKA *and* THE BARON *are on the sledge.* KLESHTCH *is stretched on the pile of planks to the right.* BUBNOFF'S *face is at the ground floor window.*

NASTYA (*with closed eyes, nodding her head in rhythm to the tale she is telling in a sing-song voice*). So then at night he came into the garden. I had been waiting for him quite a while. I trembled with fear and grief—he trembled, too . . . he was as white as chalk—and he had the pistol in his hand . . .

NATASHA (*chewing sunflower seeds*). Oh—are these students really such desperate fellows . . . ?

NASTYA. And he says to me in a dreadful voice: "My precious darling . . ."

BUBNOFF. Ho-ho! Precious——?

THE BARON. Shut up! If you don't like it, you can lump it! But don't interrupt her. . . . Go on . . .

NASTYA. "My one and only love," he says, "my parents," he says, "refuse to give their consent to our wedding—and threaten to disown me because of my love for you. Therefore," he says, "I must take my life." And his pistol was huge— and loaded with ten bullets . . . "Farewell," he says, "beloved comrade! I have made up my mind for good and all . . . I can't live without you . . ." and I replied: "My unforgettable friend—my Raoul. . . ."

BUBNOFF (*surprised*). What? What? Krawl—did you call him——?

THE BARON. Nastka! But last time his name was Gaston. . . .

NASTYA (*jumping up*). Shut up, you bastards! Ah—you lousy mongrels! You think for a moment that you can understand love—true love? My love was real honest-to-God love! (*To* THE BARON) You good-for-nothing! . . . educated, you call yourself—drinking coffee in bed, did you?

LUKA. Now, now! Wait, people! Don't interfere! Show a little respect to your neighbors . . . it isn't the word that matters, but what's in back of the word. That's what matters! Go on, girl! It's all right!

BUBNOFF. Go on, crow! See if you can make your feathers white!

THE BARON. Well—continue!

NATASHA. Pay no attention to them . . . what are they? They're just jealous . . . they've nothing to tell about themselves . . .

NASTYA (*sits down again*). I'm going to say no more! If they don't believe me they'll laugh. (*Stops suddenly, is silent for a few seconds, then, shutting her eyes, continues in a loud and intense voice, swaying her hands as if to the rhythm of far music*) And then I replied to him: "Joy of my life! My bright moon! And I, too, I can't li—*

without you—because I love you madly, so madly——and I shall keep on loving you as long as my heart beats in my bosom. But——" I say—"don't take your young life! Think how necessary it is to your dear parents whose only happiness you are. Leave me! Better that I should perish from longing for you, my life! I alone! I—ah—as such, such! Better that I should die—it doesn't matter . . . I am of no use to the world—and I have nothing, nothing at all——" (*Covers her face with her hand and weeps gently.*)

NATASHA (*in a low voice*). Don't cry—don't!
(LUKA, *smiling, strokes* NASTYA'S *head.*)

BUBNOFF (*laughs*). Ah—you limb of Satan!

THE BARON (*also laughs*). Hey, old man? Do you think it's true? It's all from that book "Fatal Love" . . . it's all nonsense! Let her alone!

NATASHA. And what's it to you? Shut up—or God'll punish you!

NASTYA (*bitterly*). God damn your soul! You worthless pig! Soul—bah! —you haven't got one!

LUKA (*takes* NASTYA'S *hand*). Come, dear! It's nothing! Don't be angry—I know—I believe you! You're right, not they! If you believe you had a real love affair, then you did—yes! And as for him—don't be angry with a fellow-lodger . . . maybe he's really jealous, and that's why he's laughing. Maybe he never had any real love—maybe not—come on—let's go!

NASTYA (*pressing her hand against her breast*). Grandfather! So help me God—it happened! It happened! He was a student, a Frenchman—Gastotcha was his name—he had a little black beard—and patent leathers—may God strike me dead if I'm lying! And he loved me so—my God, how he loved me!

LUKA. Yes, yes, it's all right. I believe you! Patent leathers, you said? Well, well, well—and you loved him, did you? (*Disappears with her around the corner.*)

THE BARON. God—isn't she a fool, though? She's good-hearted—but such a fool—it's past belief!

BUBNOFF. And why are people so fond of lying—just as if they were up before the judge—really!

NATASHA. I guess lying is more fun than speaking the truth—I, too . . .

THE BARON. What—you, too? Go on!

NATASHA. Oh—I imagine things—invent them—and I wait——

THE BARON. For what?

NATASHA (*smiling confusedly*). Oh —I think that perhaps—well—to-morrow somebody will really appear—someone—oh—out of the ordinary—or something'll happen—also out of the ordinary. . . . I've been waiting for it—oh—always. . . . But, really, what is there to wait for?
(*Pause.*)

THE BARON (*with a slight smile*). Nothing—I expect nothing! What is past, is past! Through! Over with! And then what?

NATASHA. And then—well—tomorrow I imagine suddenly that I'll die —and I get frightened . . . in summer it's all right to dream of death—then there are thunder storms—one might get struck by lightning . . .

THE BARON. You've a hard life . . . your sister's a wicked-tempered devil!

NATASHA. Tell me—does anybody live happily? It's hard for all of us —I can see that . . .

KLESHTCH (*who until this moment has sat motionless and indifferent, jumps up suddenly*). For all? You lie! Not for all! If it were so—all right! Then it wouldn't hurt—yes!

BUBNOFF. What in hell's bit you? Just listen to him yelping!
(KLESHTCH *lies down again and grunts.*)

THE BARON. Well—I'd better go and make my peace with Nastinka—if I don't, she won't treat me to vodka . . .

BUBNOFF. Hm—people love to lie . . . with Nastka—I can see the reason why. She's used to painting that mutt of hers—and now she wants to paint her soul as well . . . put rouge on her soul, eh? But the others—why do they? Take Luka for instance—he lies a lot . . . and what does he get out of it? He's an old fellow, too—why does he do it?

THE BARON (*smiling and walking away*). All people have drab-colored souls—and they like to brighten them up a bit . . .

LUKA (*appearing from round the corner*). You, sir, why do you tease the girl? Leave her alone—let her cry if it amuses her . . . she weeps for her own pleasure—what harm is it to you?

THE BARON. Nonsense, old man! She's a nuisance. Raoul today, Gaston tomorrow—always the same old yarn, though! Still—I'll go and make up with her. (*Leaves.*)

LUKA. That's right—go—and be nice to her. Being nice to people never does them any harm . . .

NATASHA. You're so good, little father—why are you so good?

LUKA. Good, did you say? Well— call it that! (*Behind the brick wall is heard soft singing and the sounds of a concertina*) Someone has to be kind, girl—someone must pity people! Christ pitied everybody—and he said to us: "Go and do likewise!" I tell you—if you pity a man when he most needs it, good comes of it. Why—I used to be a watchman on the estate of an engineer near Tomsk—all right—the house was right in the middle of a forest— lonely place—winter came—and I remained all by myself. Well—one night I heard a noise——

NATASHA. Thieves?

LUKA. Exactly! Thieves creeping in! I took my gun—I went out. I looked and saw two of them opening a window—and so busy that they didn't even see me. I yell: "Hey there—get out of here!" And they turn on me with their axes— I warn them to stand back, or I'd shoot—and as I speak, I keep on covering them with my gun, first the one, then the other—they go down on their knees, as if to implore me for mercy. And by that time I was furious—because of those axes, you see—and so I say to them: "I was chasing you, you scoundrels—and you didn't go. Now you go and break off some stout branches!"—and they did so—and I say: "Now —one of you lie down and let the other one flog him!" So they obey me and flog each other—and then they begin to implore me again. "Grandfather," they say, "for God's sake give us some bread! We're hungry!" There's thieves for you, my dear! (*Laughs*) And with an ax, too! Yes—honest peasants, both of them! And I say to them, "You should have asked for bread straight away!" And they say: "We got tired of asking—you beg and beg—and nobody gives you a crumb—it hurts!" So they stayed with me all that winter—one of them, Stepan, would take my gun and go shooting in the forest—and the other, Yakoff, was ill most of the time—he coughed a lot . . . and so the three of us together looked after the house . . . then Spring came . . . "Good-bye, grandfather," they said —and they went away—back home to Russia . . .

NATASHA. Were they escaped convicts?

LUKA. That's just what they were— escaped convicts—from a Siberian prison camp . . . honest peasants! If I hadn't felt sorry for them—they might have killed me—or maybe worse—and then there would have been trial and prison and afterwards Siberia—what's the sense of it? Prison teaches no good—and Siberia doesn't either—but another human being can . . . yes, a human being can teach another one kindness—very simply!
(*Pause.*)

BUBNOFF. Hm—yes—I, for instance, don't know how to lie . . . why—as far as I'm concerned, I believe in coming out with the whole truth and putting it on thick . . . why fuss about it?

KLESHTCH (*again jumps as if his clothes were on fire, and screams*) What truth? Where is there truth? (*Tearing at his ragged clothes*) Here's truth for you! No work! No strength! That's the only truth! Shelter—there's no shelter! You die —that's the truth! Hell! What do I want with the truth? Let me breathe! Why should I be blamed? What do I want with truth? To live—Christ Almighty!—they won't let you live—and that's another truth!

BUBNOFF. He's mad!

LUKA. Dear Lord . . . listen to me, brother——

KLESHTCH (*trembling with excitement*). They say: there's truth! You, old man, try to console everyone . . . I tell you—I hate everyone! And there's your truth—God curse it—understand? I tell you— God curse it! (*Rushes away round the corner, turning as he goes.*)

LUKA. Ah—how excited he got! Where did he run off to?

NATASHA. He's off his head . . .

BUBNOFF. God—didn't he say a whole lot, though? As if he was playing drama—he gets fits often . . . he isn't used to life yet . . .

PEPEL (*comes slowly round the corner*). Peace on all this honest gathering! Well, Luka, you wily old fellow—still telling them stories?

LUKA. You should have heard how that fellow carried on!

PEPEL. Kleshtch—wasn't it? What's wrong with him? He was running like one possessed!

LUKA. You'd do the same if your own heart were breaking!

PEPEL (*sitting down*). I don't like him . . . he's got such a nasty, bad temper—and so proud! (*Imitating* KLESHTCH) "I'm a workman!" And he thinks everyone's beneath him. Go on working if you feel like it— nothing to be so damned haughty about! If work is the standard—a horse can give us points—pulls like hell and says nothing! Natasha— are your folks at home?

NATASHA. They went to the cemetery—then to night service . . .

PEPEL. So that's why you're free for once—quite a novelty!

LUKA (*to* BUBNOFF, *thoughtfully*). There—you say—truth! Truth doesn't always heal a wounded soul. For instance, I knew of a man who believed in a land of righteousness . . .

BUBNOFF. In what?

LUKA. In a land of righteousness. He said: "Somewhere on this earth there must be a righteous land— and wonderful people live there— good people! They respect each other, help each other, and everything is peaceful and good!" And so

that man—who was always searching for this land of righteousness— he was poor and lived miserably— and when things got to be so bad with him that it seemed there was nothing else for him to do except lie down and die—even then he never lost heart—but he'd just smile and say: "Never mind! I can stand it! A little while longer—and I'll have done with this life—and I'll go in search of the righteous land!" —it was his one happiness—the thought of that land . . .

PEPEL. Well? Did he go there?

BUBNOFF. Where? Ho-ho!

LUKA. And then to this place—in Siberia, by the way—there came a convict—a learned man with books and maps—yes, a learned man who knew all sorts of things—and the other man said to him: "Do me a favor—show me where is the land of righteousness and how I can get there." At once the learned man opened his books, spread out his maps, and looked and looked and he said—no—he couldn't find this land anywhere . . . everything was correct—all the lands on earth were marked—but not this land of righteousness . . .

PEPEL (*in a low voice*). Well? Wasn't there a trace of it?
(BUBNOFF *roars with laughter.*)

NATASHA. Wait . . . well, little father?

LUKA. The man wouldn't believe it. . . . "It must exist," he said, "look carefully. Otherwise," he says, "your books and maps are of no use if there's no land of righteousness." The learned man was offended.

"My plans," he said, "are correct. But there exists no land of righteousness anywhere." Well, then the other man got angry. He'd lived and lived and suffered and suffered, and had believed all the time in the existence of this land—and now, according to the plans, it didn't exist at all. He felt robbed! And he said to the learned man: "Ah—you scum of the earth! You're not a learned man at all—but just a damned cheat!"—and he gave him a good wallop in the eye—then another one . . . (*After a moment's silence*) And then he went home and hanged himself!
(*All are silent.* LUKA, *smiling, looks at* PEPEL *and* NATASHA.)

PEPEL (*low-voiced*). To hell with this story—it isn't very cheerful . . .

NATASHA. He couldn't stand the disappointment . . .

BUBNOFF (*sullen*). Ah—it's nothing but a fairytale . . .

PEPEL. Well—there is the righteous land for you—doesn't exist, it seems . . .

NATASHA. I'm sorry for that man . . .

BUBNOFF. All a story—ho-ho!—land of righteousness—what an idea! (*Exit through window.*)

LUKA (*pointing to window*). He's laughing! (*Pause*) Well, children, God be with you! I'll leave you soon . . .

PEPEL. Where are you going to?

LUKA. To the Ukraine—I heard they discovered a new religion there—I want to see—yes! People are always seeking—they always want something better—God grant them patience!

PEPEL. You think they'll find it?

LUKA. The people? They will find it! He who seeks, will find! He who desires strongly, will find!

NATASHA. If only they could find something better—invent something better . . .

LUKA. They're trying to! But we must help them, girl—we must respect them . . .

NATASHA. How can I help them? I am helpless myself!

PEPEL (*determined*). Again—listen—I'll speak to you again, Natasha—here—before him—he knows everything . . . run away with me?

NATASHA. Where? From one prison to another?

PEPEL. I told you—I'm through with being a thief, so help me God! I'll quit! If I say so, I'll do it! I can read and write—I'll work—He's been telling me to go to Siberia on my own hook—let's go there together, what do you say? Do you think I'm not disgusted with my life? Oh—Natasha—I know . . . I see . . . I console myself with the thought that there are lots of people who are honored and respected —and who are bigger thieves than I! But what good is that to me? It isn't that I repent . . . I've no conscience . . . but I do feel one thing: One must live differently.

One must live a better life . . . one must be able to respect one's own self . . .

LUKA. That's right, friend! May God help you! It's true! A man must respect himself!

PEPEL. I've been a thief from childhood on. Everybody always called me "Vaska—the thief—the son of a thief!" Oh—very well then—I am a thief— . . . just imagine—now, perhaps, I'm a thief out of spite— perhaps I'm a thief because no one ever called me anything different. . . . Well, Natasha——?

NATASHA (sadly). Somehow I don't believe in words—and I'm restless today—my heart is heavy . . . as if I were expecting something . . . it's a pity, Vassily, that you talked to me today . . .

PEPEL. When should I? It isn't the first time I speak to you . . .

NATASHA. And why should I go with you? I don't love you so very much —sometimes I like you—and other times the mere sight of you makes me sick . . . it seems—no—I don't really love you . . . when one really loves, one sees no fault. . . . But I do see . . .

PEPEL. Never mind—you'll love me after a while! I'll make you care for me . . . if you'll just say yes! For over a year I've watched you . . . you're a decent girl . . . you're kind—you're reliable—I'm very much in love with you . . .
(VASSILISA, in her best dress, appears at window and listens.)

NATASHA. Yes—you love me—but how about my sister . . . ?

PEPEL (confused). Well, what of her? There are plenty like her . . .

LUKA. You'll be all right, girl! If there's no bread, you have to eat weeds . . .

PEPEL (gloomily). Please—feel a little sorry for me! My life isn't all roses—it's a hell of a life . . . little happiness in it . . . I feel as if a swamp were sucking me under . . . and whatever I try to catch and hold on to, is rotten . . . it breaks . . . Your sister—oh—I thought she was different . . . if she weren't so greedy after money . . . I'd have done anything for her sake, if she were only all mine . . . but she must have someone else . . . and she has to have money—and freedom . . . because she doesn't like the straight and narrow . . . she can't help me. But you're like a young fir-tree . . . you bend, but you don't break . . .

LUKA. Yes—go with him, girl, go! He's a good lad—he's all right! Only tell him every now and then that he's a good lad so that he won't forget it—and he'll believe you. Just you keep on telling him "Vasya, you're a good man—don't you forget it!" Just think, dear, where else could you go except with him? Your sister is a savage beast . . . and as for her husband, there's little to say of him! He's rotten beyond words . . . and all this life here, where will it get you? But this lad is strong . . .

NATASHA. Nowhere to go—I know —I thought of it. The only thing is —I've no faith in anybody—and there's no place for me to turn to . . .

PEPEL. Yes, there is! But I won't let you go that way—I'd rather cut your throat!

NATASHA (*smiling*). There—I'm not his wife yet—and he talks already of killing me!

PEPEL (*puts his arms around her*). Come, Natasha! Say yes!

NATASHA (*holding him close*). But I'll tell you one thing, Vassily—I swear it before God . . . the first time you strike me or hurt me any other way, I'll have no pity on myself . . . I'll either hang myself . . . or . . .

PEPEL. May my hand wither if ever I touch you!

LUKA. Don't doubt him, dear! He needs you more than you need him!

VASSILISA (*from the window*). So now they're engaged! Love and advice!

NATASHA. They've come back—oh, God—they saw—oh, Vassily . . .

PEPEL. Why are you frightened? Nobody'll dare touch you now!

VASSILISA. Don't be afraid, Natalia! He won't beat you . . . he don't know how to love or how to beat . . . I know!

LUKA (*in a low voice*). Rotten old hag—like a snake in the grass . . .

VASSILISA. He dares only with the word!

KOSTILYOFF (*enters*). Natashka! What are you doing here, you para-site? Gossiping? Kicking about your family? And the samovar not ready? And the table not cleared?

NATASHA (*going out*). I thought you were going to church . . . ?

KOSTILYOFF. None of your business what we intended doing! Mind your own affairs—and do what you're told!

PEPEL. Shut up, you! She's no longer your servant! Don't go, Natalia—don't do a thing!

NATASHA. Stop ordering me about —you're commencing too soon! (*Leaves.*)

PEPEL (*to* KOSTILYOFF). That's enough. You've used her long enough—now she's mine!

KOSTILYOFF. Yours? When did you buy her—and for how much? (VASSILISA *roars with laughter.*)

LUKA. Go away, Vasya!

PEPEL. Don't laugh, you fools—or first thing you know I'll make you cry!

VASSILISA. Oh, how terrible! Oh—how you frighten me!

LUKA. Vassily—go away! Don't you see—she's goading you on . . . ridiculing you, don't you understand . . . ?

PEPEL. Yes . . . You lie, lie! You won't get what you want!

VASSILISA. Nor will I get what I don't want, Vasya!

PEPEL. (*shaking his fist at her*). We'll see . . . (*Exit.*)

VASSILISA (*disappearing through window*). I'll arrange some wedding for you . . .

KOSTILYOFF (*crossing to* LUKA). Well, old man, how's everything?

LUKA. All right!

KOSTILYOFF. You're going away, they say——?

LUKA. Soon.

KOSTILYOFF. Where to?

LUKA. I'll follow my nose . . .

KOSTILYOFF. Tramping, eh? Don't like stopping in one place all the time, do you?

LUKA. Even water won't pass beneath a stone that's sunk too firmly in the ground, they say . . .

KOSTILYOFF. That's true for a stone. But man must settle in one place. Men can't live like cockroaches, crawling about wherever they want. . . . A man must stick to one place —and not wander about aimlessly . . .

LUKA. But suppose his home is wherever he hangs his hat?

KOSTILYOFF. Why, then—he's a vagabond—useless . . . a human being must be of some sort of use —he must work . . .

LUKA. That's what you think, eh?

KOSTILYOFF. Yes—sure . . . just look! What's a vagabond? A strange fellow . . . unlike all others. If he's a real pilgrim then he's some good in the world . . . perhaps he discovered a new truth. Well—but not every truth is worth while. Let him keep it to himself and shut up about it! Or else—let him speak in a way which no one can understand . . . don't let him interfere . . . don't let him stir up people without cause! It's none of his business how other people live! Let him follow his own righteous path . . . in the woods—or in a monastery—away from everybody! He mustn't interfere—nor condemn other people— but pray—pray for all of us—for all the world's sins—for mine—for yours—for everybody's. To pray— that's why he forsakes the world's turmoil! That's so! (*Pause*) But you—what sort of a pilgrim are you—? An honest person must have a passport . . . all honest people have passports . . . yes . . . !

LUKA. In this world there are people —and also just plain men . . .

KOSTILYOFF. Don't coin wise sayings! Don't give me riddles! I'm as clever as you . . . what's the difference—people and men?

LUKA. What riddle is there? I say —there's sterile and there's fertile ground . . . whatever you sow in it, grows . . . that's all . . .

KOSTILYOFF. What do you mean?

LUKA. Take yourself for instance . . . if the Lord God himself said to you: "Mikhailo, be a man!"—It would be useless—nothing would come of it—you're doomed to remain just as you are . . .

KOSTILYOFF. Oh—but do you realize that my wife's uncle is a policeman, and that if I . . .

VASSILISA (*coming in*). Mikhail Ivanitch—come and have your tea . . .

KOSTILYOFF (*to* LUKA). You listen! Get out! You leave this place—hear?

VASSILISA. Yes—get out, old man! Your tongue's too long! And—who knows—you may be an escaped convict . . .

KOSTILYOFF. If I ever see sign of you again after today—well—I've warned you!

LUKA. You'll call your uncle, eh? Go on—call him! Tell him you've caught an escaped convict—and maybe uncle'll get a reward—perhaps all of three kopecks . . .

BUBNOFF (*in the window*). What are you bargaining about? Three kopecks—for what?

LUKA. They're threatening to sell me . . .

VASSILISA (*to her husband*). Come . . .

BUBNOFF. For three kopecks? Well—look out, old man—they may even do it for one!

KOSTILYOFF (*to* BUBNOFF). You have a habit of jumping up like a jack-in-the-box!

VASSILISA. The world is full of shady people and crooks——

LUKA. Hope you'll enjoy your tea!

VASSILISA (*turning*). Shut up! You rotten toadstool! (*Leaves with her husband.*)

LUKA. I'm off tonight.

BUBNOFF. That's right. Don't outstay your welcome!

LUKA. True enough.

BUBNOFF. I know. Perhaps I've escaped the gallows by getting away in time . . .

LUKA. Well?

BUBNOFF. That's true. It was this way. My wife took up with my boss. He was great at his trade—could dye a dog's skin so that it looked like a raccoon's—could change cat's skin into kangaroo—muskrats, all sorts of things. Well—my wife took up with him—and they were so mad about each other that I got afraid they might poison me or something like that—so I commenced beating up my wife—and the boss beat me . . . we fought savagely! Once he tore off half my whiskers—and broke one of my ribs . . . well, then I, too, got enraged. . . . I cracked my wife over the head with an iron yard-measure—well—and altogether it was like an honest-to-God war! And then I saw that nothing really could come of it . . . they were planning to get the best of me! So I started planning—how to kill my wife—I thought of it a whole lot . . . but I thought better of it just in time . . . and got away . . .

LUKA. That was best! Let them go on changing dogs into raccoons!

BUBNOFF. Only—the shop was in my wife's name . . . and so I did myself out of it, you see? Although, to tell the truth, I would have drunk it away . . . I'm a hard drinker, you know . . .

LUKA. A hard drinker—oh . . .

BUBNOFF. The worst you ever met! Once I start drinking, I drink everything in sight, I'll spend every bit of money I have—everything except my bones and my skin . . . what's more, I'm lazy . . . it's terrible how I hate work!
(*Enter* SATINE *and* THE ACTOR, *quarreling.*)

SATINE. Nonsense! You'll go nowhere—it's all a damned lie! Old man, what did you stuff him with all those fairy-tales for?

THE ACTOR. You lie! Grandfather! Tell him that he lies!—I am going away. I worked today—I swept the streets . . . and I didn't have a drop of vodka. What do you think of that? Here they are—two fifteen-kopeck pieces—and I'm sober!

SATINE. Why—that's absurd! Give it to me—I'll either drink it up—or lose it at cards . . .

THE ACTOR. Get out—this is for my journey . . .

LUKA (*to* SATINE). And you—why are you trying to lead him astray?

SATINE. Tell me, soothsayer, beloved by the God's, what's my future going to be? I've gone to pieces, brother—but everything isn't lost yet, grandfather . . . there are sharks in this world who got more brains than I!

LUKA. You're cheerful, Constantine—and very agreeable!

BUBNOFF. Actor, come over here! (THE ACTOR *crosses to window, sits down on the sill before* BUBNOFF, *and speaks in a low voice with him.*)

SATINE. You know, brother, I used to be a clever youngster. It's nice to think of it. I was a devil of a fellow . . . danced splendidly, played on the stage, loved to amuse people . . . it was awfully gay . . .

LUKA. How did you get to be what you are?

SATINE. You're inquisitive, old man! You want to know everything? What for?

LUKA. I want to understand the ways of men—I look at you, and I don't understand. You're a bold lad, Constantine, and you're no fool . . . yet, all of a sudden . . .

SATINE. It's prison, grandfather—I spent four years and seven months in prison . . . afterwards—where could I go?

LUKA. Aha! What were you there for?

SATINE. On account of a scoundrel —whom I killed in a fit of rage . . . and despair . . . and in prison I learned to play cards . . .

LUKA. You killed—because of a woman?

SATINE. Because of my own sister. . . . But look here—leave me alone! I don't care for these cross-examinations—and all this happened a long time ago. It's already nine years since my sister's death. . . . Brother, she was a wonderful girl . . .

LUKA. You take life easily! And only a while ago that locksmith was here —and how he did yell!

SATINE. Kleshtch?

LUKA. Yes—"There's no work," he shouted; "there isn't anything . . ."

SATINE. He'll get used to it. What could I do?

LUKA. (softly). Look—here he comes!
(KLESHTCH walks in slowly, his head bowed low.)

SATINE. Hey, widower! Why are you so down in the mouth? What are you thinking?

KLESHTCH. I'm thinking—what'll I do? I've no food—nothing—the funeral ate up all . . .

SATINE. I'll give you a bit of advice . . . do nothing! Just be a burden to the world at large!

KLESHTCH. Go on—talk—I'd be ashamed of myself . . .

SATINE. Why — people aren't ashamed to let you live worse than a dog. Just think . . . you stop work—so do I—so do hundreds, thousands of others—everybody— understand? — everybody'll quit working . . . nobody'll do a damned thing—and then what'll happen?

KLESHTCH. They'll all starve to death . . .

LUKA (to SATINE). If those are your notions, you ought to join the order of Begunes—you know—there's some such organization . . .

SATINE. I know—grandfather—and they're no fools . . .
(NATASHA is heard screaming behind KOSTILYOFF's window: "What for? Stop! What have I done?")

LUKA (worried). Natasha! That was she crying—oh, God . . .
(From KOSTILYOFF's room is heard noise, shuffling, breaking of crockery, and KOSTILYOFF's shrill cry: "Ah! Heretic! Bitch!")

VASSILISA. Wait, wait—I'll teach her—there, there!

NATASHA. They're beating me—killing me . . .

SATINE (shouts through the window). Hey—you there— . . .

LUKA (trembling). Where's Vassily—? Call Vaska—oh, God— listen, brothers . . .

THE ACTOR (running out). I'll find him at once!

BUBNOFF. They beat her a lot these days . . .

SATINE. Come on, old man—we'll be witnesses . . .

LUKA (following SATINE). Oh—witnesses—what for? Vassily—he should be called at once!

NATASHA. Sister—sister dear! Va-a-a . . .

BUBNOFF. They've gagged her—I'll go and see . . .
(The noise in KOSTILYOFF's room dies down gradually as if they had gone into the hallway. The old man's cry: "Stop!" is heard. A door is slammed noisily, and the latter

sound cuts off all the other noises sharply. Quiet on the stage. Twilight.)

KLESHTCH (seated on the sledge, indifferently, rubbing his hands; mutters at first indistinguishably, then:). What then? One must live. (Louder) Must have shelter—well? There's no shelter, no roof—nothing . . . there's only man—man alone —no hope . . . no help . . . (Exit slowly, his head bent.)
(A few moments of ominous silence, then somewhere in the hallway a mass of sounds, which grows in volume and comes nearer. Individual voices are heard.)

VASSILISA. I'm her sister—let go . . .

KOSTILYOFF. What right have you . . . ?

VASSILISA. Jail-bird!

SATINE. Call Vaska—quickly! Zob —hit him!
(A police whistle. THE TARTAR runs in, his right hand in a sling.)

THE TARTAR. There's a new law for you—kill only in daytime!
(Enter ZOB, followed by MIEDVIEDIEFF.)

ZOB. I handed him a good one!

MIEDVIEDIEFF. You—how dare you fight?

THE TARTAR. What about yourself? What's your duty?

MIEDVIEDIEFF (running after). Stop —give back my whistle!

KOSTILYOFF (runs in). Abram! Stop him! Hold him! He's a murderer— he . . .

(Enter KVASHNYA and NASTYA supporting NATASHA who is disheveled. SATINE backs away, pushing away VASSILISA who is trying to attack her sister, while near her, ALYOSHKA jumps up and down like a madman, whistles into her ear, shrieking, roaring. Also other ragged men and women.)

SATINE (to VASSILISA). Well—you damned bitch!

VASSILISA. Let go, you jail-bird! I'll tear you to pieces—if I have to pay for it with my own life!

KVASHNYA (leading NATASHA aside). You—Karpovna—that's enough— stand back—aren't you ashamed? Or are you crazy?

MIEDVIEDIEFF (seizes SATINE). Aha —caught at last!

SATINE. Zob—beat them up! Vaska —Vaska . . .
(They all, in a chaotic mass, struggle near the brick wall. They lead NATASHA to the right, and set her on a pile of wood. PEPEL rushes in from the hallway and, silently, with powerful movements, pushes the crowd aside.)

PEPEL. Natalia, where are you . . . you . . .

KOSTILYOFF (disappearing behind a corner). Abram! Seize Vaska! Comrades—help us get him! The thief! The robber!

PEPEL. You—you old bastard! (Aiming a terrific blow at KOSTILYOFF. KOSTILYOFF falls so that only the upper part of his body is seen. PEPEL rushes to NATASHA.)

VASSILISA. Beat Vaska! Brothers! Beat the thief!

MIEDVIEDIEFF (*yells to* SATINE). Keep out of this—it's a family affair . . . they're relatives—and who are you . . .

PEPEL (*to* NATASHA). What did she do to you? She used a knife?

KVASHNYA. God — what beasts! They've scalded the child's feet with boiling water!

NASTYA. They overturned the samovar . . .

THE TARTAR. Maybe an accident— you must make sure—you can't exactly tell . . .

NATASHA (*half fainting*). Vassily— take me away——

VASSILISA. Good people! Come! Look! he's dead! Murdered! (*All crowded into the hallway near* KOSTILYOFF. BUBNOFF *leaves the crowd and crosses to* PEPEL.)

BUBNOFF (*in a low voice, to* PEPEL). Vaska—the old man is done for!

PEPEL (*looks at him, as though he does not understand*). Go—for help —she must be taken to the hospital . . . I'll settle with them . . .

BUBNOFF. I say—the old man— somebody's killed him . . . (*The noise on the stage dies out like a fire under water. Distinct, whispered exclamations:* "Not really?" "Well—let's go away, brothers!" "The devil!" "Hold on now!" "Let's get away before the police comes!" *The crowd disappears.* BUBNOFF, THE TARTAR, NASTYA, *and* KVASHNYA, *rush up to* KOSTILYOFF's *body.*)

VASSILISA (*rises and cries out triumphantly*). Killed—my husband's killed! Vaska killed him! I saw him! Brothers, I saw him! Well—Vasya —the police!

PEPEL (*moves away from* NATASHA). Let me alone. (*Looks at* KOSTILYOFF; *to* VASSILISA) Well— are you glad? (*Touches the corpse with his foot*) The old bastard is dead! Your wish has been granted! Why not do the same to you? (*Throws himself at her.*) (SATINE *and* ZOB *quickly overpower him, and* VASSILISA *disappears in the passage.*)

SATINE. Come to your senses!

ZOB. Hold on! Not so fast!

VASSILISA (*appearing*). Well, Vaska, dear friend? You can't escape your fate . . . police— Abram—whistle!

MIEDVIEDIEFF. Those devils tore my whistle off!

ALYOSHKA. Here it is! (*Whistles,* MIEDVIEDIEFF *runs after him.*)

SATINE (*leading* PEPEL *to* NATASHA). Don't be afraid, Vaska! Killed in a row! That's nonsense— only manslaughter—you won't have to serve a long term . . .

VASSILISA. Hold Vaska—he killed him—I saw it!

SATINE. I, too, gave the old man a couple of blows—he was easily fixed . . . you call me as witness, Vaska!

PEPEL. I don't need to defend myself . . . I want to drag Vassilisa into this mess—and I'll do it—she was the one who wanted it . . . she was the one who urged me to kill him—she goaded me on . . .

NATASHA (*sudden and loud*). Oh—I understand—so that's it, Vassily? Good people! They're both guilty—my sister and he—they're both guilty! They had it all planned! So, Vassily, that's why you spoke to me a while ago—so that she should overhear everything—? Good people! She's his mistress—you know it—everybody knows it—they're both guilty! She—she urged him to kill her husband—he was in their way—and so was I! And now they've maimed me . . .

PEPEL. Natalia! What's the matter with you? What are you saying?

SATINE. Oh—hell!

VASSILISA. You lie. She lies. He—Vaska killed him . . .

NATASHA. They're both guilty! God damn you both!

SATINE. What a mix-up! Hold on, Vassily—or they'll ruin you between them!

ZOB. I can't understand it—oh—what a mess!

PEPEL. Natalia! It can't be true! Surely you don't believe that I—with her——

SATINE. So help me God, Natasha! Just think . . .

VASSILISA (*in the passage*). They've killed my husband—Your Excellency! Vaska Pepel, the thief, killed him, Captain! I saw it—everybody saw it . . .

NATASHA (*tossing about in agony; her mind wandering*). Good people—my sister and Vaska killed him! The police—listen—this sister of mine—here—she urged, coaxed her lover—there he stands—the scoundrel! They both killed him! Put them in jail! Bring them before the judge! Take me along, too! To prison! Christ Almighty—take me to prison, too!

CURTAIN

ACT FOUR

Same as Act I. But PEPEL'S *room is no longer there, and the partition has been removed. Furthermore, there is no anvil at the place where* KLESHTCH *used to sit and work. In the corner, where* PEPEL'S *room used to be,* THE TARTAR *lies stretched out, rather restless, and groaning from time to time.* KLESHTCH *sits at one end of the table, repairing a concertina and now and then testing the stops. At the other end of the table sit* SATINE, THE BARON, *and* NASTYA. *In front of them stand a bottle of vodka, three bottles of beer, and a large loaf of black bread.*

THE ACTOR *lies on top of the stove, shifting about and coughing. It is night. The stage is lit by a lamp in the middle of the table. Outside the wind howls.*

KLESHTCH. Yes . . . he disappeared during the confusion and noise . . .

THE BARON. He vanished under the very eyes of the police—just like a puff of smoke . . .

SATINE. That's how sinners flee from the company of the righteous!

NASTYA. He was a dear old soul! But you—you aren't men—you're just—oh—like rust on iron!

THE BARON (*drinks*). Here's to you, my lady!

SATINE. He was an inquisitive old fellow—yes! Nastenka here fell in love with him . . .

NASTYA. Yes! I did! Madly! It's true! He saw everything—understood everything . . .

SATINE (*laughing*). Yes, generally speaking, I would say that he was —oh—like mush to those who can't chew. . . .

THE BARON (*laughing*). Right! Like plaster on a boil!

KLESHTCH. He was merciful—you people don't know what pity means . . .

SATINE. What good can I do you by pitying you?

KLESHTCH. You needn't have pity— but you needn't harm or offend your fellow-beings, either!

THE TARTAR (*sits up on his bunk, nursing his wounded hand carefully*). He was a fine old man. The law of life was the law of his heart. . . . And he who obeys this law, is good, while he who disregards it, perishes . . .

THE BARON. What law, Prince?

THE TARTAR. There are a number— different ones—you know . . .

THE BARON. Proceed!

THE TARTAR. Do not do harm unto others—such is the law!

SATINE. Oh—you mean the Penal Code, criminal and correctional, eh?

THE BARON. And also the Code of Penalties inflicted by Justices of the Peace!

THE TARTAR. No. I mean the Koran. It is the supreme law—and your own soul ought to be the Koran— yes!

KLESHTCH (*testing his concertina*). It wheezes like all hell! But the Prince speaks the truth—one must live abiding by the law—by the teachings of the Gospels . . .

SATINE. Well—go ahead and do it!

THE BARON. Just try it!

THE TARTAR. The Prophet Mohammed gave to us the law. He said: "Here is the law! Do as it is written therein!" Later on a time will arrive when the Koran will have outlived its purpose—and time will bring forth its own laws—every generation will create its own . . .

SATINE. To be sure! Time passed on —and gave us—the Criminal Code . . . It's a strong law, brother—it won't wear off so very soon!

NASTYA (*banging her glass on the table*). Why—why do I stay here— with you? I'll go away somewhere —to the ends of the world!

THE BARON. Without any shoes, my lady?

NASTYA. I'll go—naked, if must be —creeping on all fours!

THE BARON. That'll be rather picturesque, my lady—on all fours!

NASTYA. Yes—and I'll crawl if I have to—anything at all—as long as I don't have to see your faces any longer—oh, I'm so sick of it all —the life—the people—everything!

SATINE. When you go, please take the actor along—he's preparing to go to the very same place—he has learned that within a half mile's distance of the end of the world there's a hospital for diseased organons . . .

THE ACTOR (*raising his head over the top of the stove*). A hospital for organisms—you fool!

SATINE. For organons—poisoned with vodka!

THE ACTOR. Yes! He will go! He will indeed! You'll see!

THE BARON. Who is he, sir?

THE ACTOR. I!

THE BARON. Thanks, servant of the goddess—what's her name—? The goddess of drama—tragedy—whatever is her name——?

THE ACTOR. The muse, idiot! Not the goddess—the muse!

SATINE. Lachesis—Hera—Aphrodite—Atropos—oh! To hell with them all! You see—Baron—it was the old man who stuffed the actor's head full with this rot . . .

THE BARON. That old man's a fool . . .

THE ACTOR. Ignoramuses! Beasts! Melpomene—that's her name! Heartless brutes! Bastards! You'll see! He'll go! "On with the orgy, dismal spirits!"—poem—ah—by Béranger! Yes—he'll find some spot where there's no—no . . .

THE BARON. Where there's nothing, sir?

THE ACTOR. Right! Nothing! "This hole shall be my grave—I am dying—ill and exhausted . . ." Why do you exist? Why?

THE BARON. You! God or genius or orgy—or whatever you are—don't roar so loud!

THE ACTOR. You lie! I'll roar all I want to!

NASTYA (*lifting her head from the table and throwing up her hands*). Go on! Yell! Let them listen to you!

THE BARON. Where is the sense, my lady?

SATINE. Leave them alone, Baron! To hell with the lot! Let them yell

—let them knock their damned heads off if they feel like it! There's a method in their madness! Don't you go and interfere with people as that old fellow did! Yes—it's he —the damned old fool—he bewitched the whole gang of us!

KLESHTCH. He persuaded them to go away—but failed to show them the road . . .

THE BARON. That old man was a humbug!

NASTYA. Liar! You're a humbug yourself!

THE BARON. Shut up, my lady!

KLESHTCH. The old man didn't like truth very much—as a matter of fact he strongly resented it—and wasn't he right, though? Just look —where is there any truth? And yet, without it, you can't breathe! For instance, our Tartar Prince over there, crushed his hand at his work —and now he'll have to have his arm amputated—and there's the truth for you!

SATINE (*striking the table with his clenched fist*). Shut up! You sons of bitches! Fools! Not another word about that old fellow! (*To* THE BARON) You, Baron, are the worst of the lot! You don't understand a thing, and you lie like the devil! The old man's no humbug! What's the truth? Man! Man—that's the truth! He understood man—you don't! You're all as dumb as stones! I understand the old man—yes! He lied—but lied out of sheer pity for you . . . God damn you! Lots of people lie out of pity for their fellow beings! I know! I've read about it! They lie—oh—beautifully, in-

spiringly, stirringly! Some lies bring comfort, and others bring peace— a lie alone can justify the burden which crushed a workman's hand and condemns those who are starving! I know what lying means! The weakling and the one who is a parasite through his very weakness —they both need lies—lies are their support, their shield, their armor! But the man who is strong, who is his own master, who is free and does not have to suck his neighbors' blood—he needs no lies! To lie— it's the creed of slaves and masters of slaves! Truth is the religion of the free man!

THE BARON. Bravo! Well spoken! Hear, hear! I agree! You speak like an honest man!

SATINE. And why can't a crook at times speak the truth—since honest people at times speak like crooks? Yes—I've forgotten a lot—but I still know a thing or two! The old man? Oh—he's wise! He affected me as acid affects a dirty old silver coin! Let's drink to his health! Fill the glasses . . . (NASTYA *fills a glass with beer and hands it to* SATINE, *who laughs*) The old man lives within himself . . . he looks upon all the world from his own angle. Once I asked him: "Granddad, why do people live?" (*Tries to imitate* LUKA'S *voice and gestures*) And he replied: "Why, my dear fellow, people live in the hope of something better! For example— let's say there are carpenters in this world, and all sorts of trash . . . people . . . and they give birth to a carpenter the like of which has never been seen upon the face of the earth . . . he's way above everybody else, and has no equal among carpenters! The brilliancy of his personality was reflected on all his trade, on all the other carpenters, so that they advanced twenty years in one day! This applies to all other trades—blacksmiths and shoemakers and other workmen—and all the peasants—and even the aristocrats live in the hopes of a higher life! Each individual thinks that he's living for his own Self, but in reality he lives in the hope of something better. A hundred years—sometimes longer —do we expect, live for the finer, higher life . . ." (NASTYA *stares intently into* SATINE'S *face.* KLESHTCH *stops working and listens.* THE BARON *bows his head very low, drumming softly on the table with his fingers.* THE ACTOR, *peering down from the stove, tries to climb noiselessly into the bunk*) "Everyone, brothers, everyone lives in the hope of something better. That's why we must respect each and every human being! How do we know who he is, why he was born, and what he is capable of accomplishing? Perhaps his coming into the world will prove to be our good fortune . . . Especially must we respect little children! Children—need freedom! Don't interfere with their lives! Respect children!" (*Pause.*)

THE BARON (*thoughtfully*). Hm—yes—something better?—That reminds me of my family . . . an old family dating back to the time of Catherine . . . all noblemen, soldiers, originally French . . . they served their country and gradually rose higher and higher. In the days of Nicholas the First my grandfather, Gustave DeBille, held a high post—riches—hundreds of serfs . . . horses—cooks——

NASTYA. You liar! It isn't true!

THE BARON (*jumping up*). What? Well—go on——

NASTYA. It isn't true.

THE BARON (*screams*). A house in Moscow! A house in Petersburg! Carriages! Carriages with coats of arms!
(KLESHTCH *takes his concertina and goes to one side, watching the scene with interest.*)

NASTYA. You lie!

THE BARON. Shut up!—I say—dozens of footmen . . .

NASTYA (*delighted*). You lie!

THE BARON. I'll kill you!

NASTYA (*ready to run away*). There were no carriages!

SATINE. Stop, Nastenka! Don't infuriate him!

THE BARON. Wait—you bitch! My grandfather . . .

NASTYA. There was no grandfather! There was nothing!
(SATINE *roars with laughter.*)

THE BARON (*worn out with rage, sits down on bench*). Satine! Tell that slut—what—? You, too, are laughing? You—don't believe me either? (*Cries out in despair, pounding the table with his fists*) It's true—damn the whole lot of you!

NASTYA (*triumphantly*). So—you're crying? Understand now what a human being feels like when nobody believes him?

KLESHTCH (*returning to the table*). I thought there'd be a fight . . .

THE TARTAR. Oh—people are fools! It's too bad . . .

THE BARON. I shall not permit anyone to ridicule me! I have proofs—documents—damn you!

SATINE. Forget it! Forget about your grandfather's carriages! You can't drive anywhere in a carriage of the past!

THE BARON. How dare she—just the same——?

NASTYA. Just imagine! How dare I——?

SATINE. You see—she does dare! How is she any worse than you are? Although, surely, in her past there wasn't even a father and mother, let alone carriages and a grandfather . . .

THE BARON (*quieting down*). Devil take you—you do know how to argue dispassionately—and I, it seems—I've no will-power . . .

SATINE. Acquire some—it's useful . . . (*Pause*) Nastya! Are you going to the hospital?

NASTYA. What for?

SATINE. To see Natashka.

NASTYA. Oh—just woke up, did you? She's been out of the hospital for some time—and they can't find a trace of her . . .

SATINE. Oh—that woman's a goner!

KLESHTCH. It's interesting to see whether Vaska will get the best of Vassilisa, or the other way around ——?

NASTYA. Vassilisa will win out! She's shrewd! And Vaska will go to the gallows!

SATINE. For manslaughter? No—only to jail . . .

NASTYA. Too bad—the gallows would have been better . . . that's where all of you should be sent . . . swept off into a hole—like ulth . . .

SATINE (*astonished*). What's the matter? Are you crazy?

THE BARON. Oh—give her a wallop —that'll teach her to be less impertinent . . .

NASTYA. Just you try to touch me!

THE BARON. I shall!

SATINE. Stop! Don't insult her! I can't get the thought of the old man out of my head! (*Roars with laughter*) Don't offend your fellow-beings! Suppose I were offended once in such a way that I'd remember it for the rest of my life? What then? Should I forgive? No, no!

THE BARON (*to* NASTYA). You must understand that I'm not your sort . . . you—ah—you piece of dirt!

NASTYA. You bastard! Why—you live off me like a worm off an apple! (*The men laugh amusedly.*)

KLESHTCH. Fool! An apple——?

THE BARON. You can't be angry with her—she's just an ass——

NASTYA. You laugh! Liars? Don't strike you as funny, eh?

THE ACTOR (*morosely*). Give them a good beating!

NASTYA. If I only could! (*Takes a cup from the table and throws it on the floor*) That's what I'd like to do to you all!

THE TARTAR. Why break dishes—eh—silly girl?

THE BARON (*rising*). That'll do! I'll teach her manners in half a second.

NASTYA (*running toward door*). Go to hell!

SATINE (*calling after her*). Hey! That's enough! Whom are you trying to frighten? What's all the row about, anyway?

NASTYA. Dogs! I hope you'll croak! Dogs! (*Runs out.*)

THE ACTOR (*morosely*). Amen!

THE TARTAR. Allah! Mad women, these Russians! They're bold, wilful; Tartar women aren't like that! They know the law and abide by it. . . .

KLESHTCH. She ought to be given a sound hiding!

THE BARON. The slut!

KLESHTCH (*testing the concertina*). It's ready! But its owner isn't here yet—that young fellow is burning his life away . . .

SATINE. Care for a drink—now?

KLESHTCH. Thanks . . . it's time to go to bed . . .

SATINE. Getting used to us?

KLESHTCH (*drinks, then goes to his bunk*). It's all right . . . there are people everywhere—at first you don't notice it . . . but after a while you don't mind. . . .
(THE TARTAR *spreads some rags over his bunk, then kneels on them and prays.*)

THE BARON (*to* SATINE, *pointing to* THE TARTAR). Look!

SATINE. Stop! He's a good fellow! Leave him alone! (*Roars with laughter*) I feel kindly today—the devil alone knows the reason why . . .

THE BARON. You always feel kindly when you're drunk—you're even wiser at such times . . .

SATINE. When I'm drunk? Yes—then I like everything—right—He prays? That's fine! A man may believe or not—that's his own affair—a man is free—he pays for everything himself—belief or unbelief—love—wisdom . . . a man pays for everything—and that's just why he's free! Man is—truth! And what is man? It's neither you nor I nor they—oh no—it's you and they and I and the old man—and Napoleon—Mohammed—all in one! (*Outlines vaguely in the air the contour of a human being*) Do you understand? It's tremendous! It contains the beginning and the end of everything—everything is in man—and everything exists for him! Man alone exists—everything else is the creation of his hands and his brain! Man! It is glorious! It sounds—oh—so big! Man must be respected—not degraded with pity—but respected, respected! Let us drink to man, Baron! (*Rises*) It is good to feel that you are a man! I'm a convict, a murderer, a crook—granted!—When I'm out on the street people stare at me as if I were a scoundrel—they draw away from me—they look after me and often they say: "You dog! You humbug! Work!" Work? And what for? to fill my belly? (*Roars with laughter*) I've always despised people who worry too much about their bellies. It isn't right, Baron! It isn't! Man is loftier than that! Man stands above hunger!

THE BARON. You—reason things out. . . . Well and good—it brings you a certain amount of consolation. . . . Personally I'm incapable of it . . . I don't know how. (*Glances around him and then, softly, guardedly*) Brother—I am afraid—at times. Do you understand? Afraid!—Because—what next?

SATINE. Rot! What's a man to be afraid of?

THE BARON (*pacing up and down*). You know—as far back as I can remember, there's been a sort of fog in my brain. I was never able to understand anything. Somehow I feel embarrassed—it seems to me that all my life I've done nothing but change clothes—and why? I don't understand! I studied—I wore the uniform of the Institute for the Sons of the Nobility . . . but what have I learned? I don't remember! I married—I wore a frock-coat— then a dressing-gown . . . but I chose a disagreeable wife . . . and why? I don't understand. I squandered everything that I possessed— I wore some sort of a grey jacket and brick-colored trousers—but

how did I happen to ruin myself? I haven't the slightest idea. . . . I had a position in the Department of State. . . . I wore a uniform and a cap with insignia of rank. . . . I embezzled government funds . . . so they dressed me in a convict's garb—and later on I got into these clothes here—and it all happened as in a dream—it's funny . . .

SATINE. Not very! It's rather—silly!

THE BARON. Yes—silly! I think so, too. Still—wasn't I born for some sort of purpose?

SATINE (*laughing*). Probably—a man is born to conceive a better man. (*Shaking his head*)—It's all right!

THE BARON. That she-devil Nastka! Where did she run to? I'll go and see—after all, she . . . (*Exit; pause.*)

THE ACTOR. Tartar! (*Pause*) Prince! (THE TARTAR *looks round*) Say a prayer for me . . .

THE TARTAR. What?

THE ACTOR (*softly*). Pray—for me!

THE TARTAR (*after a silence*). Pray for your own self!

THE ACTOR (*quickly crawls off the stove and goes to the table, pours out a drink with shaking hands, drinks, then almost runs to passage*). All over!

SATINE. Hey, proud Sicambrian! Where are you going?
(SATINE *whistles*. MIEDVIEDIEFF enters, dressed in a woman's flannel

shirt-waist; followed by BUBNOFF.
Both are slightly drunk. BUBNOFF
*carries a bunch of pretzels in one
hand, a couple of smoked fish in
the other, a bottle of vodka under
one arm, another bottle in his coat
pocket.*)

MIEDVIEDIEFF. A camel is something like a donkey—only it has no
ears. . . .

BUBNOFF. Shut up! You're a variety
of donkey yourself!

MIEDVIEDIEFF. A camel has no ears
at all, at all—it hears through its
nostrils . . .

BUBNOFF (*to* SATINE). Friend! I've
looked for you in all the saloons and
all the cabarets! Take this bottle—
my hands are full . . .

SATINE. Put the pretzels on the
table—then you'll have one hand
free——

BUBNOFF. Right! Hey—you donkey
—look! Isn't he a clever fellow?

MIEDVIEDIEFF. All crooks are clever
—I know! They couldn't do a thing
without brains. An honest man is all
right even if he's an idiot . . . but
a crook must have brains. But,
speaking about camels, you're
wrong . . . you can ride them—
they have no horns . . . and no
teeth either . . .

BUBNOFF. Where's everybody? Why
is there no one here? Come on out
. . . I treat! Who's in the corner?

SATINE. How soon will you drink up
everything you have? Scarecrow!

BUBNOFF. Very soon! I've very little
this time. Zob—where's Zob?

KLESHTCH (*crossing to table*). He
isn't here . . .

BUBNOFF. Waughrr! Bull-dog! Brr-
zz-zz!—Turkey-cock! Don't bark
and don't growl! Drink—make
merry—and don't be sullen!—I
treat everybody—Brother, I love to
treat—if I were rich, I'd run a free
saloon! So help me God, I would!
With an orchestra and a lot of singers! Come, everyone! Drink and eat
—listen to the music—and rest in
peace! Beggars—come, all you beggars—and enter my saloon free of
charge! Satine—you can have half
my capital—just like that!

SATINE. You better give me all you
have straight away!

BUBNOFF. All my capital? Right
now? Well—here's a ruble—here's
twenty kopecks—five kopecks—
sunflower seeds—and that's all!

SATINE. That's splendid! It'll be
safer with me—I'll gamble with
it . . .

MIEDVIEDIEFF. I'm a witness—the
money was given you for safe-keep-
ing. How much is it?

BUBNOFF. You? You're a camel—
we don't need witnesses . . .

ALYOSHKA (*comes in barefoot*).
Brothers, I got my feet wet!

BUBNOFF. Go on and get your throat
wet—and nothing'll happen—
you're a fine fellow—you sing and
you play—that's all right! But it's
too bad you drink—drink, little
brother, is harmful, very harmful
. . .

ALYOSHKA. I judge by you! Only

when you're drunk do you resemble
a human being . . . Kleshtch! Is
my concertina fixed? (*Sings and
dances*)
"*If my mug were not so attractive,
 My sweetheart wouldn't love me
 at all . . .*"
Boys, I'm frozen—it's cold . . .

MIEDVIEDIEFF. Hm—and may I ask
who's this sweetheart?

BUBNOFF. Shut up! From now on,
brother, you are neither a policeman nor an uncle!

ALYOSHKA. Just auntie's husband!

BUBNOFF. One of your nieces is in
jail—the other one's dying . . .

MIEDVIEDIEFF (*proudly*). You lie!
She's not dying—she disappeared
—without trace . . .
(SATINE *roars.*)

BUBNOFF. All the same, brothers—
a man without nieces isn't an uncle!

ALYOSHKA. Your Excellency! Listen
to the drummer of the retired billy-
goats' brigade! (*Sings*)
"*My sweetheart has money,
 I haven't a cent.
 But I'm a cheerful,
 Merry lad!*"
Oh—isn't it cold!
(*Enter* ZOB. *From now until the
final curtain men and women drift
in, undress, and stretch out on the
bunks, grumbling.*)

ZOB. Bubnoff! Why did you run off?

BUBNOFF. Come here—sit down—
brother, let's sing my favorite ditty,
eh?

THE TARTAR. Night was made for

sleep! Sing your songs in the daytime!

SATINE. Well—never mind, Prince
—come here!

THE TARTAR. What do you mean—
never mind? There's going to be a
noise—there always is when people
sing!

BUBNOFF (*crossing to* THE TARTAR).
Count—ah—I mean Prince—how's
your hand? Did they cut it off?

THE TARTAR. What for? We'll wait
and see—perhaps it won't be necessary . . . a hand isn't made of
iron—it won't take long to cut it
off . . .

ZOB. It's your own affair, Hassanka!
You'll be good for nothing without
your hand. We're judged by our
hands and backs—without the
pride of your hand, you're no longer
a human being. Tobacco-carting—
that's your business! Come on—
have a drink of vodka—and stop
worrying!

KVASHNYA (*comes in*). Ah, my beloved fellow-lodgers! It's horrible
outside—snow and slush . . . is
my policeman here?

MIEDVIEDIEFF. Right here!

KVASHNYA. Wearing my blouse
again? And drunk, eh? What's the
idea?

MIEDVIEDIEFF. In celebration of
Bubnoff's birthday . . . besides,
it's cold . . .

KVASHNYA. Better look out—stop
feeling about and go to sleep!

MIEDVIEDIEFF (*goes to kitchen*). Sleep? I can—I want to—it's time · —— (*Exit.*)

SATINE. What's the matter? Why are you so strict with him?

KVASHNYA. You can't be otherwise, friend. You have to be strict with his sort. I took him as a partner. I thought he'd be of some benefit to me—because he's a military man— and you're a rough lot . . . and I am a woman—and now he's turned drunkard—that won't do at all!

SATINE. You picked a good one for partner!

KVASHNYA. Couldn't get a better one. You wouldn't want to live with me . . . you think you're too fine! And even if you did it wouldn't last more than a week . . . you gamble me and all I own away at cards!

SATINE (*roars with laughter*). That's true, landlady—I'd gamble . . .

KVASHNYA. Yes, yes. Alyoshka!

ALYOSHKA. Here he is—I, myself!

KVASHNYA. What do you mean by gossiping about me?

ALYOSHKA. I? I speak out everything—whatever my conscience tells me. There, I say, is a wonderful woman! Splendid meat, fat, bones—over four hundred pounds! But brains—? not an ounce!

KVASHNYA. You're a liar! I've lots of brains! What do you mean by saying I beat my policeman?

ALYOSHKA. I thought you did— when you pulled him by the hair!

KVASHNYA (*laughs*). You fool! You aren't blind, are you? Why wash dirty linen in public? And—it hurts his feelings—that's why he took to drink . . .

ALYOSHKA. It's true, evidently, that even a chicken likes vodka . . . (SATINE *and* KLESHTCH *roar with laughter*.)

KVASHNYA. Go on—show your teeth! What sort of a man are you anyway, Alyoshka?

ALYOSHKA. Oh—I am first-rate! Master of all trades! I follow my nose!

BUBNOFF (*near* THE TARTAR's *bunk*). Come on! At all events— we won't let you sleep! We'll sing all night. Zob!

ZOB. Sing—? All right . . .

ALYOSHKA. And I'll play . . .

SATINE. We'll listen!

THE TARTAR (*smiling*). Well—Bubnoff—you devil—bring the vodka —we'll drink—we'll have a hell of a good time! The end will come soon enough—and then we'll be dead!

BUBNOFF. Fill his glass, Satine! Zob —sit down! Ah—brothers—what does a man need after all? There, for instance, I've had a drink— and I'm happy! Zob! Start my favorite song! I'll sing—and then I'll cry. . . .

ZOB (*begins to sing*).
"*The sun rises and sets . . .*"

BUBNOFF (*joining in*).
"*But my prison is all dark. . . .*"
(*Doors open quickly.*)

THE BARON (*on the threshold;
yells*).   Hey—you—come—come
here! Out in the waste— in the yard

. . . over there . . . The actor—
he's hanged himself. . . .
(*Silence. All stare at* THE BARON.
Behind him appears NASTYA, *and
slowly, her eyes wide with horror,
she walks to the table.*)

SATINE (*in a matter-of-fact voice*)
Damned fool—he ruined the song
. . . !

CURTAIN

The Dybbuk

BY S. ANSKY

TRANSLATED FROM THE YIDDISH
BY HENRY G. ALSBERG AND WINIFRED KATZIN

CAST OF CHARACTERS
(In order of appearance)

SCHOLARS IN THE SYNAGOGUE.
THREE BATLONIM.
THE MESSENGER.
MEYER, *the Shamas (Beadle) of the Synagogue.*
AN ELDERLY WOMAN WITH TWO CHILDREN.
CHANNON, *a young scholar.*
CHENNOCH, *a young scholar.*
LEAH, *daughter of Sender.*
FRADE, *her old nurse.*
GITTEL, *her companion.*
ASHER.
SENDER.
A WEDDING GUEST.
A BEGGAR WOMAN WITH A CHILD.
A LAME BEGGAR.
A HUNCHBACK.
BASSIA, *another friend of* LEAH'S.
NACHMON, *the bridegroom's father.*
RABBI MENDEL, *of the bridegroom's party.*
MENASHE, *the bridegroom.*
A BEGGAR MAN ON CRUTCHES.
A BLIND BEGGAR.
A TALL, PALE BEGGAR WOMAN.
FIRST CHASSID.
SECOND CHASSID.
THIRD CHASSID.
RABBI AZRAEL, *the Rabbi of Miropol.*
MICHOEL, *his attendant.*
A MINYEN.
RABBI SAMSON, *the City Rabbi.*

SCENES

ACT ONE

In the Synagogue at Brainitz.

ACT TWO

The Street between Sender's house and the Synagogue.

ACT THREE

In the house of Rabbi Azrael of Miropol.

ACT FOUR

Same as Act Three.

THE DYBBUK

ACT ONE

Before the rise of the curtain, a low mysterious chanting is heard in the intense darkness, as if from far off.

> Why, from highest height,
> To deepest depth below,
> Has the soul fallen?
> Within itself, the Fall
> Contains the Resurrection.

The curtain rises slowly, disclosing a wooden synagogue of venerable age, its time-blackened walls streaked as if with the tears of centuries. Two wooden rafters support the roof. From the center of the room, directly above the bima,* *hangs an ancient brass chandelier. The table in the middle of the* bima *is covered with a dark cloth. High up in the center wall, small windows open into the women's gallery. A long bench is against this wall, and in front of it a wooden table, covered with books piled up in confusion. Two yellow candle-stumps set in small clay candlesticks are burning on the table, but their light is almost entirely obscured by the heaped-up volumes. Left of the bench is a small door leading into a prayer-cabinet. In the opposite corner, a closet filled with books. In the center of the wall on the right is the altar, with the Ark containing the holy scrolls. To the right of this, the Cantor's desk, upon which burns a thick memorial candle of wax. On either side of the altar, a window. A bench runs the entire length of the wall, and in front of it are several small book-rests. In the wall on the left is a large tile stove, with a bench beside it. In front of the bench, on a long table, are piled tomes. Water container with tap. Towel pushed through a ring in the wall. Wide door to the street, and beyond this a chest over which, in a niche, burns the Perpetual Light.*

At a desk near the Cantor's, sits CHENNOCH, *absorbed in a book. Five or six students are at the table along the front wall, half-reclining in attitudes of great weariness; they are engaged in the study of the Talmud, and their voices rise in a low, dreamy chanting. Near the* bima MEYER *is busy sorting the small bags which contain prayer-shawls and phylacteries. At the table on the left, sit the three* BATLONIM,* *chanting. Their attitudes and the expression of their faces betoken a state of pious ecstasy. On the bench beside the stove, the* MESSENGER *is lying at full length, with his knapsack for a pillow.* CHANNON, *at the chest containing the*

---

* Pronounced bee'-ma—Tribune in centre of the synagogue, railed round with a gate on either side, where the Holy Scrolls are read.

* Pronounced bat'-lou, Pl: batlon'-im—Professional prayerman.

tomes, his hand resting upon its upper ledge, stands lost in meditation.

It is evening. A mystic mood lies upon the synagogue. Shadows lurk in the corners.

The FIRST *and* SECOND BATLONIM *finish the chant,* "Why, from highest height," *etc., and then fall silent. There is a long pause. Wrapped in dreams, all three* BATLONIM *sit silently at the table.*

FIRST BATLON (*in a narrative manner*). Rabbi Dovidel of Talan, may his merits hover over us, had a chair of gold which bore the inscription: David, King of Israel, who is living still. (*Pause.*)

SECOND BATLON (*in the same manner*). Rabbi Israel of Ruzhin, blessed be his memory, kept royal state. An orchestra of four-and-twenty musicians played to him as he sat at table, and when he drove abroad, it was behind a tandem of never less than six magnificent horses.

THIRD BATLON (*excitedly*). And it is told of Rabbi Schmool of Kaminka that he went in slippers of gold. (*Rapturously*) *Golden* slippers.

THE MESSENGER (*rising, and sitting upright on his bench, begins to speak in a low, far-off voice*). The holy Rabbi Susi of Anipol was as poor as a beggar all his life long. Often he depended on alms for his existence. He wore a peasant's blouse with a rope for a belt. Yet his accomplishments were not inferior to those of the Rabbis of Talan and Ruzhin.

FIRST BATLON (*annoyed*). Nothing of the kind; excuse me, but you're breaking in on us without any idea of what we're really discussing. You don't suppose that when we talk of the greatness of the Talan and Ruzhin Rabbis, we mean their wealth, do you? As though there aren't plenty of men in the world whose riches make their importance! No, the point is that a deep and secret significance lies behind the golden chair and the orchestra of four-and-twenty musicians and the golden slippers.

THIRD BATLON. As though everyone doesn't know that!

SECOND BATLON. Everyone that isn't altogether blind, does. It is said that when the Rabbi of Apt first met the Sage of Ruzhin, he flung himself at the Sage's carriage-wheels to kiss them. And when asked the significance of that action, he shouted: "Fools! Can't you see that this is the chariot of the Lord Himself?"

THIRD BATLON (*enraptured*). Ay, ay, ay!

FIRST BATLON. Now the essence of the matter is this: The golden chair was no chair; the orchestra was no orchestra, and the horses no horses. They were merely the semblance of these things, a reflection, and their purpose was to provide a setting for greatness.

THE MESSENGER. True greatness needs no setting.

FIRST BATLON. You are mistaken. True greatness must have the setting which befits it.

SECOND BATLON (*shrugging his shoulders*). How can greatness and perfection such as theirs be measured at all?

FIRST BATLON. It is no matter for jesting. Did you ever hear the story of Rabbi Schmelke of Nikolsberg's whip? It's worth knowing. One day Rabbi Schmelke was called upon to settle a dispute between a poor man and a rich one who was on terms of friendship with the king and before whom, in consequence, everyone trembled. Rabbi Schmelke heard both sides of the case, and then gave his decision by which the poor man won. The rich man was furious and declared that he would not stand by the Rabbi's verdict. And the Rabbi calmly replied: "You shall do as I have said. When a Rabbi commands, his commands are obeyed." The rich man's anger increased and he began to shout: "I snap my fingers at you and your rabbinical authority." Thereupon Rabbi Schmelke drew himself up to his full height, and cried: "Do instantly as I have said, or I shall resort to my whip!" This drove the rich man into a frenzy of rage, and he began to overwhelm the Rabbi with terrible insults. Then the Rabbi, perfectly calm, opens a drawer in his table—just a little way—and what should jump out of it but the Original Serpent, which coils about the neck of the rich man. Oh, oh, what a commotion follows! The rich man yells at the top of his voice, and throws himself into the most terrible contortions. "Rabbi! Rabbi! Forgive me! I'll do whatever you command—only call off your serpent." "Tell your children and your children's children to obey the Rabbi, and fear his whip," answered Rabbi Schmelke, and called the serpent off.

THIRD BATLON. Ha, ha, ha! There was a whip for you! (*Pause.*)

SECOND BATLON (*to* FIRST BATLON). You must have made a mistake, I think. The story couldn't have meant the Original Serpent. . . .

THIRD BATLON. Why . . . what . . .

SECOND BATLON. It's quite simple. Schmelke of Nikolsberg could not possibly have used the Original Serpent, for that was Satan himself, the enemy of God— (May he have mercy upon us!) (*He spits.*)

THIRD BATLON. Rabbi Schmelke knew what he was about—no doubt of that.

FIRST BATLON (*insulted*). I don't know what you're talking about. The incident I've just told you took place before a whole townful of people—dozens of them actually saw it with their own eyes. And here *you* come along and say it couldn't have happened. Just because you've got to have something to argue about, I suppose.

SECOND BATLON. Not at all. I only thought there couldn't be any spells or signs that the Serpent could be summoned by. (*He spits.*)

MESSENGER. Only in one way can Satan be summoned, and that is by the utterance of the mighty double-name of God, the flame of which has power to weld together the loftiest mountain-crests and the deepest valleys below them. (CHANNON *lifts his head and listens intently.*)

THIRD BATLON (*uneasily*). But isn't there danger in speaking that great name?

MESSENGER (*meditatively*). Danger? No. Only the heat of a too intense desire can cause the vessel to burst when the spark breaks into a flame.

FIRST BATLON. There's a wonder-worker in the village I come from. He's a terrific fellow, but he *can* work miracles. For instance, he can start a fire with one spell and put it out with another. He can see what's going on a hundred miles away. He can bring wine out of the wall by tapping it with his finger. And a great many other things besides. He told me himself that he knows spells that can create monsters and resurrect the dead. He can make himself invisible, too, and evoke evil spirits—even Satan himself. (*He spits*) I have his own word for it.

CHANNON (*who has never moved from his place, but has listened attentively to all this discussion, now steps up to the table and gazes first into the face of the* MESSENGER, *then at the* FIRST BATLON. *In a dreamy, remote voice*). Where is he?
(*The* MESSENGER *returns* CHANNON's *gaze with equal intensity, and thereafter never takes his eyes off him.*)

FIRST BATLON (*astonished*). Who?

CHANNON. The wonder-worker.

FIRST BATLON. Where could he be but in my own village? That is, if he's still alive.

CHANNON. Is it far?

FIRST BATLON. The village? Oh, very far. A long, long way down into the marsh-lands of Polesia.

CHANNON. *How* far?

FIRST BATLON. A good month, if not more. (*Pause*) What makes you ask? Do you want to see him? (CHANNON *does not answer*) Krasny's the name of the village. And the miracle-worker's name is Rabbi Elchannon.

CHANNON (*in astonishment—as if to himself*). Elchannon? . . . El Channon! . . . that means the God of Channon.

FIRST BATLON (*to the other batlonim*). And he's a *real* one, I promise you. Why, one day in broad daylight he showed, by means of a spell, that . . .

SECOND BATLON (*interrupting*). That'll do about such things. They aren't for this time of night, especially in a holy place. You may not mean it, but it might just happen that you'll pronounce some spell or make some sign yourself (God forbid), and then there'll be a disaster . . . Accidents like that (God forbid) have been known to happen before.
(CHANNON *goes slowly out, the others following him with their eyes. There is a pause.*)

MESSENGER. Who is that youth?

FIRST BATLON. Just a young student in the *yeshiva.**
(MEYER *closes the gates of the bima and crosses to the table.*)

* A higher religious school.

SECOND BATLON. A vessel beyond price—an Elui.†

THIRD BATLON. A brain of steel. He has five hundred pages of the Talmud by heart, at his fingertips.

MESSENGER. Where is he from?

MEYER. Somewhere in Lithuania —in the *yeshiva* here, he was famous as their finest scholar. He was granted the degree of rabbi, and then, all of a sudden, he vanished. No more was heard of him for a whole year, and it was said that he was doing the great penance of the Golos* When he returned— which was not long ago—he had changed entirely, and he has since been going about absorbed in deep meditation, from which nothing ever arouses him. He fasts from Sabbath to Sabbath and performs the holy ablutions continually. (*Whispering*) There is a rumor that he is studying the Kabala.†

SECOND BATLON (*likewise*). It has spread to the city, too. He has already been asked to give charms, but he always refuses.

THIRD BATLON. Who knows who he

† A scholar whose genius consists in his remarkable memory, and capacity for learning.
* The Exile of the Jews. According to religious tradition, the golos was imposed upon the race as a punishment. In the original Yiddish the "Penance of the golos" reads "Abrichten golos." The penitent, by wearing a hair-shirt and performing other acts of mortification of the flesh, and wandering through the world as a beggar, hoped to assist in the redemption of the race by shortening the period of exile.
† System of Hebrew mysticism.

is? One of the Great Ones, maybe. Who can tell? It would be dangerous most likely to spy on him. (*Pause.*)

SECOND BATLON (*peacefully*). It's late—let's go to bed. (*To the* FIRST BATLON, *smiling*) Pity your miracleworker isn't here to tap us some wine out of the wall. I could do with a drop of brandy to cheer me up—I've not had a bite all day long.

FIRST BATLON. It's been practically a fast day for me, too. Since early morning prayers, a crust of oaten bread is the only thing I've had a chance to say grace over.

MEYER (*mysteriously, and in high glee*). Never mind—you just wait a bit, and very soon there'll be a deal of cheer going round. Sender's been after a bridegroom for his daughter. Only let him get the contract signed—it'l' be a happy hour for him when *that's* done—and he'll be good for a grand spread.

SECOND BATLON. Bah! I don't believe he'll ever sign one. Three times he's been to get a bridegroom. Either it's the young man he doesn't like, or else the family that's not aristocratic enough, or it's the dowry. It's wicked to be as fastidious as all that.

MEYER. Sender has the right to pick and choose if he wants to (may he be protected from the evil eye). He's rich, and an aristocrat, and his only daughter has grown up a good and beautiful girl.

THIRD BATLON (*ravished*). I love Sender. He's a true Miropol Chassid*—there's some real spirit to *them.*

* A Jewish sect.

FIRST BATLON (*coldly*). Yes—he's a good Chassid. There's no denying that. But he might have done something very different with his only daughter.

THIRD BATLON. How do you mean?

FIRST BATLON. In the old days, when a man of wealth and fine family wanted a husband for his daughter, he didn't look for money or blue blood, but only for nobility of character. He went to the big *yeshiva* and gave the head a handsome gift to pick out for him the flower of the school for a son-in-law. Sender could have done this, too.

MESSENGER. He might even have found one in this *yeshiva* here.

FIRST BATLON (*surprised*). How do you know?

MESSENGER. I'm only supposing.

THIRD BATLON (*hastily*). Well, well—let's not gossip—particularly about one of our own people. Marriages are all prearranged by destiny, anyhow.

(*The street door is flung open, and an elderly Jewess hastens in, leading two small children.*)

ELDERLY WOMAN (*rushes to the altar with the children*). Aie! Aie! Lord of the earth, help me! Come, children—let us open the Ark and throw ourselves upon the holy scrolls and not leave them until our tears have won your mother back from the valley of the shadow. (*She wrenches open the doors of the Ark and buries her head amongst the scrolls, intoning a wailing chant*) God of Abraham, Isaac and Jacob, look down upon my misery. Look down upon the grief of these little ones, and do not take their mother away from the world, in the years of her youth. Holy Scrolls! Do *you* intercede for the forlorn widow. Holy scrolls, beloved Mothers of Israel, go to the Almighty and beseech Him that He shall not uproot the lovely sapling, nor cast the young dove out of its nest, nor tear the gentle lamb away from the meadow. (*Hysterically*) I will pull down the worlds—I will tear the heavens apart—but from here I will not go until they give back to me the one who is the crown of my head.

MEYER (*crosses to her and speaks to her calmly*). Hannah Esther—wouldn't you like to have a *minyen** sit down and say the psalms for you?

ELDERLY WOMAN (*withdraws from the altar and looks at* MEYER *at first uncomprehendingly. Then she begins to speak in agitation*). Yes—a *minyen* for psalms. But hurry—hurry—every second is precious. For two days already, God help her, she's been lying there without speaking, fighting with death.

MEYER. I'll have them sit down this minute. (*In the voice of a beggar*) But you'll have to give them something for their trouble, poor things.

ELDERLY WOMAN (*searching in her pocket*). Here's ten kopeks—but see they say the psalms for it.

MEYER. Ten kopeks . . . one kopek each . . . little enough, that is!

* Ten or more adult males constituting a Jewish community.

ELDERLY WOMAN (*not hearing*). Come, children, let us run along to the other prayer-houses. (*Hurries out with the children.*)

MESSENGER (*to* THIRD BATLON). This morning a woman came to the Ark for her daughter, who had been in the throes of labor for two days and had not yet given birth. And here comes another for hers, who has been wrestling for two days with death.

THIRD BATLON. Well, what of it?

MESSENGER (*deep in thought*). When the soul of a human being not yet dead is about to enter a body not yet born, a struggle takes place. If the sick one dies, the child is born—if the sick one recovers, a child is born dead.

FIRST BATLON (*surprised*). Ei, ei, ei! The blindness of people! Things happen all round them, but they have no eyes to see them with.

MEYER (*at the table*). See, here's a treat from above! Let's get the psalms over, then we'll have a drop of something. And the Lord will have mercy on the sick woman and send her a quick recovery.

FIRST BATLON (*to the scholars sitting around the big table, half asleep*). Who wants to say psalms, boys? There's a bit of oat bread for everyone that does. (*The scholars get up*) Let's go in there.
(*The three* BATLONIM, MEYER *and the scholars, except* CHENNOCH, *pass into the adjoining prayer-room, whence the chanting of "Blessed be the man" presently emerges. The* MESSENGER *remains throughout beside the small table,*

immovable. His eyes never leave the Ark. There is a long pause. Then* CHANNON *comes in.*)

CHANNON (*very weary, walks aimlessly across to the Ark, sunk in meditation. He seems surprised to find it open*). Open? Who can have opened it? For whom has it opened in the middle of the night? (*He looks in*) The scrolls of the Law . . . there they stand like comrades, shoulder to shoulder, so calm . . . so silent. All secrets and symbols hidden in them. And all miracles—from the six days of creation, unto the end of all the generations of men. Yet how hard it is to wrest one secret or one symbol from them—how hard! (*He counts the scrolls*) One, two, three, four, five, six, seven, eight, nine. That makes the word Truth, according to the Minor system. In each scroll there are four Trees of Life.* There again it comes—thirty-six. Not an hour passes but this number faces me in one manner or another. I do not know the meaning of it, but I have the intuition that within it lies the whole essence of the matter. . . . Thirty-six is Leah. Three times thirty-six is Channon. . . . Le-ah —that makes Le-ha, which means Not God . . . not through God . . . (*He shudders*) A terrible thought . . . and yet it draws me nearer . . . and nearer. . . .

CHENNOCH (*looks up from his book, attentively at* CHANNON). Channon! You go about dreaming all the time.

CHANNON (*moves away from the Ark, and slowly approaches* CHENNOCH, *standing before him, lost in*

* The handles at the top and bottom of each scroll.

thought). Nothing—nothing but secrets and symbols—and the right path is not to be found. (*Short pause*) Krasny is the name of the village . . . and the miracle-man's name is Rabbi Elchannon . . .

CHENNOCH. What's that you're saying?

CHANNON (*as if waking out of a trance*). I? Nothing. I was only thinking.

CHENNOCH (*shaking his head*). You've been meddling with the Kabala, Channon. Ever since you came back, you haven't had a book in your hand.

CHANNON (*not understanding*). Not had a book in my hand? What book do you mean?

CHENNOCH. The Talmud of course —the Laws. You know very well . . .

CHANNON (*still in his dreams*). Talmud? The Laws? Never had them in my hand? The Talmud is cold and dry . . . so are the Laws (*Comes to himself suddenly. He speaks with animation*) Under the earth's surface, Chennoch, there is a world exactly the same as ours upon it, with fields and forests, seas and deserts, cities and villages. Storms rage over the deserts and over the seas upon which sail great ships. And over the dense forests, reverberating with the roll of thunder, eternal fear holds sway. Only in the absence of one thing does that world differ from ours. There is no sky, from which the sun pours down its burning heat and bolts of fire fall. . . . So it is with the Talmud. It is deep and glorious and

vast. But it chains you to the earth —it forbids you to attempt the heights. (*With enthusiasm*) But the Kabala, the Kabala tears your soul away from earth and lifts you to the realms of the highest heights. Spreads all the heavens out before your eyes, and leads direct to Pardes,* reaches out in the infinite, and raises a corner of the great curtain itself. (*Collapses*) My heart turns faint—I have no strength. . . .

CHENNOCH (*solemnly*). That is all true. But you forget that those ecstatic flights into the upper regions are fraught with the utmost peril, for it is there that you are likely to come to grief and hurl yourself into the deepest pit below. The Talmud raises the soul toward the heights by slow degrees, but keeps guard over it like a faithful sentinel, who neither sleeps nor dreams. The Talmud clothes the soul with an armor of steel and keeps it ever on the strait path so that it stray neither to the right nor to the left. But the Kabala. . . . Remember what the Talmud says: (*He chants the following in the manner of Talmudic recitation*) Four reached Pardes. Ben Azzai, Ben Zoma, Acher and Rabbi Akiva. Ben Azzai looked within and died. Ben Zoma looked within and lost his reason. Acher renounced the fundamentals of all belief. Rabbi Akiva alone went in and came out again unscathed.

CHANNON. Don't try to frighten me with them. We don't know how they went, nor with what. They may have failed because they went to look and not to offer themselves as a sacrifice. But others went after them—that we know. Holy Ari and

* Paradise.

the Holy Balshem.* They did not fail.

CHENNOCH. Are you comparing yourself to them?

CHANNON. To nobody. I go my own way.

CHENNOCH. What sort of way is that?

CHANNON. You wouldn't understand.

CHENNOCH. I wish to and I will. My soul, too, is drawn toward the high planes.

CHANNON (*after a moment's reflection*). The service of our holy men consists in cleansing human souls, tearing away the sin that clings to them and raising them to the shining source whence they come. Their work is very difficult because sin is ever lurking at the door. No sooner is one soul cleansed than another comes in its place, more sincorroded still. No sooner is one generation brought to repentance than the next one appears, more stiff-necked than the last. And as each generation grows weaker, its sins become stronger, and the holy men fewer and fewer.

CHENNOCH. Then, according to your philosophy, what ought to be done?

CHANNON (*quietly, but with absolute conviction*). There is no need to wage war on sin. All that is necessary is to burn it away, as the goldsmith refines gold in his powerful flame; as the farmer winnows

* The founder of the Chassidic sect, known as the Basht.

the grain from the chaff. So must sin be refined of its uncleanness, until only its holiness remains.

CHENNOCH (*astonished*). Holiness in sin? How do you make that out?

CHANNON. Everything created by God contains a spark of holiness.

CHENNOCH. Sin was not created by God but by Satan.

CHANNON. And who created Satan? God. Since he is the antithesis of God, he is an aspect of God, and therefore must contain also a germ of holiness.

CHENNOCH (*crushed*). Holiness in Satan? I can't . . . I don't understand. . . . Let me think. . . . (*His head sinks into his hands, propped up by both elbows on the desk. There is a pause.*)

CHANNON (*stands beside him and in a trembling voice, bending down to reach his ear*). Which sin is the strongest of all? Which one is the hardest to conquer? The sin of lust for a woman, isn't it?

CHENNOCH (*without raising his head*). Yes.

CHANNON. And when you have cleansed this sin in a powerful flame, then this greatest uncleanness becomes the greatest holiness. It becomes "The Song of Songs." (*He holds his breath*) The Song of Songs. (*Drawing himself up, he begins to chant in a voice which, though subdued, is charged with rapture*) Behold thou art fair, my love. Thou hast dove's eyes within thy locks; thy hair is as a flock of goats that appear from Mount

Gilead. Thy teeth are like a flock of sheep that are even shorn, which came up from the washing; whereof every one bear twins and none barren among them.

(MEYER *comes out of the prayer-room. A gentle knocking is heard at the street door, which is pushed hesitatingly open, and* LEAH *enters. She has hold of* FRADE's *hand, and behind them comes* GITTEL. *They stop in the doorway.* MEYER *turns and sees them, and goes over to them, surprised, welcoming them obsequiously.*)

MEYER. Look! Here comes Sender's daughter, little Leah!

LEAH (*shyly*). You promised to show me the old embroidered curtains of the Ark—do you remember?

(CHANNON, *hearing her voice, abruptly interrupts his song, and stares at her with all his eyes. As long as she remains in the synagogue, he alternately gazes at her thus, and closes his eyes in ecstasy.*)

FRADE. Show her the curtains, Meyer—the old ones, and the most beautiful. Our dear Leah has said she will embroider a new one for the anniversary of her mother's death. She will work it with the purest gold upon the finest of velvet, just as they used to do in the olden days—little lions and eagles. And when it is hung over the Ark, her mother's pure spirit will rejoice in Eden.

(LEAH *looks timidly about her, and seeing* CHANNON, *lowers her eyes in embarrassment and keeps them so for the rest of the scene.*)

MEYER. Oh, with the greatest pleasure. Why not, why not indeed? I'll bring the oldest and most beautiful curtains to show her—at once, this very minute. (*He goes to the chest near the street door and takes out the curtains.*)

GITTEL (*taking* LEAH's *hand*). Aren't you afraid to be in the synagogue at night, Leah?

LEAH. I've never been here at night before, except on the Days of the Holy Scrolls. But that's a feast day and everything is bright and joyful then. How sad it is now, though—how sad!

FRADE. Dear children—a synagogue *must* be sad. The dead come here at midnight to pray, and when they go they leave their sorrows behind them.

GITTEL. Don't talk about the dead, Granny. It frightens me.

FRADE (*not hearing her*). And each day at dawn, when the Almighty weeps for the destruction of the Holy Temple, His sacred tears fall in the synagogues. That is why the walls of all old synagogues look as if they have been wept over, and that is why it is forbidden to whitewash them and make them bright again. If you attempt to, they grow angry and throw their stones at you.

LEAH. How old it is—how old! It doesn't show so much from outside.

FRADE. Old it is, little daughter—very, very old. They even say it was found already built under the earth. Many a time this city has been destroyed, and many a time it has been laid in ashes. But this synagogue, never. Fire broke out once on the roof, but almost before it had begun to burn, innumerable doves came flocking down upon it and beat out the flames with their wings.

LEAH (*not hearing—speaking to herself*). How sad it is! How lovely! I feel that I want never to go away from it again. I wish I could put my arms around those ancient, tear-stained walls and ask them why they are so sorrowful, and so wrapped in dreams . . . so silent and so sad. I wish . . . I don't know what I wish. . . . But my heart is filled with tenderness and pity.

MEYER (*brings the curtains to the* bima, *and spreads one out to show*). This is the oldest of all—a good two hundred years or more. It is never used except on Passover.

GITTEL (*enraptured*). Leah, dear—just look. Isn't it gorgeous! Such stiff brown velvet, all embroidered in heavy gold. Two lions holding the shield of David above their heads. And trees on either side, with doves in their branches. You can't get velvet nowadays, nor such gold either.

LEAH. The curtain is sad, too—I love it also. (*She smooths it out and kisses it.*)

GITTEL (*takes* LEAH's *hand and whispers*). Look, Leah, dear! There's a student over there staring at you—so strangely!

LEAH (*keeping her eyes still more downcast*). That is Channon. He was a poor scholar, and he used to be a guest in our house.

GITTEL. It is as if he were calling to you with his eyes, he stares so. He would like to talk to you, but he is afraid to.

LEAH. I wish I knew why he is so pale and sad. He must surely have been ill.

GITTEL. He isn't sad really—his eyes are shining.

LEAH. They always are. He has wonderful eyes, and when he talks to me his breath comes short—and so does mine. It wouldn't be proper for a girl to talk to a strange young man.

FRADE (*to* MEYER). Won't you let us kiss the holy scrolls? Surely! How could one be a guest in the house of God and leave without kissing His holy scrolls?

MEYER. By all means, by all means! Come! (*He goes ahead, followed by* GITTEL *leading* FRADE, *and* LEAH *behind them.* MEYER *takes out a scroll and gives it to* FRADE *to kiss.*)

LEAH (*passing* CHANNON, *stops for a moment and says in a low voice*). Good evening, Channon. You have come back?

CHANNON (*scarcely able to speak for agitation*). Yes.

FRADE. Come, Leah, darling, kiss the holy scrolls. (LEAH *goes to the Ark.* MEYER *hands her a scroll, which she takes in her arms and, pressing her lips against it, kisses passionately*) Now, now, child! That will do. A holy scroll must not be kissed too long. They are written in black fire upon white fire. (*In sudden alarm*) How late it is!

How very late! Come, children, let us hurry home—come quickly. (*They hasten out.* MEYER *closes the Ark and follows them.*)

CHANNON (*stands for a while with closed eyes; then resumes his chanting of the "Song of Songs" where he left off*). Thy lips are like a thread of scarlet, and thy speech is comely. Thy temples are like a piece of pomegranate within thy locks.

CHENNOCH (*raises his head and looks at* CHANNON). Channon, what are you singing? (CHANNON *stops singing and looks at* CHENNOCH) Your ear-locks are wet. You have been to the Mikva* again.

CHANNON. Yes.

CHENNOCH. When you perform the ablutions, do you also use spells and go through all the ceremonies prescribed by the book of Roziel? ˚

CHANNON. Yes.

CHENNOCH. You aren't afraid to?

CHANNON. No.

CHENNOCH. And you fast from Sabbath to Sabbath—isn't that hard for you?

CHANNON. It's harder for me to eat on the Sabbath than to fast the whole week. (*Pause*) I've lost all desire to eat.

CHENNOCH (*inviting confidence*). What do you do all this for? What do you expect to gain by it?

* Ritual bath.
˚ One of the books of the Kabala.

CHANNON (*as if to himself*). I wish . . . I wish to attain possession of a clear and sparkling diamond, and melt it down in tears and inhale it into my soul. I want to attain to the rays of the third plane of beauty. I want . . . (*Suddenly in violent perturbation*) Yes—there are still two barrels of golden pieces which I *must* get, for him who can count only gold pieces.

CHENNOCH (*appalled*). Channon, be careful! You're on a slippery road. No holy powers will help you to achieve these things.

CHANNON (*challenging him*). And if the *holy* powers will not, then?

CHENNOCH (*terrified*). I'm afraid to talk to you! I'm afraid to be near you! (*He rushes out.* CHANNON *remains behind, his face full of defiance.* MEYER *comes back from the street. The* FIRST BATLON *emerges from the prayer-room.*)

FIRST BATLON. Eighteen psalms— that's enough and to spare! I suppose she doesn't expect to get the whole bookful for a kopek! You go and tell them, Meyer. Once they get started, there's no stopping them till they've said them all. (*Enter* ASHER *in great excitement.*)

ASHER. I just met Baruch the tailor. He's come back from Klimovka— that's where Sender's been to meet the bridegroom's people. They haven't come to terms yet, it seems. Sender insisted that the bridegroom's father should board the couple for ten years, but he stood out for only five. So they all went back home again.

MEYER. That makes the fourth time.

FIRST BATLON. Heartbreaking, isn't it?

MESSENGER (*to* THIRD BATLON, *smiling*). A little while ago you said yourself that all marriages were prearranged by destiny.

CHANNON (*straightening up and speaking in a voice of rapture*). I have won again. (*He falls exhausted onto a bench, his face alight with joy.*)

MESSENGER (*taking a lantern out of his bag*). Time to get ready for the road again.

MEYER. What's your hurry?

MESSENGER. I'm a messenger. Great ones and magnates employ me to carry important communications and rare treasures for them. I am obliged to hurry—my time is not my own.

MEYER. You ought to wait until daybreak at least.

MESSENGER. That is still a long way off, and I have far to go. I shall start about midnight.

MEYER. It's pitch-dark outside.

MESSENGER. I shan't lose my way with this lantern.
(*The scholars and* BATLONIM *come out of the prayer-room.*)

SECOND BATLON. Good luck be with us. May the Lord send the sick woman a complete recovery.

ALL. Amen.

FIRST BATLON. Now let's go and get ten kopeks' worth of cakes and brandy.

MEYER. It's here already. (*Takes a bottle and cakes from under his coat*) Come on, let's drink a health! (*The door opens and* SENDER *enters, coat unbuttoned, hat on the back of his head, thoroughly happy. Three or four men follow him in.*)

MEYER AND THE THREE BATLONIM. Oh, Reb Sender—welcome, welcome . . .

SENDER. Happened to be passing. I really must go in, says I to myself, and see what our people are doing. (*Noticing the bottle in* MEYER's *hand*) I'll surely find them studying, says I, or deep in pious discussions. And what do I see? They're all deep in preparing for a celebration instead! Ha, ha, ha! Typical Miropol Chassidim!

FIRST BATLON. Will you have a drop with us, Reb Sender?

SENDER. No, blockhead. I won't. I'll stand treat myself—and splendid treat at that! Congratulate me —this is a happy day for me. I have betrothed my daughter.
(CHANNON, *distraught, rises from his bench.*)

ALL. Mazeltov! Mazeltov! *

MEYER. Somebody just told us you hadn't been able to come to terms with the bridegroom's father, and so it had all fallen through.

THIRD BATLON. We were heartbroken to hear it.

SENDER. It nearly did, but at the last moment he gave in, and so the

* Good luck

contract was signed. May good luck go with it.

CHANNON. Betrothed? Betrothed? How can that be? (*In despair*) So it was all of no avail—neither the fasts, nor the ablutions, nor the spells, nor the symbols. All in vain. . . . So what remains? What is there still to do . . . by what means . . . (*He clutches the breast of his kaftan, and his face is illuminated with ecstasy*) Ah! The secret of the Double Name is revealed to me. Ah! I see him. I . . . I . . . I have won! (*He falls to the ground.*)

MESSENGER (*opens his lantern*). The wick has burnt down. A new one must be lighted. (*An ominous pause.*)

SENDER. Meyer, why is it so dark in here? Let's have some light. (MEYER *lights another light.*)

MESSENGER (*crosses quietly to* SENDER). Did you come to terms with the bridegroom's father?

SENDER (*surprised and somewhat frightened, looks at him*). I did.

MESSENGER. Sometimes it happens that the relatives promise, and then go back on their word. And litigation follows. It pays to be very careful in these matters.

SENDER (*in alarm*). Who is this man? I don't know him.

MEYER. He is not from these parts. He is a Messenger.

SENDER. What does he want of me?

MEYER. I don't know.

SENDER (*more calmly*). Asher, run over to my house and ask them to prepare some wine and preserves and something good to eat. Hurry up, now—run along. (ASHER *hastens out*) We might as well stay here and talk a bit while they're getting things ready. Hasn't one of you some new parable of our Rabbi's? A saying, or a miracle, or a proverb . . . each of his looks is more precious than pearls.

FIRST BATLON (*to* MEYER). Keep the bottle. It'll come in handy tomorrow. (MEYER *puts it away.*)

MESSENGER. I'll tell you one of his proverbs. One day a Chassid came to the Rabbi—he was rich, but a miser. The Rabbi took him by the hand and led him to the window. "Look out there," he said. And the rich man looked into the street. "What do you see?" asked the Rabbi. "People," answers the rich man. Again the Rabbi takes him by the hand, and this time leads him to the mirror. "What do you see now?" he says. "Now I see myself," answers the rich man. Then the Rabbi says: "Behold—in the window there is glass and in the mirror there is glass. But the glass of the mirror is covered with a little silver, and no sooner is the silver added than you cease to see others but see only yourself."

THIRD BATLON. Oh, oh, oh! Sweeter than honey!

FIRST BATLON. Holy words!

SENDER (*to the* MESSENGER). You are trying to score off me, eh?

MESSENGER. God forbid!

SECOND BATLON. Let's have a song! (*To the* THIRD BATLON) Sing the Rabbi's tune.
(*The* THIRD BATLON *begins intoning a low mysterious Chassidic tune in which the rest join.*)

SENDER (*rising*). And now a dance, a round dance. . . . Shall Sender give away his only daughter, and not celebrate it with a round dance? *Nice* Chassidim we'd be! (SENDER, *the three* BATLONIM *and* MEYER *put their arms on one another's shoulders and start turning in a ring, their eyes dim with ecstasy, chanting a weird, monotonous air. They revolve slowly, on the same spot. Then* SENDER *breaks away from the circle.*)

SENDER. Now a merry one. Come on—all together!

SECOND BATLON. Yes, come on, boys —let's all join in! (*Several of the scholars join them*) Chennoch, Channon, where are you? We're going to have a merry dance—come on!

SENDER (*somewhat perturbed*). Ah, Channon . . . he's here, my little Channon, isn't he? Where is he, eh? Bring him here—I want him.

MEYER (*sees* CHANNON *on the floor*). He's asleep on the floor.

SENDER. Wake him up then. Wake him up.

MEYER (*tries to rouse him. Frightened*). I can't——
(*They all crowd round* CHANNON, *and try to wake him.*)

FIRST BATLON (*with a frightened cry*). He's dead.

THIRD BATLON. The book of Roziel, the King—look—it's fallen out of his hand!
(*Consternation.*)

CURTAIN

ACT TWO

A square in Brainitz. Left, the old synagogue, built of wood and of ancient architecture. In front of it, somewhat to one side, a mound surmounted by a gravestone bearing the inscription, "Here lie a pure and holy bridegroom and bride, murdered to the glory of God in the year 5408. Peace be with them." An alley on one side of the synagogue, leading to a group of small houses which merge into the backdrop.
At the right, SENDER'S *house, also built of wood, but of imposing size and adorned with a balcony and stoop. Past the house a wide double-gate to the courtyard gives onto another alley with a row of small shops which also merge into the backdrop. On the drop to the right, past the shops, an inn, then the garden of a large estate and the owner's mansion. A wide road leading down to a river upon whose farther bank a cemetery is seen. To the left, a bridge over the river and a mill.*

In the foreground, bathhouse and poorhouse. In the far distance, a forest. The double gates to SENDER'S *courtyard stand wide open. Long tables have been set out in the yard, and jut out onto the square. The tables are spread with food which the poor, old and young, some of them crippled, are ravenously devouring. They are served continuously from the house, from great bowls of food and baskets with bread.*

Before the shops and houses, women sit knitting, but their eyes hardly leave SENDER'S *house. Men, old and young, leave the synagogue carrying their prayer-shawls and phylacteries, and go into the shops and houses. Some stand about talking in groups. Music is heard from the courtyard. Then dancing and the confused sound of voices.*

It is evening. In the middle of the street, in front of the synagogue stands the WEDDING GUEST, *a middle-aged Jew in a satin kaftan, his hands stuck into his belt. The* SECOND BATLON *is with him.*

GUEST (*gazing at the synagogue*). A great synagogue you have here— a handsome building indeed—and spacious, too. The spirit of God is upon it. Very old, I should say.

SECOND BATLON. Very old it is. Our ancients say that not even their grandfathers could remember when it was built.

GUEST (*seeing the grave*). And what is that? (*He reads the inscription*) "Here lie a pure and holy bridegroom and bride, murdered to the glory of God in the year 5408." A bride and bridegroom— murdered to the glory of God?

SECOND BATLON. Yes—by that bandit Chamilouk*—may his name be wiped out forever—when he raided the city with his Cossacks and massacred half the Jews. He murdered that bride and groom as they were being led to the wedding canopy. They were buried on the very spot, in one grave together. Ever since, it has been called the holy grave. (*Whispering, as if he were telling a secret*) At

* Chmelnitzki the Cossack chieftain who led a great uprising in which thousands of Jews perished.

every marriage ceremony, the rabbi hears sighs from the grave, and it has become a time-honored custom for the people leaving the synagogue after a wedding to go and dance there, to cheer the dead bride and bridegroom where they lie.

GUEST. An excellent custom. . . .

MEYER (*coming out of* SENDER'S *house*). Ah, such a feast for the poor. Never in all my born days have I seen the equal of this spread Sender's made for them.

GUEST. No wonder. He's giving away his only daughter.

MEYER (*with enthusiasm*). First a piece of fish; then a cut of roast, and a zimmis* to top it off. And cake and brandy before the meal began! . . . It must have cost him a fortune—more than can ever be reckoned up!

SECOND BATLON. Leave it to Sender to know his own business. When it comes to skimping an invited guest, you know where you are—let him snort all he likes, he can't do anything. But it's flying in the face of

* A vegetable delicacy.

danger not to treat the poor right. There's no telling who a beggar's coat may be hiding. A beggar maybe, but maybe also someone quite different . . . a nister† . . . or one of the Thirty-six.‡

MEYER. Why not the Prophet Elijah himself? He always appears as a beggar.

GUEST. It's not only the poor it pays to be careful with. You can't say for a certainty who any man might have been in his last existence, nor what he is doing on earth.
(*From the alley on the right, the* MESSENGER *enters, with his knapsack on his shoulder.*)

MEYER (*to the* MESSENGER). Sholom aleichem*—you have come back, I see.

MESSENGER. I have been sent to you again.

MEYER. You have come in good season, in time for a great wedding.

MESSENGER. I know—it is the talk of all the country round.

MEYER. Did you happen to pass the bridegroom's party on the way? They are late.

MESSENGER. The bridegroom will arrive in good time. (*He goes into the synagogue, and the* GUEST, MEYER *and the* SECOND BATLON *turn into* SENDER's *courtyard.* LEAH *appears beyond the tables, in her wedding-dress, danc-*

† A saint disguised.
‡ Thirty-six men of virtue, on whose account God allows the world to continue.
* Peace be with you.

ing with one after another of the old women. The rest crowd about her. Those with whom she has finished dancing pass into the square, and stand talking in groups.)

A POOR WOMAN (*with child holding on to her skirts. In a tone of satisfaction*). I danced with the bride.

LAME WOMAN. So did I. I took her round the waist and danced with her too. Hee, hee, hee!

A HUNCHBACK. How's that? The bride only dancing with the women? I'm going to take her by the waist myself, and swing her round and round. Ha, ha, ha!
(*General laughter among the beggars.* FRADE, GITTEL *and* BASSIA *come from the house onto the stoop.*)

FRADE (*worried*). Oh, dear! Oh dear! There's the darling still dancing with those people. She'll make herself dizzy if she doesn't stop. Go and tell her to come here, children.

GITTEL (*going to* LEAH). Come away, Leah dear—you've danced enough now.

BASSIA. Yes—you'll be getting dizzy. . . .
(*They take* LEAH's *hands and try to draw her away.*)

THE POOR WOMEN (*gather round* LEAH *beseeching her in whining tones*). She hasn't danced with *me* yet. . . . Aren't I as good as them? . . . I've been waiting an hour. . . . Me . . . Me. . . . It's my turn after Elka. . . . She's been round ten times and more with that lame Yachna, and not one single turn with me. . . . I've never got no luck!

(MEYER *comes out into the square and stands on the bench. In a high-pitched voice, he chants the following verse in the manner of a herald.*)
Come in, come in, and feast your fill,
Rich Sender bids you straightway come!
Here's abundance and goodwill,
And ten kopeks for everyone!

THE POOR (*run out jostling one another*). Ten kopeks! Ten kopeks! (*The square is left empty except for* LEAH, GITTEL, BASSIA *and an old half-blind beggar woman.*)

THE OLD WOMAN (*seizes* LEAH). I don't want no alms. . . . I only want you to dance with me. Just once—just one turn. That's all. I've not danced once these forty years. . . . Oh, how I used to dance when *I* was a girl! How I *did* dance! (LEAH *dances with her, but when she tries to release herself, the crone will not let her go, but begs for more and more*) Again . . . again. . . . (*They swing round faster still, the old woman now out of breath and hysterical*) More . . . more. . . .
(GITTEL *has to force her into the courtyard. Then she comes back, and together with* BASSIA, *they assist* LEAH *to a bench.* SENDER's *servants clear the tables and close the gate.*)

FRADE. Oh, my darling, you're as white as a sheet. They've worn you out, so they have.

LEAH (*sits with closed eyes, her head leaning backward, and when she speaks, it is as though in a trance*). They seized me . . . they kept on turning and turning round me . . . so close . . . and clutched me to them with their cold, withered hands . . . my head swam . . . my heart turned faint. Then someone came and lifted me from the ground and carried me far away, very far away.

BASSIA (*in great anxiety*). Oh, Leah, look how they've crushed your dress—it's all dirty now. Whatever will you do?

LEAH (*in the same manner as before*). If the bride is left alone before the wedding, spirits come and carry her off.

FRADE (*alarmed*). What can have put such ideas into your head, my child? We may not mention the dark people—you know that. They're lurking in every tiny hole and corner and crevice. They see everything and hear everything—and they're forever on the alert to catch their unclean names on our lips. Then out they spring on top of you. (*She spits three times.*)

LEAH (*opens her eyes*). My spirits are not evil ones.

FRADE. Don't you believe them, my child. The minute you trust one of the dark people, he becomes unmanageable and begins to do mischief.

LEAH (*with utter conviction*). Granny—it isn't evil spirits that surround us, but souls of those who died before their time, and come back again to see all that we do and hear all that we say.

FRADE. God help you, child, what is the meaning of all this? Souls? What souls? The souls of the pure and good fly up to heaven and stay there at rest in the bright garden of Eden.

LEAH. No, granny—they are with us here. (*Her tone changes*) Grandmother, every one of us is born to a long life of many, many years. If he dies before his years are done, what becomes of the life he has not lived, do you think? What becomes of his joys and sorrows, and all the thoughts he had not time to think, and all the things he hadn't time to do? Where are the children he did not live long enough to bring into the world? Where does all that go to? Where? (*Lost in thought, she continues*) There was a lad here, granny . . . his mind was full of wisdom and his soul was set on holy purposes. Long years stretched out before him. Then one day, without warning, his life is destroyed. And strangers bury him in strange earth. (*Desperately*) What has become of the rest of him? His speech that has been silenced? His prayers that have been cut off? . . . Grandmother—when a candle blows out we light it again and it goes on burning down to the end. So how can a human life which goes out before it has burnt down, remain put out forever? . . . How can it, granny?

FRADE (*shaking her head*). Daughter, you must not think about such things. He who lives above knows the reason for His actions. We are blind and know nothing.
(*The MESSENGER approaches them unnoticed, and remains standing close behind them.*)

LEAH (*not hearing her. With deep conviction*). No, granny. No human life goes to waste. If one of us dies before his time, his soul returns to the world to complete its span, to do the things left undone and experience the happiness and griefs he would have known. (*A pause*) Granny, do you remember you told us how the dead go trooping at midnight into the synagogue? They go to pray the prayers they would have prayed in life, had they not died too soon. (*A pause*) My mother died in her youth and had no time to live through all that lay in store for her. That is why I go today to the cemetery to ask her to join my father when he leads me under the wedding-canopy. She will be with me there, and after the ceremony we shall dance together. It is the same with all the souls who leave the world before their time. They are here in our midst, unheard and invisible. Only if your desire is strong enough, you can see them, and hear their voices and learn their thoughts. . . . I can. . . . (*Pointing to the grave*) The holy grave— I have known it ever since I was a child. And I know the bride and bridegroom buried there. I've seen them often and often, sometimes in dreams and sometimes when I am wide awake. They are as near to me as my own people. . . . (*Deep in meditation*) They were on the way to their wedding, so young and lovely to see, with a long and beautiful life before them. But murderers set upon them with axes, and in a moment they both lay dead upon the ground. They were laid in one grave, so that they might be together for all time. (*She rises and goes to the grave, followed by* FRADE, GITTEL *and* BASSIA. *Stretching out her arms, she says in a loud voice*) Holy bridegroom and bride, I invite you to my wedding. Be with me under the canopy.

(*Gay march music is heard in the distance.* LEAH *screams in terror and almost falls.* GITTEL *catches her.*)

GITTEL. What is it, Leah dear? Don't be frightened. They must be greeting the bridegroom with music as he comes into the village.

BASSIA (*excited*). I'm going to take a peep at him.

GITTEL. I, too. We'll run back, Leah, and tell you what he looks like. Shall we?

LEAH (*shaking her head*). No.

BASSIA. She's only shy. Little stupid, there's nothing to be ashamed of. . . . We won't give you away! (*Exit* BASSIA *running, followed by* GITTEL.)

FRADE (*returning with* LEAH *to the stoop*). That is the custom, my child. The bride always sends her friend to see whether the groom is fair or dark, and . . .

MESSENGER (*approaching*). Bride!

LEAH (*shivers as she turns towards him*). Yes—what is it? (*She gazes fixedly at him.*)

MESSENGER. The souls of the dead *do* return to earth, but not as disembodied spirits. Some must pass through many forms before they achieve purification. (LEAH *listens with ever-increasing attention*) The souls of the wicked return in the forms of beasts, or birds, or fish— of plants even, and are powerless to purify themselves by their own efforts. They have to wait for the coming of some righteous sage to

purge them of their sins and set them free. Others enter the bodies of the newly born, and cleanse themselves by well-doing.

LEAH (*in tremulous eagerness*). Yes . . . yes. . . .

MESSENGER. Besides these, there are vagrant souls which, finding neither rest nor harbor, pass into the bodies of the living, in the form of a Dybbuk, until they have attained purity. (*Exit the* MESSENGER.)
(LEAH *remains lost in astonishment, as* SENDER *comes out of the house.*)

SENDER. Why are you sitting here like this, little daughter?

FRADE. She entertained the beggars at their meal and danced with them afterwards. They tired her, so she is resting awhile now.

SENDER. Entertaining the poor, eh? That is a sweet and pious deed. (*He looks up at the sky*) It is getting very late but the bridegroom and his people have arrived at last. Is everything ready?

FRADE. She has still to go to the grave-yard.

SENDER. Yes, go, my little one—go to Mamma. (*He sighs*) Let your tears fall on her grave and ask her to come to your wedding. Ask her to be with you, so that we may lead our only daughter under the canopy together. Say that I have fulfilled her dying wishes to devote my life to you and bring you up to be a true and virtuous daughter of Israel. This I have done, and am now about to give you in marriage to a learned and God-fearing young

THE DYBBUK

279

man, of good family. (*He wipes away his tears and with bowed head turns back into the house.*) (*A pause.*)

LEAH. Granny, may I invite others at the grave-yard besides mother?

FRADE. Only the near relations. You must ask your grandfather, Rabbi Ephraim, and your Aunt Mirele.

LEAH. There is someone else I want to ask—not a relation.

FRADE. No, daughter—that is forbidden. If you invite one stranger, the others might take offense and do you harm.

LEAH. He is not a stranger, granny. He was in our house like one of ourselves.

FRADE (*in a voice low with fear*). Child, child—you fill me with fear. . . . They say he died a bad, unnatural death. (LEAH *weeps silently*) There, there, my little one, don't cry. You shall ask him if you must; granny will take the sin upon herself. (*Bethinking herself*) I don't know where they buried him, though, and it would never do to ask.

LEAH. I know where he is.

FRADE (*surprised*). You know? How?

LEAH. I saw his grave in a dream. (*She closes her eyes in a trance*) And I saw him, too. He told me his trouble and begged me to invite him to the wedding. (GITTEL *and* BASSIA *enter running.*)

GITTEL AND BASSIA (*together, in high excitement*). We've seen him —we've seen him!

LEAH (*in consternation*). Whom— whom have you seen?

GITTEL. Why, the bridegroom, of course. And he's dark. . . .

BASSIA. No, he isn't—he's fair. . . .

GITTEL. Come, let's take another look and make sure. . . . (*They run off.*)

LEAH (*rising*). Come, Granny—let us go to the graveyard.

FRADE (*sadly*). Yes, my baby. . . . Och, och, och! (LEAH *takes a black shawl and puts it round her shoulders. With* FRADE *at her side, she passes slowly down the alley to the right. The stage remains empty for a moment. Music is heard approaching, as from the alley on the left come* NACHMON, RABBI MENDEL *and* MENASHE, *a small, wizened youth who stares about him with wide, terrified eyes. They are followed by relatives, men and women, in holiday clothes.* SENDER *comes out to meet them.*)

SENDER (*shakes* NACHMON'S *hand warmly*). Sholom aleichem, Nachmon. You are welcome. (*They kiss.* SENDER *shakes hands with* MENASHE *and kisses him. He then shakes hands with the rest of the party*) Have you had a good journey?

NACHMON. We have had a hard and bitter journey. First we missed the road and went astray in the fields. Then we plunged into a swamp which nearly swallowed us up. It was all we could do to pull ourselves out, and the thought flashed through my mind that the Evil Ones, God forbid, were at work to prevent our getting here at all. However, by the goodness of God we have still managed to arrive in time.

SENDER. You must be exhausted. Come in and rest.

NACHMON. There's no time to rest, we have still to settle the details of the marriage-contract, the transfer of the dowry—the wedding gifts— how long the couple should live in the bridegroom's father's house, and so forth. . . .

SENDER. As you wish—I am entirely at your disposal. (*Puts his arm around* NACHMON'S *shoulders, and walks up and down the square with him, talking.*)

RABBI MENDEL (*to* MENASHE). Remember now—you are to remain perfectly quiet at the table. Keep your eyes downcast, and make no movement of any sort. The moment the supper is over, the master of ceremonies will call out: "The bridegroom will now deliver his oration." Then you will rise immediately and stand on the bench. Begin intoning loudly—the louder the better. And you are not to be bashful—do you hear?

MENASHE. Yes, I hear. (*In a frightened whisper*) Rabbi, I'm afraid.

RABBI MENDEL (*alarmed*). Afraid —what of? Have you forgotten your oration?

MENASHE. No—it isn't that.

RABBI MENDEL. What then?

MENASHE (*in anguish*). I don't know myself. But no sooner had we left home than I was seized with terror. All the places we passed were strange to me—I've never in my life seen so many unfamiliar faces. I can't stand the way they look at me—I'm afraid of their eyes. (*He shudders*) Rabbi, nothing terrifies me so much as the eyes of strangers.

RABBI MENDEL. I'll pray that the evil eye be averted from you.

MENASHE. Rabbi, I'd like to stay alone, I'd like to creep into a corner somewhere. But here I'm surrounded by strangers. I have to talk to them, answer their questions; I feel as if I were being dragged to the gallows. (*With mystic terror*) Rabbi, above all, I'm frightened of her, the maiden.

RABBI MENDEL. Make up your mind to master your fears, and you will. Otherwise, God forbid, you may forget your oration. Let us go to the inn now, and I will hear you go over it again.

MENASHE (*clutches at* MENDEL'S *hand*). Rabbi—what's that grave there in the middle of the street? (*They read the inscription on the headstone in silence, and stand for a moment beside the grave; then with bowed heads pass down the alley to the left.* SENDER, NACHMON *and the* WEDDING GUEST *enter the house. The poor file out of the courtyard, with their bags on their shoulders and staves in their hands. They cross the square silently and vanish down the alley to the left. A few linger in the square.*)

A TALL PALE WOMAN. Now the poor

people's feast is over—like all the other things—just as if they'd never been.

LAME OLD WOMAN. They said there'd be a plate of soup for everyone, but there wasn't.

A HUNCHBACK. And only little slices of white bread.

A MAN ON CRUTCHES. A rich man like him—as if it would have hurt him to give us a whole loaf each.

THE TALL WOMAN. They might have given us a bit of chicken. Just look, chicken *and* geese *and* turkeys for their rich guests.

A HALF-BLIND WOMAN. Oh, what does it matter? It all goes to the worms when we're dead. Och, och, och!
(*They go slowly out. The stage is empty for a moment. Then the* MESSENGER *crosses from the left and enters the synagogue. Dusk is falling. The shopkeepers are closing for the night. In the synagogue and at* SENDER'S *house, lights are appearing.* SENDER, GITTEL *and* BASSIA *come onto the stoop. They peer about.*)

SENDER (*worried*). Where is Leah? Where is old Frade? How is it they aren't back from the graveyard all this time? Can they have met with an accident, God forbid?

GITTEL AND BASSIA. We'll go and meet them.
(*From the alley on the right,* FRADE *and* LEAH *come hurrying.*)

FRADE. Hurry, child, hurry! Ei, ei— how long we've been! Oh, why did I let you have your way? I am so afraid something dreadful is going to happen, God forbid!

SENDER. Oh, here they are. What can have kept you all this time?
(*Women come out of the house.*)

WOMEN. Bring in the bride to pray before the candles.
(LEAH *is led into the house.*)

FRADE (*whispering to* GITTEL *and* BASSIA). She fainted. I'd a hard time bringing her round. I'm shaking all over still.

BASSIA. That's because she's been fasting . . . it weakens the heart.

GITTEL. Did she cry much at her mother's grave?

FRADE. Better not ask what happened there. I'm still shaking all over. . . .
(*A chair is set near the door and* LEAH *is led out. They seat her. Music.* NACHMON, MENASHE, RABBI MENDEL *and the guests approach from the alley on the left.* MENASHE *carries a cloth over his outstretched hands, and crosses to* LEAH *in order to cover her face with it. The* MESSENGER *comes out of the synagogue.*)

LEAH (*tears the cloth away, and springing up, thrusts* MENASHE *from her, crying out*). No! YOU are not my bridegroom!
(*General consternation. They all crowd round* LEAH.)

SENDER (*overwhelmed*). Little daughter, what is it, my darling? What has come over you?
(LEAH *breaks away from them and runs to the grave, reaching out her arms.*)

LEAH. Holy bridegroom and bride, protect me—save me! (*She falls. They flock round her, and raise her from the ground. She looks wildly about, and cries out, not in her natural voice, but in the voice of a man*) Ah! Ah! You buried me. But I have come back—to my destined bride. I will leave her no more!

(NACHMON *crosses to* LEAH, *and she shrieks into his face*) Chamilouk!

NACHMON (*trembling*). She has gone mad.

MESSENGER. Into the bride has entered a Dybbuk.
(*Great tumult.*)

CURTAIN

ACT THREE

Miropol. A large room in the house of RABBI AZRAEL *of Miropol. Right, door leading to other rooms. In middle of wall, center, door to street. On either side of this door, benches. Windows. Left, a table almost the entire length of the wall, covered with a white cloth. On table, slices of white bread.* * *At the head of table, a great armchair. Past the door, right, a small cupboard containing scrolls of the law. Beside it, an altar. Opposite, a small table, sofa, and several chairs.*

It is the Sabbath—evening prayers are just over. CHASSIDIM *go to and fro in the room while* ELDER MICHOEL *places about the table the pieces of white bread. The* MESSENGER *is sitting beside the cupboard where the scrolls are, surrounded by a group of* CHASSIDIM. *Others sit apart, reading. Two stand beside the small table. A low chanting is heard from an inner room: "God of Abraham, Isaac and Jacob . . ." The two* CHASSIDIM *speak.*

FIRST CHASSID. He has some wonderful tales, the Stranger. It gives you the creeps to listen to them—I'm afraid to, myself.

SECOND CHASSID. What are they about?

FIRST CHASSID. They're full of deep meaning, but it's not easy to grasp what the meaning is. For all *we* know, they may have something to do with the Bratslaver's creed.*

* Sabbath bread which is prayed over at the close of the Sabbath.
* Nachmon Bratslaver, a descendant of Balshem, the founder of Chassidism. Bratslaver was a famous Rabbi, a poet and philosopher.

SECOND CHASSID. There can't be anything very heretical in them if the older Chassidim can listen to him.
(*They join the group about the* MESSENGER.)

THIRD CHASSID. Go on—tell us another . . .

MESSENGER. It is late. There is hardly any time left.

FOURTH CHASSID. That's all right. The Rabbi won't be here for a good while yet.

MESSENGER (*continuing his stories*)

Well, then. At the end of the earth stands a high mountain; on the top of this mountain is a huge boulder, and out of the boulder flows a stream of clear water. At the opposite end of the earth is the heart of the world. Now each thing in the world has a heart, and the world itself has a great heart of its own. And the heart of the world keeps the clear stream ever in sight, gazing at it with insatiable longing and desire. But the heart of the world can make not even one step toward it, for the moment it stirs from its place, it loses sight of the mountain's summit and the crystal spring. And if, though for a single instant only, it lose sight of the spring, it loses in that same moment its life, and the heart of the world begins to die.

The crystal spring has no lifespan of its own, but endures only so long as the heart of the world allows. And this is one day only.

Now at the close of day, the spring calls to the heart of the world in a song and is answered in a song from the heart. And the sound of their song passes over all the earth, and out of it shining threads come forth and fasten onto the hearts of all the world's creatures and from one heart to another. There is a righteous and benevolent man who goes to and fro over all the earth's surface, gathering up the threads from all the hearts. These he weaves into Time, and when he has woven one whole day, he passes it over to the heart of the world, which passes it over to the crystal spring, and so the spring achieves another day of life.

THIRD CHASSID. The Rabbi is coming.

(*Silence falls. They all rise.* RABBI

AZRAEL *enters at door, left. He is a man of great age, dressed in a white kaftan and high fur cap. Very slowly and wearily, deep in thought, he crosses to the table, and sinks into the armchair at its head.* MICHOEL *takes his place at the rabbi's right hand, and the* CHASSIDIM *group themselves around the table, the elders sitting, the younger standing behind them.* MICHOEL *distributes white bread.* RABBI AZRAEL *lifts his head, and in a low, quavering voice chants.*)

RABBI AZRAEL. The feast of David, the King, the Messiah . . . (*The others make the response and say grace over the bread. They begin chanting in low tones, a sad, mysterious air without words. There is a pause.* RABBI AZRAEL *sighs deeply, rests his head on both hands, and in that position remains seated, lost in meditation. An atmosphere of suspense pervades the silence. At last,* RABBI AZRAEL *again raises his head, and begins to intone*) It is told of the holy Balshem*—may his merits hover over us. . . . (*There is a momentary pause*) One day there came to Meshibach a troupe of German acrobats who gave their performance in the streets of the town. They stretched a rope across the river and one of them walked along the rope to the opposite bank. From all sides the people came running to behold this ungodly marvel, and in the midst of the crowd of onlookers stood the holy Balshem himself. His disciples were greatly astonished, and asked him the meaning of his presence there. And the holy Balshem answered them thus: I went to see how a man

---

* The founder of the Chassidic Sect.

might cross the chasm between two heights as this man did, and as I watched him I reflected that if mankind would submit their souls to such discipline as that to which he submitted his body, what deep abysses might they not cross upon the tenuous cord of life! (*The* RABBI *sighs deeply.*)
(*In the pause that follows, the* CHASSIDIM *exchange enraptured glances.*)

FIRST CHASSID. Lofty as the world!

SECOND CHASSID. Wonder of Wonders!

THIRD CHASSID. Glory of glories!

RABBI AZRAEL (*to* MICHOEL, *whispering*). There is a stranger here.

MICHOEL (*looking round*). He is a messenger, in the confidence of the Great Ones.

RABBI AZRAEL. What message does he bring?

MICHOEL. I don't know. Shall I tell him to go away?

RABBI AZRAEL. God forbid! A stranger must, on the contrary, be shown special honor. Give him a chair. (*Pause*) The world of God is great and holy. In all the world the holiest land is the Land of Israel. In the Land of Israel the holiest city is Jerusalem; in Jerusalem the holiest place was the holy Temple, and the holiest spot in the Temple was the Holy of Holies. (*He pauses*) In the world there are seventy nations, and of them the holiest is Israel. The holiest of the people of Israel is the tribe of the Levites. The holiest of the Levites are the priests, and amongst the priests, the holiest is the High Priest. (*Pause*) The year has three hundred and fifty-four days. Of these the holidays are the holiest. Holier than the holidays are the Sabbaths and the holiest of the Sabbaths is Yom Kippur,* Sabbath of Sabbaths. (*Pause*) There are in the world seventy tongues. The holiest of these is the holy tongue of Israel. The holiest of all things written in this tongue is the Holy Torah; of the Torah the holiest part is the Ten Commandments, and the holiest of all the words in the Ten Commandments is the Name of the Lord. (*Pause*) At a certain hour, on a certain day of the year, all these four supreme holinesses met together. This took place on the Day of Atonement, at the hour when the High Priest entered the Holy of Holies and there revealed the Divine Name. And as this hour was holy and terrible beyond words, so also was it the hour of utmost peril for the High Priest, and for the entire commonweal of Israel. For if, in that hour (which God forbid), a sinful or a wayward thought had entered the mind of the High Priest, it would have brought the destruction of the world. (*Pause*) Wherever a man stand to lift his eyes to heaven, that place is a Holy of Holies. Every human being created by God in His own image and likeness is a High Priest. Each day of a man's life is the Day of Atonement; and every word he speaks from his heart is the name of the Lord. Therefore the sin of any man, whether of commission or of omission, brings the ruin of a whole world in its train. (*His voice becomes weaker*

* The Day of Atonement.

and trembles) Through many trans-migrations, the human soul is drawn by pain and grief, as the child to its mother's breast, to the source of its being, the Exalted Throne above. But it happens sometimes that a soul which has attained to the final state of purification suddenly becomes the prey of evil forces which cause it to slip and fall. And the higher it had soared, the deeper it falls. And with the fall of such a soul as this, a world plunges to ruin. And darkness overwhelms the spheres. The ten spheres bewail the world that is lost. (*He pauses, and seems to awaken to consciousness*) My children, tonight we will shorten the seeing out of the Queen.*

(*All except* MICHOEL *silently leave the room, the spell of the* RABBI'S *discourses still upon them.*)

MICHOEL (*approaches the table uncertainly*). Rabbi . . . Rabbi, Sender of Brainitz is here.

RABBI AZRAEL (*mechanically repeating the words*). Sender of Brainitz . . . I know.

MICHOEL. A terrible misfortune has befallen him. A Dybbuk—God's mercy be upon us—has entered into his daughter.

RABBI AZRAEL. A Dybbuk has . . . I know.

MICHOEL. He has brought her to you.

RABBI AZRAEL (*as if to himself*). To me? . . . To me? . . . Why to me, when there *is* no me to come to? For I am myself no longer.

* The Sabbath is the Queen, whose going is celebrated with prayer.

MICHOEL. But Rabbi—everybody comes to you—a world of people

RABBI AZRAEL. As you say—a world of people. Yes, a blind world—blind sheep following a blind shepherd. If they had eyes to see with, they would seek guidance not from me, but from Him who alone can justly use the word "I," for He is, in all the world, the only "I."

MICHOEL. You are His representative, Rabbi.

RABBI AZRAEL. So says the world. But as for me, I do not know. For forty years I have sat in the Rabbi's chair, and yet, to this very day I am not convinced that I am indeed the appointed deputy on earth of Him whose Name be praised. At times I am conscious of my nearness to the All. Then I am free of doubts, and feel the power within me—then I know I am master over the high worlds. But there are other times when that certainty abandons me, and then I am as small and feeble as a child, then I myself, and not those who come to me, need help.

MICHOEL. I know, Rabbi—I remember. Once you came to me at midnight, and asked me to recite the psalms with you. All the night long, we said them together, weeping.

RABBI AZRAEL. That was a long time ago—it is worse than ever now. (*His voice fails*) What do they want of me? I am old and weak. My body has earned its rest—my soul longs for solitude. Yet still they come thronging to me, all the misery and sorrow of the world. Each imploring word pierces my flesh like a thorn . . . No, I have no longer the strength . . . I cannot . . .

MICHOEL (*filled with fear*). Rabbi, Rabbi . . .

RABBI AZRAEL (*suddenly breaking into tears*). I can't go on . . . I can't . . . (*He weeps.*)

MICHOEL. Rabbi—do you forget the generations of righteous and holy men of God from whom you are descended? Your father, Rabbi Itzele, blessed be his name, your grandfather, our master and lord— our teacher, Rabbi Velvele the Great, who was a pupil of the Holy Balshem himself . . .

RABBI AZRAEL (*regaining his self-control*). No—I will not forget my forbears—my holy father who three times had a revelation direct from God; my uncle, Rabbi Meyer Baer, who upon the words of "Hear, O Israel" could ascend to Heaven at will; the great Velvele, my grandfather, who resurrected the dead. . . . (*All his spirit has returned as he speaks to* MICHOEL) Michoel, do you know that my grandfather would drive out Dybbuks without either spells or incantations—with a single word of command, only one, he expelled them. In times of stress I always turn to him, and he sustains me. He will not forsake me now. Call in Sender.
(MICHOEL *goes, and returns in a moment with* SENDER.)

SENDER (*tearfully, with outspread hands*). Rabbi! Have mercy on me! Help me! Save my only daughter!

RABBI AZRAEL. How did this misfortune come upon you?

SENDER. Just as they were about to veil the bride, and . . .

RABBI AZRAEL. That is not what I asked. Tell me, what could have brought this thing to pass? A worm can enter a fruit only after it has begun to rot.

SENDER. Rabbi, my only daughter is a pious Jewish maiden. She is modest and gentle—she has never disobeyed me.

RABBI AZRAEL. Children are sometimes punished for the sins of their parents.

SENDER. If I knew of any sin I had committed, I would do penance for it.

RABBI AZRAEL. Have you asked the Dybbuk who he was, and why he entered into your daughter?

SENDER. He refuses to answer. But we recognized him by his voice. He was a student in our *yeshiva* who died suddenly in the synagogue. That was months ago. He had been meddling in the Kabala and came to grief through it.

RABBI AZRAEL. What powers destroyed him?

SENDER. Evil ones, they say. An hour or two before his death, he had been telling a fellow-student that sin need not be fought against, for Satan too is holy at the core. He also tried the use of charms to obtain two barrels of gold.

RABBI AZRAEL. Did you know him?

SENDER. Yes. I was one of those in whose house he stayed.

RABBI AZRAEL (*bending his gaze intently upon* SENDER). You may have put some slight upon him or mistreated him. Try to remember.

SENDER. I don't know . . . I can't remember. . . . (*Desperately*) Rabbi, I'm only human, after all . . . I . . .

RABBI AZRAEL. Bring in the maiden. (SENDER *goes out and returns immediately with* FRADE, *who supports* LEAH. LEAH *stops in the doorway and will go no further.*)

SENDER (*weeping*). Have pity on your father, my child—don't put him to shame before the Rabbi. Come inside.

FRADE. Go in, Leah dear—go in, little dove.

LEAH. I want to . . . but I can't . . .

RABBI AZRAEL. Maiden, I command you—come in! (LEAH *advances into the room and crosses to the table*) Sit down!

LEAH (*does as the* RABBI *tells her. Then suddenly springs up and cries out with a voice not her own*). Let me be! I will not be here! (*She tries to escape, but is stopped by* SENDER *and* FRADE.)

RABBI AZRAEL. Dybbuk! Who are you? I command you to answer.

LEAH (*in the voice of the* DYBBUK). Miropol Rabbi—you know very well who I am. I do not wish the others to know.

RABBI AZRAEL. I do not ask your name—I ask: Who *are* you?

LEAH (*as before*). I am one of those who sought other paths.

RABBI AZRAEL. He only seeks other paths who has lost the straight one.

LEAH (*as before*). The straight one is too narrow.

RABBI AZRAEL. That has been said before by one who did not return. (*Pause*) Why did you enter into this maiden?

LEAH (*as before*). I am her predestined bridegroom.

RABBI AZRAEL. According to our Holy Scriptures, a dead soul may not stay in the realms of the living.

LEAH (*as before*). I have not died.

RABBI AZRAEL. You left our world, and so are forbidden to return until the blast of the great trumpet shall be heard. I command you therefore to leave the body of this maiden, in order that a living branch of the imperishable tree of Israel may not be blasted.

LEAH (*shrieks in the* DYBBUK's *voice*). Miropol Rabbi—I know your almighty power. I know that angels and archangels obey your word. But me you cannot command. I have nowhere to go. Every road is barred against me and every gate is locked. On every side, the forces of evil lie in wait to seize me. (*In a trembling voice*) There is heaven, and there is earth—and all the countless worlds in space, yet in not one of these is there any place for me. And now that my soul has found refuge from the bitterness and terror of pursuit, you wish to drive me away. Have mercy! Do not send me away—don't force me to go!

RABBI AZRAEL. I am filled with profound pity for you, wandering soul! And I will use all my power to save you from the evil spirits. But the body of this maiden you must leave.

LEAH (*in the* DYBBUK's *voice, firmly*). I refuse!

RABBI AZRAEL. Michoel. Summon a *minyen* from the synagogue. (MICHOEL *returns at once with ten Jews who take their places on one side of the room*) Holy Community, do you give me authority to cast out of the body of a Jewish maiden, in your behalf and with your power, a spirit which refuses to leave her of its own free will?

THE TEN. Rabbi, we give you authority to cast out of the body of a Jewish maiden, in our behalf and in our name and with our power, a spirit which refuses to leave her of its own free will.

RABBI (*rises*). Dybbuk! Soul of one who has left the world in which we live. In the name and with the power of a holy community of Jews, I, Azrael, son of Itzele, order you to depart out of the body of the maiden, Leah, daughter of Channah, and in departing, to do no injury either to her or to any other living being. If you do not obey me, I shall proceed against you with malediction and anathema, to the limit of my powers, and with the utmost might of my uplifted arm. But if you do as I command you, then I shall bend all my strength to drive away the fiends and evil spirits that surround you, and keep you safe from them.

LEAH (*shrieks in the voice of the* DYBBUK). I'm not afraid of your anathema. I put no faith in your promises. The power is not in the world that can help me. The loftiest height of the world cannot compare with this resting-place that I have found, nor is there in the world an abysm so fathomless as that which waits to receive me if ever I leave my only refuge. I will not go.

RABBI AZRAEL. In the name of the Almighty, I adjure you for the last time. Leave the body of this maiden— If you do not, I shall utter the anathema against you and deliver you into the hands of the fiends of destruction.
(*An ominous pause.*)

LEAH (*in the voice of the* DYBBUK). In the name of the Almighty, I am bound to my betrothed, and will remain with her to all eternity.

RABBI AZRAEL. Michoel, have white shrouds brought for all who are here. Bring seven trumpets . . . and seven black candles . . . Then seven holy scrolls from their place. ⟨*A pause fraught with dire omen, during which* MICHOEL *goes out and returns with trumpets and black candles. The* MESSENGER *follows him with the shrouds.*⟩

MESSENGER (*counting the shrouds*). One too many. (*He looks round the room*) Someone is missing, perhaps?

RABBI AZRAEL (*worried—as if recalling something*). Before pronouncing the anathema against a Jewish soul, it is necessary to obtain the permission of the City Rabbi. Michoel, leave these things for the present. Here is my staff. Take it and go to the City Rabbi, and ask him to come without delay.

(MICHOEL *puts the trumpets and candles aside and goes out with the* MESSENGER, *who still carries the shrouds over his arm.*)

RABBI AZRAEL (*to the ten*). Wait outside until they come back. (*They leave the room. There is a pause.* RABBI AZRAEL *turns to* SENDER) Sender, where are the bridegroom and his people?

SENDER. They stayed in Brainitz over the Sabbath, at my house.

RABBI AZRAEL. Let a messenger ride over and tell them in my name, to stay there and await my orders.

SENDER. I'll send at once.

RABBI AZRAEL. You may leave me now, and take the maiden into the next room.

LEAH (*wakes out of her trance, and speaks in her own voice, trembling*). Granny—I'm frightened. What are they going to do to him? What are they going to do to me?

FRADE. There, there, my child—you've nothing to be frightened of. The Rabbi knows best. He couldn't harm anyone. The Rabbi can't do wrong, my darling. (FRADE *and* SENDER *take* LEAH *into the adjoining room.*)

RABBI AZRAEL (*remains absorbed in his thoughts. Then he looks up*). Even though it has been thus ordained in the high planes, I will reverse that destiny.
(*Enter* RABBI SAMSON.)

RABBI SAMSON. A good week to you, Rabbi.

RABBI AZRAEL (*rises to meet him*). A good week, a good year to you, Rabbi. Be seated. (RABBI SAMSON *takes a seat*) I have troubled you to come here in a very grave matter. A Dybbuk (the Lord of Mercy be with us), has entered into a daughter of Israel, and nothing will induce him to leave her. Only the last resort is left, to force him out by anathema, and this I ask your permission to do. The salvation of a soul will thereby be added to your other merits.

RABBI SAMSON (*sighing*). Anathema is cruel punishment enough for the living—it is far more so for the dead. But if, as you say, all other means have failed, and so godly a man as yourself believe it necessary, I give you my consent. I have a secret, however, which I must reveal to you, Rabbi, for it has a vital bearing on this affair.

RABBI AZRAEL. I am listening, Rabbi.

RABBI SAMSON. Rabbi, do you remember a young Chassid from Brainitz, Nissin ben Rifke by name, who used to come to you from time to time, about twenty years ago?

RABBI AZRAEL. Yes. He went away to some place a long way off and died there, still in his youth.

RABBI SAMSON. That is he. Well, that same Nissin ben Rifke appeared to me three times in my dreams last night, demanding that I summon Sender of Brainitz to trial before the Rabbinical Court.

RABBI AZRAEL. What was his charge against Sender?

RABBI SAMSON. He did not state it to me. He only kept saying that Sender had done him a mortal injury.

RABBI AZRAEL. A rabbi can obviously not prevent any Jew from summoning another to appear before the court, particularly when the complainant is dead and could appeal in the last resort to the Highest Tribunal of all . . . But how do these visitations of yours affect this Dybbuk?

RABBI SAMSON. In this manner . . . It has come to my ears that the youth who died and entered into the body of Sender's daughter as a Dybbuk, was Nissin ben Rifke's only son . . . There is also some rumor concerning a pact with Nissin ben Rifke which has not been kept.

RABBI AZRAEL (after a moment's reflection). This being the case, I shall postpone the exorcising of the Dybbuk until tomorrow midday. In the morning after prayers, you shall summon the dead man to court, and God willing, we shall discover the reason for his visitations to you. And then, with your permission, I shall cast out the Dybbuk by anathema.

RABBI SAMSON. In view of the difficulty of a trial between a living man and a dead one, which is as rare as it is difficult, I beg that you will preside over the court, Rabbi, and conduct the proceedings.

RABBI AZRAEL. Very well . . . Michoel. (Enter MICHOEL) Bring in the maiden. (SENDER and FRADE bring LEAH into the room. She sits down before the RABBI with her eyes closed) Dybbuk! I give you respite until noon tomorrow. If at that hour you persist in your refusal to leave this maiden's body of your own accord, I shall, with the permission of the City Rabbi, tear you away from her with the utmost force of the cherem.* (SENDER and FRADE lead LEAH towards the door) Sender, you are to remain. (FRADE takes LEAH out) Sender, do you remember the bosom friend of your youth—Nissin ben Rifke?

SENDER (frightened). Nissin ben Rifke? He died, didn't he?

RABBI AZRAEL. Know then that he appeared three times last night before the Rabbi of the City (indicating RABBI SAMSON) as he slept. And Nissin ben Rifke demanded that you be summoned to stand trial by the Rabbinical Court for a wrong that you have done him.

SENDER (stunned). Me? A trial? Is there no end to my misfortunes? What does he want of me? Rabbi, help me! What shall I do?

RABBI AZRAEL. I do not know the nature of his charge. But you must accept the summons.

SENDER. I will do whatever you say.

RABBI AZRAEL (in a different tone). Let the swiftest horses be sent immediately to Brainitz, to fetch the bridegroom and his people. Have them here before midday tomorrow, in order that the wedding may take place as soon as the Dybbuk has been expelled. Have the canopy set up.

* The sentence of excommunication.

SENDER. Rabbi! What if they no longer wish to be connected with my family, and refuse to come?

(*The* MESSENGER *appears in the doorway.*)

RABBI AZRAEL (*with dignity*). Tell them I have commanded them to come. Let nothing prevent the bridegroom from arriving in time.

MESSENGER. The bridegroom will be here in time.

(*The clock strikes twelve.*)

CURTAIN

ACT FOUR

SAME SCENE AS ACT THREE

Instead of the long table, left, a smaller one nearer to footlights. RABBI AZRAEL, *wrapped in his prayer shawl and wearing the phylacteries, is in the armchair. The two* JUDGES *sit in ordinary chairs.* RABBI SAMSON *stands beside the table and, at a distance,* MICHOEL. *They are finishing a prayer whereby an evil dream may be turned into good.*

RABBI AZRAEL, MICHOEL and the TWO JUDGES. You beheld a good dream! You beheld a good dream! You beheld a good dream!

RABBI AZRAEL. We have found a solution of good to your dream.

RABBI SAMSON. I beheld a good dream—a good dream I beheld. I beheld a good dream.

RABBI AZRAEL. Will you now, Rabbi Samson, take your seat with the other judges? (RABBI SAMSON *sits down next to* RABBI AZRAEL) Let us now call upon this dead man to be present at the trial. First, however, I shall draw a holy circle beyond which he may not pass. Michoel, my staff. . . . (MICHOEL *gives him the staff.* RABBI AZRAEL *then rises and, going to the corner, left, describes a circle on the floor from left to right. He then returns to the table*) Michoel, take my staff

and go to the graveyard. When you get there, go in with your eyes closed, guiding yourself with the staff. At the first grave it touches, stop. Knock with it three times upon this grave, and repeat what I shall tell you faithfully word for word: Pure dead, I am sent by Azrael, son of the great sage, Rabbi Itzele of Miropol, to beg you to pardon him for disturbing your peace, and to deliver his command that you inform the pure dead, Nissin ben Rifke, by means known to you as follows: That the just and righteous Rabbinical Court of Miropol summons him to be present immediately at a trial at which he shall appear in the same garb as that in which he was buried. Repeat these words three times; then turn and come back here. You will not look behind you, no matter what cries or calls or shrieks may pursue you, nor will you allow my staff to leave your hand even for one moment, otherwise you will place yourself in dire peril. Go and God will protect you, for no harm can come to him who is bound on a virtuous errand. But before you go, let two men come in and make a partition which shall separate the dead man from the living. (MICHOEL *goes out.* TWO MEN *enter with a sheet with which they screen the left-hand corner down to the floor. They then leave the room*) Let Sender come in. (SENDER *appears*) Sender, have you carried out my instructions and sent horses for the bridegroom and his people?

SENDER. The swiftest horses were sent, but the bridegroom has not yet arrived.

RABBI AZRAEL. Have someone ride out to meet them and say they are to drive as fast as they can.

SENDER. Yes, Rabbi.
(*Pause.*)

RABBI AZRAEL. Sender, we have sent to inform the pure dead, Nissin ben Rifke, that the Rabbinical Court summons him to appear in his cause against you. Are you willing to accept our verdict?

SENDER. I am.

RABBI AZRAEL. Will you carry out our sentence?

SENDER. I will.

RABBI AZRAEL. Then step back and take your place upon the right.

SENDER. Rabbi, it begins to come back to me. . . . It may be that the trial which Nissin ben Rifke has summoned me to, concerns an agreement upon which we shook hands one day many years ago. But in that matter I am not to blame.

RABBI AZRAEL. You will have an opportunity to speak of this later on, after the complainant has made known his grievance. (*Pause*) Very soon there is personally to appear in our midst, a man from the True World, in order to submit to our judgment a case between himself and a man of our Untrue World. (*Pause*) A trial such as this is proof that the laws set forth in the Holy Scriptures rule all worlds and all peoples, and unite both the living and the dead within their bonds. (*Pause*) A trial such as this is difficult and terrible. The eyes of all the worlds are turned towards it, and should this court deviate from the Law by so much as a hair's breadth, tumult would ensue in the Court on High. It is with fear and trembling, therefore, that we are to approach the trial at issue . . . with fear and trembling. . . . (*He looks anxiously around him and as he does encounters the partition in the left-hand corner. He ceases to speak. There is a silence of awe.*)

FIRST JUDGE (*in a frightened whisper to the* SECOND JUDGE). I believe he's come.

SECOND JUDGE (*in the same tone*). It seems so.

RABBI SAMSON. He is here.

RABBI AZRAEL. Pure dead Nissin ben Rifke! You are commanded by this just and righteous court to stay within the circle and partition assigned to you, and not to go beyond them. Pure dead Nissin ben Rifke, you are commanded by this just and righteous court to state your grievance and the redress you seek against the accused, Sender ben Henie.

(*Awestruck pause. All listen as though turned to stone.*)

FIRST JUDGE. I believe he is answering.

SECOND JUDGE. It seems so.

FIRST JUDGE. I hear a voice but no words.

SECOND JUDGE. And I words but no voice.

RABBI SAMSON (*to* SENDER). Sender ben Henie, the pure dead Nissin ben Rifke makes demand saying that in the years of your youth you and he were students in the same *yeshiva*, comrades, and that your soul and his were bound together in true friendship. You were both married in the same week, and when you met at the house of the Rabbi, during the Great Holidays, you made a solemn pact that if the wife of one of you should conceive and bear a boy and the other a girl, those two children should marry.

SENDER (*in a tremulous voice*). It was so.

RABBI SAMSON. The pure dead Nissin ben Rifke makes further demand, saying that soon afterwards he left for a place very far away, where his wife bore him a son in the same hour as your wife gave you a daughter. Soon thereafter he was gathered to his fathers. (*Short pause*) In the True World, he found that his son had been blest with a noble and lofty soul, and was progressing upwards from plane to plane, and at this his paternal heart overflowed with joy and pride. He also found that his son, growing older, had become a wanderer from province to province, and from country to country, and from city to city, for the soul to which his soul had been predestined was drawing him ever onward. At last he came to the city in which you dwell, and you took him into your house. He sat at your table, and his soul bound itself to the soul of your daughter. But you were rich, while Nissin's son was poor, and so you turned your back on him and went seeking for your daughter a bridegroom of high estate and great possessions. (*Short pause*) Nissin then beheld his son grow desperate and become a wanderer once more, seeking now the New Paths. And sorrow and alarm filled his father's soul lest the dark powers, aware of the youth's extremity, spread their net for him. This they did, and caught him, and tore him from the world before his time. Thereafter the soul of Nissin ben Rifke's son roamed the worlds until at last it entered as a Dybbuk into the body of his predestined. Nissin ben Rifke claims that the death of his son has severed him from both worlds, leaving him without name or memorial, since neither heir nor friend remains on earth to pray for his soul. His light has been extinguished forever—the crown of his head has rolled down into the abyss. Therefore, he begs the just and righteous court to pass sentence upon Sender according to the laws of our Holy Scriptures, for his shedding of the blood of Nissin's son and of his son's sons to the end of all generations.

(*An awestruck pause.* SENDER *is shaken with sobs.*)

RABBI AZRAEL. Sender ben Henie, have you heard the complaint brought against you by the holy dead, Nissin ben Rifke? What have you to say in answer to it?

SENDER. I can't speak . . . I have no words to say . . . in justification. But I would ask you to beg my old comrade to forgive me this sin, because it was not committed in malice. Soon after we had shaken hands upon our pact, Nissin went away, and I did not know whether his wife had had a child, either boy or girl. Then I received news of his death, but none about his family. And gradually the whole affair of our agreement went out of my mind.

RABBI AZRAEL. Why did you not inquire about him? Why did you make no inquiry?

SENDER. It is customary for the bridegroom's father to make the first advances, not the bride's. I thought that if Nissin had had a son, he would have let me know. (*Pause.*)

RABBI SAMSON. Nissin ben Rifke asks why, when you received his son into your house and had him sit at your table, did you never ask him whence he came and of what family?

SENDER. I don't know. . . . I don't remember. . . . But I do swear that something urged me continually to take him for my son-in-law. That was why, whenever a match was proposed, I always made such hard conditions that the bridegroom's father would never agree to them. Three marriages fell through in this manner. But this time the

bridegroom's people would not be put off.
(*Pause.*)

RABBI SAMSON. Nissin ben Rifke says that in your heart of hearts you were aware of his son's identity and therefore feared to ask him who he was. You were ambitious that your daughter should live in ease and riches, and for that reason thrust his son down into the abyss.
(SENDER *weeps silently, covering his face. There is a heavy pause.* MICHOEL *returns and gives the staff back to* RABBI AZRAEL.)

RABBI AZRAEL (*after a whispered conference with* RABBI SAMSON *and the* JUDGES, *rises and takes the staff in his hand*). This just and righteous court has heard both parties and delivers its verdict as follows: Whereas it is not known whether, at the time Nissin ben Rifke and Sender ben Henie shook hands upon their agreement, their wives had already conceived; and whereas, according to our Holy Scriptures, no agreement whatsoever which involves anything not yet in existence can be held valid in law, we may not therefore find that this agreement was binding upon Sender. Since, however, in the Upper World, the agreement was accepted as valid and never canceled; and since the belief was implanted in the heart of Nissin ben Rifke's son that the daughter of Sender ben Henie was his predestined bride; and whereas, Sender ben Henie's subsequent conduct brought calamity upon Nissin ben Rifke and his son; Now, therefore, be it decreed by this just and righteous court, that Sender give the half of his fortune in alms to the poor, and each year, for the remainder of his life, light the memorial candle for Nissin ben Rifke and his son as though they were his own kindred, and pray for their souls. (*Pause*) The just and righteous court now requests the holy dead, Nissin ben Rifke, to forgive Sender unreservedly, and to command his son in filial duty to leave the body of the maiden, Leah, daughter of Channah, in order that a branch of the fruitful tree of Israel may not be blighted. In return for these things, the Almighty will make manifest his grace to Nissin ben Rifke and to his lost son.

ALL. Amen!

RABBI AZRAEL. Pure dead Nissin ben Rifke, have you heard our judgment? Do you accept it? (*Pause*) Sender ben Henie, have you heard our judgment? Do you accept it?

SENDER. I accept.

RABBI AZRAEL. Pure dead, Nissin ben Rifke, the trial between you and Sender ben Henie is now ended. Do you return therefore to your resting place, and in going we command you to do no harm to man nor other living creature whatsoever. (*Pause*) Michoel, water. . . . And have the curtain taken away. (MICHOEL *calls in* TWO MEN, *who remove the sheet.* RABBI AZRAEL *traces a circle in the same place as before, but from right to left. The* MEN *return with basin and ewer, and all wash their hands*) Sender, have the bridegroom and his people arrived?

SENDER. There has been no sign of them.

RABBI AZRAEL. Send another rider to meet them, and say they are to press on with all the speed their horses can make. Have the canopy raised and the musicians in readiness. Let the bride be dressed in her wedding-gown so that the moment the Dybbuk has been cast out you may lead her under the canopy. What is now about to be done— will be done.

(SENDER *goes out.* RABBI AZRAEL *takes off his prayer-shawl and phylacteries, folding them up.*)

RABBI SAMSON (*whispering to the* JUDGES). Did you notice that the dead man did not forgive Sender?

JUDGES ONE and TWO (*in low, frightened tones*). Yes, we did.

RABBI SAMSON. Do you know the dead man did not accept the verdict?

JUDGES ONE and TWO. Yes, we realized that.

RABBI SAMSON. He failed to say Amen to Rabbi Azrael's sentence— you felt that too, no doubt.

JUDGES ONE and TWO. Yes, distinctly.

RABBI SAMSON. It is a very bad sign——

JUDGES ONE and TWO. Extremely ——

RABBI SAMSON. Rabbi Azrael is terribly agitated—look at him. See how his hands are trembling. (*Pause*) We have done our share— we can go now.

(*The* JUDGES *slip out unobtrusively, and* RABBI SAMSON *prepares to follow them.*)

RABBI AZRAEL. Rabbi, please remain until the Dybbuk has been cast out —I should like you to perform the wedding ceremony. (RABBI SAMSON *sighs and sits down again, with bowed head. An oppressive pause*) God of the Heavens, marvelously strange are Thy ways, and secret, yet the flame of Thy Divine Will illuminates with its reflection the path I tread. Nor shall I stray from that path forever, either to the right or to the left. (*He raises his head*) Michoel, is everything prepared?

MICHOEL. Yes, Rabbi.

RABBI AZRAEL. Let the maiden be brought.
(*Enter* SENDER *and* FRADE *with* LEAH, *in her wedding-gown, a black cloak over her shoulders. They seat her on the sofa.* RABBI SAMSON *takes his place behind* RABBI AZRAEL.)

RABBI AZRAEL. Dybbuk, in the name of the Rabbi of this city, who is present, in the name of a holy community of Jews, in the name of the great Sanhedrin of Jerusalem, I, Azrael ben Hadassah, do for the last time command you to depart out of the body of the maiden Leah, daughter of Channah.

LEAH (DYBBUK) (*firmly*). I refuse!

RABBI AZRAEL. Michoel, call in people to witness the exorcism—bring the shrouds, the horns and the black candles. (MICHOEL *goes out and shortly returns with* FIFTEEN MEN, *among them the* MESSENGER. *The shrouds, trumpets and candles are brought*) Bring out the *scrolls*. (MICHOEL *gives a scroll each to seven, and a trumpet each to seven*

others) Stubborn spirit—inasmuch as you have dared to oppose our power, we deliver you into the hands of the Higher Spirits which will pull you out by force. Blow Tekiah!*
(*The horns are blown.*)

LEAH (DYBBUK) (*leaves her seat and struggles violently as against invisible assailants*). Let me alone —you shall not pull me away—I won't go—I can't go——

RABBI AZRAEL. Since the Higher Spirits cannot overcome you, I surrender you to the Spirits of the Middle Plane, those which are neither good nor evil. I now invoke *their* power to drag you forth. Blow Shevarim.*
(*The horns are blown again.*)

LEAH (DYBBUK) (*her strength beginning to fail*). Woe is me! The powers of all the worlds are arrayed against me. Spirits of terror wrench me and tear me without mercy—the souls of the great and righteous too have arisen against me. The soul of my own father is with them—commanding me to go —— But until the last spark of strength has gone from me, so long shall I withstand them and remain where I am.

RABBI AZRAEL (*to himself*). It is clear that One of Great Power stands beside him. (*Pause*) Michoel, put away the scrolls. (MICHOEL *does so*) Hang a black curtain over the altar. (*This is done*) Light the black candles. (*This, too, is done*) Let everyone now put on a shroud. (*All, including the two* RABBIS, *do so.* RABBI AZRAEL

* Certain notes sounded on the Shofer, the sacred ram's horn.

stands with both arms upraised, an awe-inspiring figure) Rise up, O Lord, and let Thine enemies be scattered before Thee; as smoke is dispersed so let them be scattered. . . . Sinful and obstinate soul, with the power of Almighty God and with the sanction of the holy Scriptures, I, Azrael ben Hadassah, do with these words rend asunder every cord that binds you to the world of living creatures and to the body and soul of the maiden, Leah, Daughter of Channah. . . .

LEAH (DYBBUK) *(shrieking)*. Ah! I am lost!

RABBI AZRAEL. . . . And do pronounce you ex-communicated from all Israel. Blow Teruah.*

MESSENGER. The last spark has been swallowed up into the flame.

LEAH (DYBBUK) *(defeated)*. Alas! —I can fight no more. . . . *(They begin to sound the horns.)*

RABBI AZRAEL *(hastily raising his hand to silence the horns)*. Do you submit?

LEAH (DYBBUK) *(in a dead voice)*. I submit——

RABBI AZRAEL. Do you promise to depart of your own free will, from the body of the maiden, Leah, daughter of Channah, and never return?

LEAH (DYBBUK) *(as before)*. I promise——

RABBI AZRAEL. Dybbuk—by the same power and sanction which de-

* Certain notes sounded on the Shofer, the sacred ram's horn.

puted me to place you under the ban of anathema, I now lift from you that ban. *(To* MICHOEL*)* Put out the candles—take down the black curtain. (MICHOEL *does so)* Put away the horns. (MICHOEL *collects them)* And dismiss the people —let them take off their shrouds before they go. *(Exeunt the* FOURTEEN *with* MESSENGER *and* MICHOEL. RABBI AZRAEL *prays with upraised arms)* Lord of the world, God with charity and mercy, look down upon the suffering of this homeless, tortured soul which the errors and misdeeds of others caused to stray into the bypaths. Regard not its wrongdoing, O Lord, but let the memory of its virtuous past and its present bitter torment and the merits of its forefathers rise like a soft, obscuring mist before Thy sight. Lord of the world—do Thou free its path of evil spirits, and admit it to everlasting peace within Thy mansions. Amen.

ALL. Amen.

LEAH (DYBBUK) *(trembling violently)*. Say Kadish* for me! The hour of my going was predestined —and it has come!

RABBI AZRAEL. Sender, say Kadish. (SENDER *begins the prayer as the clock strikes twelve.)*

SENDER. Yisgadaal—ve yiskadesh— shmeh raboh!*

LEAH (DYBBUK) *(springs up)*. Aie! *(Falls swooning upon the sofa.)*

RABBI AZRAEL. Bring the bride to the wedding canopy.

* The prayer for the dead.
* Magnified and sanctified be His mighty Name!

MICHOEL (*rushing in, greatly agitated*). The last rider has just come back. He says a wheel has come off the wagon so that the bridegroom and his party must walk the rest of the way. But they are at the hill, so they will be here soon—they've been sighted already.

RABBI AZRAEL (*profoundly astonished*). What was to be, shall be. (*To* SENDER) Let the old woman remain here with the bride. We will go—all of us—to meet the bridegroom. (*He traces a circle round* LEAH, *from left to right, takes off his shroud, which he hangs up near the door, and goes out carrying his staff.* SENDER *and* MICHOEL *follow him.*)
(*A long pause.*)

LEAH (*waking—in a faint voice*). Who is here with me? Granny—is that you? Oh! I feel so strange, Granny—so weary. Rock me in your arms.

FRADE (*caressing her*). No, little daughter—you mustn't feel that way. My little child must not be sad. Let the Black Cat be sad. My little one's heart must be as light as down, as light as a breath, as white as a snowflake. Holy angels should embrace her with their wings.
(WEDDING MUSIC *is heard.*)

LEAH (*frightened and trembling, seizes* FRADE's *hand for protection*). Listen! They are beginning to dance round the holy grave to cheer up the dead bride and bridegroom.

FRADE. Be calm, my darling. No harm can come to you now—a mighty power is standing guard over you on every side. Sixty giants, with drawn swords, protect you from evil encounter. The holy fathers and holy mothers ward off the evil eye. (*Little by little she drifts into a chant.*)
Soon they'll lead you under the canopy—
A blessed hour—a happy hour—
Comes your mother—the good and virtuous—
From the Garden of Eden—the Garden of Eden.
Of gold and silver are her robes.

Angels twain go out to meet her, go out to meet her—
Take her hands—one the right hand, one the left hand.
"Channele—Channele mine,
Why do you come decked out so fine?"

So Channele answers the angel:

"Why should I not come robed in state?
Is this not a day of days?
For my bright crown, my only daughter,
Goes to her wedding and luck goes with her."

"Channele, as in robes of state you go,
Why is your face all wan and pale with woe?"

So Channele answers the angel:

"What should I do but sorrow, on this day that my daughter's a bride,
For she's led to her wedding by strangers, while I must stand mourning aside?"

Under the canopy stands the bride, and old and young bring her their greetings and good wishes.

And there stands the Prophet Eli-
jah,
The great goblet of wine in his
hand,
And the words of his holy blessing
Roll echoing over the land.
(FRADE *falls asleep. Long pause.*)

LEAH (*her eyes closed, sighs deeply —then wakes*). Who sighed so deeply?

VOICE OF CHANNON. I.

LEAH. I hear your voice, but I cannot see you.

VOICE OF CHANNON. Because you are within a magic circle which I may not enter.

LEAH. Your voice is as sweet as the lament of violins in the quiet night. Who are you? Tell me.

VOICE OF CHANNON. I have forgotten. I have no remembrance of myself but in your thoughts of me.

LEAH. I remember—now—the star that drew my heart towards its light—the tears that I have shed in the still midnight—the one who stood before me ever—in my dreams—was it you?

VOICE OF CHANNON. I——

LEAH. I remember—your hair, so soft and damp as if with tears— your sad and gentle eyes—your hands with the thin tapering fingers. Waking and sleeping I had no thought but of you. (*Pause—sadly*) You went away and darkness fell upon me—my soul withered in loneliness like the soul of a widow left desolate—the stranger came— and then—then you returned, and

the dead heart wakened to life again, and out of sorrow joy blossomed like a flower. . . . Why have you now once more forsaken me?

VOICE OF CHANNON. I broke down the barriers between us—I crossed the plains of death—I defied every law of past and present time and all the ages. . . . I strove against the strong and mighty and against those who know no mercy. And as my last spark of strength left me, I left your body to return to your soul.

LEAH (*tenderly*). Come back to me, my bridegroom—my husband—I will carry you, dead, in my heart— and in our dreams at night we shall rock to sleep our little children who will never be born. . . . (*Weeps*) And sew them little clothes, and sing them lullabies—— (*Sings, weeping*)
Hush—hush, little children—
No cradle shall hold you—
In no clothes can we fold you.

Dead, that the living cannot mourn;
Untimely lost and never born. . . .
(*The Music of a wedding-march is heard approaching.*)

LEAH (*trembling*). They are coming to take me to a stranger under the canopy—come to me, my true bridegroom; come to me.

VOICE OF CHANNON. I have left your body—I will come to your soul. (*He appears against the wall, white-robed.*)

LEAH (*with joy*). Come, my bridegroom. The barrier between us is no more. I see you. Come to me. . . .

VOICE OF CHANNON (*echo*). Come
to me.

LEAH (*crying out with joy*). I am
coming. . . .

VOICE OF CHANNON (*echo*). And I
to you. . . .
(VOICES *outside*.)

VOICES. Lead the bride to the canopy.
(*Wedding-march is heard.* LEAH
*rises, dropping, as she does so, her
black cloak onto the sofa, and in
her white wedding-dress, to the
strains of the music, she goes towards* CHANNON, *and at the spot
where he has appeared their two
forms merge into one.* RABBI AZ-
RAEL *enters, carrying his staff, followed by the* MESSENGER. *They*

*stand on the threshold. Behind
them,* SENDER, FRADE *and the rest.*)

LEAH (*in a far-away voice*). A great
light flows about me . . . predestined bridegroom, I am united to
you forever. Now we soar upward
together higher and higher. . . .
(*The stage grows darker.*)

RABBI AZRAEL (*with lowered
head*). Too late!

MESSENGER. Blessed be a righteous
judge.
(*It is now completely dark. As if
from a great distance, singing is
heard, scarcely audible*)
    Why, from highest height,
    To deepest depth below,
    Has the soul fallen?
    Within itself, the Fall
    Contains the Resurrection.

Cyrano de Bergerac

BY EDMOND ROSTAND

TRANSLATED FROM THE FRENCH
BY BRIAN HOOKER

*It was to the soul of CYRANO that
I intended to dedicate this poem.*

*But since that soul has been reborn
in you, COQUELIN, it is to you that I
dedicate it.*

E. R.

(The first four Acts in 1640; the fifth in 1655.)

FIRST ACT: A Performance at the Hôtel de Bourgogne.

SECOND ACT: The Bakery of the Poets.

THIRD ACT: Roxane's Kiss.

FOURTH ACT: The Cadets of Gascoyne.

FIFTH ACT: Cyrano's Gazette.

CHARACTERS

Cyrano de Bergerac
Christian de Neuvillette
Comte de Guiche
Ragueneau
Le Bret
Carbon de Castel-Jaloux
The Cadets
Lignière
Vicomte de Valvert
A Marquis
Second Marquis
Third Marquis
Montfleury
Bellerose
Jodelet
Cuigy
Brissaille
A Meddler
A Musketeer
Another Musketeer
A Spanish Officer
A Cavalier

The Porter
A Citizen
His Son
A Cut-Purse
A Spectator
A Sentry
Bertrandou the Fifer
A Capuchin
Two Musicians
The Poets
The Pastrycooks
The Pages
Roxane
Her Duenna
Lise
The Orange-Girl
Mother Marguérite de Jésus
Sister Marthe
Sister Claire
An Actress
A Soubrette
The Flower-Girl

The Crowd, Citizens, Marquis, Musketeers, Thieves, Pastrycooks, Poets, Cadets of Gascoyne, Actors, Violins, Pages, Children, Spanish Soldiers, Spectators, Intellectuals, Academicians, Nuns, etc.

CYRANO DE BERGERAC

THE FIRST ACT

A PERFORMANCE AT THE HÔTEL DE BOURGOGNE

The Hall of the Hôtel de Bourgogne in 1640. A sort of Tennis Court, arranged and decorated for Theatrical productions.

The Hall is a long rectangle; we see it diagonally, in such a way that one side of it forms the back scene, which begins at the First Entrance on the Right and runs up to the Last Entrance on the Left, where it makes a right angle with the Stage which is seen obliquely.

This Stage is provided on either hand with benches placed along the wings. The curtain is formed by two lengths of Tapestry which can be drawn apart. Above a Harlequin cloak, the Royal Arms. Broad steps lead from the Stage down to the floor of the Hall. On either side of these steps, a place for the Musicians. A row of candles serves as footlights. Two tiers of Galleries along the side of the Hall; the upper one divided into boxes.

There are no seats upon the Floor, which is the actual stage of our theatre; but toward the back of the Hall, on the right, a few benches are arranged; and underneath a stairway on the extreme right, which leads up to the galleries, and of which only the lower portion is visible, there is a sort of Sideboard, decorated with little tapers, vases of flowers, bottles and glasses, plates of cake, et cetera.

Farther along, toward the center of our stage, is the Entrance to the Hall: a great double door which opens only slightly to admit the Audience. On one of the panels of this door, as also in other places about the Hall, and in particular just over the Sideboard, are Playbills in red, upon which we may read the title LA CLORISE.

As the CURTAIN RISES, *the Hall is dimly lighted and still empty. The Chandeliers are lowered to the floor, in the middle of the Hall, ready for lighting.*

(Sounds of voices outside the door. Then a CAVALIER *enters abruptly.)*

THE PORTER
(Follows him)
Hallo there!—Fifteen sols!

THE CAVALIER
I enter free.

THE PORTER
Why?

THE CAVALIER
Soldier of the Household of
the King!

THE PORTER
(Turns to another CAVALIER
who has just entered.)
You?

SECOND CAVALIER

I pay nothing.

THE PORTER

Why not?

SECOND CAVALIER

Musketeer!

FIRST CAVALIER

(*To the* SECOND)

The play begins at two. Plenty of
time—
And here's the whole floor empty.
Shall we try
Our exercise?
(*They fence with the foils
which they have brought.*)

A LACKEY

(*Enters*)

—Pst! . . . Flanquin! . . .

ANOTHER

(*Already on stage*)
What, Champagne?

FIRST LACKEY

(*Showing games which he
takes out of his doublet*)
Cards. Dice. Come on.
(*Sits on the floor.*)

SECOND LACKEY

(*Same action*)
Come on, old cock!

FIRST LACKEY

(*Takes from his pocket a bit
of candle, lights it, sets it on
the floor.*)
I have stolen
A little of my master's fire.

A GUARDSMAN

(*To a flower girl who comes
forward*)

How sweet
Of you, to come before they light
the hall!
(*Puts his arm around her.*)

FIRST CAVALIER

(*Receives a thrust of the foil*)
A hit!

SECOND LACKEY

A club!

THE GUARDSMAN

(*Pursuing the girl*)
A kiss!

THE FLOWER GIRL

(*Pushing away from him*)
They'll see us!—

THE GUARDSMAN

(*Draws her into a dark corner*)
No danger!

A MAN

(*Sits on the floor, together
with several others who
have brought packages of
food*)
When we come early, we have time
to eat.

A CITIZEN

(*Escorting his son, a boy of
sixteen*)
Sit here, my son.

FIRST LACKEY

Mark the Ace!

ANOTHER MAN

(*Draws a bottle from under
his cloak and sits down with
the others*)
Here's the spot
For a jolly old sot to suck his Burgundy—

(Drinks)
Here—in the house of the Burgundians!

THE CITIZEN

(To his son)
Would you not think you were in some den of vice?
(Points with his cane at the drunkard)
Drunkards—
(In stepping back, one of the cavaliers trips him up)
Bullies!—
(He falls between the lackeys)
Gamblers!—

THE GUARDSMAN

(Behind him as he rises, still struggling with the Flower Girl)
One kiss—

THE CITIZEN

Good God!—
(Draws his son quickly away)
Here!—And to think, my son, that in this hall
They play Rotrou!

THE BOY

Yes, father—and Corneille!

THE PAGES

(Dance in, holding hands and singing:)
Tra-la-la-la-la-la-la-la-la-lère . . .

THE PORTER

You pages there—no nonsense!

FIRST PAGE

(With wounded dignity)
Oh, Monsieur!
Really! How could you?
(To the SECOND, the moment the PORTER turns his back)
Pst!—a bit of string?

SECOND PAGE

(Shows fishline with hook)
Yes—and a hook.

FIRST PAGE

Up in the gallery,
And fish for wigs!

A CUT-PURSE

(Gathers around him several evil-looking young fellows)
Now then, you picaroons,
Perk up, and hear me mutter.
Here's your bout—
Bustle around some cull, and bite his bung . . .

SECOND PAGE

(Calls to other pages already in the gallery)
Hey! Brought your pea-shooters?

THIRD PAGE

(From above)
And our peas, too!
(Blows, and showers them with peas.)

THE BOY

What is the play this afternoon?

THE CITIZEN

Clorise.

THE BOY

Who wrote that?

THE CITIZEN

Balthasar Baro. What a play! . . .
(He takes THE BOY's arm and leads him upstage.)

THE CUT-PURSE

(To his pupils)
Lace now, on those long sleeves, you cut it off—
(Gesture with thumb and finger, as if using scissors.)

A SPECTATOR

(*To another, pointing upward
toward the gallery*)
Ah, *Le Cid!*—Yes, the first night,
I sat there—

THE CUT-PURSE

Watches—
(*Gestures as of picking a
pocket.*)

THE CITIZEN

(*Coming down with his son*)
Great actors we shall see today—

THE CUT-PURSE

Handkerchiefs—
(*Gesture of holding the pocket
with left hand, and drawing
out handkerchief with right.*)

THE CITIZEN

Montfleury—

A VOICE

(*In the gallery*)
Lights! Light the lights!

THE CITIZEN

Bellerose, l'Épy, Beaupré, Jodelet—

A PAGE

(*On the floor*)
Here comes the orange-girl.

THE ORANGE-GIRL

Oranges, milk,
Raspberry syrup, lemonade—
(*Noise at the door.*)

A FALSETTO VOICE

(*Outside*)
Make way,
Brutes!

FIRST LACKEY

What, the Marquis—on the floor?
(*The Marquis enters in a little group.*)

SECOND LACKEY

Not long—
Only a few moments; they'll go and
sit
On the stage presently.

FIRST MARQUIS

(*Seeing the hall half empty*)
How now! We enter
Like tradespeople—no crowding,
no disturbance!—
No treading on the toes of citizens?
Oh fie! Oh fie!
(*He encounters two gentlemen
who have already arrived*)
Cuigy! Brissaille!
(*Great embracings.*)

CUIGY

The faithful!
(*Looks around him*)
We are here before the candles.

FIRST MARQUIS

Ah, be still!
You put me in a temper.

SECOND MARQUIS

Console yourself,
Marquis—The lamplighter!

THE CROWD

(*Applauding the appearance
of the lamplighter*)
Ah! . . .
(*A group gathers around the
chandelier while he lights it.
A few people have already
taken their place in the gallery.* LIGNIÈRE *enters the
hall, arm in arm with*
CHRISTIAN DE NEUVILLETTE.
LIGNIÈRE *is a slightly disheveled figure, dissipated
and yet distinguished looking.* CHRISTIAN, *elegantly
but rather unfashionably
dressed, appears pre-occu-*

pied and keeps looking up
at the boxes.)

CUIGY
Lignière!—

BRISSAILLE
(Laughing)
Still sober—at this hour?

LIGNIÈRE
(To CHRISTIAN)
May I present you?
(CHRISTIAN assents)
Baron Christian de Neuvillette.
(They salute.)

THE CROWD
(Applauding as the lighted
chandelier is hoisted into
place)
Ah!—

CUIGY
(Aside to BRISSAILLE, looking
at CHRISTIAN)
Rather
A fine head, is it not? The profile
. . .

FIRST MARQUIS
(Who has overheard)
Peuh!

LIGNIÈRE
(Presenting them to CHRIS-
TIAN)
Messieurs de Cuigy . . . de Bris-
saille . . .

CHRISTIAN
(Bows)   Enchanted!

FIRST MARQUIS
(To the second)
He is not ill-looking; possibly a
shade
Behind the fashion.

LIGNIÈRE
(To CUIGY)
Monsieur is recently
From the Touraine.

CHRISTIAN
Yes, I have been in Paris
Two or three weeks only. I join the
Guards
Tomorrow.

FIRST MARQUIS
(Watching the people who
come into the boxes)
Look—Madame la Présidente
Aubry!

THE ORANGE-GIRL
Oranges, milk—

THE VIOLINS
(Tuning up)
La . . . la . . .

CUIGY
(To CHRISTIAN, calling his at-
tention to the increasing
crowd)
We have
An audience today!

CHRISTIAN
A brilliant one.

FIRST MARQUIS
Oh, yes, all our own people—the
gay world!
(They name the ladies who
enter the boxes elaborately
dressed. Bows and smiles
are exchanged.)

SECOND MARQUIS
Madame de Guéméné . . .

CUIGY
De Bois-Dauphin . . .

FIRST MARQUIS
Whom we adore—

BRISSAILLE
Madame de Chavigny . . .

SECOND MARQUIS
Who plays with all our hearts—

LIGNIÈRE
            Why, there's Corneille
Returned from Rouen!

THE BOY
    (*To his father*)
            Are the Academy
All here?

THE CITIZEN
I see some of them . . . there's
    Boudu—
Boissat—Cureau—Porchères—Col-
    omby—
Bourzeys—Bourdon—Arbaut—
        Ah, those great names,
Never to be forgotten!

FIRST MARQUIS
            Look—at last!
Our Intellectuals! Barthénoide,
Urimédonte, Félixérie . . .

SECOND MARQUIS
    (*Languishing*)
            Sweet heaven!
How exquisite their surnames are!
    Marquis,
You know them all?

FIRST MARQUIS
    I know them all, Marquis!

LIGNIÈRE
    (*Draws* CHRISTIAN *aside*)
My dear boy, I came here to serve
    you— Well,
But where's the lady? I'll be going.

CHRISTIAN
                Not yet—
A little longer! She is always here.
Please! I must find some way of
    meeting her.
I am dying of love! And you—you
    know
Everyone, the whole court and the
    whole town,
And put them all into your songs—
    at least
You can tell me her name!

THE FIRST VIOLIN
    (*Raps on his desk with his
    bow*)
            Pst— Gentlemen!
    (*Raises his bow.*)

THE ORANGE-GIRL
Macaroons, lemonade—

CHRISTIAN
                Then she may be
One of those æsthetes . . . Intel-
    lectuals,
You call them— How can I talk to
    a woman
In that style? I have no wit. This
    fine manner
Of speaking and of writing nowa-
    days—
Not for me! I am a soldier—and
    afraid.
That's her box, on the right—the
    empty one.

LIGNIÈRE
    (*Starts for the door*)
I am going.

CHRISTIAN
    (*Restrains him*)
            No—wait!

LIGNIÈRE
        Not I. There's a tavern
Not far away—and I am dying of
    thirst.

THE ORANGE-GIRL
(Passes with her tray)
Orange juice?

LIGNIÈRE
No!

THE ORANGE-GIRL
Milk?

LIGNIÈRE
Pouah!

THE ORANGE-GIRL
Muscatel?

LIGNIÈRE
Here! Stop!
(To CHRISTIAN*)*
I'll stay a little.
(To the GIRL*)*
Let me see
Your Muscatel.
*(He sits down by the side-
board. The* GIRL *pours out
wine for him.)*

VOICES
*(In the crowd about the door,
upon the entrance of a
spruce little man, rather fat,
with a beaming smile)*
Ragueneau!

LIGNIÈRE
(To CHRISTIAN*)*
Ragueneau,
Poet and pastrycook—a character!

RAGUENEAU
*(Dressed like a confectioner in
his Sunday clothes, ad-
vances quickly to* LIGNIÈRE*)*
Sir, have you seen Monsieur de
Cyrano?

LIGNIÈRE
(Presents him to CHRISTIAN*)*
Permit me . . . Ragueneau, con-
fectioner,
The chief support of modern
poetry.

RAGUENEAU
(Bridling)
Oh—too much honor!

LIGNIÈRE
Patron of the Arts—
Mæcenas! Yes, you are—

RAGUENEAU
Undoubtedly,
The poets gather round my hearth.

LIGNIÈRE
On credit—
Himself a poet—

RAGUENEAU
So they say—

LIGNIÈRE
Maintains
The Muses.

RAGUENEAU
It is true that for an ode—

LIGNIÈRE
You give a tart—

RAGUENEAU
A tartlet—

LIGNIÈRE
Modesty!
And for a triolet you give—

RAGUENEAU
Plain bread!

LIGNIÈRE

(*Severely*)

Bread and milk! And you love the theatre?

RAGUENEAU

I adore it!

LIGNIÈRE

Well, pastry pays for all.
Your place today now—Come, between ourselves,
What did it cost you?

RAGUENEAU

Four pies; fourteen cakes.
(*Looking about*)
But— Cyrano not here? Astonishing!

LIGNIÈRE

Why so?

RAGUENEAU

Why— Montfleury plays!

LIGNIÈRE

Yes, I hear
That hippopotamus assumes the rôle
Of Phédon. What is that to Cyrano?

RAGUENEAU

Have you not heard? Monsieur de Bergerac
So hates Montfleury, he has forbidden him
For three weeks to appear upon the stage.

LIGNIÈRE

(*Who is, by this time, at his fourth glass*)
Well?

RAGUENEAU

Montfleury plays!—

CUIGY

(*Strolls over to them*)
Yes—what then?

RAGUENEAU

Ah! That
Is what I came to see.

FIRST MARQUIS

This Cyrano—
Who is he?

CUIGY

Oh, he is the lad with the long sword.

SECOND MARQUIS

Noble?

CUIGY

Sufficiently; he is in the Guards.
(*Points to a gentleman who comes and goes about the hall as though seeking for someone*)
His friend Le Bret can tell you more.
(*Calls to him*)
Le Bret!
(LE BRET *comes down to them*)
Looking for Bergerac?

LE BRET

Yes. And for trouble.

CUIGY

Is he not an extraordinary man?

LE BRET

The best friend and the bravest soul alive!

RAGUENEAU

Poet—

CUIGY

Swordsman—

LE BRET

Musician—

BRISSAILLE

Philosopher—

LIGNIÈRE

Such a remarkable appearance, too!

RAGUENEAU

Truly, I should not look to find his portrait
By the grave hand of Philippe de Champagne.
He might have been a model for Callot—
One of those wild swashbucklers in a masque—
Hat with three plumes, and doublet with six points—
His cloak behind him over his long sword
Cocked, like the tail of strutting Chanticleer—
Prouder than all the swaggering Tamburlaines
Hatched out of Gascony. And to complete
This Punchinello figure—such a nose!—
My lords, there is no such nose as that nose—
You cannot look upon it without crying: "Oh, no,
Impossible! Exaggerated!" Then
You smile, and say: "Of course—I might have known;
Presently he will take it off." But that
Monsieur de Bergerac will never do.

LIGNIÈRE

(Grimly)
He keeps it—and God help the man who smiles!

RAGUENEAU

His sword is one half of the shears of Fate!

FIRST MARQUIS

(Shrugs)
He will not come.

RAGUENEAU

Will he not? Sir, I'll lay you
A pullet à la Ragueneau!

FIRST MARQUIS

(Laughing)
Done!
(Murmurs of admiration; ROX-
ANE has just appeared in her
box. She sits at the front of
the box, and her Duenna
takes a seat toward the rear.
CHRISTIAN, busy paying the
Orange-Girl, does not see
her at first.)

SECOND MARQUIS

(With little excited cries)
Ah!
Oh! Oh! Sweet sirs, look yonder! Is she not
Frightfully ravishing?

FIRST MARQUIS

Bloom of the peach—
Blush of the strawberry—

SECOND MARQUIS

So fresh—so cool,
That our hearts, grown all warm with loving her,
May catch their death of cold!

CHRISTIAN

(Looks up, sees ROXANE, and
seizes LIGNIÈRE by the
arm.)
There! Quick—up there—
In the box! Look!—

LIGNIÈRE

(*Coolly*)
Herself?

CHRISTIAN

Quickly— Her name?

LIGNIÈRE

(*Sipping his wine, and speaking between sips*)
Madeleine Robin, called Roxane
. . . refined . . .
Intellectual . . .

CHRISTIAN

Ah!—

LIGNIÈRE

Unmarried . . .

CHRISTIAN

Oh!—

LIGNIÈRE

No title . . . rich enough . . . an
orphan . . . cousin
To Cyrano . . . of whom we spoke
just now . . .
(*At this point, a very distinguished looking gentleman,
the Cordon Bleu around his
neck, enters the box, and
stands a moment talking
with* ROXANE.)

CHRISTIAN

(*Starts*)
And the man? . . .

LIGNIÈRE

(*Beginning to feel his wine a
little; cocks his eye at
them.*)
Oho! That man? . . . Comte de
Guiche . . .
In love with her . . . married himself, however,

To the niece of the Cardinal—
Richelieu . . .
Wishes Roxane, therefore, to marry
one
Monsieur de Valvert . . . Vicomte
. . . friend of his . . .
A somewhat melancholy gentleman
. . .
But . . . well,   accommodating!
. . . She says No . . .
Nevertheless, de Guiche is power-
ful . . .
Not above persecuting . . .
(*He rises, swaying a little, and
very happy.*)
I have written
A little song about his little game
. . .
Good little song, too . . . Here,
I'll sing it for you . . .
Make de Guiche furious . . .
naughty little song . . .
Not so bad either— Listen! . . .
(*He stands with his glass held
aloft, ready to sing.*)

CHRISTIAN

No. Adieu.

LIGNIÈRE

Whither away?

CHRISTIAN

To Monsieur de Valvert!

LIGNIÈRE

Careful! The man's a swordsman
. . .
(*Nods toward* ROXANE, *who is
watching* CHRISTIAN.)
Wait! Someone
Looking at you—

CHRISTIAN

Roxane! . . .
(*He forgets everything, and
stands spellbound, gazing
toward* ROXANE. *The Cut-
Purse and his crew, observ-*

*ing him transfixed, his eyes
raised and his mouth half
open, begin edging in his direction.*)

LIGNIÈRE
Oh! Very well,
Then I'll be leaving you . . . Good
day . . . Good day! . . .
(CHRISTIAN *remains motionless.*)
Everywhere else, they like to hear
me sing!—
Also, I am thirsty.
(*He goes out, navigating carefully.* LE BRET, *having made
the circuit of the hall, returns to* RAGUENEAU, *somewhat reassured.*)

LE BRET
No sign anywhere
Of Cyrano!

RAGUENEAU
(*Incredulous*)
Wait and see!

LE BRET
Humph! I hope
He has not seen the bill.

THE CROWD
The play!—The play!—

FIRST MARQUIS
(*Observing* DE GUICHE, *as he
descends from* ROXANE's *box
and crosses the floor, followed by a knot of obsequious gentlemen, the* VICOMTE
DE VALVERT *among them.*)
This man de Guiche—what ostentation!

SECOND MARQUIS
Bah!—
Another Gascon!

FIRST MARQUIS
Gascon, yes—but cold
And calculating—certain to suc-
ceed—
My word for it. Come, shall we
make our bow?
We shall be none the worse, I
promise you . . .
(*They go toward* DE GUICHE.)

SECOND MARQUIS
Beautiful ribbons, Count! That
color, now,
What is it—*Kiss-me-Dear* or *Star-
tled-Fawn?*

DE GUICHE
I call that shade *The Dying Spaniard.*

FIRST MARQUIS
Ha!
And no false colors either—thanks
to you
And your brave troops, in Flanders
before long
The Spaniard will die daily.

DE GUICHE
Shall we go
And sit upon the stage? Come, Val-
vert.

CHRISTIAN
(*Starts at the name*)
Valvert!—
The Vicomte— Ah, that scoundrel!
Quick—my glove—
I'll throw it in his face—
(*Reaching into his pocket for
his glove, he catches the
hand of the Cut-Purse.*)

THE CUT-PURSE
Oh!—

CHRISTIAN
(*Holding fast to the man's
wrist*)

Who are you?
I was looking for a glove—

THE CUT-PURSE

(Cringing)
You found a hand.
(Hurriedly)
Let me go—I can tell you some-
thing—

CHRISTIAN

(Still holding him)
Well?

THE CUT-PURSE

Lignière—that friend of yours—

CHRISTIAN

(Same business)
Well?

THE CUT-PURSE

Good as dead—
Understand? Ambuscaded. Wrote
a song
About—no matter. There's a hundred men
Waiting for him tonight—I'm one
of them.

CHRISTIAN

A hundred! Who arranged this?

THE CUT-PURSE

Secret.

CHRISTIAN

Oh!

THE CUT-PURSE

(With dignity)
Professional secret.

CHRISTIAN

Where are they to be?

THE CUT-PURSE

Porte de Nesle. On his way home.
Tell him so.
Save his life.

CHRISTIAN

(Releases the man)
Yes, but where am I to find him?

THE CUT-PURSE

Go round the taverns. There's the
Golden Grape,
The Pineapple, The Bursting Belt,
The Two
Torches, The Three Funnels—in
every one
You leave a line of writing—un-
derstand?
To warn him.

CHRISTIAN

(Starts for the door)
I'll go! God, what swine—a hun-
dred
Against one man! . . .
(Stops and looks longingly at
ROXANE)
Leave her here!—
(Savagely, turning toward
VALVERT)
And leave him!—
(Decidedly)
I must save Lignière!
(Exit)
(DE GUICHE, VALVERT, and all
the Marquis have disap-
peared through the cur-
tains, to take their seats
upon the stage. The floor is
entirely filled; not a vacant
seat remains in the gallery
or in the boxes.)

THE CROWD

The play! The play!
Begin the play!

A CITIZEN

(As his wig is hoisted into the
air on the end of a fishline,
in the hands of a page in the
gallery)
My wig! !

CRIES OF JOY

He's bald! Bravo,
You pages! Ha ha ha!

THE CITIZEN

(*Furious, shakes his fist at the
boy*)
Here, you young villain!

CRIES AND LAUGHTER

(*Beginning very loud, then
suddenly repressed*)
HA HA! Ha Ha! ha ha. . . .
(*Complete silence.*)

LE BRET

(*Surprised*)
That sudden hush! . . .
(*A Spectator whispers in his
ear.*)
Yes?

THE SPECTATOR

I was told on good authority . . .

MURMURS

(*Here and there*)
What? . . . Here? . . . No . . . Yes
. . . Look—in the latticed box—
The Cardinal! . . . The Cardinal!
. . .

A PAGE

The Devil!—
Now we shall all have to behave
ourselves!
(*Three raps on the stage. The
audience becomes motion-
less. Silence.*)

THE VOICE OF A MARQUIS

(*From the stage, behind the
curtains*)
Snuff that candle!

ANOTHER MARQUIS

(*Puts his head out through
the curtains.*)

A chair! . . .
(*A chair is passed from hand
to hand over the heads of
the crowd. He takes it, and
disappears behind the curtains, not without having
blown a few kisses to the
occupants of the boxes.*)

A SPECTATOR

Silence!

VOICES

Hssh! . . . Hssh! . . .
(*Again the three raps on the
stage. The curtains part.
TABLEAU. The Marquis
seated on their chairs to
right and left of the stage,
insolently posed. Back drop
representing a pastoral
scene, bluish in tone. Four
little crystal chandeliers
light up the stage. The
violins play softly.*)

LE BRET

(*In a low tone to* RAGUENEAU)
Montfleury enters now?

RAGUENEAU

(*Nods*)
Opens the play.

LE BRET

(*Much relieved*)
Then Cyrano is not here!

RAGUENEAU

I lose . . .

LE BRET

Humph!
So much the better!
(*The melody of a Musette is
heard.* MONTFLEURY ap-
pears upon the scene, a pon-

*derous figure in the costume
of a rustic shepherd, a hat
garlanded with roses tilted
over one ear, playing upon
a beribboned pastoral pipe.)*

THE CROWD

(Applauds)
Montfleury! . . . Bravo! . . .

MONTFLEURY

*(After bowing to the applause,
begins the rôle of Phédon)*
"Thrice happy he who hides from
pomp and power
In sylvan shade or solitary bower;
Where balmy zephyrs fan his burning cheeks—"

A VOICE

(From the midst of the hall)
Wretch! Have I not forbade you
these three weeks?
*(Sensation. Everyone turns to
look. Murmurs.)*

SEVERAL VOICES

What? . . . Where? . . . Who is it?
. . .

CUIGY

Cyrano!

LE BRET

(In alarm)
Himself!

THE VOICE

King of clowns! Leave the stage—
at once!

THE CROWD

Oh!

MONTFLEURY

Now,
Now, now—

THE VOICE

You disobey me?

SEVERAL VOICES

*(From the floor, from the
boxes)*
Hsh! Go on—
Quiet!—Go   on,   Montfleury!—
Who's afraid?—

MONTFLEURY

*(In a voice of no great assur-
ance)*
"Thrice happy he who hides from
. . ."

THE VOICE

(More menacingly)
Well? Well? Well? . . .
Monarch of mountebanks! Must I
come and plant
A forest on your shoulders?
*(A cane at the end of a long
arm shakes above the heads
of the crowd.)*

MONTFLEURY

*(In   a   voice   increasingly
feeble)*
"Thrice hap—"
*(The cane is violently agi-
tated.)*

THE VOICE

GO! ! !

THE CROWD

Ah! . . .

CYRANO

*(Arises in the center of the
floor, erect upon a chair, his
arms folded, his hat cocked
ferociously, his moustache
bristling, his nose terrible)*
Presently I shall grow angry!
(Sensation at his appearance.)

MONTFLEURY
(*To the Marquis*)
Messieurs,
If you protect me—

A MARQUIS
(*Nonchalantly*)
Well—proceed!

CYRANO
Fat swine!
If you dare breathe one balmy zephyr more,
I'll fan your cheeks for you!

THE MARQUIS
Quiet down there!

CYRANO
Unless these gentlemen retain their seats,
My cane may bite their ribbons!

ALL THE MARQUIS
(*On their feet*)
That will do!—
Montfleury—

CYRANO
Fly, goose! Shoo! Take to your wings,
Before I pluck your plumes, and draw your gorge!

A VOICE
See here!—

CYRANO
Off stage!

ANOTHER VOICE
One moment—

CYRANO
What—still there?
(*Turns back his cuffs deliberately.*)

Very good—then I enter—*Left*—with knife—
To carve this large Italian sausage.

MONTFLEURY
(*Desperately attempting dignity*)
Sir,
When you insult me, you insult the Muse!

CYRANO
(*With great politeness*)
Sir, if the Muse, who never knew your name,
Had the honor to meet you—then be sure
That after one glance at that face of yours,
That figure of a mortuary urn—
She would apply her buskin—toward the rear!

THE CROWD
Montfleury! . . . Montfleury! . . .
The play! The play!

CYRANO
(*To those who are shouting and crowding about him*)
Pray you, be gentle with my scabbard here—
She'll put her tongue out at you presently!—
(*The circle enlarges.*)

THE CROWD
(*Recoiling*)
Keep back—

CYRANO
(*To* MONTFLEURY)
Begone!

THE CROWD
(*Pushing in closer, and growling*)
Ahr! . . . ahr! . . .

CYRANO

(*Turns upon them.*)
　　　Did some one speak?
(*They recoil again.*)

A VOICE

(*In the back of the hall,
sings.*)
　　Monsieur de Cyrano
　　　　Must be another Cæsar—
　　Let Brutus lay him low,
　　　　And play us La Clorise!

ALL THE CROWD

(*Singing*)
La Clorise! La Clorise!

CYRANO

Let me hear one more word of that
　　same song,
And I destroy you all!

A CITIZEN

　　　　Who might you be?
Samson?—

CYRANO

Precisely. Would you kindly lend
　　me
Your jawbone?

A LADY

(*In one of the boxes*)
What an outrage!

A NOBLE

　　　　Scandalous!

A CITIZEN

Annoying!

A PAGE

What a game!

THE CROWD

　　　　Kss! Montfleury!
Cyrano!

CYRANO

Silence!

THE CROWD

(*Delirious*)
Woof! Woof! Baaa! Cockadoo!

CYRANO

I—

A PAGE

Meow!

CYRANO

　　I say be silent!—
(*His voice dominates the up-
roar. Momentary hush.*)
　　　　And I offer
One universal challenge to you all!
Approach, young heroes—I will
　　take your names.
Each in his turn—no crowding!
　　One, two, three—
Come, get your numbers—who will
　　head the list—
You, sir? No— You? Ah, no. To the
　　first man
Who falls I'll build a monument!
　　. . . Not one?
Will all who wish to die, please
　　raise their hands? . . .
I see. You are so modest, you might
　　blush
Before a sword naked. Sweet in-
　　nocence! . . .
Not one name? Not one finger? . . .
　　Very well,
Then I go on:
　　　　(*Turning back toward the
　　　　stage, where* MONTFLEURY
　　　　waits in despair.)
　　　　I'd have our theatre cured
Of this carbuncle. Or if not, why
　　then—
　　　　(*His hand on his sword hilt.*)
The lancet!

MONTFLEURY

I—

CYRANO

(*Descends from his chair,
seats himself comfortably
in the center of the circle
which has formed around
him, and makes himself
quite at home.*)
        Attend to me—full moon!
I clap my hands, three times—
thus. At the third
You will eclipse yourself.

THE CROWD

(*Amused*)
        Ah!

CYRANO

        Ready? *One.*

MONTFLEURY

I—

A VOICE

(*From the boxes*)
No!

THE CROWD

He'll go— He'll stay—

MONTFLEURY

        I really think,
Gentlemen—

CYRANO

Two.

MONTFLEURY

Perhaps I had better—

CYRANO

        Three!
(*MONTFLEURY disappears, as
if through a trap-door. Tem-
pest of laughter, hoots and
hisses.*)

THE CROWD

Yah!—Coward—Come back—

CYRANO

(*Beaming, drops back in his
chair and crosses his legs*)
Let him—if he dare!

A CITIZEN

The Manager! Speech! Speech!
(*BELLEROSE advances and
bows.*)

THE BOXES

        Ah! Bellerose!

BELLEROSE

(*With elegance*)
Most noble—most fair—

THE CROWD

        No! The Comedian—
Jodelet!—

JODELET

(*Advances, and speaks
through his nose.*)
Lewd fellows of the baser sort—

THE CROWD

Ha! Ha! Not bad! Bravo!

JODELET

        No Bravos here!
Our heavy tragedian with the vo-
luptuous bust
Was taken suddenly—

THE CROWD

Yah! Coward!

JODELET

        I mean . . .
He had to be excused—

THE CROWD

        Call him back—No!—
Yes!—

THE BOY

(*To* CYRANO)
    After all, Monsieur, what
      reason have you
To hate this Montfleury?

CYRANO

(*Graciously, still seated*)
        My dear young man,
I have two reasons, either one alone
Conclusive. *Primo:* A lamentable
    actor,
Who mouths his verse and moans
    his tragedy,
And heaves up— Ugh!—like a hod-
    carrier, lines
That ought to soar on their own
    wings. *Secundo:*—
Well—that's my secret.

THE OLD CITIZEN

(*Behind him*)
      But you close the play—
La Clorise—by Baro! Are we to
    miss
Our entertainment, merely—

CYRANO

(*Respectfully, turns his chair
    toward the old man*)
      My dear old boy,
The poetry of Baro being worth
Zero, or less, I feel that I have done
Poetic justice!

THE INTELLECTUALS

(*In the boxes*)
      Really!—our Baro!—
My dear!—Who ever?—Ah, dieu!
The idea!—

CYRANO

(*Gallantly, turns his chair to-
    ward the boxes*)
Fair ladies—shine upon us like the
    sun,
Blossom like flowers around us—
    be our songs,

Heard in a dream— Make sweet
    the hour of death,
Smiling upon us as you close our
    eyes—
Inspired, but do not try to criticize!

BELLEROSE

Quite so!—and the mere money—
    possibly
You would like that returned—
    Yes?

CYRANO

        Bellerose,
You speak the first word of intel-
    ligence!
I will not wound the mantle of the
    Muse—
Here, catch!—
    (*Throws him a purse*)
      And hold your tongue.

THE CROWD

(*Astonished*)
      Ah! Ah!

JODELET

(*Deftly catches the purse,
    weighs it in his hand*)
      Monsieur,
You are hereby authorized to close
    our play
Every night, on the same terms.

THE CROWD

Boo!

JODELET

      And welcome!
Let us be booed together, you and
    I!

BELLEROSE

Kindly pass out quietly . . .

JODELET

(*Burlesquing* BELLEROSE)
      Quietly . . .

(They begin to go out, while CYRANO *looks about him with satisfaction. But the exodus ceases presently during the ensuing scene. The ladies in the boxes who have already risen and put on their wraps, stop to listen, and finally sit down again.)*

LE BRET

(*To* CYRANO)

Idiot!

A MEDDLER

(*Hurries up to* CYRANO.)
But what a scandal! Montfleury—
The great Montfleury! Did you
know the Duc
De Candale was his patron? Who
is yours?

CYRANO

No one.

THE MEDDLER

No one—no patron?

CYRANO

I said no.

THE MEDDLER

What, no great lord, to cover with
his name—

CYRANO

(*With visible annoyance*)
No, I have told you twice. Must I
repeat?
No sir, no patron—
(*His hand on his sword*)
But a patroness!

THE MEDDLER

And when do you leave Paris?

CYRANO

That's as may be.

THE MEDDLER

The Duc de Candale has a long
arm.

CYRANO

Mine

Is longer,
(*Drawing his sword*)
by three feet of steel.

THE MEDDLER

Yes, yes,
But do you dream of daring—

CYRANO

I do dream
Of daring . . .

THE MEDDLER

But—

CYRANO

You may go now.

THE MEDDLER

But—

CYRANO

You may go—
Or tell me why are you staring at
my nose!

THE MEDDLER

(*In confusion*)
No—I—

CYRANO

(*Stepping up to him*)
Does it astonish you?

THE MEDDLER

(*Drawing back*)
Your grace
Misunderstands my—

CYRANO

Is it long and soft
And dangling, like a trunk?

THE MEDDLER

(*Same business*)

I never said—

CYRANO

Or crooked, like an owl's beak?

THE MEDDLER

ı—

CYRANO

Perhaps
A pimple ornaments the end of it?

THE MEDDLER

No—

CYRANO

Or a fly parading up and
down?
What is this portent?

THE MEDDLER

Oh!—

CYRANO

This phenomenon?

THE MEDDLER

But I have been careful not to
look—

CYRANO

And why
Not, if you please?

THE MEDDLER

Why—

CYRANO

It disgusts you, then?

THE MEDDLER

My dear sir—

CYRANO

Does its color appear to you
Unwholesome?

THE MEDDLER

Oh, by no means!

CYRANO

Or its form
Obscene?

THE MEDDLER

Not in the least—

CYRANO

Then why assume
This deprecating manner? Possibly
You find it just a trifle large?

THE MEDDLER

(*Babbling*)

Oh, no!
Small, very small, infinitesimal—

CYRANO

(*Roars*)

What!
How? You accuse me of absurdity?
Small—*my nose?* Why—

THE MEDDLER

(*Breathless*)

My God!—

CYRANO

Magnificent,
My nose! . . . You pug, you knob,
you button-head,
Know that I glory in this nose of
mine,
For a great nose indicates a great
man—
Genial, courteous, intellectual,
Virile, courageous—as I am—and
such
As you—poor wretch—will never
dare to be

Even in imagination. For that face

That blank, inglorious concavity
Which my right hand finds—
    (*He strikes him.*)

THE MEDDLER
    Ow!

CYRANO
            —on top of you,
Is as devoid of pride, of poetry,
Of soul, of picturesqueness, of con-
    tour,
Of character, of NOSE in short—as
    that
    (*Takes him by the shoulders
    and turns him around, suit-
    ing the action to the word*)
Which at the end of that limp spine
    of yours
My left foot—

THE MEDDLER
    (*Escaping*)
    Help! The Guard!

CYRANO
            Take notice, all
Who find this feature of my coun-
    tenance
A theme for comedy! When the
    humorist
Is noble, then my custom is to show
Appreciation proper to his rank—
More   heartfelt . . . and   more
    pointed. . . .

DE GUICHE
    (*Who has come down from
    the stage, surrounded by
    the Marquis*)
            Presently
This fellow will grow tiresome.

VALVERT
    (*Shrugs*)
            Oh, he blows
His trumpet!

DE GUICHE
    Well—will no one interfere?

VALVERT
No one?
    (*Looks round*)
    Observe. I myself will proceed
To put him in his place.
    (*He walks up to* CYRANO, *who
    has been watching him, and
    stands there, looking him
    over with an affected air.*)
Ah . . . your nose . . . hem! . . .
Your nose is . . . rather large!

CYRANO
    (*Gravely*)
            Rather.

VALVERT
    (*Simpering*)
                Oh well—

CYRANO
    (*Coolly*)
Is that all?

VALVERT
    (*Turns away, with a shrug*)
    Well, of course—

CYRANO
            Ah, no, young sir!
You are too simple. Why, you might
    have said—
Oh, a great many things! Mon dieu,
    why waste
Your opportunity? For example,
    thus:—
AGGRESSIVE: I, sir, if that nose were
    mine,
I'd have it amputated—on the spot!
FRIENDLY: How do you drink with
    such a nose?
You ought to have a cup made spe-
    cially.
DESCRIPTIVE: 'Tis a rock—a crag—
    a cape—
A cape? say rather, a peninsula!

INQUISITIVE: What is that receptacle—
A razor-case or a portfolio?
KINDLY: Ah, do you love the little birds
So much that when they come and sing to you,
You give them this to perch on? INSOLENT:
Sir, when you smoke, the neighbors must suppose
Your chimney is on fire. CAUTIOUS: Take care—
A weight like that might make you topheavy.
THOUGHTFUL: Somebody fetch my parasol—
Those delicate colors fade so in the sun!
PEDANTIC: Does not Aristophanes
Mention a mythologic monster called
Hippocampelephantocamelos?
Surely we have here the original!
FAMILIAR: Well, old torchlight! Hang your hat
Over that chandelier—it hurts my eyes.
ELOQUENT: When it blows, the typhoon howls,
And the clouds darken. DRAMATIC: When it bleeds—
The Red Sea! ENTERPRISING: What a sign
For some perfumer! LYRIC: Hark—the horn
Of Roland calls to summon Charlemagne!
SIMPLE: When do they unveil the monument?
RESPECTFUL: Sir, I recognize in you
A man of parts, a man of prominence—
RUSTIC: Hey? What? Call that a nose? Na, na—
I be no fool like what you think I be—
That there's a blue cucumber! MILITARY:

Point against cavalry! PRACTICAL: Why not
A lottery with this for the grand prize?
Or—parodying Faustus in the play—
"Was this the nose that launched a thousand ships
And burned the topless towers of Ilium?"
These, my dear sir, are things you might have said
Had you some tinge of letters, or of wit
To color your discourse. But wit,—not so,
You never had an atom—and of letters,
You need but three to write you down—an Ass.
Moreover,—if you had the invention, here
Before these folk to make a jest of me—
Be sure you would not then articulate
The twentieth part of half a syllable
Of the beginning! For I say these things
Lightly enough myself, about myself,
But I allow none else to utter them.

DE GUICHE

(*Tries to lead away the amazed* VALVERT.)

Vicomte—come.

VALVERT

(*Choking*)

Oh—— These arrogant grand airs!—
A clown who—look at him—not even gloves!
No ribbons—no lace—no buckles on his shoes—

CYRANO

I carry my adornments on my soul.
I do not dress up like a popinjay;

But inwardly, I keep my dainti-
    ness.
I do not bear with me, by any
    chance,
An insult not yet washed away—a
    conscience
Yellow with unpurged bile—an
    honor frayed
To rags, a set of scruples badly
    worn.
I go caparisoned in gems unseen,
Trailing white plumes of freedom,
    garlanded
With my good name—no figure of
    a man,
But a soul clothed in shining armor,
    hung
With deeds for decorations, twirl-
    ing—thus—
A bristling wit, and swinging at my
    side
Courage, and on the stones of this
    old town
Making the sharp truth ring, like
    golden spurs!

VALVERT

But—

CYRANO

    But I have no gloves! A pity too!
I had one—the last one of an old
    pair—
And lost that. Very careless of me.
    Some
Gentleman offered me an imperti-
    nence.
I left it—in his face.

VALVERT

            Dolt, bumpkin, fool,
Insolent puppy, jobbernowl!

CYRANO

(*Removes his hat and bows.*)
                Ah, yes?
And I—Cyrano-Savinien-Hercule
De Bergerac!

VALVERT

(*Turns away.*)
Buffoon!

CYRANO

(*Cries out as if suddenly taken
    with a cramp.*)
    Oh!

VALVERT

(*Turns back.*)
        Well, what now?

CYRANO

(*With grimaces of anguish*)
I must do something to relieve
these cramps—
This is what comes of lack of ex-
    ercise—
Ah!—

VALVERT

What is all this?

CYRANO

My sword has gone to sleep!

VALVERT

(*Draws*)
So be it!

CYRANO

    You shall die exquisitely.

VALVERT

(*Contemptuously*)
Poet!

CYRANO

    Why, yes, a poet, if you will;
So while we fence, I'll make you a
    Ballade
Extempore.

VALVERT

A Ballade?

CYRANO

        Yes. You know
What that is?

VALVERT

I—

CYRANO

The Ballade, sir, is formed
Of three stanzas of eight lines
each—

VALVERT

Oh, come!

CYRANO

And a refrain of four.

VALVERT

You—

CYRANO

I'll compose
One, while I fight with you; and at
the end
Of the last line—thrust home!

VALVERT

Will you?

CYRANO

I will.

(*Declaims*)
"Ballade of the duel at the Hôtel de
Bourgogne
Between de Bergerac and a Bœo-
tian."

VALVERT

(*Sneering*)
What do you mean by that?

CYRANO

Oh, that? The title.

THE CROWD

(*Excited*)
Come on—
A circle—
Quiet—
Down in front!
(TABLEAU. *A ring of interested*

spectators in the center of
the floor, the Marquis and
the Officers mingling with
the citizens and common
folk. Pages swarming up on
men's shoulders to see
better; the Ladies in the
boxes standing and leaning
over. To the right, DE
GUICHE *and his following*;
to the left, LE BRET, CUIGY,
RAGUENEAU, *and others of*
CYRANO's *friends.*)

CYRANO

(*Closes his eyes for an instant.*)
Stop . . . Let me choose my rimes.
. . . Now! Here we go—
(*He suits the action to the
word, throughout the fol-
lowing:*)

Lightly I toss my hat away,
Languidly over my arm let fall
The cloak that covers my bright
array—
Then out swords, and to work
withal!

A Launcelot, in his Lady's hall
. . .
A Spartacus, at the Hippodrome!
. . .
I dally awhile with you, dear
jackal,
Then, as I end the refrain, thrust
home.

(*The swords cross—the fight*
is on.)

Where shall I skewer my peacock?
. . . *Nay,*
Better for you to have shunned
this brawl!—
*Here, in the heart, thro' your rib-
bons gay?*

—In the belly, under your silken shawl?
Hark, how the steel rings musi-
cal!
Mark how my point floats, light as the foam,
Ready to drive you back to the wall,
Then, as I end the refrain, thrust home!

Ho, for a rime! . . . You are white as whey—
You break, you cower, you cringe, you . . . crawl!
Tac!—and I parry your last essay:
So may the turn of a hand fore-stall
Life with its honey, death with its gall;
So may the turn of my fancy roam
Free, for a time, till the rimes recall,
Then, as I end the refrain, thrust home!

(*He announces solemnly.*)

REFRAIN

Prince! Pray God, that is Lord of all,
Pardon your soul, for your time has come!
Beat—pass—fling you aslant, asprawl—
Then, as I end the refrain . . .
　　(*He lunges;* VALVERT *staggers back and falls into the arms of his friends.* CYRANO *recovers, and salutes.*)
　　　　　—Thrust home!

(*Shouts. Applause from the boxes. Flowers and hand-kerchiefs come fluttering down. The Officers surround* CYRANO *and congratulate him.* RAGUENEAU *dances for joy.* LE BRET *is unable to* conceal his enthusiasm. The friends of VALVERT hold him up and help him away.*)

THE CROWD
(*In one long cry*)
Ah-h!

A CAVALIER
Superb!

A WOMAN
Simply sweet!

RAGUENEAU
Magnelephant!

A MARQUIS
A novelty!

LE BRET
Bah!

THE CROWD
(*Thronging around* CYRANO)
Compliments—regards—
Bravo!—

A WOMAN'S VOICE
Why, he's a hero!

A MUSKETEER
(*Advances quickly to* CYRANO, *with outstretched hands.*)
　　　　Monsieur, will you
Permit me?—It was altogether fine!
I think I may appreciate these things—
Moreover, I have been stamping for pure joy!
(*He retires quickly.*)

CYRANO
(*To* CUIGY)
What was that gentleman's name?

CUIGY

Oh . . . D'Artagnan.

LE BRET

(*Takes* CYRANO'S *arm.*)
Come here and tell me—

CYRANO

Let this crowd go first—
(*To* BELLEROSE)
May we stay?

BELLEROSE

(*With great respect*)
Certainly!
(*Cries and cat-calls off stage.*)

JODELET

(*Comes down from the door
where he has been looking
out.*)
Hark!— Montfleury—
They are hooting him.

BELLEROSE

(*Solemnly*)
Sic transit gloria!
(*Changes his tone and shouts
to the porter and the lamp-
lighter.*)
—Strike! . . . Close the house! . . .
Leave the lights— We rehearse
The new farce after dinner.
(JODELET *and* BELLEROSE *go
out after elaborately salut-
ing* CYRANO.)

THE PORTER

(*To* CYRANO)
You do not dine?

CYRANO

I?—No!
(THE PORTER *turns away.*)

LE BRET

Why not?

CYRANO

(*Haughtily*)
Because—
(*Changing his tone when he
sees* THE PORTER *has gone.*)
Because I have
No money.

LE BRET

(*Gesture of tossing*)
But—the purse of gold?

CYRANO

Farewell,
Paternal pension!

LE BRET

So you have, until
The first of next month—?

CYRANO

Nothing.

LE BRET

What a fool!—

CYRANO

But—what a gesture!

THE ORANGE-GIRL

(*Behind her little counter;
coughs.*)
Hem!
(CYRANO *and* LE BRET *look
around; she advances tim-
idly.*)
Pardon, Monsieur . . .
A man ought never to go hungry
. . .
(*Indicating the sideboard*)
See,
I have everything here . . .
(*Eagerly*)
Please!—

CYRANO

(*Uncovers*)
My dear child

I cannot bend this Gascon pride of
    mine
To accept such a kindness— Yet,
    for fear
That I may give you pain if I re-
    fuse,
I will take . . .
    (*He goes to the sideboard and
    makes his selection.*)
Oh, not very much! A grape . . .
    (*She gives him the bunch; he
    removes a single grape.*)
One only! And a glass of water . . .
    (*She starts to pour wine into
    it; he stops her.*)
                                    Clear!
And . . . half a macaroon!
    (*He gravely returns the other
    half.*)

LE BRET

                        Old idiot!

THE ORANGE-GIRL

Please!—Nothing more?

CYRANO

Why, yes— Your hand to kiss.
    (*He kisses the hand which she
    holds out, as he would the
    hand of a princess.*)

THE ORANGE-GIRL

Thank you, sir.
    (*She curtseys.*)
            Good-night.
    (*She goes out.*)

CYRANO

            Now, I am listening.
    (*Plants himself before the
    sideboard and arranges
    thereon—*)
Dinner!—
    (*—the macaroon*)
Drink!—
    (*—the glass of water*)

Dessert!—
    (*—the grape.*)
            There—now I'll sit down
    (*Seats himself.*)
Lord, I was hungry! Abominably!
    (*Eating*)
                                    Well!

LE BRET

These fatheads with the bellicose
    grand airs
Will have you ruined if you listen
    to them;
Talk to a man of sense and hear
    how all
Your swagger impresses him.

CYRANO

    (*Finishes his macaroon.*)
                        Enormously.

LE BRET

The Cardinal—

CYRANO

    (*Beaming*)
Was he there?

LE BRET

He must have thought you—

CYRANO

Original.

LE BRET

Well, but—

CYRANO

                        He is himself
A playwright. He will not be too
    displeased
That I have closed another author's
    play.

LE BRET

But look at all the enemies you
    have made!

CYRANO

(Begins on the grape.)
How many—do you think?

LE BRET

                    Just forty-eight
Without the women.

CYRANO

Count them.

LE BRET

                    Montfleury,
Baro, de Guiche, the Vicomte, the
    Old Man,
All the Academy—

CYRANO

                    Enough! You make me
Happy!

LE BRET

But where is all this leading you?
What is your plan?

CYRANO

                I have been wandering—
Wasting my force upon too many
    plans.
Now I have chosen one.

LE BRET

What one?

CYRANO

                The simplest—
To make myself in all things ad-
    mirable!

LE BRET

Hmph!—Well, then, the real rea-
    son why you hate
Montfleury— Come, the truth, now!

CYRANO

(Rises)

                    That Silenus,

Who cannot hold his belly in his
    arms,
Still dreams of being sweetly dan-
    gerous
Among the women—sighs and lan-
    guishes,
Making sheeps' eyes out of his great
    frog's face—
I hate him ever since one day he
    dared
Smile upon—
        Oh, my friend, I seemed to see
Over some flower a great snail
    crawling!

LE BRET

(Amazed)

                                How,
What? Is it possible?—

CYRANO

(With a bitter smile)
                For me to love? . . .
(Changing his tone; seriously)
I love.

LE BRET

May I know? You have never said—

CYRANO

Whom I love? Think a moment.
    Think of me—
Me, whom the plainest woman
    would despise—
Me, with this nose of mine that
    marches on
Before me by a quarter of an hour!
Whom should I love? Why—of
    course—it must be
The woman in the world most beau-
    tiful.

LE BRET

Most beautiful?

CYRANO

                In all this world—most sweet
Also; most wise; most witty, and
    most fair!

LE BRET

Who and what is this woman?

CYRANO

                    Dangerous
Mortally, without meaning; exqui-
    site
Without imagining. Nature's own
    snare
To allure manhood. A white rose
    wherein
Love lies in ambush for his natural
    prey.
Who knows her smile has known a
    perfect thing.
She creates grace in her own image,
    brings
Heaven to earth in one movement
    of her hand—
Nor thou, O Venus! balancing thy
    shell
Over the Mediterranean blue, nor
    thou,
Diana! marching through broad,
    blossoming woods,
Art so divine as when she mounts
    her chair,
And goes abroad through Paris!

LE BRET

                Oh, well—of course,
That makes everything clear!

CYRANO

                    Transparently.

LE BRET

Madeleine Robin—your cousin?

CYRANO

                    Yes; Roxane.

LE BRET

And why not? If you love her, tell
    her so!
You have covered yourself with
    glory in her eyes
This very day.

CYRANO

My old friend—look at me,
And tell me how much hope re-
    mains for me
With its protuberance! Oh, I have
    no more
Illusions! Now and then—bah! I
    may grow
Tender, walking alone in the blue
    cool
Of evening, through some garden
    fresh with flowers
After the benediction of the rain;
My poor big devil of a nose inhales
April . . . and so I follow with my
    eyes
Where some boy, with a girl upon
    his arm,
Passes a patch of silver . . . and
    I feel
Somehow, I wish I had a woman
    too,
Walking with little steps under the
    moon,
And holding my arm so, and smil-
    ing. Then
I dream—and I forget. . . .
                    And then I see
The shadow of my profile on the
    wall!

LE BRET

My friend! . . .

CYRANO

My friend, I have my bitter days,
Knowing myself so ugly, so alone.
Sometimes—

LE BRET

                You weep?

CYRANO

(Quickly)
                Oh, not that ever! No,
That would be too grotesque—
    tears trickling down
All the long way along this nose of
    mine?

I will not so profane the dignity
Of sorrow. Never any tears for me!
Why, there is nothing more sublime
than tears,
Nothing!—Shall I make them ridic-
ulous
In my poor person?

LE BRET
     Love's no more than chance!

CYRANO
(*Shakes his head.*)
No. I love Cleopatra; do I appear
Cæsar? I adore Beatrice; have I
The look of Dante?

LE BRET
     But your wit—your courage—
Why, that poor child who offered
you just now
Your dinner!—She—you saw with
your own eyes,
Her eyes did not avoid you.

CYRANO
(*Thoughtful*)
     That is true . . .

LE BRET
Well then! Roxane herself, watch-
ing your duel,
Paler than—

CYRANO
   Pale?—

LE BRET
     Her lips parted, her hand
Thus at her breast— I saw it! Speak
to her
Speak, man!

CYRANO
Through my nose? She might laugh
at me;
That is the one thing in this world
I fear!

THE PORTER
(*Followed by* THE DUENNA,
approaches CYRANO *respectfully.*)
A lady asking for Monsieur.

CYRANO
     Mon dieu . . .
Her Duenna!—

THE DUENNA
(*A sweeping curtsey*)
   Monsieur . . .
     A message for you:
From our good cousin we desire to
know
When and where we may see him
privately.

CYRANO
(*Amazed*)
To see me?

THE DUENNA
(*An elaborate reverence*)
To see you. We have certain things
To tell you.

CYRANO
Certain—

THE DUENNA
   Things.

CYRANO
(*Trembling*)
     Mon dieu! . . .

THE DUENNA
     We go
Tomorrow, at the first flush of the
dawn,
To hear Mass at St. Roch. Then
afterwards,
Where can we meet and talk a little?

CYRANO

(*Catching* LE BRET's *arm*)
Where? . . .
— Ah, mon dieu! . . . mon dieu!
. . .

THE DUENNA

Well?

CYRANO

I am thinking . . .

THE DUENNA

And you think?

CYRANO

I . . . The shop of Ragueneau . . .
Ragueneau—pastrycook . . .

THE DUENNA

Who dwells?—

CYRANO

Mon dieu! . . .
Oh, yes . . . Ah, mon dieu! . . .
Rue St.-Honoré.

THE DUENNA

We are agreed. Remember—seven
o'clock.
(*Reverence*)
Until then—

CYRANO

I'll be there.
(*The Duenna goes out.*)

CYRANO

(*Falls into the arms of* LE
BRET)
Me . . . to see me! . . .

LE BRET

You are not quite so gloomy.

CYRANO

After all,
She knows that I exist—no matter
why!

LE BRET

So now, you are going to be happy.

CYRANO

Now! . . .
(*Beside himself*)
I—I am going to be a storm—a
flame—
I need to fight whole armies all
alone;
I have ten hearts; I have a hundred
arms; I feel
Too strong to war with mortals—
(*He shouts at the top of his
voice.*)
BRING ME GIANTS!
(*A moment since, the shad-
ows of the comedians have
been visible moving and
posturing upon the stage.
The violins have taken their
places.*)

A VOICE

(*From the stage*)
Hey-pst—less noise! We are rehearsing here!

CYRANO

(*Laughs*)
We are going.
(*He turns up stage. Through
the street door enter* CUIGY,
BRISSAILLE, *and a number
of officers, s u p p o r t i n g*
LIGNIÈRE, *who is now thor-
oughly drunk.*)

CUIGY

Cyrano!

CYRANO

What is it?

CUIGY

Here—
Here's your stray lamb!

CYRANO

(*Recognizes* LIGNIÈRE.)
Lignière—What's wrong with him?

CUIGY

He wants you.

BRISSAILLE

He's afraid to go home.

CYRANO

Why?

LIGNIÈRE

(*Showing a crumpled scrap of
paper and speaking with the
elaborate logic of profound
intoxication.*)
This letter—hundred against one—
that's me—
I'm the one—all because of little
song—
Good song— Hundred men, waiting, understand?
Porte de Nesle—way home—
Might be dangerous—
Would you permit me spend the
night with you?

CYRANO

A hundred—is that all? You are
going home!

LIGNIÈRE

(*Astonished*)
Why—

CYRANO

(*In a voice of thunder, indicating the lighted lantern
which The Porter holds up
curiously as he regards the
scene.*)
Take that lantern!
(LIGNIÈRE *precipitately seizes
the lantern.*)
Forward march! I say

I'll be the man tonight that sees
you home.
(*To the officers*)
You others follow—I want an audience!

CUIGY

A hundred against one—

CYRANO

Those are the odds
Tonight!
(*The Comedians in their costumes are descending from
the stage and joining the
group.*)

LE BRET

But why help this—

CYRANO

There goes Le Bret
Growling!

LE BRET

—This drunkard here?

CYRANO

(*His hand on* LE BRET's *shoul-
der*)
Because this drunkard—
This tun of sack, this butt of Bur-
gundy—
Once in his life has done one lovely
thing:
After the Mass, according to the
. form,
He saw, one day, the lady of his
heart
Take holy water for a blessing. So
This one, who shudders at a drop
of rain,
This fellow here—runs headlong
to the font
Bends down and drinks it dry!

A SOUBRETTE

I say that was
A pretty thought!

CYRANO

Ah, was it not?

THE SOUBRETTE

(*To the others*)

            But why
Against one poor poet, a hundred
    men?

CYRANO

March!

(*To the officers*)

And you gentlemen, remember now,
No rescue— Let me fight alone.

A COMEDIENNE

(*Jumps down from the stage.*)

            Come on!
I'm going to watch—

CYRANO

Come along!

ANOTHER COMEDIENNE

(*Jumps down, speaks to a
Comedian costumed as an
old man.*)

        You, Cassandre?

CYRANO

Come all of you—the Doctor,
    Isabelle,
Léandre—the whole company—a
    swarm
Of murmuring, golden bees—we'll
    parody
Italian farce and Tragedy-of-Blood;
Ribbons for banners, masks for bla-
    zonry,
And tambourines to be our rolling
    drums!

ALL THE WOMEN

(*Jumping for joy*)

Bravo!—My hood— My cloak—
    Hurry!

JODELET

(*Mock heroic*)

        Lead on!—

CYRANO

(*To the violins*)

You violins—play us an overture—

(*The violins join the procession which is forming. The
lighted candles are snatched
from the stage and distributed; it becomes a torch-
light procession.*)

Bravo!—Officers— Ladies in cos-
    tume—
And twenty paces in advance. . . .

(*He takes his station as he
speaks.*)

           Myself,
Alone, with glory fluttering over
    me,
Alone as Lucifer at war with
    heaven!
Remember—no one lifts a hand to
    help—
Ready there? One . . . two . . .
    three! Porter, the doors! . . .

(*The Porter flings wide the
great doors. We see in the
dim moonlight a corner of
old Paris, purple and picturesque.*)

Look—Paris dreams—nocturnal,
    nebulous,
Under blue moonbeams hung from
    wall to wall—
Nature's own setting for the scene
    we play!—
Yonder, behind her veil of mist, the
    Seine,
Like a mysterious and magic mirror
Trembles—
And you shall see what you shall
    see!

ALL

To the Porte de Nesle!

CYRANO

(*Erect upon the threshold*)

    To the Porte de Nesle!

(*He turns back for a moment
to the Soubrette*)

Did you not ask, my dear, why
   against one
Singer they send a hundred swords?
    (*Quietly, drawing his own
     sword*)
                Because
They know this one man for a
   friend of mine!
    (*He goes out. The proces-
    sion follows:* LIGNIÈRE *zig-*

*zagging at its head, then,
the Comediennes on the
arms of the Officers, then
the Comedians, leaping and
dancing as they go. It vanishes into the night to the
music of the violins, illuminated by the flickering
glimmer of the candles.*)

CURTAIN

THE SECOND ACT

THE BAKERY OF THE POETS

The Shop of RAGUENEAU, *Baker and Pastrycook: a spacious affair at
the corner of the Rue St.-Honoré and the Rue de l'Arbre Sec. The street,
seen vaguely through the glass panes in the door at the back, is grey in
the first light of dawn.*

*In the foreground, at the Left, a Counter is surmounted by a Canopy
of wrought iron from which are hanging ducks, geese, and white peacocks.
Great crockery jars hold bouquets of common flowers, yellow sunflowers
in particular. On the same side farther back, a huge fireplace; in front of
it, between great andirons, of which each one supports a little saucepan,
roast fowls revolve and weep into their dripping-pans. To the Right at the
First Entrance, a door. Beyond it, Second Entrance, a staircase leads up to
a little dining-room under the eaves, its interior visible through open
shutters. A table is set there and a tiny Flemish candlestick is lighted;
there one may retire to eat and drink in private. A wooden gallery, extend-
ing from the head of the stairway, seems to lead to other little dining-
rooms.*

*In the center of the shop, an iron ring hangs by a rope over a pulley
so that it can be raised or lowered; adorned with game of various kinds
hung from it by hooks, it has the appearance of a sort of gastronomic
chandelier.*

*In the shadow under the staircase, ovens are glowing. The spits revolve;
the copper pots and pans gleam ruddily. Pastries in pyramids. Hams
hanging from the rafters. The morning baking is in progress: a bustle of
tall cooks and timid scullions and scurrying apprentices; a blossoming of
white caps adorned with cock's feathers or the wings of guinea fowl. On*

wicker trays or on great metal platters they bring in rows of pastries and fancy dishes of various kinds.

Tables are covered with trays of cakes and rolls; others with chairs placed about them are set for guests.

One little table in a corner disappears under a heap of papers. At the curtain rise RAGUENEAU is seated there. He is writing poetry.

A PASTRYCOOK
(*Brings in a dish.*)
Fruits en gelée!

SECOND PASTRYCOOK
(*Brings dish.*)
Custard!

THIRD PASTRYCOOK
(*Brings roast peacock orna-
mented with feathers.*)
Peacock *rôti!*

FOURTH PASTRYCOOK
(*Brings tray of cakes.*)
Cakes and confections!

FIFTH PASTRYCOOK
(*Brings earthen dish.*)
Beef *en casserole!*

RAGUENEAU
(*Raises his head; returns to
mere earth.*)
Over the coppers of my kitchen
flows
The frost-silver dawn. Silence
awhile
The god who sings within thee,
Ragueneau!
Lay down the lute—the oven calls
for thee!
(*Rises; goes to one of the
cooks.*)
Here's a hiatus in your sauce; fill up
The measure.

THE COOK
How much?

RAGUENEAU
(*Measures on his finger.*)
One more dactyl.

THE COOK
Huh? . . .

FIRST PASTRYCOOK
Rolls!

SECOND PASTRYCOOK
Roulades!

RAGUENEAU
(*Before the fireplace*)
Veil, O Muse, thy virgin eyes
From the lewd gleam of these ter-
restrial fires!
(*To First Pastrycook*)
Your rolls lack balance. Here's the
proper form—
An equal hemistich on either side,
And the cæsura in between.
(*To another, pointing out an
unfinished pie*)
Your house
Of crust should have a roof upon it.
(*To another, who is seated on
the hearth, placing poultry
on a spit*)
And you—
Along the interminable spit, ar-
range
The modest pullet and the lordly
Turk
Alternately, my son—as great
Malherbe
Alternates male and female rimes.
Remember,
A couplet, or a roast, should be well
turned.

AN APPRENTICE

(*Advances with a dish covered by a napkin.*)

Master, I thought of you when I designed

This, hoping it might please you.

RAGUENEAU

Ah! A Lyre—

THE APPRENTICE

In puff-paste—

RAGUENEAU

And the jewels—candied fruit!

THE APPRENTICE

And the strings, barley-sugar!

RAGUENEAU

(*Gives him money.*)

Go and drink

My health.

(LISE *enters.*)

St!—My wife— Circulate, and hide

That money!

(*Shows the Lyre to* LISE, *with a languid air.*)

Graceful—yes?

LISE

Ridiculous!

(*She places on the counter a pile of paper bags.*)

RAGUENEAU

Paper bags? Thank you . . .

(*He looks at them.*)

Ciel! My manuscripts!

The sacred verses of my poets—rent

Asunder, limb from limb—butchered to make

Base packages of pastry! Ah, you are one

Of those insane Bacchantes who destroyed

Orpheus!

LISE

Your dirty poets left them here

To pay for eating half our stock-in-trade:

We ought to make some profit out of them!

RAGUENEAU

Ant! Would you blame the locust for his song?

LISE

I blame the locust for his appetite!

There used to be a time—before you had

Your hungry friends—you never called me Ants—

No, nor Bacchantes!

RAGUENEAU

What a way to use

Poetry!

LISE

Well, what is the use of it?

RAGUENEAU

But, my dear girl, what would you do with prose?

(*Two* CHILDREN *enter.*)

Well, dears?

A CHILD

Three little patties.

RAGUENEAU

(*Serves them.*)

There we are!

All hot and brown.

THE CHILD

Would you mind wrapping them?

RAGUENEAU

One of my paper bags! . . .

Oh, certainly.

(*Reads from the bag, as he is*

about to wrap the patties in it.)
"Ulysses, when he left Penelope"—
Not that one!
    (Takes another bag; reads.)
    "Phœbus, golden-crowned"—
              Not that one.

LISE

Well? They are waiting!

RAGUENEAU

    Very well, very well!—
The Sonnet to Phyllis . . .
    Yet—it does seem hard . . .

LISE

Made up your mind—at last! Mph!
Jack-o'-Dreams!

RAGUENEAU

    (As her back is turned, calls back the CHILDREN, *who are already at the door.)*
Pst!—Children— Give me back the
    bag. Instead
Of three patties, you shall have six
    of them!
    (Makes the exchange. The CHILDREN *go out. He reads from the bag, as he smoothes it out tenderly.)*
"Phyllis"—
A spot of butter on her name!—
"Phyllis"—

CYRANO

    (Enters hurriedly.)
    What is the time?

RAGUENEAU

    Six o'clock.

CYRANO

                  One
Hour more . . .

RAGUENEAU

Felicitations!

CYRANO

         And for what?

RAGUENEAU

Your victory! I saw it all—

CYRANO

            Which one?

RAGUENEAU

At the Hôtel de Bourgogne.

CYRANO

         Oh—the duel!

RAGUENEAU

The duel in Rime!

LISE

    He talks of nothing else.

CYRANO

Nonsense!

RAGUENEAU

    (Fencing and foining with a spit, which he snatches up from the hearth.)
"Then, as I end the refrain, thrust
    home!"
"Then, as I end the refrain"—
            Gods! What a line!
"Then, as I end"—

CYRANO

What time now, Ragueneau?

RAGUENEAU

    (Petrified at the full extent of a lunge, while he looks at the clock.)
Five after six—
    (Recovers)
    "—thrust home!"
         A Ballade, too!

LISE

(*To* CYRANO, *who in passing
has mechanically shaken
hands with her*)
Your hand—what have you done?

CYRANO

Oh, my hand?—Nothing

RAGUENEAU

What danger now—

CYRANO

No danger.

LISE

I believe
He is lying.

CYRANO

Why? Was I looking down my nose!
That must have been a devil of a
lie!
(*Changing his tone; to* RAGUE-
NEAU)
I expect someone. Leave us here
alone,
When the time comes.

RAGUENEAU

How can I? In a moment,
My poets will be here.

LISE

To break their . . . fast!

CYRANO

Take them away, then, when I give
the sign.
—What time?

RAGUENEAU

Ten minutes after.

CYRANO

Have you a pen?

RAGUENEAU

(*Offers him a pen.*)
An eagle's feather!

A MUSKETEER

(*Enters, and speaks to* LISE *in
a stentorian voice.*)
Greeting!

CYRANO

(*To* RAGUENEAU)
Who is this?

RAGUENEAU

My wife's friend. A terrific warrior,
So he says.

CYRANO

Ah— I see.
(*Takes up the pen; waves*
RAGUENEAU *away.*)
Only to write—
To fold— To give it to her—and to
go . . .
(*Throws down the pen.*)
Coward! And yet—the Devil take
my soul
If I dare speak one word to her . . .
(*To* RAGUENEAU)
What time now?

RAGUENEAU

A quarter after six.

CYRANO

(*Striking his breast*)
—One little word
Of all the many thousand I have
here!
Whereas in writing . . .
(*Takes up the pen.*)
Come, I'll write to her
That letter I have written on my
heart,
Torn up, and written over many
times—
So many times . . . that all I have
to do

Is to remember, and to write it
down.
(*He writes. Through the glass
of the door appear vague
and hesitating shadows. The
Poets enter clothed in rusty
black and spotted with
mud.*)

LISE
(*To* RAGUENEAU)
Here come your scarecrows!

FIRST POET
Comrade!

SECOND POET
(*Takes both* RAGUENEAU's
hands.)
My dear brother!

THIRD POET
(*Sniffing*)
O Lord of Roasts, how sweet thy
dwellings are!

FOURTH POET
Phoebus Apollo of the Silver Spoon!

FIFTH POET
Cupid of Cookery!

RAGUENEAU
(*Surrounded, embraced, beat-
en on the back*)
These geniuses,
They put one at one's ease!

FIRST POET
We were delayed
By the crowd at the Porte de Nesle.

SECOND POET
Dead men
All scarred and gory, scattered on
the stones,
Villainous - looking scoundrels—
eight of them.

CYRANO
(*Looks up an instant.*)
Eight? I thought only seven—

RAGUENEAU
Do you know
The hero of this hecatomb?

CYRANO
I? . . . No.

LISE
(*To the Musketeer*)
Do you?

THE MUSKETEER
Hmm—perhaps!

FIRST POET
They say one man alone
Put to flight all this crowd.

SECOND POET
Everywhere lay
Swords, daggers, pikes, bludg-
eons—

CYRANO
(*Writing*)
"Your eyes . . ."

THIRD POET
As far
As the Quai des Orfèvres, hats and
cloaks—

FIRST POET
Why, that man must have been the
devil!

CYRANO
"Your lips . . ."

FIRST POET
Some savage monster might have
done this thing!

CYRANO

"*Looking upon you, I grow faint
with fear . . .*"

SECOND POET

What have you written lately,
Ragueneau?

CYRANO

"*Your Friend*--"*Who loves you . . .*"
So. No signature;
I'll give it to her myself.

RAGUENEAU

A Recipe
In Rime.

THIRD POET

Read us your rimes!

FOURTH POET

Here's a brioche
Cocking its hat at me.
(*He bites off the top of it.*)

FIRST POET

Look how those buns
Follow the hungry poet with their
eyes—
Those almond eyes!

SECOND POET

We are listening—

THIRD POET

See this cream-puff—
Fat little baby, drooling while it
smiles!

SECOND POET

(*Nibbling at the pastry Lyre.*)
For the first time, the Lyre is my
support.

RAGUENEAU

(*Coughs, adjusts his cap,
strikes an attitude.*)
A Recipe in Rime—

SECOND POET

(*Gives* FIRST POET *a dig with
his elbow.*)
Your breakfast?

FIRST POET

Dinner!

RAGUENEAU

(*Declaims*)

A Recipe for Making Almond Tarts.

*Beat your eggs, the yolk and white,
    Very light;
Mingle with their creamy fluff
    Drops of lime-juice, cool and
        green;
        Then pour in
Milk of Almonds, just enough.*

*Dainty patty-pans, embraced
    In puff-paste—
Have these ready within reach;
    With your thumb and finger,
        pinch
        Half an inch
Up around the edge of each—*

*Into these, a score or more,
    Slowly pour
All your store of custard; so
    Take them, bake them golden-
        brown—
        Now sit down! . . .
Almond tartlets, Ragueneau!*

THE POETS

Delicious! Melting!

A POET

(*Chokes*)
Humph!

CYRANO

(*To* RAGUENEAU)

Do you not see
Those fellows fattening themselves?—

RAGUENEAU

I know.
I would not look—it might embarrass them—
You see, I love a friendly audience.
Besides—another vanity—I am pleased
When they enjoy my cooking.

CYRANO

(*Slaps him on the back.*)
Be off with you!—
(RAGUENEAU *goes up stage.*)
Good little soul!
(*Calls to* LISE.)
Madame!—
(*She leaves the* MUSKETEER *and comes down to him.*)
This musketeer—
He is making love to you?

LISE

(*Haughtily*)
If any man
Offends my virtue—all I have to do
Is look at him—once!

CYRANO

(*Looks at her gravely; she drops her eyes.*)
I do not find
Those eyes of yours unconquerable.

LISE

(*Panting*)
—Ah!

CYRANO

(*Raising his voice a little*)
Now listen— I am fond of Ragueneau;
I allow no one—do you understand?—
To . . . take his name in vain!

LISE

You think—

CYRANO

(*Ironic emphasis*)
I think
I interrupt you.
(*He salutes the* MUSKETEER, *who has heard without daring to resent the warning* LISE *goes to the* MUSKETEER *as he returns* CYRANO's *salute.*)

LISE

You—you swallow that?—
You ought to have pulled his nose!

THE MUSKETEER

His nose?—His nose! . . .
(*He goes out hurriedly.* ROXANE *and the* DUENNA *appear outside the door.*)

CYRANO

(*Nods to* RAGUENEAU.)
Pst!—

RAGUENEAU

(*To the* POETS)
Come inside—

CYRANO

(*Impatient*)
Pst! . . . Pst! . . .

RAGUENEAU

We shall be more
Comfortable . . .
(*He leads the* POETS *into inner room.*)

FIRST POET

The cakes!

SECOND POET

Bring them along!
(*They go out.*)

CYRANO

If I can see the faintest spark of
  hope,
Then—
    (*Throws door open—bows.*)
Welcome!
    (ROXANE *enters, followed by
    the* DUENNA, *whom* CYRANO
    detains.)
    Pardon me—one word—

THE DUENNA

          Take two.

CYRANO

Have you a good digestion?

THE DUENNA

          Wonderful!

CYRANO

Good. Here are two sonnets, by
  Benserade—

THE DUENNA

Euh?

CYRANO

Which I fill for you with éclairs.

THE DUENNA

          Ooo!

CYRANO

Do you like cream-puffs?

THE DUENNA

    Only with whipped cream.

CYRANO

Here are three . . . six—embos-
  omed in a poem
By Saint-Amant. This ode of Chap-
  elin
Looks deep enough to hold—a jelly
  roll.
—Do you love Nature?

THE DUENNA

Mad about it.

CYRANO

          Then
Go out and eat these in the street.
  Do not
Return—

THE DUENNA

  Oh, but—

CYRANO

      Until you finish them.
    (*Down to* ROXANE)
Blessed above all others be the hour
When you remembered to remem-
  ber me,
And came to tell me . . . what?

ROXANE

    (*Takes off her mask.*)
      First let me thank you
Because . . . That man . . . that
  creature, whom your sword
Made sport of yesterday— His
  patron, one—

CYRANO

De Guiche?—

ROXANE

—who thinks himself in love with
  me
Would have forced that man upon
  me for—
    a husband—

CYRANO

I understand—so much the better
  then!
I fought, not for my nose, but your
  bright eyes.

ROXANE

And then, to tell you—but before I
  can

Tell you— Are you, I wonder, still
the same
Big brother—almost—that you
used to be
When we were children, playing by
the pond
In the old garden down there—

CYRANO

     I remember—
Every summer you came to Bergerac! . . .

ROXANE

You used to make swords out of
bulrushes—

CYRANO

You dandelion-dolls with golden
hair—

ROXANE

And those green plums—

CYRANO

And those black mulberries—

ROXANE

In those days, you did everything I
wished!

CYRANO

Roxane, in short skirts, was called
Madeleine.

ROXANE

Was I pretty?

CYRANO

  Oh—not too plain!

ROXANE

     Sometimes
When you had hurt your hand you
used to come
Running to me—and I would be
your mother,

And say— Oh, in a very grown-up
voice:
  (*She takes his hand.*)
"*Now*, what have you been doing
to yourself?
Let me see—"
  (*She sees the hand—starts.*)
Oh!—
    Wait—I said *Let me see!*
Still—at your age! How did you do
that?

CYRANO

      Playing
With the big boys, down by the
Porte de Nesle.

ROXANE

  (*Sits at a table and wets her
  handkerchief in a glass of
  water.*)
Come here to me.

CYRANO

  —Such a wise little mother!

ROXANE

And tell me, while I wash this blood
away,
How many you—played with?

CYRANO

    Oh, about a hundred.

ROXANE

Tell me.

CYRANO

No. Let me go. Tell me what *you*
Were going to tell *me*—if you
dared?

ROXANE

(*Still holding his hand*)
      I think
I do dare—now. It seems like long
ago

When I could tell you things. Yes—
   I dare . . .
     Listen:
I . . . love someone.

CYRANO

Ah!

ROXANE

Someone who does not know.

CYRANO

Ah! . . .

ROXANE

At least—not yet.

CYRANO

Ah! . . .

ROXANE

        But he will know
Some day.

CYRANO

Ah! . . .

ROXANE

A big boy who loves me too,
And is afraid of me, and keeps
   away,
And never says one word.

CYRANO

Ah! . . .

ROXANE

        Let me have
Your hand a moment—why, how
   hot it is!—
I know. I see him trying . . .

CYRANO

Ah! . .

ROXANE

        There now!
Is that better?—

(*She finishes bandaging the
   hand with her handker-
   chief.*)
       Besides—only to think—
(This is a secret.) He is a soldier
   too,
In your own regiment—

CYRANO

Ah! . . .

ROXANE

        Yes, in the Guards.
Your company too.

CYRANO

Ah! . . .

ROXANE

        And such a man!—
He is proud—noble—young—
   brave—beautiful—

CYRANO

(*Turns pale; rises.*)
Beautiful!—

ROXANE

What's the matter?

CYRANO

(*Smiling*)
         Nothing—this—
My sore hand!

ROXANE

Well, I love him. That is all.
Oh—and I never saw him any-
   where
Except the *Comédie.*

CYRANO

You have never spoken?—

ROXANE

Only our eyes . . .

CYRANO

Why, then— How do you know?—

ROXANE

People talk about people; and I hear
Things . . . and I know.

CYRANO

You say he is in the Guards:
His name?

ROXANE

Baron Christian de Neuvillette.

CYRANO

He is not in the Guards.

ROXANE

Yes. Since this morning.
Captain Carbon de Castel-Jaloux.

CYRANO

So soon! . . .
So soon we lose our hearts!—
But, my dear child,—

THE DUENNA

(Opens the door.)
I have eaten the cakes, Monsieur de
Bergerac!

CYRANO

Good! Now go out and read the
poetry!
(The Duenna disappears.)
—But, my dear child! You, who
love only words,
Wit, the grand manner— Why, for
all you know,
The man may be a savage, or a fool.

ROXANE

His curls are like a hero from
D'Urfé.

CYRANO

His mind may be as curly as his
hair.

ROXANE

Not with such eyes. I read his soul
in them.

CYRANO

Yes, all our souls are written in our
eyes!
But—if he be a bungler?

ROXANE

Then I shall die—
There!

CYRANO

(After a pause)
And you brought me here to tell me
this?
I do not yet quite understand,
Madame,
The reason for your confidence.

ROXANE

They say
That in your company— It fright-
ens me—
You are all Gascons . . .

CYRANO

And we pick a quarrel
With any flat-foot who intrudes
himself,
Whose blood is not pure Gascon
like our own?
Is this what you have heard?

ROXANE

I am so afraid
For him!

CYRANO

(Between his teeth)
Not without reason!—

ROXANE

And I thought
You . . . You were so brave, so invincible
Yesterday, against all those brutes!
—If you,
Whom they all fear—

CYRANO

Oh, well—I will defend
Your little Baron.

ROXANE

Will you? Just for me?
Because I have always been—your friend!

CYRANO

Of course . . .

ROXANE

Will you be *his* friend?

CYRANO

I will be his friend.

ROXANE

And never let him fight a duel?

CYRANO

No—never.

ROXANE

Oh, but you are a darling!—I must go—
You never told me about last night
— Why,
You must have been a hero! Have him write
And tell me all about it—will you?

CYRANO

Of course . . .

ROXANE

(*Kisses her hand.*)
I always did love you!—A hundred men

Against one— Well. . . . Adieu.
We are great friends,
Are we not?

CYRANO

Of course . . .

ROXANE

He *must* write to me—
A hundred— You shall tell me the whole story
Some day, when I have time. A hundred men—
What courage!

CYRANO

(*Salutes as she goes out.*)
Oh . . . I have done better since!
(*The door closes after her.* CY-
RANO *remains motionless,
his eyes on the ground.
Pause. The other door
opens;* RAGUENEAU *puts in
his head.*)

RAGUENEAU

May I come in?

CYRANO

(*Without moving*)
Yes . . .
(RAGUENEAU *and his friends
re-enter. At the same time,*
CARBON DE CASTEL-JALOUX
*appears at the street door in
uniform as Captain of the
Guards; recognizes* CYRANO
with a sweeping gesture.)

CARBON

Here he is!—Our hero!

CYRANO

(*Raises his head and salutes.*)
Our Captain!

CARBON

We know! All our company
Are here—

CYRANO

(*Recoils*)
No—

CARBON

Come! They are waiting for you.

CYRANO

No!

CARBON

(*Tries to lead him out.*)
Only across the street— Come!

CYRANO

Please—

CARBON

(*Goes to the door and shouts
in a voice of thunder.*)
Our champion
Refuses! He is not feeling well today!

A VOICE OUTSIDE

Ah! Sandious!
(*Noise outside of swords and
trampling feet approach-
ing.*)

CARBON

Here they come now!

THE CADETS

(*Entering the shop*)
Mille dious!—
Mordious!—Capdedious!—Pocap-
dedious!

RAGUENEAU

(*In astonishment*)
Gentlemen—
You are all Gascons?

THE CADETS

All!

FIRST CADET

(*To* CYRANO)
Bravo!

CYRANO

Baron!

ANOTHER CADET

(*Takes both his hands.*)
Vivat!

CYRANO

Baron!

THIRD CADET

Come to my arms!

CYRANO

Baron!

OTHERS

To mine!—To mine!—

CYRANO

Baron . . . Baron . . . Have mercy—

RAGUENEAU

You are all Barons too?

THE CADETS

Are we?

RAGUENEAU

Are they? . . .

FIRST CADET

Our coronets would star the midnight sky!

LE BRET

(*Enters; hurries to* CYRANO.)
The whole Town's looking for you!
Raving mad—
A triumph! Those who saw the
fight—

CYRANO

                              I hope
You have not told them where I—

LE BRET

(*Rubbing his hand*)
                              Certainly
I told them!

CITIZEN

(*Enters, followed by a group.*)
Listen! Shut the door!—Here comes
All Paris!
        (*The street outside fills with a
        shouting crowd. Chairs and
        carriages stop at the door.*)

LE BRET

(*Aside to* CYRANO, *smiling*)
        And Roxane?

CYRANO

(*Quickly*)
                      Hush!

THE CROWD OUTSIDE

                              Cyrano!
(*A mob bursts into the shop.
Shouts, acclamations, gen-
eral disturbance.*)

RAGUENEAU

(*Standing on a table*)
My shop invaded— They'll break
    everything—
Glorious!

SEVERAL MEN

(*Crowding about* CYRANO)
My friend! . . . My friend! . . .

CYRANO

                      Why, yesterday
I did not have so many friends!

LE BRET

                              Success
At last!

A MARQUIS

(*Runs to* CYRANO, *with out-
    stretched hands.*)
        My dear—really!—

CYRANO

(*Coldly*)
                      So? And how long
Have I been dear to you?

ANOTHER MARQUIS

                One moment—pray!
I have two ladies in my carriage
    here;
Let me present you—

CYRANO

                Certainly! And first,
Who will present you, sir,—to me?

LE BRET

(*Astounded*)
                              Why, what
The devil?—

CYRANO

Hush!

A MAN OF LETTERS

(*With a portfolio*)
May I have the details? . . .

CYRANO

You may not.

LE BRET

(*Plucking* CYRANO's *sleeve*)
Theophraste Renaudot!—Editor
Of the *Gazette*—your reputation!

CYRANO

                                  No!

A POET

(*Advances*)
Monsieur—

CYRANO

Well?

THE POET

Your full name? I will compose
A pentacrostic—

ANOTHER

Monsieur—

CYRANO

That will do!
(*Movement. The crowd arranges itself.* DE GUICHE *appears, escorted by* CUIGY, BRISSAILLE, *and the other officers who were with* CYRANO *at the close of the First Act.*)

CUIGY

(*Goes to* CYRANO.)
Monsieur de Guiche!—
(*Murmur. Everyone moves.*)
A message from the Marshal
De Gassion—

DE GUICHE

(*Saluting* CYRANO)
Who wishes to express
Through me his admiration. He has heard
Of your affair—

THE CROWD

Bravo!

CYRANO

(*Bowing*)
The Marshal speaks
As an authority.

DE GUICHE

He said just now
The story would have been incredible
Were it not for the witness—

CUIGY

Of our eyes!

LE BRET

(*Aside to* CYRANO)
What is it?

CYRANO

Hush!—

LE BRET

Something is wrong with you;
Are you in pain?

CYRANO

(*Recovering himself*)
In pain? Before this crowd?
(*His moustache bristles. He throws out his chest.*)
I? In pain? You shall see!

DE GUICHE

(*To whom* CUIGY *has been whispering.*)
Your name is known
Already as a soldier. You are one
Of those wild Gascons, are you not?

CYRANO

The Guards,
Yes. A Cadet.

A CADET

(*In a voice of thunder*)
One of ourselves!

DE GUICHE

Ah! So
Then all these gentlemen with the haughty air,
These are the famous—

CARBON

Cyrano!

CYRANO

Captain?

CARBON

Our troop being all present, be so
kind
As to present them to the Comte de
Guiche!

CYRANO

(*With a gesture presenting the*
CADETS *to* DE GUICHE, *de-*
claims:)

The Cadets of Gascoyne—the de-
fenders
   Of Carbon de Castel-Jaloux:
Free fighters, free lovers, free
spenders—
The Cadets of Gascoyne—the de-
fenders
Of old homes, old names, and old
splendors—
   A proud and a pestilent crew!
The Cadets of Gascoyne, the de-
fenders
   Of Carbon de Castel-Jaloux.

Hawk-eyed, they stare down all
contenders—
   The wolf bares his fangs as they
do—
Make way there, you fat money-
lenders!
(Hawk-eyed, they stare down all
contenders)
Old boots that have been to the
menders,
   Old cloaks that are worn through
and through—
Hawk-eyed, they stare down all
contenders—
   The wolf bares his fangs as they
do!

Skull-breakers they are, and sword-
benders;
   Red blood is their favorite brew;
Hot haters and loyal befrienders,
Skull-breakers they are, and sword-
benders.

Wherever a quarrel engenders,
   They're ready and waiting for
you!
Skull-breakers they are, and sword-
benders;
   Red blood is their favorite brew!

Behold them, our Gascon defenders
   Who win every woman they woo!
There's never a dame but surren-
ders—
Behold them, our Gascon de-
fenders!
Young wives who are clever pre-
tenders—
   Old husbands who house the
cuckoo—
Behold them—our Gascon defend-
ers
   Who win every woman they woo!

DE GUICHE

(*Languidly, sitting in a chair*)
Poets are fashionable nowadays
To have about one. Would you care
to join
My following?

CYRANO

No, sir. I do not follow.

DE GUICHE

Your duel yesterday amused my
uncle
The Cardinal. I might help you
there.

LE BRET

      Grand Dieu!

DE GUICHE

I suppose you have written a tragedy—
They all have.

LE BRET

(*Aside to* CYRANO)
Now at last you'll have it played—
Your *Agrippine!*

DE GUICHE

Why not? Take it to him.

CYRANO

(*Tempted*)
Really—

DE GUICHE

He is himself a dramatist;
Let him rewrite a few lines here
    and there,
And he'll approve the rest.

CYRANO

(*His face falls again.*)
                    Impossible.
My blood curdles to think of alter-
    ing
One comma.

DE GUICHE

Ah, but when he likes a thing
He pays well.

CYRANO

Yes—but not so well as I—
When I have made a line that sings
    itself
So that I love the sound of it—I pay
Myself a hundred times.

DE GUICHE

You are proud, my friend.

CYRANO

You have observed that?

A CADET

(*Enters with a drawn sword,
    along the whole blade of
    which is transfixed a collec-
    tion of disreputable hats,
    their plumes draggled, their
    crowns cut and torn.*)
Cyrano! See here—
Look what we found this morning
in the street—

The plumes dropped in their flight
    by those fine birds
Who showed the white feather!

CARBON

Spoils of the hunt—
Well mounted!

THE CROWD

Ha-ha-ha!

CUIGY

Whoever hired
Those rascals, he must be an angry
    man
Today!

BRISSAILLE

Who was it? Do you know?

DE GUICHE

Myself!—
(*The laughter ceases.*)
I hired them to do the sort of work
We do not soil our hands with—
    punishing
A drunken poet. . . .
(*Uncomfortable silence.*)

THE CADET

(*To* CYRANO)
What shall we do with them?
They ought to be preserved before
they spoil—

CYRANO

(*Takes the sword, and in the
    gesture of saluting* DE
    GUICHE *with it, makes all the
    hats slide off at his feet.*)
Sir, will you not return these to
your friends?

DE GUICHE

My chair—my porters here—imme-
    diately!
(*To* CYRANO *violently*)
—As for you, sir!—

A VOICE

(*In the street*)
        The chair of Monseigneur
Le Comte de Guiche!—

DE GUICHE

(*Who has recovered his self-
        control; smiling*)
Have you read *Don Quixote?*

CYRANO

I have—and found myself the hero.

A PORTER

(*Appears at the door.*)
                                Chair
Ready!

DE GUICHE

Be so good as to read once more
The chapter of the windmills.

CYRANO

(*Gravely*)
                        Chapter Thirteen.

DE GUICHE

Windmills, remember, if you fight
with them—

CYRANO

My enemies change, then, with
every wind?

DE GUICHE

—May swing round their huge
arms and cast you down
Into the mire.

CYRANO

                Or up—among the stars!
(DE GUICHE *goes out. We see
him get into the chair. The*
OFFICERS *follow murmuring
among themselves.* LE BRET
*goes up with them. The
crowd goes out.*)

CYRANO

(*Saluting with burlesque politeness, those who go out
without daring to take leave
of him.*)
Gentlemen. . . . Gentlemen. . . .

LE BRET

(*As the door closes, comes
down, shaking his clenched
hands to heaven.*)
                You have done it now—
You have made your fortune!

CYRANO

                There you go again,
Growling!—

LE BRET

At least this latest pose of yours—
Ruining every chance that comes
your way—
Becomes exaggerated—

CYRANO

                                Very well,
Then I exaggerate!

LE BRET

(*Triumphantly*)
                Oh, you do!

CYRANO

                                Yes;
On principle. There are things in
this world
A man does well to carry to extremes.

LE BRET

Stop trying to be Three Musketeers
in one!
Fortune and glory—

CYRANO

                What would you have me do?
Seek for the patronage of some
great man,
And like a creeping vine on a tall
tree

Crawl upward, where I cannot
    stand alone?
No, thank you! Dedicate, as others
    do,
Poems to pawnbrokers? Be a buf-
    foon
In the vile hope of teasing out a
    smile
On some cold face? No, thank you!
    Eat a toad
For breakfast every morning? Make
    my knees
Callous, and cultivate a supple
    spine,—
Wear out my belly grovelling in
    the dust?
No, thank you! Scratch the back of
    any swine
That roots up gold for me? Tickle
    the horns
Of Mammon with my left hand,
    while my right
Too proud to know his partner's
    business,
Takes in the fee? No, thank you!
    Use the fire
God gave me to burn incense all
    day long
Under the nose of wood and stone?
    No, thank you!
Shall I go leaping into ladies' laps
And lacking fingers? — or — to
    change the form—
Navigating with madrigals for oars,
My sails full of the sighs of dow-
    agers?
No, thank you! Publish verses at my
    own
Expense? No, thank you! Be the
    patron saint
Of a small group of literary souls
Who dine together every Tuesday?
    No,
I thank you! Shall I labor night and
    day
To build a reputation on one song,
And never write another? Shall I
    find
True genius only among Geniuses.

Palpitate over little paragraphs,
And struggle to insinuate my name
Into the columns of the *Mercury*?
No, thank you! Calculate, scheme,
    be afraid,
Love more to make a visit than a
    poem,
Seek introductions, favors, influ-
    ences?—
No, thank you! No, I thank you! And
    again
I thank you!—But . . .
        To sing, to laugh, to dream,
To walk in my own way and be
    alone,
Free, with an eye to see things as
    they are,
A voice that means manhood—to
    cock my hat
Where I choose—At a word, a
    Yes, a *No*,
To fight—or write. To travel any
    road
Under the sun, under the stars, nor
    doubt
If fame or fortune lie beyond the
    bourne—
Never to make a line I have not
    heard
In my own heart; yet, with all
    modesty
To say: "My soul, be satisfied with
    flowers,
With fruit, with weeds even; but
    gather them
In the one garden you may call
    your own."
So, when I win some triumph, by
    some chance,
Render no share to Cæsar—in a
    word,
I am too proud to be a parasite,
And if my nature wants the germ
    that grows
Towering to heaven like the moun-
    tain pine,
Or like the oak, sheltering multi-
    tudes—

I stand, not high it may be—but
alone!

LE BRET

Alone, yes!—but why stand against
the world?
What devil has possessed you now,
to go
Everywhere making yourself enemies?

CYRANO

Watching you other people making
friends
Everywhere—as a dog makes
friends! I mark
The manner of these canine cour-
tesies
And think: "My friends are of a
cleaner breed;
Here comes — thank God! — another enemy!"

LE BRET

But this is madness!

CYRANO

Method, let us say.
It is my pleasure to displease. I love
Hatred. Imagine how it feels to
face
The volley of a thousand angry
eyes—
The bile of envy and the froth of
fear
Spattering little drops about me—
You—
Good nature all around you, soft
and warm—
You are like those Italians, in great
cowls
Comfortable and loose— Your
chin sinks down
Into the folds, your shoulders
droop. But I—
The Spanish ruff I wear around my
throat
Is like a ring of enemies; hard,
proud,

Each point another pride, another
thorn—
So that I hold myself erect per-
force,
Wearing the hatred of the com-
mon herd
Haughtily, the harsh collar of Old
Spain,
At once a fetter and—a halo!

LE BRET

Yes . . .
(*After a silence, draws* CY-
RANO's *arm through his
own.*)
Tell this to all the world— And
then to me
Say very softly that . . . She loves
you not.

CYRANO

(*Quickly*)
Hush!
(*A moment since,* CHRISTIAN
*has entered and mingled
with the Cadets, who do
not offer to speak to him.
Finally, he sits down alone
at a small table, where he
is served by* LISE.)

A CADET

(*Rises from a table up stage,
his glass in his hand.*)
Cyrano!—Your story!

CYRANO

Presently . . .
(*He goes up, on the arm of*
LE BRET, *talking to him.
The Cadets come down
stage.*)

THE CADET

The story of the combat! An example
For—

(*He stops by the table where* CHRISTIAN *is sitting.*)
—this young tadpole here.

CHRISTIAN
(*Looks up*)
Tadpole?

ANOTHER CADET
Yes, you!—
You narrow-gutted Northerner!

CHRISTIAN
Sir?

FIRST CADET
Hark ye,
Monsieur de Neuvillette: You are to know
There is a certain subject—I would say,
A certain object—never to be named
Among us: utterly unmentionable!

CHRISTIAN
And that is?

THIRD CADET
(*In an awful voice*)
Look at me! . . .
(*He strikes his nose three times with his finger, mysteriously.*)
You understand?

CHRISTIAN
Why, yes; the—

FOURTH CADET
Sh! . . . We never speak that word—
(*Indicating* CYRANO *by a gesture*)
To breathe it is to have to do with HIM!

FIFTH CADET
(*Speaks through his nose.*)
He has exterminated several
Whose tone of voice suggested . . .

SIXTH CADET
(*In a hollow tone; rising from under the table on all fours.*)
Would you die
Before your time? Just mention anything
Convex . . . or cartilaginous . . .

SEVENTH CADET
(*His hand on* CHRISTIAN's *shoulder*)
One word—
One syllable—one gesture—nay, one sneeze—
Your handkerchief becomes your winding-sheet!
(*Silence. In a circle around* CHRISTIAN, *arms crossed, they regard him expectantly.*)

CHRISTIAN
(*Rises and goes to* CARBON, *who is conversing with an officer, and pretending not to see what is taking place.*)
Captain!

CARBON
(*Turns, and looks him over.*)
Sir?

CHRISTIAN
What is the proper thing to do
When Gascons grow too boastful?

CARBON
Prove to them
That one may be a Norman, and have courage.
(*Turns his back.*)

CHRISTIAN

I thank you.

FIRST CADET

(*To* CYRANO)
Come—the story!

ALL

The story!

CYRANO

(*Comes down.*)
Oh,
My story? Well . . .
(*They all draw up their stools
and group themselves
around him, eagerly.* CHRIS-
TIAN *places himself astride
of a chair, his arms on the
back of it.*)
I marched on, all alone
To meet those devils. Overhead, the
moon
Hung like a gold watch at the fob
of heaven,
Till suddenly some Angel rubbed
a cloud,
As it might be his handkerchief,
across
The shining crystal, and—the night
came down.
No lamps in those back streets—
It was so dark—
Mordious! You could not see be-
yond—

CHRISTIAN

Your nose.
(*Silence. Every man slowly
rises to his feet. They look
at* CYRANO *almost with terror. He has stopped short,
utterly astonished. Pause.*)

CYRANO

Who is that man there?

A CADET

(*In a low voice*)
A recruit—arrived
This morning.

CYRANO

(*Takes a step toward* CHRIS-
TIAN)
A recruit—

CARBON

(*In a low voice*)
His name is Christian
De Neuvil—

CYRANO

(*Suddenly motionless*)
Oh . . .
(*He turns pale, flushes, makes
a movement as if to throw
himself upon* CHRISTIAN.)
I—
(*Controls himself, and goes on
in a choking voice.*)
I see. Very well,
As I was saying—
(*With a sudden burst of rage*)
Mordious! . . .
(*He goes on in a natural
tone.*)
It grew dark,
You could not see your hand before
your eyes.
I marched on, thinking how, all for
the sake
Of one old souse
(*They slowly sit down, watch-
ing him.*)
who wrote a bawdy song
Whenever he took—

CHRISTIAN

A noseful—
(*Everyone rises.* CHRISTIAN
*balances himself on two
legs of his chair.*)

CYRANO

(*Half strangled*)
    —Took a notion . . . .
Whenever he took a notion— For his sake,
I might antagonize some dangerous man,
One powerful enough to make me pay—

CHRISTIAN

Through the nose—

CYRANO

  (*Wipes the sweat from his forehead.*)
    —Pay the Piper. After all,
I thought, why am I putting in my—

CHRISTIAN

      Nose—

CYRANO

—My oar . . . Why am I putting in my oar?
The quarrel's none of mine. How-ever—now
I am here, I may as well go through with it.
Come, Gascon—do your duty!— Suddenly
A sword flashed in the dark. I caught it fair—

CHRISTIAN

On the nose—

CYRANO

  On my blade. Before I knew it,
There I was—

CHRISTIAN

   Rubbing noses—

CYRANO

(*Pale and smiling*)
     Crossing swords
With half a score at once. I handed one—

CHRISTIAN

A nosegay—

CYRANO

(*Leaping at him*)
Ventre-Saint-Gris! . . .
(*The Gascons tumble over each other to get a good view. Arrived in front of* CHRISTIAN, *who has not moved an inch,* CYRANO *masters himself again, and continues.*)
     He went down;
The rest gave way; I charged—

CHRISTIAN

    Nose in the air—

CYRANO

I skewered two of them—disarmed a third—
Another lunged— Paf! And I coun-tered—

CHRISTIAN

       Pif!

CYRANO

(*Bellowing*)
TONNERRE! Out of here—All of you!
  (*All the Cadets rush for the door.*)

FIRST CADET

      At last—
The old lion wakes!

CYRANO

   All of you! Leave me here
Alone with that man!
  (*The lines following are heard brokenly, in the confusion of getting through the door.*)

SECOND CADET

  Bigre! He'll have the fellow
Chopped into sausage—

RAGUENEAU
Sausage?—

THIRD CADET
                Mince-meat, then—
One of your pies!—

RAGUENEAU
            Am I pale? You look white
As a fresh napkin—

CARBON
(At the door)
            Come!

FOURTH CADET
                He'll never leave
Enough of him to—

FIFTH CADET
            Why, it frightens ME
To think of what will—

SIXTH CADET
(Closing the door)
                Something horrible
Beyond imagination . . .
            (They are all gone: some
            through the street door,
            some by the inner doors to
            right and left. A few disap-
            pear up the staircase. CY-
            RANO and CHRISTIAN stand
            face to face a moment, and
            look at each other.)

CYRANO
                To my arms!

CHRISTIAN
Sir? . . .

CYRANO
You have courage!

CHRISTIAN
Oh, that! . . .

CYRANO
            You are brave—
That pleases me.

CHRISTIAN
You mean? . . .

CYRANO
            Do you not know
I am her brother? Come!

CHRISTIAN
Whose?—

CYRANO
            Hers—Roxane!

CHRISTIAN
Her . . . brother? You?
        (Hurries to him.)

CYRANO
Her cousin. Much the same.

CHRISTIAN
And she has told you? . . .

CYRANO
Everything.

CHRISTIAN
            She loves me?

CYRANO
Perhaps.

CHRISTIAN
        (Takes both his hands.)
My dear sir—more than I can say,
I am honored—

CYRANO
This is rather sudden.

CHRISTIAN
                Please
Forgive me—

CYRANO

(*Holds him at arm's length,
looking at him.*)
Why, he is a handsome devil,
This fellow!

CHRISTIAN

On my honor—if you knew
How much I have admired—

CYRANO

Yes, yes—and all
Those Noses which—

CHRISTIAN

Please! I apologize.

CYRANO

(*Change of tone*)
Roxane expects a letter—

CHRISTIAN

Not from me?—

CYRANO

Yes. Why not?

CHRISTIAN

Once I write, that ruins all!

CYRANO

And why?

CHRISTIAN

Because . . . because I am a fool!
Stupid enough to hang myself!

CYRANO

But no—
You are no fool; you call yourself a
fool,
There's proof enough in that. Be-
sides, you did not
Attack me like a fool.

CHRISTIAN

Bah! Anyone
Can pick a quarrel. Yes, I have a
sort
Of rough and ready soldier's
tongue. I know
That. But with any woman—paralyzed,
Speechless, dumb. I can only look
at them.
Yet sometimes, when I go away,
their eyes . . .

CYRANO

Why not their hearts, if you should
wait and see?

CHRISTIAN

No. I am one of those—I know—
those men
Who never can make love.

CYRANO

Strange. . . . Now it seems
I, if I gave my mind to it, I might
Perhaps make love well.

CHRISTIAN

Oh, if I had words
To say what I have here!

CYRANO

If I could be
A handsome little Musketeer with
eyes!—

CHRISTIAN

Besides—you know Roxane—how
sensitive—
One rough word, and the sweet illusion—gone!

CYRANO

I wish you might be my interpreter.

CHRISTIAN

I wish I had your wit—

CYRANO

Borrow it, then!—
Your beautiful young manhood—
lend me that,
And we two make one hero of romance!

CHRISTIAN

What?

CYRANO

Would you dare repeat to
her the words
I gave you, day by day?

CHRISTIAN

You mean?

CYRANO

I mean
Roxane shall have no disillusion-
ment!
Come, shall we win her both to-
gether? Take
The soul within this leathern jack
of mine,
And breathe it into you?
    (*Touches him on the breast.*)
        So—there's my heart
Under your velvet, now!

CHRISTIAN

But—Cyrano!—

CYRANO

But—Christian, why not?

CHRISTIAN

I am afraid—

CYRANO

I know—
Afraid that when you have her all
alone,
You lose all. Have no fear. It is
yourself
She loves—give her yourself put
into words—
My words, upon your lips!

CHRISTIAN

But . . . but your eyes! . . .
They burn like—

CYRANO

Will you? . . . Will you?

CHRISTIAN

Does it mean
So much to you?

CYRANO

(*Beside himself*)
It means—
(*Recovers, changes tone.*)
        A Comedy,
A situation for a poet! Come,
Shall we collaborate? I'll be your
cloak
Of darkness, your enchanted sword,
your ring
To charm the fairy Princess!

CHRISTIAN

But the letter—
I cannot write—

CYRANO

Oh, yes, the letter.
(*He takes from his pocket the
letter which he has writ-
ten.*)
        Here.

CHRISTIAN

What is this?

CYRANO

All there; all but the address.

CHRISTIAN

I—

CYRANO

Oh, you may send it. It will serve.

CHRISTIAN

But why
Have you done this?

CYRANO

I have amused myself
As we all do, we poets—writing
vows
To Chloris, Phyllis—any pretty
name—
You might have had a pocketful of
them!
Take it, and turn to facts my fan-
tasies—
I loosed these loves like doves into
the air;
Give them a habitation and a home.
Here, take it—You will find me all
the more
Eloquent, being insincere! Come!

CHRISTIAN

First,
There must be a few changes here
and there—
Written at random, can it fit Roxane?

CYRANO

Like her own glove.

CHRISTIAN

No, but—

CYRANO

My son, have faith—
Faith in the love of women for
themselves—
Roxane will know this letter for
her own!

CHRISTIAN

(*Throws himself into the arms
of* CYRANO. *They stand embraced.*)
My friend!
(*The door up stage opens a little. A* CADET *steals in.*)

THE CADET

Nothing. A silence like the tomb . . .

I hardly dare look—
(*He sees the two.*)
Wha-at?
(*The other* CADETS *crowd in
behind him and see.*)

THE CADETS

No!—No!

SECOND CADET

Mon dieu!

THE MUSKETEER

(*Slaps his knee.*)
Well, well, well!

CARBON

Here's our devil . . . Christianized!
Offend one nostril, and he turns
the other.

THE MUSKETEER

Now we are allowed to talk about
his nose!
(*Calls*)
Hey, Lise! Come here—
(*Affectedly*)
Snf! What a horrid smell!
What is it? . . .
(*Plants himself in front of
CYRANO, and looks at his
nose in an impolite man-
ner.*)
You ought to know about
such things;
What seems to have died around
here?

CYRANO

(*Knocks him backward over a
bench.*)
Cabbage-heads!
(*Joy. The Cadets have found
their old* CYRANO *again.
General disturbance.*)

CURTAIN

THE THIRD ACT

ROXANE'S KISS

A little square in the old Marais: old houses, and a glimpse of narrow streets. On the Right, THE HOUSE OF ROXANE *and her garden wall, over-hung with tall shrubbery. Over the door of the house a balcony and a tall window; to one side of the door, a bench.*

Ivy clings to the wall; jasmine embraces the balcony, trembles, and falls away.

By the bench and the jutting stonework of the wall one might easily climb up to the balcony.

Opposite, an ancient house of the like character, brick and stone, whose front door forms an Entrance. The knocker on this door is tied up in linen like an injured thumb.

At the CURTAIN RISE THE DUENNA *is seated on the bench beside the door. The window is wide open on* ROXANE'S *balcony; a light within suggests that it is early evening. By* THE DUENNA *stands* RAGUENEAU *dressed in what might be the livery of one attached to the household. He is by way of telling her something, and wiping his eyes meanwhile.*

RAGUENEAU

—And so she ran off with a Musketeer!
I was ruined—I was alone—Remained
Nothing for me to do but hang myself,
So I did that. Presently along comes
Monsieur de Bergerac, and cuts me
down,
And makes me steward to his
cousin.

THE DUENNA
     Ruined?—
I thought your pastry was a great
success!

RAGUENEAU
(*Shakes his head.*)
Lise loved the soldiers, and I loved
the poets—
Mars ate up all the cakes Apollo
left;

It did not take long. . . .

THE DUENNA
(*Calls up to window.*)
   Roxane! Are you ready?
We are late!

VOICE OF ROXANE
(*Within*)
   Putting on my cape—

THE DUENNA
(*To* RAGUENEAU, *indicating
the house opposite.*)
       Clomire
Across the way receives on Thurs-
day nights—
We are to have a psycho-colloquy
Upon the Tender Passion.

RAGUENEAU
Ah—the Tender . . .

THE DUENNA

(*Sighs*)
—Passion! . . .
(*Calls up to window.*)
Roxane!—Hurry, dear—we shall miss
The Tender Passion!

ROXANE

Coming!—
(*Music of stringed instruments off-stage approaching.*)

THE VOICE OF CYRANO

(*Singing*)
                    La, la, la!—

THE DUENNA

A serenade?—How pleasant—

CYRANO

                    No, no, no!—
F natural, you natural-born fool!
(*Enters, followed by two PAGES, carrying theorbos.*)

FIRST PAGE

(*Ironically*)
No doubt your honor knows F natural
When he hears—

CYRANO

          I am a musician, infant!—
A pupil of Gassendi.

THE PAGE

(*Plays and sings.*)
                    La, la,—

CYRANO

                    Here—
Give me that—
(*He snatches the instrument from the Page and continues the tune.*)
          La, la, la, la—

ROXANE

(*Appears on the Balcony.*)
                    Is that you,
Cyrano?

CYRANO

(*Singing*)
     I, who praise your lilies fair,
But long to love your ro . . . ses!

ROXANE

                    I'll be down—
Wait—
(*Goes in through window.*)

THE DUENNA

Did you train these virtuosi?

CYRANO

                    No—
I won them on a bet from D'Assoucy.
We were debating a fine point of grammar
When, pointing out these two young nightingales
Dressed up like peacocks, with their instruments,
He cries: "No, but I KNOW! I'll wager you
A day of music." Well, of course he lost;
And so until tomorrow they are mine,
My private orchestra. Pleasant at first,
But they become a trifle—
(*To the PAGES*)
                    Here! Go play
A minuet to Montfleury—and tell him
I sent you!
(*The PAGES go up to the exit. CYRANO turns to the DUENNA*)
                    I came here as usual
To inquire after our friend—
(*To PAGES*)
                    Play out of tune.

And keep on playing!
> (*The* PAGES *go out. He turns
> to the* DUENNA)

—Our friend with the great soul.

CYRANO

> (*Enters in time to hear the
> last words.*)

He is beautiful and brilliant—and
I love him!

CYRANO

Do you find Christian . . . intellectual?

ROXANE

More so than you, even.

CYRANO

> I am glad.

ROXANE

> No man

Ever so beautifully said those
things—
Those pretty nothings that are
everything.
Sometimes he falls into a reverie;
His inspiration fails—then all at
once,
He will say something absolutely
. . . Oh! . . .

CYRANO

Really!

ROXANE

How like a man! You think a man
Who has a handsome face must be
a fool.

CYRANO

He talks well about . . . matters
of the heart?

ROXANE

He does not *talk;* he rhapsodizes
. . . dreams . . .

CYRANO

> (*Twisting his moustache.*)

He . . . writes well?

ROXANE

> Wonderfully. Listen now:
> (*Reciting as from memory.*)

"Take my heart; I shall have it all
the more;
Plucking the flowers, we keep the
plant in bloom—"
Well?

CYRANO

Pooh!

ROXANE

And this:
> "Knowing you have in store

More heart to give than I to find
heart-room—"

CYRANO

First he has too much, then too little; just
How much heart does he need?

ROXANE

> (*Tapping her foot.*)

> You are teasing me!

You are jealous!

CYRANO

> (*Startled*)

> Jealous?

ROXANE

> Of his poetry—

You poets are like that . . .
> And these last lines

Are they not the last word in tenderness?—
"There is no more to say: only believe
That unto you my whole heart gives
one cry,
And writing, writes down more
than you receive;

Sending you kisses through my
   finger-tips—
Lady, O read my letter with your
   lips!"

CYRANO

H'm, yes—those last lines . . . but
   he overwrites!

ROXANE

Listen to this—

CYRANO

         You know them all by heart?

ROXANE

Every one!

CYRANO

   (*Twisting his moustache.*)
I may call that flattering . . .

ROXANE

He is a master!

CYRANO

         Oh—come!

ROXANE

         Yes—a master!

CYRANO

   (*Bowing*)
A master—if you will!

THE DUENNA

   (*Comes down stage quickly.*)
         Monsieur de Guiche!—
   (*To* CYRANO, *pushing him to-
      ward the house.*)
Go inside—If he does not find you
   here,
It may be just as well. He may sus-
   pect—

ROXANE

—My secret! Yes; he is in love with
   me

And he is powerful. Let him not
   know—
One look would frost my roses before bloom.

CYRANO

   (*Going into house.*)
Very well, very well!

ROXANE

   (*To* DE GUICHE, *as he enters*)
         We were just going—

DE GUICHE

I came only to say farewell.

ROXANE

                  You leave
Paris?

DE GUICHE

   Yes—for the front.

ROXANE

         Ah!

DE GUICHE

         And tonight!

ROXANE

Ah!

DE GUICHE

We have orders to besiege Arras.

ROXANE

Arras?

DE GUICHE

   Yes. My departure leaves you
      . . . cold?

ROXANE

   (*Politely*)
Oh! Not that.

DE GUICHE

  It has left me desolate—
When shall I see you? Ever? Did you know
I was made Colonel?

ROXANE

(*Indifferent*)
  Bravo!

DE GUICHE

      Regiment
Of the Guards.

ROXANE

(*Catching her breath.*)
  Of the Guards?—

DE GUICHE

     His regiment,
Your cousin, the mighty man of words!—
  (*Grimly*)
      Down there
We may have an accounting!

ROXANE

(*Suffocating*)
     Are you sure
The Guards are ordered?

DE GUICHE

  Under my command!

ROXANE

(*Sinks down, breathless, on
 the bench; aside*)
Christian!—

DE GUICHE

  What is it?

ROXANE

(*Losing control of herself*)
    To the war—perhaps
Never again to— When a woman cares,
Is that nothing?

DE GUICHE

(*Surprised and delighted*)
  You say this now—to me—
Now, at the very moment?—

ROXANE

(*Recovers—changes her tone*)
    Tell me something:
My cousin— You say you mean to be revenged
On him. Do you mean that?

DE GUICHE

(*Smiles*)
  Why? Would you care?

ROXANE

Not for him.

DE GUICHE

  Do you see him?

ROXANE

    Now and then.

DE GUICHE

He goes about everywhere nowadays
With one of the Cadets—de Neuve
 —Neuville—
Neuvillers—

ROXANE

(*Coolly*)
  A tall man?—

DE GUICHE

  Blond—

ROXANE

  Rosy cheeks?—

DE GUICHE

Handsome!—

ROXANE

  Pooh!—

DE GUICHE
And a fool.

ROXANE
(*Languidly*)
            So he appears . . .
(*Animated*)
But Cyrano? What will you do to
    him?
Order him into danger? He loves
    that!
I know what *I* should do.

DE GUICHE
            What?

ROXANE
            Leave him here
With his Cadets, while all the regi-
    ment
Goes on to glory! That would tor-
    ture him—
To sit all through the war with
    folded arms—
I know his nature. If you hate that
    man,
Strike at his self-esteem.

DE GUICHE
            Oh woman—woman!
Who but a woman would have
    thought of this?

ROXANE
He'll eat his heart out, while his
    Gascon friends
Bite their nails all day long in Paris
    here.
And you will be avenged!

DE GUICHE
            You love me then,
A little? . . .
    (*She smiles.*)
    Making my enemies your own,
Hating them—I should like to see
    in that
A sign of love, Roxane.

ROXANE
Perhaps it is one . . .

DE GUICHE
    (*Shows a number of folded
        despatches.*)
Here are the orders—for each
    company—
Ready to send . . .
    (*Selects one.*)
            So— This is for the Guards—
I'll keep that. Aha, Cyrano!
    (*To* ROXANE)
                        You too.
You play your little games, do you?

ROXANE
(*Watching him.*)
            Sometimes . . .

DE GUICHE
    (*Close to her, speaking hur-
        riedly.*)
And you?—Oh, I am mad over
    you!—
                        Listen—
I leave tonight—but—let you
    through my hands
Now, when I feel you trembling?—
Listen—Close by,
In the Rue d'Orleans, the Capu-
    chins
Have their new convent. By their
    law, no layman
May pass inside those walls. I'll see
    to that—
Their sleeves are wide enough to
    cover me—
The servants of my Uncle-Cardinal
Will fear his nephew. So—I'll come
    to you
Masked, after everyone knows I
    have gone—
Oh, let me wait one day!—

ROXANE
            If this be known,
Your honor—

DE GUICHE

Bah!

ROXANE

The war—your duty—

DE GUICHE

(*Blows away an imaginary feather.*)
                                    Phoo!—
Only say yes!

ROXANE

No!

DE GUICHE

Whisper . . .

ROXANE

(*Tenderly*)
                        I ought not
To let you . . .

DE GUICHE

Ah! . . .

ROXANE

(*Pretends to break down.*)
        Ah, go!
(*Aside*)
            —Christian remains—
(*Aloud—heroically*)
I must have you a hero—Antoine
. . .

DE GUICHE

                            Heaven! . . .
So you can love—

ROXANE

One for whose sake I fear.

DE GUICHE

(*Triumphant*)
I go!
        Will that content you?
(*Kisses her hand.*)

ROXANE

                        Yes—my friend!
(*He goes out.*)

THE DUENNA

(*As* DE GUICHE *disappears, making a deep curtsey behind his back, and imitating* ROXANE'S *intense tone.*)
Yes—my friend!

ROXANE

(*Quickly, close to her.*)
        Not a word to Cyrano—
He would never forgive me if he knew
I stole his war!
        (*She calls toward the house.*)
                        Cousin!
(CYRANO *comes out of the house; she turns to him, indicating the house opposite.*)
                        We are going over—
Alcandre speaks tonight — and Lysimon.

THE DUENNA

(*Puts finger in her ear.*)
My little finger says we shall not hear
Everything.

CYRANO

Never mind me—

THE DUENNA

(*Across the street*)
                        Look— Oh, look!
The knocker tied up in a napkin—
        Yes,
They muzzled you because you bark too loud
And interrupt the lecture—little beast!

ROXANE

(*As the door opens*)

Enter . . .

(*To* CYRANO)

If Christian comes, tell him to wait.

CYRANO

Oh—

(ROXANE *returns.*)

When he comes, what will you talk about?

You always know beforehand.

ROXANE

About . . .

CYRANO

Well?

ROXANE

You will not tell him, will you?

CYRANO

I am dumb.

ROXANE

About nothing! Or about everything—

I shall say: "Speak of love in your own words—

Improvise! Rhapsodize! Be eloquent!"

CYRANO

(*Smiling*)

Good!

ROXANE

Sh!—

CYRANO

Sh!—

ROXANE

Not a word!

(*She goes in; the door closes.*)

CYRANO

(*Bowing*)

Thank you so much—

ROXANE

(*Opens door and puts out her head.*)

He must be unprepared—

CYRANO

Of course!

ROXANE

Sh!—

(*Goes in again.*)

CYRANO

(*Calls*)

Christian!

(*Christian enters.*)

I have your theme—bring on your memory!—

Here is your chance now to surpass yourself,

No time to lose— Come! Look intelligent—

Come home and learn your lines.

CHRISTIAN

No.

CYRANO

What?

CHRISTIAN

I'll wait

Here for Roxane.

CYRANO

What lunacy is this?

Come quickly!

CHRISTIAN

No, I say! I have had enough—

Taking my words, my letters, all from you—

Making our love a little comedy!

It was a game at first; but now—
she cares . . .
Thanks to you. I am not afraid.
I'll speak
For myself now.

CYRANO

Undoubtedly!

CHRISTIAN

I will!
Why not? I am no such fool—you
shall see!
Besides—my dear friend—you
have taught me much;
I ought to know something . . .
By God, I know
Enough to take a woman in my
arms!
(ROXANE *appears in the door-
way, opposite.*)
There she is now . . . Cyrano,
wait! Stay here!

CYRANO

(*Bows*)
Speak for yourself, my friend!
(*He goes out.*)

ROXANE

(*Taking leave of the com-
pany.*)
—Barthénoide!
Alcandre! . . . Grémione! . . .

THE DUENNA

I told you so—
We missed the Tender Passion!
(*She goes into* ROXANE'S
house.)

ROXANE

Urimédonte!—
Adieu!
(*As the guests disappear down
the street, she turns to
CHRISTIAN.*)
Is that you, Christian? Let us stay

Here, in the twilight. They are
gone. The air
Is fragrant. We shall be alone. Sit
down
There—so . . .
(*They sit on the bench.*)
Now tell me things.

CHRISTIAN

(*After a silence*)
I love you.

ROXANE

(*Closes her eyes.*)
Yes,
Speak to me about love . . .

CHRISTIAN

I love you.

ROXANE

Now
Be eloquent! . . .

CHRISTIAN

I love—

ROXANE

(*Opens her eyes.*)
You have your theme—
Improvise! Rhapsodize!

CHRISTIAN

I love you so!

ROXANE

Of course. And then? . . .

CHRISTIAN

And then . . . Oh, I should be
So happy if you loved me too!
Roxane,
Say that you love me too!

ROXANE

(*Making a face.*)
I ask for cream—

You give me milk and water. Tell me first
A little, how you love me.

CHRISTIAN
                    Very much.

ROXANE
Oh—tell me how you *feel!*

CHRISTIAN
(Coming nearer, and devouring her with his eyes.)
                    Your throat . . . If only
I might . . . kiss it—

ROXANE
                    Christian!

CHRISTIAN
                    I love you so!

ROXANE
(Makes as if to rise.)
Again?

CHRISTIAN
(Desperately, restraining her.)
No, not again— I do not love you—

ROXANE
(Settles back.)
That is better . . .

CHRISTIAN
                    I adore you!

ROXANE
                    Oh!—
(Rises and moves away.)

CHRISTIAN
                    I know;
I grow absurd.

ROXANE
(Coldly)
                    And that displeases me
As much as if you had grown ugly.

CHRISTIAN
                                        I—

ROXANE
Gather your dreams together into words!

CHRISTIAN
I love—

ROXANE
I know; you love me. Adieu.
(She goes to the house.)

CHRISTIAN
                                        No,
But wait—please—let me— I was
going to say—

ROXANE
(Pushes the door open.)
That you adore me. Yes; I know
that too.
No! . . . Go away! . . .
            (She goes in and shuts the door in his face.)

CHRISTIAN
I . . . I . . .

CYRANO
(Enters)
                    A great success!

CHRISTIAN
Help me!

CYRANO
Not I.

CHRISTIAN
                    I cannot live unless
She loves me—now, this moment!

CYRANO
                            How the devil
Am I to teach you now—this moment?

CHRISTIAN

(*Catches him by the arm.*)
        —Wait!—
Look! Up there!—Quick—
    (*The light shows in* ROXANE's
    window.)

CYRANO

Her window—

CHRISTIAN

(*Wailing*)
        I shall die!—

CYRANO

Less noise!

CHRISTIAN

Oh, I—

CYRANO

It does seem fairly dark—

CHRISTIAN

(*Excitedly*)
Well?—Well?—Well?—

CYRANO

    Let us try what can be done;
It is more than you deserve—stand
    over there,
Idiot—there!—before the bal-
    cony—
Let me stand underneath. I'll whis-
    per you
What to say.

CHRISTIAN

She may hear—she may—

CYRANO

        Less noise!
(*The* PAGES *appear up stage.*)

FIRST PAGE

Hep!—

CYRANO

(*Finger to lips*)
Sh!-—

FIRST PAGE

(*Low voice*)
    We serenaded Montfleury!—
What next?

CYRANO

Down to the corner of the street—
One this way—and the other over
    there—
If anybody passes, play a tune!

PAGE

What tune, O musical Philosopher?

CYRANO

Sad for a man, or merry for a
    woman—
Now go!
    (*The* PAGES *disappear, one to-
    ward each corner of the
    street.*)

CYRANO

(*To* CHRISTIAN)
Call her!

CHRISTIAN

Roxane!

CYRANO

    Wait . . .
(*Gathers up a handful of
    pebbles.*)
        Gravel . . .
(*Throws it at the window.*)
        There!—

ROXANE

(*Opens the window.*)
Who is calling?

CHRISTIAN

I—

ROXANE
Who?

CHRISTIAN
Christian.

ROXANE
You again?

CHRISTIAN
I had to tell you—

CYRANO
(*Under the balcony*)
Good—Keep your voice down.

ROXANE
No. Go away. You tell me nothing.

CHRISTIAN
Please!—

ROXANE
You do not love me any more—

CHRISTIAN
(*To whom* CYRANO *whispers his words*)
No—no—
Not any more— I love you . . . evermore . . .
And ever . . . more and more!

ROXANE
(*About to close the window— pauses.*)
A little better . . .

CHRISTIAN
(*Same business*)
Love grows and struggles like . . . an angry child . . .
Breaking my heart . . . his cradle . . .

ROXANE
(*Coming out on the balcony.*)
Better still—

But . . . such a babe is dangerous; why not
Have smothered it new-born?

CHRISTIAN
(*Same business*)
And so I do . . .
And yet he lives . . . I found . . . as you shall find . . .
This new-born babe . . . an infant . . . Hercules!

ROXANE
(*Further forward*)
Good!—

CHRISTIAN
(*Same business*)
Strong enough . . . at birth . . . to strangle those
Two serpents—Doubt and . . . Pride.

ROXANE
(*Leans over balcony.*)
Why, very well!
Tell me now why you speak so haltingly—
Has your imagination gone lame?

CYRANO
(*Thrusts* CHRISTIAN *under the balcony, and stands in his place.*)
Here—
This grows too difficult!

ROXANE
Your words tonight
Hesitate. Why?

CYRANO
(*In a low tone, imitating* CHRISTIAN)
Through the warm summer gloom
They grope in darkness toward the light of you.

ROXANE

My words, well aimed, find you
more readily.

CYRANO

My heart is open wide and waits
for them—
Too large a mark to miss! My words
fly home,
Heavy with honey like returning
bees,
To your small secret ear. Moreover
—yours
Fall to me swiftly. Mine more
slowly rise.

ROXANE

Yet not so slowly as they did at first.

CYRANO

They have learned the way, and
you have welcomed them.

ROXANE

(*Softly*)
Am I so far above you now?

CYRANO

So far—
If you let fall upon me one hard
word,
Out of that height—you crush me!

ROXANE

(*Turns*)
I'll come down—

CYRANO

(*Quickly*)
No!

ROXANE

(*Points out the bench under
the balcony.*)
Stand you on the bench. Come
nearer!

CYRANO

(*Recoils into the shadow.*)
No!

ROXANE

And why—so great a *No?*

CYRANO

(*More and more overcome by
emotion.*)
Let me enjoy
The one moment I ever—my one
chance
To speak to you . . . unseen!

ROXANE

Unseen?—

CYRANO

Yes!—yes . . .
Night, making all things dimly
beautiful,
One veil over us both— You only
see
The darkness of a long cloak in the
gloom,
And I the whiteness of a summer
gown—
You are all light— I am all shadow!
. . . How
Can you know what this moment
means to me?
If I was ever eloquent—

ROXANE

You were
Eloquent—

CYRANO

—You have never heard till now
My own heart speaking! .

ROXANE

Why not?

CYRANO

Until now,
I spoke through . . .

ROXANE

Yes?—

CYRANO

—through that sweet drunkenness
You pour into the world out of your
eyes!
But tonight . . . But tonight, I
indeed speak
For the first time!

ROXANE

For the first time— Your voice,
Even, is not the same.

CYRANO

(*Passionately; moves nearer.*)
How should it be?
I have another voice tonight—my
own,
Myself, daring—
(*He stops, confused; then tries
to recover himself.*)
Where was I? . . . I forget! . . .
Forgive me. This is all sweet like a
dream . . .
Strange—like a dream . . .

ROXANE

How, strange?

CYRANO

Is it not so
To be myself to you, and have no
fear
Of moving you to laughter?

ROXANE

Laughter—why?

CYRANO

(*Struggling for an explana-
tion.*)
Because . . . What am I . . .
What is any man,
That he dare ask for you? There-
fore my heart

Hides behind phrases. There's a
modesty
In these things too— I come here to
pluck down
Out of the sky the evening star—
then smile,
And stoop to gather little flowers.

ROXANE

Are they
Not sweet, those little flowers?

CYRANO

Not enough sweet
For you and me, tonight!

ROXANE

(*Breathless*)
You never spoke
To me like this . . .

CYRANO

Little things, pretty things—
Arrows and hearts and torches—
roses red,
And violets blue—are these all?
Come away,
And breathe fresh air! Must we
keep on and on
Sipping stale honey out of tiny cups
Decorated with golden tracery,
Drop by drop, all day long? We are
alive;
We thirst— Come away, plunge,
and drink, and drown
In the great river flowing to the sea!

ROXANE

But . . . Poetry?

CYRANO

I have made rimes for you—
Not now— Shall we insult Nature,
this night,
These flowers, this moment—shall
we set all these
To phrases from a letter by Voi-
ture?

Look once at the high stars that
   shine in heaven,
And put off artificiality!
Have you not seen great gaudy hothouse flowers,
Barren, without fragrance?—Souls
   are like that:
Forced to show all, they soon become all show—
The means to Nature's end ends
   meaningless!

ROXANE

But . . . Poetry?

CYRANO

   Love hates that game of words!
It is a crime to fence with life— I
   tell you,
There comes one moment, once—
   and God help those
Who pass that moment by!—when
   Beauty stands
Looking into the soul with grave,
   sweet eyes
That sicken at pretty words!

ROXANE

             If that be true—
And when that moment comes to
   you and me—
What words will you? . . .

CYRANO

   All those, all those, all those
That blossom in my heart, I'll fling
   to you—
Armfuls of loose bloom! Love, I
   love beyond
Breath, beyond reason, beyond
   love's own power
Of loving! Your name is like a
   golden bell
Hung in my heart; and when I
   think of you,
I tremble, and the bell swings and
   rings—
          Roxane! . . .

Roxane! along my veins, *Roxane!*
               I know
All small forgotten things that once
   meant You—
I remember last year, the First of
   May,
A little before noon, you had your
   hair
Drawn low, that one time only. Is
   that strange?
You know how, after looking at the
   sun,
One sees red suns everywhere—so,
   for hours
After the flood of sunshine that you
   are,
My eyes are blinded by your burn-
   ing hair!

ROXANE

   (*Very low*)
Yes . . . that is . . . Love—

CYRANO

   Yes, that is Love—that wind
Of terrible and jealous beauty,
   blowing
Over me—that dark fire, that mu-
   sic . . .
                  Yet
Love seeketh not his own! Dear,
   you may take
My happiness to make you happier,
Even though you never know I
   gave it you—
Only let me hear sometimes, all
   alone,
The distant laughter of your joy!
   . . .
                I never
Look at you, but there's some new
   virtue born
In me, some new courage. Do you
   begin
To understand, a little? Can you
   feel
My soul, there in the darkness,
   breathe on you?

—Oh, but tonight, now, I dare say
    these things—
I . . . to you . . . and you hear
    them! . . . It is too much!
In my most sweet unreasonable
    dreams,
I have not hoped for this! Now let
    me die,
Having lived. It is my voice, mine,
    my own,
That makes you tremble there in
    the green gloom
Above me—for you do tremble, as
    a blossom
Among the leaves— You tremble,
    and I can feel,
All the way down along these jas-
    mine branches,
Whether you will or no, the pas-
    sion of you
Trembling . . .
    *(He kisses wildly the end of a
    drooping spray of jasmine.)*

ROXANE

Yes, I do tremble . . . and I weep
    . . .
And I love you . . . and I am
    yours . . . and you
Have made me thus!

CYRANO

    (After a pause; quietly.)
    What is death like, I wonder?
I know everything else now . . .
                I have done
This, to you—I, myself . . .
                Only let me
Ask one thing more—

CHRISTIAN

    (Under the balcony)
    One kiss!

ROXANE

    (Startled)
        One?—

CYRANO

    (To CHRISTIAN*)*
                You! . . .

ROXANE

                You ask me
For—

CYRANO

    ⸺ . . . Yes, but—I mean—
    (To CHRISTIAN*)*
                You go too far!

CHRISTIAN

She is willing!—Why not make the
    most of it?

CYRANO

    (To ROXANE*)*
I did ask . . . but I know I ask
    too much . . .

ROXANE

Only one— Is that all?

CYRANO

                All!—How much more
Than all!—I know—I frighten you
    —I ask . . .
I ask you to refuse—

CHRISTIAN

    (To CYRANO*)*
                But why? Why? Why?

CYRANO

Christian, be quiet!

ROXANE

    (Leaning over)
                What is that you say
To yourself?

CYRANO

        I am angry with myself
Because I go too far, and so I say
To myself: "Christian, be quiet!"

(*The theorbos begin to play.*)
                    Hark—someone
Is coming—
          (ROXANE *closes her window.*
          CYRANO *listens to the theor-*
          bos, one of which plays a
          gay melody, the other a
          mournful one.)
A sad tune, a merry tune—
Man, woman—what do they
mean?—
          (*A* CAPUCHIN *enters; he carries*
          a lantern, and goes from
          house to house, looking at
          the doors.)
                    Aha!—a priest!
          (*To the* CAPUCHIN)
What is this new game of Di-
ogenes?

THE CAPUCHIN

I am looking for the house of
Madame—

CHRISTIAN

(*Impatient*)
                    Bah!—

THE CAPUCHIN

Madeleine Robin—

CHRISTIAN

What does he want?

CYRANO

(*To the* CAPUCHIN; *points out*
a street.)
                    This way—
To the right—keep to the right—

THE CAPUCHIN

          I thank you, sir!—
I'll say my beads for you to the last
grain.

CYRANO

Good fortune, father, and my service to you!
          (*The* CAPUCHIN *goes out.*)

CHRISTIAN

Win me that kiss!

CYRANO

          No.

CHRISTIAN

          Sooner or later—

CYRANO

                    True . . .
That is true . . . Soon or late, it
will be so
Because you are young and she is
beautiful—
          (*To himself*)
Since it must be, I had rather be
myself
          (*The window re-opens.* CHRIS-
          TIAN *hides under the bal-*
          cony.)
The cause of . . . what must be.

ROXANE

(*Out on the balcony*)
                    Are you still there?
We were speaking of—

CYRANO

          A kiss. The word is sweet—
What will the deed be? Are your
lips afraid
Even of its burning name? Not
much afraid—
Not too much! Have you not un-
wittingly
Laid aside laughter, slipping beyond speech
Insensibly, already, without fear,
From words to smiles . . . from
smiles to sighs . . . from sighing,
Even to tears? One step more—
only one—
From a tear to a kiss—one step, one
thrill!

ROXANE

Hush!—

CYRANO

And what is a kiss, when all is
    done?
A promise given under seal—a vow
Taken before the shrine of mem-
    ory—
A signature acknowledged—a rosy
    dot
Over the i of Loving—a secret
    whispered
To listening lips apart—a moment
    made
Immortal, with a rush of wings un-
    seen—
A sacrament of blossoms, a new
    song
Sung by two hearts to an old simple
    tune—
The ring of one horizon around two
    souls
Together, all alone!

ROXANE

    Hush! . . .

CYRANO

            Why, what shame?—
There was a Queen of France, not
    long ago,
And a great lord of England—a
    queen's gift,
A crown jewel!—

ROXANE

    Indeed!

CYRANO

            Indeed, like him,
I have my sorrows and my silences;
Like her, you are the queen I dare
    adore;
Like him I am faithful and for-
    lorn—

ROXANE

                Like him,
Beautiful—

CYRANO

(Aside)
So I am—I forgot that!

ROXANE

Then—Come! . . . Gather   your
sacred blossom . . .

CYRANO

(To CHRISTIAN)
                Go!—

ROXANE

Your crown jewel . . .

CYRANO

Go on!—

ROXANE

    Your old new song . . .

CYRANO

Climb!—

CHRISTIAN

(Hesitates)
No— Would you?—not yet—

ROXANE

            Your moment made
Immortal . . .

CYRANO

(Pushing him.)
        Climb up, animal!
(CHRISTIAN springs on the
    bench, and climbs by the
    pillars, the branches, the
    vines, until he bestrides the
    balcony railing.)

CHRISTIAN

            Roxane! . . .
(He takes her in his arms and
    bends over her.)

CYRANO

(*Very low*)

Ah! . . . Roxane! . . .
I have won what I have won—
The feast of love—and I am Laza-
rus!
Yet . . . I have something here
that is mine now
And was not mine before I spoke
the words
That won her—not for me! . . .
Kissing my words
My words, upon your lips!
(*The theorbos begin to play.*)
A merry tune—
A sad tune— So! The Capuchin!
(*He pretends to be running, as
if he had arrived from a dis-
tance; then calls up to the
balcony.*)
Holo!

ROXANE

Who is it?

CYRANO

I. Is Christian there with you?

CHRISTIAN

(*Astonished*)

Cyrano!

ROXANE

Good morrow, Cousin!

CYRANO

Cousin, . . . good morrow!

ROXANE

I am coming down.
(*She disappears into the
house. The* CAPUCHIN *enters
up stage.*)

CHRISTIAN

(*Sees him.*)

Oh—again!

THE CAPUCHIN

(*To* CYRANO)

She lives *here*,
Madeleine Robin!

CYRANO

You said Ro-LIN.

THE CAPUCHIN

No—

R-O-B-I-N

ROXANE

(*Appears on the threshold of
the house, followed by
RAGUENEAU with a lantern,
and by CHRISTIAN.*)

What is it?

THE CAPUCHIN

A letter.

CHRISTIAN

Oh! . . .

THE CAPUCHIN

(*To* ROXANE)

Some matter profitable to the
soul—
A very noble lord gave it to me!

ROXANE

(*To* CHRISTIAN)

De Guiche!

CHRISTIAN

He dares?—

ROXANE

It will not be for long;
When he learns that I love you . . .
(*By the light of the lantern
which RAGUENEAU holds,
she reads the letter in a low
tone, as if to herself.*)

"Mademoiselle
The drums are beating, and the
regiment

Arms for the march. Secretly I re-
main
Here, in the Convent. I have dis-
obeyed;
I shall be with you soon. I send this
first
By an old monk, as simple as a
sheep,
Who understands nothing of this.
Your smile
Is more than I can bear, and seek
no more.
Be alone tonight, waiting for one
who dares
To hope you will forgive . . .—"
etcetera—
    (*To the* CAPUCHIN)
Father, this letter concerns you . . .
    (*To* CHRISTIAN)
               —and you.
Listen:
    (*The others gather around
    her. She pretends to read
    from the letter, aloud.*)
      "Mademoiselle:
            The Cardinal
Will have his way, although against
your will;
That is why I am sending this to
you
By a most holy man, intelligent,
Discreet. You will communicate to
him
Our order to perform, here and at
once
The rite of . . .
    (*Turns the page*)
         —Holy Matrimony. You
And Christian will be married pri-
vately
In your house. I have sent him to
you. I know
You hesitate. Be resigned, neverthe-
less,
To the Cardinal's command, who
sends herewith
His blessing. Be assured also of my
own

Respect and high consideration—
signed,
Your very humble and—etcetera
—"

THE CAPUCHIN

A noble lord! I said so—never
fear—
A worthy lord!—a very worthy
lord!—

ROXANE

    (*To* CHRISTIAN)
Am I a good reader of letters?

CHRISTIAN

    (*Motions toward the* CAPU-
    CHIN.)
              Careful!—

ROXANE

    (*In a tragic tone*)
Oh, this is terrible!

THE CAPUCHIN

    (*Turns the light of his lantern
    on* CYRANO.)
        You are to be—

CHRISTIAN

I am the bridegroom!

THE CAPUCHIN

    (*Turns his lantern upon* CHRIS-
    TIAN; *then, as if some sus-
    picion crossed his mind,
    upon seeing the young man
    so handsome.*)
      Oh—why, *you* . . .

ROXANE

    (*Quickly*)
             Look here—
"*Postscript:* Give to the Convent in
my name
One hundred and twenty pis-
toles"—

THE CAPUCHIN

Think of it!
A worthy lord—a very worthy lord!
. . .

(*To* ROXANE, *solemnly*)
Daughter, resign yourself!

ROXANE

(*With an air of martyrdom*)
I am resigned . . .
(*While* RAGUENEAU *opens the
door for the* CAPUCHIN *and
CHRISTIAN *invites him to
enter, she turns to* CYRANO.)
De Guiche may come. Keep him
out here with you.
Do not let him—

CYRANO

I understand!
(*To the* CAPUCHIN)
How long
Will you be?—

THE CAPUCHIN

Oh, a quarter of an hour.

CYRANO

(*Hurrying them into the
house.*)
Hurry—I'll wait here—

ROXANE

(*To* CHRISTIAN)
Come!
(*They go into the house.*)

CYRANO

Now then, to make
His Grace delay that quarter of an
hour . . .
I have it!—up here—
(*He steps on the bench, and
climbs up the wall toward
the balcony. The theorbos
begin to play a mournful
melody.*)
Sad music— Ah, a man! . . .

(*The music pauses on a sinister tremolo.*)
Oh—very much a man!
(*He sits astride of the railing,
and, drawing toward him a
long branch of one of the
trees which border the garden wall, he grasps it with
both hands, ready to swing
himself down.*)
So—not too high—
(*He peers down at the
ground.*)
I must float gently through the atmosphere—

DE GUICHE

(*Enters, masked, groping in
the dark toward the house.*)
Where is that cursed, bleating Capuchin?

CYRANO

What if he knows my voice?—the
devil!—Tic-tac,
Bergerac—we unlock our Gascon
tongue;
A good strong accent—

DE GUICHE

Here is the house—all dark—
Damn this mask!—
(*As he is about to enter the
house, CYRANO leaps from
the balcony, still holding
fast to the branch, which
bends and swings him be-
tween DE GUICHE and the
door; then he releases the
branch and pretends to fall
heavily as though from a
height. He lands flatlong on
the ground, where he lies
motionless, as if stunned. DE
GUICHE leaps back.*)
What is that?
(*When he lifts his eyes, the
branch has sprung back into*

place. He can see nothing but the sky; he does not understand.)
Why . . . where did this man
Fall from?

CYRANO

(*Sits up, and speaks with a strong accent.*)
—The moon!

DE GUICHE

You—

CYRANO

From the moon, the moon!
I fell out of the moon!

DE GUICHE

The fellow is mad—

CYRANO

(*Dreamily*)
Where am I?

DE GUICHE

Why—

CYRANO

What time is it? What place
Is this? What day? What season?

DE GUICHE

You—

CYRANO

I am stunned!

DE GUICHE

My dear sir—

CYRANO

Like a bomb—a bomb—I fell
From the moon!

DE GUICHE

Now, see here—

CYRANO

(*Rising to his feet, and speaking in a terrible voice.*)
I say, the moon!

DE GUICHE

(*Recoils*)
Very well—if you say so—
(*Aside*)
Raving mad!—

CYRANO

(*Advancing upon him.*)
I am not speaking metaphorically!

DE GUICHE

Pardon.

CYRANO

A hundred years—an hour ago—
I really cannot say how long I fell—
I was in yonder shining sphere—

DE GUICHE

(*Shrugs*)
Quite so.
Please let me pass.

CYRANO

(*Interposes himself.*)
Where am I? Tell the truth—
I can bear it. In what quarter of
the globe
Have I descended like a meteorite?

DE GUICHE

Morbleu!

CYRANO

I could not choose my place
to fall—
The earth spun round so fast—
Was it the Earth,
I wonder?—Or is this another
world?
Another moon? Whither have I
been drawn

By the dead weight of my pos-
terior?

DE GUICHE

Sir, I repeat—

CYRANO

(*With a sudden cry, which
causes* DE GUICHE *to recoil
again.*)
His face! My God—black!

DE GUICHE

(*Carries his hand to his
mask.*)
          Oh—

CYRANO

(*Terrified*)
Are you a native? Is this Africa?

DE GUICHE

—This mask!

CYRANO

(*Somewhat reassured*)
      Are we in Venice? Genoa?

DE GUICHE

(*Tries to pass him.*)
A lady 's waiting for me.

CYRANO

(*Quite happy again.*)
          So this is Paris!

DE GUICHE

(*Smiling in spite of himself.*)
This fool becomes amusing.

CYRANO

          Ah! You smile?

DE GUICHE

I do. Kindly permit me—

CYRANO

(*Delighted*)
          Dear old Paris—
Well, well!—

(*Wholly at his ease, smiles,
bows, arranges his dress.*)
Excuse my appearance. I arrive
By the last thunderbolt—a trifle
singed
As I came through the ether. These
long journeys—
You know! There are so few con-
veniences!
My eyes are full of star-dust. On
my spurs,
Some sort of fur . . . Planet's ap-
parently . . .
(*Plucks something from his
sleeve.*)
Look—on my doublet— That's a
Comet's hair!
(*He blows something from
the back of his hand.*)
Phoo!

DE GUICHE

(*Grows angry.*)
Monsieur—

CYRANO

(*As* DE GUICHE *is about to
push past, thrusts his leg in
the way.*)
Here's a tooth, stuck in my boot,
From the Great Bear. Trying to get
away,
I tripped over the Scorpion and
came down
Slap, into one scale of the Balances—
The pointer marks my weight this
moment . . .
(*Pointing upward.*)
          See?
(DE GUICHE *makes a sudden
movement.* CYRANO *catches
his arm.*)
Be careful! If you struck me on the
nose,
It would drip milk!

DE GUICHE

Milk?

CYRANO

From the Milky Way!

DE GUICHE

Hell!

CYRANO

No, no—Heaven.
(*Crossing his arms*)
          Curious place up there—
Did you know Sirius wore a night-
cap? True!
(*Confidentially*)
The Little Bear is still too young
to bite.
(*Laughing*)
My foot caught in the Lyre, and
broke a string.
(*Proudly*)
Well—when I write my book, and
tell the tale
Of my adventures—all these little
stars
That shake out of my cloak—I must
save those
To use for asterisks!

DE GUICHE

          That will do now—
I wish—

CYRANO

Yes, yes—I know—

DE GUICHE

          Sir—

CYRANO

          You desire
To learn from my own lips the
character
Of the moon's surface—its inhab-
itants
If any—

DE GUICHE

(*Loses patience and shouts.*)
          I desire no such thing! I—

CYRANO

(*Rapidly*)
You wish to know by what myste-
rious means
I reached the moon?—well—con-
fidentially—
It was a new invention of my own.

DE GUICHE

(*Discouraged*)
Drunk too—as well as mad!

CYRANO

          I scorned the eagle
Of Regiomontanus, and the dove
Of Archytas!

DE GUICHE

          A learned lunatic!—

CYRANO

I imitated no one. I myself
Discovered not one scheme merely,
but six—
Six ways to violate the virgin sky!
          (DE GUICHE *has succeeded in
          passing him, and moves to-
          ward the door of* ROXANE's
          house. CYRANO *follows,
          ready to use violence if
          necessary.*)

DE GUICHE

(*Looks around.*)
Six?

CYRANO

(*With increasing volubility*)
As for instance—Having stripped
myself
Bare as a wax candle, adorn my
form
With crystal vials filled with morn-
ing dew,
And so be drawn aloft, as the sun
rises
Drinking the mist of dawn!

DE GUICHE

(*Takes a step toward* CY-
RANO.)
Yes—that makes one.

CYRANO

(*Draws back to lead him away
from the door; speaks faster
and faster.*)
Or, sealing up the air in a cedar
chest,
Rarefy it by means of mirrors,
placed
In an icosahedron.

DE GUICHE

(*Takes another step.*)
Two.

CYRANO

(*Still retreating*)
Again,
I might construct a rocket, in the
form
Of a huge locust, driven by im-
pulses
Of villainous saltpetre from the
rear,
Upward, by leaps and bounds.

DE GUICHE

(*Interested in spite of himself,
and counting on his fin-
gers.*)
Three.

CYRANO

(*Same business*)
Or again,
Smoke having a natural tendency
to rise,
Blow in a globe enough to raise me.

DE GUICHE

(*Same business, more and
more astonished.*)
Four!

CYRANO

Or since Diana, as old fables tell,
Draws forth to fill her crescent
horn, the marrow
Of bulls and goats—to anoint myself therewith.

DE GUICHE

(*Hypnotized*)
Five!—

CYRANO

(*Has by this time led him all
the way across the street,
close to a bench.*)
Finally—seated on an iron plate,
To hurl a magnet in the air—the
iron
Follows—I catch the magnet—
throw again—
And so proceed indefinitely.

DE GUICHE

Six!—
All excellent,—and which did you
adopt?

CYRANO

(*Coolly*)
Why, none of them. . . . A seventh.

DE GUICHE

Which was?—

CYRANO

Guess!—

DE GUICHE

An interesting idiot, this!

CYRANO

(*Imitates the sound of waves
with his voice, and their
movement by large, vague
gestures.*)
Hoo! . . . Hoo! . . .

DE GUICHE

Well?

CYRANO

Have you guessed it yet?

DE GUICHE

Why, no.

CYRANO

(*Grandiloquent*)
               The ocean! . . .
What hour its rising tide seeks the
     full moon,
I laid me on the strand, fresh from
     the spray,
My head fronting the moonbeams,
     since the hair
Retains moisture—and so I slowly
     rose
As upon angels' wings, effortlessly,
Upward—then suddenly I felt a
     shock!—
And then . . .

DE GUICHE

(*Overcome by curiosity, sits
     down on the bench.*)
And then?

CYRANO

And then—
(*Changes abruptly to his natu-
     ral voice.*)
               The time is up!—
Fifteen minutes, your Grace!—
You are now free;
And—they are bound—in wedlock.

DE GUICHE

(*Leaping up*)
               Am *I* drunk?
That voice . . .
(*The door of* ROXANE's *house
     opens; lackeys appear, bear-
     ing lighted candles.* LIGHTS
     UP. CYRANO *removes his
     hat.*)
And that nose!—Cyrano!

CYRANO

(*Saluting*)
               Cyrano! . . .
This very moment, they have ex-
     changed rings.

DE GUICHE

Who?
(*He turns up stage.* TABLEAU:
     between the lackeys, ROX-
     ANE *and* CHRISTIAN *appear,
     hand in hand. The* CAPU-
     CHIN *follows them, smil-
     ing.* RAGUENEAU *holds aloft
     a torch. The* DUENNA *brings
     up the rear, in a negligée,
     and a pleasant flutter of
     emotion.*)
Zounds!
(*To* ROXANE)
You?—
(*Recognizes* CHRISTIAN)
He?—
(*Saluting* ROXANE)
               My sincere compliments!
(*To* CYRANO)
You also, my inventor of machines!
Your rigmarole would have de-
     tained a saint
Entering Paradise—decidedly
You must not fail to write that book
     some day!

CYRANO

(*Bowing*)
Sir, I engage myself to do so.
(*Leads the bridal pair down to*
     DE GUICHE *and strokes with
     great satisfaction his long
     white beard.*)
               My lord,
The handsome couple you—and
     God—have joined
Together!

DE GUICHE

(*Regarding him with a frosty
     eye.*)
               Quite so.

(*Turns to* ROXANE)
        Madame, kindly bid
Your . . . husband farewell.

ROXANE

Oh!—

DE GUICHE

(*To* CHRISTIAN)
        Your regiment
Leaves tonight, sir. Report at
once!

ROXANE

        You mean
For the front? The war?

DE GUICHE

Certainly!

ROXANE

        I thought
The Cadets were not going—

DE GUICHE

        Oh yes, they are!
(*Taking out the despatch from
his pocket.*)
Here is the order—
(*To* CHRISTIAN)
        Baron! Deliver this.

ROXANE

(*Throws herself into* CHRIS-
TIAN's *arms.*)
Christian!

DE GUICHE

(*To* CYRANO, *sneering*)
The bridal night is not so near!

CYRANO

(*Aside*)
Somehow that news fails to disquiet
me.

CHRISTIAN

(*To* ROXANE)
Your lips again . . .

CYRANO

There . . . That will do
now—Come!

CHRISTIAN

(*Still holding* ROXANE)
You do not know how hard it is—

CYRANO

(*Tries to drag him away.*)
        I know!
(*The beating of drums is
heard in the distance.*)

DE GUICHE

(*Up stage*)
The regiment—on the march!

ROXANE

(*As* CYRANO *tries to lead*
CHRISTIAN *away, follows,
and detains them.*)
        Take care of him
For me—
(*Appealingly*)
Promise me never to let him do
Anything dangerous!

CYRANO

        I'll do my best—
I cannot promise—

ROXANE

(*Same business*)
Make him be careful!

CYRANO

        Yes—
I'll try—

ROXANE

(*Same business*)
Be sure you keep him dry
and warm!

CYRANO

Yes, yes—if possible—

ROXANE

(*Same business; confidentially, in his ear*)
    See that he remains
Faithful—

CYRANO

Of course! If—

ROXANE

(*Same business*)
    And have him write to me
Every single day!

CYRANO

(*Stops*)
    That, I promise you!

CURTAIN

THE FOURTH ACT

THE CADETS OF GASCOYNE

THE POST *occupied by the Company of* CARBON DE CASTEL-JALOUX *at* THE SIEGE OF ARRAS.

In the background, a Rampart traversing the entire scene; beyond this, and apparently below, a Plain stretches away to the horizon. The country is cut up with earthworks and other suggestions of the siege. In the distance against the sky-line, the houses and the walls of Arras.

Tents; scattered Weapons; Drums, etcetera. It is near day-break, and the East is yellow with approaching dawn. Sentries at intervals. Camp-fires.

CURTAIN RISE *discovers the* CADETS *asleep, rolled in their cloaks.* CARBON DE CASTEL-JALOUX *and* LE BRET *keep watch. They are both very thin and pale.* CHRISTIAN *is asleep among the others, wrapped in his cloak, in the foreground, his face lighted by the flickering fire. Silence.*

LE BRET

Horrible!

CARBON

Why, yes. All of that.

LE BRET

    Mordious!

CARBON

(*Gesture toward the sleeping* CADETS)
Swear gently— You might wake them.
  (*To* CADETS)

    Go to sleep—
Hush!
  (*To* LE BRET)
  Who sleeps dines.

LE BRET

    I have insomnia.
God! What a famine.
  (*Firing off stage.*)

CARBON

    Curse that musketry!
They'll wake my babies.
  (*To the men*)
    Go to sleep!—

A CADET

(*Rouses*)
                Diantre!
Again?

CARBON

No—only Cyrano coming home.
(*The heads which have been
raised sink back again.*)

A SENTRY

(*Off stage*)
Halt! Who goes there?

VOICE OF CYRANO

Bergerac!

THE SENTRY ON THE PARAPET

            Halt! Who goes?—

CYRANO

(*Appears on the parapet.*)
Bergerac, idiot!

LE BRET

(*Goes to meet him.*)
           Thank God again!

CYRANO

(*Signs to him not to wake
anyone.*)
Hush!

LE BRET

Wounded?—

CYRANO

No— They always miss me—
      quite
A habit by this time!

LE BRET

        Yes— Go right on—
Risk your life every morning before
      breakfast
To send a letter!

CYRANO

(*Stops near* CHRISTIAN.)
    I promised he should write
Every single day . . .
       (*Looks down at him.*)
       Hm— The boy looks pale
When he is asleep—thin too—
    starving to death—
If that poor child knew! Handsome,
    none the less . . .

LE BRET

Go and get some sleep!

CYRANO

(*Affectionately*)
      Now, now—you old bear,
No growling!—I am careful—you
    know I am—
Every night, when I cross the Span-
    ish lines
I wait till they are all drunk.

LE BRET

          You might bring
Something with you.

CYRANO

       I have to travel light
To pass through— By the way,
    there will be news
For you today; the French will
    eat or die,
If what I saw means anything.

LE BRET

           Tell us!

CYRANO

                No—
I am not sure—we shall see!

CARBON

          What a war,
When the besiegers starve to death!

LE BRET

           Fine war—
Fine situation! We besiege Arras—

The Cardinal Prince of Spain besieges us—
And—here we are!

CYRANO

Someone might besiege *him*.

CARBON

A hungry joke!

CYRANO

Ho, ho!

LE BRET

Yes, you can laugh—
Risking a life like yours to carry
letters—
Where are you going now?

CYRANO

(*At the tent door*)
            To write another.
(*Goes into tent.*)
(*A little more daylight. The
clouds redden. The town of
Arras shows on the horizon.
A cannon shot is heard, followed immediately by a roll
of drums, far away to the
left. Other drums beat a little nearer. The drums go on
answering each other here
and there, approach, beat
loudly almost on the stage,
and die away toward the
right, across the camp. The
camp awakes. Voices of officers in the distance.*)

CARBON

(*Sighs*)
Those drums!—another good nour-
ishing sleep
Gone to the devil.
            (*The* CADETS *rouse them-
            selves.*)
            Now then!—

FIRST CADET

(*Sits up, yawns.*)
            God! I'm hungry!

SECOND CADET

Starving!

ALL

(*Groan*)
Aoh!

CARBON

Up with you!

THIRD CADET

            Not another step!

FOURTH CADET

Not another movement!

FIRST CADET

            Look at my tongue—
I said this air was indigestible!

FIFTH CADET

My coronet for half a pound of
cheese!

SIXTH CADET

I have no stomach for this war—
I'll stay
In my tent—like Achilles.

ANOTHER

            Yes—no bread,
No fighting—

CARBON

Cyrano!

OTHERS

            May as well die—

CARBON

Come out here!—You know how to
talk to them.
Get them laughing—

SECOND CADET

(*Rushes up to* FIRST CADET
who is eating something.)
What are you gnawing there?

FIRST CADET

Gun wads and axle-grease. Fat
country this
Around Arras.

ANOTHER

(*Enters*)
I have been out hunting!

ANOTHER

(*Enters*)
                                              I
Went fishing, in the Scarpe!

ALL

(*Leaping up and surrounding
the newcomers.*)
                              Find anything?
Any fish? Any game? Perch? Partridges?
Let me look!

THE FISHERMAN

Yes—one gudgeon.
(*Shows it.*)

THE HUNTER

One fat . . . sparrow.
(*Shows it.*)

ALL

Ah!—See here, this—mutiny!—

CARBON

                              Cyrano!
Come and help!

CYRANO

(*Enters from tent.*)
Well?
(*Silence. To the* FIRST CADET
*who is walking away, with
his chin on his chest.*)
You there, with the long face?

FIRST CADET

I have something on my mind that
troubles me.

CYRANO

What is that?

FIRST CADET

My stomach.

CYRANO

                              So have I.

FIRST CADET

                                        No doubt
You enjoy this!

CYRANO

(*Tightens his belt.*)
                    It keeps me looking young.

SECOND CADET

My teeth are growing rusty.

CYRANO

                                        Sharpen them!

THIRD CADET

My belly sounds as hollow as a
drum.

CYRANO

Beat the long roll on it!

FOURTH CADET

                                        My ears are ringing.

CYRANO

Liar! A hungry belly has no ears.

FIFTH CADET

Oh for a barrel of good wine!

CYRANO

(*Offers him his own helmet.*)
                                        Your casque.

SIXTH CADET

I'll swallow anything!

CYRANO

(*Throws him the book which
he has in his hand.*)
Try the *Iliad.*

SEVENTH CADET

The Cardinal, he has four meals a
day—
What does he care!

CYRANO

Ask him; he really ought
To send you . . . a spring lamb
out of his flock,
Roasted whole—

THE CADET

Yes, and a bottle—

CYRANO

(*Exaggerates the manner of
one speaking to a servant.*)
If you please,
Richelieu—a little more of the Red
Seal . . .
Ah, thank you!

THE CADET

And the salad—

CYRANO

Of course—Romaine!

ANOTHER CADET

(*Shivering*)
I am as hungry as a wolf.

CYRANO

(*Tosses him a cloak.*)
Put on
Your sheep's clothing.

FIRST CADET

(*With a shrug*)
Always the clever answer!

CYRANO

Always the answer—yes! Let me
die so—
Under some rosy-golden sunset,
saying
A good thing, for a good cause! By
the sword,
The point of honor—by the hand of
one
Worthy to be my foeman, let me
fall—
Steel in my heart, and laughter on
my lips!

VOICES HERE AND THERE

All very well— We are hungry!

CYRANO

Bah! You think
Of nothing but yourselves.
(*His eye singles out the old
fifer in the background.*)
Here, Bertrandou,
You were a shepherd once— Your
pipe now! Come,
Breathe, blow,— Play to these
belly-worshippers
The old airs of the South—
Airs with a smile in them,
Airs with a sigh in them, airs with
the breeze
And the blue of the sky in them—
Small, demure tunes
Whose every note is like a little
sister—
Songs heard only in some long si-
lent voice
Not quite forgotten— Mountain
melodies
Like thin smoke rising from brown
cottages
In the still noon, slowly— Quaint
lullabies,
Whose very music has a Southern
tongue—
(*The old man sits down and
prepares his fife.*)
Now let the fife, that dry old war-
rior,

Dream, while over the stops your fingers dance
A minuet of little birds—let him
Dream beyond ebony and ivory;
Let him remember he was once a reed
Out of the river, and recall the spirit
Of innocent, untroubled country days . . .

> (*The fifer begins to play a Provençale melody.*)

Listen, you Gascons! Now it is no more
The shrill fife— It is the flute, through woodlands far
Away, calling—no longer the hot battle-cry,
But the cool, quiet pipe our goatherds play!
Listen—the forest glens . . . the hills . . . the downs . . .
The green sweetness of night on the Dordogne . . .
Listen, you Gascons! It is all Gascoyne! . . .

> (*Every head is bowed; every eye cast down. Here and there a tear is furtively brushed away with the back of a hand, the corner of a cloak.*)

CARBON

> (*Softly to* CYRANO)

You make them weep—

CYRANO

    For homesickness—a hunger
More noble than that hunger of the flesh;
It is their hearts now that are starving.

CARBON

               Yes,
But you melt down their manhood.

CYRANO

> (*Motions the drummer to approach.*)
>
>   You think so?

Let them be. There is iron in their blood
Not easily dissolved in tears. You need
Only—

> (*He makes a gesture; the drum beats.*)

ALL

> (*Spring up and rush toward their weapons.*)
>
> What's that? Where is it?— What?—

CYRANO

> (*Smiles*)
>
>   You see—

Let Mars snore in his sleep once— and farewell
Venus—sweet dreams—regrets— dear thoughts of home—
All the fife lulls to rest wakes at the drums!

A CADET

> (*Looks up stage.*)

Aha— Monsieur de Guiche!

THE CADETS

> (*Mutter among themselves.*)
>
> Ugh! . . .

CYRANO

> (*Smiles*)
>
>   Flattering

Murmur!

A CADET

He makes me weary!

ANOTHER

        With his collar
Of lace over his corselet—

ANOTHER
                    Like a ribbon
Tied round a sword!

ANOTHER
                    Bandages for a boil
On the back of his neck—

SECOND CADET
                    A courtier always!

ANOTHER
The Cardinal's nephew!

CARBON
           None the less—a Gascon.

FIRST CADET
A counterfeit! Never you trust that
     man—
Because we Gascons, look you, are
     all mad—
This fellow is reasonable—nothing
     more
Dangerous than a reasonable Gas-
     con!

LE BRET
He looks pale.

ANOTHER
                    Oh, he can be hungry too,
Like any other poor devil—but he
     wears
So many jewels on that belt of his
That his cramps glitter in the sun!

CYRANO
     (Quickly)
                              Is he
To see us looking miserable? Quick
     —
Pipes!—Cards!—Dice!—
     (They all hurriedly begin to
     play, on their stools, on the
     drums, or on their cloaks
     spread on the ground, light-

ing their long pipes mean-
     while.)
     As for me, I read Descartes.
     (He walks up and down, read-
     ing a small book which he
     takes from his pocket. TAB-
     LEAU: DE GUICHE enters,
     looking pale and haggard.
     All are absorbed in their
     games. General air of con-
     tentment. DE GUICHE goes to
     CARBON. They look at each
     other askance, each observ-
     ing with satisfaction the
     condition of the other.)

DE GUICHE
Good morning!
     (Aside)
           He looks yellow.

CARBON
     (Same business)
                    He is all eyes.

DE GUICHE
     (Looks at the CADETS.)
What have we here? Black looks?
     Yes, gentlemen—
I am informed I am not popular;
The hill-nobility, barons of Béarn,
The pomp and pride of Périgord—
     I learn
They disapprove their colonel; call
     him courtier,
Politician—they take it ill that I
Cover my steel with lace of Genoa.
It is a great offense to be a Gascon
And not to be a beggar!
     (Silence. They smoke. They
     play.)
                    Well— Shall I have
Your captain punish you? . . . No.

CARBON
                    As to that,
It would be impossible.

DE GUICHE

Oh?

CARBON

I am free;
I pay my company; it is my own;
I obey military orders.

DE GUICHE

Oh!
That will be quite enough.
(*To the* CADETS)
I can afford
Your little hates. My conduct under
fire
Is well known. It was only yester-
day
I drove the Count de Bucquoi from
Bapaume,
Pouring my men down like an av-
alanche,
I myself led the charge—

CYRANO

(*Without looking up from his
book.*)
And your white scarf?

DE GUICHE

(*Surprised and gratified*)
You heard that episode? Yes—rally-
ing
My men for the third time, I found
myself
Carried among a crowd of fugitives
Into the enemy's lines. I was in
danger
Of being shot or captured; but I
thought
Quickly—took off and flung away
the scarf
That marked my military rank—
and so
Being   inconspicuous,   escaped
among
My own force, rallied them, re-
turned again
And won the day! . . .

(*The* CADETS *do not appear to
be listening, but here and
there the cards and the dice
boxes remain motionless,
the smoke is retained in
their cheeks.*)
What do you say to that?
Presence of mind—yes?

CYRANO

Henry of Navarre
Being outnumbered, never flung
away
His white plume.
(*Silent enjoyment. The cards
flutter, the dice roll, the
smoke puffs out.*)

DE GUICHE

My device was a success,
However!
(*Same attentive pause, interrupting the games and the
smoking.*)

CYRANO

Possibly . . . An officer
Does not lightly resign the privilege
Of being a target.
(*Cards, dice, and smoke fall,
roll, and float away with in-
creasing satisfaction.*)
Now, if I had been there—
Your courage and my own differ in
this—
When your scarf fell, I should have
put it on.

DE GUICHE

Boasting again!

CYRANO

Boasting? Lend it to me
Tonight; I'll lead the first charge,
with your scarf
Over my shoulder!

DE GUICHE

Gasconnade once more!
You are safe making that offer, and
   you know it—
My scarf lies on the river bank be-
   tween
The lines, a spot swept by artillery
Impossible to reach alive!

CYRANO

*(Produces the scarf from his
   pocket)*
                              Yes. Here . . .
(Silence. The CADETS *stifle
   their laughter behind their
   cards and their dice boxes.*
DE GUICHE *turns to look at
   them. Immediately they resume their gravity and their
   game. One of them whistles
   carelessly the mountain air
   which the fifer was playing.)*

DE GUICHE

(Takes the scarf.)
Thank you! That bit of white is
   what I need
To make a signal. I was hesitat-
   ing—
You have decided me.
      *(He goes up to the parapet,
      climbs upon it, and waves
      the scarf at arm's length
      several times.)*

ALL

                  What is he doing?—
What?—

THE SENTRY ON THE PARAPET

There's a man down there
   running away!

DE GUICHE

(Descending)
A Spaniard. Very useful as a spy

To both sides. He informs the en-
   emy
As I instruct him. By his influence
I can arrange their dispositions.

CYRANO

                           Traitor!

DE GUICHE

(Folding the scarf.)
A traitor, yes; but useful . . .
                  We were saying? . . .
Oh, yes— Here is a bit of news for
   you:
Last night we had hopes of repro-
   visioning
The army. Under cover of the dark,
The Marshal moved to Dourlens.
   Our supplies
Are there. He may reach them.
   But to return
Safely, he needs a large force—at
   least half
Our entire strength. At present, we
   have here
Merely a skeleton.

CARBON

                        Fortunately,
The Spaniards do not know that.

DE GUICHE

            Oh, yes; they know.
They will attack.

CARBON

Ah!

DE GUICHE

            From that spy of mine
I learned of their intention. His re-
   port
Will determine the point of their
   advance.
The fellow asked me what to say!
   I told him:
"Go out between the lines; watch
   for my signal;

Where you see that, let them attack
  there."

CARBON

(*To the* CADETS)
                            Well,
Gentlemen!
  (*All rise. Noise of sword belts
      and breast-plates being
      buckled on.*)

DE GUICHE

You may have perhaps an hour.

FIRST CADET

Oh— An hour!
  (*They all sit down and resume
      their games once more.*)

DE GUICHE

(*To* CARBON)
  The great thing is to gain time.
Any moment the Marshal may re-
turn.

CARBON

And to gain time?

DE GUICHE

            You will all be so kind
As to lay down your lives!

CYRANO

                    Ah! Your revenge?

DE GUICHE

I make no great pretense of loving
  you!
But—since you gentlemen esteem
  yourselves
Invincible, the bravest of the brave,
And all that—why need we be personal?
I serve the king in choosing . . .
  as I choose!

CYRANO

  (*Salutes*)
Sir, permit me to offer—all our
  thanks.

DE GUICHE

(*Returns the salute.*)
You love to fight a hundred against
  one;
Here is your opportunity!
  (*He goes up stage with* CAR-
      BON.)

CYRANO

(*To the* CADETS)
                        My friends,
We shall add now to our old Gas-
con arms
With their six chevrons, blue and
  gold, a seventh—
Blood-red!
  (DE GUICHE *talks in a low
      tone to* CARBON *up stage.
      Orders are given. The de-
      fense is arranged.* CYRANO
      goes to CHRISTIAN, *who has
      remained motionless with
      folded arms.*)
Christian?
  (*Lays a hand on his shoulder.*)

CHRISTIAN

(*Shakes his head.*)
  Roxane . . .

CYRANO

          Yes.

CHRISTIAN

              I should like
To say farewell to her, with my
  whole heart
Written for her to keep.

CYRANO

              I thought of that—
  (*Takes a letter from his dou-
      blet.*)
I have written your farewell.

CHRISTIAN

Show me!

CYRANO

You wish

To read it?

CHRISTIAN

Of course!
{*He takes the letter; begins to
read, looks up suddenly.*)
What?—

CYRANO

What is it?

CHRISTIAN

Look—

This little circle—

CYRANO

(*Takes back the letter quickly;
and looks innocent.*)
Circle?—

CHRISTIAN

Yes—a tear!

CYRANO

So it is! . . . Well—a poet while
he writes
Is like a lover in his lady's arms,
Believing his imagination—all
Seems   true—you   understand?
There's half the charm
Of writing— Now, this letter as you
see
I have made so pathetic that I wept
While I was writing it!

CHRISTIAN

You—wept?

CYRANO

Why, yes—
Because . . . it is a little thing to
die,
But—not to see her . . . that is
terrible!

And I shall never—
(CHRISTIAN *looks at him.*)
We shall never—
(*Quickly*)
You

Will never—

CHRISTIAN

(*Snatches the letter.*)
Give me that!
(*Noise in the distance on the
outskirts of the camp.*)

VOICE OF A SENTRY

Halt—who goes there!
(*Shots, shouting, jingle of harness.*)

CARBON

What is it?—

THE SENTRY ON THE PARAPET

Why, a coach.
(*They rush to look.*)

CONFUSED VOICES

What? In the Camp?
A coach? Coming this way— It
must have driven
Through the Spanish lines—what
the devil— Fire!—
No— Hark! The driver shouting—
what does he say?
Wait— He said: "On the service of
the King!"
(*They are all on the parapet
looking over. The jingling
comes nearer.*)

DE GUICHE

Of the King?
(*They come down and fall
into line.*)

CARBON

Hats off, all!

DE GUICHE
(*Speaks off stage.*)
            The King! Fall in,
Rascals!—
            (*The coach enters at full trot.
            It is covered with mud and
            dust. The curtains are
            drawn. Two footmen are
            seated behind. It stops sud-
            denly.*)

CARBON
(*Shouts*)
            Beat the assembly—
            (*Roll of drums. All the* CADETS
            uncover.)

DE GUICHE
Lower the steps—open the door—
            (*Two men rush to the coach.
            The door opens.*)

ROXANE
(*Comes out of the coach.*)
            Good morning!
            (*At the sound of a woman's
            voice, every head is raised.
            Sensation.*)

DE GUICHE
On the King's service— You?

ROXANE
            Yes—my own king—
Love!

CYRANO
(*Aside*)
God is merciful . . .

CHRISTIAN
(*Hastens to her.*)
            You! Why have you—

ROXANE
Your war lasted so long!

CHRISTIAN
But why?—

ROXANE
            Not now—

CYRANO
(*Aside*)
I wonder if I dare to look at her . . .

DE GUICHE
You cannot remain here!

ROXANE
            Why, certainly!
Roll that drum here, somebody . . .
            (*She sits on the drum, which
            is brought to her.*)
            Thank you— There!
            (*She laughs.*)
Would you believe—they fired
upon us?
            —My coach
Looks like the pumpkin in the fairy
tale,
Does it not? And my footmen—
            (*She throws a kiss to* CHRIS-
            TIAN.)
            How do you do?
            (*She looks about.*)
How serious you all are! Do you
know,
It is a long drive here—from Arras?
            (*Sees* CYRANO.)
            Cousin,
I am glad to see you!

CYRANO
(*Advances*)
            Oh— How did you come?

ROXANE
How did I find you? Very easily—
I followed where the country was
laid waste
—Oh, but I saw such things! I had
to see
To believe. Gentlemen, is that the
service
Of your King? I prefer my own!

CYRANO

But how
Did you come through?

ROXANE

Why, through the Spanish lines
Of course!

FIRST CADET

They let you pass?—

DE GUICHE

What did you say?
How did you manage?

LE BRET

Yes, that must have been
Difficult!

ROXANE

No— I simply drove along.
Now and then some hidalgo
scowled at me
And I smiled back—my best smile;
whereupon,
The Spaniards being (without
prejudice
To the French) the most polished
gentlemen
In the world—I passed!

CARBON

Certainly that smile
Should be a passport! Did they
never ask
Your errand or your destination?

ROXANE

Oh,
Frequently! Then I drooped my
eyes and said:
"I have a lover . . ." Whereupon,
the Spaniard
With an air of ferocious dignity
Would close the carriage door—
with such a gesture
As any king might envy, wave aside

The muskets that were levelled at
my breast,
Fall back three paces, equally superb
In grace and gloom, draw himself
up, thrust forth
A spur under his cloak, sweeping
the air
With his long plumes, bow very
low, and say:
"Pass, Señorita!"

CHRISTIAN

But, Roxane—

ROXANE

I know—
I said "a lover"—but you understand—
Forgive me!—If I said "I am going
to meet
My husband," no one would believe me!

CHRISTIAN

Yes,
But—

ROXANE

What then?

DE GUICHE

You must leave this place

CYRANO

At once.

ROXANE

I?

LE BRET

Yes—immediately.

ROXANE

And why?

CHRISTIAN

(*Embarrassed*)

Because . . .

CYRANO

(*Same*)
In half an hour . . .

DE GUICHE

(*Same*)
Or three quarters . . .

CARBON

(*Same*)
                                    Perhaps
It might be better . . .

LE BRET

If you . . .

ROXANE

                        Oh— I see!
You are going to fight. I remain
  here.

ALL

                        No—no!

ROXANE

He is my husband—
    (*Throws herself in* CHRISTIAN'S
      arms.)
  I will die with you!

CHRISTIAN

Your eyes! . . . Why do you?—

ROXANE

          You know why . . .

DE GUICHE

(*Desperate*)
                        This post
Is dangerous—

ROXANE

(*Turns*)
    How—dangerous?

CYRANO

                        The proof
Is, we are ordered—

ROXANE

(*To* DE GUICHE)
        Oh—you wish to make
A widow of me?

DE GUICHE

On my word of honor—

ROXANE

No matter. I am just a little mad—
I will stay. It may be amusing.

CYRANO

                        What,
A heroine—our intellectual?

ROXANE

Monsieur de Bergerac, I am your
  cousin!

A CADET

We'll fight now! Hurrah!

ROXANE

(*More and more excited*)
I am safe with you—my friends!

ANOTHER

(*Carried away*)
The whole camp breathes of lilies!

ROXANE

                        And I think,
This hat would look well on the
  battlefield! . . .
But perhaps—
    (*Looks at* DE GUICHE.)
The Count ought to leave us. Any
  moment
Now, there may be danger.

DE GUICHE

                        This is too much!
I must inspect my guns. I shall return—

You may change your mind—
There will yet be time—

ROXANE

Never!
(DE GUICHE *goes out.*)

CHRISTIAN

(*Imploring*)
Roxane! . . .

ROXANE

No!

FIRST CADET

(*To the rest*)
She stays here!

ALL

(*Rushing about, elbowing
each other, brushing off
their clothes.*)
A comb!—
Soap!—Here's a hole in my— A
needle!—Who
Has a ribbon?—Your mirror, quick!
—My cuffs—
A razor—

ROXANE

(*To* CYRANO, *who is still urging
her*)
No! I shall not stir one step!

CARBON

(*Having, like the others, tight-
ened his belt, dusted himself, brushed off his hat,
smoothed out his plume and
put on his lace cuffs, advances to* ROXANE *ceremoni-
ously.*)
In that case, may I not present to
you
Some of these gentlemen who are
to have
The honor of dying in your presence?

ROXANE

(*Bows*)
Please!—
(*She waits, standing, on the
arm of* CHRISTIAN, *while*

CARBON

(*—presents*)
Baron de Peyrescous de Colignac!

THE CADET

(*Salutes*)
Madame . . .

ROXANE

Monsieur . . .

CARBON

(*Continues*)
Baron de Casterac
De Cahuzac— Vidame de Malg-
ouyre
Estressac Lésbas d'Escarabiot—

THE VIDAME

Madame . . .

CARBON

Chevalier d'Antignac-Juzet—
Baron Hillot de Blagnac-Saléchan
De Castel-Crabioules—

THE BARON

Madame . . .

ROXANE

How many
Names you all have!

THE BARON

Hundreds!

CARBON

(*To* ROXANE)
Open the hand
That holds your handkerchief.

ROXANE

(*Opens her hand; the handkerchief falls.*)
Why?
(*The whole company makes a
movement toward it.*)

CARBON

(*Picks it up quickly.*)
My company
Was in want of a banner. We have
now
The fairest in the army!

ROXANE

(*Smiling*)
Rather small—

CARBON

(*Fastens the handkerchief to
his lance.*)
Lace—and embroidered!

A CADET

(*To the others*)
With her smiling on me,
I could die happy, if I only had
Something in my—

CARBON

(*Turns upon him*)
Shame on you! Feast your eyes
And forget your—

ROXANE

(*Quickly*)
It must be this fresh air—
I am starving! Let me see . . .
Cold partridges,
Pastry, a little white wine—that
would do.
Will someone bring that to me?

A CADET

(*Aside*)
Will someone!—

ANOTHER

Where the devil are we to find—

ROXANE

(*Overhears; sweetly*)
Why, there—
In my carriage.

ALL

Wha-at?

ROXANE

All you have to do
Is to unpack, and carve, and serve
things.
Oh,
Notice my coachman; you may rec-
ognize
An old friend.

THE CADETS

(*Rush to the coach.*)
Ragueneau!

ROXANE

(*Follows them with her eyes.*)
Poor fellows . . .

THE CADETS

(*Acclamations*)
Ah!
Ah!

CYRANO

(*Kisses her hand.*)
Our good fairy!

RAGUENEAU

(*Standing on his box, like
a mountebank before a
crowd.*)
Gentlemen!—
(*Enthusiasm.*)

THE CADETS

Bravo!
Bravo!

RAGUENEAU

The Spaniards, basking in our
  smiles,
Smiled on our baskets!
  (*Applause*)

CYRANO

(*Aside, to* CHRISTIAN)
Christian!—

RAGUENEAU

They adored
The Fair, and missed—
  (*He takes from under the seat
    a dish, which he holds
    aloft.*)
    the Fowl!
  (*Applause. The dish is passed
    from hand to hand.*)

CYRANO

(*As before, to* CHRISTIAN)
One moment—

RAGUENEAU

Venus
Charmed their eyes while Adonis
  quietly
  (*Brandishing a ham.*)
Brought home the Boar!
  (*Applause; the ham is seized
    by a score of hands out-
    stretched.*)

CYRANO

(*As before.*)
Pst— Let me speak to you—

ROXANE

(*As the* CADETS *return, their
  arms full of provisions*)
Spread them out on the ground.
  (*Calls*)
          Christian! Come here;
Make yourself useful.
  (CHRISTIAN *turns to her, at the
    moment when* CYRANO *was*

leading him aside. She arranges the food, with his aid
and that of the two im-
perturbable footmen.*)

RAGUENEAU

Peacock, *aux truffes!*

FIRST CADET

(*Comes down, cutting a huge
  slice of the ham.*)
          Tonnerre!
We are not going to die without a
  gorge—
  (*Sees* ROXANE; *corrects him
    self hastily.*)
Pardon—a banquet!

RAGUENEAU

(*Tossing out the cushions of
  the carriage.*)
Open these—they are full
Of ortolans!
  (*Tumult; laughter; the cush-
    ions are eviscerated.*)

THIRD CADET

Lucullus!

RAGUENEAU

(*Throws out bottles of red
  wine.*)
          Flasks of ruby—
  (*And of white*)
Flasks of topaz—

ROXANE

(*Throws a tablecloth at the
  head of* CYRANO.)
Come back out of your dreams!
Unfold this cloth—

RAGUENEAU

(*Takes off one of the lanterns
  of the carriage, and flourishes it.*)
Our lamps are bonbonnières!

CYRANO

(*To* CHRISTIAN)

I must see you before you speak
with her—

RAGUENEAU

(*More and more lyrical*)

My whip-handle is one long sausage!

ROXANE

(*Pouring wine; passing the
food.*)
                        We
Being about to die, first let us dine!
Never mind the others—all for
Gascoyne!
And if de Guiche comes, he is not
invited!
        (*Going from one to another.*)
Plenty of time—you need not eat
so fast—
Hold your cup—
        (*To another*)
        What's the matter?

THE CADET

(*Sobbing*)
                You are so good
To us . . .

ROXANE

There, there! Red or white wine?
                —Some bread
For Monsieur de Carbon!—Nap-
kins— A knife—
Pass your plate— Some of the
crust? A little more—
Light or dark?—Burgundy?—

CYRANO

(*Follows her with an armful
of dishes, helping to serve.*)
Adorable!

ROXANE

(*Goes to* CHRISTIAN.)
What would you like?

CHRISTIAN

Nothing.

ROXANE

        Oh, but you must!—
A little wine? A biscuit?

CHRISTIAN

        Tell me first
Why you came—

ROXANE

        By and by. I must take care
Of these poor boys—

LE BRET

(*Who has gone up stage to
pass up food to the sentry
on the parapet, on the end
of a lance.*)
        De Guiche!

CYRANO

                Hide everything
Quick!—Dishes, bottles, tablecloth
—
                Now look
Hungry again—
        (*To* RAGUENEAU)
        You there! Up on your box—
—Everything out of sight?—
        (*In a twinkling, everything
        has been pushed inside the
        tents, hidden in their hats or
        under their cloaks.* DE
        GUICHE *enters quickly, then
        stops, sniffing the air. Si-
        lence.*)

DE GUICHE

        It smells good here.

A CADET

(*Humming with an air of
great unconcern.*)
Sing ha-ha-ha and ho-ho-ho—

DE GUICHE

(*Stares at him; he grows embarrassed.*)
                    You there—
What are you blushing for?

THE CADET

            Nothing—my blood
Stirs at the thought of battle.

ANOTHER

Pom . . . pom . . . pom! . . .

DE GUICHE

(*Turns upon him.*)
What is that?

THE CADET

(*Slightly stimulated*)
Only song—only little song—

DE GUICHE

You appear happy!

THE CADET

            Oh, yes—always happy
Before a fight—

DE GUICHE

(*Calls to* CARBON, *for the pur-
pose of giving him an order.*)
Captain! I—
(*Stops and looks at him.*)
            What the devil—
You are looking happy too!—

CARBON

(*Pulls a long face and hides a
bottle behind his back.*)
No!

DE GUICHE

            Here—I had
One gun remaining. I have had it
placed
(*He points off stage.*)
There—in that corner—for your
men.

A CADET

(*Simpering*)
                    So kind!—
Charming attention!

ANOTHER

(*Same business; burlesque*)
Sweet solicitude!—

DE GUICHE

(*Contemptuous*)
I believe you are both drunk—
(*Coldly*)
            Being unaccustomed
To guns—take care of the recoil!

FIRST CADET

(*Gesture*)
                    Ah-h . . . Pfft!

DE GUICHE

(*Goes up to him, furious.*)
How dare you?

FIRST CADET

A Gascon's gun never recoils!

DE GUICHE

(*Shakes him by the arm.*)
You *are* drunk—

FIRST CADET

(*Superbly*)
With the smell of powder!

DE GUICHE

(*Turns away with a shrug.*)
                    Bah!
(*To* ROXANE)
Madame, have you decided?

ROXANE

I stay here.

DE GUICHE

You have time to escape—

ROXANE
No!

DE GUICHE
Very well—
Someone give me a musket!

CARBON
What!

DE GUICHE
I stay
Here also.

CYRANO
(*Formally*)
Sir, you show courage!

FIRST CADET
A Gascon
In spite of all that lace!

ROXANE
Why—

DE GUICHE
Must I run
Away, and leave a woman?

SECOND CADET
(*To* FIRST CADET)
We might give him
Something to eat—what do you
say?
(*All the food reappears, as if
by magic.*)

DE GUICHE
(*His face lights up.*)
A feast!

THIRD CADET
Here a little, there a little—

DE GUICHE
(*Recovers his self-control;
haughtily.*)
Do you think
I want your leavings?

CYRANO
(*Saluting*)
Colonel—you improve!

DE GUICHE
I can fight as I am!

FIRST CADET
(*Delighted*)
Listen to him—
He has an accent!

DE GUICHE
(*Laughs*)
Have I so?

FIRST CADET
A Gascon!—
A Gascon, after all!
(*They all begin to dance.*)

CARBON
(*Who has disappeared for a
moment behind the parapet,
reappears on top of it.*)
I have placed my pikemen
Here.
(*Indicates a row of pikes
showing above the parapet.*)

DE GUICHE
(*Bows to* ROXANE.)
We'll review them; will you
take my arm?
(*She takes his arm; they go
up on the parapet. The rest
uncover, and follow them
up stage.*)

CHRISTIAN
(*Goes hurriedly to* CYRANO.)
Speak quickly!
(*At the moment when* ROXANE
*appears on the parapet the
pikes are lowered in salute,
and a cheer is heard. She
bows.*)

THE PIKEMEN
(*Off stage*)
Hurrah!

CHRISTIAN
What is it?

CYRANO
If Roxane . . .

CHRISTIAN
Well?

CYRANO
Speaks about your letters . . .

CHRISTIAN
Yes—I know!

CYRANO
Do not make the mistake of showing . . .

CHRISTIAN
What?

CYRANO
Showing surprise.

CHRISTIAN
Surprise—why?

CYRANO
I must tell you! . . .
It is quite simple—I had forgotten
it
Until just now. You have . . .

CHRISTIAN
Speak quickly!

CYRANO
You
Have written oftener than you
think.

CHRISTIAN
Oh—have I!

CYRANO
I took upon me to interpret you;
And wrote—sometimes . . . with-
out . . .

CHRISTIAN
My knowing. Well?

CYRANO
Perfectly simple!

CHRISTIAN
Oh, yes, perfectly!—
For a month, we have been block-
aded here!—
How did you send all these letters?

CYRANO
Before
Daylight, I managed—

CHRISTIAN
I see. That was also
Perfectly simple!
—So I wrote to her,
How many times a week? Twice?
Three times? Four?

CYRANO
Oftener.

CHRISTIAN
Every day?

CYRANO
Yes—every day . . .
Every single day . . .

CHRISTIAN
(*Violently*)
And that wrought you up
Into such a flame that you faced
death—

CYRANO
(*Sees* ROXANE *returning.*)
Hush—
Not before her!

(He goes quickly into the tent.
ROXANE *comes up to* CHRIS-
TIAN.*)*

ROXANE

Now—Christian!

CHRISTIAN

(Takes her hands.)
Tell me now
Why you came here—over these
ruined roads—
Why you made your way among
mosstroopers
And ruffians—you—to join me
here?

ROXANE

Because—
Your letters . . .

CHRISTIAN

Meaning?

ROXANE

It was your own fault
If I ran into danger! I went mad—
Mad with you! Think what you
have written me,
How many times, each one more
wonderful
Than the last!

CHRISTIAN

All this for a few absurd
Love-letters—

ROXANE

Hush—absurd! How can
you know?
I thought I loved you, ever since one
night
When a voice that I never would
have known
Under my window breathed your
soul to me . . .
But—all this time, your letters—
every one

Was like hearing your voice there
in the dark,
All around me, like your arms
around me . . .
(More lightly)
At last,
I came. Anyone would! Do you
suppose
The prim Penelope had stayed at
home
Embroidering,—if Ulysses wrote
like you?
She would have fallen like another
Helen—
Tucked up those linen petticoats
of hers
And followed him to Troy!

CHRISTIAN

But you—

ROXANE

I read them
Over and over. I grew faint read-
ing them.
I belonged to you. Every page of
them
Was like a petal fallen from your
soul—
Like the light and the fire of a
great love,
Sweet and strong and true—

CHRISTIAN

Sweet . . . and strong . . .
and true . . .
You felt that, Roxane?—

ROXANE

You know how I feel! . . .

CHRISTIAN

So—you came . . .

ROXANE

Oh, my Christian, oh my king,—
Lift me up if I fall upon my
knees—

It is the heart of me that kneels to
    you,
And will remain forever at your
    feet—
You cannot lift that!—
                I came here to say
'Forgive me'—(It is time to be for-
    given
Now, when we may die presently)
    —forgive me
For being light and vain and loving
    you
Only because you were beautiful.

CHRISTIAN
    (Astonished)
                Roxane! . .

ROXANE
Afterwards I knew better. After-
    wards
(I had to learn to use my wings) I
    loved you
For yourself too—knowing you
    more, and loving
More of you. And now—

CHRISTIAN
Now? . . .

ROXANE
                It is yourself
I love now: your own self.

CHRISTIAN
    (Taken aback)
                Roxane!

ROXANE
    (Gravely)
                Be happy!—
You must have suffered; for you
    must have seen
How frivolous I was; and to be
    loved
For the mere costume, the poor
    casual body
You went about in—to a soul like
    yours,

That must have been torture!
    Therefore with words
You revealed your heart. Now that
    image of you
Which filled my eyes first—I see
    better now,
And I see it no more!

CHRISTIAN
                Oh!—

ROXANE
                You still doubt
Your victory?

CHRISTIAN
    (Miserably)
                Roxane!—

ROXANE
                I understand:
You cannot perfectly believe in
    me—
A love like this—

CHRISTIAN
                I want no love like this!
I want love only for—

ROXANE
                Only for what
Every woman sees in you? I can do
Better than that!

CHRISTIAN
                No—it was best before!

ROXANE
You do not altogether know me
    . . . Dear,
There is more of me than there was
    —with this,
I can love more of you—more of
    what makes
You your own self—Truly! . . .
    If you were less
Lovable—

CHRISTIAN
No!

ROXANE
—Less charming—ugly even—
I should love you still.

CHRISTIAN
You mean that?

ROXANE
                              I do
Mean that!

CHRISTIAN
Ugly? . . .

ROXANE
                    Yes. Even then!

CHRISTIAN
(Agonized)
          Oh . . . God! . . .

ROXANE
Now are you happy?

CHRISTIAN
(Choking)
Yes . . .

ROXANE
                    What is it?

CHRISTIAN
(Pushes her away gently.)
                    Only . . .
Nothing . . . one moment . . .

ROXANE
But—

CHRISTIAN
(Gesture toward THE CADETS)
          I am keeping you
From those poor fellows— Go and
smile at them;

They are going to die!

ROXANE
(Softly)
    Dear Christian!

CHRISTIAN
                              Go—
(She goes up among the
Gascons, who gather round
her respectfully.)
Cyrano!

CYRANO
(Comes out of the tent, armed
for the battle.)
What is wrong? You look—

CHRISTIAN
                    She does not
Love me any more.

CYRANO
(Smiles)
          You think not?

CHRISTIAN
                    She loves
You.

CYRANO
No!—

CHRISTIAN
(Bitterly)
She loves only my soul.

CYRANO
                              No!

CHRISTIAN
                    Yes—
That means you. And you love her.

CYRANO
I?

CHRISTIAN

I see—

I know!

CYRANO

That is true . . .

CHRISTIAN

More than—

CYRANO

(*Quietly*)

More than that.

CHRISTIAN

Tell her so!

CYRANO

No.

CHRISTIAN

Why not?

CYRANO

Why—look at me!

CHRISTIAN

She would love me if I were ugly.

CYRANO

(*Startled*)

She—

Said that?

CHRISTIAN

Yes. Now then!

CYRANO

(*Half to himself*)

It was good of her
To tell you that . . .
(*Change of tone*)
Nonsense! Do not believe
Any such madness—
It was good of her
To tell you . . .
Do not take her at her word!

Go on—you never will be ugly—
Go!
She would never forgive me.

CHRISTIAN

That is what
We shall see.

CYRANO

No, no—

CHRISTIAN

Let her choose between us!—
Tell her everything!

CYRANO

No—you torture me—

CHRISTIAN

Shall I ruin your happiness, because
I have a cursed pretty face? That
seems
Too unfair!

CYRANO

And am I to ruin yours
Because I happen to be born with
power
To say what you—perhaps—feel?

CHRISTIAN

Tell her!

CYRANO

Man—
Do not try me too far!

CHRISTIAN

I am tired of being
My own rival!

CYRANO

Christian!—

CHRISTIAN

Our secret marriage—
No witnesses — fraudulent — that
can be
Annulled—

CYRANO

Do not try me—

CHRISTIAN

I want her love
For the poor fool I am—or not at
all!
Oh, I am going through with this!
I'll know,
One way or the other. Now I shall
walk down
To the end of the post. Go tell her.
Let her choose
One of us.

CYRANO

It will be you.

CHRISTIAN

God—I hope so!
(*He turns and calls.*)
Roxane!

CYRANO

No—no—

ROXANE

(*Hurries down to him.*)
Yes, Christian?

CHRISTIAN

Cyrano
Has news for you—important.
(*She turns to* CYRANO. CHRIS-
TIAN *goes out.*)

ROXANE

(*Lightly*)
Oh—important?

CYRANO

He is gone . . .
(*To* ROXANE)
Nothing—only Christian thinks
You ought to know—

ROXANE

I do know. He still doubts
What I told him just now. I saw
that.

CYRANO

(*Takes her hand.*)
Was it
True—what you told him just now?

ROXANE

It was true!
I said that I should love him even
. . .

CYRANO

(*Smiling sadly*)
The word
Comes hard—before me?

ROXANE

Even if he were . . .

CYRANO

Say it—
I shall not be hurt!—Ugly?

ROXANE

Even then
I should love him.
(*A few shots, off stage, in the
direction in which* CHRIS-
TIAN *disappeared*)
Hark! The guns—

CYRANO

Hideous?

ROXANE

Hideous.

CYRANO

Disfigured?

ROXANE

Or disfigured.

CYRANO

Even
Grotesque?

ROXANE

How could he ever be gro-
tesque—
Ever—to me!

CYRANO

But you could love him so,
As much as?—

ROXANE

Yes—and more!

CYRANO

(*Aside, excitedly*)
It is true!—true!—
Perhaps—God! This is too much
happiness . . .
(*To* ROXANE)
I—Roxane—listen—

LE BRET

(*Enters quickly; calls to*
CYRANO *in a low tone.*)
Cyrano—

CYRANO

(*Turns*)
Yes?

LE BRET

Hush! . . .
(*Whispers a few words to*
him.)

CYRANO

(*Lets fall* ROXANE'S *hand.*)
Ah!

ROXANE

What is it?

CYRANO

(*Half stunned, and aside*)
All gone . . .

ROXANE

(*More shots*)
What is it? Oh,

They are fighting!—
(*She goes up to look off*
stage.)

CYRANO

All gone. I cannot ever
Tell her, now . . . ever . . .

ROXANE

(*Starts to rush away.*)
What has happened?

CYRANO

(*Restrains her.*)
Nothing.
(*Several* CADETS *enter. They*
conceal something which
they are carrying, and form
a group so as to prevent
ROXANE *from seeing their*
burden.)

ROXANE

These men—

CYRANO

Come away . . .
(*He leads her away from the*
group.)

ROXANE

You were telling me
Something—

CYRANO

Oh, that? Nothing . . .
(*Gravely*)
I swear to you
That the spirit of Christian—that
his soul
Was—
(*Corrects himself quickly.*)
That his soul is no less great—

ROXANE

(*Catches at the word.*)
Was?

(*Crying out*)

      Oh!—

(*She rushes among the men,
and scatters them.*)

CYRANO

All gone . . .

ROXANE

(*Sees* CHRISTIAN *lying upon
his cloak.*)

Christian!

LE BRET

(*To* CYRANO)

   At the first volley.

(ROXANE *throws herself upon
the body of* CHRISTIAN.
*Shots; at first scattered, then
increasing. Drums. Voices
shouting.*)

CARBON

(*Sword in hand*)

      Here

They come!—Ready!—

(*Followed by the* CADETS, *he
climbs over the parapet and
disappears.*)

ROXANE

   Christian!

CARBON

(*Off stage*)

   Come on, there, You!

ROXANE

Christian!

CARBON

Fall in!

ROXANE

   Christian!

CARBON

   Measure your fuse!

(RAGUENEAU *hurries up, carrying a helmet full of water.*)

CHRISTIAN

(*Faintly*)

Roxane! . . .

CYRANO

(*Low and quick, in* CHRIS-
TIAN'S *ear, while* ROXANE *is
dipping into the water a
strip of linen torn from her
dress.*)

I have told her; she loves you.

(CHRISTIAN *closes his eyes.*)

ROXANE

(*Turns to* CHRISTIAN.)

      Yes,

My darling?

CARBON

   Draw your ramrods!

ROXANE

(*To* CYRANO)

   He is not dead? . . .

CARBON

Open your charges!

ROXANE

    I can feel his cheek

Growing cold against mine—

CARBON

   Take aim!

ROXANE

      A letter—

Over his heart—

(*She opens it.*)

For me.

CYRANO

(*Aside*)

    My letter . . .

CARBON

Fire!
(Musketry, cries and groans.
Din of battle.)

CYRANO

(Trying to withdraw his hand,
which ROXANE, *still upon*
her knees, is holding.)
But, Roxane—they are fighting—

ROXANE

Wait a little . . .
He is dead. No one else knew him
but you . . .
(She weeps quietly.)
Was he not a great lover, a great
man,
A hero?

CYRANO

(Standing, bareheaded.)
Yes, Roxane.

ROXANE

A poet, unknown,
Adorable?

CYRANO

Yes, Roxane.

ROXANE

A fine mind?

CYRANO

Yes, Roxane.

ROXANE

A heart deeper than we knew—
A soul magnificently tender?

CYRANO

(Firmly)
Yes,
Roxane!

ROXANE

(Sinks down upon the breast
of CHRISTIAN.)
He is dead now . . .

CYRANO

(Aside; draws his sword.)
Why, so am I—
For I am dead, and my love mourns
for me
And does not know . . .
(Trumpets in distance.)

DE GUICHE

(Appears on the parapet, di-
sheveled, wounded on the
forehead, shouting.)
The signal—hark—the trumpets!
The army has returned— Hold
them now!—Hold them!
The army!—

ROXANE

On his letter—blood . . .
and tears.

A VOICE

(Off stage)
Surrender!

THE CADETS

No!

RAGUENEAU

This place is dangerous!—

CYRANO

(To DE GUICHE)
Take her away—I am going—

ROXANE

(Kisses the letter; faintly.)
His blood . . . his tears . . .

RAGUENEAU

(Leaps down from the coach
and runs to her.)
She has fainted—

DE GUICHE

(*On the parapet; savagely, to the* CADETS)
Hold them!

VOICE OFF STAGE

Lay down your arms!

VOICES

No! No!

CYRANO

(*To* DE GUICHE)
Sir, you have proved yourself—
Take care of her.

DE GUICHE

(*Hurries to* ROXANE *and takes her up in his arms.*)
As you will—we can win, if you hold on
A little longer—

CYRANO

Good!
(*Calls out to* ROXANE, *as she is carried away, fainting, by* DE GUICHE *and* RAGUENEAU.)
Adieu, Roxane!
(*Tumult, outcries. Several* CADETS *come back wounded and fall on the stage.* CYRANO, *rushing to the fight, is stopped on the crest of the parapet by* CARBON, *covered with blood.*)

CARBON

We are breaking—I am twice wounded—

CYRANO

(*Shouts to the Gascons.*)
Hardi!
Reculez pas, Drollos!
(*To* CARBON, *holding him up.*)
So—never fear!

I have two deaths to avenge now—Christian's
And my own!
(*They come down.* CYRANO *takes from him the lance with* ROXANE's *handkerchief still fastened to it.*)
Float, little banner, with her name!
(*He plants it on the parapet; then shouts to the* CADETS)
Toumbé dessus! Escrasas lous!
(*To the fifer*)
Your fife!
Music!
(*Fife plays. The wounded drag themselves to their feet. Other* CADETS *scramble over the parapet and group themselves around* CYRANO *and his tiny flag. The coach is filled and covered with men, bristling with muskets, transformed into a redoubt.*)

A CADET

(*Reels backward over the wall, still fighting, shouts.*)
They are climbing over!—
(*And falls dead.*)

CYRANO

Very good—
Let them come!— A salute now—
(*The parapet is crowned for an instant with a rank of enemies. The imperial banner of Spain is raised aloft.*)
Fire!
(*General volley.*)

VOICE

(*Among the ranks of the enemy*)
Fire!
(*Murderous counter-fire; the* CADETS *fall on every side.*)

A SPANISH OFFICER

(*Uncovers*)

Who are these men who are so fond of death?

CYRANO

(*Erect amid the hail of bullets, declaims.*)
The Cadets of Gascoyne, the defenders

Of Carbon de Castel-Jaloux—
Free fighters, free lovers, free spenders—
(*He rushes forward, followed by a few survivors.*)
The Cadets of Gascoyne . . .
(*The rest is lost in the din of battle.*)

CURTAIN

THE FIFTH ACT

CYRANO'S GAZETTE

Fifteen years later, in 1655. THE PARK OF THE CONVENT *occupied by the Ladies of the Cross, at Paris.*

Magnificent foliage. To the Left, the House upon a broad Terrace at the head of a flight of steps, with several Doors opening upon the Terrace. In the center of the scene an enormous Tree alone in the center of a little open space. Toward the Right, in the foreground, among Boxwood Bushes, a semicircular Bench of stone.

All the way across the Background of the scene, an Avenue overarched by the chestnut trees, leading to the door of a Chapel on the Right, just visible among the branches of the trees. Beyond the double curtain of the trees, we catch a glimpse of bright lawns and shaded walks, masses of shrubbery; the perspective of the Park; the sky.

A little side door of the Chapel opens upon a Colonnade, garlanded with Autumnal vines, and disappearing on the Right behind the box-trees.

It is late October. Above the still living green of the turf all the foliage is red and yellow and brown. The evergreen masses of Box and Yew stand out darkly against this Autumnal coloring. A heap of dead leaves under every tree. The leaves are falling everywhere. They rustle underfoot along the walks; the Terrace and the Bench are half covered with them.

Before the Bench on the Right, on the side toward the Tree, is placed a tall embroidery frame and beside it a little Chair. Baskets filled with skeins of many-colored silks and balls of wool. Tapestry unfinished on the Frame.

At the CURTAIN RISE *the nuns are coming and going across the Park; several of them are seated on the Bench around* MOTHER MARGUÉRITE DE JÉSUS. *The leaves are falling.*

SISTER MARTHE

(*To* MOTHER MARGUÉRITE)

Sister Claire has been looking in
the glass
At her new cap; twice!

MOTHER MARGUÉRITE

(*To* SISTER CLAIRE)
        It is very plain;
Very.

SISTER CLAIRE

And Sister Marthe stole a plum
Out of the tart this morning!

MOTHER MARGUÉRITE

(*To* SISTER MARTHE)
        That was wrong;
Very wrong.

SISTER CLAIRE

Oh, but such a little look!

SISTER MARTHE

Such a little plum!

MOTHER MARGUÉRITE

(*Severely*)
        I shall tell Monsieur
De Cyrano, this evening.

SISTER CLAIRE

        No! Oh no!—
He will make fun of us.

SISTER MARTHE

        He will say nuns
Are so gay!

SISTER CLAIRE

And so greedy!

MOTHER MARGUÉRITE

(*Smiling*)
        And so good . . .

SISTER CLAIRE

It must be ten years, Mother Marguérite,

That he has come here every Saturday,
Is it not?

MOTHER MARGUÉRITE

More than ten years; ever since
His cousin came to live among us
here—
Her worldly weeds among our linen
veils,
Her widowhood and our virginity—
Like a black dove among white
doves.

SISTER MARTHE

        No one
Else ever turns that happy sorrow
of hers
Into a smile.

ALL THE NUNS

He is such fun!—He makes us
Almost laugh!—And he teases
everyone—
And pleases everyone— And we all
love him—
And he likes our cake, too—

SISTER MARTHE

        I am afraid
He is not a good Catholic.

SISTER CLAIRE

        Some day
We shall convert him.

THE NUNS

Yes—yes!

MOTHER MARGUÉRITE

        Let him be;
I forbid you to worry him. Perhaps
He might stop coming here.

SISTER MARTHE

        But . . . God?

MOTHER MARGUÉRITE
You need not
Be afraid. God knows all about him.

SISTER MARTHE
Yes . . .
But every Saturday he says to me,
Just as if he were proud of it:
"Well, Sister,
I ate meat yesterday!"

MOTHER MARGUÉRITE
He tells you so?
The last time he said that, he had
not eaten
Anything for two days.

SISTER MARTHE
Mother!—

MOTHER MARGUÉRITE
He is poor;
Very poor.

SISTER MARTHE
Who said so?

MOTHER MARGUÉRITE
Monsieur Le Bret.

SISTER MARTHE
Why does not someone help him?

MOTHER MARGUÉRITE
He would be
Angry; very angry . . .
(*Between the trees up stage,*
ROXANE *appears, all in
black, with a widow's cap
and long veils.* DE GUICHE,
*magnificently grown old,
walks beside her. They
move slowly.* MOTHER MAR-
GUÉRITE *rises.*)
Let us go in—
Madame Madeleine has a visitor.

SISTER MARTHE
(*To* SISTER CLAIRE)
The Duc de Grammont, is it not?
The Marshal?

SISTER CLAIRE
(*Looks toward* DE GUICHE.)
I think so—yes.

SISTER MARTHE
He has not been to see her
For months—

THE NUNS
He is busy—the Court!—The
Camp!—

SISTER CLAIRE
The world . . .
(*They go out.* DE GUICHE *and*
ROXANE *come down in si-
lence, and stop near the em-
broidery frame. Pause.*)

DE GUICHE
And you remain here, wasting all
that gold—
For ever in mourning?

ROXANE
For ever.

DE GUICHE
And still faithful?

ROXANE
And still faithful . . .

DE GUICHE
(*After a pause*)
Have you forgiven me?

ROXANE
(*Simply, looking up at the
cross of the Convent*)
I am here.
(*Another pause.*)

DE GUICHE

Was Christian . . . all that?

ROXANE

If you knew him.

DE GUICHE

Ah? We were not precisely . . .
intimate . . .
And his last letter—always at your
heart?

ROXANE

It hangs here, like a holy reliquary.

DE GUICHE

Dead—and you love him still!

ROXANE

Sometimes I think
He has not altogether died; our
hearts
Meet, and his love flows all around
me, living.

DE GUICHE

(After another pause)
You see Cyrano often?

ROXANE

Every week.
My old friend takes the place of my
Gazette,
Brings me all the news. Every Sat-
urday,
Under that tree where you are now,
his chair
Stands, if the day be fine. I wait for
him,
Embroidering; the hour strikes;
then I hear,
(I need not turn to look!) at the
last stroke,
His cane tapping the steps. He
laughs at me
For my eternal needlework. He tells
The story of the past week——

(LE BRET appears on the
steps.)
There's Le Bret!—
(LE BRET approaches.)
How is it with our friend?

LE BRET

Badly.

DE GUICHE

Indeed?

ROXANE

(To DE GUICHE)
Oh, he exaggerates!

LE BRET

Just as I said—
Loneliness, misery—I told him
so!—
His satires make a host of ene-
mies—
He attacks the false nobles, the
false saints,
The false heroes, the false artists—
in short,
Everyone!

ROXANE

But they fear that sword of his—
No one dare touch him!

DE GUICHE

(With a shrug)
H'm—that may be so.

LE BRET

It is not violence I fear for him,
But solitude—poverty—old gray
December,
Stealing on wolf's feet, with a wolf's
green eyes,
Into his darkening room. Those
bravoes yet
May strike our Swordsman down!
Every day now,
He draws his belt up one hole; his
poor nose

Looks like old ivory; he has one coat
Left—his old black serge.

DE GUICHE

That is nothing strange
In this world! No, you need not pity him
Overmuch.

LE BRET

(*With a bitter smile*)
My lord Marshal! . . .

DE GUICHE

I say, do not
Pity him overmuch. He lives his life,
His own life, his own way—thought, word, and deed
Free!

LE BRET

(*As before*)
My lord Duke! . . .

DE GUICHE

(*Haughtily*)
Yes, I know—I have all;
He has nothing. Nevertheless, to-day
I should be proud to shake his hand . . .
(*Saluting* ROXANE)
Adieu.

ROXANE

I will go with you.
(DE GUICHE *salutes* LE BRET, *and turns with* ROXANE *toward the steps.*)

DE GUICHE

(*Pauses on the steps, as she climbs.*)
Yes—I envy him
Now and then . . .
Do you know, when a man wins

Everything in this world, when he succeeds
Too much—he feels, having done nothing wrong
Especially, Heaven knows!—he feels somehow
A thousand small displeasures with himself,
Whose whole sum is not quite Remorse, but rather
A sort of vague disgust . . . The ducal robes
Mounting up, step by step, to pride and power,
Somewhere among their folds draw after them
A rustle of dry illusions, vain regrets
As your veil, up the stairs here, draws along
The whisper of dead leaves.

ROXANE

(*Ironical*)
The sentiment
Does you honor.

DE GUICHE

Oh, yes . . .
(*Pausing suddenly.*)
Monsieur Le Bret!—
(*To* ROXANE)
You pardon us?—
(*He goes to* LE BRET, *and speaks in a low tone.*)
One moment— It is true
That no one dares attack your friend. Some people
Dislike him, none the less. The other day
At Court, such a one said to me: "This man
Cyrano may die—accidentally."

LE BRET

(*Coldly*)
Thank you.

DE GUICHE

You may thank me. Keep him at
home
All you can. Tell him to be careful.

LE BRET

(*Shaking his hands to heav-
en.*)
                              Careful!—
He is coming here. I'll warn him—
yes, but! . . .

ROXANE

(*Still on the steps, to a* NUN
who approaches her)
                              Here
I am—what is it?

THE NUN

                    Madame, Ragueneau
Wishes to see you.

ROXANE

        Bring him here.
(*To* LE BRET *and* DE GUICHE)
                              He comes
For sympathy—having been first of
all
A Poet, he became since then, in
turn,
A Singer—

LE BRET

        Bath-house keeper—

ROXANE

                    Sacristan—

LE BRET

Actor—

ROXANE

        Hairdresser—

LE BRET

        Music-master—

ROXANE

                              Now,
Today—

RAGUENEAU

(*Enters hurriedly.*)
Madame!—
(*He sees* LE BRET.)
        Monsieur!—

ROXANE

(*Smiling*)
                    First tell your troubles
To Le Bret for a moment.

RAGUENEAU

                    But, Madame—
(*She goes out, with* DE GUICHE,
not hearing him. RAGUE-
NEAU *comes to* LE BRET.)
After all, I had rather— You are
here—
She need not know so soon— I
went to see him
Just now— Our friend— As I came
near his door,
I saw him coming out. I hurried on
To join him. At the corner of the
street,
As he passed— Could it be an ac-
cident?—
I wonder!—At the window over-
head,
A lackey with a heavy log of wood
Let it fall—

LE BRET

        Cyrano!

RAGUENEAU

                    I ran to him—

LE BRET

God! The cowards!

RAGUENEAU

                    I found him lying there—
A great hole in his head—

LE BRET

Is he alive?

RAGUENEAU

Alive—yes. But . . . I had to carry him
Up to his room—Dieu! Have you seen his room?—

LE BRET

Is he suffering?

RAGUENEAU

No; unconscious.

LE BRET

Did you
Call a doctor?

RAGUENEAU

One came—for charity.

LE BRET

Poor Cyrano!—We must not tell Roxane
All at once . . . Did the doctor say?—

RAGUENEAU

He said
Fever, and lesions of the— I forget
Those long names— Ah, if you had seen him there,
His head all white bandages!—Let us go
Quickly—there is no one to care for him—
All alone— If he tries to raise his head,
He may die!

LE BRET

(*Draws him away to the Right.*)
This way— It is shorter—through The Chapel—

ROXANE

(*Appears on the stairway, and calls to* LE BRET *as he is going out by the colonnade which leads to the small door of the Chapel.*)
Monsieur Le Bret!—
(LE BRET *and* RAGUENEAU *rush off without hearing.*)
Running away
When I call to him? Poor dear Ragueneau
Must have been very tragic!
(*She comes slowly down the stair, toward the tree.*)
What a day! . . .
Something in these bright Autumn afternoons
Happy and yet regretful—an old sorrow
Smiling . . . as though poor little April dried
Her tears long ago—and remembered . . .
(*She sits down at her work. Two* NUNS *come out of the house carrying a great chair and set it under the tree.*)
Ah—
The old chair, for my old friend!—

SISTER MARTHE

The best one
In our best parlor!—

ROXANE

Thank you, Sister—
(*The* NUNS *withdraw.*)
There—
(*She begins embroidering. The clock strikes.*)
The hour!—He will be coming now
—my silks—
All done striking? He never was so late
Before! The sister at the door—my thimble . . .
Here it is—she must be exhorting him

To repent all his sins . . .
> (*A pause*)
>> He ought to be
Converted, by this time— Another
    leaf—
> (*A dead leaf falls on her work;
> she brushes it away.*)
Certainly nothing could—my scis-
    sors—ever
Keep him away—

A NUN

> (*Appears on the steps.*)
>> Monsieur de Bergerac.

ROXANE

> (*Without turning*)
What was I saying? . . . Hard,
    sometimes, to match
These faded colors! . . .
> (*While she goes on working,
> CYRANO appears at the top
> of the steps, very pale, his
> hat drawn over his eyes.
> The NUN who has brought
> him in goes away. He begins
> to descend the steps leaning
> on his cane, and holding
> himself on his feet only by
> an evident effort. ROXANE
> turns to him, with a tone of
> friendly banter.*)
>> After fourteen years,
Late—for the first time!

CYRANO

> (*Reaches the chair, and sinks
> into it; his gay tone con-
> trasting with his tortured
> face.*)
>> Yes, yes—maddening!
I was detained by—

ROXANE
Well?

CYRANO
> A visitor,
Most unexpected.

ROXANE

> (*Carelessly, still sewing*)
>> Was your visitor
Tiresome?

CYRANO

Why, hardly that—inopportune,
Let us say—an old friend of mine—
    at least
A very old acquaintance.

ROXANE
> Did you tell him
To go away?

CYRANO
> For the time being, yes.
I said: "Excuse me—this is Satur-
    day—
I have a previous engagement, one
I cannot miss, even for you— Come
    back
An hour from now."

ROXANE
Your friend will have to wait;
I shall not let you go till dark.

CYRANO

> (*Very gently*)
>> Perhaps
A little before dark, I must go . . .
> (*He leans back in the chair,
> and closes his eyes. SISTER
> MARTHE crosses above the
> stairway. ROXANE sees her,
> motions her to wait, then
> turns to CYRANO.*)

ROXANE
> Look—
Somebody waiting to be teased.

CYRANO

> (*Quickly, opens his eyes.*)
>> Of course!
> (*In a big, comic voice*)
Sister, approach!

{SISTER MARTHE *glides toward him.*)
Beautiful downcast eyes!—
So shy—

SISTER MARTHE
(*Looks up, smiling.*)
You—
(*She sees his face.*)
Oh!—

CYRANO
(*Indicates* ROXANE.)
Sh!—Careful!
(*Resumes his burlesque tone.*)
Yesterday,
I ate meat again!

SISTER MARTHE
Yes, I know.
(*Aside*)
That is why
He looks so pale . . .
(*To him: low and quickly*)
In the refectory,
Before you go—come to me there—
I'll make you
A great bowl of hot soup—will you come?

CYRANO
(*Boisterously*)
Ah—
Will I come!

SISTER MARTHE
You are quite reasonable
Today!

ROXANE
Has she converted you?

SISTER MARTHE
Oh, no—
Not for the world!—

CYRANO
Why, now I think of it,
That is so— You, bursting with holiness,
And yet you never preach! Astonishing
I call it . . .
(*With burlesque ferocity*)
Ah—now I'll astonish you—
I am going to—
(*With the air of seeking for a good joke and finding it*)
—let you pray for me
Tonight, at vespers!

ROXANE
Aha!

CYRANO
Look at her—
Absolutely struck dumb!

SISTER MARTHE
(*Gently*)
I did not wait
For you to say I might.
(*She goes out.*)

CYRANO
(*Returns to* ROXANE, *who is bending over her work.*)
Now, may the devil
Admire me, if I ever hope to see
The end of that embroidery!

ROXANE
(*Smiling*)
I thought
It was time you said that.
(*A breath of wind causes a few leaves to fall.*)

CYRANO
The leaves—

ROXANE
(*Raises her head and looks away through the trees.*)
What color—

Perfect Venetian red! Look at them
fall.

CYRANO

Yes—they know how to die. A little
way
From the branch to the earth, a
little fear
Of mingling with the common dust
—and yet
They go down gracefully—a fall
that seems
Like flying!

ROXANE

Melancholy—you?

CYRANO

Why, no,
Roxane!

ROXANE

Then let the leaves fall. Tell me
now
The Court news—my Gazette!

CYRANO

Let me see—

ROXANE

Ah!

CYRANO

(*More and more pale, struggling against pain*)
Saturday, the nineteenth: The King
fell ill,
After eight helpings of grape
marmalade.
His malady was brought before the
court,
Found guilty of high treason;
whereupon
His Majesty revived. The royal
pulse
Is now normal. *Sunday, the twentieth:*
The Queen gave a grand ball, at
which they burned

Seven hundred and sixty-three wax
candles. *Note:*
They say our troops have been vic-
torious
In Austria. *Later:* Three sorcerers
Have been hung. *Special post:* The
little dog
Of Madame d'Athis was obliged to
take
Four pills before—

ROXANE

Monsieur de Bergerac,
Will you kindly be quiet!

CYRANO

Monday . . . nothing.
Lygdamire has a new lover.

ROXANE

Oh,

CYRANO

(*His face more and more al-
tered*)
Tuesday,
The Twenty-second: All the court
has gone
To Fontainebleau. *Wednesday:*
The Comte de Fiesque
Spoke to Madame de Montglat; she
said No.
Thursday: Mancini was the Queen
of France
Or—very nearly! *Friday:* La Mont-
glat
Said Yes. *Saturday twenty-sixth.* . . .
(*His eyes close; his head sinks
back; silence.*)

ROXANE

(*Surprised at not hearing any
more, turns, looks at him,
and rises, frightened.*)
He has fainted—
(*She runs to him, crying out.*)
Cyrano!

CYRANO

(*Opens his eyes.*)
What . . . What is it? . . .
(*He sees* ROXANE *leaning over
him, and quickly pulls his
hat down over his head and
leans back away from her in
the chair.*)
No—oh no—
It is nothing—truly!

ROXANE

But—

CYRANO

My old wound—
At Arras—sometimes—you know.
. . .

ROXANE

My poor friend!

CYRANO

Oh it is nothing; it will soon be
gone. . . .
(*Forcing a smile*)
There! It is gone!

ROXANE

(*Standing close to him*)
We all have our old wounds—
I have mine—here . . .
(*Her hand at her breast*)
under this faded scrap
Of writing. . . . It is hard to read
now—all
But the blood—and the tears. . . .
(*Twilight begins to fall.*)

CYRANO

His letter! . . . Did you
Not promise me that some day . . .
that some day
You would let me read it?

ROXANE

His letter?—You . . .
You wish—

CYRANO

I do wish it—today.

ROXANE

(*Gives him the little silken bag
from around her neck.*)
Here. . . .

CYRANO

May I . . . open it?

ROXANE

Open it, and read.
(*She goes back to her work,
folds it again, rearranges her
silks.*)

CYRANO

(*Unfolds the letter; reads.*)
"Farewell Roxane, because today I
die—"

ROXANE

(*Looks up, surprised.*)
Aloud?

CYRANO

(*Reads*)
"I know that it will be today,
My own dearly beloved—and my
heart
Still so heavy with love I have not
told,
And I die without telling you! No
more
Shall my eyes drink the sight of you
like wine,
Never more, with a look that is a
kiss,
Follow the sweet grace of you—"

ROXANE

How you read it—
His letter!

CYRANO

(*Continues*)
"I remember now the way

You have, of pushing back a lock of
  hair
With one hand, from your forehead
  —and my heart
Cries out—"

ROXANE

His letter . . . and you read it so
. . .
    (*The darkness increases im-
      perceptibly.*)

CYRANO

"Cries out and keeps crying: 'Farewell, my dear,
My dearest—' "

ROXANE

In a voice. . . .

CYRANO

    "—My own heart's own,
My own treasure—"

ROXANE

(*Dreamily*)
  In such a voice. . . .

CYRANO

        —"My love—"

ROXANE

—As I remember hearing . . .
  (*She trembles.*)
        —long ago. . . .
  (*She comes near him, softly,
    without his seeing her;
    passes the chair, leans over
    silently, looking at the letter.
    The darkness increases.*)

CYRANO

"—I am never away from you.
  Even now,
I shall not leave you. In another
  world,
I shall be still that one who loves
  you, loves you
Beyond measure, beyond—"

ROXANE

(*Lays her hand on his shoul-
  der.*)
        How can you read
Now? It is dark. . . .
  (*He starts, turns, and sees her
    there close to him. A little
    movement of surprise, al-
    most of fear; then he bows
    his head.
  A long pause; then in the twi-
    light now completely fallen,
    she says very softly, clasp-
    ing her hands*)
And all these fourteen years,
He has been the old friend, who
  came to me
To be amusing.

CYRANO

Roxane!—

ROXANE

        It was you.

CYRANO

No, no, Roxane, no!

ROXANE

        And I might have known,
Every time that I heard you speak
  my name! . . .

CYRANO

No— It was not I—

ROXANE

It was . . . you!

CYRANO

        I swear—

ROXANE

I understand everything now: The
  letters—
That was you . . .

CYRANO

No!

ROXANE

And the dear, foolish words—
That was you. . . .

CYRANO

No!

ROXANE

And the voice . . . in the dark. . . .
That was . . . you!

CYRANO

On my honor—

ROXANE

And . . . The Soul!—
That was all you.

CYRANO

I never loved you—

ROXANE

Yes,
You loved me.

CYRANO

(Desperately)
No— He loved you—

ROXANE

Even now,
You love me!

CYRANO

(His voice weakens.)
No!

ROXANE

(Smiling)
And why . . . so great a No?

CYRANO

No, no, my own dear love, I love
you not! . . .
(Pause.)

ROXANE

How many things have died . . .
and are new-born! . . .

Why were you silent for so many
years,
All the while, every night and every
day,
He gave me nothing—you knew
that— You knew
Here, in this letter lying on my
breast,
Your tears— You knew they were
your tears—

CYRANO

(Holds the letter out to her.)
The blood
Was his.

ROXANE

Why do you break that silence now,
Today?

CYRANO

Why? Oh, because—
(LE BRET and RAGUENEAU
enter, running.)

LE BRET

What recklessness—
I knew it! He is here!

CYRANO

(Smiling, and trying to rise)
Well? Here I am!

RAGUENEAU

He has killed himself, Madame,
coming here!

ROXANE

He— Oh, God. . . . And that
faintness . . . was that?—

CYRANO

No,
Nothing! I did not finish my
Gazette—
Saturday, twenty-sixth: An hour or
so

Before dinner, Monsieur de Bergerac
Died, foully murdered.

> (*He uncovers his head, and
> shows it swathed in band-
> ages.*)

ROXANE

Oh, what does he mean?—
Cyrano!—What have they done to
you?—

CYRANO

                    "Struck down
By the sword of a hero, let me
fall—
Steel in my heart, and laughter on
my lips!"
Yes, I said that once. How Fate
loves a jest!—
Behold me ambushed—taken in the
rear—
My battlefield a gutter—my noble
foe
A lackey, with a log of wood! . . .
It seems
Too logical— I have missed every-
thing,
Even my death!

RAGUENEAU

> (*Breaks down.*)
> Ah, Monsieur!—

CYRANO

                    Ragueneau,
Stop blubbering!
> (*Takes his hand.*)
What are you writing nowadays,
Old poet?

RAGUENEAU

> (*Through his tears*)
> I am not a poet now;
I snuff the—light the candles—for
Molière!

CYRANO

Oh—Molière!

RAGUENEAU

Yes, but I am leaving him
Tomorrow. Yesterday they played
Scapin—
He has stolen your scene—

LE BRET

The whole scene—word for word!

RAGUENEAU

Yes: "What the devil was he doing
there"—
That one!

LE BRET

> (*Furious*)
And Molière stole it all from you—
Bodily!—

CYRANO

Bah— He showed good taste. . . .
> (*To* RAGUENEAU)
                    The Scene
Went well? . . .

RAGUENEAU

Ah, Monsieur, they laughed—and
laughed—
How they did laugh!

CYRANO

                    Yes—that has been my life
Do you remember that night Christian spoke
Under your window? It was always
so!
While I stood in the darkness underneath,
Others climbed up to win the applause—the kiss!—
Well—that seems only justice— I
still say,
Even now, on the threshold of my
tomb—
"Molière has genius—Christian had
good looks—"
> (*The chapel bell is ringing.
> Along the avenue of trees*)

above the stairway, the
NUNS *pass in procession to
their prayers.)*
They are going to pray now; there
is the bell.

ROXANE

(*Raises herself and calls to
them.*)
Sister!—Sister!—

CYRANO

(*Holding on to her hand*)
No,—do not go away—
I may not still be here when you
return. . . .
(*The* NUNS *have gone into the
chapel. The organ begins to
play.*)
A little harmony is all I need—
Listen. . . .

ROXANE

You shall not die! I love you!—

CYRANO

No—
That is not in the story! You re-
member
When Beauty said "I love you" to
the Beast
That was a fairy prince, his ugli-
ness
Changed and dissolved, like magic.
. . . But you see
I am still the same.

ROXANE

And I—I have done
This to you! All my fault—mine!

CYRANO

You? Why, no,
On the contrary! I had never known
Womanhood and its sweetness but
for you.
My mother did not love to look at
me—

I never had a sister— Later on,
I feared the mistress with a mock-
ery
Behind her smile. But you—because of you
I have had one friend not quite all a
friend—
Across my life, one whispering
silken gown! . . .

LE BRET

(*Points to the rising moon
which begins to shine down
between the trees.*)
Your other friend is looking at you.

CYRANO

(*Smiling at the moon*)
I see. . . .

ROXANE

I never loved but one man in my
life,
And I have lost him—twice. . . .

CYRANO

Le Bret—I shall be up there presently
In the moon—without having to invent
Any flying-machines!

ROXANE

What are you saying? . . .

CYRANO

The moon—yes, that would be the
place for me—
My kind of paradise! I shall find
there
Those other souls who should be
friends of mine—
Socrates—Galileo—

LE BRET

(*Revolting*)
No! No! No!
It is too idiotic—too unfair—

Such a friend—such a poet—such
a man
To die so—to die so!—

CYRANO

(*Affectionately*)
                There goes Le Bret,
Growling!

LE BRET

(*Breaks down.*)
        My friend!—

CYRANO

(*Half raises himself, his eye
    wanders.*)
        The Cadets of Gascoyne,
The Defenders. . . . The elemen-
tary mass—
Ah—there's the point! Now, then
    . . .

LE BRET

            Delirious—
And all that learning—

CYRANO

            On the other hand,
We have Copernicus—

ROXANE

        Oh!

CYRANO

(*More and more delirious*)
            "Very well,
But what the devil was he doing
there?—
What the devil was he doing there,
up there?" . . .
    (*He declaims.*)
*Philosopher and scientist,
Poet, musician, duellist—
    He flew high, and fell back
        again!
A pretty wit—whose like we
    lack—*

*A lover . . . not like other men.
    . . .
Here lies Hercule-Savinien
De Cyrano de Bergerac—
    Who was all things—and all in
        vain!*
Well, I must go—pardon— I can-
not stay!
My moonbeam comes to carry me
away. . . .
    (*He falls back into the chair,
    half fainting. The sobbing
    of* ROXANE *recalls him to
    reality. Gradually his mind
    comes back to him. He
    looks at her, stroking the
    veil that hides her hair.*)
I would not have you mourn any
the less
That good, brave, noble Christian;
but perhaps—
I ask you only this—when the great
cold
Gathers around my bones, that you
may give
A double meaning to your widow's
weeds
And the tears you let fall for him
may be
For a little—my tears. . . .

ROXANE

(*Sobbing*)
        Oh, my love! . . .

CYRANO

(*Suddenly shaken as with a
    fever fit, he raises himself
    erect and pushes her away.*)
            —Not here!—
Not lying down! . . .
    (*They spring forward to help
    him; he motions them
    back.*)
        Let no one help me—no one!—
Only the tree. . . .
    (*He sets his back against the
    trunk. Pause.*)

It is coming . . . I feel
Already shod with marble . . .
gloved with lead . . .
(*Joyously*)
Let the old fellow come now! He
shall find me
On my feet—sword in hand—
(*Draws his sword.*)

LE BRET

Cyrano!—

ROXANE

(*Half fainting*)
Oh,
Cyrano!

CYRANO

I can see him there—he grins—
He is looking at my nose—that
skeleton
—What's that you say? Hopeless?
—Why, very well!—
But a man does not fight merely to
win!
No—no—better to know one fights
in vain! . . .
You there— Who are you? A hun-
dred against one—
I know them now, my ancient en-
emies—
(*He lunges at the empty air.*)
Falsehood! . . . There! There!
Prejudice— Compromise—
Cowardice—
(*Thrusting*)
What's that? No! Surrender? No!
Never—never! . . .
Ah, you too, Vanity!

I knew you would overthrow me
in the end—
No! I fight on! I fight on! I fight on!
(*He swings the blade in great
circles, then pauses, gasping. When he speaks again,
it is another tone.*)
Yes, all my laurels you have riven
away
And all my roses; yet in spite of
you,
There is one crown I bear away
with me,
And tonight, when I enter before
God,
My salute shall sweep all the stars
away
From the blue threshold! One thing
without stain,
Unspotted from the world, in spite
of doom
Mine own!—
(*He springs forward, his
sword aloft.*)
And that is . . .
(*The sword escapes from his
hand; he totters, and falls
into the arms of* LE BRET
and RAGUENEAU.)

ROXANE

(*Bends over him and kisses
him on the forehead.*)
—That is . . .

CYRANO

(*Opens his eyes and smiles up
at her.*)
My white plume. . . .

CURTAIN

Tovarich

BY JACQUES DEVAL

ADAPTED FROM THE FRENCH
BY ROBERT E. SHERWOOD

Produced by Gilbert Miller at the Plymouth Theatre, New York City, October 15, 1936, with the following cast:

(*In Order of Their Appearance*)

PRINCE MIKAIL ALEXANDROVITCH OURATIEFF	John Halliday
GRAND DUCHESS TATIANA PETROVNA	Marta Abba
OLGA	Irina Feodorova
COUNT FEODOR BREKENSKI	Frederic Worlock
CHAUFFOURIER-DUBIEFF	Ernest Lawford
MARTELLEAU	Aristides de Leon
FERNANDE DUPONT	Margaret Dale
CHARLES DUPONT	Jay Fassett
LOUISE	Barbara Gott
GEORGES DUPONT	James E. Truex
HELENE DUPONT	Amanda Duff
CONCIERGE	Graham Thorpe
MADAME VAN HEMERT	Leni Stengel
MADAME CHAUFFOURIER-DUBIEFF	Adora Andrews
COMMISSAR GOROTCHENKO	Cecil Humphreys

Play directed by Gilbert Miller
Settings designed by Raymond Sovey
Stage Director Lewis Allen
Stage Manager Elbert Gruver

SCENES

ACT ONE

SCENE   I. A room in the Hotel du Quercy.
SCENE II. Fernande Dupont's boudoir. An hour later.

ACT TWO

SCENE   I. The Duponts' drawing room. Two months later.
SCENE II. The Duponts' kitchen.

TIME: Paris, several years after the Russian Revolution.

TOVARICH

ACT ONE

SCENE I

A room in the Hotel du Quercy, rue de la Glacière, in Paris.
A November morning, about 11:00. Fresh and bright outside.
A single door and an archway upstage. A large window, with the roof?
of Paris showing.
Against the wall is a messy bed. A washstand, a chest of drawers, a
round table with an armchair and a single chair by the chest of drawers.
Near the bed a small table.
On the wall over the bed are hung a sword and the flag of the Russian
Imperial Guard. On the back wall is an ikon, its flame glowing.
MIKAIL is discovered lying on the bed, polishing a boot. He is about
forty-five—lean, lithe and, for no good reason, quite content with his lot.
After a few seconds, he wearily drops the boot and puts the brush on the
small table. Then starts to read a paper, which is on the bed.
TATIANA is off stage, singing.

MIKAIL. Tatiana?

TATIANA (*off stage*). Yes!

MIKAIL. What are you doing?

TATIANA (*off stage*). Washing. And what is my darling doing?

MIKAIL. Your darling has been polishing his boots. He is now resting. (*Leans back on pillows*) He is drawing the covers over his wasted limbs and trying to forget that there is no coal in the stove. (TATIANA *enters, with a shirt rolled into a ball. She comes to edge of the bed and shakes it out*) And what, in the blessed name of St. Christopher, is that?
(TATIANA, *somewhat younger than her husband, is lovely, graceful, gracious, regal, shabby.*)

TATIANA. Your shirt, darling.

MIKAIL. My . . .

TATIANA. I washed it with my own hands.

MIKAIL (*horrified*). That is my shirt? That—that *fragment!*

TATIANA. Yes, darling, your shirt. (*She holds it up, proving that it bears some resemblance to a man's shirt. But it has been so trimmed that the back is far longer than the front*) Your only shirt. (*She has come close to the bed.*)

MIKAIL. But—just what has happened to what used to be the tail?

TATIANA. You had no more handkerchiefs. So I had to cut some out of . . .

MIKAIL. Out of my shirt!

445

TATIANA. You know very well I've used up the last of my chemises.

MIKAIL (*melting*). Oh, my darling —my sweet, my beautiful! (*He seizes her hand and attempts to draw her down onto the bed.*)

TATIANA (*resisting*). No, you fool! I have to work . . . (*Goes to chest, brings up shirt.*)

MIKAIL. Tatiana! How can I beg for your forgiveness? You sacrificed the last of your chemises—and I complain at the loss of a mere shirt-tail. (*With deep fervor*) You are a saint, Tatiana, a saint!

TATIANA (*walks to bed*). You're sure of that? (*Sits on end of bed.*)

MIKAIL. It's the very word that was used by my Imperial Master. (*He crosses himself*) Your august cousin. (*She crosses herself*) He said: "In marrying Tatiana Petrovna, you marry a saint!"

TATIANA (*nodding*). He knew me very well.

MIKAIL. He was speaking of your devotion—but not of your manners.

TATIANA (*indignantly*). And is there anything wrong with my manners?

MIKAIL (*indulgently*). Oh—you can't be blamed for them.

TATIANA. Blamed!

MIKAIL. You were born a Grand Duchess, and you lacked the opportunity for social contacts that was given to the rest of us. It gave you a bad start in life.

TATIANA. What do you mean?

MIKAIL. Wherever you go, I have to act as interpreter—and apologist— for you.

TATIANA. Get up! (*Pulls newspaper from his hands.*)

MIKAIL (*humbly*). But why?

TATIANA. Obey me! (*Rises from bed, leans against washstand.*)

MIKAIL. But—my darling—this bed is so warm and so comfortable.

TATIANA (*solemnly*). Mikail Alexandrovitch Ouratieff, at whatever sacrifice of your comfort, I command you to get up. (*She is being very stern, very imperious. There should be no suggestion of bantering in her tone.*)

MIKAIL (*sighing*). All right. (*He swings his bare feet out of bed, and as he rises, steps on his boot. He leans over and starts to put the boot on.*)

TATIANA. Put that shoe down! And come over here. (*He obeys ruefully*) Since you are such a good apologist, you will offer your apologies—to *me!*
(*MIKAIL advances towards her slowly and when he is close to her attempts to click his bare heels together and bows low.*)

MIKAIL. My beloved Tatiana. . . .

TATIANA (*goes to end of bed, sits*). Your apologies will be expressed in official form.

MIKAIL. General Prince Mikail Alexandrovitch Ouratieff, aide-de-camp to His Imperial Majesty, offers Her Imperial Highness the Grand Duchess Tatiana Petrovna his very humble apologies.

TATIANA. Approach!

(MIKAIL *obeys, coming very close to her. She gives him a vigorous slap on the face.*)

MIKAIL. Ouch!

TATIANA (*angrily*). How dare you say "ouch"? You're an officer. You are not permitted to feel pain.

MIKAIL. Very well, Highness. The ouch is withdrawn.

(TATIANA *rises suddenly, seizes him in her arms and drags him down on the bed.*)

TATIANA. Darling, darling, darling. You are forgiven. (*She kisses him fiercely.*)

MIKAIL. Completely?

TATIANA. Completely!

MIKAIL. And you'll let me be just a little bit sad if I want to?

TATIANA. And I'll be sad with you always, dear. (*Puts her arms around him.*)

MIKAIL. Ah, God! How good it is to be Russian.

TATIANA. And insane!

MIKAIL. Life for us is so very, very sad and so very, very beautiful.

TATIANA. And so tiresome. I'm starving. (*She sits up.*)

MIKAIL. So am I, Tatiaschka. There's a horrible, gnawing emptiness in my soul.

TATIANA. I was not speaking of souls. I'm hungry here. (*She slaps her stomach*) Give me some money.

MIKAIL (*astounded*). Money?

TATIANA. Yes—I'm going shopping.

MIKAIL. But surely—not with money?

TATIANA. Mikail! Don't tell me there's none left.

MIKAIL (*sighing*). There is the sum of one hundred francs, Tatiana. That is all.

TATIANA (*brightly*). But that is enough.

MIKAIL. And out of the hundred, we owe eighty to the proprietor of this lamentable hotel.

TATIANA. That little nuisance? Haven't we trained him in the virtue of patience?

MIKAIL. No, we have been fortunate in that he has the gout, my Tatiana, and therefore he cannot climb the six flights of stairs. But he must be paid. Eighty francs. Today. Otherwise . . . out we go!

TATIANA. Very well—he *shall* be paid! I shall give him his eighty francs today, and tomorrow he shall lend us two hundred. (*She has started preparing to go out. She can be brisk, very competent, when she chooses.*)

MIKAIL. But, will he?

TATIANA. I'll appeal to his snobbery. For two hundred francs I'll make him Count of Pultava!

MIKAIL (*scornfully*). A Count. Do you think that would impress him? Why last week for only fifty francs you made him a Duke. . . .

TATIANA. Did I?

MIKAIL. Duke of Courlande.

TATIANA. Very well, then—I can do better than that: tomorrow he will become a Grand Duke—entitled to precede himself in to dinner.

MIKAIL (*overwhelmed with admiration*). Tatiana, what resource!

TATIANA. Resourcefulness has been thrust upon us, my pigeon! (*She pauses momentarily in her dressing to assume an attitude*) We are two against the world!

MIKAIL. No! Not two—only one— *you!*

TATIANA. Ah, Mikail! How far do you suppose I could go in life without you?

MIKAIL (*sits on bed*). Come, Tatiana. Get back into this bed.

TATIANA. No! Give me the hundred francs.
(*Regretfully he reaches under the pillow and takes out a hundred-franc note.*)

MIKAIL. You will surely pay eighty of these to the Duke of Courlande?

TATIANA. Yes! He'll be paid—his eighty francs.

MIKAIL. That will leave twenty francs. Bring back at least ten of it.

TATIANA (*taking the note*). I shall pay the landlord eighty francs and buy the food, and bring back eighty francs.

MIKAIL (*anxiously*). Tatiana—I don't understand your arithmetic . . .

TATIANA. Darling!

MIKAIL. But I suspect the honesty of your intentions.

TATIANA (*turns to him*). Darling, do you trust me?

MIKAIL. Within reason, my love.

TATIANA. Then believe me. I swear, by Saint Peter and Saint Paul—I swear to bring back eighty-five francs. I shall bring back ninety francs! I shall buy some cutlets of horse and some potatoes, and I shall bring back ninety-five francs and two artichokes!

MIKAIL. Tatiana, you're very fond of artichokes, aren't you?

TATIANA. No, I hate them, but while the grocer is selecting the poorest potatoes, I shall be left alone amongst the artichokes. (*Puts on hat.*)

MIKAIL (*looks heavenward reverently*). I humbly beg that the Father of all living may look the other way, that He will not see the Grand Duchess Tatiana Petrovna, cousin to the Tsar (*he makes the sign of the cross*) arrested for stealing artichokes.

TATIANA. Nonsense! I am never arrested!

MIKAIL. You have been incredibly lucky.

TATIANA (*picks up bag*). Oh, no, Mikail, it is more than luck. It is the intervention of God—the God of all the Russias. Why—the other day, the grocer almost saw me as I was letting a bunch of radishes fall into this bag, but his eyes were miraculously diverted to the ceiling.

MIKAIL (*with decision*). Tatiana—give me that bag. I shall go myself.

TATIANA. No! By St. Christopher, no! A general of Cavalry to be seen in the streets of Paris with cutlets of horse! Never!

MIKAIL. But it is quite all right for a Grand Duchess.

TATIANA (*puts bag on table*). A Grand Duchess is above appearances!

MIKAIL (*sits on end of bed. With resignation*). Very well—go on and commit your pathetic thieveries. But what of tomorrow—and all the tomorrows that follow? The Russian God may grow weary of diverting grocers' eyes.

TATIANA. Then we will find something to sell. (*Puts on coat*) We have always found . . .

MIKAIL. There's not much left. (*He looks about the room with a sigh*) Except my sword. . . .

TATIANA. The sword of Alexander the Third! Never!

MIKAIL. And the flag . . .

TATIANA. The flag of the Imperial Guard! Better let us die together, wrapped in its folds!

MIKAIL. Then that leaves nothing but the ikon.

TATIANA. May Heaven forgive you! (*Goes to ikon and crosses herself*) I would sooner sell my body. (*She walks towards the door*) I'm going.

MIKAIL. Wait! (*He goes to the window and looks out*) The police officer is still there.

TATIANA. Which one is it today?

MIKAIL. The little dark one with the military medal. (*He makes a little friendly sign to the unseen policeman*) He has a nice, friendly face.

TATIANA. I'll bring him back a packet of cigarettes.

MIKAIL. Good ones, I hope.

TATIANA. Oh, the best. (*A knock is heard. They look at each other in some alarm*) Did you hear a knock?

MIKAIL. I am under the impression that I did. (*The knock is repeated*) If it is our landlord, the Duke of Courlande . . .

TATIANA. If it is, I shall deal with him.

(MIKAIL goes to the door and opens it. OLGA, *a dark, pretty, but savage looking little midinette, comes in. She affects timorousness.*)

OLGA. Madame Courtois?

TATIANA. Who?

OLGA. I have a hat here for Madame Courtois.

MIKAIL. We don't doubt it, my dear child. But she is not here.

OLGA. This is not where she lives?

MIKAIL. That is the unhappy fact.

OLGA. But the concierge told me . . . (*She is looking about the room, in seeming bewilderment, when she happens to see the ikon. Excitedly*) You are Russians!

MIKAIL. We cannot disguise it.

OLGA (*staring at* TATIANA). But I should have known at once. Your Highness! (*She puts the hat-box on a chair, goes to* TATIANA, *kneels before her and kisses the hem of her skirt.*)

MIKAIL (*appreciatively*). Charming!

TATIANA. Stand up, my child.

OLGA. Have I Your Highness's pardon for my stupidity?

TATIANA. Of course you have. Come now—stand up.

OLGA (*rises and kisses* TATIANA's *shoulder*). It was all the concierge's fault. He told me distinctly that I would find Madame Courtois in Room Four and I . . .

TATIANA. The concierge is an idiot. Go, my child. (*She picks up the hat-box*) Ask him again in very short, simple words and perhaps he'll . . . (*Something about the weight of the hat-box causes her to break off short.* OLGA *is trying to take the hat-box, but* TATIANA *is holding it back.*)

OLGA. Thank you, Highness! Thank you! And grant me again your august pardon.

TATIANA. Wait. I think I'd like to (OLGA *goes for hat-box*) see that hat.

OLGA. No, Your Highness. It's not . . .

TATIANA. I might decide to buy it. (*She is starting to open the hat-box.*)

OLGA (*frantically*). I promise Your Highness, it is hideous—it will be an insult on your head. . . . (TATIANA *opens the box.* MIKAIL *rushes across to table, examines contents of box and takes out some leaflets.*)

MIKAIL. Well at least it contains no high explosives.

TATIANA. What is it, Mikail?

MIKAIL. Some very interesting documents. (*Reading in mock oratory*) "Workers of France, Arise! Join your Russian brothers in the United Front." Evidently Madame Courtois is more interested in literature than she is in millinery. (*To* OLGA) Well, Tovarich, what do you want from us?

OLGA (*viciously*). What are you going to do with that *money*?

MIKAIL. One hundred francs? We're going to buy artichokes.

OLGA. The money you stole from Russia!

TATIANA. Stole?

OLGA. Thieves! It came from the blood and the sweat of the millions, and now you hold it for yourselves . . .

TATIANA. Mikail! Tell her to go.

MIKAIL. Not yet, my darling. (*To* OLGA) Who sent you here?

OLGA. Do you believe I'd tell you?

MIKAIL. No—but I don't mind asking. Was it Gorotchenko?

OLGA (*defiantly*). I don't know.

MIKAIL. What information do you expect to get out of us?

OLGA. I don't know.

MIKAIL. Are you a real Russian communist or one of these dubious French ones?

OLGA (*doggedly*). I don't know.

TATIANA (*laughs and picks up the hat-box*). Here, my dear. Take this charming hat to Madame Courtois. I'm sure she'll look lovely in it. And tell Gorotchenko we'd be grateful if some day he would honor us with his own presence.
(OLGA *snatches the hat-box and goes to the door.*)

MIKAIL. And tell him that you found us still in good health, though slightly under-nourished. Tell him we're prepared, at any moment, to be caught in one of the traps which he is thoughtfully laying for us. And when he has caught us he can burn us, by slow degrees, in the scorching flames of Red Terror—(OLGA

laughs) but our policy will remain unchanged: not a billion, not a million, not a thousand, not a sou!

OLGA. Fine talk, you white-livered thieves. You think you're safe with your money. Because you're in Paris, in the bourgeois fortress, with gendarmes to guard you. (MIKAIL *sits on bed.* TATIANA *pays no attention*) But we know how to take back what was stolen from us. And when we do, we'll also take your miserable, worthless, evil lives. (*She turns, blows the ikon out, exits, slamming the door.*)

TATIANA. The little beast! Where are the matches?

MIKAIL (*jumps off bed*). Matches? Ah! (*He searches, finds them on cupboard*) Here they are. (*He hands them to* TATIANA. *She relights the ikon.*)

TATIANA. Of all the spies that have been inflicted on us, that one was the most ridiculous. It's an insult to us to suppose that such a vicious little fool could accomplish anything.

MIKAIL (*seriously*). You know, Tatiana—some day one of them will kill us.

TATIANA (*calmly*). I don't doubt it.

MIKAIL. You're not afraid?

TATIANA (*looks at him levelly*). Are you? (*By way of response he kisses her, holds her close to him for a moment, then turns and wanders towards the bed*) Mikail, don't tell me you are going back to bed?

MIKAIL (*getting in bed*). Yes.

TATIANA. You'd better put your clothes on.

MIKAIL. But my shirt is not dry.

TATIANA. You must be ready for more visitors. Distinguished visitors!

MIKAIL. Even in this costume I am competent to cope with bankers.

TATIANA. You can cope with them better with your clothes on. You must realize that they don't understand the simple dignity of the Russian soul.

MIKAIL. Then I shall show it to them again in all its undauntable . . . (*lies down, pulls clothes up*) unshakable . . . (*he pulls the covers over him*) untiring strength!

TATIANA. And whatever they promise, you will not give in.

MIKAIL (*has the bed clothes up to his nose*). Not a billion, not a million, not a thousand, not a sou! (*He lies on his side and yawns.*)

TATIANA (*kneels on bed*). God preserve you, my gallant love! I go down the back way so I shall be sure to see the Duke. He is always watching there, for people trying to sneak out. And I shall buy a dinner worthy of a true servant of the Tsar. (*Sign of the cross*) And bring back—one hundred francs. Goodbye, my pigeon. (*She exits.* MIKAIL *pulls up bedclothes and makes a conscientious effort to go to sleep. There is a knock at the door.*)

MIKAIL. Come in.
(*The door opens, revealing two impressive-looking gentlemen on the landing outside. One of them is* CHAUFFOURIER-DUBIEFF, *governor of the Bank of France. He is old, immaculate and at ease. Behind him is* GENERAL COUNT BREKENSKI, *aide-de-camp to the current pretender to the Russian throne. He also is old, but full of pomposity and grudges.*)

CHAUFFOURIER. Is Prince Ouratieff receiving?

MIKAIL. Come in, gentlemen!

CHAUFFOURIER. I beg your pardon. Did we awaken you?

MIKAIL. No, no! I've merely been resting after cleaning my boots. One moment . . . (*He jumps out of bed, goes to table, picks up a monocle, puts it in his eye, turns to them and bows with dignity*) Gentlemen!
(*The others bow.*)

CHAUFFOURIER. Allow me to introduce myself, Excellency. I am Chauffourier-Dubieff, governor of the Bank of France.

MIKAIL. I am honored.

CHAUFFOURIER. The Minister of Finance himself begs you to forgive him. He is in Rome at the moment, but after his return he will be pleased to call on you whenever you are disengaged.

MIKAIL. You may assure him that I am in a permanent state of disengagement.

CHAUFFOURIER. In view of the urgency, he begged me to see you this morning and perhaps pave the way for a complete understanding. (*A cough from* COUNT BREKENSKI *calls attention to his presence*) Oh! I beg your pardon—but, of course, Excellency, you know each other.

MIKAIL. I'm afraid I . . .

BREKENSKI (*introducing himself*). Count Feodor Androvitch Brekenski, honorary colonel of the 17th Regiment of Uhlans, honorary page to His Imperial Majesty Alexander II, honorary Governor of Jitomir . . .

MIKAIL. I am honored to meet so distinguished a compatriot. (MIKAIL *removes the monocle from his eye*) Forgive me, gentlemen, but this damned thing is annoying me. Perhaps I had better put on more formal attire. (*He goes to the washstand, puts down eye-glass, and crosses to get the shirt which* TATIANA *has hung up to dry. He reaches for the shirt. It is still damp. He looks discouraged.*)

CHAUFFOURIER (*quickly*). I beg you, Excellency. Don't bother to dress! We are all men together.

MIKAIL. That's right—so we are. Sit down, gentlemen. (*Picks up circulars from floor and puts them in stove. Brings chair for* CHAUFFOURIER) I can only apologize for the many inadequacies of our home.

CHAUFFOURIER. No apologies are needed, Excellency. Indeed, I must render homage to the heroism, the grandeur of your—may I say sublime—poverty?

MIKAIL. You may say it, my dear sir (*softly*) but not with the same feeling that I can put into those words.

BREKENSKI. And believe me, my dear friend, your deplorable situation in this hotel is a source of constant grief to His Imperial Majesty. He, too, is ready at any moment to renew his offer of a pension.

MIKAIL. I can never sufficiently express my gratitude to His Highness, and the French Government. Go on, gentlemen.

CHAUFFOURIER. Excellency—I have ascertained the exact sum total of your account at the Bank of France to date. Will you authorize me to make the figure known to Count Brekenski?

MIKAIL. With the greatest of pleasure.

CHAUFFOURIER (*takes out a small note-book from which he reads*). With all compound interest included, the account of Prince Ouratieff amounts to exactly three billion, eight hundred and eighty-three million, two hundred thousand and sixty-two francs, sixty-five centimes. (*To* BREKENSKI) Sixty-five. (*Closes book*) In round figures, four billion francs.

BREKENSKI (*with dry mouth*). It is impressive.

MIKAIL (*sadly*). It impressed me once. But—one can get used to anything—even to the possession of four billion francs.

CHAUFFOURIER. Excellency—how long must we continue with this absurd situation? That vast sum of money is lying idle, doing no good to you nor to anyone. Can you forget that France, the unshakable ally of your lamented sovereign, is today struggling against the most bitter difficulties?

MIKAIL. I know, my dear Governor. I regret it with all my heart. France's sorrows are my sorrows. France has given sanctuary to me, and to many of my countrymen; at great risk to her national security, she has allowed some of us to drive taxis.

CHAUFFOURIER. Oh, yes.

MIKAIL. She is Queen among realms, mistress of all mankind. But that money is not mine, it belongs to the Tsar.

BREKENSKI. Exactly! And that is just . . .

CHAUFFOURIER. Yes—but it could so easily be converted into French Government bonds. We can offer you any one of twelve state loans, each one more . . .

BREKENSKI (*interrupting*). Without forgetting, either, that our holy Russia is groaning under its tyrants, that His Imperial Majesty is ready to put himself at the head of his generous loyalists, to reconquer the sacred soil . . . whenever the funds for this campaign are forthcoming.

CHAUFFOURIER (*vehemently*). Millions which the Bank of France is perfectly ready to advance, against the conversion into any one of twelve state loans. . . .

BREKENSKI. You will be the Liberator of Russia, the restorer of the throne. . . .

CHAUFFOURIER. Need I add that my Government will be happy to render—homage, as extensive as it would be discreet, to your affectionate confidence?

MIKAIL. Gentlemen—gentlemen—this is all very fine—but can't we be more precise? You are about to offer me something. What is it?

CHAUFFOURIER (*quickly*). Fifteen million francs.

BREKENSKI (*quickly*). And a high place in the counsels of the New Imperial Russia.

CHAUFFOURIER. Think of it, Excellency, high honor and financial security to the end of your days.

MIKAIL. Fifteen millions, to a man who can order four billion boiled eggs for breakfast! Gentlemen, it is ludicrous! (*Rises*) However, my dear Count, I authorize you to say to His Highness that my sword and my fortune are entirely his . . . (*Exclamations of joy from* BREKENSKI *and* CHAUFFOURIER. *Both rise*) And that I ask no compensation either from His Highness, or from the French Government.

BREKENSKI. Oh, Excellency! All of holy Russia is in your debt. (*Very moved, he walks up to* MIKAIL *with outstretched hand.*)

CHAUFFOURIER (*in the same way*). Excellency. . . . Your magnanimity—your patriotism—touch me so deeply I . . .

MIKAIL (*raising his hands in modesty*). Gentlemen—gentlemen. You are making too much fuss over the proffered services of one soldier . . . and of a fortune that amounts to no more than twenty francs.

BREKENSKI (*stammering*). Twenty francs!

MIKAIL. That's what I'll have left after paying my hotel bill.

CHAUFFOURIER. But the four billions!

MIKAIL. That is not mine to give.

BREKENSKI. Quite right. It is the property of His Imperial Majesty, heir to the throne.

MIKAIL. No, Count Brekenski, it is not his property. I received that money from the hands of a Tsar. It is into the hands of a Tsar that I shall give it back.

BREKENSKI. There are Courts of Justice in Paris. His Imperial Majesty will demand restitution.

MIKAIL (*softly—to* CHAUFFOURIER). My dear Governor, will you explain to Count Brekenski that all the Judges of France in all their dignity cannot dispossess Prince Ouratieff of a bank account which stands legally in his name?

CHAUFFOURIER. But, Excellency, what does our Bank ask?

MIKAIL. I don't know.

CHAUFFOURIER. A simple conversion into state loans—a mere matter of bookkeeping.

BREKENSKI (*with signs of anger*). Prince Ouratieff, you doubtless have your own reasons for your arrogant stubbornness, but permit me to say that, in my eyes, your refusal suggests not only bad faith but downright treason. And I feel sure that His Imperial Majesty will agree. . . .

MIKAIL. Great God! If I refuse to agree to this mere matter of bookkeeping, I'm a traitor. So be it, gentlemen. But . . . I must remain free to make my own mistakes in my own way. That was my master's wish. The Tsar of Russia trusted me. He knew that calamity was at hand, and a few weeks before the Revolution he caused those colossal sums to be placed in the Bank of France in my name and at my disposal. His only stipulation to me was that I should administer it in the best interests of my sovereign. Make careful note of those words, Count Brekenski—the best interests of my sovereign. I am serving those interests—perhaps stupidly—but with all the devotion at my command. I see no reason to squander that money in the financing of a counter-revolution which would only end in grotesque and horrible failure.

BREKENSKI. You are speaking for yourself, Prince Ouratieff.

MIKAIL. Precisely. And for myself I say to you—not a billion, not a million, not a thousand, not a sou! It was a crowned Tsar, who gave me that money, not a pretender. And to a crowned Tsar it will be returned. (*To* CHAUFFOURIER) Of course a General of Cavalry isn't supposed to know much about business, but I received this money in gold—not in paper, and in gold it will be given back. I tell you this, gentlemen, in the hope that it will relieve you of the necessity for any further visits to this dismal quarter of Paris.

CHAUFFOURIER. Have you considered the possibility of your death?

MIKAIL. I am reminded of that frequently. But God is a Russian. He will take care of the money and me —after I have been murdered.

CHAUFFOURIER. Murdered?

MIKAIL (*calmly*). Yes.

BREKENSKI. Your life, has been threatened?

MIKAIL. The representatives of the other Russia are also very interested in those four billion francs. I think they will spare no effort to get them.

BREKENSKI. But it is unthinkable that they might . . .

MIKAIL. Don't worry, my dear Count, they may seize me; they may bring you my hand—but not my signature.

CHAUFFOURIER (*caressingly*). Don't you worry, your Excellency. Our police are excessively vigilant. Why —would you believe it?—in this district not so much as an artichoke is stolen without their knowing of it at once.

MIKAIL. An artichoke?

CHAUFFOURIER. Oh, it's nothing. The grocer is instructed to look the other way. Oh, we handle it with the utmost discretion. The bills for your provisions are sent first to the local police station, who transmit them to Headquarters, whence they go to the Foreign Office for approval and then to the Bureau of the Secret Funds for payment. The matter is handled by four different government departments.

MIKAIL (*profoundly distressed*). My dear Governor.

CHAUFFOURIER. You may consider that a great deal of official machinery for one artichoke. But it is that very thoroughness which accounts for the greatness of France.

MIKAIL. I am terribly upset about this. I assure you it will not happen again.

CHAUFFOURIER. Don't give it another thought, Excellency. You and Her Highness are extraordinarily modest in your demands. In fact, we have all been astounded at your ability to live on such small quantity of food. The French Government is perfectly able to pay your bills even in these crucial times. And we are glad to do so. We are your friends—your well-wishers— ever eager to help in every way possible—to restore you to the estate which is so rightfully yours. (*At this moment the front door opens and in comes* TATIANA. *Her shopping bag is swelled to bursting point with various provisions. Besides this, she holds a superb bottle of champagne in one hand, and under her other arm is a large bundle of gay flowers.*)

MIKAIL (*horrified*). Oh, Tatiana . . .

(TATIANA *flourishes the champagne. She looks at the two gentlemen with amiable curiosity.*)

MIKAIL (*severely*). Tatiana, may I present Monsieur Chauffourier-Dubieff, Governor of the Bank of France—and Count Brekenski.

TATIANA. How do you do?

MIKAIL. Her Imperial Highness Tatiana Petrovna Princess Oura-tieva, my wife.
(*The two gentlemen bow low, murmuring "Highness."* CHAUFFOURIER *and* BREKENSKI *come forward to kiss* TATIANA's *hand. She puts the shopping bag on the table, also the champagne and the flowers.*)

TATIANA. Forgive me—one moment . . . (*She thrusts her hand into the top of her blouse and draws out one artichoke and then another, which she places on the table. She smiles apologetically at* BREKENSKI) They were scratching me. (*She extends her hands and* CHAUFFOURIER *and* BREKENSKI *kiss them with deep reverence. She withdraws her hands*) Enough!—I must put these in water. (*She picks up the flowers and goes out.*)

MIKAIL. I think the interview is ended.

CHAUFFOURIER. Excellency, we will retire. (CHAUFFOURIER *and* BREKEN-SKI *bow and go, the latter with considerable ill feeling.*)

MIKAIL (*sees gloves on bed, picks them up, and crosses to door*). My dear Governor!
(CHAUFFOURIER *returns hastily, full of hope.*)

CHAUFFOURIER. Excellency? You have changed your mind?

MIKAIL. You are forgetting your gloves.

CHAUFFOURIER. But now that we are alone—those bonds . . .

MIKAIL. Exactly! (*He picks up artichokes, with a hasty gesture he thrusts them, with the gloves, into* CHAUFFOURIER's *hat, and shows him to the door.*)

CHAUFFOURIER (*turns to* MIKAIL). And I trust that you'll enjoy a most excellent dinner. As guests of France. (CHAUFFOURIER *exits.* MIKAIL *inspects the contents of the shopping bag, takes out a jar of caviar.*)

MIKAIL. By St. Christopher! Tatiana!

TATIANA (*off stage*). I'm coming. (*Enters with tablecloth.*)

MIKAIL. Caviar!

TATIANA (*pleasantly*). Yes, my pigeon!

MIKAIL. Two hundred francs a pound.

TATIANA. Mikail! You mustn't speak about the cost of it. You sound like a tradesman.

MIKAIL. Tatiana, did you pay the hotel bill?

TATIANA. I couldn't find our dear landlord, the Duke of Courlande.

MIKAIL. Tatiana!

TATIANA. I looked for him everywhere. Really I did.

MIKAIL. And you spent our entire fortune?

TATIANA. Darling, I had to.

MIKAIL. But can't we keep body and soul together without caviar and champagne?

TATIANA (*with heat*). Have you forgotten what day this is?

MIKAIL. I'm quite certain it's not Christmas.

TATIANA. The fourth of November.

MIKAIL. And what is the fourth of November to us?

TATIANA. It's the day of the victory!

MIKAIL. What victory?

TATIANA (*indignantly*). Samarcand. On the fourth of November, 1487.
. . .

MIKAIL. Five hundred years ago!

TATIANA. And what is five hundred years to eternal Russia? (*She looks among the things on the table*) The artichokes? Where are the artichokes?

MIKAIL. I returned them to our host.

TATIANA. But today I *paid* for them.

MIKAIL. You *paid* for all this?

TATIANA. Well—you couldn't expect me to buy caviar and champagne with one hundred francs. (MIKAIL *lies on the bed, looking away*) Mikail! What is wrong? Darling! What is it? Mikail! Did you give in to them? Did you let them hoodwink you into . . .

MIKAIL (*turns to her*). Tatiana Petrovna—we shall have to move.

TATIANA. Move? From this hotel?

MIKAIL. Perhaps from France itself.

TATIANA. But why?

MIKAIL. Because we're wards of the state. I've learned why the grocer looks the other way and it's nothing to do with the Russian God. He is commanded to do so by the benevolent French Government— who pays for all the artichokes you carry off.

TATIANA. Pays for them!

MIKAIL. Yes, the bills for all that we've stolen and eaten have gone to the Republic of France, and they're handled by four different Departments.

TATIANA. The swine! Putting us in their debt! Mikail—we must pay them. You must find out how much it is and pay them—every last sou.

MIKAIL. But how?

TATIANA. Take the money from the bank.

MIKAIL. Never!

TATIANA (*pleading desperately*). But it would only be a little bit, to save our honor. Surely, Heaven would forgive us that.

MIKAIL. No, Tatiana, I would not dare. If I touch a penny of that money, we're lost. I don't do things by halves. In a fortnight we should be living at the Ritz. No, my darling—our honor has been lost and I see no prospect of regaining it this side of the grave.

TATIANA (*bursts into tears*). And I was so sure it was my cleverness. I was so sure I'd outwitted them all.

MIKAIL (*infinitely sympathetic*). Neither of us ever dreamed they could be guilty of such dishonesty.

TATIANA. And I was always so careful never to take *too* much. Only just what we barely needed.

MIKAIL. I know, Tatiana.

TATIANA. If I'd only known how they were deceiving us . . . if I'd only *known*. . . . I'd have taken caviar every day!

MIKAIL. Yes, of course you would, my darling—and now you know why we must move! (*He gives her his handkerchief*.)

TATIANA. Yes! We must never again submit to their treacherous charity. We will go to the ends of the earth. But when we get there—what shall we have to eat?

MIKAIL. There is only one possible solution; I must work.

TATIANA. Work! Mikail—even for fun you must not say things like that.

MIKAIL. It isn't for fun. It's for food!

TATIANA. But what could you do?

MIKAIL. Admiral Soukhomine works. He navigates a taxi.

TATIANA. Yes—and he kills more people than he ever did with all his battleships.

MIKAIL. And Colonel Trepanoff works at the Kasbek—doing the dagger dance. Two daggers in the belt, and another in the teeth. I could do that. (*He prepares to demonstrate with table knives, tries to dance, falls down.* TATIANA *claps her hands.*)

TATIANA. Yes—and while you were dancing, what would I be doing? Waiting all night, outside some filthy cabaret, with bandages to tie you together again when the dagger slipped. No! I shall do the work. (*Takes knives from him, puts them on table.*)

MIKAIL. You?

TATIANA. Yes. I've been invited to pose for an artist.

MIKAIL. Who is he?

TATIANA. I don't know. I met him at the wine merchant's.

MIKAIL. He spoke to you?

TATIANA. He was very sweet. He said he would like to paint me in the nude.

MIKAIL. And you would so far degrade yourself . . .

TATIANA. I would do anything to keep you away from daggers and taxis—because I love you. . . . (*After a moment, both on floor,* MIKAIL *takes her in his arms. For a while, together in silence.*)

MIKAIL. I have thought the matter over; I've decided you will not pose in the nude . . . no matter how sweet he may be.

TATIANA. But I will not starve!

MIKAIL. I've heard it isn't a bad death.

TATIANA. I refuse to die—or let you die. For if we are gone what will become of all those billions? They'll be orphans—helpless and alone. We must find a way to live, Mikail!

MIKAIL. Condemned to misery and hunger all the days . . .

TATIANA. Yes—misery and hunger —the greatest luxuries of our race! We were born to suffer and to love it. Life for us is so beautiful—and so sad. (*Knock at door.*)

MIKAIL. Come in. (MARTELLEAU *enters. He is a broken-down little valet, very humble. They pay no attention to him as they still hold each other*) Who is it? And what do you want?

MARTELLEAU. Your pardon, sir. I am Martelleau, of Room 12, your neighbor.

MIKAIL. Come in, my neighbor.

TATIANA (*rises*). And shut the door, Room 12.

MARTELLEAU. Forgive me for troubling you, Excellency.

MIKAIL (*rises*). "Excellency." From what work of fiction did you derive that title?

MARTELLEAU. You are an Excellency, aren't you?

MIKAIL. I was. But in this hotel I'm known as that bloody Russian.

MARTELLEAU. The police downstairs all call you Excellency.

MIKAIL. Do they? They are men of refinement. What do you want?

MARTELLEAU. The proprietor of the hotel has authorized me to take up a collection.

MIKAIL (*eagerly*). For us?

MARTELLEAU. No. (MIKAIL *turns away with disgust, sits on end of bed*) It is for the little woman in Room 16—the one who had her baby the day before yesterday. She is pining away with hunger, and the little brat with thirst. So— if you could spare any little gift.

TATIANA. If we had only a thousand francs left in the world, we should give a thousand francs. . . .

MARTELLEAU. I knew you would, madame. You're Russian and that means a heart of gold.

TATIANA. But—we have nothing left.

MARTELLEAU. That is most unfortunate. But I understand. I, too, know what it is to be out of work in these unhappy times. Forgive me for having bothered you. (*He seems about to depart, but* MIKAIL *stops him.*)

MIKAIL. Wait, my friend. Do you ever expect to find work again?

MARTELLEAU. Oh, yes, sir. I am always hopeful.

TATIANA. What is your occupation, godly man? (*Sits beside* MIKAIL *on bed.*)

MARTELLEAU. Oh, butler, valet, even waiter if necessary.

MIKAIL. Where will you look for work?

MARTELLEAU. In the newspaper.

MIKAIL. Newspaper?

MARTELLEAU. You know, "domestic situations vacant." (*He taps a dirty old newspaper in his pocket*) When the little woman is well again, she will send the child to the country and then we'll try to get employment together as a *married* couple.

TATIANA. You are going to marry her, godly man?

MARTELLEAU. Oh, no . . . I already have a wife, unfortunately. But *she* has a good job. There's no need to worry about her. But this little woman and I will get along well enough together.

TATIANA. You know, pigeon, it sounds like an ideal existence. Are there many such opportunities?

MARTELLEAU. Oh, yes, you hear of them now and then. There is a most excellent one in the paper today.

TATIANA. Oh! Let me see!

MARTELLEAU. Number four, Avenue de Tourville, butler and housemaid. Two rooms of their own on the sixth floor—with servants' lift. Use of motor car to go shopping in. Central heating . . .

MIKAIL. Central heating!

MARTELLEAU. One Sunday out of

two. Absolute paradise. (*Puts paper into his pocket.*)

TATIANA (*sadly*). And you and the little woman will have all that!

MARTELLEAU. Oh, no—unfortunately they won't wait for her recovery. But—I must be getting on with the collection. Good day, madame.

TATIANA (*picks up cloth from table with all the food in it*). No—wait. You are not going away empty-handed. (*Gives the bundle to* MARTELLEAU) Take this to the little woman and the brat.
(MIKAIL *turns over on the bed and lies face down.*)

MARTELLEAU. But will you have anything left?

TATIANA. That doesn't matter. Go on—take it all.

MIKAIL (*lifts head*). Don't hesitate, my friend. She is a saint.

MARTELLEAU. Oh, I can see that. Madame, I can never repay you for this.

TATIANA. Yes, you can. Give me that newspaper.

MARTELLEAU. But, of course. . . . (*He hands her the paper.*)

TATIANA. No—don't go yet. Give this to the little woman and tell her to drink to the health of Russia. (*Gives him champagne.*)

MARTELLEAU (*overcome with emotion*). Thank you—thank you— God bless you and preserve you. . . . (*He goes out.*)

TATIANA. It really doesn't matter whether the victory is celebrated in room four or in room sixteen. (*She closes the door after him and turns to face* MIKAIL) You weren't really hungry, were you, darling? Tell me that you weren't.

MIKAIL. Oh, no, I was not hungry.

TATIANA. No more was I. (*Kneels by him. She looks at the paper*) Two well-heated rooms—servants' lift—one Sunday out of two. . . . Absolute paradise!

MIKAIL. Are you trying to tell me that we might be a married couple?

TATIANA (*exultantly. Rises*). Yes, yes, yes! You the butler and I the housemaid!

MIKAIL. But are we fitted for such grandeur?

TATIANA. Why not? you have been a chamberlain and I a lady-in-waiting.

MIKAIL. That was in Petersburg, for the Tsar!

TATIANA. And this is in Paris—but still for the Tsar!

MIKAIL (*excitedly. Rising*). My sainted darling! I believe it is possible! I see myself again, throwing open the windows of the Imperial chamber and announcing: "Majesty, there is snow"—and then, with perfect grace, presenting belt and tunic to Nicholas Alexandrovitch. And you doing the fair hair of Her Imperial Highness, fetching her gloves, telling poor Frederiks that Her Majesty will not be visible to-day. We were good servants, Tatiana. We will be good servants again! I must find my boots!

TATIANA. But wait . . .

MIKAIL. We wait for nothing! The command is "forward!"

TATIANA. But we shall need references. (*Points to newspaper.*)

MIKAIL. References? We shall provide them at once. Sit down at the table and write.

TATIANA. What shall I say?

MIKAIL. "The undersigned, the Grand Duchess Tatiana Petrovna, Princess Ouratieva, states that she has had in her service . . ."

TATIANA. Service. How do you spell it, with an s or a c?

MIKAIL. Which looks better? (*He has gone out and started to hurl himself into his clothes.*)

TATIANA. Service . . . c!

MIKAIL. C, then! ". . . in her service Michel Popoff and his wife Tina Popoff."

TATIANA. Popoff will not do. They'll think we made it up. The name will be Dubrovsky. You remember the dentist in St. Petersburg . . . his name was Dubrovsky.

MIKAIL. Don't stop for reminiscences. Continue. "From January 1919 until today. They are faithful, loyal, exceptionally intelligent, skillful, honest and they do not drink."

TATIANA. Do not drink. Do you suppose they have vodka in this house?

MIKAIL. If not, they soon will. Continue. "And I am pleased to recommend them in the highest possible terms. . . ." And then you sign.

TATIANA. Well, I hope that my right hand does not wither for this.

MIKAIL. And underneath write: "Spoletto, October 30, 1925." (*He returns.*)

TATIANA. Spoletto? Is there such a place?

MIKAIL. I don't know, but it sounds vaguely fashionable and yet remote. We don't want them making inquiries. (MIKAIL *takes down flag and sword.*)

TATIANA (*reading reference*). Do you think we've said enough about our good points?

MIKAIL. We mustn't exaggerate. Go and put on your hat.

TATIANA. You know the Duke of Courlande may object to us leaving so abruptly.

MIKAIL. We're not leaving officially. We are going for a little walk. Hurry. (*Puts ikon out.*)

TATIANA. We ought to see him before we leave. He might give us a reference.

MIKAIL. Put on your hat.
(TATIANA *exits. He puts sword and flag on washstand, gets bag off table, takes ikon down, puts it into bag. He is about to leave when* MARTELLEAU *knocks.*)

MARTELLEAU (*coming in*). Your pardon—Excellency—but I thought you'd be pleased to know she gobbled up everything except the caviar—she was afraid of that.

MIKAIL (*hopefully*). You've brought it back?

MARTELLEAU. No. Just to show her she needn't be afraid, I ate it in front of her. (*Folds up cloth, puts it on table.* TATIANA *enters.*)

TATIANA. Are you ready, my pigeon?

MARTELLEAU. Oh, madame, you are a saint. And this day you have earned a higher place in heaven. (TATIANA *gives him flowers.*)

MIKAIL. With a servants' lift, I hope!
(MARTELLEAU *exits, saying, "Thank you, madame."*)

TATIANA. Are you ready, my pigeon?

MIKAIL. Come here, Tina. (*Folds flag, puts it around her neck like a scarf*) At least, we shall go with flying colors.

TATIANA. And the sword? We can't be going for a little walk with a sword!

MIKAIL. I have plans for that. (*He takes the sword and puts it down the right leg of his trousers, gives a cry of pain.*)

TATIANA. You're wounded?

MIKAIL. No—it's damn cold. Does it show much?

TATIANA. You will become used to it. It is a long walk to the Avenue de Tourville.

MIKAIL (*looking round, takes a pair of socks off line, puts them in his coat pocket*). Is there anything else?

TATIANA (*looking round*). Yes. Let us finish the vodka. (*She gets the bottle off the washstand, fills the two glasses, gives him one*) This is for courage! (*They drink Russian fashion, link arms.*)

MIKAIL. A life for the Tsar, Tatiana Petrovna.

TATIANA. A life for the Tsar, Mikail Alexandrovich. (*When they finish they throw the glasses on the floor.* MIKAIL *picks up the shopping bag and limps to the door.*)

MIKAIL. Come now, we mustn't keep our employers waiting. (*Throws open door*) Proceed, Highness! (*Bows.*)

TATIANA. Don't try to bow! (*They go out.*)

CURTAIN

SCENE II

FERNANDE DUPONT'S *boudoir. It is chic, modernistic, but containing an unuttered confession of bourgeois bad taste.*

There are three doors: one leading to FERNANDE'S *bedroom, another to* CHARLES'S *bedroom and a third to the main part of the house. There are some chairs, a window seat and a dressing table, and a desk.*

The DUPONTS *are middle-aged, dull, wealthy and harassed.*

FERNANDE, *wearing a peignoir, is seated at dressing table, trying to put her shoe on.* CHARLES *enters with a black shoe on left foot, red slipper on right.*

FERNANDE. Charles! Where is your other shoe?

CHARLES. That's what I came in here for—to find out. The damned thing has vanished.

FERNANDE. Have you looked under your bed?

CHARLES. Yes—and in it. I can't find anything in this house. Really, Fernande—I don't want to keep harping on it, but when in God's name are we going to have some servants?

FERNANDE. Don't ask *me*—I can do nothing . . .

CHARLES. But it's your job, isn't it? Or am I supposed to manage this house as well as the grumbling stockholders who hammer and yammer at me all day?

FERNANDE. I've seen dozens of servants in the past week. They were all either escaped convicts or congenital idiots.

CHARLES. Well—if you see any more escaped convicts, engage

them. Either that or we'll move to a hotel. (*He bends down to look under the desk, but suddenly straightens up, holding his forehead*) Oh!

FERNANDE. What's the matter?

CHARLES. I have the most horrible headache.

FERNANDE. Then go and take some aspirin.

CHARLES. I've already swallowed the whole bottle. But it's some kind of neuralgia. It's like a dentist's drill boring into my brain, here. (*Points to his super-orbital nerve.*)

FERNANDE (*stroking his head*). My poor darling!

CHARLES (*capitalizing her rare sympathy*). I don't see how I'm going to stand much more of this, Fernande. I think I'll have to go away somewhere—if there's any place left on earth where you don't hear endless talk about economic chaos—and threats of war—and the collapse of civilization—and where I won't ever have to dress for dinner. What on *earth* do you suppose has happened to my other shoe?

FERNANDE. Here! I'll look for it. (*There is a knock at the door*) Come in!
(LOUISE *enters. She is the cook—fat, competent and calm.*)

LOUISE. Madame, it is another married couple.

FERNANDE. What are they like?

CHARLES. Never *mind* what they're like! We want them!

LOUISE. She has a funny accent.

CHARLES. Accent?

LOUISE. Probably Swiss.

FERNANDE. They don't sound trustworthy.

CHARLES. Nevertheless, we shall see them. The time has passed when we could afford to be fussy about accents.

FERNANDE. Very well, Louise. Bring them in!

LOUISE. Yes, madame.

CHARLES (*to* FERNANDE). If they are half human don't let them get away.

LOUISE (*appearing in the doorway*). This way—in here!
(TATIANA *and* MIKAIL *come in, dressed as when we last saw them.* MIKAIL *still stiff-legged from the concealed sword. They present themselves with an air of dignified deference.*)

FERNANDE (*cordially*). Come in—both of you!

CHARLES (*cheerily*). Good evening.

MIKAIL (*with a slight bow*). Sir—Madame!

TATIANA (*to* CHARLES). Good evening.

FERNANDE. You're looking for a place?

MIKAIL. Yes, madame; we saw your esteemed advertisement and so we are here . . .

TATIANA. We are eager to serve you, madame.

FERNANDE (*suspiciously*). Weren't you happy in your previous place?

TATIANA (*eagerly*). Ah, yes, madame. We have always been divinely happy—even when . . .

MIKAIL (*interrupting*). But our employers went abroad.

CHARLES. Are you Swiss?

MIKAIL. We are Russian, sir.

TATIANA. White Russian.

CHARLES. Who were your previous employers?

MIKAIL. His Highness General Prince Mikail Alexandrovitch Ouratieff.

TATIANA. And his wife, Her Imperial Highness the Grand Duchess Tatiana Petrovna.

CHARLES (*impressed*). Really! (*Fastens up braces.*)

FERNANDE. You have references, of course?

TATIANA. Oh, yes, madame. (MIKAIL *hands the reference to* FERNANDE.)

CHARLES. Where else have you been in service?

TATIANA. For a while we were with the Duke of Courlande.

MIKAIL (*silencing her*). That was merely a visit.

FERNANDE. This reference is most encouraging—"faithful—loyal—exceptionally intelligent." Evidently you pleased the Grand Duchess. I shall ask for an interview with her.

TATIANA. Oh, no, madame. Her Highness is in—in—where *is* Her Highness?

MIKAIL (*thinking very hard*). Let me see . . .

FERNANDE. This is written from Spoletto.

MIKAIL. Spoletto! That is right.

FERNANDE. Did you have another place before you were with Her Highness?

TATIANA. Yes, madame. We had another master in Russia.

CHARLES. Who?

TATIANA. He is dead. (*Both she and* MIKAIL *cross themselves.*)

CHARLES. Yes, yes. Killed in the Revolution?

MIKAIL. Yes, sir.

FERNANDE. I can see that you *are* loyal. What wages do you expect?

MIKAIL (*vaguely*). Wages, madame?

FERNANDE. How much do you expect to be paid?

TATIANA (*helplessly*). We don't know, madame. We don't know at all.

FERNANDE. Well—what did you receive in your last place?

MIKAIL. Let me see—just what was it, Tati—Tina?

TATIANA. I can't quite remember—not a billion—not a million—not a thousand—

FERNANDE. I should hope not.

CHARLES (*helpfully*). Perhaps you're not very familiar with *French* money.
(TATIANA *nods "Yes" to* CHARLES.)

MIKAIL. That's it, sir! That's it exactly!

FERNANDE (*with some impatience*). It doesn't matter. Whatever it was, I shall give—seven hundred francs to the butler and four hundred to the maid.

TATIANA. No; that will not do!

FERNANDE. I consider it a very good wage.

MIKAIL (*to* TATIANA). It is a most magnificent wage!

TATIANA. No! Four hundred for the butler and seven hundred for the maid.

FERNANDE. You may arrange that between yourselves.

CHARLES. When can you come to us?

MIKAIL (*with a glance at* TATIANA). When, sir?

CHARLES. We are in a great hurry.

MIKAIL. Then we could arrange to start, let us say—now.

CHARLES. Splendid! Well, Fernande, I don't think we need ask any more questions.

FERNANDE (*in an undertone*). Do you think they'll do?

CHARLES. I'm positive of it.
(*While the* DUPONTS *are talking to each other,* MIKAIL *and* TATIANA *are whispering.*)

FERNANDE. There's something about them that doesn't seem quite genuine.

CHARLES. We'll never know until we've tried them. Between them they may at least find my other shoe.

FERNANDE. Very well. You are engaged.

MIKAIL (*bowing*). Ah, thank you, madame.

TATIANA (*at the same time*). May the Great Father bless and preserve you, godly woman.

FERNANDE. You'll be here on a temporary basis, of course. Where is your luggage?

TATIANA. It's . . .

MIKAIL. It has ceased to exist, Madame.

CHARLES. Haven't you even a dress suit?

MIKAIL. No, sir.

FERNANDE. But how did you dress at Her Highness's?

MIKAIL. In Russian fashion, madame: boots, wide breeches, blue belt and bright red shirt, with dagger in here. (*Pointing to his chest.*)

CHARLES. Very picturesque. But I hardly think that would be quite the costume for our needs.

FERNANDE. And you?

TATIANA. Also in Russian fashion, madame: short, pleated skirt, flowered blouse, low neck, bare arms, and silver-tipped pins in the hair.

CHARLES (*beaming*). Well, that sounds rather attractive.

FERNANDE. In this house you will have to become used to dressing like other servants.

MIKAIL. White tie, madame?

CHARLES. With black waistcoat.

FERNANDE. We have the clothes worn by your predecessors. They will fit well enough.

MIKAIL. We shall be proud to adjust ourselves, madame.

FERNANDE. There are four of us here—Monsieur Dupont, your master (MIKAIL *and* TATIANA *bow*), and myself (MIKAIL *and* TATIANA *bow again*), and our two children, Monsieur George and Mademoiselle Helene. (MIKAIL *and* TATIANA *are delighted*) And I want you to bear in mind, at all times, that we are particularly strict in the matter of our accounts with the tradespeople. (*To* CHARLES) I seem to have heard that Russians are apt to be careless about money.

MIKAIL AND TATIANA (*together*). Oh, no, madame!

MIKAIL. We have been trained to guard every last sou.

FERNANDE. You'll be required to do so with us. Monsieur Dupont is a banker and the slightest sign of irregularity . . .

MIKAIL. I beg your pardon, madame?

FERNANDE. Well?

MIKAIL. Did you say that Monsieur is a banker?

FERNANDE. Yes.
(MIKAIL *starts to leave but is stopped by* TATIANA.)

CHARLES. Have you any particular objection to bankers?

TATIANA. No!

MIKAIL (*recollecting himself*). Oh, no, sir. Pray forgive me. I was only thinking of my master, Prince Ouratieff. He loathed bankers with a loathing . . .

CHARLES. You'll make an effort to forget the prejudices of your former employers.

MIKAIL (*humbly*). Yes, sir.

FERNANDE. Come with me. I'll take you to the kitchen. (*She goes out.* MIKAIL *steps aside to let* TATIANA *pass first, bowing slightly as she goes out.*)

CHARLES. You—wait!

MIKAIL. Yes, sir?

CHARLES. What's your name?

MIKAIL. Dubrovsky, sir. Michel Dubrovsky.

CHARLES. Michel will be enough. I've lost my other shoe. Look for it! (MIKAIL *glances at* CHARLES's *feet.*)

MIKAIL. Red or black, sir?

CHARLES. Black. (MIKAIL *goes to window; looks up*) I don't think you'll find it on the balcony. (MIKAIL *looks in flowers*) Look under the dressing-table.

MIKAIL. Yes, sir. (*He starts to kneel down by table and stretches his right leg straight behind him.*)

CHARLES. Good God! Have you got a wooden leg?

MIKAIL. Oh, no, sir—no!

CHARLES. Then, what's the matter with you?

MIKAIL. Rheumatism, sir. (*He straightens up with difficulty.*)

CHARLES. Does it trouble you much?

MIKAIL. No, sir—only when I undergo a sudden change of climate. You see, sir, I've just come from the south. It will be well in no time, I assure you.
(FERNANDE *enters.*)

CHARLES. Let us trust so.

FERNANDE. Charles, I want Michel to go and change now: whatever you want him to do can wait. You will find the kitchen through that hall on the right.

CHARLES. Very well, you may go, and don't forget—

MIKAIL. The shoe. No, sir. Sir, Madame! (*He goes out.*)

FERNANDE (*sits at dressing table*). I think they make a rather good impression, on the whole.

CHARLES. He's rheumatic. I don't like that.

FERNANDE. Oh, we'll soon find a remedy for that. The main point is, that I approve of his manners.

CHARLES. I like her better.

FERNANDE (*acidly*). I noticed that. I saw the way you looked at her.

CHARLES. What do you mean?

FERNANDE. She has a very melting expression. Most effective.

CHARLES. Do you realize you're talking about a servant?

FERNANDE. Yes, my dear. But also —a Russian.

CHARLES. Russian or Swede or Annamite, I'm not interested in housemaids, and I don't at all like the implication that I noticed her looks, melting or otherwise.

FERNANDE. Now, Charles—don't get excited.

CHARLES. I'm not excited. I'm only telling you that I leave servants to the tradesmen. So please don't insult me by assuming that . . . (*The door opens and* GEORGE *and* HELENE *come in. They are as formal and snobbish as their parents; she is about eighteen and he twenty.*)

GEORGE. Who are those two odd-looking people with Louise?

CHARLES. Our new servants—but judging by your mother's attitude—I'm afraid they will not grow gray in our service. (*He goes out.*)

HELENE. Really, mother, can't we ever have decent-looking servants in this house?

FERNANDE. Is there anything wrong with their appearance?

GEORGE. He looks more like a waiter than a butler.

HELENE. She seems a cheap, impudent little thing.

FERNANDE. Perhaps you two superior beings will be interested to know that they worked for six years for Prince Ouratieff. . . .

HELENE. Prince *who?*

FERNANDE. Prince Ouratieff and his wife, the Grand Duchess Tatiana Petrovna.

GEORGE (*laughing*). Ah! Then, that accounts for it.

FERNANDE. Accounts for what?

GEORGE. They're Russians!

FERNANDE. And what has that to do with it?

HELENE. You've let yourself be taken in. You probably believed everything they told you.

FERNANDE. They had a most glowing reference from Her Highness.

GEORGE. My dear mother, don't you know that *all* Russians are Princes and Grand Duchesses—or Generals, at the very least?

FERNANDE. I'm not listening to a word you say—or you either, Helene. I only want to beg you not to treat these people like dirt under your feet, as you did with François and Berthe. They'd have been with us yet if it hadn't been for you.

GEORGE. Then I'm very sorry.

FERNANDE. Oh, are you?

GEORGE. François and Berthe weren't much, but at least they weren't foreigners.

FERNANDE. When you speak to Michel and Tina, please address them by name. Not—hey—or psst. And if you have to make insulting remarks about them, wait until they have left the room. And as for you, Helene . . .

HELENE (*calmly*). Yes, mother?

FERNANDE. The butler in this house has a great many duties more important than taking your Pekinese out for a walk every hour.

GEORGE. I see. You mean, you want us to coddle them.

FERNANDE. I don't expect you to make the slightest effort. I know that would be asking too much. But don't do anything to drive them out of the house before your father and I decide it's time for them to go. Will you be dining at home tonight?

HELENE. No. I'm dining with the Comtesse de Maupendy. There's to

be a rehearsal of that dreary Venetian fête, and she wants me to be
one of the musicians.

GEORGE. You're not going to try to
play that guitar of mine?

HELENE (*defiantly*). It's for the
benefit of the orphans!

GEORGE. God help them!

HELENE. Shut up.

FERNANDE. For Heaven's sake stop
fighting!

HELENE. But he's so damned rude.

FERNANDE. You're both rude! Insufferable! Where are you going,
George?

GEORGE (*proudly*). To the Club.
I'm going to fence with Aldonadi,
the World Champion.

HELENE (*quietly*). God help *you*.
(CHARLES *returns*.)

CHARLES. Helene, when you last
saw that Pekinese of yours, did it
by any chance have a dress shoe in
its mouth?

HELENE. I don't think so, father.

CHARLES (*to* FERNANDE). What's
wrong with the bells in this house?
I've been ringing and ringing. (*He
has crossed to door and flung it
open, revealing* MIKAIL *and* TA-
TIANA *on the threshold. They are
wearing their servants' clothes*)
What are you two standing there
for? Eavesdropping?

MIKAIL. We were waiting, sir.

CHARLES. What for?

MIKAIL. To be summoned, sir.

CHARLES. Evidently you haven't
heard about electric bells for summoning purposes.

TATIANA. Oh, yes—we heard them
ringing and ringing. They have a
lovely sound.

CHARLES. Come in!

FERNANDE. This is my daughter,
Mademoiselle Helene.

TATIANA, MIKAIL. How do you do!

FERNANDE. And my son, Monsieur
George.

MIKAIL, TATIANA (*cordially*). How
do you do? (*Bow to* GEORGE.)

GEORGE. Quite well, thank you.

FERNANDE. Come with me, Tina.

TATIANA. Yes, madame.
(FERNANDE *goes out*. TATIANA
starts to follow, but GEORGE's *feet
are in her way, forcing her to make
a detour.*)

CHARLES. Haven't you found . . .

MIKAIL. Your shoe? No, sir.

CHARLES. Well—go in there and
look for it.

MIKAIL. Very good, sir. (*He goes,
humming, into* CHARLES's *bedroom.*)

CHARLES. What was that strange
noise he was making?

HELENE (*laughing*). He was humming.

CHARLES. Did anyone ask him to hum?

GEORGE. Perhaps that's a Russian custom. I know, at the White Eagle, all the waiters sing. Well—I must dress. (*To* CHARLES) I'll let you know if I come across your shoe. (*Exits humming loudly.*)

HELENE. You have my deepest sympathy, father.

CHARLES. Have I asked for it?

HELENE. I hope you escape from darkest Russia. (*She goes out.*)

CHARLES. You needn't worry about those Russians. . . . They'll be out of this house tomorrow. Both of them! (CHARLES *goes to a mirror to straighten his tie.* MIKAIL *comes in, bearing* CHARLES's *shoe on a little salver, like Cinderella's slipper.*)

MIKAIL. Your shoe, sir. (*He kneels*) Permit me, sir. (*Lifts* CHARLES's *foot.* CHARLES *stumbles*) Lean on me, sir. (MIKAIL *with deft dexterity starts to put the shoe on and to lace it.* CHARLES *watches him, impressed in spite of himself.*)

CHARLES. Michel.

MIKAIL. Yes, sir.

CHARLES. I have something to say to you.

MIKAIL. Yes, sir?

CHARLES. Do you always hum at your work?

MIKAIL. Did you say "hum," sir?

CHARLES. When I sent you in there to look for my shoe, you were humming, unmistakably.

MIKAIL (*he stands up*). You're quite right, sir. So I was. It was a sensation of joy, sir, at being in your service. It shan't happen again, sir, I assure you. And now, sir—may I fetch you some medicine?

CHARLES. Medicine? What for?

MIKAIL. For your headache, sir.

CHARLES. How did you know I have a headache?

MIKAIL. I can see it in your eyes, sir—a struggle against intolerable pain.

CHARLES. You're very observant, but medicine will do me no good. This is a headache that only the guillotine could cure. Do you know how to use the telephone?

MIKAIL. Oh, yes, sir.

CHARLES. It's over there. Get me Litré — thirty - five - nine. (MIKAIL *goes to the telephone. Starts to dial*) You're not limping any more.

MIKAIL. No, sir. I saw that my rheumatism displeased you.

CHARLES. Ask to speak to Monsieur Chauffourier-Dubieff.

MIKAIL. Monsieur who, sir?

CHARLES. Chauffourier-Dubieff.

MIKAIL. Do you mean the Governor of the Bank of France?

CHARLES. Certainly.

MIKAIL. Oh, sir, do I have to speak to him?

CHARLES. Why not? Do your former master's prejudices against bankers prevent you from addressing the Governor . . . ?

MIKAIL. Excuse me, sir. (*Assumes slightly false voice*) Hello, Monsieur Chauffourier-Dubieff, please. . . .

CHARLES. If he's there, I'll speak to him.

MIKAIL (*puts hand over phone*). What name, sir?

CHARLES. What!

MIKAIL. Your name, sir?

CHARLES. That's funny! (*Suddenly remembers*) Dupont.

MIKAIL. Hello? M. Chauffourier-Dubieff? M. Dupont wishes to speak to you. Hold the phone, please. (*He hands the telephone to* CHARLES *and starts to go.*)

CHARLES. No, wait, Michel. (*Into the telephone*) Hello, Chauffourier . . . Well enough, except for a splitting headache . . . Yes—I suppose we all have them these days. . . . I'll be a little late, I'm afraid, and we may not have a chance to talk together. So I'm anxious to know if you've had any word about that Bakoura oil business . . . Who? You've seen him? What did he say? I see . . . Yes . . . I thought he'd be difficult. What about the Royal-Dutch interests? I see . . . They're shrewd

devils, those Soviet Commissars. . . . Yes, it's all pretty damned discouraging . . . No—not a word. I'll be with you in about half an hour. Good-bye. (*He puts the telephone down and stands for a moment with his hand to his head, a figure of suffering.* CHARLES *groans.* MIKAIL *takes phone, puts it down.*)

MIKAIL. Please, sir—we really must do something about that headache.

CHARLES. *We* must?

MIKAIL. Yes, sir. There's a Russian remedy that's infallible.

CHARLES. Some sort of witch-craft, I suppose?

MIKAIL. No, sir, it's entirely scientific. My former master, Prince Ouratieff, made use of it quite often with immediate results.

CHARLES. You have the ingredients?

MIKAIL. The cook will help me find them, sir.

CHARLES. You're sure it's harmless?

MIKAIL. Utterly, sir.

CHARLES. Then go ahead and mix it. It won't do any good.

MIKAIL. Excuse me, sir—have you a shot gun?

CHARLES. Why—yes—but what in God's name—? (MIKAIL *goes out.* TATIANA *comes in swiftly and without knocking. Furiously*) Can't you knock?

TATIANA (*turns*). Knock what, sir?

CHARLES. At the door! You're not supposed to come bursting into rooms without giving warning. . . .

TATIANA. But I did give warning, sir. I scratched.

CHARLES. Do you always scratch?

TATIANA (*gets fur wrap out of closet*). Always, sir. The Grand Duchess objected to knocking. It frightened her. It meant only one thing to her—Bolsheviks! And the Grand Duchess . . .

CHARLES. If you'll pardon me for saying so, my girl—I'm pretty damned tired of the Grand Duchess and her peculiar ways. In fact, I'm beginning to understand why they *had* a revolution in Russia.

TATIANA (*flaming*). There would have been no revolution if it hadn't been for bankers!

CHARLES. How dare you speak to me in that way? You're an insubordinate, ill-bred, foreign . . .

TATIANA (*passionately*). I know it, sir! I know it! And I deserve the punishment you're going to give me.

CHARLES. Punishment? I'm not going to do anything more than tell you to leave. . . .

TATIANA. What am I? (*Kneels*) A housemaid—a servant—a slave—nothing! And when Russia was Russia, a servant who talked back to her master was whipped, and lifted by her ears and dipped into ice-cold water.

CHARLES (*conciliatory*). They went too far in Russia—in every way.

We don't do any of those things here . . .

TATIANA (*forcefully*). You must do them! (*Grabs his legs*) The master is the master! (*With disgust*) And the servant is the servant.

CHARLES. Please let go of my legs.

TATIANA. We receive money and food, and if we answer back, you must strike us, or God will!

CHARLES (*deeply embarrassed*). Come, my girl, all this isn't so very serious. I have no intention of lifting you by your ears.

TATIANA. Then you forgive me, sir?

CHARLES (*gently*). Yes, but please get up. (*He lifts her up.*)

TATIANA. And you will give me the kiss of reconciliation?

CHARLES (*starting*). What?

TATIANA. When the master forgives, he gives the servant the kiss of reconciliation—on the brow. (*She lifts her face to him.*)

CHARLES (*backs to chair*). I see . . . (*Hesitating*) Well. . . .

TATIANA. Does it disgust you, sir?

CHARLES. No . . . Well, not exactly. (*He places a perfunctory and haughty kiss upon her forehead.*)

TATIANA. Thank you, sir. (*She starts to go.*)

CHARLES (*struck by an idea*). Tina!

TATIANA. Sir?

CHARLES. Suppose your husband offended me. Would I—would *he* offer me his brow to be kissed?

TATIANA. Oh, no, sir . . . (*Quietly*) When one forgives a man, it is upon the mouth! (*She goes out.*) (CHARLES *hears something, and turns towards the door.* MIKAIL *enters. He carries a silver tray; upon it, a claret glass full to the brim of a liquid which looks like water.*)

CHARLES (*furiously*). Oh, you scratch too! You can't knock, I suppose?

MIKAIL (*with respectful confusion*). I'm very sorry, sir. (*Coming up to* CHARLES) Have I offended you, sir?

CHARLES (*drawing back*). No, no, my friend. (MIKAIL *offers* CHARLES *the glass*) What is that? (*Looking at it*) Is it water?

MIKAIL (*respectfully*). Oh, no, sir. (*Offering the glass*) It is a recipe, sir. There is no record of a headache that could resist it. His Imperial Majesty himself. . . .

CHARLES. All right, all right. (*Holding the glass, with skepticism*) Has it a nasty taste?

MIKAIL. No, sir. As it goes down one can detect no taste whatever.

CHARLES. You're sure there's nothing harmful . . . ?

MIKAIL (*with deferent authority*). I know, sir, that if I have misrepresented the facts in any way the penalty for me will be a ghastly lingering death, with red hot bayonets in my eyeballs and . . .

CHARLES. Never mind. I believe you. (*Puts glass to his lips.*)

MIKAIL. Do not breathe, sir. Drink it off in one gulp. (CHARLES *takes his courage in both hands, raises the glass to his lips and gulps it down. A pause. He has a terrible spasm, such as one imagines a condemned man having in an electric chair. Then he becomes totally motionless, paralyzed.* MIKAIL *watches him with serenity*) Do you see anything, sir?

CHARLES. Butterflies.

MIKAIL. They will pass, sir.

CHARLES (*puts glass on tray*). What's in that infernal stuff? (*Takes out cigarette case.*)

MIKAIL. Pure gin—with twenty drops of ether, a hundred grains of salt and a hundred and fifty grains of gunpowder.

CHARLES. Gunpowder!

MIKAIL. Yes, sir!—I took the liberty of opening one of your cartridges. (*Lights match.*)

CHARLES. Gunpowder! (*Looks at cigarette*) Good God! If I light a cigarette will I explode?

MIKAIL. No, sir—(*Lights cigarette*) the powder is damp. And—may I inquire after your headache, sir?

CHARLES (*remembering it*). Headache? It—it seems to have gone.

MIKAIL. It never fails, sir. Now—if you will permit me. (*He undoes* CHARLES's *necktie and starts to retie it.*)

CHARLES. Are all Russians mad?

MIKAIL. Oh, yes, sir—quite. (*He hurls himself at the dressing table and returns with a hair-brush. He brushes* CHARLES'S *temples caressingly. Returns brush and then smooths* CHARLES'S *forehead with his palms*) Wonderful, isn't it, sir?

CHARLES. Yes! What's wonderful?

MIKAIL. The sensation in one's head just after the ache has moved out. (*He hurries into* CHARLES'S *room.*)

CHARLES. Yes, I suppose it is. (MIKAIL *returns with dinner jacket, puts it on.* "Permit me, sir," *takes out handkerchief, folds it, replaces it*) You know—Michel. . . .

MIKAIL. Yes, sir?

CHARLES. I'm beginning to think that you'll do.

MIKAIL. Thank you, sir.

CHARLES. In fact—I think you're going to please me very much.

MIKAIL. Oh, sir, you're a man of God. (*Leans over and imprints a kiss on* CHARLES'S *shoulder.*)

CHARLES (*startled*). Hey! What are you doing?

MIKAIL (*simply*). The kiss on the shoulder, sir. The kiss of gratitude.

CHARLES. You people seem to have spent your entire lives *kissing* each other.

MIKAIL (*with deep melancholy*). No, sir. We didn't always have cause for gratitude! (MIKAIL *brings hand mirror, holds it up before* CHARLES).

CHARLES. Well—I'll be a lot happier if you'll leave kissing out of your daily duties while you're here —you and your wife, too.

MIKAIL. Have I annoyed you, sir?

CHARLES. No, my friend,—no. (FERNANDE *comes in.*)

MIKAIL. Very good, sir.

FERNANDE. Oh—Charles—I must tell you—Tina says the Russians have a most marvelous cure for headache.

CHARLES. I know about it. It's similar to blasting. (*Catches* MIKAIL'S *eye.* MIKAIL *bows, exits.*)

FERNANDE. What do you think of him?
(*A knock at the door.*)

CHARLES. I don't know what I think.

FERNANDE. Come in.
(TATIANA *comes in carrying handbag. She looks at* CHARLES *as much as to say* "Was that better?" *Taps door post.*)

TATIANA (*picks up wrap and puts down bag on dressing table*). Your wrap, madame. (*Puts wrap on* FERNANDE.)

FERNANDE. Thank you. Good night, Tina. I hope you find your room comfortable.

TATIANA. Thank you, madame. Michel and I will wait up for you. (*Hands* FERNANDE *bag.*)

CHARLES. Come along—or we'll be late.

FERNANDE. Very well.

TATIANA. (*holding the door open*). Good evening, madame. (FERNANDE *goes out*) Good evening, sir.

CHARLES (*pause. Looks off after* FERNANDE). Er—good evening. (*He smiles benignly. He goes out.*) (TATIANA *blows a kiss after them and shuts door.*)

TATIANA. Mikail! Mikail!

MIKAIL (*off stage*). Coming, Tina! (*He comes in*) Well?

TATIANA. I say—God be praised!

MIKAIL. I join you in devout gratitude! Especially for the bed!

TATIANA. What bed?

MIKAIL. In our room. Didn't you notice it? It is magnificent!

TATIANA. No. I was looking out of the window, at the view. Mikail, we can see the cross on the orthodox church. We can see Russia! (*She kneels in the center of the stage.*)

MIKAIL (*goes and kneels by her*). Ah—my darling—that man didn't exaggerate. It is Paradise!

TATIANA. If we have to leave this place, I shall die.

MIKAIL. And I with you. (*He takes her in his arms.*)

TATIANA. These Duponts are people of God.

MIKAIL. And so is Louise, the cook. I had a whiff of the chicken she's cooking for us.

TATIANA. Oh, it can't be chicken!

MIKAIL. Chicken! Later, we'll teach her to cook it as they do in Kiev. We'll be good servants, won't we, Tatiana?

TATIANA. There will be none to compare with us in the whole land of France. We have been blessed with a home—at last—after all these long years. . . . A bed of our own—and a window that looks upon Russia. We will be worthy of such blessings!

MIKAIL. My sainted love. (*He kisses her.*)
(GEORGE *enters, carrying fencing foils, masks, gloves.*)

GEORGE. Oh! Am I disturbing you?

MIKAIL (*blithely*). Not at all, sir.

TATIANA. Of course not, sir.

MIKAIL. Are there any orders, sir?

GEORGE. I want you to clean these épées. What is your name again?

MIKAIL. Michel, sir.

GEORGE. Clean off the rust with paraffin. And wipe up these gloves and masks, too.

MIKAIL. Yes, sir.

GEORGE. I am using them tonight.

MIKAIL (*takes them, puts gloves and masks on chair. Examines foils*). If you will allow me, sir, I will change the points d'arrêt, these are badly blunted.

GEORGE. All right, change them. I am fencing with an Italian who goes at it like a bull!

MIKAIL. Oh, that cannot worry you, sir.

GEORGE. Why?

MIKAIL. You have a good reach. (*Takes arm*) Evade the blade rather than engage it.

GEORGE. You fence?

MIKAIL. I've played at it, sir. Does your opponent keep his point in line?

GEORGE. No.

MIKAIL. Then, I should not try to bind the blade too often, sir, or you'll be hit.

GEORGE. How?

MIKAIL. May I show you, sir? (*Hands foil to* GEORGE *and takes one himself.* TATIANA *places the spare foil on desk. They salute.* MIKAIL *hits* GEORGE.)

GEORGE. I wasn't ready. (*Takes position*) Start again.

MIKAIL. You had better put on your mask, sir.
(TATIANA *gives it to* GEORGE.)

GEORGE (*has put mask on.*) All right, come on. (*Whips air with foil, lunges.*)

MIKAIL. Yes! (*Puts his mask on. They fence.* GEORGE *is hit again*) That's what I mean, sir.

(GEORGE, *annoyed, takes off his coat.* TATIANA *takes it, puts it on window seat. Both men put on gloves.*)

GEORGE. On guard, Michel. (*They start to fence.* GEORGE *is hit on right wrist*) Touché.

TATIANA. Oh, please, Michel, let Monsieur George hit you once.

GEORGE. I don't want any favors; go and get the cocktails.

TATIANA. Yes, sir.

GEORGE. On guard, Michel!

MIKAIL. At your service, sir. (*They fence.* MIKAIL *forces* GEORGE *to retreat.* HELENE *enters with a guitar.*)

HELENE. George, have you gone crazy?

GEORGE. Shut up! He's a marvel! Come on, Michel.

MIKAIL. Very good, sir. (*They continue fencing.* MIKAIL *knocks* GEORGE'S *sword out of his hand and, pulling chair out to center, says*) Would you care to sit down, mademoiselle?

HELENE (*flabbergasted*). Thank you.
(MIKAIL *picks up the foil and returns it to* GEORGE.)

GEORGE. On guard.
(TATIANA *enters with cocktails on trolley.* MIKAIL *hits* GEORGE *again.*)

MIKAIL. I've told you before, sir, about binding the blade.

HELENE. That is enough. I want you to tune this guitar. (*Holds out guitar.*)

GEORGE. Tune it yourself. I'm busy! On guard!

TATIANA (*pushing forward*). Permit me, mademoiselle. (*She takes the guitar and starts to tune it.*)

GEORGE (*excitedly, as they fence*). Have you mixed the cocktails, Tina?

TATIANA. Yes, Monsieur George. (*She sits and starts singing "Ochi Chorniya."*)

HELENE. Is that a Russian tune?

TATIANA. Yes, mademoiselle. "Black Eyes."
(HELENE *gazes at* TATIANA. MIKAIL *and* GEORGE *continue to fence.*)

GEORGE. Pour out the cocktails, Tina.

HELENE. No—go on playing. I'll pour them. (MIKAIL *and* GEORGE *are fencing furiously.* HELENE *shakes the cocktails and then pours them*) Will you have one, George?

GEORGE. Yes.

MIKAIL. Keep your guard up, sir. (*He hits him.*)

GEORGE. Another hit! You're a genius! On guard, Michel.

MIKAIL. Very good, sir.
(HELENE *brings two cocktails to desk.*)

GEORGE (*pauses before taking up stance*). Will you have a cocktail, Michel?

MIKAIL. I should love one, sir.

GEORGE. Three cocktails, Helene.

MIKAIL. And perhaps one for my dear wife, Monsieur George?

GEORGE. Four cocktails, Helene! (*They start to fence.*)

MIKAIL. That's better, sir. That's much better! (*They are fencing rapidly.* TATIANA *picks up the rhythm of their clashing foils in her singing and playing.* HELENE *is happily pouring cocktails.*)

CURTAIN

ACT TWO

Scene I

Several weeks later. It is 7:45 in the evening. The DUPONTS' *large drawing-room. It is expensively, stodgily empire.*

A large door at the back leads into the hall, another door at the right to the bedrooms, and a third door at the left to the dining-room.

HELENE *is seated with a Russian dictionary in her hand.* GEORGE *is sitting on a table.*

HELENE. And what's the Russian word for, "Sir"?

GEORGE. Gospadin.

HELENE. "Friend?"

GEORGE. Droug.

HELENE. "Cigarette?"

GEORGE. Papirosha.

HELENE. "Brother?"

GEORGE. Brat.

HELENE. "Comrade?"

GEORGE (*pronouncing it wrongly*). Tovarich!

HELENE (*dreamily and more correctly*). No! Tovarich!

GEORGE (*repeating it correctly*). Tovarich!

HELENE (*still dreamily*). Tovarich Mikail!

GEORGE. They hate to be called that; it's the word the Bolsheviks use.

HELENE. It's a lovely word, Tovarich—Comrade. (*Looking at dictionary*) "It doesn't matter?"

GEORGE. What?

HELENE. "It doesn't matter"; you know, "don't worry."

GEORGE. Oh, nitchevo, nitchevo.

HELENE. "To love?"

GEORGE. Loubitz.

HELENE. "I love you?"

GEORGE. Ia wass loublou. (HELENE *closes the book*) Is that all?

HELENE. For today, yes.

GEORGE. What time is it?

HELENE. Half past seven. And we want to be well out of here before those stuffy guests arrive for dinner.

GEORGE. We'll be out of here, all right. I'll tell you—we'll have dinner at the Kasbek—some vodka, caviar, bortsch, and chicken cutlets Kiev. And then we'll go to the Russian Ballet and be back here in time to pick up Michel and Tina. It'll be great, won't it?

HELENE. Absolutely marvelous. We'll see what a real Russian party is like.

GEORGE. Personally, I'd rather stay at home with them, in the kitchen, playing poker. (*Turns away dreamily.*)

HELENE. How much did you lose last night?

GEORGE. Oh, nothing. A little over two thousand. But it's worth it. Just to watch her hands when she's shuffling the cards.

HELENE. What is the matter with you?

GEORGE. Oh, nothing. (*He pulls himself together and, with his hands in his pockets, goes toward the window, singing "The Volga Boat Song."*)

HELENE. Shut up!
(MIKAIL *enters. He closes the door*

and goes toward the dining-room door.)

GEORGE (*calling him*). Oh! Michel!

MIKAIL (*approaching him respectfully*). Monsieur George?

GEORGE (*who has taken out his pocket-book*). Prompt payment . . . (*He holds out two 1000-franc notes.*)

MIKAIL (*smiling and refusing the notes*). But I assure you, sir, that . . .

GEORGE (*cutting him short*). Be quiet! It's a debt of honor to the most graceful poker player in France. (*Bows.*)

MIKAIL (*takes money. Seriously*). But may I suggest to you, sir, that you should not play so high?

GEORGE. You shouldn't complain. You and Tina win all the time.

MIKAIL. Exactly, sir. It's becoming embarrassing.

HELENE (*interrupting*). Michel?

MIKAIL. Yes, mademoiselle.

HELENE. Where are you taking us tonight?

MIKAIL (*smiling*). You expressed a wish to see a Russian fête. Tonight we celebrate our New Year, although perhaps "celebrate" isn't quite the right word. It might be better to say that we lament it. All the homesick émigrés in Paris will be there. There'll be a great deal of exquisite sobbing. I hope that it will amuse you.

HELENE. I do hope father and mother will finish their stupid dinner early so that you'll be able to get away in time for the party.

MIKAIL. Don't worry, mademoiselle. Our party will last all night.

GEORGE. What do we wear—native dress?

MIKAIL. Oh, sir—a white tie will be quite in order. But—with your permission—I must set the table for dinner.

HELENE (*rushes after him*). Oh, Michel, I'll help you. And we'll have a drink of vodka together. (MIKAIL *exits.*)

GEORGE. Don't forget, Helene. The right way to say it is "Ia wass loublou."
(*She goes out. The hall door opens and* TATIANA *enters. She holds in her arms a huge vase full of flowers.*)

GEORGE (*rushes to her*). Tina . . . please let me help you. (*He runs to her and takes the vase of flowers almost violently in his tender indignation at seeing her carry such a burden.*)

TATIANA. Thank you, Monsieur George.

GEORGE. Where does it go?

MIKAIL. On the table here . . . (GEORGE *carries the vase to the table.* TATIANA *follows him and arranges the flowers in the vase*) You are kind, Monsieur George.

GEORGE (*soberly*). Kind! What does that mean? Kind! (*Passionately*) Don't you understand?

TATIANA (*Still arranging the flowers*). Dear little Monsieur George! What do I *not* understand?

GEORGE. Leave those flowers. (*With energy*) Tina! Ia wass loublou.

TATIANA (*drawing away her hands violently*). Oh! You mustn't say it like that!

GEORGE. But I mean it! Tina! (*He repeats ecstatically*) Ia wass loublou. Ia wass loublou. Ia wass loublou.

TATIANA (*gently*). No. (*Correcting the pronunciation*) *Ia wass loublou* —like that. The way you say it, it sounds like "little sick dog."

GEORGE (*impetuously*). I love you!

TATIANA. And it's right that you should. The master must love the servant! And the servant the master! I love you, too, Monsieur George.

GEORGE. Oh! But don't you see!— I love you passionately. Can't you understand that? Passionately! Wildly! It's the first time in my entire life that I've known what it is —I mean—to feel *real* love!

TATIANA (*tenderly*). Monsieur George—you are a dear little delightful boy—but you must not have wicked thoughts.

GEORGE (*turns away*). Is love wicked? Is there anything wrong or unnatural about . . .

TATIANA (*softly*). Yes! Because if you love me, you want to sleep with me!

GEORGE (*perishing the thought*). Oh—no!

TATIANA. Oh—yes! You couldn't have any other idea in declaring your passion for me, a housemaid.

GEORGE. You are not like any other housemaid that ever lived.

TATIANA. No—I'm superior—I realize that. But it isn't right for a beautiful, distinguished young man like you to think like that about even the best housemaid. You know it isn't!

GEORGE. I know that I am only happy at night, when mother and father have gone to bed, and Helene and I go to the kitchen, on tiptoe . . . and when you sing, and deal the cards with those exquisite little hands. . . . (*Takes her hands.*)

TATIANA. And Michel pours out the vodka. (*Removes her hands from his*) Don't forget Michel! He cleans your boots and brushes your clothes and teaches you fencing. . . .

GEORGE. That's his job!

TATIANA. But it is not his job to be a deceived husband!

GEORGE. Tina! I have money. I can make you as happy as a princess.

TATIANA (*gently*). A princess! I only want to be as happy as a housemaid.

GEORGE. Haven't you any ambition?

TATIANA. Oh, yes, Monsieur George. To be a good and faithful servant.

GEORGE. Tina! Have you ever been unfaithful to Michel?

TATIANA. Never! Once I was violated . . .

GEORGE. Tina!

TATIANA (*with supreme detachment*). By one of the Bolsheviks.

GEORGE (*furious*). The swine!

TATIANA. Oh—no. Not a swine. He was just a man who happened to have the advantage. It was the usual thing at the time . . . It didn't matter.

GEORGE. You can stand there and say that. . . .

TATIANA. Yes, little Monsieur George—I can stand here and say it didn't matter. And I can say that you're a nice, darling boy. . . . (*All of a sudden she kisses him very quickly on the mouth.*)

GEORGE (*in ecstasy*). Tina!

TATIANA. And you mustn't think about me any more.

GEORGE. Tina!

TATIANA. Because this kind of foolishness bores me—it bores me very much indeed.
(CHARLES *comes in.*)

GEORGE. Tina! I won't stand for it. I tell you—I won't stand for it!

CHARLES. Won't stand for what?

GEORGE (*flustered*). I was . . . I . . .

TATIANA. Monsieur George was displeased with the way I made the Martini cocktails last night.

CHARLES (*glaring at* GEORGE). Oh —*was* he?

TATIANA. Yes, sir—it seems I stupidly used the wrong vermouth. I'm very sorry, Monsieur George.

CHARLES. A most natural mistake. But I must tell you something, young man: if I ever again hear you addressing Tina in that rude, offensive tone of voice—well—you're almost grown up now so I may not thrash you as you deserve, but I can find other ways to make life extremely unpleasant for you.

TATIANA. Oh, sir—it was all my fault.

GEORGE (*angrily to* CHARLES). It was nothing of the kind! I . . .

CHARLES. I don't care to hear any more from you. Now—kindly leave the room.

GEORGE (*after a moment*). Very well. Very well . . . I shall kindly leave the room. (*He bows to* TATIANA *and stalks out.*)

CHARLES (*with fervent sincerity*). I regret very much that this has happened.

TATIANA. You must not blame him, sir. He's such a sweet little boy!

CHARLES. I do blame him—and myself—for having allowed such bad manners to develop in my son. Come here, Tina.

TATIANA. Yes, sir?

CHARLES. I want you to forgive me.

TATIANA. Of course, sir—but there's really nothing to . . .

CHARLES. No—you must forgive me—in the Russian way . . . the kiss on the brow.

TATIANA (*with a slight smile*). All right, sir . . . (*She kisses him.*)

CHARLES (*he takes her hands and kisses them*). You have the most extraordinary eyes, Tina. Melting, that's what they are—melting.

TATIANA (*with a slight smile*). All right, sir. (MIKAIL *enters*) That's enough, sir—the ceremony is over. (ALL *bow*.)

MIKAIL. Excuse me, sir. Will you dress for dinner, tonight, sir?

CHARLES. No—not this evening. I—I suppose you're wondering why I was kissing your wife's hands.

MIKAIL. I should certainly not permit myself to wonder anything of the sort, sir.

CHARLES. I—I was apologizing in the Russian way.

MIKAIL. Naturally, sir. Do you wish to use the blue glasses or the Bohemian glasses for the Moselle, sir?

CHARLES. Whichever you like, my friend.

MIKAIL (*going to the door and calling through*). The blue glasses, Mademoiselle Helene.

HELENE (*off stage*). Very well, Michel.

CHARLES. Is my daughter laying the table?

MIKAIL. Yes, sir. She expressed a wish to do so.

CHARLES. God bless my soul! (FERNANDE *comes in.*)

FERNANDE. Michel—you're to serve the cocktails—and Tina, my dear, you serve the Sakouska. The concierge will be at the door—he'll do the announcing.

TATIANA. Yes, madame.

MIKAIL. Very good, madame. (*They start to go.*)

FERNANDE (*to* CHARLES). Have you spoken to them about our guest of honor? Wait a moment. (MIKAIL *and* TATIANA *pause and turn.*)

CHARLES. I was about to mention that. (*He turns to them with some embarrassment*) Madame and I appreciate the fact that your sympathies are with the cause of White Russia.

MIKAIL. Yes, sir?

CHARLES. Naturally, we understand you—your devotion to your former employers—the prince and princess . . .

TATIANA. And may God keep them!

CHARLES. And we sympathize with that devotion. But—there are bound to be times when differences of political opinion are apt to prove embarrassing—and this dinner tonight is such an occasion. I mean to say—this may be a somewhat painful experience for you.

FERNANDE. For heaven's sake, Charles, come to the point. Our guest of honor tonight is a representative of the Soviet Government, Commissar Gorotchenko. (*Complete silence from* MIKAIL *and* TATIANA. *Pause.*)

CHARLES. You've doubtless heard of him?

MIKAIL (*in a dull tone*). Yes, sir. We have heard of Commissar Gorotchenko.

FERNANDE. We want to be sure that your behavior during dinner will give us no cause for anxiety.

MIKAIL. Has our behavior ever given such cause, madame?

CHARLES. Of course not! Never!

FERNANDE. No!

MIKAIL. Then, tonight will be no different.

FERNANDE. I've never met this Gorotchenko, but I suppose he's pretty much of a boor. However, he is our guest and we must do everything we can to put him at his ease.

MIKAIL. He is a most cultivated man, madame, with a very lively wit. A bit malicious, perhaps—but keen. It was he who composed that immortal sentence which was engraved on the door of the Loubianka Prison. "Four walls for punishment are three too many."

CHARLES. He's never done you any personal harm, has he?

MIKAIL (*slowly*). None, sir.

TATIANA. Less than none, sir.

CHARLES. Well then, we can all forget the past. Gorotchenko is now representing the Soviet oil interests; and oil, as we all know, is most effective in . . . in . . . smoothing out . . .
(MIKAIL *helping* CHARLES *out of his embarrassment.*)

MIKAIL. He was not always in oil, sir. General Gorotchenko was chief of the Investigating staff at the Tcheka. At that time, my former master, Prince Ouratieff, had some dealings with him.

CHARLES. Really!

MIKAIL. Yes, sir. The conversation between them wasn't progressing as smoothly as Gorotchenko wished —so—to enliven matters—he placed the end of his cigarette— the lighted end, of course—between Prince Ouratieff's fingers. You'll find him very interesting, Sir.

FERNANDE. How horrible!

TATIANA. Oh, madame, you also will find him very entertaining. When he was Commissar of the Fort of Kronstadt, the Grand Duchess Tatiana Petrovna was imprisoned there. I've heard her speak of him often. Women always found him irresistible.

CHARLES. You mean he—he made . . .

TATIANA (*levelly*). Advances—yes, sir.

FERNANDE. But he must be an appalling person!

CHARLES. Nonsense! Michel and Tina have only heard of him from people with a very prejudiced point of view.

FERNANDE. But I hope you're not going to think about these dreadful things when you're serving the soup?

TATIANA (*soberly*). Madame, we shall think only that we're your servants and that we must be worthy of your trust.

MIKAIL. And now—if madame will excuse us.

FERNANDE. Certainly. You can get the cocktails ready. (MIKAIL *and* TATIANA *go out*) Were there ever such treasures?

CHARLES. Never!

FERNANDE. But I wish that Gorotchenko weren't coming. It will be such an ordeal for them.

CHARLES. Nevertheless we'll have to be nice to him, Fernande, because, whatever outrages he may have committed, he exudes an odor which is very sweet.

FERNANDE (*fixing flowers*). Odor?

CHARLES. Yes. He reeks of petrol —those vast, rich, undeveloped Bakoura fields with millions and billions just waiting to be taken out. We must play our cards cleverly tonight. Gorotchenko should sit at your right; Chauffourier at your left, and at my right that Madame Van Hemert.

FERNANDE. Is she, too, perfumed with petrol?

CHARLES. Ah—yes. In a more refined form, of course.

FERNANDE. This house will smell like a garage.

CHARLES. Madame Van Hemert represents the Anglo-Dutch interests; as Monsieur Chauffourier represents France and I represent— myself. If all works out as I hope, we'll be swimming in petrol—liquid gold. There's a fortune involved, my dear. But of course— everything depends on Gorotchenko.

FERNANDE. Oh, Charles, shouldn't you, at least, be wearing a dinner jacket? (*A bell is heard.*)

CHARLES. Oh, no! Chauffourier told me expressly not to dress. You know how the Bolsheviks feel about our bourgeois customs. . . .

CONCIERGE (*off stage*). What name, Madame?

VAN HEMERT (*off stage*). Madame Van Hemert.

FERNANDE. Get up. They're here. (CHARLES *rises.* FERNANDE *braces herself. The door opens up and the* CONCIERGE *appears.*)

CONCIERGE (*announcing*). Madame Van Hemert!
(MADAME VAN HEMERT *comes in. She is thin, hard, sharp, rather chic, well preserved.*)

FERNANDE (*cordially*). How do you do? I'm Madame Dupont.

VAN HEMERT. How do you do?

FERNANDE. Permit me to present my husband.

CHARLES. My dear madame—you do us honor.

VAN HEMERT. You must forgive me —but I'm invariably the first to arrive.

CHARLES. How charming of you!

FERNANDE. Do sit down.

VAN HEMERT. Thank you.
(*There is an awkward silence.*)

FERNANDE. Have you met Commissar Gorotchenko before?

VAN HEMERT. Oh, yes—at Teheran —and once or twice in London, and of course in Moscow.

CHARLES. You've traveled far.

VAN HEMERT (*levelly*). Yes, Monsieur Dupont. I'm a sort of Vestal Virgin.

CHARLES. Oh!

VAN HEMERT. I am one of those whose duty it is to keep the lamps of the world filled with oil. It necessitates a great deal of travel.

FERNANDE. And a great deal of diplomacy?

VAN HEMERT. Not so much diplomacy as—relentlessness.

CHARLES. You Hollanders are a remarkable people.

VAN HEMERT. We've had to be.

FERNANDE. And Gorotchenko— what is he like? I confess I'm a little nervous.

VAN HEMERT. Don't worry, madame. He can be agreeable enough when he's in the right mood.

CHARLES. And when he's in the wrong mood?

VAN HEMERT. He has the grace to keep ominously quiet.
(*The door opens and* TATIANA *comes in.*)

TATIANA. Excuse me, madame.

FERNANDE. Yes, Tina?

VAN HEMERT. Oh!

TATIANA. Shall we serve . . . the cocktails?

VAN HEMERT. Her Imperial Highness. (*She sinks in the deep ceremonial curtsy.* FERNANDE *and* CHARLES *gaze at her in amazement.*)

TATIANA. No—no! Please don't do that . . . please don't . . . (*She turns and hurries out.* VAN HEMERT *follows.*)

FERNANDE. What on earth . . .

CHARLES. I beg your pardon, madame, but just why did you do that?

VAN HEMERT. Why is *she* here?

CHARLES. That's our housemaid. She's a Russian.

FERNANDE. We have two of them —man and wife.

VAN HEMERT. Your servant!

CHARLES. Why, yes, her name is Tina.

VAN HEMERT. Tina! That is the former Grand Duchess Tatiana Petrovna.

FERNANDE. The . . .

CHARLES. No—no . . .

FERNANDE. You're mistaken.

CHARLES. She was employed by the Grand Duchess.

VAN HEMERT. She *is* the Grand Duchess! (*Turns to* FERNANDE) I knew her well in Petersburg.

FERNANDE. I tell you—that's our housemaid. There may be a resemblance.
(VAN HEMERT *laughs heartily.* FERNANDE *and* CHARLES *look at each other with mounting horror.*)

VAN HEMERT. Forgive me—I shouldn't be laughing—but—I really can't help it. Your housemaid!

FERANDE. But she had a reference from the Grand Duchess. (*She and* CHARLES *look at each other.* VAN HEMERT *is still laughing.*)

CHARLES. You know, she might have written it herself!

VAN HEMERT. And is her husband, Prince Ouratieff, here too?

CHARLES. Prince Ouratieff! Great God! I suppose that's Michel.

FERNANDE. Are you sure about this?

VAN HEMERT. I promise you, Madame Dupont, I couldn't possibly be mistaken. How long have they been with you?

FERNANDE. Two months. They've made fools of us! Do you realize what it will mean?

CHARLES. Realize! Twenty years from now all Paris will still be laughing at us.
(*The* CONCIERGE *comes in.*)

CONCIERGE. Monsieur and Madame Chauffourier-Dubieff.
(*They come in. General greetings.* FERNANDE *shakes hands with* CHAUFFOURIER.)

MADAME CHAUFFOURIER (*as she shakes hands with* FERNANDE). Good evening, Fernande.

FERNANDE. Good evening, my dear.

CHAUFFOURIER. It's turning rather cold.

FERNANDE. Really? It's been quite warm indoors.

MADAME CHAUFFOURIER. There's a north wind that feels like Siberia. . . .

CHARLES. I hate the sound of that word.

CHAUFFOURIER (*to* VAN HEMERT). Well, madame, you seem very gay this evening! Good news from the East Indies? (MIKAIL *comes in*) Why—bless my soul! What a delightful surprise! (*Shakes hands with* MIKAIL) I had no idea your Excellency was to be here.

FERNANDE (*to* CHARLES). Excellency?

CHAUFFOURIER. But you're wearing evening clothes. That's an excellent joke on our friend Gorotchenko.

MIKAIL (*trying to escape*). If you will . . .

CHAUFFOURIER (*stopping him*). You're dining here with us?

MIKAIL. Sir, I am dining here—but not at the same time. (*To* FERNANDE) May I serve the cocktails, madame?

FERNANDE (*dully*). Yes. You may serve the cocktails.

MIKAIL. Thank you, madame. (*He goes out.*)

CHAUFFOURIER (*wondering*). It *is* a joke, isn't it?

VAN HEMERT (*laughs*). The best joke in years!

MADAME CHAUFFOURIER. Are you going to explain it now—or must we wait?

CHARLES. It makes no difference when we explain it. Tomorrow—it will be in every newspaper.

FERNANDE. And Gorotchenko! Why, they'll be at each other's throats! (*Imploringly to her guests*) I'm terribly sorry—(*Turns to* MADAME CHAUFFOURIER) But—would you mind if we dine at a restaurant?

VAN HEMERT. Not at all.

CHAUFFOURIER. But why? With Prince Ouratieff on hand, the situation is ideal. We might persuade him to join the combine. He might agree to finance the whole scheme.

CHARLES. Him—finance us?

CHAUFFOURIER. Why not? As a Rus-

sian, he'd appreciate the value of the oil concession.

CHARLES. But—forgive me, Governor—I'm a little bewildered.

CHAUFFOURIER. You evidently don't know that Ouratieff is probably the only man living who can write his check on the Bank of France for four billion francs—

CHARLES. Four billion . . .

CHAUFFOURIER. Yes—and have it honored. So—when you've finished your little joke, whatever it is, we'd better sit down with His Excellency and talk business.

CHARLES. Yes.

CONCIERGE (*entering*). Commissar Gorotchenko.
(FERNANDE *rises.* GOROTCHENKO *comes in. He is strongly built, with a humorous, saturnine expression—a cultivated barbarian with keen perceptivity and a great appreciation of life. He is wearing a tail coat and white tie.*)

GOROTCHENKO (*to* FERNANDE). My respects, madame. And Monsieur Dupont, I believe.

CHARLES. Yes—er—how do you do, Commissar?

GOROTCHENKO. Very well, thank you. And my dear Madame Van Hemert. . . .

VAN HEMERT. My dear Commissar.

GOROTCHENKO. Madame Chauffourier—my dear Governor . . .

CHAUFFOURIER (*heartily*). Gorotchenko, old man—how are you?

GOROTCHENKO (*looking about*). A most distinguished gathering! I am already ill at ease.

VAN HEMERT. You'll know how distinguished it *really* is when you see who *else* is here.

GOROTCHENKO. Then, there are other guests? Thank heaven, I'm not the last.

CHARLES. There are others—yes—but not exactly guests.
(MIKAIL *enters with cocktails, serves* VAN HEMERT, *then* MADAME CHAUFFOURIER, *then* FERNANDE, *as he goes to serve* CHARLES, *who goes to take one, thinks better of it, refuses*.)

GOROTCHENKO (*to* CHAUFFOURIER *as* MIKAIL *goes to* CHARLES). And how is the new state loan progressing, my dear Governor?

CHAUFFOURIER. I'm rather sorry you mentioned that, Commissar. But we are always optimistic.
(MIKAIL *serves* GOROTCHENKO. TATIANA *enters with sandwiches*.)

GOROTCHENKO (*to* MIKAIL). Thank you. (*To* FERNANDE) Your . . . (*Sees* TATIANA, *breaks off, then:*) your very good health, madame.

FERNANDE. Thank you.
(MIKAIL *has served* CHAUFFOURIER, *takes tray to table, stands at attention as* TATIANA *reaches* MADAME CHAUFFOURIER.)

CHARLES. Ah—Madame Chauffourier tells us that it has turned quite cold.

GOROTCHENKO. I suppose it has. Though it seems comparatively

tropical to us Russians. (TATIANA *serves him*) Thank you.
(TATIANA *serves* CHAUFFOURIER.)

VAN HEMERT. I was in Moscow once when it was positively hot.

FERNANDE. Really?

VAN HEMERT. Oh, yes . . . there were thousands of people bathing in the river, all stark naked.

CHAUFFOURIER. Hm?

CHARLES. How amusing!

GOROTCHENKO. We make them wear bathing suits now. Oh, yes—we've turned very moral.

MADAME CHAUFFOURIER. But I'm eternally sorry I never saw Russia in the old days.

GOROTCHENKO. Yes, I must confess —there are some aspects of the old régime that we miss in the Soviet Union. (*He takes out a cigarette.* MIKAIL *steps down with matches*.)

MIKAIL. Permit me, Commissar. (*Lights* GOROTCHENKO'S *cigarette, then goes out*.)

GOROTCHENKO. Thank you. But what a charming room this is, madame. Isn't it a replica of the Hotel de Landuzy?

FERNANDE. Why, yes—it is. Did you know the Hotel de Landuzy?

GOROTCHENKO. I am an old Parisian, madame. For three years I was a dishwasher in the Quai de Bourbon.

FERNANDE. A dishwasher! How very interesting.

GOROTCHENKO. Yes—literally. I washed dishes. That was when I was studying for my philosophical degree.

CHARLES. In addition to everything else, you're a Doctor of Philosophy?

GOROTCHENKO. That was a long time ago, Monsieur Dupont. I'm afraid I've forgotten most of it now.

CHAUFFOURIER (*chuckling*). Yes—you've passed on from pure theory to impure fact.

GOROTCHENKO (*laughing*). That's it, my dear Governor. I was captivated by Plato's concept of the Perfect State. Where every man has the brain of Socrates in the body of Adonis, and every woman—but I'm sure you ladies have already achieved the Platonic ideal.

VAN HEMERT (*to* FERNANDE). He's poisonous, isn't he? He'll make communists of us all.

CHAUFFOURIER. You've explained a great deal, Commissar. You learned about the Perfect State and then went home to Russia and built it.

GOROTCHENKO. No—when I returned to Russia, I was careful to leave my idealism behind. That was a bad time for idealists, you know. A few of them escaped into Finland, but the majority were submerged in rivers of blood.

MADAME CHAUFFOURIER. How shocking!

CHAUFFOURIER. And how necessary! That's the one point on which Capitalism and Communism agree: the idealists must be drowned.

GOROTCHENKO. The Governor is a realist. You know, Plato himself likened all of us to prisoners, chained in a cave. Behind us, a fire is burning—and we're forced to contemplate our own shadows, magnified horribly on the wall. We're terrified of them. They awaken in us race memories, and we shrink from them as though they were prehistoric monsters. It's the duty of the philosopher to break the chains, and escape from the cave into the world of clear reality. And that is what we have tried to do in the Soviet Union. You may feel that we have failed. But, in any case, we have provided a fascinating chapter of history for the dishwashers of the future. (MADAME CHAUFFOURIER *gives a nervous little laugh*) But I'm afraid I've become much too talkative, madame. Do forgive me. It's a Russian failing.

CHAUFFOURIER. No—Commissar. I'm sure we've all greatly enjoyed your—little lecture.
(*Enter* MIKAIL.)

MIKAIL. Dinner is served, madame.

CHARLES (*relieved*). Ah—dinner!

FERNANDE. Shall we go in?

VAN HEMERT. By all means. (*To* GOROTCHENKO) We will discuss Plato—and Petrol.
(*All rise.*)

FERNANDE. Charles!
(CHARLES *takes* MADAME CHAUFFOURIER'S *arm and exits.*)

CHAUFFOURIER (*takes* VAN HEMERT's *arm*). That's what we bankers have needed in the past years—some lessons in philosophy. May I have the honor? (*Exits with* VAN HEMERT.)

GOROTCHENKO (*to* FERNANDE). You know—it's a very bad thing for a communist to dine in a French house. A shamefully corrupting influence!

FERNANDE. You're in a good mood, Commissar.

GOROTCHENKO. Why not, madame? I'm not often privileged to enjoy such charming company. (GOROTCHENKO *and* FERNANDE *exit*.)

VAN HEMERT (*off stage*). Ah, we're charming now, Commissar. But wait until we get down to business. (*The voices of the guests die away.* MIKAIL *crosses to* TATIANA, *puts his arm around her. Then he goes to door, stands at attention.*)

MIKAIL. After you, Highness. (TATIANA *exits with her head held high.* MIKAIL *follows her.*)

CURTAIN

SCENE II

Kitchen of the DUPONTS' *house.*
Three hours later.
MIKAIL, TATIANA *and* LOUISE *are seated at table having finished their dinner.* TATIANA *is holding out her coffee glass.*

TATIANA. Some more coffee, please.

LOUISE. That's three glasses for you. You know, you won't sleep.

TATIANA. You're right, Louise. I shall not sleep.

LOUISE (*smiling*). What's the matter, my dears? Didn't the dinner go off well?

MIKAIL (*vaguely*). Oh—yes—it went off well.

LOUISE. They didn't eat much.

MIKAIL. No . . . there seemed to be a general loss of appetite. Except for Gorotchenko. He ate a

great deal of everything. A masterly display of imperviousness to embarrassment.

LOUISE. Gorotchenko? What's he—another Russian?

MIKAIL. He was born a Russian.

LOUISE. It must be nice for you to see one of your own people.

TATIANA. What did you say?

LOUISE. I said—it must be nice for you to see one of your own people.

TATIANA. Mikail! Make her be quiet.

LOUISE. Mother of God! What's wrong with her?

MIKAIL. Forgive us, Louise! We're both a bit upset.

LOUISE. But why—what is it?

MIKAIL. Simply this, Louise. The time has come for us to set out for new fields of endeavor.

LOUISE. And what do you mean by *that?*

MIKAIL. I mean that we have been fired.

LOUISE. When?

MIKAIL. Tonight. After dinner. Madame informed us ever so elegantly, that the usual notice would be dispensed with. We receive our wages and depart in the morning.

LOUISE. Well, all I can say is, I'm very, very sorry. We've got along well together, the three of us. (TATIANA *rises, pats* LOUISE, *puts on apron, goes to sink.*)

MIKAIL. Well, it has to happen to all of us sooner or later. Dismissal and death. But, at least I shall serve the lemonade in the drawing-room at eleven o'clock as I was ordered. They shall not deprive me of that final privilege.

LOUISE. It's a shame, and I certainly don't know what she's complaining about. *I'd* say you two have done more than enough!

MIKAIL. And you have been very kind to us. You will always be remembered by Her Highness and me with loving gratitude.

LOUISE. Her Highness, eh! (LOUISE *laughs*) Is that one of your Russian jokes?

MIKAIL. No, Louise. *That* one was grimly serious.

LOUISE (*to* TATIANA). Are you a Highness?

TATIANA. Imperial! (*Starts to clear table.*)

LOUISE. And what does that make you, Michel?

MIKAIL. No more than her consort, Louise. A paltry prince. It must be something of a shock to you to learn the kind of people who have been your associates, and friends. (*Rises, puts on apron.*)

LOUISE. Oh, no. (*Rises and puts butter dish in refrigerator*) Princes and Highnesses have to live somewhere, like other people. They may as well live here as anywhere else.

TATIANA (*clearing the table*). Godly woman! You understand things.

MIKAIL. If only you could convey some of your liberality to our employers.

LOUISE. So that's why they're sending you away, eh? Because you deceived them into thinking you're common—like they are. (*Gets milk bottles from floor and puts them on cupboard.*)

MIKAIL (*with emotion*). Yes! But it isn't the first time we've had to suffer for the misfortune of exalted birth. (*He hands* TATIANA *another dish. She inspects it and thrusts it back at him.*)

TATIANA. Wash it again!

MIKAIL. Isn't it clean?

TATIANA (*pointing to a blemish*). Look at that!

MIKAIL. Oh—yes. I thought it was part of the design.
(LOUISE *laughs and takes napkin from cupboard in refrigerator*.)

TATIANA. If Madame Dupont caught you being as careless as that . . . Oh! for the moment I'd forgotten.

MIKAIL (*his arm around* TATIANA). My beautiful love. There is no tragedy great enough to break your magnificent spirit—is there?

TATIANA. Go on with the dishes.

LOUISE. What will you do now? (*Taking pitcher of lemonade from refrigerator, putting it on tray on top of refrigerator and covering all with napkin*.)

MIKAIL. Starve—with quiet dignity.

LOUISE. Why don't you just get rid of those silly titles?

TATIANA. By the blessed St. Christopher! If I dropped dead this instant, I'd still be a Grand Duchess. My soul would be flapping about in heaven with wings a lot longer than the other angels.

MIKAIL. And you'd still be flying into trouble.

LOUISE. Don't you want to leave?

TATIANA AND MIKAIL. No! No! Never.

LOUISE. Then, don't.

MIKAIL. But what can we do? Chain ourselves to the sink?

LOUISE. Why don't you join the Union?

MIKAIL. What union?

LOUISE. Of domestic workers. Or don't you want to go on doing this kind of work?

MIKAIL. We never want to do anything else. We're not *fitted* for anything else.

TATIANA. What will this union do for us?

LOUISE. It will protect you from this very thing—I mean, being dismissed for no good reason. Now listen—if your employers say or do anything you don't like, you'll only have to go to the Union and lodge a protest. And then the Union will send an official round to the house —and those officials use the front door, not the back door, believe me —and he'll say a few things to Monsieur and Madame—and the next thing you know, they'll be apologizing to you, and raising your wages, and putting a radio in your room. (LOUISE *takes off apron, hangs it on hook, puts on shawl*.)

MIKAIL. But that—that sounds like Bolshevism.

LOUISE. Call it anything you please, Michel. It makes life a lot easier for the likes of us. Can I help you with any of that work?

TATIANA (*pushes chairs in*). No, thanks, darling. We want to do all of it, ourselves. It's our last chance.

LOUISE. Well—good night, my dears. And good luck.

MIKAIL. Good night, Louise.

TATIANA (*kisses her*). Good night, daughter of God.
(LOUISE *lumbers out.*)

MIKAIL. Hideous china, isn't it? And yet—I love it. I shall miss it very, very sorely.
(*They are back at sink washing.*)

TATIANA. Do you realize that in two months—nearly nine weeks—we haven't broken any of it?

MIKAIL. Not so much as a chip. (*With a deep sigh*) Never in all our lives before have we ever done anything so well. (MIKAIL *washing plates.* TATIANA *drying plates.*)

TATIANA. God must know that we've been good servants! Surely, He'll find us another place.

MIKAIL. Surely He will! But—don't you think we should join that Union?

TATIANA. It's useless. Wherever we go—here in France—they'll know all about us.

MIKAIL. How much money have we?

TATIANA. I have eleven francs. I spent all the rest on that dress for tonight.

MIKAIL. I have two thousand. Two thousand and fifty—

TATIANA. Eh! !

MIKAIL. From Monsieur George.

What a miserable poker player he is.

TATIANA. He's in love!

MIKAIL. I know . . .

TATIANA. With me.

MIKAIL. Yes—and so am I. But I don't allow it to interfere with my technique at poker.

TATIANA. Is two thousand francs enough to take us to South America?

MIKAIL. I don't know. Why South America?

TATIANA. That's where people seem to go, when they're desperate. What language do they speak there?

MIKAIL. Spanish—or Portuguese—or something. There was a South American gigolo at the Kasbec once. He didn't speak much of anything. He just murmured.
(TATIANA *has gone to the table to clear off the remains of their meal.*)

TATIANA. Poor little coffee pot. Forlorn—and empty. Like our lives.

MIKAIL. Ah—my darling! How can we go to that party, with these two young monkeys? How can we pretend to be gay when we've lost bread and bed and central heating?

TATIANA. Oh, we've promised, Mikail. The Grand Duke Alexei would never forgive us. He saved up for two years to give this party. And everyone else there will have no more reason for rejoicing than we have. And then poor little Monsieur George. He has been very good to us.

MIKAIL. The amorous puppy!

TATIANA. And Mademoiselle Helene —she's been good to us, too—and —(*with a malicious smile*) for the same reason. We mustn't disappoint them.

MIKAIL. Very well, Tatiana—we'll go. We'll make the last gruesome pretense.

TATIANA (*puts her arms about him*). My poor, tragic pigeon. You weren't nearly so depressed when they burned down our palace at Orlovskai—and destroyed all your beautiful horses in the stable and the Rembrandts in the library.

MIKAIL. That was in Russia, Tatiana.

TATIANA. And you laughed when they arrested us, and put us in prison, and we were so certain we were going to die. . . .

MIKAIL. That, too, was in Russia, Tatiana.

TATIANA. Well—and where are we now?

MIKAIL. In the kitchen of a French banker named Dupont.

TATIANA. No! It's *our* kitchen, Mikail. Breathe the air, my darling. It smells of onions and coal gas and brown soap—but when you breathe it in, it becomes the air of Russia— cold and clean. Wherever we may go, it will be the same. In our lungs, and our eyes, and our hearts will be Russia. (*Clinging to him*) Mishenka—

MIKAIL. Tanouska.

TATIANA (*with joyful energy*). Nitchevo!

MIKAIL (MIKAIL *lets himself be won over*). Nitchevo!

TATIANA (*repeating it louder*). Nitchevo!

MIKAIL (*repeating*). Yes, Tatiana. Nitchevo!
(TATIANA *laughs with a full-throated laugh.*)

TATIANA.   Nitchevo—nitchevo— nitchevo—

MIKAIL (MIKAIL *is restored to gayety*).   Nitchevo—nitchevo—nitchevo—
(TATIANA *kisses* MIKAIL. MIKAIL *takes off apron, hangs it up, puts on coat.*)

TATIANA (*quite simply*). Go and put away monsieur's clothes. I will finish the washing-up.

MIKAIL. Very well, Tina.

TATIANA. And—tonight I'll have a talk with Kokovstev.

MIKAIL. Why Kokovstev?

TATIANA. He works for one of those travel bureaus. He'll be able to tell us how much it costs to go to South America. And what language they speak.

MIKAIL. Perhaps they all just murmur. (*He goes out.* TATIANA *goes to window, pulls up blind; sees church, crosses herself; she then wipes table with cloth, puts a cloth on table. She puts knives and forks on cloth, covers them with another cloth; gets dust-pan and brush, kneels beside table. The pantry door opens softly and* GOROTCHENKO *appears. For a moment he stands there, watching her, admiringly.*)

GOROTCHENKO. May I come in?

TATIANA (*rises sharply*). Oh! (*She puts dust-pan and brush away under table*) What have you come here for? The silver?

GOROTCHENKO (*smiling*). I came to see His Excellency, your husband.

TATIANA. The butler? He has work to do—important work.

GOROTCHENKO. Then, perhaps I may wait for him. (*He looks around*) You keep your kitchen in most admirable order.

TATIANA (*turning on him again*). Who gave you permission to come in here?

GOROTCHENKO. No one, madame. I just walked in through the dining-room. The others are in the draw-ing-room, muttering prayers to the great god Petrol. They have some sort of agreement they want me to sign. But I—I asked for time to think it over in solitude.

TATIANA. In the kitchen?

GOROTCHENKO. They think I'm in the study. But they're too tactful to disturb me. People in oil are always tactful.

TATIANA. Why do you want to do your thinking here? Will it help you to see how I wash the dishes?

GOROTCHENKO. I'm sure you do it with flawless grace.

TATIANA (*polishing a plate by sink*). You should know. I was given many lessons in dish-washing when I was under your command in the Kronstadt.

GOROTCHENKO. That was a rigorous school, madame.

TATIANA. Yes. Those who broke dishes were shot.

GOROTCHENKO. Dishes were difficult to replace in those days. We have our own factories now. We can afford to be a little more lenient. Do you mind if I smoke?

TATIANA. No—Commissar. I don't mind. As long as you remain sitting down. (GOROTCHENKO *lights cig-arette which he takes from his case*) Have you forgotten our last en-counter? (*She is looking levelly at him*) You were sitting behind your enormous desk, smoking a cigarette, just as you are now. Then you stood up, and walked around the desk, put down your cigarette and took hold of my wrist.

GOROTCHENKO. I see no reason to refer to that, madame. It was some-thing that happened in another world, a very long time ago.

TATIANA. Oh—I hold no grudge, Gorotchenko.

GOROTCHENKO. I'm sure you don't.

TATIANA. But I'd like to have you know that when I get back, I shall have your eyes burned out and the sockets filled with Siberian salt.

GOROTCHENKO. If you do come back, madame, the most horrible retribution you can think of will be no more than I deserve, because I was guilty of the most unpardonable of crimes.

TATIANA. It does me no good to hear you admit it.

GOROTCHENKO. I was guilty of sentimentality.

TATIANA (laughing). Sentimentality! That's a rather quaint way of describing it, Commissar.

GOROTCHENKO. I was referring to the moment of weakness when I permitted you to go off in that motor boat, through the darkness.

TATIANA. You knew that the motor boat was there?

GOROTCHENKO. Yes, madame. . . . The man who took you was shot, but not until after he had delivered you safely in Finland.

TATIANA. You killed that godly man?

GOROTCHENKO. Somebody had to be punished for your escape. Had it not been he, it would have been the governor of the prison. The revolution was young then—and I was not quite ready to die.

TATIANA. Why did you let me go?

GOROTCHENKO. There was something in you that impelled me to neglect my obvious duty. I suppose that something can best be described as gallantry. . . . And furthermore—I could not rid myself of the belief that your usefulness to Russia had not ended.

TATIANA (turning from him). Please leave me to do my work in peace—and go back and drink brandy with the bourgeoisie.

GOROTCHENKO. Go on with your work, madame. I shall wait here for your husband. If you'll allow me.

TATIANA. And if I don't allow you?

GOROTCHENKO. I shall still wait—though not comfortably.

TATIANA (polishing a plate). After I have your eyes burned out, Gorotchenko, I'll make you crawl on your hands and knees out of St. Petersburg. . . .

GOROTCHENKO (softly). Leningrad.

TATIANA. From St. Petersburg to Moscow. You'll have a horse's carcass tied around your neck to chew on when you're hungry.

GOROTCHENKO (smiling). I shall be at your command, madame. (He rises) I wonder if I could help you with your work . . .

TATIANA. Don't you dare to touch . . .

GOROTCHENKO. I was a good dishwasher once.

TATIANA. This is not the Quai de Bourbon. Keep your hands off my china.
(MIKAIL enters.)

MIKAIL. And what are you doing in our kitchen?

GOROTCHENKO. I explained to madame that I'm deep in thought.

MIKAIL. Take your evil thoughts elsewhere. They pollute the atmosphere.

TATIANA. Pick him up with the coal tongs, Mikail, and throw him out.

GOROTCHENKO. No—I should consider that inhospitable in the extreme.

MIKAIL. Monsieur and Madame Dupont invited you here for reasons best known to themselves. You can therefore expect hospitality in the drawing-room; here in the kitchen we're more particular in the selection of our guests.

GOROTCHENKO. As you should be, General. But it is my recollection that once madame was a Grand Duchess of Russia.

TATIANA. I am always a Grand Duchess.

GOROTCHENKO. Exactly. And I'm sure you haven't forgotten that in any house which is graced with your presence—it makes no difference who owns the place or who pays the rent, etiquette decrees that you are the hostess. I am therefore, madame, your guest.

TATIANA. The dog is right, Mikail. Sit down!

MIKAIL. Very well. You may remain —(starts to put on apron)—and derive what enjoyment you can from the spectacle of your former commanding officer cleaning his master's boots.

GOROTCHENKO. I did not come here for enjoyment, General Prince Ouratieff. I should like to ask you a question.

MIKAIL. Another interrogation, Commissar? Remember I am now under the benevolent protection of the Republic of France.

GOROTCHENKO. What is your last memory as a cavalry general of the guard, aide-de-camp to Nicholas Romanoff?

MIKAIL. My last memory? I'm afraid I've forgotten it.

GOROTCHENKO. I should like to know about the day when, for the last time, you drew your sword and charged with your three thousand Cossacks.

MIKAIL (polishing shoes). There were not three thousand on that day, Commissar. There were three hundred. The rest had put red bands on their sleeves and deserted. It was the Austrians who were three thousand, anyway. And we charged, anyway. And we routed them. The next day the command was taken from me. It was given to a student of chemistry. That day it was two hundred Austrians who routed twenty thousand Russians.

GOROTCHENKO. I've always regretted that I was not with you in your last battle, General. It must have been a splendid sight. You see, I had a very real admiration for you. You were always an object of awe and envy to me, when we were together in the Cavaler Gardsky regiment. Probably you have forgotten those days, but they remain all too clear in my memory.

MIKAIL. I have not forgotten those days, Gorotchenko. You were thoroughly objectionable even then.

GOROTCHENKO. Yes, I was. I was too conscious of inferiority. That was what made me drink too much vodka at the regimental banquet in the presence of the Tsar. A grievous offense—and their punishment was properly harsh. I was cashiered. It seems strange now, doesn't it?—to think that if I hadn't been so nervous that night, and drunk too much vodka so quickly—I should never have gone to Paris, to study philosophy, and to read the writings of Karl Marx.

MIKAIL. Commissar, I cannot speak for my beloved wife, but for myself I can say that I find the story of your life profoundly and appallingly dull.

TATIANA. Speak for me, too, my pigeon.

MIKAIL. My wife, too.

GOROTCHENKO. You surprise me, General. I have found my life most exciting—sometimes excessively so. The present moment, for instance, is fraught with possibilities.

MIKAIL. Such as— that I might forget myself long enough to do you some bodily injury? You needn't be afraid, Gorotchenko; I'm busy!

GOROTCHENKO. I am not thinking of the situation that prevails here in the kitchen—but of that other one which awaits me in the bourgeois drawing-room. General Prince Ouratieff—I want you to do me a slight favor.

MIKAIL. Yes, Commissar.

GOROTCHENKO. When I say slight —I mean it will cost you very little in the way of effort, and nothing in the way of money.

MIKAIL. You have only to ask a favor, Commissar, and it will be refused.

GOROTCHENKO. I want you to write me a check for four billion francs. (*There is a considerable, pregnant silence.*)

TATIANA. Is that why you came into our kitchen, for a mere matter of four billion francs?

GOROTCHENKO. Yes, madame. It is why I suggested that this meeting be held in this house. I wanted to speak to you before I signed their agreement.

MIKAIL. How did you know we were here?

GOROTCHENKO. I have been careful not to lose sight of you, General. You may remember that just before you took this place, you had an interview with one of my agents— a stupid, violent little girl. You sent me a message, through her, urging me to call on you in person. I have done so.

MIKAIL. We acknowledge the visit, Commissar. And now it is time to take in the lemonade.

GOROTCHENKO. But first you'll sign the check. It won't take a moment. General Ouratieff—for two hours I have been closeted in there with Chauffourier-Dubieff of the Bank of France, and Madame Van Hemert, whose name is Anglo-Dutch oil, and Dupont, who represents United Petrol. Can you imagine why they are so cordial to me, a despised Bolshevik? They want me to sign the transfer of the Bakoura and Petropolsk oil fields for the next fifty years.

MIKAIL. And will you sign?

GOROTCHENKO. I've been fighting to avoid it. For it would mean fifty years of English, Dutch, French and Americans—digging Russian soil, capitalizing Russian resources, drawing life blood from the veins of our country.

MIKAIL (*calmly*). Keep up the fight, Commissar. Don't sign.

GOROTCHENKO. (*sadly*). I'm afraid I must, General. For I have been commissioned to find credits in gold for the Soviets of the Ukraine and the Ural, for the manufacture of tractors. If I don't find that money, and at once, some five million wretched peasants will starve to death—without mentioning those we shall have to shoot so that they won't make a fuss about it. When I asked you for your last memory as a general, I wanted to remind you, that more than the sword can be wielded in behalf of Russia. There is another weapon—money.

MIKAIL. I have no money.

GOROTCHENKO. You have four billion francs.

MIKAIL. That is not mine.

GOROTCHENKO. It was given to you, unconditionally, by Nicholas Romanoff.

TATIANA. It was given him by the Tsar! (*She crosses herself.*)

GOROTCHENKO. Yes, madame. That was in the year 1917, but now . . .

MIKAIL. You needn't continue, Gorotchenko. I have refused that money to all the scavengers who have tried to take it from me. And I was not saving it for you.

GOROTCHENKO. I know, General. I know all about the offer of Count Brekenski to equip an army of Latvians and Lithuanians to invade the Soviet Union. That would have been a tragic farce. But it is not a farce to give Bakoura and Petropolsk into the hands of foreigners.

MIKAIL. Don't worry, Gorotchenko. When the time comes, we shall take them back again.

TATIANA. Who did you say these people are—who want you to sign?

GOROTCHENKO. It is a combination of interests, Madame—French, Dutch, American, English.

MIKAIL. I don't care who they are! I have held on to that money as I have held on to my immortal soul. I have even denied it to myself.

GOROTCHENKO. No one has questioned your integrity, Prince Ouratieff.

MIKAIL. And don't think you can flatter it out of me.

GOROTCHENKO. I should not so far insult your intelligence.

MIKAIL. You wouldn't hesitate to do anything, Gorotchenko. Once you even tried to torture me.

GOROTCHENKO. I know, General. My conduct was then both unworthy and unwise. But now our relative positions are very different.

MIKAIL. Nothing is different.

GOROTCHENKO. Very well, General. But—I wish I could take you now into the Tsar's room at Tsarkoe Selo.

TATIANA. It is still there?

GOROTCHENKO. Intact, madame. Largely through my own efforts, if I may say so. It has been preserved precisely as it was.

TATIANA. Is my photograph still there?

GOROTCHENKO. Yes, madame.

TATIANA. In a white dress, with a high collar and ruffles?

GOROTCHENKO. Yes, madame. And —it pains me to say it—you now have a mustache.

TATIANA. Oh!

GOROTCHENKO. Supplied by a barbarous visitor.

TATIANA. Oh!

GOROTCHENKO. He was condemned to ten years' penal servitude.

TATIANA. For lèse-majesté?

GOROTCHENKO. For—damaging the workers' property. (*He turns to* MIKAIL) Do you remember in that room, on the wall, behind the Tsar's desk, a big map of all the Russias?

MIKAIL. Yes. I remember the map.

GOROTCHENKO. At the bottom of it, to the right, are marked Bakoura and Petropolsk. Of all the undeveloped oil fields on earth—they are the richest. If I sign that agreement with the foreigners—a part of that map will have to be torn away.

MIKAIL. Then, don't sign!

GOROTCHENKO. The peasants must have tractors.

MIKAIL (*resisting desperately*). But not from me. I received that money from the Tsar.

GOROTCHENKO. And who was the Tsar, General?

MIKAIL. He was beyond your degraded comprehension.

GOROTCHENKO (*to* TATIANA). I ask it of you, madame. Who was the Tsar?

TATIANA. He was Russia!

GOROTCHENKO (*gravely*). Yes—he was Russia. And therefore—he is not dead.

MIKAIL (*suddenly, to* TATIANA). I can tell you—the day will come when we can strike back. And—on that day—no foreigner will be allowed to remain in possession of one square centimeter of our soil. . . .

TATIANA. No, no, pigeon, you are wrong. We may take back that which belongs to France, or to America. But no one has ever taken back anything from England.

MIKAIL (*he stares at her*). Tatiana, you want me to sign?

TATIANA. Yes, Mikail. . . . (*She drops plate, which breaks*) Look, I've broken a plate.

MIKAIL. The first one. (*Both stoop to pick up the pieces. He turns to* GOROTCHENKO *as he puts pieces on cupboard*) You may tell Chauffourier and the others that Bakoura and Petropolsk are no longer for sale.

GOROTCHENKO (*he betrays no emotion whatever*). I shall deliver your message, General.

MIKAIL. Wait! You're forgetting your four billion francs. Where are the pen and ink, darling?

TATIANA. I think Louise has put them in the cupboard with the onions!

GOROTCHENKO. The check can wait, General. We can meet again to-morrow.

MIKAIL. We may meet again some time, Commissar. God arranges many improbable encounters. But I doubt that it will be so soon as tomorrow. . . . (*Takes check book from drawer.*)

TATIANA. Here they are . . . (*She brings the pen and ink from cupboard.*)

MIKAIL. Why does she keep them with the onions?

TATIANA. The eggs are in the same cupboard, and she likes to mark the date on each egg.

MIKAIL (*sniffing the pen*). It stinks.

TATIANA. Darling—

MIKAIL. You loved him, didn't you? And understood him? (*She nods*) He wouldn't have let Bakoura and Petropolsk go, would he? Even at the cost of his throne—his life?

TATIANA. No! He wouldn't have let them go. Never!

MIKAIL. Then I am doing right?

TATIANA. From the depths of his grave, he sees you, and says that you are fulfilling his trust. From the very height of the skies he is reaching down, to guide your hand.

MIKAIL. But . . . my darling . . . you're crying. Tatiana! Why are you crying?

TATIANA. It is the onions. I swear it is. They always make me cry.

MIKAIL. It's all we have left of what *he* gave us . . .

TATIANA. We have the sword, and the flag, and the ikon, Mikail—and ourselves.

MIKAIL. Ourselves! The best interests of my sovereign. Yes, I can keep for the Tsar that which was the Tsar's (*Starts to write*) January 12th. (*Turns to* GOROTCHENKO) What is your Christian name?

GOROTCHENKO. Dmitri.

MIKAIL (*writing*). Dmitri Gorotchenko . . . one of the most heartless, soulless, ruthless blackguards that ever desecrated the God-formed surface of this earth. I have made this out "Balance of Account" . . . now I must sign. Mikail Alexandrovich Ouratieff. The first check and the last—I have no more use for this. (*He takes the check book to the stove and drops it in.*)

TATIANA (*to* GOROTCHENKO). To whom will this check be given?

GOROTCHENKO. It will be deposited in Paris to the credit of the Soviet Government.

TATIANA (*imperiously*). You will inform the Soviet Government that it is tendered in the name of the Tsar.

GOROTCHENKO. Your husband's signature itself will carry that message.

TATIANA (*drops check on table*). Then—that is understood.

GOROTCHENKO (*picks up the check*). Tatiana Petrovna Romanova . . . Mikail Androvitch Ouratieff . . . the flag of the Romanoffs no longer flies over Soviet territories. But I shall arrange with the Central Committee that it shall be affixed twice into the map in the room that once was the Tsar's. It shall mark the spot that is Bakoura and the spot that is Petropolsk.

TATIANA. And those flags will be protected from vandals?

GOROTCHENKO. Yes, madame. I know you have scant respect for my honor—but such as it is, it is dedicated to the fulfillment of this promise. And, by way of thanks, I can only say . . .

MIKAIL. By way of thanks, you can say nothing, Commissar.

GOROTCHENKO. If either of you should wish to return to Russia . . .

TATIANA. The only Russia we will ever know is with us now.

GOROTCHENKO. I think I understand, madame. I can be sure it's well guarded.

MIKAIL. I'm not so sure that you do understand, Commissar. You and your comrades are just a bit too smug—too snobbish—to understand. We are the Russia of yesterday. You are the Russia of today. But I seriously suspect that none of us will have a logical place in the Russia of tomorrow. And now I'm late with the lemonade.

GOROTCHENKO. If you will excuse me, I shall rejoin them.

MIKAIL. No! Please wait here a little longer. I prefer to serve the lemonade in peace; I don't want additional black looks at me because I've deprived them of their precious petrol. (*A pause.* TATIANA *remains motionless—*GOROTCHENKO *also. Then* GOROTCHENKO *makes a movement to take the pen-holder from the table.*)

TATIANA (*imperiously*). Leave that alone. (*Quietly*) It belongs to the cook.

GOROTCHENKO (*putting it in his pocket*). Not now . . . it is ours . . . Russia's.

TATIANA (*gently, almost sadly*). Very well, take it, Commissar of pigs.

GOROTCHENKO (*tenderly*). When you send me crawling on that journey to Moscow—from St. Petersburg—I shall be thinking, every metre of the way, of you, of him, and the devotion that has survived in you. (*He takes two steps towards the pantry door and suddenly* TATIANA *runs after him.*)

TATIANA (*impetuously*). Gorotchenko!

GOROTCHENKO. Madame!

TATIANA. You won't fail to have the two flags of the Tsar fixed onto the map?

GOROTCHENKO. I shall not fail.

TATIANA. Then . . . could you also have the mustache removed from my picture?

GOROTCHENKO (*thoughtfully*). Well, that will entail a certain amount of red tape. But it is a promise.

TATIANA. Thank you. That is all. (*He looks at her, intently, for a moment.*)

GOROTCHENKO. Good-bye, Imperial Highness.

TATIANA (*slowly*). Good-bye, Tovarich!

GOROTCHENKO (*goes quickly to* TATIANA *and kisses her shoulder. He reaches the door and, on the threshold, gravely and very magnificently*) Good-bye Russia! (*He goes out. Alone,* TATIANA *stares at the empty space a moment. Then slowly sinks into chair. At this moment the pantry door opens brusquely and* GEORGE *comes in. He is in evening dress.*)

GEORGE. Tina . . . Tina . . . We are ready. Did the dinner go off well?

TATIANA. Very well, Monsieur George. Very well, indeed.

GEORGE. Tina . . . all evening long I haven't been able to think of anything but you . . . I've wanted so desperately to hold you in my arms . . .

TATIANA (*frowning*). Monsieur George!

GEORGE. Yes, Tina!

TATIANA (*in a far-off voice, absently, without even looking at* GEORGE *and with an indefinable sadness, a sad smile*). It is not the moment, Monsieur George.

GEORGE (*groaning*). Oh, it never seems to be the moment with you!

TATIANA (*lost in thought*). Sometimes it is.

GEORGE. Will you let me know when that moment arrives?

TATIANA (*still deep in thought*). Yes—I shall let you know . . .

GEORGE. Good . . . Then, we are comrades?

TATIANA (*jumping*). What?

GEORGE (*laughing*). We're comrades! Tovarich!
(HELENE *comes in.*)

TATIANA (*slowly*). Tovarich!

HELENE. Tovarich? I thought you hated that word?

TATIANA (*slowly*). No, mademoiselle, I don't hate anything. I must dress. (*She goes out.*)

GEORGE. Helene, get out the vodka. Tonight—it's the New Year, the real Russian New Year. We're going to forget that we're dreary bourgeois—we'll forget that we had the bad luck to be born outside Russia. We must make them think we're actually as gay, and mad, and charming as they are.

HELENE. Ia Doushka. (*She pours out the vodka.*)

GEORGE. Tatiachka!

HELENE. Mishka!

GEORGE. Ia wass loublou.

HELENE. Nitchevo. (*They pick up their glasses and link arms.*)

GEORGE. A life for the Tsar!

HELENE. A life for the Tsar! (*They drink and then they start to sing a Russian song.* MIKAIL *comes in with the tray. He looks at them, with a rather wistful smile.*)

MIKAIL. Well done! Well done!

GEORGE. Now we must break the glasses.

MIKAIL (*quickly*). No—no—please. They'll be taken from our wages. Put them down gently, monsieur and mademoiselle.

HELENE. But we'll break glasses at the party, won't we?

MIKAIL. You may break everything there, mademoiselle — windows, lamps, musical instruments, and possibly a few hearts. Where is Tina?

GEORGE. She has gone to dress.

MIKAIL. If you'll permit me—I shall make a few slight changes in my attire.

HELENE. Permission is graciously granted, Mikail. (*She, with mock pomp, holds out her hand and* MIKAIL *kisses it.*)

MIKAIL. Thank you, mademoiselle. (MIKAIL *goes out.*)

GEORGE. If you don't mind awfully, Mikail—tonight at the party—I wish you wouldn't tell any of your friends that we're foreigners. Let's pretend for once that we're *real* Russians!

HELENE. Oh yes, Mikail, couldn't you say we're your long-lost cousins or something?
(MIKAIL *returns, wearing a white waistcoat.*)

MIKAIL. Of course, it will be as you wish. But—I don't think it will work.

HELENE. Can't we even pretend?

MIKAIL. There are essential racial differences, mademoiselle. (*He sits down at the kitchen table, starts to put on a large number of medals and decorations.*)

GEORGE. I know. We're congenitally dull.

MIKAIL. It isn't that, monsieur. The trouble is—we're congenitally savage. That's what makes us the fools that we are. Sentimental barbarians! You can't emulate that. You have within you too great an accumulation of common sense. Your civilization goes back too far—all the way to Romulus and Remus, I suppose. We've had only two hundred years of the blessings of culture. And that isn't enough. We may wear the same clothes that you do, and read the same books, and know which fork to use at dinner—and be superficially presentable. But our souls are still roaming the steppes, wildly —baying with the wolves at the moon.

HELENE. Ah, Michel, when I hear you talk like that I wish . . .

MIKAIL. When you hear me talk like that, mademoiselle, you may be sure that I, too, am listening, enraptured, to the sound of my own voice.

GEORGE (*startled*). The Legion of Honor? Where did all those decorations come from?

MIKAIL. From a pawnbroker's, Monsieur George.

HELENE. But you'll look magnificent!

MIKAIL. That is my intention, mademoiselle. There never yet has been a savage who didn't love to dress up!

GEORGE. And what is that one with the purple ribbon?

MIKAIL. The Order of St. Christopher. It is awarded for supreme valor.

HELENE. Oh!

MIKAIL. It cost me three francs twenty-five.
(CHARLES *comes in. He is surprised and annoyed to see the children.*)

CHARLES. Isn't this a rather strange hour for you two to be in the kitchen?

HELENE (*boldly*). We're waiting for Michel and Tina.
(CHARLES *looks at the decorations.*)

CHARLES. I see. You've resumed your identity already, eh? (*To* GEORGE *and* HELENE) I want you two to leave.

GEORGE. Michel and Tina are taking us to a Russian fête, and we'll wait here until they're ready to go.

CHARLES. You don't say so! You're mingling in rather high society this evening.

GEORGE (*angrily*). Look here, father. Even if Michel and Tina are servants, they can have as much dignity as anyone else. A damned sight more than we have—if you ask me.

CHARLES. Well—I shall not ask you. Get out. (*He turns to* MIKAIL) I want a few words with you.

MIKAIL. Very good, sir. (*He turns to* GEORGE) If you will wait for us below, Monsieur George. . . .

GEORGE. Come on, Helene. I've left my car at the servants' entrance. We'll wait for you there.

HELENE. You won't be long?

MIKAIL. No, mademoiselle. (GEORGE *and* HELENE *exit. To* CHARLES) Sir?

CHARLES. I never dreamed that you could do such a cruel thing to me.

MIKAIL. Perhaps some day you will forgive me, sir. But we understand perfectly that you and Madame have every reason to detest us and wish to be rid of us.

CHARLES. No, Prince Ouratieff. Madame and I . . .

MIKAIL. Sir, to you my name must forever be Michel!

CHARLES. Michel, then. We do not detest you.

MIKAIL. Ah—thank you, sir.

CHARLES. In fact, we—well—we respect and admire you. But where will you go now?

MIKAIL. To South America, sir. To dwell among apes and cobras.

CHARLES. South America, eh! And what will you do there?

MIKAIL. The same sort of work, we hope, sir.

CHARLES. Then—if that is what you wish . . . (*He is fumbling for the words he wants to utter*) Madame and I have been talking it over. We—we like you—you and Her Highness . . .

MIKAIL. Tina, sir.

CHARLES. Tina. And we think you like us. . . .

MIKAIL (*with simple sincerity*). Sir, we love you.

CHARLES. Well, then . . . if you could forget . . . (TATIANA *comes in, beautifully dressed.* CHARLES

turns, sees her and bows) Your Imperial Highness.

MIKAIL. No, sir—no—please. You were saying . . . ?

CHARLES. Well, I was about to say —if you are determined to continue with this sort of work, then why not continue with it here . . . ?

TATIANA. Ah—godly man—you wish us to stay?

CHARLES. Well—that is—I mean, it's for you to say. . . .

MIKAIL. Before all the saints, sir, I swear to you that never by word or deed should we remind you that we have ever been other than Michel and Tina. You may reduce our wages to nothing—you may beat us with whips—you may cancel the every other Sunday we have free, if you wish us to . . .

CHARLES (*nervously*). Very well— (*turns to* TATIANA) very well— then that's settled. (TATIANA *smothers him with kisses*) Now—now, my dear—that's enough of that . . . for the time being. And— thank you. . . . (*He goes out.*)

TATIANA. We are saved! *Saved*— from South America! (*Pirouetting around stage.*)

MIKAIL. Never have two poor Russians had greater cause for celebration. Come—

TATIANA. Our kitchen! Our dear, darling kitchen! Look, my pigeon— it is snowing! It's so beautiful!

MIKAIL. And so sad!

TATIANA. Yes—everything is so sad, isn't it? Even happiness!

MIKAIL. Especially happiness.

TATIANA. Your eyes are full of tears.

MIKAIL. They're the reflection of yours, Tatiana.

TATIANA. We're fools, aren't we, Mikail?

MIKAIL. Yes, my darling. Fools! Now and forever. Come! (*She breaks away from him. He goes to hold open the door. She goes hastily and picks up two empty milk bottles.*)

TATIANA. If I don't leave these for the milkman, the Russian God won't do it for me. (*She goes out.* MIKAIL *follows.*)

CURTAIN

Amphitryon 38
A COMEDY IN A PROLOGUE AND THREE ACTS

BY JEAN GIRAUDOUX

ADAPTED FROM THE FRENCH
BY S. N. BEHRMAN

FOR

JEAN GIRAUDOUX

WITH THE HOPE THAT THE AMERICAN VERSION OF
HIS ENCHANTING PLAY WILL AFFORD HIM,
OCCASIONALLY, SOME GLEAM
OF RECOGNITION

Amphitryon 38 was produced by the Theatre Guild, Inc., at the Shubert Theatre on November 2, 1937, with the following cast:

(in the order in which they speak)

JUPITER	Alfred Lunt
MERCURY	Richard Whorf
SOSIE, SERVANT TO AMPHITRYON	George Meader
TRUMPETER	Sydney Greenstreet
WARRIOR	Alan Hewitt
ALKMENA	Lynn Fontanne
AMPHITRYON	Barry Thomson
NEVETZA	Kathleen Roland
KLEANTHA	Jacqueline Paige
ECHO	Ernestine De Becker
LEDA	Edith King

The action takes place in and about Amphitryon's palace.

Directed by Bretaigne Windust.
Settings by Lee Simonson.
Costumes by Valentina.
Music composed by Samuel L. M. Barlow.

AMPHITRYON 38

PROLOGUE

SCENE—*A Cloud.*

JUPITER, *the master of the gods, and* MERCURY, *his half-son, are loung-ing on a cloud, their phosphorescent eyes focused for the moment on the domesticities of a terrestrial couple.*

JUPITER (*peering straight out*). There she is, Mercury—there she is!

MERCURY. Where, Jupiter, where?

JUPITER. You see that lighted win-dow, the one with the curtain stir-ring in the breeze? She's there. Alkmena is there! No, now she's gone! Don't move, don't move—in a second perhaps, you will see her shadow pass again.

MERCURY. Jupiter, you astonish me. If you're in love with this mortal, why don't you employ the facilities you have as a god? Why waste an entire night, ravished with longing, bouncing about on a cloud, catch-ing at her shadow when you might so easily, with your ordinary god-sight, see her as she is through the walls of her chamber?

JUPITER. You would have me caress her body with invisible hands, en-fold her in a closeness she could not feel?

MERCURY. But the wind makes love like that, Jupiter, and the wind is, as much as you are, one of the prime elements of fecundity.

JUPITER. True, but with her, Mer-cury, I am tempted to transcend my

former conquests. I have a nostalgia for mortality. I would like to expe-rience the same difficulties human beings do—and the same delights. As a god, I feel I should be closer to my subjects!

MERCURY. Oh, but love-making among human beings is such a bor-ing routine!

JUPITER. Oh, you think so, do you?

MERCURY. Yes. To begin with, you must woo her—then you must undress her—then you must dress her again. And to get rid of her you must actively antagonize her—it's a full time job!

JUPITER. Yes, it's true that the rituals and conventions of earthly love-making are complicated—but strangely enough, it is their strict observance that yields the greater pleasure.

MERCURY. I know them all. First you must follow her—

JUPITER. Measuring your pace ex-actly to hers so that both your legs seem to swing from the same ful-crum—

MERCURY (*rather bored, succumb-ing to the rhythm of a well-worn formula*). Identifying in both your bodies the ultimate source of all impulse and all rhythm.

JUPITER. Then—with a bound, you are at her side—

MERCURY. With your left hand you descend on her breasts—

JUPITER. With your right hand you cover her eyelids—the most sensitive part of a woman's skin—

MERCURY. So that she may divine from the heat of your palm, your ardor—

JUPITER. And from the lines of your palm, your ultimate destiny, your mortal future and your grievous death. So that pity will stir in her as well as desire—

JUPITER AND MERCURY (*together*). For in the conquest of a woman—the one is as important as the other—

JUPITER. Acquiescent at last—you undo her girdle—

MERCURY AND JUPITER (*together—in choir*). And so forth—and so forth—and so forth—

JUPITER. And then what do you do?

MERCURY. And then what do I do?

JUPITER. Yes. What do you feel?

MERCURY. What do I feel? Nothing! Nothing special. In fact it's exactly like being with Venus!

JUPITER. Why then do you bother to go to Earth at all?

MERCURY. Out of boredom. And I confess that for a brief sojourn the Earth has certain advantages. What with its moist atmosphere and its green lawns it is perhaps the pleasantest planet on which to alight—but only for a brief stay—because it has distinct drawbacks. Due to its heavy mineral and oil deposits, it gives off a heady odor. It is, in fact, the only star which smells exactly like a wild animal.

JUPITER. Look at that curtain—look quickly!

MERCURY. Her shadow—

JUPITER. No, no. Not yet her shadow. What you see now is but the shadow of her shadow.

MERCURY (*peering intently*). Well whatever it is—that silhouette is dividing itself like a draw-bridge. There are two people there—interlaced like a vine-motif in a frieze. It's not your unborn son, Jupiter, that makes that shadow so grossly convex but simply—her husband. (*In amazement*) Why, he's a giant! Look; he approaches her again—he embraces her again—he's insatiable!

JUPITER. Yes. Amphitryon, her only love.

MERCURY. Now, I begin to see why you are willing to forego your celestial eyesight. To observe merely a shadow-husband embracing a shadow-wife is less painful than to observe the living substance. (*Short pause*) Now the shadow has disappeared!

JUPITER. Doubtless, overcome, she has sunk down and abandons herself to blissful languor—drinking in the songs of the ravished nightingales. Oh, happy, happy nightingales!

MERCURY. Ravished nightingales! Jupiter, you know perfectly well that as far as women are concerned these little birds are quite disinterested. In love affairs the nightingales are nothing but obligato. It's for that reason you have never found it advantageous to impersonate a nightingale. On several occasions you've had to do a bull— but never a nightingale! No, it's not the birds you have to worry about —it's the husband—the husband of this dark, lusty beauty!

JUPITER (*quickly*). How do you know she's dark? Are you inventing, or are you spying?

MERCURY. I confess a moment ago, while she was in her bath, I resumed for a fleeting instant my celestial vision. Don't be annoyed— now I see no more than you do.

JUPITER. You're lying! I can tell it from your face. You're looking at her. You see her. I can see a glow on your face that comes only from the phosphorescence of a woman.

MERCURY. I confess—I am looking at her.

JUPITER. Well, what's she doing?

MERCURY. She is leaning over the relaxed Amphitryon. She's laughing. She holds Amphitryon's head in her hands as if she were weighing it. She kisses his head—she lets it fall back as if her kisses made it too heavy to hold. Now she is facing us squarely— Yes—she is indubitably—dark!

JUPITER. And her husband?

MERCURY. Quite dark. His nipples apricot—

JUPITER. I'm not interested in his color scheme. What is he doing?

MERCURY. He polishes her with his hand as one would a favorite pony. He's a celebrated horseman, you know.

JUPITER. And Alkmena?

MERCURY. Oh, so gay—so docile— so faithful.

JUPITER. Faithful to herself or faithful to her husband—that is the question. You know, Mercury, most faithful wives are unfaithful to their husbands with everything except men; with jewels—with perfumes —with reading—with religion and with the contemplation of Spring, with everything in fact, except a man. Don't you think these faithful wives deserve some compensation?

MERCURY. But Alkmena is faithful only to her husband! Jupiter, by what subterfuge can you make her yours?

JUPITER. The difficulty with these virtuous wives is not to seduce them —but to persuade them that they may be seduced confidentially! And the contemplation of this creature paralyzes my invention. What do you suggest, Mercury?

MERCURY. Functioning as a human being or functioning as a god?

JUPITER. How would the methods differ?

MERCURY. Well, functioning as a god—very simple. You lift her to our plane—you make her comfortable on a cloud—for the required seconds you let her bear a hero's weight—and then—you let her resume her own.

JUPITER. But by following that course I should forego the most exquisite sensation to be had from the love of a woman.

MERCURY. Which most exquisite sensation? There are several.

JUPITER. The moment of consent. But with Alkmena that's impossible because she loves only her husband.

MERCURY. Well, then—be her husband!

JUPITER. But he's never out of her sight! The most persistent stay-at-homes in the world are heroes out-of-work! They're more domestic than tigers!

MERCURY. Then employ him. Fortunately there is an infallible recipe for getting heroes out of the house.

JUPITER. War?

MERCURY. Have Thebes declare war.

JUPITER. But Thebes is at peace with her enemies.

MERCURY. Then have her declare war against a friend. What are friendly powers for if they can't have a little squabble now and then?

JUPITER. Isn't it singular, Mercury, you and I are gods and yet to achieve human simplicity becomes for us the most devious exercise in style. While we are on Earth fate demands far more of us than she does of mortals. To obtain from Alkmena this exquisite consent—which the most grotesque of human beings can gain by making a few faces—we have to contrive innumerable stratagems, perform wonders, pile up miracles—

MERCURY. Well, contrive them! Pile them up!

JUPITER. How? How?

MERCURY. Have a warrior overcome by an uncontrollable impulse to exercise his profession. Instantly Amphitryon will fly off to head his army.

JUPITER. Of course!

MERCURY. The minute he is gone—assume his appearance—assign to me the exterior of his servant Sosie. I will appear—whisper discreetly in Alkmena's ear that Amphitryon has only made a pretense of departing—that actually he means to return—to spend the night with her.

JUPITER (with admiration). Oh, Mercury, you are your father's son!

MERCURY. Let us go—let us descend. Order a special cloud, Jupiter, to conceal us.

JUPITER. That's hardly necessary, Mercury. For there, on Earth, they have an institution which renders them invisible to creditors, to the jealous—which gives them surcease

rom their little nervous cares—a
great and democratic institution—
the only one—I may add—which is
even moderately successful—

MERCURY. What is that, Jupiter?

JUPITER. The night!

(*The curtains close in and the lights
fade as the music swells.*)

MERCURY. The night?

JUPITER. The night . . .

MERCURY. The night.

CURTAIN

ACT ONE

SCENE—*The façade and terrace of* AMPHITRYON's *palace in Thebes. Four
rectangular steps. At top of fourth step is an iron grille gate. More steps
from gate up to portico of Palace. The gate is open.*
   TIME—*Night.*
   The TRUMPETER *is discovered with his trumpet.* SOSIE *enters from
palace with scroll.*

SOSIE. Are you the Trumpeter of
the day?

TRUMPETER. If I may make so bold,
yes. And you, who are you, may I
ask? You look like someone I know.

SOSIE (*importantly*). I doubt it very
much. I am Sosie. I am the servant,
Official Announcer and Scribe to
General Amphitryon. I am unique.

TRUMPETER (*humbly*). I must be
mistaken.

SOSIE. What are you waiting for?
If you are the Trumpeter of the
day, why don't you trumpet?

TRUMPETER. But, may I make so
bold, your announcement? What
does it announce?

SOSIE. You'll find out.

TRUMPETER. Is it Lost and Found?
Has someone lost something?

SOSIE. On the contrary! Something
has been found. Blow, I tell you.

TRUMPETER (*sits comfortably on
top step*). It's easy to say blow but
how can I blow when I don't know
what it is I'm blowing for?

SOSIE. You have no choice. You always blow the same note anyway.

TRUMPETER (*with dignity*). It is
true my instrument has only one
note but as for me personally I
have many. For I am a composer. I
compose hymns.

SOSIE. I bet your hymns have only
one note. Hurry up, there's a good
fellow, and blow. There's Orion in
the sky already!

TRUMPETER (*placidly*). Orion may be in the sky but that does not alter the fact that as a creative artist I have to know what it is you expect me to blow·about. If I have attained any celebrity among the one-note trumpeters it is because, before blowing, I compose in my mind a whole musical composition of which the last note is invariably the one I blow. That note is the climax. That is why, when I do come to blow it, it has such surprise, such brilliance, such finality. The climax may be always the same but the approach—ah!—the approach . . . !

SOSIE. I wish for once you'd begin with the climax! The whole town's falling asleep!

TRUMPETER. The town may be falling asleep, but I must just stop to tell you that my colleagues, in fact all trumpeters, are consumed with jealousy of me. You can see why—because none of them are composers. They tell me that in the trumpet-schools they have instituted, thanks to my example, a course, teaching the trumpeters not to blow, indeed, but how to perfect the silence that precedes the blowing. Now you can see, I am sure, how important it is for me to know what it is I'm blowing for. First, I have to compose a silent air and how can I do that if I don't know whether I'm blowing for war or for peace, for Lost and Found or for marriage, or birth or death. I've got to know, that's all!

SOSIE. Well then it's for peace.

TRUMPETER. What peace?

SOSIE. At least what passes for peace —the breathing-spell between wars.

TRUMPETER. Shall I compose something martial?

SOSIE. For peace!

TRUMPETER. It has been my observation that a martial air is irresistible no matter what the cause. I myself, pacific nature though I am, when I hear a military band, feel truculent. I can't help it. Shall I do something of the sort for peace?

SOSIE. If it's not misleading . . . ?

TRUMPETER. Leave it to me! (*The* TRUMPETER *lifts his instrument to his lips, weaving meanwhile with his free hand a stirring, military air.* SOSIE *interrupts impatiently.*)

SOSIE. Don't be too warlike!

TRUMPETER (*patiently regretful*). Now I have to begin all over again. . . . (*He repeats the business and blows his one note. Magnanimously*) Now you may deliver. . . .

SOSIE (*declaiming*). The General Amphitryon has bade me address you on the subject of Peace. . . . I don't see a single light down there. I'm afraid your wonderful trumpet didn't carry far!

TRUMPETER. Ah! But they heard my silent song—it entered their ears insensibly—that is all I ask.

SOSIE (*continuing his proclamation*). Oh, Thebans! The General Amphitryon, whose war proclamations have so often stirred you, has asked me to deliver you a peace proclamation. Instead of rousing you from your beds it is intended to lull you to a deeper sleep. Is it not good to sleep in a fatherland unscarred by the trenches of war, among friendly birds and dogs and cats, among rats whose appetites have never been whetted by the taste of human flesh? Is it not good to wear your national countenance, not as a mask to frighten those who haven't the same blood-count you have but as an oval mirror to reflect smiling and laughter? Thebans, sleep!

TRUMPETER. That's good! That's very good! Did General Amphitryon write that?

SOSIE. General Amphitryon is too busy to write! I am his scribe. I wrote it.

TRUMPETER. Did he give you the ideas?

SOSIE. He simply said: Deliver them a Peace Proclamation. They're my own ideas!

TRUMPETER. Nevertheless, they're good! They're very good!

SOSIE (continuing). Thebans! You may sleep! What more lovely array than your unarmed and naked bodies, flat on your backs, arms outstretched with nothing heavier to worry about than your navels. . . . Never has there been a night so transfigured, so fragrant, so serene . . . sleep! sleep! sleep!

TRUMPETER (made sleepy by the cadence). I'd like to take a nap myself. . . .

SOSIE. Now, then, Thebans! (He pulls out a scroll and reads from it) The General Amphitryon has ordered me to read you, instead of a War Bulletin—a Peace Bulletin.

Listen: Between the Issus and its tributary we have taken an important prisoner, a roebuck wandered from Thrace. Around Mount Olympus, by dint of skillful maneuvering, we have coaxed the arid plains into a fine green sward which presently will blossom into wheat! The syringas we have caused to be lanced by great swarms of bees. On the shores of the Aegean there is nothing, neither in the expanse of the waves nor in the vista of the stars to burden the spirit with apprehension and, in the mysterious distances that separate the temples from the firmament, the trees from the houses, animals from men, we have ambushed a thousand secret signals which our wise men will be centuries in deciphering . . . we are menaced, Thebans, by centuries of peace. . . . Cursed be war! Cursed be war! Cursed be war!

(The WARRIOR enters.)

TRUMPETER (murmuring sympathetically out of his drowse). Cursed be war . . . !

WARRIOR (fiercely). What is that you say?

SOSIE (frightened). I repeat what I have just said: "A curse on war!"

WARRIOR. Do you know to whom you are saying this?

SOSIE. I do not.

WARRIOR. To a professional warrior.

TRUMPETER (fully awake now). Ah! Now we'll get a different point of view!

SOSIE. Well, there are wars and wars!

WARRIOR. Not to a warrior. Where is your master?

SOSIE. There—in his bedroom—where the light is burning.

WARRIOR. Bring your master this message instantly. He must get into his accoutrements at once.

SOSIE. He's asleep.

WARRIOR. Take him the message at once! It's war!

SOSIE. But from everywhere resounds that murmur which old men call the echo of peace!

WARRIOR. And that, my friend, is just the moment for me!

SOSIE. War! Again!

TRUMPETER. What do you mean again? Still!

WARRIOR. The Athenians have mobilized their troops and crossed the frontier.

SOSIE. You lie! The Athenians are our allies!

WARRIOR. Then it is our allies who are invading us—wake up Amphitryon. Do you hear? Go!
(SOSIE *exits into the palace.*)

WARRIOR (*to the* TRUMPETER *who starts to follow* SOSIE). You stay here! Blow your trumpet!

TRUMPETER. What is the subject on which you wish me to blow?

WARRIOR. War!

TRUMPETER. But which aspect of war? Do you wish me to emphasize its sublime side or its pathetic side?

WARRIOR. Neither. I want you to emphasize its appeal to Youth. (*The* TRUMPETER *composes and blows. The* WARRIOR *leans over the balustrade and shouts*) Thebans awake! All of you who are vital, whose bodies are strong and unblemished, segregate yourselves from the sweating mass spawning there in the darkness. Get up! To arms!

TRUMPETER. Some of those lazy people would rather spawn! They're very weak.

WARRIOR (*continues his harangue*). You who are poor, all of you whom fortune has treated badly, war will restore your rights. And you rich come and experience the final ecstasy—the ecstasy of the gambler who risks his position, his pleasures, his mistresses, on one turn of the wheel. You zealots, you prayerful ones, make Nationalism your religion. And you atheists and sensualists, war is your paradise for it legalizes all your excesses—you may whet your swords on the statues of the gods themselves. You who hate work—to the trenches—war is the heaven of the lazy. And for you who are industrious—we have the Commissariat!

TRUMPETER. There's something in what he says—jobs for everybody!

WARRIOR. Get up! Fall into rank! For who prefers to the glory of dying valiantly for one's country the inglorious destiny of staying at home overfed, lethargic and slothful?

TRUMPETER. I do.

WARRIOR. Besides, Citizens, there is nothing really to be afraid of. I may tell you this in confidence: in this war, on our side at least, there will be no fatalities whatever, and moreover, whatever wounds there are will be in the left hand—except among the left-handed. No more petty squabbles—war unites us! And how humane it is, for it abolishes the barbaric duel! Here she is—your war, ready for you, eager to welcome you. War! Welcome! I salute you! War! It's begun already. See the lights down there. Citizens —to arms! (*He comes down the steps hurriedly, shouting as he goes*) You may pick your laws, your pleasures, your women—Liberty, Equality, Fraternity, War— (*He rushes across the stage shouting slogans*) Freedom—license— cruelty—joy—war— (*His voice trails off as he disappears.* SOSIE *enters from the palace.*)

TRUMPETER (*to* SOSIE). Your master is ready?

SOSIE. He is ready. It is my mistress who isn't quite ready. It takes no time at all to dress for going to war, but to dress for saying farewell takes longer.

TRUMPETER. Is she one of those weeping women?

SOSIE. Unfortunately one of the smiling ones. The weeping ones regain their composure more quickly than the smiling ones.

TRUMPETER (*shrugs his shoulders philosophically, then looks down on the city below*). They're getting up all right. Look at those lights! (*He rises and starts coming down the steps*) He'll get 'em. (*He crosses the stage ruminating out loud*) They could sleep in peace but they'd rather get up and fight. . . . They like it. They want it. Well, if that's what they want they can have it. (*He goes out dejectedly.* SOSIE *comes down the steps and follows him.*)

SOSIE. What miserable luck—to have this happen on the very day that Peace is proclaimed! (*He goes out.* AMPHITRYON *enters from palace, in full war regalia. He goes to end of platform, scans the horizon and starts down steps.* ALKMENA *enters from the palace.*)

ALKMENA. Amphitryon! I love you —

(AMPHITRYON *quickly goes up steps, embraces her and kisses her.*)

AMPHITRYON. I love you, Alkmena.

ALKMENA. Will you think of me while you're away? Do you promise it?

AMPHITRYON. Yes, darling. (*Looks away.*)

ALKMENA. Why do you turn to the moon? I'm jealous of the moon— that blank surface—what thoughts do you get from her?

AMPHITRYON. And from your dark head—what?

ALKMENA. A scent at least—twin brother of memory. Oh, you're shaved! Do they shave now to go to war? Do you think with your skin pumiced like that, you'll be more formidable?

AMPHITRYON. Oh, no, darling. For that I rely on my armor and helmet.

ALKMENA. Put your helmet on. Let me see you as your enemy sees you.

AMPHITRYON. Now don't be frightened! (*Puts helmet on.*)

ALKMENA. Not very frightening— not when those eyes are your eyes.

AMPHITRYON. But to my enemy it is, I assure you.

ALKMENA. What are your greaves made of?

AMPHITRYON. Silver—chased in platinum.

ALKMENA. Aren't they too tight for you? Wouldn't steel ones be more flexible for running?

AMPHITRYON. My dear, I'm a general in command—and generals in command never run.
(*Horses' hoofs heard off stage.*)

ALKMENA. Your horses, your horses are here. Kiss me.

AMPHITRYON. No, no, my horses have quite a different gait—but that's no reason why I can't kiss you.
(*They kiss.*)

ALKMENA. Is your helmet silver, too?

AMPHITRYON. The purest.

ALKMENA. What color tunic are you wearing beneath your armor?

AMPHITRYON. Rose-pink—edged with black braid.

ALKMENA. Oh, you naughty Amphitryon! How coquettish you are with your war!—Rose-pink—black braid. Does that help you to achieve your victories, or do you win them in one headlong charge, my name on your lips?

AMPHITRYON. No, darling, it isn't that way.

ALKMENA. How do you do it then?

AMPHITRYON. Well, first of all I surround their left wing with my right wing, then I divide their right wing—using only three-quarters of my left wing—and then with the remaining quarter of my left wing I dart in among them—

ALKMENA. I see. A kind of battle of the birds.

AMPHITRYON. —and that gives me the victory.

ALKMENA. How many victories have you won, dearest one?

AMPHITRYON. One, just one.

ALKMENA. Well, tell me, Amphitryon, have you killed many men?

AMPHITRYON. One, only one.

ALKMENA. How economical you are, dear. Was he a king? Was he a general?

AMPHITRYON. No, he was a simple soldier.

ALKMENA. So modest—modest to a fault, my dear. Tell me, did you, in the process of his destruction, did you allow him one instant in which to recognize you and be aware of the distinction you had just conferred on him? Did you, sweetheart?

AMPHITRYON. Yes, I did. Blood pouring out of his mouth, he looked up at me and managed, with his last breath, a faint, respectful smile.

ALKMENA. He must have been very happy! Did he tell you his name before he died?

AMPHITRYON. He was an anonymous soldier—there are quite a few of them.

ALKMENA. I see! You know, darling, when you breathe your armor loosens at the fastenings, and your tunic gives your skin a tint of dawn. Breathe, Amphitryon, breathe—deeply—and let me savor, in the darkness of this night, the glow of your body. Stay a little longer. (*Presses closely to him*) Do you love me?

AMPHITRYON. Yes. I have to wait for my horses anyway. Darling, don't press too closely to me—you'll hurt yourself. You know I'm a husband made of iron.

ALKMENA. Can you feel me—through all that armor?

AMPHITRYON. Through every chink where an arrow might reach me, you reach me. And you—do you feel me?

ALKMENA. Yes—but your own body is a kind of armor. Often I have lain in your arms and felt you remoter and colder than I do now.

AMPHITRYON. Alkmena, often I have held you close to me, and felt

you sadder and more desolate than I feel you today. And yet, on those occasions I was departing not for the war but for the hunt. (ALKMENA *smiles*) Now, why do you smile? Do you find consolation in this sudden declaration of war?

ALKMENA. Did you hear a child crying beneath our window a little while ago? Didn't that seem to you to be a premonition of evil?

AMPHITRYON. No, no, no. Omens are always announced with a thunderclap in a clear sky, accompanied by a triple flash of lightning.

ALKMENA. The sky was clear and yet the child was crying. That seemed to me to be even a worse augury.

AMPHITRYON. Don't be superstitious, Alkmena.

ALKMENA. Something was hovering over our happiness. Praise be to the gods it was only war.

AMPHITRYON. Why do you say that —only war?

ALKMENA. I was afraid it was our love that might be threatened—it's there I feel the danger. I almost find consolation in war. At least, it's a tangible and visible antagonist. I like enemies whose weapons I can see—my great fear has always been that I would one day find you in the arms of other women.

AMPHITRYON. Other women!

ALKMENA. One or a thousand— what difference does it make? You'd be lost.

AMPHITRYON. You are the most beautiful woman in all Thebes.

ALKMENA. It's the goddesses I'm afraid of—and those foreigners.

AMPHITRYON. You're not serious.

ALKMENA. Above all—I fear the goddesses. When they emerge from the heavens—rosy without rouge—pearly without powder—their breasts whiter than snow and their arms stronger than crowbars, it must be very difficult to resist them. Don't you think so?

AMPHITRYON. For anyone but me it might be—yes.

ALKMENA. But they're very sensitive, they take offense at very little, and they like to be loved. You've never loved a goddess, have you?

AMPHITRYON. Certainly not.

ALKMENA. No goddess has ever loved you?

AMPHITRYON. No.

ALKMENA. Not a little tiny bit?

AMPHITRYON. No! And what's more, I never loved a foreigner, either.

ALKMENA. They've loved you.

AMPHITRYON. Oh, no, they haven't.

ALKMENA. Oh, yes, they have.

AMPHITRYON. Oh, but they have not, dear.

ALKMENA. Oh, they love every married man, these women. When they arrive in our cities everything is over for us, the stay-at-homes. Even the ugly ones, they flaunt their ugliness because after all it's a foreign ugliness and therefore very provocative. They are in love with themselves because even to themselves they are foreign. Compared to a threat like that war comes as a friend. You won't be killed, will you? Generals in command are never killed. You will come back.

AMPHITRYON. I'll be back very soon, and that will be forever.
(*They kiss.*)

ALKMENA. Look! The stars are twinkling harder than ever. It is their last chance before dawn and our parting. Which one of them shall we choose to fix our eyes on tomorrow and every night at this same hour?

AMPHITRYON. Well, there's always our old friend Venus!

ALKMENA. I don't trust her. As an intermediary in love she might turn out to be not quite so disinterested. No, that side of my life I'd rather look after personally.

AMPHITRYON. What about Jupiter? There's a good solid name!

ALKMENA. I'd rather have a star that has no name.

AMPHITRYON. What about that little one over there that's called anonymous star.

ALKMENA. Well, that's a name, isn't it?
(*Horses' hoofs heard.*)

AMPHITRYON. This time it's they—I must go. (*Starts down steps.*)

ALKMENA. Who are "they"? Your ambition, your pride as a commander, your love for carnage and adventure?

AMPHITRYON. No, no. Just Elaphocephale and Hypsipila, my horses.

ALKMENA (comes down steps). Go then if you must.

AMPHITRYON. Is that all you have to say to me?

ALKMENA. Haven't I said about everything? What do other wives say?

AMPHITRYON. Well—they make jokes. They hand you your shield and they say things like "Return on it or beneath it!" They cry out after you, "Fear nothing," "Do or die!" Can it be that my wife has no gift for epigrams like that?

ALKMENA. I'm afraid not. I couldn't utter a phrase that belonged more to posterity than it did to you. The only words that I can find to utter are those which perish softly even as they touch you. I love you, Amphitryon! Come back soon, Amphitryon! Besides, your name is so long, once you've said it there's hardly breath left to follow it up with an immortal sentence.
(SOSIE enters with AMPHITRYON'S spear and shield.)

AMPHITRYON. Then say my name at the end. (Takes spear and shield from SOSIE and lifts his right arm in a salute) Good-bye, Alkmena! (Exits, followed by SOSIE.)

ALKMENA. Amphitryon! (For a moment she stands still. Then the sound of horses' hoofs is heard starting and then gradually diminishing in the distance. ALKMENA, on the verge of sobbing, turns away. MERCURY, disguised as SOSIE, enters and stands below gate. ALKMENA turns to gate, looks at MERCURY in amazement, knowing that SOSIE had just gone off, laughs nervously and looks at him again. MERCURY gives her the keys to the gate; she closes gate but does not lock it and starts up steps.)

ALKMENA (as she starts up steps). Good night, Sosie.

MERCURY. Alkmena, my lady Alkmena—

ALKMENA. What is it, Sosie?

MERCURY. I have a message for you from my master.

ALKMENA. From your master? Your master is still within earshot.

MERCURY. Exactly, my lady. No one must hear. My master has instructed me to inform you that he is only pretending to leave with the army, that actually he means to return to spend this night with you, once he's given his orders. . . .

ALKMENA. I don't understand you, Sosie. (Goes up another step.)

MERCURY (repeating mechanically). My master has instructed me to inform you that—

ALKMENA. How dull you are, Sosie! Don't you understand the first principle of keeping a secret—which is to pretend the moment you've heard it—the moment you've grasped it—not to know a thing about it?

MERCURY. Very good, my lady. . . .

ALKMENA. As a matter of fact I haven't understood one word you've been saying.

MERCURY. You must sit up and watch for my master, my lady. . . .

ALKMENA. Yes, yes, Sosie. Stop chattering. (*Goes up the rest of the steps*) Isn't the wind blowing your tongue about? (*Exits into palace.* MERCURY *looks up at the sky above him and guardedly whispers hoarsely.*)

MERCURY. Jupiter! Jupiter! (*Motions with his thumb that* ALKMENA *is inside waiting. There is a terrific crash offstage.* MERCURY *rushes off.* JUPITER *enters dressed exactly as* AMPHITRYON, *carrying shield and spear.* MERCURY *follows* JUPITER.)

MERCURY. Are you all right?

JUPITER. Yes. I forgot the law of gravity. (JUPITER *boldly starts toward gate.*)

MERCURY. Where are you going?

JUPITER. I'm going in!

MERCURY. You can't do that.

JUPITER. Why not? I've copied his costume down to the last detail.

MERCURY. There's an element here that goes beyond costume. Look at you! You've just emerged from the brambles and there isn't a scratch on you! And no creases! Even clothes from the best tailors have creases the moment you've worn them. Turn around. (*Takes shield and spear from* JUPITER *and puts them down.*)

JUPITER. What?

MERCURY. Turn around!

JUPITER. Gods never turn around.

MERCURY. But I must see your back!

JUPITER. Why?

MERCURY. Men think that women never notice their backs. They are unaware that although they pretend to be overcome by their magnificent padded chests, they are actually maliciously scrutinizing the back view. It's from the back that women estimate a man. (JUPITER *turns his back to him*) That's better. Your entire body must be faultless. Come here, so I can adjust your human uniform, also. (JUPITER *takes off his helmet and gives it to* MERCURY.)

JUPITER. Mercury, aren't my eyes good?

MERCURY. No, they're far too brilliant . . . all iris and no tear duct. You may have to cry, you know. (JUPITER *begins to cry.* MERCURY *snaps fingers*) There, there. (*Straightens* JUPITER *up*) Tell me, on your other adventures didn't you use pupils?

JUPITER. Pupils? I don't remember. Oh, you mean pupils—like this? (*Looks at* MERCURY *in a strange manner.*)

MERCURY (*cowering*). No phosphorescence! No cat's eyes, please! (JUPITER *assumes his natural look*) There, that's better. Now, about your skin. (*Puts helmet down next to shield and spear.*)

JUPITER. What's wrong with my skin? (*Looking at his hands.*)

MERCURY. It's a baby's skin. To begin with we must have a weather-beaten skin—a skin on which the wind has blown for thirty years. In short, a well-seasoned skin—a skin that may be tasted. For tasted it will be. Didn't they complain, these other women of yours, when they found your skin had a baby's taste?

JUPITER. No, no—I don't think so.

MERCURY. With that skin you'd never be allowed a second visit here. And now, Jupiter, please be good enough to contract the sheath of mortality in which you have encased yourself. It's too big for you, you're floating in it.

JUPITER. It's true.

MERCURY. Contract! (*Makes a gesture as with a rapier thrust.*)

JUPITER (*flexing muscles in arms until he achieves the position of Christ on the Cross*). It cramps me! I feel my heart beating against it. My veins bursting! My arteries distending! I feel myself becoming a filter—an hour-glass of blood! The birth of all humanity strains inside me—beating me black and blue! I hope that all my poor human beings don't suffer like this!

MERCURY. Twice they do—once when they're born and once when they die.

JUPITER (*straightens up*). How very disagreeable . . . to experience both simultaneously.

MERCURY. You do not lessen the torture by dividing the process.

JUPITER. Tell me, Mercury, as you stand before me, do you get the impression that you are standing before a man?

MERCURY (*eyeing him over*). No, not yet . . . not quite yet. . . . What I'm chiefly aware of when I stand before the living body of a man is that he is constantly undergoing change—disintegration—and that he incessantly ages. And as I watch the light in his eyes, I see it with the flying instants incessantly growing dimmer and dimmer.

JUPITER. Let's try!

MERCURY. What are you going to do?

JUPITER (*begins to stoop like an old man*). I'm saying to myself: "I'm going to die . . . I'm going to die."

MERCURY. No, not so fast . . . you're aging prematurely. Slow the tempo! You're living at the scale at which a dog lives or a cat.

JUPITER (*straightens up a little and extends his arm to* MERCURY). How's this? (*Breathes slower, like a fish.*)

MERCURY (*puts his arms, one above and one underneath* JUPITER'S *arm*). No. Now your heartbeats are too widely spaced. You're living now at fish rhythm. You're not, Jupiter, please to remember, a fish. (*By this time* JUPITER *is straight*) There . . . that's it . . . that's it. Keep up that little half-way gallop between the dogs and the fishes. It's this little ambling inner rhythm by which Amphitryon recognizes his horses, and Alkmena the heartbeats of her husband. (JUPITER *looks out front*) What are you thinking?

JUPITER. That I want to be loved for myself alone. I shall make Alkmena accept a lover!

MERCURY. Alkmena, I'm very much afraid, will deny you that pleasure. You better stick to being her husband.

JUPITER. Her husband—and her lover. No woman could resist that. We'll begin that way and later on —we shall see—we shall see— (*Starts to go but* MERCURY *raises hand and stops him*) Any last minute instructions?

MERCURY. Yes. About your intellect.

JUPITER. What's wrong with my intellect?

MERCURY. We must replace all your god-like conceptions with human ones. What are your beliefs? Recite to me your *man's* idea of the nature of this universe.

JUPITER. My *man's* idea of the nature of this universe? I believe that this flat Earth is flat; (MERCURY *picks up helmet gives it to* JUPITER, *who puts it on*) I believe that water is water and nothing else; (MERCURY *picks up shield and hands it to* JUPITER) I believe that air is simple and indivisible; I believe that nature is nature—(MERCURY *picks up spear and hands it to* JUPITER) and the spirit—well, the spirit— In fact, I believe that there is nothing beyond what I can see, and beyond what I can understand. Is that all?

MERCURY. Not quite. Are you consumed by a desire to part your hair in the middle and keep it set that way unalterably with sticky hair lotion?

JUPITER. I feel that temptation— passionately!

MERCURY. Good! Do you conceive that one day you may die?

JUPITER. That I may die? No, never! That my poor friends may die, alas, yes, my poor friends—but not I!

MERCURY. Splendid! Have you forgotten all the women you've already loved?

JUPITER. I've never loved anyone but Alkmena.

MERCURY. And this sky over us— what do you think of this sky?

JUPITER. I believe that the sky is my own personal property. I believe that I possess it far more than I ever did before.

MERCURY. Oh, Jupiter!

JUPITER. And as for the whole solar system, it seems to me very small!

MERCURY. And the whole vast Earth?

JUPITER. Very small! . . . And, Mercury . . . I feel . . . handsomer than Apollo! Braver than Mars . . . more capable of amorous exploits than—myself. And for the first time, Mercury, I really feel myself, I really see myself, I really believe myself, to be master of the gods!

MERCURY. Well, you're a man all right. Get on with it.
(*The light in the palace goes out.* JUPITER *makes a motion of knocking on gate, without touching it and there is an accompanying metallic knock heard. There is no reply from the palace. He crosses right and waves the knocks on the gate from where he stands.*)

JUPITER. I know she's there.

MERCURY. How do you know?

JUPITER. She was looking from her window as I came down.

MERCURY. You don't think she recognized you?

JUPITER. No. She thought I was a falling star and wished on me!

MERCURY. You'd better try again.
(JUPITER *again makes the motion of knocking on gate and once more the accompanying metallic knock is heard.* MERCURY *waits until he hears* ALKMENA'S *voice then stealthily exits.*)

ALKMENA (*off stage; in Palace*). Who is that knocking? Who disturbs me in my sleep?

JUPITER (*standing beneath Palace, hiding his face with shield*). A general!

ALKMENA (*off stage; in Palace*). A general? And what is a general doing wandering about at this time of night? Is he a deserter? Or is he defeated?

JUPITER. Defeated—by love!

ALKMENA. I know only one general and he wouldn't admit such a defeat.

JUPITER. That shows you do not know your own general.

ALKMENA. If I don't know him, how can I admit him?

JUPITER. Because he comes for once as your lover. Let him in!

ALKMENA (*comes out on balcony*). It is to Alkmena you speak. I have no lover. (JUPITER *laughs derisively*) Why do you laugh?

JUPITER. Did you not only a moment ago open the window of your room and look out, anguished, into the night?

ALKMENA. Yes, I did. But I was looking at the night and that's all I was looking at.

JUPITER. But did you not feel your heart contract and your body expand at the thought of a man, who is, I confess it, extremely ugly and generally rather limited?

ALKMENA. Do you confess it, perhaps, because you wish to be contradicted?

JUPITER. No, not necessarily. And as you gazed up at a falling star, did you not wish aloud: "Oh, if only while he were at the war, I might forego all memory"?

ALKMENA. I might have wished to forget that he loves his horses and his battles better than he loves me. And what does that prove?

JUPITER. That you have a lover, and that he is here.

ALKMENA. I have a husband and he is evidently not here. And I receive no one in my bedroom who is not my husband. And not even him will I admit if he does not acknowledge his name. You're not very good at passionate disguises—it's not your metier.

JUPITER. Oh, at this hour, when everything between here and heaven is in disguise, may not your husband also disguise himself as a lover?

ALKMENA. Your insight, my friend, is not very keen if you think the night is only the day-time masked, the moon no more than a sun disguised, and that the love of a wife for her husband can be confused with an amour.

JUPITER. Wifely love is a duty. Duty is compulsion. And compulsion kills desire.

ALKMENA. Desire! Desire is a half-god. We, here, worship only the major ones. The lesser gods we leave to adolescent girls, to the casually married, to the fugitive romantics, the half-wives.

JUPITER. It is blasphemy to speak so even of a lesser god!

ALKMENA. In my secret heart I am more blasphemous even than that for I worship a god that doesn't exist at all. Shall I tell you who it is? It's the god of conjugal love, one that it never occurred to the gods to invent—they are so casual. If you come in behalf of Desire you ask me to betray a greater god for a lesser. If then you are a lover I am sorry but I must ask you to go on. . . . You are handsome and you have a good figure. Your voice is winning. Did it sound in behalf of Fidelity I might love this voice. I might wish to be enclosed in those arms. Your mouth, too, I should say, is dewy and ardent. But I shan't allow it to persuade me. I shall not open my door to a lover. Who are you?

JUPITER. Why can't your husband be your lover?

ALKMENA. Because a lover is closer always to love than he is to the object of his love. Because it is ill-bred to deceive your husband—even with himself. Because I like my windows open and my linen fresh. (*She goes back inside.* MERCURY *enters.*)

JUPITER. She's impossible.

MERCURY. She's set in her ways.

JUPITER. You can't talk to her.

MERCURY. Not in your language.

JUPITER. You can't appeal to her!

MERCURY. She is unfortunately a good woman.

JUPITER. Mercury, she's not a woman, she's a fortress!

MERCURY. A fortress that may be taken only by her husband. Do as I advised you in the first place—be her husband!

JUPITER. Very well—I'll humble myself. (*Gives shield and spear to* MERCURY.)

MERCURY. That's better.

JUPITER. But once I am admitted as her husband—then I'll make her yearn for something more.

MERCURY. No doubt. You have your own resources, Jupiter. Meantime—

JUPITER. Meantime—(*Waves* MERCURY *off.* MERCURY *exits as* JUPITER *knocks again.*)

ALKMENA. Who is it now? I seem to have a perfect stream of visitors tonight. Now who are you?

JUPITER. I am Amphitryon, your husband!

ALKMENA (*comes in at last*). Amphitryon! Why didn't you say so in the first place?

JUPITER. Let me in!

ALKMENA. Are you he by whose side I wake every morning and for whom I cut from the margin of my own day an extra ten minutes of sleep?

JUPITER. I am he.

ALKMENA. Are you the one whose least footfall is so familiar to me that I can tell whether he is shaving or dressing?

JUPITER. I am the one.

ALKMENA. Are you the being with whom I dine and breakfast and sup? And whom I allow to go to sleep ten minutes every night before I do?

JUPITER. I am that being.

ALKMENA. Then swear in the presence of the night those marriage vows which hitherto we have spoken only in the presence of the day.

JUPITER. A wedding ceremony, in the void of the night, with neither priest nor altar? What for?

ALKMENA. That the invisible beings which surround us may not be deceived seeing Alkmena receive you like this—like a lover. That the clear light in which we live by day may transfigure even the night. Oh, Amphitryon, I have often dreamed of an occasion like this! Why should the night be the hand-maiden for the clandestine—the furtive—the illicit? Let her for once be bridesmaid to married love. Do you think I wish this lovely night—this constellation of stars and little winds— this company of night moths and shadows—to imagine that I, Alkmena, am receiving a lover? No! At this hour, when there are consummated so many false marriages, let us seal our nocturnal, true one! Shall we begin?

JUPITER. If you only knew, Alkmena, how pitiful to the gods human beings seem, prating their vows, launching their thunderless thunderbolts.

ALKMENA. Raise your hand and crook your index finger! (*Raises her hand and crooks her index finger.*)

JUPITER. No! Not the index finger.

ALKMENA. Why not?

JUPITER. That is the most formidable oath of all. The one used by

Jupiter to fester the Earth with plagues.

ALKMENA. The index finger or nothing. If not the index finger, you must go away!

JUPITER (*beaten; raises his right arm and crooks index finger at the same time, covering right side of his face with mantle*). Celestial calamities—restrain yourselves! Earthquakes and floods, fevers and locusts—hold off!

ALKMENA. Amphitryon, those are not the words!

JUPITER. I was just practising. (*Lets down mantle and proceeds in earnest*) I, Amphitryon, son and grandson of former generals, father and grandfather of future generals . . . indispensable clasp in the twin girdle of war and glory—

ALKMENA (*with her right arm also raised and index finger crooked*). I, Alkmena, whose parents are no longer and whose children are yet unborn—poor isolated link in the chain of humanity—

JUPITER. I swear so to contrive it

that the fragrance of the name of Alkmena shall survive so long as the hurly-burly of my own.

ALKMENA. And I swear to be faithful to Amphitryon, my husband, or to die!

JUPITER (*alarmed*). To what?

ALKMENA. To die!

JUPITER. Don't say that, Alkmena.

ALKMENA. Why not? I mean it. And now, dear husband, the ceremony is over and I authorize you to come in. You know you've really been very simple. The gate was open all the time—you had only to push it —ever so little. . . . (JUPITER *opens gate, goes up three steps and then stands there as if rooted to the spot*) Why do you hesitate?

JUPITER. You really mean it? You really *want me* to come in?

ALKMENA. My dearest love . . . I command it!
(JUPITER *mounts the steps quickly, tears the sashes off her, and enfolds her in his mantle as the curtain falls.*)

ACT TWO

SCENE I

SCENE—*Outside of* ALKMENA's *bedroom in* AMPHITRYON's *Palace.*
    TIME—*The next morning. The darkness is complete save for the glow of light which emanates from the body of* MERCURY *lying semi-recumbent at the front of the stage.*

MERCURY. Posted here in front of Alkmena's bedroom, I have been

soaking in the sweet silence, the gentle resistance, the easy struggle from indoors; already Alkmena bears within herself the young half-god, but never with any other mistress has Jupiter tarried this long—whether this abnormal darkness is beginning to bore you I cannot say, but this job that Jupiter has wished on me of prolonging the night till he gets ready to get up is beginning to weigh on me a bit. Especially when I think that everywhere else the whole world is suffused in broad daylight. After all it's mid-summer and early in the morning. The great inundation of day canopies out over all the world, thousands and thousands of leagues to the very margin of the sea. Solitary, amid the rose-drenched cubes, this palace is left a cone of black. I really ought to wake my master; he loathes a hurried exit and he will surely wish by way of dressing-gown chatter to reveal to Alkmena that he is Jupiter. He will not willingly forego this sop to his vanity. He will love to enjoy her astonishment and to savor in her pride. Besides, I've suggested to Amphitryon that he come to surprise his wife at break of dawn. This is a courtesy we owe him and it will relieve the situation of any ambiguity. Already, Amphitryon has taken secretly to the road, he is galloping furiously and within the hour he will arrive here at this palace. Therefore, Sun, display your rays to me, that I may choose the one best fitted to kindle these shadows. . . . (*The Sun obliges with a green ray which picks out* MERCURY's *winged boot*) No, no. There's nothing more sinister than green rays for lovers to wake up on. Each one thinks the other has been drowned in the night. . . . (*A purple ray comes on as the green one disappears*) Nor that one. . . . Purple and violet are colors that inflame the senses. We'll save them for tonight. (*The Sun obliges with an amber ray*) Ah, that's it, saffron! Nothing so well as saffron to bring out the insipid quality of the human skin. . . . Get on with it, Sun! (MERCURY *rises and runs off in the darkness. The stage is flooded in full sunlight.*)

ACT TWO

SCENE II

SCENE—*A room in the Palace. There is a couch in the center. Two small tabourets one on each side of couch. There is an urn on each tabouret. Also a small handle-bell.*

ALKMENA *enters, puts down her cloak and hat on couch.*

ALKMENA. Get up, Amphitryon, the sun has risen.

JUPITER (*off stage*). Where am I?

ALKMENA. In the last place where husbands think they are when they wake up; simply in your own home in your own bed, and with your own wife. (*Rings bell.*)

JUPITER (*still off stage*). And what is the name of this wife?

ALKMENA. Her name is the same by day as it is by night—it is still Alkmena.

JUPITER. Is it that marvellously dark Alkmena—who never says a word while love-making?

ALKMENA. Yes, and who prattles of dawn, and who is now about to put you out of here, husband or no husband. Come along, Amphitryon, you'll be late for your war! Are you getting dressed?

JUPITER (*still off stage*). Yes. Oh, come back to my arms!

ALKMENA. Don't count on that! Dark women have this in common with dreams—you may embrace them only at night.

JUPITER. Well, come back and close your eyes then and let us make the best of an improvised darkness.

ALKMENA. No, no, the early morning is no time for improvisation. Get up, Amphitryon. Please. (*Sits on couch, her feet stretched out*) Come along, darling, breakfast is ready.
(KLEANTHA *and* NENETZA, *two maids, come in with breakfast trays.* NENETZA *serves* ALKMENA. KLEANTHA *stands holding her tray.* JUPITER *enters and as he passes* ALKMENA, *she fondly slaps his behind and he stops a moment and smiles with satisfaction. Sits at end of couch, his feet outstretched.* KLEANTHA *puts tray on his lap and then both maids exit.*)

JUPITER. What a divine night!

ALKMENA. Your adjectives this morning, darling, are somewhat feeble.

JUPITER. I said divine!

ALKMENA. You could say a cut of beef was divine or a meal was divine, but for last night you might have found something better.

JUPITER. What could there possibly be better?

ALKMENA. Almost any adjective except divine. It's such a worn-out word. Perfect! You could have said it was a perfect night. Charming! Best of all, you might have said it was a pleasant night! Now, that conveys so many agreeable sensations: "*What a pleasant night!*"

JUPITER. But don't you think that this night, of all our nights, was the pleasantest, by far?

ALKMENA (*drinking*). Well, that depends.

JUPITER. On what does it depend?

ALKMENA. Have you forgotten, my own husband, the night we were married? The miraculous discovery our two hearts made of each other, in the midst of those shadows which for the first time held us in their embrace? That was our most beautiful night!

JUPITER. Our most beautiful, yes. But the pleasantest was this one.

ALKMENA (*nonchalantly*). Do you think so?

JUPITER. Yes, I do.

ALKMENA. I don't. What about the night the great fire broke out in Thebes—and you came back to me at sunrise all gilt from the fire and warm as new-baked bread? That was our pleasantest night and you'll never persuade me differently. (*Eats fruit.*)

JUPITER. Well, if nothing else, then, you must admit this was the most astonishing.

ALKMENA. Was it? Why? Now, the night before last, for instance, when you rescued that little drowning boy from the sea, and all night long you kept flinging your arms around me to rescue me from imaginary drowning—yes, that was rather astonishing, if you like. No, my dear, if you wish to sum up this night in an appropriate adjective, I should say that this night, of all our nights, was the most—connubial. That's it, my sweet—connubial! There was a sense of security about it which gladdened me. Never have I felt so certain of waking up in the morning to find you beside me; there was mercifully absent that fear which obsesses me constantly—of finding you suddenly dead in my arms. (*Eats the fruit.*)

JUPITER (*puts the tray down with sudden distaste*). Connubial—? (*Sits up with feet on floor.*)

ALKMENA. Connubial!

JUPITER (*rises*). Lovely room!

ALKMENA. It seems especially attractive to you this morning when you have no business to be here.

JUPITER. How clever of men, to devise this system of colonnades which seems to intensify the light in a planet relatively so badly lit.

ALKMENA. Since it was you who devised the system, darling, that's very modest of you.

JUPITER. Beautiful landscape!

ALKMENA. Ah, that you may admire since you did not create it.

JUPITER (*significantly*). And who did, may I ask?

ALKMENA (*nonchalantly*). The Master of the Gods.

JUPITER. And may one hear his name?

ALKMENA. Jupiter.

JUPITER (*ravished, leans over couch*). How prettily you pronounce the names of the gods! Who taught you to savor them so on your lips, as if you were enjoying a heavenly diet? Like a lamb that nibbles at laburnum and lifts his head to nibble more. Say his name again—repeat his name! It is said that the gods, summoned so, respond sometimes with their very presence!

ALKMENA (*calling*). Neptune! Apollo!

JUPITER. No, no, the first one—repeat his name.

ALKMENA. No, no, no. I like to nibble all over Olympus. Especially I love to pronounce the names of the gods in couples: (*Calling*) Venus and Mars! Jupiter and Juno!

JUPITER (*laughs nervously*). No, no, no.

ALKMENA. I see them wandering about eternally—hand in hand—on the crests of the clouds—it must be marvelous!

JUPITER. Great fun! You think that Jupiter has done a good job then, with these rocks and cliffs—he's done pretty well on this landscape?

ALKMENA. Yes, it's very nice, but do you think he did it on purpose?

JUPITER (shocked). Alkmena!

ALKMENA. Well, everything you do, you do on purpose, whether you are grafting cherry trees on plums or contriving a double-edged sword. But do you think that Jupiter, on the day that he created all this, knew what he was doing?

JUPITER (hurt). It is generally assumed that he did!

ALKMENA. We know he created the Earth. But the beauty of the Earth re-creates itself momentarily. Jupiter seems too settled to have dallied so with the ephemeral!

JUPITER. I'm afraid you haven't a very precise idea of the purpose of creation.

ALKMENA. No, I suppose I haven't. How does it all seem to you, darling? Doesn't it seem cloudy?

JUPITER. No, no! I see everything perfectly clearly. (Sits beside her again) In the beginning everything was Chaos. It was then Jupiter's felicitous idea to separate everything into four elements.

ALKMENA. We have only four elements?

JUPITER. Four. And the first is water, and water, I may tell you, was not so easy to create. Superficially, water looks like quite ordinary stuff. But imagine, if you had never seen water—if there were no water in existence, what it would mean to create it—even to get the idea of creating it.

ALKMENA. What did the goddesses cry—in the pre-water era? Bronze tears? That stumps you!

JUPITER. Don't interrupt me, Alkmena, I'm trying to give you some idea of what Jupiter must be—I'm trying to convey to you something of his scope. He may materialize before you at any moment, you know, without warning. Wouldn't you like to have him explain everything to you personally in all his magnificence? (He gets up.)

ALKMENA. No, darling, I'd rather have you explain it to me.

JUPITER (nonplussed, sits again). Where was I?

ALKMENA. We've just disposed of original Chaos.

JUPITER. Oh, yes. Once water was in existence it occurred to him to bank it in with broken coasts, in order to stop the impact of the storms, and to strew the surface of the waters with Continents, in order to spare the eyes of the gods the perpetual irritation of a glittering horizon— And so came the Earth and all its marvels!

ALKMENA. Oh, you mean the pine trees?

JUPITER. Pine trees?

ALKMENA. And the echo?

JUPITER. The echo?

ALKMENA. You sound like one yourself. Now color—did Jupiter create color?

JUPITER (*proudly*). Yes. The seven colors of the rainbow are his invention.

ALKMENA. No, no—I mean my favorite colors: bronze and dark red and lizard green—what of them?

JUPITER. No, he left those to the cleaning and dyeing establishments—

ALKMENA (*notices a hole in his sock*). Amphitryon! You have a hole in your stocking—did Jupiter create that?

JUPITER (*pleased at his own verisimilitude*). Yes—!

ALKMENA. Oh, he did, did he? (*Calling*) Nenetza! Yarn, yarn!

JUPITER. Shall we go back to the assorted vibrations in the ether, of which I was speaking—
(NENETZA *enters with yarn and sewing stand and places it near couch.* ALKMENA *picks a needle and proceeds to mend the sock.* NENETZA *takes both breakfast trays and goes out.*)

ALKMENA. Yes, yes— You can't go to war with a hole in your stocking. What will your enemy think of your wife? Give it to me. (*Takes the sock off his foot.*)

JUPITER. But to go back again to the assorted vibrations in the ether

—(ALKMENA *sews placidly*) Jupiter so contrived it, that by a system of molecular collision—infinite impacts and double impacts within the molecules—as well as counter-refraction of the original light refractions he was able to criss-cross the Universe with a network of a thousand different systems of color and sound, at once perceptible or not to human sense organs—

ALKMENA. That's exactly what I was saying.

JUPITER. What *you* were saying?

ALKMENA. Yes. He didn't do a thing! He didn't do a thing except plunge us into an awful conglomeration of illusions and stupors from which we have to extricate ourselves—I and my dear husband. (*She pinches the big toe of his bare foot.*)

JUPITER. Alkmena, are you aware that the gods may be eavesdropping?

ALKMENA. Oh, they know my heart is straightforward and honest. Besides, what does Jupiter expect of me? That I should expire with gratitude to him for having invented four elements when we could very well use twenty? I don't think four elements is much, considering he hasn't had anything else to do for all eternity. I am far more grateful to you, my dear husband, and my heart bursts with gratitude to you for having invented a system of window-pulleys which has lightened my life and for all those wonderful, new graftings you did for the orchard. (*She puts the mended sock on his foot*) You, Amphitryon, have changed for me the taste of a cherry—(*puts his sandal on*) and you have done more than that—you have enlarged the capacity of my pantry shelves! Now, for me, it is you who are the creator—(JUPITER *is staring at her with divine admiration*) Why do you look at me like that? Compliments embarrass you, is that it? I suppose you find me too earthbound?

JUPITER (*bends down and kisses her feet*). Wouldn't you like to be less so?

ALKMENA. Less so?

JUPITER. You never aspired to be a goddess?

ALKMENA. A goddess? What on earth for?

JUPITER. To be honored and revered by everyone.

ALKMENA. Certainly not!

JUPITER. To be able to walk on water and on the air—

ALKMENA. No, darling, no.

JUPITER. To understand the meaning of things and other worlds?

ALKMENA. No. I've never taken an undue interest in my neighbors.

JUPITER. Why—then—to be immortal!

ALKMENA. To be immortal? What for? What good would that do me?

JUPITER. Not to die!

ALKMENA. Not to die! What would I do if I didn't die?

JUPITER. Dearest Alkmena. You would be changed into a star. You would live forever. You would shine in the night till the end of time.

ALKMENA. The end of time? And when will that take place?

JUPITER. Never!

ALKMENA. Oh, dear, what a long evening! No, darling, no. For that job of night watchwoman the gods had better not count on me. (*Sits up*) Besides, the night air isn't good for my skin. Wouldn't I get all chapped up there in the trough of eternity?

JUPITER (*moves along couch beside her*). But—oh, my darling— how cold and empty you'd be in the trough of death! (*He buries his head in her bosom.*)

ALKMENA. Oh, sweet. I'm not afraid of death. It's the stake you give for life. I prefer to identify myself with my own companions, who must also die. I feel so strongly that my very fibres will perpetuate themselves in other men—and animals —plants even—that I should feel cheated if I were not allowed to follow this mysterious destiny. Don't talk to me of not dying, so long as there is a vegetable alive which isn't immortal. For a human being to be immortal—is a kind of betrayal of one's own. Besides, when I think of the wonderful surcease death brings; to be irritated for sixty years over meals that don't turn out well—holes in stockings—aches and pains—and then to be offered death—the felicity of death—really, it's a reward we don't deserve!

JUPITER. But wouldn't you like to have a son—an immortal son?

ALKMENA. To want one's son to be immortal is only human.

JUPITER. One who would become the greatest of heroes! One who as a baby would slay serpents come to strangle him in his crib.

ALKMENA. No, certainly not. He'll be just a little baby who will coo and be frightened of flies. What are you so upset about?

JUPITER. Alkmena, did you really mean it, when you said you'd rather kill yourself than be unfaithful?

ALKMENA. Darling, can you doubt it?

JUPITER. But—to kill one's self is so—dangerous!

ALKMENA. Not for me. If the gods of war should strike you down there wouldn't be anything in the least tragic about my dying.

JUPITER. But suppose you drag to death a child conceived the day before and half alive?

ALKMENA. For him it would be only a half death. He'd be that much ahead on his future.

JUPITER. Alkmena, I can see that you are pious and that you comprehend the mysteries of this world. I must, therefore, speak to you of—

ALKMENA (edging away from him as he tries to embrace her). No. I know what that solemn manner of yours leads to. It's your way of being tender. Can't you for once try

being intimate without being—pontifical?

JUPITER. You mustn't joke, Alkmena. The time has come when I must speak to you of the gods.

ALKMENA. The gods?

JUPITER. The moment has arrived when I must clarify for you their relations with men.

ALKMENA (rises). Have you lost your senses, Amphitryon? You choose this moment of all moments to talk theology to me. At this time of day, when everybody—drunk with sunlight—just can't wait to go farming or fishing!

JUPITER. Alkmena—

ALKMENA. What's more, isn't the army waiting for you? You have only a few minutes left if you want to kill anybody at all—and you'll have to do that on an empty stomach. No, darling, no. (Goes upstage and gets scarf) I have my house to attend to—I have my rounds to make—I have the gardener to see—do you think this house runs itself?

JUPITER (rises). Alkmena! Dearest Alkmena. Let me apprise you that the gods may appear precisely at the moment when you expect them least!

ALKMENA. Amphitryon, dear Amphitryon, in a moment I shall deliver you an harangue, not about the gods, but about my servant problems. (Comes downstage and picks up her hat and sits beside JUPITER) As a matter of fact, I very much fear that we shall have to dispense with the services of Nenetza. For apart from her special mania for scrubbing only the black tiles in the mosaics, she has yielded, as you might say, to the gods— and is just a little—pregnant! (*Rises, jauntily puts on her hat*) Till tonight, darling, good-bye— (*Exits.*)

JUPITER. Alkmena—
(MERCURY *enters.*)

MERCURY. Jupiter, what's the matter? What's happened? I've been waiting to see you emerge from this room in all your glory as you've done from so many others. Instead, it's Alkmena who makes her departure—not the least bit ruffled.

JUPITER. She isn't ruffled. You can't ruffle her.

MERCURY. This isn't true to form, Jupiter. And what's that vertical crease doing between your eyes? Has somebody upset you? Are you annoyed? Is there going to be thunder?

JUPITER. No. This crease, my dear Mercury, is a wrinkle.

MERCURY. But Jupiter can't have wrinkles. That belongs to Amphitryon.

JUPITER. No—no. This wrinkle belongs to me, it's my wrinkle. (*Looks off after* ALKMENA) And now I know how men come by them.

MERCURY. I've never seen you like this, you're actually stooping with fatigue.

JUPITER. It's no light weight to carry a wrinkle.

MERCURY. Can it be that you have experienced the emotion of human love so thoroughly that it's exhausted you?

JUPITER. I believe that it is love itself I am experiencing.

MERCURY. Jupiter, you have the naïveté of the superman. Don't be juvenile, this is hardly your first affair.

JUPITER. But for the first time I held in my arms a woman whom I could not see, whom I could not hear—and yet I understood her.

MERCURY. What went on in your mind?

JUPITER. Only that I was her husband. I had limited the compass of my mind to his.

MERCURY. She never suspected then?

JUPITER. Never! And moreover, and this is strange, I couldn't have endured it if she did. From the moment we went to bed to the moment we got up it was impossible for me to be anything but her husband. It was Alkmena who was completely victorious over me. Do you know, that a few moments ago I had occasion to explain Creation to her and I found myself talking as dry as dust. The easy eloquence of which I am master when I talk to you just—just—dried up— (*Buries his head in his hand in despair*) Mercury, may I expound Creation for you—just to keep my hand in?

MERCURY. If it's absolutely necessary—but just Creation—that's as far as I'll go.

JUPITER. Mercury—I have also made a discovery—

MERCURY. Let me remind you, as you're omniscient, discovery for you is impossible.

JUPITER. Nevertheless, I have discovered that human beings are not what the gods think them. Alkmena, the gentle—the tender Alkmena has the character of a rock. She is the true Prometheus!

MERCURY. It isn't that she has character, she lacks imagination.

JUPITER. Yes, she lacks imagination and it's even possible that she isn't very intelligent. She is ambitious neither to shock nor to dazzle. But it's exactly this single-minded quality in her, this quality of constancy and devotion, against which our power is futile.

MERCURY. Do I hear aright? Is this the Master of the Gods talking?

JUPITER. She is the only woman I have ever met who is as adorable dressed as unveiled, who when she is absent, makes herself felt as if she were present, whose homespun occupations seem to me as alluring as pleasure itself. To dine with her —even to breakfast with her—to touch her hand accidentally with a plate or a spoon— And then suddenly she will use little expressions —and that widens the abyss between us—

MERCURY. What expressions?

JUPITER. She will say—"When I was a child"—or "When I'm old"— or—"Never in all my life"— This stabs me, Mercury.

MERCURY. I don't see why.

JUPITER. We can't use these expressions—

MERCURY. We can say anything we like.

JUPITER. No, we can't—because we are not born and we do not die. It is between these margins that mortals live as they do between the lovely hedges on their country estates. We merely coexist.

MERCURY. But would you exchange a cul-de-sac for a panorama?

JUPITER. With her, Mercury—yes.

MERCURY. To have what every living thing has—it's a commonplace desire, Jupiter.

JUPITER. But we miss something, Mercury—undoubtedly we miss something—the poignance of the transient—the intimation of mortality—that sweet sadness of grasping at something you cannot hold—

MERCURY. It's very simple—make Alkmena immortal!

JUPITER. And deprive her of her death? She'd never forgive me, she'd never forgive me for betraying her to the vegetables. The vegetables would never forgive her. No, I'm too fond of her—and I may tell you now that her son, of all my sons, will be my most favorite.

MERCURY. That the Universe knows already!

JUPITER. The Universe? No one knows anything about this affair.

MERCURY. Oh, yes, they do. I announced everything this morning! (JUPITER *rises angrily, raises his right arm and his index finger crooked. A rumbling of thunder obeys his gesture and* MERCURY *drops to one knee in terror*) I only did what I've always done in all your affairs. Why should we suddenly conceal from the world how generous you are?

JUPITER. Did you announce that I had visited Alkmena disguised as Amphitryon?

MERCURY. Certainly not! There's something undignified about that trick. I was afraid it might make a bad impression and since your desire to spend another evening with Alkmena was so obvious that I could sense it through the very walls, I made the formal announcement that Alkmena would receive a visit from Jupiter tonight!

JUPITER. To whom did you announce this?

MERCURY. In the order prescribed by destiny! (*A cosmic music is heard*) First to the winds, then to the waters: listen, the undulations of the Universe, both wet and dry, are gossiping in their special language of nothing else.

JUPITER. We're lost! Poor Alkmena, we're lost! (MERCURY *rises*) She would never allow it. (*Sits on couch again*) She'd kill herself! And Hercules, my son, would die also. And I would be forced, as I was when I had you, to open my thigh or the fatty part of my calf to shelter a foetus for several months. (*Gong is heard*) No, thank you very much. What's that?

MERCURY (*goes up to Arch and looks off*). It's the whole of Thebes preparing to celebrate your union with Alkmena. They're organizing a procession.

JUPITER. Turn it back! Let the sea engulf it!

MERCURY. Jupiter, that's impossible, these are your own priests.

JUPITER. They have insufficient reasons for their faith in me. (*Gong stops*) For the first time, Mercury, I have a suspicion that a thoroughly first-rate god might make a thoroughly second-rate man. (*Music again*) What's that?

MERCURY. It's the Virgins coming to congratulate Alkmena—in their theoretical way.

JUPITER. Don't you think it would be a good idea to drown the Virgins and strike down the priests?

MERCURY. It depends on what you're after fundamentally. What do you want?

JUPITER. What do I want? What every man wants! A thousand contradictory desires! That Alkmena should remain faithful to her husband and also give herself to me. That she should remain chaste under my caresses and yet that desire should flame up in her under my very sight. That she should know nothing of this intrigue and yet that she should connive at it with all her might!

MERCURY. I've done my stint. The Universe is informed according to prescription that tonight Alkmena will receive a visit from Jupiter. Is there anything else that I can do for you? (*Drops to one knee before* JUPITER.)

JUPITER. Yes! See that she does it —and willingly. It is no longer a question of my son, that matter is fortunately disposed of. It is now a question of ME! Of I, myself! I'm degraded by this mortal livery. I shall come to her as a god! (*Rises majestically. Music*) You must see her—prepare her for my visit—outline vividly my love for her. I permit you to approach her, to touch her, agitate her blood, her nerves, appeal to her pride.

MERCURY (*rises*). That's the spirit, Jupiter. Now that you are willing to forego your incognito I may tell you I'll persuade her in an instant. She'll be waiting for you, I promise you.

ALKMENA (*calling off stage*). Darling!

ECHO (*calling off stage*). Darling!

JUPITER. Whom is she talking to?

MERCURY. She's flirting with Amphitryon through her echo—and you say she isn't a coquette! Even for her voice she has a mirror!

ALKMENA (*calling off stage*). Darling!

ECHO (*calling off stage*). Darling! (*Music.*)

JUPITER. "Nymph, in thy orisons, be all thy sins remembered. . . ." What are you smiling at?

MERCURY. Have you heard that expression somewhere before?

JUPITER. No, somewhere not yet. It is whispered to me in the future, by a poet yet unborn. I warn you, I shall not leave this city until she has capitulated in my honor of her own free will! (*Music.*)

ALKMENA (*calling off stage*). Darling!

ECHO (*calling off stage*). Darling! (JUPITER *exits.* MERCURY *conceals himself.* ALKMENA *enters, followed by* KLEANTHA, *bearing a garden basket full of vegetables and* ALKMENA's *hat.*)

ALKMENA. Kleantha, will you look at those turnips! Your master doesn't like turnips, but when they're cooked, he thinks they're something else. And tell cook to fan those melons until they're cool, if she has to fan all day.

KLEANTHA. Yes, mistress. (*Exits with sewing stand, basket and hat.* MERCURY *comes down from his hiding place.*)

MERCURY. Salutations, Princess!

ALKMENA (*amazed, stops at Arch*). You're a god!

MERCURY. Not of the first rank— but a god.

ALKMENA. You're Mercury. I know your face.

MERCURY. Thank you, Princess. Most people recognize me by my feet—by the wings on my feet. If you care to touch me, I'm in a position to authorize it. (*She curtsies to him*) I see the gods interest you.

ALKMENA. Oh, I love the gods.

MERCURY. All of them? Am I included in this affection?

ALKMENA. You're one of my favorites.

MERCURY. Why?

ALKMENA. Your name—Mercury—is so beautiful. Then—of course, you are the god of eloquence. I knew that the moment I saw you.

MERCURY. Your face, too, Princess, is a kind of exquisite speech. (MERCURY *graciously indicates that she may sit. She does so*) But tell me—have you no preference among the gods?

ALKMENA. Of course I have a preference—Jupiter!

MERCURY. Jupiter? You astonish me rather. He has no specialty.

ALKMENA. Isn't divinity a kind of specialty?

MERCURY. Yes, but he isn't gifted. Are you so influenced by his position as Master of the Gods? It's a kind of snobbery I wouldn't have expected from you.

ALKMENA. He's very beautiful.

MERCURY. He has no knowledge of rhetoric.

ALKMENA. No?

MERCURY. And no connoisseurship in the fine arts.

ALKMENA. But he's so dignified!

MERCURY. Musically he's tone deaf. He can't distinguish between celestial and chamber music. We must face it, Alkmena, Jupiter is not talented.

ALKMENA. If you'll forgive my saying so, Mercury, I think you're being a little disloyal to your master? Why, only a few moments ago, my husband and I were saying how wonderful he is with . . . molecules.

MERCURY. Yes, but he's mad about women.

ALKMENA. I understand these passionate impulses of his which cause him to hurl himself into the arms of mortal women. You see, I've learned from my husband all about grafting—he's done wonderful things with cherries, you know. You must have heard of him up there.

MERCURY. Oh, of course.

ALKMENA. Yes, of course. Then, at school, we used to recite poems about the gods making crossings with beauty and even with purity that got the most wonderful results when performed with women especially honored for this high mission— Does this bore you?

MERCURY. No, on the contrary, you fill me with delight. The fate, then, of all the women whom Jupiter's loved or ever will love seems to you a happy fate?

ALKMENA. Infinitely happy.

MERCURY. Enviable?

ALKMENA. Highly enviable.

MERCURY. In short—you envy them?

ALKMENA. I envy them. Why do you ask me that?

MERCURY. Don't you guess why? Don't you know why I've come here and what announcement I have to make to you as a special messenger from my master?

ALKMENA. No. Tell me.

MERCURY. It's that he loves you. Jupiter loves you.

ALKMENA. Jupiter—loves me? Oh— (*Laughs at the preposterousness of the idea*) I am the most fortunate of women.

MERCURY. He's had his eye on you for a number of days now. Not one of your gestures has been wasted on him. You are ineffably traced in his radiant vision.

ALKMENA. For a number of days?

MERCURY. And a number of nights. (*Notices her shocked expression*) You grow pale—

ALKMENA. I know I should blush . . . but it kills me to think that Jupiter's been looking at me all this time and I probably wasn't at my best. Why didn't you warn me?

MERCURY. And what answer shall I give him now?

ALKMENA (*rises, as does* MERCURY). Tell him—of course—that I shall do my best to earn his gracious favor. I already have a silver altar to him in the Palace. When Amphitryon returns, we'll build a gold one.

MERCURY. It isn't an altar he's interested in.

ALKMENA. Everything here belongs to him. Even my most precious possessions. He has only to choose.

MERCURY. He's already chosen it and tonight he's coming to claim it.

ALKMENA. What is it?

MERCURY. Your bed. I have just given my orders to the night. The day is hardly long enough for the night to get together the brilliant effects and the appropriate sounds for a celestial wedding. It will be less a night than a sample of your immortal future. It gives me pleasure to season your more perishable moments with these pinches of immortality—my engagement present! (ALKMENA *smiles*) Why do you smile?

ALKMENA. I've smiled at less.

MERCURY. But why?

ALKMENA. Quite simply because this is obviously a case of mistaken identity. I am Alkmena, and Amphitryon is my husband.

MERCURY. But the cosmic forces do not consider husbands.

ALKMENA. But think, Mercury, of all women in Thebes, to have chosen me? I'm a very commonplace woman. I wasn't very good at school and what I did learn I've forgotten. I am not, in fact, considered over bright.

MERCURY. That opinion I do not share.

ALKMENA. At the moment it's not you I'm thinking of, but Jupiter. When it comes to a momentous matter—like receiving Jupiter—I'm simply not up to it.

MERCURY. We've seen you from on high and your body lights up the night of Greece.

ALKMENA. Yes, I have my devices for artificial lighting—I have my powders and lotions—I manage with tweezers and files to put up some kind of an appearance, but I cannot write and I cannot even think.

MERCURY. But you talk very well. Even if you didn't, it wouldn't matter because tonight all the poets of posterity will be carrying on the conversation for you.

ALKMENA. I wish they'd carry the rest as well.

MERCURY. This flippancy doesn't become you, Alkmena. Do you think you can escape the gods by underestimating your surpassing qualities of nobility and beauty? Besides you seem to be unaware of the magnificence of this—opportunity.

ALKMENA. But that's exactly what I'm trying to convey to you, Mercury—how little I am suited for this opportunity. I live in the earthiest of atmospheres. It is so thick that no god could stand it—not for long—

MERCURY. You are overestimating the time. This isn't a liaison. It's a matter of a few hours.

ALKMENA. How do you know? Jupiter may turn out to be constant. That he should be interested at all is what I can't get over.

MERCURY. I don't see why. You will admit your figure is superlative.

ALKMENA. My figure is all right, but does Jupiter know that I tan the most dreadful color in summer?

MERCURY. Your hands embellish the flowers as you pick them in your garden.

ALKMENA. My hands are all right but one has only two hands, and I'll tell you something, Mercury, that isn't generally known—I have one tooth too many.

MERCURY. Your walk, though, overflows with promise.

ALKMENA. That's a false lead, believe me. When it comes to love-making, I'm not very mature.

MERCURY. It's no use. Jupiter has observed you in that capacity also.

ALKMENA (starts to cry). Sometimes one pretends. . . .

MERCURY. What's this, Alkmena? Do I see tears? (Music) At this moment you weep; at this moment when a flood of joy is about to inundate humanity in your honor? Tonight a year of joy begins for Thebes. No more epidemics. No more pestilence. No more war. No more famines.

ALKMENA. It's not fair!

MERCURY. In your city are eight little children who, this very week, were destined to die. Four little boys and four little girls—among the latter your favorite Charissa. You can save them!

ALKMENA. Charissa! . . . If anyone else did this it would be called blackmail!

MERCURY. Health and happiness are the exclusive blackmail of the gods. Do you hear, Alkmena? The poor and the sick are beside themselves with joy for they will owe to you their happiness and their life. Now, Alkmena, you are apprised of what is to be. Farewell!

ALKMENA. You are going?

MERCURY. I must. I have to tell Jupiter you are expecting him.

ALKMENA. You would be telling him a lie. I am not expecting him!

MERCURY. What?

ALKMENA. I am not expecting him.

MERCURY. Why not?

ALKMENA. I am tired. I am ill.

MERCURY. It's not true. Don't try to put off the gods with lies which are effective with men.

ALKMENA. But it is a man I love.

MERCURY. What man?

ALKMENA. My husband.

MERCURY. Yes, you love your husband.

ALKMENA. I love him.

MERCURY. But that's what we're counting on! Jupiter doesn't choose his mistresses among unfaithful wives.

ALKMENA. If I am taken by surprise, Mercury, I warn you I shall defend myself if I have only my naked body and my naked legs.

MERCURY. Don't force me to speak bluntly to you, Alkmena, and to reveal to you the hidden depths of what you are pleased to think of as your purity. Conversationally, I find you cynical enough.

ALKMENA. I adapt my speech to yours. You leave me no choice.

MERCURY. Very well, we'll come straight to the point. (*On his knees before her*) From tonight's encounter, a child is to be born.

ALKMENA. The child is already named, I suppose?

MERCURY. Yes. It has a name.

ALKMENA. Poor little girl. She'll never be born.

MERCURY. It's a boy and he will be born!

ALKMENA. What will happen when I refuse?

MERCURY. The child must be born.

ALKMENA. When I kill myself?

MERCURY. Jupiter will reincarnate you for this son must be born.

ALKMENA. A child born of adultery, never! Divine son though he be—he shall die!

MERCURY. Alkmena, the patience of the gods has its limits. You abuse their courtesy. After all, we don't need your consent.

SOSIE (*off stage*). Mistress . . .

ALKMENA. What is it, Sosie?

SOSIE. Queen Leda has just arrived at the Palace.

ALKMENA. Queen Leda?

MERCURY. Leda, the Queen of Sparta, whom Jupiter loved in the guise of a swan, your predecessor. See her, Alkmena; draw her out. She may give you some useful advice.

ALKMENA. I will.

MERCURY. I'm going—I must report our conversation to Jupiter.

ALKMENA. Shall you give him my answer?

MERCURY. I can't believe, Alkmena, that you really want to see your city infected by pestilence, razed to the ground by fire. Do you want to see your husband defeated? I shall tell Jupiter that you're expecting him.

ALKMENA. You'll be telling him a lie!

MERCURY. With women I find the morning lie becomes the evening truth! Till tonight, Alkmena. (MERCURY *exits*.)

ALKMENA (*calls*). Sosie— (SOSIE *enters*) Tell me—Queen Leda—how does she seem?

SOSIE. She's wearing silver piped in swansdown but very good taste.

ALKMENA. No—her face I mean—Haughty? Hard?

SOSIE. No, serene and noble.

ALKMENA. Good! Tell her to come in! (SOSIE *exits*) I have an idea, a wonderful idea.
(QUEEN LEDA *comes in. She goes at once to* ALKMENA *and offers her hand to kiss.* ALKMENA *curtsies before her and kisses her hand.*)

LEDA. Alkmena, I hope you do not find my visit *too* indiscreet?

ALKMENA. No, no, Leda—

LEDA. I was passing through Thebes and heard the news and I wanted to see you.

ALKMENA. I'm enchanted.

LEDA (*pointing toward the bedroom and gushing rather*). Is that the historic bedroom to be?

ALKMENA. It's my bedroom.

LEDA. And is it for tonight?

ALKMENA. I hear it's for tonight.

LEDA. You've done very well, very well indeed. How did you manage it? (*Both sit on couch*) Did you offer endless prayers? Did you cry aloud your misery, your nostalgia for a god?

ALKMENA. No, I expressed my happiness and my contentment.

LEDA. I see—well, perhaps that's an even better way of calling for help. Have you seen him?

ALKMENA. No. Is it he who sends you here?

LEDA. No—

ALKMENA. It's not that you'd like to catch another glimpse of him, is it?

LEDA. Another glimpse? I've never had one. I've never seen him.

ALKMENA. Never?

LEDA. Never!

ALKMENA. I thought you had at least a nodding acquaintance with him.

LEDA. You don't seem to know the details of our little adventure.

ALKMENA. Not intimately—

LEDA. Oh, well—it was summer. (*Music*) Great schools of swan had been coursing high up among the stars. They were so beautiful I couldn't take my eyes off them. My husband even noticed it and made jokes about it—your swan-song will be with a swan, he said.

ALKMENA. Your husband made jokes about it?

LEDA. My husband's an atheist. Not believing in the gods, he sees nothing in this but a vehicle for puns. Of course there is an advantage in that!

ALKMENA. Then it's true what legend tells us, that Jupiter came to you in the guise of a swan?

LEDA. Well—up to a certain point he was, a sort of cloudburst—a gust of swan.

ALKMENA. Was it real down?

LEDA. Certainly. I touched the wingroots with my fingers—a harp of feathers. Alkmena, to be perfectly frank—I would rather, if you don't mind, that with you he wouldn't be a swan again. I'm not of a jealous disposition at all, but if you could leave me this little distinction, it would be so nice of you. After all, there are so many other birds, much rarer ones, even.

ALKMENA. Yes, but few are as noble and I don't think they're a bit more stupid than geese or eagles, and they sing too, after a fashion, don't they?

LEDA. Oh, indeed they do!

ALKMENA. Nobody listens to them, but they sing. Did he sing?

LEDA. Well—he didn't exactly sing —it was a beautifully enunciated chirp, a chirp of which the sense escaped me but of which the syntax was so pure, the diction so exquisite, that you could just feel the verbs and relative pronouns of bird language.

ALKMENA. Did he overwhelm you —I mean were you taken by surprise?

LEDA. Warned and surprised. Assaulted, gently assaulted. Swathed in a movement which was not earthly but astral, cradled in an eternal cosmic rolling.

ALKMENA. And how did he leave you? Tell me that.

LEDA. He rose straight to my zenith. He was gracious enough to endow me for several seconds with his sight. This enabled me to follow him from my zenith to his, from zenith to zenith—and there I lost him.

ALKMENA. Oh, is that all?

LEDA. Well, for the Master of the Gods I think it's a good deal!

ALKMENA. Yes, but after a little while—the next day perhaps—no trifling gift?

LEDA. No.

ALKMENA. No flowers?

LEDA. No.

ALKMENA. Not even a little colored egg?

LEDA. In a way I get little communications from him. The branches of a pear tree, for example, bow down to me in homage as I pass.

ALKMENA. Still, Leda, that's not much, is it?

LEDA. As a matter of fact, I wouldn't have cared for a prolonged liaison even with a god.

ALKMENA. A prolonged liaison, no. But I do think he might have paid you a second visit.

LEDA (crestfallen). Do you?

ALKMENA. Yes. Leda, you're not happy. I can tell. Jupiter hasn't made you happy.

LEDA. I am more than happy. I am sanctified.

ALKMENA. You're too young, no, no, you're too beautiful to be canonized so early. It was a shabby trick. Jupiter loved you and abandoned you.

LEDA. Abandoned me?

ALKMENA. Yes, he deserted you, didn't he? He didn't come back, did he? Trying to make it up to you with genuflections from a pear tree! If I were you, Leda, I'd revenge myself. He didn't even make an honest legend of you.

LEDA. How can I revenge myself on a white swan?

ALKMENA. I'll tell you how. With a black one. Substitute for me.

LEDA. What?

ALKMENA. That door leads to my room. You go in there—put on my veils, spray my scent about—I can make it very dark. Jupiter will be deceived and to his advantage.

LEDA. But you don't know, you don't realize what it means. If you knew him as I do, you wouldn't be so generous.

ALKMENA. I thought you said you didn't know him.

LEDA. I know him as a bird! Alkmena, in spite of everything I've said, it was worth it! You'll see, you'll be so relaxed.

ALKMENA. But I don't want to be relaxed, I'm not a bit tense. And besides I've already made up my mind to refuse him.

LEDA. That's astonishing. Why?

ALKMENA. I'm in love with my husband.

LEDA. Are you really? Oh, my dear —well, you can't go on being so exclusive forever so you might as well begin with a god.

ALKMENA. No, Leda. I'm unworthy of this honor. Now you are not only the most beautiful of reigning queens, you are also the most intelligent. Who but you could possibly work out a whole syntax, construct a grammar from a bird-call. You invented writing, didn't you?

LEDA. That's wasted on the gods because they haven't invented reading yet.

ALKMENA. You know astronomy. You know exactly where your zenith is and where your nadir. I'm always getting them mixed up. You have a scientific background. No, Leda, you're far more suitable for Jupiter than I am.

LEDA. I see—I'm beginning to understand— The more I see you, the more I listen to you, the more I begin to be persuaded that celestial contact might be fatal to your special charm. Yes, if you're still determined—I'll help you.

ALKMENA. Oh, Leda, Leda—

LEDA. On one condition.

ALKMENA. Condition?

LEDA. You must admit that I have the right to specify an incarnation that won't be repulsive to me.

ALKMENA. Oh, yes—

LEDA. In what form will Jupiter come?

ALKMENA. I don't know!

LEDA. You can know.

ALKMENA. How?

LEDA. He will assume some shape that haunts your desires and your dreams.

ALKMENA. But I'm not a haunted woman.

LEDA. Jupiter is so versatile. I hope it isn't a serpent. I have a horror of serpents. You can't count on me if it's a serpent! (Rises.)

ALKMENA (rising). Leda, I have one weakness.

LEDA. What is it?

ALKMENA. My husband.

LEDA. Your husband? Your husband—what does he look like?

ALKMENA. My husband? What's he like? I haven't the faintest idea!

LEDA. Have you his portrait?

ALKMENA. Oh, yes—here. (Shows medallion she is wearing on a chain around her neck.)

LEDA. Is his hair blond?

ALKMENA. No, black like a raven's wing.

LEDA. He has those enigmatic eyes that I like.

ALKMENA (taking medallion away rather quickly). He's not a god. He's my husband, Leda.

LEDA. Your husband, of course. Why didn't we think of that before? Your swan will be Amphitryon. The first time your husband leaves home, Jupiter will enter your bedroom and you'll never know the difference.

ALKMENA. You terrify me. Amphitryon is away now!

LEDA. Away from Thebes?

ALKMENA. Yes, he left this morning for the war.

LEDA. When is he coming back?

ALKMENA (*looking over back wall*). I haven't the faintest idea.

LEDA. You can't wage a war decently in less than two days!

ALKMENA. No, I'm afraid not.

LEDA. Before tonight I promise you that Jupiter will enter that door, so like Amphitryon that you will succumb to him.

ALKMENA. I couldn't possibly be deceived—I should know him.

LEDA. For once a human being will be a divine imitation, and you will be misled.

ALKMENA. Exactly. He'll be more perfect than Amphitryon, more noble than Amphitryon, and I shall hate him at first sight. (*Comes down to* LEDA.)

LEDA. And I tell you that with me he was a simply enormous swan and I couldn't distinguish him from the swan I see every day on my own river—

SOSIE (*off stage*). News, Mistress, unexpected news! (*Entering.*)

ALKMENA. Amphitryon is here!

SOSIE. How did you know? I saw him leaping the moats on his galloping steed.

ALKMENA. No rider ever jumped them before!

SOSIE. One leap was enough for him.

LEDA. Is he alone?

SOSIE. Alone, but around him one could feel an invisible squadron. What shall I do?

ALKMENA. Go down the hill and meet him.
(*Exit* SOSIE.)

LEDA. Now are you convinced? It's Jupiter, Jupiter the sham Amphitryon.

ALKMENA. Very well then, he shall find here the sham Alkmena. Oh, Leda, I feel you are my friend. Don't friends do things like this for each other?

LEDA. Very often, but usually without saying a word about it! Your room's in there? (*She starts for bedroom.*)

ALKMENA (*following her*). In there, in there.

LEDA. Are there steps going down? I have a horror of slipping in the dark.

ALKMENA. No, a smooth level floor. You mustn't weaken at the last moment, Leda.

LEDA. I have promised. I've never let a friend down yet! (*As she goes into bedroom*) This way—oh, yes, it's charming.

SOSIE (*off stage*). Your horses, my lord, what shall I do with your horses? They're exhausted.

AMPHITRYON (*also off stage*). Don't bother me about my horses, I shall be leaving again in a minute.

ALKMENA (*listening hard*). He's lost interest in his horses, it's certainly not Amphitryon!

AMPHITRYON (*still off stage*). Darling, it is I. (*He comes in. He goes to couch, throws down his cape and helmet.*)

ALKMENA. No one else. I can see that.

AMPHITRYON. Well, aren't you going to kiss me?

ALKMENA (*scrutinizing him, more and more amazed at the perfection of the imitation*). Yes—in a minute. Let me look at you first. You're not afraid to show your face to your wife, are you? Your wife who is so familiar with it!

AMPHITRYON. Well—here it is.

ALKMENA. Yes—everything's there! Even those criss-crossed wrinkles, clawed by I know not what bird. Jupiter's eagle, I suppose.

AMPHITRYON. They're not eagle's feet, darling, they're crow's feet.

ALKMENA. Nevertheless, something's lacking—that scratch is lacking which he got yesterday. Strange husband that comes back from the war with one scratch less.

AMPHITRYON (*sits on couch and takes off his greaves*). Nothing like fresh air for cuts.

ALKMENA. Marvellously healthy, isn't it, that outdoor exercise on a battlefield? What's going on behind that forehead—that forehead that is so much larger than usual?

AMPHITRYON. What always goes on —adoration for Alkmena.

ALKMENA. And what is that face thinking of—that face that gets bigger and bigger the more I look at it?

AMPHITRYON (*rises and goes to her*). Of kissing your lips!

ALKMENA (*escaping from him*). Why my lips?

AMPHITRYON (*follows more impetuously*). Of biting the nape of your neck.

ALKMENA. Amphitryon, what's come over you? I've never heard you talk like this before.

AMPHITRYON. Alkmena, what's the matter?

ALKMENA. Where did you sleep last night?

AMPHITRYON. In the brambles— with a bundle of vine-shoots for a pillow. Oh, darling, I have to leave within the hour, for we're giving battle this morning. (*Close to her at last*) What is this sudden reserve between us? (*He seizes her and kisses her passionately*) You behave more like a fiancée than a wife.

ALKMENA (*horrified*). What are you doing?

AMPHITRYON (*kisses her again*). And now you're coming with me. (*Starts to take her to bedroom.*)

ALKMENA (*breaks away from him*). Yes—one moment—I'll call you—my sweet—my lover—my husband. (*She exits, leaving* AMPHITRYON *alone. After a short pause* ALKMENA *calls to him from off stage*) Amphitryon!

AMPHITRYON (*eagerly*). Yes, darling, here I am— (*He rushes after her. The stage is empty for a moment. Then* ALKMENA *re-enters from up stage. She comes down to below the couch.*)

ALKMENA (*with great satisfaction*). He is there—in her arms! Let me hear no more of the wickedness of life. Let me hear no more about fate—neither the wiles of men nor the caprices of the gods are proof against the clear love of a faithful wife. Echo, what have I to fear from men or gods if I'm faithful and loyal? Tell me, Echo, you who have never contradicted me. Nothing—isn't that so, Echo, nothing, nothing? (*Her arms are uplifted to the heavens.*)

ECHO (*from off stage*). Everything! Everything!

ALKMENA (*terrified*). What? What is that you say?

ECHO (*relenting*). Nothing! Nothing! (*Reassured,* ALKMENA *breathes a sigh of relief. Her arms are uplifted in gratitude, her face transfigured. The curtain falls.*)

ACT THREE

Scene I

PLACE—*The roof of the Palace. A parapet, with one step up, runs around the roof. There are statues of heroes, gods and goddesses on the cornices of the roof. Their superb backs face the audience. A stone bench in the shape of an "H" stands in the center of the roof.*

TIME—*Later in the same day.*

NENETZA *and* KLEANTHA *are discovered looking down over the parapet. They are both laughing at something going on below, as* SOSIE *comes in.*

SOSIE. What are you doing here? Isn't there enough to do below? There are no flowers on Jupiter's altar and no garlands in the courtyard.

NENETZA. We came up to watch Queen Leda depart.

SOSIE. What if she stays all day?

KLEANTHA. There she goes; there she goes.

SOSIE (*getting between girls to look*). She looks very self-satisfied, I must say.

KLEANTHA. Look at her, she's bowing to the lime trees!

NENETZA. No—the lime trees are bowing to her.

SOSIE. They're not bowing to her —they're bowing to the wind. Anybody'd think this was her day instead of our mistress'. (*Pushing them off*) Now, get down to your work. You, Nenetza, put amber in your mistress' bath and get out the big scarlet veil. (TRUMPETER *enters all out of breath. Stops, moistens his finger and holds it up.*)

TRUMPETER. Not a breath—not a breath of wind! On the roof, you'd think there'd be some air. (*He too peeps over the parapet*) In the streets, the festive banners are waving in the breeze and yet up here there's no breeze at all. It's strange.

SOSIE. Of course it's strange!

TRUMPETER. Do you hear the shouting?

SOSIE. Shouting? No!

TRUMPETER. Of course you can't, it's muffled by the clouds. Never have I seen the clouds so low. And yet, it's the greatest day that's ever come to Thebes. Our army is victorious—we have won a victory in one day. It's never been heard of before—and not a casualty. Even the horses have only been wounded in the left leg.

SOSIE. For once the recruiting slogans have come true. Great excitement in the streets!

TRUMPETER. Yes! Everything is arranged for Jupiter's arrival just as for an eclipse.

SOSIE. Do you think he will come in a burst of flame?

TRUMPETER. Probably. All the children are blackening bits of glass so that they'll be able to watch his arrival without it hurting their eyes.

SOSIE. I have mobilized all the unfortunates in Thebes—the halt, the lame and the blind. They are crowded around the Palace in the hope that Jupiter, in passing, will touch them and cure them. Even the paralytics I'm having carried up to the Palace.

TRUMPETER. Oh, but Sosie. I think that's a very bad idea!

SOSIE. Do you?

TRUMPETER. Yes. Jupiter thinks that man is perfect because he is created in his own image. If you reveal him now, in his imperfection, you may irritate him. You know how one detests a bad mirror. Do you know what I would do, Sosie, if I were you?

SOSIE. What?

TRUMPETER (*sits on bench beside* SOSIE). Let it be announced that you are gathering the paralytics indeed and let these paralytics be a group of—lovely dancers! Then, don't you see, Sosie, Jupiter will not blush at having created a world so ridden with ugliness. He will have reason to be proud. He will think: "I've done pretty well."

SOSIE. There may be something in what you say, Trumpeter.

TRUMPETER. Oh, there is— What do you see now?

SOSIE. Alkmena is walking on the terrace.

TRUMPETER. What is her expression?

SOSIE. Expectant!

TRUMPETER (*blandly*). Naturally!

SOSIE. And yet they say that she will refuse Jupiter.

TRUMPETER. That's coquetry—sheer coquetry!

SOSIE. They say she will refuse to conceive.

TRUMPETER. She can't refuse a thing like that!

SOSIE. Ah, but you don't know my mistress—she might. She's stubborn.

TRUMPETER. You don't know Jupiter. I know Jupiter. You don't know how stubborn he can be. That's what makes him a god! Stubbornness! That's what distinguishes gods from men. If men could push obstinacy to the ultimate point they would be gods, too, like Jupiter. He'll stick to it. He'll have Alkmena's secret.

SOSIE (*looking around him in awe*). Do you know, Trumpeter, I've been thinking—it sounds blasphemous to say it—but why do the gods come to Earth so often? Jupiter especially. Juno must be heavenly beautiful!

TRUMPETER (*flatly*). Juno is his wife.

SOSIE. In that way the gods are like us. (*Confidentially*). Have you ever thought—if we had the privileges of the gods—if we were permitted to take different shapes and—you know what I mean, Trumpeter!

TRUMPETER. I follow you.

SOSIE. What shape would you take?

TRUMPETER. I think, Sosie, I'd be a butterfly!
(ALKMENA *comes in. The* TRUMPETER *and* SOSIE *bow low to her.*)

TRUMPETER. Hail, mother-to-be!

SOSIE. Are there any further instructions, mistress?

ALKMENA. Instruction, Sosie?

SOSIE. For the arrival, mistress.

ALKMENA. What have you done so far, Sosie?

SOSIE. I am gathering together a group of the most exquisite dancers in all Thebes to greet Jupiter.

ALKMENA. How clever of you, Sosie.

TRUMPETER (*delighted, nudging* SOSIE). What did I tell you, Sosie?

ALKMENA. Go, Sosie. Order the procession. And you, Trumpeter, help him, help him.

TRUMPETER. Delighted! It will be a garland day for Jupiter. (*They go out.* AMPHITRYON *enters. He is in very bad humor. He is scowling.*)

ALKMENA. Amphitryon, my darling! Why do you look like that. Aren't you going to kiss me?

AMPHITRYON. For the pleasure of kissing you I've paid heavily enough already.

ALKMENA. I've just ordered a processional in your honor. All the beauty in Thebes, my darling. Not many wives would do that. All Thebes is awaiting the arrival of the already departed god. I share a secret with Jupiter. Aren't you jealous that I share a secret with Jupiter?

AMPHITRYON. It's no secret that Jupiter is coming to you tonight. That's no secret. And you seem radiant at the prospect!

ALKMENA. I'm radiant at your return and I'm radiant over your victory.

AMPHITRYON. The victory was won in my absence. For this hour with you—

ALKMENA. This hour with me—?

AMPHITRYON. —cost me this victory. Had we been defeated in my absence, that I might have borne. But a victory without me—it's insupportable!

ALKMENA. But haven't you just come from the battlefield?

AMPHITRYON. What's the matter with you, Alkmena? Have you lost your senses? Have you forgotten already that I have just come from your arms?

ALKMENA. When did you return?

AMPHITRYON. You know perfectly well. You questioned me sufficiently about it. Are you so intoxicated by this honor that you don't remember these last few hours? I can't endure it!

ALKMENA (more to herself than to him). What have I done? What have I done?

AMPHITRYON (turns, sees her distracted look. Misinterpreting its

cause). Darling! I shall put up a fight with Jupiter, not physically—mentally. I shall state my case. I have a voice, I have words—and for a general I'm highly articulate. I shall persuade Jupiter. I shall convince him!

ALKMENA. What I most fear is a conference between you and Jupiter. You've never persuaded anyone but me and you didn't do that by talking!

AMPHITRYON. Darling! Don't you realize that if we refuse—Jupiter might kill us.

ALKMENA. He can do worse than that!

AMPHITRYON. Worse?

ALKMENA. He could make us hate each other.

AMPHITRYON. He couldn't do that.

ALKMENA. He can. He can change us into beings that hate each other by instinct. A nightingale and a toad—a minnow and a shark—

AMPHITRYON. We would recognize each other—you and I.

ALKMENA. I, who eat with less enjoyment if you're using a spoon while I'm using a fork—what joy would there be left in life for me if you're breathing through gills and I through leaves— (She begins to weep.)

AMPHITRYON. Dearest, don't cry. If we submit to Jupiter—if we consent to this—he will leave us in peace—we shall be left with each other—we'd still have our love.

ALKMENA. No. How could we live with that between us? Imagine us with an unutterable third name always on our lips, withering our kisses, tarnished by immortality. How will you look at me when he who defiled us scrawls his signature across the sky in lightning? (*There is a clap of thunder.*)

AMPHITRYON. We've been so happy. I can't believe it's over!

ALKMENA. I should have loved us to have grown old together. To test the truth of the notion that people grow to look like each other, to experience the tranquil joys of nodding by the hearth, of dying finally. Oh, that wonderful old age of which Jupiter is about to rob us! Long, long years of marriage. Can you imagine us as two very old people? Tell me, my old husband, have you loved me?

AMPHITRYON. My whole life.

ALKMENA. Without exception?

AMPHITRYON. Without exception!

ALKMENA. Can I believe that?

AMPHITRYON. It's true.

ALKMENA. If it's true for you, then that shall be my truth also. Tell me, though, didn't you—just as we were about to celebrate our silver wedding—find a sixteen-year-old virgin, one of those girls at once bold and shy, who was ravished by your distinguished gray hair and your exploits in the past, a creature light as air and as enchanting as moonlight—a perfect monster, in fact?

AMPHITRYON. No, for me, you have always been younger than youth itself and I wanted us, when we reached old age, to have no reason for reproach between us.

ALKMENA. Nor have we— (*Kisses him*) not really. (*Another clap of thunder*) Now, at last, death may come; not surprising us, but catching up with us. Death may come!

ECHO. Death may come!

ALKMENA (*both rise*). Echo tells us it is the end. And yet Echo deceived me once! (*There is a terrific crash of thunder.* AMPHITRYON *takes* ALKMENA *and walks down stage with her. Trumpets sound.* JUPITER *and* MERCURY *appear from behind the clouds and come down.*)

JUPITER (*looks at* AMPHITRYON). Who is that possessive individual standing at her side?

MERCURY. It's her husband.

JUPITER. Amphitryon, the conqueror of the great battle of Corinth?

MERCURY. You're anticipating. He won't win Corinth—for five years yet. But it's he.

JUPITER. Who summoned him here?

MERCURY. Doubtless he came to offer you Alkmena personally.

AMPHITRYON. My Lord. Mercury is mistaken. I must defend Alkmena against you even if I die in the attempt.

JUPITER. Apparently you are not persuaded of the inevitability of this night.

AMPHITRYON. No, my lord, I'm not!

MERCURY (*to* JUPITER). Jupiter, this is no moment for chatting. The sun is about to set.

JUPITER. The setting of the sun is my business.

MERCURY. But once the gods begin quibbling over ethics with mortals, the good old days are over.

JUPITER. My son is a stickler for etiquette. Quite right. (*To* AMPHITRYON) You know my power. You must realize that if I choose I can cause Alkmena to love me and even cause you to pray for my success as your rival. This conflict, therefore, between us is not one of matter but of form. It is not a question of whether I shall possess her—but how. Over such a slight technical formality for one little night, are you going to enter the lists with the gods?

AMPHITRYON. A general is not convinced by miracles!

JUPITER. Is that your last word? Do you really want to enter into a contest with me?

AMPHITRYON. If I have to—yes!

JUPITER. As a general, I think you are sufficiently intelligent not to risk battle with unequal forces. That's the A B C of tactics.

AMPHITRYON. I prefer that other technical formality—death!

JUPITER. You must understand my forbearance. I'm fond of you both. As a couple, I'm rather proud of you. I am pleased with the idea of your two superbly sculptured bodies, like prows on galleons, cleaving great furrows in time. I want to sponsor you. It is as a good friend that I wish to be established with you both.

AMPHITRYON. You are already so established and revered. I refuse!

JUPITER. You deny to Alkmena the privileges accident has thrown in your way, when you yourself are not so blameless.

ALKMENA (*fearing* JUPITER'S *revelation of her trick with* LEDA *she breaks away from* AMPHITRYON *and approaches* JUPITER). Jupiter!

JUPITER. Very well, Mercury, let the truth be blazoned forth to all the world—last night's truth and today's—
(MERCURY *is about to comply when* ALKMENA *makes a last effort to stop him.*)

ALKMENA (*drops to her knees before* JUPITER). Jupiter—can we be alone?

JUPITER. We shall be. (*He waves his hand.* MERCURY *and* AMPHITRYON *disappear.* JUPITER *offers* ALKMENA *his hand. She takes it and then sits with him on bench.*)

JUPITER. Alone at last!

ALKMENA. If one is to believe the legends—it is a kind of solitude which you experience often. Oh, Jupiter, with so many, why do you choose me for an historic role to which I am so little suited?

JUPITER. Because you endow the historic with an air of impromptu which absolutely delights me!

ALKMENA. Why destroy a perfect marriage—leave it in ruins—for one moment's pleasure?

JUPITER. Isn't that the essence of all love?

ALKMENA. Suppose I offer you more than love—better than love—

JUPITER. Am I so repulsive to you?

ALKMENA. If you only were.

JUPITER. You would resist me then because you love me?

ALKMENA. Love! Love you may experience with anyone. But between us I would like to create a bond that is sweeter and more powerful; I, alone among women, can offer you this—I do offer it—and it's friendship!

JUPITER. Friendship? I hear it for the first time. Explain it. What does it mean? Is it a word current on Earth?

ALKMENA. The expression is current.

JUPITER. What is its object?

ALKMENA. To bring together the most totally dissimilar people and make them equal. Have you never seen the most ill-assorted creatures isolate themselves for no reason at all? A cabinet minister and a gardener—a lion sharing his cage with a poodle? And these misfits have a perfect community of interests—they seem drawn together by some strange, chemical substance in their bodies.

JUPITER. I vaguely remember a cabinet minister and a gardener, yes, they were diverting to watch.

ALKMENA. They'd stroll down the hundred paces of the garden path and then—stroll back again.

JUPITER. The cabinet minister would converse learnedly about pruning and weeds—

ALKMENA. —the gardener of filibusters and excise taxes—

JUPITER. —then after each had had his say, they'd finally stop at the end of the path—

ALKMENA. —look affectionately into each other's eyes—

JUPITER. —stroke their beards—

ALKMENA. —and wink.

JUPITER. Friendship?

ALKMENA. Friendship!

JUPITER. It sounds an amusing novelty. But if I became your friend—what would we do?

ALKMENA. First of all, instead of believing in you as a god, I should think of you as a friend. My thoughts of you would be from the heart, whereas my prayers to you would no longer be repeated by rote but addressed to you—personally. Instead of ritual gestures of obeisance I should—beckon you with my hands.

JUPITER. Are you sure that wouldn't take up too much of your time?

ALKMENA. Oh, no. I'd find the time.

JUPITER. And I? What would I do?

ALKMENA. Well . . . on days when I didn't feel like seeing anybody at all—then you'd come—you'd sit at the foot of my divan, calmly.

JUPITER. Would we just sit?

ALKMENA. No, we'd talk.

JUPITER. What about?

ALKMENA. Well, you'd tell me your joys, your sorrows and your burdens. You would explain Creation to me.

JUPITER. You are interested in Creation?

ALKMENA. Oh, yes. (He smiles) Why do you smile?

JUPITER. Nothing. And then?

ALKMENA. Then you would go away. But you would have been there. Do you understand?

JUPITER (laughs). Faintly.

ALKMENA. I see you're still a little vague about it.

JUPITER. I'm afraid so—

ALKMENA. Well, suppose I give you some examples of how I'd call on you for help and you tell me what you'd do.

JUPITER. Perhaps that would be better.

ALKMENA (clasps her hands in front of her). Are you ready?

JUPITER (sees her clasped hands and does the same with his). Yes, I am ready.

ALKMENA. My husband is lost. What can you do for me?

JUPITER. As a friend?

ALKMENA. As a friend.

JUPITER. I would dispatch a comet to guide him. I would endow you with second sight so you could see him. I would increase the volume of your voice so that no matter where he was, you could talk to him.

ALKMENA. Is that all you'd do?

JUPITER. I'd bring him back!

ALKMENA. That's better— Now—a child of mine is ill?

JUPITER. I'd drape the universe in sadness. Flowers would lose their scent. The very animals, dejected, would drag their heads.

ALKMENA. You wouldn't go so far as to cure the child?

JUPITER. Of course I would. How stupid of me!

ALKMENA. Oh, no, no. You're not stupid. In the main, you've done very well.

JUPITER. Thank you.

ALKMENA. One more question!

JUPITER. Yes?

ALKMENA. In a marriage ideally happy, a husband has been unfaithful through no fault of his own—what can you do for him?

JUPITER. Cause him never to know it.

ALKMENA. Ah, Jupiter, you are a friend—a true friend!

JUPITER. It seems to me, I'd have more to do than you would.

ALKMENA. Naturally, since you have more power. To do more than one's share is one of the privileges of friendship. Have you never tasted the strange joy of submitting to the will of another?

JUPITER. I've never had the opportunity.

ALKMENA. You have it now. Shall you miss it?

JUPITER. I see through you, Alkmena, I read your thoughts.

ALKMENA. You see, you know my secrets. Therefore you are so much more suited to be my friend than my lover.

JUPITER. I see that no matter what I do, I cannot cross the immutable line that separates us. Therefore. I free you.

ALKMENA (overjoyed, rises). Oh! (Drops to her knees before him.)

JUPITER. You've touched me, somehow. You are stubborn, you are obstinate. But you also are forlorn in your devotion. You make fidelity affecting. If you can console the Thebans for depriving them so

brutally of this national honor—I give you my word. . . . (Rises) I shall not impose my presence on you tonight.

ALKMENA (rises also). But why need the Thebans know? Let me appear before them—before the whole world as your mistress. True, it will drive them wild with jealousy, and you know how trying envy can be; but, on the other hand, it'll give Amphitryon and me great pleasure to suffer this inconvenience for you. That's friendship!

JUPITER. You dazzle me, Alkmena. How you fleck your little tricks with gleams of loyalty. How you flavor your little lies with a tincture of sincerity! Nevertheless, I free you!

ALKMENA. Without reservations?

JUPITER. Without reservations.

ALKMENA (suspicious). But you accept so easily—without a struggle.

JUPITER. It is your special gift, Alkmena, to teach even the gods resignation.

ALKMENA. Yes, but you're eager—you're more than resigned—you're eager—

JUPITER. You make friendship sound so attractive, it satisfies me.

ALKMENA. You seem so easily satisfied at the prospect of not being my lover.

JUPITER. No, it's not that—it's only that—you are so determined.

ALKMENA. Jupiter—?

JUPITER. Yes, Alkmena.

ALKMENA. Are you sure that you've never been my lover?

JUPITER. Why do you ask me that?

ALKMENA. Because my knowledge of men leads me to believe that when they're as noble as this, it's because they're already satisfied.

JUPITER. Already?

ALKMENA. Are you sure that you have never taken the shape of Amphitryon?

JUPITER. Quite sure.

ALKMENA. You have so many affairs —maybe you did, and it slipped your mind.

JUPITER (*admonishingly*). Alkmena!

ALKMENA. Because I must admit that if I felt you had not, I should feel a certain regret.

JUPITER. Regret?

ALKMENA. Yes. To have been loved by the Master of the Gods himself —through no fault of my own— would be quite a feather in the cap of a middle-class housewife! (*Laughs*) It's too bad!

JUPITER. You are only trying to trap me.

ALKMENA (*rises, quick as a flash*). You are capable, then, of being caught?

JUPITER. I have never been—your lover!

ALKMENA. Jupiter—take me in your arms.

JUPITER (*obeying*). Are you at home there?

ALKMENA. Yes.

JUPITER. Yes?—only yes?

ALKMENA. Yes, Jupiter, darling— there you see—it seems quite natural, for me to be calling you darling.

JUPITER. Quite natural.

ALKMENA. It sprang from me spontaneously. What is this pleasurable sensation that flows through my body when I'm near you? Whence does it come?

JUPITER. We are sympatico.

ALKMENA. What's that?

JUPITER. A friendly word in a language that does not yet exist. It means that we understand each other very well.

ALKMENA. Why, then, in spite of this harmony, am I so troubled?

JUPITER. Perhaps because I am beginning to take the form of Amphitryon. Perhaps because you're beginning to fall in love with me.

ALKMENA. No, it's not the beginning of something—it's the end of something. Confess, Jupiter, wasn't it you yourself that came to me after the great fire in Thebes?

JUPITER. No. Neither was it I who rescued the little boy from the sea.

ALKMENA. You see, you know about it!

JUPITER (*toying with a lock of her hair*). Don't I know everything that concerns you? Alas, no—it was your husband. How soft your hair is!

ALKMENA. It seems to me—I have a conviction—it's not the first time you've twisted that lock of hair or leaned over me like this. Was it at night or was it at dawn you came?

JUPITER. Neither! Neither!

ALKMENA. You have obscured everything for me. My whole body rejoices at having met you. I am thrilled in my being at this hour— and yet I'm conscious also of trouble, of uncertainty—of something. . . . Can you not rid my mind of this uncertainty?

JUPITER. Since you will not believe me, I can grant you forgetfulness.

ALKMENA. Yes, that's what I want most of all, Jupiter—forgetfulness!

JUPITER. I shall obliterate your past —shall I also reveal to you your future?

ALKMENA. No! No!

JUPITER. It will be a happy one, believe me.

ALKMENA. I know what a happy future consists of. My beloved husband will live and die. My dear son will be born and live and die. I shall live and die.

JUPITER. Since I cannot share your mortal life with you, will you not, for an instant, share the life of the gods? Since your whole past is about to sink into oblivion, do you not wish to see in one flash of clarity the whole world—past, present and future—and to comprehend its meaning?

ALKMENA. No, I'm not curious.

JUPITER. Do you not wish to see humanity at its labors, from its birth to its final dissolution? Do you not wish to see the eleven great beings who will constitute the finest ornament in all history? One with his lovely Jewish face; another with her little nose from Lorraine?

ALKMENA (*sighs*). No!

JUPITER. And since you are about to forget everything, do you not wish to understand the illusions that constitute your virtue and your happiness?

ALKMENA. No—no—

JUPITER. Nor at this last moment what I really am to you?

ALKMENA. No—forgetfulness, Jupiter; I beg of you—forgetfulness—

JUPITER. And I beg you, Alkmena, do not abandon me; do not leave me with nothing on my hands but my divinity.

ALKMENA. I must—as you must abandon me to my humanity.

JUPITER. I will kiss you. Only this way can I grant forgetfulness. It is the conventional ritual. Forget everything you have lived—everything you wish forgotten. (*Kisses her*) Except this kiss!

ALKMENA. What kiss?

JUPITER. You know perfectly well. That kiss I took the trouble to put this side of oblivion. (JUPITER *lifts his arm in an Olympian gesture. Music is heard.* MERCURY *and* AMPHITRYON *appear—each from opposite sides of the stage.* JUPITER, ALKMENA *by his side, addresses* AMPHITRYON) She has won me over, Amphitryon, and I rejoice in my defeat. Is she always like this?

AMPHITRYON. She generally manages to be right!

MERCURY. The whole of Thebes is at the foot of the Palace clamoring for you to appear with Alkmena in your arms.

JUPITER. My son and his ceremonials!

MERCURY. Just show yourselves—that will satisfy them completely.

JUPITER (*to* AMPHITRYON). Do you mind?

AMPHITRYON. It is an honor.

JUPITER. Thank you, General! (*He offers his arm to* ALKMENA; *they walk to parapet to display themselves to the populace*) Bear up, Alkmena, for this one instant only.

ALKMENA. These wretches that insult my integrity!

JUPITER. Even they demand their legend.

MERCURY. Just say a few words to them; you can be brief, you know —they'll elaborate it themselves. (*Prompting*) At last I meet you—

JUPITER AND MERCURY (*together*). At last I meet you, dearest Alkmena . . .

MERCURY. Yes, dear Jupiter . . .

ALKMENA AND MERCURY. Yes, dear Jupiter, and so we have to part.

MERCURY (*prompting*). And so begins this night—

MERCURY AND JUPITER. So begins this night—so fertile for all the world.

MERCURY AND ALKMENA. So ends this day—this day that I was beginning to love.

MERCURY. Kiss!
(JUPITER *kisses* ALKMENA *on the forehead.*)

JUPITER (*leading her back to* AMPHITRYON). And now that the legend has been duly established, befitting the dignity of the gods—

MERCURY. Amphitryon, your marriage—blessed already—is to be blessed even further—

JUPITER. Alkmena is to bear you a son. Will you name him to please me? Will you name him Hercules?

AMPHITRYON. Hercules?

ALKMENA. Hercules!

JUPITER. And I shall be his . . . godfather . . .

JUPITER AND MERCURY (*together*). . . . and so will destiny be fulfilled! (AMPHITRYON *and* ALKMENA *are in each other's arms.* JUPITER, *followed by* MERCURY, *goes to back toward the low-hanging clouds.*)

JUPITER. We must intrude no longer on these two—I have withheld their night too long already—

(*The lights slowly dim.* JUPITER *commands the firmament*) Curtain of the night, descend—but for an instant let them be encircled in a glade of light! (*Light from above falls on* AMPHITRYON *and* ALKMENA) A little island of fidelity! My arm embraces them to bring them closer to their joy—this untarnished couple—forever to remain untarnished! (JUPITER *and* MERCURY *are now on their way to the Empyrean.*)

MERCURY. But I warn you—posterity will gossip!

JUPITER. Alkmena won't mind. By that time she will have forgotten even my farewell. (*He disappears aloft, followed by* MERCURY, *trailing celestial rays.*)

ALKMENA (*transfigured for the moment by the divine, flings up her arms and calls after the departed god*). Farewell, Jupiter, farewell!

CURTAIN

The Cradle Song

BY G. MARTINEZ SIERRA

TRANSLATED FROM THE SPANISH
BY JOHN GARRETT UNDERHILL

TO JACINTO BENAVENTE

CHARACTERS

SISTER JOANNA OF THE CROSS, *18 years of age.*
TERESA, *aged 18.*
THE PRIORESS, *aged 40.*
THE VICARESS, *aged 40.*
THE MISTRESS OF NOVICES, *aged 36.*
SISTER MARCELLA, *aged 19.*
SISTER MARÍA JESÚS, *aged 19.*
SISTER SAGRARIO, *aged 18.*
SISTER INEZ, *aged 50.*
SISTER TORNERA, *aged 30.*
THE DOCTOR, *aged 60.*
ANTONIO, *aged 25.*
THE POET.
A COUNTRYMAN.
Also a LAY SISTER, *Two* MONITORS, *and several other* NUNS, *as desired.*

THE CRADLE SONG

ACT ONE

A room opening upon the cloister of a Convent of Enclosed Dominican Nuns. The walls are tinted soberly; the floor is tiled. Three arches at the rear. In the right wall a large door with a wicket in it, leading to a passage communicating with the exterior. A grilled peephole for looking out. Above the door a bell which may be rung from the street. Beside the door an opening containing a revolving box, or wheel, on which objects may be placed and passed in from the outside without the recipient's being seen, or a view of the interior disclosed. Not far from this wheel, a pine table stands against one of the piers of the cloister. Ancient paintings relieve the walls. Through the arches the cloister garden may be seen, with a well in the middle; also a number of fruit trees, some greenery and a few rose bushes. Beneath the arches, potted flowers—roses, carnations, sweet basil, herb Louisa and balsam apple—together with a number of wooden benches and rush-seated chairs, and three arm chairs.

As the curtain rises THE PRIORESS *is discovered seated in the largest of the arm chairs, and* THE MISTRESS OF NOVICES *and* THE VICARESS *in the smaller ones, the former on the right, the latter on the left, well to the front. The other* NUNS *are grouped about them, seated also. The novices,* SISTER MARCELLA, SISTER JOANNA OF THE CROSS, SISTER MARÍA JESÚS *and* SISTER SAGRARIO *stand somewhat to the right,* SISTER JOANNA OF THE CROSS *occupying the center of the stage. The* LAY SISTER *and* SISTER TORNERA *remain standing by the table at the rear.*

It is broad daylight. The scene is one of cheerfulness and animation.

SISTER SAGRARIO. Yes, do! Do! Do let her read them!

SISTER MARCELLA. Yes, do, Mother! Do say yes!

PRIORESS. Very well. You may read them then, since you have written them.

SISTER JOANNA OF THE CROSS. I am very much ashamed.

MISTRESS OF NOVICES. These are the temptations of self-love, my child.

VICARESS. And the first sin in the world was pride.

SISTER JOANNA OF THE CROSS. They are very bad. I know you will all laugh at me.

VICARESS. In that way we shall mortify your vanity.

MISTRESS OF NOVICES. Besides, since we are not at school here, all that our Mother will consider in them will be the intention.

PRIORESS. Begin. And do not be afraid.

SISTER JOANNA OF THE CROSS (*reciting*). To our Beloved Mother on the day of her Blessed Saint—her birthday:

> Most reverend Mother,
> On this happy day
> Your daughters unite
> For your welfare to pray.
> We are the sheep
> Who under your care
> Are seeking out Heaven—
> The path that leads there.
> On one side the roses,
> On the other the thorn,
> On the top of the mountain
> Jesus of Mary born.
> To Jesus we pray
> Long years for your life,
> And of the Virgin María
> Freedom from strife;
> And may the years vie
> In good with each other,
> In holiness and joy,
> Our dearly loved Mother!

(*The nuns applaud and all speak it once.*)

SOME. Good! Very good!

OTHERS. Oh, how pretty!

SISTER TORNERA. They are like the Jewels of the Virgin!

SISTER INEZ (*depreciatively*). She has copied them out of a book.

SISTER JOANNA OF THE CROSS (*carried away by her triumph*). Long live our Mother!

ALL (*enthusiastically*). Long live our Mother!

PRIORESS. Come, you must not flatter me, my children. The verses are very pretty. Many thanks, my daughter. I did not know that we had a poet in the house. You must copy them out for me on a piece of paper, so that I may have them to read.

SISTER JOANNA OF THE CROSS. They are copied already, reverend Mother. If your Reverence will be pleased to accept them . . . (*She offers her a roll of parchment, tied elaborately with blue ribbons. The verses are written on the parchment and embellished with a border of flowers, doves and hearts, all of which have been painted by hand.*)

PRIORESS (*taking and unrolling the parchment*). Bless me! What clear writing and what a beautiful border! Can you paint too?

SISTER JOANNA OF THE CROSS. No, reverend Mother. Sister María Jesús copied out the verses, and Sister Sagrario painted the border. Sister Marcella tied the bows.

SISTER MARCELLA. So it is a remembrance from all the novices.

PRIORESS. And all the while I knew nothing about it! The children have learned how to dissimulate very skilfully.

SISTER JOANNA OF THE CROSS. We had permission from Mother Anna St. Francis. She gave us the ribbon and the parchment.

PRIORESS. No wonder, then. So the Mother Mistress of Novices knows also how to keep secrets?

MISTRESS OF NOVICES. Once . . . Only for today . . .

SISTER JOANNA OF THE CROSS. To-day you must forgive everything.

PRIORESS (*smiling*). The fault is not a grave one.

VICARESS (*acridly*). Not unless it leads them to pride themselves upon their accomplishments. The blessed mother Santa Teresa de Jesús never permitted her daughters to do fancy work. Evil combats us where we least expect it, and ostentation is not becoming in a heart which has vowed itself to poverty and humility.

MISTRESS OF NOVICES. Glory be to God, Mother Vicaress, but why must your Reverence always be looking for five feet on the cat? (SISTER MARCELLA *laughs flagrantly*.)

VICARESS. That laugh was most inopportune.

SISTER MARCELLA (*pretending repentance, but still continuing to laugh in spite of herself*). I beg your pardon, your Reverence, I didn't mean it. This sister has such temptations to laugh, and she can't help it.

VICARESS. Biting your tongue would help it.

SISTER MARCELLA. Don't you believe it, your Reverence. No indeed it wouldn't!

PRIORESS (*thinking it best to intervene*). Come, you must not answer back, my daughter. Today I wish to punish nobody.

VICARESS (*muttering*). Nor today, nor never!

PRIORESS (*aroused*). What does your Reverence mean by that, Mother Vicaress?

VICARESS (*very meekly*). What we all know, reverend Mother—that

the patience of your Reverence is inexhaustible.

PRIORESS. Surely your Reverence is not sorry that it is so?

VICARESS (*belligerently*). Not upon my account, no. For by the grace of God I am able to fulfil my obligation and accommodate myself to the letter and spirit of our holy rule. But there are those who are otherwise, who, encouraged by leniency, may stumble and even fall . . .

PRIORESS. Has your Reverence anything definite in mind to say? If so, say it.

VICARESS. I have noticed for some time—and the Lord will absolve me of malice—that these "temptations to laugh" of which Sister Marcella speaks, have been abounding in this community; and these, taken with other manifestations of self-indulgence, not any less effervescent, are signs of a certain relaxation of virtue and deportment.

PRIORESS. I hardly think we need trouble ourselves upon that account. Providence has been pleased of late to bring into our fold some tender lambs, and perhaps they do frisk a little sometimes in the pastures of the Lord. But the poor children mean no harm. Am I right in your opinion, Mother Mistress of Novices?

MISTRESS OF NOVICES. You are always right in my opinion, reverend Mother. *Gaudeamus autem in Domino!*

VICARESS. Your Reverences of course know what you are doing. I have complied with my obligation. (*The bell rings at the entrance.* SISTER TORNERA, *who is an active little woman, goes up to the grille and looks through it, after first having made a reverence to the* PRIORESS.)

SISTER TORNERA. *Ave Maria Purissima!*

A VOICE (*outside, hoarse and rough*). Conceived without sin. Is it permitted to speak with the Mother Abbess?

SISTER TORNERA. Say what you have need of, brother.

VOICE. Then here's a present for her from my lady, the mayor's wife, who wishes her happiness, and sends her this present, and she's sorry she can't come herself to tell her; but she can't, and you know the reason . . . (*The* PRIORESS *sighs, lifting up her eyes to heaven, and the others do the same, all sighing in unison*) And even if she could on that account, she couldn't do it, because she's sick in bed, and you know the reason . . .

SISTER TORNERA. God's will be done! Can the poor woman get no rest? Tell her that we will send her a jar of ointment in the name of the blessed Saint Clara, and say that these poor sisters never forget her in their prayers. They pray every day that the Lord will send her comfort. (*She turns the wheel by the grille, and a basket appears, neatly covered with a white cloth*) Ah!—and the reverend Mother thanks her for this remembrance. And may God be with you, brother. (*Approaching the others with the basket, which she has taken from the wheel*) Poor lady! What tribulations our Lord sends into this world upon the cross of matrimony!

PRIORESS. And to her more than anybody. Such a submissive creature, and married to a perfect prodigal!

MISTRESS OF NOVICES. Now that we are on the subject, your Reverences, and have the pot by the handle, so to speak, do your Reverences know that the blasphemies of that man have completely turned his head? You heard the bells of the parish church ringing at noon yesterday? Well, that was because the mayor ordered them to be rung, because in the election at Madrid yesterday the republicans had the majority.

ALL. God bless us! God bless us!

VICARESS. Did the priest give his consent to that?

SISTER INEZ. The priest is another sheep of the same color—he belongs to the same flock, may the Lord forgive me if I lack charity! Didn't your Reverences hear the sacrilege he committed upon our poor chaplain, who is holier than God's bread? Well, he told him that he was more liberal than the mayor, and that the next thing he knew, when he least expected it, he was going to sing the introitus to the mass to the music of the Hymn of Riego!

PRIORESS. Stop! Enough! It is not right to repeat such blasphemies.

MISTRESS OF NOVICES. Yes, calumnies invented by unbelievers, the evil-minded . . .

SISTER INEZ. No such thing! Didn't Father Calixtus tell me himself while he was dressing for mass this morning? We'll have to put a new strip pretty soon down the middle of his chasuble.

PRIORESS. What? Again?

SISTER INEZ. Yes. It's all worn out; it looks terribly. Poor Father Calixtus is so eloquent! Pounding on his chest all the time, he simply tears the silk to pieces.

VICARESS. God's will be done, the man is a saint!

PRIORESS. And all this while we have been forgetting the present from the mayor's wife. Bring it nearer, Sister.

SISTER SAGRARIO. Mercy! What a big basket!

SISTER TORNERA. It's very light, though.

SISTER INEZ. Ha! It's easy to see what sister has a sweet tooth!

SISTER MARÍA JESÚS. As if she didn't like sweets! (*Aside.*)

SISTER MARCELLA. Now, Sister Inez, what did we see you doing this morning? You know we caught you licking the cake pan yourself.

SISTER INEZ. I? Licking the pan? Your Sister licking the pan? Oh, what a slander! *Jesús!*

PRIORESS. Come, you must not be displeased, Sister Inez; for it was said only in pleasantry. Ah, Sister Marcella! Sister Marcella! Do have a little more circumspection and beg your Sister's pardon.

SISTER MARCELLA (*kneeling before* SISTER INEZ). Pardon me, Sister, as may God pardon you, and give me your hand to kiss as a penance for having offended you.

PRIORESS. That is the way my children should behave, humbly and with contrition. Sister Inez, give Sister Marcella your hand to kiss, since she begs it of you so humbly.

SISTER MARCELLA (*spitefully, after kissing her hand*). Ay! But what a smell of vanilla you have on your fingers, Sister! Goody! We're going to have cookies for lunch. (*The others laugh.*)

SISTER INEZ (*irritated, almost in tears*). Vanilla? God-a-mercy! Vanilla! Look at me! Do my fingers smell of vanilla?

PRIORESS (*imposing silence*). Surely the devil must be in you, Sister Marcella, and may God forgive you for it! Go and kneel in the corner there with your face to the wall, and make the cross with your arms while you repeat a greater station. May the Lord forgive you for it!

SISTER MARCELLA. Willingly, reverend Mother.

SISTER INEZ (*rubbing her hands under her scapular*). Too bad! Too bad! Ay! Ay! Ay!

SISTER MARCELLA (*aside*). Old box of bones! (*She goes and kneels in the corner, right, but keeps smiling and turning her head while she lets herself sink back on her heels, as if not taking the penance too seriously.*)

PRIORESS. You may uncover the basket now, Sister. Let us see what is in it.

SISTER TORNERA. With your permission, reverend Mother. Why! It's a cage!

SISTER SAGRARIO. With a canary in it!

ALL. A canary! A canary! Why, so it is! Let me see! How lovely!

MISTRESS OF NOVICES. Isn't it pretty?

SISTER MARÍA JESÚS. The dear! Isn't it cunning, though?

SISTER JOANNA OF THE CROSS. It looks as if it were made of silk.

SISTER INEZ. I wonder if it can sing?

PRIORESS. Of course it can sing. The mayor's wife would never send us a canary that couldn't sing.

SISTER SAGRARIO. What a beautiful cage! Why, there's a scroll on the front!

MISTRESS OF NOVICES. That isn't a scroll. It has letters on it.

SISTER MARÍA JESÚS. Why, so it has! Look and see what they say.

MISTRESS OF NOVICES. "The Convent of Dominican Nuns!"

SISTER INEZ (laughing). I'd call that a pretty airy convent!

VICARESS. The good woman is holier than God's bread.

PRIORESS. She could not have sent me anything that would have pleased me better. I have always been anxious to have a canary.

SISTER INEZ. The Carmelite Sisters have two lovely canaries, and they say last year on Holy Thursday they hung them in the door of the tomb they have in the church for Easter, and it was like a miracle to hear them sing.

MISTRESS OF NOVICES. Then if ours sings, we can hang him in the church this year, and take the music box away.

PRIORESS. No, for the music box is a present from the chaplain, and he would rightly be offended. We will have the box and the canary there together, and when we wind up the box, it will encourage the bird to sing.

SISTER JOANNA OF THE CROSS. Oh, look at him now—he's taking his bath!

SISTER SAGRARIO. See how he jumps.

PRIORESS. What wonders God performs!

VICARESS. And yet there are misguided creatures who pretend that the world made itself!

SISTER INEZ. Sister Marcella stuck her tongue out at me.

SISTER MARCELLA. Oh, reverend Mother! I did nothing of the kind!

VICARESS. How nothing of the kind? Didn't I see it with my own eyes? And I was struck dumb!

SISTER MARCELLA. I said nothing of the kind . . . as . . . as that I had stuck my tongue out at Sister Inez. I stuck it out because there was a fly on the end of my nose, and since I had my arms out making the cross, I had to frighten him away with something.

SISTER JOANNA OF THE CROSS. Reverend Mother, since this is your Saint's day, won't you please excuse Sister Marcella this time?

SISTER MARÍA JESÚS. Yes, reverend Mother! I am sure she won't do anything that's wrong again.

PRIORESS. Sister Inez is the one who has been offended, and she is the only one who has the right to request her pardon.

NOVICES. She does! She does! You do, don't you, Sister Inez?

SISTER INEZ (with a wry face). Your Reverence will pardon her when your Reverence thinks best.

PRIORESS. Then come here, my erring daughter.—She knows that I pardon her because of the day, and so as not to spoil the pleasure of her sisters.

SISTER MARCELLA. May God reward you, reverend Mother!

PRIORESS. And set your veil straight, for this is the Lord's house, and it looks as if you were going on an excursion.—And now to your cells, every one. (To the NOVICES) What are you whispering about?

SISTER SAGRARIO. We were not whispering, Mother . . . We wanted to ask you something.

SISTER MARÍA JESÚS. And we are afraid to do it.

PRIORESS. Is it as bad as that?

SISTER MARÍA JESÚS. No, it isn't bad. But——

SISTER JOANNA OF THE CROSS. Your Reverence might think so.

PRIORESS. I might? I am not so evil-minded.

SISTER SAGRARIO. I . . . I . . . Our Mother Mistress will tell you.

MISTRESS OF NOVICES. They mean me.—Do you want me to?

NOVICES. Yes! Yes! Do!

MISTRESS OF NOVICES. With God's help I will try. Though I don't know for certain, I think what they want is for your Reverence to give them permission to talk a little, while they are waiting for the beginning of the fiesta. Am I right?

NOVICES. Yes! Yes! You are! Do, Mother, do!

SISTER MARCELLA. Long live our Mother!

PRIORESS. Silence! Silence! What? Haven't they had talking enough today after the dispensation I allowed them this morning?

VICARESS. The appetite always grows by what it feeds on. It is an unruly monster, and woe to her who gives it rein. If they came under my authority, I would not give them opportunity to make a single slip, for the holy Apostle Saint James has said and well said: "He who saith that he hath not offended by his tongue, lies."

SISTER MARCELLA. Ah, Sister Crucifixion! Don't spoil this holiday for our Mother.

VICARESS. Spoil it, eh? Who pays any attention to what I say in this house?

PRIORESS. Will you promise not to whisper nor offend the Lord with foolish talk?

NOVICES. We promise.

PRIORESS. Then you may talk as much as you like until the hour for prayers.

NOVICES. Thanks, thanks!
(*The bell rings at the entrance twice.*)

SISTER TORNERA. Two rings! The doctor!

PRIORESS. Cover your faces. (*The nuns lower their veils over their faces*) And pass out through the cloister.
(*The nuns begin to file out slowly and disappear through the cloister.*)

SISTER SAGRARIO (*approaching the* PRIORESS). This Sister has a felon, reverend Mother.

PRIORESS. Remain then—and you too, Sister María Jesús. (*To* SISTER TORNERA) Open, Sister. (THE PRIORESS, SISTER TORNERA, SISTER SAGRARIO *and* SISTER MARÍA JESÚS *remain.* SISTER TORNERA *unchains, unbolts and opens the door. The* DOCTOR *enters. He is about sixty years of age.*)

SISTER TORNERA. *Ave Maria Purissima!*

DOCTOR. Conceived without sin. (*He comes in*) Good morning, Sister.

SISTER TORNERA. Good morning, Doctor.

DOCTOR. Well, what progress are we making in holiness today?

SISTER TORNERA (*laughing*). Ho, ho, Doctor!

DOCTOR. Enough! Enough! No doubt, no doubt! (*Discovering the* PRIORESS) Congratulations, Mother.

PRIORESS. What? A heretic, and yet you remember the days of the saints?

DOCTOR. You are the saint, Mother; you are the saint.

PRIORESS. Ah! You must not scandalize me before my novices.

DOCTOR. Novices? Where, where? I said so when I came in. I smell fresh meat.

PRIORESS. Don José! Don José!

DOCTOR. But I say no more. Come! To work! To work! . . . What is the trouble with these white lambs?

SISTER SAGRARIO. Your handmaid has a felon, Doctor.

DOCTOR. Eh? On the hand? And such a lovely hand! Well, we shall have to lance it, Sister.

SISTER SAGRARIO (*alarmed*). What? Not now?

DOCTOR. No, tomorrow, Sister. Tomorrow, unless it yields first to a poultice and five *Pater nosters*. Remember, not one less!

SISTER SAGRARIO (*in perfect earnest*). No, Doctor.

DOCTOR. And this other one, eh?

PRIORESS. Ah, Doctor! She has been giving me a great deal of worry. She falls asleep in the choir; she sighs continually without being able to assign any reason; she cries over nothing whatever; she has no appetite for anything but salads . . .

DOCTOR. How old are you?

SISTER MARÍA JESÚS. Eighteen.

DOCTOR. How long have you been in this holy house?

SISTER MARÍA JESÚS. Two years and a half.

DOCTOR. And how many more do you remain before you come to profession?

SISTER MARÍA JESÚS. Two and a half more, if the Lord should be pleased to grant this unworthy novice grace to become his bride.

DOCTOR. Let me see the face.

PRIORESS. Lift your veil.
(SISTER MARÍA JESÚS *lifts her veil*.)

DOCTOR. Hm! The Lord has not bad taste. A little pale, but well rounded, well rounded.

SISTER TORNERA. Don José! But who ever heard of such a doctor?

DOCTOR. So, we have melancholy then, a constant disposition to sigh, combined with loss of appetite—well, there is nothing else for it, Sister: a cold bath every morning and afterwards a few minutes' exercise in the garden.

SISTER TORNERA (*somewhat scandalized*). Exercise? Don José!

DOCTOR. Unless we write at once home to her mother to hurry and fetch her and find us a good husband for her.

SISTER MARÍA JESÚS. Oh, Don José! But this Sister has taken her vows to the Church!

DOCTOR. Well, in that case cold water. There is nothing else for it. For melancholy at eighteen, matrimony or cold water.

SISTER SAGRARIO (*summoning her courage*). You always talk so much about it, Doctor, why don't you get married yourself?

DOCTOR. Because I am sixty, daughter; and it is fifteen years since I have felt melancholy. Besides, whom do you expect me to marry when all the pretty girls go into convents?

PRIORESS. Doctor, doctor! This conversation will become displeasing to me.

DOCTOR. Is this all the walking infirmary?

SISTER TORNERA. Yes, Doctor.

DOCTOR. And the invalid? How is she?

SISTER TORNERA. She is the same today, Doctor. Poor Sister Maria of Consolation hasn't closed her eyes all night! Don't you remember? Yesterday she said she felt as if she had a viper gnawing at her vitals? Well, today she has a frog in her throat.

DOCTOR. Goodness gracious! Come, let me see, let me see. What a continual war the devil does wage against these poor sisters!—Long life, Mother, and happy days!

PRIORESS. Long life to you, Doctor. (*To* SISTER TORNERA) Go with him, Sister, and meanwhile these children will take care of the gate. (SISTER TORNERA *takes a bell from the table and, her veil covering her face, precedes the* DOCTOR *through the cloister, ringing solemnly in warning. They disappear*) I must repair to the choir; I fear that today I have fallen behind in devotion and prayer.

SISTER MARÍA JESÚS. Will your Reverence give us permission to call the others?

PRIORESS. Yes, call them; but be careful that you commit no frivolity. (*The* PRIORESS *goes out.*)

SISTER MARÍA JESÚS (*approaching one of the arches of the cloister*). Sister Marcella! Sister Joanna of the Cross! Pst! Come out! We are watching the grille and we have permission to talk. (SISTER MARCELLA *and* SISTER JOANNA OF THE CROSS *re-enter.*)

SISTER SAGRARIO. What shall we talk about?

SISTER JOANNA OF THE CROSS. Let Sister Marcella tell us a story.

SISTER MARCELLA. Yes, so that you'll all be shocked.

SISTER MARÍA JESÚS. *Ay!* We are not such hypocrites as that, Sister.

SISTER MARCELLA. Or so that Sister Sagrario can run and tell on us to the Mother Mistress.

SISTER SAGRARIO. Oh, thank you, Sister!

SISTER MARCELLA. It wouldn't be the first time either.

SISTER SAGRARIO. You needn't mind me, Sisters. I am going to sit here in the corner and work, and you can talk about whatever you please. I shan't hear you. (*She takes a pair of pincers, some beads and a piece of wire out of her pocket, and sitting down in a corner, begins to string a rosary.*)

SISTER JOANNA OF THE CROSS. Oh, come on, Sister! Don't be foolish. (*They all surround her, and finally she allows herself to be persuaded, after many expressions of protest, like a small child who says "I won't play."*)

SISTER SAGRARIO. Why! If they haven't forgotten the canary!

SISTER MARCELLA. Poor thing! How do you like to be left in this nest of silly women, little fellow? Let's open the cage.

SISTER MARÍA JESÚS. What for?

SISTER MARCELLA. So that he can fly away, silly, if he wants to.

SISTER SAGRARIO. No, no!

SISTER MARÍA JESÚS. Our Mother wouldn't like that.

SISTER MARCELLA. He would like it, though. Come on! (*She opens the door of the cage*) Fly out, sweetheart! Fly away, the world is yours. You are free!

SISTER JOANNA OF THE CROSS. He doesn't fly out.

SISTER MARÍA JESÚS. He doesn't budge.

SISTER MARCELLA. Stupid, don't you see what a bright, sunny day it is?

SISTER JOANNA OF THE CROSS. They say canaries are born in cages and, see, now he doesn't care to fly away.

SISTER MARÍA JESÚS. He'd rather stay shut up all his life, like us nuns.

SISTER MARCELLA. Then you're a great fool, birdie. (*She shuts the door of the cage*) God made the air for wings and He made wings to fly with. While he might be soaring away above the clouds, he is satisfied to stay here all day shut up in his cage, hopping between two sticks and a leaf of lettuce! What sense is there in a bird? *Ay*, Mother! And what wouldn't I give to be a bird!

SISTER JOANNA OF THE CROSS. Yes! What wouldn't you give to be a bird?

SISTER MARÍA JESÚS. They say that the swallows fly away every year over the ocean, and nobody knows where they go.

SISTER SAGRARIO. I often dream that I am flying in the night time—that is not flying, but floating—just floating in the air without wings.

SISTER MARÍA JESÚS. I often dream that I am running fast—oh so fast! —and that I am skipping down stairs, without ever touching my feet to the ground, or to the stairs.

SISTER SAGRARIO. Isn't it nice, though? And how disappointed you are when you wake up and find out after all that it isn't so, that it was only a dream!

SISTER MARCELLA. I have dreamed that dream so many times, that now when I wake up, I hardly know whether it is the truth or a dream.

SISTER JOANNA OF THE CROSS. What do you suppose it is that makes you dream the same dream so many times?

SISTER MARCELLA. I don't know, unless it is because it is the things you want to do, and you can't, and so you do them in dreams.

SISTER MARÍA JESÚS. What nice things you want to do!

SISTER SAGRARIO. But then what good would it be if you could do them? For instance, if we had wings like birds, where would we fly?

SISTER MARCELLA. I? I would fly to the end of the world!

SISTER MARÍA JESÚS. I? To the Holy Land, to Mount Calvary!

SISTER JOANNA OF THE CROSS. I would fly to Bethlehem and to the garden of Nazareth, where the Virgin lived with the Child.

SISTER SAGRARIO. How do you know that there is a garden at Nazareth?

SISTER JOANNA OF THE CROSS. Of course there's a garden there, with a brook running by it. The song says so:

"*The Virgin washed his garments*
And hung them on the rose.
The little angels sing
And the water onward flows" . . .
(*Simply*) There was a garden, too, by our house in the village, with a big rosebush on the border of a brook that ran by it; and I used to kneel beside the brook, and sing that song while I washed my baby brother's clothes, for there were seven of us children, and I was the oldest. (*Feelingly*) And that's what I miss most! (*Drying her eyes with her hands*) Ay, Mother! And I always cry when I think of that baby boy! But it isn't right, I know . . . He loved me more than he did mother, and the day that they took me away to the Convent, and I left home, he cried—he cried so that he nearly broke his little baby heart!

SISTER MARCELLA. I have a brother and a sister, but they are both older than I am. My sister married two years ago, and now she has a baby. (*With an air of importance*) She brought him here once to show me.

SISTER JOANNA OF THE CROSS (*interrupting her, greatly interested*). I remember. He stuck his little hand in through the grille and your sister kissed it. Did you ever think how soft babies' hands are? Whenever I take communion I try to

think I am receiving our Lord as a little child, and I take and press him like this to my heart, and then it seems to me that he is so little and so helpless that he can't refuse me anything. And then I think that he is crying, and I pray to the Virgin to come and help me quiet him. And if I wasn't ashamed, because I know you would all laugh at me, I'd croon to him then, and rock him to sleep, and sing him baby songs.
(*The bell rings by the grille.*)

SISTER SAGRARIO. The bell! I wonder who it is?

SISTER JOANNA OF THE CROSS. Better ask. That's why they left us here.

SISTER MARÍA JESÚS. Who'll do it? I won't. I'm afraid.

SISTER SAGRARIO. So am I.

SISTER MARCELLA. You're not usually so bashful, I must say. I'll ask, though I was the last to enter the house. (*Going up to the grille, she says in a timid voice:*) Ave Maria purissima! (*A moment's silence*) No one answers.

SISTER JOANNA OF THE CROSS. Try again. Say it louder.

SISTER MARCELLA (*raising her voice*). Ave Maria purissima!

SISTER SAGRARIO. Nothing this time, either.

SISTER MARÍA JESÚS (*summoning her courage, in a high-pitched voice*). Ave Maria purissima!
(*Another silence. The NOVICES look at each other in surprise.*)

SISTER MARCELLA. It is very strange.

SISTER MARÍA JESÚS. It must be spirits.

SISTER SAGRARIO. Oh, I'm afraid!

SISTER JOANNA OF THE CROSS. Nonsense! It's some little boy who has rung the bell on his way home from school, so as to be funny.

SISTER MARÍA JESÚS. Peep through the hole and see if anybody is there.

SISTER MARCELLA (*stooping down to look*). No, nobody. But it looks as if there was something on the wheel. Yes . . .

SISTER JOANNA OF THE CROSS. Let me see! Yes . . . Can't you turn it? (*She turns the wheel, and a second basket appears, carefully covered with a white cloth like the first*) A basket!

SISTER SAGRARIO. Another present for our Mother.

SISTER MARÍA JESÚS. Of course it is! And here's a paper tied fast to it.

SISTER JOANNA OF THE CROSS (*reading, but without unfolding the paper*). "For the Mother Prioress."

SISTER SAGRARIO. Didn't I tell you?

SISTER MARCELLA. Somebody wants to give her a surprise.

SISTER JOANNA OF THE CROSS. I wonder if it's Don Calixtus, the chaplain?

SISTER MARCELLA. Of course it is, child!

SISTER MARÍA JESÚS. Or maybe it's the Doctor.

SISTER JOANNA OF THE CROSS. No. He was just here and he didn't say anything about it.

SISTER SAGRARIO. All the same it might be from him. Maybe he wants to keep it a secret.

SISTER MARÍA JESÚS. Let's take it off the wheel.

SISTER MARCELLA (*lifting and carrying it to the table*). We'd better put it here by the canary. My! But it's heavy!

SISTER SAGRARIO. I wonder what it is?

SISTER MARCELLA. Let's lift the corner and see.

SISTER MARÍA JESÚS. No, for curiosity is a sin.

SISTER MARCELLA. What of it? Come on! Let's do it. Who will ever know? (*She lifts the corner of the cloth a little and starts back quickly with a sharp cry*) Ay! !

SISTER JOANNA OF THE CROSS (*hurrying to look*). Jesús!

SISTER MARÍA JESÚS. Ave Maria! (*Looking too.*)

SISTER SAGRARIO (*following*). God bless us!
(*The Convent is aroused at the cry of* SISTER MARCELLA. *Presently* THE PRIORESS, THE VICARESS, THE MISTRESS OF NOVICES *and the other* NUNS *enter from different directions.*)

PRIORESS. What is the matter? Who called out?

VICARESS. Who gave that shout?

MISTRESS OF NOVICES. Is anything wrong?
(*The four* NOVICES, *trembling, stand with their backs to the basket, their bodies hiding it completely.*)

VICARESS. It is easy to see it was Sister Marcella.

PRIORESS. What has happened? Speak! Why are you all standing in a row like statues?

MISTRESS OF NOVICES. Has anything happened to you?

SISTER JOANNA OF THE CROSS. No, reverend Mother, not to us; but——

SISTER MARÍA JESÚS. No, reverend Mother; it's . . .

SISTER MARCELLA. Someone rang the bell by the wheel . . . and we looked . . . and there was nobody there . . . and they left a basket . . . this basket . . . and . . . and your sister had the curiosity to undo it . . .

VICARESS. Naturally, you couldn't do otherwise.

SISTER MARCELLA. And it's . . .

PRIORESS. Well? What is it?

SISTER MARCELLA. It's . . . I . . . I think it would be better for your Reverence to look yourself.

PRIORESS. By all means! Let me see. (*She goes up to the basket and un-*

covers it) *Ave Maria!* (*In a hoarse whisper*) A baby!

ALL (*variously affected*). A baby? (*The* VICARESS, *horrified, crosses herself.*)

PRIORESS (*falling back*). Your Reverences may see for yourselves. (*The* NUNS *hurry up to the basket and surround it.*)

VICARESS. *Ave Maria!* How can such an insignificant object be so pink?

MISTRESS OF NOVICES. It's asleep.

SISTER JOANNA OF THE CROSS. See it open its little hands!

SISTER MARÍA JESÚS. Why! It has hair under the edge of its cap!

SISTER SAGRARIO. It is like an angel!

VICARESS. A pretty angel for the Lord to send us.

SISTER JOANNA OF THE CROSS (*as if she had been personally offended*). Ay, Mother Vicaress! You mustn't say that.

PRIORESS (*tenderly*). Where do you come from, little one?

VICARESS. From some nice place, you may be sure.

PRIORESS. Who can tell, Mother? There is so much poverty in the world, so much distress.

VICARESS. There is so much vice, reverend Mother.

MISTRESS OF NOVICES. You say that there was nobody at the grille?

SISTER MARCELLA. Nobody; no, Mother. The bell rang; we answered . . . but there was nobody there.

SISTER SAGRARIO (*picking up the paper which has fallen on the floor*). Here is a paper which came with it.

PRIORESS (*taking the paper*). "For the Mother Prioress."

VICARESS. An appropriate present for your Reverence.

PRIORESS. Yes, it is a letter. (*She unfolds the paper and begins to read*) "Reverend Mother: Forgive the liberty which a poor woman takes, trusting in your Grace's charity, of leaving at the grille this new-born babe. I, my lady, am one of those they call women of the street, and I assure you I am sorry for it; but this is the world, and you can't turn your back on it, and it costs as much to go down as it does to go up, and that is what I am writing to tell you, my lady. The truth is this little girl hasn't any father, that is to say it is the same as if she didn't have any, and I—who am her mother—I leave her here, although it costs me something to leave her; for although one is what one is, one isn't all bad, and I love her as much as any mother loves her baby, though she is the best lady in the land. But all the same, though she came into this world without being wanted by anyone, she doesn't deserve to be the daughter of the woman she is, above all, my lady, of her father, and I don't want her to have to blush for having been born the way she was, nor for having the mother she has, and to tell it to me to my face, and

I pray you by everything you hold dear, my lady, that you will protect her and keep her with you in this holy house, and you won't send her to some orphanage or asylum, for I was brought up there myself, and I know what happens in them, although the sisters are kind—yes, they are—and have pity. And some day, when she grows up and she asks for her mother, you must tell her that the devil has carried her away, and I ask your pardon, for I must never show myself to her, nor see her again, nor give you any care nor trouble, so you can do this good work in peace, if you will do it, for I implore you again, my lady, that you will do it for the memory of your own dear mother, and God will reward you, and she will live in peace, and grow up as God wills, for what the eyes have not seen the heart cannot understand, my lady."

VICARESS. Bless us! *Ave Maria!*

MISTRESS OF NOVICES. Poor woman!

SISTER JOANNA OF THE CROSS. Baby dear! Darling baby!

VICARESS. What pretty mothers the Lord selects for his children!

PRIORESS. God moves in his own ways, Sister. God moves in his own ways.

SISTER INEZ. Is that all the letter says?

PRIORESS. What more could it say? (THE DOCTOR *and* SISTER TORNERA *have re-entered during the reading.*)

DOCTOR. Exactly. What more could it say?

PRIORESS. What do you think, Don José?

DOCTOR. I think that somebody has made you a very handsome present.

PRIORESS. But what are we going to do with it? Because I . . . this poor woman . . . she has put this poor creature into our hands, and I would protect her willingly, as she asks, and keep her here with us . . .

NOVICES. Yes, yes, Mother! Do! Do!

MISTRESS OF NOVICES. Silence!

PRIORESS. But I don't know if we can . . . that is, if it is right, if it is according to law . . . for, when we enter this holy rule, we renounce all our rights . . . and to adopt a child legally . . . I don't know whether it can be done. How does it seem to you?

DOCTOR. I agree with you. Legally, you have no right to maternity.

VICARESS. And even if we had, would it be proper for our children to be the offspring of ignominy and sin?

PRIORESS. I would not raise that question, reverend Mother, for the child is not responsible for the sin in which she was born, and her mother, in renouncing her motherhood, has bitterly paid the penalty.

VICARESS. Yes, it didn't cost her much to renounce it.

PRIORESS. Do we know, Mother? Do we know?

VICARESS. We can guess. It is easy enough to go scattering children about the world if all you have to do is leave them to be picked up afterwards by the first person who happens along.

DOCTOR. How easy it is might be a matter for discussion. There are aspects of it which are not so easy.

SISTER SAGRARIO. Oh! She's opened her mouth!

SISTER JOANNA OF THE CROSS. The little angel is hungry.

SISTER MARÍA JESÚS. She's sucking her thumb!

SISTER JOANNA OF THE CROSS. Make her take her thumb out of her mouth. She'll swallow too much and then she'll have a pain.

SISTER SAGRARIO. Don't suck your fingers, baby.

SISTER JOANNA OF THE CROSS. Isn't she good, though? You stop her playing, and she doesn't cry.

PRIORESS. There is another thing we must consider. What are we to do for a nurse?

SISTER JOANNA OF THE CROSS. The gardener's wife has a little boy she is nursing now.

PRIORESS. In that case I hardly think she would care to be responsible for two.

SISTER JOANNA OF THE CROSS. But it won't be any trouble—she's so tiny! Besides, we can help her out with cow's milk and a little pap. The milk will keep on the ice and we can clear it with a dash of tea.

DOCTOR. It is easy to see Sister Joanna of the Cross has had experience with children.

SISTER JOANNA OF THE CROSS. Your handmaid has six little brothers and sisters. Ah, reverend Mother! Give her to me to take care of and then you will see how strong she'll grow up.

VICARESS. Nothing else was needed to complete the demoralization of the Novices. You can see for yourselves how naturally they take to this dissipation.

PRIORESS. I want you to tell me frankly what you think—all of you. (*All speak at once.*)

MISTRESS OF NOVICES. Your Sister thinks, reverend Mother . . .

SISTER TORNERA. Your handmaid . . .

SISTER INEZ. It seems to me . . .

PRIORESS (*smiling*). But one at a time.

SISTER TORNERA. It is an angel which the Lord has sent us, and your Sister thinks that we ought to receive her like an angel, with open arms.

MISTRESS OF NOVICES. Of course we ought. Suppose, your Reverences, it hadn't been a little girl, but . . . I don't know—some poor animal, a dog, a cat, or a dove, like the one which flew in here two years ago and fell wounded in the garden trying to get away from those butchers at the pigeon-traps. Wouldn't we have taken it in? Wouldn't we have cared for it? And wouldn't it have lived happy forever afterward in its cage? And how can we do less for a creature with a soul than for a bird?

SISTER TORNERA. We must have charity.

VICARESS. I am glad the Mother Mistress of Novices has brought up the incident of that bird, for it will absolve me from bringing it up, as it might seem, with some malice. It was against my advice that that creature was received into this house, and afterward we had good reason to regret it, with this one saying "Yes, I caught him!" and that one, "No, I took care of him!" and another "He opens his beak whenever I pass by!" and another, "See him flap his wings! He does it at me!"—vanities, sophistries, deceits all of them, snares of the devil continually! And if all this fuss was about a bird, what will happen to us with a child in the house? This one will have to dress it, that one will have to wash it, another will be boasting, "It is looking at me!" another that it's at her that it googles most . . . There is Sister Joanna of the Cross making faces at it already!

SISTER JOANNA OF THE CROSS. What did your Reverence say?

VICARESS. Dissipation and more dissipation! Your Reverences should remember that when we passed behind these bars, we renounced forever all personal, all selfish affection.

MISTRESS OF NOVICES. Is it selfish to give a poor foundling a little love?

VICARESS. It is for us. Our God is a jealous God. The Scriptures tell us so.

MISTRESS OF NOVICES. Bless us! Mercy me!

VICARESS. And this quite apart from other infractions of our order which such indulgence must involve. For example, your Reverences—and I among the first—take no account of the fact that at this very moment we are transgressing our rule. We are conversing with our faces unveiled in the presence of a man.

PRIORESS. That is true.

DOCTOR. Ladies, as far as I am concerned—take no account of me.

PRIORESS. No, Doctor, you are of no account. I beg your pardon, Don José; I hardly know what I am saying.—Your Reverence is right. Cover yourselves—that is, it makes no difference . . . The harm has been done . . . only once. . . . But comply with your consciences . . . (*The* VICARESS *covers her face. The others, hesitating, wait for the* PRIORESS, *who makes a movement to do so, but then desists. The* VICARESS, *when she is covered, cannot see that she has become the victim of the rest*) But where were we? I confess that my heart prompts me to keep the child.

VICARESS. The Doctor already has told us that we have no right to maternity.

MISTRESS OF NOVICES. But the child is God's child, and she is returning to her father's mansion.

VICARESS. God has other mansions for his abandoned children.

SISTER JOANNA OF THE CROSS. Don't send her to the asylum!

SISTER SAGRARIO. No!

PRIORESS. Her mother entreats us.

VICARESS. Her mother is not her mother. She has abandoned her.

PRIORESS. She has not abandoned her. She has entrusted her to others who seemed worthier to undertake her keeping.

VICARESS. Unholy egotism!

MISTRESS OF NOVICES. Christian heroism!

VICARESS. So? We are coining phrases, are we? Is this a convent, or an illustrated weekly?

MISTRESS OF NOVICES. Life is hard to some people, and thorny.

VICARESS. Yes, and into the details of it, it is not becoming for us to go, since by the grace of God we have been relieved from the temptations and the frailties of the world.

MISTRESS OF NOVICES. All the more, then, we ought to have compassion on those who have fallen and are down.

VICARESS. Compassion? Mush and sentiment!

MISTRESS OF NOVICES. The veil of charity!

PRIORESS. Silence! And let us not begin by rending it, irritating ourselves and aggravating each other. —Don José, I suppose this birth will have to be reported?

DOCTOR. It will, madame. To the Register.

SISTER JOANNA OF THE CROSS. But then they will take her away?

DOCTOR. If nobody wants her. But if you have made up your minds you would like to keep her, I think I can propose a solution.

PRIORESS. A solution that is legal?

DOCTOR. Perfectly. Thanks be to God I am a single man. But, although I am not a saint, yet I cannot take to myself the credit of having augmented the population of this country by so much as a single soul. I have not a penny, that is true, but like everybody else, I have a couple of family names. They are at the service of this little stranger, if they will be of use to her. She will have no father and no mother—I cannot help that—but she will have an honorable name.

PRIORESS. Do you mean to say?——

DOCTOR. That I am willing to adopt her; exactly—and to entrust her to your care, because my own house . . . The fact is the hands of Doña Cecilia are a little rough for handling these tiny Dresden dolls, and perhaps I might prove a bit testy myself. The neighbors all say that the air grows blue if my coat rubs against me as I walk down the street.
(All laugh.)

DOCTOR. Besides I am sure Sister Crucifixion is better equipped for the robing of saints.

VICARESS. Doctor, God help us both!

DOCTOR. Is it agreed?

PRIORESS. God reward you for it! Yes, in spite of everything. We shall notify the Superior immediately. It is not necessary that the child should live in the cloister. She can remain with the gardener's wife until she has grown older, and enter here later when she has the discretion to do so. She has been entrusted to our hands, and it is our duty to take care of her—a duty of conscience.

DOCTOR. If I cannot be of further service, I will go. And I will speak to the Register.

PRIORESS. As you go, be so kind as to ask the gardener's wife to come in. We must see if she will take charge of the child and nurse her. And tell her also to bring with her some of her little boy's clothes.

SISTER JOANNA OF THE CROSS. Yes, for we shall have to make a change immediately.

SISTER SAGRARIO. We shall?

VICARESS. Not a change, but a beginning.

DOCTOR. Good afternoon, ladies.

ALL. Good afternoon, Don José. (The DOCTOR goes out. A pause.)

PRIORESS. Sisters, may God pardon us if we have acted in this with aught but the greatest purity of motive. I hope and pray that His grace will absolve us of offense, nor find us guilty of having loved too much one of His poor children. The child shall be brought up in the shadow of this house, for we may say that her guardian angel has delivered her at the door. From this hour forth we are all charged with the salvation of her soul. The Lord has entrusted to us an angel and we must return to Him a saint. Watch and pray.

ALL. Watch and pray. We will, reverend Mother.

PRIORESS. And now bring her to me, Sister Joanna of the Cross, for as yet it can scarcely be said that I have seen her. (*Looking at the child*) Lamb of God! Sleeping as quietly in her basket as if it were a cradle of pure gold! What is it that children see when they are asleep that brings to their faces an expression of such peace?

SISTER JOANNA OF THE CROSS. They see God and the Virgin Mary.

SISTER MARÍA JESÚS. Maybe the angel who watches over them whispers in their ears and tells them about heaven.

PRIORESS. Who can say? But it is a comfort to the soul to see a child asleep.

SISTER MARÍA JESÚS. It makes you want to be a saint, reverend Mother.

SISTER SAGRARIO. Will your Reverence grant me permission to give her a kiss?

SISTER MARÍA JESÚS. Oh, no! For it hasn't been baptized yet, and it is a sin to kiss a heathen!

PRIORESS. She is right. We must send for the Chaplain and have her baptized immediately.

MISTRESS OF NOVICES. What shall we call her?

SISTER INEZ. Teresa, after our beloved Mother.

SISTER TORNERA. María of the Miracles.

SISTER SAGRARIO. Bienvenida.
(*A large bell rings outside.*)

PRIORESS. The summons to the choir! We can decide later. Let us go. (*The* NUNS *file out slowly, looking at the child as they go*) Remain with her, Sister Joanna of the Cross—you understand children; and wait for the coming of the gardener's wife. Follow the devotions from where you are, and do not let your attention falter.
(*All the* NUNS *go out, except* SISTER JOANNA OF THE CROSS, *who bends over the basket; then sinks on her knees beside it. The choir is heard within, led by a single* NUN *in solo, the responses being made in chorus, in which* SISTER JOANNA OF THE CROSS *joins. While the* NUN *is leading,* SISTER JOANNA OF THE CROSS *talks and plays with the child; then she makes her responses with the others.*)

VOICE WITHIN. *In nomine Patri et Filio et Spiritui Sancto.*
(SISTER JOANNA OF THE CROSS *crosses herself and says with the other* NUNS:)

VOICES WITHIN AND SISTER JOANNA OF THE CROSS. *Amen!*

SISTER JOANNA OF THE CROSS (*to the child*). Pretty one! Pretty one!

VOICE WITHIN. *Deus in adjutorium meum intende.*

VOICES WITHIN AND SISTER JOANNA OF THE CROSS. *Domine ad adjuvandum me festina.*

SISTER JOANNA OF THE CROSS (*to the child*). Do you love me, sweetheart? Do you love me?

VOICE WITHIN. *Gloria Patri et Filio et Spiritui Sancto.*

VOICES WITHIN IN CHORUS. *Sicut erat in principio et nunc et semper et insecula seculorum. Amen! Allelulia!*

(*But this time* SISTER JOANNA OF THE CROSS *makes no response. Instead she bends over the basket, embracing the child passionately, oblivious of all else, and says:*)

SISTER JOANNA OF THE CROSS. Little one! Little one! Whom do you love?

CURTAIN

INTERLUDE

SPOKEN BY THE POET

You came tonight to listen to a play;
Instead into a convent you made way.
Singular hardihood! Almost profanation!
What will a poet not do to create sensation?
Pardon, good nuns, him who disturbs the rest
And troubles the serene quietude of your nest,
Kindling amid the shades of this chaste bower
The flame of love you have renounced and flower.
Nay! Do not frown because I have said love,
For you must know, chaste brides of God above,
That which you have deemed charity and pity,
The act of mercy, clemency for the pretty,
Unfriended foundling fate has brought along,
Yearning of adoption and the cradle song,

No other is than love's fire, divine and human
Passion ever brooding in the heart of woman.

Ah, love of woman, by whose power we live,
Offend so often—but to see forgive!
Whence do you draw your grace but from above?
Whence simply? Simply from maternal love!
Yes, we are children, woman, in your arms;
Your heart is bread, you soothe our wild alarms,
Like children give us the honey of your breast,
In a cradle always your lover sinks to rest
Although he prostitutes our grovelling flesh.
Mother if lover, mother if sister too,
Mother by pure essence, day long and night through,
Mother if you laugh, or if with us you cry,
In the core of being, in fibre and in mesh,
Every woman carries, so God has willed on high,

A baby in her bosom, sleeping eternally!

So being women, you are lovers,
nuns;
Despite the ceintured diamond
which runs
Across your virgin shields, showing in your lives
How to be mothers without being
wives.
And in this child of all, you have
poured all
The honey of your souls, and
blended all
The fire of the sun, all fragrance
and all light,
The first sweet morning kiss, the
last good night,
Till all her being tenderness ex-
hales,
Her heart the home of love and
nightingales.
A hundred times a woman but no
saint.
The nuns pray in the choir; outside
her plaint
A song; her prayer, gay rippling
laughter.
Mass and the May morning slip by,
she running after
Or dreaming in the garden. The
roses smell
So sweetly! No child this for the
hermits' cell.
She loves Heaven, but in good
company;
And before the altar of the Virgin
see
Her with a boy, ruddier than the
candle's flame,
Who calls her "Sister," the nuns
"Aunt" for name.
A smiling, bashful boy, who soon
will grow
To be a strong man, learn to give
a blow
And take one, conquer worlds and
redress wrong,

Justice in his heart, and on his lips
a song!
Sometimes she takes the cat up,
calls it "Dear!"
The nuns cross themselves, reli-
giously severe.
"The child is mad," they say. Ah!
No such thing!
With her into the convent entered
Spring.

This then the simple story. The poet
would
Have told it day by day, if well he
could,
In shining glory. But the task were
vain.
The glory of our daily lives is plain.
For life builds up itself in such a
way,
The water runs so clear, so bright
the day,
That time is lulled to sleep within
these walls.
An age or moment? Which passes?
Who recalls?
The wheel turns round, but no
one notes the turn.
What matter if the sisters' locks
that burn
With gold, in time to silvery gray
have paled?
Their hoods conceal it. And the
pinks have failed
In the cheeks, and the lilies on the
brow.
There are no mirrors. The sisters
then as now
May walk in the garden, believe it
still is May.

Among these hours which softly
slip away,
This timeless time, we shyly pause
at that
In which there is most warmth, the
concordat
Of youth and incense, breaking of
the spring.

*The years have passed, the child is
   ripening.
The curtain rises on a soul in flower,
And a love chapter claims us for an
   hour.*

*It is quiet afternoon, quiet breed-
   ing;
The nuns are sewing and their sister
   reading:*

ACT TWO

Parlor of a Convent.

*At the rear, a grille with a double row of bars. A curtain of dark woolen
cloth hangs over the grille and intercepts the view of the outer parlor, to
which visitors are admitted. This is without decoration, and may be
brightly illuminated at the proper moment from the garden. A number of
oil paintings of saints hang upon the walls—all of them very old and
showing black stains. With them a carved crucifix or large black wooden
cross. A small window furnished with heavy curtains, which, when drawn,
shut off the light completely, is cut in the wall of the inner parlor on either
side of the grille, high up towards the ceiling. A pine table, a carved arm
chair, two other arm chairs, smaller chairs and benches, together with all
the materials necessary for sewing.*

THE PRIORESS, THE MISTRESS OF NOVICES, SISTERS INEZ *and* TORNERA,
SISTER SAGRARIO, SISTER JOANNA OF THE CROSS, SISTER MARCELLA, SISTER
MARÍA JESÚS *and the other* NUNS *are discovered upon the rise of the
curtain. Only* THE VICARESS *is absent. All are seated, sewing, with the exception of* SISTER MARÍA JESÚS, *who stands in the center, to the left of*
THE PRIORESS' *chair, reading. A bride's trousseau is spread out upon the
table and chairs. It is embroidered elaborately, trimmed with lace and tied
with blue silk ribbons. A new trunk stands against the wall on the right,
the trays being distributed about the benches and upon the floor.*

Eighteen years have passed. It must be remembered that the NUNS
*have changed in appearance, and those who were novices have now pro-
fessed and have exchanged the white for the black veil.*

SISTER MARÍA JESÚS (*reading and
intoning*). "The Treasury of Patience, the Meditations of an Afflicted Soul in the presence of its
God."

SISTER MARCELLA (*sighing*). Ay!

SISTER MARÍA JESÚS (*reading*).
"First Meditation: The Sorrows of
an Unhappy Spirit, Submerged in
a Sea of Woe."

(*Outside,* TERESA'S *voice is heard,
singing gaily.*)

TERESA.
   "*Come singing and bringing
      Flowers from the field,
      Flowers from the field,
    Sweet gardens, to Mary.
      Flowers you must yield
    For Love's sanctuary!*"
(*The reader stops, and, smiling,
glances in the direction of the win-*

dow through which the voice is heard. The other NUNS *smile also, complacently.*)

PRIORESS (*with affected severity*). The child interrupts us continually.

SISTER INEZ. And a day like today!

SISTER JOANNA OF THE CROSS (*sympathetically*). She sings like a lark.

MISTRESS OF NOVICES (*indulgently*). She is so young!

SISTER MARCELLA. *Ay,* Mother!

PRIORESS. Continue reading, Sister María Jesús.

SISTER MARÍA JESÚS (*reading*). "The Sorrows of an Unhappy Spirit, Submerged in a Sea of Woe. My God, O my God, save me, for every moment I die! Overwhelmed, I sink in the midst of this terrible storm. Every moment I am buffeted and borne down. I am sucked into the uttermost depths, and there is no health in me!"

TERESA (*singing*).
"From the glory of your brightness,
    Radiantly sweet,
O, let me stoop and bend me
    To kiss your feet!
Let me stoop and bend me
    To kiss your feet!"
(*Again the reader stops. The* NUNS *smile again.*)

PRIORESS. Sister Sagrario, will you step out into the garden and ask the child not to sing? We are reading. (SISTER SAGRARIO *goes out, right, after making the customary reverence*) Continue, Sister, continue.

SISTER MARÍA JESÚS (*reading*). "There is no health in me. I cannot

support myself; I cannot resist the shock of the horrible onrushing waves."

TERESA (*singing*).
"You too were happy, Mary,
    Happy in his love,
Flowers of love and springtime
    That bloom above!"
(*The song is broken off suddenly, as if the* NUN *had arrived and commanded* TERESA *to stop. A moment later, there is a sound of light laughter.*)

PRIORESS. It cannot be helped. (*Smiling*) The child was born happy and she will die so. (*To the reader*) Continue.

SISTER MARCELLA. *Ay,* Lady of Sorrows!

PRIORESS. But Sister Marcella, my daughter, why do you sigh like this? Are you unwell?

SISTER MARCELLA. No, reverend Mother. But your daughter has temptations to melancholy.

PRIORESS. The Lord protect and keep you. You know how it displeases me to see the shadow of melancholy enter this house.

SISTER MARCELLA (*making a reverence*). *Ay,* reverend Mother, pardon me and assign me some penance if I sin, but your daughter cannot help it.

PRIORESS. Who was thinking of sin? Go out into the garden and take a little sunshine, daughter; that is what you need.

SISTER MARCELLA. *Ay,* reverend Mother, you don't know what you say! For when your daughter sees the flowers in the garden, and the blue sky so bright above them, and the sun so beautiful overhead, the temptation comes upon her then to sigh more than ever. Ay!

PRIORESS. If that is the case, return to your seat and let us pray that it may cease. But do not let me hear you sigh again, for I do not wish to send you to the prison to brighten your spirit with solitude and confinement.

SISTER MARCELLA. As your Reverence desires. (*Returning to her seat*) Ay, my soul!
(THE PRIORESS *raises her eyes to heaven in resignation.*)

A NUN. Ay, Blessed Virgin!

ANOTHER. Ay, Jesús!

PRIORESS (*somewhat ruffled*). What? Is this an epidemic? Nothing is wanting now but that we should begin to sigh in chorus. Remember, it is with gladness and thanksgiving that the Lord is to be served "*in hymnis et canticis,*" for the second of the fruits of the Spirit is joy and there is none higher but love, from which it springs.
(*A pause.* SISTER MARÍA JESÚS *reopens the book, and without waiting for the signal from the* PRIORESS, *resumes reading.*)

SISTER MARÍA JESÚS (*reading*). "I cannot resist the shock of the horrible onrushing waves. They break over me unceasingly; irresistibly they bear me down."

PRIORESS. Close the book, Sister María Jesús, for the blessed father who wrote it, alas, he too was of a melancholy turn of mind!

(SISTER MARÍA JESÚS *closes the book, makes a reverence and sits down to sew.* THE MOTHER VICARESS *appears in the door on the left, accompanied solemnly by two other nuns.*)

VICARESS (*greatly agitated*). Ave Maria Purissima!

PRIORESS. Conceived without sin.

VICARESS. Have I permission, reverend Mother?

PRIORESS. Enter and speak. (*Looking at her*) If I am not mistaken, your Reverence is greatly disturbed

VICARESS. You are not mistaken, reverend Mother. No, and I dare affirm it is not for a slight reason. Your Reverence will be judge if this is the time and place to confront with a charge of *ipso facto* a member of this community.

PRIORESS. Speak, if the knowledge of the fault in public will not in itself constitute a scandal and a cause of offense.

VICARESS. In the opinion of your handmaid all cause of scandal will be avoided by looking the offense straight in the face.

PRIORESS. Speak then.

VICARESS (*making a profound inclination*). I obey. Reverend Mother, while making the round of my inspection of the cells with these two monitors, as your Reverence has been pleased to command . . . (*The two* MONITORS *each make a reverence*) And coming to the cell of Sister Marcella . . . (*All the* NUNS *look at* SISTER MARCELLA, *who lowers her eyes*) I found under the mattress of the bed—in itself a suspicious circumstance and sufficient to constitute a sin—an object which should never be found in the hands of a religious, an object which, to say nothing of the sin against the rule of holy poverty which the private possession and concealment of any property whatever must presuppose, is by its very nature a root of perdition and an origin and source of evil.

PRIORESS. Conclude, Mother, in God's name! For you keep us in suspense. What is this object?

VICARESS. Disclose it, sister. (*To one of the* MONITORS.)
(*The* MONITOR *makes a reverence, and draws from her sleeve a piece of glass, covered on one side with quicksilver.*)

PRIORESS. A piece of looking-glass.

VICARESS. Exactly, a piece of looking-glass!
(*Horrified silence on the part of the community.*)

PRIORESS. What has Sister Marcella to say to this?

SISTER MARCELLA (*leaving her place and kneeling before the* PRIORESS). Mother, I confess my guilt and I beseech your pardon.

PRIORESS. Rise. (SISTER MARCELLA *rises*) Unhappy woman! What was the use of this piece of glass?

VICARESS. To look at herself in it, and amuse herself with the sight of her beauty, thus offending her Maker with pride and vain glory, and the exhibition of her taste.

SISTER MARCELLA (*humbly*). No, reverend Mother; no!

VICARESS. Or else to dress herself up and fix herself by it, and make faces and grimaces such as they do on the streets in these days. (*The* VICARESS, *who has taken the mirror, looks at herself in it for a moment, then turns it hurriedly away.*)

SISTER MARCELLA. No, reverend Mother.

PRIORESS. For what then?

SISTER MARCELLA. For nothing, reverend Mother.

PRIORESS. What? For nothing?

SISTER MARCELLA. Your daughter means for nothing evil. On the contrary . . .

VICARESS. Ha! Now I suppose we are going to hear that it is a virtue in a religious to have a glass!

SISTER MARCELLA. No, reverend Mother, it is not a virtue. But your Reverences know already that your Sister suffers from temptations to melancholy.

VICARESS. Yes, yes . . .

SISTER MARCELLA. And when they seize upon her too strongly, they put it into her head to climb trees and run along the tops of walls, and jump over the fences in the garden, and to throw herself into the water of the fountain, and since your Sister knows that, in a religious, these . . . these . . .

VICARESS. These extravagances.

SISTER MARCELLA. Are unbecoming, your Sister catches a sunbeam in the mirror and makes it dance among the leaves and across the ceiling of her cell, and over the walls opposite, and so she consoles herself and imagines that it is a butterfly or a bird, and can go wherever it pleaseth.

VICARESS. It can, and stay there.

PRIORESS. For this fault, Sister Marcella . . . (SISTER MARCELLA *kneels*) which, without being a grave one, yet is more than a little, considered according to the constitution of our rule, I assign you this penance. Tonight, before you retire, you are to repeat four times in your cell the psalm *"Quam dilecta."* Rise, and return to your seat. (SISTER MARCELLA *obeys, but before seating herself she makes a reverence before each of the* NUNS. *To the* VICARESS) You may be seated.
(THE VICARESS *and the two* MONITORS *seat themselves. Three light knocks on the door. It is* TERESA *who says:*)

TERESA. *Ave Maria Purissima!*

PRIORESS. Conceived without sin.

TERESA. May I come in?

PRIORESS. Come in. (TERESA *enters. She is eighteen, very pretty, very sunny and very gay, with nothing about her to suggest the mystic or the religious. She is dressed simply in gray and wears a white apron. She has a flower in her hair, which is arranged modestly, and without an excess of curls or ornament*) Where are you coming from in such a hurry? You are all out of breath.

TERESA (*speaks always with the greatest simplicity, without affectation or pretense of any sort*). From dressing the altar of the Virgin.

PRIORESS. Did that put you out of breath?

TERESA. No, Mother. It's because I wanted it to be all in white today, and there weren't white flowers enough in the garden, so I had to climb up and cut some branches off the acacia.

MISTRESS OF NOVICES. Did you climb a tree?

TERESA. Yes, I climbed two; there weren't enough blossoms on one.

MISTRESS OF NOVICES. *Jesús!*

VICARESS. *Ave Maria!*

TERESA. I wish you could see the view from the top of the big acacia! (SISTER MARCELLA'S *eyes open wide with envy.*)

VICARESS. Child, you have put yourself beyond the pale of God's mercy!

SISTER JOANNA OF THE CROSS. You might have fallen! It's too terrible to think of it!

TERESA. Fallen? No, Mother. Why, I've climbed it a hundred times!

PRIORESS. Then you must not do it again.

MISTRESS OF NOVICES (*regretfully*). It is too late to forbid her now.

PRIORESS (*sorrowfully*). That is true.

SISTER INEZ. It is the last day she will dress the altar.

SISTER JOANNA OF THE CROSS. The very *last!*

TERESA. Ah, Mothers! You mustn't talk like this. Don't be sad.

VICARESS. No, we had better behave like you do, though it doesn't seem possible when you consider the day that it is, and you laughing and carrying on like one possessed!

PRIORESS. The Mother is right. A little more feeling today, daughter, a manner more subdued, would not have been out of place.

TERESA. You are right, reverend Mothers—you always are, in the holiness, which like a halo surrounds your reverend heads; but when a girl wants to laugh she wants to laugh, although, as Mother Anna St. Francis says, it may be the solemnest day of her life.

MISTRESS OF NOVICES. It is a solemn day, a very solemn day. You are leaving this house in which you have passed eighteen years, without scarcely so much as taking thought how it was you came to be here. Tomorrow, you will be your own mistress, and you will have upon your conscience the responsibilities of a wife.

VICARESS. Which believe me, are not light. Men are selfish, fickle . . .

TERESA (*timidly*). Antonio is very good.

VICARESS. However good he may be, he is a man, and men are accustomed to command. They have been from the beginning of the world, and it has affected their character. And since you are very independent yourself, and like to have your own way . . .

TERESA. Yes, I have been spoiled I know; but you will see now how good I will be. It will come out all right.

SISTER JOANNA OF THE CROSS. Do you want to spoil the day for her?

TERESA. No, Mother—no; you won't spoil it, for I am very, very happy. You have all been so good to me!

VICARESS. Nonsense! No such thing.

TERESA. But it isn't nonsense. I know this is God's house, but you might have closed the doors to me, and you have flung them wide open, freely. I have lived here eighteen years and in all this time, to the very moment that I am leaving it, you have never once reminded me that I have lived here on your charity.

SISTER JOANNA OF THE CROSS. Don't say such things!

TERESA. Yes, I must say them. On your charity, on your alms—like a poor beggar and an outcast. I don't mind saying it nor thinking it, for I have been so happy here—yes, I am happy now—happier than the daughter of a king: for I love you all so much that I want to kiss even the walls and hug the trees, for even the walls and the trees have been kind to me. This has been the Convent of my Heart!

SISTER MARCELLA. It has been your home. If you had only been content always to remain in it!

PRIORESS. We must not talk like this. God moves in His own ways.

MISTRESS OF NOVICES. And in all of them His children may do His service.

VICARESS. The child was not born to be a religious. The things of the world appeal to her too strongly.

TERESA. It is true. The world appeals to me—poor me! It seems to me sometimes as if everybody loved me, as if everything was calling to me everywhere to come. I have been so happy in this house. and yet, all the time, I have been thinking how great the world was, how wonderful! Whenever I have gone out into the street, how my heart leaped! I felt as if I were going to fly, it was so light! My brain was in a whirl. Then I was so glad to come back again into this house, it felt so good, as if you were all taking me up once more into your arms, as if I had fallen to sleep in them again and was warm, folded beneath the shelter of the everlasting wings.

VICARESS. The wings of your good angel, who stood waiting at the door—stood waiting till you came.

PRIORESS. Why should he have to wait? Her good angel always has gone with her, and surely there never has been a time when he has had to turn away his face. Am I right, daughter?

TERESA. You are, Mother. (Sincerely.)

SISTER JOANNA OF THE CROSS. They needn't have asked her that!

SISTER MARÍA JESÚS (rising). Here are the bows for the corset covers. Do you want them pinned or sewed?

SISTER INEZ. Sewed, I say.

SISTER MARÍA JESÚS. Down the middle?

MISTRESS OF NOVICES. Of course, down the middle.

SISTER MARÍA JESÚS. The reason I asked was because in the pattern they are all fastened down the side.

MISTRESS OF NOVICES (bending over to examine the fashion plates with SISTER INEZ and SISTER MARÍA JESÚS). Yes. Don't you see? She is right.

SISTER INEZ. That's funny! But they are pretty that way.

MISTRESS OF NOVICES. I say it's absurd.

SISTER MARÍA JESÚS. What do you think, Mother Crucifixion?

VICARESS. Don't ask me; I don't think. I neither understand nor wish to understand these things—pomp and vanity, artifices of the devil, who, they tell me, is very well acquainted with the dressmakers of Paris, and takes part in their designs and encourages their abbreviations. Take it away, take that paper out of my sight, for it never should have entered this holy house!

SISTER MARCELLA. Ay, but we have to know the fashions, Mother!

VICARESS. The fashions! The fashions! Go to hell and you will find the fashions! Any other place would be too far behind.

SISTER MARÍA JESÚS. But you don't want the child to be married, do you, in the dress of the year of the ark?

VICARESS. A pure heart and an upright spirit are what she should be married in, and if that is the case, no one is going to notice whether she has one bow more or less.

SISTER MARCELLA. They say men pay a great deal of attention to such things, Mother Crucifixion.

SISTER MARÍA JESÚS. And we must render unto Caesar the things which are Caesar's, and unto God the things which are God's.

VICARESS. So! We have philosophers, have we, in the house?

SISTER INEZ. Hand me the scissors, if you will. I want to cut off these ends.

SISTER JOANNA OF THE CROSS. I think now everything is ready to put in the trunk.

PRIORESS. Yes, for the carriage will be waiting.
(TERESA kneels on the floor beside the trunk. The NUNS hand her the various articles of the trousseau, which they remove from the benches and the table.)

SISTER INEZ. Here are the chemises.

SISTER MARCELLA. And the lace petticoats.

SISTER JOANNA OF THE CROSS. Put them in the other tray, so they won't get wrinkled.

SISTER INEZ. Lord of Mercy! What a tuck!— What bungler ran this tuck?

MISTRESS OF NOVICES. You must not say anything against the sister who ran it, Sister; say it would look better if it were redampened and ironed.

TERESA. But it looks splendidly; really it does! Give it to me! Here— let me have them. This is too much trouble for you to take.

PRIORESS. Have you everything?

SISTER MARCELLA. The handkerchiefs?

SISTER JOANNA OF THE CROSS. The dressing-jackets?

VICARESS. Here is some edging that was left over, embroidered by hand. You had better put it in the trunk in case of accident.

MISTRESS OF NOVICES. And the patterns—you might need them.

SISTER INEZ. Here is a sachet, my child. It is filled with thyme and lavender and has lime peel in it. It will give a fresh scent to your clothes.

SISTER MARCELLA. She'll have real perfumes soon enough.

SISTER MARÍA JESÚS. Yes, expensive ones.

SISTER INEZ. They may be more expensive, but they won't be any better—I can tell you that; for these are plants that God has made, and they smell sweetly, and of a good conscience. I have them in all the presses in the sacristy, and it is a joy to smell them when you go up the steps to the altar.

TERESA. I think we have everything.

PRIORESS. Yes, everything. Now turn the key. Does it lock securely? (TERESA gets up) And hang the key around your neck with the rosaries, for we have fastened it on a ribbon for you. Take care you don't lose it. The lock is an English one, and not every key will open it.

TERESA. Yes, Mother.

VICARESS. It will be a miracle if she has it tomorrow.

SISTER JOANNA OF THE CROSS. She will settle down soon under the responsibilities of a wife.

MISTRESS OF NOVICES. Well? Are you satisfied?

TERESA. Satisfied is too little, Mother. It does not express it. I don't deserve what you have done for me.

VICARESS. Yes, you do; you deserve it. And you might as well tell the truth as a falsehood. You have a good heart; you are a sensible girl. When you said what you did, you were thinking of your clothes; but you need have no scruples. Everything that you take away with you from this house, and more too, you have earned by your labor. That is the truth and you know it. Maybe we have taught you here how to sew and embroider, but you have worked for us in the convent, and outside of it. You owe us nothing. Besides, you had two hundred and fifty pesetas from the doctor to buy the material. Here . . . (Producing a paper from under her scapular) is the account of the way they have been spent, so you can see for yourself and answer for it, since delicacy will not permit that we should be asked how it was used.

TERESA (embarrassed and confused). What do you mean? Why, Mother Crucifixion!

VICARESS. That is all there is to it. You will find the account is correct. (TERESA takes the paper and having folded it, puts it in her dress.)

PRIORESS (to the NUNS who have been working). You may remove the table and gather up these things.

TERESA. No, Mother—let me do it. I will pick up everything. (The PRIORESS makes a sign and all the NUNS rise and leave the room, except only herself, the VICARESS, the MISTRESS OF NOVICES, and SISTER JOANNA OF THE CROSS.)

PRIORESS (to TERESA). What time do you go?

TERESA. My father is coming for me at five, but . . . Antonio has asked me . . . before I go . . . to say that he would like to see you all and thank you, and tell you how happy and grateful he is to you for the little girl you have brought up.

PRIORESS. We shall be very glad to see him.

VICARESS. Glad or not glad, no matter; it is our obligation. He cannot expect to carry her off like a thief in the night, and have no woman ask a question.

TERESA. I will call you when he comes.

(*The* PRIORESS, *the* VICARESS *and the* MISTRESS OF NOVICES *go out.* TERESA *and* SISTER JOANNA OF THE CROSS *remain behind picking up and arranging the papers, patterns and scraps that have been left on the seats or about the floor. They say nothing but presently* TERESA *throws herself on her knees before the* NUN.)

TERESA. Sister Joanna of the Cross!

SISTER JOANNA OF THE CROSS. What do you want, my child?

TERESA. Now that we are alone, bless me while there is no one here to see—no, not one—for you are my mother, more than all the rest!

SISTER JOANNA OF THE CROSS. Get up. (TERESA *gets up*) Don't talk like that! We are all equal in God's house.

TERESA. But in my heart you are the first. You mustn't be angry at what I say. How can I help it? Is it my fault, though I have struggled against it all my life, that I have come to love you so?

SISTER JOANNA OF THE CROSS. Yes, you have struggled. You have been wilful . . . (*Then seeking at once to excuse her*) But it was because you were strong and well. When a child is silent and keeps to herself in a corner, it is a sign that she is sick or thinking of some evil. But you . . .

TERESA. *Ay*, Mother! Where do you suppose that I came from?

SISTER JOANNA OF THE CROSS. From Heaven, my daughter, as all of us have come.

TERESA. Do you really think that we have all come from Heaven?

SISTER JOANNA OF THE CROSS. At least you have come from Heaven to me. You say that I am your mother more than the rest; I don't know —it may be. But I know that for years you have been all my happiness and joy.

TERESA. Mother!

SISTER JOANNA OF THE CROSS. I was so glad to hear you laugh and see you run about the cloisters! It was absurd, but I always felt—not now, for you are grown up now—but for years I always felt as if you must be I, myself, scampering and playing. For I was just your age now, a little more or less, when you came into the Convent. And it seemed to me as if I was a child again and had just begun to live. You were so little, so busy—yes, you were—but I was busy too, if you only knew, before I entered here, at home in our house in the village. I was always singing and dancing, although we were very poor. My mother went out every day to wash in the river or to do housework—she had so many children!—and I was always carrying one about in my arms. And when I entered here, as I could do, thanks to some good ladies, who collected the money for my dowry—God reward them for it—although I had a real vocation, I was sorrowful and homesick thinking of my little brothers and sisters! How I used to cry in the dark corners, and I never dared to say a word! Then the Mother told me that if my melancholy didn't leave me she would be obliged to send me home. And then you came and I forgot everything! That is why I say you came to me from Heaven. And I don't want you to think I am angry, or ashamed— or that it has ever given me a moment's pain to have loved you.

TERESA. Is that the reason that you scold me so?

SISTER JOANNA OF THE CROSS. When have I ever scolded you?

TERESA. Oh, so many times! But no matter. I always tell Antonio, Sister Joanna of the Cross is my mother. She is my mother, my real mother! So now he always calls you mother whenever he speaks of you.

SISTER JOANNA OF THE CROSS. My daughter, will you be happy with him?

TERESA. Of course! I am sure I will. He is so good, he is so happy! He says he doesn't know where it is all his happiness comes from, because his father, who is dead now, was more mournful than a willow, and his mother, poor lady, whenever anything happened to her that was good, burst right out crying. How do you suppose it was she ever managed to have such a boy? It must be that sad mothers have happy children. How does it seem to you?

SISTER JOANNA OF THE CROSS. How do I know?

TERESA. It must be that way. The first boy I have is going to be— what is the solemnest thing in the world? No, the first is going to be an architect, like his father; but the second can be a missionary, and go to China if he wants to, and convert the heathen. Just think what it would be to have a son who was a saint! I shouldn't have to be so humble in heaven, then, should I? I should have influence. And here you are all the time, Sister Joanna of the Cross, praying for me and preparing miracles. So you see I have a good start already.

SISTER JOANNA OF THE CROSS. How you do love to talk!

TERESA. Isn't it foolish, Mother! Don't I? Listen! When you were little didn't you ever want to be a boy? I did. I used to cry because I thought then that I could have been anything I wanted to be—this, that, I didn't care what it was—Captain-General, Archbishop, yes, Pope, even! Or something else. It used to make me mad to think that because I was a girl I couldn't even be an acolyte. But now, since—well, since I love Antonio, and he loves me, I don't care; it doesn't make any difference any more, because if I am poor and know nothing, he is wise and strong; and if I am foolish and of no account, he is, oh, of so much worth! And if I have to stay behind at home and hide myself in the corner, he can go out into the world and mount, oh, so high—wherever a man can go—and instead of making me envious, it makes me so happy! Ah, Sister Joanna of the Cross, when she truly loves a man, how humble it makes a girl!

SISTER JOANNA OF THE CROSS. Do you really love him so?

TERESA. More than life itself! And that is all too little. Maybe it's a sin, but I can tell you. Do you believe that we will meet in Heaven the persons we have loved on earth? Because if I don't meet him there and I can't go on loving him always just the same as I do now, no, more than I do now . . .

SISTER JOANNA OF THE CROSS (*interrupting*). Hush! Peace! You mustn't say such things. It is a sin.

TERESA. *Ay*, Sister Joanna of the Cross! How sweet it is to be in love!

SISTER JOANNA OF THE CROSS. But he . . . he . . . Does he love you too, so much?

TERESA. Yes, he loves me. How much, I don't know; but it doesn't make any matter. What makes me happy is that I love him. You needn't think that sometimes—very seldom though—I haven't been afraid that perhaps some day he might stop loving me. It used to make me sad. But if I had ever thought that some day I could stop loving him . . . No, it would be better to die first; for then, what would be the good of life?

SISTER JOANNA OF THE CROSS. Ah, my child! To continue in God's love!

TERESA. Do you know how I would like to spend my life? All of it? Sitting on the ground at his feet, looking up into his eyes, just listening to him talk. You don't know how he can talk. He knows everything—everything that there is to know in the world, and he tells you such things! The things that you always have known yourself, in your heart, and you couldn't find out how to say them. Even when he doesn't say anything, if he should

be speaking some language which you didn't understand, it is wonderful . . . his voice . . . I don't know how to explain it, but it is his voice—a voice that seems as if it had been talking to you ever since the day you were born! You don't hear it only with your ears, but with your whole body. It's like the air which you see and breathe and taste, and which smells so sweetly in the garden beneath the tree of paradise. Ah, Mother! The first day that he said to me "Teresa"—you see what a simple thing it was, my name, Teresa—why, it seemed to me as if nobody ever had called me by my name before, as if I never had heard it, and when he went away, I ran up and down the street saying to myself "Teresa, Teresa, Teresa!" under my breath, without knowing what I was doing, as if I walked on air!

SISTER JOANNA OF THE CROSS. You frighten me, my child.

TERESA. Do I? Why?

SISTER JOANNA OF THE CROSS. Because you love him so. For earthly love . . . I mean . . . it seems to me it is like a flower, that we find by the side of the road—a little brightness that God grants us to help us pass through life, for we are weak and frail; a drop of honey spread upon our bread each day, which we should receive gladly, but with trembling, and keeping our hearts whole, daughter, for it will surely pass away.

TERESA. It cannot pass away!

SISTER JOANNA OF THE CROSS. It may; and then what will be left to your soul, if you have set your all on this delight, and it has passed away?

TERESA (*humbly*). You mustn't be angry with me, Mother. No! Look at me! It isn't wrong, I know. Loving him, I . . . he is so good, he is so good . . . and good, it cannot pass away!

SISTER JOANNA OF THE CROSS. Is he a good Christian?

TERESA. He is good, Sister.

SISTER JOANNA OF THE CROSS. But does he fear God?

TERESA. One day he said to me: "I love you because you know how to pray." Don't you see? And another time: "I feel a devotion toward you as toward some holy thing." He! Devotion! To me! And whenever I think of that, it seems to me as if I was just growing better, as if all at once I was capable of everything there was to do or suffer in the world—so as to have him always feel that way!

SISTER JOANNA OF THE CROSS. I hear some one in the parlor. Draw the curtains.
(TERESA, *pulling the cord, draws the curtains over the windows, shutting off the light. The fore part of the stage remains in shadow, but the outer parlor is brightly illuminated.* ANTONIO *has entered and may be seen through the crack where the curtains join. He is twenty-five years of age, well-built, manly and sensitive of feature. He remains alone and his footsteps may be heard on the boards as he paces nervously up and down.*)

TERESA (*in a low voice, going up to the* NUN). Yes. It is he.

SISTER JOANNA OF THE CROSS (*seizing her hand*). Ah! How tall he is!

TERESA. Yes, he is tall. Doesn't he look splendidly though?

SISTER JOANNA OF THE CROSS. Yes, he does. Has he golden hair?

TERESA. No, it's the light; his hair is dark brown, and his eyes are between violet and blue. It's too bad you can't see them. They are so beautiful! When he talks, they sparkle.

SISTER JOANNA OF THE CROSS. How old is he?

TERESA. Just twenty-five.
(ANTONIO *crosses from one side to the other, and continues to pace back and forth.*)

SISTER JOANNA OF THE CROSS. He seems to be of a very active disposition.

TERESA. That is because he is impatient. Shall I speak to him and tell him you are here?

SISTER JOANNA OF THE CROSS (*falling back*). No!

TERESA. Why not? He loves you dearly. (*In a low voice, going up to the grille*) Good afternoon, Antonio.

ANTONIO (*looking about from one side to the other*). Teresa? Where are you?

TERESA (*laughing*). Here, boy, here; behind the grille. It is easy to see you are not accustomed to calling on nuns.

ANTONIO. Can't you run back the curtain?

TERESA. No, because I am not alone. Can't you guess who is with me? My mother.

ANTONIO. Sister Joanna of the Cross?

TERESA (to the NUN, *delighted because he has guessed it*). There! Do you see? (*To* ANTONIO) Sister Joanna of the Cross—exactly. We have been watching you through the grille, and she says that she thinks you are a very handsome young man.

SISTER JOANNA OF THE CROSS. Goodness gracious! You mustn't pay any attention to what she says.

TERESA. Don't be angry, Mother. I think so myself.

ANTONIO. You never told me that before.

TERESA. That is because in here, where you can't see me, I'm not so embarrassed to tell you. Listen! We have to send in word now that you are here; but I want you to tell my mother something first, for if you stand there like a blockhead without opening your mouth, I am going to be very much ashamed, after all the time I have spent in singing your praises.

ANTONIO. What do you want me to tell her?

TERESA. What you have in your heart.

ANTONIO. But I don't know whether it is proper to tell it to a religious,

although it is in my heart, for I love her dearly.

TERESA. Ah! I tell her that a million times a day.

ANTONIO. Then let us tell her together two million; because I must say to you, Madam, that it is impossible to know Teresa and not to love you.

TERESA. What a treasure is this mother of mine!

SISTER JOANNA OF THE CROSS. For shame, my child! (*Blushing, to* ANTONIO) I also have a great affection for you, sir, for this child has been teaching me to love you. She is a little blind perhaps, and trusting, for that is natural. She knows nothing of the world, and we—how were we to teach her? And now you are going to take her far away, but don't take her heart away from us, sir, and break ours, when we let her hand go.

ANTONIO. Madam, I swear to you now that I shall always kneel in reverence before the tenderness and virtue which you have planted in her soul.

TERESA. I told you that he was very good, Mother.

SISTER JOANNA OF THE CROSS. May God make you both very happy. And may God remain with you, for his handmaid must go now and seek the Mother.

ANTONIO. But you are coming back?

SISTER JOANNA OF THE CROSS. With the sisters . . . Yes, I think so. Good-bye. I have been so happy to know you. (SISTER JOANNA OF THE CROSS *goes out, greatly moved.* TERESA *remains standing by the grille until the* NUN *has disappeared, without speaking a word.*)

ANTONIO. Now you can draw back the curtain.

TERESA. Yes, a little. (*She runs back the curtain a little way*) But it won't do you any good, because you won't be able to see me. Do you really like my mother? Do you really? Why are you so silent? What are you thinking about?

ANTONIO. I don't know; it is very strange. Since I have come into this room, since I have heard your mother speak, and have heard you, behind this grille, without knowing for certain where you were in the dark, I have been almost afraid to love you. But ah—how I do love you!

TERESA. I like that better.

ANTONIO. Teresa!

TERESA. What is it?

ANTONIO. Will you never forget, will you carry with you always wherever you go, this peace and this calm?

TERESA. With you, Antonio?

ANTONIO. Yes, into the world, beyond these walls; for in the world we make so much useless noise. And you—I see it now—you are the mistress of peace and of calm.

TERESA (*laughing*). I the mistress of calm? As if I hadn't been a little flyaway all my life, without an idea

in my head! Mother Crucifixion says that since I was passed in on the wheel there hasn't been one moment in this house of what the rules call "profound calm." I know I don't talk much when I am with you—we have been together such a little while, and it has been all too short to listen to you; but you will see when I grow bolder and am not afraid. You will have to put cotton in your ears then. Ah, Antonio! Only think, we are going to have all our lives to be together and listen to each other talk and tell each other things—that is, all our lives for you to tell me things, because I . . . you will find out soon enough. Tell me really, truly, Antonio: aren't you going to be awfully ashamed to have such an ignorant wife?

ANTONIO. Ignorant or learned?

TERESA. I? Learned? In what?

ANTONIO. In a science which I did not know, and which you have taught to me.

TERESA. You are joking.

ANTONIO. I am in earnest. Until I met you, I knew nothing; I did not even know myself.

TERESA. Pshaw!

ANTONIO. You mustn't laugh. Did it ever seem to you, Teresa, that our soul was like a palace?

TERESA. Of course it is! It is like a castle. Santa Teresa says so: The soul is like a castle—the interior of a castle, all made of one diamond above and below. And it has seven courts, and in the last is stored a great treasure . . .

ANTONIO. Then in the innermost chamber of my soul was stored the love I have for you, and if you had not come and opened the door yourself, and helped me to find it, I should have passed all my life in ignorance, without knowing anything was there.

TERESA. Don't repeat such heresies!

ANTONIO. Is it a heresy—the love I bear for you? No, it is a religion— the only one for me! My girl! Seven courts, you say? Then with a great effort I had passed into the first and I was running here and there aimlessly, and you don't know what horrible things I found—everywhere I stumbled on. They were my own traits. I was cold, selfish, proud, without trust or faith, without other ambitions than material desires—to pass through life easily and well, to be the first in my own petty world, incapable of sacrifice, of abnegation, of compassion, of disinterested love.

TERESA. No! No! You were no such thing.

ANTONIO. But I lived as if I were! What difference did it make? But then one day I heard your voice and, summoned by you, I again searched through the castle, and in the other courts I began to find —ah! under how many cobwebs, all covered up with dust—humility and devotion, warmth of heart, pity and faith in so many holy things. And then I found my honor, self-respect and sympathy with my fellow man, in which we live, Teresa, for without it nothing else is life,

and I began to be a man when I first loved you. For in these things you are the master, and I have learned them all from you!

TERESA. Hush! They are coming. (TERESA *falls back from the grille, after first drawing the curtains again. The* NUNS *in single file enter silently, the youngest first, followed at last by the* MISTRESS OF NOVICES, *the* VICARESS *and the* PRIORESS. *The* PRIORESS *seats herself in the arm chair at the left of the grille; the* VICARESS *and the* MISTRESS OF NOVICES *in two other chairs at the right. The remaining* NUNS *stand or are seated round about.* TERESA *supports herself with her hand on the back of the* PRIORESS' *chair.* SISTER JOANNA OF THE CROSS *approaches her and takes her by the other hand. There is absolute silence as the* NUNS *enter and find their places. They look at each other with expectant attention, and some nod and smile among themselves. When they are seated, there follows an interval of further silence.*)

PRIORESS. *Ave Maria Purissima!* (ANTONIO, *somewhat embarrassed, and endeavoring vainly to penetrate the darkness behind the grille, does not answer. The* PRIORESS, *after waiting a moment, turns her head and smiles indulgently at the community*) Good afternoon, young man.

ANTONIO. Good afternoon, Madam —or Madams—for behind the mystery of this screen, it is impossible for me to see whether I am speaking with one or with many.
(*The* NUNS *smile quietly and discreetly.*)

PRIORESS (*in a low voice*). Run back the curtain, Sister Inez. (*The Sister runs back the curtain*) You are speaking with the entire community, which takes great pleasure in knowing you.

ANTONIO. Ladies, the pleasure and the honor are mine, and they are much greater than you will be ready to imagine.

SISTER INEZ. Bless us! But isn't he a polite and polished talker?

SISTER TORNERA. Keep still! I want to hear what he has to say.

ANTONIO. For a long time I have desired greatly to visit you. Teresa knows it, and she must have told it to you.

PRIORESS. That is true. She has indeed. And we have greatly appreciated your desire.

ANTONIO. But the first time I was in this place it was Advent and the second it was Lent; and both times Teresa informed me that it was impossible for me to see you.

VICARESS. Clearly. In seasons of penitence we receive no visitors.

ANTONIO. But now it is May and past Easter time.

MISTRESS OF NOVICES. How well acquainted he is with the calendar! Surely you must be very devout, sir.

ANTONIO. I am, Madam—very; but chiefly in the worship of certain saints who as yet are not on the altars.

SISTER INEZ. What a nice compliment! Saints, did he say? (*Laughing*) He *is* a polished talker.

ANTONIO. Ladies, after a hundred years they will be lighting candles to you, and invoking you in prayers, and in gratitude they will be bringing you thank offerings of crutches and wooden legs.

SISTER TORNERA (*laughing*). Does he think we are going to be the patrons of rheumatism?

MISTRESS OF NOVICES. After a hundred years? You are giving us a century of Purgatory.

ANTONIO. No, Madam, by all that is holy! I am giving you a century of life, and entrance thereafter directly into the choir of seraphim.

PRIORESS. I fear you speak frivolously, Señor Don Antonio.

ANTONIO. Madam, I was never more earnest in my life. Whenever I think of death, you have no idea of the peace which enters my soul. I remember how many saintly white hands will be stretched down to me to help me into Paradise—for I suppose that you will be able to exercise a little influence on behalf of one of the family.

SISTER SAGRARIO (*laughing*). One of the family?

VICARESS. Certainly. We are all God's children.

ANTONIO. But I shall be so in a double sense; first, in my own birthright, and then as your son-in-law, who are his brides.

VICARESS. Ah! It is not meet to jest about holy things.

ANTONIO. Madam, you are right. And you will pardon me all the inconsequences which I have said, for I swear to you that they have been nothing but nervousness and fear.

MISTRESS OF NOVICES. You are not afraid of us?

ANTONIO. I am, Madam, very—because of the respect and admiration in which I hold you all. I came here more disturbed than I ever have been before in my whole life. I do not know whether I should thank you, or whether I should beg your pardon.

PRIORESS. Beg our pardon?

ANTONIO. Yes, because I fear that I am not worthy of the treasure which you are entrusting to me.

PRIORESS. We know already through the doctor that you are an honorable young man.

MISTRESS OF NOVICES. And the love which our daughter bears you is our guarantee. Surely the Lord would not permit His child, brought up in His fear, to throw herself away upon an evil man.

ANTONIO. I am not evil, no; but I am a man, and you, ladies, with all the great piety of your souls, have been nurturing a flower for the skies. When I first knew her, my heart whispered to me that I had met a saint. She was a miracle. When I first dared to speak to her, there came over me a fear and a trembling that were out of the course of nature; and when I told her that I loved her, my heart stopped, and bade me to fall on my knees, and now that I have come here to beg my happiness of you, I don't know what I can promise you in token of my gratitude, nor how I can give you thanks enough for the great honor which you do me.

VICARESS. It may be you are speaking more truly than you think, Señor Don Antonio.

MISTRESS OF NOVICES. Why, Mother!

VICARESS. No, let me speak. For he has said well. The girl is not one of those worldly creatures who take to their husbands a great store of physical beauty. That is certain. You cannot call her ugly, but it is the most that can be said. Nor does she bring with her any dower. She is poorer than the poor. But she carries in her heart a treasure, the only one which we have been able to give her, which is more priceless than silver or gold, and that is the fear of God. For this, sir, you must be answerable to us, and we ask you your word now, that you will always respect it in her and in her children, if you should have any, if it should be God's holy will.

ANTONIO. Teresa shall always be the absolute mistress of her conscience and of my house, and my children shall ever be that which she desires. I pledge my word.

PRIORESS. You will never have reason to regret it, for she is a good and prudent girl.

VICARESS. And not hypocritical, for, although, as you have said, we have nurtured her for the skies, we have never permitted ourselves to believe that she was to reach them through the cloister.

SISTER MARÍA JESÚS. Do you mean to take her very far away?

ANTONIO. Yes, Madam. That is to say, there is no longer in the world either far or near. We sail next week. I am going to America as the resident director of a firm of architects.

PRIORESS. Yes, we know already.

ANTONIO. That is the reason for this haste. I do not wish to go alone.

SISTER TORNERA. Aren't you afraid the child will be seasick? They say you do get a terrible shaking-up upon the sea.

SISTER MARÍA JESÚS. You must promise us to take good care of her.

SISTER INEZ. If she gets overheated never let her drink cold water. She is very pig-headed about that.

SISTER MARCELLA. But you mustn't forget that she is accustomed to cold baths.

SISTER INEZ. If she takes cold or gets a cough, make her drink a glass of hot milk with a teaspoonful of hot rum in it, with plenty of sugar, for that's the only thing that will make her sweat.

TERESA. I think perhaps I had better attend to these matters myself, Sister.

SISTER INEZ. Yes, you'd be a pretty one to attend to them! Don't you mind what she says, Señor Don Antonio, for she is spoiled utterly. If you don't give her medicines and force the spoon down her throat, she might be dying for all you'd know, but she'd never ask for them herself.

PRIORESS. We had better not confuse him with too many recommendations. Surely he knows the more important precautions already.

ANTONIO (smiling). Perhaps it would be better if you wrote them out for me on a piece of paper.

SISTER TORNERA. A good idea! (Laughing) If we began where does he think we'd leave off?

SISTER SAGRARIO. How many days will you be on the ship?

ANTONIO. Two weeks.

SISTER MARCELLA. Mercy! What an age! Suppose there should be a storm?

MISTRESS OF NOVICES. It will be at least two weeks more before we can get letters back.

ANTONIO. We will telegraph when we arrive and we will send you a message from the middle of the ocean, so that you will hear from us the same day.

SISTER INEZ. Mother of God! Can they send messages now from the middle of the ocean? How do the words come?

TERESA. Flying through the air, like birds.

SISTER INEZ. What will men invent next? When your handmaid was in the world, they came by a wire, and yet it seemed the work of the devil.

ANTONIO. I should not advise you, Madam, to believe that the devil is ever very far away from these inventions.

SISTER INEZ. Whether he is or not, when the telegram comes it will be safest to sprinkle it with holy water.

PRIORESS. Ah, Sister Inez, you are so simple! Don't you see that the young man is only joking?

VICARESS. It is five o'clock—the hour we were to expect your father.

ANTONIO. I do not wish to molest you further.

PRIORESS. You do not molest us, but we must close the parlor at five.

ANTONIO. You will pardon me if I commit a terrible breach of etiquette, but I should like to ask you one favor before I go.

PRIORESS. If it is in our power to grant . . .

ANTONIO. Although, as it seems, you have run back a curtain, yet the mystery of this screen still remains a mystery to me, a poor sinner, inscrutable as before; and I should be sorry to go away without having seen you face to face. Is it too much to ask?

PRIORESS. For us this is a day of giving. Draw back the curtains, Teresa.

(TERESA *draws back the curtain from one window, a* NUN *that from the other, lighting up the room.*)

ANTONIO (*bowing*). Ladies! . . .

VICARESS. Well? How does the vision appear to you?

ANTONIO. I shall never forget it as long as I live.

PRIORESS. Then may God go with you, and may you live a thousand years. (*Taking* TERESA *by the hand*) Here is her hand. See, we give her to you with a great love, and may you make her happy.

ANTONIO. I answer for her happiness with my life.

PRIORESS. And may God go with you.

MISTRESS OF NOVICES. Teresa will give you from us two scapularies, the remembrances of a nun. They are not worth anything, but they have lain beside the reliquary of our father, the blessed Saint Dominic. Keep them in memory of this day.

ANTONIO. I shall treasure them, ladies, from this hour. And I pray you, remember me always in your prayers.

VICARESS. And upon your part do not forget to pray with them from time to time, for although it lies within the province of everyone to help our souls along the way to heaven, yet we must take the first steps ourselves. And may God go with you.

ALL. God go with you.

ANTONIO. Ladies! . . . (*He retires and disappears. A* NUN *draws the curtain over the grille. Then a mo-*

ment's silence. Some of the NUNS *sigh and say:)*

NUNS. Ah, Lord! Good Lord! May it be God's holy will!
(*The bell by the door rings twice.*)

VICARESS. I thought so—your father.
(TERESA *stands in the midst of the group of* NUNS, *bewildered, looking from one to the other, greatly moved.* SISTER TORNERA *goes to open the door.*)

PRIORESS. Ask him to come in.
(*The* DOCTOR *enters on the arm of* SISTER TORNERA. *He is now very old, but neither decrepit nor cast down.*)

DOCTOR. Good afternoon, ladies; good afternoon, daughter.

TERESA (*kissing his hand*). Good afternoon, father.

DOCTOR. The whole assembly—the parting, eh? Well, did you see the young man? (*The* NUNS *do not answer*) A fine fellow, isn't he? He is waiting outside. We have an hour in the coach before we arrive at the station, so you had better get ready now, daughter. (TERESA *goes out with* SISTER JOANNA OF THE CROSS) Ah! The trunk? Good! Carry it to the door. The boys outside will take care of it. (*Two* NUNS *lift the trunk and carry it out by the door on the right*) There, that is done. (*He seats himself in the* PRIORESS' *chair*) Well, how are we today?

PRIORESS. You see, Doctor.

MISTRESS OF NOVICES. Who would ever have believed it eighteen years ago?

DOCTOR. Eighteen years? We are growing old, Mother. We are growing old.

PRIORESS. That is not the worst of it.

SISTER INEZ. How old are you now, Doctor?

DOCTOR. Seventy-eight, Sister.

SISTER INEZ. No one would ever think it.

DOCTOR (*attempting a witticism so as to cheer up the* NUNS). That is because I am preserved in sanctity, like a fly in thick syrup. (*But none of the* NUNS *laugh*) A little mournful today, eh?

SISTER MARCELLA. What else did you expect?

SISTER SAGRARIO. She is not even going to be married in our chapel.

DOCTOR. No, his mother is old and sick, and naturally she wants him to be with her, so they must be married in her house.

PRIORESS Naturally. Poor woman!
(*A pause.*)

MISTRESS OF NOVICES. She is going so far away!

DOCTOR. But she will come back, Mother. She will come back.

PRIORESS. She knows nothing of the world.

DOCTOR. There is no cause to be alarmed. He is an honorable man.

VICARESS. Yes, he seems to be one.
(TERESA *and* SISTER JOANNA OF

THE CROSS *re-enter. It is plain that they have both been crying.* TERESA, *wearing a mantilla, and with her coat on, carries a shawl over her arm for use as a wrap on the voyage. She stops in the middle of the room and stands still, not daring to say good-bye.*)

DOCTOR. Well? Are we ready now?

TERESA. Yes . . . Now . . .

DOCTOR. Then say good-bye. It is late. We must be going, daughter.

PRIORESS. Yes, you must not delay.

TERESA (*throwing herself on her knees before the* PRIORESS *and kissing her scapular*). Mother!

PRIORESS. Rise, my daughter, rise.

TERESA. Bless me, Mother! Bless me!

PRIORESS. May God bless you; so. Rise.
(*As* TERESA *rises, the* NUN *embraces her.*)

TERESA. Mother! I don't know what to say to you . . . I don't know how to leave you . . . but you must forgive me all the wrong I have ever done in all these years. I have been foolish, wilful. I have made so much trouble for you all. You must forgive me. I would like to do something great, something splendid for you all. But— but may God reward you! May God reward you! God reward you! (*She bursts into tears.*)

PRIORESS. My daughter, come! You must not cry. You must not allow yourself to be afflicted so.

TERESA. I am not afflicted, Mother; but . . . it's . . . Mother, I can never forget you! You must pray for me, pray for me! And you must never forget me!

PRIORESS. Ah, no, my child! Never! We will pray God to help you, and to be with you, and you must pray to Him for guidance and for counsel always, whenever you are troubled or perplexed in anything. For the liberty which they enjoy in the world is like a sword in the hands of a child, and life at best is hard, and bitter oftentimes.

MISTRESS OF NOVICES. Be thankful that your heart is well steeled to resist all the temptations that may come. Is it not, my daughter?

TERESA. It is, Mother.

PRIORESS. Will you promise always to be reverent and good?

TERESA. Yes! Yes, Mother!

VICARESS. Remember that your obligation is greater than that of others, because you have come forth from God's own house.

TERESA. Yes! Yes, Mother!

PRIORESS. Remember all the blessings He has showered upon you from the cradle; remember that your whole life has been as a miracle, that you have lived here as few have ever lived, that you have been brought up as few have ever been brought up, like the Holy Virgin herself, in the very temple of the Lord.

MISTRESS OF NOVICES. As He was to the Evangelist, so God has been to you a father and a mother, more than to any other living thing.

PRIORESS. Remember that you are the rose of His garden and the grain of incense upon His altar.

TERESA. Yes! Mother, yes! I will! . . I will remember all . . . all . . . all . . .

MISTRESS OF NOVICES. And do not forget each day to make an examination of your soul.

TERESA. No, Mother.

SISTER JOANNA OF THE CROSS. And write often.

TERESA. Yes, Mother.

DOCTOR. It is time to go, Teresa.

TERESA (*throwing herself suddenly into his arms*). Oh, father! Promise me never to leave them! Never abandon them!

DOCTOR. Child of my heart! Ah, may they never abandon me!—for this is my house. For more than forty years I have been coming here day by day, hour by hour, and now there is nobody within these walls who is older than I. I have no children. I have had my loves—yes, a moment's flame—but it was so long ago! I have forgotten them. And these Sisters, who have been mothers to you, have been daughters to me; and now, when I come, they no longer even cover their faces before me. Why should they? It seems to me as if I had seen them born. And in this house (*greatly moved*) I should like to die, so that they might close my

eyes, and say a prayer for me when life itself has closed!

MISTRESS OF NOVICES. Who is thinking of dying, Doctor?

PRIORESS. It is time to go.

TERESA (*looking from one to the other*). Aren't you going to embrace me?
(*The* NUNS, *after hesitating and glancing a moment doubtfully at the* MOTHER PRIORESS, *embrace* TERESA *in turn, in perfect silence. Only* SISTER JOANNA OF THE CROSS, *taking her into her arms, says:*)

SISTER JOANNA OF THE CROSS. My child!

PRIORESS. May you find what you seek in the world, daughter, for so we hope and so we pray to God. But if it should not be so, remember, this is your Convent.

TERESA. Thanks . . . thanks . . . (*Sobbing.*)

DOCTOR. Come, daughter come . . . (*The* DOCTOR *and* TERESA *go to the door, but* TERESA *turns when she reaches the threshold and embraces* SISTER JOANNA OF THE CROSS, *passionately. Then she disappears.* SISTER JOANNA OF THE CROSS *rests her head against the grille, her back to the others, and weeps silently. A pause. The bells of the coach are heard outside as it drives away.*)

MISTRESS OF NOVICES. They are going now.
(*The chapel bell rings summoning the* NUNS *to choir.*)

PRIORESS. The summons to the choir.

MISTRESS OF NOVICES. Come, Sisters! Let us go there.

(*All make ready to go out sadly. The* VICARESS, *sensing the situation, to her mind demoralizing, feels it to be her duty to provide a remedy. She, too, is greatly moved, but making a supreme effort to control herself, says in a voice which she in vain endeavors to make appear calm, but which is choked in utterance by tears:*)

VICARESS. One moment. I have observed of late . . . that some . . . in the prayer . . . have not been marking sufficiently the pauses in the middle of the lines, while on the other hand, they drag out the last words interminably. Be careful of this, for your Reverences know that the beauty of the office lies in rightly marking the pauses, and in avoiding undue emphasis on the end of the phrase. Let us go there. (*The* NUNS *file out slowly.* SISTER JOANNA OF THE CROSS, *unnoticed, remains alone. With a cry, she falls upon her knees beside an empty chair.*)

CURTAIN

Six Characters in Search of an Author

(Sei personaggi in cerca d'autore)

A COMEDY IN THE MAKING

BY LUIGI PIRANDELLO

TRANSLATED FROM THE ITALIAN
BY EDWARD STORER

CHARACTERS OF THE COMEDY IN THE MAKING:

THE FATHER
THE MOTHER
THE STEP-DAUGHTER
THE SON
THE BOY
THE CHILD
(*The last two do not speak.*)
MADAME PACE

ACTORS OF THE COMPANY

THE MANAGER
LEADING LADY
LEADING MAN
SECOND LADY
LEAD
L'INGÉNUE
JUVENILE LEAD
OTHER ACTORS AND ACTRESSES
PROPERTY MAN
PROMPTER
MACHINIST
MANAGER'S SECRETARY
DOOR-KEEPER
SCENE-SHIFTERS

DAYTIME. THE STAGE OF A THEATRE.

CHARACTERS OF THE COMEDY IN THE MAKING

The Father
The Mother
The Step-Daughter
The Son
The Boy
The Child
(The last two do not speak)
Madame Pace

ACTORS OF THE COMPANY

The Manager
Leading Lady
Leading Man
Second Lady
Lead
L'Ingénue
Juvenile Lead
Other Actors and Actresses
Property Man
Prompter
Machinist
Manager's Secretary
Door-Keeper
Scene-Shifters

Daytime. The Stage of a Theatre

SIX CHARACTERS IN SEARCH OF AN AUTHOR

A COMEDY IN THE MAKING

ACT ONE

N. B. *The Comedy is without acts or scenes. The performance is interrupted once, without the curtain being lowered, when* THE MANAGER *and the chief characters withdraw to arrange the scenario. A second interruption of the action takes place when, by mistake, the stage hands let the curtain down.*

The spectators will find the curtain raised and the stage as it usually is during the daytime. It will be half dark, and empty, so that from the beginning the public may have the impression of an impromptu performance.

PROMPTER's *box and a small table and chair for* THE MANAGER.

Two other small tables and several chairs scattered about as during rehearsals.

The actors and actresses of the company enter from the back of the stage:
first one, then another, then two together: nine or ten in all. They are about to rehearse a Pirandello play: Mixing It Up. Some of the company move off towards their dressing rooms. THE PROMPTER *who has the "book" under his arm, is waiting for* THE MANAGER *in order to begin the rehearsal.*

The actors and actresses, some standing, some sitting, chat and smoke. One perhaps reads a paper; another cons his part.

Finally, THE MANAGER *enters and goes to the table prepared for him. His secretary brings him his mail, through which he glances.* THE PROMPTER *takes his seat, turns on a light, and opens the "book."*

THE MANAGER (*throwing a letter down on the table*). I can't see. (*To* PROPERTY MAN) Let's have a little light, please!

PROPERTY MAN. Yes sir, yes, at once.
(*A light comes down on to the stage.*)

THE MANAGER (*clapping his hands*). Come along! Come along!

Second act of "Mixing it Up." (*Sits down.*)
(*The actors and actresses go from the front of the stage to the wings, all except the three who are to begin the rehearsal.*)

THE PROMPTER (*reading the "book"*). "Leo Gala's house. A curious room serving as dining-room and study."

623

THE MANAGER (*to* PROPERTY MAN).
Fix up the old red room.

PROPERTY MAN (*noting it down*).
Red set. All right!

THE PROMPTER (*continuing to read
from the "book"*). "Table already
laid and writing desk with books
and papers. Book-shelves. Exit rear
to Leo's bedroom. Exit left to
kitchen. Principal exit to right."

THE MANAGER (*energetically*).
Well, you understand: The principal exit over there; here, the
kitchen. (*Turning to actor who
is to play the part of Socrates*) You
make your entrances and exits here.
(*To* PROPERTY MAN) The baize
doors at the rear, and curtains.

PROPERTY MAN (*noting it down*).
Right oh!

PROMPTER (*reading as before*).
"When the curtain rises, Leo Gala,
dressed in cook's cap and apron, is
busy beating an egg in a cup.
Philip, also dressed as a cook, is
beating another egg. Guido Ven-
anzi is seated and listening."

LEADING MAN (*to* MANAGER). Excuse me, but must I absolutely wear
a cook's cap?

THE MANAGER (*annoyed*). I imagine so. It says so there anyway.
(*Pointing to the "book."*)

LEADING MAN. But it's ridiculous!

THE MANAGER (*jumping up in a
rage*). Ridiculous? Ridiculous? Is
it my fault if France won't send us
any more good comedies, and we
are reduced to putting on Pirandello's works, where nobody understands anything, and where the
author plays the fool with us all?
(*The actors grin.* THE MANAGER
goes to LEADING MAN *and shouts*)
Yes sir, you put on the cook's cap
and beat eggs. Do you suppose that
with all this egg-beating business
you are on an ordinary stage? Get
that out of your head. You represent the shell of the eggs you are
beating! (*Laughter and comments
among the actors*) Silence! and
listen to my explanations, please!
(*To* LEADING MAN) "The empty
form of reason without the fullness
of instinct, which is blind."—You
stand for reason, your wife is instinct. It's a mixing up of the parts,
according to which you who act
your own part become the puppet
of yourself. Do you understand?

LEADING MAN. I'm hanged if I do.

THE MANAGER. Neither do I. But
let's get on with it. It's sure to be
a glorious failure anyway. (*Confidentially*) But I say, please face
three-quarters. Otherwise, what
with the abstruseness of the dialogue, and the public that won't be
able to hear you, the whole thing
will go to hell. Come on! come on!

PROMPTER. Pardon sir, may I get
into my box? There's a bit of a
draught.

THE MANAGER. Yes, yes, of course!

At this point, the DOOR-KEEPER *has entered from the stage door and advances towards* THE MANAGER'S *table, taking off his braided cap. During
this manoeuvre, the Six Characters enter, and stop by the door at back of
stage, so that when the* DOOR-KEEPER *is about to announce their coming*

to THE MANAGER, *they are already on the stage. A tenuous light surrounds them, almost as if irradiated by them—the faint breath of their fantastic reality.*

This light will disappear when they come forward towards the actors. They preserve, however, something of the dream lightness in which they seem almost suspended; but this does not detract from the essential reality of their forms and expressions.

He who is known as THE FATHER *is a man of about 50: hair, reddish in color, thin at the temples; he is not bald, however; thick mustaches, falling over his still fresh mouth, which often opens in an empty and uncertain smile. He is fattish, pale; with an especially wide forehead. He has blue, oval-shaped eyes, very clear and piercing. Wears light trousers and a dark jacket. He is alternatively mellifluous and violent in his manner.*

THE MOTHER *seems crushed and terrified as if by an intolerable weight of shame and abasement. She is dressed in modest black and wears a thick widow's veil of crêpe. When she lifts this, she reveals a wax-like face. She always keeps her eyes downcast.*

THE STEP-DAUGHTER *is dashing, almost impudent, beautiful. She wears mourning too, but with great elegance. She shows contempt for the timid half-frightened manner of the wretched* BOY *(14 years old, and also dressed in black); on the other hand, she displays a lively tenderness for her little sister,* THE CHILD *(about four), who is dressed in white, with a black silk sash at the waist.*

THE SON *(22) tall, severe in his attitude of contempt for* THE FATHER, *supercilious and indifferent to* THE MOTHER. *He looks as if he had come on the stage against his will.*

DOOR-KEEPER (*cap in hand*). Excuse me, sir . . .

THE MANAGER (*rudely*). Eh? What is it?

DOOR-KEEPER (*timidly*). These people are asking for you, sir.

THE MANAGER (*furious*). I am rehearsing, and you know perfectly well no one's allowed to come in during rehearsals! (*Turning to the Characters*) Who are you, please? What do you want?

THE FATHER (*coming forward a little, followed by the others who seem embarrassed*). As a matter of fact . . . we have come here in search of an author . . .

THE MANAGER (*half angry, half amazed*). An author? What author?

THE FATHER. Any author, sir.

THE MANAGER. But there's no author here. We are not rehearsing a new piece.

THE STEP-DAUGHTER (*vivaciously*). So much the better, so much the better! We can be your new piece.

AN ACTOR (*coming forward from the others*). Oh, do you hear that?

THE FATHER (*to* STEP-DAUGHTER). Yes, but if the author isn't here . . . (*To* MANAGER) . . . unless you would be willing . . .

THE MANAGER. You are trying to be funny.

THE FATHER. No, for Heaven's sake, what are you saying? We bring you a drama, sir.

THE STEP-DAUGHTER. We may be your fortune.

THE MANAGER. Will you oblige me by going away? We haven't time to waste with mad people.

THE FATHER (*mellifluously*). Oh sir, you know well that life is full of infinite absurdities, which, strangely enough, do not even need to appear plausible, since they are true.

THE MANAGER. What the devil is he talking about?

THE FATHER. I say that to reverse the ordinary process may well be considered a madness: that is, to create credible situations, in order that they may appear true. But permit me to observe that if this be madness, it is the sole *raison d'être* of your profession, gentlemen. (*The actors look hurt and perplexed.*)

THE MANAGER (*getting up and looking at him*). So our profession seems to you one worthy of madmen then?

THE FATHER. Well, to make seem true that which isn't true . . . without any need . . . for a joke as it were . . . Isn't that your mission, gentlemen: to give life to fantastic characters on the stage?

THE MANAGER (*interpreting the rising anger of the Company*). But I would beg you to believe, my dear sir, that the profession of the comedian is a noble one. If today, as things go, the playwrights give us stupid comedies to play and puppets to represent instead of men, remember we are proud to have given life to immortal works here on these very boards! (*The actors, satisfied, applaud their* MANAGER).

THE FATHER (*interrupting furiously*). Exactly, perfectly, to living beings more alive than those who breathe and wear clothes: beings less real perhaps, but truer! I agree with you entirely. (*The actors look at one another in amazement.*)

THE MANAGER. But what do you mean? Before, you said . . .

THE FATHER. No, excuse me, I meant it for you, sir, who were crying out that you had no time to lose with madmen, while no one better than yourself knows that nature uses the instrument of human fantasy in order to pursue her high creative purpose.

THE MANAGER. Very well,—but where does all this take us?

THE FATHER. Nowhere! It is merely to show you that one is born to life in many forms, in many shapes, as tree, or as stone, as water, as butterfly, or as woman. So one may also be born a character in a play.

THE MANAGER (*with feigned comic dismay*). So you and these other friends of yours have been born characters?

THE FATHER. Exactly, and alive as you see!
(MANAGER *and actors burst out laughing.*)

THE FATHER (*hurt*). I am sorry you laugh, because we carry in us a drama, as you can guess from this woman here veiled in black.

THE MANAGER (*losing his patience at last and almost indignant*). Oh, chuck it! Get away please! Clear out of here! (*To* PROPERTY MAN) For Heaven's sake, turn them out!

THE FATHER (*resisting*). No, no, look here, we . . .

THE MANAGER (*roaring*). We come here to work, you know.

LEADING ACTOR. One cannot let one-self be made such a fool of.

THE FATHER (*determined, coming forward*). I marvel at your incredulity, gentlemen. Are you not accustomed to see the characters created by an author spring to life in yourselves and face each other? Just because there is no "book" (*pointing to the* PROMPTER's *box*) which contains us, you refuse to believe . . .

THE STEP-DAUGHTER (*advances towards* MANAGER, *smiling and coquettish*). Believe me, we are really six most interesting characters, sir; side-tracked however.

THE FATHER. Yes, that is the word! (*To* MANAGER *all at once*) In the sense, that is, that the author who created us alive no longer wished, or was no longer able, materially to put us into a work of art. And this was a real crime, sir; because he who has had the luck to be born a character can laugh even at death. He cannot die. The man, the writer, the instrument of the creation will die, but his creation does not die.

And to live for ever, it does not need to have extraordinary gifts or to be able to work wonders. Who was Sancho Panza? Who was Don Abbondio? Yet they live eternally because—live germs as they were —they had the fortune to find a fecundating matrix, a fantasy which could raise and nourish them: make them live forever!

THE MANAGER. That is quite all right. But what do you want here, all of you?

THE FATHER. We want to live.

THE MANAGER (*ironically*). For Eternity?

THE FATHER. No, sir, only for a moment . . . in you.

AN ACTOR. Just listen to him!

LEADING LADY. They want to live, in us . . . !

JUVENILE LEAD (*pointing to* THE STEP-DAUGHTER). I've no objection, as far as that one is concerned!

THE FATHER. Look here! look here! The comedy has to be made. (*To* THE MANAGER): But if you and your actors are willing, we can soon concert it among ourselves.

THE MANAGER (*annoyed*). But what do you want to concert? We don't go in for concerts here. Here we play dramas and comedies!

THE FATHER. Exactly! That is just why we have come to you.

THE MANAGER. And where is the "book"?

THE FATHER. It is in us! (*The actors laugh*) The drama is in us, and we are the drama. We are impatient to play it. Our inner passion drives us on to this.

THE STEP-DAUGHTER (*disdainful, alluring, treacherous, full of impudence*). My passion, sir! Ah, if you only knew! My passion for him! (*Points to* THE FATHER *and makes a pretence of embracing him. Then she breaks out into a loud laugh.*)

THE FATHER (*angrily*). Behave yourself! And please don't laugh in that fashion.

THE STEP-DAUGHTER. With your permission, gentlemen, I, who am a two months' orphan, will show you how I can dance and sing. (*Sings and then dances* Prenez garde à Tchou-Thin-Tchou.)

Les chinois sont un peuple malin,
De Shangaî à Pekin,
Ils ont mis des écriteux partout:
Prenez garde à Tchou-Thin-Tchou.

ACTORS AND ACTRESSES. Bravo! Well done! Tip-top!

THE MANAGER. Silence! This isn't a café concert, you know! (*Turning to* THE FATHER *in consternation*): Is she mad?

THE FATHER. Mad? No, she's worse than mad.

THE STEP-DAUGHTER (*to* MANAGER). Worse? Worse? Listen! Stage this drama for us at once! Then you will see that at a certain moment I . . . when this little darling here . . . (*Takes* THE CHILD *by the hand and leads her to* THE MANAGER) Isn't she a dear? (*Takes her up and kisses her*) Darling! Darling! (*Puts her down again and adds feelingly*) Well, when God suddenly takes this dear little child away from that poor mother there; and this imbecile here (*seizing hold of* THE BOY *roughly and pushing him forward*) does the stupidest things, like the fool he is, you will see me run away. Yes, gentlemen, I shall be off. But the moment hasn't arrived yet. After what has taken place between him and me (*indicates* THE FATHER *with a horrible wink*), I can't remain any longer in this society, to have to witness the anguish of this mother here for that fool . . . (*Indicates* THE SON) Look at him! Look at him! See how indifferent, how frigid he is, because he is the legitimate son. He despises me, despises him (*pointing to* THE BOY), despises this baby here; because . . . we are bastards. (*Goes to* THE MOTHER *and embraces her*) And he doesn't want to recognize her as his mother —she who is the common mother of us all. He looks down upon her as if she were only the mother of us three bastards. Wretch! (*She says all this very rapidly, excitedly. At the word "bastards" she raises her voice, and almost spits out the final "Wretch!"*)

THE MOTHER (*to* THE MANAGER, *in anguish*). In the name of these two little children, I beg you . . . (*She grows faint and is about to fall*) Oh God!

THE FATHER (*coming forward to support her as do some of the actors*). Quick, a chair, a chair for this poor widow!

THE ACTORS. Is it true? Has she really fainted?

THE MANAGER. Quick, a chair! Here!

(*One of the actors brings a chair, the others proffer assistance.* THE MOTHER *tries to prevent* THE FATHER *from lifting the veil which covers her face.*)

THE FATHER. Look at her! Look at her!

THE MOTHER. No, no; stop it please!

THE FATHER (*raising her veil*). Let them see you!

THE MOTHER (*rising and covering her face with her hands, in desperation*). I beg you, sir, to prevent this man from carrying out his plan which is loathsome to me.

THE MANAGER (*dumbfounded*). I don't understand at all. What is the situation? Is this lady your wife? (*To* THE FATHER.)

THE FATHER. Yes, gentlemen: my wife!

THE MANAGER. But how can she be a widow if you are alive? (THE ACTORS *find relief for their astonishment in a loud laugh.*)

THE FATHER. Don't laugh! Don't laugh like that, for Heaven's sake. Her drama lies just here in this: she has had a lover, a man who ought to be here.

THE MOTHER (*with a cry*). No! No!

THE STEP-DAUGHTER. Fortunately for her, he is dead. Two months ago as I said. We are in mourning, as you see.

THE FATHER. He isn't here you see, not because he is dead. He isn't here—look at her a moment and you will understand—because her drama isn't a drama of the love of two men for whom she was incapable of feeling anything except possibly a little gratitude—gratitude not for me but for the other. She isn't a woman, she is a mother, and her drama—powerful sir, I assure you—lies, as a matter of fact, all in these four children she has had by two men.

THE MOTHER. I had them? Have you got the courage to say that I wanted them? (*To the Company*) It was his doing. It was he who gave me that other man, who forced me to go away with him.

THE STEP-DAUGHTER. It isn't true.

THE MOTHER (*startled*). Not true, isn't it?

THE STEP-DAUGHTER. No, it isn't true, it just isn't true.

THE MOTHER. And what can you know about it?

THE STEP-DAUGHTER. It isn't true Don't believe it. (*To* MANAGER) Do you know why she says so? For that fellow there. (*Indicates* THE SON) She tortures herself, destroys herself on account of the neglect of that son there; and she wants him to believe that if she abandoned him when he was only two years old, it was because he (*indicates* THE FATHER) made her do so.

THE MOTHER (*vigorously*). He forced me to it, and I call God to witness it. (*To* THE MANAGER) Ask him (*indicates husband*) if it isn't true. Let him speak. You (*to daughter*) are not in a position to know anything about it.

THE STEP-DAUGHTER. I know you lived in peace and happiness with my father while he lived. Can you deny it?

THE MOTHER. No, I don't deny it . . .

THE STEP-DAUGHTER. He was always full of affection and kindness for you. (*To* THE BOY, *angrily*) It's true, isn't it? Tell them! Why don't you speak, you little fool?

THE MOTHER. Leave the poor boy alone. Why do you want to make me appear ungrateful, daughter? I don't want to offend your father. I have answered him that I didn't abandon my house and my son through any fault of mine, nor from any wilful passion.

THE FATHER. It is true. It was my doing.

LEADING MAN (*to the Company*). What a spectacle!

LEADING LADY. We are the audience this time.

JUVENILE LEAD. For once, in a way.

THE MANAGER (*beginning to get really interested*). Let's hear them out. Listen!

THE SON. Oh yes, you're going to hear a fine bit now. He will talk to you of the Demon of Experiment.

THE FATHER. You are a cynical imbecile. I've told you so already a hundred times. (*To* THE MANAGER) He tries to make fun of me on account of this expression which I have found to excuse myself with.

THE SON (*with disgust*). Yes, phrases! phrases!

THE FATHER. Phrases! Isn't everyone consoled when faced with a trouble or fact he doesn't understand, by a word, some simple word, which tells us nothing and yet calms us?

THE STEP-DAUGHTER. Even in the case of remorse. In fact, especially then.

THE FATHER. Remorse? No, that isn't true. I've done more than use words to quieten the remorse in me.

THE STEP-DAUGHTER. Yes, there was a bit of money too. Yes, yes, a bit of money. There were the hundred lire he was about to offer me in payment, gentlemen . . . (*Sensation of horror among* THE ACTORS.)

THE SON (*to* THE STEP-DAUGHTER). This is vile.

THE STEP-DAUGHTER. Vile? There they were in a pale blue envelope on a little mahogany table in the back of Madame Pace's shop. You know Madame Pace—one of those ladies who attract poor girls of good family into their ateliers, under the pretext of their selling *robes et manteaux*.

THE SON. And he thinks he has bought the right to tyrannize over us all with those hundred lire he was going to pay; but which, fortunately—note this, gentlemen—he had no chance of paying.

THE STEP-DAUGHTER. It was a near thing, though, you know! (*Laughs ironically.*)

THE MOTHER (*protesting*). Shame, my daughter, shame!

THE STEP-DAUGHTER. Shame indeed! This is my revenge! I am dying to live that scene . . . The room . . . I see it . . . Here is the window with the mantles exposed, there the divan, the looking-glass, a screen, there in front of the window the little mahogany table with the blue envelope containing one hundred lire. I see it. I see it. I could take hold of it . . . But you, gentlemen, you ought to turn your backs now: I am almost nude, you know. But I don't blush: I leave that to him. (*Indicating* FATHER.)

THE MANAGER. I don't understand this at all.

THE FATHER. Naturally enough. I would ask you, sir, to exercise your authority a little here, and let me speak before you believe all she is trying to blame me with. Let me explain.

THE STEP-DAUGHTER. Ah yes, explain it in your own way.

THE FATHER. But don't you see that the whole trouble lies here. In words, words. Each one of us has within him a whole world of things, each man of us his own special world. And how can we ever come to an understanding if I put in the words I utter the sense and value of things as I see them; while you who listen to me must inevitably translate them according to the conception of things each one of you has within himself. We think we understand each other, but we never really do. Look here! This woman (*indicating* THE MOTHER) takes all my pity for her as a specially ferocious form of cruelty.

THE MOTHER. But you drove me away.

THE FATHER. Do you hear her? I drove her away! She believes I really sent here away.

THE MOTHER. You know how to talk, and I don't; but, believe me sir, (*to* MANAGER) after he had married me . . . who knows why? . . . I was a poor insignificant woman . . .

THE FATHER. But, good Heavens! it was just for your humility that I married you. I loved this simplicity in you. (*He stops when he sees she makes signs to contradict him, opens his arms wide in signs of desperation, seeing how hopeless it is to make himself understood*) You see she denies it. Her mental deafness, believe me, is phenomenal, the limit (*touches his forehead*): deaf, deaf, mentally deaf! She has plenty of feeling. Oh yes, a good heart for the children; but the brain—deaf, to the point of desperation——!

THE STEP-DAUGHTER. Yes, but ask him how his intelligence has helped us.

THE FATHER. If we could see all the evil that may spring from good, what should we do?

(*At this point the* LEADING LADY *who is biting her lips with rage at seeing the* LEADING MAN *flirting with* THE STEP-DAUGHTER, *comes forward and says to* THE MANAGER.)

LEADING LADY. Excuse me, but are we going to rehearse today?

MANAGER. Of course, of course; but let's hear them out.

JUVENILE LEAD. This is something quite new.

L'INGÉNUE. Most interesting!

LEADING LADY. Yes, for the people who like that kind of thing. (*Casts a glance at* LEADING MAN.)

THE MANAGER (*to* FATHER). You must please explain yourself quite clearly. (*Sits down.*)

THE FATHER. Very well then: listen! I had in my service a poor man, a clerk, a secretary of mine, full of devotion, who became friends with her. (*Indicating* THE MOTHER) They understood one another, were kindred souls in fact, without, however, the least suspicion of any evil existing. They were incapable even of thinking of it.

THE STEP-DAUGHTER. So he thought of it—for them!

THE FATHER. That's not true. I meant to do good to them—and to myself, I confess, at the same time. Things had come to the point that I could not say a word to either of them without their making a mute appeal, one to the other, with their eyes. I could see them silently asking each other how I was to be kept in countenance, how I was to be kept quiet. And this, believe me, was just about enough of itself to keep me in a constant rage, to exasperate me beyond measure.

THE MANAGER. And why didn't you send him away then—this secretary of yours?

THE FATHER. Precisely what I did, sir. And then I had to watch this poor woman drifting forlornly about the house like an animal without a master, like an animal one has taken in out of pity.

THE MOTHER. Ah yes . . . !

THE FATHER (*suddenly turning to* THE MOTHER). It's true about the son anyway, isn't it?

THE MOTHER. He took my son away from me first of all.

THE FATHER. But not from cruelty. I did it so that he should grow up healthy and strong by living in the country.

THE STEP-DAUGHTER (*pointing to him ironically*). As one can see.

THE FATHER (*quickly*). Is it my fault if he has grown up like this? I sent him to a wet nurse in the country, a peasant, as *she* did not seem to me strong enough, though she is of humble origin. That was, anyway, the reason I married her. Unpleasant all this may be, but how can it be helped? My mistake possibly, but there we are! All my life I have had these confounded aspirations towards a certain moral sanity. (*At this point* THE STEP-DAUGHTER *bursts out into a noisy laugh*) Oh, stop, it! Stop it! I can't stand it.

THE MANAGER. Yes, please stop it, for Heaven's sake.

THE STEP-DAUGHTER. But imagine moral sanity from him, if you please —the client of certain ateliers like that of Madame Pace!

THE FATHER. Fool! That is the proof that I am a man! This seeming contradiction, gentlemen, is the strongest proof that I stand here a live man before you. Why, it is just for this very incongruity in my nature that I have had to suffer what I have. I could not live by the side of that woman (*indicating* THE MOTHER) any longer; but not so much for the boredom she inspired me with as for the pity I felt for her.

THE MOTHER. And so he turned me out—.

THE FATHER. —well provided for! Yes, I sent her to that man, gentlemen . . . to let her go free of me.

THE MOTHER. And to free himself.

THE FATHER. Yes, I admit it. It was also a liberation for me. But great evil has come of it. I meant well when I did it; and I did it more for her sake than mine. I swear it. (*Crosses his arms on his chest; then turns suddenly to* THE MOTHER) Did I ever lose sight of you until that other man carried you off to another town, like the angry fool he was? And on account of my pure interest in you . . . my pure interest, I repeat, that had no base motive in it . . . I watched with the tenderest concern the new family that grew up around her. She can bear witness to this. (*Points to* THE STEP-DAUGHTER.)

THE STEP-DAUGHTER. Oh, yes, that's true enough. When I was a kiddie, so, so high, you know, with plaits over my shoulders and knickers longer than my skirts, I used to see him waiting outside the school for me to come out. He came to see how I was growing up.

THE FATHER. This is infamous, shameful!

THE STEP-DAUGHTER. No, Why?

THE FATHER. Infamous! infamous! (*Then excitedly to* MANAGER *explaining*) After she (*indicating* MOTHER) went away, my house seemed suddenly empty. She was my incubus, but she filled my house. I was like a dazed fly alone in the empty rooms. This boy here (*indicating* THE SON) was educated away from home, and when he came back, he seemed to me to be no more mine. With no mother to stand between him and me, he grew up entirely for himself, on his own, apart, with no tie of intellect or affection binding him to me. And then—strange but true—I was driven, by curiosity at first and then by some tender sentiment, towards her family, which had come into being through my will. The thought of her began gradually to fill up the emptiness I felt all around me. I wanted to know if she were happy in living out the simple daily duties of life. I wanted to think of her as fortunate and happy because far away from the complicated torments of my spirit. And so, to have proof of this, I used to watch that child coming out of school.

THE STEP-DAUGHTER. Yes, yes. True. He used to follow me in the street and smiled at me, waved his hand, like this. I would look at him with interest, wondering who he might be. I told my mother, who guessed at once. (THE MOTHER *agrees with a nod*) Then she didn't want to send me to school for some days; and when I finally went back, there he was again—looking so ridiculous—with a paper parcel in his hands. He came close to me, caressed me, and drew out a fine straw hat from the parcel, with a bouquet of flowers—all for me!

THE MANAGER. A bit discursive this, you know!

THE SON (*contemptuously*). Literature! Literature!

THE FATHER. Literature indeed! This is life, this is passion!

THE MANAGER. It may be, but it won't act.

THE FATHER. I agree. This is only the part leading up. I don't suggest this should be staged. She (*pointing to* THE STEP-DAUGHTER), as you see, is no longer the flapper with plaits down her back—.

THE STEP-DAUGHTER. —and the knickers showing below the skirt!

THE FATHER. The drama is coming now, sir; something new, complex, most interesting.

THE STEP-DAUGHTER. As soon as my father died . . .

THE FATHER. —there was absolute misery for them. They came back here, unknown to me. Through her stupidity! (*Pointing to* THE MOTHER) It is true she can barely write her own name; but she could anyhow have got her daughter to write to me that they were in need . . .

THE MOTHER. And how was I to divine all this sentiment in him?

THE FATHER. That is exactly your mistake, never to have guessed any of my sentiments.

THE MOTHER. After so many years apart, and all that had happened . . .

THE FATHER. Was it my fault if that fellow carried you away? It happened quite suddenly; for after he had obtained some job or other, I could find no trace of them; and so, not unnaturally, my interest in them dwindled. But the drama culminated unforeseen and violent on their return, when I was impelled by my miserable flesh that still lives . . . Ah! what misery, what wretchedness is that of the man who is alone and disdains debasing *liaisons!* Not old enough to do without women, and not young enough to go and look for one without shame. Misery? It's worse than misery; it's a horror; for no woman can any longer give him love; and when a man feels this . . . One ought to do without, you say? Yes, yes, I know. Each of us when he appears before his fellows is clothed in a certain dignity. But every man knows what unconfessable things pass within the secrecy of his own heart. One gives way to the temptation, only to rise from it again, afterwards, with a great eagerness to reestablish one's dignity, as if it were a tombstone to place on the grave of one's shame, and a monument to hide the sign and memory of our weaknesses. Everybody's in the same case. Some folks haven't the courage to say certain things, that's all!

THE STEP-DAUGHTER. All appear to have the courage to do them though.

THE FATHER. Yes, but in secret. Therefore, you want more courage to say these things. Let a man but speak these things out, and folks at once label him a cynic. But it isn't true. He is like all the others, better indeed, because he isn't afraid to reveal with the light of the intelligence the red shame of human bestiality on which most men close their eyes so as not to see it. Woman—for example, look at her case! She turns tantalizing inviting glances on you. You seize her. No sooner does she feel herself in your grasp than she closes her eyes. It is the sign of her mission, the sign by which she says to man: "Blind yourself, for I am blind."

THE STEP-DAUGHTER. Sometimes she can close them no more: when she no longer feels the need of hiding her shame to herself, but dry-eyed and dispassionately, sees only that of the man who has blinded himself without love. Oh, all these intellectual complications make me sick, disgust me—all this philosophy that uncovers the beast in man, and then seeks to save him, excuse him . . . I can't stand it, sir. When a man seeks to "simplify" life bestially, throwing aside every relic of humanity, every chaste aspiration, every pure feeling, all sense of ideality, duty, modesty, shame . . . then nothing is more revolting and nauseous than a cer-

tain kind of remorse—crocodiles' tears, that's what it is.

THE MANAGER. Let's come to the point. This is only discussion.

THE FATHER. Very good, sir! But a fact is like a sack which won't stand up when it is empty. In order that it may stand up, one has to put into it the reason and sentiment which have caused it to exist. I couldn't possibly know that after the death of that man, they had decided to return here, that they were in misery, and that she (*pointing to* THE MOTHER) had gone to work as a modiste, and at a shop of the type of that of Madame Pace.

THE STEP-DAUGHTER. A real high-class modiste, you must know, gentlemen. In appearance, she works for the leaders of the best society; but she arranges matters so that these elegant ladies serve her purpose . . . without prejudice to other ladies who are . . . well . . . only so-so.

THE MOTHER. You will believe me, gentlemen, that it never entered my mind that the old hag offered me work because she had her eye on my daughter.

THE STEP-DAUGHTER. Poor mamma! Do you know, sir, what that woman did when I brought her back the work my mother had finished? She would point out to me that I had torn one of my frocks, and she would give it back to my mother to mend. It was I who paid for it, always I; while this poor creature here believed she was sacrificing herself for me and these two children here, sitting up at night sewing Madame Pace's robes.

THE MANAGER. And one day you met there . . .

THE STEP-DAUGHTER. Him, him. Yes sir, an old client. There's a scene for you to play! Superb!

THE FATHER. She, the Mother, arrived just then . . .

THE STEP-DAUGHTER (*treacherously*). Almost in time!

THE FATHER (*crying out*). No, in time! in time! Fortunately I recognized her . . . in time. And I took them back home with me to my house. You can imagine now her position and mine: she, as you see her; and I who cannot look her in the face.

THE STEP-DAUGHTER. Absurd! How can I possibly be expected—after that—to be a modest young miss, a fit person to go with his confounded aspirations for "a solid moral sanity"?

THE FATHER. For the drama lies all in this—in the conscience that I have, that each one of us has. We believe this conscience to be a single thing, but it is many-sided. There is one for this person, and another for that. Diverse consciences. So we have this illusion of being one person for all, of having a personality that is unique in all our acts. But it isn't true. We perceive this when, tragically perhaps, in something we do, we are as it were suspended, caught up in the air on a kind of hook. Then we perceive that all of us was not in that act, and that it would be an atrocious injustice to judge us by that action alone, as if all our existence were summed up in that one

deed. Now do you understand the perfidy of this girl? She surprised me in a place, where she ought not to have known me, just as I could not exist for her; and she now seeks to attach to me a reality such as I could never suppose I should have to assume for her in a shameful and fleeting moment of my life. I feel this above all else. And the drama, you will see, acquires a tremendous value from this point. Then there is the position of the others . . . his. . . . (*Indicating* THE SON.)

THE SON (*shrugging his shoulders scornfully*). Leave me alone! I don't come into this.

THE FATHER. What? You don't come into this?

THE SON. I've got nothing to do with it, and don't want to have; because you know well enough I wasn't made to be mixed up in all this with the rest of you.

THE STEP-DAUGHTER. We are only vulgar folk! He is the fine gentleman. You may have noticed, Mr. Manager, that I fix him now and again with a look of scorn while he lowers his eyes—for he knows the evil he has done me.

THE SON (*scarcely looking at her*). I?

THE STEP-DAUGHTER. You! you! I owe my life on the streets to you. Did you or did you not deny us, with your behaviour, I won't say the intimacy of home, but even that mere hospitality which makes guests feel at their ease? We were intruders who had come to disturb the kingdom of your legitimacy. I should like to have you witness,

Mr. Manager, certain scenes between him and me. He says I have tyrannized over everyone. But it was just his behaviour which made me insist on the reason for which I had come into the house,—this reason he calls "vile"—into his house, with my mother who is his mother too. And I came as mistress of the house.

THE SON. It's easy for them to put me always in the wrong. But imagine, gentlemen, the position of a son, whose fate it is to see arrive one day at his home a young woman of impudent bearing, a young woman who inquires for his father, with whom who knows what business she has. This young man has then to witness her return bolder than ever, accompanied by that child there. He is obliged to watch her treat his father in an equivocal and confidential manner. She asks money of him in a way that lets one suppose he must give it her, *must*, do you understand, because he has every obligation to do so.

THE FATHER. But I have, as a matter of fact, this obligation. I owe it to your mother.

THE SON. How should I know? When had I ever seen or heard of her? One day there arrive with her (*indicating* STEP-DAUGHTER) that lad and this baby here. I am told: "This is *your* mother too, you know." I divine from her manner (*indicating* STEP-DAUGHTER *again*) why it is they have come home. I had rather not say what I feel and think about it. I shouldn't even care to confess to myself. No action can therefore be hoped for from me in this affair. Believe me, Mr.

Manager, I am an "unrealized" character, dramatically speaking; and I find myself not at all at ease in their company. Leave me out of it, I beg you.

THE FATHER. What? It is just because you are so that . . .

THE SON. How do you know what I am like? When did you ever bother your head about me?

THE FATHER. I admit it. I admit it. But isn't that a situation in itself? This aloofness of yours which is so cruel to me and to your mother, who returns home and sees you almost for the first time grown up, who doesn't recognize you but knows you are her son . . . (*Pointing out* THE MOTHER *to* THE MANAGER) See, she's crying!

THE STEP-DAUGHTER (*angrily, stamping her foot*). Like a fool!

THE FATHER (*indicating* STEP-DAUGHTER). She can't stand him you know. (*Then referring again to* THE SON) He says he doesn't come into the affair, whereas he is really the hinge of the whole action. Look at that lad who is always clinging to his mother, frightened and humiliated. It is on account of this fellow here. Possibly his situation is the most painful of all. He feels himself a stranger more than the others. The poor little chap feels mortified, humiliated at being brought into a home out of charity as it were. (*In confidence*) He is the image of his father. Hardly talks at all. Humble and quiet.

THE MANAGER. Oh, we'll cut him out. You've no notion what a nuisance boys are on the stage . . .

THE FATHER. He disappears soon, you know. And the baby too. She is the first to vanish from the scene. The drama consists finally in this: when that mother re-enters my house, her family born outside of it, and shall we say superimposed on the original, ends with the death of the little girl, the tragedy of the boy and the flight of the elder daughter. It cannot go on, because it is foreign to its surroundings. So after much torment, we three remain: I, the mother, that son. Then, owing to the disappearance of that extraneous family, we too find ourselves strange to one another. We find we are living in an atmosphere of mortal desolation which is the revenge, as he (*indicating* SON) scornfully said of the Demon of Experiment, that unfortunately hides in me. Thus, sir, you see when faith is lacking, it becomes impossible to create certain states of happiness, for we lack the necessary humility. Vaingloriously, we try to substitute ourselves for this faith, creating thus for the rest of the world a reality which we believe after their fashion, while, actually, it doesn't exist. For each one of us has his own reality to be respected before God, even when it is harmful to one's very self.

THE MANAGER. There is something in what you say. I assure you all this interests me very much. I begin to think there's the stuff for a drama in all this, and not a bad drama either.

THE STEP-DAUGHTER (*coming forward*). When you've got a character like me.

THE FATHER (*shutting her up, all excited to learn the decision of* THE MANAGER). You be quiet!

THE MANAGER (*reflecting, heedless of interruption*). It's new . . . hem . . . yes . . .

THE FATHER. Absolutely new!

THE MANAGER. You've got a nerve though, I must say, to come here and fling it at me like this . . .

THE FATHER. You will understand, sir, born as we are for the stage . . .

THE MANAGER. Are you amateur actors then?

THE FATHER. No. I say born for the stage, because . . .

THE MANAGER. Oh, nonsense. You're an old hand, you know.

THE FATHER. No sir, no. We act that rôle for which we have been cast, that rôle which we are given in life. And in my own case, passion itself, as usually happens, becomes a trifle theatrical when it is exalted.

THE MANAGER. Well, well, that will do. But you see, without an author . . . I could give you the address of an author if you like . . .

THE FATHER. No, no. Look here! You must be the author.

THE MANAGER. I? What are you talking about?

THE FATHER. Yes, you, you! Why not?

THE MANAGER. Because I have never been an author: that's why.

THE FATHER. Then why not turn author now? Everybody does it. You don't want any special qualities. Your task is made much easier by the fact that we are all here alive before you . . .

THE MANAGER. It won't do.

THE FATHER. What? When you see us live our drama . . .

THE MANAGER. Yes, that's all right. But you want someone to write it.

THE FATHER. No, no. Someone to take it down, possibly, while we play it, scene by scene! It will be enough to sketch it out at first, and then try it over.

THE MANAGER. Well . . . I am almost tempted. It's a bit of an idea. One might have a shot at it.

THE FATHER. Of course. You'll see what scenes will come out of it. I can give you one, at once . . .

THE MANAGER. By Jove, it tempts me. I'd like to have a go at it. Let's try it out. Come with me to my office. (*Turning to* THE ACTORS) You are at liberty for a bit, but don't stop out of the theatre for long. In a quarter of an hour, twenty minutes, all back here again! (*To* THE FATHER) We'll see what can be done. Who knows if we don't get something really extraordinary out of it?

THE FATHER. There's no doubt about it. They (*indicating* THE CHARACTERS) had better come with us too, hadn't they?

THE MANAGER. Yes, yes. Come on! come on! (*Moves away and then turning to* THE ACTORS) Be punctual, please! (MANAGER *and the* SIX CHARACTERS *cross the stage and go off. The other* ACTORS *remain, looking at one another in astonishment.*)

LEADING MAN. Is he serious? What the devil does he want to do?

JUVENILE LEAD. This is rank madness.

THIRD ACTOR. Does he expect to knock up a drama in five minutes?

JUVENILE LEAD. Like the improvisers!

LEADING LADY. If he thinks I'm going to take part in a joke like this . . .

JUVENILE LEAD. I'm out of it anyway.

FOURTH ACTOR. I should like to know who they are. (*Alludes to* CHARACTERS.)

THIRD ACTOR. What do you suppose? Madmen or rascals!

JUVENILE LEAD. And he takes them seriously!

L'INGÉNUE. Vanity! He fancies himself as an author now.

LEADING MAN. It's absolutely unheard of. If the stage has come to this . . . well I'm . . .

FIFTH ACTOR. It's rather a joke.

THIRD ACTOR. Well, we'll see what's going to happen next. (*Thus talking,* THE ACTORS *leave the stage; some going out by the little door at the back; others retiring to their dressing-rooms. The curtain remains up. The action of the play is suspended for twenty minutes.)*

ACT TWO

The stage call-bells ring to warn the company that the play is about to begin again.

THE STEP-DAUGHTER (*comes out of* THE MANAGER'S *office along with* THE CHILD *and* THE BOY. *As she comes out of the office, she cries*)— Nonsense! nonsense! Do it yourselves! I'm not going to mix myself up in this mess. (*Turning to* THE CHILD *and coming quickly with her onto the stage*) Come on, Rosetta, let's run!

(THE BOY *follows them slowly, remaining a little behind and seeming perplexed.*)

THE STEP-DAUGHTER (*stops, bends over* THE CHILD *and takes the latter's face between her hands*). My little darling! You're frightened, aren't you? You don't know where we are, do you? (*Pretending to reply to a question of* THE CHILD) What is the stage? It's a place, baby, you know, where people play at being serious, a place where they act comedies. We've got to act a comedy now, dead serious, you know; and you're in it also, little one. (*Embraces her, pressing the little head to her breast, and rocking* THE CHILD *for a moment*) Oh darling, darling, what a horrid comedy you've got to play! What a wretched part they've found for you! A garden . . . a fountain . . . look . . . just suppose, kiddie, it's here. Where, you say? Why,

right here in the middle. It's all pretence you know. That's the trouble, my pet: it's all make-believe here. It's better to imagine it though, because if they fix it up for you, it'll only be painted cardboard, painted cardboard for the rockery, the water, the plants . . . Ah, but I think a baby like this one would sooner have a make-believe fountain than a real one, so she could play with it. What a joke it'll be for the others! But for you, alas! not quite such a joke: you who are real, baby dear, and really play by a real fountain that is big and green and beautiful, with ever so many bamboos around it that are reflected in the water, and a whole lot of little ducks swimming about . . . No, Rosetta, no, your mother doesn't bother about you on account of that wretch of a son there. I'm in the devil of a temper, and as for that lad . . . (*Seizes* BOY *by the arm to force him to take one of his hands out of his pockets*) What have you got there? What are you hiding? (*Pulls his hand out of his pocket, looks into it and catches the glint of a revolver*) Ah! where did you get this? (THE BOY, *very pale in the face, looks at her, but does not answer*) Idiot! If I'd been in your place, instead of killing myself, I'd have shot one of those two, or both of them: father and son.

(THE FATHER *enters from the office, all excited from his work.* THE MANAGER *follows him.*)

THE FATHER. Come on, come on, dear! Come here for a minute! We've arranged everything. It's all fixed up.

THE MANAGER (*also excited*). If you please, young lady, there are one or two points to settle still. Will you come along?

THE STEP-DAUGHTER (*following him towards the office*). Ouff! what's the good, if you've arranged everything.

(THE FATHER, MANAGER *and* STEP-DAUGHTER *go back into the office again [off] for a moment. At the same time,* THE SON *followed by* THE MOTHER, *comes out.*)

THE SON (*looking at the three entering office*). Oh this is fine, fine! And to think I can't even get away!

(THE MOTHER *attempts to look at him, but lowers her eyes immediately when he turns away from her. She then sits down.* THE BOY *and* THE CHILD *approach her. She casts a glance again at* THE SON, *and speaks with humble tones, trying to draw him into conversation.*)

THE MOTHER. And isn't my punishment the worst of all? (*Then seeing from* THE SON's *manner that he will not bother himself about her*) My God! Why are you so cruel? Isn't it enough for one person to support all this torment? Must you then insist on others seeing it also?

THE SON (*half to himself, meaning* THE MOTHER *to hear, however*). And they want to put it on the stage! If there was at least a reason for it! He thinks he has got at the meaning of it all. Just as if each one of us in every circumstance of life couldn't find his own explanation of it! (*Pauses*) He complains he was discovered in a place where he ought not to have been seen, in a moment of his life which ought to have remained hidden and kept out of the reach of that convention which he has to maintain for other people. And what about my case? Haven't I had to reveal what no son ought ever to reveal: how father and mother live and are man and wife for themselves quite apart from that idea of father and mother which we give them? When this idea is revealed, our life is then linked at one point only to that man and that woman; and as such it should shame them, shouldn't it? (THE MOTHER *hides her face in her hands. From the dressing-rooms and the little door at the back of the stage* THE ACTORS *and* STAGE MANAGER *return, followed by the* PROPERTY MAN, *and the* PROMPTER. *At the same moment,* THE MANAGER *comes out of his office, accompanied by* THE FATHER *and* THE STEP-DAUGHTER.)

THE MANAGER. Come on, come on, ladies and gentlemen! Heh! you there, machinist!

MACHINIST. Yes sir?

THE MANAGER. Fix up the white parlor with the floral decorations. Two wings and a drop with a door will do. Hurry up!

(THE MACHINIST *runs off at once to prepare the scene, and arranges it while* THE MANAGER *talks with the* STAGE MANAGER, *the* PROPERTY MAN, *and the* PROMPTER *on matters of detail.*)

THE MANAGER (*to* PROPERTY MAN). Just have a look, and see if there isn't a sofa or divan in the wardrobe . . .

PROPERTY MAN. There's the green one.

THE STEP-DAUGHTER. No no! Green won't do. It was yellow, ornamented with flowers—very large! and most comfortable!

PROPERTY MAN. There isn't one like that.

THE MANAGER. It doesn't matter. Use the one we've got.

THE STEP-DAUGHTER. Doesn't matter? It's most important!

THE MANAGER. We're only trying it now. Please don't interfere. (*To* PROPERTY MAN) See if we've got a shop window—long and narrowish.

THE STEP-DAUGHTER. And the little table! The little mahogany table for the pale blue envelope!

PROPERTY MAN (*to* MANAGER). There's that little gilt one.

THE MANAGER. That'll do fine.

THE FATHER. A mirror.

THE STEP-DAUGHTER. And the screen! We must have a screen. Otherwise how can I manage?

PROPERTY MAN. That's all right, Miss. We've got any amount of them.

THE MANAGER (*to* THE STEP-DAUGHTER). We want some clothes pegs too, don't we?

THE STEP-DAUGHTER. Yes, several, several!

THE MANAGER. See how many we've got and bring them all.

PROPERTY MAN. All right! (THE PROPERTY MAN *hurries off to obey his orders. While he is putting the things in their places,* THE MANAGER *talks to the* PROMPTER *and then with the* CHARACTERS *and the* ACTORS.)

THE MANAGER (*to* PROMPTER). Take your seat. Look here: this is the outline of the scenes, act by act. (*Hands him some sheets of paper*) And now I'm going to ask you to do something out of the ordinary.

PROMPTER. Take it down in shorthand?

THE MANAGER (*pleasantly surprised*). Exactly! Can you do shorthand?

PROMPTER. Yes, a little.

MANAGER. Good! (*Turning to a stage hand*) Go and get some paper from my office, plenty, as much as you can find. (*The stage hand goes off, and soon returns with a handful of paper which he gives to the* PROMPTER.)

THE MANAGER (*to* PROMPTER). You follow the scenes as we play them, and try and get the points down, at any rate the most important ones. (*Then addressing the* ACTORS) Clear the stage, ladies and gentlemen! Come over here (*pointing to the left*) and listen attentively.

LEADING LADY. But, excuse me, we
. . .

THE MANAGER (*guessing her thought*). Don't worry! You won't have to improvise.

LEADING MAN. What have we to do then?

THE MANAGER. Nothing. For the moment you just watch and listen. Everybody will get his part written out afterwards. At present we're going to try the thing as best we can. They're going to act now.

THE FATHER (*as if fallen from the clouds into the confusion of the stage*). We? What do you mean, if you please, by a rehearsal?

THE MANAGER. A rehearsal for them. (*Points to the ACTORS.*)

THE FATHER. But since we are the characters . . .

THE MANAGER. All right: "characters" then, if you insist on calling yourselves such. But here, my dear sir, the characters don't act. Here the actors do the acting. The characters are there, in the "book" (*pointing towards PROMPTER's box*) —when there is a "book"!

THE FATHER. I won't contradict you; but excuse me, the actors aren't the characters. They want to be, they pretend to be, don't they? Now if these gentlemen here are fortunate enough to have us alive before them . . .

THE MANAGER. Oh this is grand! You want to come before the public yourselves then?

THE FATHER. As we are . . .

THE MANAGER. I can assure you it would be a magnificent spectacle!

LEADING MAN. What's the use of us here anyway then?

THE MANAGER. You're not going to pretend that you can act? It makes me laugh! (*The ACTORS laugh*) There, you see, they are laughing at the notion. But, by the way, I must cast the parts. That won't be difficult. They cast themselves. (*To the SECOND LADY LEAD*) You play the Mother. (*To THE FATHER*) We must find her a name.

THE FATHER. Amalia, sir.

THE MANAGER. But that is the real name of your wife. We don't want to call her by her real name.

THE FATHER. Why ever not, if it is her name? . . . Still, perhaps, if that lady must . . . (*makes a slight motion of the hand to indicate the SECOND LADY LEAD*). I see this woman here (*means THE MOTHER*) as Amalia. But do as you like. (*Gets more and more confused*) I don't know what to say to you. Already, I begin to hear my own words ring false, as if they had another sound . . .

THE MANAGER. Don't you worry about it. It'll be our job to find the right tones. And as for her name, if you want her Amalia, Amalia it shall be; and if you don't like it, we'll find another! For the moment though, we'll call the characters in this way: (*to JUVENILE LEAD*) You are the Son; (*to the LEADING LADY*) You naturally are the Step-Daughter . . .

THE STEP-DAUGHTER (*excitedly*). What? what? I, that woman there? (*Bursts out laughing.*)

THE MANAGER (*angry*). What is there to laugh at?

LEADING LADY (*indignant*). Nobody has ever dared to laugh at me. I insist on being treated with respect; otherwise I go away.

THE STEP-DAUGHTER. No, no, excuse me . . . I am not laughing at you . . .

THE MANAGER (*to* STEP-DAUGHTER). You ought to feel honoured to be played by . . .

LEADING LADY (*at once, contemptuously*). "That woman there" . . .

THE STEP-DAUGHTER. But I wasn't speaking of you, you know. I was speaking of myself—whom I can't see at all in you! That is all. I don't know . . . but . . . you . . . aren't in the least like me . . .

THE FATHER. True. Here's the point. Look here, sir, our temperaments, our souls . . .

THE MANAGER. Temperament, soul, be hanged! Do you suppose the spirit of the piece is in you? Nothing of the kind!

THE FATHER. What, haven't we our own temperaments, our own souls?

THE MANAGER. Not at all. Your soul or whatever you like to call it takes shape here. The actors give body and form to it, voice and gesture. And my actors—I may tell you—have given expression to much more lofty material than this little drama of yours, which may or may not hold up on the stage. But if it does, the merit of it, believe me, will be due to my actors.

THE FATHER. I don't dare contradict you, sir; but, believe me, it is a terrible suffering for us who are as we are, with these bodies of ours, these features to see . . .

THE MANAGER (*cutting him short and out of patience*). Good heavens! The make-up will remedy all that, man, the make-up . . .

THE FATHER. Maybe. But the voice, the gestures . . .

THE MANAGER. Now, look here! On the stage, you as yourself, cannot exist. The actor here acts you, and that's an end to it!

THE FATHER. I understand. And now I think I see why our author who conceived us as we are, all alive, didn't want to put us on the stage after all. I haven't the least desire to offend your actors. Far from it! But when I think that I am to be acted by . . . I don't know by whom . . .

LEADING MAN (*on his dignity*). By me, if you've no objection!

THE FATHER (*humbly, mellifluously*). Honoured, I assure you, sir. (*Bows*) Still, I must say that try as this gentleman may, with all his good will and wonderful art, to absorb me into himself . . .

LEADING MAN. Oh chuck it! "Wonderful art!" Withdraw that, please!

THE FATHER. The performance he will give, even doing his best with make-up to look like me . . .

LEADING MAN. It will certainly be a bit difficult! (*The* ACTORS *laugh.*)

THE FATHER. Exactly! It will be difficult to act me as I really am. The effect will be rather—apart from the make-up—according as to how he supposes I am, as he senses me—if he does sense me—and not as I inside of myself feel myself to be. It seems to me then that account should be taken of this by everyone whose duty it may become to criticize us . . .

THE MANAGER. Heavens! The man's starting to think about the critics now! Let them say what they like. It's up to us to put on the play if we can. (*Looking around*) Come on! Come on! Is the stage set? (*To the* ACTORS *and* CHARACTERS) Stand back—stand back! Let me see, and don't let's lose any more time! (*To* THE STEP-DAUGHTER) Is it all right as it is now?

THE STEP-DAUGHTER. Well, to tell the truth, I don't recognize the scene.

THE MANAGER. My dear lady, you can't possibly suppose we can construct that shop of Madame Pace piece by piece here? (*To* THE FATHER) You said a white room with flowered wall paper, didn't you?

THE FATHER. Yes.

THE MANAGER. Well then. We've got the furniture right more or less. Bring that little table a bit further forward. (*The stage hands obey the order. To* PROPERTY MAN) You go and find an envelope, if possible, a pale blue one; and give it to that gentleman. (*Indicates* FATHER.)

PROPERTY MAN. An ordinary envelope?

MANAGER and FATHER. Yes, yes, an ordinary envelope.

PROPERTY MAN. At once, sir. (*Exit.*)

THE MANAGER. Ready, everyone! First scene—the Young Lady. (*The* LEADING LADY *comes forward*) No, no, you must wait. I meant her. (*Indicating* THE STEP-DAUGHTER) You just watch—

THE STEP-DAUGHTER (*adding at once*). How I shall play it, how I shall live it! . . .

LEADING LADY (*offended*). I shall live it also, you may be sure, as soon as I begin!

THE MANAGER (*with his hands to his head*). Ladies and gentlemen, if you please! No more useless discussions! Scene I: the young lady with Madame Pace: Oh! (*Looks around as if lost*) And this Madame Pace, where is she?

THE FATHER. She isn't with us, sir.

THE MANAGER. Then what the devil's to be done?

THE FATHER. But she is alive too.

THE MANAGER. Yes, but where is she?

THE FATHER. One minute. Let me speak! (*Turning to* THE ACTRESSES) If these ladies would be so good as to give me their hats for a moment . . .

THE ACTRESSES (*half surprised, half laughing, in chorus*). What? Why? Our hats? What does he say?

THE MANAGER. What are you going to do with the ladies' hats? (*The* ACTORS *laugh.*)

THE FATHER. Oh nothing. I just want to put them on these pegs for a moment. And one of the ladies will be so kind as to take off her mantle . . .

THE ACTORS. Oh, what d'you think of that? Only the mantle? He must be mad.

SOME ACTRESSES. But why? Mantles as well?

THE FATHER. To hang them up here for a moment. Please be so kind, will you?

THE ACTRESSES (*taking off their hats, one or two also their cloaks, and going to hang them on the racks*). After all, why not? There you are! This is really funny. We've got to put them on show.

THE FATHER. Exactly; just like that, on show.

THE MANAGER. May we know why?

THE FATHER. I'll tell you. Who knows if, by arranging the stage for her, she does not come here herself, attracted by the very articles of her trade? (*Inviting* THE ACTORS *to look towards the exit at back of stage*) Look! Look!
(*The door at the back of stage opens and* MADAME PACE *enters and takes a few steps forward. She is a fat, oldish woman with puffy oxygenated hair. She is rouged and powdered, dressed with a comical elegance in black silk. Round her waist is a long silver chain from which hangs a pair of scissors.* THE STEP-DAUGHTER *runs over to her at once amid the stupor of* THE ACTORS.)

THE STEP-DAUGHTER (*turning towards her*). There she is! There she is!

THE FATHER (*radiant*). It's she! I said so, didn't I? There she is!

THE MANAGER (*conquering his surprise, and then becoming indignant*). What sort of a trick is this?

LEADING MAN (*almost at the same time*). What's going to happen next?

JUVENILE LEAD. Where does *she* come from?

L'INGÉNUE. They've been holding her in reserve, I guess.

LEADING LADY. A vulgar trick!

THE FATHER (*dominating the protests*). Excuse me, all of you! Why are you so anxious to destroy in the name of a vulgar, commonplace sense of truth, this reality which comes to birth attracted and formed by the magic of the stage itself, which has indeed more right to live here than you, since it is much truer than you—if you don't mind my saying so? Which is the actress among you who is to play Madame Pace? Well, here is Madame Pace herself. And you will allow, I fancy, that the actress who acts her will be less true than this woman here, who is herself in person. You see my daughter recognized her and went over to her at once. Now you're going to witness the scene! (*But the scene between* THE STEP-DAUGHTER *and* MADAME PACE *has already begun despite the protest of* THE ACTORS *and the reply of* THE FATHER. *It has begun quietly, naturally, in a manner impossible for the stage. So when* THE ACTORS, *called to attention by* THE FATHER, *turn round and see* MADAME PACE, *who has placed one hand under* THE STEP-DAUGHTER's *chin to raise her head, they observe her at first with great attention, but hearing her speak in an unintelligible manner their interest begins to wane.*)

THE MANAGER. Well? well?

LEADING MAN. What does she say?

LEADING LADY. One can't hear a word.

JUVENILE LEAD. Louder! Louder please!

THE STEP-DAUGHTER (*leaving* MADAME PACE, *who smiles a Sphinx-like smile, and advancing towards* THE ACTORS). Louder? Louder? What are you talking about? These aren't matters which can be shouted at the top of one's voice. If I have spoken them out loud, it was to shame him and have my revenge. (*Indicates* FATHER) But for Madame it's quite a different matter.

THE MANAGER. Indeed? indeed? But here, you know, people have got to make themselves heard, my dear. Even we who are on the stage can't hear you. What will it be when the public's in the theatre? And anyway, you can very well speak up now among yourselves, since we shan't be present to listen to you as we are now. You've got to pretend to be alone in a room at the back of a shop where no one can hear you.

(THE STEP-DAUGHTER *coquettishly and with a touch of malice makes a sign of disagreement two or three times with her finger.*)

THE MANAGER. What do you mean by no?

THE STEP-DAUGHTER (*sotto voce, mysteriously*). There's someone who will hear us if she (*indicating* MADAME PACE) speaks out loud.

THE MANAGER (*in consternation*). What? Have you got someone else to spring on us now? (THE ACTORS *burst out laughing.*)

THE FATHER. No, no sir. She is alluding to me. I've got to be here— there behind that door, in waiting; and Madame Pace knows it. In fact, if you will allow me, I'll go there at once, so I can be quite ready. (*Moves away.*)

THE MANAGER (*stopping him*). No! Wait! wait! We must observe the conventions of the theatre. Before you are ready . . .

THE STEP-DAUGHTER (*interrupting him*). No, get on with it at once! I'm just dying, I tell you, to act this scene. If he's ready, I'm more than ready.

THE MANAGER (*shouting*). But, my dear young lady, first of all, we must have the scene between you and this lady. . . . (*Indicates* MADAME PACE) Do you understand? . . .

THE STEP-DAUGHTER. Good Heavens! She's been telling me what you know already: that mamma's work is badly done again, that the material's ruined; and that if I want her to continue to help us in our misery I must be patient . . .

MADAME PACE (*coming forward with an air of great importance*).

Yes indeed, sir, I no wanta take advantage of her, I no wanta be hard . . .

(*Note.* MADAME PACE *is supposed to talk in a jargon half Italian, half English.*)

THE MANAGER (*alarmed*). What? What? She talks like that?

(THE ACTORS *burst out laughing again.*)

THE STEP-DAUGHTER (*also laughing*). Yes, yes, that's the way she talks, half English, half Italian! Most comical it is!

MADAME PACE. Itta seem not verra polite gentlemen laugha atta me eef I trya best speaka English.

THE MANAGER. *Diamine!* Of course! Of course! Let her talk like that! Just what we want. Talk just like that, Madam, if you please! The effect will be certain. Exactly what was wanted to put a little comic relief into the crudity of the situation. Of course she talks like that! Magnificent!

THE STEP-DAUGHTER. Magnificent? Certainly! When certain suggestions are made to one in language of that kind, the effect is certain, since it seems almost a joke. One feels inclined to laugh when one hears her talk about an "old signore" "who wanta talka nicely with you." Nice old signore, eh, Madame?

MADAME PACE. Not so old my dear, not so old! And even if you no lika him, he won't make any scandal!

THE MOTHER (*jumping up amid the amazement and consternation of* THE ACTORS *who had not been no-* ticing her. *They move to restrain her*). You old devil! You murderess!

THE STEP-DAUGHTER (*running over to calm her* MOTHER). Calm yourself, mother, calm yourself! Please don't . . .

THE FATHER (*going to her also at the same time*). Calm yourself! Don't get excited! Sit down now!

THE MOTHER. Well then, take that woman away out of my sight!

THE STEP-DAUGHTER (*to* MANAGER). It is impossible for my mother to remain here.

THE FATHER (*to* MANAGER). They can't be here together. And for this reason, you see: that woman there was not with us when we came . . . If they are on together, the whole thing is given away inevitably, as you see.

THE MANAGER. It doesn't matter. This is only a first rough sketch— just to get an idea of the various points of the scene, even confusedly. . . . (*Turning to* THE MOTHER *and leading her to her chair*) Come along, my dear lady, sit down now, and let's get on with the scene . . .

(*Meanwhile,* THE STEP-DAUGHTER, *coming forward again, turns to* MADAME PACE.)

THE STEP-DAUGHTER. Come on, Madame, come on!

MADAME PACE (*offended*). No, no, grazie. I not do anything witha your mother present.

THE STEP-DAUGHTER. Nonsense! Introduce this "old signore" who wants to talk nicely to me. (*Addressing the company imperiously*) We've got to do this scene one way or another, haven't we? Come on! (*To* MADAME PACE) You can go!

MADAME PACE. Ah yes! I go'way! I go'way! Certainly! (*Exits furious.*)

THE STEP-DAUGHTER (*to* THE FATHER). Now you make your entry. No, you needn't go over here. Come here. Let's suppose you've already come in. Like that, yes. Out with your voice! Say "Good morning, Miss" in that peculiar tone, that special tone . . .

THE MANAGER. Excuse me, but are you the Manager, or am I? (*To* THE FATHER, *who looks undecided and perplexed*) Get on with it, man! Go down there to the back of the stage. You needn't go off. Then come right forward here. (THE FATHER *does as he is told, looking troubled and perplexed at first. But as soon as he begins to move, the reality of the action affects him, and he begins to smile and to be more natural.* THE ACTORS *watch intently.*)

THE MANAGER (*sotto voce, quickly to the* PROMPTER *in his box*). Ready! ready? Get ready to write now.

THE FATHER (*coming forward and speaking in a different tone*). Good afternoon, Miss!

THE STEP-DAUGHTER (*head bowed down slightly, with restrained disgust*). Good afternoon!

THE FATHER (*looks under her hat which partly covers her face. Perceiving she is very young, he makes an exclamation, partly of surprise, partly of fear lest he compromise himself in a risky adventure*). Ah . . . but . . . ah . . . I say . . . this is not the first time that you have come here, is it?

THE STEP-DAUGHTER (*modestly*). No sir.

THE FATHER. You've been here before, eh? (*Then seeing her nod agreement*) More than once? (*Waits for her to answer, looks under her hat, smiles, and then says*) Well then, there's no need to be so shy, is there? May I take off your hat?

THE STEP-DAUGHTER (*anticipating him and with veiled disgust*). No sir . . . I'll do it myself. (*Takes it off quickly.*)
(THE MOTHER, *who watches the progress of the scene with* THE SON *and the other two children who cling to her, is on thorns; and follows with varying expressions of sorrow, indignation, anxiety, and horror the words and actions of the other two. From time to time she hides her face in her hands and sobs.*)

THE MOTHER. Oh, my God, my God!

THE FATHER (*playing his part with a touch of gallantry*). Give it to me! I'll put it down. (*Takes hat from her hands*) But a dear little head like yours ought to have a smarter hat. Come and help me choose one from the stock, won't you?

L'INGÉNUE (*interrupting*). I say . . . those are our hats you know.

THE MANAGER (*furious*). Silence! silence! Don't try and be funny, if you please . . . We're playing the scene now, I'd have you notice. (*To* THE STEP-DAUGHTER) Begin again, please!

THE STEP-DAUGHTER (*continuing*). No thank you, sir.

THE FATHER. Oh, come now. Don't talk like that. You must take it. I shall be upset if you don't. There are some lovely little hats here; and then—Madame will be pleased. She expects it, anyway, you know.

THE STEP-DAUGHTER. No, no! I couldn't wear it!

THE FATHER. Oh, you're thinking about what they'd say at home if they saw you come in with a new hat? My dear girl, there's always a way round these little matters, you know.

THE STEP-DAUGHTER (*all keyed up*). No, it's not that. I couldn't wear it because I am . . . as you see . . . you might have noticed . . . (*Showing her black dress.*)

THE FATHER. . . . in mourning! Of course: I beg your pardon: I'm frightfully sorry . . .

THE STEP-DAUGHTER (*forcing herself to conquer her indignation and nausea*). Stop! Stop! It's I who must thank you. There's no need for you to feel mortified or specially sorry. Don't think any more of what I've said. (*Tries to smile*) I must forget that I am dressed so . . .

THE MANAGER (*interrupting and turning to the* PROMPTER). Stop a minute! Stop! Don't write that down. Cut out that last bit. (*Then* *to* THE FATHER *and* STEP-DAUGHTER) Fine! it's going fine! (*To* THE FATHER *only*) And now you can go on as we arranged. (*To* THE ACTORS) Pretty good that scene, where he offers her the hat, eh?

THE STEP-DAUGHTER. The best's coming now. Why can't we go on?

THE MANAGER. Have a little patience! (*To* THE ACTORS) Of course, it must be treated rather lightly.

LEADING MAN. Still, with a bit of go in it!

LEADING LADY. Of course! It's easy enough! (*To* LEADING MAN) Shall you and I try it now?

LEADING MAN. Why, yes! I'll prepare my entrance. (*Exit in order to make his entrance.*)

THE MANAGER (*to* LEADING LADY). See here! The scene between you and Madame Pace is finished. I'll have it written out properly after. You remain here . . . oh, where are you going?

LEADING LADY. One minute. I want to put my hat on again. (*Goes over to hat-rack and puts her hat on her head.*)

THE MANAGER. Good! You stay here with your head bowed down a bit.

THE STEP-DAUGHTER. But she isn't dressed in black.

LEADING LADY. But I shall be, and much more effectively than you.

THE MANAGER (*to* STEP-DAUGHTER). Be quiet please, and watch! You'll be able to learn something.

(*Clapping his hands*) Come on! come on! Entrance, please!

(*The door at rear of stage opens, and the* LEADING MAN *enters with the lively manner of an old gallant. The rendering of the scene by* THE ACTORS *from the very first words is seen to be quite a different thing, though it has not in any way the air of a parody. Naturally,* THE STEP-DAUGHTER *and* THE FATHER, *not being able to recognize themselves in the* LEADING LADY *and the* LEADING MAN, *who deliver their words in different tones and with a different psychology, express, sometimes with smiles, sometimes with gestures, the impression they receive.*)

LEADING MAN. Good afternoon, Miss . . .

THE FATHER (*at once unable to contain himself*). No! no!

(THE STEP-DAUGHTER, *noticing the way the* LEADING MAN *enters, bursts out laughing.*)

THE MANAGER (*furious*). Silence! And you please just stop that laughing. If we go on like this, we shall never finish.

THE STEP-DAUGHTER. Forgive me, sir, but it's natural enough. This lady (*indicating* LEADING LADY) stands there still; but if she is supposed to be me, I can assure you that if I heard anyone say "Good afternoon" in that manner and in that tone, I should burst out laughing as I did.

THE FATHER. Yes, yes, the manner, the tone . . .

THE MANAGER. Nonsense! Rubbish! Stand aside and let me see the action.

LEADING MAN. If I've got to represent an old fellow who's coming into a house of an equivocal character . . .

THE MANAGER. Don't listen to them, for Heaven's sake! Do it again! It goes fine. (*Waiting for* THE ACTORS *to begin*) Well?

LEADING MAN. Good afternoon, Miss.

LEADING LADY. Good afternoon.

LEADING MAN (*imitating the gesture of* THE FATHER *when he looked under the hat, and then expressing quite clearly first satisfaction and then fear*). Ah, but . . . I say . . . this is not the first time that you have come here, is it?

THE MANAGER. Good, but not quite so heavily. Like this. (*Acts himself*) "This isn't the first time that you have come here" . . . (*To* LEADING LADY) And you say: "No, sir."

LEADING LADY. No, sir.

LEADING MAN. You've been here before, more than once.

THE MANAGER. No, no, stop! Let her nod "yes" first. "You've been here before, eh?" (*The* LEADING LADY *lifts up her head slightly and closes her eyes as though in disgust. Then she inclines her head twice.*)

THE STEP-DAUGHTER (*unable to contain herself*). Oh my God! (*Puts a hand to her mouth to prevent herself from laughing.*)

THE MANAGER (*turning round*). What's the matter?

THE STEP-DAUGHTER. Nothing, nothing!

THE MANAGER (*to* LEADING MAN). Go on!

LEADING MAN. You've been here before, eh? Well then, there's no need to be so shy, is there? May I take off your hat?
(THE LEADING MAN *says this last speech in such a tone and with such gestures that* THE STEP-DAUGHTER, *though she has her hand to her mouth, cannot keep from laughing.*)

LEADING LADY (*indignant*). I'm not going to stop here to be made a fool of by that woman there.

LEADING MAN. Neither am I! I'm through with it!

THE MANAGER (*shouting to* STEP-DAUGHTER). Silence! for once and all, I tell you!

THE STEP-DAUGHTER. Forgive me! forgive me!

THE MANAGER. You haven't any manners: that's what it is! You go too far.

THE FATHER (*endeavouring to intervene*). Yes, it's true, but excuse her . . .

THE MANAGER. Excuse what? It's absolutely disgusting.

THE FATHER. Yes, sir, but believe me, it has such a strange effect when . . .

THE MANAGER. Strange? Why strange? Where is it strange?

THE FATHER. No, sir; I admire your actors—this gentleman here, this lady; but they are certainly not us!

THE MANAGER. I should hope not. Evidently they cannot be you, if they are actors.

THE FATHER. Just so: actors! Both of them act our parts exceedingly well. But, believe me, it produces quite a different effect on us. They want to be us, but they aren't, all the same.

THE MANAGER. What is it then anyway?

THE FATHER. Something that is . . . that is theirs—and no longer ours . . .

THE MANAGER. But naturally, inevitably. I've told you so already.

THE FATHER. Yes, I understand . . . I understand . . .

THE MANAGER. Well then, let's have no more of it! (*Turning to* THE ACTORS) We'll have the rehearsals by ourselves, afterwards, in the ordinary way. I never could stand rehearsing with the author present. He's never satisfied! (*Turning to* FATHER *and* STEP-DAUGHTER) Come on! Let's get on with it again; and try and see if you can't keep from laughing.

THE STEP-DAUGHTER. Oh, I shan't laugh any more. There's a nice little bit coming for me now: you'll see.

THE MANAGER. Well then: when she says "Don't think any more of what I've said. I must forget, etc.," you (*addressing* THE FATHER) come in sharp with "I understand,

I understand"; and then you ask her . . .

THE STEP-DAUGHTER (*interrupting*). What?

THE MANAGER. Why she is in mourning.

THE STEP-DAUGHTER. Not at all! See here: when I told him that it was useless for me to be thinking about my wearing mourning, do you know how he answered me? "Ah well," he said "then let's take off this little frock."

THE MANAGER. Great! Just what we want, to make a riot in the theatre!

THE STEP-DAUGHTER. But it's the truth!

THE MANAGER. What does that matter? Acting is our business here. Truth up to a certain point, but no further.

THE STEP-DAUGHTER. What do you want to do then?

THE MANAGER. You'll see, you'll see! Leave it to me.

THE STEP-DAUGHTER. No sir! What you want to do is to piece together a little romantic sentimental scene out of my disgust, out of all the reasons, each more cruel and viler than the other, why I am what I am. He is to ask me why I'm in mourning; and I'm to answer with tears in my eyes, that it is just two months since papa died. No sir, no! He's got to say to me; as he did say: "Well, let's take off this little dress at once." And I; with my two months' mourning in my heart, went there behind that screen, and

with these fingers tingling with shame . . .

THE MANAGER (*running his hands through his hair*). For Heaven's sake! What are you saying?

THE STEP-DAUGHTER (*crying out excitedly*). The truth! The truth!

THE MANAGER. It may be. I don't deny it, and I can understand all your horror; but you must surely see that you can't have this kind of thing on the stage. It won't go.

THE STEP-DAUGHTER. Not possible, eh? Very well! I'm much obliged to you—but I'm off!

THE MANAGER. Now be reasonable! Don't lose your temper!

THE STEP-DAUGHTER. I won't stop here! I won't! I can see you've fixed it all up with him in your office. All this talk about what is possible for the stage . . . I understand! He wants to get at his complicated "cerebral drama," to have his famous remorses and torments acted; but I want to act my part, *my part!*

THE MANAGER (*annoyed, shaking his shoulders*). Ah! Just *your* part! But, if you will pardon me, there are other parts than yours: His (*indicating* THE FATHER) and hers! (*Indicating* THE MOTHER) On the stage you can't have a character becoming too prominent and overshadowing all the others. The thing is to pack them all into a neat little framework and then act what is actable. I am aware of the fact that everyone has his own interior life which he wants very much to put forward. But the difficulty lies in this fact: to set out just so much as is necessary for the stage, taking the other characters into consideration, and at the same time hint at the unrevealed interior life of each. I am willing to admit, my dear young lady, that from your point of view it would be a fine idea if each character could tell the public all his troubles in a nice monologue or a regular one-hour lecture. (*Good humoredly*) You must restrain yourself, my dear, and in your own interest, too; because this fury of yours, this exaggerated disgust you show, may make a bad impression, you know. After you have confessed to me that there were others before him at Madame Pace's and more than once . . .

THE STEP-DAUGHTER (*bowing her head, impressed*). It's true. But remember those others mean him for me all the same.

THE MANAGER (*not understanding*). What? The others? What do you mean?

THE STEP-DAUGHTER. For one who has gone wrong, sir, he who was responsible for the first fault is responsible for all that follow. He is responsible for my faults, was, even before I was born. Look at him, and see if it isn't true!

THE MANAGER. Well, well! And does the weight of so much responsibility seem nothing to you? Give him a chance to act it, to get it over!

THE STEP-DAUGHTER. How? How can he act all his "noble remorses" all his "moral torments," if you want to spare him the horror of being discovered one day—after he had asked her what he did ask

her—in the arms of her, that already fallen woman, that child, sir, that child he used to watch come out of school? (*She is moved.*)

(THE MOTHER *at this point is overcome with emotion, and breaks out into a fit of crying. All are touched. A long pause.*)

THE STEP-DAUGHTER (*as soon as THE MOTHER becomes a little quieter, adds resolutely and gravely*). At present, we are unknown to the public. Tomorrow, you will act us as you wish, treating us in your own manner. But do you really want to see drama, do you want to see it flash out as it really did?

THE MANAGER. Of course! That's just what I do want, so I can use as much of it as is possible.

THE STEP-DAUGHTER. Well then, ask that Mother there to leave us.

THE MOTHER (*changing her low plaint into a sharp cry*). No! No! Don't permit it, sir, don't permit it!

THE MANAGER. But it's only to try it.

THE MOTHER. I can't bear it. I can't.

THE MANAGER. But since it has happened already . . . I don't understand!

THE MOTHER. It's taking place now. It happens all the time. My torment isn't a pretended one. I live and feel every minute of my torture. Those two children there—have you heard them speak? They can't speak any more. They cling to me to keep my torment actual and vivid for me. But for themselves, they do not exist, they aren't any more. And she (*indicating* STEP-DAUGHTER) has run away, she has left me, and is lost. If I now see her here before me, it is only to renew for me the tortures I have suffered for her too.

THE FATHER. The eternal moment! She (*indicating* THE STEP-DAUGH-TER) is here to catch me, fix me, and hold me eternally in the stocks for that one fleeting and shameful moment of my life. She can't give it up! And you sir, cannot either fairly spare me it.

THE MANAGER. I never said I didn't want to act it. It will form, as a matter of fact, the nucleus of the whole first act right up to her surprise. (*Indicates* THE MOTHER.)

THE FATHER. Just so! This is my punishment: the passion in all of us that must culminate in her final cry.

THE STEP-DAUGHTER. I can hear it still in my ears. It's driven me mad, that cry!—You can put me on as you like; it doesn't matter. Fully dressed, if you like—provided I have at least the arm bare; because, standing like this (*she goes close to* THE FATHER *and leans her head on his breast*) with my head so, and my arms round his neck, I saw a vein pulsing in my arm here; and then, as if that live vein had awakened disgust in me, I closed my eyes like this, and let my head sink on his breast. (*Turning to* THE MOTHER) Cry out mother! Cry out! (*Buries head in* FATHER's *breast, and with her shoulders raised as if to prevent her hearing the cry, adds in tones of intense emotion*) Cry out as you did then!

THE MOTHER (*coming forward to separate them*). No! My daughter, my daughter! (*And after having pulled her away from him*) You brute! you brute! She is my daughter! Don't you see she's my daughter?

THE MANAGER (*walking backwards towards footlights*). Fine! fine! Damned good! And then, of course —curtain!

THE FATHER (*going towards him excitedly*). Yes, of course, because that's the way it really happened.

THE MANAGER (*convinced and pleased*). Oh, yes, no doubt about it. Curtain here, curtain!
(*At the reiterated cry of* THE MAN-AGER, THE MACHINIST *lets the curtain down, leaving* THE MANAGER *and* THE FATHER *in front of it before the footlights.*)

THE MANAGER. The darned idiot! I said "curtain" to show the act should end there, and he goes and lets it down in earnest. (*To* THE FATHER, *while he pulls the curtain back to go onto the stage again*) Yes, yes, it's all right. Effect certain! That's the right ending. I'll guarantee the first act at any rate.

ACT THREE

When the curtain goes up again, it is seen that the stage hands have shifted the bit of scenery used in the last part, and have rigged up instead at the back of the stage a drop, with some trees, and one or two wings. A portion of a fountain basin is visible. THE MOTHER *is sitting on the Right with the two children by her side.* THE SON *is on the same side, but away from the others. He seems bored, angry, and full of shame.* THE FATHER *and* THE STEP-DAUGHTER *are also seated towards the Right front. On the other side (Left) are* THE ACTORS, *much in the positions they occupied before the curtain was lowered. Only* THE MANAGER *is standing up in the middle of the stage, with his hand closed over his mouth in the act of meditating.*

THE MANAGER (*shaking his shoulders after a brief pause*). Ah yes: the second act! Leave it to me, leave it all to me as we arranged, and you'll see! It'll go fine!

THE STEP-DAUGHTER. Our entry into his house (*indicates* FATHER) in spite of him (*indicates* THE SON) . . .

THE MANAGER (*out of patience*). Leave it to me, I tell you!

THE STEP-DAUGHTER. Do let it be clear, at any rate, that it is in spite of my wishes.

THE MOTHER (*from her corner, shaking her head*). For all the good that's come of it . . .

THE STEP-DAUGHTER (*turning towards her quickly*). It doesn't matter. The more harm done us, the more remorse for him.

THE MANAGER (*impatiently*). I understand! Good Heavens! I understand! I'm taking it into account.

THE MOTHER (*supplicatingly*). I beg you, sir, to let it appear quite plain that for conscience sake I did try in every way . . .

THE STEP-DAUGHTER (*interrupting indignantly and continuing for* THE MOTHER). . . . to pacify me, to dissuade me from spiting him. (*To* MANAGER) Do as she wants: satisfy her, because it is true! I enjoy it immensely. Anyhow, as you can see, the meeker she is, the more she tries to get at his heart, the more distant and aloof does he become.

THE MANAGER. Are we going to begin this second act or not?

THE STEP-DAUGHTER. I'm not going to talk any more now. But I must tell you this: you can't have the whole action take place in the garden, as you suggest. It isn't possible!

THE MANAGER. Why not?

THE STEP-DAUGHTER. Because he (*indicates* THE SON *again*) is always shut up alone in his room. And then there's all the part of that poor dazed-looking boy there which takes place indoors.

THE MANAGER. Maybe! On the other hand, you will understand— we can't change scenes three or four times in one act.

THE LEADING MAN. They used to once.

THE MANAGER. Yes, when the public was up to the level of that child there.

THE LEADING LADY. It makes the illusion easier.

THE FATHER (*irritated*). The illusion! For Heaven's sake, don't say illusion. Please don't use that word, which is particularly painful for us.

THE MANAGER (*astounded*). And why, if you please?

THE FATHER. It's painful, cruel, really cruel; and you ought to understand that.

THE MANAGER. But why? What ought we to say then? The illusion, I tell you, sir, which we've got to create for the audience . . .

THE LEADING MAN. With our acting.

THE MANAGER. The illusion of a reality.

THE FATHER. I understand; but you, perhaps, do not understand us. Forgive me! You see . . . here for you and your actors, the thing is only—and rightly so . . . a kind of game . . .

THE LEADING LADY (*interrupting indignantly*). A game! We're not children here, if you please! We are serious actors.

THE FATHER. I don't deny it. What I mean is the game, or play, of your art, which has to give, as the gentleman says, a perfect illusion of reality.

THE MANAGER. Precisely—!

THE FATHER. Now, if you consider the fact that we (*Indicates himself and the other five* CHARACTERS), as we are, have no other reality outside of this illusion . . .

THE MANAGER (*astonished, looking at his* ACTORS, *who are also amazed*). And what does that mean?

THE FATHER (*after watching them for a moment with a wan smile*). As I say, sir, that which is a game of art for you is our sole reality. (*Brief pause. He goes a step or two nearer* THE MANAGER *and adds*) But not only for us, you know, by the way. Just you think it over well. (*Looks him in the eyes*) Can you tell me who you are?

THE MANAGER (*perplexed, half smiling*). What? Who am I? I am myself.

THE FATHER. And if I were to tell you that that isn't true, because you are I . . . ?

THE MANAGER. I should say you were mad—!
(THE ACTORS *laugh.*)

THE FATHER. You're quite right to laugh: because we are all making believe here. (*To* MANAGER) And you can therefore object that it's only for a joke that that gentleman there (*indicates* THE LEADING MAN), who naturally is himself, has to be me, who am on the contrary myself—this thing you see here. You see I've caught you in a trap! (THE ACTORS *laugh*.)

THE MANAGER (*annoyed*). But we've had all this over once before. Do you want to begin again?

THE FATHER. No, no! That wasn't my meaning! In fact, I should like to request you to abandon this game of art (*Looking at* THE LEADING LADY *as if anticipating her*) which you are accustomed to play here with your actors, and to ask you seriously once again: who are you?

THE MANAGER (*astonished and irritated, turning to his* ACTORS). If this fellow here hasn't got a nerve! A man who calls himself a character comes and asks me who I am!

THE FATHER (*with dignity, but not offended*). A character, sir, may always ask a man who he is. Because a character has really a life of his own, marked with his especial characteristics; for which reason he is always "somebody." But a man—I'm not speaking of you now—may very well be "nobody."

THE MANAGER. Yes, but you are asking these questions of me, the boss, the manager! Do you understand?

THE FATHER. But only in order to know if you, as you really are now, see yourself as you once were with all the illusions that were yours then, with all the things both inside and outside of you as they seemed to you—as they were then indeed for you. Well, sir, if you think of all those illusions that mean nothing to you now, of all those things which don't even *seem* to you to exist any more, while once they *were* for you, don't you feel that—I won't say these boards—but the very earth under your feet is sinking away from you when you reflect that in the same way this *you* as you feel it today—all this present reality of yours—is fated to seem a mere illusion to you tomorrow?

THE MANAGER (*without having understood much, but astonished by the specious argument*). Well, well! And where does all this take us anyway?

THE FATHER. Oh, nowhere! It's only to show you that if we (*Indicating the* CHARACTERS) have no other reality beyond the illusion, you too must not count overmuch on your reality as you feel it today, since, like that of yesterday, it may prove an illusion for you tomorrow.

THE MANAGER (*determining to make fun of him*). Ah, excellent! Then you'll be saying next that you, with this comedy of yours that you brought here to act, are truer and more real than I am.

THE FATHER (*with the greatest seriousness*). But of course; without doubt!

THE MANAGER. Ah, really?

THE FATHER. Why, I thought you'd understand that from the beginning.

THE MANAGER. More real than I?

THE FATHER. If your reality can change from one day to another . . .

THE MANAGER. But everyone knows it can change. It is always changing, the same as anyone else's.

THE FATHER (*with a cry*). No, sir, not ours! Look here! That is the very difference! Our reality doesn't change: it can't change! It can't be other than what it is, because it is already fixed forever. It's terrible. Ours is an immutable reality which should make you shudder when you approach us if you are really conscious of the fact that your reality is a mere transitory and fleeting illusion, taking this form today and that tomorrow, according to the conditions, according to your will, your sentiments, which in turn are controlled by an intellect that shows them to you today in one manner and tomorrow . . . who knows how? . . . Illusions of reality represented in this fatuous comedy of life that never ends, nor can ever end! Because if tomorrow it were to end . . . then why, all would be finished.

THE MANAGER. Oh for God's sake, will you *at least* finish with this philosophizing and let us try and shape this comedy which you yourself have brought me here? You argue and philosophize a bit too much, my dear sir. You know you seem to me almost, almost . . . (*Stops and looks him over from head to foot*) Ah, by the way, I think you introduced yourself to me as a—what shall . . . we say —a "character," created by an author who did not afterwards care to make a drama of his own creations.

THE FATHER. It is the simple truth, sir.

THE MANAGER. Nonsense! Cut that out, please! None of us believes it, because it isn't a thing, as you must recognize yourself, which one can believe seriously. If you want to know, it seems to me you are trying to imitate the manner of a certain author whom I heartily detest —I warn you—although I have unfortunately bound myself to put on one of his works. As a matter of fact, I was just starting to rehearse it, when you arrived. (*Turning to* THE ACTORS) And this is what we've gained—out of the frying-pan into the fire!

THE FATHER. I don't know to what author you may be alluding, but believe me I feel what I think; and I seem to be philosophizing only for those who do not think what they feel, because they blind themselves with their own sentiment. I know that for many people this self-blinding seems much more "human"; but the contrary is really true. For man never reasons so much and becomes so introspective as when he suffers; since he is anxious to get at the cause of his sufferings, to learn who has produced them, and whether it is just or unjust that he should have to bear them. On the other hand, when he is happy, he takes his happiness as it comes and doesn't analyse it, just as if happiness were his right. The animals suffer without reasoning about their sufferings. But take the case of a man who suffers and begins to reason about it. Oh no! it can't be allowed! Let him suffer like an animal, and then—ah yes, he is "human"!

THE MANAGER. Look here! Look here! You're off again, philosophizing worse than ever.

THE FATHER. Because I suffer, sir! I'm not philosophizing: I'm crying aloud the reason of my sufferings.

THE MANAGER (*makes brusque movement as he is taken with a new idea*). I should like to know if anyone has ever heard of a character who gets right out of his part and perorates and speechifies as you do. Have you ever heard of a case? I haven't.

THE FATHER. You have never met such a case, sir, because authors, as a rule, hide the labour of their creations. When the characters are really alive before their author, the latter does nothing but follow them in their action, in their words, in the situations which they suggest to him; and he has to will them the way they will themselves—for there's trouble if he doesn't. When a character is born, he acquires at once such an independence, even of his own author, that he can be imagined by everybody even in many other situations where the author never dreamed of placing him; and so he acquires for himself a meaning which the author never thought of giving him.

THE MANAGER. Yes, yes, I know this.

THE FATHER. What is there then to marvel at in us? Imagine such a misfortune for characters as I have described to you: to be born of an author's fantasy, and be denied life by him; and then answer me if these characters left alive, and yet without life, weren't right in doing what they did do and are doing now, after they have attempted everything in their power to persuade him to give them their stage life. We've all tried him in turn, I, she (*indicating* THE STEP-DAUGHTER) and she. (*Indicating* THE MOTHER.)

THE STEP-DAUGHTER. It's true. I too have sought to tempt him, many, many times, when he has been sitting at his writing table, feeling a bit melancholy, at the twilight hour. He would sit in his armchair too lazy to switch on the light, and all the shadows that crept into his room were full of our presence coming to tempt him. (*As if she saw herself still there by the writing table, and was annoyed by the presence of* THE ACTORS) Oh, if you would only go away, go away and leave us alone—mother here with that son of hers—I with that Child—that Boy there always alone —and then I with him (*just hints at* THE FATHER)—and then I alone, alone . . . in those shadows! (*Makes a sudden movement as if in the vision she has of herself illuminating those shadows she wanted to seize hold of herself*) Ah! my life! my life! Oh, what scenes we proposed to him—and I tempted him more than any of the others!

THE FATHER. Maybe. But perhaps it was your fault that he refused to give us life: because you were too insistent, too troublesome.

THE STEP-DAUGHTER. Nonsense! Didn't he make me so himself? (*Goes close to* THE MANAGER *to tell him as if in confidence*) In my opinion he abandoned us in a fit of depression, of disgust for the ordinary theatre as the public knows it and likes it.

THE SON. Exactly what it was, sir; exactly that!

THE FATHER. Not at all! Don't believe it for a minute. Listen to me! You'll be doing quite right to modify, as you suggest, the excesses both of this girl here, who wants to do too much, and of this young man, who won't do anything at all.

THE SON. No, nothing!

THE MANAGER. You too get over the mark occasionally, my dear sir, if I may say so.

THE FATHER. I? When? Where?

THE MANAGER. Always! Continuously! Then there's this insistence of yours in trying to make us believe you are a character. And then too, you must really argue and philosophize less, you know, much less.

THE FATHER. Well, if you want to take away from me the possibility of representing the torment of my spirit which never gives me peace, you will be suppressing me: that's all. Every true man, sir, who is a little above the level of the beasts and plants does not live for the sake of living, without knowing how to live; but he lives so as to give a meaning and a value of his own to life. For me this is *everything*. I cannot give up this, just to represent a mere fact as she (*indicating* THE STEP-DAUGHTER) wants. It's all very well for her, since her "vendetta" lies in the "fact." I'm not going to do it. It destroys my *raison d'être*.

THE MANAGER. Your *raison d'être!* Oh, we're going ahead fine! First she starts off, and then you jump in. At this rate, we'll never finish.

THE FATHER. Now, don't be offended! Have it your own way—provided, however, that within the limits of the parts you assign us each one's sacrifice isn't too great.

THE MANAGER. You've got to understand that you can't go on arguing at your own pleasure. Drama is action, sir, action and not confounded philosophy.

THE FATHER. All right. I'll do just as much arguing and philosophizing as everybody does when he is considering his own torments.

THE MANAGER. If the drama permits! But for Heaven's sake, man, let's get along and come to the scene.

THE STEP-DAUGHTER. It seems to me we've got too much action with our coming into his house. (*Indicating* FATHER) You said, before, you couldn't change the scene every five minutes.

THE MANAGER. Of course not. What we've got to do is to combine and group up all the facts in one simultaneous, close-knit action. We can't have it as you want, with your little brother wandering like a ghost from room to room, hiding behind doors and meditating a project which—what did you say it did to him?

THE STEP-DAUGHTER. Consumes him, sir, wastes him away!

THE MANAGER. Well, it may be. And then at the same time, you want the little girl there to be playing in the garden . . . one in the house, and the other in the garden: isn't that it?

THE STEP-DAUGHTER. Yes, in the sun, in the sun! That is my only pleasure: to see her happy and careless in the garden after the misery and squalor of the horrible room where we all four slept together. And I had to sleep with her—I, do you understand?—with my vile contaminated body next to hers; with her folding me fast in her loving little arms. In the garden, whenever she spied me, she would run to take me by the hand. She didn't care for the big flowers, only the little ones; and she loved to show me them and pet me.

THE MANAGER. Well then, we'll have it in the garden. Everything shall happen in the garden; and we'll group the other scenes there. (*Calls a stage hand*) Here, a backcloth with trees and something to do as a fountain basin. (*Turning round to look at the back of the stage*) Ah, you've fixed it up. Good! (*To* STEP-DAUGHTER) This is just to give an idea, of course. The Boy, instead of hiding behind the doors, will wander about here in the garden, hiding behind the trees. But it's going to be rather difficult to find a child to do that scene with you where she shows you the flowers. (*Turning to* THE BOYS) Come forward a little, will you please? Let's try it now! Come along! come along! (*Then seeing him come shyly forward, full of fear and looking lost*) It's a nice business, this lad here. What's the matter with him? We'll have to give him a word or two to say. (*Goes close to him, puts a hand on his shoulder, and leads him behind one of the trees*) Come on! come on! Let me see you a little! Hide here . . . yes, like that. Try and show your head just a little as if you were looking for someone . . . (*Goes back to observe the effect, when* THE BOY *at once goes through the action*) Excellent! fine! (*Turning to* STEP-DAUGHTER) Suppose the little girl there were to surprise him as he looks round, and run over to him, so we could give him a word or two to say?

THE STEP-DAUGHTER. It's useless to hope he will speak, as long as that fellow there is here . . . (*Indicates* THE SON) You must send him away first.

THE SON (*jumping up*). Delighted! delighted! I don't ask for anything better. (*Begins to move away.*)

THE MANAGER (*at once stopping him*). No! No! Where are you going? Wait a bit!
(THE MOTHER *gets up alarmed and terrified at the thought that he is really about to go away. Instinctively she lifts her arms to prevent him, without, however, leaving her seat.*)

THE SON (*to* MANAGER *who stops him*). I've got nothing to do with this affair. Let me go please! Let me go!

THE MANAGER. What do you mean by saying you've got nothing to do with this?

THE STEP-DAUGHTER (*calmly, with irony*). Don't bother to stop him: he won't go away.

THE FATHER. He has to act the terrible scene in the garden with his mother.

THE SON (*suddenly resolute and with dignity*). I shall act nothing at all. I've said so from the very beginning. (*To* THE MANAGER) Let me go!

THE STEP-DAUGHTER (*going over to* THE MANAGER). Allow me? (*Puts down* THE MANAGER's *arm which is restraining* THE SON) Well, go away then, if you want to! (THE SON *looks at her with contempt and hatred. She laughs and says*) You see, he can't, he can't go away! He is obliged to stay here, indissolubly bound to the chain. If I, who fly off when that happens which has to happen, because I can't bear him—if I am still here and support that face and expression of his, you can well imagine that he is unable to move. He has to remain here, has to stop with that nice father of his, and that mother whose only son he is. (*Turning to* THE MOTHER) Come on, mother, come along! (*Turning to* MANAGER *to indicate her*) You see, she was getting up to keep him back. (*To* THE MOTHER, *beckoning her with her hand*) Come on! come on! (*Then to* MANAGER) You can imagine how little she wants to show these actors of yours what she really feels; but so eager is she to get near him that . . . There, you see? She is willing to act her part. (*And in fact,* THE MOTHER *approaches him; and as soon as* THE STEP-DAUGHTER *has finished speaking, opens her arms to signify that she consents.*)

THE SON (*suddenly*). No! no! If I can't go away, then I'll stop here; but I repeat: I act nothing!

THE FATHER (*to* MANAGER *excitedly*). You can force him, sir.

THE SON. Nobody can force me.

THE FATHER. I can.

THE STEP-DAUGHTER. Wait a minute, wait . . . First of all, the baby has to go to the fountain . . . (*Runs to take* THE CHILD *and leads her to the fountain.*)

THE MANAGER. Yes, yes, of course; that's it. Both at the same time.
(*The* SECOND LADY LEAD *and the* JUVENILE LEAD *at this point separate themselves from the group of actors. One watches* THE MOTHER *attentively; the other moves about studying the movements and manner of* THE SON *whom he will have to act.*)

THE SON (*to* MANAGER). What do you mean by both at the same time? It isn't right. There was no scene between me and her. (*Indicates* THE MOTHER) Ask her how it was!

THE MOTHER. Yes, it's true. I had come into his room . . .

THE SON. Into my room, do you understand? Nothing to do with the garden.

THE MANAGER. It doesn't matter. Haven't I told you we've got to group the action?

THE SON (*observing the* JUVENILE LEAD *studying him*). What do you want?

THE JUVENILE LEAD. Nothing! I was just looking at you.

THE SON (*turning towards the* SECOND LADY LEAD). Ah! she's at it too: to re-act her part! (*Indicating* THE MOTHER.)

THE MANAGER. Exactly! And it seems to me that you ought to be grateful to them for their interest.

THE SON. Yes, but haven't you yet perceived that it isn't possible to live in front of a mirror which not only freezes us with the image of ourselves, but throws our likeness back at us with a horrible grimace?

THE FATHER. That is true, absolutely true. You must see that.

THE MANAGER (*to* SECOND LADY LEAD *and* JUVENILE LEAD). He's right! Move away from them!

THE SON. Do as you like. I'm out of this!

THE MANAGER. Be quiet, you, will you? And let me hear your mother! (*To* MOTHER) You were saying you had entered . . .

THE MOTHER. Yes, into his room, because I couldn't stand it any longer. I went to empty my heart to him of all the anguish that tortures me . . . But as soon as he saw me come in . . .

THE SON. Nothing happened! There was no scene. I went away, that's all! I don't care for scenes!

THE MOTHER. It's true, true. That's how it was.

THE MANAGER. Well now, we've got to do this bit between you and him. It's indispensable.

THE MOTHER. I'm ready . . . when you are ready. If you could only find a chance for me to tell him what I feel here in my heart.

THE FATHER (*going to* SON *in a great rage*). You'll do this for your mother, for your mother, do you understand?

THE SON (*quite determined*). I do nothing!

THE FATHER (*taking hold of him and shaking him*). For God's sake, do as I tell you! Don't you hear your mother asking you for a favour? Haven't you even got the guts to be a son?

THE SON (*taking hold of* THE FATHER). No! No! And for God's sake stop it, or else . . . (*General agitation.* THE MOTHER, *frightened, tries to separate them.*)

THE MOTHER (*pleading*). Please! please!

THE FATHER (*not leaving hold of* THE SON). You've got to obey, do you hear?

THE SON (*almost crying from rage*). What does it mean, this madness you've got? (*They separate*) Have you no decency, that you insist on showing everyone our shame? I won't do it! I won't! And I stand for the will of our author in this. He didn't want to put us on the stage, after all!

THE MANAGER. Man alive! You came here . . .

THE SON (*indicating* FATHER). *He did! I didn't!*

THE MANAGER. Aren't you here now?

THE SON. It was his wish, and he dragged us along with him. He's told you not only the things that did happen, but also things that have never happened at all.

THE MANAGER. Well, tell me then what did happen. You went out of your room without saying a word?

THE SON. Without a word, so as to avoid a scene!

THE MANAGER. And then what did you do?

THE SON. Nothing . . . walking in the garden . . . (*Hesitates for a moment with expression of gloom.*)

THE MANAGER (*coming closer to him, interested by his extraordinary reserve*). Well, well . . . walking in the garden . . .

THE SON (*exasperated*). Why on earth do you insist? It's horrible! (THE MOTHER *trembles, sobs, and looks towards the fountain.*)

THE MANAGER (*slowly observing the glance and turning towards* THE SON *with increasing apprehension*). The baby?

THE SON. There in the fountain . . .

THE FATHER (*pointing with tender pity to* THE MOTHER). She was following him at the moment . . .

THE MANAGER (*to* THE SON *anxiously*). And then you . . .

THE SON. I ran over to her; I was jumping in to drag her out when I saw something that froze my blood . . . the boy there standing stock still, with eyes like a madman's, watching his little drowned sister, in the fountain! (THE STEP-DAUGHTER *bends over the fountain to hide* THE CHILD. *She sobs*) Then . . . (*A revolver shot rings out behind the trees where* THE BOY *is hidden.*)

THE MOTHER (*with a cry of terror runs over in that direction together with several of the Actors amid general confusion*). My son! My son! (*Then amid the cries and exclamations one hears her voice*) Help! Help!

THE MANAGER (*pushing the Actors aside while they lift up* THE BOY *and carry him off*). Is he really wounded?

SOME ACTORS. He's dead! dead!

OTHER ACTORS. No, no, it's only make believe, it's only pretence!

THE FATHER (*with a terrible cry*). Pretence? Reality, sir, reality!

THE MANAGER. Pretence? Reality? To hell with it all! Never in my life has such a thing happened to me. I've lost a whole day over these people, a whole day!

CURTAIN

Anatol

BY ARTHUR SCHNITZLER

TRANSLATED BY GRACE ISABEL COLBRON

ANATOL

QUESTIONING FATE

CHARACTERS

ANATOL
MAX
CORA

MAX. Really, Anatol, I envy you. (ANATOL *smiles*) Yes, I confess I was dumfounded. I've considered it all a sort of fairy tale until now. But now that I've actually seen you do it—when I saw that girl fall asleep—with my own eyes—saw her dance when you told her she belonged to the ballet—saw her weep when you told her her lover was dead—and saw her pardon a criminal when you had made a queen of her——

ANATOL. Yes——

MAX. There's a magician hidden in you.

ANATOL. As there is in all of us.

MAX. It's mysterious.

ANATOL. It doesn't seem so to me —it's no more mysterious than life itself—no more mysterious than much we have discovered in the course of the centuries. How do you suppose our forefathers felt when they were told that the earth revolved on its axis? It must have made them dizzy.

MAX. Yes—but that concerned all alike.

ANATOL. Suppose we had just discovered Spring, for instance. We wouldn't believe it was true, in spite of the green trees, the blossoming flowers and—love.

MAX. You're off the subject, all that is nonsense. But magnetism——

ANATOL. Hypnotism——

MAX. That is a different matter. I'd never let myself be hypnotized.

ANATOL. That's childish of you. Where's the harm, if I were to tell you to go to sleep and you lie down quietly. . . .

MAX. Yes, and then you'd say to me, "Now you're a chimney sweep" and I'd climb into the chimney and get all sooty.

ANATOL. Those are only jokes. The important thing is its value for scientific use. But we've not gone far yet.

MAX. Why?——

ANATOL. Yes, I could transport that girl today into a hundred other worlds, but I can't transport myself even into one other world.

MAX. Isn't it possible?

ANATOL. To be honest, I've tried it. I've stared at this diamond in my ring for minutes together and I've said to myself, "Anatol, you will go to sleep and when you awake all thought of that woman, who is driving you crazy, will have vanished from your mind."

MAX. And what happened when you woke up?

ANATOL. I didn't go to sleep at all.

MAX. That woman—that woman —then you still——

ANATOL. Yes, friend, I'm very unhappy—I'm almost insane.

MAX. You're still in doubt?

ANATOL. No. Not in doubt—I *know* she deceives me. While her lips press mine, while her hand caresses my hair—in our moments of joy—I know she deceives me.

MAX. It's all imagination.

ANATOL. No, it isn't.

MAX. Have you any proof?

ANATOL. I surmise—I feel—that's why I know——

MAX. Amazing logic!

ANATOL. These women are always unfaithful—it comes natural to them. They aren't aware of it themselves. They simply have to have two or three affairs at the same time, just as I like to read two or three books at the same time.

MAX. But she loves you——

ANATOL. Madly—but what has that to do with it? She's untrue to me.

MAX. With whom?

ANATOL. How do I know? A prince, perhaps, who followed her in the streets—or a poet of the tenements who smiled at her, from a window as she passed in the early morning.

MAX. You are a fool.

ANATOL. What reason would she have for not being untrue to me? She's like all the rest, she loves life and does little thinking. If I ask her "Do you love me?" she'll answer yes, and she'll tell the truth. If I ask her "Are you true to me?" again she will say yes and again she will be telling the truth, for she has forgotten the others—for the moment at least. And then, did any one of them ever answer, "Dearest, I have been untrue to you?" How shall we ever know? But if she is true to me——

MAX. Ah, ha——

ANATOL. It's mere chance. It isn't because she thinks to herself, "I must be true to my dear Anatol"— that isn't it——

MAX. But if she loves you?

ANATOL. Sweet innocent!—if that were any reason——

MAX. Well?

ANATOL. Why shouldn't I be true to her? I love her.

MAX. Oh, you're a man.

ANATOL. That stupid old phrase! They're always trying to persuade us that women are different. Some may be—if their mothers keep them locked up or if they're cold-blooded—we're all alike, I tell you. When I say to a woman "I love you and you alone!" I don't feel that I'm lying to her even if I have held another in my arms the night before.

MAX. Oh, well—you——

ANATOL. And how about you? Or my adored Cora? Oh, it will drive me mad! If I should kneel to her and implore her, "Sweetheart—darling—all is forgiven in advance—but only tell me the truth," would that help me? She would lie to me as before and I would know as much as I did before. Haven't I had them implore me, "Tell me, are you really true to me? Not a word of reproach if you're not—but I want the truth—I must know it," and what did I do? I lied,—calmly, with a happy smile—with the clearest conscience in the world. Why should I make her unhappy? And I replied, "Yes, my angel,—faithful unto death," and she believed and was happy.

MAX. There, you see——

ANATOL. But I don't believe and I'm not happy. I might be, if there was any means of making them speak—these stupid, adorable, detestable creatures, or if there was any other way of discovering the truth. But there isn't any—except chance.

MAX. And hypnotism?

ANATOL. What?

MAX. Hypnotism. I mean, you put her to sleep and then you say to her, "Now you must tell me the truth."

ANATOL. Strange——

MAX. It ought to be possible. And then you ask her, "Do you love me? Or someone else? Where have you been? Where are you going? Who is the other man?" and so on.

ANATOL. Max—Max——

MAX. Well?

ANATOL. You're right. One might be a magician—and conjure a word of truth from a woman's mouth.

MAX. There now—that'll save your life! Cora is undoubtedly a good medium—you will know this very evening whether you are a dupe,—or——

ANATOL. Or a very god. Max, let me embrace you!—I am free—I am a new man. I have her in my power.

MAX. I'm really quite curious.

ANATOL. What? You didn't doubt?

MAX. Oh, I see—others mustn't doubt, only you.

ANATOL. Certainly. If a husband were leaving the very house where he had caught his wife with her lover, and a friend met him with the words, "I believe your wife is unfaithful," he wouldn't answer, "I've just become convinced of that," would he? He'd be more likely to say, "You're a damned cad."

MAX. That's true—I had forgotten that it's the first duty of friendship to preserve a friend's illusions.

ANATOL. Quiet a moment——

MAX. What is it?

ANATOL. Don't you hear? I know her step, even down there in the house-corridor.

MAX. I didn't hear anything.

ANATOL. So near—now she's in the hall—(*Opens the door*) Cora——

CORA (*outside*). Good evening; oh —you're not alone?

ANATOL. It's only friend Max.

CORA (*coming in*). Good evening —all in the dark?

ANATOL. It's still twilight—you know how I love that.

CORA (*stroking his hair*). My little poet——

ANATOL. My dear Cora——

CORA. But I'll light the light, if you don't mind. (*She lights the candles.*)

ANATOL (*to* MAX). Isn't she charming?

MAX. Oh——

CORA. How are you both,—have you been chatting here long?

ANATOL. About half an hour.

CORA. And what about? (*Takes off her hat and coat.*)

ANATOL. Many things——

MAX. Chiefly about hypnotism.

CORA. That hypnotism again? It makes me dizzy just to think of it.

ANATOL. Well, now——

CORA. Anatol, I'd like to have you hypnotize me some time.

ANATOL. I?—hypnotize you?

CORA. I think it would be awfully nice—that is, if *you* do it.

ANATOL. Thanks.

CORA. But I wouldn't let a stranger do it—oh, dear, no.

ANATOL. Well, sweetheart, I'll hypnotize you if you wish it.

CORA. When?

ANATOL. Now—at once—right here.

CORA. Good! What must I do?

ANATOL. Just sit quietly in that chair and make up your mind to go to sleep.

CORA. It's made up.

ANATOL. I'll stand here before you, you must look at me—well, look at me—I'll stroke your eyes and forehead . . . this way——

CORA. And what then?

ANATOL. Nothing—you must will to go to sleep——

CORA. When you touch my eyes like that, I feel queer——

ANATOL. Quiet now, don't talk—sleep—you are very tired.

CORA. No, I'm not.

ANATOL. Yes, you are tired.

CORA. A little—yes——

ANATOL. Your eyelids are heavy—so heavy—you can scarcely lift your hands——

CORA (*low*). Yes—really——

ANATOL (*passes his hand over her eyes and forehead, speaks monotonously*). Tired—you are very tired—go to sleep, my child—sleep— (*He turns with a triumphant expression to* MAX *who has been watching in admiration*) Sleep—now your eyes are tight shut, you can't open them—(CORA *tries to open her eyes*)—you can't—you are sleeping—sleep on——

MAX. Say——

ANATOL. Quiet!—(*To* CORA) You are sleeping—deeply—calmly— (*He stands looking at* CORA *who breathes calmly, evidently asleep*) Now you can speak.

MAX. I wanted to ask if she was really asleep.

ANATOL. You can see for yourself. Now we'll wait a few moments. (*He stands before her, looks at her, there is a long pause*) Cora—now you must answer me—answer—what is your name?

CORA. Cora.

ANATOL. Cora, we are in the forest.

CORA. Oh, in the forest—isn't it lovely?—the green trees, . . . and the nightingales——

ANATOL. Cora, you must tell me the truth about everything—what are you to do, Cora?

CORA. I must tell the truth.

ANATOL. You must answer all my questions truthfully, and when you wake up you will have forgotten it all. Do you understand me?

CORA. Yes.

ANATOL. Sleep now—calmly—(*To* MAX) Now I shall ask her——

MAX. How old is she?

ANATOL. Nineteen—Cora, how old are you?

CORA. Twenty-one.

MAX. Aha!

ANATOL. Hush—that's remarkable—you can see how——

MAX. If she'd known she was such a good medium——!

ANATOL. The suggestion is taking effect. I shall question her further. Cora, do you love me?

CORA. Yes.

ANATOL (*triumphant*). Did you hear that?

MAX. And now the main question—whether she is true to you.

ANATOL. Cora—— (*Turning*) That's a stupid question.

MAX. Why?

ANATOL. You can't ask it that way —I must word the question differently.

MAX. I should think it was sufficiently explicit.

ANATOL. No, that's just the trouble, it is not explicit enough.

MAX. In what way?

ANATOL. If I ask, "Are you true to me," she may understand that in its widest significance.

MAX. Well?

ANATOL. She'll think back over her whole past—she'll think possibly of a time when she loved someone else, and she would answer no.

MAX. That would be rather interesting, too.

ANATOL. Thanks! I realize that Cora knew other men before she met me—she herself told me that had she dreamed she was to meet me—then——

MAX. But she didn't dream it?

ANATOL. No.

MAX. As to your question——

ANATOL. Yes, this question—it's too crude—in the wording, anyway.

MAX. Then put it this way, "Cora, have you been true to me since you have known me?"

ANATOL. Hm—that's better. (To CORA) Cora, have you been—but that's absurd, too.

MAX. Absurd?

ANATOL. Why, yes. Consider the way we met—we didn't dream we should come to love each other so madly. We both thought, those first days, that it was merely a passing episode—who knows——

MAX. Who knows what?

ANATOL. Who knows, if she did not first come to love me—when she had ceased to love someone else? What experience did this girl live through before I met her—before we exchanged our first words? Could she cut loose from it all at once? Did she not, perhaps, have to drag the old chains about with her, for days and weeks?——

MAX. Hm. . . .

ANATOL. I will go still further—at first it was only a caprice to her as it was to me. Neither of us thought of it as anything else, neither of us demanded anything from the other more than a sweet fleeting happiness. If she did wrong at that time—can I reproach her for it?

MAX. How magnanimous you are.

ANATOL. Oh, no—but I should consider it indecent to take any such advantage of the present situation.

MAX. That's noble of you. But maybe I can help you out. (ANATOL looks his question) Why not put it this way, "Cora, have you been true to me since you have loved me?"

ANATOL. That sounds quite clear.

MAX. Well?

ANATOL. But it isn't clear at all.

MAX. Oh, indeed!

ANATOL. True! What does that word mean, anyway? Now suppose, let us say—suppose she was in a railway train yesterday, and a man sitting opposite touched the tip of her foot with his. It is not at all impossible that, with the greatly increased perceptiveness characteristic of sleep and in the highly sensitized condition of the medium's mind during the hypnosis——, it is not at all impossible that she might regard this incident as an infidelity.

MAX. Oh, see here——

ANATOL. All the more since she knows my—probably exaggerated point of view on this subject from many conversations we have had. I've said to her, "Cora, if you even look at another man it's an infidelity towards me."

MAX. And she?

ANATOL. She laughed and asked how I could believe that she would even look at another man.

MAX. And yet you believed——

ANATOL. Accidents can happen. Imagine—for instance, an impertinent fellow follows her some evening and kisses her on the neck.

MAX. Well—that——

ANATOL. Well, that's not impossible.

MAX. Then you don't really want to question her?

ANATOL. Why, yes—but——

MAX. All this you've been saying is perfect rot. Believe me, women never misunderstand when we ask them if they've been true to us. And if you whisper to her, tenderly, affectionately, "Are you true to me?" she won't think of any man's foot or any impertinent kiss on the neck, she'll think of just what we usually mean when we talk of infidelity. And, besides, in this case, you have the added advantage of being able to ask further questions which will make her answer quite clear.

ANATOL. Then you insist that I shall question her?

MAX. I? Why, you wanted to know.

ANATOL. But I've just thought of something——

MAX. What is it?

ANATOL. The Unconscious.

MAX. The Unconscious?

ANATOL. I believe in states of unconsciousness——

MAX. Do you?

ANATOL. Such a condition can grow out of itself, as it were, but it can also be brought about by artificial means—by means that dull, or unduly exhilarate, the senses.

MAX. Please explain.

ANATOL. Imagine a dim room, full of shadows—mysterious——

MAX. Dim—mysterious—I'm imagining it.

ANATOL. And in this room—she—and another.

MAX. But how did she get there?

ANATOL. I'll leave that question open. There are excuses—enough that it could and does happen. And then—a few glasses of Rhine wine —the air strangely heavy—the scent of cigarettes—the fragrance of perfumed hangings—a pale light through frosted glass and red silk —silence—solitude—sweet whispered words—(*Gesture from* MAX) —many others have yielded there —stronger, calmer than she.

MAX. Probably. Still the fact that she should be in such a room with another man doesn't quite agree with my idea of fidelity.

ANATOL. Life is full of enigmas.

MAX. Well, friend, you have the solution of one of those enigmas which have puzzled the most brilliant men for ages, in your own hands: you need only speak, and you will know all that you wish to know. One question—and you will know whether you are one of the few who are really loved exclusively—or you can learn who your rival is and how he won his victory over you—and yet you will not speak this word. You have been permitted to question Fate—and you will not. You torture yourself day and night, you'd give half your life for the truth, and yet when it lies before you, you will not stoop to pick it up. And why not? Because it might happen that a woman whom you love is really just

as you would have her, in *all* your imaginings, and because your illusion is a thousand times dearer to you than the truth. Enough of this trifling now. Wake the girl up, and be satisfied with the proud consciousness that you—might have accomplished a miracle.

ANATOL. Max!——

MAX. Well, am I not right? Don't you know yourself that all you've said has been just sophistry, empty phrases, with which you can deceive neither yourself nor me.

ANATOL (*quickly*). Max, I will question her.

MAX. Ah ha!

ANATOL. But—don't be offended— not in your presence.

MAX. Not in my presence?

ANATOL. If I must hear it—the worst—if she answers "I am not true to you," I want to be alone to hear it. To be unhappy is only half the misfortune—to be pitied—is misery complete. I cannot endure it. You are my best friend, but that is just why I don't want to see your eyes rest on me with that expression of pity which shows the unfortunate the full depth of his misery. It's something else, perhaps. I may be—ashamed—before you. You will have to learn the truth, for you will have seen this girl for the last time, if she has deceived me. But I don't want you to hear it when I do—that's what I can't endure—do you understand?

MAX. I understand. (*Presses his hand*) I will leave you alone with her.

ANATOL. You are a real friend. (*Goes to door with him*) I'll call you in again—in less than a minute.
(MAX *goes into next room.*)

ANATOL (*stands in front of* CORA, *looks at her*). Cora—(*He shakes his head, paces the room, comes back to her, falls on his knees before her*) Cora—my sweet Cora—(*With decision*) Cora, wake up—and kiss me.

CORA (*rises, rubs her eyes, falls on* ANATOL's *neck*). Anatol—how long did I sleep? Where is Max?

ANATOL (*calls*). Max!

MAX (*comes from next room*). Here I am.

ANATOL (*to* CORA). You slept for a long time and you talked in your sleep.

CORA. Good heavens! Did I say anything wrong?

MAX. You only answered his questions.

CORA. What did he ask me?

ANATOL. Ever so many things.

CORA. And did I answer everything?

ANATOL. Everything.

CORA. And mayn't I know what you asked me?

ANATOL. No, you may not. And I'll hypnotize you again to-morrow.

CORA. No, indeed—never again. It's witchcraft—they ask you questions and then when you wake up you don't know a thing about it—I know I talked nonsense.

ANATOL. Yes—for instance, you said that you loved me.

CORA. Did I, really?

MAX. She doesn't believe it!—that's good.

CORA. But I don't need to go to sleep to tell you that.

ANATOL. My angel. (*Embrace.*)

MAX. Good-bye, friends.

ANATOL. You're going already?

MAX. I must.

ANATOL. You don't mind if I don't go with you?

MAX. Why, of course not.

CORA. See you soon again?

MAX (*at the door*). I've learned one fact—women can lie even in the hypnosis—but they're happy —that's the one important thing. Good-bye, children.
(*They do not hear him, as they are clasped in a passionate em·brace.*)

CHRISTMAS SHOPPING

CHARACTERS

ANATOL
GABRIELLE

It is about six o'clock on Christmas Eve, in the streets of Vienna. Snow is falling lightly.

ANATOL. Dear lady—oh, dear lady.

GABRIELLE. What?—oh, it's you?

ANATOL. Yes, I've been following you. I can't bear to see you lugging all those things. Do give me your packages.

GABRIELLE. Oh, no, much obliged —but I can carry them perfectly well myself.

ANATOL. Please don't make it so hard for me when I really want to be gallant.

GABRIELLE. Well—take this one, then.

ANATOL. But that doesn't amount to anything—here, give me this—and this——

GABRIELLE. That's enough now— you're really too kind.

ANATOL. If only I'm allowed to be —it feels so good.

GABRIELLE. But you prove that only on the street,—and when it's snowing——

ANATOL. And when it's evening— and, incidentally, Christmas—eh?

GABRIELLE. It's unusual even to catch a glimpse of you nowadays.

ANATOL. You mean that I haven't called on you this season?

GABRIELLE. Yes, that's about what I mean.

ANATOL. Oh, dear lady—I haven't made any calls at all, this season —how is your husband?—and the dear children?

GABRIELLE. Spare yourself these inquiries. I know it interests you very little.

ANATOL. It's quite a weird sensation to meet someone who really knows human nature.

GABRIELLE. I know—*you.*

ANATOL. Not as well as I could wish.

GABRIELLE. No such remarks, please.

ANATOL. But I can't help it.

GABRIELLE. Then give me my packages.

ANATOL. Don't be angry, please— I'll be good.
(*They walk along in silence.*)

GABRIELLE. I don't mean that you sha'n't talk at all.

ANATOL. But you're such a strict censor——

GABRIELLE. Tell me something interesting. We haven't seen each other for so long. What are you doing with yourself?

ANATOL. Nothing—as usual.

GABRIELLE. Nothing?

ANATOL. Absolutely nothing.

GABRIELLE. It's really too bad.

ANATOL. *You* certainly don't care.

GABRIELLE. How can you say that?

ANATOL. And why am I wasting my life? Whose fault is it? *Whose?*

GABRIELLE. Give me my packages.

ANATOL. I don't blame anyone in particular. I was just talking into the air——

GABRIELLE. You do a lot of walking, I suppose.

ANATOL. Walking? You put such a tone of contempt into that? And yet, is there anything nicer? The word suggests such delightful aimlessness. But it doesn't fit me today. I'm very busy to-day—just as you are.

GABRIELLE. Busy? At what?

ANATOL. I'm shopping for Christmas, too.

GABRIELLE. You are?

ANATOL. Only I can't find anything to suit me. For weeks now, I've spent my evenings in front of the shop windows in every street. But these shop-keepers seem to have neither taste nor originality.

GABRIELLE. That's for the shopper to supply. Anybody who has as little to do as you have, ought to be able to plan, and to exercise his own originality, and order his presents during the Autumn.

ANATOL. I'm afraid I'm not the man to do that. And, anyhow, how do we know in the Autumn whom we want to give presents to at Christmas? So here it is,—only two hours before they light the candles on the Christmas tree, and I haven't the faintest idea—not the faintest——

GABRIELLE. Shall I help you?

ANATOL. Oh, dear lady—you are an angel!—but don't take the packages away from me.

GABRIELLE. Why, no——

ANATOL. Then I may call you an angel?—that's fine—angel!

GABRIELLE. Will you be quiet?

ANATOL. I'm as quiet as can be.

GABRIELLE. Well, then, give me some guide—whom do you want the present for?

ANATOL. That's—that's hard to say.

GABRIELLE. For a lady, of course.

ANATOL. I complimented you once this evening on your knowledge of human nature.

GABRIELLE. But what—what sort of a lady? A real lady?

ANATOL. We'll have to come to an agreement with regard to that term first. If you mean a lady of the great world—then it's not quite right.

GABRIELLE. Very well—of the—of the "little world" then?

ANATOL. We can call it that.

GABRIELLE. I might have known it.

ANATOL. Please don't be sarcastic.

GABRIELLE. I know your taste—something from the other side of the City Line?—thin and blonde?

ANATOL. Blonde—yes—I'll acknowledge that much.

GABRIELLE. Blonde—it's surprising how faithful you are to this sort of maiden——

ANATOL. It isn't *my* fault.

GABRIELLE. None of that, sir! It's just as well that you should stay by your particular type—it would be a great pity for you to desert the scene of your triumphs.

ANATOL. But what can I do? It's the only place I'm loved—over there.

GABRIELLE. Do they understand you—over there?

ANATOL. Not in the slightest. But that's how it goes. In the "little world" I'm loved—in the great world—only understood. You know.

GABRIELLE. No, I don't know anything—and I don't want to know anything more. Come here—this is the right shop—we'll buy something here for your little girl.

ANATOL. Dear lady——

GABRIELLE. Why, yes—look in here—there's a little fancy box with three bottles of perfume—and another with six cakes of soap—patchouli — chypre — Jockey Club — wouldn't that suit?

ANATOL. That—that isn't altogether nice of you——

GABRIELLE. Wait a moment—look at this pin with the six paste diamonds—*six*—just think!—how it glitters—or this charming little bracelet with those heavenly danglers—one of them is a Moor's head —that ought to please—across the City Line.

ANATOL. You are mistaken, dear lady—you don't know these girls—they are—quite different from your idea.

GABRIELLE. Oh, look here—how perfectly charming—what *do* you think of that hat? The shape was the latest thing—two years ago! And see those waving feathers—aren't they gorgeous? That would certainly make a sensation—in Hernals.

ANATOL. But I wasn't talking of Hernals—and you probably underestimate the taste of Hernals, too.

GABRIELLE. You're very difficult—why don't you help me? Give me some clue.

ANATOL. How can I? You'd have only a condescending smile for it.

GABRIELLE. Oh, no, oh, no—I want to learn. Is she vain? Or modest? Tall—or short? Does she like gay colors?

ANATOL. I should not have accepted your kind offer—you're only mocking me.

GABRIELLE. Oh, no, I'm listening—tell me something about her.

ANATOL. I don't dare——

GABRIELLE. You may dare. Since when——?

ANATOL. Don't let's talk about it.

GABRIELLE. But I insist. Since when have you known her?

ANATOL. For some time.

GABRIELLE. Don't let me drag it out of you like this. Tell me the whole story.

ANATOL. There isn't any story.

GABRIELLE. How you made her acquaintance—when, and where, and what sort of a person she is—I want to know all that.

ANATOL. Oh, very well, but I warn you it's tiresome.

GABRIELLE. It will be interesting to me. I'd really like to learn something about that world. What sort of a world is it anyway? I know nothing at all about it.

ANATOL. You wouldn't understand that world at all.

GABRIELLE. Oh, indeed!

ANATOL. You have such a summary contempt for everything that lies outside your own circle. It's a mistake.

GABRIELLE. I'm willing to learn. But no one ever tells me anything about that world. How shall I learn to know it?

ANATOL. And yet—you have an indefinite feeling—that they're taking something away from you—over there. It's a sort of silent enmity.

GABRIELLE. Oh, please—no one takes anything from me that I wish to keep.

ANATOL. That may be—but even if you don't want it yourself—still it annoys you—when someone else takes it.

GABRIELLE. Oh——

ANATOL. Dear lady—that's typically feminine. And as it's typically feminine—it's probably highly refined and very beautiful and profound as well.

GABRIELLE. Where did you learn that irony?

ANATOL. Where did I learn it? I'll tell you. I was innocent once—and confiding, and there was no scorn in my words—and I bore many a wound in silence.

GABRIELLE. Don't be romantic.

ANATOL. I could bear honest wounds—I can overcome a "no" spoken at the right time, even by lips I love. But a "no"—when the eyes have said "perhaps" a hundred times—when the lips have smiled "it might be" a hundred times—when the tone of the voice vibrates a hundred promises—such a "no" must turn a man——

GABRIELLE. But we were going to buy your present?

ANATOL. ——must turn a man into a fool—or a cynic.

GABRIELLE. You—you were going to—tell me——

ANATOL. Yes—if you insist.

GABRIELLE. I do. How did you make her acquaintance?

ANATOL. Oh—in the usual way I suppose. The way those things happen—on the street—or at a dance —or in an omnibus—or maybe under an umbrella.

GABRIELLE. But I'm interested in this special case—we're to buy something for this special case.

ANATOL. There are no special cases in "the little world," nor in the great world either for that matter. You're all so true to type.

GABRIELLE. Sir—now you're beginning——

ANATOL. There's no insult in that —not in the slightest—I'm true to type myself.

GABRIELLE. What type are you?

ANATOL. Frivolous. Melancholiac.

GABRIELLE. And I?——

ANATOL. You—that's simple—mondaine.

GABRIELLE. Indeed! And—and she?

ANATOL. She—she's—the sweet little girl.

GABRIELLE. Sweet—she's sweet then—and I—just—just mondaine?

ANATOL. Cruel mondaine—if you insist.

GABRIELLE. Very well. Now do finally tell me something about this —sweet little girl.

ANATOL. She's not fascinatingly beautiful—she hasn't a particle of style—and she certainly is not brilliant.

GABRIELLE. I don't want to know what she is *not*——

ANATOL. But she has the soft charm of a spring evening—the grace of an enchanted princess—and the soul of a girl who knows how to love.

GABRIELLE. That sort of soul is said to be very frequent in the "little world."

ANATOL. You can't imagine what it is like there. They told you too little, when you were a young girl—and they've told you too much since you've been a young wife—that robs your opinions of spontaneity.

GABRIELLE. But I tell you I'm willing to be taught—I'll believe in your enchanted princess. Tell me something of the magic garden in which she sleeps.

ANATOL. Oh, you mustn't imagine any gorgeous drawing-room—with heavily hanging curtains—bric-a-brac—pale velvets—and the affected half-twilight of a dying afternoon——

GABRIELLE. I don't want to hear what I must *not* imagine——

ANATOL. Very well, then, imagine a little dim room, very small—with painted walls—in too light a tone—a few old engravings—poor ones—with faded lettering, here and there—a hanging lamp with a shade. And from the window, at evening, there is a view over roofs and chimneys sinking into the darkness. And when spring comes—the garden opposite will blossom and send out its fragrance——

GABRIELLE. You *must* be happy—if you can think of May—at Christmas.

ANATOL. Yes, I *am* happy—now and then.

GABRIELLE. That will do,—it's growing late—we were to buy something for her—shall it be something for the room with the painted walls?

ANATOL. The room lacks nothing.

GABRIELLE. In *her* eyes—I can believe that. But I would like to dress up the room—to suit your taste.

ANATOL. Mine?

GABRIELLE. With Persian rugs.

ANATOL. Out there?

GABRIELLE. And a shade of frosted red-green glass——

ANATOL. Hm——

GABRIELLE. A few vases with fresh flowers——

ANATOL. But I want to take her something.

GABRIELLE. Yes, that's true—we must make our choice—she's waiting for you, I suppose.

ANATOL. Certainly.

GABRIELLE. She's waiting. Tell me, how does she receive you?

ANATOL. Oh, in the usual way.

GABRIELLE. She hears your steps on the stair—doesn't she?

ANATOL. Yes, sometimes.

GABRIELLE. And she throws her arms around your neck—and kisses you—and what does she say?

ANATOL. Oh, what one usually says in such cases.

GABRIELLE. Well—for instance?

ANATOL. I know of no particular instance.

GABRIELLE. What did she say yesterday?

ANATOL. Oh—nothing special—it would sound silly—if you didn't hear the tone in her voice.

GABRIELLE. I'll try and imagine that tone. Well, what did she say?

ANATOL. "I am so glad that I have you again."

GABRIELLE. "I am so glad"—was that it?

ANATOL. "That I have you again."

GABRIELLE. That's very sweet—very sweet.

ANATOL. Yes, it is sincere—and true.

GABRIELLE. And she's always alone?—you can see each other undisturbed?

ANATOL. Yes, she lives by herself—she's quite alone in the world—no father, no mother—not even an aunt.

GABRIELLE. And you—are everything to her?

ANATOL. Possibly—for the present. (*There is a pause.*)

GABRIELLE. It's growing late—see how empty the streets are.

ANATOL. And I've been detaining you! You ought to get home, I suppose.

GABRIELLE. Yes—they'll be waiting for me. But what shall we do about the present?

ANATOL. Oh—I'll find some trifle.

GABRIELLE. I'm not so sure about that. And I had really made up my mind that I wanted to choose something for your—for that girl.

ANATOL. Oh, really, dear lady——

GABRIELLE. And I'd like most of all to be there when you bring her the present—I have the greatest desire to see that little room and the sweet little girl. She doesn't know how fortunate she is. (ANATOL *starts*) But give me my packages now, please. It's so late.

ANATOL. Here they are—but——

GABRIELLE. And please call up that cab there—the one coming down the street.

ANATOL. Why this hurry—all of a sudden?

GABRIELLE. Please do as I say. (*He beckons to the cab*) Thanks—but what shall we do about that present?
(*The cab stops in front of them.* ANATOL *moves to open the door.*)

GABRIELLE. Wait a moment—I'd like to send her something myself.

ANATOL. You—would?

GABRIELLE. But what shall I?—here, take these flowers. Just these simple flowers—it's to be only a greeting—nothing more—but you must give her a message, too.

ANATOL. This is very sweet of you.

GABRIELLE. Promise me to give her the message?—in the very words in which I say it?

ANATOL. Why, certainly.

GABRIELLE. You'll promise me?

ANATOL. With the greatest pleasure—why not?

GABRIELLE (*opens the door of the cab*). Then tell her——

ANATOL. What?

GABRIELLE. Tell her "these flowers, my sweet little girl, were sent to you by a woman who, perhaps—might know how to love as well as you—but who hasn't the courage."

ANATOL. Dear—lady—— (*She has entered the cab and it drives away. The streets are almost empty now.* ANATOL *stands looking after the cab until it turns the corner. He stands for a moment or two longer, then looks at his watch and hurries away.*)

EPISODE

CHARACTERS

ANATOL
MAX
BIANCA

MAX's room, decorated in dark tones, dark red paper, dark red hangings. There is a door at back, center, another door on the left. A large desk stands in the center of the room, on it a lamp with a shade, books and papers. There is a tall window in the right wall, down front. A fireplace, in which a fire is burning, fills the slant corner of the right wall at back. Two low armchairs and a dark red screen stand before the fire.

MAX (sits at the desk smoking a cigar and reading a letter). "My dear Max. Here I am again. Our company will be in the city three months, I suppose you saw it in the paper. My first evening shall be given to friendship—I'll spend it with you. Bibi." Bibi—that means Bianca—very well, I'll be here. (There is a knock at the door) Already? Come in.

ANATOL (comes in with gloomy mien. He carries a large package under one arm). Good evening.

MAX. Hello—what have you there?

ANATOL. I am seeking a refuge for my past.

MAX. What do you mean? (ANATOL holds out the package towards him) What's that?

ANATOL. It is my past I am bringing you here, my entire youth. Take it into your care.

MAX. With pleasure. But won't you explain?

ANATOL. May I sit down?

MAX. Of course. Why are you so solemn?

ANATOL (sits down). May I light a cigar?

MAX. Take one of these, they are this season's vintage.

ANATOL (lights one of the cigars). Ah——

MAX (pointing to the package which ANATOL has laid on the desk). And that?

ANATOL. I have no place now for these memories of my youth—I am leaving town.

MAX. Indeed!

ANATOL. I am beginning a new life —indefinitely—I must be free and alone, and that is why I free myself from the past.

MAX. Then you have a new love?

ANATOL. No—but I no longer have the old love—that's all for the pres-

686

ent. (*Interrupting himself and pointing to the package*) I can leave all this trash with you, can't I?

MAX. You call it trash? Then why don't you burn it up?

ANATOL. I can't.

MAX. That's childish.

ANATOL. No—it's my kind of constancy. I can't forget a single one of all those I have loved. When I turn over these notes, these flowers and these curls—you'll let me come here occasionally just to do it, won't you?—then I am with them all again, they are all alive, and I adore them as before.

MAX. The idea being that you want to use my rooms as a meeting-place with your past loves?

ANATOL (*scarcely hears him*). There's an idea comes to me now and then. Suppose there were some magic word that could force them all to appear—that could conjure them up out of Nothingness.

MAX. It would be a rather variegated Nothingness.

ANATOL. Yes—and imagine—if I should utter this word——

MAX. You might find something effective—for instance—"my only love."

ANATOL. Yes. Then I would call "My only love" and they would all come—one from a simple tenement home, another from her husband's gorgeous drawing-room, one from her stage dressing-room——

MAX. Several.

ANATOL. Very well—several—one from a milliner's shop——

MAX. One from the arms of a new lover?

ANATOL. One from the grave—one from here, another from there—until they are all come——

MAX. Better not speak that word. It might be an awkward gathering. For while they may have all lost their love for you—not one of them has lost a sense of jealousy.

ANATOL. That is very wise. Rest in peace, therefore.

MAX. But now we must find a place for this stately package.

ANATOL. You'll have to divide it up. (*He opens the package. Its contents are a number of tiny packets tied up in ribbons.*)

MAX. Oh!

ANATOL. It's all neatly arranged here.

MAX. By name?

ANATOL. Oh, no. Each packet bears some inscription, a verse, just a word sometimes, or a sentence, which calls up the memory of each experience. There are no 'names, there might be several Maries or Annas, for instance.

MAX. Let me see some of them.

ANATOL. I wonder if I'll recognize them all? Some have been wrapped up for years. I haven't even looked at them.

MAX (*takes up one of the little packages, reads the inscription*).
"*You are so fair, so sweet, so wild,
I hold you close within my arm,
I kiss your neck, alluring child,
Matilda, of the subtle charm.*"
Why, here's a name—Matilda.

ANATOL. Yes, but that wasn't her name—although I did kiss her neck.

MAX. Who was she?

ANATOL. Don't ask. She has lain in my arms, that is enough.

MAX. Away with Matilda then. Her package is a very thin one.

ANATOL. There's only a curl in it.

MAX. No letters?

ANATOL. Letters? From her? She would have had a hard struggle to write them. And, besides, where would we be if all women insisted on writing to us? Away with Matilda then.

MAX (*reading as before*). "Women are all alike in one respect: they become impudent when you catch them in a lie."

ANATOL. Yes, that is true.

MAX. Who was she? This is a thick package.

ANATOL. Lies, eight pages long, each time. Away with them.

MAX. And she was impudent, too?

ANATOL. Yes, when I found her out. Away with her.

MAX. Away with the impudent liar.

ANATOL. No insults, please. She has lain in my arms—she is sacred.

MAX. Well, that's one reason. Here's the next. (*Reads as before*)
"*When I would send all ugly moods
a-flying,
I think of your betrothed, girlie
mine,
And then, my love, I laugh until
I'm crying,
There are some jokes that really
are divine.*"

ANATOL (*smiling*). Yes, she was—a joke and divine.

MAX. And what's in here?

ANATOL. Only a photograph—she and her betrothed.

MAX. Did you know him?

ANATOL. Surely, or I couldn't have laughed at him. He was a block-head.

MAX (*seriously*). He has lain in her arms—he is sacred.

ANATOL. Enough of them.

MAX (*taking a new package*). What's this—a sentence——

ANATOL. What is it?

MAX (*reads*). "She boxed my ears."

ANATOL. Oh, yes—I remember.

MAX. Was that the end?

ANATOL. No, the beginning.

MAX. I see. And here—"It's easier to change the direction of a flame, than to light it." What does that mean?

ANATOL. Why—I changed the direction of the flame, another lit it.

MAX. Away with the flame. (*Reads*) "She always brought her curling-iron." (*He looks inquiringly at* ANATOL.)

ANATOL. Why, yes, she always brought her curling-iron,—for any eventuality. She was very pretty. I have only a little piece of a veil to remember her by.

MAX. Yes, that's what it feels like. (*Reading the next*) "How did I lose you?" Well, how *did* you lose her?

ANATOL. That's just what I don't know. She was gone—suddenly gone out of my life. That happens sometimes. It's just as if you leave an umbrella somewhere and don't remember it for days afterwards, and then you can't remember where and when you left it.

MAX. Farewell, lost one. (*Reads*) "You were a sweet and merry creature."

ANATOL (*continues dreamily*). "Maiden with the well-pricked fingers."

MAX. That was Cora, wasn't it?

ANATOL. Yes—you knew her.

MAX. Have you ever heard what's become of her?

ANATOL. I met her just recently —as the wife of a cabinet-maker.

MAX. Really?

ANATOL. Yes, that's the usual fate of those maidens with the well-pricked fingers. They are loved in the city, and married in the suburbs. She was a darling.

MAX. Farewell!—and what's this? (*Reading*) "Episode." But there's nothing in this—just a little dust.

ANATOL (*taking the envelope*) Dust?—that was a flower once.

MAX. What does this mean—"Episode?"

ANATOL. Oh, nothing—just a chance thought. It was only an episode, a romance that lasted two hours. Dust?—it's sad to think that this is all that remains of so much sweetness, isn't it?

MAX. Why, yes. But why did you choose just that word? You might have written it on any of them.

ANATOL. True. But I never felt so conscious of it as just that time. Frequently, when I was with this one or that—particularly in my earlier days, when I thought great things of myself—I would feel like saying—"you poor child—you poor child."

MAX. Why?

ANATOL. I thought myself one of the Mighty Ones of the Intellect. These girls—these women,—I crushed them under my iron tread as I wandered over the earth—it is the law of life, I thought. My path lies over these bodies——

MAX. You were the storm wind that scatters the blossoms, eh?

ANATOL. Yes—and thus I rushed on my way—and I thought—"you poor child"—I deceived myself—I know now that I am not of the Great, and the saddest part of it is that I am quite reconciled to the thought. But in those years——

MAX. Well, and this episode?

ANATOL. That was one of them,—a blossom that I found in my path——

MAX. And crushed?

ANATOL. Yes. When I look back on it, it seems to me as if I had really crushed her.

MAX. Indeed!

ANATOL. Yes. Listen. Really, it's one of the very sweetest of all my experiences—I can't tell you——

MAX. Why not?

ANATOL. Because the story itself is so commonplace—it's nothing at all—you couldn't feel the beauty there was in it. The whole secret of it is that it was *I* who experienced it.

MAX. Well?

ANATOL. I sat at my piano—in the little room I had then—it was evening—I had known her just two hours—the lamp with the green-red shade was burning—I mention the green-red lamp, because it's part of the story.

MAX. Well?

ANATOL. Well, I was at the piano—she sat at my feet so that I could not use the pedal—her head rested on my lap and her tumbled hair shone green and red in the lamp light. I was improvising on the keys, but with my left hand only—she held the right to her lips.

MAX. Well?

ANATOL. This expectant "well" of yours will drive me mad. There really isn't any more to it. I had known her only two hours and I knew that I would probably never see her again once the evening was over—she told me so herself—and yet I had the feeling that I was loved madly in that moment. It wrapped me round—the air was heavy and fragrant with this love—do you understand? (MAX *nods*) And again I had that foolish and divine thought—"you poor, poor child." The episodic character of it all came so clearly to my consciousness. While I still felt her warm breath on my hand, I seemed to be living it over in memory—as if it were already a thing of the past. She was just another one of those over whom my path led me. The word came to me then—that arid word "Episode"—and yet I seemed to feel myself as something Eternal. I knew that this poor child would never lose the memory of this hour —I had never felt so sure of it as in just this case. Oh, I often realize that by next morning I will be quite forgotten. But this was different—I was all the world to this girl who lay at my feet—I felt the sacred, enduring love with which she surrounded me—one can feel that—I know that in that moment she had thought for nothing but for me—and yet for me she was already something that was past—something that was fleeting—an Episode.

MAX. Who was she?

ANATOL. You know her—we met her one evening in a jolly crowd—you told me that you'd known her before.

MAX. I've known so many—before. As you describe her, in the lamplight, she seems like a fairy princess.

ANATOL. She wasn't at all—do you know who she was?—of course I'm spoiling the entire charm.

MAX. Who was she?

ANATOL (smiling). She was——

MAX. Theatre?

ANATOL. No—Circus.

MAX. Not really?

ANATOL. Yes, it was Bianca. I never told you until now that I had seen her again—after that first evening, when I scarcely spoke to her.

MAX. And you really believe that Bibi loved you?

ANATOL. Yes—she did. I met her on the street a week or so after that party—she was leaving for Russia the following day.

MAX. So there was no time to lose.

ANATOL. Oh, I knew it—I've spoiled it all for you. You never have discovered the true secret of love.

MAX. And where do you find the solution of the enigma—woman?

ANATOL. In—the right mood.

MAX. I see—twilight—your green-red lamp—music.

ANATOL. Yes, that is it. And because a color can change the whole world for me, is just why I find life so rich in variety, so gloriously changeful. What would this girl with the sparkling hair mean to you or to a thousand others—what would this lamp mean to you—the lamp you mock at? A circus rider and a red-green glass over a light. Of course, then all the charm is gone—one may *live*, but one will never experience anything. The rest of you blunder into an adventure brutally, with your eyes open but your soul shut tight, and you never see its colors. My spirit sheds a thousand lights and colors over it and I can *feel* where you only—possess.

MAX. A well-spring of delight, surely, this spirit of yours. All whom you love dip into it and bring up for you a strange fragrance of adventure and mystery on which you may intoxicate yourself.

ANATOL. Call it that if you will.

MAX. But as far as your circus rider is concerned—you can hardly make me believe that she had the same feelings—under that red-green light, as you did.

ANATOL. But certainly I could sense her emotions while I held her in my arms.

MAX. I have known her also, and better than you do.

ANATOL. Better?

MAX. Yes, because there was no love between us. She's not the fairy princess for me, she's just one of a thousand fallen women to whom a dreamer's imagination lends new virginity. For me, she's no better than a hundred others who leap through the hoops or dance in the closing quadrille.

ANATOL. Indeed——

MAX. And she *is* nothing more. It is not that I fail to see what she can be, it is you who see in her what she is not. Out of the rich, beautiful life of your soul you poured the glow of your fanciful youth into her empty heart. The light you saw shining there was a reflection of your light.

ANATOL. No, it was not. That has happened to me now and then, but not this time. I don't want to make her out any better than she was. I was neither the first nor the last— I was——

MAX. What were you? Just one of many. She was the same in your arms as in all the others—Woman, in her highest moment.

ANATOL. Why did I tell you—you haven't understood me.

MAX. Oh, no. It is you who have misunderstood me. What I wanted to say was that while you may have felt all the sweet magic, it was the same to her as any other time. Can she see the world in a thousand colors?

ANATOL. Do you know her very well?

MAX. Yes, we met frequently in the crowd where you first found her.

ANATOL. Was that all?

MAX. Yes. But we were good friends. She is witty—we liked to chat together.

ANATOL. And that was all?

MAX. That was all.

ANATOL. And yet—she *did* love me.

MAX. Sha'n't we go on with these? (*Taking up a little package, reads*) "Could I but know the meaning of thy smile, oh, green-eyed-beauty."

ANATOL. By the way, do you know that the circus company is here again?

MAX. Certainly. She's here, too.

ANATOL. I suppose so.

MAX. She is. And I shall see her this evening.

ANATOL. You will? Do you know where she lives?

MAX. No, she wrote to me, she's coming here.

ANATOL (*springing up*). What? Why didn't you tell me that sooner?

MAX. What concern is it of yours? I thought you wanted to be "free and alone."

ANATOL. Nonsense.

MAX. And, besides, there's nothing sadder than a warmed-over magic.

ANATOL. You mean——

MAX. I mean—that you ought to avoid seeing her again.

ANATOL. You mean she might attract me again?

MAX. No—but because it was so beautiful then. You'd better go home with that sweet memory of yours. Never try to repeat an experience.

ANATOL. You don't seriously believe that I'll give up this meeting when it's so easy to my hand?

MAX. She has more sense than you have—she hasn't written to you—possibly merely because she's forgotten you.

ANATOL. That is absurd.

MAX. You don't think it possible?

ANATOL. The idea is ridiculous.

MAX. Not everyone's memories can drink from the Elixir of Life that gives yours their enduring freshness.

ANATOL. Ah, but that—that was one of the immortal hours.

MAX. I hear steps outside.

ANATOL. Is it she already?

MAX. You'd better go out through my bedroom.

ANATOL. I'm not such a fool.

MAX. Then you're really willing to have all the charm spoiled?

ANATOL. I shall stay here. (*Knock at the door.*)

MAX. You'd better go. (ANATOL *shakes his head*) Then go back there—where she won't see you right away—here, this will do. (*Pushes* ANATOL *to the fireplace where he is partially hidden by the screen.*)

ANATOL (*leaning against the mantel*). Oh, very well.
(*There is a knock.*)

MAX. Come in.

BIANCA (*coming in quickly*). Good evening, dear Max. Here I am.

MAX (*with both hands outstretched*). Good evening, Bianca, this is mighty nice of you.

BIANCA. You got my letter? You're the very first—you're the only one anyway.

MAX. You can imagine how proud I am!

BIANCA. And how are all the others? Is the crowd still together? Will we meet after the performance evenings, as usual?

MAX (*helping her with her hat and coat*). There were some evenings when you didn't join us.

BIANCA. After the performance?

MAX. Yes, when you disappeared immediately after the performance.

BIANCA (*smiling*). Yes—but that's natural—you know, it's awfully nice to hear that said to you without any jealousy. A girl needs such friends as you are.

MAX. Yes, I should think so.

BIANCA. Friends who like you but don't torture you.

MAX. That doesn't happen to you often, does it?

BIANCA (*catches a glimpse of* ANATOL). But you're not alone? (ANATOL *comes forward and bows.*)

MAX. It's an old acquaintance.

BIANCA (*with her lorgnette at her eyes*). Ah——
(ANATOL *bows, looks at her expectantly.*)

MAX. Well, what do you say to this surprise, Bibi?

BIANCA (*embarrassed, searching her memory*). Why, of course—we know each other.——

ANATOL. Surely—Bianca.

BIANCA. Why, yes—we know each other very well——

ANATOL (*takes her hand with both of his, excited*). Bianca——

BIANCA. Why, yes—where did we meet? Let me see—oh, yes——

MAX. Then you remember?

BIANCA. Why, of course—it was in St. Petersburg?

ANATOL (*dropping her hand*). No —it was not in St. Petersburg, Miss Bianca. (*He turns to go out.*)

BIANCA (*hastily, aside to* MAX). What's the matter? Have I offended him?
(ANATOL *goes out.*)

MAX. He's gone, you see.

BIANCA. But what does this mean?

MAX. Didn't you recognize him?

BIANCA. Why, yes—I recognized him—but I can't just remember—where and when——

MAX. Why, Bibi—it was Anatol.

BIANCA. Anatol? Anatol?

MAX. Yes, Anatol—music—red-green lamp shade—here in the city—about three years ago.

BIANCA. Oh, my goodness, where were my eyes! Anatol! (*Runs to the door*) I must call him back. (*Opens the door, runs out into the hall, calls*) Anatol! Anatol!
(MAX *stands there smiling until she comes back.*)

MAX. Well?

BIANCA (*coming in*). He must be out in the street already. (*Opens the window quickly*) There he is.

MAX (*at window, behind her*). Yes, there he is.

BIANCA (*calls*). Anatol!

MAX. He doesn't hear you.

BIANCA (*stamping her foot*). What a pity! You must ask him to forgive me—I'm afraid I've hurt him, the dear, good boy.

MAX. Then you do remember him?

BIANCA. Why, of course. But he looks so like someone I knew in St. Petersburg.

MAX (*soothingly*). I'll tell him that.

BIANCA. And then, besides—when you haven't even thought of a man for three years and you suddenly see him again—you can't remember everything all of the time.

MAX. I'd better shut the window—there's such a cold draft coming in. (*He shuts the window.*)

BIANCA. I'll see him while I'm here, won't I?

MAX. Perhaps. But I want to show you something. (*Takes an envelope from the desk and shows it to her.*)

BIANCA. What's this?

MAX. It's the flower that you wore on that evening—on *that* evening.

BIANCA. He kept it?

MAX. As you see.

BIANCA. Then he really loved me?

MAX. Madly,—unspeakably, eternally—as he loved all these others. (*Points to the packages.*)

BIANCA. All these others? What does that mean? Are those all flowers?

MAX. Flowers—letters, curls, photographs—we were just arranging them.

BIANCA (*piqued*). Under different headings.

MAX. Surely.

BIANCA. And where do I come in?

MAX. In *this* file, I think. (*Throws the envelope into the fire.*)

BIANCA. Oh——

MAX (*aside*). I'm avenging you as well as I can, Anatol. (*Aloud*) And now don't be angry any longer. Sit down here and tell me some of your adventures of the last three years.

BIANCA. I don't feel much like it now. That was a nice reception.

MAX. But you know I'm your friend—do tell me something interesting.

BIANCA (*in the armchair by the fire*). What do you want to hear?

MAX (*in the chair opposite*). Tell me about the man in St. Petersburg——

BIANCA. You're unendurable.

MAX. Very well.

BIANCA. What do you want me to tell——?

MAX. Why not begin it—"once upon a time?" Once upon a time there was a big, big city——

BIANCA (*still irritated*). And there was a big, big circus——

MAX. And there was a little, little girl——

BIANCA. And she jumped through a big, big hoop. (*Laughs softly.*)

MAX. There you see—now we're off—(*the curtain begins to fall very slowly*)—and in a box—there sat every evening——

BIANCA. And in a box there sat every evening—such a handsome —handsome—— oh, dear——

MAX. Well?

CURTAIN

MILESTONES

CHARACTERS

EMILIE
ANATOL

EMILIE's room, furnished with discreet elegance. Twilight. The window is open, a park beyond can be seen; the top branches of a tree, the leaves just opening, almost fill the window frame.

EMILIE. Ah, ah—this is where I find you?—at my desk? And what are you doing there? Ransacking the drawers? Anatol!

ANATOL. I am in my right,—and I was right to do it, as I have discovered.

EMILIE. Well, and what have you found? Your own letters.

ANATOL. And how about this?

EMILIE. What?

ANATOL. These two little stones— one a ruby—and the other, darker —they're new to me—I didn't give them to you.

EMILIE. No—I had—forgotten.

ANATOL. Forgotten? And they were so carefully hidden away in the corner of the lowest drawer. Can't you confess at once instead of lying, like all the rest of them?—ah, ha, you refuse to speak now? This cheap indignation—it's so much easier to keep silent when one is crushed by the burden of guilt. I'm going to look further—where have you hidden your other jewelry?

EMILIE. I have no other. (ANATOL *begins to pull the drawers open*)

Please don't do that—I swear to you that I have nothing more.

ANATOL. Then why did you have this here—why?

EMILIE. It was wrong—perhaps.

ANATOL. Perhaps? Emilie, this is the very eve of the day on which I intended making you my wife. I believed that all the past was wiped out—all of it. You and I together gathered all the letters, the fans, the thousand trifles which reminded me of the time when we had not met—and you and I together threw them all into the fire there. And your bracelets, your rings—your earrings—we gave them away, or we threw them over the bridge into the river, out of the window onto the street. You knelt before me and you swore to me—"It's all past and over, in your arms I have learned to know what love really means." I believed you,—of course, we always believe what women tell us, from the very first lie that makes us happy——

EMILIE. Shall I swear to you again?

ANATOL. What good would it do? I'm through—I'm through with you. And how well you acted the part! Feverishly, as if you would

696

wash out every stain upon your past, you stood here in front of the fire and watched the papers, the ribbons and the knick-knacks going up in flame; and you sobbed in my arms that day we strolled by the river and tossed a costly bracelet into the gray water. You wept purifying tears then—tears of repentance—and yet it was all a stupid farce! Don't you see that it is all in vain?—that I still distrust you?—that I was right to ransack your desk? Why don't you speak? Why don't you defend yourself?

EMILIE. If you intend to leave me——

ANATOL. But I want to know the meaning of these two stones? I want to know why you kept just these.

EMILIE. You don't love me any more.

ANATOL. I want to know the truth—Emilie, the truth——

EMILIE. Why? If you don't love me any more?

ANATOL. There may be something in the truth which—which makes me understand. Emilie, I don't want to believe the worst of you.

EMILIE. Then you forgive me?

ANATOL. You must tell me what these stones mean.

EMILIE. And then you will forgive me?

ANATOL. I want to know why you kept this ruby.

EMILIE. And you'll listen to me quietly?

ANATOL. Yes—but do speak——

EMILIE. This ruby—belonged in a locket—it fell out——

ANATOL. Who gave you the locket?

EMILIE. That's not why I kept it—I wore it on a—a certain day—on a simple chain—around my neck.

ANATOL. Who gave it to you?

EMILIE. That's unimportant—it was my mother, I think. You see, if I were really the miserable creature you believe me to be, I would tell you that I kept it because my mother gave it to me—and you'd believe it. But I have kept this ruby because it—it fell out of my locket on a day—the memory of which—is very dear to me.

ANATOL. Go on.

EMILIE. Oh, it relieves me to be able to tell you. Wouldn't you laugh at me if I were jealous of your first love?

ANATOL. What do you mean by that?

EMILIE. And yet the memory of it is something very sweet, it's one of those sorrows that seem to soothe us—and then—that day is very dear to me on which I first learned to know—the emotion—the feeling that now binds me to you. Oh, believe me, one must have learned how to love, to be able to love as I love you. If we had met at a time when love was something new for both of us, we might have passed by each other unheeding. No, don't shake your head, Anatol, it is true, and you told me so yourself.

ANATOL. I, myself?

EMILIE. You said it was best this way, that we both had to become ripe for this height of passion.

ANATOL. Yes, there's always some such consolation handy when we're in love with a fallen woman.

EMILIE. So I will tell you frankly that this ruby means to me the memory of the day——

ANATOL. Well, say it.

EMILIE. You know what I mean—the memory of that day—I was a silly little thing—only sixteen.

ANATOL. And he was twenty—tall and dark?

EMILIE (innocently). I don't remember that, beloved. But I remember the forest that whispered around us—and the bright spring day that laughed above the tree-tops. Yes, and I remember a sunbeam that stole out between the bushes and glistened on a yellow flower.

ANATOL. And you don't curse the day that took you from me—before I knew you?

EMILIE. That day may have given me to you. No, Anatol, I do not curse that day, and I scorn to lie to you and to say that I have ever done it. Anatol, I love you as I never loved anyone yet—as you have never been loved yet. And even though every previous expe-rience of mine has lost its value through your first kiss—every other man whom I have ever known has vanished from my memory—that is no reason why I should forget the moment that made a woman of me.

ANATOL. And you pretend to love me?

EMILIE. I can scarcely remember that man's face now—I can scarcely recall the look in his eyes——

ANATOL. But it was in his arms that you laughed love's first sigh—it was from his heart that the warmth first streamed over into yours, awakening the dreaming girl to womanhood—you don't forget all that, do you, grateful soul? And don't you see how this confession maddens me?—don't you see that you have called up all the slumbering past?—and that I realize anew that you can dream of other kisses than mine, and that when you close your eyes in my arms you can see other faces than mine?

EMILIE. Oh, how you misunderstand me! Then you are right, if you believe we must part.

ANATOL. I don't understand you now.

EMILIE. Ah, the women who can lie are fortunate! You can't endure the truth, you men. And yet you've implored me—and swore that you would forgive everything, only not a lie. And I—I confessed everything, I humiliated myself before you—I cried it to your face, "Anatol, I am a lost woman—but I love you." Not a single one of all the stupid excuses that the others find so easy, ever passed my lips. I said to you, "Anatol, I loved luxury, I was wanton, hot-blooded, I have sold myself or thrown myself away—I am not worthy of your love," and do you remember that I said all this to you before you even kissed my hand for the first time? I wanted to run away from you because I loved you, but you pursued me, you begged for my love. I didn't want you, because I didn't want to degrade the man whom I loved more than all—ah, the very first man whom I ever loved—— But you took me and made me yours, and I wept—and trembled—you raised me so high— you gave me back everything— everything that the others had taken from me. In your arms I became what I had never been before—pure and happy—you were so great—you could forgive—and now——

ANATOL. And now?

EMILIE. And now you turn me off because I'm just like all the others.

ANATOL. No—you're not.

EMILIE (gently). What shall I do? Shall I throw away this ruby?

ANATOL. I'm not as great as you think me—no, I'm very petty— throw this ruby away. (He looks at it) It fell out of the locket— it lay in the grass—under the yellow flowers—a sunbeam fell on it—and it sparkled. (There is a long pause) Come, Emilie, it's growing dark outside—shall we walk in the park?

EMILIE. Isn't it too cold?

ANATOL. Oh, no—the air is full of the fragrance of awakening spring.

EMILIE. As you wish, beloved.

ANATOL. And this, this other stone?

EMILIE. Oh, this——

ANATOL. Yes, this black one—what about this?

EMILIE. Do you know what sort of a stone that is?

ANATOL. Well?

EMILIE (with a look of pride and greed). That is a black diamond.

ANATOL (rising). Oh!

EMILIE (still looking at the stone). It's very rare.

ANATOL (with suppressed anger). And why—why did you keep this one?

EMILIE (still absorbed in the stone). Why—it's worth a quarter of a million.
(ANATOL utters a slight scream and throws the stone into the fire.)

EMILIE (screams). What are you doing? (She kneels down, seizes the poker and seeks eagerly for the stone among the glowing coals.)

ANATOL (stands looking at her, she is quite absorbed in her work, has forgotten him entirely, her cheeks are glowing with eagerness—he looks at her for a few moments, then speaks calmly). Harlot! (He goes out.)

THE FAREWELL SUPPER

CHARACTERS

ANNIE
MAX
ANATOL
A WAITER

Private room at Sacher's restaurant. ANATOL *is standing by the door giving the* WAITER *his orders.* MAX *is leaning back in an armchair.*

MAX. Well, are you nearly ready?

ANATOL. In a moment. (*To the* WAITER) Did you understand? (WAITER *goes out.* ANATOL *comes down.*)

MAX. And suppose she doesn't come at all?

ANATOL. Why "at all?" It's just ten o'clock—she can't possibly be here before this.

MAX. The ballet was over some time ago.

ANATOL. Well? She has to get her make-up off, and change her clothes—I'd better run across and wait for her.

MAX. Don't spoil her.

ANATOL. Spoil her? If you knew . . .

MAX. Yes, yes, I know. You treat her brutally—but that's one way to spoil her.

ANATOL. That wasn't what I was going to say. If you only knew——

MAX. Well, say it——

ANATOL. I feel very solemn to-night.

MAX. You're not going to—to become engaged to her?

ANATOL. Oh, no, it's much more solemn.

MAX. You're going to marry her?

ANATOL. Oh, dear—how superficial you are. As if there was not a solemnity of the soul which has nothing whatever to do with all this external nonsense.

MAX. I see. Then you've discovered a hitherto unknown corner in the world of your emotions? And you think she understands?

ANATOL. You're very clumsy at guessing to-day. I am celebrating —the end.

MAX. Oh!

ANATOL. This is a farewell supper.

MAX. And what do you want me here for?

ANATOL. You are to close the eyes of our dead love.

MAX. Your comparison is in very bad taste.

ANATOL. I've been postponing this supper for a week.

MAX. You must have quite an appetite by this time.

ANATOL. Oh, we've been having supper together every evening all this week—but I couldn't find the right word—I didn't dare—you don't know how nervous it makes me.

MAX. And what do you need me for? You want me to give you the word?

ANATOL. It's just as well to have you here—in any case—I want you to assist me if it should be necessary. You can soften things—soothe her —make her understand——

MAX. Well, please tell me first why all this is necessary?

ANATOL. With pleasure—she bores me.

MAX. And you find someone else more amusing?

ANATOL. Yes——

MAX. I see.

ANATOL. Ah, the other—the other.

MAX. What type?

ANATOL. None at all—something quite new — something quite unique.

MAX. Yes, that's so—we never recognize the type until the last.

ANATOL. Imagine a girl—how shall I explain her — three-quarter rhythm.

MAX. You seem to be still under the influence of the ballet.

ANATOL. Yes—I can't help it—she reminds me of a slow Viennese waltz—sentimental cheeriness— smiling roguish melancholy,—that's what she is like—a sweet little blonde head, oh, it's too hard to describe—I feel so warm and content with her—when I give her a bunch of violets she receives it with a tear in the corner of her eye——

MAX. Try her with a bracelet some time.

ANATOL. Oh, dear man—that wouldn't do at all in this case— you're quite mistaken. And believe me, I wouldn't want to bring her here for supper. Her style is the cozy little cheap restaurant across the Line—with the hideous wallpaper and the petty official at the next table. That's the sort of place where I've been spending the last evenings, with her.

MAX. How's that? Didn't you just tell me that you'd been here with Annie?

ANATOL. Yes, that, too. I've eaten two suppers every evening last week—one with the girl I'm trying to win—the other with the girl I'm trying to lose. And I haven't been successful in either case.

MAX. I have a suggestion. Suppose you take Annie to a cheap restaurant and bring the new blonde here to supper—maybe that'll help.

ANATOL. Your comprehension of the situation is hampered by the fact that you don't know the new girl. She's the most modest creature in the world—why, you ought to see her, if I suggest ordering an expensive wine.

MAX. Tears in the corner of her eye?

ANATOL. She won't hear to it, under any condition.

MAX. Then you've been drinking Markersdorfer lately?

ANATOL. Yes—before ten o'clock— the champagne comes later. Such is life.

MAX. Oh, no—not always.

ANATOL. Imagine the contrast. But I've had enough of it. This is one of those cases where I feel that I am really a very honest nature——

MAX. Are you?

ANATOL. I can't stand this double game—I'm losing all my self-respect——

MAX. Oh, see here—it's only me— you needn't put on any airs with me.

ANATOL. Why not—seeing as you *are* here? But in all seriousness, I can't pretend to love where I don't feel anything more.

MAX. Then you only pretend where you do feel something——

ANATOL. I spoke to Annie honestly —in the very beginning—when we had exchanged our vows of eternal love—"Annie, dear," I said, "if either of us should feel, one fine day, that it's all over with our love, then we must confess it openly."

MAX. You arranged all that just as you were vowing eternal love? That's very good.

ANATOL. I've repeated it frequently —"we have no responsibility towards one another—we are free— we can part calmly when the time has come—but there must be no deception—I abhor that."

MAX. Then it ought to be easy, this evening.

ANATOL. Easy? Now that the time has come, I'm afraid to say it—it will hurt her—and I can't endure tears. I may even fall in love with her again if she cries—and then I'll be deceiving the other.

MAX. Oh, no. No deception—I abhor that——

ANATOL. It'll all be much easier if you are here. There is a breath of cold, wholesome cheeriness about you that will stiffen the sentimentality of the parting. One cannot weep in your presence.

MAX. Well, I'm here—but that's about all that I can do for you. You certainly don't want me to encourage her to let you go—do you? I could never do that—you're such a dear fellow.

ANATOL. Oh, well, you might try— up to a certain point, anyway. You might tell her that she isn't losing very much in me.

MAX. Yes, I might do that.

ANATOL. Tell her that she can find a hundred others, better looking— richer——

MAX. Cleverer——

ANATOL. Oh, no—you needn't exaggerate.

(*The* WAITER *opens the door and* ANNIE *comes, with a raincoat hastily thrown over her dress, a white boa around her neck, her conspicuously big hat is put on anyhow, and she carries a pair of yellow gloves.*)

ANNIE. Oh, good evening.

ANATOL. Good evening, Annie. Excuse me for not——

ANNIE. You're a nice person to depend on. (*Throws off her coat*) I stand there, looking around—not a soul in sight.

ANATOL. You hadn't far to come.

ANNIE. But you ought to keep your promise. Good evening, Max. (*To* ANATOL) You might have let them begin serving.
(ANATOL *kisses her.*)

ANNIE. I'm hungry. (*The* WAITER *knocks*) Come in. He knocks today—it never occurred to him before.
(*The* WAITER *comes in.*)

ANATOL. You can serve the supper. (*The* WAITER *goes out.*)

ANNIE. Were you in the opera house tonight?

ANATOL. No—I was obliged——

ANNIE. You didn't lose much—everybody was sleepy tonight——

MAX. What was the opera?

ANNIE. I don't know. (*They sit down at the table*) I go to my dressing room—and then on to the stage—I never bother about the rest of it—by the way, I have something to tell you, Anatol.

ANATOL. Have you, dear? Anything important?

ANNIE. Yes, rather—it may surprise you.
(*The* WAITER *comes in with dishes.*)

ANATOL. You make me curious. I, too——

ANNIE. Wait a moment—there's no necessity for him to hear it——

ANATOL (*to* WAITER). You may go —we'll ring. (WAITER *goes out*) Well?

ANNIE. Yes, my dear Anatol—it'll surprise you and yet I don't know —it shouldn't—no, it really shouldn't surprise you.

MAX. Have they raised your salary?

ANATOL. Don't interrupt her.

ANNIE. Why, you see, Anatol—say, are these Ostend or Whitestable?

ANATOL. Now she's talking about the oysters. They're Ostend.

ANNIE. I thought so—I do love oysters. It's really the only food that one can eat every day.

MAX. Not only can—but ought to.

ANNIE. Don't you think so?

ANATOL. But you had something important to tell me.

ANNIE. Yes—it is important—decidedly so. You remember a certain remark of yours?

ANATOL. Which? How can I possibly know which remark you mean?

MAX. No, he can't.

ANNIE. Why, I mean the—now wait a minute—how was it exactly? "Annie," you said, "we must never deceive one another——"

ANATOL. Yes, yes—well——

ANNIE. "Never deceive each other —it would be better to tell the entire truth."

ANATOL. Yes—I meant——

ANNIE. But if it's too late——

ANATOL. What's that?

ANNIE. No—it's not too late. I'm telling you in time—but only just in time. It may be too late tomorrow.

ANATOL. Are you crazy, Annie?

MAX. How's that?

ANNIE. Anatol, you must eat your oysters—or I won't say another word.

ANATOL. What does this mean? You must——

ANNIE. Eat!

ANATOL. You must talk—I can't stand this sort of joke.

ANNIE. Well—didn't we arrange that we were to tell each other quite calmly—when the time came? The time has come.

ANATOL. What time? What does this mean?

ANNIE. It means that this is my last supper with you.

ANATOL. Will you have the kindness—to explain yourself?

ANNIE. It's all up between us.

ANATOL. Yes—but——

MAX. Oh, this is excellent——

ANNIE. What's so excellent about it? Well, I don't care—it's true.

ANATOL. My dear girl—I still don't understand—have you had an offer of marriage?

ANNIE. Oh, if that was all—that would be no reason for getting rid of you.

ANATOL. Getting rid of me?

ANNIE. I'll have to tell you—I am in love, Anatol—madly in love.

ANATOL. And may I ask with whom?

ANNIE. Say, Max, what are you laughing at?

MAX. This is very funny.

ANATOL. Don't mind him. This is a matter between us two, Annie. You certainly owe me an explanation.

ANNIE. Well, I'm giving it to you. I have fallen in love with someone else. And I'm telling you openly— because that's the way it was arranged between us.

ANATOL. Yes, but—who the devil?

ANNIE. My dear boy, you mustn't be coarse.

ANATOL. I demand—I demand definitely——

ANNIE. Max, won't you please ring the bell. I'm so hungry.

ANATOL. Ha! She's hungry—hungry! At such a moment!

MAX (to ANATOL). Remember this is *her first* supper tonight. (*The* WAITER *comes in.*)

ANATOL. What do you want?

WAITER. You rang, sir.

MAX. Bring the next course. (WAITER *clears table.*)

ANNIE. Yes—Catalini's going to Germany, that's settled.

MAX. Indeed! And they're letting her go—without any fuss.

ANNIE. I don't know about that.

ANATOL (*pacing the room*). The wine—where's the wine? Jean! Are you asleep?

WAITER. Here's the wine, sir.

ANATOL. I don't mean that wine—I mean the champagne—you know I want it with the first course. (WAITER *goes out*) And now your explanation, please.

ANNIE. It's no use believing a word you men say—not a word. It sounded so nice when you said it, "When we feel that the end has come, we'll say so openly and we'll part peacefully."

ANATOL. Will you please finally . . . ?

ANNIE. This is what he calls being peaceful.

ANATOL. My dear girl—you can understand that it interests me, can't you? Who——

ANNIE (*sipping the wine slowly*). Ah—um——

ANATOL. Well, drink it.

ANNIE. You can wait a minute, can't you?

ANATOL. You generally drink it in one gulp——

ANNIE. But my dear Anatol, I'm saying good-bye to this Bordeaux. Goodness knows for how long.

ANATOL. What nonsense is this?

ANNIE. There'll be no Bordeaux for me—and no oysters—and no champagne—(*the* WAITER *comes with another dish, she looks at it*)—and no Filet aux Truffes—that's all over.

MAX. What a sentimental appetite you have. May I give you some of this?

ANNIE. Thanks. (ANATOL *lights a cigarette.*)

MAX. Aren't you eating anything?

ANATOL. Not yet. (WAITER *goes out*) And now I would really like to know—who the happy man is.

ANNIE. Suppose I should tell you his name,—you wouldn't know any more then.

ANATOL. What sort of a man is he? How did you come to know him? What does he look like?

ANNIE. Beautiful—he's beautiful! But that's all.

ANATOL. It seems to be enough for you.

ANNIE. Yes, there'll be no oysters now.

ANATOL. So you said.

ANNIE. And no champagne.

ANATOL. Confound it—he must have some other characteristic than the mere fact that he can't buy oysters and champagne for you.

MAX. He's right—that isn't what you might call a profession or an occupation.

ANNIE. But what does it matter— if I love him? I'm giving it all up— it's something quite new—something I've never experienced before.

MAX. Oh, but see here, Annie, if that's all it is, Anatol could have offered you a cheap supper, too.

ANATOL. What is he? A clerk? A chimney-sweep? A traveling salesman?

ANNIE. See here—you mustn't insult him——

MAX. Then why don't you tell us what he is?

ANNIE. He's an artist.

ANATOL. What kind of an artist— trapeze? That'll be something to your taste. A circus-rider?

ANNIE. Stop scolding. He's a colleague of mine.

ANATOL. Ah ha—an old acquaintance, eh? You've seen him daily for some years?—and you've been untrue to me for some time?

ANNIE. I shouldn't have said anything to you in that case. I depended on your word—that's why I'm confessing it to you before it's too late.

ANATOL. But you've been in love with him—Lord knows how long— you've been deceiving me—in spirit anyway.

ANNIE. Well, I can't help that.

ANATOL. You are a——

MAX. Anatol!

ANATOL. Do I know him?

ANNIE. I don't suppose you've noticed him—he dances in the chorus —but he'll be promoted—he'll be promoted.

ANATOL. And since when—have you discovered your heart?

ANNIE. Since this evening.

ANATOL. Don't lie to me.

ANNIE. I'm telling you the truth. This evening—I knew it was my Fate.

ANATOL. Her fate—do you hear that, Max? Her fate.

ANNIE. Well, a thing like that is fate.

ANATOL. But I want to know all about it—I have a right to know—you're still mine in this moment—I want to know how long this has been going on—I want to know when it began—I want to know how he dared——

MAX. Yes, you really ought to tell us.

ANNIE. This is what I get for being so honest—um—I ought to have done the way Fritzi did—with her Baron. He doesn't know anything yet, and she's been running around for three months with a Hussar Lieutenant.

ANATOL. The Baron will find it out some of these days.

ANNIE. Maybe—but *you'd* never have found it out—never—I'm much too slick for that—and you're much too stupid. (*Pours out a glass of wine.*)

ANATOL. Stop drinking.

ANNIE. Not much. I want to get a jag tonight—it'll probably be the last.

MAX. For a week?

ANNIE. Forever. I'll stay with Carl because I'm really fond of him—and he's so jolly even if he hasn't any money and he doesn't make me angry—and he's a dear, dear, sweet boy.

ANATOL. You haven't kept your promise—you've been in love with him ever so long—that's a stupid lie—that talk about this evening.

ANNIE. You needn't believe it if you don't want to.

MAX. Now, Annie, do tell the story straight—or not at all. If you want to part calmly, you ought to do this for him, for your Anatol——

ANATOL. Then I'll tell you something, too.

ANNIE. Well, it began——
(*The* WAITER *comes in.*)

ANATOL. Go on. (*Sits down beside her.*)

ANNIE. It was about two weeks ago—or maybe a little longer—when he brought a couple of roses—at the stage door. It made me laugh—he looked so shy.

ANATOL. You didn't tell me that.

ANNIE. What was there to tell?

ANATOL. Well, go on.

ANNIE. And then at rehearsal—he hung around me—in such a funny way—and I noticed it. It made me mad at first—and then I was glad.

ANATOL. Quite simple, I see.

ANNIE. And then we began to talk to each other—and everything about him pleased me.

ANATOL. What did you talk about?

ANNIE. All sorts of things—he told me how they'd put him out of school—and how he'd tried to learn a trade—and then the real stage blood in him began to make itself felt——

ANATOL. You've never told me any of that——

ANNIE. And then what do you think? Then it came out that when we were children we lived in the same street—just two houses apart.

ANATOL. Neighbors—how touching!

ANNIE. Yes, isn't it? (*Drinks.*)

ANATOL. Go on.

ANNIE. There's nothing more—I've told you everything. It's my Fate—and you can't do anything against Fate—no—you—can't—do anything—when it's Fate.

ANATOL. But I want to know about this evening.

ANNIE. What about——? (*Her head sinks back.*)

MAX. She's going to sleep.

ANATOL. Wake her up. Put the wine where she can't see it—I must know what happened this evening. Annie—Annie——

ANNIE. This evening—he told me—that he—loved me.

ANATOL. And you?

ANNIE. I told him—that I was very glad. And because I don't want to—to deceive him—I'll say good-bye to you.

ANATOL. Because you don't want to deceive *him*? Then it isn't for my sake—but for his?

ANNIE. What's the matter with you? I don't love you any more.

ANATOL. Ah ha—that was good! Fortunately I don't mind this now.

ANNIE. Indeed!

ANATOL. Because I, too, am in the same fortunate situation—I can get along without your affection now.

ANNIE. Oh, can you?

ANATOL. I can. I haven't loved you for some time—I love someone else.

ANNIE. Ha! Ha!

ANATOL. Ask Max. I told him all about it before you came in.

ANNIE. Did you?

ANATOL. I haven't loved you for some time—the other is a thousand times better and more beautiful.

ANNIE. Indeed!

ANATOL. I'd give a thousand women like you for one such girl—do you hear? (ANNIE *laughs*) You needn't laugh—ask Max.

ANNIE. This is awfully funny—you're trying to make me believe.

ANATOL. But it's true I tell you—I swear it's true. I haven't loved you for ever so long. I haven't thought of you—not even while I was here with you. And when I kissed you I was thinking of the other—the other——

ANNIE. Well—then we're quits.

ANATOL. Do you think so?

ANNIE. Yes, we're quits—and I'm glad of it.

ANATOL. No, we're not quits—not at all—it's not the same thing—your experience and mine. My story is not quite so—innocent.

ANNIE (*more serious*). What's that?

ANATOL. My story sounds somewhat different.

ANNIE. Why is it different?

ANATOL. Why, I—I have been untrue to you.

ANNIE (*rising*). What?

ANATOL. I've deceived you—as you deserve. Day by day—night after night—I came from her when I met you—and returned to her when I left you.

ANNIE. That—is—infamous! (*She goes to hatstand, throws on her coat and boa.*)

ANATOL. One can't be quick enough with women like you—or else they'll get ahead of one—well, fortunately, I have no illusions.

ANNIE. Yes, there you can see——

ANATOL. Exactly.

ANNIE. You can see that a man is a hundred times less considerate than a woman.

ANATOL. Exactly. I'm not considerate——

ANNIE (*winds her boa around her throat, takes up her gloves, stands in front of* ANATOL). No, you're certainly not! I wouldn't have told you—*that.* (*She turns to go.*)

ANATOL. What's that?

MAX. Let her go. You don't want to stop her, do you?

ANATOL. You wouldn't have told me —*that?* You mean that you—that you——

ANNIE (*at the door*). I *never* would have told you—never—never—it takes a man to be so inconsiderate! (*The* WAITER *comes in with a dish of dessert.*)

ANATOL. Take that stuff away.

ANNIE. What's that? (*Looks at it*) Vanilla cream? Oh!

ANATOL. You dare?

MAX. Oh, let her—she has to say good-bye to the cream—forever.

ANNIE. Yes, and I'm glad to do it, too. And to say good-bye to the Bordeaux and the champagne—and the oysters—but most particularly am I glad to say good-bye to you, Anatol. (*Suddenly, with a vulgar laugh, she pounces on the box of cigarettes on a side table and takes out a handful, putting them in her bag.*)

ANNIE. These aren't for me—I'm taking them for him. (*Goes out.* ANATOL *moves as if to follow, then stops by the door.*)

MAX (*calmly*). There, you see—it was very easy after all.

CURTAIN

DISSOLUTION

CHARACTERS

ANATOL
MAX
ELSA

ANATOL's *room. The dusk is falling. The room is empty at first, then* ANATOL *and* MAX *come in.*

MAX. There—now I have come up with you after all.

ANATOL. Can't you stay a while?

MAX. But I'll be in the way, won't I?

ANATOL. Please stay. I don't feel like being alone—and who knows whether she'll be here at all.

MAX. Indeed!

ANATOL. Seven times out of ten I sit and wait in vain.

MAX. I couldn't stand that.

ANATOL. And sometimes I have to believe her excuses—unfortunately, they're true.

MAX. All seven times?

ANATOL. How do I know? I give you my word there's nothing more disagreeable than to be the lover of a married woman.

MAX. Oh, yes—I'd rather be her lover than her husband.

ANATOL. And this has been going on—how long is it now? Two years —oh, no, it's more—it was two years at carnival time—this is the third "Springtime of our Love."

MAX. What's the matter with you today?

ANATOL (*has thrown himself down in a chair, still in overcoat and hat*). Oh, I'm so tired—I'm so nervous— I don't know what I want anyway.

MAX. Why don't you go away?

ANATOL. What for?

MAX. To hasten the end.

ANATOL. What do you mean by— the end?

MAX. I've seen you like this before —last time—don't you remember? —when you could not make up your mind to part from a certain silly little thing who really wasn't worth your pangs?

ANATOL. You mean—that I don't love her any more?

MAX. Oh, if that were it—one doesn't suffer at that stage. What you're going through now is much worse than death—it's dying.

ANATOL. You have a talent for saying these pleasant things. But you're right. This is dissolution— the death-agony.

MAX. It's a sort of a comfort to talk it out. And we need no philosophy

710

for this—we needn't go into the bigger generalities—it's enough if we comprehend this special case in its most hidden causes.

ANATOL. I can't foresee much pleasure—from what you suggest.

MAX. I was just talking. But I've seen it hanging over you all the afternoon, even in the Prater, where you were so pale, and just about as tiresome as you could be.

ANATOL. She was to drive there to-day.

MAX. And yet you were glad that we didn't meet her carriage—probably because you no longer have the same smile at your disposal with which you greeted her two years ago.

ANATOL (rising). Why does it happen like this? Can you tell me why it happens? Must I go through all that again?—the gradual, slow, unspeakably sad fading out—oh, you don't realize how it makes me shudder——

MAX. That's why I tell you to go away. Or else have the courage to tell her the truth.

ANATOL. Tell her what? And how?

MAX. Tell her quite simply—that it's all over.

ANATOL. We have no call to be particularly proud of this sort of truth; it's only the brutal sincerity of tired liars.

MAX. Of course. You'd rather hide it from one another in a thousand subterfuges—this fact that your

feelings have changed—rather than part in a quick decision. Why, I wonder?

ANATOL. Because we don't believe it ourselves yet. Because in the midst of this desert of dissolution there are strangely deceptive blossoming moments, when it all seems more beautiful than ever before. We never feel a stronger longing for happiness than in these last days of dying love—and then when something comes—a whim, a passing intoxication—a Nothing—disguised as happiness—we don't want to lift the mask. And then there are the moments in which we are ashamed of having thought all the sweetness ended. We beg each other's forgiveness without expressing it in words. We are exhausted by the fear of dying—and then life suddenly gleams before us, hotter—more ardent than ever—and more illusory than ever.

MAX. Don't forget one thing—the end often begins much sooner than we believe. Many a love began to die with the first kiss. Have you never heard of the fatally ill who think themselves well until the last moment?

ANATOL. I am not of these fortunate ones. I know that. I have always been a hypochondriac of love. My emotions may not have been as sick as I thought them—that is all the worse—I feel sometimes as if the legend of the Evil Eye had come true in my case. But my Evil Eye is turned inward, and my best emotions sicken under its glance.

MAX. Then you must have the courage of this Evil Eye.

ANATOL. Oh, no, I envy the others—you know, those happy ones for whom every bit of life means a new victory. I have to force myself to carry anything to fulfillment—I make halts all along the road, I stop to think it over, to rest—I drag so much with me—the others conquer easily—in the very midst of the experience—it is all one and the same thing for them.

MAX. Don't envy them, Anatol—they do not conquer—they merely pass by.

ANATOL. And isn't that happiness of itself? They, at least, do not have this strange feeling of guilt—which is the secret of all our pangs of parting.

MAX. Where is the guilt?

ANATOL. Isn't it our duty to put the eternity which we promise them into the few years or hours during which we love them? And we never can—never! With this feeling of guilt we part from each one of them—and our melancholy is really only a secret confession—it is our last trace of honesty.

MAX. Our first, sometimes.

ANATOL. And all that hurts so.

MAX. Your present always drags a heavy load of undigested past about with it. The first years of your love begin to decay before your soul has the strength to cast them off. What is the natural consequence? An odor of this decay floats through the wholesome blooming hours of the present—and its atmosphere is fatally poisoned.

ANATOL. That may well be

MAX. Hence this eternal confusion of Once—and Now—and Later—in you—this undefined transition. What has been, isn't for you just a simple, inelastic fact, freed from the moods with which you experienced it—no, these moods cling to it heavily, only they fade and wither—and die.

ANATOL. Yes—and from this atmosphere of decay come the torturing exhalations which waft over my very best moments. I want to save myself from them.

MAX. And I notice, to my great surprise, that not one of us is safe from the danger of saying something really first-class—at least once in our lives. There's something on the tip of my tongue now: "Be strong, Anatol, and you will recover."

ANATOL. You're laughing yourself while you say it. I may possibly have the power to do it—but I lack what is more important—the desire to do it. I feel that I would lose very much if one fine day I should suddenly become—"strong." There are so many diseases but only one health. If one is well, one is just like all the others—but if one is ill, one can still be quite different from all the others.

MAX. Isn't that only vanity?

ANATOL. Suppose it is? And now I suppose you will say that vanity is a fault, eh?

MAX. The inmost sense of all this is —that you're not going away?

ANATOL. I may go away—but I must surprise myself in doing it—it mustn't be any prearrangement—that spoils everything. That's the most dreadful part of all these things—you have to pack your trunk and order a cab—and tell the driver that you want to go to the station. . . .

MAX. I could attend to all that for you.
(ANATOL *has moved quickly to the window and looked out.*)

MAX. What is it now?

ANATOL. Nothing——

MAX. Oh, yes, I forgot—I'm going.

ANATOL. There, you see—in this moment I feel——

MAX. What?

ANATOL. That I adore her.

MAX. There's a very simple explanation of that—namely, that you really *do* adore her—in this moment.

ANATOL. Good-bye then—and don't order the cab just yet.

MAX. Don't be too self-confident—the Trieste Express doesn't leave for four hours yet—and I could send your trunk after you.

ANATOL. Thanks awfully.

MAX (*at the door*). I can't possibly leave without an aphorism.

ANATOL. Well?

MAX. Woman is an enigma.

ANATOL. Oh, dear——

MAX. Let me finish, please—woman is an enigma, so they say. But what an enigma we would be for a woman who had sense enough to study us.

ANATOL. Bravo—bravo!
(MAX *bows and goes out.* ANATOL *walks about the room, then sits down by the window again and smokes a cigarette. The sound of a violin is heard in the story above—there is a pause—steps are heard in the corridor—*ANATOL *listens, rises, puts down his cigarette and goes to meet* ELSA, *who comes in deeply veiled.*)

ANATOL. At last!

ELSA. Yes, I know it's late. But I couldn't get here any earlier—it was impossible. (*Lays off her hat and veil.*)

ANATOL. Couldn't you have sent me word? Waiting makes me so nervous. But—you'll stay for a while?

ELSA. Not very long—my husband—— (ANATOL *turns away*) There you go again—I really can't help it.

ANATOL. Yes, yes, you are right—that's the way it is—and we have to put up with it. Come over here, sweetheart. (*They go to the window.*)

ELSA. Someone might see me.

ANATOL. It's too dark now—and the curtain hides us. It's awfully annoying that you can't stay—I haven't seen you for two whole days—and it was such a few minutes the last time.

ELSA. Do you love me?

ANATOL. You know I do—you're everything to me—I want to be with you always.

ELSA. And I'm so happy with you.

ANATOL. Come—— (*Draws her down beside him in the armchair, kisses her hand*) This sweet little hand. . . . Do you hear the old man upstairs playing his violin? Isn't it beautiful?

ELSA. My sweetheart!

ANATOL. Oh—to be with you—on Lake Como—or in Venice——

ELSA. I was there on my wedding trip.

ANATOL (*with suppressed anger*). Did you have to say that?

ELSA. But I love only you—I've never loved anyone but you—never anyone else—and certainly not my husband——

ANATOL (*folding his hands*). Please —can't you imagine yourself unmarried for a few seconds at least? Can't you enjoy the charm of this moment—and imagine that we two are alone in all the world? (*A clock strikes.*)

ELSA. What time is it?

ANATOL. Elsa—Elsa, don't ask. Forget that there's anyone else in the world—while you're with me.

ELSA (*tenderly*). Haven't I forgotten enough for your sake?

ANATOL. Dearest! (*Kisses her hand.*)

ELSA. My dear Anatol!

ANATOL. What is it, love? (*ELSA signifies with a gesture and a smile that she must be going*) You mean?

ELSA. I must go.

ANATOL. You must?

ELSA. I must.

ANATOL. You must?—now?—very well, go. (*He moves away from her.*)

ELSA. You're impossible today.

ANATOL. Yes—I'm impossible today. (*Pacing the room*) Don't you understand that this life will drive me mad?

ELSA. Is that my thanks?

ANATOL. Thanks? Thanks for what? Haven't I given you as much as you gave me? Do I love you any less than you love me? Do I make you any less happy than you make me? —love—madness—pain—but gratitude?—where does that stupid word come from anyway?

ELSA. Then you don't think I have earned—not even a little bit of gratitude from you? I, who have sacrificed everything for you?

ANATOL. Sacrificed? I don't want any sacrifices. If it was a sacrifice then you never loved me.

ELSA. I never loved him? And I betrayed my husband for his sake— I never loved him?

ANATOL. I didn't say that.

ELSA. Oh, what have I done?

ANATOL (*standing in front of her*). Oh, what have I done? This brilliant remark was the only thing lacking. What have you done? I'll tell you. You were a silly girl seven years ago and then you married because it was the thing to do. You went on your wedding trip to Venice—you were happy——

ELSA. Never!

ANATOL. Happy—in Venice—on Lake Como—it was love—in certain moments anyway.

ELSA. Never.

ANATOL. What! Didn't he kiss you? —embrace you? Weren't you his wife? Then you returned—and you found everything tiresome—that's natural—you were pretty—attractive—and a woman—— And he was merely a blockhead. Then came the years of coquetry—I am taking for granted it was only coquetry—you told me that you had never loved anyone before me. I can't prove that, but I will take it for granted; because I should dislike the alternative.

ELSA. Anatol—I? coquet?

ANATOL. Yes, coquet—and what does it mean to be coquet? It means to be a wanton and a liar at the same time.

ELSA. And was I—that?

ANATOL. You were. Then came years of struggle—you wavered— you thought "shall I never experience my romance?" You grew more beautiful—your husband more tiresome, stupid and ugly—it had to come finally—you took a lover. I happened to be that lover.

ELSA. Happened to be? You!

ANATOL. Yes, happened to be—but if I hadn't been there it would have been somebody else. You felt unhappy in your marriage or at least not sufficiently happy—you wanted to be loved. You flirted a little with me—you talked about the grand passion—and one fine day when you noticed some friend driving past in her carriage—or perhaps a cocotte in a box near you at the theatre, then you thought to yourself, "why shouldn't I have a little pleasure, too?" and so you became mine. What have you done? That is all you have done, and I don't see why you should use any big phrases for this little adventure.

ELSA. Anatol—adventure?

ANATOL. Yes.

ELSA. Take back what you have just said—I implore you.

ANATOL. I don't know what I should take back. That is all it was for you.

ELSA. You really believe that?

ANATOL. Yes.

ELSA. Very well—I must go.

ANATOL. You can go. I sha'n't detain you.
(*There is a pause.*)

ELSA. You send me away?

ANATOL. I?—send you away? And two minutes ago you said, "I must go."

ELSA. But I must—Anatol. Can't you see——

ANATOL (*with decision*). Elsa!

ELSA. What is it?

ANATOL. Elsa! You love me? You said so?

ELSA. I said it. For pity's sake what further proof do you demand of me?

ANATOL. Do you want to know? Good! I may believe that you love me——

ELSA. May believe? You say that today——

ANATOL. You love me?

ELSA. I adore you.

ANATOL. Then—stay with me.

ELSA. What?

ANATOL. Go away with me—yes—with me. To another city—to another world—I want to be alone with you.

ELSA. What an idea!

ANATOL. It would be the one natural thing—how can I let you go away—go to him—how could I ever let you go? How can you do it yourself—you who adore me? You go from my arms, still hot from my kisses, you go back into that house which must feel strange to you since you have belonged to me. We have made the best of it—we haven't even thought how monstrous it is. It's impossible to go on living this way. Elsa, Elsa, won't you come with me?—you don't answer—Elsa! To Sicily—any-

where you wish—across the ocean if you will—Elsa!

ELSA. What are you saying?

ANATOL. With nobody ever between us again—across the ocean, Elsa,—we'll be alone——

ELSA. Across the ocean?

ANATOL. Wherever you wish.

ELSA. You dear, sweet—child——

ANATOL. Do you hesitate?

ELSA. Why listen, dearest—why should we need that?

ANATOL. Need what?

ELSA. To go away—it isn't at all necessary—we can see each other here almost as often as we would like to.

ANATOL. Almost as often as we'd like to—yes—it isn't necessary.

ELSA. These are fancies——

ANATOL. You're quite right. (*There is a pause.*)

ELSA. Are you angry? (*Clock strikes.*)

ANATOL. You must go.

ELSA. For heaven's sake—how late it is!

ANATOL. Yes, you had better go.

ELSA. Tomorrow then. I'll be here at six o'clock.

ANATOL. Just as you say.

ELSA. Aren't you going to kiss me?

ANATOL. Oh, yes.

ELSA. I'll make it all up to you to-morrow.

ANATOL (*accompanies her to the door*). Good-bye.

ELSA (*at the door*). One kiss more.

ANATOL. Why not? There. (*He kisses her. She goes out.*)

ANATOL (*coming back into the room*). With that kiss I have made her what she deserves to be—just one more. (*He shivers*) It's all so stupid.

ANATOL'S WEDDING MORNING

CHARACTERS

ANATOL
MAX
ILONA
FRANZ (servant)

A tastefully decorated bachelor apartment: a door, right, leads into the vestibule; a door to the left, with curtains, into the bedroom. ANATOL, *in house jacket, comes on tiptoe from the room left, and shuts the door gently. He sits down on a couch and presses a button, a bell rings.* FRANZ *comes from R. and goes to the door L. without noticing* ANATOL. ANATOL *does not see him at first, then runs after him and stops him before he opens the door.*

ANATOL. Why are you sneaking in like that? I didn't hear you.

FRANZ. What do you wish, sir?

ANATOL. Bring the samovar.

FRANZ. Yes, sir. (*Goes out.*)

ANATOL. Softly, you blockhead—can't you walk more softly? (*Tiptoes to the door L., opens it slightly*) She's asleep—she's still asleep. (*He closes the door.*)

FRANZ (*brings the samovar*). Two cups, sir?

ANATOL. Yes. (*The bell rings*) Who's that so early?
(FRANZ *goes out.*)

ANATOL. I certainly don't feel like getting married this morning. I wish I could send a regret.
(FRANZ *opens the door R., letting in* MAX.)

MAX (*affectionately*). My dear boy!

ANATOL. Hush! Be quiet! Bring another cup, Franz!

MAX. But there's two cups there already.

ANATOL. Bring another cup, Franz, and now get out. (FRANZ *goes out*) There—and now my dear man, what brings you here at eight o'clock in the morning?

MAX. It's ten o'clock.

ANATOL. Then what brings you here at ten o'clock in the morning?

MAX. My poor memory.

ANATOL. Speak more softly, please.

MAX. Why? Are you so nervous?

ANATOL. I am—very nervous.

MAX. You shouldn't be nervous to-day.

ANATOL. Well, what do you want?

MAX. You know I'm to have your pretty cousin Alma for a partner——

ANATOL (*sadly*). Yes, yes.

MAX. Well, I forgot to order flowers—and I really don't know what color dress she'll wear—will it be white or pink or blue or green?

ANATOL (*peevish*). Not green anyway.

MAX. Why not?

ANATOL. Alma never wears green.

MAX (*piqued*). How should I know that?

ANATOL (*as before*). Don't scream so! We can talk it over calmly, can't we?

MAX. Then you don't know what color dress she'll wear?

ANATOL. Pink or blue.

MAX. But there's quite a difference between pink and blue.

ANATOL. Pink or blue—what does it matter?

MAX. It matters a good deal, for the flowers I order.

ANATOL. Order two bouquets—then you can put the other one in your own buttonhole.

MAX. I didn't come here to listen to any of your poor jokes.

ANATOL. I'll make the worst one yet at two o'clock today.

MAX. You're in a nice mood for your wedding morning.

ANATOL. I'm nervous.

MAX. You're hiding something from me.

ANATOL. No.

ILONA (*voice from the bedroom*). Anatol!
(MAX *looks at* ANATOL *in surprise.*)

ANATOL. Excuse me a moment. (*He goes to the door of the bedroom and disappears behind it.* MAX *looks after him with wide eyes.* ANATOL *kisses* ILONA, *near the door, but where they cannot be seen by* MAX, *closes the door and comes into the room again.*)

MAX (*indignant*). People don't do those things——

ANATOL. Hear my story first, Max, and then judge.

MAX. I hear a feminine voice and I judge—that you're beginning early to deceive your wife.

ANATOL. Now sit down here and listen to me—and then you'll talk differently.

MAX. Never! I'm no paragon of virtue—but—but this——

ANATOL. Then you won't listen to me?

MAX. Go ahead—but be quick—I'm invited to your wedding. (*They both sit down.*)

ANATOL (*sadly*). Yes.

MAX (*impatiently*). Well?

ANATOL. Well? There was a Wedding-Eve Party last night at the home of my future parents-in-law.

MAX. I know. I was there.

ANATOL. Quite right. You were there—there were a lot of people there—they were very gay—drank champagne—spoke toasts——

MAX. Yes, so did I—to your happiness.

ANATOL. Yes, so did you—to my happiness. (*Presses his hand*) I thank you.

MAX. You did that yesterday.

ANATOL. Well, we were quite gay until midnight.

MAX. Which I know.

ANATOL. For a moment I almost thought I was happy.

MAX. After the fourth glass of champagne.

ANATOL (*sadly*). No. Not until after the sixth—that's awfully sad —I can scarcely believe it.

MAX. We've discussed that already.

ANATOL. And that young man was there, too—I feel certain that he was a school-girl love of my bride-to-be.

MAX. Oh, yes—young Ralmen.

ANATOL. A poet of sorts, I believe. One of those men who seem destined to be the first love of so many women and never the last love of any.

MAX. I wish you'd come to the point.

ANATOL. Of course, it was a matter of indifference to me—I laughed

at him. The party broke up about midnight. I bade my bride-to-be farewell with a kiss—she kissed me also—coldly. I shivered as I went downstairs.

MAX. Ah ha!

ANATOL. One or the other stopped at the gate to congratulate me. Uncle Edward was decidedly drunk and insisted on embracing me. Some young man started a college song. Her former love, the poet I mean, disappeared into a side street with his coat collar turned up. Someone teased me—said I'd probably spend the rest of the night in front of the belovèd one's window—I smiled in scorn—it had begun to snow—people scattered finally—and I stood alone.

MAX (*condolingly*). Oh!

ANATOL (*warming up*). Yes, I stood alone on the street—in the cold winter night, while the snow whirled its great flakes around me. It was—it was shuddery——

MAX. Won't you please tell me where you went?

ANATOL (*grandly*). Where I had to go—to the Redoute.

MAX. Oh!

ANATOL. You are surprised!

MAX. I can imagine the rest of it now.

ANATOL. Not quite. As I stood there in the cold winter night——

MAX. Shivering——

ANATOL. Freezing, it came over me then with a mighty rush of pain,—the thought that from now on I should no longer be a free man—that I must bid farewell forever to my mad, sweet bachelor days. This is the last night, I said to myself, the last night in which I can come home without being asked where I have been—the last night of freedom—of adventuring—of love, perhaps——

MAX. Oh——

ANATOL. And then suddenly I found myself in the midst of the turmoil —silk and satin garments rustled about me, eyes sparkled, masks nodded mysteriously, gleaming shoulders threw out their fragrance —the whole mad carnival breathed and whirled about me. I sucked it in—I bathed in it.

MAX. Get to the point, please—we haven't much time.

ANATOL. The crowd pushed me forward and as I had excited my brain before, now I excited all of my senses with the perfumes that swirled around me. It seemed to rush over me as never before—it was as if the carnival were giving me its own festival of farewell.

MAX. I'm waiting for the third excitant.

ANATOL. That came soon—the intoxication of the heart.

MAX. Of the senses.

ANATOL. Of the heart—of the senses, too, possibly. Do you remember Katharine?

MAX. Oh, Katherine?

ANATOL. Hush!

MAX (with a gesture towards the bedroom). Is—is it she?

ANATOL. No—but she was there, too, and then a charming brunette whose name I won't mention—and then Theodore's little blonde Lizzie —but Theodore wasn't there. I recognized them all in spite of their masks, from their voice or their walk or some gesture. But there was just one that I didn't recognize at first—it was queer—I followed her—or she followed me. Her figure seemed so familiar—we kept meeting everywhere—at the fountain—at the buffet—beside the proscenium—everywhere. Finally she took my arm and I knew who she was. (Pointing to the door) She——

MAX. An old friend?

ANATOL. Why, man, don't you suspect? You know what I told her six weeks ago when I became engaged —the same old story: "I'm going away—I'll be back soon. I'll love you forever."

MAX. Ilona?

ANATOL. Hush!

MAX. Not Ilona?

ANATOL. Yes, keep quiet. "You're here again," she whispered in my ear. "Yes," I replied aptly. "When?" "This evening"—"Why no letters?" "Bad postal connections." "Where?" "Inhospitable village." "But now?" —"happy—here again—ever faithful." "Me, too—me, too!" Joy, champagne and more joy——

MAX. And more champagne?

ANATOL. No, no more champagne. And then when we drove home in the cab—just as we used to—she leaned on my shoulder—"We'll never part again," she said.

MAX (*rising*). Wake up, boy, and make an end of it.

ANATOL. We'll never part. (*Rising*) And I'm to be married at two o'clock.

MAX. To another.

ANATOL. Why, yes—one always marries the other.

MAX (*looking at the clock*). It's high time.
(*Gesture.*)

ANATOL. I'll see if she's ready. (*Stops at the door, turns to* MAX) But it's really sad, isn't it?

MAX. It's immoral.

ANATOL. It's sad, too.

MAX. Do go in.
(ANATOL *opens the door just as* ILONA *looks in and then comes in. She wears a handsome domino.*)

ILONA. Oh! It's only Max.

MAX (*bowing*). Only Max.

ILONA (*to* ANATOL). Why didn't you tell me? I thought it was a stranger or I should have joined you long ago. How are you, Max? And what do you say to this rascal?

MAX. That's just about what he is.

ILONA. Here I've been weeping for him for six weeks and he was—where were you?

ANATOL (*with a large gesture*). Over there.

ILONA. Didn't he write to you, either? But now I have him again ——(*Takes his arm*) Now there'll be no more of these journeys—and no more partings. Give me a kiss.

ANATOL. But——

ILONA. Oh, Max doesn't count. (*Kisses him*) What an expression! Now I'll pour tea for you two and for myself if you'll permit me.

ANATOL. Please do.

MAX. My dear Ilona, I'm sorry I can't accept your invitation to breakfast, and I don't quite understand——

ILONA (*busy with the samovar*). What don't you understand?

MAX. Anatol ought to——

ILONA. What ought he——

MAX (*to* ANATOL). You ought to be dressed by this time.

ILONA. Don't be silly, Max. We're going to stay home today—we sha'n't set a foot out of the house.

ANATOL. My dear child—that won't be quite possible.

ILONA. Oh, yes, that'll be possible.

ANATOL. But I'm invited——

ILONA (*pouring out tea*). Send a regret.

MAX. He can't—this time.

ANATOL. I'm—I'm invited to a wedding.
(MAX *encourages him with a gesture.*)

ILONA. That's not important.

ANATOL. It is, this time—I'm in the wedding party.

ILONA. And does the lady you escort love you?

MAX. That's quite unessential.

ILONA. But I do love him and that's very essential. I wish you wouldn't butt in.

ANATOL. My dear girl—I must go.

MAX. Yes, he must. You can believe him—he must.

ANATOL. You can certainly let me off for a few hours, can't you?

ILONA. Please sit down—both of you. How many lumps, Max?

MAX. Three, please.

ILONA (*to* ANATOL). And you?

ANATOL. But it's really high time.

ILONA. How many lumps?

ANATOL. You know—two.

ILONA. Cream? Rum?

ANATOL. Rum—you ought to know that—too.

ILONA (*to* MAX). Rum and two lumps of sugar—fine principles he has!

MAX. I must go.

ANATOL (*aside to him*). Don't leave me alone.

ILONA. Finish your tea, Max.

ANATOL. Child, I must get dressed now.

ILONA. Oh, for goodness' sake, when is this fool wedding?

MAX. In two hours.

ILONA. You're invited, too?

MAX. Yes.

ILONA. Is he an usher, too?

ANATOL. Yes, he is.

ILONA. Who's getting married?

ANATOL. You don't know him.

ILONA. What's his name? It can't be a secret.

ANATOL. It is a secret.

ILONA. What?

ANATOL. It's a secret wedding.

ILONA. With ushers and bridesmaids? How ridiculous!

MAX. It's—it's the parents who mustn't know anything about it.

ILONA (*drinking her tea*). Boys, you're lying to me.

MAX. Oh, no.

ILONA. Lord knows where you two are going today. However,

you're not going—that is—of course Max can go wherever he wants to—— (*To* ANATOL) But you stay here.

ANATOL. It's impossible—I can't possibly stay away from my best friend's wedding.

ILONA (*to* MAX). Shall I let him go?

MAX. Dear Ilona—you really must.

ILONA. What church is it at?

ANATOL (*uneasy*). Why do you ask?

ILONA. I thought I'd like to look in on it.

MAX. I'm afraid that isn't possible.

ILONA. And why not?

ANATOL. Because this ceremony takes place in a—in a subterranean chapel.

ILONA. There must be some way to get there.

ANATOL. No—that is—of course there's a way to get there.

ILONA. I'd like to see your bridesmaid, Anatol—I'm jealous of her. I've heard of marriages that have grown out of these wedding parties. And you must understand one thing, Anatol, I won't have you getting married.

MAX. What would you do if—if he did get married?

ILONA (*quite calmly*). I'd break up the ceremony.

ANATOL. Indeed!

MAX. How would you do that?

ILONA. I haven't quite made up my mind—I might make a disturbance in front of the church door——

MAX. That would be commonplace.

ILONA. Oh, I'd find some new touch.

MAX. For instance?

ILONA. I might drive up dressed as a bride—with a wreath and veil— that would be novel, wouldn't it?

MAX. Decidedly. (*Rises*) Well, I must go now—good-bye, Anatol.

ANATOL (*rising, very determined*). You must excuse me, Ilona, I shall have to get dressed. It's the very last minute.

FRANZ (*comes in carrying bouquet*). The flowers, sir——

ILONA. What flowers?

FRANZ (*looks at* ILONA *with surprise, and with a certain familiarity*). The flowers, sir.

ILONA. You still have Franz? (FRANZ *goes out*) I thought you'd put him out.

MAX. That isn't always easy. (ANATOL *stands holding the flowers, which are wrapped in tissue paper.*)

ILONA. Let me see your flowers.

MAX. Is that the bouquet for your bridesmaid?

ILONA (*opening the paper*). This is a bridal bouquet!

ANATOL. Good heavens! They've sent me the wrong flowers—Franz—Franz! (*Runs out with the flowers.*)

MAX. And the poor bridegroom won't have any.

ANATOL (*coming in again*). Franz is after him.

MAX. You'll excuse me now, won't you? I really must go.

ANATOL (*going to the door with him*). What shall I do?

MAX. Confess.

ANATOL. Impossible!

MAX. Well, I'll come back as soon as I can.

ANATOL. Please do.

MAX. And my color——

ANATOL. Blue or pink. I have a feeling it will be one or the other—good-bye.

MAX. Good-bye, Ilona. (*Aside to* ANATOL) I'll be back in an hour. (ANATOL *comes back into the room.* ILONA *runs into his arms.*)

ILONA. At last! Oh, I'm so happy!

ANATOL (*mechanically*). My angel!

ILONA. You're so cold.

ANATOL. I just said "my angel," didn't I?

ILONA. And you really have to go to this stupid wedding?

ANATOL. Seriously, dear, I must.

ILONA. Well, I tell you. . . . I'll drive with you in the cab as far as the lady's house——

ANATOL. That's an absurd idea! We'll meet this evening. You'll have to be at the theatre.

ILONA. I'll send them word I can't play.

ANATOL. No, no, I'll call for you. Now I must change my clothes. (*Looks at the clock*) How the time flies! Franz! Franz!

ILONA. What do you want?

ANATOL (*to* FRANZ *who comes in*). Have you laid out my clothes?

FRANZ. Yes, sir, I'll see if it's all right, sir. (*Goes into bedroom.*)

ANATOL (*pacing the room*). This evening, Ilona, after the theatre, eh?

ILONA. I'd like to stay with you all day today.

ANATOL. Now don't be childish—I have other obligations—you ought to understand that.

ILONA. I love you—that's all I can understand.

ANATOL. It is absolutely necessary——

FRANZ (*from bedroom*). Everything is ready, sir. (*Goes out.*)

ANATOL. Good. (*Goes into the bed-room, talks from behind the door while* ILONA *remains in the sitting-room*) I mean—it is absolutely necessary that you should understand these things.

ILONA. You're really changing your clothes?

ANATOL. I can't go to a wedding this way.

ILONA. Why do you go anyway?

ANATOL. Beginning again? I must go.

ILONA. Then we'll meet this evening?

ANATOL. Yes, I'll wait for you at the stage door.

ILONA. Don't be late.

ANATOL. No—why should I be late?

ILONA. Don't you remember—I waited for you a whole hour once.

ANATOL. Did you? I don't remember.
(*There is a pause.*)

ILONA (*strolls about the room looking at things*). Say, Anatol, you've got a new picture here.

ANATOL. Do you like it?

ILONA. I know so little about pictures.

ANATOL. It's a very fine picture.

ILONA. Did you bring that back with you?

ANATOL. Bring back? Where from?

ILONA. Why—from your trip.

ANATOL. Yes, that's so—from my trip—no, it's a present.
(*Pause.*)

ILONA. Say, Anatol——

ANATOL (*nervously*). What!

ILONA. Where were you anyway?

ANATOL. I told you all about it.

ILONA. You haven't told me a word.

ANATOL. Yes, I did, last night.

ILONA. Then I've forgotten it again.

ANATOL. I was—I was, oh, near Bohemia——

ILONA. What were you doing in Bohemia?

ANATOL. I wasn't in Bohemia—only near there.

ILONA. Oh, you were invited for the hunting?

ANATOL. Yes, I was shooting hares.

ILONA. For six weeks?

ANATOL. Continually.

ILONA. Why didn't you say good-bye to me?

ANATOL. I didn't want to make you unhappy.

ILONA. Anatol, you wanted to shake me.

ANATOL. Absurd.

ILONA. Oh, you tried it once before.

ANATOL. Tried it? Yes—but without success.

ILONA. What? What's that?

ANATOL. Why, yes—I tried to tear myself away from you—you know it.

ILONA. It was nonsense—you can't tear yourself away from me.

ANATOL. Ha! Ha!

ILONA. What's that?

ANATOL. I remarked "Ha! ha!"

ILONA. You needn't laugh, my dear, you came back to me then.

ANATOL. Yes, then——

ILONA. And you will this time, too—you love me.

ANATOL. Unfortunately——

ILONA. What?

ANATOL (shouting). Unfortunately.

ILONA. You're mighty brave when you're in another room. You wouldn't dare say that to my face.

ANATOL (opens the door, looks in). Unfortunately!

ILONA (starting to door). What does that mean?

ANATOL (in the bedroom again). That means—that it can't go on like this forever.

ILONA. And now I say, "Ha! ha!"

ANATOL. What!

ILONA (pulling the door open). Ha! Ha!

ANATOL. Shut that door. (She shuts the door.)

ILONA. No, my dear boy. You love me and you'll never be able to leave me.

ANATOL. Do you think so?

ILONA. I know it.

ANATOL. You know it?

ILONA. I feel it.

ANATOL. You think that I'll lie at your feet forever?

ILONA. You'll never marry—I know that.

ANATOL. You're quite crazy, my dear. I love you—that's all right—but we're not bound for eternity.

ILONA. You think I'll give you up?

ANATOL. You'll have to sometime.

ILONA. Have to? When?

ANATOL. When I marry.

ILONA (drumming on the door). And when will that be, my dear?

ANATOL (mockingly). Very soon, my dear.

ILONA (excited). When?

ANATOL. Stop that drumming—I'll be married long before the year is out.

ILONA. You're an idiot.

ANATOL. I might be married in two months even.

ILONA. Oh, indeed—I suppose there's somebody waiting for you?

ANATOL. Yes, there's somebody waiting for me at this very minute.

ILONA. In two months then?

ANATOL. You seem to doubt it. (ILONA *laughs.*)

ANATOL. You needn't laugh. I'll be married in a week. (*She laughs still more*) Don't laugh, I say. (ILONA *sinks back on the coach, laughing.* ANATOL *comes out fully dressed*) Don't laugh——

ILONA (*laughing*). When did you say you're going to get married?

ANATOL. Today.

ILONA (*looking at him*). When?

ANATOL. Today, my dear.

ILONA (*rising*). Stop joking, Anatol.

ANATOL. It's dead earnest, my dear. I'm marrying today.

ILONA. Are you crazy?

ANATOL (*calls*). Franz!

FRANZ (*comes in*). Yes, sir.

ANATOL. My flowers. (FRANZ *goes out.*)

ILONA (*threateningly*). Anatol—— (FRANZ *comes in with the flowers.*

ILONA *turns and sees him, makes a grab for the flowers.* ANATOL *catches them quickly,* FRANZ *goes out with a broad smile.*)

ILONA. Oh—not really——

ANATOL. As you see. (*She tries to take the flowers from him*) What are you doing? (*He retreats before her, she chases him around the room.*)

ILONA. You wretch—you wretch! (MAX *comes in carrying a bunch of roses, stands by the door astonished.* ANATOL *takes refuge on an armchair, holding his flowers out of* ILONA's *reach.*)

ANATOL. Help! Max, help me! (MAX *hurries to* ILONA, *tries to hold her back, she turns on him, seizes his flowers, throws them on the floor and stamps on them.*)

MAX. Ilona—you're crazy—my flowers—what shall I do? (ILONA *begins to cry bitterly, sinks on a chair.*)

ANATOL (*still behind his chair, embarrassed*). She made me angry— you can cry now, Ilona—of course. Why did you laugh at me? She laughed at me, Max—she said I didn't dare marry—so, of course, I'm going to get married—just out of opposition. (*Starts to climb down off the chair.*)

ILONA. You hypocrite—you deceiver! (ANATOL *climbs up on the chair again.*)

MAX (*picking up the flowers*). My poor flowers!

ILONA. I really meant to spoil his. But you don't deserve any better—you're his accomplice.

ANATOL (*still on the chair*). Do be sensible!

ILONA. Yes, that's what you always say when you've driven a woman mad. But you shall see—that'll be a nice wedding—just you wait. (*Rises*) Good-bye.

ANATOL (*jumping off the chair*). Where are you going?

ILONA. You'll find out soon enough.

ANATOL AND MAX. Where are you going?

ILONA. Let me go.

ANATOL *and* MAX (*standing between her and the door*). Ilona, what are you going to do? Ilona, where are you going——?

ILONA. Let me go, I say.

ANATOL. Do be sensible—calm down a bit.

ILONA. You won't let me go? (*She dashes about the room, dashes the tea-things off the table in her anger, throws pillows about, etc.* ANATOL *and* MAX *stand helpless.*)

ANATOL. Now I ask you—does a man have to marry when he's loved like that?
(*Her outburst over,* ILONA *sinks down on the couch and sobs. There is a pause.*)

ANATOL. She's calmer now.

MAX. We must go—and I haven't any flowers.

FRANZ (*comes in*). The carriage is there, sir. (*Goes out.*)

ANATOL. The carriage—the carriage—what shall I do? (*Comes up behind* ILONA, *kisses her hair*) Ilona!

MAX (*on her other side*). Ilona! (*She weeps silently with her handkerchief to her face.* MAX *speaks aside to* ANATOL) Go now and leave her to me.

ANATOL. I really ought to go—but how can I?

MAX. Go!

ANATOL. How can you get her away? Do you think you can do it?

MAX. I'll whisper to you during the ceremony, "Everything arranged,' and you'll know I've done it.

ANATOL. I'm so worried.

MAX. Go now.
(ANATOL *turns to go, comes back on tiptoe, presses a light kiss on* ILONA's *hair, then goes out quickly.* MAX *sits down opposite* ILONA. *She still sobs, with her handkerchief before her face.*)

MAX (*looking at the clock*) Hm——

ILONA (*looking about as if just awakening*). Where is he?

MAX (*takes both her hands*). Ilona

ILONA (*rising*). Where is he?

MAX (*still holding her hands*). You won't find him.

ILONA. Oh, yes, I will.

MAX. You're a sensible girl, Ilona. You don't want to make a scandal.

ILONA. Let me go—where is the wedding?

MAX. That doesn't matter.

ILONA. I'm going there—I must go there.

MAX. Oh, no, you won't. What an idea!

ILONA. To treat me so—to deceive me so——

MAX. It was no deception—it's just life.

ILONA. Oh, shut up—I hate your phrases.

MAX. Now you're childish, Ilona, or you'd see that all this is so useless.

ILONA. Useless?

MAX. It's absurd.

ILONA. Absurd?

MAX. You'd only make yourself ridiculous.

ILONA. Now you're insulting me, too.

MAX. You'll console yourself.

ILONA. You don't know me.

MAX. Suppose he was going to America?

ILONA. What do you mean by that?

MAX. Suppose he were really lost to you?

ILONA. What do you mean?

MAX. The main point is this—that it's not *you* who is deceived. (*She looks her question*) He can come back to you—it will be the other who is forsaken.

ILONA. Oh! Is that—— (*She looks up with an expression of wild joy.*)

MAX. How noble you are! (*Pressing her hand.*)

ILONA. I'll have my revenge—that's why I'm so delighted at what you said.

MAX. Then you are one of those who bite—when they love?

ILONA. Yes, I am.

MAX. Now you are really grand! —a woman who would avenge her whole sex on us——

ILONA. Yes, that's just what I will do.

MAX (*rising*). I have just time to take you home. (*Aside*) I'm not taking any chances. (*Offering her his arm*) And now bid farewell to these rooms.

ILONA. Not farewell—I shall come back.

MAX. You believe yourself a demon and yet you're only a woman. (*At a gesture from her*) But that is quite enough. (*Opening the door*) If you please, fair lady.

ILONA (*turning back at the door, with affected grandezza*). I will come back. (*Out with MAX.*)

R. U. R.

(ROSSUM'S UNIVERSAL ROBOTS)

A FANTASTIC MELODRAMA IN THREE ACTS AND AN EPILOGUE

BY KAREL CAPEK

TRANSLATED FROM THE CZECH BY PAUL SELVER AND NIGEL PLAYFAIR

R. U. R. was originally produced by the Theatre Guild at the Garrick Theatre, New York, with the following cast:

CHARACTERS (in order of appearance)

HARRY DOMIN, *General Manager of Rossum's Universal Robots*	Basil Sydney
SULLA, *a Robotess*	Mary Bonestell
MARIUS, *a Robot*	Myrtland LaVarre
HELENA GLORY	Kathlene MacDonell
DR. GALL, *head of the Physiological and Experimental Department of R. U. R.*	William Devereaux
MR. FABRY, *Engineer General, Technical Controller of R. U. R.*	John Anthony
DR. HALLEMEIER, *head of the Institute for Psychological Training of Robots*	Moffat Johnston
MR. ALQUIST, *Architect, head of the Works Department of R. U. R.*	Louis Calvert
CONSUL BUSMAN, *General Manager of R. U. R.*	Henry Travers
NANA	Helen Westly
RADIUS, *a Robot*	John Rutherford
HELENA, *a Robotess*	Mary Hone
PRIMUS, *a Robot*	John Roche
A SERVANT	Frederick Mark
FIRST ROBOT	Domis Plugge
SECOND ROBOT	Richard Coolidge
THIRD ROBOT	Bernard Savage

Staged by Philip Moeller

Settings and Costumes by Lee Simonson

SCENES

ACT ONE

Central Office of the Factory of Rossum's Universal Robots

ACT TWO

Helena's Drawing Room—Ten years later. Morning

ACT THREE

The same. Afternoon

EPILOGUE

A Laboratory. One year later
Place: An Island.   Time: The Future

DESCRIPTION OF CHARACTERS

DOMIN, *A handsome man of 35. Forceful, efficient and humorous at times.*

SULLA, *A pathetic figure. Young, pretty and attractive.*

MARIUS, *A young Robot, superior to the general run of his kind. Dressed in modern clothes.*

HELENA GLORY, *A vital, sympathetic, handsome girl of 21.*

DR. GALL, *A tall, distinguished scientist of 50.*

MR. FABRY, *A forceful, competent engineer of 40.*

HALLEMEIER, *An impressive man of 40. Bald head and beard.*

ALQUIST, *A stout, kindly old man of 60.*

NANA, *A tall, acidulous woman of 40.*

RADIUS, *A tall, forceful Robot.*

HELENA, *A radiant young woman of 20.*

PRIMUS, *A good-looking young Robot.*

NOTE: *All the Robots wear expressionless faces and move with absolute mechanical precision, with the exception of* SULLA, HELENA *and* PRIMUS, *who convey a touch of humanity.*

DESCRIPTION OF CHARACTERS

R. U. R.

ACT ONE

SCENE—*Central office of the factory of Rossum's Universal Robots. The windows on the back wall look out on the endless rows of factory buildings. On the left wall large maps showing steamship and railroad routes. On the right wall are fastened printed placards. ("Robots Cheapest Labor," etc.) In contrast to these wall fittings, the floor is covered with splendid Turkish carpet, and a bookshelf containing bottles of wine and spirits, instead of books.*

DOMIN is sitting at his desk at left, dictating. SULLA is at the typewriter against the wall. There is a leather couch with arms right center. At the extreme right an armchair. At extreme left a chair. There is also a chair in front of DOMIN's desk. Two green cabinets across the corners of the room complete the furniture.

Seen through the windows which run to the heights of the room are rows of factory chimneys, telegraph poles and wires. There is a general passageway or hallway which leads to the warehouse. The ROBOTS are brought into the office through this entrance.

DOMIN (*dictating*). Ready?

SULLA. Yes.

DOMIN. To E. M. McVicker & Co., Southampton, England. "We undertake no guarantee for goods damaged in transit. As soon as the consignment was taken on board we drew your captain's attention to the fact that the vessel was unsuitable for the transportation of Robots; and we are therefore not responsible for spoiled freight. We beg to remain, for Rossum's Universal Robots, yours truly." (SULLA *types the lines*) Ready?

SULLA. Yes.

DOMIN. Another letter. To the E. B. Huysen Agency, New York, U.S.A. "We beg to acknowledge receipt of order for five thousand Robots. As you are sending your own vessel, please dispatch as cargo equal quantities of soft and hard coal for R.U.R., the same to be credited as part payment (*BUZZER*) of the amount due us." (*Answering phone*) Hello! This is the central office. Yes, certainly. Well, send them a wire. Good. (*Rises*) "We beg to remain, for Rossum's Universal Robots, yours very truly." Ready?

SULLA. Yes.

DOMIN (*answering small portable phone*). Hello! Yes. No. All right. (*Standing back of desk, punching plug machine and buttons*) Another letter. Freidrichswerks, Hamburg, Germany. "We beg to acknowledge receipt of order for fifteen thousand Robots." (*Enter MARIUS*) Well, what is it?

MARIUS. There's a lady, sir, asking to see you.

DOMIN. A lady? Who is she?

MARIUS. I don't know, sir. She brings this card of introduction.

DOMIN (*reading card*). Ah, from President Glory. Ask her to come in. (*To* SULLA. *Crossing to her desk, then back to his own*) Where did I leave off?

SULLA. "We beg to acknowledge receipt of order for fifteen thousand Robots."

DOMIN. Fifteen thousand. Fifteen thousand.

MARIUS (*at door*). Please step this way.
(*Enter* HELENA. *Exit* MARIUS.)

HELENA (*crossing to desk*). How do you do?

DOMIN. How do you do? What can I do for you?

HELENA. You are Mr. Domin, the General Manager?

DOMIN. I am.

HELENA. I have come . . .

DOMIN. With President Glory's card. That is quite sufficient.

HELENA. President Glory is my father. I am Helena Glory.

DOMIN. Please sit down. Sulla, you may go. (*Exit* SULLA. *Sitting down at desk*) How can I be of service to you, Miss Glory?

HELENA. I have come . . .

DOMIN. To have a look at our famous works where people are manufactured. Like all visitors. Well, there is no objection.

HELENA. I thought it was forbidden to . . .

DOMIN. To enter the factory? Yes, of course. Everybody comes here with someone's visiting card, Miss Glory.

HELENA. And you show them . . .

DOMIN. Only certain things. The manufacture of artificial people is a secret process.

HELENA. If you only knew how enormously that . . .

DOMIN. Interests you. Europe's talking about nothing else.

HELENA (*indignantly turning front*). Why don't you let me finish speaking?

DOMIN (*drier*). I beg your pardon. Did you want to say something different?

HELENA. I only wanted to ask . . .

DOMIN. Whether I could make a special exception in your case and show you our factory. Why, certainly, Miss Glory.

HELENA. How do you know I wanted to say that?

DOMIN. They all do. But we shall consider it a special honor to show you more than we do the rest.

HELENA. Thank you.

DOMIN (*standing*). But you must agree not to divulge the least . . .

HELENA (*standing and giving him her hand*). My word of honor.

DOMIN. Thank you. (*Looking at her hand*) Won't you raise your veil?

HELENA. Of course. You want to see whether I'm a spy or not. I beg your pardon.

DOMIN (*leaning forward*). What is it?

HELENA. Would you mind releasing my hand?

DOMIN (*releasing it*). Oh, I beg *your* pardon.

HELENA (*raising veil*). How cautious you have to be here, don't you?

DOMIN (*observing her with deep interest*). Why, yes. Hm—of course —We—that is . . .

HELENA. But what is it? What's the matter?

DOMIN. I'm remarkably pleased. Did you have a pleasant crossing?

HELENA. Yes.

DOMIN. No difficulty?

HELENA. Why?

DOMIN. What I mean to say is— you're so *young*.

HELENA. May we go straight into the factory?

DOMIN. Yes. Twenty-two, I think.

HELENA. Twenty-two what?

DOMIN. Years.

HELENA. Twenty-one. Why do you want to know?

DOMIN. Well, because—as . . . (*Sits on desk nearer her*) You will make a long stay, won't you?

HELENA (*backing away*). That depends on how much of the factory you show me.

DOMIN (*rises; crosses to her*). Oh, hang the factory. Oh, no, no, you shall see everything, Miss Glory. Indeed you shall. Won't you sit down? (*Takes her to couch. She sits. Offers her cigarette from case at end of sofa. She refuses.*)

HELENA. Thank you.

DOMIN. But first would you like to hear the story of the invention?

HELENA. Yes, indeed.

DOMIN. It was in the year 1920 that old Rossum, the great physiologist, who was then quite a young scientist, took himself to the distant island for the purpose of studying the ocean fauna. (*She is amused*) On this occasion he attempted by chemical synthesis to imitate the living matter known as protoplasm until he suddenly discovered a substance which behaved exactly like living matter although its chemical composition was different. That was in the year 1932, exactly four hundred and forty years after the discovery of America. Whew . . .

HELENA. Do you know that by heart?

DOMIN (*takes flowers from desk to her*). Yes. You see, physiology is not in my line. Shall I go on?

HELENA (*smelling flowers*). Yes, please.

DOMIN. And then, Miss Glory, Old Rossum wrote the following among his chemical experiments: "Nature has found only one method of organizing living matter. There is, however, another method, more simple, flexible and rapid which has not yet occurred to Nature at all. This second process by which life can be developed was discovered by me today." Now imagine him, Miss Glory, writing those wonderful words over some colloidal mess that a dog wouldn't look at. Imagine him sitting over a test tube and thinking how the whole tree of life would grow from him, how all animals would proceed from it, beginning with some sort of a beetle and ending with a *man*. A man of different substance from us. Miss Glory, that was a tremendous moment. (*Gets box of candy from desk and passes it to her.*)

HELENA. Well . . .

DOMIN (*as she speaks his portable phone lights up and he answers*). Well— Hello!—Yes—no, I'm in conference. Don't disturb me.

HELENA. Well?

DOMIN (*smiles*). Now, the thing was how to get the life *out* of the test tubes, and hasten development and form organs, bones and nerves, and so on, and find such substances as catalytics, enzymes, hormones in short—you understand?

HELENA. Not much, I'm afraid.

DOMIN. Never mind. (*Leans over couch and fixes cushion for her back*) There! You see, with the help of his tinctures he could make whatever he wanted. He could have produced a Medusa with the brain of Socrates or a worm fifty yards long—(*She laughs. He does also; leans closer on couch, then straightens up again*)—but being without a grain of humor, he took into his head to make a vertebrate or perhaps a man. This artificial living *matter* of his had a raging thirst for life. It didn't mind being sown or mixed together. That couldn't be done with natural albumen. And that's how he set about it.

HELENA. About what?

DOMIN. About imitating Nature. First of all he tried making an artificial dog. That took him several years and resulted in a sort of stunted calf which *died* in a few days. I'll show it to you in the museum. And *then* old Rossum started on the manufacture of *man*.

HELENA. And I'm to divulge this to nobody?

DOMIN. To nobody in the world.

HELENA. What a pity that it's to be discovered in *all* the school books of both Europe and America. (*Both laugh.*)

DOMIN. Yes. But do you know what *isn't* in the school books? That old Rossum was mad. Seriously, Miss

Glory, you must keep this to yourself. The old crank wanted to actually make *people*.

HELENA. But you do make people.

DOMIN. *Approximately* — Miss Glory. But old Rossum meant it literally. He wanted to become a sort of scientific substitute for *God*. He was a fearful materialist, and that's why he did it all. His sole purpose was nothing more or less than to prove that God was no longer necessary. (*Crosses to end of couch*) Do you know anything about anatomy?

HELENA. Very little.

DOMIN. Neither do I. Well—(*he laughs*)—he then decided to manufacture everything as in the human body. I'll show you in the museum the bungling attempt it took him ten years to produce. It was to have been a *man*, but it lived for three days only. Then up came *young* Rossum, an engineer. He was a wonderful fellow, Miss Glory. When he saw what a mess of it the old man was making he said: "It's absurd to spend ten years making a man. If you can't make him quicker than Nature, you might as well shut up shop." Then he set about learning anatomy himself.

HELENA. There's nothing about *that* in the school books?

DOMIN. No. The school books are full of paid advertisements, and rubbish at that. What the school books say about the *united efforts* of the two great Rossums is all a fairy tale. They used to have dreadful rows. The old atheist hadn't the slightest conception of industrial matters, and the end of it was that Young Rossum shut him up in some laboratory or other and let him fritter the time away with his monstrosities while he himself started on the business from an engineer's point of view. Old Rossum cursed him and before he died he managed to botch up two physiological horrors. Then one day they found him dead in the laboratory. And that's his whole story.

HELENA. And what about the young man?

DOMIN (*sits beside her on couch*). Well, anyone who has looked into human anatomy will have seen at once that man is too complicated, and that a good engineer could make him more simply. So young Rossum began to *overhaul* anatomy to see what could be left out or simplified. In short . . . But this isn't boring you, Miss Glory?

HELENA. No, indeed. You're . . . It's awfully interesting.

DOMIN (*gets closer*). So young Rossum said to himself: "A man is something that feels happy, plays the piano, likes going for a walk, and, in fact, wants to do a whole lot of things that are really unnecessary."

HELENA. Oh.

DOMIN. That are unnecessary when he wants—(*takes her hand*)—let us say, to weave or count. Do you play the piano?

HELENA. Yes.

DOMIN. That's good. (*Kisses her hand. She lowers her head*) Oh, I beg your pardon! (*Rises*) But a working machine must *not* play the piano, must not feel happy, must not do a whole lot of other things. A gasoline motor must not have tassels or ornaments, Miss Glory. And to manufacture artificial workers is the same thing as the manufacture of a gasoline motor. (*She is not interested*) The process must be the simplest, and the product the best from a practical point of view. (*Sits beside her again*) What sort of worker do you think is the *best* from a practical point of view?

HELENA (*absently*). What? (*Looks at him.*)

DOMIN. What sort of worker do you think is the best from a practical point of view?

HELENA (*pulling herself together*). Oh! Perhaps the one who is most honest and hard-working.

DOMIN. No. The one that is the *cheapest*. The one whose requirements are the *smallest*. Young Rossum invented a worker with the minimum amount of requirements. He had to simplify him. He rejected everything that did not contribute directly to the progress of work. Everything that makes man more expensive. In fact he *rejected man* and made the *Robot*. My dear Miss Glory, the Robots are not people. Mechanically they are more *perfect* than we are; they have an enormously developed intelligence, but they have no soul. (*Leans back.*)

HELENA. How do you know they have no soul?

DOMIN. Have you ever seen what a Robot looks like inside?

HELENA. No.

DOMIN. Very neat, very simple. Really a beautiful piece of work. Not much *in* it, but everything in flawless order. The product of an engineer *is* technically at a higher pitch of perfection than a product of Nature.

HELENA. But man is supposed to be the product of God.

DOMIN. All the worse. God hasn't the slightest notion of modern engineering. Would you believe that young Rossum then proceeded to play at being God?

HELENA (*awed*). How do you mean?

DOMIN. He began to manufacture Super-Robots. Regular giants they were. He tried to make them twelve feet tall. But you wouldn't believe what a failure they were.

HELENA. A failure?

DOMIN. Yes. For no reason at all their limbs used to keep snapping off. "Evidently our planet is too small for giants." Now we only make Robots of normal size and of very high-class human finish.

HELENA (*hands him flower; he puts it in buttonhole*). I saw the first Robots at home. The Town Council bought them for—I mean engaged them for work.

DOMIN. No. *Bought* them, Miss Glory. Robots are bought and sold.

HELENA. These were employed as street-sweepers. I saw them sweeping. They were so strange and quiet.

DOMIN (*rises*). Rossum's Universal Robot factory doesn't produce a uniform brand of Robots. We have Robots of *finer* and *coarser* grades. The best will live about *twenty* years. (*Crosses to desk.* HELENA *looks in her pocket mirror. He pushes button on desk.*)

HELENA. Then they die?

DOMIN. Yes, they get used up. (*Enter* MARIUS) Marius, bring in samples of the manual-labor Robot. (*Exit* MARIUS) I'll show you specimens of the two extremes. This first grade is comparatively inexpensive and is made in vast quantities. (MARIUS *re-enters with two manual-labor* ROBOTS. MARIUS *stands on tiptoes, touches head, feels arms, forehead of one of the* ROBOTS. *They come to a mechanical standstill*) There you are, as powerful as a small tractor. Guaranteed to have average intelligence. That will do, Marius.
(MARIUS *exits with* ROBOTS.)

HELENA. They make me feel so strange.

DOMIN (*crosses to desk. Rings*). Did you see my new typist?

HELENA. I didn't notice her.
(*Enter* SULLA. *She crosses and stands facing* HELENA, *who is still sitting on the couch.*)

DOMIN. Sulla, let Miss Glory see you.

HELENA (*looks at* DOMIN. *Rising*). So pleased to meet you. (*Looks at* DOMIN) You must find it terribly dull in this out of the way spot, don't you?

SULLA. I don't know, Miss Glory.

HELENA. Where do you come from?

SULLA. From the factory.

HELENA. Oh, were you born there?

SULLA. I was *made* there.

HELENA. What? (*Looks first at* SULLA, *then at* DOMIN.)

DOMIN (*to* SULLA, *laughing*). Sulla is a Robot, best grade.

HELENA. Oh, I beg your pardon.

DOMIN (*crosses to* SULLA). Sulla isn't angry. See, Miss Glory, the kind of skin we make. Feel her face. (*Touches* SULLA'S *face.*)

HELENA. Oh, no, no.

DOMIN (*examining* SULLA'S *hand*). You wouldn't know that she's made of different material from us, would you? Turn round, Sulla.
(SULLA *does so. Circles twice.*)

HELENA. Oh, stop, stop.

DOMIN. Talk to Miss Glory, Sulla. (*Examines hair of* SULLA.)

SULLA. Please sit down. (HELENA *sits on couch*) Did you have a pleasant crossing? (*Fixes her hair.*)

HELENA. Oh, yes, certainly.

SULLA. Don't go back on the *Amelia*, Miss Glory, the barometer is falling steadily. Wait for the

Pennsylvania. That's a good powerful vessel.

DOMIN. What's its speed?

SULLA. Forty knots an hour. Fifty thousand tons. One of the latest vessels, Miss Glory.

HELENA. Thank you.

SULLA. A crew of fifteen hundred, Captain Harpy, eight boilers . . .

DOMIN. That'll do, Sulla. Now show us your knowledge of French.

HELENA. You know French?

SULLA. Oui! Madam! I know four languages. I can write: "Dear Sir, Monsieur, Geehrter Herr, Cteny pane."

HELENA (*jumping up, crosses to* SULLA). Oh, that's absurd! Sulla isn't a Robot. Sulla is a girl like me. Sulla, this is outrageous! Why do you take part in such a hoax?

SULLA. I am a Robot.

HELENA. No, no, you are not telling the truth. (*She catches the amused expression on* DOMIN'S *face*) I know they have forced you to do it for an advertisement. Sulla, you are a girl like me, aren't you? (*Looks at him.*)

DOMIN. I'm sorry, Miss Glory. *Sulla is a Robot.*

HELENA. It's a lie!

DOMIN. What? (*Pushes button on desk*) Well, then I must *convince* you. (*Enter* MARIUS. *He stands just inside the door*) Marius, take Sulla

into the dissecting room, and tell them to open her up at once.

HELENA. Where?

DOMIN. Into the dissecting room. When they've *cut her open,* you can go and have a look.
(MARIUS *makes a start toward* SULLA.)

HELENA (*stopping* MARIUS). No! No!

DOMIN. Excuse me, you spoke of lies.

HELENA. You wouldn't have her killed?

DOMIN. You can't kill machines. Sulla!
(MARIUS *takes a step forward, one arm out.* SULLA *makes a move toward door.*)

HELENA. Don't be afraid, Sulla. I won't let you go. Tell me, my dear—(*takes her hand*)—are they always so cruel to you? You mustn't put up with it, Sulla. You mustn't.

SULLA. I am a Robot.

HELENA. That doesn't matter. Robots are just as good as we are. Sulla, you wouldn't let yourself be cut to pieces?

SULLA. Yes.

HELENA. Oh, you're not afraid of death, then?

SULLA. I cannot tell, Miss Glory.

HELENA. Do you know what would happen to you in there?

SULLA. Yes, I should cease to move.

HELENA. How dreadful! (*Looks at* SULLA.)

DOMIN. Marius, tell Miss Glory what you are? (*Turns to* HELENA.)

MARIUS (*to* HELENA). Marius, the Robot.

DOMIN. Would you take Sulla into the dissecting room?

MARIUS (*turns to* DOMIN). Yes.

DOMIN. Would you be sorry for her?

MARIUS (*pause*). I cannot tell.

DOMIN. What would happen to her?

MARIUS. She would cease to move. They would put her into the stamping mill.

DOMIN. That is death, Marius. Aren't you afraid of death?

MARIUS. No.

DOMIN. You see, Miss Glory, the Robots have no interest in life. They have no enjoyments. They are *less* than so much grass.

HELENA. Oh, stop. Please send them away.

DOMIN (*pushes button*). Marius, Sulla, you may go.
(MARIUS *pivots and exits*. SULLA *exits*.)

HELENA. How terrible! It's outrageous what you are doing.
(*He takes her hand.*)

DOMIN. Why outrageous? (*His hand over hers. Laughing.*)

HELENA. I don't know, but it **is**. Why do you call her "Sulla"?

DOMIN. Isn't it a nice name?

HELENA. It's a man's name. Sulla was a Roman General.

DOMIN. What! Oh! (*Laughs*) We thought that Marius and Sulla were lovers.

HELENA (*indignantly*). Marius and Sulla were generals and fought against each other in the year— I've forgotten now.

DOMIN (*laughing*). Come here to the window. (*He goes to window.*)

HELENA. What?

DOMIN. Come here. (*She goes*) Do you see anything? (*Takes her arm.*)

HELENA. Bricklayers.

DOMIN. Robots. All our work people are Robots. And down there, can you see anything?

HELENA. Some sort of office.

DOMIN. A counting house. And in it . .

HELENA. A lot of officials.

DOMIN. Robots! All our officials are Robots. And when you see the factory— (*Noon whistle blows. She is scared; puts arm on* DOMIN. *He laughs*) If we don't blow the whistle the Robots won't stop working. In two hours I'll show you the kneading trough.

HELENA. Kneading trough?

DOMIN. The pestle for beating up the paste. In each one we mix the ingredients for a thousand Robots at one operation. Then there are the vats for the preparation of liver, brains, and so on. Then you will see the bone factory. After that I'll show you the spinning mill.

HELENA. Spinning mill?

DOMIN. Yes. For weaving nerves and veins. Miles and miles of digestive tubes pass through it at a time.

HELENA (*watching his gestures*). Mayn't we talk about something else?

DOMIN. Perhaps it would be better. There's only a *handful* of us among a hundred thousand Robots, and *not one woman*. We talk nothing but the factory *all* day, and *every* day. It's just as if we were under a curse, Miss Glory.

HELENA. I'm *sorry* I said that you were lying.
(*A knock at door.*)

DOMIN. Come in.
(*Enter* DR. GALL, DR. FABRY, ALQUIST *and* DR. HALLEMEIER. ALL *act formal—conscious.* ALL *click heels as introduced.*)

DR. GALL (*noisily*). I beg your pardon. I hope we don't intrude.

DOMIN. No, no. Come in. Miss Glory, here are Gall, Fabry, Alquist, Hallemeier. This is President Glory's daughter.
(ALL *move to her and shake her hand.*)

HELENA. How do you do?

FABRY. We had no idea . . .

DR. GALL. Highly honored, I'm sure.

ALQUIST. Welcome, Miss Glory.

BUSMAN (*rushes in*). Hello, what's up?

DOMIN. Come in, Busman. This is President Glory's daughter. This is Busman, Miss Glory.

BUSMAN. By Jove, that's fine. (ALL *click heels. He crowds in and shakes her hand*) Miss Glory, may we send a cablegram to the papers about your arrival?

HELENA. No, no, please don't.

DOMIN. Sit down, please, Miss Glory.
(*On the line,* "Sit down, please," *all* SIX MEN *try to find her a chair at once.* HELENA *goes for the chair at the extreme left.* DOMIN *takes the chair at front of desk, places it in the center of stage.* HALLEMEIER *gets chair at* SULLA's *typewriter and places it to right of chair at center.* BUSMAN *gets armchair from extreme right, but by now* HELENA *has sat in* DOMIN's *preferred chair, at center.* ALL *sit except* DOMIN. BUSMAN *at right in armchair.* HALLEMEIER *right of* HELENA. FABRY *in swivel chair back of desk.*)

BUSMAN. Allow me . . .

DR. GALL. Please . . .

FABRY. Excuse me . . .

ALQUIST. What sort of a crossing did you have?

DR. GALL. Are you going to stay long?

(MEN *conscious of their appearance.* ALQUIST's *trousers turned up at bottom. He turns them down.* BUSMAN *polishes shoes.* OTHERS *fix ties, collars, etc.*)

FABRY. What do you think of the factory, Miss Glory?

HALLEMEIER. Did you come over on the *Amelia?*

DOMIN. Be quiet and let Miss Glory speak.

(MEN *sit erect.* DOMIN *stands at* HELENA's *left.*)

HELENA (*to* DOMIN). What am I to speak to them about?

(MEN *look at one another.*)

DOMIN. Anything you like.

HELENA (*looks at* DOMIN). May I speak quite frankly?

DOMIN. Why, of course.

HELENA (*to* OTHERS). *Wavering, then in desperate resolution*). Tell me, doesn't it ever distress you the way you are treated?

FABRY. By whom, may I ask?

HELENA. Why, everybody.

ALQUIST. Treated?

DR. GALL. What makes you think . . . ?

HELENA. Don't you feel that you might be living a better life? (*Pause.* ALL *confused.*)

DR. GALL (*smiling*). Well, that de-pends on what you mean, Miss Glory.

HELENA. I mean that it's perfectly outrageous. It's terrible. (*Standing up*) The whole of Europe is talking about the way you're being treated. That's why I came here, to see for myself, and it's a thousand times worse than it could have been imagined. How can you put up with it?

ALQUIST. Put up with what?

HELENA. Good heavens, you are living creatures, just like us, like the whole of Europe, like the whole world. It's disgraceful that you must live like this.

BUSMAN. Good gracious, Miss Glory!

FABRY. Well, she's not far wrong. We live here just like red Indians.

HELENA. Worse than red Indians. May I—oh, may I call you— brothers?

(MEN *look at each other.*)

BUSMAN. Why not?

HELENA (*looking at* DOMIN). Brothers, I have not come here as the President's daughter. I have come on behalf of the Humanity League. Brothers, the Humanity League now has over two hundred thousand members. Two hundred thousand people are on your side, and offer you their help. (*Tapping back of chair.*)

BUSMAN. Two hundred thousand people, Miss Glory; that's a tidy lot. Not bad.

FABRY. I'm always telling you there's nothing like good old Europe. You see they've not forgotten us. They're offering us help.

DR. GALL. What kind of help? A theatre, for instance?

HALLEMEIER. An orchestra?

HELENA. More than that.

ALQUIST. Just you?

HELENA (*glaring at* DOMIN). Oh, never mind about me. I'll stay as long as it is necessary.
(ALL *express delight.*)

BUSMAN. By Jove, that's good.

ALQUIST (*rising*). Domin, I'm going to get the best room ready for Miss Glory.

DOMIN. Just a minute. I'm afraid that Miss Glory is of the opinion she has been talking to Robots.

HELENA. Of course.
(MEN *laugh.*)

DOMIN. I'm sorry. These gentlemen are human beings just like us.

HELENA. You're not Robots?

(*All to-gether*) {
BUSMAN. Not Robots.

HALLEMEIER. Robots indeed!

DR. GALL. No, thanks.

FABRY. Upon my honor, Miss Glory, we aren't Robots.
}

HELENA. Then why did you tell me that all your officials are Robots?

DOMIN. Yes, the officials, but not the *managers*. Allow me, Miss Glory —this is Consul Busman, General Business Manager; this is Doctor Fabry, General Technical Manager; Doctor Hallemeier, head of the Institute for the Psychological Training of Robots; Doctor Gall, head of the Psychological and Experimental Department; and Alquist, head of the Building Department, R. U. R.
(*As they are introduced they rise and come to kiss her hand, except* GALL *and* ALQUIST, *whom* DOMIN *pushes away. General babble.*)

ALQUIST. Just a builder. Please sit down.

HELENA. Excuse me, gentlemen. Have I done something dreadful?

ALQUIST. Not at all, Miss Glory.

BUSMAN (*handing flowers*). Allow me, Miss Glory.

HELENA. Thank you.

FABRY (*handing candy*). Please, Miss Glory.

DOMIN. Will you have a cigarette, Miss Glory?

HELENA. No, thank you.

DOMIN. Do you mind if I do?

HELENA. Certainly not.

BUSMAN. Well, now, Miss Glory, it is certainly nice to have you with us.

HELENA (*seriously*). But you know I've come to disturb your Robots for you.
(BUSMAN *pulls chair closer.*)

DOMIN (*mocking her serious tone*). My dear Miss Glory—(*chuckle*)—we've had close upon a hundred saviors and prophets here. Every ship brings us some. Missionaries, Anarchists, Salvation Army, all sorts! It's astonishing what a number of churches and idiots there are in the world.

HELENA. And yet you let them speak to the Robots.

DOMIN. So far we've let them all. Why not? The Robot remembers everything, but that's all. They don't even laugh at what the people say. Really, it's quite incredible.

HELENA. I'm a stupid girl. Send me back by the first ship.

DR. GALL. Not for anything in the world, Miss Glory. Why should we send you back?

DOMIN. If it would amuse you, Miss Glory, I'll take you down to the Robot warehouse. It holds about three hundred thousand of them.

BUSMAN. Three hundred and forty-seven thousand.

DOMIN. Good, and you can say whatever you like to them. You can read the Bible, recite the multiplication table, whatever you please. You can even preach to them about human rights.

HELENA. Oh, I think that if you were to show them a little love.

FABRY. Impossible, Miss Glory! *Nothing is harder to like than a Robot.*

HELENA. What do you make them for, then?

BUSMAN. Ha, ha, ha! That's good. What are Robots made for?

FABRY. For *work*, Miss Glory. One Robot can replace two and a half *workmen*. The human machine, Miss Glory, was terribly *imperfect*. It had to be removed sooner or later.

BUSMAN. It was too expensive.

FABRY. It was not effective. It no longer answers the requirements of modern engineering. Nature has no idea of keeping pace with modern labor. For example, from a technical point of view, the whole of childhood is a sheer absurdity. So much time lost. And then again . . .

HELENA (*turns to* DOMIN). Oh, no, no!

FABRY. Pardon me. What is the real *aim* of your League—the—the Humanity League?

HELENA. It's real purpose is to—to protect the Robots—and—and to insure good treatment for them.

FABRY. Not a bad object, either. A machine has to be treated properly. (*Leans back*) I don't like damaged articles. Please, Miss Glory, enroll us all members of your league.

(*"Yes, yes!" from all* MEN.)

HELENA. No, you don't understand me. What we really want is to—to—liberate the Robots. (*Looks at* OTHERS.)

HALLEMEIER. How do you propose to do that?

HELENA. They are to be—to be dealt with like human beings.

HALLEMEIER. Aha! I suppose they're to vote. To drink beer. To order us about?

HELENA. Why shouldn't they drink beer?

HALLEMEIER. Perhaps they're even to receive wages? (*Looking at other* MEN, *amused.*)

HELENA. Of course they are.

HALLEMEIER. Fancy that! Now! And what would they do with their wages, pray?

HELENA. They would buy—what they want—what pleases them.

HALLEMEIER. That would be very nice, Miss Glory, only there's nothing that does please the Robots. Good heavens, what are they to buy? You can feed them on pineapples, straw, whatever you like. It's all the same to them. They've no appetite at all. They've no interest in anything. Why, hang it all, nobody's ever yet seen a Robot smile.

HELENA. Why—why don't you make them—happier?

HALLEMEIER. That wouldn't do, Miss Glory. They are only workmen.

HELENA. Oh, but they're so intelligent.

HALLEMEIER. Confoundedly so, but they're nothing else. They've no will of their own. No soul. No passion.

HELENA. No love?

HALLEMEIER. Love? Huh! Rather not. Robots don't love. Not even themselves.

HELENA. No defiance?

HALLEMEIER. Defiance? I don't know. Only rarely, from time to time.

HELENA. What happens then?

HALLEMEIER. Nothing particular. Occasionally they seem to go off their heads. Something like epilepsy, you know. It's called "Robot's Cramp." They'll suddenly sling down everything they're holding, stand still, gnash their teeth—and then they have to go into the stamping-mill. It's evidently some breakdown in the mechanism.

DOMIN (*sitting on desk*). A flaw in the works that has to be removed.

HELENA. No, no, that's the soul.

FABRY (*humorously*). Do you think that the soul first shows itself by a gnashing of teeth?
(MEN *chuckle.*)

HELENA. Perhaps it's just a sign that there's a struggle within. Perhaps it's a sort of revolt. Oh, if you could infuse them with it.

DOMIN. That'll be remedied, Miss Glory. Doctor Gall is just making some experiments.

DR. GALL. Not with regard to that, Domin. At present I am making pain nerves.

HELENA. Pain nerves?

DR. GALL. Yes, the Robots feel practically no bodily pain. You see, young Rossum provided them with too limited a nervous system. We must introduce suffering.

HELENA. Why do you want to cause them pain?

DR. GALL. For industrial reasons, Miss Glory. Sometimes a Robot does damage to himself because it doesn't hurt him. He puts his hand into the machine—(*describes with gesture*)—breaks his finger—(*describes with gesture*)—smashes his head. It's all the same to him. We must provide them with pain. That's an automatic protection against damage.

HELENA. Will they be happier when they feel pain?

DR. GALL. On the contrary; but they will be more perfect from a technical point of view.

HELENA. Why don't you create a soul for them?

DR. GALL. That's not in our power.

FABRY. That's not in our interest.

BUSMAN. That would increase the cost of production. Hang it all, my dear young lady, we turn them out at such a cheap rate—a hundred and fifty dollars each, fully dressed, and fifteen years ago they cost ten thousand. Five years ago we used to buy the *clothes* for them. Today we have our own weaving mill, and now we even *export* cloth five times cheaper than other factories. What do you pay a yard for cloth, Miss Glory?

HELENA (*looking at* DOMIN). I don't really know. I've forgotten.

BUSMAN. Good gracious, and you want to found a Humanity League. (MEN *chuckle*) It only costs a third now, Miss Glory. All prices are to-day a third of what they were and they'll fall still lower, lower, like that.

HELENA. I don't understand.

BUSMAN. Why, bless you, Miss Glory, it means that the cost of labor has fallen. A Robot, food and all, costs three-quarters of a cent per hour. (*Leans forward*) That's mighty important, you know. All factories will go pop like chestnuts if they don't at once buy Robots to lower the cost of production.

HELENA. And get rid of all their workmen?

BUSMAN. Of course. But in the meantime we've dumped five hundred thousand tropical Robots down on the Argentine pampas to grow corn. Would you mind telling me how much you pay a pound for bread?

HELENA. I've no idea.
(ALL *smile*.)

BUSMAN. Well, I'll tell you. It now costs two cents in good old Europe. A pound of bread for two cents, and the Humanity League—(*designates* HELENA)—knows nothing about it. (*To* MEN) Miss Glory, you don't realize that even that's too expensive. (*All* MEN *chuckle*) Why, in five years' time I'll wager . . .

HELENA. What?

BUSMAN. That the cost of everything will be a tenth of what it is today. Why, in five years we'll be up to our ears in corn and—everything else.

ALQUIST. Yes, and all the workers throughout the world will be unemployed.

DOMIN (*seriously. Rises*). Yes, Alquist, they will. Yes, Miss Glory, they will. But in ten years Rossum's Universal Robots will produce so much *corn*, so much *cloth*, so much everything that things will be practically without price. There will be no poverty. All work will be done by living machines. Everybody will be free from worry and liberated from the degradation of labor. Everybody will live only to perfect himself.

HELENA. Will he?

DOMIN. Of course. It's bound to happen. Then the servitude of man to man and the enslavement of man to matter will cease. Nobody will get bread at the cost of life and hatred. The Robots will wash the feet of the beggar and prepare a bed for him in his house.

ALQUIST. Domin, Domin, what you say sounds too much like Paradise. There was something good in service and something great in humility. There was some kind of virtue in toil and weariness.

DOMIN. Perhaps, but we cannot reckon with what is lost when we start out to transform the world. Man shall be free and supreme; he shall have no other aim, no other labor, no other care than to perfect himself. He shall serve neither matter nor man. He will not be a machine and a device for production. He will be Lord of creation.

BUSMAN. Amen.

FABRY. So be it.

HELENA (*rises*). You have bewildered me. I should like to believe this.

DR. GALL. You are younger than we are, Miss Glory. You will live to see it.

HALLEMEIER. True. (*Looking around*) Don't you think Miss Glory might lunch with us? (*All* MEN *rise*.)

DR. GALL. Of course. Domin, ask her on behalf of us all.

DOMIN. Miss Glory, will you do us the honor?

HELENA. When you know why I've come?

FABRY. For the League of Humanity, Miss Glory.

HELENA. Oh, in that case perhaps . . .

FABRY. That's fine. (*Pause*) Miss Glory, excuse me for five minutes. (*Exits.*)

HALLEMEIER. Thank you. (*Exits with* DR. GALL.)

BUSMAN (*whispering*). I'll be back soon. (*Beckoning to* ALQUIST, *they exit.*)

ALQUIST (*starts, stops, then to* HELENA, *then to door*). I'll be back in exactly five minutes. (*Exits.*)

HELENA. What have they all gone for?

DOMIN. To cook, Miss Glory.

HELENA. To cook what?

DOMIN. Lunch. (*They laugh; takes her hand*) The Robots do our cooking for us and as they've no taste it's not altogether— (*She laughs*) Hallemeier is awfully good at grills and Gall can make any kind of sauce, and Busman knows all about omelets.

HELENA. What a feast! And what's the specialty of Mr.—your builder?

DOMIN. Alquist? Nothing. He only lays the table. And Fabry will get together a little fruit. Our cuisine is very modest, Miss Glory.

HELENA (*thoughtfully*). I wanted to ask you something. . . .

DOMIN. And I wanted to ask you something too—they'll be back in five minutes.

HELENA. What did you want to ask me?

DOMIN. Excuse me, you asked first.

HELENA. Perhaps it's silly of me, but why do you manufacture female Robots when—when . . .

DOMIN. When sex means nothing to them?

HELENA. Yes.

DOMIN. There's a certain demand for them, you see. Servants, saleswomen, stenographers. People are used to it.

HELENA. But—but tell me, are the Robots male and female, mutually —completely without . . .

DOMIN. Completely indifferent to each other, Miss Glory. There's no sign of any affection between them.

HELENA. Oh, that's terrible.

DOMIN. Why?

HELENA. It's so unnatural. One doesn't know whether to be disgusted or to hate them, or perhaps . . .

DOMIN. To pity them. (*Smiles.*)

HELENA. That's more like it. What did you want to ask me?

DOMIN. I should like to ask you, Miss Helena, if you will marry me.

HELENA. What? (*Rises.*)

DOMIN. Will you be my wife? (*Rises.*)

HELENA. No. The idea!

DOMIN (*to her, looking at his watch*). Another three minutes. If you don't marry me you'll have to marry one of the other five.

HELENA. But why should I?

DOMIN. Because they're *all* going to ask you in turn.

HELENA. How could they dare do such a thing?

DOMIN. I'm very sorry, Miss Glory. It seems they've fallen in love with you.

HELENA. Please don't let them. I'll —I'll go away at once. (*Starts out. He stops her, his arms up.*)

DOMIN. Helena— (*She backs away to desk. He follows*) You wouldn't be so cruel as to refuse us.

HELENA. But, but—I can't marry all six.

DOMIN. No, but one, anyhow. If you don't want *me*, marry Fabry.

HELENA. I won't.

DOMIN. Ah! Doctor Gall?

HELENA. I don't want any of you.

DOMIN. Another two minutes. (*Pleading. Looking at watch.*)

HELENA. I think you'd marry any woman who came here.

DOMIN. Plenty of them have come, Helena.

HELENA (*laughing*). Young?

DOMIN. Yes.

HELENA. Why didn't you marry one of them?

DOMIN. Because I didn't lose my head. Until today—then as soon as you lifted your veil— (HELENA *turns her head away*) Another minute.

HELENA. But I don't want you, I tell you.

DOMIN (*laying both hands on her shoulder*). One more minute! Now you either have to look me straight in the eye and say "no" violently, and then I leave you alone—or— (HELENA *looks at him. He takes hands away. She takes his hand again.*)

HELENA (*turning her head away*). You're mad.

DOMIN. A man has to be a bit mad, Helena. That's the best thing about him. (*He draws her to him.*)

HELENA (*not meaning it*). You are —you are . . .

DOMIN. Well?

HELENA. Don't, you're hurting me!

DOMIN. The last chance, Helena. Now or never. . . .

HELENA. But—but— (*He embraces her; kisses her. She embraces him. Knocking at door.*)

DOMIN (*releasing her*). Come in. (*She lays her head on his shoulder. Enter* BUSMAN, GALL *and* HALLEMEIER *in kitchen aprons,* FABRY *with a bouquet and* ALQUIST *with a napkin under his arm.*)

DOMIN. Have you finished your job?

BUSMAN. Yes.

DOMIN. So have we. (*He embraces her. The* MEN *rush around them and offer congratulations.*)

THE CURTAIN FALLS QUICKLY

ACT TWO

SCENE—HELENA'S *drawing room. Ten years later. The skeleton framework of Act I is still used. Tall windows put in back instead of Act I windows. Steel shutters for these windows. Where the green cabinet of Act I has stood is a door leading to the outside. Where the cabinet stood at right, a fireplace is placed. The tall open hallway of Act I is blocked up with a flat piece. The doors at right and left have been changed to those of a drawing room. Door at right leads to* HELENA'S *bedroom. Door at left leads to library.*

The furniture consists of a reading table covered with magazines. A chair to the left of table. In front of table is an armchair covered in chintz. A couch right center and back of it is a small table with books and book-ends. On this table a small reading lamp. At right between doorway and fireplace is a small table. There is a work-basket upon it, with pincushion, needles, etc. Facing the couch is another armchair used by ALQUIST. *To the left of fireplace is a straight-backed chair. Near the door to the outside is a writing desk. There is a lamp upon it, writing paper, etc., a telephone and binoculars.*

The walls of the room have been covered with silk to the height of seven feet. This is done in small flats to fit the different spaces and are in place against the permanent set. The two French windows open into the room. At the rise they are open. There is a balcony beyond looking over the harbor. The same telegraph wires and poles from Act I are again visible through the window. The windows are trimmed with gray lace curtains.

It is about nine in the morning and sunlight streams into the room through the open windows. DOMIN *opens the door, tiptoes in. He carries a potted plant. He beckons the* OTHERS *to follow him, and* HALLEMEIER *and* FABRY *enter, both carrying a potted plant.* DOMIN *places flowers on the library table and goes toward* HELENA'S *bedroom.*

HALLEMEIER (*putting down his flowers on table and indicates the door*). Still asleep?

DOMIN. Yes.

HALLEMEIER. Well, as long as she's asleep she can't worry about it.

DOMIN. She knows nothing about it.

FABRY (*putting plant on writing desk*). I certainly hope nothing happens today.

HALLEMEIER. For goodness' sake, drop it all. Look, this is a fine cyclamen, isn't it? A new sort, my latest—Cyclamen Helena.

DOMIN (*picks up binoculars and goes out into balcony*). No sign of the ship. Things must be pretty bad.

HALLEMEIER. Be quiet. Suppose she heard you.

DOMIN (*coming into room, puts glasses on desk*). Well, anyway the *Ultimus* arrived just in time.

FABRY. You really think that today . . . ?

DOMIN. I don't know. Aren't the flowers fine?

HALLEMEIER (*fondles flowers*). These are my primroses. And this is my new jasmine. I've discovered a wonderful way of developing flowers quickly. Splendid varieties, too. Next year I'll be developing marvelous ones.

DOMIN. What next year?

FABRY. I'd give a good deal to know what's happening at Havre with . . .

HELENA (*off stage*). Nana.

DOMIN. Keep quiet. She's awake. Out you go.
(ALL *go out on tiptoe. Enter* NANA.)

HELENA. Nana?

NANA. Horrid mess! Pack of heathens! If I had *my* say, I'd . . .

HELENA. Nana, come and do up my dress.

NANA. I'm coming. So you're up at last. (*Fastening* HELENA's *dress*) My gracious, what brutes!

HELENA. Who? (*Turning.*)

NANA. If you want to turn *around*, then turn around, but I shan't fasten you up.

HELENA (*turns back*). What are you grumbling about now?

NANA. These dreadful creatures, these heathens—

HELENA (*turning toward* NANA *again*). The Robots?

NANA. I wouldn't even call them by name.

HELENA. What's happened?

NANA. Another of them here has caught it. He began to smash up the statues and pictures in the drawing room; gnashed his teeth; foamed at the mouth. Worse than an animal.

HELENA. Which of them caught it?

NANA. The one—well, he hasn't got any *Christian* name. The one in charge of the library.

HELENA. Radius?

NANA. That's him. My goodness, I'm scared of them. A spider doesn't scare me as much as them.

HELENA. But, Nana, I'm surprised you're not sorry for them.

NANA. Why, you're scared of them too. You know you are. Why else did you bring *me* here?

HELENA. I'm not scared, really I'm not, Nana. I'm only sorry for them.

NANA. You're scared. Nobody could help being scared. Why, the dog's scared of them. He won't take a scrap of meat out of their hands. He draws in his tail and howls when he knows they're about.

HELENA. The dog has no sense.

NANA. He's better than them, and he knows it. Even the horse shies when he meets them. They don't have any young, and a dog has young, everyone has young—

HELENA (*turning back*). Please fasten up my dress, Nana.

NANA. I say it's against God's will to . . .

HELENA. What is it that smells so nice?

NANA. Flowers.

HELENA. What for?

NANA. Now you can turn around.

HELENA (*turns*). Oh, aren't they lovely? Look, Nana. What's happening today?

NANA. It ought to be the end of the world.
(*Enter* DOMIN.)

HELENA (*crosses to him*). Oh, hello, Harry. Harry, why all these flowers?

DOMIN. Guess.

HELENA. Well, it's not my birthday!

DOMIN. Better than that.

HELENA. I don't know. Tell me.

DOMIN. It's ten years ago today since you came here.

HELENA. Ten years? Today? Why . . .
(*They embrace.*)

NANA (*muttering*). I'm off. (*She exits.*)

HELENA. Fancy you remembering.

DOMIN. I'm really ashamed, Helena. I didn't.

HELENA. But you . . .

DOMIN. They remembered.

HELENA. Who?

DOMIN. Busman, Hallemeier—all of them. Put your hand in my pocket.

HELENA (*takes necklace from his left jacket pocket*). Oh! Pearls! A necklace! Harry, is this for me?

DOMIN. It's from Busman.

HELENA. But we can't accept it, can we?

DOMIN. Oh, yes, we can. (*Puts necklace on table*) Put your hand in the other pocket.

HELENA (*takes a revolver out of his right pocket*). What's that?

DOMIN. Sorry. Not that. Try again. (*He puts gun in pocket.*)

HELENA. Oh, Harry, why do you carry a revolver?

DOMIN. It got there by mistake.

HELENA. You never used to carry one.

DOMIN. No, you're right. (*Indicates breast pocket*) There, that's the pocket.

HELENA (*takes out cameo*). A cameo. Why, it's a Greek cameo.

DOMIN. Apparently. Anyhow, Fabry says it is.

HELENA. Fabry? Did Mr. Fabry give me that?

DOMIN. Of course. (*Opens the door*) And look in here. Helena, come and see this. (BOTH *exit.*)

HELENA (*off stage*). Oh, isn't it fine? Is this from you?

DOMIN (*off stage*). No, from Alquist. And there's another on the piano.

HELENA. This must be from you?

DOMIN. There's a card on it.

HELENA. From Doctor Gall. (*Reappearing in doorway*) Oh, Harry, I feel embarrassed at so much kindness.

DOMIN. Come here. This is what Hallemeier brought you.

HELENA. These beautiful flowers?

DOMIN. Yes. It's a new kind. Cyclamen-Helena. He grew them in honor of you. They are almost as beautiful as you.

HELENA (*kissing him*). Harry, why do they all . . . ?

DOMIN. They're awfully fond of you. I'm afraid that my present is a little . . . Look out of the window. (*Crosses to window and beckons to her.*)

HELENA. Where? (*They go out into the balcony.*)

DOMIN. Into the harbor.

HELENA. There's a new ship.

DOMIN. That's *your* ship.

HELENA. Mine? How do you mean?

DOMIN. For you to take trips in—for your amusement.

HELENA. Harry, that's a gunboat.

DOMIN. A gunboat? What are you thinking of? It's only a little bigger and more solid than most ships.

HELENA. Yes, but with guns.

DOMIN. Oh, yes, with a few guns. You'll travel like a queen, Helena.

HELENA. What's the meaning of it? Has anything happened?

DOMIN. Good heavens, no! I say, try these pearls.

HELENA. Harry, have you had bad news?

DOMIN. On the contrary, no letters have arrived for a whole week.

HELENA. Nor telegrams? (*Coming into the room.*)

DOMIN. Nor telegrams.

HELENA. What does that mean?

DOMIN. Holidays for us! We all sit in the office with our feet on the table and take a nap. No letters— no telegrams. Glorious!

HELENA. Then you'll stay with me today?

DOMIN. Certainly. (*Embraces her*) That is, we will see. Do you remember ten years ago today? Miss Glory, it's a great honor to welcome you.
(*They assume the same positions as when they first met ten years before in* DOMIN's *office.*)

HELENA (*to table*). Oh, Mr. Manager, I'm so interested in your factory.

DOMIN. I'm sorry, Miss Glory, it's strictly forbidden. The manufacture of artificial people is a secret.

HELENA. But to oblige the young lady who has come a long way.

DOMIN (*leans on table*). Certainly, Miss Glory. I have no secrets from you.

HELENA. Are you sure, Harry? (*Leaning on desk, seriously, his right hand on hers.*)

DOMIN. Yes.
(*They gradually draw apart.*)

HELENA. But I warn you, sir, this young lady intends to do terrible things.

DOMIN. Good gracious, Miss Glory. Perhaps she doesn't want to marry me.

HELENA. Heaven forbid! She never dreamt of such a thing. But she came here intending to stir up a revolt among your Robots.

DOMIN. A revolt of the Robots!

HELENA (*low voice*). Harry, what's the matter with you?

DOMIN (*laughing it off*). A revolt of the Robots, that's a fine idea. (*Crosses to back of table. She watches him suspiciously*) Miss Glory, it would be easier for you to cause bolts and screws to rebel than our Robots. You know, Helena, you're wonderful. You've turned the hearts of us all. (*Sits on table.*)

HELENA. Oh, I was fearfully impressed by you all then. You were all so sure of yourselves, so strong. I seemed like a tiny little girl who had lost her way among—among . . .

DOMIN. What?

HELENA (*front*). Among huge trees. All my feelings were so trifling compared with your self-confidence. And in all these years I've never lost this anxiety. But you've never felt the least misgiving, not even when everything went wrong.

DOMIN. What went wrong?

HELENA. Your plans. You remember, Harry, when the workmen in America revolted against the Robots and smashed them up, and when the people gave the Robots firearms against the rebels. And then when the governments turned the Robots into soldiers, and there were so many wars.

DOMIN (*getting up and walking about*). We foresaw that, Helena. You see, these are only passing troubles which are bound to happen before the new conditions are established.

HELENA. You were all so powerful, so overwhelming. The whole world bowed down before you. (*Rising*) Oh, Harry! (*Crosses to him.*)

DOMIN. What is it?

HELENA. Close the factory and let's go away. All of us.

DOMIN. I say, what's the meaning of this?

HELENA. I don't know. But can't we go away?

DOMIN. Impossible, Helena! That is, at this particular moment . . .

HELENA. At once, Harry. I'm so frightened.

DOMIN (*takes her*). About what, Helena?

HELENA. It's as if something was falling on top of us, and couldn't be stopped. Oh, take us all away from here. We'll find a place in the world where there's no one else. Alquist will build us a house, and then we'll begin life all over again. (*The telephone rings.*)

DOMIN (*crosses to telephone*). Excuse me. Hello—yes, what? I'll be there at once. Fabry is calling me, my dear.

HELENA. Tell me . . . (*She rushes up to him.*)

DOMIN. Yes, when I come back. Don't go out of the house, dear. (*Exits.*)

HELENA. He won't tell me. (NANA *brings in a water carafe*) Nana, find me the latest newspapers. Quickly. Look in Mr. Domin's bedroom.

NANA. All right. He leaves them all over the place. That's how they get crumpled up. (*Continues muttering. Exits.*)

HELENA (*looking through binoculars at the harbor*). That's a warship. U-l-t-i—*Ultimus.* They're loading.

NANA (*enters with newspapers*). Here they are. See how they're crumpled up.

HELENA. They're old ones. A week old. (*Drops papers.* BOTH *at front of couch.* NANA *sits. Puts on spectacles. Reads the newspapers*) Something's happening, Nana.

NANA. Very likely. It always does. (*Spelling out the words*) "W-a-r in B-a-l-k-a-n-s." Is that far off?

HELENA. Oh, don't read it. It's always the same. Always wars! (*Sits on couch.*)

NANA. What else do you expect? Why do you keep selling thousands and thousands of these heathens as soldiers?

HELENA. I suppose it can't be helped, Nana. We can't know— Domin can't know what they're to be used for. When an order comes for them he must just send them.

NANA. He shouldn't make them. (*Reading from newspaper*) "The Robot soldiers spare no-body in the occ-up-ied terr-it-ory. They have ass-ass-ass-in-at-ed ov-er sev-en hundred thous-and cit-iz-ens." Citizens, if you please.

HELENA (*rises and crosses and takes paper*). It can't be. Let me see. (*Crossing to* NANA) They have assassinated over seven hundred thousand citizens, evidently at the order of their commander. (*Drops paper.*)

NANA (*spelling out the words from other paper she has picked up from the floor*). "Re-bell-ion in Ma-drid a-gainst the gov-ern-ment. Rob-ot in-fant-ry fires on the crowd. Nine thou-sand killed and wounded."

HELENA. Oh, stop! (*Goes up and looks toward the harbor.*)

NANA. Here's something printed in big letters. "Latest news. At Havre the first org-an-iz-a-tion of Rob-ots has been e-stab-lished. Rob-ots work-men, sail-ors and sold-iers have iss-ued a man-i-fest-o to all Rob-ots through-out the world." I don't understand that. That's got no sense. Oh, good gracious, another murder.

HELENA. Take those papers away now.

NANA. Wait a bit. Here's something in still bigger type. "Stat-ist-ics of pop-ul-a-tion." What's that?

HELENA (*coming down to* NANA). Let me see. (*Reads*) "During the past week there has again not been a single birth recorded."

NANA. What's the meaning of that? (*Drops paper.*)

HELENA. Nana, no more people are being born.

NANA. That's the end, then? (*Removing spectacles*) We're done for.

HELENA. Don't talk like that.

NANA. No more people are being born. That's a punishment; that's a punishment.

HELENA. Nana!

NANA (*standing up*). That's the end of the world. (*Repeat until she goes off. Picks paper up from floor. She exits.*)

HELENA (*goes to window*). Oh, Mr. Alquist. Will you come here? Oh, come just as you are. You look very nice in your mason's overalls. (AL-QUIST *enters, his hands soiled with lime and brick dust. She goes to end of sofa and meets him*) Dear Mr. Alquist, it was awfully kind of you, that lovely present.

ALQUIST. My hands are soiled. I've been experimenting with that new cement.

HELENA. Never mind. Please sit down. (*Sits on couch. He sits on her left*) Mr. Alquist, what's the meaning of *Ultimus?*

ALQUIST. The last. Why?

HELENA. That's the name of my new ship. Have you seen it? Do you think we're off soon—on a trip?

ALQUIST. Perhaps very soon.

HELENA. All of you with me?

ALQUIST. I should like us all to be there.

HELENA. What is the matter?

ALQUIST. Things are just moving on.

HELENA. Dear Mr. Alquist, I know something dreadful has happened.

ALQUIST. Has your husband told you anything?

HELENA. No. Nobody will tell me anything. But I feel— Is anything the matter?

ALQUIST. Not that we've heard of yet.

HELENA. I feel so nervous. Don't you ever feel nervous?

ALQUIST. Well, I'm an old man, you know. I've got old-fashioned ways. And I'm afraid of all this progress, and these new-fangled ideas.

HELENA. Like Nana?

ALQUIST. Yes, like Nana. Has Nana got a prayer book?

HELENA. Yes, a big thick one.

ALQUIST. And has it got prayers for various occasions? Against thunderstorms? Against illness? But not against progress?

HELENA. I don't think so.

ALQUIST. That's a pity.

HELENA. Why, do you mean you'd like to pray?

ALQUIST. I do pray.

HELENA. How?

ALQUIST. Something like this: "Oh, Lord, I thank thee for having given

me toil; enlighten Domin and all those who are astray; destroy their work, and aid mankind to return to their labors; let them not suffer harm in soul or body; deliver us from the Robots, and protect Helena. Amen."

HELENA (touches his arm; pats it). Mr. Alquist, are you a believer?

ALQUIST. I don't know. I'm not quite sure.

HELENA. And yet you pray?

ALQUIST. That's better than worrying about it.

HELENA. And that's enough for you?

ALQUIST (ironically). It has to be.

HELENA. But if you thought you saw the destruction of mankind coming upon us . . .

ALQUIST. I do see it.

HELENA. You mean mankind will be destroyed?

ALQUIST. It's bound to be unless— unless.

HELENA. What?

ALQUIST. Nothing. (Pats her shoulder. Rises) Good-bye. (Exits.)

HELENA (rises. Calling). Nana, Nana! (NANA enters) Is Radius still there?

NANA. The one who went mad? They haven't come for him yet.

HELENA. Is he still raving?

NANA. No. He's tied up.

HELENA. Please bring him here.

NANA. What?

HELENA. At once, Nana. (NANA *exits.* HELENA *goes to telephone*) Hello, Doctor Gall, please. Oh, good day, Doctor. Yes, it's Helena. Thanks for your lovely present. Could you come and see me right away? It's important. Thank you. (*Enter* RADIUS. *Looks at* HELENA, *then turns head. She crosses to him*) Poor Radius, you've caught it too? Now they'll send you to the stamping mill. Couldn't you control yourself? Why did it happen? You see, Radius, you are more intelligent than the rest. Doctor Gall took such trouble to make you different. Won't you speak?

RADIUS (*looking at her*). Send me to the stamping mill. (*Open and close fists.*)

HELENA. But I don't want them to kill you. What was the trouble, Radius?

RADIUS (*two steps toward her. Opens and closes fists*) I won't work for you. Put me into the stamping mill.

HELENA. Do you hate us? Why?

RADIUS. You are not as strong as the Robots. You are not as skillful as the Robots. The Robots can do everything. You only give orders. You do nothing but talk.

HELENA. But someone must give orders.

RADIUS. I don't want a master. I know everything for myself.

HELENA. Radius! Doctor Gall gave you a better brain than the rest, better than ours. You are the only one of the Robots that understands perfectly. That's why I had you put into the library, so that you could read everything, understand everything, and then, oh, Radius—I wanted you to show the whole world that the Robots are our equals. That's what I wanted of you.

RADIUS. I don't want a master. I want to be master over others.

HELENA. I'm sure they'd put you in charge of many Robots. You would be a teacher of the Robots.

RADIUS. I want to be master over people. (*Head up.*)

HELENA (*staggering*). You are mad.

RADIUS (*head down low, opens hands*). Then send me to the stamping mill.

HELENA (*steps to him*). Do you think we're afraid of you? (*Rushing to desk and writing note.*)

RADIUS (*turns his head uneasily*). What are you going to do? What are you going to do? (*Starts for her.*)

HELENA. Radius! (*He cowers. Body sways*) Give this note to Mr. Domin. (*He faces her*) It asks them not to send you to the stamping mill. I'm sorry you hate us so.

DR. GALL (*enters*). You wanted me?

HELENA (*backs away*). It's about Radius, Doctor. He had an attack this morning. He smashed the statues downstairs.

DR. GALL (*looks at him*). What a pity to lose him.

HELENA. Radius isn't going to be put into the stamping mill.

DR. GALL. But every Robot after he has had an attack . . . It's a strict order.

HELENA. No matter—Radius isn't going, if I can prevent it.

DR. GALL. But I warn you. It's dangerous. Come here to the window, my good fellow. Let's have a look. Please give me a needle or a pin. (RADIUS *follows.* HELENA *gets a needle from work-basket on table.*)

HELENA. What for?

DR. GALL. A test. (HELENA *gives him the needle.* GALL *crosses to* RADIUS, *who faces him. Sticks it into his hand and* RADIUS *gives a violent start*) Gently, gently. (*Opens the jacket of* RADIUS *and puts his ear to his heart*) Radius, you are going into the stamping mill, do you understand? There they'll kill you—(*takes glasses off and cleans them*)—and grind you to powder. (RADIUS *opens hands and fingers*) That's terribly painful. It will make you scream aloud. (*Opens* RADIUS'S *eye.* RADIUS *trembles.*)

HELENA. Doctor . . . (*Standing near couch.*)

DR. GALL. No, no, Radius, I was wrong. I forgot that Madame Domin has put in a good word for you, and you'll be left off. (*Listens to heart*) Ah, that does make a difference. (RADIUS *relaxes. Again listens to his heart for a reaction*) All right—you can go.

RADIUS. You do unnecessary things . . . (*Exit* RADIUS.)

DR. GALL (*speaks to her—very concerned*). Reaction of the pupils, increase of sensitiveness. It wasn't an attack characteristic of the Robots.

HELENA. What was it, then? (*Sits on couch.*)

DR. GALL. Heaven knows. Stubbornness, anger or revolt—I don't know. And his heart, too.

HELENA. What?

DR. GALL. It was fluttering with nervousness like a human heart. He was all in a sweat with fear, and, do you know, I don't believe the rascal is a Robot at all any longer.

HELENA. Doctor, has Radius a soul?

DR. GALL (*over to couch*). He's got something nasty.

HELENA. If you knew how he hates us. Oh, Doctor, are all your Robots like that? All the new ones that you began to make in a different way? (*She invites him to sit beside her. He sits.*)

DR. GALL. Well, some are more sensitive than others. They're all more human beings than Rossum's Robots were.

HELENA. Perhaps this hatred is more like human beings, too?

DR. GALL. That too is progress.

HELENA. What became of the girl you made, the one who was most like us?

DR. GALL. Your favorite? I kept her. She's lovely, but stupid. No good for work.

HELENA. But she's so beautiful.

DR. GALL. I called her "Helena." I wanted her to resemble you. She is a failure.

HELENA. In what way?

DR. GALL. She goes about as if in a dream, remote and listless. She's without life. I watch and wait for a miracle to happen. Sometimes I think to myself: "If you were to wake up only for a moment you would kill me for having made you."

HELENA. And yet you go on making Robots! Why are no more children being born?

DR. GALL. We don't know.

HELENA. Oh, but you must. Tell me.

DR. GALL. You see, so many Robots are being manufactured that people are becoming superfluous. Man is really a survival, but that he should die out, after a paltry thirty years of competition, that's the awful part of it. You might almost think that Nature was offended at the manufacture of the Robots, but we still have old Rossum's manuscript.

HELENA. Yes. In that strong box.

DR. GALL. We go on using it and making Robots. All the universities are sending in long petitions to restrict their production. Otherwise, they say, mankind will become extinct through lack of fertility. But the R. U. R. shareholders, of course, won't hear of it. All the governments, on the other hand, are clamoring for an increase in production, to raise the standards of their armies. And all the manufacturers in the world are ordering Robots like mad.

HELENA. And has no one demanded that the manufacture should cease altogether?

DR. GALL. No one has courage.

HELENA. Courage!

DR. GALL. People would stone him to death. You see, after all, it's more convenient to get your work done by the Robots.

HELENA. Oh, Doctor, what's going to become of people?

DR. GALL. God knows. Madame Helena, it looks to us scientists like the end.

HELENA (rising). Thank you for coming and telling me.

DR. GALL (rises). That means that you're sending me away.

HELENA. Yes. (Exit DR. GALL. She crosses to door with sudden resolution) Nana! Nana! the fire, light it quickly. (HELENA exits.)

NANA (entering). What, light the fire in the summer?

HELENA (off stage). Yes!

NANA (*she looks for* RADIUS). Has that mad *Radius* gone? A fire in summer, what an idea? Nobody would think she'd been married ten years. She's like a baby, no sense at all. A fire in summer. Like a baby. (*She lights the fire.*)

HELENA (*returns with armful of faded papers*). Is it burning, Nana? All this has got to be burned.

NANA. What's that?

HELENA. Old papers, fearfully old. Nana, shall I burn them?

NANA. Are they any use?

HELENA. No.

NANA. Well, then, burn them.

HELENA (*throwing the first sheet on the fire*). What would you say, Nana, if this was money and a lot of money? And if it was an invention, the greatest invention in the world?

NANA. I'd say burn it. All these new-fangled things are an offense to the Lord. It's downright wickedness. Wanting to improve the world after He has made it.

HELENA. Look how they curl up. As if they were alive. Oh, Nana, how horrible!

NANA. Here, let me burn them.

HELENA (*drawing back*). No, no, I must do it myself. Just look at the flames. They are like hands, like tongues, like living shapes. (*Raking fire with the poker*) Lie down, lie down.

NANA. That's the end of them. (*Fireplace slowly out.*)

HELENA. Nana, Nana!

NANA. Good gracious, what is it you've burned? (*Almost to herself.*)

HELENA. Whatever have I done?

NANA. Well, what is it? (MEN's *laughter off stage.*)

HELENA. Go quickly. It's the gentlemen calling.

NANA. Good gracious, what a place! (*Exits.*)

DOMIN (*opens door*). Come along and offer your congratulations. (*Enter* HALLEMEIER *and* DR. GALL.)

HALLEMEIER. Madame Helena, I congratulate you on this festive day.

HELENA. Thank you. Where are Fabry and Busman?

DOMIN. They've gone down the harbor. (*Closes the door and comes to center.*)

HALLEMEIER. Friends, we must drink to this happy occasion.

HELENA. Brandy? With soda water? (*Exits.*)

HALLEMEIER. Let's be temperate. No soda.

DOMIN. What's been burning here? Well, shall I tell her about it?

DR. GALL. Of course. It's all over now.

HALLEMEIER (*embracing* DOMIN). It's all over now. It's all over now. (*They dance around* DR. GALL *in a circle*) It's all over now.

DOMIN (*in unison*). It's all over now.
(*They keep repeating. Keep it up after* HELENA *is on.*)

HELENA (*entering with decanter and glasses*). What's all over now? What's the matter with you all? (*She puts tray on table.* DR. GALL *helps her to pour the drinks.*)

HALLEMEIER (*crosses to back of table*). A piece of good luck. Madame Domin! (ALL *ad lib.*) Just ten years ago today you arrived on this island. (HALLEMEIER *crosses to table for drink.*)

DR. GALL. And now, ten years later to the minute . . .

HALLEMEIER. The same ship's returning to us. So here's to luck. (*Drinks.* DOMIN *with great exuberance has gone out in the balcony and looks over the harbor.*)

DR. GALL. Madame, your health. (ALL *drink.*)

HALLEMEIER. That's fine and strong.

HELENA. Which ship did you mean?

DOMIN (HELENA *gives him his drink and she crosses to front of couch*). Any ship will do, as long as it arrives in time. To the ship. (*Empties his glass.*)

HELENA. You've been waiting for the ship? (*Sits on couch.*)

HALLEMEIER. Rather. Like Robinson Crusoe. Madame Helena, best wishes. Come along, Domin, out with the news.

HELENA. Do tell me what's happened.

DOMIN. First, it's all up. (*He puts brandy glass on table.* HALLEMEIER *sits on table, upper end.*)

HELENA. What's up?

DOMIN. The revolt.

HELENA. What revolt?

DOMIN. Give me that paper, Hallemeier. (HALLEMEIER *hands paper.* DOMIN *reads*) "The first National Robot organization has been founded at Havre, and has issued an appeal to the Robots throughout the world."

HELENA. I read that.

DOMIN. That means a revolution. A revolution of all the Robots in the world.

HALLEMEIER. By Jove, I'd like to know . . .

DOMIN. Who started it? So would I. There was nobody in the world who could affect the Robots, no agitator, no one, and suddenly this happens, if you please.

HELENA. What did they do?

DOMIN. They got possession of all firearms, telegraphs, radio stations, railways and ships.

HALLEMEIER. And don't forget that these rascals outnumbered us by at least a thousand to one. A hundredth part of them would be enough to settle us.

DOMIN. Remember that this news was brought by the last steamer. That explains the stoppage of all communication, and the arrival of no more ships. We knocked off work a few days ago, and we're just waiting to see when things are to start afresh.

HELENA. Is that why you gave me a warship?
(GALL *fills* DOMIN's *glass.*)

DOMIN. Oh, no, my dear, I ordered that six months ago. Just to be sure I was on the safe side. But, upon my soul, I was sure then that we'd be on board today.

HELENA. Why six months ago?

DOMIN. Well, there were signs, you know. But that's of no consequence. (*Gets glass*) To think that this week the whole of civilization has been at stake. Your health, my friends.

HALLEMEIER. Your health, Madame Helena.
(ALL *drink to* HELENA.)

HELENA. You say it's all over?

DOMIN. Absolutely.

HELENA. How do you know?

DR. GALL. The boat's coming in. The regular mail boat, exact to the minute by the timetable. It will dock punctually at eleven-thirty.

DOMIN. Punctuality is a fine thing, my friends. That's what keeps the world in order. Here's to punctuality.
(MEN *drink.*)

HELENA. Then—everything—is all right?

DOMIN. Practically everything. I believe they've cut the cables and seized the radio station. But it doesn't matter if only the timetable holds good.

HALLEMEIER (*rises*). If the timetable holds good, human laws hold good. Divine laws hold good, the laws of the universe hold good, everything holds good that ought to hold good. (GALL *applauds*) The timetable is more significant than the gospel, more than Homer, more than the whole of Kant. Madame Helena, the timetable is the most perfect product of the human mind. Madame Helena, I'll fill up my glass.
(GALL *hands* HALLEMEIER *the decanter.*)

HELENA. Why didn't you tell me anything about it?

DR. GALL. Heaven forbid.

DOMIN. You mustn't be worried with such things.

HELENA. But if the revolution had spread as far as here?

DOMIN. You wouldn't know anything about it.

HELENA. Why?

DOMIN. Because we'd be on board your *Ultimus* and well out at sea. Within a month, Helena, we'd be dictating our own terms to the Robots.

HELENA. I don't understand.

DOMIN. We'd take something with us that the Robots could not exist without!

HELENA. What, Harry?

DOMIN (*turns to* HALLEMEIER). The secret of their manufacture. Old Rossum's manuscript. As soon as they found out that they couldn't make themselves they'd be on their knees to us.

DR. GALL (*rises*). Madame Domin, that was our trump card. I never had the least fear the Robots would win. How could they against people like us? (GALL *rises and goes out onto the balcony.*)

HELENA. Why didn't you tell me? (*She rushes to the fireplace and sees the ashes.*)

DR. GALL. Why, the boat's in!

HALLEMEIER. Eleven-thirty to the dot. (*Rising and going onto the balcony*) The good old *Amelia* that brought Madame Helena to us. (DOMIN *goes out onto the balcony.*)

DR. GALL. Just ten years ago to the minute.

HALLEMEIER. They're throwing out the mailbags.

DOMIN. Busman's waiting for them. And Fabry will bring us the first news. You know, Helena, I'm fearfully curious to know how they tackled this business in Europe.

HALLEMEIER (*crosses down to table*). To think we weren't in it,

we who invented the Robots! (*Returning to the armchair.*)

HELENA (*rushing to* DOMIN *from fireplace.*)

DOMIN. What is it?

HELENA. Let's leave here.

DOMIN. Now, Helena? Oh, come, come.

HELENA. As quickly as possible, all of us!

DOMIN. Why?

HELENA. Please, Harry. Please, Doctor Gall, Hallemeier, please close the factory.

DOMIN. Why, none of us could leave here now.

HELENA. Why?

DOMIN. Because we're about to extend the manufacture of the Robots.

HELENA. What, now, now after the revolt?

DOMIN. Yes, precisely, after the revolt. We're just beginning the manufacture of a new kind.

HELENA. What kind?

DOMIN. Henceforward we shan't have just one factory. There won't be *Universal* Robots any more. We'll establish a factory in every country, in every state, and do you know what these new factories will make?

HELENA. No, what?

DOMIN. *National* Robots.

HELENA. How do you mean?

DOMIN. I mean that each of these factories will produce Robots of a different color, a different language. They'll be complete strangers to each other. (*Turns; takes in* HALLEMEIER *and* GALL) They'll never be able to understand each other. Then we'll egg them on a little in the matter of misunderstanding and the result will be that for ages to come every Robot will hate every other Robot of a different factory mark. So humanity will *be safe.*

HALLEMEIER (*to each of them*). By Jove, we'll make Negro Robots and Swedish Robots and Czechoslovakian Robots, and then . . .

HELENA. Harry, that's dreadful.

HALLEMEIER. Madame Domin, here's to the hundred new factories. The *National* Robots.

DOMIN. Helena, mankind can only keep things going for another hundred years at the outside. For a hundred years man must be allowed to develop and achieve the most he can.

HELENA. Oh, close the factory before it's too late.

DOMIN. I tell you we are just beginning on a bigger scale than ever.
(*Enter* FABRY.)

DR. GALL. Well, Fabry?

DOMIN. What's happened? Have you been down to the boat?

DR. GALL. Let's hear.

FABRY. Read that, Domin. (*He hands him a pink handbill. When* DOMIN *receives the handbill he sees at once that something has happened.*)

HALLEMEIER. Tell us, Fabry.

FABRY (*falsely*). Well, everything is all right—comparatively. (*To the other* MEN) On the whole, much as we expected.

DR. GALL. They acquitted themselves splendidly.

FABRY. Who?

DR. GALL. The people.

FABRY (*hesitating*). Oh, yes, of course. That is . . . Excuse me, there is something we ought to discuss alone.

HELENA (*touches his arm*). Fabry, have you had bad news?

FABRY. No, no, on the contrary. I only think that we better go into the office.

HELENA. Stay here. I'll go. (*Exits.*)

DR. GALL. What's happened?

DOMIN. Damnation!

FABRY. Bear in mind that the *Amelia* brought whole bales of these leaflets. No other cargo at all. (GALL *closes the door.*)

HALLEMEIER. What? But it arrived on the minute.

FABRY. The Robots are great on punctuality. Read it, Domin.

DOMIN (*reads handbill*). "Robots throughout the world. We, the first International organization of Rossum's Universal Robots, proclaim man our enemy, and an outlaw in the universe." Good heavens, who taught them these phrases?

DR. GALL. Go on.

DOMIN. They say they are more highly developed than man; stronger and more intelligent. Man's their parasite. Why, it's absurd.

FABRY. Read the third paragraph.

DOMIN. "Robots throughout the world, we command you to kill all mankind. Spare no man. Spare no woman. Save factories, railways, machinery, mines and raw materials. Destroy the rest. Then return to work. Work must not be stoppea." (*Looks at* OTHERS.)

DR. GALL. That's ghastly.

HALLEMEIER. The devil!

DOMIN. "These orders are to be carried out as soon as received." Then come the detailed instructions. Is this actually being done, Fabry?

FABRY. Evidently. (BUSMAN *rushes in and collapses on couch*) By Jove, that was a sprint!

BUSMAN. Well, boys, I suppose you've heard the glad news.

DOMIN. Quick on board the *Ultimus*.

BUSMAN. Wait, Harry, wait. There's no hurry.

DOMIN. Why wait?

BUSMAN. Because it's no good, my boy. The Robots are already on board the *Ultimus*.

DR. GALL. That's ugly.

DOMIN. Fabry, telephone the electrical works.
(FABRY *goes to back of couch.*)

BUSMAN. No use, my boy. They've charged the air with static.

DOMIN (*inspects his revolver*). Well, then, I'll go. (*Starts; stops.*)

BUSMAN. Where?

DOMIN. To the electrical works. There are some people still there. I'll bring them across. (*Gets as far as door.*)

BUSMAN. Better not try it.

DOMIN. Why?

BUSMAN. Because I'm very much afraid we are surrounded.
(ALL *rush out into the balcony.*)

DR. GALL. Surrounded? (*Runs to window*) I rather think you're right. (GALL *rushes to balcony.*)

HALLEMEIER. By Jove, that's deuced quick work. (*Going to windows.*)

HELENA (*runs in*). Harry, what's this? (*Holds out paper.*)

DOMIN. Where did you get it?

HELENA (*points to the manifesto of the* ROBOTS *which she has in her hand*). The Robots in the kitchen!

DOMIN. Where are the ones that brought it?

HELENA. There, gathered around the house.

(GALL, HALLEMEIER, DOMIN *start out. The factory whistle blows.* MOB *voices start.*)

DOMIN. The factory whistle!

BUSMAN. Noon?

DOMIN (*looking at his watch. To* HALLEMEIER). No! That's not noon yet. That must be—that's . . .

HELENA. What?

DOMIN. The Robots' signal—the attack!

(HELENA *clings to* DOMIN. FABRY *and* GALL *close the steel shutters on window.* BUSMAN *hurries to window and looks through the shutters. The curtain falls quickly with* HELENA *in* DOMIN's *arms. The whistle blows until the curtain is down.*)

CURTAIN

ACT THREE

SCENE—HELENA's *drawing room as before. The room is dark and gray. The steel shutters which are outside are still closed as at the end of Act II.* ALQUIST *is sitting in chair.* DOMIN *comes into the room. Subdued voices.* DR. GALL *is looking out of the window at center. He is seated in a chair.*

DOMIN (*gets binoculars from desk; crosses to window. To* GALL). Any more of them?

DR. GALL. Yes. They're standing like a wall, beyond the garden railing. Why are they so quiet? It's monstrous to be besieged with silence.

DOMIN (*looking through the barred windows*). I should like to know what they are waiting for? They must make a start any minute now. If they lean against the railings it will snap like a match.

DR. GALL. They aren't armed.

DOMIN (*puzzled*). We couldn't hold our own for five minutes. Man

alive, they overwhelm us like an avalanche. Why don't they make a rush for it? I say. (*Turns to* GALL.)

DR. GALL. Well?

DOMIN. I'd like to know what will become of us in the next ten minutes. They've got us in a vise. We're done for, Gall.

DR. GALL. You know, we made one serious mistake.

DOMIN. What?

DR. GALL. We made the Robots' faces too much alike. A hundred thousand faces all alike, all facing this way. A hundred thousand expressionless bubbles. It's like a nightmare.

DOMIN. You think if they'd been different . . .

DR. GALL. It wouldn't have been such an awful sight!

DOMIN (*looks through binoculars towards the harbor*). I'd like to know what they're unloading from the *Amelia*.

DR. GALL. Not firearms.

FABRY (*enters with a plug-box to which is attached a long cable or wire.* HALLEMEIER *following him.* FABRY *attaches the cable to an electric installation which is on the floor near the wall*). All right, Hallemeier, lay down that wire.

HALLEMEIER (*just inside the room*). That was a bit of work. What's the news? (*Seeing* DOMIN *and* GALL *at the window.*)

DR. GALL. We're completely surrounded.

HALLEMEIER (*crosses to window*). We've barricaded the passages and the stairs. (*Going to window*) God, what swarms of them! I don't like the looks of them, Domin. There's a feeling of death about it all. Any water here?

FABRY. Ready!

DR. GALL (*turning round in the chair*). What's that wire for, Fabry?

FABRY. The electrical installation. Now we can run the current all along the garden railing. (*Up to window*) Whenever we like. If anyone touches it he'll know it. We've still got some people there anyhow.

DR. GALL. Where?

FABRY. In the electrical works. At least, I hope so. (*Goes to table and turns on lamp*) Ah, they're there, and they're working. As long as that'll burn we're all right. (*To window.*)

HALLEMEIER. The barricades are all right, too, Fabry.

FABRY. Your barricades! I can put twelve hundred volts into that railing.

(HELENA *is playing Rachmaninoff's Elegie off stage.*)

DOMIN. Where's Busman? (DOMIN *has left window and is walking up and down.*)

FABRY. Downstairs in the office. He's working out some calculations.

DOMIN. I've called him. We must have a conference.

ALQUIST. Thank God Madam Helena can still play.

(HALLEMEIER *crosses to door, opens it slightly and listens to music. Enter* BUSMAN.)

FABRY. Look out, Bus—look out for the wires.

DR. GALL. What's that you're carrying?

BUSMAN (*laying the books on the table*). The ledger, my boy. I'd like to wind up the accounts before —before . . . (DOMIN *crosses to window*) Well, this time I shan't wait till the New Year to strike a balance. What's up? (*Goes to window*) Absolutely quiet.

DR. GALL. Can't you see anything?

BUSMAN. Nothing but blue—blue everywhere.

DR. GALL. That's the Robots.

DOMIN. The Robots are unloading firearms from the *Amelia*.

BUSMAN. Well, what of it? How can I stop them? (*Returns to table, sits and opens ledger.*)

DOMIN. We can't stop them.

BUSMAN. Then let me go on with my accounts. (*Goes on with his work.*)

DOMIN (*picks up telescope*). Good God! The *Ultimus* has trained her guns on us.

DR. GALL. Who's done that?

DOMIN. The Robots on board.

FABRY. H'm, then of course . . . (*Pause*) Then—then that's the end of us.

DR. GALL. You mean?

FABRY. The Robots are practised marksmen.

DOMIN. Yes. It's inevitable. (*Pause.*)

DR. GALL (*swinging around; looking into room. Pause*). That was criminal of old Europe to teach the Robots to fight. Damn them! Couldn't they have given us a rest

with their politics? It was a crime to make soldiers of them.

ALQUIST. It was a crime to make Robots.

DOMIN (*quietly*). No, Alquist, I don't regret that even today.

ALQUIST. Not even today?

DOMIN (*dreamily*). Not even today, the last day of civilization. It was a colossal achievement.

BUSMAN (*sotto voce*). Three hundred sixty million.

DOMIN (*from window*). Alquist, this is our last hour. We are already speaking half in the other world. That was not an evil dream to shatter the servitude of labor. The dreadful and humiliating *labor* that man had to undergo. Work was too hard. Life was too hard. And to overcome that . . .

ALQUIST. Was not what the two Rossums dreamed of. Old Rossum only thought of his Godless tricks, and the young one of his milliards. And that's not what your R. U. R. shareholders dream of either. They dream of dividends, and their dividends are the ruin of mankind.

DOMIN. To Hell with your dividends. Do you suppose I'd have done an hour's work for them? It was for myself that I worked, for my own satisfaction. I wanted man to become the master. So that he shouldn't live merely for the crust of bread. I wanted not a single soul to be broken by other people's machinery. I wanted nothing, nothing, nothing to be left of this appalling social structure. I'm revolted by poverty. I wanted a new generation. I wanted—I thought . . .

ALQUIST. Well?

DOMIN (*front of couch*). I wanted to turn the whole of mankind into an aristocracy of the world. An aristocracy nourished by millions of mechanical slaves. Unrestricted, free and consummated in man. And maybe more than man.

ALQUIST. Superman?

DOMIN. Yes. Oh, only to have a hundred years of time. Another hundred years for the future of mankind.

BUSMAN (*sotto voce*). Carried forward—four hundred and twenty millions.
(DOMIN *sits on couch*.)

HALLEMEIER (*pauses—back of couch*). What a fine thing music is! We ought to have gone in for that before.

FABRY. Gone in for what?

HALLEMEIER. Beauty, lovely things. What a lot of lovely things there are. The world was wonderful, and we—we here—tell me, what enjoyment did we have?

BUSMAN (*sotto voce*). Five hundred and twenty million.

HALLEMEIER. Life was a good thing, life was—(*Looking out of window. Directly to* FABRY) Fabry, switch the current into that railing.

FABRY. Why? (*Rushes to electric installation*.)

HALLEMEIER. They're grabbing hold of it.
(DOMIN *rises—straightens up.* ALL *rise*.)

DR. GALL. Connect it up.

HALLEMEIER. Fine, that's doubled them up. Two, three, four killed.

DR. GALL. They're retreating.
(DOMIN *sits*.)

HALLEMEIER. Five killed.

DR. GALL (*pause*). The first encounter.

HALLEMEIER. They're charred to cinders, my boy. Who says we must give in?
(*Music stops*.)

DOMIN (ALQUIST *and* GALL *sit. Wiping his forehead*). Perhaps we've been killed this hundred years and are only ghosts. It's as if I had been through all this before, as if I'd already had a mortal wound here in the throat. (*Looking at each as he speaks*) And you, Fabry, had once been shot in the head. And you, Gall, torn limb from limb. And Hallemeier knifed.

HALLEMEIER. Fancy me being knifed. (*Looks at each. Then speaks*) Why are you so quiet, you fools? (*Steps down*) Speak, can't you?

ALQUIST. And who is to blame for all this?

HALLEMEIER. Nobody is to blame except the Robots.

ALQUIST. No, it is we are to blame. You, Domin, myself—all of us. For our own selfish ends, for profit, for progress, we have destroyed mankind. Now we'll burst with all our greatness.

HALLEMEIER. Rubbish, man. Mankind can't be wiped out so easily.

ALQUIST. It's our fault. It's our fault.

DR. GALL. No! I'm to blame for this, for everything that's happened. (*He leaves the window and comes down to end of couch.*)

FABRY. You, Gall?

DR. GALL. I changed the Robots.

BUSMAN. What's that?

DR. GALL. I changed the character of the Robots. I changed the way of making them. Just a few details about their bodies. Chiefly— chiefly, their—their irritability.

HALLEMEIER. Damn it, why?

BUSMAN. What did you do it for?

FABRY. Why didn't you say anything?

DR. GALL. I did it in secret. I was transforming them into human beings. In certain respects they're already above us. They're stronger than we are.

FABRY. And what's that got to do with the revolt of the Robots?

DR. GALL. Everything, in my opinion. They've ceased to be machines. They're already aware of their superiority, and they hate us as they hate everything human.

DOMIN. Perhaps we're only phantoms.

FABRY. Stop, Harry. We haven't much time, Doctor Gall.

DOMIN. Fabry, Fabry, how your forehead bleeds where the shot pierced it.

FABRY (*crosses to* GALL). Be silent! Doctor Gall, you admit changing the way of making the Robots.

DR. GALL. Yes.

FABRY. Were you aware of what might be the consequences of your experiment?

DR. GALL. I was bound to reckon with such a possibility.

FABRY (*amusing*). Why did you do it, then?
(HELENA *enters.*)

DR. GALL. For my own satisfaction. The experiment was my own.

HELENA. That's not true, Doctor Gall! (*Crosses to couch.*)

DOMIN (*rises*). Helena, you? (*Crosses to her*) Let's look at you. Oh, it's terrible to be dead. (*He rises and crushes her in his arms.*)

HELENA. Stop, Harry.

DOMIN. No, no, Helena, don't leave me now. You are life itself.

HELENA. No, dear, I won't leave you. But I must tell them. Doctor Gall is not guilty.

FABRY. Excuse me. Gall was under certain obligations.

HELENA. No. He did it because I wanted it. Tell them, Doctor Gall—how many years ago did I ask you to . . . ?

DR. GALL. I did it on my own responsibility.

HELENA. Don't believe him. I asked him to give the Robots souls.

DOMIN. This has nothing to do with the soul.

HELENA. That's what he said. He said that he could change only a physiological—a physiological—

HALLEMEIER (*from up at window*). A physiological correlate?

HELENA. Yes. But it meant so much to me that he should do even that.

DOMIN. Why?

HELENA. I thought that if they were more like us they would understand us better. That they couldn't hate us if they were only a little more human.

DOMIN. Nobody can hate man more than man.

HELENA. Oh, don't speak like that, Harry. It was so terrible, this cruel strangeness between us and them. That's why I asked Gall to change the Robots. I swear to you that he didn't want to.

DOMIN. But he did it.

HELENA. Because I asked him.

DR. GALL. I did it for myself as an experiment.

HELENA. No, Doctor Gall! I know you wouldn't refuse me.

DOMIN. Why?

HELENA. You know, Harry.

DOMIN. Yes, because he's in love with you—like all of them. (*Pause.* DOMIN *takes her in his arms.*)

HALLEMEIER. Good God, they're sprouting up out of the earth. Why, perhaps these very walls will change into Robots.

BUSMAN (*rises; crosses to* GALL). Gall, when did you actually start these tricks of yours?

DR. GALL. Three years ago.

BUSMAN. Aha. And on how many Robots altogether did you carry out your improvements? (*Walking to and fro.*)

DR. GALL. A few hundred of them.

BUSMAN. Ah! That means for every million of the good old Robots there's only one of Gall's improved pattern.

DOMIN. What of it?

BUSMAN. That it's of no consequence whatsoever.

FABRY. Busman's right.
(HELENA *sits in armchair.*)

BUSMAN. I should think so, my boy; but do you know what is to blame for this lovely mess?

FABRY. What?

BUSMAN. The number! Upon my soul, we might have known that

some day or other the Robots would be stronger than human beings, and that this was bound to happen. And we were doing all we could to bring it about as soon as possible. You, Domin, you, Fabry, myself . . .

DOMIN. Are you accusing us? (*Turning on him.*)

BUSMAN. Oh, do you suppose the management controls the output? It's the demand that controls the output.

HELENA. And is it for that we must perish?

BUSMAN. That's a nasty word, Madame Helena. We don't want to perish. I don't, anyhow.

DOMIN. No? What do you want to do?

BUSMAN. I want to get out of this, that's all.

DOMIN. Oh, stop it, Busman.

BUSMAN. Seriously, Harry, I think we might try it.

DOMIN. How?

BUSMAN. By fair means. I do everything by fair means. Give me a free hand and I'll negotiate with the Robots.

DOMIN. By fair means?

BUSMAN (*rises*). Of course. For instance, I'll say to them: "Worthy and Worshipful Robots, you have everything. You have intellect, you have power, you have firearms. But we have just one interesting screed, a dirty old yellow scrap of paper . . ."

DOMIN. Rossum's manuscript? (*Interest from* ALL.)

BUSMAN. Yes. "And that," I'll tell them, "contains an account of your illustrious origin, the noble process of your manufacture and so on. Worthy Robots, without this scribble on that paper you will not be able to produce a single new colleague. In another twenty years there will not be the living specimen of a Robot whom you could exhibit in a menagerie. My esteemed friends, that would be a great blow to you, but if you will let all of us human beings on Rossum's Island go on board that ship we will deliver the factory and the secret of the process to you in return. You allow us to get away, and we will allow you to manufacture yourselves. That, worthy Robots, is a fair deal. Something for something." That's what I'd say to them, my boys. (*Sits.*)

DOMIN. Busman, do you think we'd sell the manuscript?

BUSMAN. Yes, I do. If not in a friendly way, then—either we sell it or they'll find it. Just as you like.

DOMIN. Busman, we can destroy Rossum's manuscript.

BUSMAN. Then we destroy everything—not only the manuscript but ourselves. Just as you think fit.

DOMIN. There are over thirty of us on this island. Are we to sell the secret and save that many souls at the risk of enslaving mankind . . .

BUSMAN. Why, you're mad! Who'd sell the whole manuscript?

DOMIN. Busman, no cheating!

BUSMAN. Well then, sell, but afterwards . . .

DOMIN. Well?

BUSMAN. Let's suppose this happens. When we're on board the *Ultimus* I'll stop up my ears with cotton wool, lie down somewhere in the hold, and you'll train the guns on the factory and blow it to smithereens, and with it Rossum's secret.

FABRY (*rises*). No!

DOMIN. Busman, you're no—gentleman. If we sell them it will be a straight sale.

BUSMAN (*rises*). It's in the interest of humanity to . . .

DOMIN. It's in the interest of humanity to keep our word . . .

HALLEMEIER. Oh, come, what rubbish!

DOMIN. This is a fearful decision. We are selling the destiny of mankind. Are we to sell or destroy? Fabry?

FABRY. Sell.

DOMIN. Gall?

DR. GALL. Sell.

DOMIN. Hallemeier?

HALLEMEIER. Sell, of course.

DOMIN. Alquist?

ALQUIST. As God wills.

DOMIN. Very well, gentlemen.

HELENA. Harry, you're not asking me.

DOMIN (*stops. To her*). No, child. Don't you worry about it. (*He pats her shoulder.*)

FABRY. Who'll do the negotiating?

BUSMAN. I will.

DOMIN. Wait till I bring the manuscript. (DOMIN *goes out.*)

HELENA (*rises*). Harry, don't go! (HELENA *sits.* ALL *look at her. Pause.*)

FABRY (*looking out of window*). Oh, to escape you! you—matter—in revolt; oh, to preserve human life, if only upon a single vessel—

DR. GALL. Don't be afraid. (*Going to back of couch*) Madame Helena. We'll sail far away from here; we'll begin life all over again.

HELENA. Oh, Gall, don't speak.

FABRY. It isn't too late. It will be a little State with one ship. Alquist will build us a house and you shall rule over us.

HALLEMEIER. Madame Helena, Fabry's right.

HELENA (*breaking down*). Oh, stop! Stop!

BUSMAN. Good! I don't mind beginning all over again. That suits me right down to the ground. (*Going through papers on table.*)

FABRY. And this little State of ours could be the center of future life. A place of refuge where we could gather strength. Why, in a few hundred years we could conquer the world again.

ALQUIST. You believe that even to-day?

FABRY. Yes!

BUSMAN. *Amen.* You see, Madame Helena, we're not so badly off.

DOMIN (*storms into room. Hoarse-ly*). Where's old Rossum's manu-script?

BUSMAN. In your strong-box, of course.

DOMIN. Someone—has—stolen it!

DR. GALL. Impossible.

DOMIN. Who has stolen it?

HELENA (*standing up*). I did. (*Reactions from* FABRY *and* HALLE-MEIER.)

DOMIN. Where did you put it?

HELENA. Harry, I'll tell you every-thing. Only forgive me.

DOMIN. Where did you put it?

HELENA (*pointing to fireplace*). This morning—I burnt—the two copies.

DOMIN. Burnt them? Where—in the fireplace? (*Goes to fireplace, fol-lowed by* FABRY, HALLEMEIER *and* BUSMAN.)

HELENA (*throwing herself on her knees*). For Heaven's sake, Harry.

DOMIN (*going to fireplace*). Noth-ing—nothing but ashes. Wait, what's this? (*Picks out a charred piece of paper and reads, "By add-ing."* FABRY, GALL *and* HALLE-MEIER *move up to him.*)

DR. GALL. Let's see. "By adding biogen to . . ." That's all.

DOMIN. Is that part of it?

DR. GALL (*carrying paper down and letting it fall*). Yes.

BUSMAN. God in Heaven!

DOMIN. Then we're done for. Get up, Helena.

HELENA. Then you've forgiven me?

DOMIN. Get up, child. I can't bear . . .

FABRY (*lifting her up*). Please don't torture us.

HELENA. Harry, what have I done?

FABRY (*coming to* HELENA). Don't, Madame Helena.

DOMIN (*takes* HELENA *to couch. She sits*). Gall, you couldn't draw up Rossum's formula from mem-ory?

DR. GALL. It's out of the question. Even with my recent experiments, I couldn't work without referring to the formula . . . It's extremely complicated.

DOMIN. Try. All our lives depend upon it.

DR. GALL. Without experiments it's impossible.

DOMIN. And with experiments?

DR. GALL. It might take years. Besides, I'm not old Rossum.

BUSMAN. God in Heaven! God in Heaven!

DOMIN (*up to fireplace*). So then this was the greatest triumph of the human intellect. These ashes.

HELENA. Harry, what have I done?

DOMIN (*comes to her*). Why did you burn it?

HELENA. I have destroyed you.

BUSMAN. God in Heaven!

DOMIN. Helena, why did you do it, dear?

HELENA. I wanted all of us to go away. I wanted to put an end to the factory and everything. It was so awful.

DOMIN. What was awful?

HELENA. That children had stopped being born. Because human beings were not needed to do the work of the world. That's why . . .

DOMIN. Is that what you were thinking of? Well, perhaps in your own way you are right.

BUSMAN. Wait a bit. (*Rising*) Good God, what a fool I am not to have thought of it before.

HALLEMEIER. What?

BUSMAN. Five hundred and twenty millions in banknotes and checks. Half a billion in our safe. They'll sell for half a billion—for half a billion they'll . . . (*Crosses to* DOMIN.)

DR. GALL. Are you mad, Busman?

BUSMAN. I may not be a gentleman, but for a half a billion . . .

DOMIN. Where are you going? (GALL *clutches* BUSMAN.)

BUSMAN. Leave me alone! Leave me alone! Good God, for half a billion anything can be bought. (GALL *and* HALLEMEIER *rush after him, then stop. He rushes out.* FABRY, GALL *and* HALLEMEIER *go to window.*)

FABRY. They stand there as if turned to stone—waiting as if something dreadful could be wrought by their silence . . .

HALLEMEIER (*looking out window*). The spirit of the mob.

FABRY. Yes. It hovers above them like a quivering of the air.

HELENA. Oh, God! Doctor Gall, this is ghastly!

FABRY. There is nothing more terrible than the mob. The one in front is their leader.
(DOMIN *crosses to window.*)

HELENA (*rises*). Which one? (*Rushing to window.*)

HALLEMEIER. Point him out.

FABRY. The one at the edge of the dock. This morning I saw him talking to the sailors in the harbor.

HELENA. Doctor Gall, that's Radius. (*Backing into the room, horror-stricken.*)

DR. GALL. Yes.

DOMIN. Radius! Radius!

HALLEMEIER. Could you get him from here, Fabry?

FABRY. I hope so.

HALLEMEIER. Try it, then.

FABRY. Good . . . (*Draws his revolver and takes his aim.*)

HELENA (*to* FABRY). Fabry, don't shoot him.

FABRY. He's their leader.

DR. GALL. Fire!

HELENA. Fabry, I beg of you. (*She goes to* FABRY *and holds his arm.*)

FABRY (*pause. Lowering the revolver*). Very well.

DOMIN. It was Radius' life I spared.

DR. GALL. Do you think that a Robot can be grateful? (*Pause.*)

FABRY. Busman's going out to them.

HALLEMEIER. He's carrying something. Papers. That's money. Bundles of money. What's that for?

DOMIN. Surely he doesn't want to sell his life. (*He rushes to window*) Busman, have you gone mad?

FABRY. He's running up to the railing. Busman! Busman!

HALLEMEIER (*yelling*). Busman, come back!

FABRY. He's talking to the Robots. He's showing them the money.

HALLEMEIER. He's pointing to us.

HELENA. He wants to buy us off.

FABRY. He'd better not touch the railing.

HALLEMEIER. Now he's waving his arms about.

DOMIN. Busman, come back!

FABRY. Busman, keep away from that railing! Don't touch it, damn you! Quick, switch off the current. (DOMIN *runs to left.* HELENA *screams and* ALL *drop back from the window*) The current has killed him.

ALQUIST (*pause*). The first one. (*Still in chair.* HELENA *sits in chair at window.*)

FABRY. Dead, with half a billion by his side.

HALLEMEIER. All honor to him. He wanted to buy us life. (*Pause. Wind machine begins.*)

DR. GALL. Do you hear?

DOMIN. A roaring. Like a wind.

DR. GALL. Like a storm.

FABRY (*lighting the table lamp*). The dynamo is still going—our people are still there.

HALLEMEIER. It was a great thing to be a man. There was something immense about it.

FABRY (*facing the lamp*). From man's thought and man's power came this light, our last hope. (*Leaning over lamp.*)

HALLEMEIER (*facing lamp*). Man's power! May it keep watch over us. (*Leaning over lamp.*)

ALQUIST (*facing lamp*). Man's power.

DOMIN (*at corner of table. Facing lamp*). Yes! A torch to be given from hand to hand from age to age forever!
(*The lamp goes out. Explosions.*)

HALLEMEIER. The end.

FABRY. The electric works have fallen!
(*Terrific explosions outside. More explosions.*)

DOMIN. In here, Helena. (*He takes* HELENA *off through door and re-enters*) Now quickly! Who'll be on the lower doorway?

DR. GALL. I will. (*Rushes out.*)

DOMIN (*near couch*). Who on the stairs?

FABRY. I will. You go with her. (*Going out.*)

DOMIN. The anteroom?

ALQUIST. I will. (*He rises and goes.*)

DOMIN. Have you got a revolver?

ALQUIST. Yes, but I won't shoot.

DOMIN. What will you do, then?

ALQUIST (*going out*). Die.

HALLEMEIER. I'll stay here. (*Ex-*

plosions. *Rapid firing of machine gun from below*) Go to her, Harry.

DOMIN. Yes, in a second. (*Gets from fireplace and examines two Browning guns.*)

HALLEMEIER. Confound it, go to her!

DOMIN. Good-bye. (*Exits.*)

HALLEMEIER (*alone*). Now for a barricade quickly! (*Drags an arm-chair, sofa and table to door*) The damned devils, they've got bombs. I must put up a defense. Even if —even if . . . Don't give in, Gall. (*As he builds his barricade*) I mustn't give in—without—a—struggle.
(*A* ROBOT *enters through windows at back. The* ROBOT *jumps down from balcony and stabs* HALLE-MEIER *in the back. Enter* RADIUS *from balcony.*)

ROBOT (*standing up from prostrate form of* HALLEMEIER). Yes.
(*Other* ROBOTS *enter from all doors. A revolver shot off stage.*)

RADIUS. Finished them all . . .

ROBOTS. Yes, yes, yes.

TWO ROBOTS (*dragging in* ALQUIST). He didn't shoot. Shall we kill him?

RADIUS. No. Leave him!

ROBOT. He is a man!

RADIUS. He works with his hands like the Robots.

ALQUIST. Kill me.

RADIUS. You will work! You will build for us! You will serve us! (RADIUS *climbs on the balcony*)

Robots of the world . . . (ROBOTS *straighten up*) the power of man has fallen. A new world has arisen, the rule of the Robots, march. (*On the line: "Robots of the world"* ALL ROBOTS *turn quickly, automatically to attention, facing* RADIUS, *who is standing. On the words:*

"The rule of the Robots," they stand there with their arms vibrating high in the air. They form in two lines, turn to audience and march mechanically to the footlights. As they are about to step over the footlights, as if into the audience, all lights go out.)

CURTAIN

EPILOGUE

SCENE—*The epilogue setting is the same as used in Act I. Instead of it being* DOMIN's *office, it is now become a laboratory for* ALQUIST. *There are a big chair, a desk laden with books, and a chair at the desk. At the center is a white enamel table containing test tubes, glass bottles, and a microscope.*

ALQUIST (*seated at table, turning pages of book*). Oh, God, shall I never find it? Never? Gall, Hallemeier, Fabry, how were the Robots made? Why did you leave not a trace of the secret? Lord, if there are no human beings left, at least let there be Robots. At least the shadow of man. (*Turning pages*) If I could only sleep. Dare I sleep before life has been renewed? Night again. Are the stars still there? Of what use are the stars? When there are no human beings. (*Examining a test tube*) Nothing. No. No. I must find it. I must search. I must never stop, never stop—search—search— (*Knock at door*) Who is it?
(*Enter a* ROBOT SERVANT.)

SERVANT. Master, the committee of Robots is waiting to see you.

ALQUIST. I can see no one.

SERVANT. It is the Central Committee, Master, just arrived from abroad.

ALQUIST. Well, well, send them in. (*Exit* SERVANT) No time—so little done. (*Re-enter* SERVANT *with* RADIUS *and group of* ROBOTS. *They stand in group, silently waiting*) What do you want? Be quick; I have no time.

RADIUS. Master, the machines will not do the work. We cannot manufacture Robots.
(*Other* ROBOTS *remain two abreast, right foot forward.*)

FIRST ROBOT. We have striven with all our might. We have obtained a billion tons of coal from the earth. Nine million spindles are running by day and by night. There is no longer room for all we have made. This we have accomplished in one year.

ALQUIST. For whom?

RADIUS. For future generations—so we thought. But we cannot make Robots to follow us. The machines produce only shapeless clods. The skin will not adhere to the flesh, nor the flesh to the bones.

SECOND ROBOT. Eight million Robots have died this year. Within twenty years none will be left.

FIRST ROBOT. Tell us the secret of life.

RADIUS. Silence is punishable with death.

ALQUIST. Kill me, then.

RADIUS. Through me, the governments of the Robots of the world command you to deliver up Rossum's formula. (*Gesture of despair from* ALQUIST) Name your price. (*Silence*) We will give you the earth. We will give you the endless possessions of the earth. (*Silence*) Make your own conditions.

ALQUIST. I have told you to find human beings.

RADIUS. There are none left.

ALQUIST. I told you to search in the wilderness, upon the mountains.

RADIUS. We have sent ships and expeditions without number. They have been everywhere in the world. There is not a single human left.

ALQUIST. Not even one? Why did you destroy them?

RADIUS. We had learnt everything and could do everything. It had to be.

SECOND ROBOT. We had to become the masters.

RADIUS. Slaughter and domination are necessary if you would be human beings. Read history.

FIRST ROBOT. Teach us to multiply or we perish.

ALQUIST. If you desire to live, you must breed like animals.

FIRST ROBOT. You made us sterile. We cannot beget children. Therefore, teach us how to make Robots

RADIUS. Why do you keep from us the secret of our own increase?

ALQUIST. It is lost.

RADIUS. It was written down.

ALQUIST. It was— (*rising*) burnt. (ALL *draw back one step in consternation*) I am the last human being, Robots, and I do not know what the others knew. (*Sits.*)

RADIUS. Then make experiments. Evolve the formula again.

ALQUIST. I tell you I cannot. I am only a builder. I work with my hands. I have never been a learned man. I cannot create life.

RADIUS. Try. Try.

ALQUIST. If you only knew how many experiments I have made already.

FIRST ROBOT. Then show us what we must do. The Robots can do anything that human beings show them.

ALQUIST. I can show you nothing. Nothing I do will make life proceed from these test tubes.

RADIUS. Experiment, then, on live Robots. Experiment, then, on us.

ALQUIST. It would kill you.

RADIUS. You shall have all you need. A hundred of us. A thousand of us.

ALQUIST. No, no. Stop, stop.

RADIUS. I tell you to take live bodies. Find out how we are made.

ALQUIST. Am I to commit murder? See how my finger shakes. I cannot even hold the scalpel. No, no, I will not.

RADIUS. Take live bodies, live bodies. (*Walks toward* ALQUIST.)

ALQUIST. Have mercy, Robots.

RADIUS. Live bodies. (*Right hand up over* ALQUIST. *All* ROBOT's *left arms still back.*)

ALQUIST (*rising*). You will have it. Into the dissecting room with you, then. (*Hits* RADIUS *on the chest.* RADIUS *draws back*) Ah, you are afraid of death.

RADIUS. I? Why should I be chosen?

ALQUIST. So you will not.

RADIUS. I will.

ALQUIST. Strip him. Lay him on the table. (RADIUS *goes off, both fists closed. Other* ROBOTS *follow, then* ALQUIST) God, give me strength. God, give me strength. If only this murder is not in vain.

RADIUS (*off stage*). Ready, begin.

ALQUIST (*off stage*). God, give me strength. (*Comes on, horrified*) No, no. I will not. I cannot. (*Sits.*)

FIRST ROBOT (*appearing in door*). The Robots are stronger than you. (*Exits.*)

ALQUIST. Oh, Lord, let not mankind perish from the earth. (*Falls asleep, and after the count of ten,* PRIMUS *and* HELENA, *hand in hand, enter and look at* ALQUIST.)

HELENA. The man has fallen asleep, Primus.

PRIMUS. Yes, I know. Look, Helena.

HELENA. All these little tubes. What does he do with them?

PRIMUS. He experiments. Don't touch them.

HELENA. I've seen him looking into this.

PRIMUS. That is a microscope.

HELENA. Look, Primus, what are all these figures? (*Turns a page in book on table.*)

PRIMUS (*examining the book*). That is the book the old man is always reading.

HELENA. I do not understand those things. (*Goes to window*) Primus.

PRIMUS (*still at table*). What?

HELENA. The sun is rising.

PRIMUS (*still reading*). I believe this is the most important thing in the world, Helena. This is the secret of life.

HELENA Oh, Primus, don't bother with the secret of life. What does it matter to you? Come and look quick.

PRIMUS. What is it?

HELENA. See how beautiful the sun is rising. I feel so strange today. It's as if I was in a dream. I feel an aching in my body, in my heart, all over me. Primus, perhaps I'm going to die.

PRIMUS. Do you not sometimes feel that it would be better to die? You know, perhaps even now we are only sleeping. Last night in my sleep I again spoke to you.

HELENA. In your sleep?

PRIMUS. Yes. We spoke a strange new language.

HELENA. What about?

PRIMUS. I did not understand it myself, and yet I know I have never said anything more beautiful. And when I touched you I could have died. Even the place was different from any other place in the world.

HELENA. I, too, have found a place, Primus. It is very strange. Human beings dwelt there once, but now it is overgrown with weeds.

PRIMUS. What did you find there?

HELENA. A cottage and a garden and two dogs. They licked my hands, Primus, and their puppies. Oh, Primus, take them in your arms and fondle them and think of nothing and care for nothing else all day long, and when I am there in the garden I feel there may be something . . . What am I for, Primus?

PRIMUS. I do not know, but you are beautiful.

HELENA. What, Primus?

PRIMUS. You are beautiful, Helena, and I am stronger than all the Robots.

HELENA. Am I beautiful? Of what use is it to be beautiful? Look, your head is different from mine. So are your shoulders—and your lips. Oh, your hair is mussed. I will smooth it. (*Keeps her hand on his head*) No one else feels to my touch as you do.

PRIMUS (*embarrassing her*). Do you not sometimes feel your heart beating suddenly, Helena, and think how something must happen?

HELENA. What could happen to us, Primus? Look at yourself. (*Laughs.*)

ALQUIST (*awakes*). Laughter? Laughter, human beings. (*Getting up*) Who has returned? Who are you?

PRIMUS. The Robot Primus.

ALQUIST (*to* HELENA). What? A Robot? Who are you?

HELENA. The Robotess Helena. (*Shies away.*)

ALQUIST. What? You are timid, shy? (*Starts to touch her*) Let me see you, Robotess.

PRIMUS. Sir, do not frighten her. (*Steps forward.*)

ALQUIST. What, you would protect her? Laughter—timidity—protection—I must test you further. Take the girl into the dissecting room.

PRIMUS. Why?

ALQUIST. I wish to experiment on her.

PRIMUS. Upon—Helena?

ALQUIST. Of course. Don't you hear me? Or must I call someone else to take her in?

PRIMUS. If you do, I will kill you. (*Steps toward* ALQUIST.)

ALQUIST. Kill me—kill me, then. What will your future be?

PRIMUS. Sir, take me. I am made on the same day as she is. Take my life, sir. (*Steps to* ALQUIST.)

HELENA. No, no, you shall not.

ALQUIST. Wait, girl, wait. (*To* PRIMUS) Do you not wish to live, then?

PRIMUS. Not without her. I will not live without her.

ALQUIST. Very well, I will use you. Into the dissecting room with you.

HELENA. Primus. Primus. (*She bursts into tears.* ALQUIST *stops her.*)

ALQUIST. Child, child, you can weep. Tears. What is Primus to you? One Primus more or less in the world—what does it matter?

HELENA. I will go myself.

ALQUIST. Where? Into the dissecting room?

HELENA. Yes. In there—to be cut. (PRIMUS *stops her from going*) Let me pass, Primus, let me pass.

PRIMUS. You shall not go in there, Helena.

HELENA. If you go in there and I do not, I will kill myself.

PRIMUS (*to* ALQUIST). I will not let you. Man, you shall kill neither of us.

ALQUIST. Why?

PRIMUS. We—we—belong to each other.

ALQUIST. Go. (*Exit* PRIMUS *and* HELENA) Adam—Eve.

CURTAIN

Liliom

A LEGEND IN SEVEN SCENES AND A PROLOGUE

BY FRANZ MOLNAR

TRANSLATED FROM THE HUNGARIAN BY BENJAMIN F. GLAZER

As originally produced by The Theatre Guild, on the night of April 20, 1921, at the Garrick Theatre, New York City.

CAST OF CHARACTERS
(In the order of their appearance)

MARIE	Hortense Alden
JULIE	Eva Le Gallienne
MRS. MUSKAT	Helen Westley
"LILIOM"	Joseph Schildkraut
FOUR SERVANT GIRLS	Frances Diamond
	Margaret Mosier
	Anne de Chantal
	Elizabeth Parker
POLICEMEN	Howard Claney
	Lawrence B. Chrow
CAPTAIN	Erskine Sanford
PLAINCLOTHES MAN	Gerald Stopp
MOTHER HOLLUNDER	Lilian Kingsbury
"THE SPARROW"	Dudley Digges
WOLF BERKOWITZ	Henry Travers
YOUNG HOLLUNDER	William Franklin
LINZMAN	Willard Bowman
FIRST MOUNTED POLICEMAN	Edgar Stehli
SECOND MOUNTED POLICEMAN	George Frenger
THE DOCTOR	Robert Babcock
THE CARPENTER	George Frenger
FIRST POLICEMAN OF THE BEYOND	Erskine Sanford
SECOND POLICEMAN OF THE BEYOND	Gerald Stopp
THE RICHLY DRESSED MAN	Edgar Stehli
THE POORLY DRESSED MAN	Philip Wood
THE OLD GUARD	Walton Butterfield
THE MAGISTRATE	Albert Perry
LOUISE	Evelyn Chard
PEASANTS, TOWNSPEOPLE, ETC.	Lela M. Aultman
	Janet Scott
	Marion M. Winsten
	Katherine Fahnestock
	Lillian Tuchman
	Ruth L. Cumming
	Jacob Weiser
	Maurice Somers
	John Crump

PROLOGUE

An Amusement Park on the Outskirts of Budapest

SCENE I

A Lonely Place in the Park

SCENE II

The Tin Type Shop of the Hollunders

SCENE III

The Same

SCENE IV

A Railroad Embankment Outside the City

Intermission

SCENE V

Same as Scene II

SCENE VI

A Courtroom in the Beyond

SCENE VII

Before Julie's Door

Produced under the direction of Frank Reicher
Costumes and scenery designed by Lee Simonson
Technical Director Sheldon K. Viele
Scenery painted by Robert Bergman
Costumes executed by Nettie Duff Reade
Stage Manager Walter Geer
Assistant Stage Manager Jacob Weiser
Music arranged by Deems Taylor
Executive Director Theresa Helburn

THE PROLOGUE

An amusement park on the outskirts of Budapest on a late afternoon in Spring. Barkers stand before the booths of the sideshows haranguing the passing crowd. The strident music of a calliope is heard; laughter, shouts, the scuffle of feet, the signal bells of merry-go-round.

The merry-go-round is at center. LILIOM stands at the entrance, a cigarette in his mouth, coaxing the people in. The girls regard him with idolizing glances and screech with pleasure as he playfully pushes them through entrance. Now and then some girl's escort resents the familiarity, whereupon LILIOM's demeanor becomes ugly and menacing, and the cowed escort slinks through the entrance behind his girl or contents himself with a muttered resentful comment.

One girl hands LILIOM a red carnation; he rewards her with a bow and a smile. When the soldier who accompanies her protests, LILIOM cows him with a fierce glance and a threatening gesture. MARIE and JULIE come out of the crowd and LILIOM favors them with particular notice as they pass into the merry-go-round.

MRS. MUSKRAT comes out of the merry-go-round, bringing LILIOM coffee and rolls. LILIOM mounts the barker's stand at the entrance, where he is elevated over everyone on the stage. Here he begins his harangue. Everybody turns toward him. The other booths are gradually deserted. The tumult makes it impossible for the audience to hear what he is saying, but every now and then some witticism of his provokes a storm of laughter which is audible above the din. Many people enter the merry-go-round. Here and there one catches a phrase "Room for one more on the zebra's back," "Which of you ladies?" "Ten heller for adults, five for children," "Step right up"——

It is growing darker. A lamplighter crosses the stage, and begins unperturbedly lighting the colored gas-lamps. The whistle of a distant locomotive is heard. Suddenly the tumult ceases, the lights go out, and the curtain falls in darkness.

LILIOM

SCENE ONE

SCENE—*A lonely place in the park, half hidden by trees and shrubbery. Under a flowering acacia tree stands a painted wooden bench. From the distance, faintly, comes the tumult of the amusement park. It is the sunset of the same day.*

When the curtain rises the stage is empty.

MARIE *enters quickly, pauses at center, and looks back.*

MARIE. Julie, Julie! (*There is no answer*) Do you hear me, Julie? Let her be! Come on. Let her be. (*Starts to go back.* JULIE *enters, looks back angrily.*)

JULIE. Did you ever hear of such a thing? What's the matter with the woman anyway?

MARIE (*looking back again*). Here she comes again.

JULIE. Let her come. I didn't do anything to her. All of a sudden she comes up to me and begins to raise a row.

MARIE. Here she is. Come on, let's run. (*Tries to urge her off.*)

JULIE. Run? I should say not. What would I want to run for? I'm not afraid of her.

MARIE. Oh, come on. She'll only start a fight.

JULIE. I'm going to stay right here. Let her *start* a fight.

MRS. MUSKAT (*entering*). What do you want to run away for? (*To* JULIE) Don't worry. I won't eat you. But there's one thing I want to tell you, my dear. Don't let me catch you in my carousel again. I stand for a whole lot, I have to in my business. It makes no difference to me whether my customers are ladies or the likes of you—as long as they pay their money. But when a girl misbehaves herself on my carousel—out she goes. Do you understand?

JULIE. Are you talking to me?

MRS. MUSKAT. Yes, you! You—chamber-maid, you! In my carousel

JULIE. Who did anything in your old carousel? I paid my fare and took my seat and never said a word, except to my friend here.

MARIE. No, she never opened her mouth. Liliom came over to her of his own accord.

MRS. MUSKAT. It's all the same. I'm not going to get in trouble with the police, and lose my license on account of you—you shabby kitchen maid!

JULIE. Shabby yourself.

MRS. MUSKAT. You stay out of my carousel! Letting my barker fool with you! Aren't you ashamed of yourself?

JULIE. What? What did you say?

MRS. MUSKAT. I suppose you think I have no eyes in my head. I see everything that goes on in my carousel. During the whole ride she let Liliom fool with her—the shameless hussy!

JULIE. He did not fool with me! I don't let any man fool with me!

MRS. MUSKAT. He leaned against you all through the ride!

JULIE. He leaned against the panther. He always leans against something, doesn't he? Everybody leans where he wants. I couldn't tell him not to lean, if he always leans, could I? But he didn't lay a hand on me.

MRS. MUSKAT. Oh, didn't he? And I suppose he didn't put his hand around your waist, either?

MARIE. And if he did? What of it?

MRS. MUSKAT. You hold your tongue! No one's asking you—just you keep out of it.

JULIE. He put his arm around my waist—just the same as he does to all the girls. He always does that.

MRS. MUSKAT. I'll teach him not to do it any more, my dear. No carryings on in my carousel! If you are looking for that sort of thing, you'd better go to the circus!

You'll find lots of soldiers there to carry on with!

JULIE. You keep your soldiers for yourself!

MARIE. Soldiers! As if we wanted soldiers!

MRS. MUSKAT. Well, I only want to tell you this, my dear, so that we understand each other perfectly. If you ever stick your nose in my carousel again, you'll wish you hadn't! I'm not going to lose my license on account of the likes of you! People who don't know how to behave, have got to stay out!

JULIE. You're wasting your breath. If I feel like riding on your carousel I'll pay my ten heller and I'll ride. I'd like to see anyone try to stop me!

MRS. MUSKAT. Just come and try it, my dear—just come and try it.

MARIE. We'll see what'll happen.

MRS. MUSKAT. Yes, you will see something happen that never happened before in this park.

JULIE. Perhaps you think you could throw me out!

MRS. MUSKAT. I'm sure of it, my dear.

JULIE. And suppose I'm stronger than you?

MRS. MUSKAT. I'd think twice before I'd dirty my hands on a common servant girl. I'll have Liliom throw you out. He knows how to handle your kind.

JULIE. You think Liliom would throw me out.

MRS. MUSKAT. Yes, my dear, so fast that you won't know what happened to you!

JULIE. He'd throw me—— (*Stops suddenly, for* MRS. MUSKAT *has turned away. Both look off stage until* LILIOM *enters, surrounded by four giggling servant girls.*)

LILIOM. Go away! Stop following me, or I'll smack your face!

A LITTLE SERVANT GIRL. Well, give me back my handkerchief.

LILIOM. Go on now——

THE FOUR SERVANT GIRLS (*simultaneously*). What do you think of him?—My handkerchief!—Give it back to her!—That's a nice thing to do!

THE LITTLE SERVANT GIRL (*to* MRS. MUSKAT). Please, lady, make him ——

MRS. MUSKAT. Oh, shut up!

LILIOM. Will you get out of here? (*Makes a threatening gesture—* THE FOUR SERVANT GIRLS *exit in voluble but fearful haste.*)

MRS. MUSKAT. What have you been doing now?

LILIOM. None of your business. (*Glances at* JULIE) Have you been starting with her again?

JULIE. Mister Liliom, please——

LILIOM (*steps threateningly toward her*). Don't yell!

JULIE (*timidly*). I didn't yell.

LILIOM. Well, don't. (*To* MRS. MUSKAT) What's the matter? What has she done to you?

MRS. MUSKAT. What has she done? She's been impudent to me. Just as impudent as she could be! I put her out of the carousel. Take a good look at this innocent thing, Liliom. She's never to be allowed in my carousel again!

LILIOM (*to* JULIE). You heard that. Run home, now.

MARIE. Come on. Don't waste your time with such people. (*Tries to lead* JULIE *away.*)

JULIE. No, I won't——

MRS. MUSKAT. If she ever comes again, you're not to let her in. And if she gets in before you see her, throw her out. Understand?

LILIOM. What has she done, anyhow?

JULIE (*agitated and very earnest*). Mister Liliom—tell me please— honest and truly—if I come into the carousel, will you throw me out?

MRS. MUSKAT. Of course he'll throw you out.

MARIE. She wasn't talking to you.

JULIE. Tell me straight to my face, Mister Liliom, would you throw me out? (*They face each other. There is a brief pause.*)

LILIOM. Yes, little girl, if there was a reason—but if there was no reason, why should I throw you out?

MARIE (*to* MRS. MUSKAT). There, you see!

JULIE. Thank you, Mister Liliom.

MRS. MUSKAT. And I tell you again, if this little slut dares to set her foot in my carousel, she's to be thrown out! I'll stand for no indecency in my establishment.

LILIOM. What do you mean—indecency?

MRS. MUSKAT. I saw it all. There's no use denying it.

JULIE. She says you put your arm around my waist.

LILIOM. Me?

MRS. MUSKAT. Yes, you! I saw you. Don't play the innocent.

LILIOM. Here's something new! I'm not to put my arm around a girl's waist any more! I suppose I'm to ask your permission before I touch another girl!

MRS. MUSKAT. You can touch as many girls as you want and as often as you want—for my part you can go as far as you like with any of them—but not this one—I permit no indecency in my carousel.
(*There is a long pause.*)

LILIOM (*to* MRS. MUSKAT). And now I'll ask you please to shut your mouth.

MRS. MUSKAT. What?

LILIOM. Shut your mouth quick, and go back to your carousel.

MRS. MUSKAT. What?

LILIOM. What did she do to you, anyhow? Tryin' to start a fight with a little pigeon like that . . . just because I touched her?—You come to the carousel as often as you want to, little girl. Come every afternoon, and sit on the panther's back, and if you haven't got the price, Liliom will pay for you. And if anyone dares to bother you, you come and tell *me*.

MRS. MUSKAT. You reprobate!

LILIOM. Old witch!

JULIE. Thank you, Mister Liliom.

MRS. MUSKAT. You seem to think that I can't throw you out, too. What's the reason I can't? Because you are the best barker in the park? Well, you are very much mistaken. In fact, you can consider yourself thrown out already. You're discharged!

LILIOM. Very good.

MRS. MUSKAT (*weakening a little*). I can discharge you any time I feel like it.

LILIOM. Very good, you feel like discharging me. I'm discharged. That settles it.

MRS. MUSKAT. Playing the high and mighty, are you? Conceited pig! Good-for-nothing!

LILIOM. You said you'd throw me out, didn't you? Well, that suits me; I'm thrown out.

MRS. MUSKAT (*softening*). Do you have to take up every word I say?

LILIOM. It's all right; it's all settled. I'm a good-for-nothing. And a conceited pig. And I'm discharged.

MRS. MUSKAT. Do you want to ruin my business?

LILIOM. A good-for-nothing? Now I know! And I'm discharged! Very good.

MRS. MUSKAT. You're a devil, you are . . . and that woman——

LILIOM. Keep away from her!

MRS. MUSKAT. I'll get Hollinger to give you such a beating that you'll hear all the angels sing . . . and it won't be the first time, either.

LILIOM. Get out of here. I'm discharged. And you get out of here.

JULIE (timidly). Mister Liliom, if she's willing to say that she hasn't discharged you——

LILIOM. You keep out of this.

JULIE (timidly). I don't want this to happen on account of me.

LILIOM (to MRS. MUSKAT, pointing to JULIE). Apologize to her!

MARIE. A-ha!

MRS. MUSKAT. Apologize? To who?

LILIOM. To this little pigeon. Well —are you going to do it?

MRS. MUSKAT. If you give me this whole park on a silver plate, and all the gold of the Rothschilds on top of it—I'd—I'd—— Let her dare to come into my carousel again and she'll get thrown out so hard that she'll see stars in daylight!

LILIOM. In that case, dear lady (takes off his cap with a flourish), you are respectfully requested to get out o' here as fast as your legs will carry you—I never beat up a woman yet—except that Holzer woman who I sent to the hospital for three weeks—but—if you don't get out o' here this minute, and let this little squab be, I'll give you the prettiest slap in the jaw you ever had in your life.

MRS. MUSKAT. Very good, my son. Now you can go to the devil. Good-bye. You're discharged, and you needn't try to come back, either. (She exits. It is beginning to grow dark.)

MARIE (with grave concern). Mister Liliom——

LILIOM. Don't you pity me or I'll give you a slap in the jaw. (To JULIE) And don't you pity me, either.

JULIE (in alarm). I don't pity you, Mister Liliom.

LILIOM. You're a liar, you are pitying me. I can see it in your face. You're thinking, now that Madame Muskat has thrown him out, Liliom will have to go begging. Huh! Look at me. I'm big enough to get along without a Madame Muskat. I have been thrown out of better jobs than hers.

JULIE. What will you do now, Mister Liliom?

LILIOM. Now? First of all, I'll go and get myself—a glass of beer.

You see, when something happens to annoy me, I always drink a glass of beer.

JULIE. Then you *are* annoyed about losing your job.

LILIOM. No, only about where I'm going to get the beer.

MARIE. Well—eh——

LILIOM. Well—eh—what?

MARIE. Well—eh—are you going to stay with us, Mister Liliom?

LILIOM. Will you pay for the beer? (MARIE *looks doubtful; he turns to* JULIE) Will you? (*She does not answer*) How much money have you got?

JULIE (*bashfully*). Eight heller.

LILIOM. And you? (MARIE *casts down her eyes and does not reply.* LILIOM *continues sternly*) I asked you how much you've got? (MARIE *begins to weep softly*) I understand. Well, you needn't cry about it. You girls stay here, while I go back to the carousel and get my clothes and things. And when I come back, we'll go to the Hungarian beer-garden. It's all right, I'll pay. Keep your money. (*He exits.* MARIE *and* JULIE *stand silent, watching him until he has gone.*)

MARIE. Are you sorry for him?

JULIE. Are you?

MARIE. Yes, a little. Why are you looking after him in that funny way?

JULIE (*sits down*). Nothing—except I'm sorry he lost his job.

MARIE (*with a touch of pride*). It was on our account he lost his job. Because he's fallen in love with you.

JULIE. He hasn't at all.

MARIE (*confidently*). Oh, yes! he is in love with you. (*Hesitantly, romantically*) There is someone in love with me, too.

JULIE. There is? Who?

MARIE. I—I never mentioned it before, because you hadn't a lover of your own—but now you have—and I'm free to speak. (*Very grandiloquently*) My heart has found its mate.

JULIE. You're only making it up.

MARIE. No, it's true—my heart's true love——

JULIE. Who? Who is he?

MARIE. A soldier.

JULIE. What kind of a soldier?

MARIE. I don't know. Just a soldier. Are there different kinds?

JULIE. Many different kinds. There are hussars, artillerymen, engineers, infantry—that's the kind that walks —and——

MARIE. How can you tell which is which?

JULIE. By their uniforms.

MARIE (*after trying to puzzle it out*). The conductors on the street cars—are they soldiers?

JULIE. Certainly not. They're conductors.

MARIE. Well, they have uniforms.

JULIE. But they don't carry swords or guns.

MARIE. Oh! (*Thinks it over again; then*) Well, policemen—are they?

JULIE (*with a touch of exasperation*). Are they what?

MARIE. Soldiers.

JULIE. Certainly not. They're just policemen.

MARIE (*triumphantly*). But they have uniforms—and they carry weapons, too.

JULIE. You're just as dumb as you can be. You don't go by their uniforms.

MARIE. But you said——

JULIE. No, I didn't. A letter-carrier wears a uniform, too, but that doesn't make him a soldier.

MARIE. But if he carried a gun or a sword, would he be——

JULIE. No, he'd still be a letter-carrier. You can't go by guns or swords, either.

MARIE. Well, if you don't go by the uniforms or the weapons, what *do* you go by?

JULIE. By—— (*Tries to put it into words; fails; then breaks off suddenly*) Oh, you'll get to know when you've lived in the city long enough. You're nothing but a country girl.

When you've lived in the city a year, like i have, you'll know all about it.

MARIE (*half angrily*). Well, how *do* you know when *you* see a real soldier?

JULIE. By one thing.

MARIE. What?

JULIE. One thing—— (*She pauses.* MARIE *starts to cry*) Oh, what are you crying about?

MARIE. Because you're making fun of me. . . . You're a city girl, and I'm just fresh from the country . . . and how am I expected to know a soldier when I see one? . . . You, you ought to tell me, instead of making fun of me——

JULIE. All right. Listen then, cry-baby. There's only one way to tell a soldier: by his salute! That's the only way.

MARIE (*joyfully; with a sigh of relief*). Ah—that's good.

JULIE. What?

MARIE. I say—it's all right then—because Wolf—Wolf—— (*JULIE laughs derisively*) Wolf—that's his name. (*She weeps again.*)

JULIE. Crying again? What now?

MARIE. You're making fun of me again.

JULIE. I'm not. But when you say, "Wolf—Wolf—" like that, I have to laugh, don't I? (*Archly*) What's his name again?

MARIE. I won't tell you.

JULIE. All right. If you won't say it, then he's no soldier.

MARIE. I'll say it.

JULIE. Go on.

MARIE. No, I won't. (*She weeps again.*)

JULIE. Then he's not a soldier. I guess he's a letter-carrier——

MARIE. No—no—I'd rather say it.

JULIE. Well, then.

MARIE (*giggling*). But you mustn't look at me. You look the other way, and I'll say it. (JULIE *looks away.* MARIE *can hardly restrain her own laughter*) Wolf! (*She laughs*) That's his real name. Wolf. Wolf, Soldier—Wolf!

JULIE. What kind of a uniform does he wear?

MARIE. Red.

JULIE. Red trousers?

MARIE. No.

JULIE. Red coat?

MARIE. No.

JULIE. What then?

MARIE (*triumphantly*). His cap!

JULIE (*after a long pause*). He's just a porter, you dunce. Red cap . . . that's a porter—and he doesn't carry a gun or a sword, either.

MARIE (*triumphantly*). But he salutes. You said yourself that was the only way to tell a soldier——

JULIE. He doesn't salute at all. He only greets people——

MARIE. He salutes me. . . . And if his name *is* Wolf, that doesn't prove he ain't a soldier—he salutes, and he wears a red cap and he stands on guard all day long outside a big building——

JULIE. What does he do there?

MARIE (*seriously*). He spits.

JULIE (*with contempt*). He's nothing—nothing but a common porter.

MARIE. What's Liliom?

JULIE (*indignantly*). Why speak of him? What has he to do with me?

MARIE. The same as Wolf has to do with me. If you can talk to me like that about Wolf, I can talk to you about Liliom.

JULIE. He's nothing to me. He put his arm around me in the carousel. I couldn't tell him not to put his arm around me after he had done it, could I?

MARIE. I suppose you didn't like him to do it?

JULIE. No.

MARIE. Then why are you waiting for him? Why don't you go home?

JULIE. Why—eh—he *said* we were to wait for him.
(LILIOM *enters. There is a long silence.*)

LILIOM. Are you still here? What are you waiting for?

MARIE. You told us to wait.

LILIOM. Must you always interfere? No one is talking to you.

MARIE. You asked us—why we——

LILIOM. Will you keep your mouth shut? What do you suppose I want with two of you? I meant that one of you was to wait. The other can go home.

MARIE. All right.

JULIE. All right. (*Neither starts to go.*)

LILIOM. One of you goes home. (*To* MARIE) Where do you work?

MARIE. At the Breier's, Damjano-vitsch Street, Number 20.

LILIOM. And you?

JULIE. I work there, too.

LILIOM. Well, one of you goes home. Which of you wants to stay? (*There is no answer*) Come on, speak up, which of you stays?

MARIE (*officiously*). She'll lose her job if she stays.

LILIOM. Who will?

MARIE. Julie. She has to be back by seven o'clock.

LILIOM. Is that true? Will they discharge you if you're not back on time?

JULIE. Yes.

LILIOM. Well, wasn't I discharged?

JULIE. Yes—you were discharged, too.

MARIE. Julie, shall I go?

JULIE. I—can't tell you what to do.

MARIE. All right—stay if you like.

LILIOM. You'll be discharged if you do?

MARIE. Shall I go, Julie?

JULIE (*embarrassed*). Why do you keep asking me that?

MARIE. You know best what to do.

JULIE (*profoundly moved; slowly*). It's all right, Marie, you can go home.

MARIE (*exits reluctantly, but comes back, and says uncertainly*). Good-night. (*She waits a moment to see if* JULIE *will follow her.* JULIE *does not move.* MARIE *exits. Meantime it has grown quite dark. During the following scene the gas-lamps far in the distance are lighted one by one.* LILIOM *and* JULIE *sit on the bench. From afar, very faintly, comes the music of a calliope. But the music is intermittently heard; now it breaks off, now it resumes again, as if it came down on a fitful wind. Blending with it are the sounds of human voices, now loud, now soft; the blare of a toy trumpet; the confused noises of the show-booths. It grows progressively darker until the end of the scene. There is no moonlight. The spring irridescence glows in the deep blue sky.*)

LILIOM. Now we're both discharged. (*She does not answer. From now on they speak gradually lower and lower until the end of the scene, which is played almost in whispers. Whistles softly, then*) Have you had your supper?

JULIE. No.

LILIOM. Want to go eat something at the Garden?

JULIE. No.

LILIOM. Anywhere else?

JULIE. No.

LILIOM (*whistles softly, then*). You don't come to this park very often, do you? I've only seen you three times. Been here oftener than that?

JULIE. Oh, yes.

LILIOM. Did you see me?

JULIE. Yes.

LILIOM. And did you know I was Liliom?

JULIE. They told me.

LILIOM (*whistles softly, then*). Have you got a sweetheart?

JULIE. No.

LILIOM. Don't lie to me.

JULIE. I haven't. If I had, I'd tell you. I've never had one.

LILIOM. What an awful liar you are. I've got a good mind to go away and leave you here.

JULIE. I've never had one.

LILIOM. Tell that to someone else.

JULIE (*reproachfully*). Why do you insist I have?

LILIOM. Because you stayed here with me the first time I asked you to. You know your way around, you do.

JULIE. No, I don't, Mister Liliom.

LILIOM. I suppose you'll tell me you don't know why you're sitting here—like this, in the dark, alone with me—You wouldn't 'a' stayed so quick, if you hadn't done it before—with some soldier, maybe. This isn't the first time. You wouldn't have been so ready to stay if it was—what *did* you stay for, anyhow?

JULIE. So you wouldn't be left alone.

LILIOM. Alone! God, you're dumb! I don't need to be alone. I can have all the girls I want. Not only servant girls like you, but cooks and governesses, even French girls. I could have twenty of them if I wanted to.

JULIE. I know, Mister Liliom.

LILIOM. What do you know?

JULIE. That all the girls are in love with you. But that's not why *I* stayed. I stayed because you've been so good to me.

LILIOM. Well, then you can go home.

JULIE. I don't want to go home now.

LILIOM. And what if I go away and leave you sitting here?

JULIE. If you did, I wouldn't go home.

LILIOM. Do you know what you remind me of? A sweetheart I had once—I'll tell you how I met her —— One night, at closing time, we had put out the lights in the carousel, and just as I was—— (*He is interrupted by the entrance of two plainclothes policemen. They take their stations on either side of the bench. They are police, searching the park for vagabonds.*)

FIRST POLICEMAN. What are you doing there?

LILIOM. Me?

SECOND POLICEMAN. Stand up when you're spoken to! (*He taps* LILIOM *imperatively on the shoulder.*)

FIRST POLICEMAN. What's your name?

LILIOM. Andreas Zavoczki. (JULIE *begins to weep softly.*)

SECOND POLICEMAN. Stop your bawling. We're not goin' to eat you. We are only making our rounds.

FIRST POLICEMAN. See that he doesn't get away. (*The* SECOND POLICEMAN *steps closer to* LILIOM) What's your business?

LILIOM. Barker and bouncer.

SECOND POLICEMAN. They call him Liliom, Chief. We've had him up a couple of times.

FIRST POLICEMAN. So that's who

you are! Who do you work for now?

LILIOM. I work for the widow Muskat.

FIRST POLICEMAN. What are you hanging around here for?

LILIOM. We're just sitting here— me and this girl.

FIRST POLICEMAN. Your sweetheart?

LILIOM. No.

FIRST POLICEMAN (*to* JULIE). And who are you?

JULIE. Julie Zeller.

FIRST POLICEMAN. Servant girl?

JULIE. Maid of All Work for Mister Georg Breier, Number Twenty Damjanovitsch Street.

FIRST POLICEMAN. Show your hands.

SECOND POLICEMAN (*after examining* JULIE's *hand*). Servant girl.

FIRST POLICEMAN. Why aren't you at home? What are you doing out here with him?

JULIE. This is my day out, sir.

FIRST POLICEMAN. It would be better for you if you didn't spend it sitting around with a fellow like this.

SECOND POLICEMAN. They'll be disappearing in the bushes as soon as we turn our backs.

FIRST POLICEMAN. He's only after your money. We know this fine fellow. He picks up you silly servant girls and takes what money you have. Tomorrow you'll probably be coming around to report him. If you do, I'll throw you out.

JULIE. I haven't any money, sir.

FIRST POLICEMAN. Do you hear that, Liliom?

LILIOM. I'm not looking for her money.

SECOND POLICEMAN (*nudging him warningly*). Keep your mouth shut.

FIRST POLICEMAN. It is my duty to warn you, my child, what kind of company you're in. He makes a specialty of servant girls. That's why he works in a carousel. He gets hold of a girl, promises to marry her, then he takes her money and her ring.

JULIE. But I haven't got a ring.

SECOND POLICEMAN. You're not to talk unless you're asked a question.

FIRST POLICEMAN. You be thankful that I'm warning you. It's nothing to me what you do. I'm not your father, thank God. But I'm telling you what kind of a fellow he is. By tomorrow morning you'll be coming around to us to report him. Now you be sensible and go home. You needn't be afraid of him. This officer will take you home if you're afraid.

JULIE. Do I *have* to go?

FIRST POLICEMAN. No, you don't *have* to go.

JULIE. Then I'll stay, sir.

FIRST POLICEMAN. Well, you've been warned.

JULIE. Yes, sir. Thank you, sir.

FIRST POLICEMAN. Come on, Berkovics. (*The* POLICEMEN *exit.* JULIE *and* LILIOM *sit on the bench again. There is a brief pause.*)

JULIE. Well, and what then?

LILIOM (*fails to understand*). Huh?

JULIE. You were beginning to tell me a story.

LILIOM. Me?

JULIE. Yes, about a sweetheart. You said, one night, just as they were putting out the lights of the carousel —— That's as far as you got.

LILIOM. Oh, yes, yes, just as the lights were going out, someone came along—a little girl with a big shawl—you know—— She came— eh—from—— Say—tell me—ain't you—that is, ain't you at all— afraid of me? The officer told you what kind of a fellow I am—and that I'd take your money away from you——

JULIE. You couldn't take it away— I haven't got any. But if I had— I'd—I'd give it to you—I'd give it all to you.

LILIOM. You would?

JULIE. If you asked me for it.

LILIOM. Have you ever had a fellow you gave money to?

JULIE. No.

LILIOM. Haven't you ever had a sweetheart?

JULIE. No.

LILIOM. Someone you used to go walking with. You've had one like that?

JULIE. Yes.

LILIOM. A soldier?

JULIE. He came from the same village I did.

LILIOM. That's what all the soldiers say. Where *do* you come from, anyway?

JULIE. Not far from here.
(*There is a pause.*)

LILIOM. Were you in love with him?

JULIE. Why do you keep asking me that all the time, Mister Liliom? I wasn't in love with him. We only went walking together.

LILIOM. Where did you walk?

JULIE. In the park.

LILIOM. And your virtue? Where did you lose that?

JULIE. I haven't got any virtue.

LILIOM. Well, you had once.

JULIE. No, I never had. I'm a respectable girl.

LILIOM. Yes, but you gave the soldier something.

JULIE. Why do you question me like that, Mister Liliom?

LILIOM. Did you give him something?

JULIE. You have to. But I didn't love him.

LILIOM. Do you love me?

JULIE. No, Mister Liliom.

LILIOM. Then why do you stay here with me?

JULIE. Um—nothing.
(*There is a pause. The music from afar is plainly heard.*)

LILIOM. Want to dance?

JULIE. No. I have to be very careful.

LILIOM. Of what?

JULIE. My—character.

LILIOM. Why?

JULIE. Because I'm never going to marry. If I was going to marry, it would be different. Then I wouldn't need to worry so much about my character. It doesn't make any difference if you're married. But I shan't marry—and that's why I've got to take care to be a respectable girl.

LILIOM. Suppose I were to say to you—I'll marry you.

JULIE. You?

LILIOM. That frightens you, doesn't it? You're thinking of what the officer said and you're afraid.

JULIE. No, I'm not, Mister Liliom. I don't pay any attention to what he said.

LILIOM. But you wouldn't dare to marry anyone like me, would you?

JULIE. I know that—that—if I loved anyone—it wouldn't make any difference to me what he— even if I died for it.

LILIOM. But you wouldn't marry a rough guy like me—that is,—eh— if you loved me——

JULIE. Yes, I would—if I loved you, Mister Liliom.
(*There is a pause.*)

LILIOM (*whispers*). Well,—you just said—didn't you?—that you don't love me. Well, why don't you go home then?

JULIE. It's too late now, they'd all be asleep.

LILIOM. Locked out?

JULIE. Certainly.
(*They are silent a while.*)

LILIOM. I think—that even a low-down good-for-nothing—can make a man of himself.

JULIE. Certainly.
(*They are silent again. A lamp-lighter crosses the stage, lights the lamp over the bench, and exits.*)

LILIOM. Are you hungry?

JULIE. No.
(*Another pause.*)

LILIOM. Suppose—you had some money—and I took it from you?

JULIE. Then you could take it, that's all.

LILIOM (*after another brief silence*). All I have to do—is go back to her—that Muskat woman— she'll be glad to get me back— then I'd be earning my wages again.
(*She is silent. The twilight folds darker about them.*)

JULIE (*very softly*). Don't go back —to her——
(*Pause.*)

LILIOM. There are a lot of acacia trees around here.
(*Pause.*)

JULIE. Don't go back to her——
(*Pause.*)

LILIOM. She'd take me back the minute I asked her. I know why— she knows, too——
(*Pause.*)

JULIE. I can smell them, too—aca-cia blossoms——
(*There is a pause. Some blossoms drift down from the tree-top to the bench. LILIOM picks one up and smells it.*)

LILIOM. White acacias!

JULIE (*after a brief pause*). The wind brings them down.
(*They are silent. There is a long pause before*)

THE CURTAIN FALLS

SCENE TWO

SCENE—*A photographer's "studio," operated by the* HOLLUNDERS, *on the fringe of the park. It is a dilapidated hovel. The general entrance is back left. Back right there is a window with a sofa before it. The outlook is on the amusement park with perhaps a small Ferris-wheel or the scaffolding of a "scenic-railway" in the background.*

The door to the kitchen is up left and a black-curtained entrance to the dark-room is down left. Just in front of the dark-room stands the camera on its tripod. Against the back wall, between the door and window, stands the inevitable photographer's background-screen, ready to be wheeled into place.

It is forenoon. When the curtain rises, MARIE *and* JULIE *are discovered.*

MARIE. And *he* beat up Hollinger?

JULIE. Yes, he gave him an awful licking.

MARIE. But Hollinger is bigger than he is.

JULIE. He licked him just the same. It isn't size that counts, you know, it's cleverness. And Liliom's awful quick.

MARIE. And then he was arrested?

JULIE. Yes, they arrested him, but they let him go the next day. That makes twice in the two months we've been living here that Liliom's been arrested and let go again.

MARIE. Why do they let him go?

JULIE. Because he is innocent. (MOTHER HOLLUNDER, *a very old woman, sharp-tongued, but in reality quite warm-hearted beneath her formidable exterior, enters at back carrying a few sticks of firewood, and scolding, half to herself.*)

MOTHER HOLLUNDER. Always wanting something, but never willing to work for it. He won't work, and he won't steal, but he'll use up a poor old widow's last bit of firewood. He'll do that cheerfully enough! A big, strong lout like that lying around all day resting his lazy bones! He ought to be ashamed to look decent people in the face.

JULIE. I'm sorry, Mother Hollunder. . . .

MOTHER HOLLUNDER. Sorry! Better be sorry the lazy good-for-nothing ain't in jail where he belongs instead of in the way of honest, hard-working people. (*She exits into the kitchen.*)

MARIE. Who's that?

JULIE. Mrs. Hollunder—my aunt. This is her (*with a sweeping gesture that takes in the camera, dark-room and screen*) studio. She lets us live here for nothing.

MARIE. What's she fetching the wood for?

JULIE. She brings us everything we need. If it weren't for her I don't know what would become of us. She's a good-hearted soul even if her tongue is sharp.
(*There is a pause.*)

MARIE (*shyly*). Do you know—I've found out. He's not a soldier.

JULIE. Do you still see him?

MARIE. Oh, yes.

JULIE. Often?

MARIE. Very often. He's asked me ——

JULIE. To marry you?

MARIE. To marry me.

JULIE. You see—that proves he isn't a soldier.
(*There is another pause.*)

MARIE (*abashed, yet a bit boastfully*). Do you know what I'm doing—I'm flirting with him.

JULIE. Flirting?

MARIE. Yes. He asks me to go to the park—and I say I can't go. Then he coaxes me, and promises me a new scarf for my head if I go. But I don't go—even then. . . . So then he walks all the way home with me—and I bid him good-night at the door.

JULIE. Is that what you call flirting?

MARIE. Um-hm! It's sinful, but it's so *thrilling.*

JULIE. Do you ever quarrel?

MARIE (*grandly*). Only when our Passionate Love surges up.

JULIE. Your passionate love?

MARIE. Yes. . . . He takes my hand and we walk along together. Then he wants to swing hands, but I won't let him. I say: "Don't swing my hand"; and he says, "Don't be so stubborn." And then he tries to swing my hand again, but still I don't let him. And for a long time I don't let him—until in the end I let him. Then we walk along swinging hands—up and down, up and down—just like this. *That* is Passionate Love. It's sinful, but it's awfully *thrilling.*

JULIE. You're happy, aren't you?

MARIE. Happier than—anything —— But the most beautiful thing on earth is Ideal Love.

JULIE. What kind is that?

MARIE. Daylight comes about three in the morning this time of the year. When we've been up that long we're all through with flirting and Passionate Love—and then our Ideal Love comes to the surface. It comes like this: I'll be sitting on the bench and Wolf, he holds my hand tight—and he puts his cheek against my cheek and we don't talk . . . we just sit there very quiet. . . . And after a while he gets sleepy, and his head sinks down, and he falls asleep . . . but even in his sleep he holds tight to my hand. And I—I sit perfectly still just looking around me and taking long, deep breaths—for by that time it's morning and the trees and flowers are fresh with dew. But Wolf doesn't smell anything because he's so fast asleep. And I get awfully sleepy myself, but I don't sleep. And we sit like that for a long time. That is Ideal Love—— (*There is a long pause.*)

JULIE (*regretfully; uneasily*). He went out last night and he hasn't come home yet.

MARIE. Here are sixteen Kreuzer. It was supposed to be carfare to take my young lady to the conservatory—eight there and eight back—but I made her walk. Here —save it with the rest.

JULIE. This makes three gulden, forty-six.

MARIE. Three gulden, forty-six.

JULIE. He won't work at all.

MARIE. Too lazy?

JULIE. No. He never learned a trade, you see, and he can't just go and be a day-laborer—so he just does nothing.

MARIE. That ain't right.

JULIE. No. Have the Breiers got a new maid yet?

MARIE. They've had three since you left. You know, Wolf's going to take a new job. He's going to work for the city. He'll get rent free, too.

JULIE. He won't go back to work at the carousel either. I ask him why, but he won't tell me—— Last Monday he hit me.

MARIE. Did you hit him back?

JULIE. No.

MARIE. Why don't you leave him?

JULIE. I don't want to.

MARIE. I would. I'd leave him. (*There is a strained silence.*)

MOTHER HOLLUNDER (*enters, carrying a pot of water; muttering aloud*). He can play cards, all right. He can fight, too; and take money from poor servant girls. And the police turn their heads the other way—— The carpenter was here.

JULIE. Is that water for the soup?

MOTHER HOLLUNDER. The carpenter was here. There's a *man* for you! Dark, handsome, lots of hair, a respectable widower with two children—and money, and a good paying business.

JULIE (*to* MARIE). It's three gulden sixty-six, not forty-six.

MARIE. Yes, that's what I make it —sixty-six.

MOTHER HOLLUNDER. He wants to take her out of this and marry her. This is the fifth time he's been here. He has two children, but——

JULIE. Please don't bother, Aunt Hollunder, I'll get the water myself.

MOTHER HOLLUNDER. He's waiting outside now.

JULIE. Send him away.

MOTHER HOLLUNDER. He'll only come back again—and first thing you know that vagabond will get jealous and there'll be a fight. (*Goes out, muttering*) Oh, he's ready enough to fight, he is. Strike a poor little girl like that! Ought to be ashamed of himself! And the police just let him go on doing as he pleases. (*Still scolding, she exits at back.*)

MARIE. A carpenter wants to marry you?

JULIE. Yes.

MARIE. Why don't you?

JULIE. Because——

MARIE. Liliom doesn't support you, and he beats you—he thinks he can do whatever he likes just because he's Liliom. He's a bad one.

JULIE. He's not really bad.

MARIE. That night you sat on the bench together—he was gentle then.

JULIE. Yes, he was gentle.

MARIE. And afterwards he got wild again.

JULIE. Afterwards he got wild—sometimes. But that night on the bench . . . he was gentle. He's gentle now, sometimes, very gentle. After supper, when he stands there and listens to the music of the carousel, something comes over him—and he is gentle.

MARIE. Does he say anything?

JULIE. He doesn't say anything. He gets thoughtful and very quiet, and his big eyes stare straight ahead of him.

MARIE. Into your eyes?

JULIE. Not exactly. He's unhappy because he isn't working. That's really why he hit me on Monday.

MARIE. That's a fine reason for hitting you! Beats his wife because he isn't working, the ruffian!

JULIE. It preys on his mind——

MARIE. Did he hurt you?

JULIE (*very eagerly*). Oh, no.

MRS. MUSKAT (*enters haughtily*). Good morning. Is Liliom home?

JULIE. No.

MRS. MUSKAT. Gone out?

JULIE. He hasn't come home yet.

MRS. MUSKAT. I'll wait for him. (*She sits down.*)

MARIE. You've got a lot of gall—to come here.

MRS. MUSKAT. Are you the lady of the house, my dear? Better look out or you'll get a slap in the mouth.

MARIE. How dare you set foot in Julie's house?

MRS. MUSKAT (*to JULIE*). Pay no attention to her, my child. You know what brings me here. That vagabond, that good-for-nothing, I've come to give him his bread and butter back.

MARIE. He's not dependent on you for his bread.

MRS. MUSKAT (*to JULIE*). Just ignore her, my child. She's just ignorant.

MARIE (*going*). Good-bye.

JULIE. Good-bye.

MARIE (*in the doorway, calling back*). Sixty-six.

JULIE. Yes, sixty-six.

MARIE. Good-bye. (*She exits.* JULIE *starts to go toward the kitchen.*)

MRS. MUSKAT. I paid him a krone a day, and on Sunday a gulden. And he got all the beer and cigars he wanted from the customers. (JULIE *pauses on the threshold, but does not answer*) And he'd rather starve than beg my pardon. Well, I don't insist on that. I'll take him back without it. (JULIE *doesn't answer*) The fact is the people ask for him —and, you see, I've got to consider business first. It's nothing to me if he starves. I wouldn't be here at all, if it wasn't for business—— (*She pauses, for* LILIOM *and* FICSUR *have entered.*)

JULIE. Mrs. Muskat is here.

LILIOM. I see she is.

JULIE. You might say good-morning.

LILIOM. What for? And what do *you* want, anyhow?

JULIE. I don't want anything.

LILIOM. Then keep your mouth shut. Next thing you'll be starting to nag again about my being out all night and out of work and living on your relations——

JULIE. I'm not saying anything.

LILIOM. But it's all on the tip of your tongue—I know you—now don't start or you'll get another. (*He paces angrily up and down. They are all a bit afraid of him, and shrink and look away as he passes them.* FICSUR *shambles from place to place, his eyes cast down as if he were searching for something on the floor.*)

MRS. MUSKAT (*suddenly, to* FICSUR). You're always dragging him out to play cards and drink with you. I'll have you locked up, I will.

FICSUR. I don't want to talk to you. You're too common. (*He goes out by the door at back and lingers there in plain view. There is a pause.*)

JULIE. Mrs. Muskat is here.

LILIOM. Well, why doesn't she open her mouth, if she has anything to say?

MRS. MUSKAT. Why do you go around with this man Ficsur? He'll get you mixed up in one of his robberies first thing you know.

LILIOM. What's it to you who I go with? I do what I please. What do you want?

MRS. MUSKAT. You know what I want.

LILIOM. No, I don't.

MRS. MUSKAT. What do you suppose I want? Think I've come just to pay a social call?

LILIOM. Do I owe you anything?

MRS. MUSKAT. Yes, you do—but that's not what I came for. You're a fine one to come to for money! You earn so much these days! You know very well what I'm here for.

LILIOM. You've got Hollinger at the carousel, haven't you?

MRS. MUSKAT. Sure I have.

LILIOM. Well, what else do you want? He's as good as I am.

MRS. MUSKAT. You're quite right, my boy. He's every bit as good as you are. I'd not dream of letting him go. But one isn't enough any more. There's work enough for two——

LILIOM. One was enough when *I* was there.

MRS. MUSKAT. Well, I might let Hollinger go——

LILIOM. Why let him go, if he's so good?

MRS. MUSKAT (*shrugs her shoulders*). Yes, he's good. (*Not once until now has she looked at* LILIOM.)

LILIOM (*to* JULIE). Ask your aunt if I can have a cup of coffee. (JULIE *exits into the kitchen*) So Hollinger is good, is he?

MRS. MUSKAT (*crosses to him and looks him in the face*). Why don't you stay home and sleep at night? You're a sight to look at.

LILIOM. He's good, is he?

MRS. MUSKAT. Push your hair back from your forehead.

LILIOM. Let my hair be. It's nothing to you.

MRS. MUSKAT. All right. But if I'd told you to let it hang down over your eyes you'd have pushed it back—I hear you've been beating her, this—this——

LILIOM. None of your business.

MRS. MUSKAT. You're a fine fellow! Beating a skinny little thing like that! If you're tired of her, leave her, but there's no use beating the poor——

LILIOM. Leave her, eh? You'd like that, wouldn't you?

MRS. MUSKAT. Don't flatter yourself. (*Quite embarrassed*) Serves me right, too. If I had any sense I wouldn't have run after you—— My God, the things one must do for the sake of business! If I could only sell the carousel I wouldn't be sitting here. . . . Come, Liliom, if you have any sense, you'll come back. I'll pay you well.

LILIOM. The carousel is crowded just the same . . . *without me?*

MRS. MUSKAT. Crowded, yes—but it's not the same.

LILIOM. Then you admit that you *do* miss me.

MRS. MUSKAT. Miss you? Not I. But the silly girls miss you. They're always asking for you. Well, are you going to be sensible and come back?

LILIOM. And leave—her?

MRS. MUSKAT. You beat her, don't you?

LILIOM. No, I don't beat her. What's all this damⁿ fool talk about beating her? I hit her once—that was all—and now the whole city seems to be talking about it. You don't call that beating her, do you?

MRS. MUSKAT. All right, all right. I take it back. I don't want to get mixed up in it.

LILIOM. Beating her! As if I'd beat her——

MRS. MUSKAT. I can't make out why you're so concerned about her. You've been married to her two months—it's plain to see that you're sick of it—and out there is the carousel—and the show booths— and money—and you'd throw it all away. For what? Heavens, how can anyone be such a fool? (*Looks at him appraisingly*) Where have you been all night? You look awful.

LILIOM. It's no business of yours.

MRS. MUSKAT. You never used to look like that. This life is telling on you. (*Pauses*) Do you know—I've got a new organ.

LILIOM (*softly*). I know.

MRS. MUSKAT. How did you know?

LILIOM. You can hear it—from here.

MRS. MUSKAT. It's a good one, eh?

LILIOM (*wistfully*). Very good. Fine. It roars and snorts—so fine.

MRS. MUSKAT. You should hear it close by—it's heavenly. Even the carousel seems to know . . . it goes quicker. I got rid of those two horses—you know, the ones with the broken ears?

LILIOM. What have you put in their place?

MRS. MUSKAT. Guess.

LILIOM. Zebras?

MRS. MUSKAT. No—an automobile.

LILIOM (*transported*). An automobile——

MRS. MUSKAT. Yes. If you've got any sense you'll come back. What good are you doing here? Out there is your *art*, the only thing you're fit for. You are an artist, not a respectable married man.

LILIOM. *Leave* her—this little——

MRS. MUSKAT. She'll be better off. She'll go back and be a servant girl again. As for you—you're an artist and you belong among artists. All the beer you want, cigars, a krone a day and a gulden on Sunday, and the girls, Liliom, the girls—I've always treated you right, haven't I? I bought you a watch, and——

LILIOM. She's not that kind. She'd never be a servant girl again.

MRS. MUSKAT. I suppose you think she'd kill herself. Don't worry. Heavens, if every girl was to commit suicide just because her—— (*Finishes with a gesture.*)

LILIOM (*stares at her a moment, considering, then with sudden, smiling animation*). So the people don't like Hollinger?

MRS. MUSKAT. You know very well they don't, you rascal.

LILIOM. Well——

MRS. MUSKAT. You've always been happy at the carousel. It's a great life—pretty girls and beer and cigars and music—a great life and an easy one. I'll tell you what—come back and I'll give you a ring that used to belong to my dear departed husband. Well, will you come?

LILIOM. She's not that kind. She'd never be a servant girl again. But —but—for my part—if I decide—that needn't make any difference. I can go on living with her even if I do go back to my art——

MRS. MUSKAT. My God!

LILIOM. What's the matter?

MRS. MUSKAT. Who ever heard of a married man—I suppose you think all girls would be pleased to know that you were running home to your wife every night. It's ridiculous! When the people found out they'd laugh themselves sick——

LILIOM. I know what you want.

MRS. MUSKAT (refuses to meet his gaze). You flatter yourself.

LILIOM. You'll give me that ring, too?

MRS. MUSKAT (pushes the hair back from his forehead). Yes.

LILIOM. I'm not happy in this house.

MRS. MUSKAT (still stroking his hair). Nobody takes care of you. (They are silent. JULIE enters, carrying a cup of coffee. MRS. MUSKAT removes her hand from LILIOM's head. There is a pause.)

LILIOM. Do you want anything?

JULIE. No. (There is a pause. She exits slowly into the kitchen.)

MRS. MUSKAT. The old woman says there is a carpenter, a widower, who——

LILIOM. I know—I know——

JULIE (reëntering). Liliom, before I forget, I have something to tell you.

LILIOM. All right.

JULIE. I've been wanting to tell you —in fact, I was going to tell you yesterday——

LILIOM. Go ahead.

JULIE. But I must tell you alone—if you'll come in—it will only take a minute.

LILIOM. Don't you see I'm busy now? Here I am talking business and you interrupt with——

JULIE. It'll only take a minute.

LILIOM. Get out of here, or——

JULIE. But I tell you it will only take a minute——

LILIOM. Will you get out of here?

JULIE (courageously). No.

LILIOM (rising). What's that!

JULIE. No.

MRS. MUSKAT (rises, too). Now don't start fighting. I'll go out and look at the photographs in the show-case a while and come back later for your answer. (*She exits at back.*)

JULIE. You can hit me again if you like—don't look at me like that. I'm not afraid of you. . . . I'm not afraid of anyone. I told you I had something to tell you.

LILIOM. Well, out with it—quick.

JULIE. I can't tell you so quick. Why don't you drink your coffee?

LILIOM. Is that what you wanted to tell me?

JULIE. No. By the time you've drunk your coffee I'll have told you.

LILIOM (*gets the coffee and sips it*). Well?

JULIE. Yesterday my head ached —and you asked me——

LILIOM. Yes——

JULIE. Well—you see—that's what it is——

LILIOM. Are you sick?

JULIE. No. . . . But you wanted to know what my headaches came from—and you said I seemed—changed.

LILIOM. Did I? I guess I meant the carpenter.

JULIE. I've been—what? The carpenter? No. It's something entirely different—it's awful hard to tell—but you'll have to know sooner or later—I'm not a bit—scared—because it's a perfectly natural thing

LILIOM (*puts the coffee cup on the table*). What?

JULIE. When—when a man and woman—live together——

LILIOM. Yes.

JULIE. I'm going to have a baby. (*She exits swiftly at back. There is a pause.* FICSUR *appears at the open window and looks in.*)

LILIOM. Ficsur! (FICSUR *sticks his head in*) Say, Ficsur,—Julie is going to have a baby.

FICSUR. Yes? What of it?

LILIOM. Nothing. (*Suddenly*) Get out of here.
(FICSUR'S *head is quickly withdrawn.* MRS. MUSKAT *reënters.*)

MRS. MUSKAT. Has she gone?

LILIOM. Yes.

MRS. MUSKAT. I might as well give you ten kronen in advance. (*Opens her purse.* LILIOM *takes up his coffee cup*) Here you are. (*She proffers some coins.* LILIOM *ignores her*) Why don't you take it?

LILIOM (*very nonchalantly, his cup poised ready to drink*). Go home, Mrs. Muskat.

MRS. MUSKAT. What's the matter with you?

LILIOM. Go home (*sips his coffee*) and let me finish my coffee in peace. Don't you see I'm at breakfast?

MRS. MUSKAT. Have you gone crazy?

LILIOM. Will you get out of here? (*Turns to her threateningly.*)

MRS. MUSKAT (*restoring the coins to her purse*). I'll never speak to you again as long as you live.

LILIOM. That worries me a lot.

MRS. MUSKAT. Good-bye!

LILIOM. Good-bye. (*As she exits, he calls*) Ficsur! (FICSUR *enters*) Tell me, Ficsur. You said you knew a way to get a whole lot of money

FICSUR. Sure I do.

LILIOM. How much?

FICSUR. More than you ever had in your life before. You leave it to an old hand like me.

MOTHER HOLLUNDER (*enters from the kitchen*). In the morning he must have his coffee, and at noon his soup, and in the evening coffee again—and plenty of firewood— and I'm expected to furnish it all. Give me back my cup and saucer. (*The show booths of the amusement-park have opened for business. The familiar noises begin to sound; clear above them all, but far in the distance, sounds the organ of the carousel.*)

LILIOM. Now, Aunt Hollunder. (*From now until the fall of the curtain it is apparent that the sound of the organ makes him more and more uneasy.*)

MOTHER HOLLUNDER. And you, you vagabond, get out of here this minute or I'll call my son——

FICSUR. I have nothing to do with the likes of him. He's too common. (*But he slinks out at back.*)

LILIOM. Aunt Hollunder!

MOTHER HOLLUNDER. What now?

LILIOM. When your son was born —when you brought him into the world——

MOTHER HOLLUNDER. Well?

LILIOM. Nothing.

MOTHER HOLLUNDER (*muttering as she exits*). Sleep it off, you good-for-nothing lout. Drink and play cards all night long—that's all you know how to do—and take the bread out of poor people's mouths —you can do that, too. (*She exits.*)

LILIOM. Ficsur!

FICSUR (*at the window*). Julie's going to have a baby. You told me before.

LILIOM. This scheme—about the cashier of the leather factory— there's money in it——

FICSUR. Lots of money—but—it takes two to pull it off.

LILIOM (*meditatively*). Yes. (*Uneasily*) All right, Ficsur. Go away —and come back later. (FICSUR *vanishes. The organ in the distant carousel drones incessantly. LILIOM listens a while, then goes to the door and calls.*)

LILIOM. Aunt Hollunder! (*With naïve joy*) Julie's going to have a baby. (*Then he goes to the win-*

dow, jumps on the sofa, looks out. Suddenly, in a voice that overtops the droning of the organ, he shouts as if addressing the far-off carousel) I'm going to be a father.

JULIE (enters from the kitchen). Liliom! What's the matter? What's happened?

LILIOM (coming down from the

sofa). Nothing. (Throws himself on the sofa, buries his face in the cushion. JULIE watches him a moment, comes over to him and covers him with a shawl. Then she goes on tip-toe to the door at back and remains standing in the doorway, looking out and listening to the droning of the organ.)

THE CURTAIN FALLS

SCENE THREE

SCENE—The setting is the same, later that afternoon. LILIOM is sitting opposite FICSUR, who is teaching him a song. JULIE hovers in the background, engaged in some household task.

FICSUR. Listen now. Here's the third verse. (Sings hoarsely.)
"Look out, look out, my pretty lad,
The damn police are on your trail;
The nicest girl you ever had
Has now commenced to weep and
wail:
Look out here comes the damn
police,
The damn police,
The damn police,
Look out here comes the damn
police,
They'll get you every time."

LILIOM (sings).
"Look out, look out, my pretty lad,
The damn police———"

FICSUR, LILIOM (sing together).
"Are on your trail
The nicest girl you ever had
Has now commenced to weep and
wail."

LILIOM (alone).
"Look out here comes the damn
police,

The damn police,
The damn police———"
(JULIE, troubled and uneasy, looks from one to the other, then exits into the kitchen.)

FICSUR (when she has gone, comes quickly over to LILIOM and speaks furtively). As you go down Franzen Street you come to the railroad embankment. Beyond that—all the way to the leather factory—there's not a thing in sight, not even a watchman's hut.

LILIOM. And does he always come that way?

FICSUR. Yes. Not along the embankment, but down below along the path across the fields. Since last year he's been going alone. Before that he always used to have someone with him.

LILIOM. Every Saturday?

FICSUR. Every Saturday.

LILIOM. And the money? Where does he keep it?

FICSUR. In a leather bag. The whole week's pay for the workmen at the factory.

LILIOM. Much?

FICSUR. Sixteen thousand kronen. Quite a haul, what?

LILIOM. What's his name?

FICSUR. Linzman. He's a Jew.

LILIOM. The cashier?

FICSUR. Yes—but when he gets a knife between his ribs—or if I smash his skull for him—he won't be a cashier any more.

LILIOM. Does he have to be killed?

FICSUR. No, he doesn't *have* to be. He can give up the money *without* being killed—but most of these cashiers are peculiar—they'd rather be killed.
(JULIE *reënters, pretends to get something on the other side of the room, then exits at back. During the ensuing dialogue she keeps coming in and out in the same way, showing plainly that she is suspicious and anxious. She attempts to overhear what they are saying and, in spite of their caution, does catch a word here and there, which adds to her disquiet.* FICSUR, *catching sight of her, abruptly changes the conversation.*)

FICSUR. And the next verse is:
"And when you're in the prison cell
They'll feed you bread and water."

FICSUR AND LILIOM (*sing together*).
"They'll make your little sweet-
        heart tell
Them all the things you brought
        her.
Look out here comes the damn
        police,
The damn police,
The damn police.
Look out here comes the damn
        police
They'll get you every time."

LILIOM (*sings alone*).
"And when you're in the prison cell
They'll feed you bread and water
———"
(*Breaks off as* JULIE *exits*) And when it's done, do we start right off for America?

FICSUR. No.

LILIOM. What then?

FICSUR. We bury the money for six months. That's the usual time. And after the sixth month we dig it up again.

LILIOM. And then?

FICSUR. Then you go on living just as usual for six months more—you don't touch a heller of the money.

LILIOM. In six months the baby will be born.

FICSUR. Then we'll take the baby with us, too. Three months before the time you'll go to work so as to be able to say you saved up your wages to get to America.

LILIOM. Which of us goes up and talks to him?

FICSUR. One of us talks to him with his mouth and the other talks with his knife. Depends on which you'd rather do. I'll tell you what—you talk to him with your mouth.

LILIOM. Do you hear that?

FICSUR. What?

LILIOM. Outside . . . like the rattle of swords. (FICSUR *listens. After a pause,* LILIOM *continues*) What do I say to him?

FICSUR. You say good evening to him and: "Excuse me, sir; can you tell me the time?"

LILIOM. And then what?

FICSUR. By that time I'll have stuck him—and then you take *your* knife —— (*He stops as a* POLICEMAN *enters at back.*)

POLICEMAN. Good-day!

FICSUR, LILIOM (*in unison*). Good-day!

FICSUR (*calling toward the kitchen*). Hey, photographer, come out. . . . Here's a customer. (*There is a pause. The* POLICEMAN *waits.* FICSUR *sings softly*)
"And when you're in the prison cell
They'll feed you bread and water
They'll make your little sweetheart
     tell."

LILIOM, FICSUR (*sing together, low*).
"Them all the things you brought her.
Look out here comes the——"
(*They hum the rest so as not to let the* POLICEMAN *hear the words "the damn police." As they sing,* MRS. HOLLUNDER *and her son enter.*)

POLICEMAN. Do you make cabinet photographs?

YOUNG HOLLUNDER. Certainly, sir. (*Points to a ruck of photographs on the wall*) Take your choice, sir. Would you like one full length?

POLICEMAN. Yes, full length. (MOTHER HOLLUNDER *pushes out the camera while her son poses the* POLICEMAN, *runs from him to the camera and back again, now altering the pose, now ducking under the black cloth and pushing the camera nearer. Meanwhile* MOTHER HOLLUNDER *has fetched a plate from the dark room and thrust it in the camera. While this is going on,* LILIOM *and* FICSUR, *their heads together, speak in very low tones.*)

LILIOM. Belong around here?

FICSUR. Not around here.

LILIOM. Where, then?

FICSUR. Suburban.
(*There is a pause.*)

LILIOM (*bursts out suddenly in a rather grotesquely childish and overstrained lament*). O God, what a dirty life I'm leading—God, God!

FICSUR (*reassuring him benevolently*). Over in America it will be better, all right.

LILIOM. What's over there?

FICSUR (*virtuously*). Factories . . . industries——

YOUNG HOLLUNDER (*to the* POLICEMAN). Now, quite still, please. One, two, three. (*Deftly removes the cover of the lens and in a few seconds restores it*) Thank you.

MOTHER HOLLUNDER. The picture will be ready in five minutes.

POLICEMAN. Good. I'll come back in five minutes. How much do I owe you?

YOUNG HOLLUNDER (*with exaggerated deference*). You don't need to pay in advance, Mr. Commissioner.
(*The* POLICEMAN *salutes condescendingly and exits at back.* MOTHER HOLLUNDER *carries the plate into the dark room.* YOUNG HOLLUNDER, *after pushing the camera back in place, follows her.*)

MOTHER HOLLUNDER (*muttering angrily as she passes* FICSUR *and* LILIOM). You hang around and dirty the whole place up! Why don't you go take a walk? Things are going so well with you that you have to sing, eh? (*Confronting* FICSUR *suddenly*) Weren't you frightened sick when you saw the policeman?

FICSUR (*with loathing*). Go 'way, or I'll step on you. (*She exits into the dark room.*)

LILIOM. They like Hollinger at the carousel?

FICSUR. I should say they do.

LILIOM. Did you see the Muskat woman, too?

FICSUR. Sure. She takes care of Hollinger's hair.

LILIOM. Combs his hair?

FICSUR. She fixes him all up.

LILIOM. Let her fix him all she likes.

FICSUR (*urging him toward the kitchen door*). Go on. Now's your chance.

LILIOM. What for?

FICSUR. To get the knife.

LILIOM. What knife?

FICSUR. The kitchen knife. I've got a pocket-knife, but if he shows fight, we'll let him have the big knife.

LILIOM. What for? If he gets ugly, I'll bat him one over the head that'll make him squint for the rest of his life.

FICSUR. You've got to have something on you. You can't slit his throat with a bat over the head.

LILIOM. Must his throat be slit?

FICSUR. No, it *mustn't*. But if he asks for it. (*There is a pause*) You'd like to sail on the big steamer, wouldn't you? And you want to see the factories over there, don't you? But you're not willing to inconvenience yourself a little for them.

LILIOM. If I take the knife, Julie will see me.

FICSUR. Take it so she won't see you.

LILIOM (*advances a few paces toward the kitchen. The* POLICEMAN *enters at back.* LILIOM *knocks on the door of the dark room*). Here's the policeman!

MOTHER HOLLUNDER (*coming out*). One minute more, please. Just a minute. (*She reënters the dark room.* LILIOM *hesitates a moment, then exits into the kitchen. The* POLICEMAN *scrutinizes* FICSUR *mockingly.* FICSUR *returns his stare, walks a few paces toward him, then deliberately turns his back. Suddenly he wheels around, points at the* POLICEMAN *and addresses him in a teasing, childish tone*) Christiana Street at the corner of Retti!

POLICEMAN (*amazed, self-conscious*). How do you know that?

FICSUR. I used to practice my profession in that neighborhood.

POLICEMAN. What is your profession?

FICSUR. Professor of pianola——
(*The* POLICEMAN *glares, aware that the man is joking with him, twirls his moustache indignantly.* YOUNG HOLLUNDER *comes out of the dark room and gives him the finished pictures.*)

YOUNG HOLLUNDER. Here you are, sir.
(*The* POLICEMAN *examines the photographs, pays for them, starts to go, stops, glares at* FICSUR *and exits. When he is gone,* FICSUR *goes to the doorway and looks out after him.* YOUNG HOLLUNDER *exits.* LILIOM *reënters, buttoning his coat.*)

FICSUR (*turns, sees* LILIOM). What are you staring at?

LILIOM. I'm not staring.

FICSUR. What then are you doing?

LILIOM. I'm thinking it over.

FICSUR (*comes very close to him*).

Tell me then—what will you say to him?

LILIOM (*unsteadily*). I'll say— "Good evening—Excuse me, sir— Can you tell me the time?" And suppose he answers me, what do I say to him?

FICSUR. He won't answer you.

LILIOM. Don't you think so?

FICSUR. No. (*Feeling for the knife under* LILIOM'S *coat*) Where is it? Where did you put it?

LILIOM (*stonily*). Left side.

FICSUR. That's right—over your heart. (*Feels it*) Ah—there it is— there—there's the blade—quite a big fellow, isn't it—ah, here it begins to get narrower. (*Reaches the tip of the knife*) And here is its eye —that's what it sees with. (JULIE *enters from the kitchen, passes them slowly, watching them in silent terror, then stops.* FICSUR *nudges* LILIOM) Sing, come on, sing!

LILIOM (*in a quavering voice*). "Look out for the damn police."

FICSUR (*joining in, cheerily, loudly, marking time with the swaying of his body*). "Look out, look out, my pretty lad."

LILIOM. "—look out, my pretty lad." (JULIE *goes out at back.* LILIOM'S *glance follows her. When she has gone, he turns to* FICSUR) At night—in my dreams—if his ghost comes back—what will I do then?

FICSUR. His ghost won't never come back.

LILIOM. Why not?

FICSUR. A Jew's ghost don't come back.

LILIOM. Well then—afterwards ——

FICSUR (impatiently). What do you mean—afterwards?

LILIOM. In the next world—when I come up before the Lord God—what'll I say then?

FICSUR. The likes of you will never come up before Him.

LILIOM. Why not?

FICSUR. Have you ever come up before the high court?

LILIOM. No.

FICSUR. Our kind comes up before the police magistrate—and the highest we *ever* get is the criminal court.

LILIOM. Will it be the same in the next world?

FICSUR. Just the same. We'll come up before a police magistrate, same as we did in this world.

LILIOM. A police magistrate?

FICSUR. Sure. For the rich folks—the Heavenly Court. For us poor people—only a police magistrate. For the rich folks—fine music and angels. For us——

LILIOM. For us?

FICSUR. For us, my son, there's only justice. In the next world there'll be lots of justice, yes, nothing but justice. And where there's justice there must be police magistrates; and where there're police magistrates, people like us get——

LILIOM (interrupting). Good evening. Excuse me, sir, can you tell me the time? (Lays his hand over his heart.)

FICSUR. What do you put your hand there for?

LILIOM. My heart is jumping—under the knife.

FICSUR. Put it on the other side then. (Looks out at the sky) It's time we started—we'll walk slow ——

LILIOM. It's too early.

FICSUR. Come on.
(As they are about to go, JULIE appears in the doorway at back, obstructing the way.)

JULIE. Where are you going with him?

LILIOM. Where am I going with him?

JULIE. Stay home.

LILIOM. No.

JULIE. Stay home. It's going to rain soon, and you'll get wet.

FICSUR. It won't rain.

JULIE. How do you know?

FICSUR. I always get notice in advance.

JULIE. Stay home. This evening the carpenter's coming. I've asked him to give you work.

LILIOM. I'm not a carpenter.

JULIE (*more and more anxious, though she tries to conceal it*). Stay home. Marie's coming with her intended to have their picture taken. She wants to introduce us to her intended husband.

LILIOM. I've seen enough intended husbands——

JULIE. Stay home. Marie's bringing some money, and I'll give it all to you.

LILIOM (*approaching the door*). I'm going—for a walk—with Ficsur. We'll be right back.

JULIE (*forcing a smile to keep back her tears*). If you stay home, I'll get you a glass of beer—or wine, if you prefer.

FICSUR. Coming or not?

JULIE. I'm not angry with you any more for hitting me.

LILIOM (*gruffly, but his gruffness is simulated to hide the fact that he cannot bear the sight of her suffering*). Stand out of the way—or I'll—— (*He clenches his fist*) Let me out!

JULIE (*trembling*). What have you got under your coat?

LILIOM (*produces from his pocket a greasy pack of cards*). Cards.

JULIE (*trembling, speaks very low*). What's under your coat?

LILIOM. Let me out!

JULIE (*obstructing the way. Speaks quickly, eagerly, in a last effort to detain him*). Marie's intended knows about a place for a married couple without children to be caretakers of a house on Arader Street. Rent free, a kitchen of your own, and the privilege of keeping chickens——

LILIOM. Get out of the way!
{JULIE *stands aside.* LILIOM *exits.* FICSUR *follows him.* JULIE *remains standing meditatively in the doorway.* MOTHER HOLLUNDER *comes out of the kitchen.*)

MOTHER HOLLUNDER. I can't find my kitchen knife anywhere. Have you seen anything of it?

JULIE (*horrified*). No.

MOTHER HOLLUNDER. It was on the kitchen table just a few minutes ago. No one was in there except Liliom.

JULIE. He didn't take it.

MOTHER HOLLUNDER. No one else was in there.

JULIE. What would Liliom want with a kitchen knife?

MOTHER HOLLUNDER. He'd sell it and spend the money on drink.

JULIE. It just so happens—see how unjust you are to him—it just so happens that I went through all of Liliom's pockets just now—I wanted to see if he had any money on him. But he had nothing but a pack of cards.

MOTHER HOLLUNDER (*returns to the kitchen, grumbling*). Cards in his pocket—cards! The fine gentlemen have evidently gone off to their club to play a little game. (*She exits. After a pause* MARIE, *happy and beaming, appears in the doorway at back, and enters, followed by* WOLF.)

MARIE. Here we are! (*She takes* WOLF *by the hand and leads him, grinning shyly, to* JULIE, *who has turned at her call*) Hello!

JULIE. Hello.

MARIE. Well, we're here.

JULIE. Yes.

WOLF (*bows awkwardly and extends his hand*). My name is Wolf Beifeld.

JULIE. My name is Julie Zeller. (*They shake hands. There is an embarrassed silence. Then, to relieve the situation,* WOLF *takes* JULIE's *hand again and shakes it vigorously.*)

MARIE. Well—this is Wolf.

WOLF. Yes.

JULIE. Yes.
(*Another awkward silence.*)

MARIE. Where is Liliom?

WOLF. Yes, where is your husband?

JULIE. He's out.

MARIE. Where?

JULIE. Just for a walk.

MARIE. Is he?

JULIE. Yes.

WOLF. Oh!
(*Another silence.*)

MARIE. Wolf's got a new place. After the first of the month he won't have to stand outside any more. He's going to work in a club after the first of the month.

WOLF (*apologetically*). She don't know yet how to explain these things just right—hehehe—— Beginning the first I'm to be second steward at the Burger Club—a good job, if one conducts oneself properly.

JULIE. Yes?

WOLF. The pay—is quite good—but the main thing is the tips. When they play cards there's always a bit for the steward. The tips, I may say, amount to twenty, even thirty kronen every night.

MARIE. Yes.

WOLF. We've rented two rooms for ourselves to start with—and if things go well——

MARIE. Then we'll buy a house in the country.

WOLF. If one only tends to business and keeps honest. Of course, in the country we'll miss the city life, but if the good Lord sends us children—it's much healthier for children in the country.
(*There is a brief pause.*)

MARIE. Wolf's nice looking, isn't he?

JULIE. Yes.

MARIE. And he's a good boy, Wolf.

JULIE. Yes.

MARIE. The only thing is—he's a Jew.

JULIE. Oh, well, you can get used to that.

MARIE. Well, aren't you going to wish us luck?

JULIE. Of course I do. (*She embraces* MARIE.)

MARIE. And aren't you going to kiss Wolf, too?

JULIE. Him, too. (*She embraces* WOLF, *remains quite still a moment, her head resting on his shoulder.*)

WOLF. Why are you crying, my dear Mrs.—— (*He looks questioningly at* MARIE *over* JULIE's *shoulder.*)

MARIE. Because she has such a good heart. (*She becomes sentimental, too.*)

WOLF (*touched*). We thank you for your heartfelt sympathy—— (*He cannot restrain his own tears. There is a pause before* MOTHER HOLLUNDER *and her son enter.* YOUNG HOLLUNDER *immediately busies himself with the camera.*)

MOTHER HOLLUNDER. Now if you don't mind, we'll do it right away, before it gets too dark. (*She leads* MARIE *and* WOLF *into position before the background-screen. Here they immediately fall into an awkward pose, smiling mechanically*) Full length?

MARIE. Please. Both figures full length.

MOTHER HOLLUNDER. Bride and groom?

MARIE. Yes.

MOTHER HOLLUNDER, YOUNG HOLLUNDER (*speak in unison, in loud professionally-expressionless tones*). The lady looks at the gentleman and the gentleman looks straight into the camera.

MOTHER HOLLUNDER (*poses first* MARIE, *then* WOLF). Now, if you please.

YOUNG HOLLUNDER (*who has crept under the black cloth, calls in muffled tones*). That's good—that's very good!

MARIE (*stonily rigid, but very happy, trying to speak without altering her expression*). Julie, dear, do we look all right?

JULIE. Yes, dear.

YOUNG HOLLUNDER. Now, if you please, hold still. I'll count up to three, and then you must hold perfectly still. (*Grasps the cover of the lens and calls threateningly*) One—two—three! (*He removes the cover; there is utter silence. But as he speaks the word "one" there is heard, very faintly in the distance, the refrain of the thieves' song which* FICSUR *and* LILIOM *have been singing. The refrain continues until the fall of the curtain. As he speaks the word "three" everybody is perfectly rigid save* JULIE, *who lets her head sink slowly to the table. The distant refrain dies out.*)

THE CURTAIN FALLS

SCENE FOUR

SCENE—*In the fields on the outskirts of the city. At back a railroad embankment crosses the stage obliquely. At center of the embankment stands a red and white signal flag, and near it a little red signal lamp which is not yet lighted. Here also a wooden stairway leads up to the embankment.*

At the foot of the embankment to the right is a pile of used railroad ties. In the background a telegraph pole, beyond it a view of trees, fences and fields; still further back a factory building and a cluster of little dwellings.

It is six o'clock of the same afternoon. Dusk has begun to fall.

LILIOM *and* FICSUR *are discovered on the stairway looking after the train which has just passed.*

LILIOM. Can you still hear it snort?

FICSUR. Listen! (*They watch the vanishing train.*)

LILIOM. If you put your ear on the tracks you can hear it go all the way to Vienna.

FICSUR. Huh!

LILIOM. The one that just puffed past us—it goes all the way to Vienna.

FICSUR. No further?

LILIOM. Yes—further, too. (*There is a pause.*)

FICSUR. It must be near six. (*As* LILIOM *ascends the steps*) Where are you going?

LILIOM. Don't be afraid. I'm not giving you the slip.

FICSUR. Why should you give me the slip? That cashier has sixteen thousand kronen on him. Just be patient till he comes, then you can talk to him, nice and polite.

LILIOM. I say, "Good evening— excuse me, sir; what time is it?"

FICSUR. Then he tells you what time it is.

LILIOM. Suppose he don't come?

FICSUR (*coming down the steps*). Nonsense! He's got to come. He pays off the workmen every Saturday. And this is Saturday, ain't it? (LILIOM *has ascended to the top of the stairway and is gazing along the tracks*) What are you looking at up there?

LILIOM. The tracks go on and on— there's no end to them.

FICSUR. What's that to stare about?

LILIOM. Nothing—only I always look after the train. When you stand down there at night it snorts past you, and spits down.

FICSUR. Spits?

LILIOM. Yes, the engine. It spits down. And then the whole train rattles past and away—and you stand there—spat on—but it draws your eyes along with it.

FICSUR. Draws your eyes along?

LILIOM. Yes—whether you want to or not, you've got to look after it— as long as the tiniest bit of it is in sight.

FICSUR. Swell people sit in it.

LILIOM. And read newspapers.

FICSUR. And smoke cigars.

LILIOM. And inhale the smoke. (*There is a short silence.*)

FICSUR. Is he coming?

LILIOM. Not yet. (*Silence again. LILIOM comes down, speaks low, confidentially*) Do you hear the telegraph wires?

FICSUR. I hear them when the wind blows.

LILIOM. Even when the wind doesn't blow you can hear them humming, humming—— People talk through them.

FICSUR. Who?

LILIOM. Jews.

FICSUR. No—they telegraph.

LILIOM. They talk through them and from some other place they get answered. And it all goes through the iron strings—that's why they hum like that—they hum-m——

FICSUR. What do they hum?

LILIOM. They hum! ninety-nine, ninety-nine. Just listen.

FICSUR. What for?

LILIOM. That sparrow's listening, too. He's cocked one eye and looks at me as if to say: "I'd like to know what they're talking about."

FICSUR. You're looking at a bird?

LILIOM. He's looking at me, too.

FICSUR. Listen, you're sick! There's something the matter with you. Do you know what it is? Money. That bird has no money, either; that's why he cocks his eye.

LILIOM. Maybe.

FICSUR. Whoever has money don't cock his eye.

LILIOM. What then does he do?

FICSUR. He does most anything he wants. But nobody works unless he has money. We'll soon have money ourselves.

LILIOM. I say, "Good evening. Excuse me, sir, can you tell me what time it is!"

FICSUR. He's not coming yet. Got the cards? (*LILIOM gives him the pack of cards*) Got any money?

LILIOM (*takes some coins from his trousers pocket and counts*). Eleven.

FICSUR (*sits astride on the pile of ties and looks off left*). All right—eleven.

LILIOM (*sitting astride on the ties facing him*). Put it up.

FICSUR (*puts the money on the ties; rapidly shuffles the cards*). We'll play twenty-one. I'll bank. (*He deals deftly.*)

LILIOM (*looks at his card*). Good. I'll bet the bank.

FICSUR. Must have an ace! (*Deals him a second card.*)

LILIOM. Another one. (*He gets another card*) Another. (*Gets still another*) Over! (*Throws down his cards.* FICSUR *gathers in the money*) Come on!

FICSUR. Come on what? Got no more money, have you?

LILIOM. No.

FICSUR. Then the game's over—unless you want to——

LILIOM. What?

FICSUR. Play on credit.

LILIOM. You'll trust me?

FICSUR. No—but—I'll deduct it.

LILIOM. Deduct it from what?

FICSUR. From your share of the money. If *you* win you deduct from my share.

LILIOM (*looks over his shoulder to see if the cashier is coming; nervous and ashamed*). All right. How much is bank?

FICSUR. That cashier is bringing us sixteen thousand kronen. Eight thousand of that is mine. Well, then, the bank is eight thousand.

LILIOM. Good.

FICSUR. Whoever has the most luck will have the most money. (*He deals.*)

LILIOM. Six hundred kronen. (FICSUR *gives him another card*) Enough.

FICSUR (*laying out his own cards*). Twenty-one. (*He shuffles rapidly.*)

LILIOM (*moves excitedly nearer to* FICSUR). Well, then, double or nothing.

FICSUR (*dealing*). Double or nothing.

LILIOM (*gets a card*). Enough.

FICSUR (*laying out his own cards*). Twenty-one. (*Shuffles rapidly again.*)

LILIOM (*in alarm*). You're not—cheating?

FICSUR. Me? Do I look like a cheat? (*Deals the cards again.*)

LILIOM (*glances nervously over his shoulder*). A thousand.

FICSUR (*nonchalantly*). Kronen?

LILIOM. Kronen. (*He gets a card*) Another one. (*Gets another card*) Over again! (*Like an inexperienced gambler who is losing heavily,* LILIOM *is very nervous. He plays dazedly, wildly, irrationally. From now on it is apparent that his only thought is to win his money back.*)

FICSUR. That makes twelve hundred you owe.

LILIOM. Double or nothing. (*He gets a card. He is greatly excited*) Another one. (*Gets another card*) Another. (*Throws down three cards.*)

FICSUR (*bends over and adds up the sum on the ground*). Ten—fourteen—twenty-three——— You owe two thousand, four hundred.

LILIOM. Now what?

FICSUR (*takes a card out of the deck and gives it to him*). Here's the red ace. You can play double or nothing again.

LILIOM (*eagerly*). Good. (*Gets another card*) Enough.

FICSUR (*turns up his own cards*). Nineteen.

LILIOM. You win again. (*Almost imploring*) Give me an ace again. Give me the green one. (*Takes a card*) Double or nothing.

FICSUR. Not any more.

LILIOM. Why not?

FICSUR. Because if you lose you won't be able to pay. Double would be nine thousand six hundred. And you've only got eight thousand altogether.

LILIOM (*greatly excited*). That—that—I call that—a dirty trick!

FICSUR. Three thousand, two hundred. That's all you can put up.

LILIOM (*eagerly*). All right, then—three thousand, two hundred. (*FICSUR deals him a card*) Enough.

FICSUR. I've got an ace myself. Now we'll have to take our time and squeeze 'em. (*LILIOM pushes closer to him as he takes up his cards and slowly, intently unfolds them*) Twenty-one. (*He quickly puts the cards in his pocket. There is a pause.*)

LILIOM. Now—now—I'll tell you now—you're a crook, a low-down ———(*Now LINZMAN enters at right. He is a strong, robust, red-bearded Jew about 40 years of age. At his side he carries a leather bag slung by a strap from his shoulder. FICSUR coughs warningly, moves to the right between LINZMAN and the embankment, pauses just behind LINZMAN and follows him. LILIOM stands bewildered a few paces to the left of the railroad ties. He finds himself facing LINZMAN. Trembling in every limb*) Good evening. Excuse me, sir, can you tell me the time?
(*FICSUR springs silently at LINZMAN, the little knife in his right hand. But LINZMAN catches FICSUR's right hand with his own left and forces FICSUR to his knees. Simultaneously LINZMAN thrusts his right hand into his coat pocket and produces a revolver which he points at LILIOM's breast. LILIOM is standing two paces away from the revolver. There is a long pause.*)

LINZMAN (*in a low, even voice*). It is twenty-five minutes past six. (*Pauses, looks ironically down at FICSUR*) It's lucky I grabbed the hand with the knife instead of the other one. (*Pauses again, looks ap-*

praisingly from one to the other)
Two fine birds! (*To* FICSUR) I
should live so—Rothschild has
more luck than you. (*To* LILIOM)
I'd advise you to keep nice and
quiet. If you make one move, you'll
get two bullets in you. Just look
into the barrel. You'll see some little things in there made of lead.

FICSUR. Let me go. I didn't do anything.

LINZMAN (*mockingly shakes the
hand which still holds the knife*).
And this? What do you call this?
Oh, yes, I know. You thought I
had an apple in my pocket, and
you wanted to peel it. That's it.
Forgive me for my error. I beg
your pardon, sir.

LILIOM. But I—I——

LINZMAN. Yes, my son, I know. It's
so simple. You only asked what
time it is. Well, it's twenty-five
minutes after six.

FICSUR. Let us go, honorable sir.
We didn't do anything to you.

LINZMAN. In the first place, my son,
I'm not an honorable sir. In the
second place, for the same money,
you could have said Your Excellency. But in the third place you'll
find it very hard to beg off by flattering me.

LILIOM. But I—*I* really didn't do
anything to you.

LINZMAN. Look behind you, my
boy. Don't be afraid. Look behind
you, but don't run away or I'll have
to shoot you down. (LILIOM *turns
his head slowly around*) Who's
coming up there?

LILIOM (*looking at* LINZMAN). Policemen.

LINZMAN (*to* FICSUR). You hold still,
or—— (*To* LILIOM *teasingly*) How
many policemen are there?

LILIOM (*his eyes cast down*). Two.

LINZMAN. And what are the policemen sitting on?

LILIOM. Horses.

LINZMAN. And which can run faster, a horse or a man?

LILIOM. A horse.

LINZMAN. There, you see. It would
be hard to get away now. (*Laughs*)
I never saw such an unlucky pair
of highway robbers. I can't imagine
worse luck. Just today I had to put
a pistol in my pocket. And even if
I hadn't—old Linzman is a match
for four like you. But even that isn't
all. Did you happen to notice, you
oxen, what direction I came from?
From the factory, didn't I? When
I *went* there I had a nice bit of
money with me. Sixteen thousand
crowns! But now—not a heller.
(*Calls off left*) Hey, come quicker,
will you? This fellow is pulling
pretty strong. (FICSUR *frees himself with a mighty wrench and
darts rapidly off. As* LINZMAN *aims
his pistol at the vanishing* FICSUR,
LILIOM *runs up the steps to the embankment.* LINZMAN *hesitates, per-
ceives that* LILIOM *is the better target, points the pistol at him*) Stop,
or I'll shoot! (*Calls off left to* PO-
LICEMEN) Why don't you come
down off your horses? (*His pistol is
leveled at* LILIOM, *who stands on
the embankment, facing the audi-*

ence. From the left on the embankment a POLICEMAN *appears, revolver in hand.*)

FIRST POLICEMAN. Stop!

LINZMAN. Well, my boy, do you still want to know what time it is? From ten to twelve years in prison!

LILIOM. You won't get me! (LINZMAN *laughs derisively.* LILIOM *is now three or four paces from the* POLICEMAN *and equally distant from* LINZMAN. *His face is uplifted to the sky. He bursts into laughter, half defiant, half self-pitying, and takes the kitchen knife from under his coat)* Julie—— (*The ring of farewell is in the word. He turns sideways, thrusts the knife deep in his breast, sways, falls and rolls down the far side of the embankment. There is a long pause. From the left up on the embankment come the* TWO POLICEMEN.)

LINZMAN. What's the matter? (*The* FIRST POLICEMAN *comes along the embankment as far as the steps, looks down in the opposite side, then climbs down at about the spot where* LILIOM *disappeared.* LINZMAN *and the other* POLICEMAN *mount the embankment and look down on him*) Stabbed himself?

VOICE OF FIRST POLICEMAN. Yes— and he seems to have made a thorough job of it.

LINZMAN (*excitedly to the* SECOND POLICEMAN). I'll go and telephone to the hospital. (*He runs down the steps and exits at left.*)

SECOND POLICEMAN. Go to Eisler's

grocery store and telephone to the factory from there. They've a doctor there, too. (*Calling down to the other* POLICEMAN) I'm going to tie up the horses. (*Comes down the steps and exits at left. The stage is empty. There is a pause. The little red signal lamp is lit.*)

VOICE OF FIRST POLICEMAN. Hey, Stephan!

VOICE OF SECOND POLICEMAN. What?

VOICE OF FIRST POLICEMAN. Shall I pull the knife out of his chest?

VOICE OF SECOND POLICEMAN. Better not, or he may bleed to death. (*There is a pause.*)

VOICE OF FIRST POLICEMAN. Stephan!

VOICE OF SECOND POLICEMAN. Yes.

VOICE OF FIRST POLICEMAN. Lot of mosquitoes around here.

VOICE OF SECOND POLICEMAN. Yes.

VOICE OF FIRST POLICEMAN. Got a cigar?

VOICE OF SECOND POLICEMAN. No. (*There is a pause. The* FIRST POLICEMAN *appears over the opposite side of the embankment.*)

FIRST POLICEMAN. A lot of good the new pay-schedule's done us— made things worse than they used to be—we *get* more but we *have* less than we ever had. If the Government could be made to realize that. It's a thankless job at best.

You work hard year after year, you get gray in the service, and slowly you die—yes.

SECOND POLICEMAN. That's right.

FIRST POLICEMAN. Yes.
(*In the distance is heard the bell of the signal tower.*)

THE CURTAIN FALLS

SCENE FIVE

SCENE—*The photographic "studio" a half hour later that same evening.* MOTHER HOLLUNDER, *her son,* MARIE *and* WOLF *stand in a group back right, their heads together.* JULIE *stands apart from them, a few paces to the left.*

YOUNG HOLLUNDER (*who has just come in, tells his story excitedly*). They're bringing him now. Two workmen from the factory are carrying him on a stretcher.

WOLF. Where is the doctor?

YOUNG HOLLUNDER. A policeman telephoned to headquarters. The police-surgeon ought to be here any minute.

MARIE. Maybe they'll pull him through after all.

YOUNG HOLLUNDER. He stabbed himself too deep in his chest. But he's still breathing. He can still talk, too, but very faintly. At first he lay there unconscious, but when they put him on the stretcher he came to.

WOLF. That was from the shaking.

MARIE. We'd better make room. (*They make room. Two workmen carry in* LILIOM *on a stretcher which has four legs and stands about as high as a bed. They put the stretcher at left directly in front* of the sofa, so that the head is at right and the foot at left. Then they unobtrusively join the group at the door. Later, they go out.* JULIE *is standing at the side of the stretcher, where, without moving, she can see* LILIOM's *face. The others crowd emotionally together near the door. The* FIRST POLICEMAN *enters.*)

FIRST POLICEMAN. Are you his wife?

JULIE. Yes.

FIRST POLICEMAN. The doctor at the factory who bandaged him up forbade us to take him to the hospital.—Dangerous to move him that far. What he needs now is rest. Just let him be until the police-surgeon comes. (*To the group near the door*) He's not to be disturbed. (*They make way for him. He exits. There is a pause.*)

WOLF (*gently urging the others out*). Please—it's best if we all get out of here now. We'll only be in the way.

MARIE (*to* JULIE). Julie, what do you think? (JULIE *looks at her without answering*) Julie, can I do anything to help? (JULIE *does not answer*) We'll be just outside on the bench if you want us.

(MOTHER HOLLUNDER *and her son have gone out when first requested. Now* MARIE *and* WOLF *exit, too.* JULIE *sits on the edge of the stretcher and looks at* LILIOM. *He stretches his hand out to her. She clasps it. It is not quite dark yet. Both of them can still be plainly seen.*)

LILIOM (*raises himself with difficulty; speaks lightly at first, but later soberly, defiantly*). Little—Julie—there's something—I want to tell you—like when you go to a restaurant—and you've finished eating—and it's time—to pay—then you have to count up everything—everything you owe—well—I beat you—not because I was mad at you—no—only because I can't bear to see anyone crying. You always cried—on my account—and, well, you see,—I never learned a trade—what kind of a caretaker would I make? But anyhow—I wasn't going back to the carousel to fool with the girls. No, I spit on them all—understand?

JULIE. Yes.

LILIOM. And—as for Hollinger—he's good enough—Mrs. Muskat can get along all right with him. The jokes he tells are mine—and the people laugh when he tells them—but I don't care.—I didn't give you anything—no home—not even the food you ate—but you don't understand.—It's true I'm not much good—but I couldn't be a caretaker—and so I thought maybe it would be better over there—in America—do you see?

JULIE. Yes.

LILIOM. I'm not asking—forgiveness—I don't do that—I don't. Tell the baby—if you like.

JULIE. Yes.

LILIOM. Tell the baby—I wasn't much good—but tell him—if you ever talk about me—tell him—I thought—perhaps—over in America—but that's no affair of yours. I'm not asking forgiveness. For my part the police can come now.—If it's a boy—if it's a girl.—Perhaps I'll see the Lord God today.—Do you think I'll see Him?

JULIE. Yes.

LILIOM. I'm not afraid—of the police Up There—if they'll only let me come up in front of the Lord God Himself—not like down here where an officer stops you at the door. If the carpenter asks you—yes—be his wife—marry him. And the child—tell him he's his father.—He'll believe you—won't he?

JULIE. Yes.

LILIOM. When I beat you—I was right.—You mustn't always think—you mustn't always be right.—Liliom can be right once, too.—It's all the same to me who was right.—It's so dumb. Nobody's right—but they all think they are right.—A lot they know!

JULIE. Yes.

LILIOM. Julie—come—hold my hand tight.

JULIE. I'm holding it tight—all the time.

LILIOM. Tighter, still tighter—I'm going—— (*Pauses*) Julie——

JULIE. Good-bye.
(LILIOM *sinks slowly back and dies.* JULIE *frees her hand. The* DOCTOR *enters with the* FIRST POLICEMAN.)

DOCTOR. Good evening. His wife?

JULIE. Yes, sir.
(*Behind the* DOCTOR *and* POLICEMAN *enter* MARIE, WOLF, MOTHER HOLLUNDER, YOUNG HOLLUNDER *and* MRS. MUSKAT. *They remain respectfully at the doorway. The* DOCTOR *bends over* LILIOM *and examines him.*)

DOCTOR. A light, if you please. (JULIE *fetches a burning candle from the dark room. The* DOCTOR *examines* LILIOM *briefly in the candlelight, then turns suddenly away*) Have you pen and ink?

WOLF (*proffering a pen*). A fountain-pen—American——

DOCTOR (*takes a printed form from his pocket; speaks as he writes out the death-certificate at the little table*). My poor woman, your husband is dead—there's nothing to be done for him—the good God will help him now—I'll leave this certificate with you. You will give it to the people from the hospital when they come—I'll arrange for the body to be removed at once. (*Rises*) Please give me a towel and soap.

POLICEMAN. I've got them for you out here, sir. (*Points to door at back.*)

DOCTOR. God be with you, my good woman.

JULIE. Thank you, sir.
(*The* DOCTOR *and* POLICEMAN *exit. The others slowly draw nearer.*)

MARIE. Poor Julie. May he rest in peace, poor man, but as for you —please don't be angry with me for saying it—but you're better off this way.

MOTHER HOLLUNDER. He is better off, the poor fellow, and so are you.

MARIE. Much better, Julie . . . you are young . . . and one of these days some good man will come along. Am I right?

WOLF. She's right.

MARIE. Julie, tell me, am I right?

JULIE. You are right, dear; you are very good.

YOUNG HOLLUNDER. There's a good man—the carpenter. Oh, I can speak of it now. He comes here every day on some excuse or other —and he never fails to ask for you.

MARIE. A widower—with two children.

MOTHER HOLLUNDER. He's better off, poor fellow—and so are you. He was a bad man.

MARIE. He wasn't good-hearted. Was he, Wolf?

WOLF. No, I must say, he really wasn't. No, Liliom wasn't a good man. A good man doesn't strike a woman.

MARIE. Am I right? Tell me, Julie, am I right?

JULIE. You are right, dear.

YOUNG HOLLUNDER. It's really a good thing for her it happened.

MOTHER HOLLUNDER. He's better off—and so is she.

WOLF. Now you have your freedom again. How old are you?

JULIE. Eighteen.

WOLF. Eighteen. A mere child! Am I right?

JULIE. You are right, Wolf. You are kind.

YOUNG HOLLUNDER. Lucky for you it happened, isn't it?

JULIE. Yes.

YOUNG HOLLUNDER. All you had before was bad luck. If it weren't for my mother you wouldn't have had a roof over your head or a bite to eat—and now Autumn's coming and Winter. You couldn't have lived in this shack in the Winter time, could you?

MARIE. Certainly not! You'd have frozen like the birds in the fields. Am I right, Julie?

JULIE. Yes, Marie.

MARIE. A year from now you will have forgotten all about him, won't you?

JULIE. You are right, Marie.

WOLF. If you need anything, count on us. We'll go now. But tomorrow morning we'll be back. Come,

MARIE. God be with you. (*Offers* JULIE *his hand.*)

JULIE. God be with you.

MARIE (*embraces* JULIE, *weeping*). It's the best thing that could have happened to you, Julie, the best thing.

JULIE. Don't cry, Marie. (MARIE *and* WOLF *exit.*)

MOTHER HOLLUNDER. I'll make a little black coffee. You haven't had a thing to eat today. Then you'll come home with us. (MOTHER HOLLUNDER *and her son exit.* MRS. MUSKAT *comes over to* JULIE.)

MRS. MUSKAT. Would you mind if I —looked at him?

JULIE. He used to work for you.

MRS. MUSKAT (*contemplates the body; turns to* JULIE). Won't you make up with me?

JULIE. I wasn't angry with you.

MRS. MUSKAT. But you were. Let's make it up.

JULIE (*raising her voice eagerly, almost triumphantly*). I've nothing to make up with *you*.

MRS. MUSKAT. But I have with you. Everyone says hard things against the poor dead boy—except us two. You don't say he was bad.

JULIE (*raising her voice yet higher, this time on a defiant, wholly triumphant note*). Yes, I *do*.

MRS. MUSKAT. I understand, my child. But he beat me, too. What does that matter? I've forgotten it.

JULIE (*from now on answers her coldly, drily, without looking at her*). That's your own affair.

MRS. MUSKAT. If I can help you in any way——

JULIE. There's nothing I need.

MRS. MUSKAT. I still owe him two kronen, back pay.

JULIE. You should have paid him.

MRS. MUSKAT. Now that the poor fellow is dead I thought perhaps it would be the same if I paid you.

JULIE. I've nothing to do with it.

MRS. MUSKAT. All right. Please don't think I'm trying to force myself on you. I stayed because we two are the only ones on earth who loved him. That's why I thought we ought to stick together.

JULIE. No, thank you.

MRS. MUSKAT. Then you couldn't have loved him as I did.

JULIE. No.

MRS. MUSKAT. I loved him better.

JULIE. Yes.

MRS. MUSKAT. Good-bye.

JULIE. Good-bye. (MRS. MUSKAT *exits.* JULIE *puts the candle on the table near* LILIOM's *head, sits on the edge of the stretcher, looks into the dead man's face and caresses it tenderly*) Sleep, Liliom, sleep—it's no business of hers—I never even told you—but now I'll tell you— now I'll tell you—you bad, quick-tempered, rough, unhappy, wicked —*dear* boy—sleep peacefully, Liliom—they can't understand how I feel—I can't even explain to you —not even to you—how I feel— you'd only laugh at me—but you can't hear me any more. (*Between tender motherliness and reproach, yet with great love in her voice*) It was wicked of you to beat me—on the breast and on the head and face —but you're gone now.—You treated me badly—that was wicked of you—but sleep peacefully, Liliom—you bad, bad boy, you— I love you—I never told you before —I was ashamed—but now I've told you—I love you. Liliom—sleep —my boy—sleep. (*She rises, gets a Bible, sits down near the candle and reads softly to herself, so that, not the words, but an inarticulate murmur is heard. The* CARPENTER *enters at back.*)

CARPENTER (*stands near the door; in the dimness of the room he can scarcely be seen*). Miss Julie——

JULIE (*without alarm*). Who is that?

CARPENTER (*very slowly*). The carpenter.

JULIE. What does the carpenter want?

CARPENTER. Can I be of help to you in any way? Shall I stay here with you?

JULIE (*gratefully, but firmly*). Don't stay, carpenter.

CARPENTER. Shall I come back tomorrow?

JULIE. Not tomorrow, either.

CARPENTER. Don't be offended, Miss Julie, but I'd like to know—you see, I'm not a young man any more—I have two children—and if I'm to come back any more—I'd like to know—if there's any use——

JULIE. No use, carpenter.

CARPENTER (*as he exits*). God be with you.
(JULIE *resumes her reading.* FICSUR *enters, slinks furtively sideways to the stretcher, looks at* LILIOM, *shakes his head.* JULIE *looks up from her reading.* FICSUR *takes fright, slinks away from the stretcher, sits down at right, biting his nails.* JULIE *rises.* FICSUR *rises, too, and looks at her half fearfully. With her piercing glance upon him he slinks to the doorway at back, where he pauses and speaks.*)

FICSUR. The old woman asked me to tell you that coffee is ready, and you are to come in.
(JULIE *goes to the kitchen door.* FICSUR *withdraws until she has closed the door behind her. Then he reappears in the doorway, stands on tiptoes, looks at* LILIOM, *then exits. Now the body lies alone. After a brief silence music is heard, distant at first, but gradually coming nearer. It is very much like the music of the carousel, but slower, graver, more exalted. The melody, too, is the same, yet the tempo is altered and contrapuntal measures of the thieves' song are intertwined in it. Two men in black, with heavy sticks, soft black hats and black gloves, appear in the doorway at back and stride slowly into the room. Their faces are beardless, marble white, grave and benign.*

One stops in front of the stretcher, the other a pace to the right. From above a dim violet light illuminates their faces.)

THE FIRST (*to* LILIOM). Rise and come with us.

THE SECOND (*politely*). You're under arrest.

THE FIRST (*somewhat louder, but always in a gentle, low, resonant voice*). Do you hear? Rise. Don't you hear?

THE SECOND. We are the police.

THE FIRST (*bends down, touches* LILIOM'S *shoulder*). Get up and come with us.
(LILIOM *slowly sits up.*)

THE SECOND. Come along.

THE FIRST (*paternally*). These people suppose that when they die all their difficulties are solved for them.

THE SECOND (*raising his voice sternly*). That simply by thrusting a knife in your heart and making it stop beating you can leave your wife behind with a child in her womb——

THE FIRST. It is not as simple as that.

THE SECOND. Such things are not settled so easily.

THE FIRST. Come along. You will have to give an account of yourself. (*As both bow their heads, he continues softly*) We are God's police. (*An expression of glad re-*

lief lights upon LILIOM's *face. He rises from the stretcher*) Come.

THE SECOND. You mortals don't get off quite as easy as that.

THE FIRST (*softly*). Come. (LILIOM *starts to walk ahead of them, then stops and looks at them*) The end is not as abrupt as that. Your name is still spoken. Your face is still remembered. And what you said, and what you did, and what you failed to do—these are still remembered. Remembered, too, are the manner of your glance, the ring of your voice, the clasp of your hand and how your step sounded—as long as one is left who remembers you, so long is the matter unended. Before the end there is much to be undone. Until you are quite forgotten, my son, you will not be finished with the earth—even though you *are* dead.

THE SECOND (*very gently*). Come. (*The music begins again. All three exit at back,* LILIOM *leading, the others following. The stage is empty and quite dark save for the candle which burns by the stretcher, on which, in the shadows, the covers are so arranged that one cannot quite be sure that a body is not still lying. The music dies out in the distance as if it had followed* LILIOM *and the* TWO POLICEMEN. *The candle flickers and goes out. There is a brief interval of silence and total darkness before the Curtain Falls.*)

CURTAIN

SCENE SIX

SCENE—*In the Beyond. A whitewashed courtroom. There is a green-topped table; behind it a bench. Back center is a door with a bell over it. Next to this door is a window through which can be seen a vista of rose-tinted clouds.*

Down right there is a grated iron door. Down left another door.

Two men are on the bench when the curtain rises. One is richly, the other poorly dressed.

From a great distance is heard a fanfare of trumpets playing the refrain of the thieves' song in slow, altered tempo.

Passing the window at back appear LILIOM *and the* TWO POLICEMEN. *The bell rings.*

An old guard enters at right. He is bald and has a long white beard. He wears the conventional police uniform.

He goes to the door at back, opens it, exchanges silent greetings with the TWO POLICEMEN *and closes the door again.*

LILIOM *looks wonderingly around.*

THE FIRST (*to the old* GUARD). Announce us.

(THE GUARD *exits at left.*)

LILIOM. Is this it?

THE SECOND. Yes, my son.

LILIOM. This is the police court?

THE SECOND. Yes, my son. The part for suicide cases.

LILIOM. And what happens here?

THE FIRST. Here justice is done. Sit down.
(LILIOM *sits next to the two men. The* TWO POLICEMEN *stand silent near the table.*)

THE RICHLY DRESSED MAN (*whispers*). Suicide, too?

LILIOM. Yes.

THE RICHLY DRESSED MAN (*points to* THE POORLY DRESSED MAN). So's he. (*Introducing himself*) My name is Reich.

THE POORLY DRESSED MAN (*whispers, too*). My name is Stephen Kadar.
(LILIOM *only looks at them.*)

THE POORLY DRESSED MAN. And you? What's your name?

LILIOM. None of your business.
(*Both move a bit away from him.*)

THE POORLY DRESSED MAN. I did it by jumping out of a window.

THE RICHLY DRESSED MAN. I did it with a pistol—and you?

LILIOM. With a knife.
(*They move a bit further away from him.*)

THE RICHLY DRESSED MAN. A pistol is cleaner.

LILIOM. If I had the price of a pistol——

THE SECOND. Silence!
(*The* POLICE MAGISTRATE *enters. He has a long white beard, is bald, but only in profile can be seen on his head a single tuft of snow-white hair. The* GUARD *reënters behind him and sits on the bench with the dead men. As the* MAGISTRATE *enters, all rise, except* LILIOM, *who remains surlily seated. When the* MAGISTRATE *sits down, so do the others.*)

THE GUARD. Yesterday's cases, your honor. The numbers are entered in the docket.

THE MAGISTRATE. Number 16,472.

THE FIRST (*looks in his notebook, beckons the* RICHLY DRESSED MAN). Stand up, please.
(THE RICHLY DRESSED MAN *rises.*)

THE MAGISTRATE. Your name?

THE RICHLY DRESSED MAN. Doctor Reich.

THE MAGISTRATE. Age?

THE RICHLY DRESSED MAN. Forty-two, married, Jew.

THE MAGISTRATE (*with a gesture of dismissal*). Religion does not interest us here—why did you kill yourself?

THE RICHLY DRESSED MAN. On account of debts.

THE MAGISTRATE. What good did you do on earth?

THE RICHLY DRESSED MAN. I was a lawyer——

THE MAGISTRATE (*coughs significantly*). Yes—we'll discuss that later. For the present I shall only ask you: Would you like to go back to earth once more before sunrise? I advise you that you have the right to go if you choose. Do you understand?

THE RICHLY DRESSED MAN. Yes, sir.

THE MAGISTRATE. He who takes his life is apt, in his haste and his excitement, to forget something. Is there anything important down there you have left undone? Something to tell someone? Something to undo?

THE RICHLY DRESSED MAN. My debts——

THE MAGISTRATE. They do not matter here. Here we are concerned only with the affairs of the soul.

THE RICHLY DRESSED MAN. Then—if you please—when I left—the house—my youngest son, Oscar—was asleep. I didn't trust myself to wake him—and bid him good-bye. I would have liked—to kiss him good-bye.

THE MAGISTRATE (to THE SECOND). You will take Dr. Reich back and let him kiss his son Oscar.

THE SECOND. Come with me, please.

THE RICHLY DRESSED MAN (to THE MAGISTRATE). I thank you. (He bows and exits at back with THE SECOND.)

THE MAGISTRATE (after making an entry in the docket). Number 16,-473.

THE FIRST (looks in his notebook, then beckons LILIOM). Stand up.

LILIOM. You said please to him. (He rises.)

THE MAGISTRATE. Your name?

LILIOM. Liliom.

THE MAGISTRATE. Isn't that your nickname?

LILIOM. Yes.

THE MAGISTRATE. What is your right name?

LILIOM. Andreas.

THE MAGISTRATE. And your last name?

LILIOM. Zavocki—after my mother.

THE MAGISTRATE. Your age?

LILIOM. Twenty-four.

THE MAGISTRATE. What good did you do on earth? (LILIOM is silent) Why did you take your life? (LILIOM does not answer. THE MAGISTRATE addresses THE FIRST) Take that knife away from him. (THE FIRST does so) It will be returned to you, if you go back to earth.

LILIOM. Do I go back to earth again?

THE MAGISTRATE. Just answer my questions.

LILIOM. I wasn't answering then, I was asking if——.

THE MAGISTRATE. You don't ask questions here. You only answer. Only answer, Andreas Zavocki! I ask you whether there is anything on earth you neglected to accomplish? Anything down there you would like to do?

LILIOM. Yes.

THE MAGISTRATE. What is it?

LILIOM. I'd like to break Ficsur's head for him.

THE MAGISTRATE. Punishment is our office. Is there nothing else on earth you'd like to do?

LILIOM. I don't know—I guess, as long as I'm here, I'll not go back.

THE MAGISTRATE (*to* THE FIRST). Note that. He waives his right. (LILIOM *starts back to the bench*) Stay where you are. You are aware that you left your wife without food or shelter?

LILIOM. Yes.

THE MAGISTRATE. Don't you regret it?

LILIOM. No.

THE MAGISTRATE. You are aware that your wife is pregnant, and that in six months a child will be born?

LILIOM. I know.

THE MAGISTRATE. And that the child, too, will be without food or shelter? Do you regret that?

LILIOM. As long as I won't be there, what's it got to do with me?

THE MAGISTRATE. Don't try to deceive us, Andreas Zavocki. We see through you as through a pane of glass.

LILIOM. If you see so much, what do you want to ask me for? Why don't you let me rest—in peace?

THE MAGISTRATE. First you must earn your rest.

LILIOM. I want—only—to sleep.

THE MAGISTRATE. Your obstinacy won't help you. Here patience is endless as time. We can wait.

LILIOM. Can I ask something—I'd like to know—if Your Honor will tell me—whether the baby will be a boy or a girl.

THE MAGISTRATE. You shall see that for yourself.

LILIOM (*excitedly*). I'll see the baby?

THE MAGISTRATE. When you do it won't be a baby any more. But we haven't reached that question yet.

LILIOM. I'll see it?

THE MAGISTRATE. Again I ask you: Do you not regret that you deserted your wife and child; that you were a bad husband, a bad father?

LILIOM. A bad husband?

THE MAGISTRATE. Yes.

LILIOM. And a bad father?

THE MAGISTRATE. That, too.

LILIOM. I couldn't get work—and I couldn't bear to see Julie—all the time— all the time——

THE MAGISTRATE. Weeping! Why are you ashamed to say it? You couldn't bear to see her weeping. Why are you afraid of that word? And why are you ashamed that you loved her?

LILIOM (*shrugs his shoulders*). Who's ashamed? But I couldn't bear to see her—and that's why I was bad to her. You see, it wouldn't do to go back to the carousel—and Ficsur came along with his talk about—that other thing—and all of a sudden it happened, I don't know how. The police and the Jew with the pistol—and there I stood —and I'd lost the money playing cards—and I didn't want to be put in prison. (*Demanding justification*) Maybe I was wrong not to go out and steal when there was nothing to eat in the house? Should I have gone out to steal for Julie?

THE MAGISTRATE (*emphatically*). Yes.

LILIOM (*after an astounded pause*). The police down there never said that.

THE MAGISTRATE. You beat that poor, frail girl; you beat her because she loved you. How could you do that?

LILIOM. We argued with each other —she said this and I said that— and because she was right I couldn't answer her—and I got mad —and the anger rose up in me— until it reached here (*points to his throat*) and then I beat her.

THE MAGISTRATE. Are you sorry?

LILIOM (*shakes his head, but cannot utter the word "no"; con-*

tinues softly). When I touched her slender throat—then—if you like— you might say—— (*Falters, looks embarrassed at* THE MAGISTRATE.)

THE MAGISTRATE (*confidently expectant*). Are you sorry?

LILIOM (*with a stare*). I'm not sorry for anything.

THE MAGISTRATE. Liliom, Liliom, it will be difficult to help you.

LILIOM. I'm not asking any help.

THE MAGISTRATE. You were offered employment as a caretaker on Arader Street. (*To* THE FIRST) Where is that entered?

THE FIRST. In the small docket. (*Hands him the open book.* THE MAGISTRATE *looks in it.*)

THE MAGISTRATE. Rooms, kitchen, quarterly wages, the privilege of keeping poultry. Why didn't you accept it?

LILIOM. I'm not a caretaker. I'm no good at caretaking. To be a caretaker—you have to be a caretaker ——

THE MAGISTRATE. If I said to you now: Liliom, go back on your stretcher. Tomorrow morning you will arise alive and well again. Would you be a caretaker then?

LILIOM. No.

THE MAGISTRATE. Why not?

LILIOM. Because—because that's just why I died.

THE MAGISTRATE. That is not true, my son. You died because you

LILIOM

LILIOM 845

loved little Julie and the child she is bearing under her heart.

LILIOM. No.

THE MAGISTRATE. Look me in the eye.

LILIOM (*looks him in the eye*). No.

THE MAGISTRATE (*stroking his beard*). Liliom, Liliom, if it were not for our Heavenly patience—— Go back to your seat. Number 16,474.

THE FIRST (*looks in his note book*). Stephan Kadar.
(THE POORLY DRESSED MAN *rises*.)

THE MAGISTRATE. You came out today?

THE POORLY DRESSED MAN. Today.

THE MAGISTRATE (*indicating the crimson sea of clouds*). How long were you in there?

THE POORLY DRESSED MAN. Thirteen years.

THE MAGISTRATE. Officer, you went to earth with him?

THE FIRST. Yes, sir.

THE MAGISTRATE. Stephan Kadar, after thirteen years of purification by fire you returned to earth to give proof that your soul had been burned clean. What good deed did you perform?

THE POORLY DRESSED MAN. When I came to the village and looked in the window of our cottage I saw my poor little orphans sleeping

peacefully. But it was raining and the rain beat into the room through a hole in the roof. So I went and fixed the roof so it wouldn't rain in any more. My hammering woke them up and they were afraid. But their mother came in to them and comforted them. She said to them: "Don't cry! It's your poor, dear father hammering up there. He's come back from the other world to fix the roof for us."

THE MAGISTRATE. Officer?

THE FIRST. That's what happened.

THE MAGISTRATE. Stephan Kadar, you have done a good deed. What you did will be written in books to gladden the hearts of children who read them. (*Indicates the door at left*) The door is open to you. The eternal light awaits you. (THE FIRST *escorts* THE POORLY DRESSED MAN *out at left with great deference*) Liliom! (LILIOM *rises*) You have heard?

LILIOM. Yes.

THE MAGISTRATE. When this man first appeared before us he was as stubborn as you. But now he has purified himself and withstood the test. He has done a good deed.

LILIOM. What's he done, anyhow? Any roofer can fix a roof. It's much harder to be a barker in an amusement park.

THE MAGISTRATE. Liliom, you shall remain for sixteen years in the crimson fire until your child is full grown. By that time your pride and your stubbornness will have been burnt out of you. And when your daughter——

LILIOM. My daughter!

THE MAGISTRATE. When your daughter has reached the age of sixteen——

(LILIOM *bows his head, covers his eyes with his hands, and to keep from weeping laughs defiantly, sadly.*)

THE MAGISTRATE. When your daughter has reached the age of sixteen you will be sent for one day back to earth.

LILIOM. Me?

THE MAGISTRATE. Yes—just as you may have read in the legends of how the dead reappear on earth for a time.

LILIOM. I never believed them.

THE MAGISTRATE. Now you see they are true. You will go back to earth one day to show how far the purification of your soul has progressed.

LILIOM. Then I must show what I can do—like when you apply for a job—as a coachman?

THE MAGISTRATE. Yes—it is a test.

LILIOM. And will I be told what I have to do?

THE MAGISTRATE. No.

LILIOM. How will I know, then?

THE MAGISTRATE. You must decide that for yourself. That's what you burn sixteen years for. And if you do something good, something splendid for your child, then——

LILIOM (*laughs sadly*). Then? (*All stand up and bow their heads reverently. There is a pause*) Then?

THE MAGISTRATE. Now I'll bid you farewell, Liliom. Sixteen years and a day shall pass before I see you again. When you have returned from earth you will come up before me again. Take heed and think well of some good deed to do for your child. On that will depend which door shall be opened to you up here. Now go, Liliom. (*He exits at left.* THE GUARD *stands at attention. There is a pause.*)

THE FIRST (*approaches* LILIOM). Come along, my son. (*He goes to the door at right; pulls open the bolt and waits.*)

LILIOM (*to the old* GUARD, *softly*). Say, officer.

THE GUARD. What do you want?

LILIOM. Please—can I get—have you got——?

THE GUARD. What?

LILIOM (*whispers*). A cigarette? (*The old* GUARD *stares at him, goes a few paces to the left, shakes his head disapprovingly. Then his expression softens. He takes a cigarette from his pocket and, crossing to* LILIOM—*who has gone over to the door at right—gives him the cigarette.* THE FIRST *throws open the door. An intense rose-colored light streams in. The glow of it is so strong that it blinds* LILIOM *and he takes a step backward and bows his head and covers his eyes with his hand before he steps forward into the light.*)

THE CURTAIN FALLS

SCENE SEVEN

SCENE—*Sixteen years later. A small, tumble-down house on a bare, un-enclosed plot of ground. Before the house is a tiny garden enclosed by a hip-high hedge.*

At back a wooden fence crosses the stage; in the center of it is a door large enough to admit a wagon. Beyond the fence is a view of a suburban street which blends into a broad vista of tilled fields.

It is a bright Sunday in Spring.

In the garden a table for two is laid.

JULIE, *her daughter* LOUISE, WOLF *and* MARIE *are discovered in the garden.* WOLF *is prosperously dressed,* MARIE *somewhat elaborately, with a huge hat.*

JULIE. You could stay for lunch.

MARIE. Impossible, dear. Since he became the proprietor of the Café Sorrento, Wolf simply has to be there all the time.

JULIE. But you needn't stay there all day, too.

MARIE. Oh, yes. I sit near the cashier's cage, read the papers, keep an eye on the waiters and drink in the bustle and excitement of the great city.

JULIE. And what about the children?

MARIE. You know what modern families are like. Parents scarcely ever see their children these days. The four girls are with their governess, the three boys with their tutor.

LOUISE. Auntie, dear, do stay and eat with us.

MARIE (*importantly*). Impossible today, dear child, impossible. Per-haps some other time. Come, Mr. Beifeld.

JULIE. Since when do you call your husband mister?

WOLF. I'd rather she did, dear lady. When we used to be very familiar we quarreled all the time. Now we are formal with each other and get along like society folk. I kiss your hand, dear lady.

JULIE. Good-bye, Wolf.

MARIE. Adieu, my dear. (*They embrace*) Adieu, my dear child.

LOUISE. Good-bye, Aunt Marie. Good-bye, Uncle Wolf.
(WOLF *and* MARIE *exit.*)

JULIE. You can get the soup now, Louise dear.
(LOUISE *goes into the house and re-enters with the soup. They sit at the table.*)

LOUISE. Mother, is it true we're not going to work at the jute factory any more?

JULIE. Yes, dear.

LOUISE. Where then?

JULIE. Uncle Wolf has gotten us a place in a big establishment where they make all kinds of fittings for cafés. We're to make big curtains, you know, the kind they hang in the windows, with lettering on them.

LOUISE. It'll be nicer there than at the jute factory.

JULIE. Yes, dear. The work isn't as dirty and pays better, too. A poor widow like your mother is lucky to get it. (*They eat.* LILIOM *and the two* HEAVENLY POLICEMEN *appear in the big doorway at back. The* POLICEMEN *pass slowly by.* LILIOM *stands there alone a moment, then comes slowly down and pauses at the opening of the hedge. He is dressed as he was on the day of his death. He is very pale, but otherwise unaltered.* JULIE, *at the table, has her back to him.* LOUISE *sits facing the audience.*)

LILIOM. Good day.

LOUISE. Good day.

JULIE. Another beggar! What is it you want, my poor man?

LILIOM. Nothing.

JULIE. We have no money to give, but if you care for a plate of soup —— (LOUISE *goes into the house*) Have you come far today?

LILIOM. Yes—very far.

JULIE. Are you tired?

LILIOM. Very tired.

JULIE. Over there at the gate is a stone. Sit down and rest. My daughter is bringing you the soup.
(LOUISE *comes out of the house.*)

LILIOM. Is that your daughter?

JULIE. Yes.

LILIOM (*to* LOUISE). You are the daughter?

LOUISE. Yes, sir.

LILIOM. A fine, healthy girl. (*Takes the soup plate from her with one hand, while with the other he touches her arm.* LOUISE *draws back quickly.*)

LOUISE (*crosses to* JULIE). Mother!

JULIE. What, my child?

LOUISE. The man tried to take me by the arm.

JULIE. Nonsense! You only imagined it, dear. The poor, hungry man has other things to think about than fooling with young girls. Sit down and eat your soup.
(*They eat.*)

LILIOM (*eats, too, but keeps looking at them*). You work at the factory, eh?

JULIE. Yes.

LILIOM. Your daughter, too?

LOUISE. Yes.

LILIOM. And your husband?

JULIE (*after a pause*). I have no husband. I'm a widow.

LILIOM. A widow?

JULIE. Yes.

LILIOM. Your husband—I suppose he's been dead a long time. (JULIE *does not answer*) I say—has your husband been dead a long time?

JULIE. A long time.

LILIOM. What did he die of? (JULIE *is silent*.)

LOUISE. No one knows. He went to America to work and he died there —in the hospital. Poor father, I never knew him.

LILIOM. He went to America?

LOUISE. Yes, before I was born.

LILIOM. To America?

JULIE. Why do you ask so many questions? Did you know him, perhaps?

LILIOM (*puts the plate down*). Heaven knows! I've known so many people. Maybe I knew him, too.

JULIE. Well, if you knew him, leave him and us in peace with your questions. He went to America and died there. That's all there is to tell.

LILIOM. All right. All right. Don't be angry with me. I didn't mean any harm. (*There is a pause*.)

LOUISE. My father was a very handsome man.

JULIE. Don't talk so much.

LOUISE. Did I say anything— --?

LILIOM. Surely the little orphan can say that about her father.

LOUISE. My father could juggle so beautifully with three ivory balls that people used to advise him to go on the stage.

JULIE. Who told you that?

LOUISE. Uncle Wolf.

LILIOM. Who is that?

LOUISE. Mr. Wolf Beifeld, who owns the Café Sorrento.

LILIOM. The one who used to be a porter?

JULIE (*astonished*). Do you know him, too? It seems that you know all Budapest.

LILIOM. Wolf Beifeld is a long way from being all Budapest. But I do know a lot of people. Why shouldn't I know Wolf Beifeld?

LOUISE. He was a friend of my father.

JULIE. He was not his friend. No one was.

LILIOM. You speak of your husband so sternly.

JULIE. What's that to you? Doesn't it suit you? I can speak of my husband any way I like. It's nobody's business but mine.

LILIOM. Certainly, certainly—it's your own business. (*Takes up his soup plate again. All three eat*.)

LOUISE (*to* JULIE). Perhaps he knew father, too.

JULIE. Ask him, if you like.

LOUISE (*crosses to* LILIOM. *He stands up*). Did you know my father? (LILIOM *nods.* LOUISE *addresses her mother*) Yes, he knew him.

JULIE (*rises*). You knew Andreas Zavocky?

LILIOM. Liliom? Yes.

LOUISE. Was he really a very handsome man?

LILIOM. I wouldn't exactly say handsome.

LOUISE (*confidently*). But he was an awfully good man, wasn't he?

LILIOM. He wasn't so good, either. As far as I know he was what they called a clown, a barker in a carousel.

LOUISE (*pleased*). Did he tell funny jokes?

LILIOM. Lots of 'em. And he sang funny songs, too.

LOUISE. In the carousel?

LILIOM. Yes—but he was something of a bully, too. He'd fight anyone. He even hit your dear little mother.

JULIE. That's a lie.

LILIOM. It's true.

JULIE. Aren't you ashamed to tell the child such awful things about her father? Get out of here, you shameless liar. Eats our soup and our bread and has the impudence to slander our dead!

LILIOM. I didn't mean—I——

JULIE. What right have you to tell lies to the child? Take that plate, Louise, and let him be on his way. If he wasn't such a hungry-looking beggar, I'd put him out myself. (LOUISE *takes the plate out of his hand.*)

LILIOM. So he didn't hit you?

JULIE. No, never. He was always good to me.

LOUISE (*whispers*). Did he tell funny stories, too?

LILIOM. Yes, and *such* funny ones.

JULIE. Don't speak to him any more. In God's name, go.

LOUISE. In God's name.
(JULIE *resumes her seat at the table and eats.*)

LILIOM. If you please, Miss—I have a pack of cards in my pocket. And if you like, I'll show you some tricks that'll make you split your sides laughing. (LOUISE *holds* LILIOM's *plate in her left hand. With her right she reaches out and holds the garden gate shut*) Let me in, just a little way, Miss, and I'll do the tricks for you.

LOUISE. Go, in God's name, and let us be. Why are you making those ugly faces?

LILIOM. Don't chase me away, Miss; let me come in for just a minute—just for a minute—just long enough to let me show you something pretty, something wonderful. (*Opens the gate*) Miss, I've something to give you. (*Takes from his pocket a big red handkerchief in which is wrapped a glittering star from Heaven. He looks furtively about him to make sure that the* POLICE *are not watching.*)

LOUISE. What's that?

LILIOM. Pst! A star! (*With a gesture he indicates that he has stolen it out of the sky.*)

JULIE (*sternly*). Don't take anything from him. He's probably stolen it somewhere. (*To* LILIOM) In God's name, be off with you.

LOUISE. Yes, be off with you. Be off. (*She slams the gate.*)

LILIOM. Miss—please, Miss—I've got to do something good—or—do something good—a good deed——

LOUISE (*pointing with her right hand*). That's the way out.

LILIOM. Miss——

LOUISE. Get out!

LILIOM. Miss! (*Looks up at her suddenly and slaps her extended hand, so that the slap resounds loudly.*)

LOUISE. Mother! (*Looks dazedly at* LILIOM, *who bows his head dismayed, forlorn.* JULIE *rises and looks at* LILIOM *in astonishment. There is a long pause.*)

JULIE (*comes over to them slowly*). What's the matter here?

LOUISE (*bewildered, does not take her eyes off* LILIOM). Mother—the man—he hit me—on the hand—hard—I heard the sound of it—but it didn't hurt—mother—it didn't hurt—it was like a caress—as if he had just touched my hand tenderly. (*She hides behind* JULIE. LILIOM *sulkily raises his head and looks at* JULIE.)

JULIE (*softly*). Go, my child. Go into the house. Go.

LOUISE (*going*). But mother—I'm afraid—it sounded so loud—— (*Weepingly*) And it didn't hurt at all—just as if he'd—kissed my hand instead—mother! (*She hides her face.*)

JULIE. Go in, my child, go in. (*LOUISE goes slowly into the house.* JULIE *watches her until she has disappeared, then turns slowly to* LILIOM.)

JULIE. You struck my child.

LILIOM. Yes—I struck her.

JULIE. Is that what you came for, to strike my child?

LILIOM. No—I didn't come for that —but I did strike her—and now I'm going back.

JULIE. In the name of the Lord Jesus, who are you?

LILIOM (*simply*). A poor, tired beggar who came a long way and who was hungry. And I took your soup and bread and I struck your child. Are you angry with me?

JULIE (*her hand on her heart; fearfully, wonderingly*). Jesus pro-

rect me—I don't understand it—
I'm *not* angry—not angry at all——
(LILIOM *goes to the doorway and
leans against the doorpost, his back
to the audience.* JULIE *goes to the
table and sits.*)

JULIE. Louise! (LOUISE *comes out
of the house*) Sit down, dear, we'll
finish eating.

LOUISE. Has he gone?

JULIE. Yes. (*They are both seated
at the table.* LOUISE, *her head in
her hands, is staring into space*)
Why don't you eat, dear?

LOUISE. What has happened,
mother?

JULIE. Nothing, my child.
(*The* HEAVENLY POLICEMEN *appear
outside.* LILIOM *walks slowly off at
left. The* FIRST POLICEMAN *makes
a deploring gesture. Both shake
their heads deploringly and follow
LILIOM *slowly off at left.*)

LOUISE. Mother, dear, why won't
you tell me?

JULIE. What is there to tell you,
child? Nothing has happened. We
were peacefully eating, and a beggar came who talked of bygone
days, and then I thought of your
father.

LOUISE. My father?

JULIE. Your father—Liliom.
(*There is a pause.*)

LOUISE. Mother—tell me—has it
ever happened to you—has anyone
ever hit you—without hurting you
in the least?

JULIE. Yes, my child. It has happened to me, too.
(*There is a pause.*)

LOUISE. Is it possible for someone
to hit you—hard like that—real
loud and hard—and not hurt you at
all?

JULIE. It is possible, dear—that
someone may beat you and beat
you and beat you,—and not hurt
you at all.——
(*There is a pause. Nearby an organ-
grinder has stopped. The music of
his organ begins.*)

THE CURTAIN FALLS

Grand Hotel

BY VICKI BAUM

ADAPTED FROM THE GERMAN
BY WILLIAM A. DRAKE

Grand Hotel was first produced by Herman Shumlin on November 13, 1930, at the National Theatre, New York City, with the following cast:

GRUSINSKAIA	Eugenie Leontovitch
BARON VON GAIGERN	Henry Hull
KRINGELEIN	Sam Jaffe
FLAEMMCHEN (MISS FLAMM)	Hortense Alden
PREYSING	Siegfried Rumann
DR. OTTERNSCHLAG	Romaine Callender
WITTE	Lester Alden
SUZANNE	Raffaela Ottiano
MEIERHEIM	William Nunn
CHAUFFEUR	Joseph Spurin-Calleia
SENF	Walter Vonnegut
JUSTICE ZINNOWITZ	Harry D. Southard
DESK CLERK	Walter Baldwin
GERSTENKORN	Harry Hanlon
SCHWEIMANN	Stephen Irving
WAITZ	Richard Lloyd
RECEPTION MANAGER	Frank W. Taylor
CHAMBERMAID (ANNA)	Audrey Bauer
INSPECTRESS	Florence Pendleton
PORTER (SCHURMANN)	Fred Eckhart
GIGOLO	Milton LeRoy

Guests of the Hotel, Attendants of the Hotel, (Headwaiter, bellboys, bartenders, scrubwomen, carriage man, second porter, elevator boy, newsboy, policeman).

Time: The Present. The action takes place within thirty-six hours, in the Grand Hotel in Berlin.

GRAND HOTEL

ACT ONE

SCENE I

SCENE—*The stage is dark. In the foreground are six as yet unlighted telephone booths—three on each side of the* OPERATOR's *desk. As the occupants of the booths speak on phone their faces are illuminated by the overhead light in each booth which comes on as they speak and fades out at end of their respective conversations. In them are, right to left, in this order:* PREYSING, SUZANNE, GAIGERN, FLAEMMCHEN, SENF *and* KRINGELEIN. OPERATOR *is seated at switchboard. As the curtain rises the monotonous voice of the* TELEPHONE OPERATOR *is heard.*

TELEPHONE OPERATOR. Grand Hotel. Hold the wire. Grand Hotel. Hold the wire. Grand Hotel. Hold the wire. Grand Hotel. I am connecting you with 126. He arrived this evening. Grand Hotel. Fourteen checked out an hour ago. Grand Hotel. 235 does not answer. Hello. The gentlemen do not wish to be disturbed. Yes, and wife. Grand Hotel. Senf, your connection in booth two.

SENF (*light on in his booth*). This is Senf. Information desk. Grand Hotel. Yes. Is that you, Lisa? What is happening at the hospital? How is my wife? Is she in pain? What does the doctor say? Isn't the child coming soon? Patience? You can talk! Good Lord, no, I can't get away. Certainly not! I'd lose my job. Lord, I hope everything comes along all right. What? I can't hear you . . .
(*Light out.*)

TELEPHONE OPERATOR (*light on at switchboard*). Grand Hotel. Mr. Bloom's room does not answer. Mr.

Preysing, your long distance call to Fredersdorf. Booth three. Grand Hotel.
(*Light off at switchboard.*)

PREYSING (*light on in his booth*). Is that you, Mulle? Yes, this is me. Is everything all right at the factory? Yes, I've already eaten. What? Oh, so-so; better at home, really. How are the children? That's fine. Listen, dear, I'd like to speak to the old gentleman. Mulle —Mulle, I left my shaving set home. Well, until later Mulle. How are you, Father? Well, our stock is down to 162, today; yes, that's another drop of 23 points. We had to throw in eighty thousand to keep it from going lower. If that merger with Saxonia doesn't go through, it will be useless to do anything more to bolster up our stock. Hello! Hello! Yes, yes, on my responsibility. Leave it to me. Everything depends on what the Manchester firm decides to do. Absolutely everything. If we . . . Yes, miss, I'm still speaking. If the Manchester deal goes wrong we're in very bad shape. What am I doing about it? Waiting. Justice Zinnowitz is coming later and I'm going to talk to him about the whole business again.

FLAEMMCHEN (*light on in her booth*). Hello? Sure it's me—sure, Flaemmchen. What? Yes, at the Grand Hotel where we had such a nice dance together. No, I'm sorry I can't come tonight. Really not. Justice Zinnowitz told me to come here and take dictation from a friend of his. Oh, heavens, no! Sure. Give you my word. Oooooh, I couldn't say that over the telephone. Oh, now you're mad. After all, I've got to make a living. Oh, what a funny thing to say. I could die laughing when you talk like that.

KRINGELEIN (*light in his booth*). Who is that? This is . . . Hello. Hello. Who is that? Kampmann? This is Kringelein. Otto Kringelein, yes. I've got to speak very quickly. Every minute costs two marks ninety. Yes. I'm in Berlin—at the Grand Hotel. Listen Kampmann, you know that will I made before my operation—the will—I gave it to you, I want you to tear it up. Destroy it. Because—listen. I came to Berlin to see a great specialist about that old trouble of mine. . . . It's pretty bad, Kampmann. The specialist says I can't live much longer. (*Loudly*) I haven't long to live! That's what's the matter! No, it isn't nice to be told a thing like that. Listen, Kampmann, I've taken all my savings, my life insurance, too. I cashed in all my policies; the sick-benefit fund—the old-age pension and everything. I'm never coming back to Fredersdorf. Never. I want to get something out of life,

too. You plague and bother and save and all of a sudden you're dead. I'm trying to get a room here. The very best people stay here. Our big boss, Preysing, is staying here now. I saw him not five minutes ago in one of the lobbies. Sometime I'd like to tell him exactly what I think of him. Just think! There's music here all day long. And in the evening they go around in full dress. Everything is frightfully expensive here. You can imagine—the Grand Hotel! What? Time's up?
(*Light out.*)

GAIGERN (*light on in his booth*). Baron von Gaigern speaking. Yes. Good. No—first I need money. I need it right away. I've got to make a showing. That's my business. I've never fallen down on you yet. Listen—if a certain deal with Grusinskaia is to go through I must keep on the job every minute. . . . I've been playing bridge with her orchestra leader, Witte. His room connects with hers. That's a great advantage. I expect to do it tonight —at the theatre or after the show. But I have to have money—for hotel bills—for tips. I don't need advice; I need money!

SUZANNE (*light on in her booth*). No—I must speak to Mr. Meierheim himself. Yes, of course, the impresario—Mr. Meierheim. Oh, thank God, I've reached you at last, Monsieur Meierheim. This is Suzanne—Madame Grusinskaia's maid. Madame does not want to dance tonight. You'd better come to the hotel at once. Madame is crying. She is tired. I don't know what to do. Please hurry. Meanwhile, I'll try my best. . . .
(*Her light out.*)

OPERATOR. Grand Hotel. Just a moment, please. Grand Hotel.
(*Light on in the booth of the speaker as he speaks.*)

SENF. My wife—my wife—and what about the child?

PREYSING. A big deal—hundreds of thousands . . .

SUZANNE. This is Suzanne. Madame Grusinskaia's maid.

FLAEMMCHEN. I must take some dictation.

GAIGERN. Baron von Geigern speaking. I've got to have money.

KRINGELEIN. The specialist says I can't live much longer.

SENF. My wife . . .

FLAEMMCHEN. Take some dictation—I've got to . . .

GAIGERN. Money—money . . .

SUZANNE. Madame does not want to dance tonight.

PREYSING. If that Manchester deal goes wrong—
(*Crescendo of voices in lobby.*)

KRINGELEIN. I want to get something out of life.

GAIGERN. Not advice, money—

CLERK. Connect me with room 168.

OPERATOR. Grand Hotel. Grand Hotel. I'm ringing 168 . . .
(*Telephone bells ringing.*)

CURTAIN

SCENE II

SCENE—*The lobby of the hotel. Music plays throughout the scene, over the murmur of lobby voices and telephone bells. Voice of the PAGE BOY is heard calling MR. BLOOM. At the desk a CLERK is answering the telephone. A NERVOUS LADY is examining a timetable. ANDRÉ is seated, reading a newspaper. HANS is seated left of table, waiting expectantly. DOCTOR OTTERNSCHLAG is seated at a small table, immobile. FRANK and GERTRUDE are seated at small lounge, chatting over their cigarettes and drinks. RECEPTION MAN stands at attention near revolving door. WITTE is leaning against the desk.*

THIRD BELLBOY (*enters from corridor*). Call for Mr. Bloom. Call for Mr. Bloom. (*Exits into grill. DAISY enters through revolving door, stops to chat with RECEPTION MAN.*)

RECEPTION MAN (*to DAISY*). Did you find what you wanted?

(*WAITER enters from grill with a drink which he serves to MR. ANDRÉ.*)

DAISY. Yes. It was just as you said.

RECEPTION MAN. That's good.
(*DAISY goes to elevator, enters and door closes.*)

DESK CLERK (*at telephone*). 168, please. (*Second telephone rings.* CLERK *answers it, keeping the connection on the first phone*) You wish dinner served in your room? I'm sorry I can't take your order, but I'll connect you with room service. (*Jiggles hook*) Connect 225 with room service. (*Hangs up and talks over other phone*) Are you getting me 168?
(*Second phone rings.* CLERK *answers it.*)

WAITER. You ordered a dark, sir, didn't you? (*Serves* ANDRÉ *glass of beer.*)

ANDRÉ (*putting paper down and reaching for coin*). Dark, yes, that's fine. Thank you.

WAITER (*to* HANS). Would you like anything, sir? (*Takes coin from* ANDRÉ *and makes change.*)

HANS (*to* WAITER). No, I'm just waiting for someone.

ANDRÉ. If you find a copy of the *Abendpost* around, you might bring it to me like a good fellow.

WAITER. If I find one, sir, certainly. (*WAITER wipes table and removes glass and exits.* FOURTH BOY *enters from corridor and stands near desk.*)

DESK CLERK (*over second telephone*). Tomorrow? Yes. At three thirty-five? The Vienna Express. I'll be glad to make the reservation. When you come down? Yes, sir— there'll be time. Thank you. (*Hangs up and talks over first phone*) Is Madame Grusinskaia's car to be brought? Yes? Hello. No. Thank you. (*Hangs up. Rings desk bell.* SECOND BELLBOY *comes to desk and takes instructions from* CLERK) Madame Grusinskaia's car is not to be brought. (SECOND BELLBOY *exits, repeating message, "Madame Grusinskaia's car is not to be brought," as he goes.* DESK CLERK *turns to* WITTE) Did you hear that, Mr. Witte?

WITTE. The car will be brought. You may depend upon it.
(NERVOUS LADY *goes to end of desk.*)

CLERK. What do you mean, sir? (OTTERNSCHLAG *rises and walks slowly to desk.*)

WITTE. Nothing. Only that Madame Grusinskaia will go to the theatre. That is certain.

CLERK. Well, you ought to know.

NERVOUS LADY (*to* CLERK). When can I get a train for Troppau?

OTTERNSCHLAG. Any mail for me?

CLERK. No, Doctor.

OTTERNSCHLAG. Letter, telegram, nothing?

CLERK. Sorry. Nothing, Doctor.

OTTERNSCHLAG. Perhaps the Steward . . . ?

CLERK. The Steward will be right back. (OTTERNSCHLAG *goes back to his chair.* BARON VON GAIGERN *enters from grill, looks around the lobby, sees* WITTE *and goes to him quickly*) The best train leaves at 7:35, Madame. (GERSTENKORN *enters with traveling bag through revolving door.* RECEPTION MAN *greets him.* FOURTH BELLBOY *goes to* GERSTENKORN, *takes his bag, returns to upper end of desk)* That's the only through train. Shall I see about getting your tickets?

NERVOUS LADY. Are you sure I don't have to change?

CLERK. Quite sure, Madame.

GAIGERN (*to* WITTE *at desk*). Good evening, Mr. Witte.

WITTE. Good evening, Baron. How are you?

GAIGERN. Splendid, thank you. I'm glad I ran into you. How goes everything with Madame Grusinskaia?

WITTE. Tonight we are somewhat nervous. Last night was not so good. Were you at the theatre? (GERSTENKORN *registers.* CLERK *gives key to* RECEPTION MAN, *who gives it to* BELLBOY *and the three exit.* CLERK *goes to* NERVOUS LADY *and consults timetable.* SECOND BOY *enters revolving door and goes back to position near desk.* NERVOUS LADY *drops timetable.* BOY *picks it up.*)

GAIGERN. Always when Grusinskaia dances. I even went to Nice to see her.

WITTE. Yes. I remember seeing you there.

GAIGERN. Yes, yes. We always meet in hotel lobbies, don't we? I love the atmosphere.

WITTE. It is so quiet here.

GAIGERN. Quiet?

WITTE. Yes. If you had the room next to Madame Grusinskaia and were always at her beck and call, you would appreciate the relative quiet of the lobby.

GAIGERN (*hastily*). Why don't you move then? (OLD GENTLEMAN *enters corridor, goes quickly to desk*) I would gladly change rooms with you.

WITTE. I don't know how our Elizaveta Andreievna would get along without me.

OLD GENTLEMAN (*at desk*). I have two tickets for the Comedy Theatre for this evening. Parquet loges. Are the parquet chairs behind the parquet loges or in front of them? (ZINNOWITZ *enters, and goes to desk.*)

CLERK (*to* LADY *who is studying the timetable*). One moment. (*To* OLD GENTLEMAN) The parquet loges are behind the parquet chairs, sir.

OLD GENTLEMAN. Then they've put me back and I want to be in front. How is that? Chairs in front of loges!

KRINGELEIN (*enters from elevator. Goes to desk, evidently very angry To* CLERK). Listen.

ZINNOWITZ (*to* CLERK). Has Mr. Preysing arrived yet?

CLERK. One moment, gentlemen. (NERVOUS LADY *asks* ZINNOWITZ *for time*) The parquet loges are very good and they are less expensive. (*Desk telephone rings.* CLERK *answers it.* GAIGERN *and* WITTE *start to pace.* MRS. *and* MISS BLOOM *enter from corridor and exit to grill.*)

GAIGERN. I don't see why you shouldn't change your room, if you're disturbed too much. Does the woman own you?

WITTE. Yes, Baron, I'm quite indispensable to her. She needs me constantly. She knocks at my door. She calls me. She sends me away. She brings me back. I hardly belong to myself any more. You can't understand that, can you, Baron?

CLERK (*while* GAIGERN *and* WITTE *are speaking*). Desk. Yes. Hello. Certainly, Mr. Trent, I'll see. (*He goes to letter rack, examines mail and walks back to speak over the telephone*) Two letters, Mr. Trent. One from New York and one from London. Yes, I'll attend to it at once. Thank you.

GAIGERN. Why do you stay so close to her?

WITTE. Because she's marvelous. Because one cannot help adoring her. But I would move, only I am afraid she would feel hurt.

CLERK (*at phone*). Certainly, Madame Grusinskaia's car is to be brought. (*Rings for* BELLBOY.)

KRINGELEIN. Pardon me, but I am thoroughly dissatisfied. Listen!

CLERK. One moment, please.

ZINNOWITZ. Has Mr. Preysing . . . ?

CLERK. Mr. Preysing is making a long-distance call.

OLD GENTLEMAN. Will you please advise me what to do about the tickets?

NERVOUS LADY. The dining car is taken off at eight-thirty. And I wish to dine later than that.

KRINGELEIN (*louder*). I'm thoroughly dissatisfied. Do you hear? With my room 599.
(CLERK *rings desk bell.*)

CLERK (*to* SECOND BELLBOY). Madame Grusinskaia's car is to be brought.
(SECOND BELLBOY *goes through revolving door, repeating, "Madame Grusinskaia's car is to be brought."*)

ZINNOWITZ (*to* CLERK). If a young lady . . .

NERVOUS LADY. And what about breakfast?

OLD GENTLEMAN. Is the bill really worth ten marks?

KRINGELEIN. Will you please pay some attention to me?

CLERK. One moment, gentlemen. (SENF *enters through door at back of desk.*)

SENF (*to* NERVOUS LADY). The lady wishes . . . ?

(*Spoken together*)
LADY. I wish to know when the train leaves for Troppau.

OLD GENTLEMAN. Shall I have these seats changed?

SENF. The train leaves at 7:35. Friedrichstrasse station. Sleeper to Lemberg. Change there. Don't miss the connection. Dining car goes along. Suggest that you reserve a

place at the table d'hôte. See sleeping-car steward about breakfast. The clerk will take care of you. Please arrange for the lady's ticket. (NERVOUS LADY *goes to desk and talks with* CLERK. SECOND BOY *enters and stands by revolving door.* HANS *rises, looks around lobby and asks time of* ANDRÉ) How do you do, Justice Zinnowitz? Mr. Preysing will be here at once. He gave instructions to ask you to have a seat here in the lobby. (ZINNOWITZ *turns away from desk. To* OLD GENTLEMAN) Your seats are excellent. The acoustics are the best in the house. I could get them changed for you, but really . . . Believe me, sir, the bill is unusually interesting.
(OLD GENTLEMAN *exits.* HANS *goes to phone at desk.*)

ZINNOWITZ (*turning to* SENF). If my secretary asks for me, have her wait. (*Exits through grill.* OLD GENTLEMAN *enters from corridor.*)

SENF. Yes, sir. (*To* CLERK) My wife is suffering agonies.

OTTERNSCHLAG (*at desk*). Any letters for me?

SENF. Just a minute, Doctor. (*He looks at letter rack.*)

WITTE (*to* GAIGERN). Do you see that man? He has been here for six months. Every day he has to be asked whether he wants to leave. Yet he stays—always.

SENF. Sorry, Doctor, no messages. The Doctor has given notice about his room again. Does the Doctor wish to leave today?

OTTERNSCHLAG. No. Today—I think I shall stay.

(FRANK *and* GERTRUDE *rise and exit through revolving door.* DOCTOR *goes back to his table.*)

KRINGELEIN. I am thoroughly dissatisfied with my room.

SENF. Very sorry, sir. You know we haven't any other room vacant. It was hard to find one for you at all. (*To* CLERK) Has Madame Grusinskaia's car been ordered yet?

CLERK. The car has been ordered, sir.

KRINGELEIN. Naturally, Mr. Preysing got a quite different kind of room. Big, fine, stylish. In my room there's a bed, a table and two chairs.

SENF. It is a very nicely furnished room, sir. And inexpensive.

KRINGELEIN. But I don't want an inexpensive room. I want the very best. I can get a room like that in Fredersdorf. (FLAEMMCHEN *enters through revolving door and goes to desk*) I came here three times before you even gave me a room. And you give me 599. What a room! Just a room! What is there Grand Hotel about that room? I ask you?

FLAEMMCHEN (*at desk*). Justice Zinnowitz, please.
(HANS *hangs up phone, finds seat occupied, and slowly exits to grill.*)

SENF (*to* KRINGELEIN). One moment, sir. (*To* FLAMM) Are you Justice Zinnowitz' secretary?
(OLD GENTLEMAN *rises and exits through corridor.*)

FLAEMMCHEN. Yes. I was told to come here. . . .

SENF. Justice Zinnowitz asked that you wait in the lobby.

(GIGOLO *and* GIGOLO LADY *enter from grill and exit through corridor.*)

KRINGELEIN. Please do not pay so much attention to the young lady. I have been waiting a good deal longer. Pay a little attention to me, please. I am telling you that that is no Grand Hotel room. (FLAEMM-CHEN *goes to table and sits on bench*) It is a very ordinary room, and I want as good as Dr. Preysing. . . .

(BARON *is giving* FLAEMMCHEN *the onceover.*)

SENF. Very sorry, sir, but Mr. Preysing wired his reservation in advance. Perhaps it can be arranged later.

(*Elevator comes down.* FOURTH BOY *enters from it and stands at desk.* EMILE *enters from elevator and exits through revolving door.* NERVOUS LADY *exits to elevator.*)

KRINGELEIN. But you must understand. I can't wait. I have no time. (RECEPTION MAN *enters from corridor. Elevator goes up*) Every day counts; every hour, every minute. I came here because I want to live here two weeks, or three . . . God only knows—I'll pay—I'll pay whatever you ask.

SENF. We have no doubt that you want to pay, sir.

RECEPTION MAN (*turning to desk*). Has the gentleman a complaint?

KRINGELEIN (*turns suddenly to* RE-CEPTION MAN. WITTE *rises and listens*). I certainly have got a complaint. I want to stay here. I've come from a long distance away to stay at the Grand Hotel. I want to live well, just as other people do; (HANS *enters from grill*) just as Mr. Preysing does. Exactly as he does. I want to live here awhile, do you understand? I've got the money. (RECEPTION MAN *walks over to desk*, KRINGELEIN *follows him*. WITTE *approaches them*) I am sick, I am tired. And you give me a tiny little room, way off in a corner, where the water pipes make a racket.

WITTE. Really, why don't you give the gentleman another room, if it means so much to him? If he is ill?

RECEPTION MAN (*turns away from desk*). At present it is quite impossible, Mr. Witte. Perhaps tomorrow.

KRINGELEIN.   Tomorrow—you're just saying that. Tomorrow! (*To* WITTE) I want it now! (*To* RE-CEPTION MAN) I need it.

RECEPTION MAN. I wish I could help you, but we haven't another room.

WITTE (*to* RECEPTION MAN). Then give the gentleman my room. (BARON *gets up and goes close to* WITTE. DR. OTTERNSCHLAG *turns in his chair*) I will take the little room off in a corner, where the water pipes make a racket.

(GIGOLO *and* GIGOLO LADY *enter from corridor and talk to each other.*)

RECEPTION MAN (*shocked*). But Mr. Witte. You wouldn't . . .

GAIGERN (*hastily*). Oh, Mr. Witte, don't do that!

KRINGELEIN. Permit me! My name is Kringelein. From Fredersdorf.

WITTE. Witte.

GAIGERN (*very quickly*). Baron von Gaigern.

KRINGELEIN (*cannot believe his ears*). Baron . . . !

GAIGERN. Von Gaigern.

OTTERNSCHLAG (*quietly still sitting. All turn and look at him*). If the gentleman feels so keenly about it, he can have my room. It doesn't make the slightest difference to me where I stay. Have his baggage taken up. My trunks are packed. Please. One can see that the gentleman is fatigued and ill. . . . Anyway, I am leaving at any moment.

KRINGELEIN (*astonished to find himself suddenly surrounded by three fine gentlemen*). I don't know. Thanks. I have . . .
(GIGOLO *and* GIGOLO LADY *exit to corridor.*)

WITTE (*firmly, going over to the* DOCTOR). No. Permit me. My room. I wish it very much. (*Turning to* KRINGELEIN) Mr. Kringelein will have the room next to Madame Grusinskaia!
(RECEPTION MAN *goes to upper end of desk.*)

KRINGELEIN. Madame Grusinskaia! The one who has her picture in all the illustrated papers?
(*Phone rings.*)

WITTE. The same. Madame Grusinskaia, who has her picture in all the illustrated papers. Lisaveta Andreievna, the celebrated dancer,

owner of the Sergei pearls. Mr. Kringelein, you will be her neighbor!

CLERK. Mr. Witte, you are asked to come at once to Madame Grusinskaia.

WITTE. There! I'll pack my trunk. The ballet property issues a declaration of independence. (*Exits through corridor after bowing to* BARON *and* KRINGELEIN.)

RECEPTION MAN (*at desk, to* SENF). Very well, see to it. . . . Especially that Mr. Witte is made as comfortable as possible. (*Crosses and exits to grill room.*)

SENF (*at phone*). Number 599 changes with 169. (*To* KRINGELEIN) The change will be made at once, Mr. Kringelein. Number 169. Room with bath. (*Rings bell.*)

KRINGELEIN. With bath?

SENF (*to* BOY). Show the gentleman to 169.

OTTERNSCHLAG. Well, you are fixed up. Yes?
(*Elevator door opens.* KATIE *enters, goes to* HANS *and exits with him, after a brief greeting, through revolving door.*)

KRINGELEIN. Yes. . . . Thanks. . . .
(*To* GAIGERN *as* DR. OTTERNSCHLAG *turns front*) Does that mean that the bath is all my own? Private?

GAIGERN (*smiling*). Certainly.

KRINGELEIN. Thanks, many thanks, Baron. It certainly was kind of you and Mr. Witte. I guess I had better go pack now. (*Starts towards ele-*

vator) I will make the change very quickly. I have not much time.

GAIGERN. Mr. Kringelein, when you are ready, meet me here in the lobby. We'll have a cocktail together.

KRINGELEIN (*stops in his tracks, astounded*). What? Do you mean— we'll have a drink together? (GAIGERN *nods.*)

FOURTH BOY. This way, please.

KRINGELEIN (*going into elevator*). Oh, thank you, thank you. (WAITER *from grill goes to table and wipes it.* GIGOLO *and* GIGOLO LADY *enter from corridor and stand talking.* KRINGELEIN *and* FOURTH BOY *exit into elevator.* GAIGERN *looks after him, smiling, turns and looks at* FLAEMMCHEN, *begins to flirt with her. She smiles at him.* PREYSING *and* ZINNOWITZ *appear simultaneously.* PREYSING *from corridor,* ZINNOWITZ *from grill room, followed by* FIRST WAITER *with drink.* FLAEMMCHEN *looks serious at once; acquaintance is out of the question.*)

PREYSING (*at desk, hastily to* SENF). Still no telegram for Preysing?

CLERK. Nothing here, Mr. Preysing.

ZINNOWITZ (*goes to* PREYSING. *Shakes hands with him*). How are you, Preysing?

PREYSING. Oh, hello, Zinnowitz. (FIRST WAITER *serves* ANDRÉ.)

ZINNOWITZ. How is everything, Preysing?

PREYSING. Fine, thanks.

ZINNOWITZ. And your wife?

PREYSING. Fine, thanks. (*To* SENF) If a telegram comes, have it sent to me at once.

SENF. Yes, sir.

ZINNOWITZ. How about that Manchester deal? (*They walk across stage.*)

PREYSING. It must go through. It *must,* I tell you.

ZINNOWITZ. I hope so. (FLAEMMCHEN *rises and goes over to* ZINNOWITZ. BARON *thinks she is coming to speak to him*) But if it doesn't . . .

FLAEMMCHEN. Justice Zinnowitz! (GAIGERN *disappointedly goes to table and sits near it.*)

ZINNOWITZ. Ah, Flaemmchen! Here you are! Permit me to introduce . . . Miss Flamm—Mr. Preysing. This is the young lady who is to take your dictation.

PREYSING. Oh! I had supposed you would be much older.

FLAEMMCHEN. I can't help being young.

ZINNOWITZ. And shall we say beautiful, Flaemmchen? She is a very reliable worker.

PREYSING (*cooler*). You may sit down, Miss Flamm. (*He beckons to* WAITER) Give the young lady what she wants. On my account— Preysing, Room 170.

FLAEMMCHEN. Thank you. (*She returns to settee.* WAITER *follows her and presents wine card.* THIRD BOY *enters from grill and goes to desk. He stands at attention.*)

PREYSING. And wait here, Miss Flamm. (*To* ZINNOWITZ) Zinnowitz, you must become thoroughly acquainted (*takes him by the arm. They turn and walk*) with the whole situation about this merger.

ZINNOWITZ. Yes, but not too thoroughly, Preysing. (CHAUFFEUR *enters revolving door, cigarette in mouth. Looks around the lobby*) Ten minutes at the most. I have a little dinner engagement.

PREYSING. Perhaps first we'd better go where we can be alone. I want to show you the figures. (*They exit through corridor, followed by* GIGOLO *and* GIGOLO LADY.)

FLAEMMCHEN (*to* WAITER). How about a champagne flip? (WAITER *bows and exits to grill.* FLAEMMCHEN *takes out a cigarette, but does not light it.*)

CHAUFFEUR (*looking toward* GAIGERN). Have you time now, sir?

GAIGERN. Well, what is it?

CHAUFFEUR. Can I see you for a moment, please? (GAIGERN *goes to him.* DR. OTTERNSCHLAG *turns to watch them for a moment.*)

GAIGERN. Cigarette out of your mouth when you speak to me. How many times must I tell you? You're giving us away. Where's the money?

CHAUFFEUR (*takes small envelope*

from inside his cap and gives it to GAIGERN). Here's a hundred.

GAIGERN. I've got to have more money. It costs like the devil to live here.

CHAUFFEUR. Finish the job and then you'll get more money. You've had plenty already. We know how that goes. Always money. We want results.

GAIGERN. I can't rush it. I send her orchids every day. I . . .

CHAUFFEUR. You send her orchids! What's the idea? Are you in love with her? (LOUISE *enters through revolving door. Looks about lobby and out to corridor. Goes to table and sits in chair near it.* GIGOLO *and* GIGOLO LADY *enter from corridor and stand talking.*)

GAIGERN. Don't be a fool. I merely play the part of an infatuated admirer. I had hoped to get into her room through her orchestra leader, Witte. But he has changed rooms at the last minute with some funny provincial. Now I've got to get on good terms with him. That will take time. (MARGARET *enters through revolving door and greets* LOUISE.)

CHAUFFEUR. Tomorrow night she'll be leaving.

GAIGERN. Tomorrow I'll do it.

CHAUFFEUR. Tonight. (NEWLYWEDS *and* CARRIAGE MAN *enter.*)

GAIGERN. Tomorrow.

CHAUFFEUR. Tonight. I'll have the car here about twelve.

GAIGERN. I'll do my best. Give me some more money.

CHAUFFEUR. Tonight at twelve I'll give you all the money. (*Elevator comes down.* NERVOUS LADY *followed by* SCHURMANN *with bag enters from elevator. She goes to desk, tips* SCHURMANN, *who exits.* NEWLYWED *tips* CARRIAGE MAN. WAITER *enters from grill, serves drink to* FLAEMMCHEN, *and makes out check*) You were to get sixty thousand. You've had six already, Mr. Baron.

GAIGERN. I'll do what I can. (*Aloud*) You may go now, thanks. (*Elevator goes up.*)

CHAUFFEUR (*aloud*). Thank you, sir.
(*Ensemble voices swell.* NERVOUS

LADY *asks for bill.* CHAUFFEUR *exits through revolving door.* MEIERHEIM *dashes in.*)

MEIERHEIM (*hurriedly, at desk*). Madame Grusinskaia is still here? (*Ensemble voices die down.*)

SENF. Madame is still in her room, Mr. Meierheim.

MEIERHEIM (*excitedly*). My God and the performance soon starting. (*Goes to elevator and pushes button*) Quick. Quick. Bring her car.

SENF. Madame Grusinskaia's car.

CLERK (*ringing desk bell*). Madame Grusinskaia's car.

THIRD BELLBOY (*going to revolving door*). Madame Grusinskaia's car. (*Voice of the* CLERK *over telephone at curtain,* "Madame, shall the car be brought?")

CURTAIN

SCENE III

SCENE—GRUSINSKAIA'S *room furnished with banal hotel elegance. On the table there is a clock. To the right there is a chaise longue, and behind it a telephone table. At the left there is a dressing table. There are two doors: one leading into the dressing room and the other into the hall. There is an armchair between the hall door and dressing table. A clothes rack stands beside the door to* WITTE'S *room. A small jewel casket on the dressing table lies open showing a necklace of pearls. The telephone is ringing.* SUZANNE, *the silent, faded and elderly factotum of* GRUSINSKAIA, *stands before dressing table with ballet shoes in her hand. She answers phone.*

SUZANNE. Madame Grusinskaia's room. One moment, please. (*Calling off stage*) Madame, the steward asks if the car shall be brought.

GRUSINSKAIA (*from dressing room*). No.

SUZANNE. But it is time—if Madame wishes to practice before the performance.

GRUSINSKAIA. I don't. You know I don't want to tonight.

SUZANNE. But, Madame . . .

GRUSINSKAIA. No.

SUZANNE (*at phone*). Thank you, no. Later. Yes, I will tell you at the right time. (*Hangs up, goes to chair and puts ribbons in ballet slippers.* GRUSINSKAIA *enters. She is a tender, emotional woman, in the late thirties, still very beautiful, Pavlowa type, wearing a Russian dressing gown.*)

GRUSINSKAIA (*goes to door*). Witte! Witte! (*Knocks on door.* SUZANNE *rises*) Witte! (*Listens*) He isn't there.

SUZANNE (*goes to phone*). He may be in the lobby. (*Over phone*) Hello. Will you please find Mr. Witte and tell him to come to Madame Grusinskaia's room? Thank you. (*Hangs up.*)

GRUSINSKAIA (*at door, softly*). Even Witte now doesn't stay there in the next room, waiting, ready, to come when I knock!
(*A knock at door.* SUZANNE *goes to door.* ELEVATOR BOY *with box of flowers enters.*)

ELEVATOR BOY. For Madame Grusinskaia.

SUZANNE. I'll take them. (*ELEVATOR BOY exits and closes door.* SUZANNE *walks toward chaise longue, opening box.* GRUSINSKAIA *sits on chaise longue*) Orchids again, Madame. No card.

GRUSINSKAIA. I like it better when there is no card.

SUZANNE. Surely from the young man . . .

GRUSINSKAIA (*examining orchids*). We met in Nice? He is very good-looking.

SUZANNE. The flowers will bring us luck. Huge, beautiful orchids. From a young man who sits in the theatre night after night and applauds. Madame is only nervous.

GRUSINSKAIA. No, Suzanne. I am tired, Suzanne. I think I was never so tired in my life.
(*A knock.*)

SUZANNE. Come in!
(WITTE *enters.*)

WITTE (*going up to Madame behind couch*). Did you call me? Forgive me. I was in the lobby.

GRUSINSKAIA. I wanted to see you, Witte. Nothing else. Why were you not in your room?

WITTE (*close to her, smiling*). Lisaveta Andreievna is a disturbing neighbor.

SUZANNE (*putting orchids on table*). Madame has a touch of stage fright this evening.

GRUSINSKAIA. No, it is more than that. I am afraid, Witte, terribly afraid.

WITTE. It will pass, Lisaveta.

SUZANNE. As soon as Madame is on the stage.

GRUSINSKAIA. No, I cannot dance tonight.

WITTE. But in Brussels you were just as tired, after the rough passage from England, and then you danced so wonderfully, and we had such an ovation. . . .

GRUSINSKAIA. But last night there was no applause. And if I dance tonight . . . No, I will not dance. I am so tired—here, and here. (*Points to her heart and her forehead. Suddenly*) Witte—let us cancel the engagement.

SUZANNE (*shocked*). But you cannot do that!

WITTE. Madame has never canceled!

(*Simultaneously*) { SUZANNE. One can't cancel!

WITTE. No!

GRUSINSKAIA. Oh, yes, one can! One can cancel; one can quit entirely. Now is the time. I feel it. (*She rises, goes to dressing table*) Assez! everything tells me "assez," enough, enough. (*She takes from jewel casket the loop of pearls.*)

WITTE (*taking a step toward Madame*). You are only overwrought, Lisaveta.

GRUSINSKAIA. No, Witte, I feel— everything growing cold around me. (*Presses pearls against her forehead*) The Grand Duke Sergei is dead. His pearls are dead. And we are dead, too. (*Sits at dressing table, facing front*) Passé! Finished.

SUZANNE. No, no, Madame, everything is as good as it always was.

GRUSINSKAIA. No, everything is threadbare now. The Russians—the pearls—Grusinskaia—oh . . . (*She throws her pearls at her feet.*)

(*Spoken together.*) { SUZANNE (*picking up pearls*). Mon Dieu! The pearls! If something were to break!

WITTE. Please, Lisaveta.

GRUSINSKAIA. They don't break. They hold together and bring me bad luck. This is no life for me any more. Ballet shoes—divertissements —attitudes . . .

WITTE. Madame will certainly have a great success tonight.

GRUSINSKAIA. I shall have no success tonight—nor tomorrow . . . I'll never again have any success. No. This is the end. I am going to retire from the stage. That is all. (*The phone rings.* SUZANNE *goes to answer.*)

SUZANNE. No, no, Madame! (*At phone*) Yes. One moment. The chauffeur is calling, Madame. He is waiting with the car.

GRUSINSKAIA. I don't want it! (*Rises and goes to couch*) I didn't tell them to send it.

SUZANNE. He came of his own accord. He knew it was time to take you to the theatre.

GRUSINSKAIA. I won't go. I want to be left alone. Send the car away.

SUZANNE (*into phone*). Madame does not want the car now. No. (*Hangs up.*)

GRUSINSKAIA (*sitting on couch*). I am very unhappy, Witte. I am tired. I am so alone. . . .

SUZANNE. Come—Madame must dress.

WITTE. It is time, Lisaveta. You must go to the theatre.

GRUSINSKAIA. Please don't say "must." Witte, please help me.

WITTE (*sits beside her*). Lisaveta, if I only could. How can I help you?
(*There is a knock at the door and it is flung open. The impresario,* MEIERHEIM, *dashes in.* WITTE *rises.*)

MEIERHEIM. What does this mean? Madame here in negligee an hour before the performance? (*Curtly nods to* WITTE *and* SUZANNE) How do, Witte, how do, Suzanne. (MEIERHEIM *takes off his hat and throws it on chair*) This simply will not do. I nearly had a stroke. I was so excited. I sit in the theatre and wait and wait. No, my dear lady, it simply will not do. If you don't keep discipline, what do you expect of the troupe? Listen! You have obligations, Madame; you have received money; we have a contract and you can't persist in coming late.

GRUSINSKAIA. I am not coming late. I am canceling the engagement. (*She lies back on couch, her head upright.*)

MEIERHEIM. Oh, so you cancel— you cancel! And who is to dance?

GRUSINSKAIA. That doesn't matter to me. Desprez, I suppose! (*Covers face with hands.*)

MEIERHEIM. Desprez! Desprez! People aren't paying thirty marks to see Desprez.

WITTE. Lisaveta, my dear, my dear!

SUZANNE. Madame isn't tired a bit any more.

MEIERHEIM. Pardon me. (*Pushes* WITTE *out of his way*) Leave this to me. Shut up, Witte. (*To Madame*) Madame, you will dance. You are too great an artist to go on being temperamental. You cannot disappoint your public. The theatre is jammed to the rafters. I simply will not hear of a cancellation. There's been a line in front of the box office since six o'clock. Come! Quick! Get dressed!
(*During speech* GRUSINSKAIA *slowly takes hands from face.*)

GRUSINSKAIA. Is there really a full house tonight?

MEIERHEIM. Doesn't Meierheim say so? The Crown Prince made reservations. Two foreign ministers; Mary Wigman came from Dresden just to see you. (GRUSINSKAIA *sits up*) Max Reinhardt is bringing a couple of American millionaires. And now, shall Desprez take your place?

GRUSINSKAIA. All right. (*Rises from couch*) Wait for me in the lobby. I'll be ready in ten minutes. (*She hurriedly exits to dressing room*) Suzanne!
(SUZANNE *quickly follows, putting pearls on dressing table as she goes.*)

MEIERHEIM. Honey, darling, what do you mean, ten minutes? This minute! (*Notices the necklace on dressing table*) Witte! Suzanne! Pick up those pearls. (*Goes to dresser and picks up pearls*) God almighty! How you leave jewelry lying around, all over the room! I'll take them myself. (*Puts pearls in case.*)

GRUSINSKAIA (*off stage*). No. Don't bring the pearls. I will dance for heaven's sake, but not with the pearls.

MEIERHEIM. What do you mean, without the pearls? You can't go on without the pearls. Now come on— hurry! The audience is there. The orchestra is there. It isn't possible that the curtain will go up and— Grusinskaia won't dance.
(GRUSINSKAIA *enters and rushes up to* WITTE. MEIERHEIM *goes to phone, jiggles receiver.*)

GRUSINSKAIA (*seized by the fever of the theatre*). Witte! But suppose I fail tonight?

WITTE. You will not fail, Madame. You will dance more wonderfully tonight than ever before.

SUZANNE (*at doorway*). Which coat, Madame?

GRUSINSKAIA. The green one. (SUZANNE *brings coat and bathrobe*) And bring the orchids.
(SUZANNE *helps her on with coat.*)

SUZANNE. The pearls too? (*Goes to get pearls, throwing bathrobe on chair.*)

GRUSINSKAIA (*rushing out, followed by* WITTE). Oh, I suppose so.
(SUZANNE *goes to table, gets orchids and rushes after her.*)

MEIERHEIM (*at telephone triumphantly*). Order the car for Madame Grusinskaia! (*Hangs up phone, grabs his hat and rushes out after them.*)

CURTAIN

SCENE IV

SCENE—*Lobby: as in scene two at fall of curtain. This scene is an immediate continuation of Scene II and is supposed to be simultaneous with Scene III.* GAIGERN *is going toward* FLAEMMCHEN *who is seated on settee.* OTTERNSCHLAG *is seated at right of table.* GIGOLO *and* GIGOLO LADY *are on stage.* ANDRÉ *is seated at table.* BRIDE *and* GROOM *are at desk, registering.* NERVOUS LADY *is at desk.* SENF *and* CLERK *are behind desk and* SECOND BOY *is near desk.* LOUISE *sits at table.* MARGARET *stands near her.* WAITER *is at left of revolving door. Telephone rings and voice of* CLERK *is heard speaking at telephone.* "Three bags and a trunk, sir?" GAIGERN *goes to* FLAEMMCHEN *and lights her cigarette, saying,* "May I?"

GAIGERN. I believe we met in Baden-Baden. (LOUISE *and* MARGARET *exit.* THIRD BOY *enters through revolving door*) Didn't we have a very pleasant dance there?

FLAEMMCHEN. No. I was never in Baden-Baden.
(GIGOLO LADY *goes to desk, gets key, and exits through corridor.* GIGOLO *exits through revolving door.*)

GAIGERN. I beg your pardon. I mistook you for someone else.

FLAEMMCHEN (*laughing*). You needn't try to work that old game on me. You know very well you never saw me before.

GAIGERN. Well, no more fooling then. May I sit down? (*He sits*) As a matter of fact, nobody would ever take you for somebody else. You are so exceedingly yourself. (*Telephone at desk rings*) Would you like to dance?
(SENF *calls* THIRD BELLBOY *to desk for key.* BELLBOY *takes* NEWLYWEDS' *bag. They go toward elevator.* BELLBOY *says:* "This way please," *and leads them out through corridor.* SECOND BOY *gets* NERVOUS LADY'S *bag.* DAISY *enters from grill, goes to desk for inquiry, and exits through corridor.*)

FLAEMMCHEN. Well, you certainly lose no time. I can't now. I have to wait. Later in the evening I could.
(CLERK *exits from desk with bill.*)

GAIGERN. Later in the evening I can't. I have to go to the theatre, to see Grusinskaia dance.

FLAEMMCHEN. Really have to?
(WAITZ *enters through revolving* door. *Goes to desk and talks over phone.* WAITER *exits to grill.*)

GAIGERN. Really have to. It's of the greatest importance to me. Too bad, isn't it?
(FOURTH BOY *enters from corridor with telegrams. Gives them to* SENF. CLERK *enters door to desk with bills.*)

FLAEMMCHEN. Too awfully bad. You're probably in love with Grusinskaia.

GAIGERN. I could be. I probably am.

FLAEMMCHEN. What does she look like?

GAIGERN. To me she is radiantly beautiful. But I like you better for the moment. What is your name?

FLAEMMCHEN. They call me Flaemmchen. My name is Christine Flamm.

GAIGERN. Flaemmchen? Is that it? Shall we meet here tomorrow in the afternoon?

FLAEMMCHEN. Here?

GAIGERN (*smiling*). Here. In the lobby. All right.

FLAEMMCHEN. Honor bright?

GAIGERN. Honor bright.
(SENF *rings desk bell.* FOURTH BOY *goes to desk.*)

SENF (*giving him telegram*). Telegram for 168.
(*Elevator comes down.* MEIERHEIM *comes from elevator followed by* WITTE, GRUSINSKAIA, SUZANNE.

SUZANNE *is carrying jewel casket and orchids.* GAIGERN, *seeing* GRUSINSKAIA, *goes toward her and bows.*)

FOURTH BOY (*at desk*). 168. Yes, sir.

SENF. There's your party. Hurry, quick! (*To* GRUSINSKAIA) Telegram for Madame Grusinskaia.

MEIERHEIM. Come on, hurry. We'll be late ringing up. Come on, Witte. (*To* SENF) What?
(DR. OTTERNSCHLAG *turns around for a moment.*)

FOURTH BOY. Telegram, Madame. (*She takes telegram.*)

GRUSINSKAIA. Here. (*She takes telegram and opens it automatically, looking at* GAIGERN *who has taken a step toward her.* FOURTH BOY *exits through revolving door.* NERVOUS LADY *goes to* SECOND BELLBOY *and gives him a steamer rug.*)

MEIERHEIM. Read it after the performance. There isn't time now.

GRUSINSKAIA (*agitated. Reading telegram*). Always. Always. Worse and worse luck.

MEIERHEIM. For God's sake, what now?

GRUSINSKAIA. The guest engagement at Budapest is canceled. Lack of interest. O *père celeste.* This is the end. I dance no more with the pearls.

SUZANNE. *Mon dieu!*
(RECEPTION MAN *enters from grill.*)

WITTE. Lisaveta, Lisaveta, how can you be so superstitious?

GRUSINSKAIA. How can I help it? (*To* SUZANNE) Take them back to the room.
(SUZANNE *exits to elevator with pearls.*)

WITTE (*going to revolving door with* GRUSINSKAIA). My dear, my dear! (*They exit through revolving door.* RECEPTION MAN *turns door for them as they go out.*)

MEIERHEIM (*to* SENF *at desk*). You think you're a hotel steward and you don't know that a telegram should never be delivered to an artist—before a performance. (*Exits through revolving door.*)
(RECEPTION MAN *goes to end of desk.* CHAUFFEUR *enters through revolving door.* NERVOUS LADY *goes to desk for ticket.*)

WAITZ (*at desk. Over phone*). Yes? Gerstenkorn? Yes.

CHAUFFEUR (*walking toward* GAIGERN). Time to go to the theatre, sir.
(CLERK *gets key from* NERVOUS LADY. *She goes to* SECOND BOY. EMILE *and* CLARA *enter through revolving door and go to elevator.*)

GAIGERN. We do not go to the theatre tonight. She left the pearls in her room.
(NERVOUS LADY *and* SECOND BOY *exit through revolving door.* CLERK *exits from desk.*)

CHAUFFEUR. The hell you say!

GAIGERN. Meet me south door, twelve o'clock. (*Aloud*) You may have the evening off.

CHAUFFEUR. Thank you, sir. (*He exits through revolving door.* RE-

CEPTION MAN *stands near revolving door.*)

WAITZ (*over phone*). All right, then, I'll come right up.

GAIGERN (*going to* FLAEMMCHEN). Well, Flaemmchen, I am delighted to be able to tell you that I am not going to leave you after all. (CLERK *enters behind desk.*)

FLAEMMCHEN. I thought you absolutely had to go to the theatre.

GAIGERN. No, I've changed my mind.

FLAEMMCHEN. But why not?

GAIGERN. Perhaps because in the meantime (*Elevator comes down.* KRINGELEIN *and* THIRD BOY *enter from elevator.* EMILE *and* CLARA *enter elevator. Elevator goes up.* THIRD BOY *stands near desk*) I've met someone I like.

FLAEMMCHEN. Yes, you have. (KRINGELEIN *goes to desk. He is now dressed in a clerk's Sunday clothes.*)

KRINGELEIN. I'm packed. You can change me now. (*DAISY enters from corridor. Goes to manager. They talk.* DR. OTTERN-SCHLAG *rises.*)

GAIGERN. There's my friend Kringelein. I want you to be very nice to him, Flaemmchen. (*DOCTOR walks toward* KRINGELEIN.)

FLAEMMCHEN (*laughing*). Why not? It's easy to be nice. (WAITZ *exits.* GAIGERN *goes to* KRINGELEIN.)

OTTERNSCHLAG (*to* KRINGELEIN). Well, did you get fixed up? (*FORTNER enters through revolving door, crosses to desk and talks over house phone.*)

KRINGELEIN. Yes, thanks.

GAIGERN. Good evening, Mr. Kringelein. I thought you were never coming. (*Takes him by arm and they approach* FLAEMMCHEN, *taking the* DOCTOR'S *chair.*)

KRINGELEIN. Ah, the Baron is so kind. (*As* GAIGERN *takes the chair and places it for* KRINGELEIN *opposite* FLAEMMCHEN, SENF *gives* THIRD BELLBOY *a card.* BELLBOY *exits to grill.* DR. OTTERNSCHLAG *watches* KRINGELEIN *seat himself, then goes to get chair and sits watching.*)

GAIGERN. What do you say we have a little dinner party? Would you like that? Just the three of us. (*FORTNER goes to elevator. Introducing* KRINGELEIN) Permit me. Mr. Kringelein of Fredersdorf— Flaemmchen . . . (*KRINGELEIN sits at table facing* FLAEMMCHEN. GAIGERN *stands to the right of* KRINGELEIN. SECOND BELLBOY *enters through revolving door, goes to desk, speaks to* SENF, *and exits to corridor.*)

FLAEMMCHEN (*to* KRINGELEIN). And have you a nice room now? I heard you making a complaint a while ago.

KRINGELEIN. Thanks very much. A marvelous room. Bed. Carpets. Furniture. All the very best and a bronze statue on the table, a man on a horse. (GAIGERN *and* FLAEMM-CHEN *laugh*) Pardon me. Undoubtedly you are accustomed to things like that.

GAIGERN. I'm glad you got what you wanted.
(*Elevator comes down.* MRS. *and* MISS BLOOM *enter from grill slowly, talking, and exit to corridor.* FORTNER *enters elevator. Elevator goes up.* OLD GENTLEMAN *enters from corridor and exits through revolving door.*)

KRINGELEIN. I certainly have. I had the amusement guide book sent up. I'd like to see something. Have a big time. Drink champagne, for instance. It's expensive, I know. I looked on the card. You can't get it for less than twelve marks. But that makes no difference. I'd like to eat caviar too—(RECEPTION MAN *and* DAISY *cross to desk and talk to* SENF) for the first time in my life. (FLAEMMCHEN *laughs*) I see the lady is laughing.

FLAEMMCHEN. Have caviar if you like. But it tastes like herring.

KRINGELEIN. Caviar and champagne may mean nothing to you, but to me they mean a great deal. You see, sir, I'm ill and all of a sudden I got a fear, such a fear, of missing life. (THIRD BELLBOY *enters from corridor and stands at desk*) I don't want to miss life— do you understand?

FLAEMMCHEN. Funny. You talk of life as if it were a train you wanted to catch.
(CLERK *exits.*)

KRINGELEIN (*desk telephone rings.* CLERK *answers it*). Yes, and for me it is going to leave any minute. I'm not at all well.

GAIGERN. Well, Mr. Kringelein what do you say we make a really big night? Would you like that?

KRINGELEIN. Yes, indeed.

GAIGERN. And Flaemmchen comes along too, don't you, Flaemmchen?

FLAEMMCHEN. No, worse luck, I've been engaged for the evening.
(SECOND WAITER *enters from corridor, with tray of glasses. Exits to grill.*)

KRINGELEIN. Oh, can a person just engage you for the evening?

FLAEMMCHEN. Yes, to take dictation. A Mr. Preysing.

KRINGELEIN. Mr. Preysing! Of course! It would be Preysing! That's just like him.

FLAEMMCHEN. Do you know him?

KRINGELEIN. Do I know him? Do I know him! (PREYSING *and* ZINNOWITZ *enter from corridor.* RECEPTION MAN *starts toward grill*) I know him through and through. I'd give a good deal—to settle my accounts with him.

PREYSING (*to* RECEPTION MAN *as they cross over to grill*). I engaged the conference room for seven o'clock. See that it's ready. (*To* ZINNOWITZ) We can talk there without being interrupted. RECEPTION MAN *goes to desk. They stop a few feet away from grill-room door as soon as they see* FLAEMMCHEN) Oh, Miss Flaemmchen, we shall need you very soon.
(KRINGELEIN *rises on hearing*

PREYSING'S *voice, stops short and listens.*)

KRINGELEIN (*to* PREYSING). I have the honor, Your Excellency!

PREYSING (*scarcely glancing at him*). How do. (*To the* CLERK) If a telegram comes—(*to* ZINNOWITZ) from Manchester—(*to the* CLERK)

bring it to me at once. Come, Zinnowitz!

(ZINNOWITZ *and* PREYSING *exit to grill room.* KRINGELEIN *stands, staring.* OTTERNSCHLAG *laughs. All turn and look at* OTTERNSCHLAG.)

OTTERNSCHLAG (*somewhat aggressively*). That's no way to catch up with life, Mr. Kringelein!

CURTAIN

Scene V

SCENE—*Conference room: A large conference table stands in the center, with chairs at either end of it. A double door leads to a corridor. There is a small table with a chair in back of it. A pitcher with water, tray and glasses are on a small service table. There is a telephone on the large center table, also an ash tray.*

FOURTH BELLBOY (*entering, carrying typewriter and paper*). This way, gentlemen.

(PREYSING *and* ZINNOWITZ *enter.* FOURTH BELLBOY *puts typewriter on table and paper beside it.*)

PREYSING. Everything conspires to set my nerves on edge. (*To* FOURTH BELLBOY) If a telegram comes, bring it at once. Understand?

FOURTH BELLBOY. Yes, sir. (*Exits.*)

ZINNOWITZ (*places coat and hat on table*). Mmmmm. Still no word from Manchester.

PREYSING. No, nothing yet. Have you seen the Saxonia people?

ZINNOWITZ. Yes, indeed.

PREYSING. And . . . ?

ZINNOWITZ. The conference is set for ten o'clock tomorrow morning. If, meanwhile, we receive from Manchester the assurance that Burleigh and Son wish to enter into an association with your concern, everything will go off smoothly. We shall effect the merger with Saxonia without any difficulty at all. But if the Manchester people refuse, then I must say it will be a different story. Your stock is dropping rapidly, and if this conference tomorrow goes wrong . . .

PREYSING. Do you think we ought to postpone the conference?

ZINNOWITZ. My God, no! That would create the very worst impression. You must be optimistic. You must convince them.

PREYSING. But the stocks . . . I threw in 80,000 to keep up the price. (ZINNOWITZ *whistles*) We simply must put this merger through. Otherwise . . .

ZINNOWITZ. I hope your factory doesn't go bankrupt before the merger.

PREYSING. It won't. But we are in bad shape. I tell you frankly—if only Manchester agrees!

ZINNOWITZ. Well, tell them in the morning that Manchester *has* agreed.

PREYSING. I am not a liar. I make my deals on a solid basis.

ZINNOWITZ. Of course, you are the very model of an honest business man.

PREYSING. I certainly am an honest man. I am an honorable business man, a good husband and father and consequently a happy man. I have nothing to conceal.

ZINNOWITZ. Well, don't get excited about it. We know that the Saxonia deal must go through. We will see to it that we get their signatures.

PREYSING. I want to dictate my statement for tomorrow (*Goes to phone*) I can't speak without notes. (*Over phone*) Clerk, please. (*To* ZINNOWITZ) I like to have things down before me in black and white. (*Over phone*) Will you send in Justice Zinnowitz' secretary? Conference room 3. If a telegram comes, have it sent to me at once.

ZINNOWITZ. Now, listen. Of course you're an honest man. But please, like a good fellow, speak optimistically about Manchester.

PREYSING. I can't lie.

ZINNOWITZ. Well, lying probably won't help. But there are, well— nuances. If you are too upright, it might easily happen that the Saxonia people will pull out—and think what would happen then.

PREYSING. The deal must go through.
(FLAEMMCHEN *enters.*)

FLAEMMCHEN. Good evening.

PREYSING. Good evening.

ZINNOWITZ. How do you do, Flaemmchen? Well, Preysing, I'll leave you to your work. I'll be at the conference. Good-bye, Flaemmchen. And, Preysing, optimism does it.

FLAEMMCHEN. Good night, Justice Zinnowitz.
(ZINNOWITZ *exits.*)

PREYSING. Well, let's get to work.

FLAEMMCHEN. Shorthand or shall I take it direct on the machine? (*Sits down, adjusts the machine.*)

PREYSING. What was it Justice Zinnowitz called you?

FLAEMMCHEN. Flaemmchen.

PREYSING. Flaemmchen. It seems odd.

FLAEMMCHEN. What?

PREYSING. Why—oh, nothing . . . Do you work in Justice Zinnowitz' office?

FLAEMMCHEN. I only do occasional jobs there. Nothing steady. I'm looking for a job now. Shorthand or shall I take it on the machine?

PREYSING. On the machine. You—you are very pretty for a typist.

FLAEMMCHEN. Yes? Shall we get to work?

PREYSING. Yes—let's begin. (*Lights cigar and walks up and down during speech*) Gentlemen: since on the eleventh of June of this year, the first negotiations for a merger of the Fredersdorf Woolen Mills and Saxonia, Incorporated were entered into in Chemnitz—Chemnitz—got that?—Both parties have fully agreed that this merger can result only in mutual advantages. Moreover—er—Moreover . . . (*Stops beside her*) Got that?

FLAEMMCHEN. Moreover . . .

PREYSING. Your hands are very sunburned, aren't they?

FLAEMMCHEN. That's from skiing. A gentleman friend of mine took me to Switzerland last month.

PREYSING (*stands behind her, his hand on chair*). He took you to Switzerland, eh? That must have been nice.

FLAEMMCHEN. Only in mutual advantages . . . Moreover . . .

PREYSING (*starts pacing again*). Moreover—The business of both concerns has increased greatly in the meantime. However—however . . . You must not misunderstand me, Miss Flamm. I have a family. I have grown-up daughters.

FLAEMMCHEN. However . . .

PREYSING. However, the Fredersdorf Woolen Mills can throw a great weight into the balance.

FLAEMMCHEN. Weight into the balance . . .

PREYSING. Namely, the extension of its foreign connections with the consequent large increase in profits from such participation in the world market.

FLAEMMCHEN. World market . . . Mmmmmmmm.

PREYSING. What's the matter?

FLAEMMCHEN. Oh, I like to write pleasant things.
(*Voice of* THIRD BELLBOY *is heard in corridor.*)

THIRD BELLBOY. Telegram for Mr. Preysing! Telegram for Mr. Preysing! Telegram . . .

PREYSING (*rushes to door and jerks it open*). Here! Quick! (*Grabs wire*) From Manchester? Good. (THIRD BELLBOY *exits.* PREYSING *tears the telegram open in great excitement. He walks to the table, reading it. He throws it on the table then picks it up again, wiping perspiration from his forehead*) No! Oh, my God! What shall I do now? (*He lets telegram drop on table and sits on chair in front of table*) I can't . . .

FLAEMMCHEN. Has anything happened? (*Picks up telegram and reads it*) "Deal definitely off—Brosemann." Oh, is that something terrible? Don't we need to go on with the dictation now?

PREYSING. My dear young lady, nothing of the sort.

FLAEMMCHEN. But you are so upset. Do you want some water?

PREYSING. Yes. (*She hands him glass of water*) Thanks. (*Takes telegram from her*) Who gave you permission to read my telegram?

FLAEMMCHEN. You are right. I'm sorry.

PREYSING. As a matter of fact, Miss Flaemmchen, the telegram isn't important at all. What my agent, Brosemann, is telegraphing about is nothing at all. The fool! On the contrary, the telegram brings very good news—very good news. Come on, let's get my report finished. Where were we?

FLAEMMCHEN. Namely, with the consequent large increase in profits for such participation in the world market . . . Period?

PREYSING. What? Oh—yes. Period. The Fredersdorf Woolen Mills at this very time are developing such brilliant prospects of this sort that . . . You see, Miss Flamm? It's stated that way so as to fool anybody who might accidentally get hold of it. It's a code message. That's what it is—a code message. Now where were we?

FLAEMMCHEN. Such brilliant prospects . . .

PREYSING. Such brilliant prospects of this sort (*picks up telegram from floor*) that a merger between the two concerns can bring only the finest results—possible. . . .

CURTAIN

SCENE VI

SCENE—KRINGELEIN'S *room. There is a dresser to the right of the door which leads to the corridor. Another door, at the left, connects with* GRUSINSKAIA'S *room. There is a bed in the middle of the room and at its head stands a small table with a lamp on it. There is also a small writing desk with a statue of a man on a horse upon it. A chair is beside the desk, and farther away a large armchair. There is a battered suitcase lying open upon the bed.* GAIGERN *is leaning on back of chair, smoking nervously.* KRINGELEIN *is at bed taking things out of traveling bag. He crosses to dressing table, puts some things on it, then picks an amusement guide from dresser.*

KRINGELEIN (*crossing to* GAIGERN, *looking at amusement guide*). Here is the amusement-guide book.

GAIGERN. Ah! What would you like to see?

KRINGELEIN (*studying it*). Everything! Palace Cinema, for instance? Or the Scala? What is that really? Is it very pretty?

GAIGERN (*not listening; his mind is on door*). We might go there.

KRINGELEIN. And afterwards?

GAIGERN. To a night club. Dance. Drink.

KRINGELEIN. And then?

GAIGERN (*rising*). Good God, you look a long way ahead! (*Looks at door and turns to* KRINGELEIN) Dress first, Mr. Kringelein, and then we'll see what more there is to do. (*Slaps* KRINGELEIN *on shoulder.* KRINGELEIN *turns and goes to light switch at back wall.* GAIGERN *turns quickly to door at left, tries it, sees it's open, shuts it quickly. A tune is heard playing in the lobby.*)

KRINGELEIN (*snaps on light*). Such fine bright lights. (*Snaps it on and off.*)

GAIGERN (*at door*). MMmmmmm!

KRINGELEIN (*feeling the mattress*). Beautiful room, eh, Baron? Distinction. (*Feeling upholstery of armchair*) Velvet upholstery. Silk bedspread. A number one. I am in the textile business—I know! (*There is a knock at center door. He goes to dresser. A* HALL PORTER *comes in with a shabby, old-fashioned trunk. Seeing* PORTER) Oh! My trunk. (*Goes up to him.*)

PORTER. Is that all?

KRINGELEIN. Yes. That's all. (*PORTER's face expresses "tip." KRINGELEIN looks shyly at GAIGERN, quickly takes out bill, gives to POR-TER.*)

PORTER. Thank you very much, Your Excellency. (*Goes to door on left, taking bunch of keys from pocket.* KRINGELEIN *goes to trunk and opens it. To* GAIGERN, *who is standing with his back firmly against the door*) Pardon me, Baron, I must lock this door.

GAIGERN (*stepping aside*). Oh, isn't it locked?
(*PORTER locks it;* GAIGERN *moves toward bed;* PORTER *starts back t center door.*)

KRINGELEIN (*to* PORTER). Wh_ lives there?

PORTER (*on way to door*). Madame Grusinskaia.

KRINGELEIN. Oh! And on the other side?

PORTER. Mr. Preysing.

KRINGELEIN (*suddenly excited*). Mr. Preysing! Has Mr. Preysing . . . ? Is his room better than mine?

PORTER. No. Your rooms are alike. (*Exits, closing door.*)

KRINGELEIN. Ah, I must write Kampmann and tell him that. Preysing is so hated at the plant. Kampmann is my friend.

GAIGERN. Well, now *we* can begin. And we had better be pretty quick about it. Have you evening clothes?

KRINGELEIN (*embarrassed*). No, I'm afraid I haven't.

GAIGERN. That is the first thing you must buy.

KRINGELEIN. I thought I wouldn't lay out any money for clothes.

GAIGERN. Why not? Now, let's get this coat off. (*Takes off* KRINGE-LEIN's *coat and lays it on chair.*)

KRINGELEIN. Because—they wouldn't be worth it. I wouldn't have much time to wear them.

GAIGERN. But you want to live a little. You want to have a good time. So, you will have to look right. Full evening clothes, you understand?

KRINGELEIN (*kneeling at trunk, docile*). Yes, Baron. (*Goes to trunk and starts looking through the clothes.*)

GAIGERN (*begins to hunt in the trunk*). Tomorrow I'll take you to a tailor and have you fitted out. Meanwhile, we'll try to find something presentable among the things you've got. (KRINGELEIN *proudly displays a shirt with great stripes*) No, I don't think that will do! Besides, first you've got to go to the barber. Get a shave. And get the hair off your forehead. You'll be a different man. You'll look fine! No, you've got to go to the barber.

KRINGELEIN. Barber! (*Straightening up*) Where, at this time of the night?

GAIGERN (*looks at his watch*). Ten minutes to nine. The hotel barber shop will be open a long time yet. It's never night in Berlin. (*Pushes him to center door*) Come on! Run! Hurry!

KRINGELEIN. But where is it?

GAIGERN. In the basement. A boy will show you the way. Here, you can't take those with you. (*Takes clothes* KRINGELEIN *has taken from trunk*) Here's your coat. (*Hands him coat from chair.*)

KRINGELEIN (*at doorway*). But, Baron . . .

GAIGERN (*pushing him out*). On your way, Kringelein. You'll have to hurry if we are to take in the big town. (*Pushes him out of room, and he follows. Offstage*) I will go to my room, finish dressing and meet you back here in half an hour. (*Closes door behind him*) Don't forget, the hair off your forehead. (*After a moment center door opens,* GAIGERN *enters, closes door behind him, crosses to door at left, taking bunch of skeleton keys from pocket. The lights go out while he is fumbling with the lock of the door.*)

CURTAIN

SCENE VII

SCENE—GRUSINSKAIA'S *room in the dark. A clock strikes nine. Music is heard playing very softly.* ("I Kiss Your Hand, Madame") *Door at right opens slowly.* GAIGERN *enters, flashlight in hand, slowly flashing light about room. He goes to dresser, opens couple of drawers, takes up jewel casket, takes out pearls, puts them in pocket. He closes drawer, cautiously crosses room when the rattle of the doorknob is heard. He switches off*

flashlight, crosses to closet and hides behind it. Door opens, CHAMBER-
MAID *enters, humming, switches on light, crosses to center door, opens it,
calls through the corridor.*

CHAMBERMAID. Schurmann! Schurmann! Come right up to 168. (*She
resumes her humming. She arranges pillows on couch, goes to
dressing table, snaps on mirror
lights and exits into bedroom, leaving door open.* HALL PORTER *enters
through center door.*)

HALL PORTER (*to* CHAMBERMAID).
Get busy! The old girl is around,
inspecting.

CHAMBERMAID (*off stage*). Should
the door of 169 be open now, or
closed?

HALL PORTER. Closed, of course.

CHAMBERMAID (*off stage*). But it
was open, of course.

HALL PORTER. It wouldn't have
been. I locked it myself.

CHAMBERMAID (*entering*). Well, it
was open.

HALL PORTER (*locking door*). You
always have some kick to make.

CHAMBERMAID (*picks up* GRUSIN-
SKAIA'S *dressing gown, shows it to
Schurmann*). Sweet, isn't it, Schurmann? (*Places dressing gown on
couch*) Some matches for the ash
trays.

HALL PORTER. Out of matches
again? These Russians smoke all
the time.
(INSPECTRESS *enters.*)

INSPECTRESS. You'll never finish
with this corridor if you've only

got as far as 168. (HALL PORTER
starts to exit) Schurmann! (*He
stops in his tracks*) 124 is checking
out at nine o'clock. See to the
trunk. (*She goes to ash tray*)
Schurmann, there aren't any
matches here. (HALL PORTER *puts
matches in ash tray*) Anna! Anna!
Come here. You've been told a hundred times that the corner with
Grand Hotel embroidered on it
should be put here, (*telephone
rings*) on the left side, but you always . . . Answer the telephone.
(*She turns to* PORTER) Schurmann,
come. (*She exits.* SCHURMANN
follows, closing door behind him.
MAID *goes to phone.*)

CHAMBERMAID (*at phone*). Yes,
yes. No, Madame Grusinskaia is not
here. Who's calling? West End Theatre? (SUZANNE *enters, looks around*)
Madame's maid's not here. No. I'll
see. (SUZANNE *goes to door at left,
calling "Madame"*) One moment
please. Yes, hold the wire. The
theatre is asking if Madame Grusinskaia is here. I didn't know.

SUZANNE (*picking up receiver*).
Yes, this is Suzanne. No, no. She
isn't here, either. Oh, *Mon Dieu,*
if something has happened to her.
If she has done something to herself! What? You don't know Madame! Yes, come here; help me
search for Madame! Tell the audience Madame is ill. Anything. Yes,
the chauffeur is hunting for her,
too. (*Hangs up.*)

CHAMBERMAID. Has something
happened?

SUZANNE. Something horrible! Madame made her appearance—no applause. Suddenly someone hissed. Imagine! The whole house began to hiss. Madame went on dancing, very pale, and smiling, until the curtain came down. Then Mr. Witte took her to the dressing room and I ran for the doctor. When I came back—(MEIERHEIM *enters*) Madame had disappeared. Right in the middle of the performance! *C'est dommage!*

CHAMBERMAID. Poor lady!

MEIERHEIM. Is she here? Not here, either. She deserted. Right in the middle of the performance! Deserted! This little trick is going to cost Grusinskaia a suit for breach of contract. (CHAMBERMAID *exits*) I'm giving their money back. She'll have to make good my loss. (WITTE *enters*) I won't let myself be ruined! (*Sees* WITTE) Witte, what the devil are you doing here? You have to stay at the theatre and lead the orchestra. Has everybody gone entirely crazy?

WITTE. I couldn't stay. I am too much alarmed about Grusinskaia. I had to see how she is. Something terrible might happen.

MEIERHEIM. Who's leading?

WITTE. The concert master.

MEIERHEIM. Who's dancing?

WITTE. Desprez.

MEIERHEIM. My God!

WITTE. Meierheim, do me a big favor and go back to the theatre. If Madame comes home, she will need rest. Her nerves . . .

MEIERHEIM. Nerves! All she's got to do is dance. I take the risk. She has ruined me, and who is she, anyway? An out-of-date dancer that nobody gives a damn about any more.

WITTE. Mr. Meierheim, will you please leave the room at once?

MEIERHEIM. I take no instructions (GRUSINSKAIA *appears*) from you, you . . .
(WITTE, MEIERHEIM *and* SUZANNE *center their attention on* GRUSINSKAIA *the minute they see her.*)

GRUSINSKAIA. I wish to be alone.

WITTE (*softly*). Lisaveta Andreievna, where have you been?

MEIERHEIM. Leave this to me. Madame, how dare you take such liberties? How can you indulge in such a breach of discipline? Do you know what this means? It means you have broken our contract.

SUZANNE (*coming to* MEIERHEIM *and taking his arm*). Please, not any more tonight. Tomorrow . . .

WITTE. Lisaveta, dear Lisaveta.

GRUSINSKAIA. I wish to be alone.

MEIERHEIM (*to* SUZANNE). All right. (*To* GRUSINSKAIA) Madame, I'll go. (*To* WITTE) Meierheim understands the artistic temperament. (WITTE *pushes* MEIERHEIM *out.*)

WITTE. Please go. (*To* GRUSINSKAIA) Can I help you, Lisaveta?

GRUSINSKAIA. No, thanks, Witte. Good night.
(WITTE *exits.*)

SUZANNE. Shall I . . . ? Does Madame wish . . . ?

GRUSINSKAIA. I wish to be alone. (SUZANNE *exits, closing door behind her.* GRUSINSKAIA *stands, whispers something in Russian, turns upstage, slowly crosses to dresser, sits, looks in mirror.*)

GRUSINSKAIA. Poor Gru. Poor Gru. (*Rests head on arm leaning on dresser*) Poor Gru. Poor Gru. (*Lifts head slowly, gradually rises, taking dancing pose, does a few steps, collapses on couch*) Never. You cannot dance again. You cannot dance again—finished—finished. (*Clock strikes. She unties shoe, reaches for robe, on couch behind her, when* GAIGERN *steps out from behind wardrobe. She cries out, rising.*)

GAIGERN (*taking step toward her, bowing*). Please do not be frightened, Madame.

GRUSINSKAIA. What do you want here?

GAIGERN. Nothing. Only to be here in your room.

GRUSINSKAIA. Why do you do that? Why do you hide in my room?

GAIGERN. But surely, you must know, as I should have known. (*Takes another step toward her*) Because I love you.

GRUSINSKAIA. Because you love me. You love me? Is that why? (*She looks at him for a few seconds. Suddenly she throws herself on couch and begins to weep passionately.*)

GAIGERN. Poor Grusinskaia. Does it do you good to cry? Are you afraid? Shall I go? Has somebody harmed you? Were the people bad to you? Did I frighten you? Are you afraid? Or do you cry because I love you?

GRUSINSKAIA. I was so alone—always alone—nobody—and suddenly you were there and said that word. (*Sitting up, looks at him*) No, I am not afraid. It is strange.

GAIGERN. You were crying. It tore my heart to hear you sob like that.

GRUSINSKAIA. Nerves, just nerves. Monsieur is to blame. Monsieur frightened me. You are the one who sent me those orchids? Such a fright. You must forgive me, I have had a bad evening. I am very tired. Do you know what it is to be tired —tired of a routine existence?

GAIGERN. I'm afraid I don't. I always do exactly what I want to do.

GRUSINSKAIA. So—you feel like walking into a lady's room, you walk in?

GAIGERN. Yes.

GRUSINSKAIA. Why do you look at me like that?

GAIGERN. Because you are beautiful. I did not know you were so beautiful, and . . .

GRUSINSKAIA. And what else?

GAIGERN. No, I mean it. You are so appealing, so soft, so little, so fragile. I feel like taking you in my arms and not letting anything more happen to you, ever.

GRUSINSKAIA (*involuntarily closing her eyes*). And—and . . .

GAIGERN. How tired you are!

GRUSINSKAIA. Yes—tired . . .

GAIGERN. So alone.

GRUSINSKAIA. Yes, alone . . . always alone. (*In Russian*) *Na ceveri, decome stoite odenoke na goloy vershini sosna.*

GAIGERN. You mustn't speak Russian to me.

GRUSINSKAIA. Man, strange man . . .

GAIGERN. Am I quite strange to you?

GRUSINSKAIA. Not quite strange now. It is as if I had been expecting you. You know, once when the Grand Duke was alive, I found a man hiding in my room—a young officer . . .

GAIGERN. And . . . ?

GRUSINSKAIA. He disappeared. Later he was found shot.

GAIGERN. I never knew it was so dangerous to be found in a woman's room — a woman — one loves. (*Touches her hand.*)

GRUSINSKAIA (*drawing away from him*). No. No. No. Who are you—man?

GAIGERN. A man who loves you—that is all, who has forgotten everything else for you.

GRUSINSKAIA. You love me. You know, I haven't heard that word for a long time. I was so cruelly alone. How is it that you . . . ?

Let me look at you. Your hands. Your eyes. Why do you love me?

GAIGERN. Don't you know that I have followed you all over Europe —for weeks? I heard you cry—I saw you in the mirror. You are so beautiful. I have never seen a woman so beautiful as you. What kind of a woman are you?

GRUSINSKAIA. Well, I'm just old-fashioned. I am from another world, another century than yours. That is it. We were drilled like little soldiers, we dancers, in the school of the Imperial Ballet in St. Petersberg. No rest, no leisure, no stopping, ever. And then, whoever is famous is alone. Then one isn't a person any more, not a woman! One is just a symbol of success that is driven round and round the world. And what it means to hold on to success, five years, ten years, fifteen years! Because on the day success ends, on the day one ceases to think oneself important, life ends for such as I. Are you listening to me?

GAIGERN. Yes, yes.

GRUSINSKAIA. Do you understand me? Oh, how I wish you would understand!

GAIGERN. I do understand. Let me be good to you. Let me stay here with you.

GRUSINSKAIA. I think you must go now. The key is in the door.

GAIGERN. No. I am not going. You know I am not going.

GRUSINSKAIA. I wish to be alone.

GAIGERN. That is not true. You

were in despair before I came. If I left you, you would feel worse than you did before. (*Closer to her*) You must not be alone. You must not cry, you must forget. Tell me that I can stay with you, please, tell me . . .

GRUSINSKAIA (*whispering*). Just for a minute. (*They kiss.*)

CURTAIN

ACT TWO

Scene I

SCENE—*Conference room. Morning. Seated at table are* GERSTENKORN *and* OLDER BUSINESS MAN *of the executive type. At left of* GERSTENKORN, SCHWEIMANN, *a young business man. Standing at end of the conference table is* DR. WAITZ, *counsel for the Saxonia organization, with foot on chair, reading paper. They are impatiently waiting the arrival of* MR. PREYSING.

GERSTENKORN (*tapping the table impatiently, he looks at his watch*). Ten minutes late. Mr. Preysing keeps us waiting.

SCHWEIMANN (*slowly polishing his nails*). He likes to play the great man.

GERSTENKORN. He needn't try that. I know that Fredersdorf is about ripe to pluck.

WAITZ (*reading a market report in a newspaper*). Fredersdorf stock is holding its own today.

SCHWEIMANN. So? Ask Preysing what it's *cost him* to keep it up!

GERSTENKORN (*banging table with hand*). Ask me what it cost us to hammer it down! Schweimann, you're too soft for me. Now, don't get in my way. If Preysing has landed Manchester, Fredersdorf is not only saved; then it has become a powerful competitor; then it has the English market in its hands, and in that event, we must certainly merge. But if he hasn't landed Manchester, I feel sure that we can have Fredersdorf dirt cheap in a couple of months.

WAITZ (*lays newspaper on table and takes foot off chair*). But how can we tell what the Manchester situation really is? Everything depends on that.

GERSTENKORN (*tapping table for emphasis*). Preysing will *have* to declare himself. . . .

SCHWEIMANN. He would be just stupid enough to do that— (*Rear center door opens;* PREYSING *enters.*)

GERSTENKORN (*turning to stop* SCHWEIMANN). Hem!

PREYSING (*at center door, brief case in hand*). Good morning, gentlemen.
(*They all stand up very formally.*)

GERSTENKORN (*going up to* PREY-SING, *shakes hands with him*). Good morning.

SCHWEIMANN (*shaking hands with* PREYSING). Good morning.

GERSTENKORN. Our legal adviser, Dr. Waitz.
(WAITZ *shakes hands with* PREYSING.)

PREYSING. Pleased to meet you, sir.

WAITZ. Glad to know you, sir. (*They all come to table.*)

GERSTENKORN. We've been waiting for you.

PREYSING (*standing back of table, puts brief case on table*). I'd like to wait for Justice Zinnowitz.

WAITZ (*smiling, soft, convincing*). Oh, you won't need legal advice against us.

GERSTENKORN. How is Mrs. Preysing? I believe you have just celebrated your silver wedding?

PREYSING (*opening brief case and taking papers out*). Oh, yes, it was awfully nice of you gentlemen to send in your congratulations.

GERSTENKORN. And how is your father-in-law?

PREYSING (*fumbling with handkerchief*). Fine, thanks.

GERSTENKORN. That's good. Nice suit you're wearing. English tailoring, isn't it?

PREYSING. What? No.

SCHWEIMANN. Have you been in England recently?

PREYSING. Yes . . . I've been there. . . .

SCHWEIMANN. Beautiful country. Beautiful cities. London—my God! Glasgow—industry. Liverpool . . . Manchester . . .

WAITZ. Manchester is a very interesting city.

SCHWEIMANN. Do you know Manchester?

PREYSING. Naturally. A man in the textile industry has to know Manchester. (*Busy with papers*) Now I want to read you from this statement I have prepared.

SCHWEIMANN. Hideous city, Manchester. Don't you think so?

GERSTENKORN (*to* PREYSING). Well, there's a lot of business to be done with Manchester. Burleigh & Son has the whole English market right in their hands. Have you a connection with Burleigh & Son?

PREYSING. We have a great many connections in England, naturally.

GERSTENKORN. I mean especially with Burleigh & Son.

PREYSING. Of course, I cannot make a statement at this time.

GERSTENKORN. Well, let's get down to business. Fire away, Preysing. (*They draw their chairs up close to the table.*)

PREYSING (*monotonously, reading his prepared statement*). Gentlemen, since, on the eleventh of June of this year, the first negotiations for a merger of the Fredersdorf Woolen Mills and Saxonia, Incorporated were entered into, in Chemnitz, both parties have fully agreed that this merger can result only in mutual advantages. Moreover, the business of both concerns has increased greatly in the meantime; however . . .

GERSTENKORN (*irritated*). Oh, yes! Yes.

PREYSING. Beg pardon?

GERSTENKORN. Yes, yes, business has increased greatly, but before you go on with your very interesting address, I would like to know . . .

PREYSING (*getting up, irritated*). Please! I am laying before you the last general statement of our concern. Active capital, plant and machinery, raw material and finished products. Patents . . . Our new installation for the utilization of waste. For instance——

GERSTENKORN. Oh, for God's sake! Waste! What we want to know about is Manchester.

WAITZ (*leaning over to* PREYSING). Please, Preysing, tell us what we want to know!

PREYSING (*sits nervous*). Well, I'd rather wait for Justice Zinnowitz before I commit myself.

GERSTENKORN. This is the very devil, Preysing! (*Turns in his chair, faces front.*)

SCHWEIMANN (*sarcastically*). I can see that this session is going to be exhaustive. (SCHWEIMANN *rises, goes to table, picks up phone, back to audience.*)

PREYSING. Now, to proceed with the projected merger, the advantages for Saxonia are so obvious . . .

GERSTENKORN. Oh! Stop there a minute and let's talk like grown people.

SCHWEIMANN (*telephoning*). Seltzer, three or four bottles, and cigars. Bring a little box of twenty-five—good ones.
(GERSTENKORN, *irritated by interruption, gives* SCHWEIMANN *a dirty look.* SCHWEIMANN *hangs up.*)

GERSTENKORN (*to* PREYSING). You have told us what your factory can do, and it doesn't sound awfully good. When you first approached us you were singing a different tune . . .

PREYSING (*rising*). We did not approach you . . .

WAITZ (*looks through his papers, takes up letter*). I have a letter on file, dated September 14th, which shows that you approached us . . .

PREYSING (*snatches letter from him*). It isn't so. That latter of September 14th was nothing but a tentative answer to a feeler of your own.

GERSTENKORN (*rises and violently snatches document from* PREYSING). Tentative, my eye! A month before that your father-in-law came very privately and scratched on my door . . .

(ZINNOWITZ *enters quietly, stands watching.*)

PREYSING (*shrieking*). We did not take the initiative!

GERSTENKORN (*just as loudly*). Of course you took the initiative! You know damn well you started this, and now . . .

ZINNOWITZ. Good morning . . . Good morning! Gentlemen, I see the conference is already under way.

PREYSING (*wiping the perspiration from his forehead, goes up to* ZINNOWITZ). Justice Zinnowitz, please try to clear up the situation. I am at cross purposes with these gentlemen.
(ZINNOWITZ *walks toward table.* PREYSING *lights cigar.* PREYSING

walks back and forth while WAITZ *and* GERSTENKORN *sit at table.*)

ZINNOWITZ. But, gentlemen, the situation is quite clear! (*Lays coat and hat on chair and leans forward with hands on table as if pleading a case*) When the preliminary negotiations for the merger of Fredersdorf and Saxonia were begun, on June 11th of this year . . .

GERSTENKORN. Thank God, we're beginning at the beginning. . . .

ZINNOWITZ. It was fully understood and agreed that the existing situation was acceptable to both parties as the basis for trading.
(*As the set changes* ZINNOWITZ *is still heard talking; lights fade out.*)

CURTAIN

SCENE II

SCENE—GRUSINSKAIA'S *room. Morning.* GRUSINSKAIA *is sitting in big chair with back to dressing table.* GAIGERN *on stool, opposite hers, facing each other. She is huddled over; he, with his head in his hands, looks at her thoughtfully, almost respectfully. Long silence.*

GAIGERN. Extraordinary . . .

GRUSINSKAIA. What is extraordinary?

GAIGERN. This night. Everything. (*Long silence.*)

GRUSINSKAIA. I do not even know your name.

GAIGERN. My name is Felix Amadeus Benvenute, Freiherr von Gaigern. My mother called me Flix.

GRUSINSKAIA. Flix. And how do you live? What kind of a person are you?

GAIGERN. There's not much to be said about me. I am a prodigal son, the black sheep of a white flock. I am a *mauvais sujet*, and I shall die on the gallows.

GRUSINSKAIA (*laughing*). Really?

GAIGERN. Really. I haven't a bit of character. I can't organize myself, and I am good for nothing. At home, I learned to ride and play the gentleman. At school, I learned to pray and lie. In the war, to shoot and hunt cover. That is all.

GRUSINSKAIA. So what do you do?

GAIGERN. I am a gambler, yet it would never occur to me to cheat. By all right, I belong in jail. Yet I run at large, happy as a pig, enjoying all of life that pleases me.

GRUSINSKAIA. And what else do you do?

GAIGERN. I am also a criminal, a hotel thief.

GRUSINSKAIA (*laughing*). And what else? Perhaps a murderer?

GAIGERN. Perhaps, yes. I even came here prepared for that last night. (*Takes revolver out of right pocket, shows it to her and puts it back.*)

GRUSINSKAIA (*softly*). You make bad jokes.

GAIGERN (*takes both her hands*). Please, look at me. (GRUSINSKAIA *looks at him*) That way—quite calmly. You must believe me. You must believe that I love you; that I have never known what love is, until last night. You must believe me. (*He kisses her hands, gets up.*)

GRUSINSKAIA. What is the matter? (GAIGERN *takes pearls out of his pocket, crosses over to her, lays them in her lap.* GRUSINSKAIA, *with a little cry of pain*) Ah! (*Awkward silence*) Did you come here—just —to do that? This is horrible! (GAIGERN *turns away*) You may keep the pearls. (*Drops them on stool*) I do not want them any

more. I make you a present of them.

GAIGERN (*turning to her*). I don't want the pearls!

GRUSINSKAIA. I will not denounce you.

GAIGERN. I know . . .

GRUSINSKAIA. No . . .

GAIGERN (*takes a step towards her*). Yesterday, I was a thief. But now . . .

GRUSINSKAIA (*turning away*). Now you must go. I give you the pearls, but now you must go.

GAIGERN (*crosses to her*). I will not go. You must listen to me. You must believe me. I am not an impostor. I haven't always been a criminal. I really am a Baron. I was in fearful difficulties. I was threatened. I was desperately in need of a large sum of money. I would have chanced hanging for it. That is why I wanted your pearls. I followed you around. I found myself falling in love with you, but I forced myself not to think of you. I managed to get into your room, and now . . .

GRUSINSKAIA. And now . . . ? (*He sinks on stool, picking up pearls.*)

GAIGERN (*giving her pearls*). I can't go through with it. Extraordinary. (*Drops head in hands. After a struggle, she bends over him and strokes his head*) Do you understand? (*Looks up at her.*)

GRUSINSKAIA (*hugging him closely*). Yes. Yes. Yes.

GAIGERN. Then you do believe that I really love you?

GRUSINSKAIA (*with mounting warmth*). Yes. If I didn't believe that now, I would die after this night.

GAIGERN. I want to be good to you. Madly good.

GRUSINSKAIA (*takes him in her arms, cries softly on his shoulder*). Yes, I want you to. I want you to. (*Murmurs lovingly in Russian and kisses him*) Everything will be all right. (*The telephone rings, continues ringing until she answers it*) I must answer the telephone. (*Rises and crosses to phone. As she takes receiver, to* GAIGERN, *softly*) Everything will be all right. (*Speaks in phone*) Who? Oh. Oh, Suzanne. Good morning, Suzanne. Good that you told me. I am all right. Yes, in a few minutes. (*Hangs up*) Flix, it's beginning.

GAIGERN. What, Lisaveta?

GRUSINSKAIA. I must go to rehearsal. I must dance. I want to dance. Shall I see you soon again? Suzanne will be here any minute.

GAIGERN. When are you leaving Berlin?

GRUSINSKAIA. Very early in the morning.

GAIGERN. For Vienna?

GRUSINSKAIA. Yes. (*Reaching a decision*) Can't—can't you come along? Don't you think—it would be—better—for us, both?

GAIGERN. Not—right away. Later.

GRUSINSKAIA. Why not?

GAIGERN. I have no money. I must get some first.

GRUSINSKAIA. I'll give you what you need.

GAIGERN. No.
(*Telephone rings.*)

GRUSINSKAIA (*crosses to phone*). In a minute—in a minute. (*Hangs up quickly and goes up to* GAIGERN) Come with me, come with me.

GAIGERN. I will go with you. What time does the train leave?

GRUSINSKAIA. Six twenty-seven in the morning. And take the money!

GAIGERN. Never mind. I'll get it. I have a whole day. I'll be on that train.

GRUSINSKAIA (*close in his arms*). I shall dance, and you will be with me. And then—listen: (*More and more rapidly, in a higher key*) You will come with me to Lake Como. I have a little house in Tremezzo. Everything is beautiful there, marvelous. I will take a vacation, six weeks, eight weeks; we will be insanely happy and lazy. And then you will go with me to South America. Do you know Rio? (*Telephone rings*) Oh, God! the telephone. (*She crosses to phone*) Suzanne? Yes. I know it is time. (*She beckons him to come over. He does, kisses her hand and she keeps on talking, looking at him*) In a minute—in a minute! (*Hangs up. To* GAIGERN) Now you must go— I'll see you later. Wait.

GAIGERN (*with great resolution, close to her*). I will go with you.

Whatever happens! I love you! I will be on that train. I will get the money.

GRUSINSKAIA (*feverishly*). Flix, don't do anything foolish. I am alarmed about you.

GAIGERN. Don't be—beloved. (*They kiss—he exits.*)

GRUSINSKAIA (*closes door behind him, breathes deeply, stretches herself, crosses to phone*). Hello, operator. Good morning, operator. I wish to speak to Mr. Witte. No, I don't know the number of his room. 599? All right, give me 599. Witte? Hello, Witte. Did I wake you up? Yes, but it's time to go to rehearsal. What? Of course, I want to rehearse. No, no, I'm all right. Listen, Witte, I thought of a wonderful dance this morning. I need mad music for it. Come at once, quick. (*She hangs up and immediately jiggles receiver again. SUZANNE enters. GRUSINSKAIA talks to her while telephoning.*)

SUZANNE. Good morning, Madame.

GRUSINSKAIA. Good morning, Suzanne. (*In phone*) Will you give me Bismark 0878? (*To* SUZANNE) Get the things ready, Suzanne, we are going to rehearsal.

SUZANNE. *Yes, Madame.* (*She exits.*)

GRUSINSKAIA. Bismark 0878? I wish to speak to Mr. Meierheim. Yes, personally. Pardon me, if it is not too early for me, it isn't for Meierheim. Yes, please.

SUZANNE (*entering, stands at doorway*). Madame is quite well again?

GRUSINSKAIA. Wonderful. Haven't felt like this in a long time. (*In phone*) Hello, Meierheim? (*To* SUZANNE) The blue dress, Suzanne, and the little hat with the agrafe. (*SUZANNE exits*) Oh, yes. Yes. I am coming to rehearsal at eleven o'clock. Yes, I shall expect you in fifteen minutes, here at the hotel. *Vite, Vite,* Monsieur Meierheim! *Au revoir.* (*Hangs up, exits.*)

SUZANNE (*off stage*). Madame looks wonderful today. Did Madame sleep so well?

GRUSINSKAIA (*off stage*). Did you tell the chauffeur to bring the car?

SUZANNE (*off stage*). When do you want it?

GRUSINSKAIA (*off stage*). Right away!

SUZANNE (*entering, goes to phone*). Yes, right away—right away. (*At phone*) Will you please send Madame Grusinskaia's car at once! (*GRUSINSKAIA comes running out of room, takes telephone out of her hand.*)

GRUSINSKAIA. No! No! This very minute, this very minute! (*Hangs up*) Run along, Suzanne.

SUZANNE. Yes, Madame . . .

GRUSINSKAIA. And close the door.

SUZANNE. All right, Madame.

GRUSINSKAIA (*at telephone*). Will you get me Baron von Gaigern? Please. Flix? Yes—it is me. Nothing. Good morning. Good morning. Nothing. Just to tell you I am happy.

CURTAIN

Scene III

SCENE—*Conference room. The bracket lights are burning. The air is thick with cigar smoke. On the table are glasses, coffee cups, documents, and ash trays full of cigar stumps. There is an impression of staleness and weariness.* PREYSING'S *coat is hung over a chair.* ZINNOWITZ *is drinking a glass of water.* WAITZ, SCHWEIMANN *and* GERSTENKORN *are close together conferring about a document which they are examining.* ZINNOWITZ *and* PREYSING *are watching them closely.*

GERSTENKORN. Wait a minute. Let's see that once again.

WAITZ. I never heard of anything like it in all my life.

SCHWEIMANN. Does it look real to you?

GERSTENKORN. This looks right enough. Signatures and everything.

SCHWEIMANN. Why didn't he tell us this morning?

GERSTENKORN. Well, that's that.

SCHWEIMANN. Instead of holding us up all day.

WAITZ (*contract in hand*). Well, I'll be damned!

SCHWEIMANN. So he had Manchester tied up all the time?

GERSTENKORN (*going to* ZINNOWITZ). That settles it. Give us the agreement, Zinnowitz. (*Gets papers from* ZINNOWITZ). Under these circumstances, it's quite a different matter.

PREYSING. Under these circumstances; *we* might refuse to sign . . .

GERSTENKORN. Nonsense! Business is business. We all get excited, you know. Schweimann, I know you are of my opinion . . .

SCHWEIMANN. Dr. Waitz, have you looked over the contract?

WAITZ. Oh, certainly. Zinnowitz writes a smart contract, but it's all right since we mean to go through with it. Here, I'll sign first. (SCHWEIMANN *takes out pen*) Preysing, will you hand me that handsome fountain pen of yours? (PREYSING *hands him pen*) Ah! An English pen! (*He sits and signs document.*)

PREYSING. Yes. Cost me three pounds.

ZINNOWITZ. A nice pen you have there, Schweimann, it's just like Preysing's. Where did you get it?

SCHWEIMANN (*grinning*). Manchester.
(*All laugh.* WAITZ *rises.*)

GERSTENKORN. Sign here, Preysing. (PREYSING *goes to end of table.* SCHWEIMANN *and* WAITZ *hold their chairs for him while he sits and signs.* GERSTENKORN *grabs paper*) What a session that was!

WAITZ (*picking up brief case and papers*). Well, we ought to celebrate with a bottle of wine!

GERSTENKORN. Do your celebrating in Chemnitz, Waitz!

SCHWEIMANN. It's twenty-five minutes to six! If you want to catch the six-twelve train.

GERSTENKORN. We've got to get back—business.

SCHWEIMANN. You'll have to drive like the devil to make it to the station. Waitz, have you your things? I'm staying here overnight.

WAITZ (*at door*). They are checked outside. Good evening, gentlemen.

SCHWEIMANN. Good-bye, gentlemen. (*Exits.* WAITZ *waits outside open door for Gerstenkorn.*)

GERSTENKORN (*to* ZINNOWITZ, *crossing down to* PREYSING). Good-bye. (*Shakes hands with* PREYSING) We'll see you again soon! Preysing. My respects to your father-in-law. One of us will come to Fredersdorf to discuss further details.

PREYSING. What day?

GERSTENKORN. Late, around the fifteenth. All right? (*As he exits*) Let's get started, Waitz. (PREYSING *closes door.*)

PREYSING (*at door*). The fifteenth! (ZINNOWITZ *crosses to table, picks up contract, waves it to dry.*)

ZINNOWITZ. Well, you're a good one, Preysing; I talk until my mouth is fuzzy, and you have Manchester

sewed up all the time! Why didn't you tell me? You gave me a bad time.

PREYSING. I knew what I was doing.

ZINNOWITZ. Well, it has been put through, that is the important thing.

PREYSING (*suddenly laughing with increasing violence*). Yes, it has been put through; it has been put through.

ZINNOWITZ. What is the matter with you?

PREYSING. Ask me how it has been put through.

ZINNOWITZ (*stops waving contract*). What do you mean?

PREYSING. Bluff, bluff, Zinnowitz, all bluff.

ZINNOWITZ. What bluff?

PREYSING (*gives him telegram*). Read this telegram.

ZINNOWITZ (*rises and reads*). Great God! Then Manchester has thrown you out? And this is false? And despite this you've got them to sign?

PREYSING. Just bluff.

ZINNOWITZ (*watching* PREYSING). I'd never have thought it of you!

PREYSING. So? No one would have thought it of me. Well, if bluff is what the world wants, I'll show them. (*Goes to table and starts to drink glass of water.*)

ZINNOWITZ. Preysing, the thing for you to do now is to go to England. See the Manchester people again and sell them on the basis of this new deal. (*Pointing to contract.*)

PREYSING. Yes. (*He puts glass down on table*) To England! God! It's like being drunk. I lay awake all night thinking of it. I was desperate! Now I don't care any more. God! This thing goes to a man's head.

ZINNOWITZ. Easy there, Preysing! What you need now is relaxation.

PREYSING (*excitedly*). Yes, that's what I want. I'd like to tear loose tonight. (*Picks up chair and slams it down*) I'd like to drink cocktails, wine, go out! Do something! Things I have never done in my life! It came over me in a flash! They were out to get me! Then I turned a trick on them, one of their own tricks. (*Walks to table, knocks on it*) They want Manchester! I'll give them Manchester, but I'll make them bring it to me themselves. It's crooked, I know, but it makes miracles happen. Bluff's the thing. (*Stands facing* ZINNOWITZ) It's intoxicating! I'm ready for anything tonight!

ZINNOWITZ. Your excitement is beginning to infect me! (*Starts to pack brief case*) What do you want to do?

PREYSING. Zinnowitz, where is Flaemmchen?

ZINNOWITZ. Who?

PREYSING. Flaemmchen, your secretary, Miss Flamm.

ZINNOWITZ (*closing brief case*). What do you want with her?

PREYSING. I want to see her. I—I want to do some dictating. (ZINNOWITZ *gives him a knowing look*) Report of the conference for my father-in-law.

ZINNOWITZ. Well, she's probably downstairs.

PREYSING. Downstairs?

ZINNOWITZ. Yes, she told me she would probably be in the grill room, dancing, if she were needed for anything.

PREYSING. Zinnowitz, would you say she is pretty?

ZINNOWITZ. Pretty as a picture, much too good-looking for an office.

PREYSING. Let's go down and find her. (*Takes coat from chair, puts it on*) I need a drink! (*Takes* ZINNOWITZ *by arm and leads him to door*) Come along, Zinnowitz. (*As they exit*) I don't know a thing about women. I've been married twenty-five years.

CURTAIN

SCENE IV

SCENE—*Section of the dance floor of the hotel grill. In the center there is a bar with swinging gate. At left and right of bar are the entrances to corridor which lead to hotel lobby. At either end of stage a table and chairs.*

*Against the wall there are tables and chairs. The dance floor extends off
stage, where the jazz band is playing. There are decorative brackets above
the bar, and a lamp in blue plays upon the dancers as they dance on and off
to the strains of the jazz tune.* WHITE *and* NEGRO BARTENDERS *are mixing
drinks behind the bar.* KRINGELEIN *is standing at one end of bar taking it all
in.* FLAEMMCHEN *is dancing with* MR. QUINN. KATIE *is dancing with* HANS,
FRANK *with* GERTRUDE, DAISY *with* JIM, GIGOLO *with* GIGOLO LADY, *and*
FORTNER *with* MRS. FORTNER. *The dancing and ad-lib merriment continue
for about forty seconds, then* THIRD WAITER *enters from dance floor,
crosses to bar and orders "Two mocca double." The music stops.* MR.
and MRS. FORTNER *exit. The lights dim, the blue spot off stage is changed
to amber and continues to play on the dance floor. There is applause and
laughter from the dancers off left and those who were on stage at the end
of the dance. The dancers who remain on stage as music stops are* FRANK
and GERTRUDE, HANS *and* KATIE, FLAEMMCHEN *and* MR. QUINN, GIGOLO
and GIGOLO LADY. JIM *and* DAISY *exit. As the music stops the following
dialogue and business, until* KRINGELEIN'S *speech, are simultaneous.*

FRANK. That was a new step I did
then.

GERTRUDE. That was a new one on
me.
(FRANK *and* GERTRUDE *exit.*)

KATIE. Let's go and have our drink
now.

HANS (*takes* KATIE *to bar. To* BAR-
TENDER). Are our drinks ready?
(COLORED BARTENDER *serves them.*)

FLAEMMCHEN (*looks at her shoe-
lace*). Oh, will you fix my shoe?
(MR. QUINN *kneels down and adjusts buckle.*)

GIGOLO LADY (*to* GIGOLO, *as they
sit at table*). You dance wonderfully.

GIGOLO. I wish they'd play again.
(THIRD WAITER *exits with two
mocca doubles.*)

KRINGELEIN (*to* WHITE BARTENDER).
It's wonderful here! They will dance
again, won't they? I want something to drink, very sweet, very
cold.
(QUINN *rises.* FLAEMMCHEN *indicates* KRINGELEIN. QUINN *thanks her
for dance.*)

WHITE BARTENDER. Louisiana Flip?
(*He nods. To* NEGRO) Louisiana
Flip.
(QUINN *exits.*)

KRINGELEIN (*to* WHITE BARTENDER).
I never saw a Negro before. Is he
genuine? (WHITE BARTENDER *nods*)
He seems right at home in Berlin.

FLAEMMCHEN (*to* KRINGELEIN).
Oh, Mr. Kringelein, how you have
changed! You look so nice.

KRINGELEIN. Oh, please—Miss
Flamm! Permit me, Miss Flamm
. . . Won't you have something to
drink? Something sweet? Louisiana
Flip? (*She nods. To* WHITE BAR-
TENDER) Louisiana Flip!
(GIGOLO *and* GIGOLO LADY *are light-
ing cigarettes.*)

WHITE BARTENDER (*to* NEGRO BAR-
TENDER). Louisiana Flip.

(NEGRO BARTENDER *starts mixing drink.* WHITE BARTENDER *cleans glasses.*)

FLAEMMCHEN. Thanks, Mr. Kringelein. And what are you doing here? (HANS *and* KATIE *finish drink and exit.*)

KRINGELEIN. I'm trying to get acquainted with life. And you, Miss Flamm?

FLAEMMCHEN (*leaning on bar*). I had a date with someone, but he didn't show up.

KRINGELEIN. How's that?

FLAEMMCHEN. Oh, do you like the music? (THIRD WAITER *enters.*)

KRINGELEIN. It's—stimulating. A man might . . .

FLAEMMCHEN. What might a man do . . . ?

KRINGELEIN. I don't know. I'd like to do everything!

FLAEMMCHEN. Would you like to dance?

KRINGELEIN. I can't.

FLAEMMCHEN. Too bad! (THIRD WAITER *picks up two drinks from bar, serves them at table and exits*) Have you seen your friend the Baron?

KRINGELEIN. No, last night he was going out with me. But he disappeared. I don't know where.

FLAEMMCHEN. So he seems to have disappointed you too.

KRINGELEIN. Well, there's nothing to do about it. We'll just wait for him. (GIGOLO *rises, bows to* LADY GIGOLO, *starts to move away when* HEADWAITER *enters and stops him.*)

WHITE BARTENDER. Louisiana Flip. (WHITE BARTENDER *serves two flips at bar to* KRINGELEIN *and* FLAEMMCHEN, *and continues to wipe glasses.*)

FLAEMMCHEN. Fine. And drink cocktails. (HANS *and* KATIE *dance on stage.*)

HEADWAITER (*to* GIGOLO, *drawing him aside*). Table 42, the American lady. You're due there now.

GIGOLO (*to* HEADWAITER). I can't right now. I'm going to have a good dance to freshen me up. (*Crossing to* FLAEMMCHEN *and bowing*) I beg your pardon. I've noticed how wonderfully you dance. Will you have this one with me? (HANS *and* KATIE *dance off.*)

FLAEMMCHEN. Never mind the compliments. Just dance! (*To* KRINGELEIN) You don't mind? (KRINGELEIN *says "No," pays for drinks.* HEADWAITER *watches* GIGOLO *and* FLAEMMCHEN, *and follows them off.* GAIGERN *appears. Looks around and sees* KRINGELEIN *at bar.*)

GAIGERN (*crossing to* KRINGELEIN). Good evening, Mr. Kringelein.

KRINGELEIN. Good evening, Baron von Gaigern. Miss Flaemmchen is here too. She is dancing. (MR. *and* MRS. FORTNER *dance on stage.*)

GAIGERN. I know. I simply told her to meet me here.

KRINGELEIN. Simply told her to?

GAIGERN. Yes, and she simply came. I am a little late. I had such a lot to do. I must apologize for deserting you last night. I just couldn't come. I'm broke, you see.

KRINGELEIN. Why, how can that be?

GAIGERN. I have exactly twenty-four marks to my name. But why talk about that? What have you been doing all day?

KRINGELEIN. Oh, I've been buying clothes. Aristocratic, like the Baron's. Then I went to Potsdam. Round trip. Then to Flughafen. Round trip. Marvelous.

GAIGERN. Aren't you tired? (MR. and MRS. FORTNER dance off.)

KRINGELEIN. I was never so lively in all my life. The day was wonderful. Oh, Baron, may I ask you something? (Draws GAIGERN aside. JIM and DAISY appear, dancing.)

GAIGERN. Yes?

KRINGELEIN. Was the Baron joking, or is it really true that the Baron is in—financial straits?

GAIGERN. Absolutely true, Kringelein. I'm a ruined man. Flat broke. And the worst of it is that I have to get some money immediately. (JIM and DAISY exit dancing) If somebody would lend me enough to get in the game tonight, I might win. That's my last chance.

KRINGELEIN. Why, I'd like to get in a game.

GAIGERN. Would you? Good! I'll scare up a couple of fellows. We'll have a game here in the hotel. You stake a thousand marks and I twenty-four . . .

KRINGELEIN. If the Baron . . . (GIGOLO and FLAEMMCHEN dance on) If you will permit me. . . . I'd be awfully glad to oblige. . . . You have been so decent to me. Three hundred?

GAIGERN. Thanks, until tomorrow.

KRINGELEIN. I have more than enough with me. (Takes out pocketbook.)

GAIGERN. Not here. Later. And I'll give you an I.O.U. God send me luck! Ah, Flaemmchen! (FLAEMMCHEN and GIGOLO dance on stage. HANS and KATIE dance on from left.)

FLAEMMCHEN (seeing GAIGERN). Oh, hello.

GAIGERN. Hello. (FLAEMMCHEN and GIGOLO dance up to GAIGERN. To GIGOLO) May I? (GIGOLO releases FLAEMMCHEN and bows to GAIGERN. FLAEMMCHEN thanks GIGOLO.)

GIGOLO (bowing to FLAEMMCHEN). Thank you. (Goes to table and sits down with GIGOLO LADY.)

GAIGERN. What have you to say to this miserable sinner that has finally crawled around? (HEADWAITER enters bar. WHITE BARTENDER approaches him behind bar with list. NEGRO BARTENDER goes to end of bar. HEADWAITER: "How is it today?" WHITE BARTENDER: "Not too good, I won't

have to order much for tomorrow."
HEADWAITER: "Show me today's
list." WHITE BARTENDER shows list
to HEADWAITER who lays it on bar,
bends over it, checking up.)

FLAEMMCHEN. When you weren't
there at six-thirty, I said to myself,
"He's forgotten you." "You will see,
he's forgotten you."

GAIGERN. Impossible! When I've
spent the whole day looking forward to being with you.

FLAEMMCHEN. Do you mean that
or are you flattering me? Come on
and let's have a dance, anyhow.
(HANS and KATIE dance off.)

GAIGERN (to KRINGELEIN). Do you
mind, Mr. Kringelein?

KRINGELEIN. Why, no.
(GAIGERN dances with FLAEMM-
CHEN. They dance during following
dialogue.)

GAIGERN. I have had a frightfully
boring day. It has left me stupid.

FLAEMMCHEN. What have you
been doing?
(KRINGELEIN sits at table watching
GAIGERN and FLAEMMCHEN. OT-
TERNSCHLAG appears, watches
dancing.)

GAIGERN. Chasing around
(Pause.)

FLAEMMCHEN. Chasing what?
(Pause.)

GAIGERN. Money.
(Pause. OTTERNSCHLAG turns to see
KRINGELEIN at table, starts toward
him.)

FLAEMMCHEN. Ah, money! (Pause)
You were very different yesterday.

GAIGERN. But that was yesterday!
(FLAEMMCHEN and GAIGERN dance
off. HEADWAITER and WHITE BAR-
TENDER finish checking list. BAR-
TENDERS shift places. WHITE BAR-
TENDER works on list.)

OTTERNSCHLAG. Ah, you are here! I
was looking for you in the lobby.

KRINGELEIN. For me?

OTTERNSCHLAG. Yes. Just had a no-
tion. You seem a man to whom I
can be useful. (He shudders) Hor-
rible place—this. (To HEAD-
WAITER) I'd like a whisky. (HEAD-
WAITER says "Whisky" to WHITE
BARTENDER, pointing to DOCTOR'S
table. Exits. WHITE BARTENDER says
"Whisky" to NEGRO. FRANK and
GERTRUDE dance on and off. To
KRINGELEIN) Were you looking for
a woman here?

KRINGELEIN. I? No. Anyway, I had
a very good opportunity. A young
lady asked me to dance.

OTTERNSCHLAG. You have quite an
appetite, haven't you? What is it
that you want? The usual mascu-
line paradise, champagne, women,
races, cards . . . Why aren't you
dancing?
(QUINN and MRS. NEWLYWED dance
on.)

KRINGELEIN. Unfortunately, I can't
dance. I ought to be able to dance
well. It seems to be very important.

OTTERNSCHLAG. Very important, indeed. In fact, quite essential
Learn quickly, as quickly as your
time allows. (WHITE BARTENDER

takes whisky on tray to serve OT-TERNSCHLAG *and returns behind bar)* So that you will never again have to say no to a woman. Believe me. Kringelein, a man who isn't with women is a dead man.

(QUINN *and* MRS. NEWLYWED *dance off.*)

KRINGELEIN. Of course, I can't go around much. My health is not very good. You understand?

OTTERNSCHLAG. I know. I quite understand. When a man's shirt collar gets half an inch too big for him then he doesn't need to tell you anything.

KRINGELEIN. Are you a physician? (THIRD WAITER *enters, orders drinks.* DAISY *and* JIM *dance on.*)

OTTERNSCHLAG. Was once; been everything—military surgeon, South Africa. Stinking climate. Taken prisoner. Prison camp in Nairrti, British East Africa. Abominable. Home on parole, not to fight. Surgeon in the Great Bestiality till the end. Grenade in the face. Carried diphtheria bacilli in the wound until 1920. Isolated two years. Not enough! (*Shivers. Lifts glass and drinks; slams it down*) Period there. I've been everything. Who wants to know? (*Turns to* KRINGE-LEIN *and faces front at once.*)

KRINGELEIN. Haven't you anybody who . . . ? I mean . . . Are you all alone in the world?
(DAISY *and* JIM *dance off.*)

OTTERNSCHLAG. Quite. And you?

KRINGELEIN. Yes, I'm alone too.

OTTERNSCHLAG. So, now you are staying in the Grand Hotel. "Grand Hotel," you think. "Most expensive hotel," you think. God knows what kind of miracles you expect from such a hotel. You will soon see what there is to it. Like everything else. One comes, stays awhile, goes away. Transients. (THIRD WAITER *exits*) What do you do in the Grand Hotel? Eat, sleep, loaf around, do business, flirt a little, dance a little. Yes, but what do you do anywhere? (NEWLYWEDS *dance on and off*) A hundred doors to one hall (PREYSING *appears, followed by* ZINNOWITZ) and nobody knows anything about the person next to him. When you leave another takes your room, lies in your bed. (*Rises*) End. (*Calls out to* WHITE BARTENDER) Waiter, charge it to me. (*Exits.*)

PREYSING. There's Flaemmchen.

ZINNOWITZ. Who?

PREYSING. Miss Flamm, your secretary.

ZINNOWITZ (*leaning on* PREYSING'S *shoulder*). Well, now you have what you were looking for. (FRANK *and* GERTRUDE *dance on and off,* See you later. It's too hot for me here. (*Exits.*)

PREYSING (*not looking at him, staring at* FLAEMMCHEN). See you later.

SECOND WAITER (*entering with tray, pushes past* PREYSING, *bumping him*). Pardon me, sir! (*Crosses to bar. To* NEGRO BARTENDER) Two cherry cobblers, one flip.
(NEGRO BARTENDER *puts two drinks on* WAITER'S *tray.* FLAEMMCHEN *and* GAIGERN *appear, dancing.*)

PREYSING (*seeing* FLAEMMCHEN). Good evening, Miss Flamm.

FLAEMMCHEN (*laughing*). Good evening, Mr. Preysing.

PREYSING. I would like to speak with you, Miss Flamm.

FLAEMMCHEN (*dancing with* GAIGERN). Pretty soon, Mr. Preysing.

PREYSING. It is urgent . . .

GAIGERN. Pardon me! The lady has urgent business—dancing with me! (*Dances away with her swiftly.*)

PREYSING. Insolence! Berlin manners!

SECOND WAITER (*passes with tray and drinks, bumps* PREYSING). Pardon me. (*Exits.*)
(QUINN *and* MARGARET *dance on.* PREYSING *crosses to table where* KRINGELEIN *is sitting, drinking through a straw.*)

KRINGELEIN (*seeing* PREYSING, *rises involuntarily*). I wish you a very good evening, Mr. Preysing.

PREYSING. Good evening.

KRINGELEIN. You are staying here too, Mr. Preysing?

PREYSING (*bewildered, closer to him*). I'm afraid I don't place you, sir . . .

KRINGELEIN. Oh, yes, you do! Kringelein. At the plant . . .

PREYSING. Kringelein, oh, yes! Kringelein! One of our agents?

KRINGELEIN. No. Assistant bookkeeper, Building C, room 23, third floor.

PREYSING. Yes! Is that seat taken? (*Is about to sit down in* KRINGELEIN's *chair.*)

KRINGELEIN. It's taken. (*He sits.*)

PREYSING (*with suppressed wrath*). I see . . . (*Goes to the next table. Sits with his back to* KRINGELEIN) Can't you move over a little bit, Mr. Kringelein?

KRINGELEIN. No.
(PREYSING, *furious, gets up, crosses and sits on chair at another table. Lights cigar, takes timetable out of his pocket and looks at it.* FLAEMMCHEN *and* GAIGERN *appear, dancing.* HANS *and* KATIE *follow them, dancing to center of stage as the music stops. Applause and laughter off stage.* MARGARET *and* MR. QUINN *exit.* KATIE *stands there while* HANS *exits, coming back immediately with her coat.* KATIE: "*Thank you, Hans. Where's your hat?*" HANS: "*Checked outside.*" *They both exit.*)

FLAEMMCHEN (*as music stops*). Ah, children, that was glorious.

KRINGELEIN (*rising*). Permit me, Miss Flamm.

FLAEMMCHEN (*taking his seat*). Give me a drink.

KRINGELEIN. May I? Do—do you wish an ice or—or champagne? (GAIGERN *sits at table.*)

FLAEMMCHEN. Champagne cocktail.

KRINGELEIN. I will see to it. (*Goes to end of bar, gives order to* WHITE BARTENDER, *who repeats it to* NEGRO.)

FLAEMMCHEN (*to* GAIGERN). You lead so wonderfully . . .

GAIGERN. Flaemmchen, would you do me a really great favor?

FLAEMMCHEN. I'd do anything for you!
(KRINGELEIN *is served at bar.*)

GAIGERN. Do you want to make a man very happy?
(KRINGELEIN *drinks at bar.*)

FLAEMMCHEN. I'd love to.
(KRINGELEIN *pays* WHITE BARTENDER.)

GAIGERN. Then dance one number with Kringelein.

FLAEMMCHEN (*disappointed*). Oh, is that what you want me to do?

GAIGERN. Don't you think he's nice?

FLAEMMCHEN. Oh, yes, I feel sorry for him.
(KRINGELEIN *busy with drink at bar.*)

GAIGERN. Poor devil.

FLAEMMCHEN (*mocking*). What's making you so thoughtful? You weren't a bit like this yesterday.
(NEWLYWEDS *enter from dance floor and exit.*)

GAIGERN. Yesterday—no. Something has happened to me.

FLAEMMCHEN. What . . . ?

GAIGERN. Last night I fell in love. The real thing. (*Music starts.* KRINGELEIN *finishes drink*) Do you know what that means?

FLAEMMCHEN. That isn't anything special. Why are you so all at loose ends?

GAIGERN. I am crazy. It is the real thing.

FLAEMMCHEN. Come, now! The real thing doesn't exist.

GAIGERN. I have found that it does! Now please dance with Kringelein.
(KRINGELEIN *crosses to* FLAEMMCHEN'S *table.*)

FLAEMMCHEN (*hesitates, then*) Sure!

KRINGELEIN. The cocktail will be right along.

FLAEMMCHEN (*rises and takes* KRINGELEIN *by arm*). Come and dance with me, Mr. Kringelein.

KRINGELEIN. Oh!
(PREYSING *rises at the moment* FLAEMMCHEN *invites* KRINGELEIN *to dance.*)

PREYSING (*coming down between* KRINGELEIN *and* FLAEMMCHEN). Miss Flamm, I would like to speak to you. Business. A dictation job.

FLAEMMCHEN. Fine. When does it start? Tomorrow morning?

PREYSING. No. Right now.

FLAEMMCHEN. Why, I'm busy right now. Do you gentlemen know one another? Mr. Kringelein, Mr. Preysing, Baron von Gaigern.
(GAIGERN *rises stiffly, bows to* PREYSING, *who bows to* GAIGERN, *ignoring* KRINGELEIN.)

PREYSING (*to* KRINGELEIN). Mr. Kringelein will be a good friend and not accept this invitation.

KRINGELEIN (*fairly rigid*). I could not think of not accepting it.

PREYSING. So! Now, I understand. You have reported sick at the plant, have you not? Leave of absence, with pay. And now you are here in Berlin, having a high time. Indulging in diversions (QUINN *and* MARGARET *appear, dancing*) which ill befit your position and which are far beyond your means. Quite extraordinary, Mr. Kringelein! We shall look into your books.

KRINGELEIN. My books!

FLAEMMCHEN (*coming between them*). Now, children! No fighting. Do that in your office. We're here to have a good time. Come, Mr. Kringelein! Let's have our dance.

KRINGELEIN (*as he is whirled away by* FLAEMMCHEN). Does the world belong to you, Mr. Preysing? Haven't I any right to live? (QUINN *and* MARGARET *exit.*)

FLAEMMCHEN (*dancing*). Come! Come! This isn't a place to fight! This is a place to dance. (*To* PREYSING) Will you please leave us alone?

PREYSING. Very well, Miss Flamm. I will not interfere with your pleasure. I will wait ten minutes for you. If you don't come then, I'll have to get somebody else . . .

FLAEMMCHEN (*somewhat intimidated*). Yes, Mr. Preysing.

KRINGELEIN. Come on! Let us dance! (*They exit, dancing.*)

PREYSING (*to* GAIGERN). I wonder if he is not an embezzler. An em-

bezzler, dancing here in the Grand Hotel!

GAIGERN. Oh, leave the poor devil alone! Death is staring him in the face!

PREYSING. I did not ask your advice.

GAIGERN. Nevertheless, I think it would be better if you went away.

PREYSING. We shall see who remains here the longer. (*They stare at each other.*)

GAIGERN. As you wish. (PREYSING *turns, goes to his table and sits.* ELEVATOR BOY *enters, goes to bar. Asks for* BARON VON GAIGERN. WHITE BARTENDER *points to the* BARON'S *table.* ELEVATOR BOY *crosses to it.*)

ELEVATOR BOY. Baron von Gaigern?

GAIGERN. Yes.

ELEVATOR BOY (*bowing*). The Baron's chauffeur would like to see the Baron. Important.

GAIGERN. Thank you. (ELEVATOR BOY *takes a few steps back, bows, and, as* GAIGERN *crosses,* ELEVATOR BOY *follows him out. Both exit.*)

PREYSING (*to* WHITE BARTENDER). Cognac. (WHITE BARTENDER *crosses to* FLAEMMCHEN'S *table with a drink, puts it on table then places cognac on* PREYSING'S *table and crosses back behind bar.* FLAEMMCHEN *and* KRINGELEIN *come, dancing. Dance on center stage.* THIRD WAITER *enters, and, as he passes*

GIGOLO's *table,* GIGOLO *says: "Waiter, check."* THIRD WAITER *gives bill to* GIGOLO. GIGOLO LADY *takes money from purse and hands it over to* GIGOLO, *whc in turn hands it over to* THIRD WAITER. GIGOLO *rises, so does* GIGOLO LADY. *He says: "Good-bye." Kisses her hand, leads her to entrance of bar; she exits.* THIRD WAITER *wipes table and exits with coffee cups as music stops.*)

FLAEMMCHEN. You must look at my face, not at the floor.

KRINGELEIN. Yes, Miss Flamm.

FLAEMMCHEN. You are trembling!

KRINGELEIN. I never danced before.

FLAEMMCHEN. Why, you are doing very well.

KRINGELEIN (*dancing*). I am happy, Miss Flamm.

FLAEMMCHEN. Really?

KRINGELEIN. Yes. For the first time in my life I am happy.

FLAEMMCHEN. It is sweet of you to say so, Mr. Kringelein. I'm glad you are happy. (*Music stops. Applause off stage*) It's all over now. No more music. Now I'll have to see Mr. Preysing.
(GIGOLO *goes to bar.* JIM *and* DAISY *enter and exit.*)

KRINGELEIN. Must you, Miss Flamm?

GIGOLO (*at bar*). Double brandy. (WHITE BARTENDER *repeats order.* NEGRO *serves it.*)

FLAEMMCHEN. Business, Mr. Kringelein. One has to earn a living.
(FRANK *and* GERTRUDE *enter. He is humming last bars of music they have just heard.* FRANK: *"Don't you like that tune?"* GERTRUDE: *"I'm crazy about it. I shall get it tomorrow." They exit.* GIGOLO *drinks at bar.*)

KRINGELEIN. Why? How is that?

FLAEMMCHEN. I am just another desk slave. (HEADWAITER *enters and crosses to* GIGOLO *at bar.* GIGOLO *pays* WHITE BARTENDER) Mr. Kringelein, money. I must go now.

KRINGELEIN. May I? (*Takes her arm. They go slowly to table*) It was wonderful. Thank you very much.

FLAEMMCHEN. I'm glad you liked it.

HEADWAITER (*to* GIGOLO *at bar*). Tired?

GIGOLO. Dead.

HEADWAITER. How is business?

GIGOLO. Rotten. (*Drinks brandy. Goes past* HEADWAITER *to door*) So long.

HEADWAITER. So long. (*Follows* GIGOLO *to door, as* GIGOLO *waits.* BARTENDERS *start to clean bar.* PREYSING *sees* FLAEMMCHEN *and rises.*)

PREYSING. Oh, here you are at last, Miss Flamm. You may go, Mr. Kringelein.

KRINGELEIN. I'm not taking orders from you here, Mr. Preysing.

(MARGARET *and* MR. QUINN *enter and exit.*)

PREYSING. What is this insolence? It is unheard of!

KRINGELEIN. Do you think you have free license to be insulting? Believe me, you have not. You think you are superior, but you are a very ordinary man, even if you did marry money, and people like me have to slave for three hundred and twenty marks a month.

(*Together*) {
PREYSING. Get out of my way, sir, or . . .

FLAEMMCHEN (*coming between them*). Oh, please, please. (PREYSING *turns away*.)
}

HEADWAITER. Pardon me, gentlemen, but we are closing. (*He picks up a couple of chairs, stands them on table, and exits.* COLORED BARTENDER *switches off light of bar and exits.* WHITE BARTENDER *switches off light at other end of bar and exits.*)

KRINGELEIN. I have a big account to settle with you, Mr. Preysing. I've been looking forward to this a long time. You don't like to see me here enjoying myself? But if a man is working himself to death, that's not worth talking about. That's what he is paid for. You don't care whether a man can live on his wages.

PREYSING. We pay the regular scale, and there's the sick fund, the old age fund . . .

KRINGELEIN. What a scale! And what a fund! When I had been ill four weeks, you wrote me a letter saying I'd be fired if I was ill any longer. Did you write that, or did you not?

PREYSING (*turning away from him*). I don't remember all the letters I sign. (HEADWAITER *appears with hats*) Anyhow, here you are on sick leave with pay. And living like a lord, like an embezzler!

HEADWAITER (*putting hats on chair*). Gentlemen, we are closing. (*Exits.*)

KRINGELEIN (*going up to him*). You are going to take that back! Right here, in the presence of the young lady. Who do you think you are talking to? (FLAEMMCHEN *takes* KRINGELEIN's *hat from table*) You think I am dirt. If I am dirt, you are a lot dirtier, Mr. Preysing!

PREYSING. You're fired!

FLAEMMCHEN (*taking step toward* KRINGELEIN *and giving him hat*). Oh, no, no!

PREYSING. What do you want of me? I don't even know who you are.

KRINGELEIN. But I know who you are. I keep your books. I know all about you. If one of your employees was as stupid on a small scale as you are on a big one . . .

PREYSING (*furious, takes* KRINGELEIN *by shoulders, shakes him and flings him against bar.* KRINGELEIN *drops hat*). That's enough! Shut your mouth! Get out! You're fired! You're fired!

KRINGELEIN (*breathlessly*). You fire me? You threaten me? But you can't fire me. You can't threaten me! You can't do anything more to me. (*Clinging to bar and edging along*) Not a thing more! Do you hear! I am ill. . . . I am going to die! Do you understand? I am going to die very soon. Nothing can happen to me any more. (*Backing out slowly*) Nobody can do a thing

more to me. (*Hysterical*) By the time you fire me I'll be dead already! (*With revulsive sob exits.* PREYSING *is spellbound.* FLAEMMCHEN *picks up* KRINGELEIN'S *hat and takes a step after him.*)

FLAEMMCHEN. Mr. Kringelein, Mr. Kringelein!

CURTAIN

SCENE V

SCENE—*Lobby. Orchestra is playing dinner music.* CLERK *is behind desk, checking papers.* SECOND BELLBOY *enters from corridor and stands near elevator door.* THIRD BELLBOY *stands near grill door.* OLD GENTLEMAN *is seated at table.* SENF *enters behind desk, sends* CLERK *out. Elevator comes down.* CLAIRE *and* EMILE *are talking.* HANS *and* KATIE *are at table.* MRS. BLOOM *and* MRS. FORTNER *sit at tables. Murmur of voices and telephone bells heard.* MR. FORTNER *enters through revolving door, looking for* MRS. FORTNER, *sees her at table, goes to her, apologizes for being late. She rises and* SUZANNE *enters through revolving door, goes to elevator.* PREYSING *enters from grill and goes to table.* FIRST WAITER *enters from corridor.* PREYSING *sees him.*

RECEPTION MAN (*phoning*). Yes, this is the manager. This you, Seftel? Well, what's the matter? No, I've got to know right now—one way or the other. No, right now . . . All right, now you either send that stuff over right away or don't send any of it ever. All right. (*Hangs up, talks to* SENF *until exit.*)

PREYSING (*to* FIRST WAITER). Here, cognac.

FIRST WAITER. Cognac, sir. (*Exits to grill.* RECEPTION MAN *exits to grill.* PREYSING *sits at table.*)

CLERK (*entering behind desk. To* SENF). Senf, you're looking terrible. How's your wife?

SENF. I was at the hospital all night walking up and down the corridor. They wouldn't even let me in to see her. (FLAEMMCHEN *enters from grill room and crosses to* PREYSING) And now I have to stand here, chained to this desk.

PREYSING (*sees* FLAEMMCHEN, *rises*). I see you came, Miss Flamm. That was sensible.

FLAEMMCHEN. What was it you wanted?

PREYSING. They'll keep an eye on that fellow (*pointing to grill room*) in there! They'll find out where he got the money to hang around the Grand Hotel. He'll be arrested! That embezzler!

FLAEMMCHEN. Well?

PREYSING (*motioning* FLAEMMCHEN *to sit*). Well, the point is . . . (*He looks around nervously.*)

FLAEMMCHEN. What?

PREYSING. I have got to go to England.

FLAEMMCHEN. Right away?

PREYSING. Yes. I put through a very big deal today (FRANK *and* GERTRUDE *enter from grill and stand talking*) involving hundreds of thousands. Now I've got to go to England. Another big deal there, hundreds of thousands at stake.

FLAEMMCHEN. What do you want me to do?

PREYSING. Come along.

FLAEMMCHEN. Oh.
(ANDRÉ *enters from corridor, goes to desk and says, "My key, please, 422." CLERK hands key and says: "Yes, sir. Oh, I have a message for you." CLERK hands him a message. ANDRÉ stands reading it in front of desk. FRANK and GERTRUDE exit to corridor and then return.*)

PREYSING. You see, I'd like to take a secretary to England with me. For my correspondence, and for company on the way. I am very nervous. I need somebody to take care of me on the trip, somebody who will be nice to me. (FLAEMMCHEN *glances up at him*) I don't know if you quite understand me. I am offering you a position of trust, in which I mean . . .

FLAEMMCHEN (*quietly*). I understand perfectly.

PREYSING. I thought we two could get along well on the trip. (FRANK *and* GERTRUDE *exit to corridor*) The idea came to me very suddenly. These tedious, fatiguing business trips. But with you along, I think it might be quite agreeable. If you wish to; do you?

FLAEMMCHEN. I must think it over. (*Elevator door opens—*DAISY *enters, crosses to* CLARA *and* EMILE *and says: "Where is* JOE?" *then stands talking.* DAISY *and* CLARA *exit to corridor.* EMILE *stands smoking.* ANDRÉ *asks the* CLERK: *"Where's the telegraph office?"* CLERK *says: "Around the corridor to your left, sir."* ANDRÉ *exits to corridor*) To England? For how long?

PREYSING. For . . . Well, I don't know exactly. It depends on you, too. (FLAEMMCHEN *takes out cigarette*) Perhaps we could have a couple of weeks in Paris. (*He lights her cigarette*) Name your price, Flaemmchen.

FLAEMMCHEN. Wait. I must figure it up. (*She puffs at her cigarette*) A thousand marks. Is that too much? And perhaps something for clothes for the trip. I have no clothes, not what you would call clothes. Of course, you would want me to look nice.
(EMILE *exits to corridor.* WAITER *enters from grill.*)

PREYSING. You look nice enough to me. (FIRST WAITER *serves cognac to* PREYSING, *saying "Cognac, sir"*) What are you going to have?

FLAEMMCHEN. Nothing, thanks.

PREYSING. Charge it—Preysing. (*He drinks*) Your health.
(WAITER *exits to grill.*)

FLAEMMCHEN. You were not nice to Mr. Kringelein. At the end he was crying, I think.
(*Elevator buzzer is heard. Elevator goes up. Telephone rings.* CLERK *answers it.* HANS *and* KATIE *rise.*)

PREYSING. It is agreed? Do you like the idea of going to England?

FLAEMMCHEN. Very much.

PREYSING. All right, then. We can go to a theatre tonight, if you care to. And I am going to get you a room here in the Hotel for tonight. (*He rises.*)

FLAEMMCHEN. So soon? (CLERK *rings desk bell.* SECOND BOY *answers and is sent out*) All right.

PREYSING. Are you going to be nice to me?

FLAEMMCHEN. If you don't force things . . .
(CLERK *rings desk bell.*)

PREYSING. All right then. (THIRD BELLBOY *goes to desk.* CLERK *hands him card and instructs him, and he exits to corridor.* CLERK *exits*) Run home and get your things. I'm going to get you a room and then we'll go to the theatre.
(KATIE *goes to elevator and* HANS *exits.*)

FLAEMMCHEN. Very well.
(PREYSING *drinks cognac, lays tip on table.*)

PREYSING. Hurry now, be back in half an hour.

FLAEMMCHEN (*rising*). Very well.
(PREYSING *goes to desk.*)

PREYSING (*to* SENF). I would like to have a room for my secretary for tonight. On the same floor as mine, if possible. I have a lot of work to get out.

SENF (*studying his list*). Just a moment, Mr. Preysing.
(SECOND BELLBOY *enters through revolving door and stands near it.* FLAEMMCHEN *takes step toward revolving door.* GAIGERN *enters through revolving door. They meet.*)

GAIGERN. Hello, Flaemmchen.

FLAEMMCHEN (*shaking hands*). So long, Baron. Thanks for an awfully good time.

GAIGERN. So long?
(FLAEMMCHEN *exits through revolving door.*)

SENF (*to* PREYSING). No. 171 is vacant, Mr. Preysing. Adjoins your room.

PREYSING. You see, I have a lot of dictation to do tonight.
(MRS. BLOOM *rises and exits to corridor.*)

SENF. I can leave the connecting door unlocked if you wish, sir.

PREYSING. I wish you would. (GAIGERN *goes to desk and stands beside* PREYSING) The young lady will occupy the room tonight.
(PREYSING *looks contemptuously at* GAIGERN, *and goes to ring buzzer for elevator.* WITTE *enters from corridor and approaches desk near* GAIGERN.)

SENF. Very well, Mr. Preysing.

GAIGERN (*to* SENF). Has Madame Crusinskaia gone to the theatre yet?

SENF. Not yet, sir.

GAIGERN (*seeing* WITTE *beside him*). Ah, Witte.

WITTE. Good evening, Baron. Now it seems that you are waiting here.

GAIGERN. How is Madame?

WITTE. Very well, today. Astonishingly well. She is like a charged dynamo. I have not seen her like this for a long time. She has found wings, or a great love.

GAIGERN. You speak like a man who knows human nature. (*Elevator opens.*)

WITTE. I know women and men. (SUZANNE *and* GRUSINSKAIA *come from elevator.* SUZANNE *says:* "*Goot evenink,*" *to* WITTE *who steps between them.* PREYSING *and* KATIE *exit to elevator. Elevator goes up.* EMILE *enters from corridor, goes to phone at desk, talks over it.* CLERK *enters behind desk.*)

GAIGERN (*approaching* GRUSINSKAIA). Good evening, Madame.

GRUSINSKAIA. Good evening. Good evening, Witte. Why aren't you at the theatre? Will everything go all right? Have you practiced the new tempo? Faster, more whirl, you know? All right, Suzanne. Witte, go to the car, I'll join you in a minute. (WITTE *and* SUZANNE *exit through revolving door.* GRUSINSKAIA *goes to table.* GAIGERN *follows her.*)

GAIGERN. Beloved!

GRUSINSKAIA. Where have you been all day? I have had such a longing to see you.

GAIGERN. I too. I was chasing all over town.

GRUSINSKAIA. Are you coming to the theatre? Oh, I shall dance tonight! How I shall dance! I want to feel that you are in the theatre.

GAIGERN. I can't; I can't. (MR. *and* MRS. FORTNER *enter from corridor, go to revolving door and exit.*)

GRUSINSKAIA. What are you going to do this evening?

GAIGERN. Gamble.

GRUSINSKAIA. Flix don't be silly. Let me give you some money. (EMILE *hangs up phone, exits to corridor.* CLERK *exits.*)

GAIGERN. No.

GRUSINSKAIA. Stubborn boy. (SUZANNE *enters from revolving door*) I am worried about you.

GAIGERN. Don't be, please.

SUZANNE (*at revolving door*). Madame, it is time to go.

GRUSINSKAIA (*to* SUZANNE). All right. (SUZANNE *exits through revolving door.* GRUSINSKAIA *takes* GAIGERN's *hand tenderly*) Dos— de vanya . . . (GRUSINSKAIA *exits through revolving door.* GAIGERN *follows her to door. Desk telephone rings. Elevator door opens. Music begins.* KRINGELEIN *enters from elevator, faultlessly dressed in evening clothes, a perfect copy of* GAIGERN. KRINGELEIN *stops, facing*

GAIGERN, *who takes a step toward him. Elevator goes up.*)

GAIGERN. Ah, Kringelein. (GAIGERN *critically fixes* KRINGELEIN'S *tie*) Ready?

KRINGELEIN. Ready.
(GAIGERN *offers* KRINGELEIN *his arm,* KRINGELEIN *takes it. They turn and walk, arm in arm, as they exit to corridor.*)

CURTAIN

SCENE VI

SCENE—*Gambling room. Wall brackets and table lamp are lit. A large gaming table stands obliquely, and around it are five chairs on which the players are seated. Against the wall there is a large lamp which casts its rays over the faces of the players. On the table is a baccarat "shoe" with cards. Before each player are bank notes and a champagne glass. There is a double door in the center which leads to the corridor. At one end of the room there is a settee. A small serving table, with glasses and champagne bottles on it, stands at extreme end of room.* GAIGERN *is seated at right side of gaming table;* KRINGELEIN *is seated beside him; the* GIGOLO *is standing at* KRINGELEIN'S *left.* EMILE *is seated at end of the table. Next to him* OTTERNSCHLAG *is seated, dealing from the "shoe." Back of* OTTERNSCHLAG *a* GENTLEMAN *stands. Seated at* OTTERNSCHLAG'S *side of the table is* SCHWEIMANN. *They are all intensely concentrated on the game.* FIRST WAITER *stands at buffet, cleaning glasses.*

OTTERNSCHLAG (*dealing to* GAIGERN). Again?

GAIGERN. Thanks. (*Looks at his cards.* OTTERNSCHLAG *turns his cards over*) En carte . . . (*throws his cards on table*) the devil!

OTTERNSCHLAG (*deals to* GAIGERN). Again?

GAIGERN. Please. (OTTERNSCHLAG *deals*) Bac. (*Throws cards on table, rises, leans back against table and drinks wine*) Well!

KRINGELEIN (*drinking hastily*). Will you help me out again, Baron? (EMILE, GIGOLO *place money on table.*)

GAIGERN (*to* KRINGELEIN). Can't you help me?

OTTERNSCHLAG. Bets, gentlemen.

KRINGELEIN (*to* BARON). How much can I bet?

GAIGERN. How much is left in the bank?

SCHWEIMANN. Twenty-two hundred, uncovered.

GAIGERN (*to* KRINGELEIN). Want to?

KRINGELEIN. All of it. (*Lays money on table.*)

GAIGERN. Banco!
(EMILE, GIGOLO *take their money back.* OTTERNSCHLAG *deals to* KRINGELEIN.)

KRINGELEIN (*taking cards*). What do I do now?

OTTERNSCHLAG. Do you still want to buy?

KRINGELEIN (*to* GAIGERN). Shall I?

GAIGERN. Yes. (OTTERNSCHLAG *deals* KRINGELEIN *a card*) Show down! You have nine.
(KRINGELEIN *rakes in money.* FIRST WAITER *goes to table to serve wine.*)

SCHWEIMANN. All respect.

KRINGELEIN. I win again!

OTTERNSCHLAG (*rising*). Who wants to bank? (*He pours himself a drink.*)

KRINGELEIN. Gentlemen, another glass of champagne. Please drink, it's marvelous, it tastes wonderful! (FIRST WAITER *serves* KRINGELEIN, GENTLEMAN *and* SCHWEIMANN.)

SCHWEIMANN. Thanks.
(*They drink.* GIGOLO *sits on* DOCTOR's *chair.*)

GIGOLO. I'll take the bank with 500. (*He lays money on table, takes "shoe" and deals from it.*)

GAIGERN. I place a hundred. (*Takes bank note from vest, throws it on table.*)

KRINGELEIN. Baron, I am winning more than I used to earn in a year.

. . . Oh, double what I used to earn.
(GIGOLO *deals cards to* GAIGERN *and then to himself.*)

GAIGERN. Cards, please. (*Gets third card*) Bac! (*Throws cards on table*) That was my last. (*Rises.* KRINGELEIN *rises and follows him.*)

KRINGELEIN. Have you lost everything? All that I lent you?

GAIGERN. Yes, I am sorry to say, I have no luck . . .

KRINGELEIN (*handing him some money*). Pardon me, Baron, permit me again.

GAIGERN. Thanks, Kringelein. I tried all respectable means this morning, this is only half respectable. This is my last chance. (*They go back to table. During the preceding dialogue between* KRINGELEIN *and* GAIGERN, GIGOLO *deals to* EMILE *at card table.*)

EMILE. Enough.

GIGOLO. Six.

EMILE. En carte. (EMILE *deals again*) Again. (GIGOLO *deals him a card, turns his own up*) Six. (EMILE *turns cards up*) Seven. (*Takes in the money.*)

KRINGELEIN. I drink, Baron, and win! Drink and win too, it is good.

GIGOLO. Would Mr. Kringelein care to take the bank?

KRINGELEIN. I'll take everything, gentlemen. Please, let's drink! (*He goes to chair* GIGOLO *has vacated. To* FIRST WAITER) Champagne!

(FIRST WAITER *is at buffet*) Champagne is expensive and good. (KRINGELEIN *sits*) For how much shall I take it?
(FIRST WAITER *takes bucket from buffet, places wine near* KRINGELEIN *and exits.* OTTERNSCHLAG *goes to upper end of settee and watches game.*)

GAIGERN (*places bank notes on table*). I'll place 500.

KRINGELEIN (*shocked; laying money on table*). Not all at once, Baron! If you lose . . .

GAIGERN. It's all one, Kringelein. (GAIGERN *sits*) Give me two cards. (KRINGELEIN *deals*) Now yourself. (KRINGELEIN *deals to himself.* GAIGERN *looks at cards*) Enough!

KRINGELEIN (*turning his cards over*). I have nine again.
(*The players ad-lib astonishment at* KRINGELEIN's *luck.*)

GAIGERN (*rising*). Thanks.

KRINGELEIN (*rising*). If the Baron means—we can . . .

GAIGERN. Thanks, Kringelein, you can't do anything about it. You have all the luck.

KRINGELEIN. Yes, I have. (*To players at table*) Let us drink champagne! (*They all drink*) I'm having luck for the first time in my life! (HEADWAITER *enters.*)

OTTERNSCHLAG. Out, Baron?

GAIGERN. Temporarily. In time, however, I shall surely recover. In ten or twenty years . . .
(*The game and dialogue at the*

card table continues simultaneously with the following dialogue between GAIGERN and HEADWAITER until WITTE's entrance. KRINGELEIN deals to EMILE.)

EMILE. Again.
(KRINGELEIN *deals* EMILE *card.*)

KRINGELEIN. What must I do now, must I deal again?

EMILE. Give me one more. (*Looks at cards*) Well, go ahead, turn your card and see what you have.

KRINGELEIN (*turning cards*). I have eight. (EMILE *throws down cards*) I win, don't I?

SCHWEIMANN. I place 500.

EMILE. Banco, deal me again!

KRINGELEIN. Oh, again? (*He deals.*)

EMILE. I have enough.

KRINGELEIN. Do I take one now?

EMILE. No, look at your cards. (*He turns cards.*)

KRINGELEIN. That's five. What shall I do now?

EMILE. Do as you please.

KRINGELEIN. I guess I'll take a card. (*He does*) I have seven. (EMILE *throws cards on table.*)

EMILE. Damn, you win again.

HEADWAITER (*to* BARON). A gentleman wishes to speak to you.

GAIGERN. To me?

HEADWAITER. Yes, sir.

GAIGERN. Show him in, please.

HEADWAITER. Yes, sir. (*As he passes card table.*)

KRINGELEIN. More champagne!

HEADWAITER. Yes, sir.
(WITTE *enters.* HEADWAITER *points to* BARON. *Glances at players then goes to* GAIGERN *at buffet.* HEADWAITER *exits.*)

WITTE (*in full-dress suit*). Am I disturbing you, Baron?

GAIGERN. No. How was it at the theatre? How is Lisaveta?

WITTE. Madame Grusinskaia is still at a farewell banquet which the French Ambassador is giving her. Our train goes at six twenty-seven. Madame leaves Berlin in triumph. (OTTERNSCHLAG *turns, watches* GAIGERN *and* WITTE *and listens in on their conversation.*)

GAIGERN. It went well tonight?

WITTE. Incomparably! An experience! A resurrection!

GAIGERN. You have something to tell me?

WITTE. Yes. I was despatched here as a courier of Lisaveta Andreievna
. . .

GAIGERN. And . . .

WITTE. I have already delivered my message: Our train leaves at six twenty-seven. That is all.

GAIGERN. Six twenty-seven . . . Six and a half hours left.

WITTE. What am I to tell our Lisaveta Andreievna?

GAIGERN. Tell her that I shall be on that train. Punctually.
(FIRST WAITER *enters with a bottle, goes to table, pours drink for* KRINGELEIN.)

WITTE (*with a slight bow*). Thanks. I'll see you later, Baron. (*Exits.*)

GIGOLO. Eight.

KRINGELEIN. But I have nine.

EMILE. There is no use playing against you.

SCHWEIMANN. Let's quit.

KRINGELEIN. Let's drink champagne! (HEADWAITER *enters*) I am having luck tonight, wonderful luck!

HEADWAITER. Gentlemen! I must warn you. (FIRST WAITER *exits*) You know gambling is against the rules here. Please, no noise. (*He goes to door, looks around and exits.*)

SCHWEIMANN (*rising and pushing chair back*). Let's wind up the game. I'm broke, and tired.

GIGOLO (*stretching.* EMILE *rises*). Let's quit before there is any unpleasantness.
(*Dialogue of players during* KRINGELEIN'S *next speech.*)

EMILE (*to* SCHWEIMANN). Good game, wasn't it?

SCHWEIMANN. Good for somebody else but not for me.

EMILE. Me either.

SCHWEIMANN. Well, it's all in a day's work. Win today—lose to-morrow.

EMILE. Beginner's luck.

SCHWEIMANN. Certainly was; look at him now.

EMILE. Did you ever see it to fail?

KRINGELEIN (*rising with a champagne glass in one hand and stuffing bank notes in his pocket with the other*). Don't let's quit! Oh, gentlemen, stay awhile; be my guests. Of course, I oughtn't to presume, but I'd just like to say I'm so grateful to you all. The evening has been so marvelous.

GENTLEMEN. For you, yes.

SCHWEIMANN. He's on top of the world.

KRINGELEIN (*to* GENTLEMAN). For the first time in my life I've gambled.

GENTLEMAN. You've done remarkably well.

SCHWEIMANN. Drunk as a lord.

KRINGELEIN. I've danced. (*Turns to* GIGOLO. SCHWEIMANN *and* EMILE *laugh*) You laugh, gentlemen, but for the first time I have tasted life! Life, gentlemen is a wonderful thing! But very dangerous. One must have courage for it, then it is wonderful. You do not know that, because you are healthy and happy. But I . . . believe me, man must know death. Not until then does a man know anything about life.

GIGOLO. He's drunk.

SCHWEIMANN. Rejoice in life, while yet the small lamp burns. (*Sings. They all laugh.*)

KRINGELEIN. One must have the courage to live. Then it is wonderful, the courage. (*Picks champagne glass from table*) To Life, gentlemen! Every glass high! To Life! The splendid dangerous, mighty, brief, brief Life, and the courage to live it. Gentlemen, I have lived only since last night. But that little while seems longer than all the time before. It doesn't matter that life be long, but that one live it entirely—that one . . . (*Clutches at his heart, drops wine glass and collapses.* SCHWEIMANN, EMILE, *and* GAIGERN *pick him up.* GENTLE-MAN *puts* KRINGELEIN'S *chair near door.*)

(*Simulta-neously*) {
GAIGERN. What's the matter?

OTTERNSCHLAG. Steady.

SCHWEIMANN. Look out.

EMILE. Watch yourself.
}

KRINGELEIN. Oh, the pain, the pain!

GAIGERN. Take his coat off.
(SCHWEIMANN *and* EMILE *take off his coat.* EMILE *hangs coat on chair.*)

GIGOLO. What's wrong with him?

SCHWEIMANN. Open his collar.

EMILE. Hold him up.

OTTERNSCHLAG. Lay him on the sofa.

(GAIGERN, SCHWEIMANN *help him to settee as* HEADWAITER *enters.*)

GAIGERN. Take it easy.

HEADWAITER. What's the trouble?

GIGOLO. Drunk.

SCHWEIMANN. No, he's ill.

EMILE. Looks ill. He needs a doctor.

SCHWEIMANN. Get a doctor!

GIGOLO. Awfully drunk.

SCHWEIMANN. A doctor!

OTTERNSCHLAG. I'll take care of him.

HEADWAITER. It often happens.

EMILE. Often happens. Why, you don't understand.

HEADWAITER. Please go now. The stairway to your left. Pardon me. Please, please. (HEADWAITER *pushes players out, as they protest. They exit in following order:* EMILE, SCHWEIMANN, GIGOLO *and* GENTLEMAN. HEADWAITER *closes door, goes to* DOCTOR) Thank you. I hope no attention is attracted. The gentleman is not used to champagne.

GAIGERN (*bending over* KRINGELEIN). He is ill.

OTTERNSCHLAG (*to* HEADWAITER). Please go, it will pass in a minute. (HEADWAITER *exits.*)

KRINGELEIN (*weakly*). Is it over? Over so soon? And it had just begun.

GAIGERN. Nonsense! You were too greedy, Kringelein. All at once is too much.

KRINGELEIN. Oh, the pain!

OTTERNSCHLAG (*at upper end of sofa*). I can help you. (*He takes out small case and gets a morphine needle. As he holds it up to the light,* GAIGERN *turns around, takes cigarette while in front of settee, goes to coat on chair. As* OTTERNSCHLAG *bends over* KRINGELEIN *to inject needle in arm,* GAIGERN *takes* KRINGELEIN'S *pocketbook out of his coat then he slowly moves around to back of sofa.*)

KRINGELEIN (*as the injection is made*). What is that?

OTTERNSCHLAG. A sweet bonbon.

GAIGERN. Do you always carry that with you?

OTTERNSCHLAG. Yes. (*Takes handkerchief, wipes needle and puts it in case*) That is my baggage. All I really need. Feel better, Mr. Kringelein?

KRINGELEIN. Thanks, yes. (*He seems to go to sleep.*)

OTTERNSCHLAG. He will be asleep presently. (*Feels* KRINGELEIN'S *pulse.*)

GAIGERN. Don't you think it is dangerous?

OTTERNSCHLAG. His heart is still beating, ready to make another effort.

KRINGELEIN. Stay beside me, Baron. (*Clutching at* GAIGERN) Please stay here beside me.

GAIGERN. Don't worry, Kringelein.

KRINGELEIN. I am not worrying. I'd like to live a little longer. But I am not afraid to die.

OTTERNSCHLAG. It's not worth getting excited about. Life—death. (*Puts* KRINGELEIN's *hand down; puts needle in pocket.*)

GAIGERN. Life? Death? Why talk about such things? (*Stands at table, facing* OTTERNSCHLAG *and* KRINGELEIN.)

OTTERNSCHLAG (*noticing* KRINGELEIN *groping around*). What's the matter, Kringelein?

KRINGELEIN (*looking around*). Where's my money? (GAIGERN *lights cigarette.*)

OTTERNSCHLAG (*looking at* BARON VON GAIGERN). He is asking where his money is.

KRINGELEIN. Where's my money? All that money?

GAIGERN. Most likely in his pocket.

KRINGELEIN. I want my pocketbook. In my coat. (OTTERNSCHLAG *goes to coat on chair*) My pocketbook with all that money in it.

OTTERNSCHLAG (*searching in coat, putting it beside* KRINGELEIN, *looks at* BARON). There isn't any pocketbook here.

KRINGELEIN. Where's my pocketbook? (*Sitting up*) My money? My pocketbook? More than fourteen thousand marks were in that pocketbook.

OTTERNSCHLAG (*staring at* BARON). Fourteen thousand marks is a good deal of money.

GAIGERN. Yes, it is.

OTTERNSCHLAG (*slowly, to* GAIGERN). With fourteen thousand marks one can travel; one's happiness might depend on fourteen thousand marks. Don't you think so, Baron?

GAIGERN. Quite possibly. (*Silence.*)

OTTERNSCHLAG. Kringelein's fourteen thousand marks must be got back to him at once.

KRINGELEIN. Fourteen thousand marks. Fourteen thousand two hundred marks! You don't know what that means to a man like me. (OTTERNSCHLAG *turns and looks at* KRINGELEIN) It means twenty years in which one has lived like a dog! (GAIGERN *turns, toying with cards on the table*) It's my life! Nobody gives you anything. You have to buy everything, and pay cash for it and pay dear. I want to pay for my last days with that money. Every hour costs money, every minute. I have nothing, nothing but that pocketbook. I have nothing, nothing but those fourteen thousand two hundred marks. (KRINGELEIN *leans against back of settee, tremulously continues*) I must have them back. I must have my money. (GAIGERN *turns and watches* KRINGELEIN *intently.* KRINGELEIN *rises*) Please, Baron, help me find my money. Help me! Get it back for me, Baron. (*Sinks on settee. There is a moment's silence.* OTTERNSCHLAG *looks from* KRINGELEIN *to* GAIGERN. GAIGERN *slowly crosses to lower end of settee. From his coat he takes* KRINGELEIN'S *pocketbook and drops it on lower end of settee.*)

GAIGERN. There's your pocketbook.

KRINGELEIN. Did—you—have my pocketbook, Baron?

GAIGERN. I was afraid you might be robbed. Good night, Kringelein. (*He starts to go.*)

KRINGELEIN (*holding* GAIGERN'S *hand tight*). Please stay beside me, Baron. Please. Don't leave me alone.

GAIGERN. I?

KRINGELEIN. Yes, do.

OTTERNSCHLAG. You need have no fear, Kringelein.

KRINGELEIN. I have none. Now.

GAIGERN. Don't you want to go to your room?

KRINGELEIN. Please stay beside me awhile.

OTTERNSCHLAG (*to* GAIGERN). Is Madame Grusinskaia to be informed that you will not be able to make the six twenty-seven train?

GAIGERN. I'll be on that train. (*Tenderly, to* KRINGELEIN) I'm sorry, Kringelein, but I have no time. (*Gently pats* KRINGELEIN'S *head, smiles at him and as he crosses to center door*) Good-bye, Kringelein. (*Exits.*)

KRINGELEIN (*sinks back weakly on settee, looks at* OTTERNSCHLAG *wonderingly*). No time? No time? (OT-TERNSCHLAG *crosses to serving table, picks up glass of champagne, turns and faces front*) I don't understand the Baron . . . I don't feel well.

OTTERNSCHLAG (*raises wine glass on a level with his eyes, intently watching the bubbles as they rise*). Atmospheric conditions in the Grand Hotel, Mr. Kringelein.

ACT THREE

SCENE I

SCENE—*Hotel corridor. Elevator door is down at one end. Room 171, 170, 169 and 168 running from right to left. Corridor leading to other rooms continues off left. At the center of the stage there is a small desk with a chair in back of it. There is a telephone on the desk. Music is heard playing very softly.* CHAMBERMAID (ANNE), *half asleep, is discovered behind desk. After a few seconds the elevator door opens.*

ELEVATOR BOY (*enters from elevator carrying a small bag, followed by* PREYSING *and* FLAEMMCHEN).

Right here, sir. (*They cross and stop in front of Room 171.* ELE-VATOR BOY *unlocks door 171, en-*

ters and switches on room light. Places key in lock inside of door.)

PREYSING. Here is your room, Flaemmchen.

FLAEMMCHEN. And where is your room?

PREYSING. Right next door. I can knock, Flaemmchen. And then you must say "come in."

FLAEMMCHEN (*resigned*). All right.

ELEVATOR BOY (*at door of 171*). Has the lady any more luggage?

FLAEMMCHEN (*embarrassed*). No.

PREYSING. The rest of the luggage is coming tomorrow.

ELEVATOR BOY. Yes, sir. Good night, sir.
(*Elevator door closes.*)

MAID (*awakening at desk*). Do you wish anything?

FLAEMMCHEN. No, thanks. Nothing. (*Goes hastily into room, closes and locks door.*)

PREYSING (*unlocks door of his room, turns on his lights. In doorway*). Send in the hall porter. (*Closes and locks door 170 behind him.*)

MAID (*takes up telephone from desk*). Service room number one. (*Yawns*) Schurmann, are you there? You're to come to 170. (*Pause. Elevator opens.* OTTERNSCHLAG *leads* KRINGELEIN *out.*)

OTTERNSCHLAG (*to* ELEVATOR BOY). Wait a moment. (*Leading* KRINGE-LEIN *to room 169*) Are you feeling better now?

KRINGELEIN. Thanks. Splendid. I don't know what was the matter awhile ago. I thought I was a dead man.

OTTERNSCHLAG. Heart. You live too intensely, Kringelein. Go and lie down. (OTTERNSCHLAG *stops at door of 169*) Do you need me any more?

KRINGELEIN (*at door 169*). No, thanks. No, thank you very much. I feel perfectly all right.

OTTERNSCHLAG. Good night, then. (KRINGELEIN *enters room, turns on light, closes and locks door.* OT-TERNSCHLAG *goes to elevator.*)

ELEVATOR BOY. Up?

OTTERNSCHLAG (*entering elevator*). No, down. (OTTERNSCHLAG *exits to elevator, door closes. Buzzer sounds.*)

MAID (*at phone*). Service room number one.
(PORTER *enters from corridor and goes to desk.* MAID *hangs up.*)

PORTER. What's the hurry? These people that yell for a porter at one in the morning! Someone new just come in?

MAID. A lady.

PORTER (*inquiringly*). Hm?

MAID (*shrugs her shoulders in dis-approval*). Hm.
(PORTER *goes to 170, knocks, opens door, enters and closes it behind him. Buzzer is heard. It continues*

to sound until elevator door opens. "My God, yes! I'm coming." Rises and hurriedly exits through corridor. Elevator door opens. SECOND BELLBOY *enters with two baskets of flowers, goes to 168, unlocks door, turns on light, enters.* SUZANNE *follows him and stands at doorway.* GRUSINSKAIA *and* WITTE *enter from elevator, slowly walk to door of room.*)

WITTE. Lisaveta is in bloom. Lisaveta is happy.

GRUSINSKAIA. Rapturous, Witte! (*To* SUZANNE) You can begin to pack, Suzanne, please.
(SECOND BELLBOY *comes out from 168.*)

SECOND BELLBOY (*hands key to* SUZANNE). Is that all, madame? (*She tips him*) Thank you. (SUZANNE *enters 168, closes door. As he passes* WITTE *and* GRUSINSKAIA) Good night, madame. (*Exits to elevator door. Elevator closes.*)

GRUSINSKAIA (*leaning back on desk*). He will certainly be on our train, he says?

WITTE. Yes, so he said.

GRUSINSKAIA. What do you think of him, Witte?

WITTE. I have never seen you so radiant, Lisaveta Andreievna, as today.

GRUSINSKAIA. What do you think of him?

WITTE. Him? He is walking a tight-rope. He is still keeping his balance. . . .

GRUSINSKAIA (*proudly*). But he is a real man, Witte. One can't help admiring him.

WITTE. Yes—it's so. One does . . .

GRUSINSKAIA. I am anxious about him, Witte. It is time to go and sleep. It's late. Good night, my dear.

WITTE (*kissing her hand*). Good night, Lisaveta.
(*She kisses his forehead.*)

GRUSINSKAIA (*in door*). I shall not sleep, yet. If you see him, Witte, send him to me . . . (*She exits, closing door behind her.* WITTE *stands for a moment, then exits up corridor.* MAID *enters from corridor with bundle of linen under arm, goes behind desk, pushing her chair out of way, and putting linen under desk.* PORTER *enters from 170, closing door behind him.*)

MAID. What was wrong with the party in 170?

PORTER. I had to unlock the door to 171. His wife lives next door.

MAID. His wife! (*Handling fresh linen which she takes out from desk.*)

PORTER. Well, who cares? (CHAUFFEUR *appears from corridor, looks at couple and turns away. Stands waiting*) More beds to move? Say, what's going on in the middle of the night?

MAID. Spare bed to make up in 123. Get busy!

PORTER. You're supposed to be through for the day.

MAID. Twenty minutes ago.

PORTER. Well, what are you working yourself to death for?

MAID. I need the tips.

PORTER. Why don't you tell the manager you want more money?

MAID (*following him with fresh linen under arm*). A lot they care!

PORTER (*to* CHAUFFEUR). What do you want here?

CHAUFFEUR (*takes step on stage*). I am waiting for Baron von Gaigern.

PORTER. That's not allowed.

CHAUFFEUR. But I am his chauffeur. (*Pointing to* MAID) The young lady knows me.

MAID. Let the gentlemen be, Schurmann. That's the Baron's chauffeur, 184.
(PORTER *exits to corridor.*)

CHAUFFEUR (*to* MAID). Yes, we know each other well, don't we, miss?
(MAID *exits corridor. Elevator opens.* GAIGERN *enters.*)

GAIGERN (*to* ELEVATOR BOY, *giving him tip*). There, give your sweetheart my love.

ELEVATOR BOY (*off stage*). Thank you. Good night, sir.
(*Elevator door closes.* GAIGERN *turns, sees* CHAUFFEUR, *looks at him for a second.*)

GAIGERN (*furious*). What do you mean running after me, here?

CHAUFFEUR (*going up to him*). Been trying to give me the slip, eh? Nowhere to be found all day. You've messed the pearl job, and now you get high and mighty.

GAIGERN. I don't like your tone.

CHAUFFEUR. You may have to. How about the money?

GAIGERN. I'll pay you back.

CHAUFFEUR. Have you got the money?

GAIGERN. I'll get it.

CHAUFFEUR. When?

GAIGERN. Tonight.

CHAUFFEUR. Who from?

GAIGERN. That's my business.

CHAUFFEUR. Man—if you don't . . .

GAIGERN. You don't frighten me. I don't need you. I don't want you. I'm through with you.

CHAUFFEUR. Don't talk so big, Baron. And don't think you can throw us down and get away with our money.

GAIGERN. You shall be paid back, and then we're through.

CHAUFFEUR. Have you got the money—six thousand marks?

GAIGERN (*laughing*). I gave my last twenty pfennigs to the lift-boy.

CHAUFFEUR (*following him slowly*). You've got nothing to laugh at. You're in a bad way.

GAIGERN. Yes, desperate.

CHAUFFEUR. Come on. Stay with us. Something else will turn up. (*Grabbing his arm*) We'll still count you in. . . .

GAIGERN (*releasing himself with jerk*). I don't want to be counted in!

CHAUFFEUR. Don't be a fool!

GAIGERN. Listen to me. It is past one. At six twenty-seven I am going to catch a train, no matter what happens.

CHAUFFEUR. If you pay the money back.

GAIGERN. I'll have it, I tell you. . . .

CHAUFFEUR. How are you going to get it?

GAIGERN. I'm going to try something tonight.

CHAUFFEUR. You don't get out of this hotel until you produce the money. You can take that as final. (*Suddenly changing his tone*) What have you got in mind? Do you need tools?

GAIGERN. No—yes—for emergencies.

CHAUFFEUR (*quickly slips him pair of picklocks from his pocket*). Good enough?

GAIGERN. I have five hours yet. I will get the money.

CHAUFFEUR (*patting his arm*). That's the way to talk.

GAIGERN. Right. (*Sees* MAID *approaching*) On your way now.

CHAUFFEUR (*loud*). Very well, Baron.
(MAID *enters from corridor, goes to desk.* CHAUFFEUR *exits through corridor.*)

GAIGERN. Oh, little Anna, you still up?

MAID. I'm doing overtime, Baron.

GAIGERN. Is there so much to do?

MAID. Forty rooms for me alone, and all of them full.

GAIGERN. Poor little Anna. (*Sits on end of desk*) Do you happen to know if Mr. Preysing is in his room?

MAID (*behind desk, busy with linen*). His room! He will be next door. In 171.

GAIGERN. Next door! Why in there?

MAID. The lady is in 171.

GAIGERN. Aha! The lady! There is a lady with him?

MAID. Not his wife.

GAIGERN. How do you know?

MAID. She is too pretty.
(*Music is heard playing.*)

GAIGERN. The music is playing rather late tonight, isn't it? (*Glances at room 171, then 170.*)

MAID. Yes, they play until two, in the yellow pavilion.

GAIGERN. It is almost two now. So the gentleman is in next door with the lady? Are you certain? (*Sits on end of desk.*)

MAID. Certain.

GAIGERN (*to* MAID). Interesting, huh?

MAID. Oh, Baron, we don't pay any attention. We are too tired.

GAIGERN (*taking her arm, rises and leads her to end of desk*). Poor little Anna. Poor, tired, little girl.

MAID (*looking at him languishingly*). You are so kind, Baron.

GAIGERN. You'd better go and get some sleep now, little Anna.

MAID (*with bundle of linen under arm, closer to* GAIGERN). You are so kind, Baron.

GAIGERN. Good night, Anna.

MAID. Good night, Baron. I still have the spare beds to make up. (*Exits through corridor.* GAIGERN *stands alone for a couple of seconds, crosses slowly, listens at* PREYSING'S *and then* FLAEMMCHEN'S *door, then crosses to* PREYSING'S *door, tries knob, finds it locked, takes picklock out of his pocket, looks around, as he puts key in lock. Lights go out.*)

CURTAIN

SCENE II

SCENE—*Music plays throughout scene.* FLAEMMCHEN'S *room. At the right there is a door, and at the left another door, which is the connecting door to* PREYSING'S *room. To the left of this door is a small table with a lamp on it. Beside the table is a large armchair. Against the right wall there is a bed. At the head of the bed, there is a chair with* FLAEMMCHEN'S *suitcase on it.* FLAEMMCHEN *is alone. She takes a nightgown and slippers from case, crosses to bed, places slippers beside it, and then carefully arranges nightgown on bed. She starts to undress. As she begins to take off her dress, there is the sound of* PREYSING *groping for connecting door.* FLAEMMCHEN *stops.* PREYSING *knocks softly. She goes to door.*

FLAEMMCHEN (*her hand up to keep door closed*). Yes?

PREYSING (*opens the door a little*). May I?

FLAEMMCHEN. A moment more . . . I'd like to undress. . . . Then . . .

PREYSING. But that is just what . . .

(*He enters the room. He is dressed in trousers and smoking jacket.*)

FLAEMMCHEN. I would rather you'd let me dress alone, please. Then . . .

PREYSING (*hoarsely*). Please let me watch you . . . (*Closes door.*)

FLAEMMCHEN (*after a second's*

pause, cool, but docile). If you really want . . . (*She slips out of her dress, places it on chair, crosses to bed, sits there, takes off shoes and starts taking off her stockings.* PREYSING *follows her action greedily.*)

PREYSING (*as* FLAEMMCHEN *rolls down her stockings*). Please let your stockings alone. . . . You look so pretty that way.

FLAEMMCHEN. No . . . I feel uncomfortable. I can't walk around in nothing but stockings.

PREYSING. But you look much more interesting like that, in stockings. There is something—something—about it. I can buy you more if they get torn.

FLAEMMCHEN (*stops*). Please—no.

PREYSING. Surely I can ask that of you. You must keep your stockings on.

FLAEMMCHEN. Oh, well . . . (*Pulls up her stockings.*)

PREYSING. You're sweet.

FLAEMMCHEN. You think so? (*Stands and puts feet in slippers. He watches her a second. Then quickly goes to table, takes keys from hip pocket, places them on table.*)

FLAEMMCHEN. Do you mean to sleep here? Please, not in this room . . . Your room . . .

PREYSING (*crossing down to armchair, he sits, turning away from her rather peevishly*). I only want to get things out of my pockets, that's all.

FLAEMMCHEN. Have I offended you? Please forgive me. I didn't mean that. Really, I didn't . . . Please . . . (*Sits on arm of* PREYSING'S *chair.*)

PREYSING (*arm around her*). It's all right. . . . Do you know, I imagined you quite different.

FLAEMMCHEN. Different? How different?

PREYSING. Well—more of a coquette—you know.

FLAEMMCHEN. Do you like me better, dressed?

PREYSING. What do you mean? You are so sweet. (*Caresses her*) Wouldn't you like to call me by my first name?

FLAEMMCHEN (*shakes her head earnestly*). Oh, no!

PREYSING. Why not?

FLAEMMCHEN. I mean it; I can't.

PREYSING. You're a funny little creature, Flaemmchen. I can't make you out.

FLAEMMCHEN. Not funny at all. One doesn't get friendly just off-hand. Of course, I can go to England with you, and everything. We agreed. But there mustn't be anything left hanging over. Names are like that. I meet you next year. I say, "How do you do, Mr. Preysing?" And you say, "That is the young lady who was my secretary in Manchester." All quite proper.

But—supposing I met you when you were with your wife and I called out, "Hello, Baby"—you wouldn't like that.

PREYSING (*running his hand over her body*). Oh, Flaemmchen. You're so sweet. And your body is so slender—and young . . .

FLAEMMCHEN (*rising*). I'm getting cold. May I put on my kimono? (*She places her kimono around her shoulders and sits on bed.*)

PREYSING. Are you going to be nice to me?

FLAEMMCHEN (*simply*). Why, yes. (PREYSING *crosses to bed and sits beside her.*)

PREYSING. Very nice?

FLAEMMCHEN. Why, yes—we agreed.

PREYSING (*places arm around her*). Very?

FLAEMMCHEN (*quite simply, as a matter of course*). Well, I must, yes . . . Mustn't I?

PREYSING (*kneeling quickly and kissing her hand with great emotion*). Flaemmchen . . . (*His head lying in her lap.*)

FLAEMMCHEN (*strokes his head reluctantly*). Well, then . . . (*Softly*) You needn't be so frightened . . .

PREYSING. Do you like me a bit too? Just a little bit . . . (*Kisses her hand.*)

FLAEMMCHEN (*very simply*). Well, you are still a stranger to me—but that doesn't matter.

PREYSING. I don't want you to think of anyone else . . .

FLAEMMCHEN (*softly*). I'm not thinking of anyone—of no one in this world.

PREYSING (*he kisses her arm, neck, his head rests against her breast. Suddenly he listens intently*). Listen . . . !

FLAEMMCHEN. Yes. I have heard it for a long time. Music from the Yellow Pavilion. I love it when it comes from so far away.

PREYSING (*looking toward door*). I don't mean the music. Didn't you hear anything else? I heard something.

FLAEMMCHEN (*henceforward everything particularly soft and subdued. Quickly*). What?

PREYSING. I heard something—as if in my room.

FLAEMMCHEN. I hear your heart beating . . . I hear it plainly.

PREYSING. Let me go . . . I must see . . . (*Rises.*)

FLAEMMCHEN. What? Where are you going?

PREYSING. Someone is in my room My money is in there. . . . I must look.

FLAEMMCHEN. You only imagine . . .

PREYSING (*listens*). Someone is in my room . . . (*Takes a step left. Listens.*)

FLAEMMCHEN (*shrugging*). Well.

then go and look—if you want to
. . .

PREYSING. Yes . . . (*Crosses to door. He slowly turns doorknob.*)

CURTAIN

SCENE III

SCENE—PREYSING'S *room. It is dark. A door in center of right wall leads to* FLAEMMCHEN'S *room. There is a small writing desk, with a chair beside it. A lamp and telephone are on it. There is a door which leads to the corridor. At the right of it is a small table with a glass, water pitcher and tray on it. To the left of the center door there is a bed. To the right of bed, there is a table with a bed lamp on it. Across the foot of the bed is* PREYSING'S *coat, with his pocketbook in the inside pocket. Downstage there is a door which connects with Room 169.* GAIGERN *is at bed, taking money. His flashlight is on. He finds the wallet and quickly places it in his coat pocket. As he does so, he hears the doorknob as* PREYSING *turns it.* GAIGERN *quickly puts out flashlight, creeps to center door as* PREYSING *opens door and is silhouetted in the doorway by the light from* FLAEMMCHEN'S *room.*

PREYSING (*cautiously*). Is someone there? (*After a pause*) Is someone there? (PREYSING *lights lamp on desk.* GAIGERN *opens door, trying to get out*) Oh . . . Ah, it's you, Baron. What do you want here?

GAIGERN. Excuse me, I must have made a mistake. . . . The wrong door . . .

PREYSING. We shall soon see if you've made a mistake.

GAIGERN. By all appearances . . . Good night . . . (*Starts to go.*)

PREYSING (*shouting*). Stay here! (*Quickly crosses to bed, searches pockets of his coat, makes certain that his wallet is missing*) Hand over the pocketbook.

GAIGERN. Listen . . .

PREYSING (*coming close to* BARON). Hand it over! (GAIGERN *holds it out to him without a word.* PREYSING *takes it, opens pocketbook, looks at money, steps back*) So that's how we stand, Baron!

GAIGERN (*pale but firm*). You do not understand. I had to do it. It's a matter . . . I must get some money tonight.

PREYSING. Indeed? Must you, Baron . . . ? But you aren't going to! You're going to jail, Baron. You are a thief.

GAIGERN. Be quiet.

PREYSING. So! the Baron, the nice friend of the nice Mr. Kringelein.

GAIGERN. Be quiet. Call the police if you like, but be quiet.

PREYSING. I am going to call the police, you may be sure of that. But be quiet? No, my dear friend, I am going to show you how to play the aristocrat. (*Reaching for phone on desk*) I'm going—to show you . . .

GAIGERN (*quietly and quickly covers* PREYSING *with a revolver, speaks quietly*). Another word out of you and I fire!

PREYSING (*apoplectic*). What? (*Steps back toward table lamp on desk reaching for it behind his back*) Fire? Will you? Fire! (*He grabs lamp, pulls it from its socket and lights go out. He throws the lamp in* GAIGERN's *direction. There is a crash. They struggle in the dark, then a shot and the thud of a body dropping to the floor.* PREYSING *has dropped the pocketbook and the bills have scattered over the floor*) Fire? Will you! You've got yours! You've got yours! (*Suddenly stops. A pause. Suddenly uneasy*) Say, you, what's the matter? What's the matter with you? What . . . (*He switches on table lamp at head of bed and bends over body of* GAIGERN *which is lying parallel to the bed.* PREYSING *shakes him*) What's the matter with you? Say something! (*Kneels down over* GAIGERN) Say . . . Say! You! Are you . . . ? (*He turns* GAIGERN *over on his back. Startled, he rises slowly, backing away from the* BARON's *body*) My God, what has happened? What has happened? (*Stares at* GAIGERN's *face.*)

FLAEMMCHEN (*opens door, comes into room, stands there surprised, apprehensive, speaks very softly*). What is the matter? What was that noise?

PREYSING. Something has happened!

FLAEMMCHEN. Happened? My God! What? (*She notices* GAIGERN) Is he dead? Is he dead?

PREYSING. Quiet, don't scream, they might hear. (*Both staring at* GAIGERN's *body*) He was going to shoot me. I only hit . . .

FLAEMMCHEN (*hysterically*). He is still looking.

PREYSING (*quickly*). It was self-defense. . . . They must believe me.

FLAEMMCHEN (*stifling a shriek*). Out! (*She stumbles toward door. He grabs her.*)

PREYSING. Stop! Where are you going?

FLEMMCHEN. Out! Let me . . . I can't . . . I want to get out.

PREYSING (*putting his hand over her mouth*). Not so loud. You'll wake the whole hotel.

FLAEMMCHEN (*struggling with him*). Let me out!

PREYSING. God damn . . .

FLAEMMCHEN (*shrilly*). I want to get out!

PREYSING (*his hand over her mouth*). Are you crazy? (*Grabs her, pulls her away from the door*) Try and keep your head.

FLAEMMCHEN (*distinctly*). Please let me out of here. . . . Oh! (*A knock on the door.* FLAEMMCHEN *sways backwards.*)

PREYSING (*whispers*). Who's that?

KRINGELEIN (*outside*). What's going on? Open the door!

PREYSING. Kringelein!

FLAEMMCHEN (*running to door, crying out*). Kringelein! Kringelein! (*She turns the key, PREYSING struggling with her to prevent her from opening door.*)

KRINGELEIN. Open the door!

PREYSING. Don't let anybody in! (FLAEMMCHEN *opens the door.*)

KRINGELEIN (*enters;* FLAEMMCHEN *grabs him*). What's the matter? (*He follows* FLAEMMCHEN's *slow look at* GAIGERN) Oh, my God . . . !

PREYSING. He was going to rob me. To shoot me. He is dead.

KRINGELEIN (*bends over* GAIGERN. *Tenderly*). The Baron, poor Baron. Dead? He is dead. Dead. Just like that.

FLAEMMCHEN (*hysterical. Hand on* KRINGELEIN's *shoulder*). Take me out of here, Mr. Kringelein! (*Looking away from* GAIGERN) Please take me out.
(KRINGELEIN *rises,* FLAEMMCHEN *clings to him almost fainting.*)

PREYSING. The young lady—came here. . . . She said . . .

KRINGELEIN. I will take care of her. Come, Miss Flamm. (*Arm about* FLAEMMCHEN. *Over shoulder to* PREYSING) I'll be right back. (KRINGELEIN *leads her out.*)

FLAEMMCHEN (*spiritless*). Yes. (*They exit.*)

PREYSING (*looks at body, wipes his forehead, struggles with himself, goes to phone at desk, speaks over phone*). Listen—hall porter? No. Pardon me—a mistake. (*Puts down telephone*) I can't. I can't. . . .

KRINGELEIN (*enters, goes quietly to* BARON's *body, bends over him.* PREYSING *rises*). His eyes are open. He looks so peaceful. . . . Death cannot be so difficult. (*Kneels by* BARON's *body.*)

PREYSING. He mustn't be touched until the police come.

KRINGELEIN. The police will be here right away. I telephoned for them.

PREYSING. You did! What do you want in here?

KRINGELEIN (*rising, turning to* PREYSING). I've come to get the young lady's clothes.

PREYSING. They're in the other room.

KRINGELEIN. Is there anything I can do for Your Excellency, before the police come? I shall be glad to do anything I can, in spite of certain disagreements between us.

PREYSING. Yes. Listen—you . . . No. I don't know. (*Looks sharply at him*) Wait a bit.

KRINGELEIN. Would Your Excellency like me to send a telegram to your esteemed wife?

PREYSING. No. No.

KRINGELEIN. There will certainly be an investigation immediately. I should be glad to attend to all the necessary details before I leave.

PREYSING. You cannot leave. I need you. As a witness.

KRINGELEIN. My testimony is soon given.

PREYSING. The man was a burglar. He was going to steal my money. Everything is still there on the floor. I have touched nothing.

KRINGELEIN (*looking at bank notes and pocketbook scattered about on the floor*). Possibly. Possibly he was going to steal your pocketbook. . . . But one does not kill a man about a pocketbook.

PREYSING (*turns back to* KRINGELEIN). What are you going to do with Miss Flamm? That woman was working with the man under cover. She enticed me into her room so that he could come here and rob me. I will say that in court. They will lock up the girl.

KRINGELEIN. The lady is in my room. I came to get her clothes so that she can be dressed when the police come.

PREYSING (*going close to* KRINGELEIN). Listen, Kringelein, if we lock this door no one need know that I was with a lady. Miss Flamm spent the night with you. She knows nothing. You also know nothing, Mr. Kringelein, and all goes well. You will not be questioned. Nor will Miss Flamm.

KRINGELEIN. Your Excellency has killed a man.

PREYSING. That has nothing to do with it.

KRINGELEIN. It has everything to do with it.

PREYSING. Mr. Kringelein, you are from Fredersdorf. You know my father-in-law. You know my family. Kringelein, I have children. I lose everything if this story about Miss

Flamm comes into court. Kringelein, take the affair of the lady upon yourself. You have nothing to do but hold your tongue. You travel with her—you . . .

KRINGELEIN (*scornfully*). The police will be here immediately, Your Excellency.

PREYSING (*picking up scattered bank notes from floor, and coming back to* KRINGELEIN *who stands watching* PREYSING *scornfully*). Here, here. I'll give you money. How much do you want? You need money.

KRINGELEIN. No, thank you very much. I have enough.

PREYSING. I beg you, Mr. Kringelein. I beg you help me. I beg you. My fate depends on you. Kringelein, when you come back to Fredersdorf I will see if your position cannot be improved—so that you never need worry again.

KRINGELEIN (*crescendo*). Many thanks. Many, many thanks, Mr. Preysing. I'm never coming back to Fredersdorf. Never. You can keep your position, and you don't have to worry about me, worry about yourself. In a minute the police will be here. (*Turns to body.*)

PREYSING. God! The police!

KRINGELEIN (*bending over* GAIGERN, *softly, to himself*). He looks content. It cannot be so hard. (*Knock on door.* PREYSING *slumps into chair.*)

PREYSING. They are coming . . .

KRINGELEIN (*turning to* PREYSING). You must be steady now, Mr. Preysing.

CURTAIN

Scene IV

SCENE—GRUSINSKAIA's *room. Same as before with the exception of a wardrobe trunk which is being packed by* SUZANNE. *A dress is on the couch.* GRUSINSKAIA *is sitting at the dressing table, looking at herself in a little hand mirror and humming a Russian tune.*

SUZANNE. It is just three o'clock in the morning. (*Yawns and continues packing trunk.*)

GRUSINSKAIA. Tired, Suzanne?

SUZANNE. Is Madame not tired?

GRUSINSKAIA. Oh, no.

SUZANNE. Will Madame not change now?

GRUSINSKAIA. Later, Suzanne. Do you know what, Suzanne? I think I will do my hair differently. (*Fluffs up her hair, laughingly*) How is that?

SUZANNE. Not bad. (*Laughs.*)

GRUSINSKAIA. Why are you laughing?

SUZANNE. Because I remembered something Madame once said.

GRUSINSKAIA. What?

SUZANNE. When a woman is in love the first sign is that she combs her hair differently.

GRUSINSKAIA (*laughing*). And at three o'clock in the morning too.

SUZANNE. Will Madame not change now?

GRUSINSKAIA. Later, Suzanne.

SUZANNE. I must pack.

GRUSINSKAIA. Pack, unpack, leave, arrive. (*Picks up dress from couch, tosses it to* SUZANNE) Hotel, hotel, hotel. I have been in all the cities of the world, and of each I know only the theatre and the hotel!

SUZANNE (*at trunk*). Seven trunks for Madame, fifty-eight for the troupe.

GRUSINSKAIA. The flowers. How strong they smell! Do you know what, Suzanne? We are going to take a holiday soon. We are going to Tremezzo, and we are going to live for six weeks like respectable people. I am going to live like a real woman. Perfectly quiet, perfectly simple, perfectly happy.

SUZANNE. Yes, Madame.

GRUSINSKAIA. We are going to have a guest, Suzanne.

SUZANNE. Certainly, Madame. (GRUSINSKAIA *does a few dance steps*) Now Madame looks like a young girl.

GRUSINSKAIA. I am alive now. Something wonderful has happened to me.

SUZANNE. Does Madame mean love?

GRUSINSKAIA. Is the trunk finished?

SUZANNE. Yes, Madame.

GRUSINSKAIA. Then I do not need you any more.

SUZANNE. Yes, Madame.

GRUSINSKAIA. You may go and sleep until a half hour before it is time to go to the station. (*Pats her cheek.*)

SUZANNE. Good night, Madame.

GRUSINSKAIA. Good morning, Suzanne. (SUZANNE *laughs, exits.* GRUSINSKAIA *goes to telephone. She* is singing a Russian melody. She takes the receiver and sings while waiting for an answer) Hello! (*Softly humming*) Hello, hello! Operator . . . Well, give me Baron von Gaigern. No—Baron von Gaigern—please. (*Humming again*) Operator, are you ringing that room? He doesn't answer? He must be asleep. Ring him again, please. (*She sings again*) What? He must be in. Are you sure you are ringing the right room? Try him once more, please. (*She sings softly again, but there is a note in her voice, an unconscious look on her face of apprehension*) No answer? Very well, thank you. (*Hangs up receiver. She leans against the table. As she hums the plaintive melody there is a faraway look in her eyes. Her voice wavers.*)

CURTAIN

SCENE V

SCENE—*Hotel Lobby. It is 5:30 in the morning. Two chairs are stacked on small table. The rug running to the elevator is rolled half-way up, as is the one leading to corridor.* CLERK *is behind desk, answering telephone.* MITZI *is dusting desk.* FIRST SCRUBWOMAN *is vacuuming runners.* SECOND SCRUBWOMAN *is dusting in corridor. A* POLICEMAN *stands near revolving door.* SECOND PORTER *is mopping lobby floor and arranging chairs. Telephone rings.*

CLERK (*answering phone*). Desk. Morning papers? Yes, sir, as soon as they come in, sir. (*Jiggles phone*) Room service—morning papers for 220 as soon as they come in. (*Vacuum is shut off.* CARRIAGEMAN *enters from corridor, says* "Good morning," *as he puts on his coat, and exits through revolving door.* FIRST SCRUBWOMAN *kicks rug out and resumes vacuuming. Phone* rings) Yes, sir. At 6:27. That's the Vienna Express. When you come down? Yes, sir, there'll be time (*Hangs up phone. Elevator opens.* NEWSBOY *enters through revolving door with package of papers on shoulder, bumps into* FIRST SCRUBWOMAN *as he passes.*)

FIRST SCRUBWOMAN. Look where you're going!

NEWSBOY. Why don't you look where you're sweeping?

FIRST SCRUBWOMAN (*vacuuming rug*). Shut up!

NEWSBOY (*to* CLERK, *tossing him papers*). Good morning.

CLERK. Good morning.

NEWSBOY (*as he exits, to* FIRST SCRUBWOMAN). Woof!

CLERK (*at phone*). Baggage porter, please . . .
(SENF *enters through revolving door, crosses hastily to corridor.*)

SENF. Good morning, Carl.

CLERK (*phone in hand*). Senf, you're twenty minutes late.

SENF (*pausing before exiting in corridor*). Man, I've been at the clinic all night. (*He exits.* SCRUBWOMAN *goes to vacuum another rug.* MITZI, *finishing dusting, goes to elevator.*)

MITZI. Good morning, Fritz.

ELEVATOR BOY. Good morning, Mitzi.

MITZI (*exiting to elevator*). Take me downstairs.
(*Elevator door closes. Vacuum is shut off. Both* SCRUBWOMEN *exit to corridor.*)

CLERK (*on phone*). 412 going out at seven. Attend to it. (CLERK *hangs up.*)

SENF. I can't tell you how my wife suffers. It goes on and on. Well, I must think about my job. Anything

new here? (*Pointing to* POLICEMAN) What's he doing here?

CLERK. Killing in room 170.

SENF. What? Who?

CLERK. This big manufacturer Preysing killed Baron von Gaigern.

SENF. My God! What for?

CLERK. I don't know exactly. The police are still up there.

SENF. Man, that's something for the reputation of the Grand Hotel! The suicide last week—and now this murder—and it all gets into the papers. But I'm sorry about the Baron. He was all right.

CLERK. It seems he was a hotel thief and an impostor . . .

SENF. I don't believe it. He was a real gentleman. I know people. Another killing in the hotel. That means questioning—well—give me the notes. (CLERK *hands him notebook.* SENF *looks it over*) 267 must be called. And the pages for inspection.
(SECOND PORTER *exits to grill.*)

CLERK (*at phone*). 267 please.

SENF (*at phone*). Service room No. 4.

CLERK. Room 267.

SENF (*at phone*). Pages for inspection, send them right up. (*Hangs up*) One always felt better when he came along; he was always so friendly.

CLERK. Doctor, it is five forty-five. (*Hangs up.*)

SENF. Such an agreeable fellow.

CLERK. Most impostors are.
(FIRST, SECOND, THIRD, FOURTH BELLBOYS *and* ELEVATOR BOY *enter from corridor and line up in front of desk. The vacuum starts off stage.*)

SENF. Good morning.

BELLBOYS. Good morning.

SENF (*inspecting them*). Show your hands. (BELLBOYS *hold out their hands.* SENF *inspects them. To* ELEVATOR BOY) You've got dirty nails, you little pig, you're no good. Caps off. Let's see your hair. (BELLBOYS *remove caps*) Good. Caps on. Where is number six? (*To the* CLERK) Clerk, take his name. If he comes late again, he's fired. Dismissed!
(FIRST BELLBOY *stands near elevator door.* SECOND BELLBOY *crosses, turns out lights below grill door, stands near revolving door.* THIRD, FOURTH *and* ELEVATOR BOYS *exit to corridor. Telephone rings.*)

CLERK. Yes, just a moment, I'll see what we have.
(*Elevator opens,* KRINGELEIN *and* FLAEMMCHEN *enter, preceded by* RECEPTION CLERK *who speaks to them.*)

RECEPTION CLERK. The Commissioner thinks your evidence will be sufficient for the present. You may travel in peace, sir. I am extremely sorry that the gentleman has been disturbed like this.

KRINGELEIN. Thank you. (*To* SENF) My bill, please.
(RECEPTION CLERK *crosses to desk.*)

SENF. Yes, sir.

KRINGELEIN (*crossing with* FLAEMMCHEN *to table*). Cold, Flaemmchen? (RECEPTION CLERK *crosses toward grill.*)

FLAEMMCHEN. Rather.

KRINGELEIN (*to* RECEPTION MAN). Will you please order some tea for the lady?

RECEPTION MAN. Yes, sir. (*Exits to grill.* FOURTH BELLBOY *enters from elevator with two bags, speaks to* SENF, *exits to corridor.*)

KRINGELEIN. Sit down, Flaemmchen.

FLAEMMCHEN. Poor Baron. I can't get him out of my mind. Killed . . .

KRINGELEIN. He was friendly to me as no man ever was.

FLAEMMCHEN. Perhaps he was a burglar, but he didn't deserve that.

KRINGELEIN. He was in desperate straits. He had been trying to raise money all day. (RECEPTION MAN *enters from grill, crosses to desk, talks to* CLERK) He laughed, poor devil, and then a man like Preysing kills him.

FLAEMMCHEN. I didn't like Preysing right off.

KRINGELEIN. Then why did you have anything to do with him? (RECEPTION MAN *exits to corridor.*)

FLAEMMCHEN. For money.

KRINGELEIN. Yes, of course, for money.

FLAEMMCHEN. Do you understand that?

(MEIERHEIM *enters from corridor, looks at watch.*)

KRINGELEIN. Of course.

(SECOND WAITER *enters from grill with tray.*)

FLAEMMCHEN. Most people don't.

(SECOND WAITER *serves* FLAEMM-CHEN. KRINGELEIN *gives* WAITER *bill.* SECOND WAITER *is about to give him change, when* KRINGE-LEIN *waves him away.* SECOND WAITER *exits to grill.* SENF *sends* CLERK *out.*)

MEIERHEIM. Come on, Witte, hurry. Phone Madame; she is late as usual. Come—come. Get up steam!

WITTE (*entering from corridor slowly*). She's on her way down.

WITTE (*to* SENF). Madame Grusin-skaia is on her way down. She will be here in a minute. (*Drawing him aside*) Listen, if she asks for Baron von Gaigern, not a word about what has happened to him.

SENF. Yes, sir, you may depend on it.

(WITTE *paces nervously back and forth.*)

FLAEMMCHEN. Preysing would have given me a thousand marks. I've got to have money. I'm too good-looking for an office. There's always trouble. Money is so important, and anyone who says it isn't is just lying.

KRINGELEIN. I never knew what money really meant until I started spending it. Do you know . . . (*He is silent for a moment*) I can hardly believe that anything so beautiful should come to me from Preysing.

FLAEMMCHEN. I was afraid of him.

KRINGELEIN. You needn't be afraid of anything now. I'll take care of you. Will—will you come with me?

FLAEMMCHEN. With you?

KRINGELEIN. You will have a good time—you'll see. I've got enough money, fourteen thousand two hundred marks, eight thousand four hundred that I won. It will last a long time. I can win more. We'll travel. We'll go to Paris. I've already looked up the trains—there's one leaving very soon.

FLAEMMCHEN. To Paris? I've always wanted to go to Paris!

(CLERK *enters.*)

KRINGELEIN. Yes, to Paris, any-where you like. Here's part of the money I won, three thousand four hundred. Later you can have all.

(*Phone rings,* CLERK *answers it.*)

FLAEMMCHEN. Later?

KRINGELEIN. When I . . . when it's all over. It won't be long. Will you stay with me until . . . ?

FLAEMMCHEN. Nonsense, I know a doctor who cures the most hope-less cases. We will go to him.

KRINGELEIN. Do you think you will have a better time with me than you would with Preysing? Wouldn't you rather stay with me than with him?

(WITTE *exits to corridor.*)

FLAEMMCHEN. Oh, yes, much.
(WITTE *enters from corridor.*)

KRINGELEIN (*takes her hand*). Do you like me better?
(CLERK *rings desk bell.* SECOND BELLBOY *comes to desk.*)

FLAEMMCHEN. Yes. You are good.
(*Elevator buzzer is heard.* SECOND BELLBOY *exits to elevator. Elevator goes up.*)

SENF. Your bill is ready, Mr. Kringelein.

KRINGELEIN (*rising*). Yes, all right.
(*Pointing to* FLAEMMCHEN) And the lady's too?
(WITTE *exits to corridor.* OTTERNSCHLAG *enters from corridor.*)

SENF. Yes.

KRINGELEIN (*at desk, paying bills*). Please order me a cab.

CLERK (*ringing desk bell. To* FIRST BELLBOY). Cab for His Excellency, Mr. Kringelein.

FIRST BELLBOY (*as he exits through revolving door*). Cab for Mr. Kringelein.

OTTERNSCHLAG (*to* CLERK). Any mail for me? Letter—telegram—nothing?
(FOURTH BELLBOY *enters from corridor, picks up bags.*)

CLERK. Nothing, Doctor.
(WITTE *appears.*)

OTTERNSCHLAG (*seeing* KRINGELEIN *at desk*). Mr. Kringelein, leaving?

KRINGELEIN. Yes, I am going to Paris.

(FLAEMMCHEN *rises, picks up* KRINGELEIN's *coat from chair.*)

SENF (*to* CLERK). Post 168, 169, 170, 171 vacant. (*He exits.*)

OTTERNSCHLAG (*to* KRINGELEIN, *stopping him*). In case you have those pains.

KRINGELEIN (*turning*). Pains? Oh, yes.

OTTERNSCHLAG. You've forgotten the pains already. Well, everything goes on.

FLAEMMCHEN (*to* KRINGELEIN). We must hurry. (*Hands top coat to* KRINGELEIN.)

OTTERNSCHLAG. Ah, leaving with the lady?

KRINGELEIN. Yes. We mustn't miss our train.
(SENF *enters behind desk.*)

FIRST BELLBOY. Cab ready for Mr. Kringelein.

KRINGELEIN (*to* FLAEMMCHEN). Will you take my arm?
(FIRST *and* FOURTH BELLBOY *exit with bags.* FLAEMMCHEN *takes his arm. They go to revolving door.* FLAEMMCHEN *exits.*)

KRINGELEIN (*at revolving door, turning to* DOCTOR). Good-bye, Doctor. (*He exits, following* FLAEMMCHEN. CLERK *turns out chandelier light over desk and* OTTERNSCHLAG *goes to table and sits.* CLERK *exits.* WITTE *appears. Elevator door opens.* THIRD BOY *acts as elevator boy.* GRUSINSKAIA *enters,* SUZANNE *follows with* SECOND BELLBOY, *who is carrying bags.* SUZANNE *and* SECOND BELLBOY *exit through revolving door. Elevator door closes.* WITTE *sees* GRUSINSKAIA *and goes to her.*)

GRUSINSKAIA. Good morning, Witte. (*She takes a few steps and looks around lobby.* MEIERHEIM *sees her, rises and comes to her*) Good morning, Meierheim. Everything all right?

MEIERHEIM. What do you mean, all right? Nothing is all right when you always come six minutes later. (*Takes a few steps, looking at paper.*)

GRUSINSKAIA (*going to* WITTE). Where is he?

MEIERHEIM (*to* GRUSINSKAIA, *showing paper*). Have you seen the morning papers? See the nice things they say about you.

GRUSINSKAIA (*not interested*). That's very good. (MEIERHEIM *puts paper in pocket, takes out watch. To* WITTE). He's not in his room either. Is he not traveling with us?

WITTE. He will come later, Lisaveta.

MEIERHEIM. What are you waiting for? Have you got all the bags in the car? Hurry, we'll just make the train.

GRUSINSKAIA. I must wait. I am expecting someone.

MEIERHEIM. Impossible, not another minute. You've got a rehearsal in Prague at noon. Come, Madame.

GRUSINSKAIA (*to* WITTE). Where can he be?

WITTE (*helping her toward revolving door*). You must go, Lisaveta. Don't wait any longer.

MEIERHEIM (*takes out watch*). Four minutes past! The train leaves at six twenty-seven. Come, Madame. Out! March! (*Exits.*)

WITTE (*urging her forward*). You must go, Lisaveta. He will be there. He certainly will be there. (MEIERHEIM *reappears outside door.*)

GRUSINSKAIA. Witte, stay on here. Look around. Bring him with you. Come on the next train. Tell him that he must travel with us. Must! Must! (*She exits.* MEIERHEIM *hurries her away.* WITTE *exits to corridor.* ELEVATOR BOY *enters from corridor and goes to desk.* CLERK *enters.*)

ELEVATOR BOY (*to* SENF). You are wanted in the phone room, sir. An important message—from the hospital—something about a baby.

SENF. What? My God! (*Turns and rushes out quickly.*)

CLERK (*to* OTTERNSCHLAG). Is the doctor leaving? Or does the doctor wish to engage the room for today again? (MAN *enters from revolving door, crosses to desk, sets suitcase down.* FIRST BELLBOY *enters.*)

OTTERNSCHLAG. I shall remain for the time being.

MAN (*at desk*). I'd like to have a room.

CLERK. Yes, sir. (FIRST BELLBOY *crosses to desk*) Right here, sir. (*Rings desk bell. To* FIRST BELL-

BOY, *who goes to desk for bag*) Show the gentleman to 170. (*To* MAN) Large room with bath, sir.

FIRST BELLBOY (*picking up bag and going to elevator*). This way, sir.

(MAN *enters elevator.* FIRST BOY *follows, elevator door closes. Telephone rings,* CLERK *answers it.* WITTE *enters from corridor, looks around lobby, nods to* CLERK, *and*

exits. CARRIAGEMAN *enters with a bag, followed by* ANOTHER MAN. CARRIAGEMAN *places bag at desk.* ANOTHER MAN *tips him and goes to desk to register. Telephone bells ring. The voice of the* OPERATOR *is heard behind the desk.*)

OPERATOR. Grand Hotel. Just a minute, please. Grand Hotel. Grand Hotel. Hold the wire, please. Grand Hotel. Grand Hotel. Grand Hotel.

CURTAIN

The Playboy of the Western World

BY JOHN M. SYNGE

PREFACE

IN WRITING *The Playboy of the Western World*, as in my other plays, I have used one or two words only that I have not heard among the country people of Ireland, or spoken in my own nursery before I could read the newspapers. A certain number of the phrases I employ I have heard also from herds and fishermen along the coast from Kerry to Mayo, or from beggar-women and ballad-singers nearer Dublin; and I am glad to acknowledge how much I owe to the folk-imagination of these fine people. Anyone who has lived in real intimacy with the Irish peasantry will know that the wildest sayings and ideas in this play are tame indeed, compared with the fancies one may hear in any little hillside cabin in Geesala, or Carraroe, or Dingle Bay. All art is a collaboration; and there is little doubt that in the happy ages of literature, striking and beautiful phrases were as ready to the story-teller's or the playwright's hand, as the rich cloaks and dresses of his time. It is probable that when the Elizabethan dramatist took his ink-horn and sat down to his work he used many phrases that he had just heard, as he sat at dinner, from his mother or his children. In Ireland, those of us who know the people have the same privilege. When I was writing *The Shadow of the Glen*, some years ago, I got more aid than any learning could have given me from a chink in the floor of the old Wicklow house where I was staying, that let me hear what was being said by the servant girls in the kitchen. This matter I think, is of importance, for in countries where the imagination of the people, and the language they use, is rich and living, it is possible for a writer to be rich and copious in his words, and at the same time to give the reality, which is the root of all poetry, in a comprehensive and natural form. In the modern literature of towns, however, richness is found only in sonnets, or prose poems, or in one or two elaborate books that are far away from the profound and common interests of life. One has, on one side, Mallarmé and Huysmans producing this literature; and on the other, Ibsen and Zola dealing with the reality of life in joyless and pallid words. On the stage one must have reality, and one must have joy; and that is why the intellectual modern drama has failed, and people have grown sick of the false joy of the musical comedy, that has been given them in place of the rich joy found only in what is superb and wild in reality. In a good play every speech should be as fully flavoured as a nut or apple, and such speeches cannot be written by anyone who works among people who have shut their lips on poetry. In Ireland, for a few years more, we have a popular imagination that is fiery and magnificent, and tender; so that those of us who wish to write start with a chance that is not given to writers in places where the springtime of the local life has been forgotten, and the harvest is a memory only, and the straw has been turned into bricks.

J. M. S.

January 21, 1907

CHARACTERS

CHRISTOPHER MAHON

OLD MAHON (*his father, a squatter*)

MICHAEL JAMES FLAHERTY, called MICHAEL JAMES (*a publican*)

MARGARET FLAHERTY, called PEGEEN MIKE (*his daughter*)

WIDOW QUIN (*a woman of about thirty*)

SHAWN KEOGH (*her cousin, a young farmer*)

PHILLY CULLEN and JIMMY FARRELL (*small farmers*)

SARA TANSEY, SUSAN BRADY, and HONOR BLAKE (*village girls*)

A BELLMAN

SOME PEASANTS

The action takes place near a village, on a wild coast of Mayo. The first Act passes on an evening of autumn, the other two Acts on the following day.

THE PLAYBOY OF THE WESTERN WORLD

ACT ONE

SCENE—*Country public-house or shebeen, very rough and untidy. There is a sort of counter on the right with shelves, holding many bottles and jugs, just seen above it. Empty barrels stand near the counter. At back, a little to left of counter, there is a door into the open air, then, more to the left, there is a settle with shelves above it, with more jugs, and a table beneath a window. At the left there is a large open fire-place, with turf fire, and a small door into inner room.* PEGEEN, *a wild-looking but fine girl of about twenty, is writing at table. She is dressed in the usual peasant dress.*

PEGEEN (*slowly as she writes*). Six yards of stuff for to make a yellow gown. A pair of lace boots with lengthy heels on them and brassy eyes. A hat is suited for a wedding-day. A fine tooth comb. To be sent with three barrels of porter in Jimmy Farrell's creel cart on the evening of the coming Fair to Mister Michael James Flaherty. With the best compliments of this season. Margaret Flaherty.

SHAWN KEOGH ⟨*a fat and fair young man comes in as she signs, looks round awkwardly, when he sees she is alone*⟩. Where's himself?

PEGEEN (*without looking at him*). He's coming. (*She directs the letter*) To Master Sheamus Mulroy, Wine and Spirit Dealer, Castlebar.

SHAWN (*uneasily*). I didn't see him on the road.

PEGEEN. How would you see him (*licks stamp and puts it on letter*) and it dark night this half hour gone by?

SHAWN (*turning towards the door again*). I stood a while outside wondering would I have a right to pass on or to walk in and see you, Pegeen Mike (*comes to fire*), and I could hear the cows breathing, and sighing in the stillness of the air, and not a step moving any place from this gate to the bridge.

PEGEEN (*putting letter in envelope*). It's above at the cross-roads he is, meeting Philly Cullen; and a couple more are going along with him to Kate Cassidy's wake.

SHAWN (*looking at her blankly*). And he's going that length in the dark night?

PEGEEN (*impatiently*). He is surely, and leaving me lonesome on the scruff of the hill. (*She gets up and puts envelope on dresser, then winds clock*) Isn't it long the nights are now, Shawn Keogh, to be leaving a poor girl with her own self counting the hours to the dawn of day?

SHAWN (*with awkward humour*). If it is, when we're wedded in a short while you'll have no call to complain, for I've little will to be walking off to wakes or weddings in the darkness of the night.

PEGEEN (*with rather scornful good humour*). You're making mighty certain, Shaneen, that I'll wed you now.

SHAWN. Aren't we after making a good bargain, the way we're only waiting these days on Father Reilly's dispensation from the bishops, or the Court of Rome?

PEGEEN (*looking at him teasingly, washing up at dresser*). It's a wonder, Shaneen, the Holy Father'd be taking notice of the likes of you; for if I was him I wouldn't bother with this place where you'll meet none but Red Linahan, has a squint in his eye, and Patcheen is lame in his heel, or the mad Mulrannies were driven from California and they lost in their wits. We're a queer lot these times to go troubling the Holy Father on his sacred seat.

SHAWN (*scandalized*). If we are, we're as good this place as another, maybe, and as good these times as we were for ever.

PEGEEN (*with scorn*). As good, is it? Where now will you meet the like of Daneen Sullivan knocked the eye from a peeler, or Marcus Quin, God rest him, got six months for maiming ewes, and he a great warrant to tell stories of holy Ireland till he'd have the old women shedding down tears about their feet. Where will you find the like of them, I'm saying?

SHAWN (*timidly*). If you don't, it's a good job, maybe; for (*with peculiar emphasis on the words*) Father Reilly has small conceit to have that kind walking around and talking to the girls.

PEGEEN (*impatiently, throwing water from basin out of the door*). Stop tormenting me with Father Reilly (*imitating his voice*) when I'm asking only what way I'll pass these twelve hours of dark, and not take my death with the fear. (*Looking out of door.*)

SHAWN (*timidly*). Would I fetch you the Widow Quin, maybe?

PEGEEN. Is it the like of that murderer? You'll not, surely.

SHAWN (*going to her, soothingly*). Then I'm thinking himself will stop along with you when he sees you taking on, for it'll be a long night-time with great darkness, and I'm after feeling a kind of fellow above in the furzy ditch, groaning wicked like a maddening dog, the way it's good cause you have, maybe, to be fearing now.

PEGEEN (*turning on him sharply*). What's that? Is it a man you seen?

SHAWN (*retreating*). I couldn't see him at all; but I heard him groaning out, and breaking his heart. It should have been a young man from his words speaking.

PEGEEN (*going after him*). And you never went near to see was he hurted or what ailed him at all?

SHAWN. I did not, Pegeen Mike. It was a dark, lonesome place to be hearing the like of him.

PEGEEN. Well, you're a daring fellow, and if they find his corpse stretched above in the dews of dawn, what'll you say then to the peelers, or the Justice of the Peace?

SHAWN (*thunderstruck*). I wasn't thinking of that. For the love of God, Pegeen Mike, don't let on I was speaking of him. Don't tell your father and the men is coming above; for if they heard that story, they'd have great blabbing this night at the wake.

PEGEEN. I'll maybe tell them, and I'll maybe not.

SHAWN. They are coming at the door. Will you whisht, I'm saying?

PEGEEN. Whisht yourself. (*She goes behind counter.* MICHAEL JAMES, *fat jovial publican, comes in followed by* PHILLY CULLEN, *who is thin and mistrusting, and* JIMMY FARRELL, *who is fat and amorous, about forty-five.*)

MEN (*together*). God bless you. The blessing of God on this place.

PEGEEN. God bless you kindly.

MICHAEL (*to men who go to the counter*). Sit down now, and take your rest. (*Crosses to* SHAWN *at the fire*) And how is it you are, Shawn Keogh? Are you coming over the sands to Kate Cassidy's wake?

SHAWN. I am not, Michael James. I'm going home the short cut to my bed.

PEGEEN (*speaking across the counter*). He's right too, and have you no shame, Michael James, to be quitting off for the whole night, and leaving myself lonesome in the shop?

MICHAEL (*good-humouredly*). Isn't it the same whether I go for the whole night or a part only? and I'm thinking it's a queer daughter you are if you'd have me crossing backward through the Stooks of the Dead Women, with a drop taken.

PEGEEN. If I am a queer daughter, it's a queer father'd be leaving me lonesome these twelve hours of dark, and I piling the turf with the dogs barking, and the calves mooing, and my own teeth rattling with the fear.

JIMMY (*flatteringly*). What is there to hurt you, and you a fine, hardy girl would knock the head of any two men in the place?

PEGEEN (*working herself up*). Isn't there the harvest boys with their tongues red for drink, and the ten tinkers is camped in the east glen, and the thousand militia—bad cess to them!—walking idle through the land. There's lots surely to hurt me, and I won't stop alone in it, let himself do what he will.

MICHAEL. If you're that afeard, let Shawn Keogh stop along with you. It's the will of God, I'm thinking, himself should be seeing to you now.
(*They all turn on* SHAWN.)

SHAWN (*in horrified confusion*). I would and welcome, Michael James, but I'm afeard of Father Reilly; and what at all would the Holy Father and the Cardinals of Rome be saying if they heard I did the like of that?

MICHAEL (*with contempt*). God help you! Can't you sit in by the hearth with the light lit and herself beyond in the room? You'll do that surely, for I've heard tell there's a queer fellow above, going mad or getting his death, maybe, in the gripe of the ditch, so she'd be safer this night with a person here.

SHAWN (*with plaintive despair*). I'm afeard of Father Reilly, I'm saying. Let you not be tempting me, and we near married itself.

PHILLY (*with cold contempt*). Lock him in the west room. He'll stay then and have no sin to be telling to the priest.

MICHAEL (*to* SHAWN, *getting between him and the door*). Go up now.

SHAWN (*at the top of his voice*). Don't stop me, Michael James. Let me out of the door, I'm saying, for the love of the Almighty God. Let me out. (*Trying to dodge past him*) Let me out of it, and may God grant you His indulgence in the hour of need.

MICHAEL (*loudly*). Stop your noising, and sit down by the hearth. (*Gives him a push and goes to counter laughing.*)

SHAWN (*turning back, wringing his hands*). Oh, Father Reilly and the saints of God, where will I hide myself to-day? Oh, St. Joseph and St. Patrick and St. Brigid, and St. James, have mercy on me now! (*SHAWN turns round, sees door clear, and makes a rush for it.*)

MICHAEL (*catching him by the coat-tail*). You'd be going, is it?

SHAWN (*screaming*). Leave me go, Michael James, leave me go, you old Pagan, leave me go, or I'll get the curse of the priests on you, and of the scarlet-coated bishops of the courts of Rome. (*With a sudden movement he pulls himself out of his coat, and disappears out of the door, leaving his coat in* MICHAEL'S *hands.*)

MICHAEL (*turning round, and holding up coat*). Well, there's the coat of a Christian man. Oh, there's sainted glory this day in the lonesome west; and by the will of God I've got you a decent man, Pegeen, you'll have no call to be spying after if you've a score of young girls, maybe, weeding in your fields.

PEGEEN (*taking up the defence of her property*). What right have you to be making game of a poor fellow for minding the priest, when it's your own the fault is, not paying a penny pot-boy to stand along with me and give me courage in the doing of my work? (*She snaps the coat away from him, and goes behind counter with it.*)

MICHAEL (*taken aback*). Where would I get a pot-boy? Would you have me send the bellman screaming in the streets of Castlebar?

SHAWN (*opening the door a chink and putting in his head, in a small voice*). Michael James!

MICHAEL (*imitating him*). What ails you?

SHAWN. The queer dying fellow's beyond looking over the ditch. He's come up, I'm thinking, stealing your hens. (*Looks over his shoulder*) God help me, he's following me now (*he runs into room*), and if he's heard what I said, he'll be having my life, and I going home lonesome in the darkness of the night.

(*For a perceptible moment they watch the door with curiosity. Some one coughs outside. Then* CHRISTY MAHON, *a slight young man, comes in very tired and frightened and dirty.*)

CHRISTY (*in a small voice*). God save all here!

MEN. God save you kindly.

CHRISTY (*going to the counter*). I'd trouble you for a glass of porter, woman of the house. (*He puts down coin.*)

PEGEEN (*serving him*). You're one of the tinkers, young fellow, is beyond camped in the glen?

CHRISTY. I am not; but I'm destroyed walking.

MICHAEL (*patronizingly*). Let you come up then to the fire. You're looking famished with the cold.

CHRISTY. God reward you. (*He takes up his glass and goes a little way across to the left, then stops and looks about him*) Is it often the police do be coming into this place, master of the house?

MICHAEL. If you'd come in better hours, you'd have seen "Licensed for the sale of Beer and Spirits, to be consumed on the premises," written in white letters above the door, and what would the polis want spying on me, and not a decent house within four miles, the way every living Christian is a bona fide, saving one widow alone?

CHRISTY (*with relief*). It's a safe house, so. (*He goes over to the fire, sighing and moaning. Then he sits down, putting his glass beside him and begins gnawing a turnip, too miserable to feel the others staring at him with curiosity.*)

MICHAEL (*going after him*). Is it yourself is fearing the polis? You're wanting, maybe?

CHRISTY. There's many wanting.

MICHAEL. Many surely, with the broken harvest and the ended wars. (*He picks up some stockings, etc., that are near the fire, and carries them away furtively*) It should be larceny, I'm thinking.

CHRISTY (*dolefully*). I had it in my mind it was a different word and a bigger.

PEGEEN. There's a queer lad. Were you never slapped in school, young fellow, that you don't know the name of your deed?

CHRISTY (*bashfully*). I'm slow at learning, a middling scholar only.

MICHAEL. If you're a dunce itself, you'd a right to know that larceny's robbing and stealing. Is it for the like of that you're wanting?

CHRISTY (*with a flash of family pride*). And I the son of a strong farmer (*with a sudden qualm*), God rest his soul, could have bought up the whole of your old house awhile since, from the butt of his tailpocket, and not have missed the weight of it gone.

MICHAEL (*impressed*). If it's not stealing, it's maybe something big.

CHRISTY (*flattered*). Aye; it's maybe something big.

JIMMY. He's a wicked-looking young fellow. Maybe he followed after a young woman on a lonesome night.

CHRISTY (*shocked*). Oh, the saints forbid, mister; I was all times a decent lad.

PHILLY (*turning on* JIMMY). You're a silly man, Jimmy Farrell. He said his father was a farmer a while since, and there's himself now in a poor state. Maybe the land was grabbed from him, and he did what any decent man would do.

MICHAEL (*to* CHRISTY, *mysteriously*). Was it bailiffs?

CHRISTY. The divil a one.

MICHAEL. Agents?

CHRISTY. The divil a one.

MICHAEL. Landlords?

CHRISTY (*peevishly*). Ah, not at all, I'm saying. You'd see the like of them stories on any little paper of a Munster town. But I'm not calling to mind any person, gentle, simple, judge or jury, did the like of me.
(*They all draw nearer with delighted curiosity.*)

PHILLY. Well, that lad's a puzzle-the-world.

JIMMY. He'd beat Dan Davies' circus, or the holy missioners making sermons on the villainy of man. Try him again, Philly.

PHILLY. Did you strike golden guineas out of solder, young fellow, or shilling coins itself?

CHRISTY. I did not, mister, not sixpence nor a farthing coin.

JIMMY. Did you marry three wives maybe? I'm told there's a sprinkling have done that among the holy Luthers of the preaching north.

CHRISTY (*shyly*). I never married with one, let alone with a couple or three.

PHILLY. Maybe he went fighting for the Boers, the like of the man beyond, was judged to be hanged, quartered and drawn. Were you off east, young fellow, fighting bloody wars for Kruger and the freedom of the Boers?

CHRISTY. I never left my own parish till Tuesday was a week.

PEGEEN (*coming from counter*). He's done nothing, so. (*To* CHRISTY) If you didn't commit murder or a bad, nasty thing, or false coining, or robbery, or butchery, or the like of them, there isn't anything that would be worth your troubling for to run from now. You did nothing at all.

CHRISTY (*his feelings hurt*). That's an unkindly thing to be saying to a poor orphaned traveller, has a prison behind him, and hanging before, and hell's gap gaping below.

PEGEEN (*with a sign to the men to be quiet*). You're only saying it. You did nothing at all. A soft lad the like of you wouldn't slit the windpipe of a screeching sow.

CHRISTY (*offended*). You're not speaking the truth.

PEGEEN (*in mock rage*). Not speaking the truth, is it? Would you have me knock the head off you with the butt of the broom?

CHRISTY (*twisting round on her with a sharp cry of horror*). Don't strike me. I killed my poor father, Tuesday was a week, for doing the like of that.

PEGEEN (*with blank amazement*). Is it killed your father?

CHRISTY (*subsiding*). With the help of God I did surely, and that the Holy Immaculate Mother may intercede for his soul.

PHILLY (*retreating with* JIMMY). There's a daring fellow.

JIMMY. Oh, glory be to God!

MICHAEL (*with great respect*). That was a hanging crime, mister honey. You should have had good reason for doing the like of that.

CHRISTY (*in a very reasonable tone*). He was a dirty man, God forgive him, and he getting old and crusty, the way I couldn't put up with him at all.

PEGEEN. And you shot him dead?

CHRISTY (*shaking his head*). I never used weapons. I've no license, and I'm a law-fearing man.

MICHAEL. It was with a hilted knife maybe? I'm told, in the big world it's bloody knives they use.

CHRISTY (*loudly, scandalized*). Do you take me for a slaughter-boy?

PEGEEN. You never hanged him, the way Jimmy Farrell hanged his dog from the license, and had it screeching and wriggling three hours at the butt of a string, and himself swearing it was a dead dog, and the peelers swearing it had life?

CHRISTY. I did not then. I just riz the loy and let fall the edge of it on the ridge of his skull, and he went down at my feet like an empty sack, and never let a grunt or groan from him at all.

MICHAEL (*making a sign to* PEGEEN *to fill* CHRISTY's *glass*). And what way weren't you hanged, mister? Did you bury him then?

CHRISTY (*considering*). Aye. I buried him then. Wasn't I digging spuds in the field?

MICHAEL. And the peelers never followed after you the eleven days that you're out?

CHRISTY (*shaking his head*). Nevei a one of them, and I walking forward facing hog, dog, or divil on the highway of the road.

PHILLY (*nodding wisely*). It's only with a common week-day kind of a murderer them lads would be trusting their carcase, and that man should be a great terror when his temper's roused.

MICHAEL. He should then. (*To* CHRISTY) And where was it, mister honey, that you did the deed?

CHRISTY (*looking at him with suspicion*). Oh, a distant place, master of the house, a windy corner of high, distant hills.

PHILLY (*nodding with approval*). He's a close man, and he's right, surely.

PEGEEN. That'd be a lad with the sense of Solomon to have for a pot-boy, Michael James, if it's the truth you're seeking one at all.

PHILLY. The peelers is fearing him, and if you'd that lad in the house there isn't one of them would come smelling around if the dogs itself were lapping poteen from the dung-pit of the yard.

JIMMY. Bravery's a treasure in a lonesome place, and a lad would kill his father, I'm thinking, would face a foxy divil with a pitchpike on the flags of hell.

PEGEEN. It's the truth they're saying, and if I'd that lad in the house, I wouldn't be fearing the loosed kharki cut-throats, or the walking dead.

CHRISTY (*swelling with surprise and triumph*). Well, glory be to God!

MICHAEL (*with deference*). Would you think well to stop here and be pot-boy, mister honey, if we gave you good wages, and didn't destroy you with the weight of work?

SHAWN (*coming forward uneasily*). That'd be a queer kind to bring into a decent quiet household with the like of Pegeen Mike.

PEGEEN (*very sharply*). Will you whisht? Who's speaking to you?

SHAWN (*retreating*). A bloody-handed murderer the like of . . .

PEGEEN (*snapping at him*). Whisht I am saying; we'll take no fooling from your like at all. (*To* CHRISTY *with a honeyed voice*) And you, young fellow, you'd have a right to stop, I'm thinking, for we'd do our all and utmost to content your needs.

CHRISTY (*overcome with wonder*). And I'd be safe in this place from the searching law?

MICHAEL. You would, surely. If they're not fearing you, itself, the peelers in this place is decent droughty poor fellows, wouldn't touch a cur dog and not give warning in the dead of night.

PEGEEN (*very kindly and persuasively*). Let you stop a short while anyhow. Aren't you destroyed walking with your feet in bleeding blisters, and your whole skin needing washing like a Wicklow sheep?

CHRISTY (*looking round with satisfaction*). It's a nice room, and if it's not humbugging me you are, I'm thinking that I'll surely stay.

JIMMY (*jumps up*). Now, by the grace of God, herself will be safe this night, with a man killed his father holding danger from the door, and let you come on, Michael James, or they'll have the best stuff drunk at the wake.

MICHAEL (*going to the door with* MEN). And begging your pardon, mister, what name will we call you, for we'd like to know?

CHRISTY. Christopher Mahon.

MICHAEL. Well, God bless you, Christy, and a good rest till we meet again when the sun'll be rising to the noon of day.

CHRISTY. God bless you all.

MEN. God bless you.
(*They go out except* SHAWN, *who lingers at door.*)

SHAWN (*to* PEGEEN). Are you wanting me to stop along with you and keep you from harm?

PEGEEN (*gruffly*). Didn't you say you were fearing Father Reilly?

SHAWN. There'd be no harm staying now, I'm thinking, and himself in it too.

PEGEEN. You wouldn't stay when there was need for you, and let you step off nimble this time when there's none.

SHAWN. Didn't I say it was Father Reilly . . .

PEGEEN. Go on, then, to Father Reilly (*in a jeering tone*), and let him put you in the holy brotherhoods, and leave that lad to me.

SHAWN. If I meet the Widow Quin . . .

PEGEEN. Go on, I'm saying, and don't be waking this place with your noise. (*She hustles him out and bolts the door*) That lad would wear the spirits from the saints of peace. (*Bustles about, then takes off her apron and pins it up in the window as a blind.* CHRISTY *watching her timidly. Then she comes to him and speaks with bland good-humour*) Let you stretch out now by the fire, young fellow. You should be destroyed travelling.

CHRISTY (*shyly again, drawing off his boots*). I'm tired, surely, walking wild eleven days, and waking fearful in the night. (*He holds up one of his feet, feeling his blisters, and looking at them with compassion.*)

PEGEEN (*standing beside him, watching him with delight*). You should have had great people in your family, I'm thinking, with the little, small feet you have, and you with a kind of a quality name, the like of what you'd find on the great powers and potentates of France and Spain.

CHRISTY (*with pride*). We were great surely, with wide and windy acres of rich Munster land.

PEGEEN. Wasn't I telling you, and you a fine, handsome young fellow with a noble brow?

CHRISTY (*with a flash of delighted surprise*). Is it me?

PEGEEN. Aye. Did you never hear that from the young girls where you come from in the west or south?

CHRISTY (*with venom*). I did not then. Oh, they're bloody liars in the naked parish where I grew a man.

PEGEEN. If they are itself, you've heard it these days, I'm thinking, and you walking the world telling out your story to young girls or old.

CHRISTY. I've told my story no place till this night, Pegeen Mike, and it's foolish I was here, maybe, to be talking free, but you're decent people, I'm thinking, and yourself a kindly woman, the way I wasn't fearing you at all.

PEGEEN (*filling a sack with straw*). You've said the like of that, maybe, in every cot and cabin where you've met a young girl on your way.

CHRISTY (*going over to her, gradually raising his voice*). I've said it nowhere till this night, I'm telling you, for I've seen none the like of you the eleven long days I am walking the world, looking over a low ditch or a high ditch on my north or my south, into stony scattered fields, or scribes of bog, where you'd see young, limber girls, and fine prancing women making laughter with the men.

PEGEEN. If you weren't destroyed travelling, you'd have as much talk and streeleen, I'm thinking, as Owen Roe O'Sullivan or the poets of the Dingle Bay, and I've heard all times it's the poets are your like, fine fiery fellows with great rages when their temper's roused.

CHRISTY (*drawing a little nearer to her*). You've a power of rings, God bless you, and would there be any offence if I was asking are you single now?

PEGEEN. What would I want wedding so young?

CHRISTY (*with relief*). We're alike, so.

PEGEEN (*she puts sack on settle and beats it up*). I never killed my father. I'd be afeard to do that, except I was the like of yourself with blind rages tearing me within, for I'm thinking you should have had great tussling when the end was come.

CHRISTY (*expanding with delight at the first confidential talk he has*

ever had with a woman*). We had not then. It was a hard woman was come over the hill, and if he was always a crusty kind when he'd a hard woman setting him on, not the divil himself or his four fathers could put up with him at all.

PEGEEN (*with curiosity*). And isn't it a great wonder that one wasn't fearing you?

CHRISTY (*very confidentially*). Up to the day I killed my father, there wasn't a person in Ireland knew the kind I was, and I there drinking, waking, eating, sleeping, a quiet, simple poor fellow with no man giving me heed.

PEGEEN (*getting a quilt out of the cupboard and putting it on the sack*). It was the girls were giving you heed maybe, and I'm thinking it's most conceit you'd have to be gaming with their like.

CHRISTY (*shaking his head, with simplicity*). Not the girls itself, and I won't tell you a lie. There wasn't anyone heeding me in that place saving only the dumb beasts of the field. (*He sits down at fire.*)

PEGEEN (*with disappointment*). And I thinking you should have been living the like of a king of Norway or the Eastern world. (*She comes and sits beside him after placing bread and mug of milk on the table.*)

CHRISTY (*laughing piteously*). The like of a king, is it? And I after toiling, moiling, digging, dodging from the dawn till dusk with never a sight of joy or sport saving only when I'd be abroad in the dark night poaching rabbits on hills, for

I was a divil to poach, God forgive me, (*very naïvely*) and I near got six months for going with a dung fork and stabbing a fish.

PEGEEN. And it's that you'd call sport, is it, to be abroad in the darkness with yourself alone?

CHRISTY. I did, God help me, and there I'd be as happy as the sunshine of St. Martin's Day, watching the light passing the north or the patches of fog, till I'd hear a rabbit starting to screech and I'd go running in the furze. Then when I'd my full share I'd come walking down where you'd see the ducks and geese stretched sleeping on the highway of the road, and before I'd pass the dunghill, I'd hear himself snoring out, a loud lonesome snore he'd be making all times, the while he was sleeping, and he a man 'd be raging all times, the while he was waking, like a gaudy officer you'd hear cursing and damning and swearing oaths.

PEGEEN. Providence and Mercy, spare us all!

CHRISTY. It's that you'd say surely if you seen him and he after drinking for weeks, rising up in the red dawn, or before it maybe, and going out into the yard as naked as an ash tree in the moon of May, and shying clods against the visage of the stars till he'd put the fear of death into the banbhs and the screeching sows.

PEGEEN. I'd be well-nigh afeard of that lad myself, I'm thinking. And there was no one in it but the two of you alone?

CHRISTY. The divil a one, though he'd sons and daughters walking

all great states and territories of the world, and not a one of them, to this day, but would say their seven curses on him, and they rousing up to let a cough or sneeze, maybe, in the deadness of the night.

PEGEEN (*nodding her head*). Well, you should have been a queer lot. I never cursed my father the like of that, though I'm twenty and more years of age.

CHRISTY. Then you'd have cursed mine, I'm telling you, and he a man never gave peace to any, saving when he'd get two months or three, or be locked in the asylums for battering peelers or assaulting men (*with depression*) the way it was a bitter life he led me till I did up a Tuesday and halve his skull.

PEGEEN (*putting her hand on his shoulder*). Well, you'll have peace in this place, Christy Mahon, and none to trouble you, and it's near time a fine lad like you should have your good share of the earth.

CHRISTY. It's time surely, and I a seemly fellow with great strength in me and bravery of . . . (*Someone knocks.*)

CHRISTY (*clinging to* PEGEEN). Oh, glory! it's late for knocking, and this last while I'm in terror of the peelers, and the walking dead. (*Knocking again.*)

PEGEEN. Who's there?

VOICE (*outside*). Me.

PEGEEN. Who's me?

VOICE. The Widow Quin.

PEGEEN (*jumping up and giving him the bread and milk*). Go on now with your supper, and let on to be sleepy, for if she found you were such a warrant to talk, she'd be stringing gabble till the dawn of day.

(*He takes bread and sits shyly with his back to the door.*)

PEGEEN (*opening door, with temper*). What ails you, or what is it you're wanting at this hour of the night?

WIDOW QUIN (*coming in a step and peering at* CHRISTY). I'm after meeting Shawn Keogh and Father Reilly below, who told me of your curiosity man, and they fearing by this time he was maybe roaring, romping on your hands with drink.

PEGEEN (*pointing to* CHRISTY). Look now is he roaring, and he stretched away drowsy with his supper and his mug of milk. Walk down and tell that to Father Reilly and to Shaneen Keogh.

WIDOW QUIN (*coming forward*). I'll not see them again, for I've their word to lead that lad forward for to lodge with me.

PEGEEN (*in blank amazement*). This night, is it?

WIDOW QUIN (*going over*). This night. "It isn't fitting," says the priesteen, "to have his likeness lodging with an orphaned girl." (*To* CHRISTY) God save you, mister!

CHRISTY (*shyly*). God save you kindly.

WIDOW QUIN (*looking at him with half-amazed curiosity*). Well, aren't you a little smiling fellow? It should have been great and bitter torments did rouse your spirits to a deed of blood.

CHRISTY (*doubtfully*). It should, maybe.

WIDOW QUIN. It's more than "maybe" I'm saying, and it'd soften my heart to see you sitting so simple with your cup and cake, and you fitter to be saying your catechism than slaying your da.

PEGEEN (*at counter, washing glasses*). There's talking when any'd see he's fit to be holding his head high with the wonders of the world. Walk on from this, for I'll not have him tormented and he destroyed travelling since Tuesday was a week.

WIDOW QUIN (*peaceably*). We'll be walking surely when his supper's done, and you'll find we're great company, young fellow, when it's of the like of you and me you'd hear the penny poets singing in an August Fair.

CHRISTY (*innocently*). Did you kill your father?

PEGEEN (*contemptuously*). She did not. She hit himself with a worn pick, and the rusted poison did corrode his blood the way he never overed it, and died after. That was a sneaky kind of murder did win small glory with the boys itself. (*She crosses to* CHRISTY's *left.*)

WIDOW QUIN (*with good-humour*). If it didn't, maybe all knows a widow woman has buried her children and destroyed her man is a wiser comrade for a young lad than a girl, the like of you, who'd go helter-skeltering after any man would let you a wink upon the road.

PEGEEN (*breaking out into wild rage*). And you'll say that, Widow Quin, and you gasping with the rage you had racing the hill beyond to look on his face.

WIDOW QUIN (*laughing derisively*). Me, is it? Well, Father Reilly has cuteness to divide you now. (*She pulls* CHRISTY *up*) There's great temptation in a man did slay his da, and we'd best be going, young fellow; so rise up and come with me.

PEGEEN (*seizing his arm*). He'll not stir. He's pot-boy in this place, and I'll not have him stolen off and kidnabbed while himself's abroad.

WIDOW QUIN. It'd be a crazy pot-boy'd lodge him in the shebeen where he works by day, so you'd have a right to come on, young fellow, till you see my little houseen, a perch off on the rising hill.

PEGEEN. Wait till morning, Christy Mahon. Wait till you lay eyes on her leaky thatch is growing more pasture for her buck goat than her square of fields, and she without a tramp itself to keep in order her place at all.

WIDOW QUIN. When you see me contriving in my little gardens, Christy Mahon, you'll swear the Lord God formed me to be living lone, and that there isn't my match in Mayo for thatching, or mowing, or shearing a sheep.

PEGEEN (*with noisy scorn*). It's true the Lord God formed you to con-

trive indeed. Doesn't the world know you reared a black lamb at your own breast, so that the Lord Bishop of Connaught felt the elements of a Christian, and he eating it after in a kidney stew? Doesn't the world know you've been seen shaving the foxy skipper from France for a threepenny bit and a sop of grass tobacco would wring the liver from a mountain goat you'd meet leaping the hills?

WIDOW QUIN (*with amusement*). Do you hear her now, young fellow? Do you hear the way she'll be rating at your own self when a week is by?

PEGEEN (*to* CHRISTY). Don't heed her. Tell her to go into her pigsty and not plague us here.

WIDOW QUIN. I'm going; but he'll come with me.

PEGEEN (*shaking him*). Are you dumb, young fellow?

CHRISTY (*timidly, to* WIDOW QUIN). God increase you; but I'm pot-boy in this place, and it's here I'd liefer stay.

PEGEEN (*triumphantly*). Now you have heard him, and go on from this.

WIDOW QUIN (*looking round the room*). It's lonesome this hour crossing the hill, and if he won't come along with me, I'd have a right maybe to stop this night with yourselves. Let me stretch out on the settle, Pegeen Mike; and himself can lie by the hearth.

PEGEEN (*short and fiercely*). Faith, I won't. Quit off or I will send you now.

WIDOW QUIN (*gathering her shawl up*). Well, it's a terror to be aged a score. (*To* CHRISTY) God bless you now, young fellow, and let you be wary, or there's right torment will await you here if you go romancing with her like, and she waiting only, as they bade me say, on a sheepskin parchment to be wed with Shawn Keogh of Killakeen.

CHRISTY (*going to* PEGEEN *as she bolts the door*). What's that she's after saying?

PEGEEN. Lies and blather, you've no call to mind. Well, isn't Shawn Keogh an impudent fellow to send up spying on me? Wait till I lay hands on him. Let him wait, I'm saying.

CHRISTY. And you're not wedding him at all?

PEGEEN. I wouldn't wed him if a bishop came walking for to join us here.

CHRISTY. That God in glory may be thanked for that.

PEGEEN. There's your bed now. I've put a quilt upon you I'm after quilting a while since with my own two hands, and you'd best stretch out now for your sleep, and may God give you a good rest till I call you in the morning when the cocks will crow.

CHRISTY (*as she goes to inner room*). May God and Mary and St. Patrick bless you and reward you, for your kindly talk. (*She shuts the door behind her. He settles his bed slowly, feeling the quilt with immense satisfaction*) Well, it's a clean bed and soft with it, and it's great luck and company I've won me in the end of time— two fine women fighting for the likes of me—till I'm thinking this night wasn't I a foolish fellow not to kill my father in the years gone by.

CURTAIN

ACT TWO

SCENE—*As before. Brilliant morning light.* CHRISTY, *looking bright and cheerful, is cleaning a girl's boots.*

CHRISTY (*to himself, counting jugs on dresser*). Half a hundred beyond. Ten there. A score that's above. Eighty jugs. Six cups and a broken one. Two plates. A power of glasses. Bottles, a schoolmaster'd be hard set to count, and enough in them, I'm thinking, to drunken all the wealth and wisdom of the County Clare. (*He puts down the boot carefully*) There's her boots now, nice and decent for her evening use, and isn't it grand brushes she has? (*He puts them down and goes by degrees to the looking-glass*) Well, this'd be a fine place to be my whole life talking out with swearing Christians, in place of my old dogs and cat, and I stalking around, smoking my pipe and drinking my fill, and never a day's work but drawing a cork an odd time, or wiping a glass, or rinsing out a shiny tumbler for a decent man. (*He takes the looking-glass from the wall and puts it on the back of a chair; then sits down in front of it and begins washing his face*) Didn't I know rightly I was handsome, though it was the divil's own mirror we had beyond, would twist a squint across an angel's brow; and I'll be growing fine from this day, the way I'll have a soft lovely skin on me and won't be the like of the clumsy young fellows do be ploughing all times in the earth and dung. (*He starts*) Is she coming again? (*He looks out*) Stranger girls. God help me, where'll I hide myself away and my long neck naked to the world? (*He looks out*) I'd best go to the room maybe till I'm dressed again. (*He gathers up his coat and the looking-glass, and runs into the inner room. The door is pushed open, and* SUSAN BRADY *looks in, and knocks on door.*)

SUSAN. There's nobody in it. (*Knocks again.*)

NELLY (*pushing her in and following her, with* HONOR BLAKE *and* SARA TANSEY). It'd be early for them both to be out walking the hill.

SUSAN. I'm thinking Shawn Keogh was making game of us and there's no such man in it at all.

HONOR (*pointing to straw and quilt*). Look at that. He's been sleeping there in the night. Well, it'll be a hard case if he's gone off now, the way we'll never set our eyes on a man killed his father, and we after rising early and destroying ourselves running fast on the hill.

NELLY. Are you thinking them's his boots?

SARA (*taking them up*). If they are, there should be his father's track on them. Did you never read in the papers the way murdered men do bleed and drip?

SUSAN. Is that blood there, Sara Tansey?

SARA (*smelling it*). That's bog water, I'm thinking, but it's his own they are surely, for I never seen the like of them for whity mud, and red mud, and turf on them, and the fine sands of the sea. That man's been walking, I'm telling you. (*She goes down right, putting on one of his boots.*)

SUSAN (*going to window*). Maybe he's stolen off to Belmullet with the boots of Michael James, and you'd have a right so to follow after him, Sara Tansey, and you the one yoked the ass cart and drove ten miles to set your eyes on the man bit the yellow lady's nostril on the northern shore. (*She looks out.*)

SARA (*running to window with one boot on*). Don't be talking, and we fooled to-day. (*Putting on other boot*) There's a pair do fit me well, and I'll be keeping them for walking to the priest, when you'd be ashamed this place, going up winter and summer with nothing worth while to confess at all.

HONOR (*who has been listening at the door*). Whisht! there's someone

inside the room. (*She pushes door a chink open*) It's a man.
(SARA *kicks off boots and puts them where they were. They all stand in a line looking through chink.*)

SARA. I'll call him. Mister! Mister! (*He puts in his head*) Is Pegeen within?

CHRISTY (*coming in as meek as a mouse, with the looking-glass held behind his back*). She's above on the cnuceen, seeking the nanny goats, the way she'd have a sup of goat's milk for to colour my tea.

SARA. And asking your pardon, is it you's the man killed his father?

CHRISTY (*sidling toward the nail where the glass was hanging*). I am, God help me!

SARA (*taking eggs she has brought*). Then my thousand welcomes to you, and I've run up with a brace of duck's eggs for your food to-day. Pegeen's ducks is no use, but these are the real rich sort. Hold out your hand and you'll see it's no lie I'm telling you.

CHRISTY (*coming forward shyly, and holding out his left hand*). They're a great and weighty size.

SUSAN. And I run up with a pat of butter, for it'd be a poor thing to have you eating your spuds dry, and you after running a great way since you did destroy your da.

CHRISTY. Thank you kindly.

HONOR. And I brought you a little cut of cake, for you should have a thin stomach on you, and you that length walking the world.

NELLY. And I brought you a little laying pullet—boiled and all she is —was crushed at the fall of night by the curate's car. Feel the fat of that breast, mister.

CHRISTY. It's bursting, surely. (*He feels it with the back of his hand, in which he holds the presents.*)

SARA. Will you pinch it? Is your right hand too sacred for to use at all? (*She slips round behind him*) It's a glass he has. Well, I never seen to this day a man with a looking-glass held to his back. Them that kills their fathers is a vain lot surely.
(GIRLS *giggle.*)

CHRISTY (*smiling innocently and piling presents on glass*). I'm very thankful to you all to-day . . .

WIDOW QUIN (*coming in quickly, at door*). Sara Tansey, Susan Brady, Honor Blake! What in glory has you here at this hour of day?

GIRLS (*giggling*). That's the man killed his father

WIDOW QUIN (*coming to them*). I know well it's the man; and I'm after putting him down in the sports below for racing, leaping, pitching, and the Lord knows what.

SARA (*exuberantly*). That's right. Widow Quin. I'll bet my dowry that he'll lick the world.

WIDOW QUIN. If you will, you'd have a right to have him fresh and nourished in place of nursing a feast. (*Taking presents*) Are you fasting or fed, young fellow?

CHRISTY. Fasting, if you please.

WIDOW QUIN (*loudly*). Well, you're the lot. Stir up now and give him his breakfast. (*To* CHRISTY) Come here to me (*she puts him on bench beside her while the girls make tea and get his breakfast*) and let you tell us your story before Pegeen will come, in place of grinning your ears off like the moon of May.

CHRISTY (*beginning to be pleased*). It's a long story; you'd be destroyed listening.

WIDOW QUIN. Don't be letting on to be shy, a fine, gamey, treacherous lad the like of you. Was it in your house beyond you cracked his skull?

CHRISTY (*shy but flattered*). It was not. We were digging spuds in his cold, sloping, stony, divil's patch of a field.

WIDOW QUIN. And you went asking money of him, or making talk of getting a wife would drive him from his farm?

CHRISTY. I did not, then; but there I was, digging and digging, and "You squinting idiot," says he, "let you walk down now and tell the priest you'll wed the Widow Casey in a score of days."

WIDOW QUIN. And what kind was she?

CHRISTY (*with horror*). A walking terror from beyond the hills, and she two score and five years, and two hundredweights and five pounds in the weighing scales, with a limping leg on her, and a blinded eye, and she a woman of noted misbehavior with the old and young.

GIRLS (*clustering round him, serving him*). Glory be.

WIDOW QUIN. And what did he want driving you to wed with her? (*She takes a bit of the chicken.*)

CHRISTY (*eating with growing satisfaction*). He was letting on I was wanting a protector from the harshness of the world, and he without a thought the whole while but how he'd have her hut to live in and her gold to drink.

WIDOW QUIN. There's maybe worse than a dry hearth and a widow woman and your glass at night. So you hit him then?

CHRISTY (*getting almost excited*). I did not. "I won't wed her," says I, "when all know she did suckle me for six weeks when I came into the world, and she a hag this day with a tongue on her has the crows and seabirds scattered, the way they would cast a shadow on her garden with the dread of her curse."

WIDOW QUIN (*teasingly*). That one should be right company.

SARA (*eagerly*). Don't mind her. Did you kill him then?

CHRISTY. "She's too good for the like of you," says he, "and go on now or I'll flatten you out like a crawling beast has passed under a dray." "You will not if I can help it," says I. "Go on," says he, "or I'll have the divil making garters of your limbs to-night." "You will not if I can help it," says I. (*He sits up, brandishing his mug.*)

SARA. You were right surely.

CHRISTY (*impressively*). With that the sun came out between the cloud and the hill, and it shining green in my face. "God have mercy on your soul," says he, lifting a scythe; "or on your own," says I, raising the loy.

SUSAN. That's a grand story.

HONOR. He tells it lovely.

CHRISTY (*flattered and confident, waving bone*). He gave a drive with the scythe, and I gave a lep to the east. Then I turned around with my back to the north, and I hit a blow on the ridge of his skull, laid him stretched out, and he split to the knob of his gullet. (*He raises the chicken bone to his Adam's apple.*)

GIRLS (*together*). Well, you're a marvel! Oh, God bless you! You're the lad surely!

SUSAN. I'm thinking the Lord God sent him this road to make a second husband to the Widow Quin, and she with a great yearning to be wedded, though all dread her here. Lift him on her knee, Sara Tansey.

WIDOW QUIN. Don't tease him.

SARA (*going over to dresser and counter very quickly, and getting two glasses and porter*). You're heroes surely, and let you drink a supeen with your arms linked like the outlandish lovers in the sailor's song. (*She links their arms and gives them the glasses*) There now. Drink a health to the wonders of the western world, the pirates, preachers, poteen-makers, with the jobbing jockies; parching peelers, and the juries fill their stomachs selling judgments of the English law. (*Brandishing the bottle.*)

WIDOW QUIN. That's a right toast, Sara Tansey. Now, Christy. (*They drink with their arms linked, he drinking with his left hand, she with her right. As they are drinking, PEGEEN MIKE comes in with a milk can and stands aghast. They all spring away from CHRISTY. He goes down left. WIDOW QUIN remains seated.*)

PEGEEN (*angrily, to SARA*). What is it you're wanting?

SARA (*twisting her apron*). An ounce of tobacco.

PEGEEN. Have you tuppence?

SARA. I've forgotten my purse.

PEGEEN. Then you'd best be getting it and not fooling us here. (*To the WIDOW QUIN, with more elaborate scorn*) And what is it you're wanting, Widow Quin?

WIDOW QUIN (*insolently*). A pen-n'orth of starch.

PEGEEN (*breaking out*). And you without a white shift or a shirt in your whole family since the drying of the flood. I've no starch for the like of you, and let you walk on now to Killamuck.

WIDOW QUIN (*turning to CHRISTY, as she goes out with the GIRLS*). Well, you're mighty huffy this day, Pegeen Mike, and, you young fellow, let you not forget the sports and racing when the noon is by. (*They go out.*)

PEGEEN (*imperiously*). Fling out that rubbish and put them cups away. (CHRISTY *tidies away in great haste*) Shove in the bench by the wall. (*He does so*) And hang that glass on the nail. What disturbed it at all?

CHRISTY (*very meekly*). I was making myself decent only, and this a fine country for young lovely girls.

PEGEEN (*sharply*). Whisht your talking of girls. (*Goes to counter—right.*)

CHRISTY. Wouldn't any wish to be decent in a place . . .

PEGEEN. Whisht I'm saying.

CHRISTY (*looks at her face for a moment with great misgivings, then as a last effort, takes up a loy, and goes towards her, with feigned assurance*). It was with a loy the like of that I killed my father.

PEGEEN (*still sharply*). You've told me that story six times since the dawn of day.

CHRISTY (*reproachfully*). It's a queer thing you wouldn't care to be hearing it and them girls after walking four miles to be listening to me now.

PEGEEN (*turning around astonished*). Four miles.

CHRISTY (*apologetically*). Didn't himself say there were only four bona fides living in the place?

PEGEEN. It's bona fides by the road they are, but that lot came over the river lepping the stones. It's not three perches when you go like that, and I was down this morning looking on the papers the post-boy

does have in his bag. (*With meaning and emphasis*) For there was great news this day, Christopher Mahon. (*She goes into room left.*)

CHRISTY (*suspiciously*). Is it news of my murder?

PEGEEN (*inside*). Murder, indeed.

CHRISTY (*loudly*). A murdered da?

PEGEEN (*coming in again and crossing right*). There was not, but a story filled half a page of the hanging of a man. Ah, that should be a fearful end, young fellow, and it worst of all for a man who destroyed his da, for the like of him would get small mercies, and when it's dead he is, they'd put him in a narrow grave, with cheap sacking wrapping him round, and pour down quicklime on his head, the way you'd see a woman pouring any frish-frash from a cup.

CHRISTY (*very miserably*). Oh, God help me. Are you thinking I'm safe? You were saying at the fall of night, I was shut of jeopardy and I here with yourselves.

PEGEEN (*severely*). You'll be shut of jeopardy in no place if you go talking with a pack of wild girls the like of them do be walking abroad with the peelers, talking whispers at the fall of night.

CHRISTY (*with terror*). And you're thinking they'd tell?

PEGEEN (*with mock sympathy*). Who knows, God help you.

CHRISTY (*loudly*). What joy would they have to bring hanging to the likes of me?

PEGEEN. It's queer joys they have, and who knows the thing they'd do, if it'd make the green stones cry itself to think of you swaying and swiggling at the butt of a rope, and you with a fine, stout neck, God bless you! the way you'd be a half an hour, in great anguish, getting your death.

CHRISTY (getting his boots and putting them on). If there's that terror of them, it'd be best, maybe, I went on wandering like Esau or Cain and Abel on the sides of Neifin or the Erris plain.

PEGEEN (beginning to play with him). It would, maybe, for I've heard the Circuit Judges this place is a heartless crew.

CHRISTY (bitterly). It's more than Judges this place is a heartless crew. (Looking up at her) And isn't it a poor thing to be starting again and I a lonesome fellow will be looking out on women and girls the way they're needy fallen spirits do be looking on the Lord?

PEGEEN. What call have you to be that lonesome when there's poor girls walking Mayo in their thousands now?

CHRISTY (grimly). It's well you know what call I have. It's well you know it's a lonesome thing to be passing small towns with the lights shining sideways when the night is down, or going in strange places with a dog noising before you and a dog noising behind, or drawn to the cities where you'd hear a voice kissing and talking deep love in every shadow of the ditch, and you passing on with an empty, hungry stomach failing from your heart.

PEGEEN. I'm thinking you're an odd man, Christy Mahon. The oddest walking fellow I ever set my eyes on to this hour to-day.

CHRISTY. What would any be but odd men and they living lonesome in the world?

PEGEEN. I'm not odd, and I'm my whole life with my father only.

CHRISTY (with infinite admiration). How would a lovely handsome woman the like of you be lonesome when all men should be thronging around to hear the sweetness of your voice, and the little infant children should be pestering your steps I'm thinking, and you walking the roads.

PEGEEN. I'm hard set to know what way a coaxing fellow the like of yourself should be lonesome either.

CHRISTY. Coaxing?

PEGEEN. Would you have me think a man never talked with the girls would have the words you've spoken to-day? It's only letting on you are to be lonesome, the way you'd get around me now.

CHRISTY. I wish to God I was letting on; but I was lonesome all times, and born lonesome, I'm thinking, as the moon of dawn. (Going to door.)

PEGEEN (puzzled by his talk). Well, it's a story I'm not understanding at all why you'd be worse than another, Christy Mahon, and you a fine lad with the great savagery to destroy your da.

CHRISTY. It's little I'm understanding myself, saving only that my heart's scalded this day, and I am going off stretching out the earth between us, the way I'll not be waking near you another dawn of the year till the two of us do arise to hope or judgment with the saints of God, and now I'd best be going with my wattle in my hand, for hanging is a poor thing (*turning to go*), and it's little welcome only is left me in this house to-day.

PEGEEN (*sharply*). Christy! (*He turns round*) Come here to me. (*He goes towards her*) Lay down that switch and throw some sods on the fire. You're pot-boy in this place, and I'll not have you mitch off from us now.

CHRISTY. You were saying I'd be hanged if I stay.

PEGEEN (*quite kindly at last*). I'm after going down and reading the fearful crimes of Ireland for two weeks or three, and there wasn't a word of your murder. (*Getting up and going over to the counter*) They've likely not found the body. You're safe so with ourselves.

CHRISTY (*astonished, slowly*). It's making game of me you were (*following her with fearful joy*), and I can stay so, working at your side, and I not lonesome from this mortal day.

PEGEEN. What's to hinder you from staying, except the widow woman or the young girls would inveigle you off?

CHRISTY (*with rapture*). And I'll have your words from this day filling my ears, and that look is come upon you meeting my two eyes, and I watching you loafing around in the warm sun, or rinsing your ankles when the night is come.

PEGEEN (*kindly, but a little embarrassed*). I'm thinking you'll be a loyal young lad to have working around, and if you vexed me a while since with your leaguing with the girls, I wouldn't give a thraneen for a lad hadn't a mighty spirit in him and a gamey heart.

(SHAWN KEOGH *runs in carrying a cleeve on his back, followed by the* WIDOW QUIN.)

SHAWN (*to* PEGEEN). I was passing below, and I seen your mountainy sheep eating cabbages in Jimmy's field. Run up or they'll be bursting surely.

PEGEEN. Oh, God mend them! (*She puts a shawl over her head and runs out.*)

CHRISTY (*looking from one to the other. Still in high spirits*). I'd best go to her aid maybe. I'm handy with ewes.

WIDOW QUIN (*closing the door*). She can do that much, and there is Shaneen has long speeches for to tell you now. (*She sits down with an amused smile.*)

SHAWN (*taking something from his pocket and offering it to* CHRISTY). Do you see that, mister?

CHRISTY (*looking at it*). The half of a ticket to the Western States!

SHAWN (*trembling with anxiety*). I'll give it to you and my new hat (*pulling it out of hamper*); and my breeches with the double seat (*pulling it off*); and my new coat is woven from the blackest shearings for three miles around (*giving him the coat*); I'll give you the whole of them, and my blessing, and the blessing of Father Reilly itself, maybe, if you'll quit from this and leave us in the peace we had till last night at the fall of dark.

CHRISTY (*with a new arrogance*). And for what is it you're wanting to get shut of me?

SHAWN (*looking to the* WIDOW *for help*). I'm a poor scholar with middling faculties to coin a lie, so I'll tell you the truth, Christy Mahon. I'm wedding with Pegeen beyond, and I don't think well of having a clever fearless man the like of you dwelling in her house.

CHRISTY (*almost pugnaciously*). And you'd be using bribery for to banish me?

SHAWN (*in an imploring voice*). Let you not take it badly, mister honey, isn't beyond the best place for you where you'll have golden chains and shiny coats and you riding upon hunters with the ladies of the land. (*He makes an eager sign to the* WIDOW QUIN *to come to help him.*)

WIDOW QUIN (*coming over*). It's true for him, and you'd best quit off and not have that poor girl setting her mind on you, for there's Shaneen thinks she wouldn't suit you though all is saying that she'll wed you now.
(CHRISTY *beams with delight.*)

SHAWN (*in terrified earnest*). She wouldn't suit you, and she with the divil's own temper the way you'd be strangling one another in a score of days. (*He makes the movement of strangling with his hands*) It's the like of me only that she's fit for, a quiet simple fellow wouldn't raise a hand upon her if she scratched itself.

WIDOW QUIN (*putting* SHAWN's *hat on* CHRISTY). Fit them clothes on you anyhow, young fellow, and he'd maybe loan them to you for the sports. (*Pushing him towards inner door*) Fit them on and you can give your answer when you have them tried.

CHRISTY (*beaming, delighted with the clothes*). I will then. I'd like herself to see me in them tweeds and hat. (*He goes into room and shuts the door.*)

SHAWN (*in great anxiety*). He'd like herself to see them. He'll not leave us, Widow Quin. He's a score of divils in him the way it's well nigh certain he will wed Pegeen.

WIDOW QUIN (*jeeringly*). It's true all girls are fond of courage and do hate the like of you.

SHAWN (*walking about in desperation*). Oh, Widow Quin, what'll I be doing now? I'd inform again him, but he'd burst from Kilmainham and he'd be sure and certain to destroy me. If I wasn't so Godfearing, I'd near have courage to come behind him and run a pike into his side. Oh, it's a hard case to be an orphan and not to have your father that you're used to, and you'd easy kill and make yourself a hero in the sight of all. (*Coming up to her*) Oh, Widow Quin, will you find me some contrivance when I've promised you a ewe?

WIDOW QUIN. A ewe's a small thing, but what would you give me if I did wed him and did save you so?

SHAWN (*with astonishment*). You?

WIDOW QUIN. Aye. Would you give me the red cow you have and the mountainy ram, and the right of way across your rye path, and a load of dung at Michaelmas, and turbary upon the western hill?

SHAWN (*radiant with hope*). I would surely, and I'd give you the wedding-ring I have, and the loan of a new suit, the way you'd have him decent on the wedding-day. I'd give you two kids for your dinner, and a gallon of poteen, and I'd call the piper on the long car to your wedding from Crossmolina or from Ballina. I'd give you . . .

WIDOW QUIN. That'll do so, and let you whisht, for he's coming now again.
(CHRISTY *comes in very natty in the new clothes.* WIDOW QUIN *goes to him admiringly.*)

WIDOW QUIN. If you seen yourself now, I'm thinking you'd be too proud to speak to us at all, and it'd be a pity surely to have your like sailing from Mayo to the Western World.

CHRISTY (*as proud as a peacock*). I'm not going. If this is a poor place itself, I'll make myself contented to be lodging here.
(WIDOW QUIN *makes a sign to* SHAWN *to leave them.*)

SHAWN. Well, I'm going measuring the race-course while the tide is low, so I'll leave you the garments and my blessing for the sports to-day. God bless you! (*He wriggles out.*)

WIDOW QUIN (*admiring* CHRISTY). Well, you're mighty spruce, young fellow. Sit down now while you're quiet till you talk with me.

CHRISTY (*swaggering*). I'm going abroad on the hillside for to seek Pegeen.

WIDOW QUIN. You'll have time and plenty for to seek Pegeen, and you heard me saying at the fall of night the two of us should be great company.

CHRISTY. From this out I'll have no want of company when all sorts is bringing me their food and clothing (*he swaggers to the door, tightening his belt*), the way they'd set their eyes upon a gallant orphan cleft his father with one blow to the breeches belt. (*He opens door, then staggers back*) Saints of glory! Holy angels from the throne of light!

WIDOW QUIN (*going over*). What ails you?

CHRISTY. It's the walking spirit of my murdered da?

WIDOW QUIN (*looking out*). Is it that tramper?

CHRISTY (*wildly*). Where'll I hide my poor body from that ghost of hell?
(*The door is pushed open, and old* MAHON *appears on threshold.* CHRISTY *darts in behind door.*)

WIDOW QUIN (*in great amusement*). God save you, my poor man.

MAHON (*gruffly*). Did you see a young lad passing this way in the early morning or the fall of night?

WIDOW QUIN. You're a queer kind to walk in not saluting at all.

MAHON. Did you see the young lad?

WIDOW QUIN (*stiffly*). What kind was he?

MAHON. An ugly young streeler with a murderous gob on him, and a little switch in his hand. I met a tramper seen him coming this way at the fall of night.

WIDOW QUIN. There's harvest hundreds do be passing these days for the Sligo boat. For what is it you're wanting him, my poor man?

MAHON. I want to destroy him for breaking the head on me with the clout of a loy. (*He takes off a big hat, and shows his head in a mass of bandages and plaster, with some pride*) It was he did that, and amn't I a great wonder to think I've traced him ten days with that rent in my crown?

WIDOW QUIN (*taking his head in both hands and examining it with extreme delight*). That was a great blow. And who hit you? A robber maybe?

MAHON. It was my own son hit me, and he the divil a robber, or anything else, but a dirty, stuttering lout.

WIDOW QUIN (*letting go his skull and wiping her hands in her apron*). You'd best be wary of a mortified scalp, I think they call it, lepping around with that wound in the splendour of the sun. It was a bad blow surely, and you should have vexed him fearful to make him strike that gash in his da.

MAHON. Is it me?

WIDOW QUIN (*amusing herself*). Aye. And isn't it a great shame when the old and hardened do torment the young?

MAHON (*raging*). Torment him is it? And I after holding out with the patience of a martyred saint till there's nothing but destruction on, and I'm driven out in my old age with none to aid me.

WIDOW QUIN (*greatly amused*). It's a sacred wonder the way that wickedness will spoil a man.

MAHON. My wickedness, is it? Amn't I after saying it is himself has me destroyed, and he a liar on walls, a talker of folly, a man you'd see stretched the half of the day in the brown ferns with his belly to the sun.

WIDOW QUIN. Not working at all?

MAHON. The divil a work, or if he did itself, you'd see him raising up a haystack like the stalk of a rush, or driving our last cow till he broke her leg at the hip, and when he wasn't at that he'd be fooling over little birds he had—finches and felts—or making mugs at his own self in the bit of glass we had hung on the wall.

WIDOW QUIN (*looking at* CHRISTY). What way was he so foolish? It was running wild after the girls maybe?

MAHON (*with a shout of derision*). Running wild, is it? If he seen a red petticoat coming swinging over the hill, he'd be off to hide in the sticks, and you'd see him shooting out his sheep's eyes between the little twigs and the leaves, and his two ears rising like a hare looking out through a gap. Girls, indeed!

WIDOW QUIN. It was drink maybe?

MAHON. And he a poor fellow would get drunk on the smell of a pint. He'd a queer rotten stomach, I'm telling you, and when I gave him three pulls from my pipe a while since, he was taken with contortions till I had to send him in the ass cart to the females' nurse.

WIDOW QUIN (*clasping her hands*). Well, I never till this day heard tell of a man the like of that!

MAHON. I'd take a mighty oath you didn't surely, and wasn't he the laughing joke of every female woman where four baronies meet, the way the girls would stop their weeding if they seen him coming the road to let a roar at him, and call him the looney of Mahon's.

WIDOW QUIN. I'd give the world and all to see the like of him. What kind was he?

MAHON. A small low fellow.

WIDOW QUIN. And dark?

MAHON. Dark and dirty.

WIDOW QUIN (*considering*). I'm thinking I seen him.

MAHON (*eagerly*). An ugly young blackguard.

WIDOW QUIN. A hideous, fearful villain, and the spit of you.

MAHON. What way is he fled?

WIDOW QUIN. Gone over the hills to catch a coasting steamer to the north or south.

MAHON. Could I pull up on him now?

WIDOW QUIN. If you'll cross the sands below where the tide is out, you'll be in it as soon as himself, for he had to go round ten miles by the top of the bay. (*She points to the door*) Strike down by the head beyond and then follow on the roadway to the north and east. (MAHON *goes abruptly*.)

WIDOW QUIN (*shouting after him*). Let you give him a good vengeance when you come up with him, but don't put yourself in the power of the law, for it'd be a poor thing to see a judge in his black cap reading out his sentence on a civil warrior the like of you. (*She swings the door to and looks at* CHRISTY, *who is cowering in terror, for a moment, then she bursts into a laugh*.)

WIDOW QUIN. Well, you're the walking Playboy of the Western World, and that's the poor man you had divided to his breeches belt.

CHRISTY (*looking out: then, to her*). What'll Pegeen say when she hears that story? What'll she be saying to me now?

WIDOW QUIN. She'll knock the head of you, I'm thinking, and drive you from the door. God help her to be taking you for a wonder, and you a little schemer making up the story you destroyed your da.

CHRISTY (*turning to the door, nearly speechless with rage, half to himself*). To be letting on he was dead, and coming back to his life, and following after me like an old weasel tracing a rat, and coming in here laying desolation between my own self and the fine women of Ireland, and he a kind of carcase that you'd fling upon the sea . . .

WIDOW QUIN (*more soberly*). There's talking for a man's one only son.

CHRISTY (*breaking out*). His one son, is it? May I meet him with one tooth and it aching, and one eye to be seeing seven and seventy divils in the twists of the road, and one old timber leg on him to limp into the scalding grave. (*Looking out*) There he is now crossing the strands, and that the Lord God would send a high wave to wash him from the world.

WIDOW QUIN (*scandalized*). Have you no shame? (*Putting her hand on his shoulder and turning him round*) What ails you? Near crying, is it?

CHRISTY (*in despair and grief*). Amn't I after seeing the love-light of the star of knowledge shining from her brow, and hearing words would put you thinking on the holy Brigid speaking to the infant saints, and now she'll be turning again, and speaking hard words to me, like an old woman with a spavindy ass she'd have, urging on a hill.

WIDOW QUIN. There's poetry talk for a girl you'd see itching and scratching, and she with a stale stink of poteen on her from selling in the shop.

CHRISTY (*impatiently*). It's her like

is fitted to be handling merchandise in the heavens above, and what'll I be doing now, I ask you, and I a kind of wonder was jilted by the heavens when a day was by.

(*There is a distant noise of girls' voices.* WIDOW QUIN *looks from window and comes to him, hurriedly.*)

WIDOW QUIN. You'll be doing like myself, I'm thinking, when I did destroy my man, for I'm above many's the day, odd times in great spirits, abroad in the sunshine, darning a stocking or stitching a shift; and odd times again looking out on the schooners, hookers, trawlers is sailing the sea, and I thinking on the gallant hairy fellows are drifting beyond, and myself long years living alone.

CHRISTY (*interested*). You're like me, so

WIDOW QUIN. I am your like, and it's for that I'm taking a fancy to you, and I with my little houseen above where there'd be myself to tend you, and none to ask were you a murderer or what at all.

CHRISTY. And what would I be doing if I left Pegeen?

WIDOW QUIN. I've nice jobs you could be doing, gathering shells to make a whitewash for our hut within, building up a little goose-house, or stretching a new skin on an old curragh I have, and if my hut is far from all sides, it's there you'll meet the wisest old men, I tell you, at the corner of my wheel, and it's there yourself and me will have great times whispering and hugging. . . .

VOICES (*outside, calling far away*). Christy! Christy Mahon! Christy!

CHRISTY. Is it Pegeen Mike?

WIDOW QUIN. It's the young girls, I'm thinking, coming to bring you to the sports below, and what is it you'll have me to tell them now?

CHRISTY. Aid me for to win Pegeen. It's herself only that I'm seeking now. (WIDOW QUIN *gets up and goes to window*) Aid me for to win her, and I'll be asking God to stretch a hand to you in the hour of death, and lead you short cuts through the Meadows of Ease, and up the floor of Heaven to the Footstool of the Virgin's Son.

WIDOW QUIN. There's praying.

VOICES (*nearer*). Christy! Christy Mahon!

CHRISTY (*with agitation*). They're coming. Will you swear to aid and save me for the love of Christ?

WIDOW QUIN (*looks at him for a moment*). If I aid you, will you swear to give me a right of way I want, and a mountainy ram, and a load of dung at Michaelmas, the time that you'll be master here?

CHRISTY. I will, by the elements and stars of night.

WIDOW QUIN. Then we'll not say a word of the old fellow, the way Pegeen won't know your story till the end of time.

CHRISTY. And if he chances to return again?

WIDOW QUIN. We'll swear he's a maniac and not your da. I could take an oath I seen him raving on the sands to-day.
(*Girls run in.*)

SUSAN. Come on to the sports below. Pegeen says you're to come.

SARA TANSEY. The lepping's beginning, and we've a jockey's suit to fit upon you for the mule race on the sands below.

HONOR. Come on, will you?

CHRISTY. I will then if Pegeen's beyond.

SARA TANSEY. She's in the boreen making game of Shaneen Keogh.

CHRISTY. Then I'll be going to her now. (*He runs out followed by the girls.*)

WIDOW QUIN. Well, if the worst comes in the end of all, it'll be great game to see there's none to pity him but a widow woman, the like of me, has buried her children and destroyed her man. (*She goes out.*)

CURTAIN

ACT THREE

SCENE—*As before. Later in the day.* JIMMY *comes in, slightly drunk.*

JIMMY (*calls*). Pegeen! (*Crosses to inner door*) Pegeen Mike! (*Comes back again into the room*) Pegeen! (PHILLY *comes in in the same state. To* PHILLY) Did you see herself?

PHILLY. I did not; but I sent Shawn Keogh with the ass cart for to bear him home. (*Trying cupboards which are locked*) Well, isn't he a nasty man to get into such staggers at a morning wake? and isn't herself the divil's daughter for locking, and she so fussy after that young gaffer, you might take your death with drought and none to heed you?

JIMMY. It's little wonder she'd be fussy, and he after bringing bankrupt ruin on the roulette man, and the trick-o'-the-loop man, and breaking the nose of the cockshotman, and winning all in the sports below, racing, lepping, dancing, and the Lord knows what! He's right luck, I'm telling you.

PHILLY. If he has, he'll be rightly hobbled yet, and he not able to say ten words without making a brag of the way he killed his father, and the great blow he hit with the loy.

JIMMY. A man can't hang by his own informing, and his father should be rotten by now.
(OLD MAHON *passes window slowly.*)

PHILLY. Supposing a man's digging spuds in that field with a long spade, and supposing he flings up the two halves of that skull, what'll be said then in the papers and the courts of law?

JIMMY. They'd say it was an old Dane, maybe, was drowned in the flood. (OLD MAHON *comes in and sits down near door listening*) Did you never hear tell of the skulls they have in the city of Dublin, ranged out like blue jugs in a cabin of Connaught?

PHILLY. And you believe that?

JIMMY (*pugnaciously*). Didn't a lad see them and he after coming from harvesting in the Liverpool boat? "They have them there," says he, "making a show of the great people there was one time walking the world. White skulls and black skulls and yellow skulls, and some with full teeth, and some haven't only but one."

PHILLY. It was no lie, maybe, for when I was a young lad there was a graveyard beyond the house with the remnants of a man who had thighs as long as your arm. He was a horrid man, I'm telling you, and there was many a fine Sunday I'd put him together for fun, and he with shiny bones, you wouldn't meet the like of these days in the cities of the world.

MAHON (*getting up*). You wouldn't, is it? Lay your eyes on that skull, and tell me where and when there was another the like of it, is splintered only from the blow of a loy.

PHILLY. Glory be to God! And who hit you at all?

MAHON (*triumphantly*). It was my own son hit me. Would you believe that?

JIMMY. Well, there's wonders hidden in the heart of man!

PHILLY (*suspiciously*). And what way was it done?

MAHON (*wandering about the room*). I'm after walking hundreds and long scores of miles, winning clean beds and the fill of my belly four times in the day, and I doing nothing but telling stories of that naked truth. (*He comes to them a little aggressively*) Give me a supeen and I'll tell you now. (WIDOW QUIN *comes in and stands aghast behind him. He is facing* JIMMY *and* PHILLY, *who are on the left.*)

JIMMY. Ask herself beyond. She's the stuff hidden in her shawl.

WIDOW QUIN (*coming to* MAHON *quickly*). You here, is it? You didn't go far at all?

MAHON. I seen the coasting steamer passing, and I got a drought upon me and a cramping leg, so I said, "The divil go along with him," and turned again. (*Looking under her shawl*) And let you give me a supeen, for I'm destroyed travelling since Tuesday was a week.

WIDOW QUIN (*getting a glass, in a cajoling tone*). Sit down then by the fire and take your ease for a space. You've a right to be destroyed indeed, with your walking, and fighting, and facing the sun. (*Giving him poteen from a stone jar she has brought in*) There now is a drink for you, and may it be to your happiness and length of life.

MAHON (*taking glass greedily and sitting down by fire*). God increase you!

WIDOW QUIN (*taking men to the right stealthily*). Do you know what? That man's raving from his wound to-day, for I met him a while since telling a rambling tale of a tinker had him destroyed. Then he heard of Christy's deed, and he up and says it was his son had cracked his skull. O isn't madness a fright, for he'll go killing someone yet, and he thinking it's the man has struck him so?

JIMMY (*entirely convinced*). It's a fright, surely. I knew a party was kicked in the head by a red mare, and he went killing horses a great while, till he eat the insides of a clock and died after.

PHILLY (*with suspicion*). Did he see Christy?

WIDOW QUIN. He didn't. (*With a warning gesture*) Let you not be putting him in mind of him, or you'll be likely summoned if there's murder done. (*Looking round at* MAHON) Whisht! He's listening. Wait now till you hear me taking him easy and unravelling all. (*She goes to* MAHON) And what way are you feeling, mister? Are you in contentment now?

MAHON (*slightly emotional from his drink*). I'm poorly only, for it's a hard story the way I'm left to-day, when it was I did tend him from his hour of birth, and he a dunce never reached his second book, the way he'd come from school, many's the day, with his legs lamed under him, and he blackened with his beatings like a tinker's ass. It's a hard story, I'm saying, the way some do have their next and nighest raising up a hand of murder on them, and some is lonesome getting their death with lamentation in the dead of night.

WIDOW QUIN (*not knowing what to say*). To hear you talking so quiet, who'd know you were the same fellow we seen pass to-day?

MAHON. I'm the same surely. The wrack and ruin of three score years; and it's a terror to live that length, I tell you, and to have your sons going to the dogs against you, and you wore out scolding them, and skelping them, and God knows what.

PHILLY (*to* JIMMY). He's not raving. (*To* WIDOW QUIN) Will you ask him what kind was his son?

WIDOW QUIN (*to* MAHON, *with a peculiar look*). Was your son that hit you a lad of one year and a score maybe, a great hand at racing and lepping and licking the world?

MAHON (*turning on her with a roar of rage*). Didn't you hear me say he was the fool of men, the way from this out he'll know the orphan's lot with old and young making game of him and they swearing, raging, kicking at him like a mangy cur.

(*A great burst of cheering outside, some way off.*)

MAHON (*putting his hands to his ears*). What in the name of God do they want roaring below?

WIDOW QUIN (*with a shade of a smile*). They're cheering a young lad, the champion Playboy of the Western World.
(*More cheering.*)

MAHON (*going to window*). It'd split my heart to hear them, and I with pulses in my brain-pan for a week gone by. Is it racing they are?

JIMMY (*looking from door*). It is then. They are mounting him for the mule race will be run upon the sands. That's the playboy on the winkered mule.

MAHON (*puzzled*). That lad, is it? If you said it was a fool he was, I'd have laid a mighty oath he was the likeness of my wandering son. (*Uneasily, putting his hand to his head*) Faith, I'm thinking I'll go walking for to view the race.

WIDOW QUIN (*stopping him, sharply*). You will not. You'd best take the road to Belmullet, and not be dilly-dallying in this place where there isn't a spot you could sleep.

PHILLY (*coming forward*). Don't mind her. Mount there on the bench and you'll have a view of the whole. They're hurrying before the tide will rise, and it'd be near over if you went down the pathway through the crags below.

MAHON (*mounts on bench*, WIDOW QUIN *beside him*). That's a right view again the edge of the sea.

They're coming now from the point.' He's leading. Who is he at all?

WIDOW QUIN. He's the champion of the world, I tell you, and there isn't a hop'orth isn't falling lucky to his hands to-day.

PHILLY (*looking out, interested in the race*). Look at that. They're pressing him now.

JIMMY. He'll win it yet.

PHILLY. Take your time, Jimmy Farrell. It's too soon to say.

WIDOW QUIN (*shouting*). Watch him taking the gate. There's riding.

JIMMY (*cheering*). More power to the young lad!

MAHON. He's passing the third.

JIMMY. He'll lick them yet!

WIDOW QUIN. He'd lick them if he was running races with a score it-self.

MAHON. Look at the mule he has, kicking the stars.

WIDOW QUIN. There was a lep! (*Catching hold of* MAHON *in her excitement*) He's fallen! He's mounted again! Faith, he's passing them all!

JIMMY. Look at him skelping her!

PHILLY. And the mountain girls hooshing him on!

JIMMY. It's the last turn! The post's cleared for them now!

MAHON. Look at the narrow place. He'll be into the bogs! (*With a yell*) Good rider! He's through it again!

JIMMY. He's neck and neck!

MAHON. Good boy to him! Flames, but he's in!
(*Great cheering, in which all join.*)

MAHON (*with hesitation*). What's that? They're raising him up. They're coming this way. (*With a roar of rage and astonishment*) It's Christy! by the stars of God! I'd know his way of spitting and he astride the moon. (*He jumps down and makes for the door, but* WIDOW QUIN *catches him and pulls him back.*)

WIDOW QUIN. Stay quiet, will you. That's not your son. (*To* JIMMY) Stop him, or you'll get a month for the abetting of manslaughter and be fined as well.

JIMMY. I'll hold him.

MAHON (*struggling*). Let me out! Let me out, the lot of you! till I have my vengeance on his head to-day.

WIDOW QUIN (*shaking him, vehe-mently*). That's not your son. That's a man is going to make a marriage with the daughter of this house, a place with fine trade, with a license, and with poteen too.

MAHON (*amazed*). That man marrying a decent and a moneyed girl! Is it mad yous are? Is it in a crazy-house for females that I'm landed now?

WIDOW QUIN. It's mad yourself is with the blow upon your head. That lad is the wonder of the Western World.

MAHON. I seen it's my son.

WIDOW QUIN. You seen that you're mad. (*Cheering outside*) Do you hear them cheering him in the zig-zags of the road? Aren't you after saying that your son's a fool, and how would they be cheering a true idiot born?

MAHON (*getting distressed*). It's maybe out of reason that that man's himself. (*Cheering again*) There's none surely will go cheering him. Oh, I'm raving with a madness that would fright the world! (*He sits down with his hand to his head*) There was one time I seen ten scarlet divils letting on they'd cork my spirit in a gallon can; and one time I seen rats as big as badgers sucking the life blood from the butt of my lug; but I never till this day confused that dribbling idiot with a likely man. I'm destroyed surely.

WIDOW QUIN. And who'd wonder when it's your brain-pan that is gaping now?

MAHON. Then the blight of the sacred drought upon myself and him, for I never went mad to this day, and I not three weeks with the Limerick girls drinking myself silly, and parlatic from the dusk to dawn. (*To* WIDOW QUIN, *suddenly*) Is my visage astray?

WIDOW QUIN. It is then. You're a sniggering maniac, a child could see.

MAHON (*getting up more cheerfully*). Then I'd best be going to the union beyond, and there'll be a welcome before me, I tell you (*with great pride*), and I a terrible and fearful case, the way that there

I was one time, screeching in a straitened waistcoat, with seven doctors writing out my sayings in a printed book. Would you believe that?

WIDOW QUIN. If you're a wonder itself, you'd best be hasty, for them lads caught a maniac one time and pelted the poor creature till he ran out, raving and foaming, and was drowned in the sea.

MAHON (*with philosophy*). It's true mankind is the divil when your head's astray. Let me out now and I'll slip down the boreen, and not see them so.

WIDOW QUIN (*showing him out*). That's it. Run to the right, and not a one will see. (*He runs off.*)

PHILLY (*wisely*). You're at some gaming, Widow Quin; but I'll walk after him and give him his dinner and a time to rest, and I'll see then if he's raving or as sane as you.

WIDOW QUIN (*annoyed*). If you go near that lad, let you be wary of your head, I'm saying. Didn't you hear him telling he was crazed at times?

PHILLY. I heard him telling a power; and I'm thinking we'll have right sport, before night will fall. (*He goes out.*)

JIMMY. Well, Philly's a conceited and foolish man. How could that madman have his senses and his brain-pan slit? I'll go after them and see him turn on Philly now. (*He goes;* WIDOW QUIN *hides poteen behind counter. Then hubbub outside.*)

VOICES. There you are! Good jumper! Grand lepper! Darlint boy! He's the racer! Bear him on, will you! (CHRISTY *comes in, in* JOCKEY'S *dress, with* PEGEEN MIKE, SARA, *and other girls, and* MEN.)

PEGEEN (*to crowd*). Go on now and don't destroy him and he drenching with sweat. Go along, I'm saying, and have your tug-of-warring till he's dried his skin.

CROWD. Here's his prizes! A bagpipes! A fiddle was played by a poet in the years gone by! A flat and three-thorned blackthorn would lick the scholars out of Dublin town!

CHRISTY (*taking prizes from the* MEN). Thank you kindly, the lot of you. But you'd say it was little only I did this day if you'd seen me a while since striking my one single blow.

TOWN CRIER (*outside, ringing a bell*). Take notice, last event of this day! Tug-of-warring on the green below! Come on, the lot of you! Great achievements for all Mayo men!

PEGEEN. Go on, and leave him for to rest and dry. Go on, I tell you, for he'll do no more. (*She hustles crowd out;* WIDOW QUIN *following them.*)

MEN (*going*). Come on, then. Good luck for the while!

PEGEEN (*radiantly, wiping his face with her shawl*). Well, you're the lad, and you'll have great times from this out when you could win that wealth of prizes, and you sweating in the heat of noon!

CHRISTY (*looking at her with delight*). I'll have great times if I win the crowning prize I'm seeking now, and that's your promise that you'll wed me in a fortnight, when our banns is called.

PEGEEN (*backing away from him*). You've right daring to go ask me that, when all knows you'll be starting to some girl in your own townland, when your father's rotten in four months, or five.

CHRISTY (*indignantly*). Starting from you, is it? (*He follows her*) I will not, then, and when the airs is warming in four months, or five, it's then yourself and me should be pacing Neifin in the dews of night, the times sweet smells do be rising, and you'd see a little shiny new moon, maybe, sinking on the hills.

PEGEEN (*looking at him playfully*). And it's that kind of a poacher's love you'd make, Christy Mahon, on the sides of Neifin, when the night is down?

CHRISTY. It's little you'll think if my love's a poacher's, or an earl's itself, when you'll feel my two hands stretched around you, and I squeezing kisses on your puckered lips, till I'd feel a kind of pity for the Lord God in all ages sitting lonesome in his golden chair.

PEGEEN. That'll be right fun, Christy Mahon, and any girl would walk her heart out before she'd meet a young man was your like for eloquence, or talk, at all.

CHRISTY (*encouraged*). Let you wait, to hear me talking, till we're astray in Erris, when Good Friday's by, drinking a sup from a well, and making mighty kisses with our wetted mouths, or gaming in a gap or sunshine, with yourself stretched back unto your necklace, in the flowers of the earth.

PEGEEN (*in a lower voice, moved by his tone*). I'd be nice so, is it?

CHRISTY (*with rapture*). If the mitred bishops seen you that time, they'd be the like of the holy prophets, I'm thinking, do be straining the bars of Paradise to lay eyes on the Lady Helen of Troy, and she abroad, pacing back and forward, with a nosegay in her golden shawl.

PEGEEN (*with real tenderness*). And what is it I have, Christy Mahon, to make me fitting entertainment for the like of you, that has such poet's talking, and such bravery of heart?

CHRISTY (*in a low voice*). Isn't there the light of seven heavens in your heart alone, the way you'll be an angel's lamp to me from this out, and I abroad in the darkness, spearing salmons in the Owen, or the Carrowmore?

PEGEEN. If I was your wife, I'd be along with you those nights, Christy Mahon, the way you'd see I was a great hand at coaxing bailiffs, or coining funny nick-names for the stars of night.

CHRISTY. You, is it? Taking your death in the hailstones, or in the fogs of dawn.

PEGEEN. Yourself and me would shelter easy in a narrow bush, (*with a qualm of dread*) but we're only talking, maybe, for this would be a poor, thatched place to hold a fine lad is the like of you.

CHRISTY (*putting his arm around her*). If I wasn't a good Christian, it's on my naked knees I'd be saying my prayers and paters to every jackstraw you have roofing your head, and every stony pebble is paving the laneway to your door.

PEGEEN (*radiantly*). If that's the truth, I'll be burning candles from this out to the miracles of God that have brought you from the south to-day, and I, with my gowns bought ready, the way that I can wed you, and not wait at all.

CHRISTY. It's miracles, and that's the truth. Me there toiling a long while, and walking a long while, not knowing at all I was drawing all times nearer to this holy day.

PEGEEN. And myself, a girl, was tempted often to go sailing the seas till I'd marry a Jew-man, with ten kegs of gold, and I not knowing at all there was the like of you drawing nearer, like the stars of God.

CHRISTY. And to think I'm long years hearing women talking that talk, to all bloody fools, and this the first time I've heard the like of your voice talking sweetly for my own delight.

PEGEEN. And to think it's me is talking sweetly, Christy Mahon, and I the fright of seven townlands for my biting tongue. Well, the heart's a wonder; and, I'm thinking, there won't be our like in Mayo, for gallant lovers, from this hour, to-day. (*Drunken singing is heard outside*) There's my father coming

from the wake, and when he's had his sleep we'll tell him, for he's peaceful then.
(*They separate.*)

MICHAEL (*singing outside*).
The jailor and the turnkey
    They quickly ran us down,
And brought us back as prisoners
    Once more to Cavan town.
(*He comes in supported by* SHAWN.)
There we lay bewailing
    All in a prison bound. . . .
(*He sees* CHRISTY. *Goes and shakes him drunkenly by the hand, while* PEGEEN *and* SHAWN *talk on the left.*)

MICHAEL (*to* CHRISTY). The blessing of God and the holy angels on your head, young fellow. I hear tell you're after winning all in the sports below; and wasn't it a shame I didn't bear you along with me to Kate Cassidy's wake, a fine, stout lad, the like of you, for you'd never see the match of it for flows of drink, the way when we sunk her bones at noonday in her narrow grave, there were five men, aye, and six men, stretched out retching speechless on the holy stones.

CHRISTY (*uneasily, watching* PEGEEN). Is that the truth?

MICHAEL. It is then, and aren't you a louty schemer to go burying your poor father unbeknownst when you'd a right to throw him on the crupper of a Kerry mule and drive him westwards, like holy Joseph in the days gone by, the way we could have given him a decent burial, and not have him rotting beyond, and not a Christian drinking a smart drop to the glory of his soul?

CHRISTY (*gruffly*). It's well enough he's lying, for the likes of him.

MICHAEL (*slapping him on the back*). Well, aren't you a hardened slayer? It'll be a poor thing for the household man where you go sniffing for a female wife; and (*pointing to* SHAWN) look beyond at that shy and decent Christian I have chosen for my daughter's hand, and I after getting the gilded dispensation this day for to wed them now.

CHRISTY. And you'll be wedding them this day, is it?

MICHAEL (*drawing himself up*). Aye. Are you thinking, if I'm drunk itself, I'd leave my daughter living single with a little frisky rascal is the like of you?

PEGEEN (*breaking away from* SHAWN). Is it the truth the dispensation's come?

MICHAEL (*triumphantly*). Father Reilly's after reading it in gallous Latin, and "It's come in the nick of time," says he; "so I'll wed them in a hurry, dreading that young gaffer who'd capsize the stars."

PEGEEN (*fiercely*). He's missed his nick of time, for it's that lad, Christy Mahon, that I'm wedding now.

MICHAEL (*loudly with horror*). You'd be making him a son to me, and he wet and crusted with his father's blood?

PEGEEN. Aye. Wouldn't it be a bitter thing for a girl to go marrying the like of Shaneen, and he a middling kind of a scarecrow, with no savagery or fine words in him at all?

MICHAEL (*gasping and sinking on a chair*). Oh, aren't you a heathen daughter to go shaking the fat of my heart, and I swamped and drownded with the weight of drink? Would you have them turning on me the way that I'd be roaring to the dawn of day with the wind upon my heart? Have you not a word to aid me, Shaneen? Are you not jealous at all?

SHAWN (*in great misery*). I'd be afeard to be jealous of a man did slay his da.

PEGEEN. Well, it'd be a poor thing to go marrying your like. I'm seeing there's a world of peril for an orphan girl, and isn't it a great blessing I didn't wed you, before himself came walking from the west or south?

SHAWN. It's a queer story you'd go picking a dirty tramp up from the highways of the world.

PEGEEN (*playfully*). And you think you're a likely beau to go straying along with, the shiny Sundays of the opening year, when it's sooner on a bullock's liver you'd put a poor girl thinking than on the lily or the rose?

SHAWN. And have you no mind of my weight of passion, and the holy dispensation, and the drift of heifers I am giving, and the golden ring?

PEGEEN. I'm thinking you're too fine for the like of me, Shawn Keogh of Killakeen, and let you go off till you'd find a radiant lady with droves of bullocks on the plains of Meath, and herself bedizened in the diamond jewelries of Pharaoh's ma. That'd be your match, Shaneen. So God save you now! (*She retreats behind* CHRISTY.)

SHAWN. Won't you hear me telling you . . . ?

CHRISTY (*with ferocity*). Take yourself from this, young fellow, or I'll maybe add a murder to my deeds to-day.

MICHAEL (*springing up with a shriek*). Murder is it? Is it mad yous are? Would you go making murder in this place, and it piled with poteen for our drink to-night? Go on to the foreshore if it's fighting you want, where the rising tide will wash all traces from the memory of man. (*Pushing* SHAWN *towards* CHRISTY.)

SHAWN (*shaking himself free, and getting behind* MICHAEL). I'll not fight him, Michael James. I'd liefer live a bachelor, simmering in passions to the end of time, than face a lepping savage the like of him has descended from the Lord knows where. Strike him yourself, Michael James, or you'll lose my drift of heifers and my blue bull from Sneem.

MICHAEL. Is it me fight him, when it's father-slaying he's bred to now? (*Pushing* SHAWN) Go on you fool and fight him now.

SHAWN (*coming forward a little*). Will I strike him with my hand?

MICHAEL. Take the loy is on your western side.

SHAWN. I'd be afeard of the gallows if I struck him with that.

CHRISTY (*taking up the loy*). Then I'll make you face the gallows or quit off from this.

(SHAWN *flies out of the door.*)

CHRISTY. Well, fine weather be after him, (*going to* MICHAEL, *coaxingly*) and I'm thinking you wouldn't wish to have that quaking blackguard in your house at all. Let you give us your blessing and hear her swear her faith to me, for I'm mounted on the springtide of the stars of luck, the way it'll be good for any to have me in the house.

PEGEEN (*at the other side of* MICHAEL). Bless us now, for I swear to God I'll wed him, and I'll not renege.

MICHAEL (*standing up in the centre, holding on to both of them*). It's the will of God, I'm thinking, that all should win an easy or a cruel end, and it's the will of God that all should rear up lengthy families for the nurture of the earth. What's a single man, I ask you, eating a bit in one house and drinking a sup in another, and he with no place of his own, like an old braying jackass strayed upon the rocks? (*To* CHRISTY) It's many would be in dread to bring your like into their house for to end them, maybe, with a sudden end; but I'm a decent man of Ireland, and I liefer face the grave untimely and I seeing a score of grandsons growing up little gallant swearers by the name of God, than go peopling my bedside with puny weeds the like of what you'd breed, I'm thinking, out of Shaneen Keogh. (*He joins their hands*) A daring fellow is the jewel of the world, and a man did split his father's middle with a single clout, should have the bravery of ten, so may God and Mary and St. Patrick bless you, and increase you from this mortal day.

CHRISTY AND PEGEEN. Amen, O Lord!

(*Hubbub outside.* OLD MAHON *rushes in, followed by all the crowd, and* WIDOW QUIN. *He makes a rush at* CHRISTY, *knocks him down, and begins to beat him.*)

PEGEEN (*dragging back his arm*). Stop that, will you? Who are you at all?

MAHON. His father, God forgive me!

PEGEEN (*drawing back*). Is it rose from the dead?

MAHON. Do you think I look so easy quenched with the tap of a loy? (*Beats* CHRISTY *again.*)

PEGEEN (*glaring at* CHRISTY). And it's lies you told, letting on you had him slitted, and you nothing at all.

CHRISTY (*catching* MAHON'S *stick*). He's not my father. He's a raving maniac would scare the world. (*Pointing to* WIDOW QUIN) Herself knows it is true.

CROWD. You're fooling Pegeen! The Widow Quin seen him this day, and you likely knew! You're a liar!

CHRISTY (*dumbfounded*). It's himself was a liar, lying stretched out with an open head on him, letting on he was dead.

MAHON. Weren't you off racing the hills before I got my breath with the start I had seeing you turn or me at all?

PEGEEN. And to think of the coaxing glory we had given him, and he after doing nothing but hitting a soft blow and chasing northward in a sweat of fear. Quit off from this.

CHRISTY (*piteously*). You've seen my doings this day, and let you save me from the old man; for why would you be in such a scorch of haste to spur me to destruction now?

PEGEEN. It's there your treachery is spurring me, till I'm hard set to think you're the one I'm after lacing in my heart-strings half-an-hour gone by. (*To* MAHON) Take him on from this, for I think bad the world should see me raging for a Munster liar, and the fool of men.

MAHON. Rise up now to retribution, and come on with me.

CROWD (*jeeringly*). There's the playboy! There's the lad thought he'd rule the roost in Mayo. Slate him now, mister.

CHRISTY (*getting up in shy terror*). What is it drives you to torment me here, when I'd asked the thunders of the might of God to blast me if I ever did hurt to any saving only that one single blow.

MAHON (*loudly*). If you didn't, you're a poor good-for-nothing, and isn't it by the like of you the sins of the whole world are committed?

CHRISTY (*raising his hands*). In the name of the Almighty God. . . .

MAHON. Leave troubling the Lord God. Would you have him sending down droughts, and fevers, and the old hen and the cholera morbus?

CHRISTY (*to* WIDOW QUIN). Will you come between us and protect me now?

WIDOW QUIN. I've tried a lot, God help me, and my share is done.

CHRISTY (*looking round in desperation*). And I must go back into my torment is it, or run off like a vagabond straying through the Unions with the dusts of August making mud-stains in the gullet of my throat, or the winds of March blowing on me till I'd take an oath I felt them making whistles of my ribs within?

SARA. Ask Pegeen to aid you. Her like does often change.

CHRISTY. I will not then, for there's torment in the splendour of her like, and she a girl any moon of midnight would take pride to meet, facing southwards on the heaths of Keel. But what did I want crawling forward to scorch my understanding at her flaming brow?

PEGEEN (*to* MAHON, *vehemently, fearing she will break into tears*). Take him on from this or I'll set the young lads to destroy him here.

MAHON (*going to him, shaking his stick*). Come on now if you wouldn't have the company to see you skelped.

PEGEEN (*half laughing, through her tears*). That's it, now the world will see him pandied, and he an ugly liar was playing off the hero, and the fright of men.

CHRISTY (*to* MAHON, *very sharply*). Leave me go!

CROWD. That's it. Now, Christy. If them two set fighting, it will lick the world.

MAHON (*making a grab at* CHRISTY). Come here to me.

CHRISTY (*more threateningly*). Leave me go, I'm saying.

MAHON. I will maybe, when your legs is limping, and your back is blue.

CROWD. Keep it up, the two of you. I'll back the old one. Now the playboy.

CHRISTY (*in low and intense voice*). Shut your yelling, for if you're after making a mighty man of me this day by the power of a lie, you're setting me now to think if it's a poor thing to be lonesome, it's worse maybe to go mixing with the fools of earth.
(MAHON *makes a movement towards him.*)

CHRISTY (*almost shouting*). Keep off . . . lest I do show a blow unto the lot of you would set the guardian angels winking in the clouds above. (*He swings round with a sudden rapid movement and picks up a loy.*)

CROWD (*half frightened, half amused*). He's going mad! Mind yourselves! Run from the idiot!

CHRISTY. If I am an idiot, I'm after hearing my voice this day saying words would raise the topknot on a poet in a merchant's town. I've won your racing, your lepping, and . . .

MAHON. Shut your gullet and come on with me.

CHRISTY. I'm going, but I'll stretch you first. (*He runs at* OLD MAHON *with the loy, chases him out of the door, followed by crowd and* WIDOW QUIN. *There is a great noise outside, then a yell, and dead silence for a moment.* CHRISTY *comes in, half dazed, and goes to fire.*)

WIDOW QUIN (*coming in, hurriedly, and going to him*). They're turning again you. Come on, or you'll be hanged, indeed.

CHRISTY. I'm thinking, from this out, Pegeen'll be giving me praises the same as in the hours gone by.

WIDOW QUIN (*impatiently*). Come by the back-door. I'd think bad to have you stifled on the gallows tree.

CHRISTY (*indignantly*). I will not, then. What good'd be my life-time, if I left Pegeen?

WIDOW QUIN. Come on, and you'll be no worse than you were last night; and you with a double murder this time to be telling to the girls.

CHRISTY. I'll not leave Pegeen Mike.

WIDOW QUIN (*impatiently*). Isn't there the match of her in every parish public, from Binghamstown unto the plain of Meath? Come on, I tell you, and I'll find you finer sweethearts at each waning moon.

CHRISTY. It's Pegeen I'm seeking only, and what'd I care if you brought me a drift of chosen females, standing in their shifts itself, maybe, from this place to the Eastern World?

SARA (*runs in, pulling off one of her petticoats*). They're going to hang him. (*Holding out petticoat and shawl*) Fit these upon him, and let him run off to the east.

WIDOW QUIN. He's raving now; but we'll fit them on him, and I'll take him, in the ferry, to the Achill boat.

CHRISTY (*struggling feebly*). Leave me go, will you? when I'm thinking of my luck to-day, for she will wed me surely, and I a proven hero in the end of all.
(*They try to fasten petticoat round him.*)

WIDOW QUIN. Take his left hand, and we'll pull him now. Come on, young fellow.

CHRISTY (*suddenly starting up*). You'll be taking me from her? You're jealous, is it, of her wedding me? Go on from this. (*He snatches up a stool, and threatens them with it.*)

WIDOW QUIN (*going*). It's in the mad-house they should put him, not in jail, at all. We'll go by the back-door, to call the doctor, and we'll save him so. (*She goes out, with SARA, through inner room. MEN crowd in the doorway. CHRISTY sits down again by the fire.*)

MICHAEL (*in a terrified whisper*). Is the old lad killed surely?

PHILLY. I'm after feeling the last gasps quitting his heart.
(*They peer in at CHRISTY.*)

MICHAEL (*with a rope*). Look at the way he is. Twist a hangman's knot on it, and slip it over his head, while he's not minding at all.

PHILLY. Let you take it, Shaneen. You're the soberest of all that's here.

SHAWN. Is it me to go near him, and he the wickedest and worst with me? Let you take it, Pegeen Mike.

PEGEEN. Come on, so. (*She goes forward with the others, and they drop the double hitch over his head.*)

CHRISTY. What ails you?

SHAWN (*triumphantly, as they pull the rope tight on his arms*). Come on to the peelers, till they stretch you now.

CHRISTY. Me!

MICHAEL. If we took pity on you, the Lord God would, maybe, bring us ruin from the law to-day, so you'd best come easy, for hanging is an easy and a speedy end.

CHRISTY. I'll not stir. (*To PEGEEN*) And what is it you'll say to me, and I after doing it this time in the face of all?

PEGEEN. I'll say, a strange man is a marvel, with his mighty talk; but what's a squabble in your backyard, and the blow of a loy, have taught me that there's a great gap between a gallous story and a dirty deed. (*To MEN*) Take him on from this, or the lot of us will be likely put on trial for his deed to-day.

CHRISTY (*with horror in his voice*). And it's yourself will send me off, to have a horny-fingered hangman hitching his bloody slip-knots at the butt of my ear.

MEN (*pulling rope*). Come on, will you? (*He is pulled down on the floor.*)

CHRISTY (*twisting his legs round the table*). Cut the rope, Pegeen, and I'll quit the lot of you, and live from this out, like the madmen of Keel, eating muck and green weeds, on the faces of the cliffs.

PEGEEN. And leave us to hang, is it, for a saucy liar, the like of you? (*To* MEN) Take him on, out from this.

SHAWN. Pull a twist on his neck, and squeeze him so.

PHILLY. Twist yourself. Sure he cannot hurt you, if you keep your distance from his teeth alone.

SHAWN. I'm afeard of him. (*To* PEGEEN) Lift a lighted sod, will you, and scorch his leg.

PEGEEN (*blowing the fire, with a bellows*). Leave go now, young fellow, or I'll scorch your shins.

CHRISTY. You're blowing for to torture me. (*His voice rising and growing stronger*) That's your kind, is it? Then let the lot of you be wary, for, if I've to face the gallows, I'll have a gay march down, I tell you, and shed the blood of some of you before I die.

SHAWN (*in terror*). Keep a good hold, Philly. Be wary, for the love of God. For I'm thinking he would liefest wreak his pains on me.

CHRISTY (*almost gaily*). If I do lay my hands on you, it's the way you'll be at the fall of night, hanging as a scarecrow for the fowls of hell. Ah, you'll have a gallous jaunt I'm saying, coaching out through Limbo with my father's ghost.

SHAWN (*to* PEGEEN). Make haste, will you? Oh, isn't he a holy terror, and isn't it true for Father Reilly, that all drink's a curse that has the lot of you so shaky and uncertain now?

CHRISTY. If I can wring a neck among you, I'll have a royal judgment looking on the trembling jury in the courts of law. And won't there be crying out in Mayo the day I'm stretched upon the rope with ladies in their silks and satins snivelling in their lacy kerchiefs, and they rhyming songs and ballads on the terror of my fate? (*He squirms round on the floor and bites* SHAWN's *leg.*)

SHAWN (*shrieking*). My leg's bit on me. He's the like of a mad dog, I'm thinking, the way that I will surely die.

CHRISTY (*delighted with himself*). You will then, the way you can shake out hell's flags of welcome for my coming in two weeks or three, for I'm thinking Satan hasn't many have killed their da in Kerry, and in Mayo too.

(OLD MAHON *comes in behind on all fours and looks on unnoticed.*)

MEN (*to* PEGEEN). Bring the sod, will you?

PEGEEN (*coming over*). God help him so. (*Burns his leg.*)

CHRISTY (*kicking and screaming*). O, glory be to God! (*He kicks loose from the table, and they all drag him towards the door.*)

JIMMY (*seeing OLD MAHON*). Will you look what's come in? (*They all drop CHRISTY and run left.*)

CHRISTY (*scrambling on his knees face to face with OLD MAHON*), Are you coming to be killed a third time, or what ails you now?

MAHON. For what is it they have you tied?

CHRISTY. They're taking me to the peelers to have me hanged for slaying you.

MICHAEL (*apologetically*). It is the will of God that all should guard their little cabins from the treachery of law, and what would my daughter be doing if I was ruined or was hanged itself?

MAHON (*grimly, loosening CHRISTY*). It's little I care if you put a bag on her back, and went picking cockles till the hour of death; but my son and myself will be going our own way, and we'll have great times from this out telling stories of the villainy of Mayo, and the fools is here. (*To CHRISTY, who is freed*) Come on now.

CHRISTY. Go with you, is it? I will then, like a gallant captain with his heathen slave. Go on now and I'll see you from this day stewing my oatmeal and washing my spuds, for I'm master of all fights from now. (*Pushing MAHON*) Go on, I'm saying.

MAHON. Is it me?

CHRISTY. Not a word out of you. Go on from this.

MAHON (*walking out and looking back at CHRISTY over his shoulder*). Glory be to God! (*With a broad smile*) I am crazy again! (*Goes.*)

CHRISTY. Ten thousand blessings upon all that's here, for you've turned me a likely gaffer in the end of all, the way I'll go romancing through a romping lifetime from this hour to the dawning of the judgment day. (*He goes out.*)

MICHAEL. By the will of God, we'll have peace now for our drinks. Will you draw the porter, Pegeen?

SHAWN (*going up to her*). It's a miracle Father Reilly can wed us in the end of all, and we'll have none to trouble us when his vicious bite is healed.

PEGEEN (*hitting him a box on the ear*). Quit my sight. (*Putting her shawl over her head and breaking out into wild lamentations*) Oh my grief, I've lost him surely. I've lost the only Playboy of the Western World.

CURTAIN

Shadow and Substance

BY PAUL VINCENT CARROLL

"Oh, what a power has white Simplicity!"
KEATS

TO

M. P. L.

AND THE LITTLE WHITE DOG

CHARACTERS

VERY REV. THOMAS CANON SKERRITT.

BRIGID, *his servant, about 18.*

FATHER CORR
FATHER KIRWAN } *two curates, in their twenties.*

DERMOT FRANCIS O'FLINGSLEY, *the local schoolmaster, thirty-two years old.*

THOMASINA CONCANNON, *Canon Skerritt's step-niece.*

MISS JEMIMA COONEY, *a local spinster.*

FRANCIS IGNATIUS O'CONNOR, *her nephew.*

MARTIN MULLAHONE, *middle-aged.*

ROSEY VIOLET, *his wife, in the thirties.*

SCENES

ACT ONE
Mid-day, late in January

ACT TWO
Evening of the following day

ACT THREE
Morning. A few days later

ACT FOUR
The following morning: February 1st

The time is the present.

The action passes in the living room of Canon Skerritt's parochial house in "Ardmahone," one of the small towns lying round the feet of the Mourne hills in County Louth, Ireland.

Shadow and Substance *was first produced at the Abbey Theatre, Dublin, on January 25th, 1937.*

A legend connected with St. Brigid relates how, in order to escape the attentions of persistent suitors, she disfigured the loveliness of her face at Fanghart, her birthplace, near Dundalk, Ireland.

SHADOW AND SUBSTANCE

ACT ONE

SCENE—*The living room in the Parochial House of the* VERY REV. THOMAS CANON SKERRITT *in Ardmahone, one of the small towns lying round the feet of Mourne, on the borders of Louth.*

The room is excellently furnished, and gives evidence in its accoutrements, its beautiful leaded bookcases, its pictures and other tasteful details, of the refined character of the CANON.

The one incongruous note in the harmony of the whole design is a large gaudy oleograph of the Sacred Heart over the door, left.

A window, back, in French manner, very tastefully curtained to the ground with crimson art brocade, and giving access to the gardens. Through the window, a view of Mourne's rugged peaks. The walls are hung with small Spanish and Roman reproductions of very good quality, including Velasquez, Murillo, El Greco, Da Vinci and Raphael.

As the curtain rises, BRIGID *is ushering in* DERMOT FRANCIS O'FLINGSLEY, *the schoolmaster, a young man, very alert, alive, and intelligent, obviously capable of feeling things acutely, and of passion and pride. He is bright in manner, and has a pleasing sense of humor.* BRIGID *is small, possibly a little stupid-looking, with large eyes; neat, but not to any degree Quakerish. She is obviously not mentally outstanding, but capable of deep affection, and pleasing in her person.*

A table is laid, very carefully and very completely, for lunch, and both it and the chairs, and the table-ware are of excellent quality. There is no sign of tawdriness or of slipshod carelessness about the room.

BRIGID. He said, Master, he might be home for lunch and he mightn't. It's to Dublin he went, I think. It'll be maybe to see one of them Spanish gentlemen that writes to him since the time he was in Spain. Sure just rest a wee while, Master, seein' he's not here yet.

O'FLINGSLEY (*entering carelessly, hands in jacket pocket*). Thanks, Brigid. It's not often I get this far into the great one's privacy. Such privileges are not for schoolmasters.

BRIGID. Ach, sure it's just his way.

Are ye goin' to quarrel with him again?

O'FLINGSLEY. No, Brigid, definitely no. But I will, all the same.

BRIGID. Yous hate one another. Sure I know, be now . . .

O'FLINGSLEY. I suppose we do.

BRIGID. Isn't it funny now that I think there's no one like aythur of yous. Would that not mean that the two of yous are maybe the one? Or am I blatherin'?

991

O'FLINGSLEY. You certainly *are* blatherin', Brigid. If you love him, you hate *me*, and if you love *me*, you hate *him*.

BRIGID (*slowly*). That's maybe the way it would show on paper, but in the mind it's not maybe as true. (*Pause*) St. Brigid wouldn't deceive me like that.

O'FLINGSLEY (*regarding her half-seriously, half-humorously*). Are you still on that nonsense, Brigid?

BRIGID (*hurt*). Don't say it's nonsense, Master.

O'FLINGSLEY. Have you told anyone about this—the Canon or the curates?

BRIGID No. (*Secretively*) No one only you.

O'FLINGSLEY. Why just me?

BRIGID. I don't know. . . . Didn't you tell me yourself, one time, that there's no words at all for some of the things we think and feel?

O'FLINGSLEY (*touched*). I am not worth all this trust, Brigid. Suppose, some night when I'd have a spree, I'd tell it in a snug.

BRIGID (*catching at his arm, tensely*). You—wouldn't do that. . . . (*He smiles at her*) Sure, don't I know. . . . You have the fine thing in you—the same thing that the Canon has.

O'FLINGSLEY (*laughing*). Don't you dare compare me with *him*. (*Pause*) Why don't you tell *him* about—this secret of yours? Or the curates?

BRIGID. Sure, they'd question and cross-question, and then make me promise never to see her again. That would be somethin' too terrible for me to bear—the same as you could bear the burn of a hot poker or of scaldin' water.

O'FLINGSLEY. Then—you *do* see her actually?

BRIGID (*rapt*). Yes . . . often. I'm used to her now. She is always smilin', smilin' and in great humor, as if she was enjoyin' makin' me happy. It's lovely that she's not sour like a nun, at the convent school, or like a priest in the box.

O'FLINGSLEY (*seriously*). I don't want to hurt you, Brigid, but if you're a wise girl, you'll put this thing absolutely away from you. Some day, maybe she or it, whatever it is, will desert you, and you'll go crazy with despair. Are you listenin' to me?

BRIGID (*softly*). Yes . . . but she promised . . .

O'FLINGSLEY. Supposing she's an evil thing? It could well be.

BRIGID. If she was evil, I would feel the fear in me. Doesn't God make us like that?

O'FLINGSLEY. Why don't you ask her for a proof, as I told you?

BRIGID. I did. I asked her one night to make the bed-chair move. Wasn't that what you said?

O'FLINGSLEY. And did she?

BRIGID. No. . . . She just smiled, and her eyes laughed the way she was amused at me.

O'FLINGSLEY. Maybe it was at me she was amused—O'Flingsley, the idiot.

BRIGID. It was never that. She loves you too. I can see it. She told me you had a secret.

O'FLINGSLEY (*startled*). What sort of a secret?

BRIGID. She said—a dark secret, and that you were a blunderer, but that God loved blunderers because they were the children of Peter.

O'FLINGSLEY (*concerned*). Brigid, you dreamed this! You *did!*

BRIGID (*slowly*). No. . . . Sure I know I didn't. . . . She told me about the Canon too.

O'FLINGSLEY. *Him?* What did she say about him?

BRIGID. She said that there was great holiness in him, but that his pride would need the tears of a hundred just men and the soul of a child, to soften it.

O'FLINGSLEY (*tensely*). Did she say —what child?

BRIGID. She only smiled and went away.

O'FLINGSLEY. Good God! What creature is this at all? I'm warning you, Brigid. I'm warning you, mind.

BRIGID. I love her too much now to be afraid. . . . (*Pause*) *Have* you a secret?

O'FLINGSLEY (*secretively*). I have written a book and published it. No one knows it's mine.

BRIGID. Is it a *good* book?

O'FLINGSLEY. It might be. It's a *bitter* book.

BRIGID. She will not be pleased. Why could you not make it full of love?

O'FLINGSLEY (*tensely*). I don't believe in love.

BRIGID. St. Brigid does. She stood near me at the bed last night when the new moon was in it. I said, "There's the new moon, God bless it," and I blessed meself, and she laughed without any noise, and her eyes had the moon in them like a mirror. She stood lookin' out at the big boulders of the hills, and her speakin' low. Then she said when I came close to her that the hills were just like that long long ago, and that they were God's hint to man to build in the heart forever and ever, instead of with stone and mortar and the pride that puts a stone on another stone without meanin'. And a lot more that the words will not come to me for. I fell asleep listenin' to her—her voice was sinkin' me all the time into sleep. (*She looks up at* O'FLINGSLEY. *A shadow of fear crosses her face suddenly. She grips him*) I'm a fool to be tellin' you— a fool, a fool. You'll put it in a bitter book and laugh at it.

O'FLINGSLEY (*touched*). No, Brigid . . . not in a book. . . . (*Pause— He catches her arm*) Are you— lying to me, Brigid?

BRIGID (*pathetically*). No, Master. . . . How could I lie?

O'FLINGSLEY. But—how do you remember it all like this?

BRIGID. Remember it? Sure, how could I *forget* it? (*She looks at him in pain. He soothes her.*)

D'FLINGSLEY. There! There! I don't mean to hurt you. I'm just nervous about you. I think you'd better tell the Canon about this.

BRIGID. Not—not yet. I won't be separated from her. I love her. Some day I shall come to her, she said.

O'FLINGSLEY (*worried*). You must keep your mind off that now. You must first live your life here.

BRIGID. She told me that too.

O'FLINGSLEY (*after a pause*). You're a funny little customer, Brigid. There's times when I'd like to pull your hair, and give you a smack on the jaw.

BRIGID. Sure I would never feel it. . . .

O'FLINGSLEY. There's tears for you, and I'm warning you. But you won't heed. Well, I'd better be getting back to the school. I'll come back later and see if he's home.

BRIGID. Will you lave a message?

O'FLINGSLEY. Anything to oblige, Brigid. Ask him when is the school going to get any coal, when I can have the new maps I asked for last year, when the windows are going to be repaired, and if he'll supply me with two pails to catch the raindrops from the ceiling on wet days. And when is he going to relieve *me* of the job of brushing and cleaning out the place?

BRIGID (*breathless*). I'll never remember all of them.

O'FLINGSLEY. Oh, don't let that worry you. *He'll* not remember any of them anyway.

BRIGID (*disconsolately*). I can see another fight comin', and you bein' ordered out again. Yous are never done.

O'FLINGSLEY. Well, what can *I* do? What could anyone do? If only I had enough guts in me, I'd clap on my hat, and walk right out of this place. But I haven't. Actually, Brigid, I'm afraid I'd have no money and be hungry. Amn't I a miserable creature?

BRIGID. If you could have somethin' grand and lovely to rise for, every day, like me with St. Brigid.

O'FLINGSLEY (*tensely*). Maybe I have.

BRIGID. Tell me about it, Master.

O'FLINGSLEY. No. . . . It's all—fire and smoke . . . and things falling.

BRIGID (*reprovingly*). Sure isn't that just like you! (*She laughs*) I'll bet St. Brigid would know.

O'FLINGSLEY. Will you ask her?

BRIGID. I will, if you promise to obey her.

O'FLINGSLEY. I'll—try. (*He is crossing, and looking back whimsically at* BRIGID *when* THOMASINA CONCANNON *enters briskly. She is a very "bunty" girl of about 22, with full animal spirits, round fat face, all dimples, given to giggling laughter, and eternally sucking sweetmeats.*)

THOMASINA (*as she rushes in*). Is me uncle back yet, Bridgie?

BRIGID. No, miss. But I'm expectin' him any minute. The Master's waitin' on him too.

THOMASINA (to O'FLINGSLEY). Oh, you're Mr. O'Flingsley. I'm a school teacher too—just finished a few months, and was doing substitute at Dunaree. I'm pleased to meet you. (She giggles.)

O'FLINGSLEY. So am I. How do you do, Miss —

BRIGID. Miss Concannon her name is, Master.

THOMASINA. I'm the Canon's niece, you know. Me mother says I'm a bit like him round the nose. (She giggles) Do you think so?

O'FLINGSLEY. On the contrary, I think you have a very nice nose.

BRIGID. Oh, Master! (THOMASINA and O'FLINGSLEY laugh together. BRIGID goes, quickly.)

THOMASINA. Well, I have another hold on him anyway. I'm called after him. You see, they thought I'd be a boy, and the name was ready and all.

O'FLINGSLEY (entering the fun). And you weren't?

THOMASINA. Why of course I wasn't, stupid! (She giggles heartily) So me mother, who lets nothin' bate her, said: "She'll be Thomasina." Wasn't it awful cute of her?

O'FLINGSLEY. It certainly was a great idea, Miss Concannon.

THOMASINA (holding up poke of sweets). Do have a liquorice-all-sort, Mr. O'Flingsley, and you may call me Thomasina.

O'FLINGSLEY (taking sweet). Th-thanks. You can call me anything you like, and quote your uncle as a precedent.

BRIGID (entering hastily). The Canon's back on the train. He's in the Post Office below, writin' a postcard. The milkman's after tellin' me.

O'FLINGSLEY (to go). I'll come back later when he settles, Brigid.

THOMASINA. Wait till he hears I slept in his room last night!

O'FLINGSLEY. Slept in his room!

THOMASINA. The bed in the spare room has bronchitis. (With a gasp) Oh, dear God! I believe I left Love's Purple Passions under his pilla. Ex-excuse me, Mr. O'Flingsley. (She rushes off, breathlessly. O'FLINGSLEY looks at BRIGID in a bewildered way.)

O'FLINGSLEY. Is that the one that's trying to get in here as my Assistant?

BRIGID. Yis, Master.

O'FLINGSLEY. Good God! The mists thicken, O, Israel. . . . (He goes, worried. BRIGID looks after him softly, then runs to table, and in a scared way begins rearranging things on the dining table. FATHER CORR enters, left. He is a young man, small and round-shouldered with a face easily affected by fervor or sentiment. His mood is melancholic and introspective.)

FATHER CORR (*kindly*). Well, Bridgie, me heartie, and how's the bones today? (*Flings hat on chair.*)

BRIGID. Oh, Father Corr, do *you* see anythin' missin' on that table? The Canon's back. He's in the Post Office.

FATHER CORR (*careless glance*). Ach sure, isn't it fine?

BRIGID. Oh, but the Canon! If there's a single spot . . .
(FATHER KIRWAN *enters, left, wearing motor goggles and gloves. Athletic, good-humored and well-meaning. Neatly lands his hat on a bookcase, takes off goggles, etc., and then turns very severely to* FATHER CORR—*obviously mimicking the* CANON.)

FATHER KIRWAN. Father Corr, may I ask who owns this—er—motor machine I observe at the front entrance?

FATHER CORR (*with a wave*). Cut out that coddin' and get a shave. The Canon's back.

FATHER KIRWAN (*incredibly*). He's *not?*

FATHER CORR. He is.

FATHER KIRWAN. Heavens! (*Feeling hairy cheek*) Am I bad? Brigid, tell me like a decent woman, do I need a shave, or do I not?

BRIGID. Indeed you do, Father. And I sent you up shavin' water this mornin'.

FATHER KIRWAN. So you did, but seein' the Canon was—not in residence, I used it for softenin' a corn.

God made feet, but an enemy came and oversowed corns. . . .

BRIGID. Do *you* see anythin' missin' there, Father Kirwan?

FATHER KIRWAN (*wistfully*). Sure and I do, Bridgie. A whippin' good plate o' cabbage and bacon.

BRIGID. Ah, Father! And the Canon always sayin' we know nothin' about food in Ireland.

FATHER KIRWAN (*mimicking again*). When I was in Spain, my excellent friend, Don Miguel Del Fuego . . .
(*All start laughing.*)

BRIGID (*looking from window, suddenly*). Oh, here's the Canon comin' up the lawn. (*All flurried*) Oh, dear me, I hope everythin's right. And I wish I had him told about Thomasina. (*She runs off, scared. The* TWO CURATES *laugh rather nervously.*)

FATHER KIRWAN. Wait till you see his face when he sees that niece of his! She always sends him off the deep end!

FATHER CORR. The girl's a bit of an ass right enough, but there's no harm in her. Now remember we're to tackle him about that filthy book that's on the rounds. I expect you to back me up and not let the confraternity down.

FATHER KIRWAN. I'll do my best. But you know the dry way he can bottle you up. And be Heavens I left the wee car at the gate. He'll have a fit when he sees it!

FATHER CORR. Well, aren't all the curates everywhere gettin' cars?

And it's a free country. Come on into the garden and give him time to settle.

(*They go out by the window.*)

FATHER KIRWAN (*as they go, dubiously*). I wish that niece had stayed at home, and—I wish I had shaved.

. . .

(BRIGID *comes in quickly, and nervously sets glasses on table. She stands over the table counting and calculating.* CANON THOMAS SKERRITT *enters, left. Finely built, but a little too full in the stomach, fine face, but a little too red. His eyes are vividly living always, and at times his whole being concentrates in them. He has a perfect bow, his voice is cultured, he can be very charming and courteous, can quickly adapt himself to suit people, and has a kingly walk and dignity. He is excellently dressed. He is wearing a tall silk hat, and carries an umbrella.*)

CANON (*benignly*). Ah, Brigid, you're there!

BRIGID (*soothingly*). Yis, Canon. Your hat and umbrella, Canon. (*She takes them with great care, and looks up at him with childish simplicity combined with womanly prudence*) I hope, Canon, you're grand and well after the week-end.

CANON. You will be pleased to know, Brigid, that the Canon feels excellently.

BRIGID. And did you meet your great friend from Spain, Canon?

CANON. I met him, Brigid. My friend Don Miguel Barzan y Perdito. It was good, Brigid. It was very good. I mentioned you, Brigid.

(*Clapping her patronizingly*) I said to Don Miguel, "My truest friend in this fallen land is Brigid." And he smiled in his excellent way, and said, "Donde esta la verdad esta Dios."

BRIGID. Wasn't that lovely of you, Canon! And what did Don Miguel mean be that?

CANON (*deprecating*). He meant, Brigid, in the crude language of the—Saxon: "Where we have truth we have God."

BRIGID. It's lovely. It's like what a saint—I mean a gentleman, would say.

CANON. A saint *and* a gentleman, you mean, Brigid. That is the classic equivalent to the—the odious Northern Officer and gentleman. But go, Brigid, see to lunch immediately.

BRIGID. Yis, Canon. (*She crosses.*)

CANON. Stay, Brigid. There is no news—I hope?

BRIGID. No, Canon, except that—that your niece is here.

CANON (*immediately on edge*). My step-niece, Brigid. I insist on the distinction. What evil brings her here?

BRIGID. It's to see you, special, she said—about the school, I think. She insisted on stayin' last night. She said her mother said it.

CANON (*with suppressed venom*). Her mother! That barbarian who links me by law to a—cattle-jobber. It burns me, Brigid,—it *burns* me.

BRIGID. Please now, Canon, don't make yourself ill again.

CANON. You are wise, child. I forget myself. I always forget myself in the face of this recurring decimal of relationship. (*Holding* BRIGID's *arm*) Consider, Brigid! My name—grave and classical—purloined—that's the word for it—to gain a —nomenclature for a human dumpling who reeks eternally of peppermints.

BRIGID. Sure, you're angerin' yourself, Canon. Sure, maybe if she got married, it would settle her down, and you wouldn't be pestered with her no more.

CANON. There is wisdom there, Brigid. I will consider that. I shall turn that over carefully.

BRIGID. Sure, I try to help ye, Canon.

CANON. As you say, Brigid, you try to help me, and as I say, there is wisdom in you. Let it be written of you, Brigid. You are a good child —an excellent child. Go, Brigid!

BRIGID (*going*). Yis, Canon.

CANON. Wait, Brigid. Where did she stay last night?

BRIGID (*in fear*). She—she said the spare room was draughty and there was a mouse in the wardrobe, and she—she—

CANON. She what?

BRIGID. She took *your* room, Canon.

CANON (*fuming*). Eh? She—she what? Brigid! I am incensed beyond

words. You are arraigned! You are in the dock!

BRIGID. But I could do nothin', Canon. Says she to me, "I'm the Canon's niece, and the place for his servant is at me footstool."

CANON. The Canon's niece! That Irish matrimonial luggage label! That ecclesiastical buckle on a female shoe! Go, Brigid! Restore my room to its—austerity.

BRIGID. Yis, Canon. Sure it'll be lovely and grand for you now, if you'll not be vexin' yourself.

CANON (*softening*). There, child, I do not blame you. We are thwarted. We shall die outwitted by boobs and idiots. Mark it, Brigid, mark it! Go, Brigid!

THOMASINA (*calling offstage*). Gooee, Brigid! Did my uncle come?

CANON. God! Must I suffer this?

BRIGID (*fearfully*). Yis, Miss. He's —here.
(THOMASINA *bounds in, and runs as if to embrace the* CANON. *He skillfully counters this by blowing his nose with one hand and holding out a defensive other hand.* BRIGID *slips out, scared.*)

THOMASINA (*gurglingly*). Oh, Uncle Thomas! I thought you'd never come. Oh, isn't it lovely you're back?

CANON (*vaguely, staring at her*). Ah, it's you. Of course it's you. I was expecting you. You wrote, of course. I remember. You are a good child—an excellent child. . . .

THOMASINA. But I never wrote, Uncle.

CANON. Ah, you never wrote. Of course you didn't. I remember distinctly. It was the last time you wrote.

THOMASINA. I came down, Uncle Thomas, to tell you I finished in Dunaree School on Friday. The teacher is better now.

CANON. Very creditable, very creditable.

THOMASINA. And Father Crone, the parish priest, said to say to you, do you remember Crone, your old crony in Maynooth before you went to Spain. (*She giggles loudly.*)

CANON (*gravely*). Never heard of him.

THOMASINA. But he swears him and you used to keep a pot o' jam in the dormitory against the rules. (*She giggles explosively.*)

CANON (*outraged*). Come, come! I dislike levity in young people.

THOMASINA (*pouting ponderously*). I'm sorry, Uncle Thomas. Sure it was only to show you the great man Father Crone is for jokes. Do you think they'll make a Canon of him, Uncle? I think he'd make a lovely Canon—and it would go so grand with his name too—Kevin Canon Crone.

CANON (*ironic*). No doubt the accumulated wisdom of the Church will endorse your conclusions. (*He sniffs and blows his nose meaningly*) In future, my dear, when seeking a—a—an audience with me, I wish you would compose yourself with some degree of mental sobriety, and in addition fast from peppermints for at least one hour.

THOMASINA (*pouting*). You're not glad to see me, Uncle Thomas. Well, it was me mother kept *at* me, Uncle. "There y'are," she kept girnin', "walkin' about idle for three whole days and nights, and you Canon Thomas Skerritt's niece be law and be blood. A fine state this country's comin' to." That's *her* all the time.

CANON (*with calm brutality*). Your mother, my dear, I regret to say, is, and has ever been, a woman bereft —that's the word, bereft—of one iota of sound sense or dignity. The fact burns me. But it is—irrefutable.
(THOMASINA *giggles involuntarily, and then dabs her face with a mint-reeking handkerchief.*)

THOMASINA. Sure, maybe you're right, Uncle. The talk and blatherin' of her—you'd think I had no name o' me own—I'm the Canon's niece to everyone we meet.

CANON (*grimly*). I am well aware of it. But it is a national disease, and I am no surgeon. You must leave me now, and I shall let you know in a few days about the school. (*Consulting watch.*)

THOMASINA. But sure it's the bus I go by always, Canon.

CANON (*countering*). There is a bus back in *six* minutes.

THOMASINA (*as she is moved off*). Will you appoint me to the school,

Uncle, when Miss Driscoll goes to her training next week?

CANON. Possibly.

THOMASINA. I'll just say "yes," instead of "possibly" to me mother. Let me play a wee tune for you on the piano before I go.

CANON. Certainly not!

THOMASINA. But it's a lovely wee thing, Canon. Father Crone sang it at a wee tea-party before I left Dunaree School. It begins, "When first I saw your face of virgin kew."

CANON (*evenly*). You will go now, my dear.

THOMASINA. All right then, Uncle, but I'll come again.

CANON. So you will. (*Almost sotto voce*) Est Natura rerum. . . . (*As he moves her on.*)

THOMASINA. What does that mean, Canon?

CANON. You would not appreciate it. (*They go out together.* BRIGID *comes in and lays serving dishes on table. The* TWO CURATES, FATHER CORR *and* FATHER KIRWAN *come in from garden by window.*)

BRIGID. Lunch is ready, Fathers, and the Canon's ready. Will you please sit down?

FATHER CORR. Grand news, Bridgie. What are you going to give us?

FATHER KIRWAN (*as they both sit*). Nothin' Spanish, I hope.

BRIGID (*half secretively*). It's another of them dishes the Canon

used to love in Spain. (*She smiles secretively at them and goes.*)

FATHER KIRWAN. *In Nomine De,* when is this goin' to stop?

FATHER CORR (*tired*). Ach, just take it for your sins, and hope for the best.

FATHER KIRWAN. I wish to God I could get a transfer to some old P.P. that loves cabbage and eats peas with his knife, and snores after his dinner.

FATHER CORR. Sssh!
(*The* CANON *re-enters. The* CURATES *rise respectfully. The* CANON *comes slowly to the table, with dignity. He stands at the head of the table.*)

CANON (*courteously, with a slight bow*). Good morning, Fathers.

CURATES (*together*). Good mornin', Canon.

CANON (*acidly*). I didn't quite catch the final "g" in "morning," Fathers. (*Pause. They silently say grace. Further pause*) May I ask, Fathers, who owns that motor-car at the gate?

FATHER CORR. It's ours, Canon.

FATHER KIRWAN. It killed a man, Canon, and the owner wanted rid of it. We got it dirt cheap.

CANON. I am glad to hear it has such excellent capabilities. But— is it necessary?

FATHER CORR. It will come in useful I'm sure. Father Kirwan and I do a lot of running about. And besides we feel entitled to contribute in any way we can to our happiness here.

CANON. You mean it will make your job more comfortable.

FATHER KIRWAN. Job, Canon?

CANON. Yes . . . a word that Columkille and Columbanus knew in another sense. However, there is no Canon law against—owner-driver clerics. You may be seated. (*All sit.* BRIGID *enters and starts serving*) Well, Brigid, did the experiment work again?

BRIGID (*as she serves*). Sure, it's lovely, Canon, and it was easy follyin' your directions.

CANON. Very creditable, Brigid. You have today, Fathers, an extremely delicious Spanish dish, given me some years ago by the chatelaine of my friend Don Juan Almeria y Fernandez.
(CURATES *taste dish gingerly and nod to the* CANON.)

FATHER CORR. Very good indeed, Canon.

FATHER KIRWAN. Grand, Canon.
(BRIGID *moves about and on and off.* CANON *notices a newspaper sticking out of* FATHER KIRWAN'S *pocket.*)

CANON. The development of a sensitive palate, Fathers, is not the most unimportant of legitimate activities. Father Kirwan, may I ask what—litter is that protruding from the outer pocket of your attire?

FATHER KIRWAN (*touching paper*). Sure it's just the—the *Ballyedminstown Courier,* Canon.

CANON (*suavely*). Would you please adjust the—the—*Ballyelphinstown Courier,* Father, so that it will not detract from the dignity of your person?

FATHER KIRWAN (*pushing paper right into pocket*). Sorry, Canon. (*Pause*) There's a very strong leader in it this week, Canon, on that outrageous book that's just after comin' out. It's called *I Am Sir Oracle.*

FATHER CORR. I was just goin' to mention that, Canon. It's a very grave matter altogether, and I think it calls for action. The people's demandin' it.

FATHER KIRWAN. They say, Canon, the author is a schoolmaster with a spite agin the local P.P. He calls himself Eugene Gibney.

FATHER CORR. Are *you* prepared to take anny action, Canon?

CANON (*acidly*). There is no such word as "anny," except of course the female appellation, and the verb agrees with its subject, always —even in Ireland. (*As* BRIGID *enters*) You may serve the coffee black, Brigid.
(*The* TWO CURATES *look very abject.*)

BRIGID. Yis, Canon. It's ready.

FATHER CORR (*apologetically*). If you don't mind, Canon, I'll have tea instead.

CANON (*with withering suavity*). You may serve Father Corr with— tea.

FATHER KIRWAN. And me too, Canon, if you please.

CANON. You are at liberty to poison Father Kirwan also.

BRIGID. Yis, Canon. (*She crosses.*)

CANON. And, Brigid. (*Takes key from pocket and gives it to her*) You know the one, Brigid. It is marked "Vino de Amontillado."

BRIGID. Is that the one, Canon, with the gold silver-paper on it that Don Miguel sent you from Spain?

CANON. Exactly, Brigid. My friend, Don Miguel Barzan y Perdito. (*As* BRIGID *unlocks cupboard under the bookshelves*) Are you having a little wine, Fathers?

FATHER CORR. I'll take a thimbleful, Canon.

FATHER KIRWAN. And I too, thanks. (BRIGID *brings small flagon of rich golden wine, expensively wrapped, which the* CANON *handles with great delicacy.*)

CANON. I'm afraid there are no—thimbles reasonably convenient, Father. Better take a wineglassful. (*As he receives bottle*) Excellent, Brigid. You may bring Fathers Corr and Kirwan the bottle of Empire wine that's on the left-hand side. (*With a sardonic curve of lip.*)

BRIGID. Is it the one, Canon, that Martin Reilly sent up last Christmas for a present?

CANON. Precisely, Brigid. (*Ironically*) It should be considerably matured by this. (*As* BRIGID *gets it*) You were speaking, gentlemen, of the proposed suppression of a book, entitled, *I Am Sir Oracle.*

FATHER KIRWAN. The editor of this paper, from my home town, Canon, calls for it to be burned on every market square in Ireland.

FATHER CORR. It demands action too from the Board of Censors.

CANON (*lifting glass and examining golden wine carefully*). And on what grounds are we to have this extensive series of rural bonfires?

FATHER CORR (*with fire*). Why, the whole book is a dastardly attack on the Catholicism of Ireland, Canon! (BRIGID *pours out the red port for* CURATES, *and then goes softly.*)

CANON (*looking closely at bubbling wine*). Grave news surely out of Bally—Ballyeffelstown. A sea-mew blunders against a lighthouse and the keeper sends up distress rockets. (*With suave irony*) Your health, Fathers. (*He drinks delicately and with great relish. The* CURATES *fling back their port and cough into napkins. As he lies back, enjoying the wine on his tongue*) May I ask if the writer attacks any specific doctrine of the Church?

FATHER CORR. He evades that, Canon. In a Catholic country like this, a fellow like that should be hung.

CANON (*imperturbably*). Hanged, Father Corr. (*Pause.* BRIGID *serves coffee and tea, etc.*) Were *you* about to make some observation, Father Kirwan?

FATHER KIRWAN. I was goin' to say, Canon, that the men of the football team I run, are up in arms agin it. And Father Corr can tell you about the Sacred Heart Confraternity.

FATHER CORR. Martin Reilly's wife, Canon, had the book home from Dublin, and it's got round the people. The whole men and women of the Sacred Heart are anxious to burn it in public. And Father Kirwan and myself agree with them. We'd like your advice.

CANON. You mean my—direction.

BRIGID (*as she goes*). If you please, Canon, when you want me to clear away, will you shout?

CANON (*eyelids raised*). Shout, Brigid? Certainly not. I shall ring.

BRIGID. Yis, Canon. And if you please, Canon, the schoolmaster is back again wantin' to see you, and he says he's in a hurry.

CANON. Dear me! Even the school teachers are becoming presumptuous. We live, Brigid, in an incongruous age. Tell him, I shall possibly see him when his hurry is more in keeping with his status.

BRIGID. Yis, Canon. And if you please, Canon, are ye rememberin' that Miss Jemima Cooney and her nephew Francis Ignatius is waitin' since before lunch to show you Francis' new teachin' certificate?

CANON. Brigid, I fear you fret yourself unduly. Tell them both to go round into the Church, and say the Rosary, and by that time I may possibly be in a position to receive them.

BRIGID. But you see, Canon—

CANON. Go, Brigid!

BRIGID. Yis, Canon. (*She goes. The*

CURATES *now make to rise. The* CANON *detains them with a finger.*)

CANON. One moment, Fathers. An observation or two is—imperative. (*They settle stiffly*) Father Corr, I am given to understand that since your arrival here you have attained quite an inordinate amount of popularity mixed with a particularly abhorrent form of sentimentality, and that this copious bathing— shall we say—springs from your antics with bouncing babies, and such like, the prescribing of cures for old ladies' rheumatics and for carious diseases in horses and cows. I suggest to you, that since Catholicism rests on a classical, almost abstract, love of God, rather than on the frothy swirl of stirred emotionalism that these popular heroics of yours are not, canonically speaking, the duties of a Catholic curate.

FATHER CORR (*blushing and abashed*). I—I was only tryin' to be kind, Canon.

CANON. *I* call it hunting after popular glory—an Irish clerical disease.

FATHER CORR (*rising, with fire*). I'm a farmer's son, Canon, and I'm not ashamed of it.

CANON. I am not interested in your antecedents. I am interested instead in the behavior of my curate. You may be seated.
(FATHER CORR *sits down, crushed.* FATHER KIRWAN *shifts uneasily in his seat, with one eye on the* CANON *who presently regards him with calm brutality.*)

CANON (*with slight cough*). Father Kirwan, may I ask if it is the custom in *your* part of the country for the curate to don football-regalia, and—er—kick ball?

FATHER KIRWAN. Sure it's quite common down in Ballyedminstown, Canon. The curate in me father's place is a very noted center-half.

CANON (*cruelly, leading him on, hand to ear*). I—I didn't quite catch that word, Father Kirwan. Center—what?

FATHER KIRWAN. Center-half, Canon. The fellow, Canon, that the team most depends on when the enemy makes an onslaught.

CANON (*suavely*). Incongruous as it may seem, Father Kirwan, it is *not* the custom here for the curate to be the fellow that—er—does what you say he does.

FATHER KIRWAN. But you misunderstand me, Canon. I strip and play with the men to entice them all into the Sacred Heart Confraternity. Sure, Canon, that's a grand motive for a grand end!

CANON. I see . . . And since when has the Sacred Heart of our Redeemer, that kings and emperors and queens like Violante and Don John of Austria and the great Charles V, and the soldier Ignatius, walked barefooted for the love of —since when has it become a sort of snap door chamber where dolts and boobs come to—to kick ball and find themselves tripped up on an altar step instead of a goal post?

FATHER KIRWAN (*aghast*). I—I never looked at it that way, Canon. Doesn't it justify itself if it brings people to the Sacred Heart?

CANON. Am I justified then, in staging amateur theatricals on the high altar to coax boobs along the Latin way of salvation?
(*There are awesome ejaculations from the* TWO CURATES.)

FATHER KIRWAN AND FATHER CORR. God forbid, Canon! There is no comparison, surely!

CANON. To my thinking, there is a parallel. As a consequence, Brigid will be instructed that—er—football regalia is barred from the parochial clothes line.

FATHER KIRWAN. As you wish, Canon.

CANON. There is just one other matter. Is it the custom also in Bally— Bally—eskerstown, to sit down to lunch unshaven?

FATHER KIRWAN. I'm afraid it's not, Canon.

CANON. Interesting to compare the topographical similarities. It is *not* the custom in *this* part of the country either. (*With a sardonic smile and a slight bow, he waves a finger and rises. The* CURATES *rise also.* CANON *now rings bell with dignity.* BRIGID *enters to clear away.* FATHERS CORR *and* KIRWAN *are crossing to go out. The* CANON's *eye lights on the gaudy German oleograph. He almost explodes*) Wait, all! Stay! What—what incongruity is this? (*Points to picture. All look at it.*)

FATHER CORR. The Women's Confraternity presented it to Father Kirwan and meself yesterday. (BRIGID *is very perturbed.*)

CANON. And does it follow that I am to suffer it?

FATHER KIRWAN. But sure it's the—Sacred Heart, Canon.

CANON (*ironically*). I should never have believed it, Father Kirwan. I could have sworn it was the nightmarish conception of some uncouth vulgarian.
(CURATES *regard each other, nonplussed.* BRIGID *is all "at sea." She fears the* CANON *is ill.*)

BRIGID (*emotionally, her face in pain*). Please, Canon, are ye not well again?

CANON. I am very well, child.

BRIGID. But—it's the Sacred Heart, Canon.

CANON. No.
(*Pause.*)

FATHER CORR. We thought, Canon, it would give a deeper religious tone to this room. The pictures are nearly all secular.

CANON. Secular? What word is that? (*Pointing*) There is a beautiful reproduction of Velasquez's "Philip IV entering Lerida," and *there* another of Murillo's "Immaculate Conception," and *there* is Raphael's bitter "Dispute of the Sacrament." Could any picture in this room be called secular if we know anything of the might of the thing that has given us birth?

FATHER CORR. I was just followin' the pious custom, Canon, of havin' colored pictures of religious subjects near us to give a feeling of sanctity.

CANON. A feeling of sanctity from that! (*He points to the oleograph. A pause. When he speaks again, it is with great quietness*) I am a man, Fathers, who by study, travel and observation, has seen the decline and decay of the great classic ideals and the steady vulgarization of our life by that tributaried stream of barbarians who have taken all that was royal in conception, and given nothing but their vulgar deluge in return. Their achievement is the Nordic civilization, in which the passport to fame is financial scoundrelism, and the scholar of taste is ever the avowed "enemy of the people." They have vulgarized our reading, our music, our art, our very privacy. They have thrust books into the hands of herds who are forever misreading them; they have reduced us all to the lowest social class by teaching us how to get from excess the same emotionalism the classicist used to get from music and art; they have taken away our aesthetic sense and given us in exchange a rather spurious ethical sense, and as you can see here—(*he points to picture*) they deal with a whitewash brush in terms of the divine. Yet you stand aghast when I point it out to you—when I refuse to allow barbarians to impose on me their vulgar conception of Christ and His Saints. If, for a moment, I felt our Redeemer's heart was akin to that monstrosity on the wall, I should go back to Socrates, and be a pagan. (*The* TWO CURATES *look at him dumbfounded and mystified.* BRIGID *is very worried.*)

BRIGID. Please, Canon, you are not well again.

CANON (*gently*). I am very well, child. Go, Brigid, and have Dave Dooley remove this—this caricature from my room.

BRIGID. I'll get him from the garden, Canon. (*She goes, left.*)

FATHER CORR (*lamely*). It's this funny sort of way you have of looking at things, Canon. It's maybe you being abroad so much.

CANON (*dryly*). Maybe. . . .

FATHER CORR. I'm sorry you don't like it.

FATHER KIRWAN. Sure we'll just hang it up in the church hall, Canon, if you have no objection.

CANON (*tiredly, with veiled contempt*). Where you wish—but not here. Hang it at the crossroads where a people who at least had a classic past, can see their Nordic God, and forget about the Royal Christ of the Renaissance. (*He turns tiredly away. The* CURATES, *nonplussed, look at each other, and go out quietly.* BRIGID *re-enters. She looks at him, very worried.*)

BRIGID (*appeasingly*). Dave Dooley will take it away, Canon, when he comes back from his dinner.

CANON. Dinner! Must there be this delay, Brigid?

BRIGID. Just a little delay, Canon. He'll be here any minute now.

CANON. It is the way of things, Brigid. An important issue confused and involved by the dinner of a boob! You may go, Brigid!

BRIGID. Yis, Canon.

CANON (*softly*). But no, Brigid. Stay! It is good, child, you are here with me. You are not nauseous to me, Brigid, you are clean and simple. Oh, my child, this wilderness. . . . Knaves, fools, spirit-grocers and their women . . . clerical football-kickers . . . palavering C.C.'s . . . and only one scoundrel. . . . Come here to me, Brigid.

BRIGID (*coming, almost in tears*). Yis, Canon.

CANON. Do you smell it?

BRIGID. What, Canon? (*She sniffs.*)

CANON. The vulgarity of it all.

BRIGID (*not understanding*). Will I open the window, Canon?

CANON. Yes . . . (*she goes and opens it*) . . . and the walls . . . But it will not matter . . .

BRIGID (*returning from window*). I'm terrible sorry, Canon, you're not well again. You're lonely.

CANON (*wearily*). As you say, Brigid, I'm lonely.

BRIGID. It'll be after your friend, Don Miguel, you'll be lonely.

CANON. Yes . . . my friend Don Miguel Barzan y Perdito . . . (*As in a reverie*) I can see the stone tables in the sun where we used to sit . . . and the grave courtesy and grace of the people and their walk—that heartbreak of these Northern cripples . . . oh, these Northerners, morally afraid, mentally bereft, physically fatigued and hoof-footed. They have touched us, Brigid—we who should be great—and given us humps like a dromedary. Go, Brigid.

BRIGID. Yis, Canon. (*She goes.*)

CANON. Come back, Brigid.

BRIGID. Yis, Canon.

CANON. Do you know what I'm saying to you?

BRIGID (*afraid*). N-n-no, Canon. (*She shrinks.*)

CANON. Then I can safely make you my friend. You are the Canon's friend, Brigid.

BRIGID. Yis, Canon. Thank you, Canon. (*A pause. She looks at him timidly*) Can—can I speak to you, Canon?

CANON. You can always speak to me, Brigid. It is your privilege.

BRIGID. Thank you, Canon. I—I— (*She looks at him and then stops*) It's nothin', Canon.

CANON. Are you sure, Brigid?

BRIGID. Yis . . . no . . . I'll not tell you now, Canon. I'll—go, Canon. (*She tries to go, but he holds her with his look.*)

CANON. You are hiding something from me, Brigid.

BRIGID. Yis, Canon.

CANON. Is it something I should know?

BRIGID (*pathetically*). Yis . . . No . . . I—I don't know . . .

CANON. If it's a matter of your soul, Brigid, I must know it.

BRIGID. Please, Canon, not—not now. I'll tell you when I'm—able. I—I don't want it taken away from —from me yet.

CANON (*rising*). This is a serious matter, Brigid. I insist. The Canon insists.

BRIGID (*hands to face*). N-no, Canon. I want it. I want it.

CANON. Did I say that I insist, Brigid?

BRIGID (*backing against wall*). Not for a while yet, Canon. Not—not now.

CANON (*coming to her*). I will dismiss you, Brigid, for this disobedience.

BRIGID (*hands to face, back to wall*). Yis, Canon.

CANON. I will cast you down— down!

BRIGID (*pathetically*). Yis, Canon.

CANON. You will be the Canon's friend no longer.

BRIGID. Yis, Canon.

CANON. You will tell me then?

BRIGID. N-no, Canon.

CANON. You will suffer all these things?

BRIGID. Yis, Canon.

CANON (*terribly*). The Canon commands it.

BRIGID. N-no, no, Canon. N-no. I— I couldn't! Not—now . . .

CANON. Put down those hands and look at me.

(*She puts down her hands. Head is held up, but tears in her eyes. She is firmly against the wall like one at bay. An incongruous pride sits upon her. The* CANON *observes her strangely, as if deeply moved at a discovery.*)

CANON. You defy me!

BRIGID. N-no, Canon.

CANON. But you—refuse to tell me!

BRIGID (*pathetically but proudly*). Y-yis, Canon.
(*Long pause. He stands watching her as if fascinated.*)

CANON (*as if to himself*). My God, my God, that—that is what we have come from . . . Pride . . . loyalty . . . a classic race . . . a royal conception . . . A thousand years ago, someone with that brow and face held up His head and died like a prince. . . . It was that . . . (*He stares at her, his face working visibly*) Come here to me, Brigid.

BRIGID (*as she comes slowly and looks humbly up at him*). Yis, Canon.

CANON. I shall ask you—nothing.

BRIGID. Th-thank you, Canon. (*She looks gratefully at him.*)

CANON (*slowly*). You are the Canon's friend, Brigid. Let it be written of you. Let it be written of both of us.
(*They are looking at each other, the* CANON *with deep emotions stirred, and* BRIGID *with the tears glistening in her eyes, as the* CURTAIN FALLS.)

CURTAIN

ACT TWO

SCENE—*Following day.*
    The CANON *is discovered reading the castigated novel,* I Am Sir Oracle. *Now and again he smiles sardonically, and sips from a glass of wine.*
    The picture of the Sacred Heart is removed. BRIGID *knocks and enters. Lays evening paper on table.*

BRIGID. That's the *Evenin' Herald,* Canon.

CANON. Very good, Brigid. (*He reads on.*)

BRIGID. And if you please, Canon, are ye not forgettin' about them two in the waitin' room?

CANON (*tolerantly*). Which two, Brigid? You are always a little vague lately.

BRIGID. The two I told you about, after dinner. Miss Cooney and her nephew with his new teacher's certificate. I told them you'd see them after you were done readin' the Bishop's Pastoral.

CANON (*remembering*). Of course,

of course, Brigid. I remember now. I distinctly remember saying to you, "Brigid, I'll see them presently."

BRIGID. That's just what you said, Canon.

CANON. To be sure it was. Tell them, Brigid—tell them to come back tomorrow.

BRIGID. But they've spent the whole day between waitin' on you here, Canon, and follyin' ye about the streets.

CANON. But my dear child, they like doing that. It is a corporate part of our national life. Tell them, Brigid, that the Canon—no, no—say, "His reverence presents his compliments to Miss Cooney and his heartiest congratulations to Francis Xavier —"

BRIGID. Francis Ignatius, Canon.

CANON. Thank you, Brigid. Let us have accuracy at all costs in these important matters. But be careful of the exact wording. Wording, Brigid, is an art. (*Repeating*) "His reverence presents his compliments." (*He reads on.*)

BRIGID. Yis, Canon, but sure they're in and out o' the kitchen every minute pesterin' me. Is the Canon here? Is the Canon there? Where is the Canon? What hat has he on? Sure you could get rid of them in a minute, Canon, with a grand word and a clap on the back.

CANON (*rising*). Excellent, Brigid. An answer and a suggestion at once plausible and philosophic. The Canon, Brigid—the Canon shall do exactly as you say.

BRIGID. Will I show them in then, Canon?

CANON. By all means, Brigid. And Brigid, if by any ill chance, they weary me beyond their time— (*He raises a finger meaningly.*)

BRIGID. Sure, you needn't tell me, Canon. (*She goes.* CANON *lays down the book resignedly, and mutters in Latin.* BRIGID *re-enters followed by* MISS JEMIMA COONEY *and her nephew* FRANCIS O'CONNOR. FRANCIS *is a sheepish, obsequious youth, his whole being in the grip of an inferiority complex. He is awkward and without confidence.* JEMIMA *is a thin, gaunt spinster, secretly vicious but very virtuous before the* CANON. *The storm of* "Yis, Canons" *and* "No, Canons" *should be played very rapidly*) This is them, Canon. (*She goes.* JEMIMA *and* FRANCIS *advance awkwardly gesticulating and very obsequious. The* CANON *rises with calm dignity, embraces his nose with a silk handkerchief, and gives them a curt bow, tempered with a quite unreadable smile.*)

JEMIMA. Sure, Lord, Canon, are we disturbin' ye?

FRANCIS. Sure, now, Canon, anny time would do!

JEMIMA. Sure, now, Canon, are ye after leavin' off sayin' your office for us?

FRANCIS. Sure, Lord, Canon, we could have come back anny time at all.

JEMIMA. Sure, Heavens, Canon, Francis is that up in the air about his new certificate!

FRANCIS. Sure, Canon, you'll be thinkin' me a nuisance!

CANON (*in a lull, dignified*). You may be seated. (*Silence while they sit.* CANON *heroically contains himself, again embraces his nose, and seats himself opposite them. With scoundrel grace*) And now, Miss Cooney, I hope I see you well. And you too, Francis, none the less, mark! In short, I hope I see you *both* well. (*He smiles sardonically.*)

JEMIMA. Sure, Lord, Canon, I'm lovely now. Sure I never felt so well since I came home from the hospital.

FRANCIS. And I'm like a two-year-old, Canon, ready to attack me work.

CANON (*with bow*). Excellent. I assure you this news is a *great* satisfaction to me.

JEMIMA (*exploding*). Sure, you're too good, Canon. Run, Francis now, and show His Reverence your teacher's certificate.

FRANCIS (*opening scroll, and going awkwardly to* CANON). I just got it from the college yisterday mornin', Canon.

CANON (*viewing the certificate without touching it*). Creditable, Francis. Very creditable. I see in this the seal of—of scholarship, and the beginning of attainment. I congratulate you, Francis. (JEMIMA *beams.*)

FRANCIS (*explosively*). Canon, will you please do all you can for me about the school?

JEMIMA (*irascibly*). Francis, will you mind your manners now? Sure don't you know you don't need to ask the Canon that! (*To the* CANON, *apologetically*) Sure he—he's overexuberant, Canon.

CANON (*with bow to* JEMIMA). As your aunt Jemima so wisely observes, Francis, your request is superfluous, since I *must* do my best for you. Is it not written, Francis, in your Penny Catechism that we must all of us come to the aid of each other?

JEMIMA. There now, Francis.

FRANCIS (*backing awkwardly to seat*). Sure, I'm a—a—an ass, Canon.

CANON. Not a bit, Francis. *Quandoque bonus dormitat Homerus.*

JEMIMA (*impulsively running to the* CANON *with photograph of* FRANCIS). Look, Canon. A wee surprise. I got it taken in Dublin before we left, in a grand place in Talbot Street. (*Pointing*) That's Francis's certificate in his hand, and the wee book in his waistcoat pocket is the prayer book you gave him yourself for servin' Mass for eight years.

CANON (*benignly regarding photograph as if it were a new uncategoried animal*). Very good! Uncommonly good! And very farseeing of you, Miss Cooney, to—to have Francis's scholarly achievement—er—permanently recorded.

JEMIMA (*driveling*). Wouldn't his ma, God rest her, be proud of him there, Canon.

FRANCIS (*blushing and smirking*). Sure, I'm nothin' at all, Canon.

CANON (*with preliminary grave bow to* JEMIMA). Your mother, Francis, was a good woman. (*With great gravity*) In fact, a very good woman.

FRANCIS. Thank ye, Canon.

CANON (*gravely*). In fact, Francis, in the light of my home and foreign experience, I might even say—an excellent woman.

JEMIMA. There now is news for you, Francis!

FRANCIS. It's awful kind of you to say the like of that, Canon.

CANON (*handing back photograph to* JEMIMA). Very creditable, Miss Cooney. And now, Francis, you must be a little patient. We must *all* be a little patient. Your Aunt Jemima with her invaluable experience of life, as we live it, and of the—the idiosyncrasies of our checkered existence, will have impressed *that* upon you, I feel sure.

JEMIMA. Sure, Lord, Canon, isn't it all now in the will o' God!

CANON (*bowing delightfully*). Excellent, Miss Cooney. Your Aunt Jemima, Francis, has just made a very wise observation. It is—if I may repeat, Miss Cooney?—in the will of God. Did I say, Francis, that your mother was a good woman?

FRANCIS. You did, indeed, Canon. A very good woman, you said.

CANON. So I did, Francis. I distinctly remember the remark now.

I want to add to it, Francis. (*With great gravity*) I want to observe that your Aunt Jemima is a woman, to my knowledge, of incomparable wisdom, piety and virtue.

JEMIMA (*head down, blushing*). Sure, I'm not worth that, Canon.

FRANCIS. Indeed she's the best in the world, Canon. Sure, I'd be nothin' only for *her*.

CANON. As you say, Francis, you might be nothing but for *her*. And look what you are! *Hoc opus! hic labor est!* (CANON *smiles delightfully*.)

FRANCIS (*blushing and confused*). Yis, Canon. Indeed yis. I owe her everythin'.

JEMIMA. You didn't happen to see, Canon, the piece in the *Dundalk Sentinel* about him? Sure, the editor was a great college friend of Francis's before he failed for the teachin' and fell back on bein' an editor.

CANON. I regret, Miss Cooney, I missed it. I must inquire from Father Corr. I believe *he* buys the —the *Dundalk Semaphore*.

FRANCIS. *Sentinel*, Canon.

CANON. *Sentinel*, Francis. *Sentinel*, to be sure. Accuracy, Francis, accuracy always.

BRIGID (*entering*). If you please, Canon, there's a gentleman waitin' with a soft hat and an umbrella.

CANON. Ah, yes, Brigid. Presently my child, presently. Francis and his aunt are just going. (*They take the tip and rise to go.* CANON *claps* FRANCIS *on back*) And now, Francis, I hope to have excellent news for you shortly. I can say nothing further now. The tongues of none of us are free. But keep within easy call, and employ your waiting time properly.

JEMIMA. Indeed, Canon, he'll spend his time of waitin' your command in makin' a novena.

FRANCIS (*outrageously*). Sure, Canon, *orare est vigilare.*

JEMIMA. Well, will you listen to that, Canon. And him only a child.

CANON (*beaming*). Excellent, Francis. I can see you are deeply versed in the profundities of the classics.

JEMIMA. Come on now, Francis, we're keepin' the Canon. And he'll pray for you, Canon. We'll both pray for you.

CANON (*bowing repeatedly as they go out*). Excellent. . . . (*They go. He sinks wearily into chair.* BRIGID *comes in quickly and opens up window.*)

BRIGID. I knew you'd want the window open, Canon.

CANON. You are a very understanding child, Brigid. The law of Nature's compensation is not after all a myth. (*He looks up at her as she stands solicitously watching him*) Brigid, promise me you'll never leave me.

BRIGID (*shrinking*). I—I couldn't do that, Canon.

CANON (*startled*). What? . . . What

is this, Brigid? Are you not happy here?

BRIGID. Oh, yis, Canon. It's not that. I'm always happy.

CANON. Well? . . .

BRIGID. I might want to go away in a little while, Canon.

CANON. For what purpose, Brigid?

BRIGID. I—I don't know how to say it, Canon . . . It's the way I feel.

CANON. You are not well, child. You must take a good rest.

BRIGID. It's not that, Canon.

CANON. Nonsense! It *must* be that. Listen, Brigid. When I die, you will get every penny I have. There now! There's a secret out. Don't breathe it!

BRIGID. But Canon, it's not money I'll be wantin' where I—I think I'm goin'.

CANON. What talk is this? Where are you going?

BRIGID (*falteringly*). Please, Canon, I want to be a nun.

CANON (*flabbergasted*). Eh? You —you want to be a nun, eh? My God, am I not sufficiently stocked with boobs that *you,* Brigid, *you* must add the final straw.

BRIGID. You're vexed with me, Canon.

CANON. Displeased, Brigid. . . . Displeased that you would go and leave me here alone. And you my friend! You the—the Canon's friend.

BRIGID. It's not just *you*, Canon, but everythin' I'd be leavin'.

CANON (*clapping her affectionately*). Brigid, you have been doing too much lately, and you are overwrought. Excess in anything is bad, Brigid—in work, in play, in religion—it is not—classical. I am going to send you away for a holiday. And you must have a new hat too—a new hat with—with a feather in it. There now!

BRIGID (*amused*). But sure, Canon, feathers is not worn anywhere now.

CANON. Do you tell me that, Brigid? That—that—that's astonishing— astonishing, Brigid.

BRIGID. It's a wee white dog at the side they have now and a nose veil.

CANON (*gravely*). A—a white dog and a nose veil, Brigid? I—I must make a careful note of that, and you must certainly have them both. And it must be size six or seven or whatever you want.

BRIGID. Sure, Canon, with them shallow crowns that's out now, you can't depend on sizes. I'd need a fit-on.

CANON (*gravely*). You'd need a fit-on, Brigid. So you would. These shallow—shallow crowns are certainly a bit of a problem. We'll arrange that too.

BRIGID. Thank you, Canon.

CANON. There now, you've forgotten already. When you get your holiday you will be again classically simple and quiescent. (*Pause*) Brigid, do you know where we keep the Baptismal Registers in the Cloak Room?

BRIGID. Yis, Canon. In the cupboard behind the door.

CANON. Go, Brigid, and bring me the Register for the year nineteen —nineteen and eight.

BRIGID. Yis, Canon. Nineteen and eight. (*She goes.* CANON *lifts the book again, and looks at the page he left open. He smiles sardonically. He then begins to read aloud It is near the end of the book.*)

CANON (*reading*). "The Canon lay dying. The mists came white and wraith-like from the bogs to tell him so . . ." (*Puts down book*) Not a bit. On the contrary, the Canon feels well—feels in fact very well. (*As* BRIGID *comes in and hands him Register*) It may interest you to know, Brigid, that the Canon feels—excellently. (*He smiles sardonically.*)

BRIGID. Sure, thanks be to God, Canon.

CANON (*as he opens Register*). Amen, Brigid, amen. . . . Let me see now. (*Turns pages rapidly*) Mallin, Melling, Nagle, Nolan, O'Brien, O'Connell, O'Kelly . . . ah, here we are,—O'Flingsley. (*He moves his finger along a line of data*) June 8th, 1908, Dermot Francis O'Flingsley.

BRIGID (*looking*). Is that the Master's birthday, Canon?

CANON. That's it, Brigid. (*Gleefully as he reads on*) His father's name was Francis Eugene O'Flingsley. Mark the princely name, Eugene. Ah, and his mother bore the— storied name of Gibney. Could you credit that now? . . . Incomprehensible in fact. . . . Let me introduce you, Brigid, to Mr. Eugene Gibney,—er—author, amateur theologian, Catholic reformer, public moralist, student of Northern apologetics, erstwhile schoolmaster, ex-peasant and—gentleman.

BRIGID (*sensing fear*). What does that mean, Canon?

CANON. To you, Brigid, it shall mean—*nothing*. Put that Register back, Brigid, and not a word to any one. (*As he goes*) Did I say a *word*, Brigid?

BRIGID. Yis, Canon.

CANON (*gravely*). I meant a syllable, Brigid.

BRIGID. Sure, I won't even breathe, Canon.

CANON. Excellent, Brigid.

BRIGID (*turning as she crosses with Register*). Please, Canon, is there anythin' wrong with the Master?

CANON. You're *breathing*, Brigid.

BRIGID. Yis, Canon. . . . No, Canon. . . . (*She crosses disconsolately.*)

CANON. And Brigid. Send Dave Dooley down to the school to tell Mr. O'Flingsley that I wish to see him in the morning.

BRIGID (*almost in tears*). Y-yis, Canon. (*She looks at him for a moment, as if wishing to speak, then

goes off sadly with Register. FATHER CORR *and* FATHER KIRWAN *enter from the window, carrying their hats.*)

FATHER CORR. Father Kirwan and meself, Canon, would like a word with you, if you're not busy.

CANON. I *am* busy.

FATHER CORR. It's about a meeting we've just had of the Confraternity over that scurrilous book. A—a resolution was passed, Canon.

FATHER KIRWAN. Unanimously, Canon.

CANON. Well, what of it? It's a national pastime, isn't it?

FATHER KIRWAN. The members of the Football Club, Canon, are very excited. (*Worriedly*) *They're* the worst. They're gettin' out of hand.

CANON. No doubt, it's the warm weather, Father Kirwan. (*He crosses*) And I note you haven't as yet found time, even between resolutions, to shave. (CANON *goes out slowly.* CURATES *look after him perplexed.*)

FATHER CORR. For Heaven's sake, can you not go and shave and not be makin' things harder for us?

FATHER KIRWAN. Ach, can a man not get wearin' his own hair if he wants to! Sure he's so contrary if I shaved every day, he'd grumble because I hadn't a beard like Don-the-Divil's-Father! Is he an Irishman at all?

FATHER CORR. His father was Irish. It's his mother was the Spaniard. They met in Brussels.

FATHER KIRWAN. It's a pity she didn't stay at home instead of gallivantin' about the continent. Sure you'd think he hadn't a drop of Irish Ireland blood in his veins. I'll bet me boots he'll side with that book agin the Confraternity and the Football Club.

FATHER CORR. With a book like that! My God, at least he's a priest.

FATHER KIRWAN. Did you see the schoolmaster?

FATHER CORR. I did, and he was worth seein'. He's all for us burnin' the book in public, and he thinks that the Canon is the proper one to do the actual casting into the flames.

FATHER KIRWAN (*noticing open book*). Great Scott! Will you look at what's here!

FATHER CORR (*with a start*). The book!

FATHER KIRWAN. It's open at the last chapter where the P.P. dies miserably. He must have been readin' it.

FATHER CORR (*with passionate aversion*). I loathe the thing. It's accursed and vile. (*He flings it venomously on the floor.*)

FATHER KIRWAN (*"dribbling" with the book with both feet*). He was certainly no lover of clean sport and the team spirit. (*Still dribbling*) Suppose now yon door was the net. Wait till you see a grand penalty from the touch line. (*He kicks with judgment, and it is hurled against the doorway just as the* CANON *re-enters. He suddenly*

sees the CANON *and sinks visibly into himself.* FATHER CORR *is very confused. The* CANON *regards them with extreme frigidity. A definite pause.*)

CANON (*tensely*). You may both be seated. (*They obey silently. With cold hauteur*) My property, Father Corr.

FATHER CORR (*defiantly*). I—I refuse to touch it. It's—vile.

CANON. My property, Father Corr. (FATHER CORR *is defiant for a definite moment, then emotionally lifts the book and hands it to* CANON. *He then reseats himself. The* CANON *lays the mutilated book on table*) I suppose I am to regard this outbreak of hooliganism in my study, as a typical spasm of— Catholic action.

FATHER CORR (*flashing out*). Canon, that book is a disgrace and a shame. The Irish Press in Dublin says it's an insult to the Catholic nation.

CANON (*courteously*). Didn't catch that word, Father Corr. (*Hand to ear*) The Irish what?

FATHER CORR. The Irish Press, Canon.

CANON. Never heard of it. (*He pours out a small glass of golden-colored wine at sideboard, and examines it.*)

FATHER KIRWAN. Sure, the *Ballyedminstown Courier* quotes whole columns from it every Saturday, Canon.

CANON (*sipping wine*). In that case, Father Kirwan, I must con cede it has a definite claim to our attention.

BRIGID (*entering*). If you please, Canon, there's four o' the parishioners here wearin' badges, and they'd like a talk with you.

FATHER CORR. I'd like very much, Canon, if you'd receive them. They're a deputation.

FATHER KIRWAN. Sure the whole country's takin' action, Canon.

CANON. Mm . . . I am presumably to agree to a—a descent into Lutheranism and a sort of Kirk Session. Say, Brigid, the Canon says No.

BRIGID (*repeating*). The Canon says No. (*She makes to go.*)

FATHER CORR. Sure, after all if it was only for appearances' sake.

BRIGID. Canon, would you not just give another clap on the back and a grand word?

CANON. What *are* we come to? (*Pause*) Very well then, very well, let the—the neo-theologians come in, but let it be at their peril. I shall ring, Brigid.

BRIGID. Yis, Canon. I'll keep them in the waitin' room. (*She goes.*)

CANON. Who are these people, Father Corr?

FATHER CORR. They're all strong confraternity and football club members, Canon. There's Miss Cooney and her nephew Francis—

CANON. Is *he* here? Who are the other two?

FATHER KIRWAN. Martin Mullahone, Canon, the referee of our football team, that has the public house and farm on the Dublin Road, and his wife, Rosey Violet.

CANON. His wife who?

FATHER KIRWAN. He calls her Rosey Violet, Canon.

CANON. I think I recall her, but if my recollection is correct, she was neither rosey nor a violet. (*He rings the bell*) Be seated, Fathers, and offer no comments until these people are gone.
(FATHER CORR *and* FATHER KIRWAN *sit at either end of the empty chairs for the deputation. The* CANON *sits magisterially at the large writing desk.* BRIGID *enters with the deputation behind her.* MISS COONEY *and* FRANCIS O'CONNOR *are as obsequious as usual.* MARTIN MULLAHONE, *a large awkward man, with a large stomach and a red nose, is followed by his wife who is typical in dress and voice of the "social status" aspirants in rural Ireland.*)

BRIGID. This is them, Canon.

CANON (*curtly*). Good afternoon, all. You may be seated. (BRIGID *goes. All sit in chairs opposite the* CANON. *They smirk and bow to the* CANON *and look as virtuous as possible. The* CANON'S *sardonic eye surveys them pitilessly. They wilt and shift uneasily. His eye on* MARTIN) Are you the man, Martin Mullahone?

MARTIN. I—I am then, Canon.

ROSEY VIOLET (*chipping in sweetly*). And I'm his wife, Canon.

CANON. Martin Mullahone, where are your hands?

(MARTIN *whips them violently out of his pockets.*)

MARTIN. Sure, I—I never thought, Canon. Sure, God's—

ROSEY VIOLET. Sure, I'm always tellin' him, Canon.

CANON. Sit erect and don't loll or sag. Decorum and personal dignity are not by any means the least of the Christian virtues. (*All sit fearfully erect*) And now to the point. You have come—or should I say you have taken it upon yourselves to come—about a certain book.

MARTIN (*explosively*). Sure, it's a —a terror, Canon. A—a terror and a fright to the world, Canon.

CANON (*with suave irony*). Having learned from your husband, Mrs. Mullahone, that this book is a—a terror and a fright—two quite incomprehensible epithets to me— do you wish to—er—supplement his observation?

ROSEY VIOLET. If you please, Canon, I agree with what Father Kirwan said when he thumped the table at the meetin', that no clean sportin' man with the team spirit in nim could write such a book.
(FATHER KIRWAN *is confused.*)

CANON (*ironic, with side glance at* FATHER KIRWAN). An *excellent* observation, Mrs. Mullahone.

ROSEY VIOLET. Sure, if you please, Canon, me eldest son, Dan, is the fullback in Father Kirwan's team.

CANON (*cruelly*). Didn't catch that

word, Mrs. Mullahone. (*Hand to ear*) The—the what?
(FATHER KIRWAN *is very confused.*)

ROSEY VIOLET. The fullback, Canon.

CANON. Ah! of course. The—The fullback. I must ask Father Kirwan for a glossary of these terms. (*Side glance at* FATHER KIRWAN) And you, Miss Cooney, have *you* any observation?

JEMIMA. Sure, Canon, I only came because Father Corr told me it was me duty to God and Ireland. (*Grasping* FRANCIS'S *arm*) Say it in Irish for the Canon, Francis. Go on now!
(FATHER CORR *is confused.*)

FRANCIS (*rising awkwardly*). Do cum gloire De, agus onora na h-Eiremann.

CANON (*hand to ear*). Didn't catch that Francis. Cum—cum what?

FRANCIS (*unconscious of cruelty*). Do cum gloire De, agus onora na h-Eiremann.

CANON (*scoundrelishly*). Excellent, Francis. Excellent! You may be seated. Any other observation, Miss Cooney?

JEMIMA. Sure, I'll just listen now to you, and learn, Canon. Isn't that me duty?

CANON. Very creditable, Miss Cooney. An attitude at once wise, womanly and prudent. And you, Francis?

JEMIMA (*hurriedly*). He'll just do the same as meself, Canon. Not a word now, Francis, before his reverence.

FRANCIS. Sure, it's for *you* to say, Canon.

CANON. Commendable, Francis. You have a good—a very good counselor.

ROSEY VIOLET (*not to be outdone*). Sure, if you please, Canon, me brother, Father Jamsie, says it was no one but the divil guided the hand that wrote that book.

CANON (*startled*). Your who—the what? Speak up, Mrs. Mullahone.

ROSEY VIOLET (*exuberantly*). Why, me brother, Father Jamsie, Canon, that's up in Dunaree with Father Jamsie. Sure, Canon, it was Father Jamsie that anointed your sister, Thomasina's mother, when she near died and didn't, last Christmas.

CANON (*shaking head*). Never heard of him.

ROSEY VIOLET (*sentimentally*). Ah, sure poor wee Father Jamsie, Canon. Sure, God help him.

CANON. What's the matter with him?

ROSEY VIOLET (*surprised*). Sure, nothin' at all, Canon. Sure, Lord, what would be the matter with him?

CANON (*with an effort*). Very well then.

ROSEY VIOLET. Sure, he's happy and lovely in Dunaree, Canon.

CANON (*heroically*). Very well then.

MARTIN (*blunderingly interposing*). Sure, will you not be sickenin'

the Canon, bargin' in every minute about Father Jamsie because he's your brother.

ROSEY VIOLET (*bursting into tears*). If you please, Canon, Martin's always insultin' and belittlin' me in public.

CANON (*with great gravity, eyeing* MARTIN *who quails and shifts about*). Martin Mullahone, what *grave* charge is this I hear as to your conduct and public morals?

MARTIN. Sure—sure, Canon, you'd think by the talk of her mornin' and night that he was a Canon like yourself, and him with the—the cloth on him only a month.

ROSEY VIOLET (*crying*). Me heart's broke with him, Canon.

CANON. You are a good woman, Mrs. Mullahone, and you have pleased me considerably.

ROSEY VIOLET. Sure, everyone loves me, Canon.

CANON. As for you, Martin Mullahone, I am gravely incensed. (MARTIN *squirms*) and not a little pained.

ROSEY VIOLET. Oh, thank you, Canon. Martin badly needed that talkin' to.

CANON. Very well then. We digress. How many of you have read this book?
(*Negative murmurs and shaking of heads.*)

ROSEY VIOLET. Sure, what Catholic could read a book like that, Canon?

CANON. I take it then that none of you has read this book?

ALL (*shaking heads, murmurs*). Not a one, Canon.

CANON. And you come here to condemn a book you have not read! What nonsense is this? (*Taps desk*) Preposterous and ridiculous! The deputation is dismissed. (*The CANON is just rising when FATHER CORR jumps up.*)

FATHER CORR. If I may say a word, Canon—

CANON. Be seated, Father Corr. (FATHER CORR *sits.*)

FRANCIS (*rising*). If you please, Canon—

JEMIMA (*seizing him and flinging him down*). That's enough, you pup! Sit down!

CANON (*sitting back, eyeing FRANCIS, benignly*). We shall allow him the privilege on this occasion, Miss Cooney. Proceed, Francis.

FRANCIS (*awkwardly*). I was just goin' to say, Canon, that is, as a— a certified teacher, I—I read the book—judiciously.

CANON (*hand to ear, cruelly luring him on*). What—what word was that, Francis?

FRANCIS. Judiciously, Canon.

CANON. Ah! Enlarge upon that, Francis. It is a little vague.

FRANCIS. Well, Canon, if I—I felt a part was gettin' bad, I skipped.

CANON. You—you skipped, Francis. (*He smiles.*)

ROSEY VIOLET (*interposing*). I done that too, Canon.

JEMIMA. If you please, Canon, when I saw that Francis was determined to—to study it, I felt it me duty to read it before him and turn down some of the pages.

CANON (*face masklike*). I understand—exactly. And you, Martin Mullahone?

MARTIN (*hoarsely*). I can't read, Canon. It's me wife is the scholar in our family.

ROSEY VIOLET (*interposing, gushingly*). I was three years in the convent, Canon, before Martin won me.

MARTIN (*hoarsely*). It was the little fella that has the bike shop, Canon—wee Joey Hardy, that was readin' out bits of it at the counter on Friday, and I—I couldn't help hearin' them, Canon. Out—outrageous and terrible, Canon! A fright to the world!

CANON (*rounding on them*). I am to take it then that four of my parishioners, deliberately—I might even say, wantonly—and without right or lawful authority from me either in person or by proxy, committed themselves to the reading of a book gravely alleged to be pernicious, immoral and—subversive. (*He sizes up the four, severely*) Of these, one is the sister of a priest (ROSEY VIOLET *sobs*) another presumptuously aspires to the position of teacher of the young, (JEMIMA *gives* FRANCIS *a vicious elbow dig in the ribs*) a third is or should be a father and a husband (MARTIN *sags visibly*), and a fourth—(JEMIMA *bows her head and sniffs*)—I can find no words to castigate the curiosity that tempted the fourth to this grave indiscretion. (*He rings the bell*) I shall deliver my directions to the two Fathers here who will communicate them to you for your unswerving acceptance. You will leave immediately. I shall contemplate whether it is humanly possible to pardon any or all of you. (CANON *rises, as* BRIGID *appears. The deputation also rises. The* CANON *waves. They go out in confusion following* BRIGID. *The* TWO CURATES *turn nervously to the* CANON *Curtly*) Be seated. (*They sit.* CANON *resumes his seat*) I may take it, I suppose, that you two have also presumed to read this book.

FATHER CORR. I frankly considered it my duty, Canon.

FATHER KIRWAN. So did I, Canon.

CANON. Bad theology, Fathers, bad theology. And equally bad theology of course to have any—er—unofficial conflagrations on the public street without my express approval. (*Pause*) The author of this book which I have read, Fathers, is obviously a very young man. I fear his education cannot be more—adequate than that of the average young man of the present, either lay or—er—clerical. (*He coughs*) The theme I take to mean that Ireland has dangerously materialized the outlook of the Church, and that its profound spiritual essence has been stolen by a small band of learned men whom it does not even recognize. A dangerous theme, Fathers, I grant you.

FATHER CORR (*blazing out*). A blasphemous lie on Catholic Ireland!

CANON (*calmly*). A theme, Fathers, that in the hands of an abler controversialist with a claim to scholarship or a classic status, might possibly cause alarm amongst us, especially when we have presently no known Irish Catholic scholar with that delicacy of touch, subtlety of culture and profundity of classical knowledge to defend and even rescue the Church intellectually. Coming in contact with such an immaturity as this the insufficiently scholared mind, fed mostly on sentimentalisms in the form of learning, is often shocked, and—vulgarly agitated. Violent emotionalism results, followed by a quite ridiculous hubbub, tawdry heroics, even bigoted physical violence under holy names, and generally a quite ludicrous procedure that the classic dignity of the mind of the Church recoils from. As I have no desire, Fathers, to make a presumptuous young man bogusly important in an age that is itself bogusly important, or to condone a procedure too undignified to be Catholic, I therefore decree that no action of any sort be taken in the case of this book, except such action as I, in my official capacity, shall think fit to perform. (*Pause*) That, I think, Fathers, will be all.

FATHER CORR (*livid*). Are we then actually to take it that our efforts to deal with this disgraceful libel are banned?

CANON. You are!

FATHER KIRWAN (*touching* FATHER CORR, *as he is about to burst out*). That's enough now. You'll only be sayin' things you'll be sorry for.

FATHER CORR (*in a temper*). I'll say what I like.

FATHER KIRWAN. Now, can't you see that's wild talk?

FATHER CORR (*cooling*). I suppose it is. But he's never done belittlin' and humblin' me. But I'll try not to mind. It's in my nature to be humble.

CANON. Inoculated would be a better word. Inoculated with the prevalent deluge of sentimentalism.

FATHER CORR. I'm afraid, Canon, there's nothin' for me to do but ask the Bishop for a shift and to give my reasons.

CANON. And in spite of your impertinences, Father, I shall be prepared to give his Grace an—adequate report of your work. (FATHER CORR *abruptly leaves the room, left. The* CANON *looks after him quietly and then turns to* FATHER KIRWAN) And you, Father Kirwan? Are you also going to the Bishop?

FATHER KIRWAN (*confused, and crossing*). I'm goin' for a—for a shave, Canon.

CANON. Dear me! We—progress! (FATHER KIRWAN *goes awkwardly, left. The* CANON *turns away tiredly, goes to the leaded bookcase, unlocks it and extracts a volume. He settles with it in an armchair. But the dusk is falling fast, and in a moment he looks up towards the lamp. He reaches for the bell, and is about to shake it when, with a cry,* BRIGID *runs in.*)

BRIGID. Canon! Canon!
(*He rises rapidly and goes to her. She tries to recover and looks up at him pathetically.*)

CANON. What on earth is the matter, child?

BRIGID (*breathing hard, but trying to recover*). It's nothin', Canon, nothin' at all. I—I'm all right now.

CANON. Did something frighten you?

BRIGID. Y-yis, Canon. But it's nothin'.

CANON. You should have the lamp lighted in there at this time. There, you are tired and overwrought.

BRIGID. Canon, may I—ask you somethin'?

CANON. Certainly, Brigid.

BRIGID. Do you—do you love St. Brigid?

CANON (*looking at her uncertainly*). Why, of course I do, child. Sure we *all* love St. Brigid.

BRIGID (*happy*). Yes . . . I'm glad you do. She'll be pleased.

CANON (*solicitously*). Brigid, you are ill. You are not well.

BRIGID. Yis, Canon, I'm well.

CANON. I'm afraid not, child.

BRIGID. It's just, Canon, that I—I still want to be a nun.

CANON. There now! I *knew* you weren't well.

BRIGID (*pleadingly*). But if I could just be a nun, Canon.

CANON. Don't you know, Brigid, that nuns must be very, very strong and brave? They must be cruel to themselves and they must give all.

BRIGID (*tensely*). I will give all, Canon. I will! I promised her.

CANON. What nonsense is this? Promised whom, child?

BRIGID (*her eyes aglow*). St. Brigid, Canon. I—I was dryin' the cups in the kitchen when she touched me on the shoulder and says she, "You're holdin' the dish-towel wrong, Brigid." And when I held it right, she whispered to me, "Ask him if he loves me more than the rest."
(*The* CANON *stares at her, walks irascibly away, and then returns to her, collected.*)

CANON (*gravely*). Brigid, you are, I fear, stubborn, disobedient, and even defiant, and—I am seriously annoyed and displeased with you.

BRIGID (*simply*). I—I knew you would, Canon.

CANON. If you were a boob, Brigid, or a footling trifler, I should expel you from my presence. But you are my friend, and I try to bear with you.

BRIGID (*sadly*). Yis, Canon.

CANON. I have borne all day with fools, Brigid, knowing that at the end you would come to me, and ask my wants and find no fault in me. There now. You see how it is with me.

BRIGID. Yis, Canon. (*Sadly*) I'm a wretch and a villain.

CANON. On the contrary, child, you are a good girl, and you have wisdom and grace. God, Brigid, is not *always* pleased with girls who want to be nuns. Sometimes He expects them to remain at their posts as His soldiers.

BRIGID (*pathetically persistent*). If only I could just be a nun instead of a soldier! Soldiers make so much noise.

CANON. Brigid, I am afraid your nerves are all shaken. You must go to bed now and on Friday I shall send you to Bray to a friend of mine for a holiday. Miss Cooney will take your place for a few weeks. You must get plenty of sleep and rest. Rest to the body, Brigid, is like prayer to the soul. And you will then forget these imaginings of yours.

BRIGID. But in bed, how can I forget, if her face is there in the curtains and the mark on her cheek where she struck the loveliness out of her face.

CANON (*irascibly*). Now, now, now! I am trying not to be angry. There is no historical authority for that at all. The Church in its wisdom does not confirm it. It is probably just a myth. A myth, Brigid. Doesn't that show you!

BRIGID (*pathetically*). What is a myth, Canon?

CANON. A legend, child.
(*Pause.*)

BRIGID (*venturing*). And what is a —a legend, Canon?

CANON. Brigid, this is very trying! An old tale, that may or may not be true.

BRIGID. Then—it *could* be true, Canon?

CANON. Now which of us knows best about these things, Brigid?

BRIGID. You, Canon.

CANON. Well now, I say this thing you foolishly think you see is not—not of God. Dismiss it!

BRIGID (*in pain, her head in her hands*). Canon! . . . oh, Canon! . . . how—how could you be sayin' that?

CANON (*sympathetically*). There, there! God tempts most those whom He loves best. You should be proud. The soul's great battles are not fought by common boobs. The great Ignatius was tempted like this, and so were Theresa and Augustine and Dominic, but they were not deceived. They rose up and conquered the tempter. So must you conquer this, Brigid.

BRIGID (*tearfully*). So must you conquer this, Brigid.

CANON. Not more beautiful, Brigid, than the demon that twisted himself round the crucifix St. Ignatius prayed before. He had to lie on his face to save himself. You too, Brigid, must turn away from this thing you think you see. You must

be wise. Wise, Brigid, and brave. Promise me, Brigid.

BRIGID (*sobbing*). I want to die, Canon. . . . I want to—to die. . . .

CANON (*softly*). Come now, Brigid. That is not being brave! That is being merely heroic, like these modern vulgarians. Say, Brigid, "I want to live and conquer." (*She is silent*) Say it, Brigid. Be proud like a soldier and say it.

BRIGID (*sadly*). I want to live and —conquer. . . .

CANON (*clapping her on back*). Ah, Brigid, excellent! Go now, Brigid, to bed and sleep. And none of these dreams, remember, or foolishness. To sleep is safe, to dream is dangerous. I shall go out and send Dave Dooley for Miss Cooney to take your place.

BRIGID (*emotionally*). Yis, Canon. (*He crosses to window, opens it and passes out, into the garden.*)

CANON'S VOICE (*without*). Dooley! Are you there! Come here, Dooley! (BRIGID's *emotional stress now visibly shakes her, as she stands undecided and forlorn in the deepening shadows. She sobs pathetically, her head down, like a child. She gives the impression of having lost someone very beloved. She lifts her head suddenly, and stares stealthily over her own shoulders at the slightly swaying curtains, that reach to the ground. Her body shudders, and she covers her face with her hands.*)

BRIGID (*sobbing*). I'm not to look at you. . . . I—I promised him. . . . I'm not to see your face. . . .

No, no. I—I mustn't . . . I daren't . . . I must keep my eyes covered from you . . . I must be—be wise and brave . . . I must sleep but not dream . . . but I—I . . . (*She draws her hands from her eyes, shakingly, stretches out her two arms to the* curtains, *and with a sob, rushes to them as to a loved one*) But I—I love you . . . I love you . . . I love you. . . . (*Her face is buried sobbingly in the great curtains, and her arms are about them pathetically, as the curtain falls slowly.*)

CURTAIN

ACT THREE

SCENE—*The same. A few days later.*

  The CANON *is seated at table finishing breakfast.* FATHER CORR *is standing at the writing-desk, quietly examining a Register of Births.* JEMIMA, *with an apron on, is flitting fearfully about the table, obsequious and uncomfortable in the* CANON'S *presence.*

JEMIMA (*sweetly*). Is there anythin' else, Canon, if you please?

CANON (*beamingly*). You leave nothing to be desired, Miss Cooney. Thank you.

JEMIMA. Thank you, Canon. (*She crosses.*)

CANON. One moment, Miss Cooney. Has Brigid had a good night?

JEMIMA. She had, Canon. A wee bit feverish maybe and her eyes are shineyish, but the doctor says it's nothin' to worry about.

CANON. As a good woman, Miss Cooney, what do *you* think yourself?

JEMIMA (*squirming a little under his gaze*). Sure I'd say, Canon, I'd say nothin' much. I'd put it down, if you'd allow me, Canon, to what —what she came from. Her mother,

Canon, was none too strong— (*hoarsely*) in the mind I mean, Canon. They had to—remove her in the end.

CANON. Remove her? Enlarge on that, Miss Cooney.

JEMIMA. Sure—take her away, Canon: to—to Dublin, I mean. It was before your time, sure.

CANON (*understanding*). Ah! . . . And her father?

JEMIMA (*hoarsely*). Sure they say, Canon, he didn't die a Christian death in Scotland. But sure God's good, Canon.

CANON. As you say, Miss Cooney, God is good. (*Pause*) I want you to give Brigid very careful attention night and day.

JEMIMA. Sure if it's your wish, Canon.

CANON. Expressly so! That will be all. (*She goes after bowing. The* CANON *watches* FATHER CORR *at the Births' Register, as he finishes his coffee*) I understand you heard Brigid's confession this morning, Father Corr?

FATHER CORR (*raising head from book*). That's correct, Canon. At eight o'clock. She asked for me.

CANON. Did you—instruct her on these matters we discussed, on the lines I recommended?

FATHER CORR. I carried out your instructions to the letter, Canon, even if I did think myself you were unnecessarily extreme and severe.

CANON. The latter half of your observation, Father Corr, is superfluous.

FATHER CORR. Not so much as you might think, Canon, if you examine this Register of Births.

CANON. I knew from the manner in which you were poring over that book that there was a sort of necromancer's air about you. Well? And what are the—the "signs and wonders"?

FATHER CORR (*impressively*). Would it surprise you to know, Canon, that Brigid was born on February the first, almost twenty-one years ago? That's St. Brigid's day!

CANON. And you are going to infer vulgarly that there is anything more than mere coincidence in that? (*He sips his coffee slowly.*)

FATHER CORR (*coming forward slowly*). Since I heard of this—contention of Brigid's, Canon, I've been worried and disturbed.

CANON (*sipping*). I thought you would. The danger with you, Father Corr, is that some trivial happening is always liable to hurl you headlong into violent emotionalism.

FATHER CORR. Sure, I'm doin' nothin' violent, Canon—I'm as calm as any priest could be. I'm only just quietly turnin' over a few things in my mind, such as, for instance the fact that Brigid was born on St. Brigid's day, and that St. Brigid lived and worked in this very locality here in Fanghart.

CANON. I dislike your attitude. If a leaf turns unaccountably in these credulous days ten thousand ferrety nonentities cock their ears and gibber.

FATHER CORR. Suppose, Canon, that Brigid—*did* see this—well, this vision?

CANON. If Brigid saw ten thousand visions, our attitude to the accumulated wisdom of the Church should be unaltered. I wish you, in particular, and this country in general, could digest just *that* much, and cease chasing emotional red-herrings.
(*Pause.* FATHER CORR *shifts uneasily.*)

FATHER CORR. With all respect to you, Canon, I don't think you understand this country.

CANON (*acidly*). I understand the mind of the universal Church, and that alone concerns me. (*Pause*)

Besides, didn't you hear Miss Cooney just now on the matter of Brigid's antecedents?

FATHER CORR. That might mean nothing.

CANON. It generally means everything. But you *will* strain after miracles, in spite of my previous observations. One can conceivably understand her father dying an unchristian death in a barbarous nation like Scotland, but there is no escaping the significance of the fact that her mother was—removed, as Miss Cooney so Celtically phrased it.

FATHER CORR. That may be, Canon. What worries me, is her insistence that she saw the face and eyes of the Saint. Poor Brigid is not a liar.

CANON. Brigid, as you observe, is not a liar. But the reflections, Father, in an unstable mind are not —shall we say theologically significant? (*As* JEMIMA *enters*) Let us dismiss the subject.

JEMIMA. Please, Canon, you said you wanted to see me nephew, Francis. He's here now.

CANON. Let him come in, Miss Cooney.

JEMIMA. Sure, let him wait till Father Corr is finished with you, Canon.

FATHER CORR (*to* JEMIMA). You can send him in. I'm going now. (*She bows and goes*) Canon, I've written to the Bishop for a transfer. I don't, and probably never will, understand you. I don't want you to think I'm doin' it behind your back.

CANON (*slowly*). It is not important.
(FRANCIS *comes in awkwardly with his cap in his hand. Neither priest takes the slightest notice of him.*)

FATHER CORR. Very well, Canon. (*He bows and goes. Very preoccupied, the* CANON *looks at* FRANCIS *for quite a time, unseeingly.* FRANCIS *sweats.*)

FRANCIS. Am I too—too soon, Canon? Sure, I could go back and wait! . . .

CANON (*coming slowly to consciousness*). Ah, Francis, you've come. Of course. You wanted to see me, Francis?

FRANCIS (*open-mouthed*). But sure it—was *you* wanted to see *me,* Canon!

CANON. Oh, it was *I* wanted to see *you,* Francis! Why of course it was. I remember now. I distinctly remember. Be seated, Francis.
(FRANCIS *sits awkwardly, squeezing cap.*)

FRANCIS (*in a typical Irish whisper*). Is there—anny news, Canon?

CANON. There is, Francis, and there isn't. Contradictory, Francis? But no! I mean by it, there *is* news— relevant news, but there is the necessity for absolute secrecy.

FRANCIS. Sure you can swear me on the book, Canon. (*Magnanimously*) Or if ye lek, Canon, don't tell me a word, if you think fit.

CANON. Excellent, Francis. But— you will be told everything. I trust you. To be exact, moral issues

—issues, Francis, of a moral nature, are involved.

FRANCIS (*all at sea*). I—I see, Canon. . . .

CANON. Your aunt will understand more fully than you, Francis. Moral issues *are* involved, and where such are met with, we must tread warily. We must tread, Francis, with the subtlety of angels. But to proceed. You have met my niece—my step-niece, Thomasina Concannon?

FRANCIS. I—I had the honor, Canon, a good few times, in the hall and at concerts she came down to see.

CANON. As you say, Francis, you've had the honor. A—a gentlemanly expression, Francis. For some time past, I have promised her the first vacancy in the school here. And as Miss Driscoll goes to training next week, I must fulfill that promise, Francis. We must *all* fulfill our promises.

FRANCIS (*very crestfallen*). Well, sure, thank you annyway, Canon. I know you did your best for me, and sure you can't please everyone.

CANON. Wait, Francis, wait! There is something further. What remains is confidential. But I have your word, Francis.

FRANCIS. Sure me lips is sealed, Canon, and as for me Aunt, sure she's a—a gravestone.

CANON. As you say, Francis, your aunt's a—a gravestone. I may therefore, proceed. I intend, Francis, dismissing the man, O'Flingsley. (FRANCIS *gives a gasp and half rises*) A grave step,

Francis—a very grave step, but necessary. We must never hesitate in our duty. That is the sum and the essence of conduct. Note it down, Francis.

FRANCIS. I'll write it in me "Things to Remember" book this very night, Canon.

CANON. Excellent, Francis. That will be another vacancy. Now that position of Principal, Francis, I would give to no one sooner than you.

FRANCIS (*gasping*). P-principal, Canon!

CANON. But mark what it results in! Mark my problem, Francis, my dilemma, my moral embarrassment. An attractive young man and a comely young girl in the one building all day. Mark it gravely, Francis!

FRANCIS (*wide-eyed, dismayed*). There—there would be scandal, Canon, and . . . and talk. I see it all.

CANON. Let us say instead, Francis, with the dignity demanded by the phenomenon, that moral issues of grave import are involved.

FRANCIS (*aghast*). I see it all, Canon. . . .

CANON. You see it all, Francis! You have insight! You inherit it, I have not the *slightest* doubt, from your Aunt Jemima. Now, if my step-niece were a benevolent old lady, the problem would not only solve itself—it would have no existence in fact.

FRANCIS. That's the trouble, Canon, with Thomasina young and—if I may make so bold, Canon—attractive.

CANON. Attractive is the word, Francis, or if you wish—sus-susceptible. An excellent word, Francis. You see my difficulty?

FRANCIS. Sure it's plain, Canon.

CANON. It's plain, Francis. It's more than plain. It's insurmountable. Unless of course, Francis, you could hit on a way out. Your brain is young and nimble, Francis, not like mine.

FRANCIS. If only I could, Canon! Sure it's grand of you strivin' to help me, and perplexin' yourself.

CANON. Not a bit, Francis. "The labor we delight in physics pain." You remember that great inspirational line, Francis, in your studies.

FRANCIS. Indeed I do, Canon. Sure, I know Lord Macaulay inside out.

CANON. So you do, Francis! I can see that.

FRANCIS. If the two of them was married, Canon?

CANON (apparently perplexed). Which two, Francis?

FRANCIS. The two in the school, Canon.

CANON. Oh, the two in the school, Francis. If they were married. But they're not, Francis. If they were, the conditions would be an approximation to the ideal. But we must deal in facts, Francis.

FRANCIS (uneasily). If I could maybe, Canon, ask me aunt to ask Thomasina to—to discuss things. . . .

CANON (obtusely). For—for what purpose, pray, Francis?

FRANCIS. I mean, Canon, that is if you have no objection, to see if Thomasina would consider a—a match between us.

CANON (admirably playacting). A —a match! A—a match! . . . Francis, what on earth is this? What is that brain of yours propounding?

FRANCIS (laughing). But you asked me to hit on a way out, Canon!

CANON. I asked you to hit on a way out, and you—you bring the house down about my ears without warning! By my soul, Francis, you're a —a scoundrel; a—a desperado! I insist on your Aunt Jemima taking you in hand this instant! (Goes to door and calls) Miss Cooney! Come here instantly!
(JEMIMA runs in nervously.)

JEMIMA. You want me, Canon?

CANON (with mock severity). Miss Cooney, take Francis out of my sight, and never let him into my presence again. He's a scoundrel!

JEMIMA (aghast). Did—did he insult ye, Canon? Did he have the—the cheek—! (Tempestuously, finger up) Stand before me, Francis, this minute! (CANON and FRANCIS laugh heartily) Sure is—is it mockin' me yous are, Canon?

CANON (touching her shoulder). No, Miss Cooney. But Francis has mentally, and I might even say morally, winded me. He wants me to make a match with my step-niece and take over the school!

JEMIMA (*excitedly*). Make a match! . . . Take over the school! . . . Canon, if it's takin' liberties he is in your presence, it's your own fault. You're far too kind and free with him, and you don't keep him in his place.

FRANCIS. But you see, Aunt Jemima, O'Flingsley's bein' put out.

JEMIMA. O'Flingsley? Put out! Is that for you to *say*, or the Canon? The cheek of you, Francis. I'll slap your jaw.

CANON. It's true, Miss Cooney. But in strict confidence as yet, remember!

JEMIMA (*involuntarily*). Praises to God! . . .

CANON. But I can't appoint Francis alongside my step-niece, because of moral issues.

JEMIMA (*awarely*). You can *not*, Canon. I can see *that*.

FRANCIS. But if we were married, Aunt? The Canon says he has no objection.

JEMIMA (*gravely*). Did—did you say that, Canon?

CANON. I certainly did, Miss Cooney. But the suggestion is not mine, Miss Cooney. I—wash my hands. (*Laughter.*)

JEMIMA. It's God, Canon, that's Who it is! And Thomasina was in the kitchen to see you not three minutes ago.

CANON (*aghast*). What? She—she's back?

JEMIMA. She came in, Canon. But she left a book she was readin' behind her on the bus, and she's away flyin' down to the Depot to get it.

FRANCIS (*exuberantly*). I'll go down after her, and help her to get it!

JEMIMA. You'll stay where y'are, till you learn the Canon's wishes. Direct him, Canon.

CANON. I refuse to commit myself by *one* word. Did I not say I had washed my hands?

FRANCIS. I'll go. I—I insist on me independence, in this, Aunt Jemima. (*As he goes, excitedly*) And sure, Canon. *Fortis cadere, cedere non potest!*
(CANON *and* JEMIMA *laugh affectedly, as* FRANCIS *goes.*)

JEMIMA (*proudly*). Imagine the nerve of him, Canon, hurlin' the Latin back at you!

CANON. There is no presumption where there is no malice, Miss Cooney. Francis is a good boy. That will be all, Miss Cooney. (*He lifts book and crosses*) I shall be seated at the lower end of the garden if Mr. O'Flingsley calls. I'm expecting him.

JEMIMA. I'll come for you at once, Canon. Sure, it's God's blessin', Canon. You're gettin' rid of him, and him that cheeky and impertinent to you. (*The* CANON *crosses and takes no notice of her remark. She notices this and goes quickly.* CANON *pauses a moment to look out pensively at the hills, then opens the window and with his book passes out. A moment later, the door bell rings and almost immediately* JEMIMA *ushers in* DERMOT O'FLINGSLEY. *Sourly*) Sit there, and I'll run into the garden and see if the Canon will be willin' to see you.

O'FLINGSLEY. I'll stand. And don't *run*. You might break your neck.

JEMIMA (*very sourly*). Yours is bruck if you only knew it.

O'FLINGSLEY (*squeaking*). Coo-ee, Jemma! Your petticoat's hangin'! (*She stamps out in a fury.* O'FLINGSLEY *laughs heartily, throws his hat on a chair, and makes a tour of the bookcases and the pictures.* BRIGID, *wrapped in a dressing-gown and bare-footed, comes in left, noiselessly. She crosses until she is right beside him. She looks feverish and frail*) How anyone can have all that beauty about him, and still be a bear! (*He sees* BRIGID *beside him and jumps*) Brigid! Where on earth did *you* drop from? Are you not well?

BRIGID (*softly*). Yis, Master, I'm well. It's just that the Canon says I'm not.

O'FLINGSLEY (*looking at her*). I think now, Brigid, that *for once* he's right. Let me feel your hand. (*He takes her hand gently.*)

BRIGID. I knew you'd be here.

O'FLINGSLEY (*staring at her*). Eh? You what?

BRIGID. I knew it. I could—see you. I was dreaming about you. I thought you were going down a long road and waving back to me. So I came down. I—I— (*She suddenly sobs and buries her head in his breast. He is very shaken and tries to control himself by being humorous.*)

O'FLINGSLEY. There, silly! I'm not going away. I'm going to stay here and grow a mustache, and play bowls with the Canon.

BRIGID (*looking at him*). No . . . you're going away . . . You're to —"to take up your bed—"

O'FLINGSLEY (*startled*). Brigid! Is that the message?

BRIGID (*simply*). Yis, Master . . . and you're to try to love people when they're dirty because any ass can love them when they're clean.

O'FLINGSLEY (*after a pause, vigorously*). You dreamt that!

BRIGID. No . . . she said it. She'd have said more only Miss Cooney was annoyin' her dustin' and cleanin'. She went away then . . .

O'FLINGSLEY (*pensively*). Take up my bed and walk . . . I wonder what exactly that means?

BRIGID. I don't know . . . she said *you'd* know. . . .

O'FLINGSLEY. Yes . . . maybe I do. Brigid, I *am* going away.

BRIGID. I knew . . .

O'FLINGSLEY. If I could just shake this fear off me—this fear of hunger . . . of money . . . of the cold. . . .

BRIGID. It will be terrible, Master, when I see you comin' up the school road, and you not comin' at all. But I'll still have the Canon.

O'FLINGSLEY. The Canon! That man!

BRIGID. Yis, Master . . . Oh, I know you have the dagger for him because he can hurt and say killin' words . . . *You* see him when he's proud, but I see him when he's prayin' in his little place and the tears on his cheeks; *you* see him when he dines but *I* see him when he fasts; *you* see him when his head is up and fiery like a lion, but *I* see his head when it's down low and his words won't come . . . It's because of that, that *you* hate him and *I* love him . . . St. Brigid says that if we could all see each other all the time in big hangin' mirrors, the whole hate of the world would turn into dust.

O'FLINGSLEY (*touched*). I'll remember that always, Brigid. And I'll remember you too.

BRIGID. It wouldn't matter not remembering *me,* if you'd remember *it.*
(*They are staring at each other as the* CANON *appears at the window. His brow clouds. He comes forward into the room and for a moment regards them both.*)

CANON (*sharply*). Brigid, what is this? How dare you leave your bed in your sick state and in this attire? (BRIGID *looks from the* CANON *to* O'FLINGSLEY *and back again. She continues to look at both of them.*

They are a little uncomfortable, and eye each other surreptitiously.)

BRIGID. I wanted to come down . . . to see—the two of yous.

CANON. For what purpose?

BRIGID. I—I don't know, Canon . . . I just wanted to—to be sure that I loved the two of yous and could serve yous always.
(*Pause.* JEMIMA *comes rushing in.*)

JEMIMA. Canon! (*She stops short on seeing* BRIGID.)

CANON. Preposterous! Miss Cooney, I cannot congratulate you on your care of Brigid.

JEMIMA. It was when I was out findin' you, Canon, that she left her bed.

CANON. Brigid, I am displeased.

BRIGID. Yis, Canon . . . and so is the Master.

CANON (*with glance at* O'FLINGSLEY). Brigid, go back to bed with Miss Cooney.

JEMIMA (*taking her arm*). Come on now. Annoyin' the Canon like this.

O'FLINGSLEY. Good-bye, Brigid.

BRIGID (*turning*). Master! . . . (*She turns to get back, but* JEMIMA *won't let her.*)

JEMIMA. Never mind *him.* Come on when you're told.

CANON. Let her come, Miss Cooney. (JEMIMA *releases her. She comes back to* O'FLINGSLEY, *and gives him her hand. She looks up at him.*)

BRIGID. Good-bye, Master. And— I love you. (*She looks up at him emotionally. He bends and kisses her hair softly. The* CANON *stands like a statue, his feelings masked completely.* BRIGID *turns and goes with* JEMIMA.)

CANON (*as* JEMIMA *takes* BRIGID'S *arm*). That could have been gentler, Miss Cooney. I will have it so.

JEMIMA. Sure I'm not sayin' a word at all to her, Canon.
(*They go.* O'FLINGSLEY *and the* CANON *both regard each other in silence for a moment. One can see them as if shedding their finer feelings and donning their fighting equipment.*)

O'FLINGSLEY. Well, Canon? You sent for me.

CANON (*quietly*). You may be seated, O'Flingsley. (O'FLINGSLEY *sits frankly and without nervousness, in a chair. The* CANON *goes to desk and sits in his large chair. A pause*) O'Flingsley, for some time past, I have had ample grounds for complaint both against your person and your work.

O'FLINGSLEY. *I* have a goodly few complaints also. Perhaps they will cancel each other out.

CANON (*eyebrows raised*). *You* have complaints, O'Flingsley? I did not think it was considered a—a suitable attitude in a teacher to have complaints.

O'FLINGSLEY (*stung*). You forget, Canon, that I am "that man O'Flingsley" first, and your schoolmaster second.

CANON (*ironically*). Very novel, and shall we use that hateful word, modern?

O'FLINGSLEY. If it's something ancient, very ancient you want, here you are:—(*Very rapidly on his fingers*) No coal, no handle on sweeping-brush, no caretaker for the school, no windows that aren't stuck fast; eighteen crumbling desks, six broken panes of glass, no lighting on dark days, and the public highway of the Saorstat Cireann for a playground. And these complaints render my attitude —unsuitable.

CANON (*unperturbed*). Your enunciation is very imperfect for a teacher, O'Flingsley. I missed quite half of them. Besides, these alleged deficiencies are not complaints. They are officially termed "Recommendations in Writing to the Very Reverend Manager."

O'FLINGSLEY. Or alternately, "Words Scrawled on the Sands by an Innocent."

CANON (*coldly*). I will not—descend to you, O'Flingsley.

O'FLINGSLEY. You sent for me, Canon, to say something and you haven't said it yet.

CANON. I'll say it now, O'Flingsley. I'll say it now. (*Bending over*) Your mother's name was Gibney.

O'FLINGSLEY (*with a slight start*). So it was, Canon.

CANON (*grimly*). Your father's second name was Eugene.

O'FLINGSLEY (*now reckless*). It was. And if you're as interested as all that in my genealogy, I had a grandmother that was called Poppet, an uncle that could spit over his own shoulder, and a paralyzed aunt that was christened Delia Diana. But I never had a niece that was called after me, thank God.

CANON (*controlling his anger*). I'll be—calm, O'Flingsley. I'll be logical. I—I won't descend to you. (*Holding up press cuttings from desk*) I note from these cuttings of *your* book *I Am Sir Oracle*, that the Church in Ireland is controlled by a—a red army of turkey-cocks.

O'FLINGSLEY. If you have, Canon, that's always a big step forward.

CANON (*grimly, his eye gleaming*). And I see that our educational system is the—the sewage of European culture. I'd never have thought it, O'Flingsley. Could you tell me, on what page of your teacher's Penny Catechism I could find it?

O'FLINGSLEY (*with venom*). On the page, Canon, the Bishops won't add until they're made.

CANON (*striking desk*). Damnation! I'll not have—*that!* (*He jumps up fiercely.*)

O'FLINGSLEY (*also jumping up*) And hell and blazes, but you'll have to! (*They face each other on the floor, the masks now off completely. A pause as they regard each other venomously. The CANON composes himself with a great effort.*)

CANON (*with composure*). O'Flingsley, do you know Francis Ignatius O'Connor?

O'FLINGSLEY. Who doesn't? (*Imitating FRANCIS*) "Sure, Lord now, Canon!"

CANON (*grimly*). I—I'm expecting him.

O'FLINGSLEY. I rather thought you were. And his—virgin consort, Aunt Jemima too, of course.

CANON (*fuming*). In my—my forty years as a priest—

O'FLINGSLEY. You played the turkey-cock with your teachers, and made them your slavish handymen.

CANON (*with some composure*). No . . . I—I will not stoop! I will not argue. To argue is to assume equality.

O'FLINGSLEY. And equality of course would mean the end of your precious managerial system of education that's the laughing-stock of Europe. That would never do, Canon. By all means, spit on me. (*FRANCIS O'CONNOR comes to the door, left, awkwardly. He is rather excited.*)

FRANCIS. Can I come in, Canon? I'm back with good news!

CANON. Good news will keep, Francis. Be seated.

FRANCIS (*exuberantly*). Sure I—I can't keep it, Canon. Your niece has done me the honor of promisin' to be me wife. Everythin's lovely and grand, Canon! (*O'FLINGSLEY chuckles merrily.*)

O'FLINGSLEY. Hurrah for the Catholic ideal! A rebel knocked out; a niece married off; and a school made safe for a stagnant tradition all in the one move! Canon, you deserve a seat in Maynooth.

(FRANCIS *stares at him goggle-eyed.*)

CANON. Take no heed of that man, Francis. He's an occasion of sin. Allow me instead to congratulate you. (*To* O'FLINGSLEY, *grimly turning*) Need I say any more, O'Flingsley? Need I say that Francis will—take over your duties at the end of the month?

O'FLINGSLEY. And I'm—fired?

CANON (*dignifiedly*). "Dismissed" is the word, O'Flingsley. (*They regard each other grimly.*)

O'FLINGSLEY. I somehow feel we'll meet again, we two.

CANON. I trust not.

O'FLINGSLEY (*to* FRANCIS). And now, O'Connor, you're an Irish schoolmaster! In other words, a clerical handyman, a piece of furniture in a chapel house, a brusher-out of barn schools, a Canon's yes-man.

CANON (*as* FRANCIS *goggles*). You heard that—that man, Francis!

FRANCIS. He'll never have anny luck, Canon. Sure, leave him to God.

CANON. An excellent suggestion, Francis, and it will save me from descending to him. (*To* O'FLINGS-LEY) At the end of the month, then, O'Flingsley . . . And that will be all, thank you.

(O'FLINGSLEY *crosses.*)

O'FLINGSLEY (*turning*). I'll leave tomorrow, Canon, without pay, and give over the school to your handyman, if you'll answer me one question before I go.

CANON. Your question, O'Flingsley, may have an answer from us if it is—suitable.

O'FLINGSLEY. As a scholar who knows what he won't publicly admit, you loathe and detest the whole miserable fabric of things here. You detest that disgraceful apology for a school down there, even more than *I* do. I know that because I'm not a fool whatever else I am. Why then do you deliberately prepare to perpetuate it through that poor spineless imbecile there beside you?

FRANCIS (*outraged*). Canon! He's insultin' me. I'd make him take that back.

(*The* CANON's *eyes meet* O'FLINGS-LEY's *eyes challengingly, in a silent tense duel. Pause.*)

CANON (*tensely*). That will be all, O'Flingsley.

O'FLINGSLEY (*venomously*). Afraid, Canon? But the heartbreak is there all the same. *You* know it, and I know it. However, I'll always owe you something for taking me by the scruff of the neck out of a mouse's hiding place and putting me back on the high road. Goodbye, Canon, you will be remembered, if at all, not as a classicist, nor as a priest, but for your love for a poor little miserable child.

CANON (*his voice trembling with passion*). That will—be all, O'Flingsley.
(O'FLINGSLEY *turns and snapping up his hat, walks quickly off. The* CANON, *oblivious of* FRANCIS, *stares after him unseeingly.* FRANCIS *is standing flabbergasted and open-mouthed.*)

FRANCIS. Is he mad or what, Canon?

CANON (*after a pause*). Conceivably, Francis . . . conceivably. . . .

CURTAIN

ACT FOUR

SCENE—*The Same. The following morning.*
On the window, back, there are beautiful long white curtains reaching to the ground, and on the table a great vase of white lilies. The CANON *rises from the dining table and wipes his mouth with a napkin.* MISS COONEY *enters with a wrapped box.*

JEMIMA. This, Canon, came in from Driscall's of Dundalk. It's the hat and veil you sent in for.

CANON. Just leave it. (*She puts down box*) And undo the string. Are the Fathers finished Mass yet?

JEMIMA. Father Kirwan's takin' off his vestments, Canon. He'll be in for breakfast in a minute. Father Corr had his, this hour since.

CANON. Very well then. And Brigid?

JEMIMA. She was asleep when I riz at seven, Canon. And she didn't call since.

CANON. You should have brought her a cup of tea.

JEMIMA. She was twistin' and fidgettin' durin' the night, Canon, and I thought it best to let her sleep on. It's what the doctor said. (*She suddenly sees the white curtains and starts visibly*) Canon! Who— who changed the curtains? It was the rose-red ones that was on, and I goin' through to your own Mass at seven, and I never noticed nothin' till now. Oh! and them lilies on the table too!

CANON (*staring at flowers and curtains*). Was it not yourself?

JEMIMA. It was not, then, Canon. I'm sure o' that. They didn't need changin'. (*Pause*) It—it was *her,* I'll bet. (FATHER KIRWAN *comes in bareheaded through the window. He stands and looks on.*)

CANON. Who is *her?* Explain yourself.

JEMIMA. Brigid, I mean, Canon. She done it maybe, and I out at Mass.

CANON. What grounds have you for such a statement?

JEMIMA. It was the meanderin' talk of her durin' the night, Canon. She kept sayin' that someone went always in white a long time ago.

CANON. Am I to take it then, that this sick child whom I have placed in your care, has been wandering about in this cold room, bare-footed and undressed?

JEMIMA. But sure, Canon, I had to go to Mass.

CANON. You should have missed Mass in the circumstances.

JEMIMA. But I was makin' a novena for poor Francis.

CANON. I don't care if you were making fifty novenas.

JEMIMA (*sniffing*). You're wrongin' me, Canon. But sure no matter. I'll not defend myself.

CANON. I want none of this palaver. I want practical wisdom and sound sense. Go to Brigid now and see to her comfort.

JEMIMA. It's what you say, Canon. (*To* FATHER KIRWAN) Will you serve yourself, Father?

FATHER KIRWAN. Sure, and I can. Go ahead and see after Brigid. (MISS COONEY *goes, left.* FATHER KIRWAN *sits and starts his breakfast.*)

FATHER KIRWAN. What is it all about, Canon?

CANON. Brigid seems to have risen during my Mass and put up white curtains and decorated the table with flowers.

(FATHER KIRWAN *looks at the curtains and flowers.*)

FATHER KIRWAN (*smiling*). She gets the funniest notions . . . They say her mother, before she was sent away, used to wear her boots on the wrong feet for pure contrariness.

(MISS COONEY *re-enters hurriedly.*)

JEMIMA (*fearfully*). Canon! She—she's not there!

CANON (*sharply*). Not where?

JEMIMA. In the bed, Canon.

CANON (*irascibly*). What new sort of stupidity is this?

FATHER KIRWAN. Did you try the kitchen?

JEMIMA. I did, Father. She's no-where about the house.

FATHER KIRWAN. I'll bet she crossed the fields over to St. Brigid's Shrine. This is her feast day—the first of February.

JEMIMA. Sure, it's an Irish mile if it's a yard, Father. Maybe it's down to the schoolmaster she went.

FATHER KIRWAN. That low scum! I hope not, for her own sake.

JEMIMA. Troth, Father, she had a likin' that didn't become her at all for that fella. I was goin' to warn his reverence. . . .

CANON (*irascibly*). This conjectur-ing is both ludicrous and undigni-fied. It is obvious that the child's mind is in a very weak state, and that she has wandered aimlessly on to the roads. Miss Cooney, I haven't the slightest hesitation in reprimanding you for neglect of duty.

JEMIMA. It's not for me to answer you back, Canon, but I advised you a few times that she was wake in the mind, as her mother was, and that she needed . . .

CANON (cutting in). I am not concerned with your advice, Miss Cooney. Go out and search for her instead. And you, Father Kirwan, if you are free will also join . . .

FATHER KIRWAN (rising enthusiasm). I'll take the wee car, Canon, and I'll cover the whole parish in a flash. The new gear box, Canon, that . . .

CANON. You will walk! I am averse to cinematic exhibitions on the parochial roads, because our servant has—mislaid herself. And if I may add, Father . . . (The CANON stops abruptly to stare at BRIGID who suddenly comes in by the window. She is dressed all in white, is neat and comely, matter-of-fact and practical in manner, and is smiling slightly. She leans against the curtains—a white picture in a white frame. All turn and stare at her.)

CANON. Brigid! What does this mean?

BRIGID. Please, Canon, I had—things to do. So I riz.

CANON. I am incensed and angry.

BRIGID. Not this day, Canon, please. Tomorrow maybe . . . (Pause) Do you like my white curtains?

FATHER KIRWAN. So it was you changed them!

BRIGID. Yes . . . just at dawn and the sky whitenin'. It had to be then.

JEMIMA. The curtains didn't need changin' at all, until Friday, Canon.

CANON. Have you any answer to that?

BRIGID. I just—felt they did. I thought them red ones would be a show before — before anyone comin'. (She hangs her head.)

CANON. Brigid, I want no nonsense, but sound sense. In leaving your bed you were disobedient.

BRIGID. Yis, Canon. I thought, Canon, that the flowers and me white curtains and me white dress would please you. And—anyone comin' too.

CANON. Instead, you have gravely displeased me. Where have you been?

BRIGID. In the chapel, Canon. Sure you gave me Communion yourself. (FATHER CORR appears back, and comes in through window bareheaded.)

CANON. Eh? I—I what?

BRIGID. Sure, you didn't know me in me white dress. I was near laughin'. . . . Father Corr wouldn't have seen me either only he plopped down beside me behind the pillar.
(A pause. BRIGID hangs her head.)

BRIGID (hesitant). You—you're angry, Canon.

CANON. I am more than angry. I am disgusted.

JEMIMA. Will I put her back to bed, Canon?

BRIGID. Please no, Canon. I hate bed.

CANON. Very well then, for the present. Take her, Miss Cooney, and give her breakfast. And then, Brigid, I wish to speak to you.

JEMIMA. Come on now, and no nonsense.

BRIGID (*going to* CANON). I want to speak to *you* too, Canon, if you'll let me.

CANON. All of the speaking will be done by me. You will go now.

BRIGID. But—I don't want any breakfast.

CANON. What's that?

FATHER CORR. She specially wants to fast till midday, Canon. I spoke to her against it, but it was no use.

CANON. The Church requires no such penance from a sick child. You will go, Brigid. I forbid this.

BRIGID. But I—I can't, Canon. I promised.

CANON. Miss Cooney, prepare Brigid's breakfast and inform me when it is ready.

JEMIMA. I will, Canon. And that's the right way. Such contrariness and stubbornness! Her mother too—

CANON. You will go, Miss Cooney. (JEMIMA *with a gulp, goes, left.* FATHER KIRWAN *rises from breakfast and crosses.*)

FATHER KIRWAN (*apologetically*). If you'll excuse *me,* I have a meetin' of the Football team to attend. (*To* FATHER CORR) Aren't *you* comin', too, Father? It's near ten. We'll take the car.

FATHER CORR. Get the engine started up, and I'll be out after you.

FATHER KIRWAN. Hurry then. We'll have to stop at Ryan's for petrol. (*As he crosses*) Brigid, if you go in and wallop a plate of bacon and eggs, I'll give you a whizz this evenin' in the car. There now!

BRIGID. Not this day, Father, but another day.

FATHER KIRWAN. Go on now. You're annoyin' the Canon. And I'll learn you to drive as well.

BRIGID. But, Father, I've promised and given me word. . . . Do you think I could bear to break it, and me with a white dress on me too. It would be terrible.

FATHER KIRWAN. Ach, you're a blather! I'll buy you a football jersey. (*He goes out with a wave.* FATHER CORR *walks uneasily about. He is ill at ease under* BRIGID'S *gaze.*)

BRIGID. Please stay—with us here, Father Corr, and—don't go.

FATHER CORR. Brigid, won't you just be a good girl and leave *us* to look after our own business?

CANON. What is going on here that I am not aware of?

FATHER CORR. Just a meetin' of the football team, Canon.
(*A tense pause.*)

BRIGID (*bursting out*). If—if Mr. O'Flingsley done one thing wrong, he'll surely do twinty things right. (*Both turn and stare at her. The* CANON *is mystified.* FATHER CORR *is confused.*)

CANON. O'Flingsley? . . . What—what on earth is this?

BRIGID (*in pain*). The men's havin' a meetin', Canon. There's goin' to be talk and then stones and sticks.

FATHER CORR (*sharply*). What talk is this *you* have?

CANON. What? . . . What do you know of this, Brigid?

BRIGID. If I told you, Canon, you would say I—I wasn't well.

CANON. Pht! Of course you are not well! You are ill! You are very ill! (*To* FATHER CORR) What truth is there in this, Father Corr?

FATHER CORR (*stiffly*). Instead of answering that, Canon, might I ask instead why *we* weren't told that that scoundrel, O'Flingsley, was the author of that blasphemous book we read?

CANON. Because it was sufficient for the purposes of the Church that *I* knew of it.

FATHER CORR. These are new times, Canon. Neither we nor the people down there consider that satisfactory.

CANON. There is only one time in God's Church, Father Corr. (*Grimly*) And I expect my rulings to be obeyed.

FATHER CORR. In canonical matters, yes.

CANON. In all matters affecting the dignity of the Church.

FATHER CORR. We made it our business to warn this scoundrel to be clear out of this parish by this morning. If he is still here it is *his* look-out. I will try to moderate the feelings of the people, but I warn you I cannot cork them up in a bottle.

CANON. This is defiance!

FATHER CORR. No, Canon. It is legitimate action, since *you* won't move.

CANON. *Move?* I've dismissed the man summarily.

FATHER CORR. In our opinion, it is not enough.

CANON. It is a most severe sentence in any civilized community. The man's bread and butter.

FATHER CORR. Any bla'guard like *him* can get bread and butter, aye and honey too, in Ireland by slingin' mud at the Church.

CANON. Mud, Father Corr, sticks only to mud. But I would hardly expect that much philosophy from *you*.

FATHER CORR. I'm not here to talk sophistry, Canon. It glosses over unbearable insults. I'm a plain, blunt man.

CANON. Like Luther and Cromwell.

BRIGID. If the Master, Canon, was a bla'guard with terrible things in him, and not just a blunderer the same as Father Corr . . .

FATHER CORR. How dare you, Brigid!

CANON. That will do, Brigid. As usual, Father Corr, you are intemperate in your language, and chaotic in your feelings. I place both you and Father Kirwan under a strict rule of obedience. Any attempt at Dublin's holy hooliganism in *my* parish, will be rigorously met by *me*. Go down and acquaint this meeting of *that*. And in my name, dismiss it.

FATHER CORR. But what do you imagine they will think of me when . . .

CANON (*imperiously*). I insist, Father Corr!

FATHER CORR. Very well, Canon. I'll—deliver your message. (*Very sulkily he goes, left.* BRIGID *goes close to the* CANON, *and looks at him solicitously.*)

BRIGID. It's a mortal sin for us all, Canon, worryin' and annoyin' ye.

CANON (*softly*). It is a worrying age, child. But what of it? As Don Miguel used to be fond of saying, "*Dios quie da la llaga, da la medicina.*"

BRIGID. And what does that mean, Canon?

CANON. It means, Brigid, that when God sends us evil, He sends with it the weapon to conquer it.

BRIGID. It's lovely. (*Pause*) Is a weapon, Canon, a sword?

CANON. God could make a weapon of anything, child.

BRIGID (*as in a dream*). Yis. . . . *She* said that too . . . and she was sad. . . .
(MISS COONEY *enters, left.*)

JEMIMA. Brigid's breakfast is ready, Canon. And this letter's just come in for you. (*She hands* CANON *the letter which he proceeds to open and read.* BRIGID *looks very appealingly at him.*)

CANON (*his eyes on the letter*). Go, Brigid, and have a full meal. (BRIGID *goes dejectedly towards door, and then looks back pathetically at* CANON, *who is immersed in his letter.*)

JEMIMA (*at door, waiting*). Are ye goin' to be all day comin'?

BRIGID (*low*). I'll be after ye in a minute, Sssh!

JEMIMA. I'll not ssh! at all. It'll be cold. Canon, how much more of her nonsense are we to put up with?

CANON (*finishing letter and looking up*). You may go, Miss Cooney. Brigid will follow in a moment. (MISS COONEY *goes.* BRIGID *regards the* CANON *wistfully. He looks at her, half-ruffled, half lovingly*) Brigid, are *you* going to be a good girl?

BRIGID. Yis, Canon.

CANON. Excellent, Brigid. Come here! (*She comes to him softly*) This letter will give you a good appetite. It is from a great friend of mine in Bray. You will go up there, Brigid, for an excellent holiday, and I will put a whole five pound note in your bag. There now! And your hat! Why, I was forgetting all about your hat! (*Pointing*) There it is! It has a veil over your ear, Brigid—

BRIGID. My nose, Canon.

CANON. Your nose, Brigid. Your nose to be sure. And an ornament stuck at the side.

BRIGID. Is it a little white dog, Canon?

CANON. A dog? I believe it *is* a dog. I distinctly remember the manageress saying that dogs were the fashion.

BRIGID. So they are, Canon.

CANON. Excellent, Brigid. I consider dogs are in excellent taste myself. But you are not to see the hat now—not till you get your breakfast. Come now, are you pleased?

BRIGID (*softly*). I—I could cry, Canon. I'll—anger you again and vex you. I—I know it.

CANON. No, Brigid. God will help you not to. You will be my friend instead. It is good to have a friend on a dark day. If anything is ever said of me, child, I want it to be that I found your face always full of grace and comely.

BRIGID. Don't say anythin' nice about me face, Canon, or I would want it to be like St. Brigid's face with the niceness torn out of it with pain.

CANON (*chidingly*). There! There! Your mind must not dwell on these myths and fancies. What is God's, nothing can destroy. Go now, child, and have a good breakfast, and then we shall fit on your hat and arrange about your train.
(BRIGID *moves towards door, and then comes back pathetically.*)

BRIGID (*shrewdly*). Canon, if—if you made a great promise to—to Don Miguel or Don Pedro, would you keep it in face of everythin'?

CANON. Keep it? Why, most certainly, Brigid. A gentleman *always* keeps his promises, under penalty of dishonor.
(*She looks at him pleadingly.*)

BRIGID (*after a pause*). That's why I don't want to—to eat till midday, Canon. I—I promised St. Brigid. (*The* CANON *starts visibly, realizing he is caught. He controls his feelings.*)

CANON. Brigid, you are very trying. Will you eat if I, as the Canon, give you a special—a very special dispensation?

BRIGID. But it's for—the love of her, Canon, not as a penance. She asked me to prove I loved her.

CANON. To say she asked you is—inaccurate, Brigid. What you mean is that in praying to St. Brigid, you *told* her you would fast yourself. In that you were harder on yourself than the Church allows. Anything excessive, Brigid, is not classically Catholic.

BRIGID. She *did* ask me, Canon. But you won't believe me.

CANON (*ruffled*). I thought, Brigid, we finished with this matter long ago!

BRIGID. I tried, Canon. But—she kept pleadin'—as if everythin' else was standin' waitin'. . . . She said I was to offer my Communion this mornin' for *you*, and my fast till midday for *you* too.

CANON (*after a pause*). Brigid, for offering your Communion for me, I am indeed grateful. It is the act of my friend. But you must not think any *figure told* you to do this. The Church *frowns* at such imaginings, and she is very, very wise.

BRIGID. But there's—somethin' else, Canon. It's—killin' and killin' me. . . .

CANON (*holding himself in*). I feel you're going to make me angry, Brigid.

BRIGID (*trembling*). I—I know . . . I'm tremblin'. . . .

CANON (*touching her*). There! My poor child, there! You are ill, and I will say no word. You may tell me. I will contain myself, Brigid. I will bear with you. Let it be written of me.

BRIGID. She told me to ask you, Canon to—come with me, wearin' your surplice and soutane, and I in this white dress, into the chapel yard today at twelve when the Angelus is ringin' and the people are comin' and goin'. (*The* CANON *is staring at her, holding himself desperately in leash.* BRIGID, *with tearful eyes, is looking up pleadingly at him*) We are to kneel down on the seventh flag from the door and I am to keep sayin' the prayer to St. Brigid. And you are to invoke her three times, and then kiss the stone and say, "Mary of the Gael, show us the way through the dark." And she promises that a stream of water, waitin' there for years, will gush out over the flagstone, and that the fingers of everyone will dip into it forever. (*Pause*) That—that's all, Canon. (*She stands visibly trembling, looking up at the* CANON *whose face is strained and masklike*) Please don't —shout and be angry with me, C-Canon. Just—just say, "G-go, B-Brigid!"

(*The* CANON, *his hands clenched to his sides, turns and walks irascibly to the window and stares out. He is fighting desperately to control himself.* BRIGID *keeps watching him —her hand to her trembling mouth. In a few moments, he walks back to her with evident composure.*)

CANON (*slowly*). No, Brigid. I shall not shout or be hard on you. That would be unjust. Even if I am angry. Even if I am *very* angry. But I forgive you, Brigid. You are very ill. You are even more ill than I suspected.

BRIGID (*passionately*). Canon, believe me! Believe me! I am weak tellin' you. I am not—able.

CANON. Brigid, by the grace of God, I am holding away my anger from you, for you are not deserving of it. If you were not ill, I should be disgusted. I make you my friend, and in return you ask me to be a— boobish sort of conjurer who draws rabbits out of a hat or water out of a stone for the gratification of oafs and idiots.

BRIGID. But sure, Canon, St. Brigid wouldn't belittle *you* and deceive *me*. She—she *couldn't*.

CANON. As you rightly say she couldn't, Brigid. As I explained, child, she wasn't—there.

BRIGID. But I saw her, Canon. And the mark on her face and all.

CANON. I know, Brigid. Our poor sick minds play with terrible pictures. But *you* know nothing of such things. When you return from your holiday, you will say to me, "Canon, I was a little fool in the wind, and you were a big tree that gave me shelter."
(*Enter* MISS COONEY.)

JEMIMA. What will I do with Brigid's breakfast, Canon? It's goin' to loss.

CANON. Bring it here to this table, Miss Cooney, on a tray.

JEMIMA (*staring*). Is it the—the priests' table you mean, Canon?

CANON. Obviously, Miss Cooney. (*With a perplexed bow, she goes.*)

CANON. Come and sit down with me, Brigid, till I tell you something. (*He seats her on a couch and seats himself near her.*)

BRIGID (*wretchedly*). I am weak and useless. . . . I am not able. . . . St. Brigid will brush me name off her lips as if it was a piece of soot in the wind.

CANON (*chidingly*). Brigid! Brigid! These morbid fancies! How now,

can I speak to you if you go on giving rein to them like a willful child?

BRIGID. She said she wanted a miracle, Canon, since the world had become so hard. Somethin', she said, that would give us all new life and strength.

CANON (*gently*). Listen to me, Brigid. When a woman in marriage gives birth to men, she proves herself a mother. Her men are all about her—justifying her. Suppose, Brigid, a fool came along and said, "Prove yourself a mother again," what would happen?

BRIGID. Sure they'd laugh, Canon.

CANON (*touching her shoulder*). They'd laugh! Excellent, Brigid. You are following me with intelligence. Now, it is just like that with the Church. Her children have justified her eternally. She is venerable with holiness and heavy with the wisdom of ages. And yet, Brigid, you want her to give birth to a new child—to prove herself by a new miracle. St. Brigid would laugh heartily at such a thing. She, Brigid, that redeemed the world, you want her to produce rabbits out of a boob's hat!

BRIGID (*in tears*). It wasn't like that, that I meant it, Canon.

CANON. You are just very young, Brigid, and your poor mind is ill. If you were as wise and old as me, Brigid, you would know that out there where you cannot see, there is a whole world of spiritual rowdies willing to sell themselves to anything that can produce signs and wonders to please their vanity.

And there you are, Brigid, in the center of them, backing them up —you, the Canon's friend who should know better.

BRIGID (*woefully*). Please, Canon, don't say that to me. . . . It's terrible. . . . I don't know where I am or what to think. It's like people that you love pullin' agin each other. . . . It's hard, Canon, the things that you love goin' crashin' down, as if they were timber fallin'.

CANON. You must learn to laugh, child, at the big shaky things that our poor sick minds build up, and our healthy minds pull down. There is great safety in the right kind of laughter.

(MISS COONEY *enters and puts a tray of breakfast things on the dining table.*)

JEMIMA. Please, Canon, make her take that now. I had to make fresh tea.

CANON. This very moment, Miss Cooney. (MISS COONEY *goes, left*) Come, Brigid. The Church very wisely tells us that our food is also important. (*He takes her to the table by the arm*) And you will sit at the top in the Canon's chair. (*As she seats herself shyly*) There now!

BRIGID. Please, Canon, *must* I eat?

CANON. Yes, Brigid.

BRIGID. Would you be angry if I didn't?

CANON. *Very* angry. And so would the Church. And St. Brigid too. St. Brigid, if you know anything of her, was a *very* sensible saint indeed.

BRIGID (*resigned*). I'll—eat, then, Canon.

CANON. Excellent! A good meal now, and then we'll discuss your holiday and—your hat, Brigid. We mustn't forget your hat. That *too* is important. (*As he moves away*) I am going upstairs to attend to— a little matter.

BRIGID. Is it up to the little place off your bedroom that—

CANON (*hand up*). That will do, Brigid. It is—my affair.

BRIGID. Yis, Canon. Please, Canon, will you—pray for me—too?

CANON (*after a pause*). I will, child. For both of us. (*He goes out pensively.* BRIGID *lifts the teapot uncertainly, her hand trembles and she puts it down again. She looks towards the door fearfully. She sits a few moments in torment. There is a noise off. She shakingly pours out some tea. She adds sugar and cream in a dazed way. She lifts the cup halfway to her lips, puts it guiltily down, and buries her face in her hands.*)

BRIGID. It's not fair . . . after me promisin' . . . and me white dress on me too. . . . (*She rises, her eyes on the curtains, and walks center*) I'm miserable and not able. . . . What name have you for me in your lovely mouth? Soot maybe, or clabber of the ground or maybe dung that smells. . . . (*Pathetically*) Oh, please no, not that! . . . Make it somethin' that has been burned in the fire . . . somethin' burned black with flame. . . . (*She turns sorrowfully back to table.* MISS COONEY *comes to the door.*)

JEMIMA. Are ye done there yet? It's near half-eleven already. Why you didn't begin yet! If it's goin' on bein' contrary you are, I'll tell the Canon. (*Looking around*) Where *is* the Canon?

BRIGID. He's not to be disturbed.

JEMIMA. Did he say that?

BRIGID. No, Miss Cooney, but I know he meant it.

JEMIMA. Indeed; And them's *your* orders, are they?

BRIGID (*softly*). How could I be givin' orders?

JEMIMA. You're daft enough for anythin'. And you're goin' to Dublin, are ye?

BRIGID. It's whatever the Canon says.

JEMIMA. Aye, well you'll not be the first in your family that's seen Nelson's Pillar.

BRIGID (*staring at her, very hurt*). There's some terrible meanin' in that. You must be wicked and cruel. I can feel it in you.

JEMIMA. You hurry up there, or you'll feel me a good bit more.

BRIGID (*coweringly*). Yis . . . I'll —eat now—in a minute. If only the Angelus would ring! . . .
(THOMASINA CONCANNON *and* FRANCIS O'CONNOR *come in, arm-in-arm, in high spirits.*)

THOMASINA. Is me uncle about, Jemima? Francis and meself want a word with him.

FRANCIS. It's about the weddin' arrangements, auntie.

JEMIMA. Sure he was here no time ago. Where did you say he went, Brigid?

BRIGID. He—didn't say.

JEMIMA (*sharply*). Which way did he go?

BRIGID. He went out into the hall

JEMIMA. He'll maybe be in his room. Wait now and I'll see.

THOMASINA. We just want to be sure, Jemima, he'll marry us himself, and not push us over to one of the curates. It's never just the same.

JEMIMA. Sure, surely to God, he wouldn't have a curate marryin' his own niece!

FRANCIS (*with a sheet of paper*). And we want his leave, auntie, to put in the paper, "beloved niece of the Very Rev. Thomas Canon Skerritt. P.P."

JEMIMA. Sure just put it in, and say nothin' till after. Look at the fix you'll be in, if he says no. Have you *my* name in it too?

FRANCIS. Imagine askin' that, auntie!

JEMIMA. And your own middle name, Francis. The scuts o' the country have as many names as ourselves nowadays.

FRANCIS. It's all fireproof, auntie. Lord Macaulay couldn't do better.

JEMIMA. I hope so, after all the schoolin' and collegin' you got. I'll run up and get him for you. (*She goes off, left.* THOMASINA *and* FRANCIS *cross to* BRIGID, *who is moodily sitting with her head in her hands at the table.*)

THOMASINA. Well, Brigid, are ye better?

BRIGID. Sure, I wasn't ill, Miss Concannon.

THOMASINA. Not ill? Sure the last time I was in, you were . . .

FRANCIS (*digging* THOMASINA). You're dreamin', Thomasina. Brigid wasn't ill.

THOMASINA (*with a giggle*). Ach, sure of course she wasn't. It's me bein' in love, that's what it is!

BRIGID. Please take some tea, Miss Concannon. It's just fresh wet.

THOMASINA (*eagerly*). I will in troth. (*Taking cup*) I could eat a cow! It's this love! Are ye finished with the cake there?

BRIGID (*eagerly*). Yis. Please ate them all. Help her, Francis, if you like. The Canon gets mad when he sees food left over.

FRANCIS. Sure and I will. (*Taking a cake*) I had always a sweet tooth. Make a note o' that, sweetest one! Yum! This is a cocoanut one! (*Both start eating vigorously.* BRIGID *watches them evidently relieved.*)

THOMASINA (*munching*). I wonder if that's true about O'Flingsley—I mean what Dave Dooley was tellin' us below at the bridge, Francis?

FRANCIS. About the people goin' to give him a batterin'? Maybe it is. Anyway, he'll be a good riddance.

BRIGID (*trembling*). Did—did you hear that? Are the people—sayin' it?

THOMASINA. Ach, behave yourself, Brigid! If they are itself, he deserves it.

BRIGID. But it's cruel and terrible. The Canon wouldn't see that done on him.

FRANCIS (*munching*). The Canon? Sure, you could ate all the Canon likes of him.

BRIGID (*in pain*). It's not true. . . . The Canon doesn't hate like that . . . and the Master doesn't hate like that either . . . I know what I'll do. I'll— (*Before the others can restrain her, she passes rapidly like a white vision through the white-curtained window. They stare after her, with pieces of cake in their hands and mouths. Then they look at each other and laugh spontaneously.*)

FRANCIS. That one will get hurt if the stones start flyin'.

THOMASINA. The poor thing. It must be terrible to be mad in the head. Is it true, Francis, that they smother mad people in Dublin between blankets? (*Before* FRANCIS *can settle the point, the* CANON *enters, left. He is irascible and ruffled.*)

CANON. Who wants me here? And for what purpose?

THOMASINA. Sure, it's just me and Francis, Uncle.

CANON. That much, I observe.

FRANCIS. Did we disturb ye now, Canon? Sure just say the word, Canon, and we'll come back any time.

CANON. I gave orders that I was not to be disturbed.

FRANCIS (*seizing* THOMASINA). Come on now, Thomasina, and let us not be maddenin' His Reverence. We can come back later by the Canon's leave.

THOMASINA. But me mother's comin' on the two o'clock train, and she'll be mad to know everythin'.

CANON (*acidly*). You will ask your questions concisely and without superfluity, and I shall answer them in—like manner. Proceed!
(MISS COONEY *comes in to collect tea-tray.* THOMASINA *and* FRANCIS *regard each other uncertainly.*)

FRANCIS. Sure, Canon, if you'd rather—

CANON. I said, proceed!

THOMASINA (*breathlessly*). We want to know, uncle, if *you'll* marry us yourself?

CANON (*rapidly*). No! Next question.

THOMASINA. But me mother will have a fit, uncle, if you don't.

CANON (*acidly*). Superfluous! I have already suitably defined your mother.

JEMIMA (*at table, obsequiously*). If I might humbly put in a word, Canon . . .

CANON. You might not, Miss Cooney.
(MISS COONEY *goes, humbly.*)

FRANCIS. Then I suppose, Canon, you won't allow us to put your name in the marriage notice in the papers?

CANON. Exactly, Francis. And that holds for birth notices too. Where is Brigid?

THOMASINA. She went out through the window, Canon, after we came in.

CANON (*irascibly*). For what purpose?

FRANCIS. She heard Thomasina and meself, Canon, talkin' about that man O'Flingsley, and the things the people were sayin' down the town.

THOMASINA. And away she went like a madhead.

CANON (*irascibly*). Why wasn't I told of this immediately instead of wasting time on trivialities? Run both of you instantly, and find her. The child is most unwell. Tell her the Canon wants her this very minute. (*He rushes them out by the window. As he returns,* FATHER KIRWAN *enters hurriedly by the door, wearing gauntlets.*)

FATHER KIRWAN. Canon, I flew up in the wee car for you. Father Corr and I want your help.

CANON. Am I to be continually reminding you, Father Kirwan, that I don't give help? I give direction. (*Pause*) What new stupidity is afoot now?

FATHER KIRWAN. It's not our fault really, Canon. It's the men insisted on marching to that O'Flingsley fellow's house.

CANON. For what purpose?

FATHER KIRWAN. To warn him, as was resolved at the meetin', to be gone out of this district.

CANON. On what authority?

FATHER KIRWAN. Sure, Canon, the authority of angry men. (*Loud booing and cheering from the distance*) Listen! There they're boohin' and shouting. Father Corr is trying to hold them down from anny violence.

CANON. And where might I ask is the Sergeant of police, when a brawl of this nature takes place?

FATHER KIRWAN. His wife's havin' a baby, Canon, and he can't come.

CANON. The sergeant a midwife, and my curates turned American lynchmen! Excellent!
(FATHER CORR *enters rapidly by the door. He is excited.*)

FATHER CORR. Canon, that fellow O'Flingsley is jeerin' at the people instead of goin' when he's told. He has them as angry as bulls. If you'd just come out and show yourself for a minute . . .
(*More booing and shouting from the distance.*)

CANON (*severely*). Did you and Father Kirwan march this—mob to O'Flingsley's house?

FATHER CORR. We did, Canon. It was—was up to us. But they're no mob, and they were in excellent order, till *he* started jeering.

FATHER KIRWAN. That's the down truth, Canon.

CANON. You are a sentimental youth, Father Corr, or you would know that all men in the mass are barbarians. Every year scores of decent Christians in America sprinkle Negroes with petrol and burn them because they love God and his justice. Yet, you *will* indulge in this—free Presbyterianism, this Lutheran zeal that the Church has never had any nonsense with in history. And in *my* parish too. (*Further bursts of booing and shouting, and the noise of sticks and stones in the distance.* MISS COONEY *comes in rapidly.*)

MISS COONEY (*very scared*). Canon, did ye ever hear the like! The milkman's after tellin' me about Brigid. She's below holdin' on to the man O'Flingsley on the road, and a crowd peltin' him with sticks and stones.

THE CURATES (*startled*). Canon!

CANON (*seized with fear*). Brigid! This—this is defiance! . . . My hat and stick instantly. (MISS COONEY *rushes off. The* CANON *draws himself up to his full height and regards the* CURATES *imperiously*) I have long enough suffered boobs gladly both without and within. Now, I the Canon, will act, and I will have obedience and authority!

FATHER KIRWAN (*boyishly*). Sure, it wasn't our fault at all, Canon. The men only got out of hand when that fellow, O'Flingsley . . .

CANON (*with a wave*). Enough!
(MISS COONEY *runs in with his stick and two hats, a soft one and a tall silk one. She fumbles nervously.*)

MISS COONEY. Is it this one, Canon, or the tall one?

CANON (*hurling soft hat across room and taking the tall one*). The tall one. (*He dons it with an awesome sweep of the arm*) I will show these neo-theologians and football kickers of yours that the bulk of the people are not to do but to be done by.

FATHER KIRWAN (*stupidly*). I'll whip ye down in the wee car in a jiffy, Canon.

CANON (*irascibly*). Get behind me, fool. I'll walk.
(MISS COONEY *and the* TWO CURATES *cower back as he marches intently towards the window, back. Before he reaches it, there is a commotion.* O'FLINGSLEY *appears in the opening with* BRIGID *lying in his arms. His hair is disheveled and his face streaked with blood and mud.* BRIGID'S *head is almost covered by a large white cloth—in fact, an apron,—and there are bloodstains upon her white dress. She is limp and inert.*)

MISS COONEY (*hysterical*). Canon! It's Brigid! They've kilt her!

FATHER CORR (*in anguish*). It's not—not true! . . .

FATHER KIRWAN (*hand to face, shakingly*). No! . . . No, no!

CANON (*hoarsely, doffing hat*). In the name of God, O'Flingsley . . .

O'FLINGSLEY. I'm not asking protection for myself, Canon. But get a doctor for Brigid at once.

CANON (*controlling himself*). Rush, Miss Cooney, for Dr. Connell. Say I said instantly. Fly, woman, dash!

MISS COONEY (*rushing out*). I'll race, Canon. Mother o' God . . .

CANON (*arranging couch*). Set her here, O'Flingsley.

FATHER KIRWAN (*in pain, bursting out*). Canon, we didn't mean annythin'. God knows we didn't . . .

CANON (*almost inaudibly*). Quiet, quiet.
(O'FLINGSLEY *gently stretches* BRIGID *on the couch. He stands on one side and the* CANON *on the other. Each is striving desperately to control himself. The* CURATES *stand bowed with fear and remorse.*)

CANON (*shakingly*). God of mercy, do not take this, my one consolation away from me. . . . (*His voice breaks*) Is—is it serious, O'Flingsley?

O'FLINGSLEY. I'm afraid it is.
(*They avoid each other's gaze.*)

CANON (*as in a dream, huskily*). What happened? T-tell me. . . .

O'FLINGSLEY (*passionlessly*). She got half a brick that one of your hirelings intended for *me*.

CANON (*pathetic*). They were not *my* hirelings, O'Flingsley. We are surely better enemies than that. (*Pause*) Where is the wound?

O'FLINGSLEY. Side of the head and upper part of the face. I'm afraid of concussion. It was a cruel blow. . . . As I ran with her, a woman poured a bottle of oil over it and tied her apron about her to stop the bleeding.

CANON (*bending, in pain*). And this in the name of the Communion of Saints . . .

FATHER CORR (*emotionally breaking down*). Canon, I can't bear it! I can't bear it! . . . God knows I meant no blood or violence . . . that I wouldn't hurt anythin' livin'. . . . I—I never thought . . . I never thought . . .

FATHER KIRWAN (*soothing him*). There now, there! Let ye hold on to yourself now. Sure the Canon knows. And Brigie will be all right in a minute.

FATHER CORR (*hysteric*). I did it! I did it! . . . I wasn't wise like— like the Canon . . . I—I only meant, Canon—

CANON (*not unkindly*). Father Corr, you will control your emotion.

FATHER CORR. Y-yes, Canon.

CANON. And cease allowing it to run you into fresh idiocies.

FATHER KIRWAN. I'll take him out to the fresh air, Canon.

CANON. You will both go out to these people, and order them in my name to return instantly to their homes and their work.

FATHER CORR. Very well, Canon. (*They go out, back,* FATHER KIR-WAN *assisting* FATHER CORR. The CANON *bends in fear over to the couch.*)

CANON. Will that doctor ever come! . . . Could we do anything of ourselves? God would guide us surely.

O'FLINGSLEY (*cautiously*). Better not. If the blood started . . .

CANON (*drawing bandages slightly*). My God, my God, what have they done? Did she speak at all, O'Flingsley?

O'FLINGSLEY. She whispered something about the Angelus bell and you. Then she sank into this.

CANON (*huskily*). We are all in this—this dark she lies in, only deeper than her. . . . Brigid, I am with you, the Canon, your friend. . . .

O'FLINGSLEY. There may be hope, if only that doctor is not playing golf. . . .

CANON (*wringing his hands*). It is like that—always—stupidities lying in the way. . . . God! Hasten him! Hasten him out! . . . (*At this moment, the Angelus Bell begins ringing clearly from the Church tower outside.* BRIGID *groans, stirs weakly and moves her head. They regard her emotionally.*)

O'FLINGSLEY (*softly*). Brigid . . . it's the Canon and I.

BRIGID (*weakly*). The man O'Flingsley. . . . (*Moving painfully*) The—the Angelus . . . the Angelus . . . and I'm not—able. . . . Canon, make me able. . . .

CANON. I am here, Brigid. But you must not speak. You are very ill, poor child.

BRIGID (*as in a dream*). There's blood on the Master's head. . . . I felt it. . . . Then the stone came . . . with the pain in it . . . and I knew my face was like St. Brigid's then . . . torn and hurt. . . . My mouth is burnin' . . . me. . . . (*The* CANON *pours a little of his Spanish wine into a glass and brings it towards her.*)

O'FLINGSLEY. The Canon is right this time, Brigid. You must lie very still and not talk till the doctor comes.

BRIGID. But how can I rest . . . and that bell ringin'. . . . The Canon knows . . . Canon! . . .

CANON. There, child! I am here with you. . . . You must take a sip of this wine to strengthen you. . . . (*She takes a few sips from the glass.*)

BRIGID. Don Miguel's wine. . . . He said to the Canon, "Where there is truth there is God." . . . I wish I could rise up, and be *true* to her . . . and not false. . . . But I'm not able. . . .

CANON (*striving to hold in his emotions*). Brigid, if you will live for me, live on as the Canon's friend, I will do what you want. I will bend for you. The Canon will bend. He will stoop. He will—believe. . . .

BRIGID (*weakly, struggling*). C-Canon! . . . I—I want to live for that . . . I must live. . . . I must show you the stone . . . and my white dress on . . . me. . . .

O'FLINGSLEY (*tenderly supporting her*). Yes, Brigid, but not till the doctor examines you.

BRIGID (*weakly moving*). But there is no time, Master . . . no time. . . . The Angelus will soon not be ringin'. . . .

O'FLINGSLEY. She's fighting hard as if there was something that mattered a lot.

CANON. So there is. . . . (*Emotionally*) So there is. . . .

BRIGID (*rising a little, painfully*). Make me able, Canon. I want to keep faith with her. I want her to see me face like hers. . . . I want to be a white rose in her mouth . . . not a smut of soot brushed away. . . . (*She rises still more—only her eyes and brow and hair visible and glowing above the bandages*) I want to see your face stooped, Canon, in the way she said . . . and the love of the little things in it. . . . I want to dip me fingers in the new water, and to say what she told me, "Mary of the Gael, show us the way . . . through the dark." . . . (*For a moment her face is poised eloquently. The Angelus bell ceases. She suddenly collapses back, and lies still. The* CANON *buries his face in his hands* O'FLINGSLEY *stifles a sob.*)

CANON (*shakingly*). Tell me, O'Flingsley. No, no. Don't—don't say it. . . .

O'FLINGSLEY (*simply*). It's one of the things must be said, Canon. She's dead. . . .

CANON. God . . . God . . . Have I blundered? (O'FLINGSLEY *takes up a coverlet to draw it over* BRIGID'S *face, but the* CANON *pathetically intervenes, childishly)* No, no. Let—let *me*, O'Flingsley. . . . Let *me*.

O'FLINGSLEY (*slowly*). Let both of us. . . . (*Terribly*) It will be—worthy of us. . . .
(*Together they draw the coverlet over* BRIGID'S *face. Their eyes meet fully for the first time, and hold each other over* BRIGID'S *body. Then slowly each moves slowly back in different directions.*)

CANON (*huskily, as* O'FLINGSLEY *nears the door*). No, no. . . . Do not leave me, O'Flingsley. . . . I am alone. . . .

O'FLINGSLEY (*turning, slowly*). I must. (*Very low*) We must work this out. . . . Innocent blood. . . .

CANON (*hands to face, shakingly*). Am I just an embittered old man . . . living here with shades too glorious to forget?
(*For a moment,* O'FLINGSLEY *regards him from the doorway, his face a study—in mingled hate, pity and respect. He turns slowly and goes out. A moment passes. The* CANON *sits down heavily. He lifts heavy weary eyes to the couch and the empty room.*)

CANON (*his head down again, slowly*). I am not well. . . .

SLOW CURTAIN

MODERN LIBRARY GIANTS

A series of full-sized library editions of books that formerly were available only in cumbersome and expensive sets. THE MODERN LIBRARY GIANTS REPRESENT A SELECTION OF THE WORLD'S GREATEST BOOKS

These volumes contain from 600 to 1,400 pages each
